TIRUMANTIRAM

A Tamil scriptural Classic

By

Tirumular

Tamil Text with English Translation and Notes

By

Dr. B. Natarajan

General Editor

Dr. N. Mahalingam

SRI RAMAKRISHNA MATH
31, Ramakrishna Mutt Road
Mylapore, Chennai—600004

Published by
Adhyaksha
Sri Ramakrishna Math
#31, Ramakrishna Mutt Road
Mylapore, Chennai–600004
✉ publication@chennaimath.org
Online store: *istore.chennaimath.org*
Ebooks: *vedantaebooks.org*

First Edition, September 1991
Thirteenth Print, April 2025
1000 copies

ISBN: 978-81-7120-383-3

Printed in India at
Sri Ramakrishna Math Printing Press
Mylapore, Chennai–4

PUBLISHER'S NOTE

We have great pleasure in presenting before our readers this edition of Tirumular's scriptural classic *Tirumantiram* with. Tamil Text, English translation and notes.

Very little is known of the legendary Tirumular who is traditionally considered to be a Siva Yogi hailing from the North and settled down in the south at Thiruvavaduthurai. We do not know how and when the 3,000 verses were recorded but it is acknowledged that they form the nucleus for the Saiva Siddhanta that developed in Tamil Nadu. Besides the tenets found in Saiva Siddhanta, we find in *Tirumantiram* doctrines common to Tantras. On the whole, the vision of *Tirumantiram* is liberal and is as relevant today as when the work was first composed. It equates Love with Godhead in the famous Mantra 'Anbe Sivam'. It preaches that God is One and so is mankind too. This is a splendid echo of the Rig Vedic dictum *Ekam sat viprā bahudhā Vadanti* — Reality is One, though the sages speak of it variously. This non-sectarian approach to the Ultimate Reality is happily the tradition of the South as much as of the North.

The English translation and part of the notes are by the late Dr. B. Natarajan who was not only a profound Tamil scholar, but also a noted economist. Sri M. Sundararaj IRAS has furnished a running commentary on the verses which we have incorporated in the Introduction. He has also supplied critical notes in addition to those written by Dr. Natarajan.

We are very thankful to Dr. N. Mahalingam, the generous industrialist and Tamil-lover, who has not only functioned as the General Editor of this book but has also substantially subsidized the publication.

We hope that this great scriptural text will enable the readers to feel the touch of the One in the play of the many.

Sri Ramakrishna Math
Madras
March 1991

Publisher

June 1991

CONTENTS

PUBLISHER'S NOTE iii

INTRODUCTION vii

PROLOGUE **1**

IN PRAISE OF GOD **3**

Special Introduction - 3, Greatness of Vedas - 9, The Greatness of the Agamas - 10, The Guru Hierarchy - 11, History of Tirumular - 12, In Humility - 15, The Glory of the Holy Hymns Three Thousand - 15, The Spiritual Hierarchy - 16, The Three Gods - 16

1. TANTRA ONE **18**

Divine Instruction - 18, Transitoriness of Body - 22, Transitoriness of Wealth - 26, Transitoriness of Youth - 27, Transitoriness of Life - 29, Non-Violence - 30, Meat Eating—Forbidden - 31, Not Committing Adultery - 31, Evil Women is Ignominy - 31, In Vain Pursuit of Accumulation - 32, Relating to Sacrificial Fire - 33, Dharma of Brahmins - 34, The Path of Kings - 37, The Glory of Rains - 38, The Glory of Giving - 39, In Praise of the Charitable - 39, Way of the Uncharitable - 40, To be Love-Possessed - 42, Siva Knows Those Who Love Him - 43, Learning - 45, Listening and Thus Containing - 46, Non-Learning - 47, The Middle Path - 49, Abstaining from Drink - 49

2. TANTRA TWO **52**

Agastyam - 52, Eight Heroic Deeds of Siva - 52, Linga Puranam - 54, Daksha's Sacrifice - 55, Deluge - 57, Gift of the Discus - 57, Skeleton and Skull - 58, In Search of Crown and Feet of Siva - 58, Creation — Microcosmic - 59, Sustenance - 63, Destruction - 66, Obscuration - 67, Bestowal of Grace - 68, Creation Microcosm - 70, The Three Categories of Jivas - 75, The Worthy Souls - 77, The Unworthy Souls - 78, Holy Waters - 79, Consequence of Damaging the Holy Temple - 80, Darshan of Downward-Looking Face - 81, Abuse of Siva - 82, Abuse of Guru - 82, Abuse of Siva Jnani (Mahesvara) - 83, Patience - 84, To Seek the Company of the Holy - 84

3. TANTRA THREE **86**

Ashtanga Yogam - 86, Iyama - 86, Niyama - 87, Asanas - 88, Pranayama - 89, Pratyahara - 91, Dharana - 93, Dhyana - 94, Samadhi - 97, Fruits of Eight-Limbed Yoga - 99, The Eight Great Siddhis - 100, Kala Unwavering - 112, Way to Kayasiddhi - 113, Wheel of Time or Kala Chakra - 116, Measurement of Life Span - 120, Breath Rhythm in Days of the Week - 124, Hostile Week Days - 126, Kechari Yoga - 126, Pariyanga Yoga - 131, Amuri Dharana - 134, Chandra Yoga - 136

4. TANTRA FOUR 141

Ajapa - 141, Thiru Ambala Chakra - 146, Archana - 158, Navagundam (Nine Sacrificial Pits) - 160, Sakti-Bheda — Tiripurai Chakra - 164, Bhairavi Mantra - 169, Purna Sakti - 176, Support-Supported - 180, Eroli Chakram (Chakra of Supreme Light) - 194, Bhairava Chakra - 200, Sambhavi Mandala Chakra - 201, Bhuvanapathi Chakra - 202, Navakkari Chakra - 204

5. TANTRA FIVE 219

Suddha Saivam - 219, Asuddha Saivam - 220, San Marga Saivam - 221, Rigorous Suddha Saivam 223, Chariya - 223, Kriya - 225, Yoga - 226, Jnana - 227, Sanmarga (Path of Knowledge) - 229, Sahamarga (Path of Yoga) - 230, Satputra Marga (Path of Kriya) - 231, Dasa Marga (Path of Devotion) - 233, Salokam (In God's World) - 234, Samipam (In God's Proximity) - 234, Sarupam (In God's Form) - 234, Sayujyam (One in God) - 235, Sathinipadam (Descent of Grace) - 235, Arusamaya Pinakkam (A Critique of Formal Religions) - 238, Niracharam (Dissension Refuted) - 241, Inner Faiths - 242

6. TANTRA SIX 246

Darshan of Siva Guru - 246, Grace of Guru's Feet - 248, Jnathru, Jnana, Jneya (Knower, Knowledge and Known) - 251, Renunciation - 252, Tapas - 254, Abuse of Tapas - 255, Jnana Flows from God's Grace - 257, False Robes - 259, Robes of Tapas - 260, Holy Ashes - 260, Robes of Jnana - 261, Siva Robe - 262, The Unfit - 263, The Fit Disciple - 264

7. TANTRA SEVEN 267

The Six Adharas - 267, The Cosmic Lingam - 268, Microcosmic (Pinda) Linga - 270, Sadasiva Lingam - 271, Atma Lingam - 275, Jnana Lingam - 276, Siva Lingam - 278, Sampradaya (Holy Tradition) - 278, Placing of Grace - 280, Light of Grace - 283, Siva Puja - 285, Guru Puja - 288, Maheswara Puja (Worship of Devotees) - 290, Greatness of Holy Men - 292, Rules for Feeding Holy Men - 295, Rules for Receiving Alms - 295, Mudra Variations - 296, The Samadhi called the Path to the Perfect Cave - 298, Samadhi Rituals - 299, Rise of Bindu - 301, Conquest of Bindu — Regulation of Bindu Flow - 304, The Sun's Position — The Cosmic Sun - 310, The Microcosmic Sun - 311, Mind's Sun - 312, Jnana-Sun - 312, Siva-Sun - 314, Nature of Jiva Prana - 315, Purusha - 315, Jiva (Soul) - 316, Jiva (Pasu) 316, Bodhan (Lord as Giver of Light of Jnana) - 317, Importance of Controlling the Five Indriyas (Senses) - 318, How to Control Senses (Way of Sublimation) - 319, Ways of Unholy Guru - 321, Ways of Holy Guru - 322, Unholy Conduct - 324, In Compassion for Men's Evil Lot - 326, Salutary Instruction - 329

8. TANTRA EIGHT 332

Five Divisions of the Body - 332, Giving Up Body - 334, Avasta Differences — Lower Avasta - 335, Mid-Jagrat-Avasta - 339, Adhvas (Higher Steps) - 342, Suddha Jagrat and Other States - 342, Kevala, Sakala, Suddha - 349, Para-Avasta - 355, Triple Gunas and Nirguna (Sans Gunas) - 359, Cosmic Divisions - 359, The Eleventh State is also Avasta - 360, Uniting and Exiting - 360, Pure Avasta (Devoid of Malas) - 361, Dawn of Jnana - 368, The Six Essences - 370, Pati-Pasu-Pasam Non-Difference - 375, Head-And-Foot Knowledge - 378, Three Blemishes - 379, Three States (Padas) of Realization - 380, Three Paras - 381, Attributes of Para - 382, Three Turiyas - 384, Three Muktis - 385, Triple Svarupa - 386, Mukkaranam - 387, Three Spaces and Tvam-Tat-Asi - 387, Three Spaces - 388, Caused-Causal Experiences - 389, Upasantam - 390, Refraining from Vain Speech - 390,

Experience in the Eight-Petalled Sphere - 393, Nine Avastas and Nine Aspirants - 394, Suddha-Asuddham - 395, Scron of Mukti - 397, Lakshana Trayam - 398, Tattvamasivakyam - 399, Viswa-Grasam (Total Absorption) - 401, Truth - 402, Ways of Jnani - 404, Sundering of Desires - 405, To be Possessed of Bhakti - 406, To be in Mukti - 407, Experimentation - 408

9. TANTRA NINE 410

Darshan of Guru Monastery - 410, Darshan of Jnana Guru - 411, Pranava Samadhi - 413, Light - 414, Sthula (Articulate) Panchakshara - 416, Sukshma (Inarticulate) Panchakshara - 418, Ati-Sukshma (Super Subtle) Panchakshara - 419, Darshan of Holy Dance - 419, Attainment of Akasa (Space) Within - 431, Jnanodayam (Dawn of Jnana) - 432, Satya Jnananandam (Sat-Chit-Ananda) - 434, Svarupa Udayam (Dawn of Manifestness) - 435, Fate - 437, Darshan of Siva - 438, Darshan of Siva Svarupa (Manifestness) - 438, Mukti Bheda and Karma Nirvana (Gradations of Liberation) - 440, Sunya Sambhashana (Dialogue of Symbolism) - 440, Mauna Samadhi (Transcendental) - 451, Greatness of Limitlessness Beyond - 453, Greatness of the Realized - 454, Laudation - 457, The All-Pervasive - 463, Benediction - 465

INTRODUCTION

The Author:

The author of this treatise, Tirumular, was originaly a Yogi called Sundarar residing in the Mount Kailas. Once he undertook a journey to the south to meet his friend and fellow-disciple Agastyar, who was living in Pothiya mountains. One evening he found himself in the outskirts of the Sathanur village. He was deeply moved to notice a herd of cows lowing miserably round the dead body of their cowherd, Mulan. The Yogi who gave us the famous dictum 'Anbe Sivam', 'God is love,' thought it his duty to do something to help the dumb creatures. By virtue of his Yogic Power he abandoned his body and entered the body of the dead cowherd. The cows were overjoyed to see their master coming alive. The asecetic in the cowherd's body led the cattle to the village, and leaving them there, returned to the spot where he had left his own body. He was surprised to find that the body had disappeared. It was an act of grace of Lord Siva, who had a mission to fulfil through His devotee. So, the Yogi had to continue to remain in the cowherd's body. He was immersed in Tapas under a peepul tree in Thiruvavaduthurai, a neighbouring Saivite centre. He came to be known as Thirumular. Soon disciples flocked to him. He was usually in Samadhi. But now and then he uttered a verse which was recorded. Thus 3000 verses came to be recorded and these now form the text of the Tirumandiram.

Saiva Siddhanta:

The religious and spiritual path blazed by Tirumular broadened later into the highway of devotion known as Saiva Siddhantam. Nurtured by the Nayanmars, it has played an important role in the development of Tamil culture. Before we go into the contribution of Tirumular, it would be useful to have a bird's eye view of the Saiva Siddhanta doctrines.

Central to the Saiva Siddhanta system is the Pati-Pasu-Pasa triangle. Pati or the Master stands for God. Pasu is the individual soul in ignorance. And Pasa is the bondage of Maya that ties down the individual soul. All these three entities are real and hence Saiva Siddhanta looks like pluralistic realism. But it calls itself Suddhadvaita. 'Suddha' here means 'unqualified' and 'Advaita' is 'dvaita devoid of duality.' The difference between the three entities is real in existence, but they are inseparably united with Him who is the Supreme Reality. Here we notice the influence of Sri Ramanuja's *Aprtak Siddhi.* But while for Ramanuja, the Jivas and the Jagat are attributes of God, in the Siddhanta, they have a substantive existence as in Madhva's philosophy.

Siva, the Pati, is also called Hara, Isa, Natha, Nandi, etc. He is the First Cause even as the potter who fashions the pot. Just as the staff and the wheel are the instrumental causes in the case of the pot, Sakti is the instrumental cause in creation. Just as clay is the material cause for the pot, Maya or Prakriti is the material cause for the world. Siva and Sakti have Tadatmya or identity represented by the form of Ardhanareeswara. Sakti is conscious, unchanging, eternal energy, the Svarupa Sakti of the Lord. As in Ramanuja's system, a distinction is made between pure matter (Suddha or Sattvika jagat) and defiled matter (Asuddha or Prakrita Jagat). The material cause of pure creation is Mahamaya (Bindu or Vidya) while that of defiled creation is Maya or Asuddha Bindu. Both Mahamaya and Maya are Jada (inert) and different from the Svarupa Sakti which is the essence of the Lord. The Lord Himself is omnipotent, omnipresent and omniscient. Siva is not just one of the Trimurtis of the Puranas. He is the source from which the Trimurtis emanate. He is both immanent and transcendent. He is called Visvarupa and Visvadhika — universal in form and beyond the universe. Again, He is Sarupa and Arupa, with form and without form. This is symbolized by the Linga which is a formless form. He is said to be Ashtamurti — embodied as the five elements, the sun, the moon and man. He has eight qualities — innocence, purity, self-knowledge, omniscience, freedom from Malas or stains, benevolence, omnipotence and bliss. He is said to be Nirguna, not in the sense of having no quality, but in the sense that he is not tainted by the Gunas of Prakriti. He has five functions — Pancha kritya — creation (Srishti), preservation (Sthiti), destruction (Samhara), obscuration (Tirodhana), and liberation (Anugraha). Unlike Maha Vishnu, Siva does not take Avataras. But how can He keep away when devotees need Him? So, He assumes ad hoc embodiments, 'plays' with the devotees for a while, and then vanishes.

The individual soul in the Siddhanta is called Pasu, because like cattle he is bound to the world by the rope of Avidya. The soul is all-pervading, eternal and a conscious agent capable of enjoyment (iccha-jnana-kriya yuktah). He is distinct from the gross and subtle bodies he inhabits. Bound souls suffer because they mistake themselves to be finite, limited in thought, will and action; but when liberated they get restored to their original nature.

The Pasas or fetters that bind the Pasu, are of three types. They are called Malas or stains — Anava Mala, Karma Mala and Maya Mala. The Anava Mala corresponds to the original sin or Mula-avidya. It is the same in all and is beginningless. Anava means of the nature of Anu or atom. The reference is not to size but to finiteness. The soul feels confined and limited to the body and the sense organs. The Anava Mala makes the Jiva ignorant of his real glory and power. Under the influence of Anava, the soul indulges in all manner of actions, acquires merits and demerits and becomes subject to birth and death. This is Karma Mala. It causes the union of the conscious and unconscious. The third Mala is due to Maya, the material cause. It gives the soul the means and objects of enjoyment. Through spiritual disciplines and love of God the Maya Mala, and Karma Mala can be effaced. But Anava mala can be removed only by the grace of God. According to the Malas lingering, the souls are divided into three kinds. The Sakalas have all the three Malas. The Pralayakalas have got rid of Maya Mala, but are subject to Karma and Anava; while the Vijnanakalas, who are the highest evolved, have only Anava Mala, from which they can get free only through total surrender to the Lord and His grace. The wind of God's grace, as Sri Ramakrishna observes, is always blowing, only we have to be sensitive and avail ourselves of it.

When all the Malas are removed, the Jiva becomes one with Siva. He becomes co-pervasive with Siva and shares all His glory and greatness. He has not lost his individuality, but because of the overwhelming bliss, he is not aware of it. Meikantar compares this to salt dissoved in water. But the Pancha Kritya belongs only to the Lord, the Mukta Jiva is not empowered for it. What is stressed is that when the Jiva identifies itself with matter, it becomes bound, and when it identifies itself with Siva it becomes Mukta.

Four approaches to the Ultimate are blue-printed in the Siddhanta. The first is Charya which involves doing service in the shrines like cleaning the premises, gathering flowers for worship etc. This is Dasa Marga, the path of the servitor. It leads to Salokya Mukti, i.e., the devotee abides in the sphere of the Lord. The second path is called Kriya. It consists of ritualistic worship. It is termed Satputra Marga, the path of the Lord's child. It leads to Samipya mukti — the devotee is close to the Lord. The third approach is that of Yoga, calling for contemplation. This is called Sakha marga, the path of the Lord's friend. It leads to Sarupya Mukti. The devotee attains the form and the various insignia of the Lord. These three approaches are considered preliminary. They are the rungs in the ladder which lead to Jnana or direct realization. It is called Sanmarga and culminates in Sayujya Mukti, complete union with the Lord. But, as we have already mentioned, the individuality is not lost. The Siddhanta does not say "There are not two", but it asserts "They are not two"

Place of Tirumantiram in Saiva Siddhanta:

Tirumantiram provides many of the Mahavakyas of Saivism. The most sublime statement is 'Anbe Sivam' 'God is Love'. In fact all the Nayanmars are living commentaries on this statement. Many of them are singer-saints inebriated with Siva Bhakti. They had no other concern in life except adoration of the Lord and service of His servitors. It was this over-mastering devotion to the Lord that expressed itself in the various inspiring deeds they performed. When we read the hymns spontaneously pouring out of their sacred lips, we can feel how their burning love of the Lord makes every word come out like a thunderbolt. Love of the Lord implies for the Nayanmars Love of all the devotees. This Tirumular stressed by the declaration, "Yan petra Inbam Peruka Ivvaiyakam" — "May this world share the bliss that I have had,". The devotee does not believe in enjoying even the Lord's grace exclusively by himself. Bliss shared is bliss multiplied. A third dictum which illumines the essence of true religion is 'Ontre kulamum Oruvane Devanum' - The whole mankind is one family and the Lord we worship is only one. This shows how catholic was the vision of the Nayanmars. Tirumular goes on to declare "Udampule Uthaman Koil Kondanentu Udambinai Yanirundu Ompukintrene.' Our body is the Temple of the Lord. So it is not to be despised but taken care of as a sacred trust. How keen and transcendent Tirumular's insight was can be seen from the verse:

Marathai Maraithathu mamatha yanai
marathin maraintathu mamatha yanai
parathai maraithathu parmutharputham
parathin marainthathu parmutharputhame.

—A child looks at a toy elephant carved from wood. It sees only the elephant and is not aware of the wood. A carpenter, on the other hand, looks at the quality of the wood and is not bothered about the figure carved. Similarly, we ignorant children are aware only of the world constituted of the five elements and not of the Lord who has manifested as the world. A Jnani, on the other hand, sees only God in everything, living and non-living. He is not aware of the material world as we see it. For the devotee of Siva everything is pervaded by Siva. Tirumular thus exemplifies Sanmarga, the path of Gnosis.

A bird's eye view of Tirumantiram:

I *PROLOGUE*

The literary convention in India is that in every treatise there should be an introductory section in praise of the subject matter of the treatise, who in this text happens to be Siva, the Lord of the Universe. Accordingly, his Payiram, or Prologue, describes the powers, the acts of grace, the immanence and transcendence and various other aspects of the Lord, in verses brimming with Bhakti. To some extent, the material is drawn from the Puranas, but essentially, it is a spontaneous outpouring of the Soul in the presence of the majesty and the grandeur of the omnipotence, omniscience and omni-presence of the Lord. It is theology couched in exquisite poetic lines.

The first verse (1) is capable of being interpreted in many ways, and in the items listed as one to seven are encapsulated many concepts which, centuries later, find their way as fundamental concepts in Saiva Siddhanta. Such is also the case with many of the phrases in the verses of the Prologue. What is particularly to be noticed is the way that monotheism slides imperceptibly into dualism, in this very first verse. It is the characteristic of Saiva Siddhanta to term the active arm of the monotheistic divine as Grace (Karuna).

In verse 9, we find Siva being described as "Nandi", Bull (corresponding to Vrsabha of the Vedas), which in iconography appears as the Vahana of Siva. Tirumular, like most Saivites, is very much attached to this designation. Siva is in verse 22 said to be the "Lord of Maya-land that has its rise in the mind", which makes Maya a Principle of Illusion.

Verse 49 introduces the concept of "Pasu-Pasa", two of the three principles (the third being "Pati",) which constitute the essence of the Pasupata system.

In sections 2 and 3 of the Prologue are discussed respectively the nature and import of the Vedas and the Agamas, the two systems of religious modes in Hinduism.

Sections 4 deals with the important role of Gurus, termed Natha here.

In verse 79, while giving us in section 5, some insight into biographical details of his life, Tirumular mentions that he conducted his Tapas under a Bodhi tree in Avaduthurai. As against this, we have in verses 337 and 338 of Tantra Two an eulogium on Agastya, implying his role as the Leader who was the pioneer in bringing down Saivism from the North, and consequently being the Supreme Guru of all Tamil Saivites, including Tirumular himself. As is well-known, the location of the Agastya monastery in ancient times was deemed to be the Podigai Hills on the southern-most border of Tamil and Kerala lands. Also, the Tamil Siddhars, of whom Tirumular is the acknowledged chief, are by nature lovers of forests, from where they would only occasionally sally into inhabited territory.

Verse 90 of section 5 introduces us to the terms, "Jneya, Jnana, Jnathru, Maya, Paryaya, Mamaya, Siva and Agochara Veeya," which are some of the terms which play an important part in Tamil Saiva Siddhanta, and whose significance the Tirumantiram itself expounds, though not fully, at some length in later verses.

In two verses of section 8 of the Payiram, some details are given of the spiritual hierarchy and of the Mutts (Monasteries) established by them. They are said to be seven, a number often resorted to in respect of various aspects of Agamas and Tantras from the days of the Atharva Veda. It is not, however, possible to determine the location of the seven mutts referred to by Mular in this section, nor do we know anything more about the disciples except those Mular mentions here.

Verse 111 informs us that the ONE has become MANY, that is to say, the Saivite theology is both monistic (like Sankara's Advaita,) and is also pluralistic (like Madhva's Dvaita).

In verse 112, the Lord, Sadasiva, appears as the Unmoved Mover, One part of Him is in heaven, and the other abides on earth.

II *TANTRA ONE*

From this Tantra, Tirumular launches out in full force on Saivite philosophy, mostly in the form of theology. The two approaches are so completely inter-mixed that it is practically impossible to separate purely metaphysical (ontological and epistemological) matter from the corresponding theological view points. However, mostly it is a case of the name of Siva being super-imposed parenthetically as the hidden power-entity on what would appear to be purely secular concepts. Since the large bulk of the verses are merely repetitive, it is proposed to direct attention only to what are of metaphysical (philsophical) importance.

The concept of Grace, a theological concept, pervades practically the whole of the text and it would be tedious to refer to it in comments upon each and every verse.

Verse 115, initiates the discussion on the three basic terms, "Pati, Pasu and Pasa"

Verse 119 is an important metaphysical concept. The essential aspect common to both Siva and Jiva is said to be "consciousness", the former being the "higher" and the latter, the "lower", as in Sankara's Vedanta. The "Cit-Acit" is also another aspect of this same concept, the "Acit" (the ignorance of the Jiva) having to be broken asunder before merging in the Cit (the Self-Knowledge of Siva).

Verse 135 starts the discussion, which is elaborated in detail in later verses, about the five senses (sight, sound, touch, smell and taste) which create the Acit that stands barred from Cit.

It is, as verses 121 et seq. mention, the sundering of this bondage in the Turiya state (a term to be explained in later verses) which leads to the Jivan-mukta state of the Siva yogin or the Siddha.

Verses 124 to 129 tell us what the nature of Siva-Siddhas is and how many "Tattvas" there are which they have to ascend to reach that state. First, verse 125 tells us that Saiva Siddhanta recognises 36 "Tattvas", (Tattvas being of the nature of categories that go to make up the manifested world). The various systems of Indian philosophy differ amongst themselves in the number of Tattvas recognised by them.

Verse 129 implies that the Ultimate (here Siva) is of the nature of Cosmic Space (Ether, Akasa or Void), and the essence of Jiva lies in the self-same Space in microcosmic condition.

The remaining sections 3 to 24 (verses 168 to 336), of this Tantra are in the nature of the Agamic "carya" preparing the novice for the higher stages of the path to Moksha. But in the midst of the commonplace advice are to be found some special gems.

The condemnation of Vama Tantra forms of Worship in verses 326 and 327 is to be specially noticed.

III *TANTRA TWO*

The two verses 337 and 338 which speak of Agastya do not appear, on a first consideration, to have anything to do with the other material in the text, but a more careful examination indicates the importance of the Agastyan cult to the founding of the Tamil Saiva Siddhanta system.

Verses 339 to 380 are in the nature of theology whose foundation lies in Puranic myths, especially the Linga Purana. From 381 to 450 onwards, however, the verses describe what are essentially pure, that is non-theological, speculations, but their theological nature is never over-looked, and is ensured by verses which here and there bring in the name of Siva, and the connected Puranic myths.

Siva's activities are by his devotees classified under five heads, and these appear in verses 381 to 450. These are Creation (381 to 410), Sustenance (411 to 420), Destruction (421 to 430), Obstruction, "Tirodhana" (431-440), and Pervasion or Salvation (441 to 450).

The verses that describe Creation (381-410) explain the following terms that are encountered in Tamil Saiva Siddhanta Philosophy. There are: Paraparam, Consciousness, Paraparai, Param, Parai, Nada (381), Bindu, Siva, Sakti, Jnana, Kriya, Iccha (382), Maya (383), Mana Sakti (the Substratum of Matter), the Five elements (385), the source of Creation (Sadasiva) (386), and Five Elements (Fire, Water, Light, Sound, and Earth (388). Thereafter, the text goes on to describe the process and nature of creation thus: (1) Creation is an Act of Pure Consciousness by the Primal One (390), (2) He is the First Cause (391), (3) (the term adopted is "dayabharan" which is synonymous with "one who is full of Karuna", (4) The Lord animates the Body (394), (5) Creation is the Play of He-She (396), (6) The Five Gods were born of Anava Sakti when united with Bindu, (7) Creation was the Play of the Ultimate, Maya being born of the three Mayas (Suddha, Asuddha, and Prakriti), the Bindu itself having been born of Nada, and Nada of Parai, and all this in the play of Parasiva, the Ultimate (399), (8) The Five Gods were born to perform the Five Duties, such as Creation, Preservation, etc. (400), (9) It is Maya Sakti that is born of Bindu who Performs the Five Acts (401), the Five Names of Maya Sakti being Manonmani, Mangali, Varani, Arani, Mohini and Poorani, in which Cause-Effect are conjoined and She remains as Consciousness beyond Consciousness (402), (10) He pervades All Creation (409) as Life Within, and finally (11) the Varieties of Creation, the Sun, Moon, Agni, etc. (410).

Nandi supports everything in the World (411-420).

His destructive aspects are described in 421-430. These are, it appears, 4 Forms of death: daily death, fated death, Pure death and Redeemed death (425-428). The beginning and the End of all things is Void (429),.

The Lord is the creator of mysteries (431-440).

The Lord pervades everything (450). He created all, Himself being the Param Uncreated (446).

Verses 451 to 491 explain how the body is created, and the principle of life placed within it.

The Tattvas are 25 (454) that make up the Purusha within the body. They are grouped in sets of five (455), the elements five, the tanmatras five, the sense organs five, the gross sense organs five, and the subtle organs five, being the four congnising organs, Mind, Intellect, will and Egoity, and the Centre of Forehead. The role of the 3 gunas in the body is described (458). In the quiescent (Turiya) state in the womb, Maya confers Consciousness and the eight, Desire and the rest, are evolved (460). Then 35 Tattvas are introduced into the body by the Lord (467) (compare 454). There are six Adharas (469), and the Divine Jnana is in the cranium (470).

Verses 492 to 500 describe the categories of the JIVA. JIVA is originally in pure Kevala state in Turiya, when Maya envelopes him and the Lord enters into him (492). There are 3 categories forming 10 classes, Vignanars 4, Prayakalas, 3, and Sakalars 3 (493). The 4 classes of Vignanars, viz., Kevala state, 8 Vidyeswaras, and 7 Gross Mantra Nayakas, all devoid of Egoity Impure. The three classes of Pralayakala's, are Mukti-attained malas (Egoity and Karma) bound, and 108 Rudras, all Sakalas with 3 malas (495). The 3 classes of Sakalas are those who have attained Siddhis, and Muktis respectively and those who have attained neither, all powerless to conquer Malas (496). There are 5 malas hard to get rid of (497). There are 9 gradations of Jivas, Vijnanakalas (3 classes), those in quiescent Anava State (3 classes) and Sakalas (3 classes) (498). The way for Sakalas and Jivas to attain Siva is described in 499.

The nature of Worthy and Unworthy Souls is described in 501 to 508.

The Human Body has within itself Holy Water and is also the Holy Temple (509-519). Consequently, Worship (Kriya) can be performed internally.

Kriya, Worship, is to be performed to the Downward Looking Face of Siva, "Adhomukha" (520-525). This, the 6th face of Siva, is an innovation of Tirumular, and is drawn in the image of Avalokitesvara (also meaning Downward-looking) who in Mahayana Buddhism is the One of Supreme Compassion even as Adhomukha of Siva is, having consumed poison out of compassion for the Devas at the time of Amritamathana.

Verses 526-548 are in the nature of Cariya advice.

IV *TANTRA THREE*

Verses 549 to 631 describe how Ashtanga Yoga is to be performed, and verses 632 to 639 tell us what are the Fruits of the Yoga. Similarly, in verses 640 to 740 are to be found descriptions of the Eight Great Siddhis and the manner of their operation. The Sadhaka's state in Samadhi, the action of Kundalini turning the Body into a Temple of Siva, the attainment of Immortality through Samadhi Yoga, and such other achievements by Yoga practice and Kaya Siddhi are all described.

The varieties of relationships between Time and Yoga are spelt out in detail in 741 to 798.

Then come discourses on special types of Yoga.

First, verses 799 to 824 describe Kecari Yoga, the Supreme state of Yogic Bliss and the highest achievement in Yoga discipline.

Next, we have in verses 825 to 844, the Paryanga Yoga, the literal meaning of the term being "Bedside Yoga". The Sanskrit terminology is Vamacara or the Left-handed Yoga. Here, sexual techiniques and practices are adopted for practising yoga. Puritanical purdery bars such practices, but there is reason to believe that it is wide-spread and much resorted to in secrecy.

Verses 845-850, which advocate the imbibing of urine as a form of medical therapeutics, give us a glimpse of Siddha medical practices.

Chandra Yoga as another type of special Yoga for achieveing immortality is the subject matter of 851-883.

Tirumular discusses Yoga more fully, completely and with greater frankness than Patanjali. He cannot be said to have borrowed his ideas from Patanjali. Quite obviously, Tirumular goes the full length of Yoga as known in his time, whereas Patanjali stops short of it.

V TANTRA FOUR

Tantra Four is concerned mainly with Mantras and Yantras (Mandalas).

Verses 884 to 913 refer mostly to "Ajapa", the silent mantras (Ajapas), Aum and Sivayanama. They mention also the Dance of Siva (902 & 913) and the "Tiru Ambala Chakra" (904). This latter is a Yantra, and the term "Ambala" is a Tamilised form of Sanskrit "Ambaram", meaning "sky, atmosphere, ether, etc.", and is a synonym for "akasa", the Void that is, the Supreme. Hence, this is a most important Mandala, and it may be noted that the "25 squares" mentioned in 904 has its counterpart in the 25 Tattvas of the Saiva Siddhanta.

Verses 914 to 1002 are devoted entirely to the Ambala Chakra and to mysticism of the letters of the alphabet, as well as to the Sivayanama and Aum mantras. The Panchakshara comes in 908, and we have in (987) the six letter mantra "Om Namasivaya". The 51 letters of 924 are of the Sanskrit Language. These mantras and yantras give, it is said, the vision of Siva's Dance (vide 944).

Kriya (of Agama) is the subject matter of verses 1003 to 1004. The Puja form (1003, for example) is the Kriya dealt with here, and it is connected with the Bija mantras.

The Kriya of section 4 (verses 1015 to 1074) does not refer to the external Vedic sacrificial system, but the inner Tapasic and Tantric form.

Section 5 (verses 1045 to 1074) establishes the role of Sakti in Tantra as Tiripurai. In 1063, the two namely Siva and Sakti are conjoined as Siva-Sakti, and in 1070, she is said to pervade the sixteen Kalas, and to be the Grace within Nada and Nadanta.

Verses 1075 to 1124 of Section 6 are devoted to the Bhairavi Mantra, the Mantra of Sakti, which is the natural sequence to the previous section.

The various roles of Sakti in Tantra, as Purna Sakti, are enumerated (parasakti) in verses 1125 to 1144. We are told of the Lotuses of Sakti. She was One with Siva in the Primal Act of Creation(1137).

Section 8 (verses 1155 to 1254) continues with the subject of Sakti now in the role of "Support-Supported", where she is the Support of the Adharas (Tantric). She is Kriya Sakti, Bhoga Sakti, and Parasakti (1170).

In Siva-Sakti Union, Maya, Bindu and Nada arise. 1194 describes Sakti's attributes. "She is the Vine from Visuddha to Sahasrara" (1196), "She Stood Beyond Tattvas Thirty-Six" (1218), etc.

The subject of Tantric Chakras is continued in Section 9 (1255 to 1290), 10 (1291 to 1296), 11 (1297 to 1306), 12 (1307 to 1318), and 13 (1319 to 1416). They deal respectively with Eroli Chakram (Chakra of Radiant Light), Bhairavi Chakra, Sambhavi Chakra, Bhuvanapathi Chakra, and Navakkari Chakra of 9 Rounds, [the term "Navakkari" (Navakshari) meaning nine aksharas or bija mantras]. The central point in these sections is to relate the concerned Yantra (or Mandala) with the related Bija mantra. In 1269, et seq., we find astrological concepts also linked with these yantras. The purpose of the whole is the obtaining of Siddhis, especially the highest of them, namely Samadhi. The relative Bija mantra, namely Srim, Klim, Hrim, etc., are also given.

IV *TANTRA FIVE*

This Tantra provides a guidance to the attainment to Saiva Siddhanta. The first 4 sections of the Fifth Tantra (verses 1419 to 1442) deal with the nature of Saiva Siddhanta or Suddha Saivam as verses 1419 and 1420 term it. The last verse (1420) describes the characteristics of those who "tread the path of Suddha Saivam........hearts intent on Eternal Para, transcending Worlds of Pure and Impure Maya, where Pure Intelligence consorts not with base Ignorance, and the lines that divide Real, Unreal and Real-Unreal which are discerned sharp", 1420). 1421 says Suddha Saivam is Saiva Siddhanta, and it goes on to say that only after acquiring all knowledge (Jnana), practising all aspects of Yoga, passing into the World of Formless Sound, and getting rid of impurities can one envision the Supreme, the self-created and be a true Saiva Siddhantin. 1422 adds that Saiva Siddhanta is Vedanta, and that in the Unwavering Vision, one comprehends the Tattvas of elemental matter to the finite end of Jnana (Bhodanta) to attain perfection in Nadanta and become ardent seekers of Jnānna.

Chariya, Kriya, Yoga and Jnana are said to be the four main stages in the path to Saiva Siddhanta (1423 to 1426). This is Agama doctrine.

The Jnana Path is San Marga Saivam (1427-1437) and the end of Siddhanta is Union with Siva (1437).

It is through Section 4 (verses 1438 to 1442) that we are taught the true lessons of Saiva Siddhanta, and here it is Siva, not Brahman (unlike 1435), who is the final goal. (There is a world of difference between Brahman of Sankara's Vedanta and of Saiva Siddhanta).

The four stages of Chariya, Kriya, Yoga and Jnana are the subject of 1443 to 1506. It is interesting to note the emphasis placed on Bhakti as a Kriya in 1453 and 1454. The Path of knowledge is Sanmarga (1477 to 1487), and it leads to the Svarupa State (1486). The Path of Yoga is Sakhamarga (1488 to 1494), and the Path of Kriya (to which Chariya also leads, 1501) is Satputra Marga (1495 to 1501), as also Dasamarga, the Path of Devotion (1502 to 1506).

Verse 1507 says that there are 4 stages of attainment (in Saiva Siddhanta), namely, Saloka, Samipa, Sarupa, and Sayujya, and the starting point is Chariya. They stand respectively for God's World, God's proximity, Gods Form, and Being One with God. (1507 to 1513). Grace is an essential aid for this (1514 to 1529); it illumines (1517) and descends either at a low pace (1518 to 1522) or rapidly (1523 to 1526) or very rapidly (1527 to 1529).

It is not an unusal practice in Indian Philosophical systems to refute other systems as a concomitant step to establishing the presumed true faith. It is in accordance with this practice that the Tirumantiram criticising six other systems (1530 to 1549), refutes their arguments (1550 to 1556) before proceeding to establish the truth of its own inner Faith (1557 to 1572).

VIII *TANTRA SIX*

Verses 1573 to 1604 are in praise of the Siva Guru, which is the summit of the Saiva Siddhantin's upward journey. It is the ultimate aim of the Jnana stage and, therefore, constitutes the climax of the discussions of the previous (5th) Tantra.

Verses 1605 to 1613 establish the unity of the Knower, the knowledge and the object of the knowledge which is achieved in Siva, the Supreme.

Verses 1614 to 1632 talk of Renunciation and Tapas, which also provide a path to the Ultimate, but which were not touched upon earlier when discussing the various Margas. Tapas in a way is perhaps to be considered an extra-ordinary path in Saiva Siddhanta.

Verses 1633 to 1703 discuss the correct way of practising Tapas, and the misuses to which it is sometimes put. That even in Tapas, the Lord's Grace is indispensible is the message of verses 1645 to 1654. The meaning of the Holy Ashes (Vibhuti) is brought out in 1655 to 1667.

Finally, in section 14, verses 1690 to 1703, indicate the characteristics of the "Fit" Disciple, that is one who is on the right path. Verse 1702 also talks of the "Siddhanta-Vedanta" way.

VIII *TANTRA SEVEN*

This Tantra is in the main concerned with aspects of Yoga and Kriya, but in common with other parts of the text, there are frequent but short divergences from the main topic.

In verses 1704 to 1711, the Adharas (of Yoga and Tantra) are dealt with under the symbolism of the Lotus, a much favoured symbol in Hinduism.

Another symbolic object, namely the Linga, in its various characteristics of Cosmic, Microcosmic (Pinda), Sadasiva, Atma, Jnana and Siva is the subject of discourse in verses 1712 to 1777. The most important point to be noted in these verses is the nature of "Sadasiva" as distinct from Siva. Verses 1713, 1715, 1716, 1723, 1728, 1730, 1731, 1734, 1735 to 1744, 1746 to 1748 and 1764 to 1768 are the more important of the verses which deal with Sadasiva. It appears that Tirumular distinguishes between Sadasiva and Siva, treating the former as the Ultimate, Formless (and beyond Sound) Power, and the latter as being not free of these attributes. Siva has to be the object of Union. This is a sort of distinction which resembles, but is not exactly the same as, the Saguna and Nirguna Brahman of the Vedanta, with its Higher and Lower knowledge. It does not necessarily follow that there has been borrowing of ideas of one from the other. Various ways of looking at things seem to have been floating about in the polemics of those times. Sakti also plays an important role in these verses. As is to be expected, She merges in Sadasiva, but remains as separate entity, but all the same closely united with Siva. At the micro-cosmic level, Sadasiva is seated in Sahasrara (1746).

There are some very important verses dispersed throughout sections 2 to 7 which require special individual attention as throwing much light on Tirumular's metaphysics, epistemology and theology. In 1713, Sakti is found to be the first manifestation of Sadasiva, and in 1714, the 36 Tattvas come next as well as the Six Adhvas of the Agamas. Sadasiva is the Light of the Life of all the Devas (1716); He pervades all Space (Akasa) according to 1723; He is the Lord of the sense gates of the body; He has five forms (1730), whose Five Colours are described in 1735; Sakti first evolves from Him (1732) and then she in turn evolves the Six Vedangas, the Four Vedas, the Four Agamic Paths (commencing with Chariya), and finally the "Saiva Truth" (by which is probably meant Siva Himself) (1733). Proceeding further are evolved from Sakti, the Avastas, the Rasis (!), the Tattvas and the Truth Supreme (1734); Sakti is the Kinetic and Siva the Potential Aspect of God (1737); the Five Saktis, namely Jnana, Para, Adi, Iccha and Kriya are seated in Sadasiva (1744) who in turn is seated in Sahasrara (1746). He is in the Body (1747 and 1748); Sadasiva is Form-Formless (1764); all creation is Siva-Sakti play (1772); Siva is Immanent and Transcendent (1733), and the only way of knowing Him is Worship as One Being (1744-1775), but the Tantric path of rousing Kundalini is also recommended in 1777.

Section 8 (1778 to 1791) places Siva as the first Guru in the Sampradaya, union with whom is the Supreme objective of Kriya Worship.

Section 9 and 10 (verses 1792 to 1822) are all about the Lord's Grace, a most important tenet of Saiva Siddhanta.

From verses 1723 to 1867 (sections 11 to 14), the importance of Kriya Puja to Siva, Guru and Mahesvara (Devotees) is emphasized.

Sections 14 to 16 (verses 1868 to 1891) concern themselves with Holy Men and the hospitablity to be extended to them, an act which has both Chariya and Kriya characteristics.

From section 17 to Section 19 (verses 1892 to 1922), concepts pertaining to Kundalini Yoga make their appearance. First of all, we are told what Mudras are and how they are to be practised (1892 to 1901). This is a matter which is very rarely revealed in other Tantric literature. Verses 1902 to 1922 prescribe the special procedures to be adopted in performing Samadhi rituals for a fully accomplished Siddha.

Verses 1923 to 1974 (Section 20 and 21) belong to that branch of Tantra, known as Vamacara. Handling a subject such as this in practice or theory is a very onerous task. Both ways, it advocates a way of life considered, under a misunderstanding of the purpose of the teaching by non-practitioners on all counts, as immoral and depraved. Nevertheless, it is practised as a tantric ritual by some sects. The Tirumantiram does no more than describe the ritual and the consequences to be expected of it with due warning as to the evils arising from making it a licentious act. Verses 2023 to 2043 which come later prescribe the techiniques to be adopted for such control. Verses 2044 to 2121 describe in great detail the Gurus and the types of instructions imparted by them which on the one hand lead to good results, and on the other to evil.

The above discussion has skipped sections 22 to 31 (verses 1975 to 2022), whose subject matter is philosophical and, therefore, not related to the empiricisms of the sections discussed there. The central point of these verses, namely 1975 to 2022 is contained in verses 1976 and 1978, which clearly state that the "Sun is the Primal Energy", which makes it Sakti in short. It is interesting to note Tirumular referring (1976) to the Sun in this capacity of the source Energy as Vishnu.

As Primal energy whose acquisition and control is the objective of all Tantras, the Sun's role in Tantric categories, such as the Tattvas, Chakras, Kalas, Adharas, etc., and his path inside the human body in verses 1978 to 1987 become clear. The relationship between the Sun and the Moon philosophically conceived is described in 1988 to 1992. From this, it is natural to view the Sun as the giver of Jnana and as manifested Power of Sadasiva (1993 to 2004). Verses 2002 to 2004 signify this aspect when they call the Sun, "Sivaditya", a term that recalls the word Aditya, born of Aditi, as related in the Rg Veda.

From 2005 to 2022, some aspects of the relationship between Siva and Jiva are considered. They are two swans (2006); the Lord is the Purusha, who, acting on Sakti, Jnana, and Kriya, makes Tattvas, Maya and Vaikhari all illusory

(2007); He is an Atom-within-Atom (2008); His Dance destroys all Pasas (2009); and He and Jiva, in the Ultimate, commingle and stand as one (2010).

Jiva as Soul (2011 to 2014) and as Pasu (2015 and 2016) are next dealt with.

The Lord is the Giver of Jnana, Light (Bodha), to the Jiva (2017 to 2022), in the form of Grace, and as such stands beyond the thirtysix Tattvas (2020).

Section 37 (verses 2084 to 2101) is captioned "In Compassion for Men's Evil Lot" referring undoubtedly to the Lord's Grace. Such Supreme compasion is not of Vedic provenance, and as a concept, its origin must be traced to other influences.

IX *TANTRA EIGHT*

The nature of knowledge at various levels is the subject matter of this Tantra.

The first two sections (verses 2122 to 2141) of this Tantra deal with the nature of the human body, its essential ingredients and its experience in various states. In terms of verse 2123, there are two bodies, the gross and the substle (Sukshma, Soul). The former has 8 constituents, viz., sound, touch, shape, taste and smell, Buddhi (Intellect), Man (Mind and Ahankara (Egoity), and subtle Puriashta. There are 5 Indriyas, (External Sense Organs) and three Karanas (Internal Sense Organs) (2124). There are 24 Tattvas (2126 and 2127); Jiva has five (5) experiences (Avastas), viz., Jagra, Swapna, Sushupti, Turiya and Turiyatita (2128); there are 6 Adharas, 9 Orifices and 18 Kalas (2129).

The Gross, Subtle and Causal bodies merge in Para (2130); Jiva Incarnates in many bodies (reincarnations) (2131 and 2133).

Siva is the ground (Dhanu) of Jnani's body, which is Siva's body; Yogi's body is Nada and Bindu; and the Mauni's Body is Mukti beyond SPACES Three.

Body substrates of Jivas are in Three Stages of Evolution. Anava (Egoity) is the (Dharma) ground of Vijnanis, Maya of Pralayakalas and Karma of Sakalas. Siva is the ground of Jnanas Three.

In the 4 states of Jiva Awareness (Avasthas), the position of the Tattvas varies (2142).

The Instruments of Experience are:

a) Ten Indriyas (5 sensory organs and 5 motor organs); b) Ten Tanmatras (subtle potent elements of Indriyas), c) Ten Vayus (winds), d) Four Antahkaranas (inner seats of thought), and e) Purusha, the Experiencing Jiva (2144). There are 5 elements with the Body, viz., a) Earth of Golden colour, b) White Water, c) Red Fire, d) dark Wind, and e) Smoky Space (2415).

There are 96 Tattvas in all, (2146). In working state, the Jiva is with 24 Tatvas (2147). There are 16 Kalas (2150). Out of the 5 elements are born the 5 senses (2152).

In Deep Sleep are 3 Tattvas a) Chitta (Will), b) Prana (Vital breath), and c) Sentience of Self (2156).

In Turiya or 4th state, he remains in Mauna (Silence) (2157).

In Turiyatita, Jiva is by Aum pervaded with the Five Senses withdrawn (2158).

Consciousness begins with Egoity (2162), and Maya awakens Soul from Primordial (Kevala) Slumber (2163).

Section 4 (2167 to 2163) deals with "*Mid-Jagrat-Avasta*" a) In the Waking State, Maya is Tirodai, b) In the Dream State, She is Mamaya (Impure); c) In the state of Deep Sleep, She is Kamya (of Self-delusion): and d) In Turiya-Maya (Pure) (2167).

In Turiya, Kalas and Raga are roused by Maya (2169) God placed 25 Tattvas for Jiva (2171).

Vedanta reckons Tattvas differently as 28 (2172).

24 Tattvas + Purusha = 25 Tattvas.

But in Vedanta,

25+Purusha+Void (Vyoma) + Para=28 (2172).

By Breath Control Tattvas subside within Body (2178) and Malas (5) are got rid of (2177).

The Malas are 5; for Brahma (5) (Anava (Egoity) and the rest, that is, Maya, Karma, Mayeyam and Tirodayi,

b) For Vishnu - 4 (Mayeyam absent),

c) For Rudra 3 (Mayeyam and Tirodayi excepted),

d) Two for Mahesa, (Only Anava and Karma); and

e) One alone (Anava) for Sadasiva.

Section 5 deals with Adhvas (higher Steps).

(2184) Tattvas - 36;
Mantras - 7 Crores;
Varnas (letter) - 51;
Bhuvanas - 224;
Padas Primal - 81
Kalas - 5

(2186) The 5th State of Turiyatita - They watch the Dance of the Lord and become Siva by the Grace - Fruit of Siva.

In the five (5) states of Awareness, the following Limitations of Awareness are suffered by the Jiva:

1. In Turiyatita State -Consciousness of Self

2. In Turiya State -Consciousness of Self through spoken word comprehended still burns;

3. In the Sushupti State -Maya binds the Jiva, and the Desire-Potency afterwards to speak exists;

4. In the Waking State and the Dream State experiences in diverse ways exist.

(2195 to 2212)

According to 2213, Mala contamination is the Root of All Evil. Turiya in Turiya is Para Turiya; Beyond is Turiyatita (2225).

Section 6 to 42 (verses 2187 to 2648) are full of metaphysical and theological speculations and are, therefore, of very great importance.

It is Bindu Power which permeates the Tattvas (2187). Paraparam evolves as Siva, Sakti, Sadasiva (!), Isa Pure, Vidya Tattvas, Bodha, Kalas, Time, Niyati, and Mamaya (2190). Jiva ascends through Purusha, Mahamaya, Niyati, knowledge (Bodha), Time (kala), Kalas, Ragas, Pure Vidya, Maheswara, Sadasivam, Sakti and Siva to reach Paraparam (2191). Three Malas (Impurities) plague the Jiva; they are Anava (Egoity), Maya (Ignorance), and Kama (Action). (2192). Jiva is a prey to Tattvas and Pasa (2194).

Section 7 (verses 2227 to 2268) describes the Kevala, Sakala, Suddha states.

He who congnises the Self is in Suddha state; he who is not is in Kevala, he who cognises in distracting differences is in Sakala. They respectively conjoin in Sat (Real), Asat (Unreal) and Sat-Asat (Real-Unreal) states. This concept is further elaborated in verses 2233 to 2265.

Verse 2266 states that beyond Turiyatita lies Void and explains how this is so.

Section 8 (verses 2269 to 2295) deals with Para-Avastha, that is experience at the highest level.

The Lord is the Para (2269), Saktis are Dynamic aspects of Static Parapara; they are Para, Chit and Iccha, Jnana, and Kriya Saktis (2270). Beyond Tattvas is Divine Bliss (2271); Beyond Turiya is Turiya-Turiya or Para Turiya and Para-atita Turiya is further Beyond (2273). From Turiya to Turiyatit (2276). Beyond Four states in Turiya is Para Turiya (2281). End of Para Turiya is Siva Turiya (2282).

Beyond the Ten Avastas in Jiva Turiya, Para Turiya and Siva Turiya is the Eleventh State of Consciousness of Para Nandi (Siva) (2284).

Further Beyond Para Siva State is Paramam (Brahman),, Paramparam and Para Maha Sivam (2285).

There are 9 Manifestations of Para Siva (2286).

True Knowledge and the Way of Self-Knowledge through Thought Process are discussed in 2287 and 2289.

Knowledge of Siva, Sakti and Jiva (Sivaya) constitues Liberation (2291).

Experiences in Pure Turiya, (2292) and Pure (Suddha) Experience and Supreme (Para) Experience are beyond Jiva Experiences (2293).

The State of Suddha Avasta (Pure Experience) is described in 2294, and in 2295 it is said that the Lordly Guru, the NATHA, guides the Soul in its journey.

Verses 2297 which talks of Space as God's Seat and 2298 which talks of Bliss beyond Tattvas repeat ideas already conveyed many times over in earlier verses.

Verse 2299 grades the Higher Experiences (Para Avasta) thus:

In the Fifth State (Jiva Turiyatita) is Ambrosia;
In the Seventh State (Para Turiya-Jagrat) is Bliss;
In the Ninth State (Para-Turiya-Sushupti) is Aum;
In the Eleventh State (Siva Turiya), Jiva Stands illumined; abiding there He attains the Divine Body.

(The doctrine is presented as if it is spoken by Siva to Parvati)

This is further elaborated in verses 2300 to 2303. According to them, "even in the Atita Turiya State, 6 Tattvas abide, namely, Purusha with Chitta, and 5 formless Tattvas; in the Sushupti State of Atita Turiya are the rest eight; only in the Eleventh State, nothing of Tattva remains", (meaning presumably that here in the 11th Turiyatita, it is all Void). Beyond Kevala, Sakala and Self-Realisation States is Suddha Avasta which is Pure and is Jagratita State (2303) and that is the Void State.

Section 13 (verses 2304 to 2354) describes the state of Pure Avasta which is totally devoid of Malas. The role of Grace in achieving this state, and the attainment of Pure Knowledge, Jnana, the actions of Siva who is seated within the Jiva, etc., are other topics of these verses. Verses 2326 pronounces a Maha Vakyam which conveys the message of the Jnana enjoyed in the Samadhi State. The topic of Jnana is further dwelt upon in verses 2355 to 2369.

Elsewhere Tirumular repeatedly talks of the Six Ends (antas), namely Vedanta, Siddhanta, Nadanta, Bodhanta, Yoganta and Kalanta in general terms. In Section 15 (verses 2370 to 2404), the subject is discussed at length, providing an insight into the various aspects of these 6 antas, which all lead in different ways to the complete elimination of Malas (2371). Verse 2372 is interesting in that it makes clear one of the fundamental differences between Vedanta and Siddhanta. "I am the Supreme One", Says the former, whereas the latter hold: "I shall become the Supreme One", that is to say, Siddhanta more clearly lays out a simple path for the soul's journey. Verses 2374 to 2377 deal with Nadanta, Bodhanta, Yoganta and Kalanta.

There are, says 2378, five other ways "dear to Siva". They are Mantra, Tantra, Serenity (Samadhi Yoga), Upadesa and Jnana and 2379 gives some details of these. They are to be found, in Agamas (also called Vedas), according to which Tantra preaches action, Mantra is in th mind and beyond the body and Upadesa is the teaching of Siva-Jnana. These details are supplemented in verses 2380 to 2382.

Verse 2382, discussing the Kalas, states that 'Unmanai Kala ends in the Sixteenth, and Unmanai Kalanta ends beyond the Seventeenth, the Kala being Nadanta'. Both Vedanta and Nadanta are revelations of the Lord, and their joint truth (there is no difference between them 2386) is the Truth of the Agamas, which lies beyond the Prakriti Maya (Impure) and Mamaya (Pure-Impure). 2397 which repeats 2384, refers to the Veda as general and Agama as special.

The Vedantic formula "Tat Tvam Asi" is played upon in different ways in 2387, 2392, 2404.

Verses 2403, 2404 and others are repetitions of earler verses on the subject of Vedanta and Siddhanta.

There are 5 verses in this section, which, while discussing the nature of the 6 antas, maintain that Vedanta - Siddhanta both of which teach the same doctrines are at the same time superior to the other four antas.

Section 14 (2405 to 2474) is concerned wholly whith the Pati-Pasu-Pasam concepts using different imageries. 2404 talks of Four Tapasvins. Who are they? We are not told.

Verses 2425 to 2434 talk of "Head-and-Foot-Knowledge", a curious caption for what is basically a reference both to Puranic stories (of the Lingam) (2427), and of Kundalini Yoga (2426). It also seems to imply the equal validity of the two paths of Jnana (Head) and Bhakti (service to the Lord's Feet.).

The number Three (3) dominates in various ways the concepts in verses 2435 to 2500. Lust, Anger, and Ignorance are the three main obstacles to Liberation (2435 to 2436). The three syllables of the mantra, "Tat Tvam Asi", provide the inspiration for viewing in various combinations the three states (Padas) of Realization (2437 to 2444). The Para state is also three in kind (2445 to 2451). This leads on to further descriptions of the Para state in verses 2452 to 2465. The Turiyas are also said (2466 to 2473) to be Three in nature, though elsewhere they are even counted upto eleven. The Muktis (2474 to 2477) are also three in kind, namely Atita Jiva-Mukti (Beyond Consciousness State), Upasanta Para-Mukti (Divine Peace), and Ananda Siva-Mukti (Divine Bliss). "All three are Svarupa Muktis, branching from Nadanta, where Pranava (AUM) is to be found" (2474).

The Divine Svarupa is also triplefold (2478 to 2483), and Kundalini Yoga leads one on to the highest of these (2484).

Led on by tantric exercise (2486) and with the help of Sakti Grace (2487), one reaches the Jiva, Para and Siva which are one in three places (2485).

The mantras "Tat-Tvam-Asi" (2488) and "Sivayanama" (2499) help the Soul's journey on to the Ultimate "Void" (2488 to 2500). The Saktis are Maya, Parai and Santhi (Kala) (2492); the Gunas are three, and so also are the Malas (Kamya, etc) (2494).

The phenomena of Cause and Consequential Experiences are rather briefly, too briefly, and cryptically, touched upon, in 2501 to 2505.

The State of Upasanta is the seed of Sakti, even as that of Siva Becoming is that of Siddhi, and of 'Adoration meek' is that of Bhakti and of Knowledge of the Primal One is Mukti (2505). The state and conditions of Upasantam are discussed in greater detail in 2506 to 2511.

Section 30, (verses 2512 to 2516) emphasizes the importance of Tapas (in silence) for attaining Siva-hood. This is Tantra whose importance under the symbolism of 8-petalled Lotus is further dwelt upon in 2527 to 2536.

The goal of Siddhanta is declared in 2545 to be to reach the Three Turiya states of nine Categories, as a climax to the discourse on the subject in verses 2537 to 25245.

The removal of Asuddham leading on to the attainment of Suddha-Saivism through Tantra-yoga forms the subject matter of section 33 (2546 to 2577).

Denial of the value of Mukti (2558 to 2565) is the sign of evil and folly in men (2562=and 2565), and the Void, Upasanta and Nadanta are the Lakshanatrayam of the opposite kind (2566 to 2567).

The Mahavakyam, "Tat-Tvam-Asi", provides guidance to attaining Para-hood (2568 to 2586). and helps to attain Viswa-Grasam or Total Absorption (2587 to 2594). That is the Vaymai, the Truth of the Universe (2595 to 2609).

Jnanis' ways are described in sections 39 to 42 (verses 2610 to 2634). They are able to destroy Karma (2610 to 2612), surrender Desires (2613 to 2622), be possessed of Bhakti (2623 to 2632), and then abide in Mukti. (263 to 2634).

The 14 verses 2635 to 2648 (section 43) sum up the whole process of Living, Knowing, attaining Moksha, etc., as a Divine Experimentation.

X *TANTRA NINE*

The mahin purpose of Tantra nine (2649-3045) seems to be to present a picture of the Divine Vision which is the ultimate aim of seeking Moksha. It is demonstrated in variouys ways. Guru, Monastery (the abode of the Lord), Jnana Guru (the Knowledge Form of the Lord), Pranava Samadhi (the Lord in Tantric Yoga state of Mantra form), Divine Light (Jyoti), Sthula (Articulate), Sukshma, (Inarticulate), Ati-Sukshma (Super Subtle), Sound manifestations in the 5-syllabled Panchakshara, (2649 to 2721) and in the Dancing Posture are the various aspects of the Darshan. The Dances of the Lord are of many kinds. They are the Sivananda (Siva Bliss), the Sundara (Beauty), the Golden Tillai performed in the Golden Hall, and the Adbudha (Wonder), all performed on the stage of Akasa, (which is Space within men's heart, and outside in the Cosmos) (2722 to 2812).

The Darshan thus revealed to the devotee leads to his attaining Jnanodayam (Dawn of Jnana) (2813 to 2824), to the Bliss of Sat-Chit-Ananda (2825 to 2834), and to Svarupa Udayam (Dawn of World Manifestness). It destroys Fate (Niyati or Karma) (2487 to 2863).

There is some more of Siva Darshan in verses 2853 to 2856, and it also confers Knowledge of Siva Svarupa (Manifestion) (2856 to 2863).

Such a Siva Darshan confers the gift of Liberation, termed Karma Nirvana (2864 and 2865). Nirvana is a word borrowed from Buddhism, but used in a sense different fom the original source. There, it is the complete shedding of all accretions that conceal the Ultimate Truth which is Sunya (not complete vacuity but an inexpressible and inexplicable state) whereas in Tamil Saiva Siddhanta and Vedanta, it is a synonym for Moksha which does not possess the non-substantial character of Sunyata.

In Section 17 (2866 to 2935), Tirumular reverts to the style of poetry peculiar to Tamil Siddhars, whose nearest, though very faint, counter-part can be traced only in the Sandha Bhasha of Bengali Baul bards. The Tamil Siddhars are a peculiar brand of wandering ascetics generally atheistic in their attitude though most of them view Siva as their Guru or Natha. They go about living on alms and singing deeply esoteric songs which superficially attacked material values in language which often seemed vulgar or even obscene, but were in reality deeply mystic. They practise a very highly systematised science of medicine, called Siddha medicine, whose constituents were herbal, though intermixed with mercury, gold, iron and other metals in some cases.

In Sections 18, 19 and 20 (verses 2936 to 2981), the text reverts to the glorification of Samadhi and mystic realization.

The work ends in a note of grand paean of religious passion over Siva in Sections 21 and 22 (2982 to 3045) and verse 3047.

TIRUMANTIRAM

A Tamil scriptural Classic

TIRUMANTIRAM

PROLOGUE

The Prologue commences with an invocation to Ganesa in the traditional manner. Ganesa, the Elder Son of Siva, is the Elephant-Faced God, who removes by His grace all obstacles that may arise in the course of any undertaking. Among the Gods of the Hindu pantheon He is always worshipped first.

Then the work proper starts with a "Prayer to God," or "In the Praise of God" in 50 mantras (verses). Here the author, Saint Tirumular, dwells at length on the attributes of God.

"God is One." That is Tirumular's first and foremost message. "Yet is He two—the static and the kinetic aspects of the One Being. The static aspect is Sivam; the kinetic aspect is His sweet Grace, His love for all creation, the Sakti. The One God is three too, when He pervades Brahma in the act of creation, Vishnu in the act of preservation and Rudra in the act of dissolution. He conquered the five senses. He filled the six faiths. He pervaded the seven Worlds; permeated the eight cardinal directions. Yet He remained unchanged, cognising all and being everywhere. Such a God I worship and you too do so." Thus exclaims Tirumular in these 50 mantras that are soul-stirring. It is both devout prayer and a distillate of pure philosophy at once.

All schools of the Hindu faith believe in the revelation of the four *Vedas — Rk, Yajus, Sama* and *Atharvana.* And so does the Saiva Siddhanta school of Agamic philosophy which Tirumular expounds in the *Tirumantiram* of 3,000 verses categorized into nine Tantras. God is enshrined in the *Vedas*; and there is no Dharma, barring what the *Vedas* prescribe; and Siddhanta's pure path is the end of Vedanta.

Equally revealed by God are the *Agamas.* Siva/Sakti expounded them to 66 saints who sought Him. The *Agamas* thus expounded are countless in number, and are couched in the 18 languages known to pandits. Of these, nine *Agamas,* revealed in Sanskrit and Tamil at once, are the primal ones. They were handed down from Siva to Sakti, from Sakti to Sadasiva, Mahesvara, Rudra, Vishnu and Brahma in that order. These nine primal *Agamas* are: *Karana, Kamika, Veeram, Chintam, Vadulam, Vyamalam, Kalottaram, Subhram and Makutam.*

In this Agamic tradition, Nandi Supreme stands as the head of the Guru lineage. He had for his direct disciples the four sages—Sanaka, Sanantana, Sanatana and Sanatkumara—all bearing the title of Nandi. Besides them were Sivayoga Muni, Patanjali, Vyaghrapada and Tirumular himself. All these eight were the spiritual leaders of one of the initial Agamic schools and were known as Nathas. Of them, the first four Nathas received the Lord's special Grace and were commanded by Him to disperse themselves in the four directions, and carry the message of the *Agamas.* Once at their appointed destinations they practised intense Yoga in the Agamic way—through sun and rain, hail and storm—and in time ascended to celestial status.

Of the latter four, Tirumular, the author of this inspired work, in turn had seven disciples: Malangan, Indiran, Soman, Brahman, Rudran, Kalangi and Kanjamalayan. Often in this work, he addresses one or another of these disciples to convey certain messages.

Tirumular, after having thus received the precepts of Sivagama from the Lord, reached Thillai (Chidambaram) and witnessed the Lord's Cosmic Dance. There he stayed on at the Feet of the Lord for an indefinite length of time (poetically for 10 million years) in devotional contemplation of Siva/Sakti (Bhuvaneswari). It was there that he realised that he was blessed with this particular life, body and longevity to fulfil a special mission—the rendering of the Agamic truths in Tamil, so that many more people of the world may imbibe some of what he had come to know through the truths of the *Agamas* including the categories of Jneya (known) Jnana (knowledge), Jnata (knower); of Maya and Mamaya (pure and impure); the primal sound potential of Nada and its manifestations; of Bindu—the primal point of light/energy that is beyond words—and of Siva, who is above them all. Having thus composed the *Tirumantiram* (originally titled Mantra Mala—Garland of Mantras), he travelled through space back to Kailas, sought the Primal One and attained the Sadasiva (form/formless) state realising divine Jnana and grace. And so he remained immortal and eternally youthful. His work too remains immortal and eternally fresh, condensing the entirety of Agamic wisdom in these Nine Tantras.

His seven disciples each established their own monastery to teach and propagate the Agamic truths contained in the *Tirumantiram*. Of these, in the line of Kalanga, came Aghora, Maligai Deva, Nadanta, Paramananda and Bhoga Deva—all fully realised souls in the Agamic doctrines as taught by Tirumular.

Finally, the Prologue returns to the question of the nature of the God-head with which it commenced. What is the order of precedence among the three Gods, Brahma the Creator, Vishnu the Preserver and Rudra the Destroyer? Considering limitless youth, finality, survival at the end, and time duration, Rudra is the most qualified candidate. But his devotees invest Brahma and Vishnu too with infinite greatness. In fact, all the three Gods are One from the point of continuity. It is the ignorant world which invests superiority on the one or the other. God is beyond all Karmas (actions). He is the seed of all creation. They who contend, "This the God", "That the God" are of muddled thinking.

Siva is the formless Primal Being; then are three Saktis: Ichcha, Kriya and Jnana. From them evolve the five Gods: Brahma, Vishnu, Rudra, Sadasiva and Maheswara. Nada and Bindu are also evolutes of the Primal Being. All these are but the different names of Siva, the One Being Original. Thus considered, neither Brahma nor Vishnu, nor Rudra is a distinct God; they are but aspects of the Three-Eyed Sadasiva. Neither man nor celestials exist but with the Grace of the Supreme Being, Siva. To consider any other being as supreme is to run after beings mortal. And that One Supreme Being is formless, form/formless and formed; pulsating as Jiva and as the Self-God in all bodies.

NOTES

'Tiru' in Tamil means holy. The word, 'mantiram' (Skt.Mantra), is used in two senses: general and special. In the general sense, it conveys the meaning of devotional prayer composed of special words, e.g. Vedic hymns. In the special sense a Mantra is that which is composed of certain letters arranged in a definite sequence of sounds of which the letters are the representative signs. In this usage a Mantra may, or may not, convey its meaning on its face. Bija or seed Mantras such as aim, klim, and hrim have no meaning according to the ordinary use of language.

Tirumular uses the word, Mantra, in both senses. The title he gave his book originally was "Mantra Mala" or "Garland of Mantras." Here it conveys the sense of being a volume of hymns. Later, in subsequent Tantras, he elaborately speaks of specific Mantras for specific deities and special rituals, and expounds in full the meaning of the primal Mantra, Aum, and the five-lettered Siva mantra—Namasivaya—explaining the ways of intoning it in different contexts.

Literally, Mantra is composed of two syllables: 'man' mind, and 'tra', protects—that is, Mantra protects when contemplated upon.

விநாயகர் காப்பு
INVOCATION OF VINAYAKA

ஐந்து கரத்தனை யானை முகத்தனை
இந்தின் இளம்பிறை போலும் எயிற்றனை
நந்தி மகன்தனை ஞானக் கொழுந்தினைப்
புந்தியில் வைத்தடி போற்றுகின் றேனே.

Adoration to the Holy Feet enshrined in my Consciousness
The Feet of His whose arms are five,
Whose face has the Elephant's majesty,
Whose single tusk rivals the crescent moon,
Who is the darling child of Nandi
And who is wisdom pure and overflowing.

This verse does not appear to have been an integral part of the original work by Tirumular. Sekkizhar in his *Periyapuranam*, where he recounts the life of Saint Tirumular, says the *Tirumantiram* commences with the mantram, "Onravan Tane," which follows the Vinayaka invocation, and forms the first verse in the work. The "Invocation to Vinayaka" therefore appears to be a later addition by some one who thought no work can conventionally commence without first paying obeisance to the Elephant-Faced God.

கடவுள் வாழ்த்து
IN PRAISE OF GOD

ஒன்றவன் தானே இரண்டவன் இன்னருள்
நின்றனன் மூன்றினுள் நான்குணர்ந் தான்ஐந்து
வென்றனன் ஆறு விரிந்தனன் ஏழும்பர்ச்
சென்றனன் தானிருந் தானுணர்ந் தெட்டே. 1

One is Many

The One is He, the Two His sweet Grace,
In Three He stood, in all the Four witnessed,
The Five He conquered, the Six He filled,
The Seven Worlds pervades, manifests the Eight
And so remains.

---

1. The One—The Uncreated Eternal Being—Sivam.
2. The Two—Siva/Sakti. Sakti is the dynamic aspect of static Sivam. She confers grace on the Jivas.
3. The Three—Triads are many:
a) Primal Sakti evolves into three subsidiary Saktis: Ichcha (desire), Jnana (knowledge), and Kriya (action).
b) The three Gods: Brahma or Aya (of creation), Vishnu or Mal (of preservation), and Siva or Rudra (of dissolution).
c) The three primal gunas: Rajas, Tamas, and Sattva.
d) The entire creation represented by the three genders: he, she and it.
e) The three theological categories Pati, pasu and pasam.
4) The Four—
a) The *four Vedas: Rk, Yajus, Sama, Atharvana.*
b) The four steps to God-realization: Charya and Kriya, Yoga and Jnana.
5) The Five—
a) The five senses.
b) The five acts: creation, preservation, dissolution, obfuscation, and liberation.
6) The Six—
a) The six schools of philosophy.
b) The six Adhvas or steps to final realization: padam (sound), ezhuthu (letter), mantram (syllable), kalai (light), tattvam (principles of matter), and bhuvanam (world).
c) The six adharas or plexuses (chakras): i) muladhara, ii) svadhishthana, iii) manipuraka, iv) anahata, v) visuddhi, vi) ajna.
7) The Seven—
a) Seven Worlds: Bhuloka, Bhuvarloka, Svarloka, Maharloka, Tapoloka, Satyaloka, and Sivaloka. For an elaborate and esoteric account of the lokas (worlds), see the Vishnu, Bhagavata, Vayu and other *Puranas.* Q.V. "Introduction to Tantra Sastra" by Sir John Woodroffe (Ganesh & Co., Madras) pp.25. ff.
b) The seventh chakra—sahasrara located in the cranium.
8) The Eight—pervasiveness through earth, water, fire, air, sky, sun, moon and Jiva.

1. சிறப்புப் பாயிரம்
SPECIAL INTRODUCTION

போற்றிசைத் தின்னுயிர் மன்னும் புனிதனை
நாற்றிசைக் கும்நல்ல மாதுக்கு நாதனை
மேற்றிசைக் குள்தென் திசைக்கொரு வேந்தனாங்
கூற்றுதைத் தானையான் கூறுகின் றேனே. 2

Defies Death

The Holy One who all life sustains,
Lord of Her, Beloved of all the world,
He who spurned Yama, the Southern Quarter's King
Of Him I sing, He glory and praise.

Yama is the god of death. When that god came to seize Siva's devotee Markandeya on the appointed day, Siva spurned the Death-God. The implication is that neither Siva nor his devotees are subject to the process of death. They are immortal and eternal.

ஒக்கநின் றானை உலப்பிலிதேவர்கள்
நக்கனென் றேத்திடு நாதனை நாடொறும்
பக்கநின் றார்அறியாத பரமனைப்,
புக்குநின் றுன்னியான் போற்றிசெய் வேனே. 3

Immortal Gods Adore

He who stands the same to all,
The Pure One, whom immortal gods adore,
Whom, even they, that daily stand beside, know not,
Him I seek, praise, and on Him I meditate.

The word "நக்கன்" literally means the "naked," unclothed one (from Sanskrit nagna). Both the Jain Arhat, and Siva are usually described thus.

அகலிடத் தார்மெய்யை அண்டத்து வித்தைப்
புகலிடத் தென்றனைப் போதவிட் டானைப்
பகலிடத் தும்இர வும்பணிந் தேத்தி
இகலிடத் தேஇருள் நீங்கிநின் றேனே. 4

Dispels Gloom

The Truth of Spaces Vast, Seed of the Universe orb,
Our Haven of Refuge, He bade me seek and find,
Him I praised by night and day,
And praising thus, gloom-dispelled,
I held firm in this world of strifes.

"அண்டத்து வித்தை" may also refer to the "Hiranya Garbha" and Agni described as "retas" descending from the antariksa in the RgVeda.

சிவனொடொக் குந்தெய்வந் தேடினும் இல்லை
அவனொடொப் பார்இங்கு யாவரும் இல்லை
புவனங் கடந்தன்று பொன்னொளி மின்னுந்
தவனச் சடைமுடித் தாமரை யானே. 5

Siva Is Nonpareil

Search where ye will, there's no God like Siva,
None here below to equal Him in glory;
Lotus-like, He, of gleaming matted locks,
Fiery in splendour, beyond the worlds, apart.

அவனை ஒழிய அமரரும் இல்லை
அவனன்றிச் செய்யும் அருந்தவம் இல்லை
அவனன்றி மூவரால் ஆவதொன் றில்லை
அவனன்றி ஊர்புகு மாறறி யேனே. 6

Omni-Competent

Without Him, there be Celestials none,
Without Him, penance is not,
Without Him, naught the Three accomplish,
Without Him, I know not how to enter the City's Gate.

City's Gate - liberation.

முன்னையொப் பாயுள்ள மூவர்க்கு மூத்தவன்
தன்னையொப் பாயொன்றும் இல்லாத் தலைமகன்
தன்னையப் பாஎனில் அப்பனு மாய்உளன்
பொன்னையொப் பாகின்ற போதகத் தானே. 7

Divine Father

Primal First is He, older than the Co-eval Three
But the Lord is He peerless, unequalled;
Call Him "Father," and Father He to thee
Inside you He flames in the Lotus of Golden Hue.

The Lotus is a very important and very frequently adopted symbol in Hindu and Buddhist literature. Amongst other things it stands for the primeval evolution of the Universe from the One, as well as for the Energy (Sakti) thus released. It is not only the One, all pervasive Power, but also the individual separate items that constitute the essence of Life, whose location in the human body is deemed to be the heart chakra. The Brahma- randra of the cranium is also often referred to as a thousand petalled LOTUS. There are other concepts also which are symbolized by the LOTUS.

Co-eval three = These are the three I namely, Brahma, the creator, Vishnu, the protector, and Rudra, the destroyer, respectively.

தீயினும் வெய்யன் புனலினுந் தண்ணியன்
ஆயினும் ஈசன் அருளறி வார்இல்லை
சேயினும் நல்லன் அணியன்நல் அன்பர்க்குத்
தாயினும் நல்லன் தாழ்சடை யோனே. 8

Kinder Than Mother

Hotter is He than fire, cooler than water;
And yet none knows of His Grace abounding;
Far away, yet very close to the good,
Kinder than the mother is He, of the flowing matted locks.

பொன்னாற் புரிந்திட்ட பொற்சடை யென்னப்
பின்னாற் பிறங்க இருந்தவன் பேர்நந்தி
என்னால் தொழப்படும் எம்இறை மற்றவன்
தன்னால் தொழப்படு வாரில்லை தானே. 9

All Worship Him

Gold-bewrought, His matted locks fall back and gleam
Nandi, His name,
My Lord is He, ever by me worshipt;
But none there be whom He worships.

Siva is also frequently referred to as Nandi by Tirumular Nandi is a synonym for Sadasiva - the form/formless aspect of Siva. Nandi literally means the Bull of Siva.

தானே இருநிலந் தாங்கிவிண் ணாய்நிற்குந்
தானே சுடும்அங்கி ஞாயிறுந் திங்களுந்
தானே மழைபொழி தையலு மாய்நிற்குந்
தானே தடவரை தண்கட லாமே. 10

Omnium Gatherum

Holding the worlds apart, as the Heavens high He spreads;
Himself the scorching Fire, Sun and Moon,
Himself the Mother that sends down the rains
Himself the mountains strong and oceans cold.

அயலும் புடையும்எம் ஆதியை நோக்கில்
இயலும் பெருந்தெய்வம் யாதுமொன் றில்லை
முயலும் முயலில் முடிவுமற் றாங்கே
பெயலும் மழைமுகிற் பேர்நந்தி தானே. 11

Effort And Fruit

Near and far I look; but around the Being First,
No other God, I see, mightier than He;
Himself the effort, and Himself, too, effort's end;
Himself the rains, Himself the clouds rain-laden,
The Nandi-named.

கண்ணுத லான்ஒரு காதலின் நிற்கவும்
எண்ணிலி தேவர் இறந்தார் எனப்பலர்
மண்ணுறு வார்களும் வானுறு வார்களும்
அண்ணல் இவன்என் றறியகி.லார்களே. 12

Beyond Comprehension

Humans and celestials go after gods who pass away
They do not realize that He of the fore-head eye is the Supreme,
One-pointed in His concern for His devotees.

மண்ணளந் தான்மல ரோன்முதல் தேவர்கள்
எண்ணளந் தின்ன நினைக்கிலார் ஈசனை
விண்ணளந்தான்தன்னை மேல்அளந் தாரில்லை
கண்ணளந் தெங்குங் கடந்துநின் றானே. 13

Immeasurable

Mal who spanned the earth and Brahma the Lotus-seated one,
And others of the gods fathomed Him not;
There be none to measure Him that measured the Heav'ns
Transcending He stands, bestowing everything with a glance.

Mal - Vishnu.

கடந்துநின் றான்கம லம்மல ராதி
கடந்துநின் றான்கடல் வண்ணம்எம் மாயன்
கடந்துநின் றான்அவர்க் கப்புறம் ஈசன்
கடந்துநின் றான்எங்கும் கண்டுநின் றானே. 14

Transcends All

Transcended He Brahma on the lotus-seat,
Transcended Mayan, the ocean-hued,
Transcended He, Isan, who transcends all,
Transcended He space infinite, witnessing all.

Māyan-Vishnu
Isan-Rudra
In all these cases, 'Siva is considered as different from and superior to Hara, Isan, Maheśvara, etc., names otherwise applied to Śiva, for the ultimate God-head, Śiva, transcends all His own manifestations.

ஆதியு மாய்அர னாய்உட லுள்நின்ற
வேதியு மாய்விரிந் தார்ந்திருந் தான்அருட்
சோதியு மாய்ச்சுருங் காததோர் தன்மையுள்
நீதியு மாய்நித்த மாகிநின் றானே. 15

Blossoms As All

He is Brahma, He is Hara and is seated in every heart,
He blossoms as Divine Effulgence which knows no contraction
And he is the Order Eternal.

Hara-Rudra

கோது குலாவிய கொன்றைக் குழற்சடை
மாது குலாவிய வாணுதல் பாகனை
யாது குலாவி அமரருந் தேவருங்
கோது குலாவிக் குணம்பயில் வாரே. 16

Confers Everything On Gods

Him of the matted locks fragrant with Konrai flowers,
Him who is with the Divine Mother,
Him the Devas and the celestials,
Adore for anything they require.

காயம் இரண்டுங் கலந்துகொதிக்கினும்
ஆயங் கத்தூரி யதுமிகும் அவ்வழி.
தேசங் கலந்தொரு தேவனென் றெண்ணினும்
ஈசன் உறவுக் கெதிரில்லை தானே. 17

Love Profound

The body and soul may intermingle,
But the soul's effulgence predominates,
God infils the whole universe,
But His love for us stands supreme.

அதிபதி செய்து அளகை வேந்தனை
நிதிபதி செய்த நிறைதவ நோக்கி
அதுபதி யாதரித் தாக்கம தாக்கின்
இதுபதி கொள்ளென்ற எம்பெரு மானே. 18

Munificent

Seeing the devout penance of the King of Alagai,
The Supreme Lord made him the lord,
Bestowed on him riches galore, and
Commanded him to abide there and reign.

Alagai King: Kubera, the god of wealth and sovereign of the land of Alagapuri.

இதுபதி ஏலங் கமழ்பொழில் ஏழும்
முதுபதி செய்தவன் மூத்தறி வாளன்
விதுபதி செய்தவன் மெய்த்தவம் நோக்கி
அதுபதி யாக அமருகின் றானே. 19

Created Universe

All the fragrant seven worlds are His,
But He chooses to remain in the cremation ground,
If we do sincere penance,
He is sure to abide in our hearts.

முடிவும் பிறப்பையும் முன்னே படைத்த
அடிகள் உறையும் அறநெறி நாடில்
இடியும் முழக்கமும் ஈசர் உருவங்
கடிமலர்க் குன்ற மலையது தானே. 20

In Mount Kailas

If we pursue the path that leads to the Abode,
Of Him who of yore created birth and death,
We shall find Him in the holy hill of Kailas
Resonant with thunders and fragrant with flowers.

வானப் பெருங்கொண்டல் மாலயன் வானவர்
ஊனப் பிறவி ஒழிக்கும் ஒருவனைக்
கானக் களிறு கதறப் பிளந்தஎங்
கோனைப் புகழுமின் கூடலு மாமே. 21

Comes Speeding

Sing His praise and become one with Him,
The Lord, who is the source of all compassion,
Who rescues Vishnu, Brahma and the celestials from birth,
And who killed the trumpeting wild elephant.

Reference is to the destruction of Gaja Mukhasura—the elephant-faced monster who challenged Siva's supremacy. This is one of the eight heroic deeds of Siva referred to later in Tantra Two.

மனத்தில் எழுகின்ற மாயநன் னாடன்
நினைத்த தறிவ னெனில்தான் நினைக்கிலர்
எனக்கிறை அன்பிலன் என்பர் இறைவன்
பிழைக்கநின் றார்பக்கம் பேணிநின் றானே. 22

Seek Him, He Seeks You

This Lord of Maya-world that has its rise in the mind,
He, knows yet all our thoughts but we do not think of Him;
Some be who groan, "God is not favourable to me;"
But, sure, God seeks those who seek their souls to save.

வல்லவன் வன்னிக் கிறையிடை வாரண
நில்லென நிற்பித்த நீதியுள் ஈசனை
இல்லென வேண்டா இறையவர் தம்முதல்
அல்லும் பகலும் அருளுகின் றானே. 23

Infinite Grace

The God of Fire, was set amidst the seas by The Mighty Lord
Do not say He is not
He, the Lord of the Heavenly Beings all,
Who, day and night, pours forth His Divine Grace.

The God of fire, who at one time threatened to engulf the world, was contained in the northern seas.

போற்றிசைத் தும்புகழ்ந் தும்புனி தன்னடி
தேற்றுமின் என்றுஞ் சிவனடிக் கேசெல்வ
மாற்றிய தென்று மயலுற்ற சிந்தையை
மாற்றிநின் றார்வழி மன்னிநின் றானே. 24

Firm In Minds Firm

Sing His praise, sing of His Holy Feet!
Pour all your treasures at Siva's Sacred Feet!
And they who shake off the clouded eye and disturbed mind,
With them He ever stood, benignantly firm.

பிறப்பிலி பிஞ்ஞகன் பேரரு ளாளன்
இறப்பிலி யாவர்க்கும் இன்பம் அருளும்
துறப்பிலி தன்னைத் தொழுமின் தொழுதால்
மறப்பிலி மாயா விருத்தமும் ஆமே. 25

Illusions Vanish

Birthless is He, of plated locks, and of compassion vast,
Deathless is He, who never deserts those who come to Him,
Granter of Joys entire
To Him kneel, and, kneeling, shall find
Naught becomes Maya, the bond immemorial.

தொடர்ந்துநின் றானைத் தொழுமின் தொழுதால்
படர்ந்துநின் றான்பரி பாரக முற்றுங்
கடந்துநின் றான்கம லம்மலர் மேலே
உடந்திருந் தானடிப் புண்ணிய மாமே. 26

Attain Grace

Adore the Lord, who in unbroken continuity stood,
The Lord who protecting over all earth expanded,
Transcending all He stood; on the lotus of the heart,
In smiling glory He sat; Holy be His feet!

சந்தி எனத்தக்க தாமரை வாண்முகத்
தந்தமில் ஈசன் அருள்நமக் கேயென்று
நந்தியை நாளும் வணங்கப் படும்அவர்
புந்தியி னுள்ளே புகுந்துநின் றானே. 27

He Enters Into You

The Infinite of Lotus-Face, rivalling the rose of sunset,
May ours be His Grace Divine!
And they who thus Nandi daily beseech,
Into their Heart He walks in and abides.

இணங்கிநின் றான்எங்கு மாகிநின் றானும்
பிணங்கிநின் றான்பின்முன் னாகிநின் றானும்
உணங்கிநின் றான்அம ராபதி நாதன்
வணங்கிநின் றார்க்கே வழித்துணை யாமே. 28

Your Guide

Beckoning He stood, He, the All-pervading;
Invisible to most but

To those who freely give themselves to the Lord on High,
To them is He the certain, immutable Guide.

காணநில் லாயடி யேற்குற வாருளர்
நாணநில் லேன்உன்னை நான்தழு விக்கொளக்
கோணநில் லாத குணத்தடி யார்மனத்
தாணிய னாகிஅமர்ந்துநின் றானே. 29

Axle-Pin

Oh! who else is kin to me but You?
Come to me that I may see you
Let me not feel shy to embrace Your feet!
For to the heart of Your servant, pure and true
You ever stood even as the axle-pin.

வானின் றழைக்கும் மழைபோல் இறைவனுந்
தானின் றழைக்குங்கொல் என்று தயங்குவார்·
ஆனின் றழைக்கு மதுபோல்என் நந்தியை •
நானின் றழைப்பது ஞானங் கருதியே. 30

Yearn For Him

As the Heavens draw the rains;
Even so will my Lord draw me to Him?
Thus, doubting, many ask.
But like a calf lowing for its mother
I cry for Nandi for the sake of knowledge.

மண்ணகத் தான்ஒக்கும் வானகத் தான்ஒக்கும்
விண்ணகத் தான்ஒக்கும் வேதகத்தான்ஒக்கும்
பண்ணகத் தின்னிசை பாடலுற் றானுக்கே
கண்ணகத் தேநின்று காதலித் தேனே. 31

Seek Him In Love

The Earth is He, the sky is He! Well He be!
The Heaven is He, truest gold is He! Well He be!
Sweetest song's inmost rapture is He!
Him my love besought, from heart's central core.

தேவர் பிரான்நம் பிரான்திசை பத்தையும்
மேவு பிரான்விரி நீருல கேழையுந்
தாவு பிரான்தன்மை தானறி வாரில்லை
பாவு பிரான்அருட் பாடலு மாமே. 32

Sing Of Him

The Lord of Gods, and of ours too,
The Lord who all space pervades,
And the seven Worlds, ocean-bound, transcends;
None do know His nature true,
May we sing His Grace Divine!

பதிபல வாயது பண்டிவ் வுலகம்
விதிபல செய்தொன்று மெய்ம்மை உணரார்
துதிபல தோத்திரஞ் சொல்லவல் லாரும்
மதியிலர் நெஞ்சினுள் வாடுகின் றாரே. 33

Adore Him

Many the gods this hoary world adores,
Many the rituals; many the songs they sing;
But knowing not the One Truth, of Wisdom bereft
Unillumined, they can but droop at heart.

சாந்து கமழுங் கவரியின் கந்தம்போல்
வேந்தன் அமரர்க் கருளிய மெய்ந்நெறி
ஆர்ந்த சுடரன்ன ஆயிர நாமமும்
போந்தும் இருந்தும் புகழுகின் றேனே. 34

Chant His Names Thousand

Like the fragrance of the musk the musk-deer constant emits,
Is the True Path which the Lord to Celestials imparts.
Sitting or moving, I chant the rich essence of His Name,
His thousand Names that are like spark divine.

'Thousand' implies numerous, The 69th chapter of the *Siva Purana*, and the 7th chapter of *Anusasana-Parvan* of the *Mahabharata* gives 1008 names. Also see the *Agni, Padma, Bhavisyothara, Varaha, Kurma. and Vamana Puranas*, the *Linga Purana* and the "Kasikhanda" of the *Skanda Purana*. V. "Introduction to Tantra Sastra" by Sir John Woodroffe pp.ii, and iin.

ஆற்றுகி லாவழி யாகும் இறைவனைப்
போற்றுமின் போற்றிப் புகழ்மின் புகழ்ந்திடில்
மேற்றிசைக் குங்கிழக் குத்திசை எட்டொடு
மாற்றுவன் அப்படி யாட்டவு மாமே. 35

Path Crossed

If we tread the path of goodness shown by Him,
And sing His praise and adore Him,
He, the Lord of all ten directions,
Will protect and impel us in the right direction.

அப்பனை நந்தியை ஆரா அமுதினை
ஒப்பிலி வள்ளலை ஊழி முதல்வனை
எப்பரி சாயினும் ஏத்துமின் ஏத்தினால்
அப்பரிசீசன் அருள்பெற லாமே. 36

Praise And Be Blessed

Heavenly Father, Nandi, the unsurfeiting nectar sweet,
Bounteous One, Unequalled, First of Time!
Praise Him ever; and even as you praise,
So thine reward will also be.

நானும்நின் றேத்துவன் நாடொறும் நந்தியைத்
தானும்நின் றான்தழல் தானொக்கு மேனியன்
வானில்நின் றார்மதி போல்உடல் உள்ளுவந்
தூனில்நின் றாங்கே உயிர்க்கின்ற வாறே. 37

Throbs Within

Daily I kneel and chant Nandi's holy Name;
Envisioned, He stands, the Fire-hued One,
Flaming like the moon in sky; into me He comes,
And throbs and breathes through my mortal flesh.

பிதற்றொழி யேன்பெரி யான்அரி யானைப்
பிதற்றொழி யேன்பிற வாஉரு வானைப்
பிதற்றொழி யேன்எங்கள் பேர்நந்தி தன்னைப்
பிதற்றொழி யேன்பெரு மைத்தவன் யானே. 38

Greatness Unceasing

I will not cease to speak of Him, the Great, the Rare,
I will not cease to prate of Him, the Form Unborn,
I will not cease to talk of Nandi, the Mighty,
I will never cease, for pure and great am I then!

வாழ்த்தவல் லார்மனத் துள்ளுறு சோதியைத்
தீர்த்தனை அங்கே திளைக்கின்ற தேவனை
ஏத்தியும் எம்பெரு மான்என் றிறைஞ்சியும்
ஆத்தஞ்செய் தீசன் அருள்பெற லாமே. 39

Adore And Attain Grace

He, the Divine Light, shining bright in devotee's heart
He, the pure One, sporting therein
Him shall we praise, Him call, "Our Lord",
And, thus adoring, His Grace attain.

குறைந்தடைந் தீசன் குரைகழல் நாடும்
நிறைந்தடை செம்பொனின் நேரொளி ஒக்கும்
மறைஞ்சடைஞ் செய்யாது வாழ்த்தவல் லார்க்குப்
புறஞ்சடஞ் செய்வான் புகுந்துநின் றானே. 40

In The Heart Of The Pure

Humbled and meek, seek thou the Feet of the Lord,
Who equals the rays of purest gold serene;
Praise Him with songs of the humble heart
And unpenurious tongue;
Into such He enters, the all-fashioning Lord.

சினஞ்செய்த நஞ்சுண்ட தேவர் பிரானைப்
புனஞ்செய்த நெஞ்சிடை போற்றவல் லார்க்குக்
கனஞ்செய்த வாணுதல் பாகனும் அங்கே
இனஞ்செய்த மான்போல் இணங்கிநின் றானே. 41

In Depths Of Devotee's Heart

To them He comes, who, in heart's deep confines
Treasure His Name,
The Lord who consumed the deadly poison of hatred born,
He the Consort of Her of the gleaming brow,
He comes like a deer to its fold.

The reference is to the story of Siva devouring poison. Once upon a time the devas (celestials) and asuras (demons) made a joint effort to churn the 'milky ocean' to produce the elixir of life. They used the Mandara mountain for the churning rod and the formidable giant serpent Vasuki for the cord. When they churned hard, Vasuki unable to bear the strain vomited poison. The poison spread over the entire atmosphere and threatened to kill all life. Siva in His mercy swallowed the poison and saved creation from total destruction. His consort Parvati, afraid the poison might endanger Her beloved, held His throat tight and there the poison remains ever, earning Him the appellation "Blue Throated." The symbolism and significance of this legendary event, known as Samudra-Manthan, is that divine compassion is unparalleled.

போயரன் தன்னைப் புகழ்வார் பெறுவது
நாயக னான்முடி செய்தது வேநல்கு
மாயகஞ் சூழ்ந்து வரவல்ல ராகிலும்
வேயன தோளிக்கு வேந்தொன்றுந் தானே. 42

Grants All

To Those who seek Him, the Lord's grace flows umimpeded
Even if one is able to orbit the world,
He cannot achieve anything without the grace of
The Lord, the consort of the Mother of shoulders reed-shaped.

அரனடி சொல்லி அரற்றி அழுது
பரனடி நாடியே பாவிப்ப நாளும்
உரனடி செய்தங் கொதுங்கவல் லார்க்கு
நிரனடி செய்து நிறைந்துநின் றானே. 43

Eternal Grace

To them that speak of Hara's Holy Feet and weep,
To them that daily muse at the Great One's mighty feet
To them that, in deep devotion fixed, wait to serve,
To them comes the Eternal's all-filling Grace.

போற்றிஎன் பார்அம ரர்புனி தன்அடி
போற்றிஎன் பார்அசு ரர்புனி தன்அடி
போற்றிஎன் பார்மனி தர்புனி தன்அடி
போற்றிஎன் அன்புள் பொலியவைத் தேனே. 44

Shines In Love

"Glory to the Holy Feet," the Devas chant,
"Glory to the Holy Feet," the Asuras hymn,
"Glory to the Holy Feet," the humans, too echo,
Thus I gloried Him, and in my love He shone.

விதிவழி அல்லதிவ் வேலை உலகம்
விதிவழி இன்பம் விருத்தமும் இல்லை
துதிவழி நித்தலுஞ் சோதிப் பிரானும்
பதிவழி காட்டும் பகலவ னாமே. 45

Divine Path

Except according to the Law, this sea-girt world survives not,
Except according to the Law, happiness does not follow,
Nothing can work against the Law,
If we adore Him, the light effulgent
He will guide us on the Path to liberation like the sun.

அந்திவண் ணாஅர னேசிவ னேஎன்று
சிந்தைசெய் வண்ணந் திருந்தடி யார்தொழ
முந்திவண் ணாமுதல் வாபர னேஎன்று
வந்திவ் வண்ணன்எம் மனம்புகுந் தானே. 46

In Heart's Centre

"You of the Twilight Hue! O! Hara! O! Siva!"
Thus, His Holy Feet devotees praise and sing;
He of the Primary Hue, the First, the Infinite
Entered my being, my heart's centre held.

மனையுள் இருந்தவர் மாதவர் ஒப்பர்
நினைவுள் இருந்தவர் நேசத்துள் நிற்பர்
பனையுள் இருந்த பருந்தது போல
நினையாத வர்க்கில்லை நின்இன்பந் தானே. 47

Bliss Denied

They who enshrine Him in themselves equal great sages,
Contemplating Him in their hearts, they will love and adore Him,
Those who do not think Him do not get happiness,
Even as the kite sitting on a palm tree does not enjoy the palm fruit.

அடியார் பரவும் அமரர் பிரானை
முடியால் வணங்கி முதல்வனை முன்னிப்
படியார் அருளும் பரம்பரன் எந்தை
விடியா விளக்கென்று மேவிநின் றேனே. 48

Unflickering Lamp

The Lord of gods, whom the pious adore,
To Him I bend my knees and His Grace invoke,
The Lord, Our Father, blessing us of earth,
The Lamp that flickers not, Him I seek.

பரைபசு பாசத்து நாதனை உள்ளி
உரைபசு பாசத் தொருங்கவல் லார்க்குத்
திரைபசு பாவச் செழுங்கடல் நீந்திக்
கரைபசு பாசங் கடந்தெய்த லாமே. 49

Sea Of Bondage

They who adore the Lord of soul and its limitation,
And released from the bondage,
Are able to cross the ocean of samsara
And reach the other shore of it.

Pasu—soul; Pasa—bondage. Pasu-pasa is the eternal bondage that is inherent in the soul. Pati, the Lord, alone sunders this bondage, and then pasu becomes one with Pati. Pati, pasu and pasa are denoted as three eternal categories in Saiva Siddhanta philosophical literature. Pasu literally means cow; Pati means cowherd, and pasa, the lead string that binds.

சூடுவன் நெஞ்சிடை வைப்பன் பிரான்என்று
பாடுவன் பன்மலர் தூவிப் பணிந்துநின்
றாடுவன் ஆடி அமரர்பி ரான்என்று
நாடுவன் யானின் றறிவது தானே. 50

Seeking Is All

I'll adore Him I'll keep Him in my heart;
I'll sing His Name and dance with gift of flowers,
Singing and dancing seek the Lord;
This alone I know, only too well I know.

2. வேதச் சிறப்பு

GREATNESS OF VEDAS

வேதத்தை விட்ட அறம்இல்லை வேதத்தின்
ஓதத் தகும்அறம் எல்லாம் உளதர்க்க
வாதத்தை விட்டு மதிஞர் வளமுற்ற
வேதத்தை ஓதியே வீடுபெற்றார்களே. 51.

Vedas Proclaim Dharma

No Dharma is, barring what the Vedas say;
Its central core the Vedas proclaim;
And the Wise ones ceased contentious brawls,.
Intoned the lofty strains and Freedom's battle won.

வேதம் உரைத்தானும் வேதிய னாகிலன்
வேதம் உரைத்தானும் வேதா விளங்கிட
வேதம் உரைத்தானும் வேதியர் வேள்விக்காய்
வேதம் உரைத்தானும் மெய்ப்பொருள் காட்டவே. 52.

Truth Of Maker

Brahma spoke the Vedas, but Himself is not the author thereof;
He spoke the Vedas only the great Maker to reveal;
He spoke them for the Holy, sacrifices to perform,
He spoke them, the True One to manifest

இருக்குரு வாம்எழில் வேதத்தி னுள்ளே
உருக்குணர் வாயுணர் வேதத்துள் ஓங்கி
வெருக்குரு வாகிய வேதியர் சொல்லுங்
கருக்குரு வாய்நின்ற கண்ணனு மாமே. 53

Moving Mood

In the beauteous Veda, aptly named the Rik
As the moving mood behind, He stood;
In the thrilling chant of the Vedic priests He stood,
Himself the Eye of vision Central.

திருநெறி யாவது சித்தசித் தன்றிப்
பெருநெறி யாய பிரானை நினைந்து
குருநெறி யாஞ்சிவ மாநெறி கூடும்
ஒருநெறி ஒன்றாக வேதாந்தம் ஓதுமே. 54

Supreme Path

The Lord is neither cit not acit; He is the path Supreme,
If we meditate on Him He will bestow on us grace,
This is the only path, Supreme path, says Vedanta.

Vedanta—end of the *Vedas* — usually refers to the conclusions of philosophy in the *Upanishads.*

ஆறங்க மாய்வரு மாமறை ஓதியைக்
கூறங்க மாகக் குணம்பயில் வாரில்லை
வேறங்க மாக விளைவுசெய் தப்புறம்
பேறங்க மாகப் பெருக்குகின் றாரே. 55

One In Several

The Vedas and the six Vedangas proclaim only Him,
Few bother about it,
Others follow many other gods and
Consider it a privilege and thus waste their time.

The six divisions of Vedangas or auxiliaries of the Vedas are: (1)Siksha (2)Vyakarana, (3)Chandas (4)Nirukta (5)Kalpa (6)Jyotisha

Siksha:lays down the rules for correct chanting of Vedic hymns.

Vyakarana:lays down the grammar of the Vedic language

Chandas:deals with the cadence and numbers of Vedic hymns.

Nirukta:gives the interpretation of Vedic syllables.

Kalpa:lays down the rules for their performance.

Jyotisha:prescribes the appropriate times for performing Vedic rites and sacrifices.

பாட்டும் ஒலியும் பரக்குங் கணிகையர்
ஆட்டும் அறாத அவனியின் மாட்டாதார்
வேட்டு விருப்பார் விரதமில் லாதவர்
ஈட்டும் இடஞ்சென் றிகலலுற்றாரே. 56

Vedic Sacrifices

Those who do not participate in The singing and dancing
Of the women dedicated to the Lord,
And do not perform sacrifices or observe vows,
Go to their destiny and become miserable.

3. ஆகமச் சிறப்பு

THE GREATNESS OF THE AGAMAS

அஞ்சன மேனி அரிவையோர் பாகத்தன்
அஞ்சொ டிருபத்து மூன்றுள ஆகமம்
அஞ்சலி கூப்பி அறுபத் தறுவரும்
அஞ்சா முகத்தில் அரும்பொருள் கேட்டதே. 57

Agamas From The Fifth Face Of Siva

The Lord that consorts with his blue-hued half
Has the Agamas twenty-five and three;
Bowing low, the six and sixty heard
His Fifth-Face the Agamas expound.

(1) The 28 Agamas are:

1. Kamigam
2. Yogajam
3. Sivithiam
4. Karanam
5. Ajitham
6. Deeptham
7. Sukshmam
8. Sahasram
9. Hamsumam
10. Suprabhedam
11. Vijayam
12. Niswasam
13. Swayambhuvam
14. Agneyam
15. Veeram
16. Rauravam
17. Makutam
18. Vishalam
19. Chandra Jnanam
20. Mukha Bimbam
21. Purotgeetham
22. Lalitam
23. Siddham
24. Santanam
25. Sarvoktam
26. Parameswaram
27. Karanam
28. Vathulam

Tradition regarding these 66 sages is not clear.

Fifth Face - Siva has five faces — four facing the four directions, and the fifth facing upward. The westward looking Face is known as Sadyojatam, the eastward as Tatpurusham, the northward as Vamadevam, the southward as Aghoram, and the upward as Isanam. The first four faces revealed the four *Vedas* and the fifth face, Isanam, revealed the *Agamas.*

அண்ணல் அருளால் அருளுஞ் சிவாகமம்
எண்ணில் இருபத்தெண் கோடிநூ றாயிரம்
விண்ணவர் ஈசன் விழுப்பம் உரைத்தனர்
எண்ணிநின் றப்பொருள் ஏத்துவன் யானே. 58

Agamas Innumerable

The Sivagamas the Lord by Grace revealed;
In number a billion-million-twenty-eight

In them the Celestials the Lord's greatness gloried;
Him, I too shall muse and praise.

பண்டித ராவார் பதினெட்டுப் பாடையுங்
கண்டவர் கூறுங் கருத்தறி வார்என்க
பண்டிதர் தங்கள் பதினெட்டுப் பாடையும்
அண்ட முதலான் அறஞ்சொன்ன வாறே. 59

Agamic Truths in 18 Languages

In eighteen various tongues they speak
The thoughts which Pandits alone know;
The Pandits' tongues numbering ten and eight
Are but what the Primal Lord declared.

What the Lord declared scholars expressed in 18 languages.

அண்ணல் அருளால் அருளுந்திவ் யாகமம்
விண்ணில் அமரர் தமக்கும் விளங்கரி
தெண்ணில் எழுபது கோடிநூ றாயிரம்
எண்ணிலும் நீர்மேல் எழுத்தது ஆகுமே. 60

Agamas Deep in Content

The Agamas sublime, the Lord by Grace revealed,
Deep and baffling even to the gods in Heaven;
Seventy billion-millions though they be;
Like writing on the waters, eluding grasp.

பரனாய்ப் பராபரங் காட்டி உலகிற்
றரனாய்ச் சிவதன்மந் தானேசொல் காலத்
தரனாய் அமரர்கள் அர்ச்சிக்கு நந்தி
உரனாகி ஆகமம் ஓங்கிநின் றானே. 61

Agamas Revealed

The Infinite Siva revealing the Infinite Vast,
Came down to earth, His Dharma to proclaim,
The immortals, then, Him as Nandi adored,
And He stood forth as the Agamas entire.

சிவமாம் பரத்தினிற் சத்தி சதாசிவம்
உவமா மகேசர் உருத்திர தேவர்
தவமால் பிரமீசர் தம்மில்தாம் பெற்ற
நவஆ கமம்எங்கள் நந்திபெற் றானே. 62

Agamas Transmitted

From Siva the Infinite to Sakti and Sadasiva,
To Maheswara the Joyous, to Rudra Deva to
Holy Vishnu and to Brahmisa
So in succession unto Himself from Himself,
The nine Agamas our Nandi begot.

பெற்றநல் ஆகமங் காரணங் காமிகம்
உற்றநல் வீரம் உயர்சிந்தம் வாதுளம்
மற்றவ் வியாமள மாகுங்கா லோத்தரந்
துற்றநற் சுப்பிரஞ் சொல்லு மகுடமே. 63

Nine Agamas

The Agamas so received are Karanam, kamigam,
The Veeram good, the Sindam high and Vadulam,
Vyamalam the other, and Kalottaram,
The Subram pure and Makutam to crown.

அண்ணல் அருளால் அருளுஞ் சிவாகமம்
எண்ணிலி கோடி தொகுத்திடு மாயினும்
அண்ணல் அறைந்த அறிவறி யாவிடின்
எண்ணிலி கோடியும் நீர்மேல் எழுத்தே. 64

Import Of Agamas

Numberless the Sivagamas composed,
The Lord by His Grace revealed;
Yet if they know not the wisdom He taught;
Like writing on water, the unnumbered fade.

மாரியும் கோடையும் வார்பனி தூங்கநின்
றேரியு நின்றங் கிளைக்கின்ற காலத்து
ஆரிய முந்தமி ழும்உட னேசொல்லிக்
காரிகை யார்க்குக் கருணைசெய் தானே. 65

Revealed Alike In Sanskrit and Tamil

When rain and summer and long drawn dews stay occuring,
And when they sustain the lakes,
Then did He in Sanskrit and Tamil at once,
Reveal the rich treasure of His compassion to our Mother Great.

அவிழ்க்கின்ற வாறும் அதுகட்டு மாறுஞ்
சிமிட்டலைப் பட்டுயிர் போகின்ற வாறுந்
தமிழ்ச்சொல் வடசொல் எனும்இவ் விரண்டும்
உணர்த்தும் அவனை உணரலு மாமே. 66

Key To Mystery Of Life

Life takes its birth, stands preserved awhile,
And then its departure takes; caught
In that momentary wave of flux, Him we glimpse,
The Lord who in Tamil sweet and northern tongue
Life's mystery revealed.

4. குரு பாரம்பரியம்

THE GURU HIERARCHY

நந்தி அருள்பெற்ற நாதரை நாடிடின்
நந்திகள் நால்வர் சிவயோக மாமுனி
மன்று தொழுத பதஞ்சலி வியாக்ரமர்
என்றிவர் என்வோ டெண்மரு மாமே. 67

Eight Masters

Seekest thou the Masters who Nandi's grace received
First the Nandis Four, Sivayoga the Holy next;

Patanjali and Vyaghrapada, who in Sabha's holy precincts worshipt
And including me to complete the number Eight.

நந்தி அருளாலே நாதனாம் பேர்பெற்றோம்
நந்தி அருளாலே மூலனை நாடினோம்
நந்தி அருளாவ தென்செயும் நாட்டினில்
நந்தி வழிகாட்ட யானிருந்தேனே. 68

Eight Nathas

By Nandi's grace I, became Nathan,
By Nandi's grace I, entered into Moolan,
By Nandi's grace, what can I perform not?
Nandi guiding, I here below remained.

Tirumular explains how he got his name and became one of the eight Nathas.

மந்திரம் பெற்ற வழிமுறை மாலாங்கன்
இந்திரன் சோமன் பிரமன் உருத்திரன்
கந்துருக் காலாங்கி கஞ்ச மலையனோ
டிந்த எழுவரும் என்வழி யாமே. 69

Seven Disciples

Through instruction imparting
Malangan, Indiran, Soman and Brahman,
Rudran, Kalangi and Kancha malayan,
Come as my disciples in succession.

நால்வரும் நாலு திசைக்கொன்று நாதர்கள்
நால்வரும் நானா விதப்பொருள் கைக்கொண்டு
நால்வரும் யான்பெற்ற தெல்லாம் பெறுகென
நால்வருந் தேவராய் நாதரா னார்களே. 70

Four Nandis

The Four, each in his corner, as Master ruled,
The Four, each his diverse spiritual treasure held
Each gave to the world whatever they had attained,
And thus, the four Immortals and Masters became.

மொழிந்தது மூவர்க்கும் நால்வர்க்கும் ஈசன்
ஒழிந்த பெருமை இறப்பும் பிறப்புஞ்
செழுஞ்சுடர் மூன்றொளி யாகிய தேவன்
கழிந்த பெருமையைக் காட்டகி லானே. 71

Lord Transcends What He Revealed

The Lord who is beyond birth and death,
Inspired me to instruct the three and four,
Yet, the surpassing greatness of Him, of the three radiant lights,
Is never fully revealed.

எழுந்துநீர் பெய்யினும் எட்டுத் திசையுஞ்
செழுந்தண் நியமங்கள் செய்மினென் றண்ணல்
கொழுந்தண் பவளக் குளிர்சடை யோடே
அழுந்திய நால்வர்க் கருள்புரிந் தானே. 72

Nandis Attain Celestial State

"The Heavens in eight directions may rain,
Yet shall you the Holy rites and pure perform;"
So spoke He of the cool matted locks and coral hue,
And His Grace conferred on the steadfast Four.

5. திருமூலர் வரலாறு
HISTORY OF TIRUMULAR

நந்தி இணையடி யான்தலை மேற்கொண்டு
புந்தியின் உள்ளே புகப்பெய்து போற்றிசெய்
தந்தி மதிபுனை அரனடி நாடொறுஞ்
சிந்தைசெய் தாகமஞ் செப்பலுற் றேனே. 73

In Meekness And Prayer

High on my bowed head Nandi's sacred Pair of Feet I bore,
Intoning loud His Name in my heart's deepest core,
Daily musing on Hara wearing high the crescent moon,
Thus I ventured the Agamas to compose.

செப்புஞ் சிவாகமம் என்னும்அப் பேர்பெற்றும்
அப்படி நல்கும் அருள்நந்தி தாள்பெற்றுத்
தப்பிலா மன்றில் தனிக்கூத்துக் கண்டபின்
ஒப்பில் எழுகோடி யுகம்இருந் தேனே. 74

Witnessed Divine Dance

Flashed in my mind the mystic name of Sivagama;
Straight I rose to Arul Nandi's Holy Feet;
These eyes witnessed, enthralled,
The surpassing Dance in Holy Sabha;
Thus I lived and joyed for seven crore Yugas.

The Dance of Siva, which symbolises the manifestations of the Universe as an activity of Siva, is the most fascinating and unique characteristic of Tamil Saivite religion and is repeatedly stressed by Tirumular in this work. The deep impact it has made on Tamil mind is reflected in every branch of literature and art, music, painting, bronze casting, sculpture etc. The bronze castings are especially popular all over the world. Ananda Coomaraswamy's superb article on the "Dance of Siva" leaves an indelible impression about the greatness of the theme.

இருந்தவக் காரணங் கேளிந் திரனே
பொருந்திய செல்வப் பவனா பதியாம்
அருந்தவச் செல்வியைச் சேவித் தடியேன்
பரிந்துடன் வந்தனன் பத்தியி னாலே. 75

Lost In Sakti Devotion

Hear O! Indra, what urged me thus to stay?
She the Holy One, Divine Daughter of austerity of the Universe, rich in penance,

In devotion deep and true, Her I adored
And with ardour unceasing, here I pursued.

Divine Daughter: Parvati Devi.

சதாசிவந் தத்துவம் முத்தமிழ் வேதம்
மிதாசனி யாதிருந் தேனின்ற காலம்
இதாசனி யாதிருந் தேன்மன நீங்கி
உதாசனி யாதுடனே உணர்ந் தோமால். 76

Mystic Truths Flashed

Sadasiva, Tattva, the Muthamil and Vedas
Them I sought not while here I fasted;
I held them not in the heart; but soon my mind turned,
And indifference abandoning, realised them all

மாலாங்க னேயிங்கு யான்வந்த காரணம்
நீலாங்க மேனியள் நேரிழை யாளொடு
மூலாங்க மாக மொழிந்த திருக்கூத்தின்
சீலாங்க வேகத்தைச் செப்பவந் தேனே. 77

Import Of Siva's Dance

This it was, O Malanga, urged me here to come,
The Veda to expound and the Dance Divine's deep import;
These mysteries occult the Lord first unveiled
To Her of the azure hue and jewels bright.

நேரிழை யாவாள் நிரதிச யானந்தப்
பேருடை யாளென் பிறப்பறுத் தாண்டவள்
சீருடை யாள்சிவ னாவடு தண்டுறை
சீருடை யாள்பதஞ் சேர்ந்திருந் தேனே. 78

Devotion To Sakti

Bright jewelled, the Eternal Bliss named,
She my Saviour, sundering all bonds of birth;
Siva's treasure, Mistress of Avaduthurai cool,
Her Feet I reached and in devotion fast remained.

சேர்ந்திருந் தேன்சிவ மங்கைதன் பங்கனைச்
சேர்ந்திருந் தேன்சிவ னாவடு தண்டுறை
சேர்ந்திருந் தேன்சிவ போதியின் நீழலிற்
சேர்ந்திருந் தேன்சிவன் நாமங்கள் ஓதியே. 79

Under The Sacred Bodhi Tree

Fixed in devotion fast I clung to Him, Parvati's Half,
Rooted firm to Siva who in Avaduthurai
In devotion fast sought repose under Siva Bodhi's shade,
In devotion fast I chanted
The lyric spell of His countless names.

This refers to the legend that Tirumular as he traversed through space from Kailas and came near Tiruvavaduthurai (now in Tanjavur District of Tamil Nadu, India, where the holy monastery Tiruvavaduthurai Aadheenam now is) he saw a herd of cows moaning for their master, Mula, who was lying dead. Unable to bear the sufferings of the herd of cows Tirumular, by his miraculous Siddhi power, transmigrated into the body of the cowherd Mula, concealing his own original body in the hollow of a tree. The herd of cows seeing their master, Mula, come back to life, frisked and bellowed in joy. The saint, now in the guise of the cowherd, Mula, drove the cows safely back home. There, the wife of the cowherd suspected that her husband was not his usual self because he was behaving strangely. The news soon reached the village, and people began to wonder. The saint then reached the Bodhi tree in the village and there remained in deep meditation. So passed 3,000 years. Each year he composed one mantra expounding the essence of Agamic truths. Thus in 3,000 years the 3,000 mantras of the Tirumantiram came to be composed. This would mean that while Tirumular realised the truths of the Agama while at Thillai witnessing the Cosmic Dance and contemplating Siva/Sakti, he actually composed the work Tirumantiram under the shade of the Bodhi tree at Tiruvavaduthurai; and he acquired the name Mular, because he entered the body of the cowherd, Mula.

இருந்தேன் இக்காயத்தே எண்ணிலிகோடி
இருந்தேன் இராப்பகல் அற்ற இடத்தே
இருந்தேன் இமையவர் ஏத்தும் பதத்தே
இருந்தேன் என்நந்தி இணையடிக் கீழே. 80

Countless Years In Mortal Body

Remained thus prisoned in mortal coil for ages beyond count;
Remained in space where not day nor darkeness is;
Remained at the feet where Devas offer praise,
Remained immutably fixed, at my Nandi's holy

பின்னைநின் றென்னே பிறவி பெறுவது
முன்னைநன் றாக முயல்தவஞ்செய்கிலர்
என்னைநன் றாகஇறைவன் படைத்தனன்
தன்னைநன் றாகத் தமிழ்ச்செய்யு மாறே. 81

Agamic Truths In Tamil

If in a former birth one does not do penance,
Who can say what the next birth will be.
The Lord, however, gave me a good birth
So that I may sing His glory in sweet Tamil.

ஞானத் தலைவிதன் நந்தி நகர்புக்கு
ஊனமில் ஒன்பதுகோடி யுகந்தனுள்
ஞானப்பா லாட்டி நாதனை அர்ச்சித்து
யானும் இருந்தேன்நற் போதியின் கீழே. 82

Through Ninety Million Yugas

Entering the city of Nandi, the Lord of the goddess of wisdom
I sat under the Bodhi tree for ninety million Yugas
Worshipping the Lord with the milk of wisdom

செல்கின்ற வாறறி சிவமுனி சித்தசன்
வெல்கின்ற ஞானத்து மிக்கோர் முனிவராய்ப்

பல்கின்ற தேவர் அசுரர்நரர் தம்பால்
ஒல்கின்ற வான்வழி யூடுவந் தேனே. 83

From Kailas To Earth

I sought the way countless Devas, Asuras, humans take
To scale the heights; all wisdom conquered;
Thus a Shiva Muni I grew and Siddha true,
Came down here through the cerulean blue.

சித்தத்தின் உள்ளே சிறக்கின்ற நூல்களில்
உத்தம மாகவே ஓதியவேதத்தின்
ஒத்த உடலையும் உள்நின்ற உற்பத்தி
அத்தன் எனக்கிங் கருளால் அளித்ததே. 84

Scriptures

By the grace of the Lord I came to realize
The inner meaning of the Agamas
Which are on a par with the Vedas,
The greatest of the scriptures that thrill the heart.

யான்பெற்ற இன்பம் பெறுகஇவ் வையகம்
வான்பற்றி நின்ற மறைப்பொருள் சொல்லிடின்
ஊன்பற்றி நின்ற உணர்வுறு மந்திரந்
தான்பற்றப் பற்றத் தலைப்படுந் தானே. 85

Bliss To Humanity

All the world may well attain the bliss I have received,
If the name of the Lord chanted by the great ones is repeated,
Within the heart will arise a thrilling unstruck sound
Which, when practised, will lead to. realization.

பிறப்பிலி நாதனைப் பேர்நந்தி தன்னைச்
சிறப்பொடு வானவர் சென்றுகை கூப்பி
மறப்பிலர் நெஞ்சினுள் மந்திர மாலை
உறைப்பொடுங் கூடிநின் றோதலு மாமே. 86

Garland Of Mantras

The Heavenly Beings with folded hands approach
Nandi, the Lord above and free of the bonds of birth;
Deep in their hearts the Holy Hymns revolve
Forget not to chant the chain of holy hymns.

அங்கிமி காமைவைத் தானுடல் வைத்தான்
எங்குமி காமைவைத் தானுல கேழையுந்
தங்கிமி காமைவைத் தான்தமிழ்ச் சாத்திரம்
பொங்கிமி காமைவைத் தான்பொருள் தானுமே. 87

Splendour Of Tamil Agamas

In the human body He placed the digesting fire.
To prevent the flooding of the seven worlds He placed a cosmic fire,
To prevent the eruption of egoism He has given us
the Tamil. Sastras,
He who gave all these is the Supreme.

அடிமுடி காண்பார் அயன்மால் இருவர்
படிகண் டிலர்மீண்டும் பார்மிசைக் கூடி
அடிகண் டிலேன்என் றச்சுதன் சொல்ல
முடிகண்டேன் என்றயன் பொய்மொழிந் தானே. 88

Baffling Quest Of Brahma And Vishnu

Ayan and Mal, His Head and Foot toiling sought,
Baffled in their quest, again on earth they met;
"I saw not the Foot," Achutha plained
"The Head I saw," Ayan falsely claimed.

பெற்றமும் மானும் மழுவும் பிறிவற்ற
தற்பரன் கற்பனை யாகுஞ் சராசரத்
தற்றமும் நல்கி அடியேன் சிரத்தினில்
நற்பத மும்அளித் தான்எங்கள் நந்தியே. 89

Lord Blessed Tirumular

Our Nandi, who ever holds the bull, deer and axe
The infinite God, whose imagination is this earth
Containing moving and non-moving things has granted me this opportunity.
And on my head He planted His Holy feet!

ஞேயத்தை ஞானத்தை ஞாதுரு வத்தினை
மாயத்தை மாமாயை தன்னில் வரும்பரை
யாயத்தை யச்சிவன் தன்னை யகோசர
வீயத்தை முற்றும் விளக்கியிட் டேனே. 90

Basic Spiritual Categories.

So impelled, streamed out of me in measures full
The Jneya, the Jnana, and the Jnathru,
The Maya, and the Parayaya that in Mamaya arise,
The Siva and the Agochara Veeya.

Tirumular claims in line 4 (Tamil) that he has explained in full in this text all the categories mentioned in this verse. These are the core essentials of Saiva Siddhanta philosophy. They are Sanskrit words in Tamilised form and it may be helpful to explain the terms briefly. "Jñeya" is "that which is to be known", "Jñāna" is "knowledge" and "Jñāṭr" is the "knower" (subject). In Saiva Siddhanta "Māyā" is not "illusion" but a kind of "purity" (mala) which hides 'Pati", the Lord, from the vision of the imperfect "Paśu" (soul). It is of two kinds, "Śuddha māyā" and "aśuddha māyā"; the evolutes from the former are five in kind, known as "parāyaya; and "agochara veeya" stands for "Śiva's splendours" here.

விளக்கிப் பரமாகும் மெய்ஞ்ஞானச் சோதி
அளப்பில் பெருமையன் ஆனந்த நந்தி
துளக்கறும் ஆனந்தக் கூத்தன்சொற் போந்து
வளப்பில் கயிலை வழியில்வந் தேனே. 91

From Siva's Seat To Earth

I have come by the great path of Kailas,
In the line of the Lord who expounded the above truths,
Who is eternal, Truth effulgent, limitless;
Nandi, the Blissful One who dances joyously.

நந்தி அருளாலே மூலனை நாடிப்பின்
நந்தி அருளாலே சதாசிவ னாயினேன்
நந்தி அருளால்மெய்ஞ் ஞானத்துள் நண்ணினேன்
நந்தி அருளாலே நானிருந் தேனே. 92

Form-Formless Sadasiva State

With Nandi's Grace I sought Moolan,
With Nandi's Grace I Sadasiva became,
With Nandi's Grace Truth Divine attained,
With Nandi's Grace I so remained.

இருக்கில் இருக்கும் எண்ணிலி கோடி
அருக்கின்ற மூலத்துள் அங்கே இருக்கும்
அருக்கனுஞ் சோமனும் ஆரழல் வீச
உருக்கிய ரோமம் ஒளிவிடுந் தானே. 93

God Within Vedic Hymns

In the countless measures that are in Veda Rig,
He indwells with His radiant locks;
The Sun and Moon with their splendid argent rays,
In vain they melt the waxing lustre of His glowing locks.

பிதற்றுகின் றேன்என்றும் பேர்நந்தி தன்னை
இயற்றுவன் நெஞ்சத் திரவும் பகலும்
முயற்றுவன் ஓங்கொளி வண்ணன்எம் மானை
இயற்றி சோதி இறைவனு மாமே. 94

Night And Day Yearn For Him

Unceasing, I prattle daily Nandi's name.
By day praise Him in thought and by night as well,
Daily I yearn for my Master, the Light-hued,
The Lord of the uncreated Radiant Flame.

6. அவையடக்கம்

IN HUMILITY

ஆரறி வார்எங்கள் அண்ணல் பெருமையை
யாரறி வார்இந்த அகலமும் நீளமும்
பேரறி யாத பெருஞ்சுடர் ஒன்றதின்
வேரறி யாமை விளம்புகின் றேனே. 95

Infinite Greatness!

Who can know the greatness of our Lord!
Who can measure His length and breadth!
He is the mighty nameless Flame;
Whose unknown beginnings I venture to speak.

பாடல்வல் லார்நெறி பாட அறிகிலேன்
ஆடவல் லார்நெறி ஆட அறிகிலேன்
நாடவல் லார்நெறி நாட அறிகிலேன்
தேடவல் லார்நெறி தேடகில் லேனே. 96

Poor Qualifications

I know not the way singers sing,
I know not the way dancers dance,
I know not the way seekers seek,
I know not the way searchers search.

மன்னிய வாய்மொழி யாலும் மதித்தவர்
இன்னிசை உள்ளே எழுகின்ற ஈசனைப்
பின்னை உலகம் படைத்த பிரமனும்
உன்னும் அவனை உணரலு மாமே. 97

Power Of Prayer

By words spoken in Truth's luminous accents
Rising on sweetest music's pious heights
Even Brahma who after Him created this our world,
All, all, seek His imperishable Light.

தத்துவ ஞானம் உரைத்தது தாழ்வரை
முத்திக் கிருந்த முனிவருந் தேவரும்
ஒத்துடன் வேறா யிருந்து துதிசெயும்
பத்திமை யால்இப் பயனறி யாரே. 98

God's Deep Mystery

The saints and celestials seeking liberation,
Listen to His exposition at the sacred foothill,
And singing His glory gain realization.
Others indifferent do not.

7. திருமந்திரத் தொகைச் சிறப்பு

THE GLORY OF THE HOLY HYMNS THREE THOUSAND

மூலன் உரைசெய்த மூவா யிரந்தமிழ்
ஞாலம் அறியவே நந்தி அருளது
காலை எழுந்து கருத்தறிந் தோதிடின்
ஞாலத் தலைவனை நண்ணுவ ரன்றே.

Path To God

Three Thousand Holy Hymns, Mula in Tamil composed,

Did he, Nandi, reveal for all the world to know,
Those who wake early at dawn and sing understanding the meaning
Will win the splendid soft repose
Of the Bosom of the Lord.

வைத்த பரிசே வகைவகை நன்னூலின்
முத்தி முடிவிது மூவா யிரத்திலே
புத்திசெய்து பூர்வத்து மூவா யிரம்பொது
வைத்த சிறப்புத் தருமிவை தானே. 100

General And Specialised Knowledge

In the Holy Three Thousand is the Salvation Fine
Of the diverse works, true and good;
In the Divine Three Thousand, original and wise,
All knowledge is, special and general.

8. குருமட வரலாறு

THE SPIRITUAL HIERARCHY

வந்த மடமேழு மன்னுஞ்சன் மார்க்கத்தின்
முந்தி உதிக்கின்ற மூலன் மடவரை
தந்திரம் ஒன்பது சார்வு வாயிரஞ்
சுந்தர ஆகமச் சொல்மொழிந் தானே. 101

Seven Holy Orders

Seven are the Holy Orders, spiritual and true;
Mula, of the first, from the Himalayas sprung,
In the Tantras Nine and Hymns Three thousand
Propounds the Word of Agama in beauty dight.

For the seven monasteries, see Mantra 102. Tirumula's Agamic school of Saiva Siddhanta was replicated by his disciples.

கலந்தருள் காலாங்கர் தம்பால கோரர்
நலந்தரு மாளிகைத் தேவர்நா தாந்தர்
புலங்கொள் பரமானந் தர்போக தேவர்
நிலந்திகழ் மூலர் நிராமயத் தோரே. 102

Heads Of Seven Orders

Kalanga immanent-living, Agora his very next,
Maligai Deva the good and the holy Nadanta,
Paramananda, who the senses conquered and Bhogadeva,
And Mula here breathing—of the Eternal are they all.

9. மும்மூர்த்திகள் முறைமை

THE THREE GODS

அளவில் இளமையும் அந்தமும் ஈறும்
அளவியல் காலமும் நானும் உணரில்
தளர்விலன் சங்கரன் தன்னடி யார்சொல்
அளவில் பெருமை அரிஅயற்காமே. 103

Hara, Hari And Aya

However much I may think for ages and ages
Of Him whose youth is eternal,
Him who has no beginning or end, I cannot succeed
He too remains everywhere, however much Brahma and Vishnu
May describe His glory.

ஆதிப் பிரானும் அணிமணி வண்ணனும்
ஆதிக் கமலத் தலர்மிசை யானுஞ்
சோதிக்கில் மூன்றுந் தொடர்ச்சியில் ஒன்றெனார்
பேதித் துலகம் பிணங்குகின் றார்களே. 104.

Trinity—One Continuity

He, the Being First, and He, the Emerald-hued,
And He of the glowing, original Lotus-seat—
Though the three form an integral whole
The world considers them separate and quarrel.

ஈசன் இருக்கும் இருவினைக் கப்புறம்
பீசம் உலகிற் பெருந்தெய்வ மானது
ஈசன் அதுஇது என்பார் நினைப்பிலார்
தூசு பிடித்தவர் தூரறிந் தார்களே. 105

God Is One

Beyond the Two Karmas[1] is Isa seated,
The seed of this world, the mighty God become;
"This" and "That" is Isa[2]—so the thoughtless contend,
The dross but know the basest sediment low.

(1) Good and evil deeds.
(2) Isa — Siva

சிவன்முதல் மூவரோ டைவர் சிறந்த
அவைமுதல் ஆறிரண் டொன்றொடொன் றாகும்
அவைமுதல் விந்துவும் நாதமும் ஓங்கச்
சவைமுதற் சங்கரன் தன்பெயர் தானே. 106

Nine Aspects Of One Being

Siva the First, then the Three[1], and the following,

With whom flourished Bindu and Nada,
Nine are they all, yet one and the same—
All these but names of Sankara First.

---

(1) Sakti, Nada and Bindu — the first three evolutes.
(2) Brahma, Vishnu, Rudra, Mahesvara, Sadasiva.

பயன்அறிந் தவ்வழி எண்ணும் அளவில்
அயனொடு மால்நமக் கன்னியம் இல்லை
நயனங்கள் மூன்றுடை நந்தி தமாரம்
வயனம் பெறுவீர்அவ் வானவ ராலே. *107*

Trinity Are Kin

But if we thus the soul of truth probe and bare,
Aya or Mal to us no alien Beings are!
But Indissolubly kin to Nandi, the Three Eyed!
Blessed be ye all by the Heavenly Three!

ஓலக்கஞ் சூழ்ந்த உலப்பிலி தேவர்கள்
பாலொத்த மேனி பணிந்தடி யேன்தொழ
மாலுக்கும் ஆதிப் பிரமற்கும் ஒப்புநீ
ஞாலத்து நம்மடி நல்கிடென் றானே. *108*

Trinity Are Co-Equals

Lying prostrate I adored the Milk-hued One,
While countless Devas stood around in melting prayers lost;
Then spoke the Lord to me:
"To Vishnu and Brahma am I equal;
Be it Yours to give the world
The Grace of My Feet."

வானவர் என்றும் மனிதர்இவர் என்றுந்
தேனமர் கொன்றைச் சிவனருள் அல்லது
தானமர்ந் தோருந் தனித்தெய்வம் மற்றில்லை
ஊனமர்ந் தோரை உணர்வது தானே. *109*

All Gods Are But The One Siva

It is only by the grace of Siva decked with konrai flowers,
That the celestials and the humans who are in essence the same exist.
There is no God except He,
Our only duty is to enshrine Him in our heart.

சோதித்த பேரொளி மூன்றைந் தெனநின்ற
ஆதிக்கண் ஆவ தறிகிலர் ஆதர்கள்
நீதிக்கண் ஈசன் நெடுமால் அயன்என்று
பேதித் தவரைப் பிதற்றுகின் றாரே. *110*

Assign Not Ranks To Trinity

The ignorant know not from the First did leap
The Light that flamed into Three and Five;
So blindly groping, lost in maze of words,
Isa, Mal and Aya, to graded ranks assign.

பரத்திலே ஒன்றாய்உள் ளாய்ப்புறமாகி
வரத்தினுள் மாயவ னாய்அய னாகித்
தரத்தினுள் தான்பல தன்மைய னாகிக்
கரத்தினுள் நின்று கழிவுசெய் தானே. *111*

One And Many

The Supreme is one, Absolute without lapse,
In descent thereof, Mal and Aya becoming;
Thus He, the One into many ranked;
By conscious choice a Self-deduction made.

தானொரு கூறு சதாசிவன் எம்இறை
வானொரு கூறு மருவியும் அங்குவான்
கோனொரு கூறுடல் உள்நின் றுயிர்க்கின்ற
தானொரு கூறு சலமய னாமே. *112*

Siva Is Jiva

In one Part, He, Sadasiva my Lord;
One heavenly Part in Heaven resides;
One Kingly Part, the spirit that the body heaves;
One His Part to all motion transformed.

Special Introduction Concluded

முதல் தந்திரம்
TANTRA ONE

1. உபதேசம்

DIVINE INSTRUCTION

விண்ணின் றிழிந்து வினைக்கீடாய் மெய்கொண்டு
தண்ணின்ற தாளைத் தலைக்காவல் முன்வைத்து
உண்ணின் றுருக்கியொ ரொப்பிலா ஆனந்தக்
கண்ணின்று காட்டிக் களிம்பறுத் தானே. 113

He Descended From Heaven and Filled Me With Grace

He came down from Heaven, clothed in body,
Karma to match, stretched forth His cool Feet of Grace, form time immemorial
And lo! inside me He stood, melting my yielding heart;
And filled my eyes with peerless bliss, past all compare,
All impurity dispelled.

Divine Nandi, Siva's form/formless aspect of Sadasiva, assumed human form and planted His Feet of Grace on Tirumular. In so doing, Tirumular's primordial impurities vanished. He became pure as crystal at the touch of the Lord's coral red Feet. Tirumular's inner eye opened and he perceived the divine Truths.

களிம்பறுத் தான்எங்கள் கண்ணுதல் நந்தி
களிம்பறுத் தான்அருட் கண்விழிப் பித்துக்
களிம்பணு காத கதிரொளி காட்டிப்
பளிங்கிற் பவளம் பதித்தான் பதியே. 114

He Planted His Feet on My Heart

All impurity He shattered—our Nandi, Forehead-eyed,
Shattered to pieces by His opening Eye of Grace,
His Eye; at whose radiant light impurity quails;
So transfixed He His Coral Feet on heart of mine,
Crystal turned.

The Fore-head eye of Siva is also the "Eye of Grace", that which sheds Grace; besides being the fierce one which burns up all offending objects, such as Tripura and Kama. Since Sakti is the one through whom Siva confers grace, and is also the wielder of Siva's Power, paranthetically the third-eye stands for Sakti.

பதிபசு பாசம் எனப்பகர் மூன்றிற்
பதியினைப் போற்பசு பாசம் அனாதி
பதியினைச் சென்றணு காப்பசு பாசம்
பதியணு கிற்பசு பாசநில் லாவே. 115

Pati (God), Pasu (Soul) and Pasa (Bondage) are Eternal

They speak of the Three—Pati, Pasu and Pasa;
Beginningless as Pati, Pasu and Pasa are:
But the Pasu-Pasa nears not the Pati supreme:
Let but Pati touch! the Pasu-Pasa is as naught.

Three categories are eternal: Pati (Lord), pasu (soul) and pasam (bondage). But Pati is untouched by pasam (bondage). Pasam binds pasu only. But when Pati nears pasu, pasam will not stand.

வேயின் எழுங்கனல் போலேஇம் மெய்யெனுங்
கோயி லிருந்து குடிகொண்ட கோன்நந்தி
தாயினும் மும்மலம் மாற்றித் தயாஎன்னுந்
தோயம தாய்எழுஞ் சூரிய னாமே. 116

He Shattered Impurities Three—Egoity, Illusion and Karma

Like the rising spark that within the bamboo indwells,
So Lord Nandi abides in this body-temple
With sweet compassion gentler than a mother's,
He shattered the Impurities Three,
And like unto the sun on the ocean of mercy arose.

Like the music that issues from the flute, from within the body rises Nandi's divinity. In infinite maternal compassion, He dispels the impurities within, as the sun dispels darkness.

சூரிய காந்தமுஞ் சூழ்பஞ்சும் போலவே
சூரிய காந்தஞ் சூழ்பஞ்சைச் சுட்டிடா
சூரியன் சந்நிதி யிற்சுடு மாறுபோல்
ஆரியன் தோற்றமுன் அற்ற மலங்களே. 117

At His Glance, Impurities Vanish

The sunstone sleeps in cotton enclosed,
The sunstone burns not the fragile stuff;
Let but the sun's rays fall! How it shrivels and flames!
Even so the impure wilts before the Lord's cathartic glance.

Well may the sun-stone be surrounded by cotton wool. The stone by itself burns, not the wool; but when the sun beats on it, the cotton blazes into fire and turns into ash. So too the impurities before the Lord's cathartic glance.

மலங்களைந் தாமென மாற்றி அருளித்
தலங்களைந் தானற் சதாசிவ மான
புலங்களைந் தானப் பொதுவினுள் நந்தி
நலங்களைந் தானுள் நயந்தான் அறிந்தே. 118

He Broke Into My Soul's Silent Depths

All our impurities He removes,
Our worldly existence He transmutes into spiritual life,
And dancing in the citsabha He controls our sensual passions
Knowing the purity of the soul He has come to reside there.

Thus did Nandi descending from His Sadasiva state enter the dance hall of the soul, poured His Grace, destroyed the passions that bind the senses, and removed all impurities.

அறிவைம் புலனுட னேநான் றதாகி
நெறியறி யாதுற்ற நீராழம் போல
அறிவறி வுள்ளே அழிந்தது போலக்
குறியறி விப்பான் குருபர னாமே. 119

Supreme Consciousness

Our intelligence entangled in the senses,
Finds itself in very deep waters,
But inside our consciousness is a deeper Consciousness,
Which the Supreme grace stimulates.

Consciousness is entangled with the senses knowing not its true course. But when the Gurupara, the Master Supreme, entered in me, consciousness was drowned in the deeper waters of superconsciousness.

ஆமேவு பால்நீர் பிறிக்கின்ற அன்னம்போல்
தாமே தனிமன்றில் தன்னந் தனிநித்தந்
தீமேவு பல்கர ணங்களுள் உற்றன
தாமேழ் பிறப்பெரி சார்ந்தவித் தாமே. 120

He Roasted the Seeds of Recurring Births

Like unto the swan that from cow's milk the water parts,
So the Lord, Himself, alone, in this Sabha unique,
Grasped the senses many that scorch like fire,
And thus the Seven Births unto roasted seeds rendered.

Like unto the swan that separates water from the milk — in the dance hall of awareness, He separated the impurities that lay intermixed in the senses, and scorched for ever the seed of birth.

வித்தைக் கெடுத்து வியாக்கிரத் தேமிகச்
சுத்தத் துரியம் பிறந்து துடக்கற்ற
ஒத்துப் புலனுயிர் ஒன்றாய் உடம்பொடு
செத்திட்டிருப்பர் சிவயோகி யார்களே. 121

Sivayogins Attain Turiya State in Mortal Body

Sivayogins are they that the seed destroy,
Who, in waking state, the pure awareness induce;
Who in harmony unbroken, achieve the tranced breath,
When life, senses, body — alike simulate death.

They destroy the seed of birth; and reach the turiya state of superconsciousness becoming dead to the body, senses and life, as it were, although remaining alive —this is the state of Siva- yogis.

Siva yogin is a Jīvan Mukta or a Saivite bhakta who, by obeying strictly the injunctions of his faith in worship, yoga, etc., has attained that condition, and has become 'liberated'. Man's consciousness, in Vedāntic thought, operates differently in four different states, namely, waking, sleep with dreams, dreamless sleep, and finally in the fourth or Turiya state completely liberated from bodily bonds. In this state, man is, 'dead' to material circumstances, and even while alive, he is fully spiritual.

சிவயோக மாவது சித்தசித் தென்று
தவயோகத் துள்புக்குத் தன்னொளி தானாய்
அவயோகஞ் சாரா தவன்பதி போக
நவயோக நந்தி நமக்களித் தானே. 122

Sivayoga is to Attain Self-Illumination

Sivayoga it is to know the Cit-Acit,
And for the Yoga-Penance qualify;
Self-light becoming Self,
To enter undeviating, His lordly domain;
He granted me this — Nandi of the Nine Yogas.

Cognising cit (spiritual) and acit (material) as distinct and different, entering samadhi yoga, attaining self-illumination, skirting the false paths, and reaching the Lord world — this, Siva yoga true. And Nandi of the blessed nine yogas imparted this.

'Cit' is a Sanskrit word meaning Mind or Consciousness; hence, 'Acit' is the opposite of it. When Cit is made fully operative through yoga and tapas, the Self becomes enlightened, and liberation is attained.

அளித்தான் உலகெங்குந் தானான உண்மை
அளித்தான் அமரர் அறியா உலகம்
அளித்தான் திருமன்றுள் ஆடுந் திருத்தாள்
அளித்தான் பேரின்பத் தருள்வெளி தானே. 123

He Granted Me Bliss Supreme

He made me see the truth that He pervades all.
Granted me the vision of the world that even Devas know not,
The vision of the Sacred Feet in Holy Sabha's cosmic dance,
Granted me His infinite Grace and the Bliss supreme.

These He granted: the truth of His all-pervasiveness; the world that even celestials know not; the Feet of Grace that danceth forever in the holy hall; the Grace of infinite bliss that is the space vast.

Holy Sabha, a term which frequently makes its appearance in this text, refers to the Universe in its totality, or more specifically 'akasa' or Space which is void and the operating ground of the Divine. In another sense, it is the mind of the human being, which, when purified, becomes one with the Universal Mind, that is 'akasa'. In Tamil culture the counter part on earth of the Holy Sabha is "Thillai" or the temple at Chidambaram.

வெளியில் வெளிபோய் விரவிய வாறும்
அளியில் அளிபோய் அடங்கிய வாறும்
ஒளியில் ஒளிபோய் ஒடுங்கிய வாறும்
தெளியும் அவரே சிவ சித்தர் தாமே. 124

Who Are the Siva-Siddhas

Space intermingling with space,
Nectar drowning in nectar,
Light dissolving in light
The elect are they, the Siva-Siddhas,
Who attain this glorious state.

Space merges in space; love in love; light in light — they who realise this alone, are Siva-siddhas.
A Siva-Siddha is, it is said in this verse, one whose 'cit' has attained the conditions referred in the notes on the preceding three verses.

சித்தர் சிவலோகம் இங்கே தெரிசித்தோர்
சத்தமுஞ் சத்த முடிவுந்தம் முள்கொண்டோர்
நித்தர் நிமலர் நிராமயர் நீள்பர
முத்தர்தம் முத்தி முதல்முப்பத் தாறே. 125

Siddhas Ascend the Thirty-Six Tattvas

Siddhas they that Siva's world here visioned,
Nada and Nadanta deep in them realized,
The Eternal, the Pure, reposing in Bliss unalloyed, —
Thirty and Six the steps to Liberation leading.

They are siddhas who perceive Siva's world here below; who transcend nada (sound principle) and nadanta (the ultimate sound); they are immortal; the beings pure; are in eternal bliss; attain transcendental liberation, beyond the 36 tattvas.
Tattvas are the fundamental principles of existence. The Saiva Siddhanta School of philosophy postulates them as thirty-six; the five Siva tattvas, the seven vidya tattvas, and the twenty-four prakriti tattvas — also known as atma tattvas. The Siva tattvas arise in the 'pure maya' sphere, the vidya tattvas in the 'impure maya' sphere and the prakriti tattvas in the 'prakriti maya' sphere. These three spheres may be approximated to the 'pure immaterial', 'material/immaterial', and 'pure material' concepts. For a further account of the tattvas and their evolution, see Tantra II.

முப்பதும் ஆறும் படிமுத்தி ஏணியாய்
ஒப்பிலா ஆனந்தத் துள்ளொளி புக்குச்
செப்ப அரிய சிவங்கண்டு தான்தெளிந்
தப்பரி சாக அமர்ந்திருந் தாரே. 126

They Walk Into Light of Siva

Ascending thus the steps,
Thirty and six of Freedom's ladder high,
Into the peerless Light of Bliss they walked;
And Siva, the inexplicable, they saw—
Having seen, realized and so stayed.

They remain pervasive as Sivam, witnessing all of Siva's works. Perceiving the three tenses — the past, present and future; they remain lost in divine tranquility.

இருந்தார் சிவமாகி எங்குந் தாமாகி
இருந்தார் சிவன்செயல் யாவையும் நோக்கி
இருந்தார் முக்காலத் தியல்பைக் குறித்தங்
கிருந்தார் இழவுவந் தெய்திய சோம்பே. 127

Siddhas Lose Themselves in Divine Tranquillity

In Siva they remained, seeing themselves in all,
Remained thus mutely gazing at Siva's works manifold,
In silence witnessing Time's three tenses,
They remained, lost, in Divine tranquillity.

In divine tranquillity they remain. Realization of divine tranquillity is the end of all knowledge. They who realise it sleep in absolute knowledge.

சோம்பர் இருப்பது சுத்த வெளியிலே
சோம்பர் கிடப்பதுஞ் சுத்த வெளியிலே
சோம்பர் உணர்வு சுருதி முடிந்திடஞ்
சோம்பர்கண் டாரச் சுருதிக்கண் தூக்கமே. 128

Nature of Divine Tranquillity

In space pure is tranquillity seated
In space pure It does repose,
Tranquillity begins where Vedas end;
There in self-realization they quietly abide.

தூங்கிக்கண் டார்சிவ லோகமும் தம்உள்ளே
தூங்கிக்கண் டார்சிவ யோகமும் தம்உள்ளே
தூங்கிக்கண் டார்சிவ போகமும் தம்உள்ளே
தூங்கிக் கண்டார்நிலை சொல்வதெவ் வாறே. 129

Sleeping Still They Perceive

Sleeping, in themselves they saw Siva's World,
Sleeping, in themselves they saw Siva's Yoga,
Sleeping, in themselves they saw Siva's Bhoga,
How then describe the minds
Of those who sleeping saw?

They who 'sleep' thus vision the world of Siva within them. Within them they realise Siva yoga; within them they enjoy Siva bhoga. Their state is indeed beyond description.

எவ்வாறு காண்பான் அறிவு தனக்கெல்லை
அவ்வாறருட் செய்வன் ஆதியரன் தானும்

ஒவ்வாத மன்றுள் உமைகாண ஆடிடுஞ்
செவ்வானிற் செய்ய செழுஞ்சுடர் மாணிக்கம். 130

As Much as You Strive, So Much is His Grace Bestowed

Even as you strive to reach Wisdom's bounds,
Even so on you, Hara, the Being First, His Grace bestows,
In Sabha unique He dances for Uma to behold,
Like a Flaming Ruby in the Flaming Sky.

The Lord is the Flaming Ruby that dances in the arena of space for Sakti to witness. And as you near the frontiers of awareness, so does He grant His Grace.

Siva's Grace matches human endeavour. In Akasa is His dance, played for his Sakti, Uma, to behold and enjoy.

மாணிக்கத் துள்ளே மரகதச் சோதியாய்
மாணிக்கத் துள்ளே மரகத மாடமாய்
ஆணிப்பொன் மன்றினில் ஆடுந்திருக்கூத்தைப்
பேணித் தொழுதென்ன பேறுபெற் றாரே. 131

The Glorious Beauty of Divine Dance

Inside the ruby like the emerald flaming
Inside the ruby like the emerald inset,
He dances the Holy Dance in the Sabha of purest gold
What Oh, the reward, to those who Him adored!

As luminous emerald green within the ruby red, as storied terrace within the ruby red, He dances in the purest Hall of Gold. What did they get — those who witnessed that Dance? Infinite rapture.

பெற்றார் உலகிற் பிரியாப் பெருநெறி
பெற்றார் உலகிற் பிறவாப் பெரும்பயன்
பெற்றார் அம் மன்றிற் பிரியாப் பெரும்பேறு
பெற்றார் உலகுடன் பேசாப் பெருமையே. 132

Attainment of Deathlessness and Birthlessness

In this world they received the Deathless Way great
In this world they attained the Birthless End great
The Gift unique of non-separateness from the Sabha pure
The ineffable rapture, of non-communication with the world.

பெருமை சிறுமை அறிந்தெம் பிரான்போல்
அருமை எளிமை அறிந்தறி வாரார்
ஒருமையுள் ஆமைபோல் உள்ளைந் தடக்கி
இருமையுங் கேட்டிருந் தார்புரை அற்றே. 133

Senses Controlled, They Saw This World and Next

Who there be who, like our Lord, distinct know
The great and the small, the difficult and the facile?
They, like unto tortoise, drawing in senses five under the shell,
They heard and saw This and Next, all impurities dispelled.

Who else but He has the knowledge of human greatness and littleness? They, who, turtle-like, withdraw their senses within, know this world and That.

The simile of the tortoise and the five senses is a favourite one in Hinduism. The Goraknaths (Khānpata Yogis) of the 14th Cent. A.D. onwards seem to have adopted the tortoise as their symbol and emblematic mascot.

புரைஅற்ற பாலினுள் நெய்கலந் தாற்போல்
திரைஅற்ற சிந்தைநல் ஆரியன் செப்பும்
உரையற் றுணர்வோர் உடம்பிங் கொழிந்தாற்
கரையற்ற சோதி கலந்தசத் தாமே. 134

Silence of Waveless Thought

Like the ghee subtly latent in purest milk,
Into the waveless Thought the Lord in silence speaks;
They who, in silence realise, this mortal coil shuffled,
Purity they become, in Limitless Light mingling.

Latent as the ghee within pure milk is waveless thought for the Pure Lord. They who grasp its entire inner meaning will merge as pure spirit in divine light.

சத்த முதல்ஐந்துந் தன்வழித் தான்சாரில்
சித்துக்குச் சித்தன்றிச் சேர்விடம் வேறுண்டோ
சுத்த வெளியிற் சுடரிற் சுடர்சேரும்
அத்தம் இதுகுறித் தாண்டுகொள் அப்பிலே. 135

When the Five Senses Take Cit's Way, They Reach Cit

When the five senses commencing with sound, retrace their evolution
Where shall the consciousness merge but in the cosmic mind?
When one light merges in another there will be only light,
Understand this crystal clear.

அப்பினிற் கூர்மை ஆதித்தன் வெம்மையால்
உப்பெனப் பேர்பெற் றுருச்செய்த அவ்வுரு
அப்பினிற் கூடிய தொன்றாகு மாறுபோற்
செப்பினிற் சீவன் சிவத்துள் அடங்குமே. 136

Jiva Lies Enclosed in Siva

The fierce rays of the sun beating upon the water,
The dissolved salt does in crystal shapes emerge;
That salt in the water dissolved becomes liquid again,
So does Jiva in Siva get redissolved.

அடங்குபே ரண்டத் தணுஅண் டஞ் சென்றங்
கிடங்கொண் ட தில்லை இதுவன்றி வேறுண் டோ
கடந்தொறும் நின்ற உயிர்கரை காணில்
திடம்பெற நின்றான் திருவடி தானே. 137

As Atom Merges in the Vast, Jiva Merges in Siva

The tiny atom, swimming in the Universe vast,
Merges in the Vast—no separate existence knows;
So the Spirit abiding in each body
At sight of His Holy Feet, discovers its Ancient Home.

திருவடி யேசிவ மாவது தேரில்
திருவடி யேசிவ லோகஞ் சிந்திக்கில்
திருவடி யேசெல் கதியது செப்பில்
திருவடி யேதஞ்சம் உள்தெளி வார்க்கே. 138

Lord's Feet are the Final Refuge of Souls Illumined

The Holy Feet is Siva, if you but know,
The Holy Feet is Siva's world, if you but think,
The Holy Feet is Freedom's bliss, realize,
There is the final refuge for souls illumed.

The Lord's Holy Feet are Sivam; the Lord's Holy Feet are Siva's world; the Holy Feet are life's goal; the Holy Feet are the sure refuge.

தெளிவு குருவின் திருமேனி காண்டல்
தெளிவு குருவின் திருநாமஞ் செப்பல்
தெளிவு குருவின் திருவார்த்தை கேட்டல்
தெளிவு குருவுரு சிந்தித்தல் தானே. 139

Guru's Role in Soul's Illumination

It is but to see the Guru's Holy Form,
It is but to chant the Guru's Holy Name
It is but to hear the Guru's Holy Word,
It is but to muse on the Guru's Holy Being,
Thus it is the soul its illumination receives.

Seek the Darsana of the holy Guru; chant the name of the holy Guru; listen to the teachings of the holy Guru; and meditate on the form of the holy Guru.

தானே புலன்ஐந்துந் தன்வச மாயிடும்
தானே புலன்ஐந்துந் தன்வசம் போயிடும்
தானே புலன்ஐந்துந் தன்னில் மடைமாறும்
தானே தனித்தெம் பிரான்தனைச் சந்தித்தே. 140

Seek His Grace, the Senses Get Controlled

Surely then the senses five under your control come,
Surely then the senses five back to their native homes retreat,
Surely then the senses five turn inward
When the soul meets the Lord.

சந்திப் பதுநந்தி தன்திருத் தாளிணை
சிந்திப் பதுநந்தி செய்ய திருமேனி
வந்திப் பதுநந்தி நாமம்என் வாய்மையால்
புந்திக்குள் நிற்பது நந்திபொற் போதமே. 141

Fill Thy Thoughts With Nandi

All I see is Nandi's Holy Feet twain,
All I think is Nandi's Holy Form divine,
All I chant is Nandi's Name, I trow,
In all my thoughts Nandi's golden Words and wise.

போதந் தரும்எங்கள் புண்ணிய நந்தியைப்
போதந் தனில்வைத்துப் புண்ணிய ராயினார்
நாதன் நடத்தால் நயனங் களிகூர
வேதந் துதித்திடப் போயடைந் தார் விண்ணே. 142

Thus They Reached Heaven

Who, in their minds, kept our Nandi's Holy Name,
Nandi, Wisdom's Lord, — they holy became;
As the Lord danced, they beheld Him with eyes enthralled,
While the Vedas sang in praise,
Reached Heaven's sacred shores.

Having thus imparted the essence of "Divine Instruction" (Upadesam) in 30 verses, which sum up the final teachings of the Tirumantiram's 3,000 verses, Tirumular proceeds to lay down the ground rules that have to be observed by the Sadhaka — the spiritual aspirant.

He first dwells on the ephemeral nature of this body and the certainty of death laying its icy hands on all living things.

2. யாக்கை நிலையாமை

TRANSITORINESS OF BODY

மண்ணொன்று கண்டீர் இருவகைப் பாத்திரந்
திண்ணென் றிருந்தது தீவினை சேர்ந்தது
விண்ணின்று நீர்விழின் மீண்டுமண் ணானாற்போல்
எண்ணின்றி மாந்தர் இறக்கின்ற வாறே. 143

Dust Into Dust-That is Body's Way

At first it was clay, then it divided into two,
It was keeping well when evil entered,
Even as clear water falling from the skies,
Mixed with the mud becomes muddy,
Men degenerated and became subject to birth and death.

This body of mortal clay is driven by twain Karmas, good and bad. When the rains pour incessantly the mud pot turns to mud again. So, too death brings destruction; and when the body-roof in time caves in, neither wife nor children accompany it. Only the austerities and knowledge the man acquired go with him. They gather—the kith and kin—wail aloud, no longer call him by his name, but as a corpse carry him to the burning ground and having burnt the body, wash their own bodies and think no more of it.

பண்டம்பெய் கூரைபழகி விழுந்தக்கால்
உண்டஅப் பெண்டிரும் மக்களும் பின்செலார்
கொண்ட விரதமும் ஞானமும் அல்லது
மண்டி அவருடன் வழிநட வாதே. 144

Vigil and Wisdom Alone Accompany the Departing Soul

This roof of delights, when by use, to pieces falls,
Wife nor children who all enjoyed follow the parting Soul
Only the holy vigils kept and wisdom gained
Remain to save—others dwindle and desert us all.

ஊரெலாங் கூடி ஒலிக்க அழுதிட்டுப்
பேரினை நீக்கிப் பிணமென்று பேரிட்டுச்
சூரையங் காட்டிடைக் கொண்டுபோய்ச் சுட்டிட்டு
நீரினில் மூழ்கி நினைப்பொழிந் தார்களே. 145

How Soon the Dead are Forgotten

The neighbours gathered together wailing loud and long,
Denied him now a name, called him corpse,
And bore him to the burning ghat and the body burnt,
Then did a ceremonial dip—and memory of him fades away.

காலும் இரண்டு முகட்டலக் கொன்றுள
பாலுள் பருங்கழி முப்பத் திரண்டுள
மேலுள கூரை பிரியும் பிரிந்தால்முன்
போலுயிர் மீளப் புகஅறி யாதே. 146

When Body Roof Falls, It Falls Forever

Two pillars support this roof and one single beam,
Thirty and two the rafters extend sideways,
But as the roof above decays and breaks,
Back to its mansion the breath of life fails its way to trace.

The body is a fleshy frame with two legs, a central column, and 32 siderial skeletal bones. When the roof above falls, the life that departed doesn't re-enter.

சீக்கை விளைந்தது செய்வினை மூட்டிற்ற
ஆக்கை பிரிந்த தலகு பழுத்தது
மூக்கினிற் கைவைத்து மூடிட்டுக் கொண்டுபோய்க்
காக்கைக் குப்பலி காட்டிய வாறே. 147

Body Dead is to be cremated

The body rots with gangrene and phlegm, the Prarabdhas leave the body,
The bones turn fragile,
After verifying death by feeling the nostrils with the fingers.
They cover the body and perform the cremation which includes the offering to the ravens.

அடப்பண்ணி வைத்தார் அடிசிலை உண்டார்
மடக்கொடி யாரொடு மந்தணங் கொண்டார்
இடப்பக்க மேஇறை நொந்தது என்றார்
கிடக்கப் படுத்தார் கிடந்தொழிந் தாரே. 148

Death Comes Sudden

The rich repast was laid and he dined and joyed,
With damsels sweet in amorous dalliance toyed;
''A little, little pain — on the left'' he moaned
And laid himself to rest to be gathered to dust.

The cake was baked. He ate the meal; enjoyed with his winsome damsels; complained of a slight pain on the left; went to repose; and for ever slept.

மன்றத்தே நம்பி மாடம் எடுத்தது
மன்றத்தே நம்பி சிவிகைபெற் றேறினான்
மன்றத்தே நம்பி முக்கோடி வழங்கினான்
சென்றத்தா வென்னத் திரிந்திலன் தானே. 149

Pomp and Glory Lead But to the Grave

In pride of pomp a stately mansion he built,
In rage of wealth into the palanquin he stept,
In vain excess gave away largesses in crores,
But, he ne'er went to say, 'Oh! God'' and roamed.

He raised a towering mansion; he rode the stately palanquin; he distributed largesses; but never called the name of God.

வாசந்தி பேசி மணம்புணர்ந் தப்பதி
நேசந் தெவிட்டி நினைப்பொழி வார்பின்னை
ஆசந்தி மேல்வைத் தமைய அழுதிட்டுப்
பாசந்திச் சுட்டுப் பலியட்டி னார்களே. 150

Alive They Embraced the Body, Dead They Consigned it to Flames

Lips met lips, bodies locked in close embrace,
And love in surfeit cloyed—then died memories long cherished,
Soon the body on bier was set while mourners mourned;
All passsion spent, the body in the leaping flames perished.

கைவிட்டு நாடிக் கருத்தழிந் தச்சற
நெய்யட்டிச் சோறுண்ணும் ஐவரும் போயினார்
மையிட்ட கண்ணாளும் மாடும் இருக்கவே
மெய்விட்டுப் போக விடைகொள்ளு மாறே. 151

Nothing Remains, When Life Departs

The pulse failed, the mind lost its axle-hold,
The senses five, that buttered sweets enjoyed, left their home;

The fair-eyed beloved and dear treasures remained to stay,
But the spark of life for ever quitted.

பந்தல் பிரிந்தது பண்டாரங் கட்டற்ற
ஒன்பது வாசலும் ஒக்க அடைத்தன
துன்புறு காலந் துரிசுவர மேன்மேல்
அன்புடை யார்கள் அழுதகன் றார்களே. 152

Kith and Kin Wept and Left

The roof to pieces went, the bonds of life broke loose,
The mansion's nine gates closed fast for ever and aye,
Time's painful march fast gaining apace,
One by one weeping they left him as the hours passed by.

நாட்டுக்கு நாயகன் நம்மூர்த் தலைமகன்
காட்டுச் சிவிகையொன் றேறிக் கடைமுறை
நாட்டார்கள் பின்செல்ல முன்னே பறைகொட்ட
நாட்டுக்கு நம்பி நடக்கின்ற வாறே. 153

Final Procession to Grave

Lord was he of our land, sole leader of our place,
Mounted now on palanquin for the ultimate journey's end;
Mourners walked behind, clashing drums beat afore;
Thus did the solemn show in ample length, extend.

முப்பதும் முப்பதும் முப்பத் தறுவருஞ்
செப்ப மதிளுடைக் கோயிலுள் வாழ்பவர்
செப்ப மதிளுடைக் கோயில் சிதைந்தபின்
ஒப்ப அனைவரும் ஓட்டெடுத் தார்களே. 154

The Body Temple Crumbled; the Ninety-Six Tattvas Fled

The thirty and thirty and thirty-six they say,
They that behind temple walls safely dwelt.
They saw the temple walls crash and crumble,
And all alike, without a trace, thence did run.

The 96 tattvas dwelt within the fortress of the body - temple; and when the body-temple crashed down, all of them fled in haste.

The ninety-six tattvas comprised the thirty-six internal tattvas referred to in Mantra 124 above, plus sixty external tattvas consisting of the twenty-five manifestations of the five elements: earth, water, fire, air and space; the ten nadis; the ten vayus (airs); the three desires; the five modes of speech; the three gunas; and the four sound forms. The specific names of the ninety-six tattvas are given below:

Ninety-Six Tattvas

1. Manifestations of the five elements in the body (25)

(1) Earth, Skin, Bone, Tendon, Flesh, Hair, (2) Water, Blood, Fat, Brain, Semen, (3) Fire, Food, Sleep, Fear, Coition, Sloth, (4) Wind, Running, Walking, Standing, Sitting, Lying (5) Space, Anger, Miserliness, Avarice, Obstinacy, Malice.

2. Nadis in the Body (10)

Ida, Pingala, Sushumna, Gandhari, Hasti, Singhavi, Alambutai, Purushan, Gugu, Sangini

3. Vayus (airs) in the body (10)

Prana, Apana, Udana, Vyana, Samana, Naga, Kurma, Girihara, Devadatta, Dhananjaya.

4. Desires (3)

Wealth, Children, World

5. Speech (5)

Talking, Memorising, Singing, Weeping, Exulting.

6. Gunas (3)

Sattva, Rajas, Tamas

7. Sound (4)

Sukshma (subtle), Pasyanti (incoherent speech), **Madhyama** (emanating from throat), Vaikhari (articulate)

மதுவூர் குழலியும் மாடும் மனையும்
இதுவூர் ஒழிய இதணம தேறிப்
பொதுவூர் புறஞ்சுடு காடது நோக்கி
மதுவூர வாங்கியே வைத்தகன் றார்களே. 155

They Hurried the Body to Flames

Death strikes from life's enchanted cup
Honeyed delights of wife, cherished treasures of heart;
Kinsmen bore him on bier to the common burning ghat,
And the burden discharged, hurried home,
Having done their part.

The dear wife, and wealth and home remained behind. They mounted the corpse on the bier and sped it towards the burning ground.

வைச்சகல் வுற்றது கண்டு மனிதர்கள்
அச்சக லாதென நாடும் அரும்பொருள்
பிச்சது வாய்ப்பின் தொடர்வுறு மற்றவர்
எச்சக லாநின் றிளைக்கின்ற வாறே. 156

We do not learn from the death of others

Witnessing the corpse from which the spirit has departed,
Men think it will not happen to them,
They pursue the tinsels of the world,

And degenerate without any Karma getting extinguished.

ஆர்த்தெழு சுற்றமும் பெண்டிரும் மக்களும்
ஊர்த்துறைக் காலே ஒழிவர் ஒழிந்தபின்
வேர்த்தலை போக்கி விறகிட் டெரிமூட்டி
நீர்த்தலை மூழ்குவர் நீதியி லோரே. 157

They Too Finally Depart Cleansing Themselves by a Bath

Mourning friends, weeping spouse, dear children all,
They but followed him to the river's edge—not a step beyond;
Then sorrow dropped its mark, quick the pyre was lit,
Then they plunge in water, heart-whole they, the graceless band.

வளத்திடை முற்றத்தோர் மாநிலம் முற்றுங்
குளத்தின் மண்கொண்டு குயவன் வனைந்தான்
குடமுடைந் தால்அவை ஓடென்று வைப்பர்
உடலுடைந் தால்இறைப் போதும் வையாரே. 158

When Body-Pot Breaks None Cares To Retain It

This universe entire of treasures vast compact
The Great Potter from watery clay wrought to shape;
If the moulded pot breaks, men keep the pieces still,
But if the body cracks, who even a whit cares to keep?

ஐந்து தலைப்பறி யாறு சடையுள
சந்தவை முப்பது சார்வு பதினெட்டுப்
பந்தலும் ஒன்பது பந்தி பதினைந்து
வெந்து கிடந்தது மேலறி யோமே. 159

Body is Burnt to Ashes; Beyond That We Know Not

Five the senses, six the chakras
Thirty the joints, eighteen the sides,
Nine the ligaments, fifteen the rows—
All to ashes burnt—no more we know beside.

The body fashioned out of numerous constituents— hair, bones, flesh, blood and lymph—dressed in diverse styles was finally consigned to flames, and turned to ashes. Beyond that we know nothing.

அத்திப் பழமும் அறைக்கீரை நல்வித்துங்
கொத்திஉலைப்பெய்து கூழட்டு வைத்தனர்
அத்திப் பழத்தை அறைக்கீரை வித்துண்ணக்
கத்தி எடுத்தவர் காடுபுக் காரே. 160

Body is Karmic Fruit

Fruit of fig and seeds of green to pieces chopped,
In a pot they placed, mixed and ground to paste;
Seeds of green the fruit of fig consumed,
Loud they wailed, and bore the body in haste.

Seeds of green are symbolic of unending karmas. The particular green (arai keerai) referred to grows the more you cut it.

The body is described as a fig fruit, as the word 'athi' (Tamil form of Sanskrit word 'ashti') means bone, as well as fig.

மேலும் முகடில்லை கீழும் வடிம்பில்லை
காலும் இரண்டு முகட்டலக் கொன்றுண்டு
ஓலையான் மேய்ந்தவ ரூடு வரியாமை
வேலையான் மேய்ந்ததோர் வெள்ளித் தளிகையே. 161

Body is Fragile Frame

No roofing above, no standing ground below,
Two legs to suppport and a central beam athwart
Rudely thatched on top but unlined within,
An empty vessel in Karmic garb enwrapt.

An ill-designed habitat is this body. Roof above it has none; nor foundation below. Pillars it has two, and central beam as well; but no cross beam exists; and the thatch is flimsy. Of such incompleteness is this handiwork.

கூடங் கிடந்தது கோலங்கள் இங்கில்லை
ஆடும் இலையமும் அற்ற தறுதலும்
பாடுகின் றார்சிலர் பண்ணில் அழுதிட்டுத்
தேடிய தீயினில் தீயவைத் தார்களே. 162

The Lute Lay in Dust; the Music Ceased

Deserted the banquet-hall, unlit, unadorned,
Gone the dancer's swaying shape and flashing feet;
Another song now they sang to a wailing tune,
And, seeking fire, flung the body to its consuming heat.

The hall lay empty; no decorations remained; dance and music ceased. However, some do still sing plaintive tunes, after consigning the body to the flame and turning it to ashes.

முட்டை பிறந்தது முந்நூறு நாளினில்
இட்டது தானிலை ஏதேனும் ஏழைகாள்
பட்டது பார்மணம் பன்னிரண் டாண்டினிற்
கெட்ட தெழுபதிற் கேடறி யீரே. 163

What Did the Body Leave Behind?

When three hundred days are gone, the foetus emerged,
Naught remains of it now, dear friends, you know;
In twelve years' time it learned to smell the rich odours of life,
At seventy it turned to dust—thus briefly ends the show.

In 300 days the egg in the mother's womb hatched in the body. At the age of 12 it began to smell the odours of adult life; at 70 it turned to dust. What did it leave behind?

இடிஞ்சில் இருக்க விளக்கெரி கொண்டான்
முடிஞ்ச தறியார் முழங்குவர் மூடர்
விடிஞ்சிரு ளாவ தறியா உலகம்
படிஞ்சு கிடந்து பதைக்கின்ற வாறே. 164

Lamp Remained; Flame Died

The lamp remains but the flame is out,
Loud the fools lament unaware that the oil is spent,
Night follows day—this they fail to grasp,
And thus immersed fall and moan,
Ever sobbing more and more.

மடல்விரி கொன்றையன் மாயன் படைத்த
உடலும் உயிரும் உருவந் தொழாமல்
இடர்படர்ந் தேழா நரகிற் கிடப்பர்
குடர்பட வெந்தமர் கூப்பிடு மாறே. 165

Those Who Do Not Adore the Lord, Lie writhing in the Seventh Hell

While the body the Lord of blooming Konrai wrought
And Life worshipping not the Divine,
In the Seventh hell, neglected lie,
Writhing in pain and wordless agony keen,
The kith and kin, widely crying, did shout and howl and sigh

The body and soul that worshipped not the Lord, who created all, writhes in the seventh hell. Of what avail are kith and kin, all weeping and shouting?

குடையுங் குதிரையுங் கொற்றவா ளுங்கொண்
டிடையுமக் காலம் இருந்து நடுவே
புடையு மனிதனார் போகும்அப் போதே
அடையும் இடம்வலம் ஆருயி ராமே. 166

Life's Procession Leads But to the Grave

With horse and sword and canopy outspread,
Man fills his fugitive years with pride of life;
But even as the grand cavalcade sweeps past,
Circling from left to right, expires the breath of life.

Man marches in triumphant procession as a hero at the head of a victorious army. But even as the cavalcade passes, life ebbs away without warning. How very transitory is it all!

காக்கை கவரிலென் கண்டார் பழிக்கிலென்
பாற்றுளி பெய்யிலென் பல்லோர் பழிச்சிலென்
தோற்பையுள் நின்றுதொழிலறச் செய்தூட்டுங்
கூத்தன் புறப்பட்டுப் போனஇக்கூட்டையே. 167

Nothing Can Lure Back the Life that Left

When the energising soul leaves this leather bag of the body,
What does it matter if the ravens feed on it, or the bystanders scorn,
Or drops of milk are poured on it and praise.

3. செல்வம் நிலையாமை

TRANSITORINESS OF WEALTH

அருளும் அரசனும் ஆனையுந் தேரும்
பொருளும் பிறர்கொள்ளப் போவதன் முன்னந்
தெருளும் உயிரொடுஞ் செல்வனைச் சேரின்
மருளும் பினையவன் மாதவ மன்றே. 168

Kingly regalia, domains and riches are impermanent

Before others seize and away your riches take,
Your elephant and car, your kingship and grace,
Even while life pulses, if you the Lord's asylum seek,
You need not do any other austerities.

இயக்குறு திங்கள் இருட்பிழம் பொக்குந்
துயக்குறு செல்வத்தைச் சொல்லவும் வேண்டா
மயக்கற நாடுமின் வானவர் கோனைப்
பெயற்கொண்டல் போலப் பெருஞ்செல்வமாமே. 169

Wealth waxes and wanes like the moon

The radiant moon that life animates into massive darkness turns;
Why then speak of riches which no better fate can meet?
If the Heaven's King, you unwaveringly seek,
Like pouring clouds choicest treasures fall at your feet.

Even the luminous moon is devoured by darkness. The wealth we accumulate is far more ephemeral. Seek the Lord of the Heavenly Hosts. You shall receive indestructible treasures, as from the pouring clouds.

தன்னது சாயை தனக்குத வாதுகண்
டென்னது மாடென் றிருப்பார்கள் ஏழைகள்
உன்னுயிர் போம்உடல் ஒக்கப் பிறந்தது
கண்ணது காணொளி கண்டுகொளீரே. 170

Your Shadow is With You, Does it help You? How About Wealth Then?

Foolish they who claim their wealth their own,
Seeing their own shadows to them useless though nearby;

The life that with the body comes as surely departs;
They see not; the light that lends lustre to the seeing eye.

Your own shadow is so much with you; yet it offers no shelter to you. How is it then you cling on to possessions? It is vain hope that it will afford you security. With your body, life too departs. Seek that which imparts light to all.

ஈட்டிய தேன்பூ மணங்கண் டிரதமும்
கூட்டிக் கொணர்ந்தொரு கொம்பிடை வைத்திடும்
ஓட்டித் துரந்திட் டதுவலி யார்கொளக்
காட்டிக் கொடுத்தது கைவிட்ட வாறே. 171

The Bee Stores Honey Only to be Appropriated by Others; So is Your Hoarded Wealth

The industrious bee from flower to flower hops,
Seeking, scenting, gathering, its store of honey sweet;
But soon the subtle thief digs and steals the hoarded wealth;
Likewise, our earthly treasures the same story repeat.

The bee gathers honey industriously. But someone else steals it and enjoys. So it is with your wealth.

தேற்றத் தெளிமின் தெளிந்தீர் கலங்கன்மின்
ஆற்றுப் பெருக்கிற் கலக்கி மலக்காதே
மாற்றிக் களைவீர் மறுத்துங்கள் செல்வத்தைக்
கூற்றன் வருங்கால் குதிக்கலுமாமே. 172

Wealth is a Flood that Ebbs and Flows

Weigh well the pros and cons, and having weighed, waver not.
Lose not your bearings, caught in wealth's eddy;
Fling aside the transient trappings of earthly treasures
And thus when the Pale Sergeant comes, for the great leap be ready.

Wealth comes like the flood of waters and flour away. Put not your trust in it. Fling it aside and think of the Lord. You can defy death in triumphant joy.

மகிழ்கின்ற செல்வமும் மாடும் உடனே
கவிழ்கின்ற நீர்மிசைச் செல்லுங் கலம்போல்
அவிழ்கின்ற ஆக்கைக்கோர் வீடுபே றாகச்
சிமிழொன்று வைத்தமை தேர்ந்தறி யாரே. 173

Wealth is a Boat in Dangerous Waters

How fast we cling to stock of cattle and riches gay
Less stable even than the boat which midstream upturns!
Likewise a bond ties the body to soul,
When it will give away no one knows.

வாழ்வும் மனைவியும் மக்கள் உடன்பிறந்
தாரு மளவே தெமக்கென்பர் ஒண்பொருள்
மேவு மதனை விரிவுசெய் வார்கட்குக்
கூவுந் துணையொன்று கூடலு மாமே. 174

Earthly Treasures are Fleeting

However much of treasure we may leave,
Our wife, children, brothers and sisters will only exclaim "What has he left for us?"
If we devote our life merely for such treasure,
At the end when we are in agony no one will come for help.

வேட்கை மிகுத்தது மெய்கொள்வார் இங்கிலை
பூட்டுந் தறியொன்று போம்வழி ஒன்பது
நாட்டிய தாய்தமர் வந்து வணங்கிப்பின்
காட்டிக் கொடுத்தவர் கைவிட்ட வாறே. 175

Worldly Desires are Never-Ending

Our desires grow, but none the truth to find;
There's one stake to hold but nine exits to leave;
The old familiar faces come smiling to greet and bow;
Deceivers ever, they abandon us without a reprieve.

உடம்பொ டுயிரிடை விட்டோடும் போது
அடும்பரி சொன்றில்லை அண்ணலை எண்ணும்
விடும்பரி சாய்நின்ற மெய்ந்நமன் தூதர்
சுடும்பரி சத்தையுஞ் சூழகி லாரே. 176

All Your Wealth Cannot Bribe Death Away

When the vital spark leaves this mortal mould,
Bribe there is none to lure it back; think, think of the Lord;
Death's loyal servants on restless mission bent,
Do nothing consider that with hot breath you pulse.

When life takes its flight from the body, think of the Lord. You cannot bribe death to stay his hands. The Lord alone shall be our refuge then.

4. இளமை நிலையாமை

TRANSITORINESS OF YOUTH

கிழக்கெழுந் தோடிய ஞாயிறு மேற்கே
விழக்கண்டுந் தேறார் விழியிலா மாந்தர்
குழக்கன்று மூத்தெரு தாய்ச்சில நாளில்
விழக்கண்டுந் தேறார் வியனுல கோரே. 177

Rising Sun Sets; Glowing Youth Fades

They see the sun rises in the east and sets in the west.
Yet blind of eye, the truth they ne'er apprehend.

The tender calf grows, fattens for a while and dies;
But this wonder-pageant of the world they do not comprehend.

Morning after morning the sun rises in the east; blazes through the noonday sky and sets in the western horizon. The tender calf grows into the fat bull and in a few years dies. They see all these; yet they do not realise how very emphemeral youth is!

ஆண்டு பலவுங் கழிந்தன அப்பனைப்
பூண்டுகொண் டாரும் புகுந்தறி வார்இல்லை
நீண்டன காலங்கள் நீண்டு கொடுக்கினுந்
தூண்டு விளக்கின் சுடரறி யாரே. 178

Even a Life-time is not Enough to Know Him

The years roll on; but none the Lord in his bosom holds,
None to probe and perceive Him profound;
Even if Time's thread be to the utmost stretched,
Still they know not the spark that kindles all the lamps around.

தேய்ந்தற் றொழிந்த இளமை கடைமுறை
ஆய்ந்தற்ற பின்னை அரிய கருமங்கள்
பாய்ந்தற்ற கங்கைப் படர்சடை நந்தியை
ஓர்ந்துற்றுக் கொள்ளும் உயிருள்ள போதே. 179

While Life Still Throbs, Fix Your Mind on the Lord

When youth had danced its way to palsied age,
Scarce the chance to fill the years with good deeds more and more;
So while life still throbs, fix your mind on Nandi,
Into whose spreading locks
The holy waters of Ganga eternally pour.

விரும்புவர் முன்னென்னை மெல்லியன் மாதர்
கரும்பு தகர்த்துக் கடைக்கொண்ட நீர்போல்
அரும்பொத்த மென்முலை ஆயிழை யார்க்குக்
கரும்பொத்துக் காஞ்சிரங் காயும்ஒத் தேனே. 180

Youth is Sugar-cane; Age is Nux Vomica

Time was when fond damsels on him their love bestowed;
Like cane's sugary juice, slow sucked, was to them,
The idol of wenches with budding breasts and jewelled shapes;
But now the sweetest cane has bitter nux vomica become.

In youth, man is the cynosure of women's eyes; but when palsied age advances, he becomes an object of repulsion to them. He who was like sugarcane to them now becomes bitter nux-vomica. Such is youth's brief dazzle of glory.

பாலன் இளையன் விருத்தன் எனநின்ற
காலங் கழிவன கண்டும் அறிகிலார்
ஞாலங் கடந்தண்டம் ஊடறுத் தானடி
மேலுங் கிடந்து விரும்புவன் யானே. 181

Time Fleets, So Centre yourself on the Lord

The boy grows to youth, and youth as surely to old age decays,
But time's changes teach them not that nothing abides;
And so, in ceaseless pursuit, His Sacred Feet, I seek
Him who, transcending this world, beyond the universe presides.

From the cradle to the grave man passes through the seven stages of life; and none of the seven stages lasts. Youth passes into age and then to senile decay.

காலை எழுந்தவர் நித்தலும் நித்தலும்
மாலை படுவதும் வாணாள் கழிவதுஞ்
சாலும்அவ் வீசன் சலவிய னாகிலும்
ஏல நினைப்பவர்க் கின்பஞ்செய் தானே. 182

Think of the Lord Through Time's Cycles

Day after day we wake to greet the morn,
Day after day we seek the nightly couch;
Even though God, good and great, may frown in wrath,
True devotees ne'er miss His great Love's guarantee.

Man rises with the sun and goes to sleep at night. Day after day, night after night this happens and thus life fleets away

பருவூசி ஐந்துமோர் பையினுள் வாழும்
பருவூசி ஐந்தும் பறக்கும் விருகம்
பருவூசி ஐந்தும் பனித்தலைப் பட்டாற்
பருவூசிப் பையும் பறக்கின்ற வாறே. 183

The Body Perishes with the senses

The five senses dwell inside the body,
They may leave it any time,
If the five senses become unsteady,
The body which is the container of the senses also perishes.

கண்ணதுங் காய்கதி ரோனும் உலகினை
உண்ணின் றளக்கின்ற தொன்றும் அறிகிலார்
விண்ணுற வாரையும் வினையுறு வாரையும்
எண்ணுறும் முப்பதில் ஈர்ந்தொழிந் தாரே. 184

Know Him the Eye of the eye

We perceive only the external sun and the eye with which we see it,
We do not realise the Lord within who stimulates both the eye and the sun,
Not knowing Him we pass from heaven to hell again and again,
We pass away in the spring of our youth.

ஒன்றிய ஈரெண் கலையும் உடனுற
நின்றது கண்டு நினைக்கிலர் நீசர்கள்
கன்றிய காலன் கருக்குழி வைத்தபின்
சென்றதில் வீழ்வர் திகைப்பொழி யாரே. 185

The Sixteen Kalas are Within; Why Then the Grave?

We pitiable creatures do not think,
Of the Lord who dwells within with sixteen Kalas
Then we wonder why we enter the mother's womb,
And later pass away again and again.

Kala— a part; also a digit of the moon. The 16 Kalas are:

1) Krpa (mercy), 2) mrduta (gentleness) 3) Dhairyam (patience, composure), 4) vairagya (dispassion), 5) dhrti (constancy), 6) sampat (prosperity i.e.,spiritual) 7) trasya (cheerfulness), 8) romanca (rapture), 9) vinaya (sense of propriety, humility), 10) dhyana (meditation), 11) susthirata (quietude, restfulness),12) gambhirya (gravity of demeanour), 13) udyama (enterprise, effort), 14) akshoba (emotionlessness), 15) audarya (magnanimity), 16) ekagrata (concentration)

These are in the *Sahasra Padma.*

Vide "Introduction to Tantra Sastra, "by Sir John Woodroffe, p.57

எய்திய நாளில் இளமை கழியாமை
எய்திய நாளில் இசையினால் ஏத்துமின்
எய்திய நாளில் எறிய தறியாமல்
எய்திய நாளில் இருந்துகண் டேனே. 186

Before Youth Passes, Praise Him in Songs

In the days assigned to you, before youth passes,
In songs of praise to the Lord, pour out your heart;
In the days to me assigned, wasting not the minutes away,
In the days to me assigned, I, seeing all, remained apart.

5. உயிர் நிலையாமை

TRANSITORINESS OF LIFE

தழைக்கின்ற செந்தளிர்த் தண்மலர்க்கொம்பில்
இழைக்கின்ற தெல்லாம் இறக்கின்ற கண்டும்
பிழைப்பின்றி எம்பெரு மானடி ஏத்தார்
அழைக்கின்ற போதறி யாரவர் தாமே. 187

The Bud Blossoms and Fades; So does Human Life

They see in the sprouting wanton buds on tender twigs
Which all soon they flash their beauty and die;
Yet they praise not the Holy Feet;
Alas! they know not when the sure call comes from High.

ஐவர்க் கொருசெய் விளைந்து கிடந்தது
ஐவரும் அச்செய்யைக் காத்து வருவார்கள்
ஐவர்க்கு நாயகன் ஓலை வருதலால்
ஐவரும் அச்செய்யைக் காவல்விட் டாரே. 188

When Death's Summons Come, the Five Senses Desert the Body

One field lay ready and ripe for the Five Senses to work,
The Five, that one field watched and tilled;
But when the grim summons came from the Lord of death,
All the Five for ever fled and quit the field.

The five senses ruled the body-field. When death's grim summons came, they fled and quit that field.

மத்தளி ஒன்றுள தாளம்இ ரண்டுள
அத்துள்ளே வாழும் அரசரும் அஞ்சுள்ள
அத்துள்ளே வாழும் அரசனும் அங்குளன்
மத்தளி மண்ணாய் மயங்கிய வாறே. 189

Life's Drum Shattered to Pieces

One this body-drum, two the rhythms keeping time,
Five the masters who, inside, make display;
But when the great king, indwelling departed,
The drum lay shattered, a heap of inert clay.

The body is like unto a musical drum. It has two rhythms, the right and left breaths; five its players, the senses; and one the king within—the Jiva. When he departs the drum is as dead as clay.

வேங்கட நாதனை வேதாந்தக் கூத்தனை
வேங்கடத் துள்ளே விளையாடு நந்தியை
வேங்கடம் என்றே விரகறி யாதவர்
தாங்கவல் லாருயிர் தாமறி யாரே. 190

Body is an Empty Vessel

The Lord of this body frail that to ashes turns, the Lord of Vedanta dance
Nandi He is, who in this crumbling frame disports
They, who know not what an empty vessel this body is,
They know not what the life sustains and supports.

சென்றுணர் வான்திசை பத்துந் திவாகரன்
அன்றுணர் வால்அளக் கின்ற தறிகிலர்
நின்றுண ரார்இந் நிலத்தின் மனிதர்கள்
பொன்றுணர் வாரிற் புணர்க்கின்ற மாயமே. 191

Our Days are Numbered

The sun's rays visit all the quarters ten,
But men measuring with their little sense know this not;
They ponder not nor on the deep mystery muse,
These men on earth — subject to birth and death.

மாறு திருத்தி வரம்பிட்ட பட்டிகை
பீறு மதனைப் பெரிதுணர்ந் தாரிலை
கூறும் கருமயிர் வெண்மயி ராவது
ஈறும் பிறப்புமொ ராண்டெனும் நீரே. 192

Everything decays

Even a fine woven cloth gets torn after a time,
The dark locks turn grey,
The year begins and ends,
This truth we do not realize,

துடுப்பிடு பானைக்கும் ஒன்றே அரிசி
அடுப்பிடு மூன்றிற்கும் அஞ்செரி கொள்ளி
அடுத்தெரி யாமற் கொடுமின் அரிசி
விடுத்தன நாள்களும் மேற்சென் றனவே. 193

Extract the food of Nectar

The cooking pot of body contains the rice of nectar,
The three fires are the sun, moon and agni and the five firewoods are the pranas,
Without wasting time get the rice of nectar cooked,
The days are passing away fast.

இன்புறு வண்டிங் கினமலர் மேற்போய்
உண்பது வாச மதுபோல் உயிர்நிலை
இன்புற நாடி நினைக்கிலு மூன்றொளி
கண்புற நின்ற கருத்துள்நில் லானே. 194

Lord is the Light Beyond Visible Reach

The bee, that nectar seeks, flies high for its flower on top
And there, alone, it sucks the fragrant juice;
Even so, they who seek the blessed grace divine,
Aspire for the Light beyond visible reach of eyes.

The bee flies high and drinks the nectar invisible. Ascend high in spirit and vision the light. It is invisible to the naked eye.

ஆம்விதி நாடி அறஞ்செய்மின் அந்நிலம்
போம்விதி நாடிப் புனிதனைப் போற்றுமின்
நாம்விதி வேண்டும தென்சொலின் மானிடர்
ஆம்விதி பெற்ற அருமைவல் லார்க்கே. 195

Pray and Perform Noble Deeds—This is the Law of Life Eternal

Perform thou noble deeds, good Karma to shape,
Praise thou the Holy One, the Holy Land to reach;
This is the law we need, this the law for men,
Who, blessed with earthly life, seek the Life eternal.

அவ்வியம் பேசி அறங்கெட நில்லன்மின்
வெவ்விய னாகிப் பிறர்பொருள் வவ்வன்மின்.
செவ்விய னாகிச் சிறந்துண்ணும் போதொரு
தவ்விக்கொ டுண்மின் தலைப்பட்ட போதே. 196

Share With Others Before You Eat

Speak not in envy, stray not from the Dharmic way,
Covet not other's riches with lustful greedy glances;
With heart to pity attuned, as you sit down to eat,
Share with others before the feast commences.

Speak not in envy; stray not from the dharmic path; covet not other's possessions; share your goodly things with others. Let compassion fill your heart.

6. கொல்லாமை

NON-VIOLENCE

பற்றாய நற்குரு பூசைக்கும் பன்மலர்
மற்றோர் அணுக்களைக் கொல்லாமை ஒண்மலர்
நற்றார் நடுக்கற்ற தீபமுஞ் சித்தமும்
உற்றாரும் ஆவி அமர்ந்திடம் உச்சியே. 197

Don't Kill Even an Atom of Life

For the worship of the Lord many flowers are available,
But the best is not killing even an atom of life,
The best steady flame is the tranquil mind,
The best place for worship is the heart where the soul resides.

கொல்லிடு குத்தென்று கூறிய மாக்களை
வல்லடிக் காரர் வலிக்கயிற் றாற்கட்டிச்
செல்லிடு நில்லென்று தீவாய் நரகிடை
நில்லிடும் என்று நிறுத்துவர் தாமே. 198.

They Who Kill Reach Hell

The men who shouted, "Kill and stab,"
Them with strong ropes Death's ruffians bind;
And stationing them at the fire-gates of Hell,
The agents yell, "Stand, go; and in the fire pit roast."

They who kill reach but hell; in turn to be tortured and roasted in hell fire by Death's messengers.

7. புலால் மறுத்தல்

MEAT EATING—FORBIDDEN

பொல்லாப் புலாலை நுகரும் புலையரை
எல்லாருங் காண இயமன்றன் தூதுவர்
செல்லாகப் பற்றித் தீவாய் நரகத்தில்
மல்லாக்கத் தள்ளி மறித்துவைப் பாரே. 199

Meat Eaters Will Have to Face Hell's Torments

The ignoble ones who base flesh do eat,
Death's agents bind them fast for all to see;
And push them quick into the fiery jaws of hell,
And fling them down there for ever to be.

கொலையே களவுகட் காமம் பொய்கூறல்
மலைவான பாதக,மாம் அவை நீக்கித்
தலையாஞ் சிவனடி சார்ந்தின்பஞ் சார்ந்தோர்க்
கிலையாம் இவைஞானா னந்தத் திருத்தலே. 200

Shun Sinful Living

Killing, thieving, drinking, lusting, lying—
These horrid sins detest and shun; to those
Who Siva's Holy Feet attain and the Bliss eternal,
They come not; such men in Wisdom's bliss ever repose.

8. பிறன்மனை நயவாமை

NOT COMMITTING ADULTERY

ஆத்த மனையாள் அகத்தில் இருக்கவே
காத்த மனையாளைக் காமுறுங் காளையர்
காய்ச்ச பலாவின் கனியுண்ண மாட்டாமல்
ஈச்சம் பழத்துக் கிடருற்ற வாறே. 201

Seek not the Thorny Date; Ripened Jack-Fruit is at Hand

The dear, wedded wife pines within the home,
But the lusting youth covets the guarded neighbour's mate;
Even as one, declining the luscious ripeness of the jack,
Yearns for the tamer taste of the thorny date

The luscious jackfruit is ready at home. Why then climb the thorny date tree?

திருத்தி வளர்த்ததோர் தேமாங் கனியை
அருத்தமென் றெண்ணி அறையிற் புதைத்துப்
பொருத்தமி லாத புளிமாங் கொம்பேறிக்
கருத்தறி யாதவர் காலற்ற வாறே. 202

Seek Not the Sour Tamarind: Sweet Mango is at Hand

The sweet, ripe mango, tended with loving care,
They bury deep, deeming it unripe still;
And up the gnarled tamarind they climb for the sour fruit,
Only to break their limbs—they whom the senses beguile.

The sweet mango stands for one's dear wife. The tamarind stands for other women.

பொருள்கொண்ட கண்டனும் போதகை யாளும்
இருள்கொண்ட மின்வெளி கொண்டுநின் றோரும்
மருள்கொண்ட மாதர் மயலுறு வார்கள்
மருள்கொண்ட சிந்தையை மாற்றகில் லாரே. 203

Adulterers Rush to Doom

Only those who are rolling in wealth,
And those whose intelligence is obscured by ignorance,
Such yield to woman's sensuous charms;
It is impossible to transform the minds of such men

Do not yield to the sensuous charms of other men's wives. You are only rushing to your doom. Hoarders of wealth, rulers of kingdoms, and souls of great learning—have all perished that way.

9. மகளிர் இழிவு

EVIL WOMEN IS IGNOMINY

இலைநல வாயினும் எட்டி பழுத்தாற்
குலைநல வாங்கனி கொண்டுண லாகா
முலைநலங் கொண்டு முறுவல்செய் வார்மேல்
விலகுறு நெஞ்சினை வெய்துகொள் ளீரே. 204

Pledge not Your Heart to Lust

Fine though the leaves be of the nux vomica tree,
Its wealth of fruit is bitter on tongue, unfit to eat;

To them with rounded breasts and luring smile,
Pledge not your wavering heart in passion's heat.

Do not be lured by temptresses. Lovely the fruits of nux vomica look when full ripe. But how very bitter and unfit they are to eat!

மனைபுகு வார்கள் மனைவியை நாடில்
சுனைபுகு நீர்போற் சுழித்துடன் வாங்குங்
கனவது போலக் கசிந்தெழும் இன்பம்
நனவது போலவும் நாடவொண் ணாதே. 205

Incontinent Passion Spells Ruin

The worldly folk who seek connubial delights
Are, like eddying water, sucked into whirling pool;
Such is passion, incontinent, fleeting as a dream;
Real it is not; let not its siren spell you befool.

The delight that women of easy virtue give you is like eddying water. You are sucked forever into passion's whirls.

இயலுறும் வாழ்க்கை இளம்பிடி மாதர்
புயலுறப் புல்லிப் புணர்ந்தவர் எய்தும்
மயலுறும் வானவர் சார்விது என்பார்
அயலுறப் பேசி அகன்றொழிந் தாரே. 206

Women's Charms unreliable

A damsel full of charm and tempting like a she-elephant;
May embrace a lover with the ardour of grass that has received rain
But if another looking more handsome like a celestial,
She will ask the first lover to wait and desert him.

வையகத் தேமட வாரொடுங் கூடியென்
மெய்யகத் தோருளம் வைத்த விதியது
கையகத் தேகரும் பாலையின் சாறுகொள்
மெய்யகத் தேபெறு வேம்பது வாமே. 207

Sweet Beginning, Bitter End

"What are the joys that in woman's charms we seek or find?"
The truly wise of heart pronounce thus their course;
"In the hand like the sugary juice from crushing mills,
But in the body bitterer than bitterest neem.

Momentarily their embrace tastes sugary sweet. But in the end it is bitter neem.

கோழை ஒழுக்கங் குளமூடு பாசியில்
ஆழ நடுவார் அளப்புறு வார்களைத்
தாழத் துடக்கித் தடுக்ககில் லாவிடில்
பூழை நுழைந்தவர் போகின்ற வாறே. 208

Irretrievable Loss in Lust

Those unfirm of mind who, in folly vain,
Indulge in sex
If such betimes we bind not and restrain,
Irretrievably lost are they in lust of sex, sordid and rank.

Indulgence in lust gets you into irretrievable waters. The deeper you plunge, the surer you perish.

10. நல்குரவு

IN VAIN PURSUIT OF ACCUMULATION

புடைவை கிழிந்தது போயிற்று வாழ்க்கை
அடையப்பட் டார்களும் அன்பில ரானார்
கொடையில்லை கோளில்லை கொண்டாட்ட மில்லை
நடையில்லை நாட்டில் இயங்குகின் றார்கட்கே. 209

Misery of Making a Living

Garments to tatters torn, life a joyless desert becomes;
Loved ones and dear friends forsake, with no more love to spare;
Nothing more to give or ask, void of glory and pomp,
Neglected, like automatons they walk, sad and men.

Incessantly, you work for making a living and to accumulate riches. But when the riches are gone, no one cares for you. Even your loved ones forsake you. In loneliness you walk, bereft of pomp and glory.

பொய்க்குழி தூர்ப்பான் புலரி புலருதென்
றக்குழி தூர்க்கும் அரும்பண்டந் தேடுவீர்
எக்குழி தூர்த்தும் இறைவனை ஏத்துமின்
அக்குழி தூரும்அழுக்கற்ற போதே. 210

Pre-Occupation With Filling the Stomach-Pit

Even as the day dawns, men strive the stomach-pit to fill;
With needed tools, they seek hard the hungry void to stop;
But our only way is to praise Him whatever the way of life we pursue;
Sure then that pit is filled when, what in us is impure, is swept off.

Your striving for making a living is pathetic. You stop at nothing to fill the stomach pit. But you do not think of filling up the birth pit. Adore God and be rid of impurities.

கற்குழி தூரக் கனகமுந் தேடுவர்
அக்குழி தூர்க்கை யாவர்க்கும் அரியது
அக்குழி தூர்க்கும் அறிவை அறிந்தபின்
அக்குழி தூரும் அழுக்கற்ற வாறே. 211

Seek not to Fill the Stomach - Pit; Fill the Birth Pit

To fill the stomach's stony pit, they seek the precious gold;
But little do they know how hard it is to fill birth's pit;
Only when true wisdom you attain that pit to rule,
Then that pit is filled, when life is washed clean and rendered fit.

You seek gold to fill the stomach's stony pit. But the birth pit cannot be so filled. Seek the Wisdom True; then that pit will be filled up and you shall forever be cleansed of primordial impurities.

தொடர்ந்தெழு சுற்றம் வினையினுந் தீய
கடந்தோர் ஆவி கழிவதன் முன்னே
உடந்தொரு காலத் துணர்விளக் கேற்றித்
தொடர்ந்துநின் றவ்வழி தூர்க்கலு மாமே. 212

Light Wisdom's Lamp in Good Time

Our kith and kin, unrelenting, more than Karma stern,
Unrelaxing us pursue; so, ere life from body goes,
In good time, light thou Wisdom's lamp,
And intent thus, to that new-lit track, keep close.

Do not trust in kith and kin. The bondage they forge is relentless as Karma. So in good time light wisdom's lamp, and guided by it, close the track to birth.

அறுத்தன ஆறினும் ஆனின மேவி
அறுத்தனர் ஐவரும் எண்ணிலி துன்பம்
ஒறுத்தன வல்வினை ஒன்றல்ல வாழ்வை
வெறுத்தனன் ஈசனை வேண்டிநின் றானே. 213

Lord Alone is Refuge from Harrying Births

Him the Six tastes harried
Him the Five senses maligned, countless miseries giving,
Him Karma tortured through birth after birth pursuing—
Thus he learned to despise life—in the Lord alone refuge finding.

The six tastes harry; the five senses torture: the karmas in cluster malign; the miseries crowd without count. "No more this birth for me" — thus you pray to the Lord.

11. அக்கினி காரியம்

RELATING TO SACRIFICIAL FIRE

வசையில் விழுப்பொருள் வானும் நிலனுந்
திசையுந் திசைபெறு தேவர் குழாமும்
விசையம் பெருகிய வேத முதலாம்
அசைவிலா அந்தணர் ஆகுதி வேட்கிலே. 214

Prosperity Springs From Sacrifice

Riches from obloquy free, the spreading sky and earth,
The directions all, and the godly hosts who there hold sway,
All flourish in Victory's wake when Brahmins true,
With Vedas commencing pursue the sacrificial way

ஆகுதி வேட்கும் அருமறை அந்தணர்
போகதி நாடிப் புறங்கொடுத் துண்ணுவர்
தாம்விதி வேண்டித் தலைப்படு மெய்ந்நெறி
தாமறி வாலே தலைப்பட்ட வாறே. 215

They Give Before They Eat

The Vedic Brahmins who holy sacrifices perform,
On Salvation intent, give before they eat;
Even as in knowledge true, supreme they stand,
So in conduct they lead—to the One Goal headed straight.

Such Brahmins are elevated in knowledge and conduct. They feed others before they feed themselves.

அணைதுணை அந்தணர் அங்கியுள் அங்கி
அணைதுணை வைத்ததின் உட்பொரு ளான
இணைதுணை யாமத் தியங்கும் பொழுது
துணையணை யாயதோர் தூய்நெறி யாமே. 216

Sacrifices Lead to Heaven

When the sacrificer in the company of his consort,
Offers oblations to the outer fire and the inner fire,
Maintaining the discipline of yama etc
They proceed along the correct yogic path.

போதிரண் டோதிப் புரிந்தருள் செய்திட்டு
மாதிரண் டாகி மகிழ்ந்துட னேநிற்குந்
தாதிரண் டாகிய தண்ணம் பறவைகள்
வேதிரண் டாகி வெறிக்கின்ற வாறே. 217

Karmas Depart When Mantras are Chanted

Morn and eve, when in devotion rapt they chant,
The two goddesses (Gayatri and Savitri) with them in smiling grace stand;
Then do the two birds of one seed sprung
Karmas, good and bad, fluttering in haste depart.

நெய்நின் றெரியும் நெடுஞ்சுட ரேசென்று
மைநின் றெரியும் வகையறி வார்கட்கு
மைநின் றவிழ்தரு மத்தின மாம் என்றுஞ்
செய்நின்ற செல்வம் தீயது வாமே. 218

Sacrificial Fires Consume Sins

The flame emerging from the sacrificial fire fed with ghee,
When it enters our heart the egoism is burnt away,
The moment this truth is realized, salvation dawns,
This is the path supreme.

பாழி அகலும் எரியுந் திரிபோலிட்
டூழி அகலும் உறுவினை நோய்பல
வாழிசெய் தங்கி உதிக்க அவைவிழும்
வீழிசெய் தங்கி வினைசுடு மாமே. 219

It Scorches Karmic Evils

All sins fly like wick fast consumed in flame,
All diseases fade that Karma brings in its wake;
They fade and fall in the rising sacrificial fire,
And all evils are scorched that our Karmas make.

In the sacrificial fire, all sins are burnt; all Karma is scorched and all diseases that Karma brings in its train fade.

பெருஞ்செல்வங் கேடென்று முன்னே படைத்த
வருஞ்செல்வம் தந்த தலைவனை நாடும்
வருஞ்செல்வத் தின்பம் வரவிருந் தெண்ணி
அருஞ்செல்வத் தாகுதி வேட்கநின் றாரே. 220

Sacrifices Give Wealth Imperishable

Firmly holding that vast riches are a grievous curse
They hungered for the Lord who to us richest treasure gave;
Hoping and dreaming they waited for the immortal prize,
All sacrifices performed, the undying wealth to achieve.

Riches bring unending grief. Sacrifices lead to undying riches.

ஒண்சுட ரானை உலப்பிலி நாதனை
ஒண்சுட ராகிஎன் னுள்ளத் திருக்கின்ற
கண்சுட ரோன்உல கேழுங் கடந்தஅத்
தண்சுட ரோமத் தலைவனு மாமே. 221

Lord is the Sacrificial Flame of the Heart

The Pure Flame is He, the immortal Lord is He,
The Radiant Flame who in my heart's core resides,
The Lord whose eyes are the Three Fires,
Who the Seven Worlds transcends,
The Lord of Homa's Cool Flame, and my heart's kin besides.

The Lord is Pure Flame. He resides as the pure flame in our hearts. His eyes are of the three flames—the sun, moon, and fire. He is the transcendental Lord of the seven worlds. He is the Master of Holy Sacrifices.

ஓமத்துள் அங்கியின் உள்ளுளன் எம்இறை
ஈமத்துள் அங்கி இரதங்கொள் வானுளன்
வேமத்துள் அங்கி விளைவு வினைக்கடல்
கோமத்துள் அங்கி குரைகடல் தானே. 222

He is the Fire Within All Fires

Inside the Fire of the Homa is my Lord,
Inside too is He seated in the flame of the funeral pyre
The two Fires in the sky, the Sun and the Moon, are He.
The Fire of the Homa checks the sea of Karma from expanding.
The Fire, that the mighty Churner in the sea begot, abides.

He who is inside the fire of sacrificial homa is also the flame of the funeral pyre. He who is the flame that scorches Karma is also the fire that was contained by the Lord in the northern seas, when the Devas and Asuras churned the ocean for ambrosia.

அங்கி நிறுத்தும் அருந்தவர் ஆரணத்
தங்கி இருக்கும் வகையருள் செய்தவர்
எங்கும் நிறுத்தி இளைப்பப் பெரும்பதி
பொங்கி நிறுத்தும் புகழது வாமே. 223

Sacrificial Flame is Undying

In true penance striving, to Vedic rites conforming
They, who everywhere raise the sacrificial flame,
Tireless, unsparing in kindling the Holy Fire—
Theirs the true flame eternal, theirs the undying name.

They who kindle the Vedic fire and tend it in tireless continuity have kindled the eternal flame. They become immortals.

12. அந்தணரொழுக்கம்

DHARMA OF BRAHMINS

அந்தண ராவோர் அறுதொழில் பூண்டுளோர்
செந்தழல் ஓம்பிமுப் போதும் நியமஞ்செய்
தந்தவ நற்கரு மத்துநின் றாங்கிட்டுச்
சந்தியும் ஓதிச் சடங்கறுப் போர்களே. 224

Brahmins Stand in Holy Path

Brahmins are they who the six duties perform,
Tend the glowing fire and thrice daily pray,

Stand fixt in the Holy Path and chant the Vedic hymns,
Morn and eve and perform the rituals.

Six are the duties of Brahmins—to learn, to instruct, to give alms, to receive gifts, to perform sacrifices and to persuade others to perform sacrifices. They tend the holy fire morn, noon and evening. They chant the Vedic mantras at dawn and dusk. They stand constant on the holy path.

வேதாந்தங் கேட்க விருப்பொடு முப்பதப்
போதாந்த மான பிரணவத் துள்புக்கு
நாதாந்த வேதாந்த போதாந்த நாதனை
ஈதாந்தம் எனாதுகண் டின்புறு வோர்களே. 225

Through Vedanta They Seek the Endless Bliss

Intensely eager, Vedanta's noble doctrine to imbibe,
They merge into Pranava, which transcends the three syallables.
And having the vision of the Lord who is Nadanta, Vedanta and Bhodanta,
Merge in Him and be in eternal bliss.
Vision the Lord that is the Finite End,
And there into unending bliss they grow.

Nadanta = transcending sound
Vedanta = beyond the upanishad
Bhodanta = transcending the Pasu-Pati-Pasa complex.

காயத் திரியே கருதுசா வித்திரி
ஆய்தற் குவப்பர் மந்திரமாங் குன்னி
நேயத் தேரேறி நினைவுற்று நேயத்தாய்
மாயத்துள் தோயா மறையோர்கள் தாமே. 226

They Incessant Chant Gayatri and Savitri Mantras

Minds centered in Gayatri holy and Savitri mysterious,
They chant the noble hymns, the heart of Truth to seek;
Mounted on Love's Chariot, lost in Love's sweet ecstasy,
They drown not in Maya — the holy Brahmins meek.

They seek to know the inner meaning of the mantras, Gayatri and Savitri. Chanting the mantras, and mounted on devotion's chariot, they triumph over Maya's temptations.

Gayatri Mantra—Gayatri is the most sacred of all Vaidik mantras. The *Vedas* lie embedded in it, as in a seed. It runs: Om bhur—bhuvah—svah: tat savitur varenyam bhargo devasya dhimahi dhiyo yo nah pracodayat.

Meaning: "Om Let us contemplate the adorable spirit of the Divine Creator (Savitr) of the earth, atmosphere, and celestial spheres. May He illumine our intellect. Om."

The above is the Vaidik Gayatri. The Tantra has its own Gayatri which may be chanted by all. It is called 'Brahma Gayatri', and is given as follows in the *Mahanirvana Tantra* (Chapter III, Verses 109-111):

"Paramesvaraya Vidmahe; Pasa-tattvaya dhimahi; tan no Brahma pracodayat"

Meaning: "May we know the Supreme Lord: let us contemplate the Supreme Essence; and may that Brahman direct us — "Introduction to Tantra Sastras" by Sir John Woodroffe, pp.92-93.

Tirumular's reference here seems to be the Vaidik Gayatri,

பெருநெறி யான பிரணவம் ஓர்ந்து
குருநெறி யாலுரை கூடிநால் வேதத்
திருநெறி யான கிரியை யிருந்து
சொருபம தானோர் துகளில்பார்ப் பாரே. 227

They attained the Manifest State of God

Deep they pondered on Pranava's great holy way,
By Guru's grace inspired, they recited the mystic lay,
The rituals performed by the four Vedas prescribed,
And thus attained pure, pristine Manifestation—the spotless Brahmins they.

Having realised the truth of Pranava (Aum), guided by the Guru, they perform the rituals prescribed in the four *Vedas* and realise the pure form of self-manifest existence (Svarupa).

சத்திய முந்தவம் தான் அவன் ஆதலும்
எய்த்தகும் இந்தியம் ஈட்டியே வாட்டலும்
ஒத்த உயிர்கள் உண்டா யுணர்வுற்றுப்
பெத்தம் அறுத்தலு மாகும் பிரமமே. 228

To Sunder Birth's Bonds is to Realize Brahmam

The Truth, penance, the realization that He and we are one,
Intense control of the senses and
Getting rid of the body-mind complex—
These help to attain the Brahmic state.

வேதாந்தங் கேட்க விரும்பிய வேதியர்
வேதாந்தங் கேட்டுந்தம் வேட்கை ஒழிந்திலர்
வேதாந்த மாவது வேட்கை ஒழிந்திடம்
வேதாந்தங் கேட்டவர் வேட்கைவிட் டாரே. 229

Vedanta is to be Rid of Desires

The Brahmins who yearned for Vedanta's mystic truths,
Heard and listened they yielded still to desire's sway;
True Vedanta it is when earth-born desires all are crushed;
Those who Vedanta truly grasped, all desires burnt away.

நூலுஞ் சிகையும் நுவலிற் பிரமமோ
நூலது கார்ப்பாச நுண்சிகை கேசமாம்

நூலது வேதாந்தம் நுண்சிகை ஞானமாம்
நூலுடை அந்தணர் காண நுவலிலே. 230

Tuft and Thread Alone do not Make a Brahmin

Do thread and tuft alone prove the Brahmin state?
The thread is but cotton and the tuft but hair;
The true thread Vedanta is, the true tuft knowledge
These the Brahmins truly see, these virtues to them belong.

சத்தியம் இன்றித் தனிஞானந் தானின்றி
ஒத்த விடையம்விட் டோரும் உணர்வின்றிப்
பத்தியும் இன்றிப் பரன் உண்மை யின்றிப்
பித்தேறும் மூடர் பிராமணர் தாம்அன்றே. 231

Attributes of True Brahmins

Of Truth devoid, of pure Wisdom bereft,
Lacking sense-control, spiritually inert,
Empty of devotion or grasp of Truth divine;
Mad fools are they—not Brahmins, I assert.

திருநெறி யாகிய சித்தசித் தின்றிக்
குருநெறி யாலே குருபதஞ் சேர்ந்து
கரும நியமாதி கைவிட்டுக் காணுந்
துரிய சமாதியாந் தூய்மறை யோர்க்கே. 232

They Seek Samadhi State

The Holy Path neither Chit nor Achit is;
Along the Guru-led way, they reach the blessed Holy State;
And all action and rituals abandoning,
The pure Brahmins glide into Turiya Samadhi State.

The true brahmins transcend the chit/achit (real/unreal) state of consciousness. Guided by the holy Guru they attain the grace of his feet. They give up all rituals and sacraments; and finally attain Turiya Samadhi state.

மறையோது வாரே மறையவ ரானால்
மறையோர்தம் வேதாந்த வாய்மையில் தூய்மை
குறையோர்தல் மற்றுள்ள கோலாகலமென்
றறிவோர் மறைதெரிந் தந்தண ராமே. 233

They Stand Firm in Vedanta Truth

Only those who chant the Vedas are true Brahmins.
It is only the Vedanta preached by true Brahmins that is lofty.
If other texts which are defective are read it is only for show,
The true Brahmins realize this.

அந்தண்மை பூண்ட அருமறை அந்தத்துச்
சிந்தைசெய் அந்தணர் சேருஞ் செழும்புவி
நந்துதல் இல்லை நரபதி நன்றாகும்
அந்தியுஞ் சந்தியும் ஆகுதி பண்ணுமே. 234

True Brahmins Bring Prosperity to Earth

The holy Brahmins who the pure life embrace,
And ponder well on truths that mark the Vedas' end,
Their land wanes not, their king's earthly empire ever grows,
If morn and eve the sacrificial fire they tend.

Where brahmins truly tend the sacrificial fire morn and evening, where they embrace the pure life, where they meditate on the teachings of Vedanta—there, in that land is no scarcity. The kingdom flourishes and affluence abounds.

வேதாந்த ஞானம் விளங்க விதியிலோர்
நாதாந்த போதம் நணுகிய போக்கது
போதாந்த மாம்பரன் பாற்புகப் புக்கதால்
நாதாந்த முத்தியுஞ் சித்தியும் நண்ணுமே. 235

Through Vedanta They Scale the Heights of Siddhanta

When the Light of Vedanta dawns, from Karma are they freed;
Then, up the path to the Light of Nadanta they scale;
When thus they reach the Lord of Bodhanta Light,
Salvation they attain—and Siddhis come to them.

ஒன்றும் இரண்டும் ஒடுங்கிய காலத்து
நன்றும் இருந்தும் நலம்பல பேசினும்
வென்று விளங்கும் விகிர்தனை நாடுவர்
சென்று வணங்குந் திருவுடை யோரே. 236

They Seek Merger in Lord

When 'You' and 'I'merge in one and the truth they see,
Then seek they the Lord triumphant, seated firm, serene,
Past all babbling words of sweet-sounding praise·
Such alone the true, worshipful grace attain.

தானே விடும்பற் றிரண்டுந் தரித்திட
யானே விடப்படு மேதொன்றை நாடாது
பூமேவு நான்முகன் புண்ணிய போகனாய்
ஓமேவும் ஓரா குதிஅவி உண்ணவே. 237

They Vision Brahman in Aum

The attachment internal and external vanishes,
Egoism goes and mind ceases to wander elsewhere,
Like Brahma seated in the lotus they enjoy bliss.
Who partake only the havis offered in the homa.

13. அரசாட்சி முறை
THE PATH OF KINGS

கல்லா அரசனுங் காலனும் நேரொப்பர்
கல்லா அரசனிற் காலன் மிகநல்லன்
கல்லா அரசன் அறம்ஓரான் கொல்லென்பான்
நல்லாரைக் காலன் நணுகநில் லானே. 238

Death Fairer Than the Tyrant

The ignorant king and Death are cast in equal mould;
Nay, truth to tell, more justly than foolish King, Death claims his due;
The Witless tyrant no law obeys but in murderous fury kills
But Death, cast in finer mould, nears not the good men true.

A tyrant is as bad as death; nay worse. Death does not approach the truly devout; but the tyrant obeys no laws and kills in murderous fury.

நாடோறும் மன்னவன் நாட்டில் தவநெறி
நாடோறும் நாடி அவன்நெறி நாடானேல்
நாடோறும் நாடு கெடுமுட நண்ணுமால்
நாடோறுஞ் செல்வம் நரபதி குன்றுமே. 239

Let the Ruler Observe Holy Law;

The Holy Law daily in strictness observe
If he who rules the state fails to seek the Divine Way
Day by day that land decays in folly envelopt,
Day by day that ruler's wealth declines and dwindles away.

Let the ruler observe the laws of divine dharma. If he fails, the land falls a prey to destruction.

வேட நெறிநில்லார் வேடம்பூண் டென்பயன்
வேட நெறிநிற்போர் வேடம்மெய் வேடமே
வேட நெறிநில்லார் தம்மை விறல்வேந்தன்
வேட நெறிசெய்தால் வீடது வாமே. 240

Ruler's Duty Towards Men of False Garb

What avails the holy garb if the holy life you refuse?
Theirs the truest garb when outer guise and mind accord;
If the king justly rules and restrains these who go off the holy way
Then he and they attain salvation.

It is the duty of the ruler to spot out the men of false garb, and make them walk the path of purity.

மூடங் கெடாதோர் சிகைநூல் முதற்கொள்ளில்
வாடும் புவியும் பெருவாழ்வு மன்னனும்
பீடொன் றிலனாகும் ஆதலாற் பேர்த்துணர்ந்
தாடம் பரநூற் சிகையறுத் தால்நன்றே. 241

Ruler's Duty to Impious Brahmins

If Brahmins, from folly unredeemed, flaunt the tuft and thread,
That land droops and fades, its ruler's glory runs to waste;
So, scanning deep in Wisdom's light, the King shall clip
The thread and tuft for empty show kept and possessed.

If brahmins flaunting the thread and tuft lead an unholy life, the ruler has a duty to put them back on the straight path. So too with those pretenders who don the holy garb and practise evil ways.

ஞானமி லாதார் சடைசிகை நூல்நண்ணி
ஞானிகள் போல நடிக்கின் றவர்தம்மை
ஞானிக ளாலே நரபதி சோதித்து
ஞானமுண் டாக்குதல் நலமாகும் நாட்டிற்கே. 242

Ruler's Duty to Impart Wisdom to Erring Brahmins

The senseless fools donning sacred thread and matted locks,
And with chanting phrases pretend to wisdom unpossessed,
Them, the ruler of state shall, with wise men's help, take and test,
And, for the country's good, impart words in wisdom drest.

ஆவையும் பாவையும் மற்றற வோரையுந்
தேவர்கள் போற்றுந் திருவேடத் தாரையுங்
காவலன் காப்பவன் காவா தொழிவனேல்
மேவும் மறுமைக்கு மீளா நரகமே. 243

Ruler's Duty to Protect Cows, Women and Brahmins

The cow, the woman, the sacred Brahmins true,
And men in holy garb whom the Devas acclaim,
These the king shall protect; if that duty he ignores,
Irredeemable his hell shall be, cursed ever his name.

It is the duty of the ruler to protect the cow, the woman, the brahmins true and the devout true. If he fails, he shall surely be condemned to hell.

திறந்தரு முத்தியுஞ் செல்வமும் வேண்டின்
மறந்தும் அறநெறி யேஆற்றல் வேண்டும்
சிறந்தநீர் ஞாலஞ் செய்தொழில் யாவையும்
அறைந்திடில் வேந்தனுக் காறிலொன் றாமே. 244

Ruler's Share—One-Sixth of the Subject's Produce

If salvation high and treasures true you seek,
Then, awake or asleep, unceasing, the holy way pursue;
Know that of labour done in this sea-girt world,
To the King, in truth, one share in six is due.

The ruler has a claim to one-sixth of the produce of his subjects. Let him not go beyond this. That is not the dharmic way.

வேந்தன் உலகை மிகநன்று காப்பது
வாய்ந்த மனிதர்கள் அவ்வழி யாநிற்பர்
பேர்ந்திவ் வுலகைப் பிறர்கொள்ளத் தாங்கொள்ளப்
பாய்ந்த புலியன்ன பாவகத் தானே. 245

Ruler's Duty to Defend the Territory

If the ruler exceeding well his state protects,
The subjects, in duty bound, to that same end incline;
When the enemy, in lust of pride, the state invades,
Then, like a leopard, leaps the king to defend his domain.

It is the duty of the ruler to defend his people. Like a tiger he should spring on the invader. The ruler who protects his people wins the loyalty of his subjects.

கால்கொண்டு கட்டிக் கனல்கொண்டு மேலேற்றிப்
பால்கொண்டு சோமன் முகம்பற்றி உண்ணாதோர்
மால்கொண்டு தேறலை உண்ணும் மருளரை
மேல்கொண்டு தண்டஞ்செய் வேந்தன் கடனே. 246

Ruler to Punish Drunkards

Breath in control held, letting inward fire upward rise,
Mind turned to Samadhi moon-sprung nectar—if they drink not,
But, like inebriates, heady liquors madly consume,
Then, such shall by ruler to just punishment be brought.

It is the duty of the ruler to punish those who indulge in inebriate drinking. True drinking is to reach the moon in samadhi and quaff of the divine nectar that flows from there.

தத்தஞ் சமயத் தகுதிநில் லாதாரை
அத்தன் சிவன்சொன்ன ஆகம நூல்நெறி
எத்தண் டமுஞ்செயும் அம்மையில் இம்மைக்கே
மெய்த்தண்டஞ் செய்வதவ் வேந்தன் கடனே. 247

Ruler to Punish Those Who Deviate From Their Professed Faiths

Who, by their professed faiths, do not abide,
Beside the judgement they receive in the life beyond,
In terms of Agamic law by Siva revealed,
Punished they shall be on earth by the just ruler of the land.

Let each one stand constant in his own ordained faith. If they deviate, the ruler should not fail to punish them according to the laws laid down in the *Agamas*.

14. வானச் சிறப்பு

THE GLORY OF RAINS

அமுதூறு மாமழை நீரத னாலே
அமுதூறும் பன்மரம் பார்மிசை தோற்றுங்
கமுகூறு தெங்கு கரும்பொடு வாழை
அமுதூறுங் காஞ்சிரை ஆங்கது வாமே. 248

Vegetation Blooms

The fertilising flood of rains outpouring
Makes trees and plants bloom enriched with sap;
The areca palm, coconut, cane and plantain green.
And nux vomica — stand laden rich with crop.

The rains fertilise the earth. All nature wears a green mantle. The trees grow and plants bloom enriched with sap. The palms, the coconut and areca, rise tall and high. The cane gets its sugary sucrose; the plantain yields its delicious fruits. Even the bitter nux vomica so dear to yogic practices flourish because of rain.

வரையிடை நின்றிழி வான்நீர் அருவி
உரையில்லை உள்ளத் தகத்துநின் றூறு
நுரையில்லை மாசில்லை நுண்ணிய தெண்ணீர்க்
கரையில்லை எந்தை கழுமணியாறே. 249

Clear Stream

The mountain torrent rushes down from the heights,
Boundless like the love from the pure heart,
Foamless, stainless, clear and crystalline,
It is fit for bathing the Lord.

15. தானச் சிறப்பு

THE GLORY OF GIVING

ஆர்க்கும் இடுமின் அவரிவர் என்னன்மின்
பார்த்திருந் துண்மின் பழம்பொருள் போற்றன்மின்
வேட்கையுடையீர் விரைந்தொல்லை உண்ணன்மின்
காக்கை கரைந்துண்ணுங் காலம் அறிமினே. 250

Share Your Food With Others

Give freely to all; discriminate not o'er much;
See that food is served to others ere sitting down to eat;
Do not hoard, eat not in greedy haste;
The crow calls its brood to share its food, howe'er sweet.

16. அறஞ்செய்வான் திறம்

IN PRAISE OF THE CHARITABLE

தாமறி வாரண்ணல் தாள்பணி வாரவர்
தாமறி வாரறந் தாங்கிநின் றாரவர்
தாமறி வார்சிவ தத்துவ ராவர்கள்
தாமறி வார்க்குத் தமர்பர னாமே. 251

The Charitable Realize the Self

Who the self realise, seek and adore the Feet of the I ord;
Who the self realise, most freely give in charity;
Who the self realise, Lord of Tattvas become;
Who the self realise, kin they become to the Lord in dear amity.

They who adore the Feet of the Lord realise the Self; they who give freely in charity realise the Self; they who cognise the Tattvas realise the Self. The Lord is kin to those who realise the Self.

Śiva is the 'Lord of the Tattvas'.

யாவர்க்கு மாம்இறை வற்கொரு பச்சிலை
யாவர்க்கு மாம்பசு வுக்கொரு வாயுறை
யாவர்க்கு மாம்உண்ணும் போதொரு கைப்பிடி
யாவர்க்கு மாம்பிறர்க் கின்னுரை தானே. 252

Charity is Within the Reach of All

Easy for all to offer in worship a green leaf to the Lord,
Easy for all to give a mouthful to the cow,
Easy for all to give a handful of food to others before sitting down to eat,
Easy for all, good, kind words on others to bestow.

அற்றுநின் றாருண்ணும் ஊணே அறனென்னுங்
கற்றன போதங் கமழ்பவர் மானிடர்
உற்றுநின் றாங்கொரு கூவற் குளத்தினிற்
பற்றிவந் துண்ணும் பயன்அறி யாரே. 253

Evils of Hoarding

The food that feeds the needy—that alone true charity is;
True men they who that simple truth do find;
But they who hoard, like water in pool past access,
To eat and gorge—to Charity's ways are they blind.

That alone is true charity, when the needy are fed. They who hoard in silence as in a deep concealed pool and gorge themselves alone without giving do not know what wealth is for. This a simple truth, that true men know.

அழுக்கினை ஓட்டி அறிவை நிறையீர்
தழுக்கிய நாளில் தருமமுஞ் செய்யீர்
விழித்திருந் தென்செய்வீர் வெம்மை பரந்து
விழிக்கவன் றென்செய்வீர் ஏழைநெஞ் சீரே. 254

Give Charity When You Have

Driving away ignorance, if with Wisdom you fill not your mind
In days of plenty, you will not give in charity.
What avails it, though wide awake, if hell-fire spreads around,
What avails it, then, if impoverished of heart you are?

தன்னை அறியாது தானல என்னாதிங்
கின்மை யறியா திளையரென் றோராது
வன்மையில் வந்திடுங் கூற்றம் வருமுன்னந்
தன்மையின் நல்ல தவஞ்செய்யும் நீரே. 255

Give Charity Here and Now

Of yourself knowing little, caring naught for your good,

Unmindful e'en of poverty of tender youth taking no care,
Before Death's stern, relentless summons arrives,
Let noble charities your redeeming goodness declare

When death steals upon you, does he care who you are; what is good for you; whether you are rich or poor? Before he arrives, perform charitable deeds.

துறந்தான் வழிமுதற் சுற்றமும் இல்லை
இறந்தான் வழிமுதல் இன்பமும் இல்லை
மறந்தான் வழிமுதல் வந்திலன் ஈசன்
அறந்தான் அறியும் அளவறி வாரே. 256

By Your Charities the Lord Knows You

To him who renounces, no kith or kin has he;
To him who is dead no delights has he;
To him who charityless is, the Lord denies His Presence;
By the measure of thy charity done, the Lord is known to thee.

The Lord denies His presence to him who has not given in charity. Only by the measure of your charity does the Lord know you. Except charity, what kith and kin can a man have after death?

தான்தவஞ் செய்வதாஞ் செய்தவத் தவ்வழி
மான்தெய்வ மாக மதிக்கும் மனிதர்கள்
ஊன்தெய்வ மாக உயிர்க்கின்ற பல்லுயிர்
நான்தெய்வம் என்று நமன்வரு வானே. 257

Charity Leads to Life Eternal

Some in charity overflow; by such noble deeds done,
Noble gods they become in human being's high esteem;
And the many who hold this fleshly body their dear God,
To them comes Death, saying; "I am, your God supreme."

Men who give in charity are esteemed as gods on earth. To others death comes saying "I am your God."

திளைக்கும் வினைக்கடல் தீர்வுறு தோணி
இளைப்பினை நீக்கும் இருவழி உண்டு
கிளைக்குந் தனக்கும்அக் கேடில் புகழோன்
விளைக்குந் தவம்அறம் மேற்றுணை யாமே. 258

Charity and Devotion Twin Escorts to Heaven

Our life's boat across the foaming sea of Karma flies;
Twin the pathways to dispel the labourious strain;
Glory giving tapas and charity the heavenly escorts,
To us and our dear kin from life's battle vain.

There are only two ways of crossing the foaming sea of karma; perform penance and give in charity.

பற்றது வாய்நின்ற பற்றினைப் பார்மிசை
அற்றம் உரையான் அறநெறிக் கல்லது
உற்றுங் களால்ஒன்றும் ஈந்தது வேதுணை
மற்றண்ணல் வைத்த வழிகொள்ளு மாறே. 259

Charity is Your Life's Prop

Earthly desires to worldly objects attached,
No end know; but in charity's noble way,
E'en the little things you give, sure props provide;
All the rest meekly take as the Lord's gift for the day.

Your desires have no end. Only two things can be your prop for the life hereafter; your acts of charity, and your godly way of life.

17. அறஞ்செயான் திறம்

WAY OF THE UNCHARITABLE

எட்டி பழுத்த இருங்கனி வீழ்ந்தன
ஒட்டிய நல்லறஞ் செய்யா தவர்செல்வம்
வட்டிகொண் டீட்டியே மண்ணின் முகந்திடும்
பட்டிப் பதகர் பயன்அறி யாரே. 260

The Hoarders are Sinners

The ripening nux vomica falls profitless on the ground;
Such the barren wealth of those who charities deny;
With usurious greed they bury deep their treasures,
The hardened sinners know not the Truth.

The way of the uncharitable is to accumulate wealth and die leaving all. They are like the bitter nux vomica which drops profitless to the ground.

ஒழிந்தன காலங்கள் ஊழியும் போயின
கழிந்தன கற்பனை நாளுங் குறுகிப்
பிழிந்தன போலத்தம் பேரிடர் ஆக்கை
அழிந்தன கண்டும் அறம்அறி யாரே. 261

Life is Fleeting; Give While You Live

The aeons pass, the unreturning ages fly;
The allotted span of life daily dwindles away;
This irksome body, as if squeezed by some power unknown,
Perishes: seeing this yet, they learn not charity's way.

Even when they are aware that they are daily nearing the grave's edge, men do not think of giving in charity; nor of walking in the path of God.

அறம்அறி யார்அண்ணல் பாதம் நினையுந்
திறம்அறி யார்சிவ லோக நகர்க்குப்
புறம்அறி யார்பலர் பொய்ம்மொழி கேட்டு
மறம்அறி வார்பகை மன்னிநின் றாரே. 262

Give and Escape Hell

Charity denying they know not the Lord's Feet to priase,
Nor enter they the precincts of the City of Siva's Grace;
Their ears inclined to those who falsehoods preach,
They stand to sin enslaved, condemned to hell's hot embrace.

இருமலுஞ் சோகையும் ஈளையும் வெப்புந்
தருமஞ்செய் யாதவர் தம்பால தாகும்
உருமிடி நாகமு ரோணி கழலை
தருமஞ்செய் வார்பக்கல் தாழகி லாவே. 263

All Ailments Assail, If in Charity You Fail

Consumption and anaemia, asthma and colic pain—
Such the lot of those who nothing in charity give;
Snake and thunder, sore throat and fleshly ills,
Approach not them that other's needs relieve

Fell diseases make a prey of misers — but they do not approach the charitable man.

பரவப் படுவான் பரமனை ஏத்தார்
இரவலர்க் கீதலை யாயினும் ஈயார்
கரகத்தால் நீரட்டிக் காவை வளர்க்கார்
நரகத்தில் நிற்றிரோ நாள்எஞ்சி னீரே. 264

End is Nigh; Do not Deny

The Lord adored by all the world, yet they praise not,
To the needy poor, even the smallest bit they deny,
Nor'll they tend the grove e'en with one potful of water;
Will they for ever stand in Hell? they whose end is nigh.

Hell is gaping its mouth for those who neither give to the poor, nor adore God.

வழிநடப் பாரின்றி வானோர் உலகங்
கழிநடப் பார்நடந் தார்கரும் பாரும்
மழிநடக் கும்வினை மாசற வோட்டிட
வழிநடக் கும்மள வீழ்ந்தொழிந் தாரே. 265

Loneliness Comes of Denial

Unescorted, alone, the charity-less their last journey make,
And miss their track, journeying thus, in birth-cycle caught in the world,
They know not how the binding Karmas to dispel,
And so slip and fall to be irretrievably lost.

They journey in loneliness through life, to be caught in the recurring birth cycle, and to be irretrievably lost in the vortex of karma.

கனிந்தவர் ஈசன் கழலடி காண்பர்
துணிந்தவர் ஈசன் துறக்கம தாள்வர்
மலிந்தவர் மாளுந் துணையுமொன் றின்றி
மெலிந்த சினத்தினுள் வீழ்ந்தொழிந் தாரே. 266

Compassion Leads to God

They, whose hearts melt in charity, see the Feet of the Lord,
The steadfast of faith attain Swarga's might,
But those sinful ones of charity bereft, helpless, forsaken,
Engulfed in passions low, pass into eternal night.

They whose heart melt in charity vision the Lord's Feet. They who are steadfast in devotion reach the world of light. They who do not give in charity reach the eternal night.

இன்பம் இடரென் றிரண்டுற வைத்தது
முன்பவர் செய்கையி னாலே முடிந்தது
இன்பம் அதுகண்டும் ஈகிலாப் பேதைகள்
அன்பிலார் சிந்தை அறம்அறி யாரே. 267

Denial Leads to Misery

Bliss and pain — these two woven into the web of life,
Result from deeds of our own devising;
The bliss of giving they knew, and yet the fools gave not,.
The shrivelled of heart, to charity unwise, its glory unknowing.

Everything results from your past actions — bliss or pain. Even having seen that bliss flows from charity, they do not give, but remain shrivelled of heart.

கெடுவது மாவதுங் கேடில் புகழோன்
நடுவல்ல செய்தின்ப நாடவும் ஒட்டான்
இடுவதும் ஈவதும் எண்ணுமின் இன்பம்
படுவது செய்யிற் பசுவது வாமே. 268

Denial Leads to Sinful State

The Lord of blemishless glory, from death and birth immune,
Permits none to enjoy bliss, unearned by worthy deed;
Giving and gifting — of these always think;

Deny and cause pain;
You stand condemned as animals.

Think constantly of giving and gifting. That alone is pure pleasure. Denial causes pain and a continued human state of existence, subject to recurring birth and death.

செல்வங் கருதிச் சிலர்பலர் வாழ்வெனும்
புல்லறி வாளரைப் போற்றிப் புலராமல்
இல்லங் கருதி இறைவனை ஏத்துமின்
வில்லி இலக்கெய்த விற்குறி யாமே. 269

Giving is Aiming True

Seek not wealth that many reckon as life indeed,
Nor waste your days on silly minded fools, of wisdom dark,
But turn your feet to the eternal Home and praise the Lord,
Then true bowman you prove, hitting straight the mark.

Do not go after accumulation of wealth as if it is all to life; nor waste your days flattering fools of dark wisdom. Praise the Lord. You shall reach His home. Be a true marksman.

18. அன்புடைமை
TO BE LOVE-POSSESSED

அன்பும் சிவமும்இரண் டென்பர் அறிவிலார்
அன்பே சிவமாவ தாரும் அறிகிலார்
அன்பே சிவமாவ தாரும் அறிந்தபின்
அன்பே சிவமாய் அமர்ந்திருந் தாரே. 270

Love and Siva are One

The ignorant prate that Love and Siva are two,
But none do know that Love alone is Siva
When men but know that Love and Siva are the same,
Love as Siva, they e'er remain.

Love and Siva are not two. Only the ignorant say so. Love alone is Siva. When that realisation dawns, they remain in love of Siva.

பொன்னைக் கடந்திலங் கும்புலித் தோலினன்
மின்னிக் கிடந்து மிளிரும் இளம்பிறை
துன்னிக் கிடந்த சுடுபொடி யாடிக்குப்
பின்னிக் கிடந்ததென் பேரன்பு தானே. 271

Lay Love's Garland at the Lord's Feet

He of the leopard skin, gleaming brighter than gold,
His tender crescent flashing rich with argent ray,
The Great Dancer, with burnt ashes smeared thick;
At His Feet, my Love, I lay.

I remained in love of Siva, the Great Dancer, who wears the tiger skin, is adorned by the crescent moon and gleams with burnt ashes.

என்பே விறகா இறைச்சி அறுத்திட்டுப்
பொன்போற் கனலிற் பொரிய வறுப்பினும்
அன்போ டுருகி அகங்குழை வார்க்கன்றி
என்போல் மணியினை எய்தவொண் ணாதே. 272

Melt in Love and Possess Him

You may turn your bone to fuel, your flesh to meat,
And let them roast and sizzle to the gold-red blaze;
But unless your heart melts in the sweet ecstasy of Love,
My Lord, my Treasure-trove, you ne'er can

Well may you roast your bones to fuel, your flesh to meat; but unless your heart melts in the ecstasy of love, by these unnecessary austerities you cannot possess the Lord.

ஆர்வம் உடையவர் காண்பர் அரன்தன்னை
ஈரம் உடையவர் காண்பார் இணையடி
பாரம் உடையவர் காண்பார் பவந்தன்னைக்
கோர நெறிகொடு கொங்குபுக் காரே. 273

Love Hara and See Him

They, of intense love, Hara surely see,
They, of the compassionate heart, see the Holy Feet to praise;
The world-burdened see only life's revolving wheel,
And, in horror's mazes lost, enter Hell's trackless ways.

They of intense love will surely vision Hara; they of compassionate heart attain His Feet of Grace. They who wallow in selfish ways reach hell, caught in the wheel of birth-death.

என்னன் புருக்கி இறைவனை ஏத்துமின்
முன்னன் புருக்கி முதல்வனை நாடுமின்
பின்னன் புருக்கிப் பெருந்தகை நந்தியுந்
தன்னன் பெனக்கே தலைநின்ற வாறே. 274

Love Him, He Loves You

Worship the Lord with heart melted in love;
Seek the Lord, with love

When we direct our love to God
He too approaches us with love.

Adore the Lord melting in love; He is the source of all Love. To me He showed His infinite love.

தானொரு காலஞ் சயம்புவென் றேத்தினும்
வானொரு காலம் வழித்துணை யாய்நிற்குந்
தேனொரு பால்திகழ் கொன்றை அணிசிவன்
தானொரு வண்ணம்என் அன்பில்நின் றானே. 275

He is Enthroned in Love

The Lord who sports on His Head honeyed with Kontrai flowers,
Who was self-born before the beginning of time
And who abides even after the pralaya
He came to me out of His great compassion.

முன்படைத் தின்பம் படைத்த முதலிடை
அன்படைத் தெம்பெரு மானை அறிகிலார்
வன்படைத் திந்த அகலிடம் வாழ்வினில்
அன்படைத் தான்தன் அகலிடத் தானே. 276

His Love is Unending

Many know not Him who first wrought this world,
And wrapt in infinite Love, born of His lordly Grace;
In this world, evil-ridden, He filled our life
With His love unending, He, the Lord of limitless space.

Out of infinite love for us He created this world, that by that love we may know bliss true. Of limitless dimensions He is; and yet He contains Himself in the love of our tiny heart.

கருத்துறு செம்பொன்செய் காய்கதிர்ச் சோதி
இருத்தியும் வைத்தும் இறைவஎன் றேத்தியும்
அருத்தியுள் ஈசனை யாரருள் வேண்டில்
விருத்தி கொடுத்திடும் விண்ணவர் கோனே. 277

His Love is Blessings All

The Light Refulgent emits beams of purest gold;
Plant that deep and firm in heart; raising worship thus,
If you, in yearning song, seek Isan's Grace,
Then, sure, no end be to His blessings copious.

நித்தலுந் துஞ்சும் பிறப்பையுஞ் செய்தவன்
வைத்த பரிசறிந் தேயு மனிதர்கள்
இச்சையு ளேவைப்பர் எந்தை பிரான்என்று
நச்சியே அண்ணலை நாடுகி லாரே. 278

Seek in Love the Heavenly Father

Birth He caused, and Death, too, in its wake;
This mystery we daily see; and yet mankind
Cling in deep desire to life, but call not on Him,
Nor seek Him, saying, "Our Father, great and kind."

அன்பினுள் ளான்புறத் தானுட லாயுளான்
முன்பினுள் ளான்முனி வர்க்கும் பிரானவன்
அன்பினுள் ளாகி அமரும் அரும்பொருள்
அன்பினுள் ளார்க்கே அணைதுணை யாமே. 279

He is Our Refuge

Inside Love is He; in outer Nature is He; as body also is He;
The past and future is He; the Lord of Rishis is He;
The Precious One who inside Love resides,
Only those, who in Love reside, find in Him the Refuge free.

19. அன்பு செய்வாரை அறிவன் சிவன்

SIVA KNOWS THOSE WHO LOVE HIM

இகழ்ந்ததும் பெற்றதும் ஈசன் அறியும்
உகந்தருள் செய்திடும் உத்தம நாதன்
கொழுந்தன்பு செய்தருள் கூரவல் லார்க்கு
மகிழ்ந்தன்பு செய்யு மருளது வாமே. 280

Lord Rewards as Merit Befits

What we scorned and what we gained, He knows;
The righteous Lord in Love rewards as merit befits;
Who, with burning zeal, seek Him with heart of love
To such, well-pleased, He His Grace awards.

Siva rewards us as our love for Him merits. In His love He gave us this world. Will He not in His love also extricate us from birth's cycle, if we seek Him?

இன்பப் பிறவிக் கியல்வது செய்தவன்
துன்பப் பிறவித் தொழில்பல என்னினும்
அன்பிற் கலவிசெய் தாதிப் பிரான்வைத்த
முன்பிப் பிறவி முடிவது தானே. 281

Lord Blends Life With Love

The Lord gave us this life to attain supreme bliss,
But we spent it in deeds that bring misery
Yet if we have love for Him
He will put an end to our rebirths.

அன்புறு சிந்தையின் மேலெழும் அவ்வொளி
இன்புறு கண்ணியொ டேற்க இசைந்தன

துன்புறு கண்ணியைந் தாடுந் துடக்கற்று
நண்புறு சிந்தையை நாடுமின் நீரே. 282

Divine Light in God-Love

If we have love there will be spiritual glory, and
The grace of the Mother will come to us,
So give up attachment to the body-mind complex,
And seek the Lord ardently.

புணர்ச்சியுள் ஆயிழை மேல்அன்பு போல
உணர்ச்சியுள் ஆங்கே ஒடுங்கவல் லார்க்கு
உணர்ச்சியில் லாது குலாவி உலாவி
அணைத்தலும் இன்பம் அதுவிது வாமே. 283

Surrender in Love

Like the sweet love in sex-act experienced,
So, in the Great Love, let yourself to Him succumb;
Thus in Love sublimed, all your senses stilled,
Bounding in Bliss Supreme, That this becomes

உற்றுநின் றாரொடு மத்தகு சோதியைச்
சித்தர்கள் என்றுந் தெரிந்தறி வார்இல்லை
பத்திமை யாலே பணிந்தடி யார்தொழ
முத்தி கொடுத்தவர் முன்புநின் றானே. 284

Devotion Leads to Liberation

Even the Siddhas, standing close in banded group,
Knew not the Light Supreme in splendorous glow;
But He gave Salvation's bliss and the Vision splendid,
To them whose hearts did in intense devotion overflow.

Even enlightened Siddhas have not visioned the Divine Light; but in intense love He is envisioned.

கண்டேன் கமழ்தரு கொன்றையி னான்அடி
கண்டேன் கரியுரி யான்றன் கழலிணை
கண்டேன் கமல மலர்உறை வானடி
கண்டேன் கழலதென் அன்பினுள் யானே. 285

His Feet Visioned in Love

I saw the Feet of the Lord, deckt in odorous Konrai blooms,
I saw the Feet of the Lord, dark-dressed in elephant-skin,
I saw the Feet of the Lord, on lotus-blossom abiding
I saw the Feet of the Lord, my heart-core's love within.

I visioned Him in the intense love of heart's core. In that love I visioned Him decked in konrai blossoms, dressed in dark-elephant skin, and abiding on a lotus blossom.

நம்பனை நானா விதப்பொரு ளாகுமென்
றும்பரில் வானவர் ஓதுந் தலைவனை
இன்பனை இன்பத் திடைநின்றிரதிக்கும்
அன்பனை யாரும் அறியகி லாரே. 286

His Love is Inscrutable

My Lord God whom the heavenly beings praise
As one into myriad forms and things outspread,
The Great Lover who inside love savours love's tributes;
Sad indeed that few seek Him, or to Him are led.

The celestial beings seek Him in diverse forms; but He savours in love's tributes.

முன்பு பிறப்பும் இறப்பும் அறியாதார்
அன்பில் இறைவனை யாம்அறி வோம்என்பர்
இன்புப் பிறப்பும் இறப்பும் இலான்நந்தி
அன்பிலவனை அறியகி லாரே. 287

Seek Him in Love

Those who know nothing but the cycle of birth and death
Think that through worldly love they can attain the Lord,
But the Lord is beyond birth and death,
Only through true devotion can He be attained.

ஈசன் அறியும் இராப்பக லுந்தன்னைப்
பாசத்துள் வைத்துப் பரிவுசெய் வார்களைத்
தேசுற் றறிந்து செயலற் றிருந்திடில்
ஈசன்வந் தெம்மிடை ஈட்டிநின் றானே. 288

Seek Him, He Seeks You

The Lord God knows them who, by night and day,
Seat Him in heart's core, and in love exalted adore;
To them wise with inner light, actionless in trance,
He comes, and, in close proximity, stands before.

He knows them who night and day seat Him in the heart's core in exalted love. He stands before them as inner light as they love him in actionless trance.

விட்டுப் பிடிப்பதென் மேதகு சோதியைத்
தொட்டுத் தொடர்வன தொலையாப் பெருமையை
எட்டுமென் னாருயி ராய்நின்ற ஈசனை
மட்டுக் கலப்பது மஞ்சன மாமே. 289

Be Steadfast in Devotion

It little profits if, intermittently, you pursue the Divine Light;
Unceasing, I will seek the Greatness that has no end,
My Lord, my heart's precious Life and treasured Delight;
In Him to merge is the holy bath.

20. கல்வி
LEARNING

குறிப்பறிந் தேனுடல் உயிரது கூடிச்
செறிப்பறிந் தேன்மிகு தேவர் பிரானை
மறிப்பறி யாதுவந் துள்ளம் புகுந்தான்
கறிப்பறி யாமிகுங் கல்விகற் றேனே. 290

True Learning Leads to Liberation

The meaning I knew of life and body in union knit;
In the depth of my being I knew of the Lord of Devas untold;
Denying naught, He stept straight into my yearning heart;
Thus I gained the Learning Great, freeing us from fleshy fold.

I learned the meaning of life and its union in the body. I sought Him in close proximity and knew it all. The Lord stepped into the inner core of my yearning heart; and I acquired the great learning of being free from fleshy bondage.

கற்றறி வாளர் கருதிய காலத்துக்
கற்றறி வாளர் கருத்திலோர் கண்ணுண்டு
கற்றறி வாளர் கருதி உரைசெய்யுங்
கற்றறி காட்டக் கயலுள வாக்குமே. 291

Illumined Souls Get the Inner Eye

When the Learned-wise in deep meditation sat,
In their deep, illumined souls was an Inner Eye;
What in contemplation they saw and spoke,
In turn opened others' eyes leading to Wisdom high.

The deeply learned sit in Samadhi. There, they obtain the inner eye; and what they saw in deep contemplation they imparted to others; and opened their inner eye in turn.

நிற்கின்ற போதே நிலையுடை யான்கழல்
கற்கின்ற செய்மின் கழிந்தறும் பாவங்கள்
சொற்குன்றல் இன்றித் தொழுமின் தொழுதபின்
மற்றொன் றிலாதமணி விளக் காமே. 292

Learning Purifies

While yet life subsists, the Lord of existence adore;
In action prove what you learn all sins to clear;
In accents unfaltering worship the Lord, and thiswise,
A jewelled lamp It'll be, beyond compare.

Prove in action what you learn; in unfaltering accents adore the Lord. While life exists, adore the Lord of Existence. Be rid of impurities, you will behold that bejewelled lamp, beyond compare.

கல்வி யுடையார் கழிந்தோடிப் போகின்றார்
பல்லி யுடையார் பாம்பரிந் துண்கின்றார்
எல்லியுங் காலையும் ஏத்தும் இறைவனை
வல்லியுள் வாதித்த காயமு மாமே. 293

Learning Leads to Renunciation

Men of Learning abandon the fettering, worldly ways
The firm of mind flourish high on coiling snake-like Kundalini
Night and day, unremitting praise the Lord,
And so your body, as on herbs alchemised, with glory of youth will be.

The truly learned abandon the worldly fetters. In firmness they practise Kundalini yoga and achieve the glow of youth.

துணையது வாய்வருந் தூயநற் சோதி
துணையது வாய்வருந் தூயநற் சொல்லாந்
துணையது வாய்வருந் தூயநற் கந்தம்
துணையது வாய்வருந் தூயநற் கல்வியே. 294

Pure Knowledge is Guardian Angel

As our Guardian Angel comes the pure Light from high
As our Guardian Angel, the Pure word in beauty drest,
As our Guardian Angel comes the Pure Fragrance rich,
As our Guardian Angel comes the Pure Knowledge best.

Pure knowledge is our guardian angel. It is that which leads to the pure word, the pure fragrance and the pure light.

நூலொன்று பற்றி நுனியேற மாட்டாதார்
பாலொன்று பற்றினாற் பண்பின் பயன்கெடுங்
கோலொன்று பற்றினாற் கூடா பறவைகள்
மாலொன்று பற்றி மயங்குகின் றார்களே. 295

Holy Books Help Scale Spiritual Heights

Those who fail to scale the heights with holy books to guide,
If to outer things of life they yield, fruitless is all the lore;
On rod of Vairagya lean, and away fly the Birds of Desire;
And yet, men to Ignorance clinging in stupor ever lie

Holy books are our guide to scale the heights of pure knowledge. Fruitless is that learning which leads to outer things of life. Lean on the rod of Vairagya. The birds of desire fly away. Men of ignorance cling to them and forever lie in stupor.

ஆய்ந்துகொள் வார்க்கரன் அங்கே வெளிப்படும்
தோய்ந்த நெருப்பது தூய்மணி சிந்திடும்
ஏய்ந்த இளமதி எட்டவல் லார்கட்கு
வாய்ந்த மனமல்கு நூலேணி யாமே. 296

Hara Stands Revealed to the Truly Learned

Those who meditate on the Lord become effulgent,
Even as the sunstone radiates luminous sparks,
The education we acquire will help us
To meditate in the spiritual field of the moon.

வழித்துணை யாய்மருந் தாயிருந் தார்முன்
கழித்துணை யாங்கற் றிலாதவர் சிந்தை
ஒழித்துணை யாம்உம் பராய்உல கேழும்
வழித்துணை யாம்பெருந் தன்மைவல் லானே. 297

Lord is no Support to the Ignorant

In life's journey a Support and Elixir rare is He,
An unfailing Guide — but to the ignorant of mind,
No support He — in all the seven Heavenly globes,
Sure prop is He, the Mighty being. Great and Kind.

பற்றது பற்றிற் பரமனைப் பற்றுமின்
முற்றது எல்லா முதல்வன் அருள்பெறில்
கிற்ற விரகிற் கிளரொளி வானவர்
கற்றவர் பேரின்பம் உற்றுநின் றாரே. 298

The Truly Learned Attain Bliss

If desire you must, the Lord in desire seize,
If the Lord's Grace you get, all things are obtained;
Like the deep-skilled Devas of flaming Light;
The truly learned Heavenly Bliss attained.

கடலுடை யான்மலை யானைந்து பூதத்
துடலுடை யான்பல ஊழிதொ றூழி
அடல்விடை யேறும் அமரர்கள் நாதன்
இடமுடை யார்நெஞ்சத் தில்லிருந் தானே. 299

He Resides in Learned Devotees' Hearts

The seas He owns and the mountains high;
His Body shaped of the elements five;
The Lord of Immortals who, through endless ages,
Mounts the powerful Bull, at devotees' heart to arrive.

21. கேள்வி கேட்டமைதல்

LISTENING AND THUS CONTAINING

அறங்கேட்டும் அந்தணர் வாய்மொழி கேட்டும்
மறங்கேட்டும் வானவர் மந்திரங் கேட்டும்
புறங்கேட்டும் பொன்னுரை மேனியெம் ஈசன்
திறங்கேட்டும் பெற்ற சிவகதி தானே. 300

Listen to Words of Siva's Glory.

Listening to Dharma and to the words of the Holy,
Listening to God's valorous acts and the Devas' mantras many,
Listening to loud reports and the deeds peerless of the Lord,
The Lord whose body gleaming bright as gold
are all to attain the Siva State.

தேவர் பிரான்தனைத் திவ்விய மூர்த்தியை
யாவர் ஒருவர் அறிவார் அறிந்தபின்
ஓதுமின் கேள்மின் உணர்மின் உணர்ந்தபின்
ஓதி உணர்ந்தவர் ஓங்கி நின்றாரே. 301

Listening to Holy Words Leads to Realization

The Lord of all Devas, the Supreme Being Divine,
Who is there who knows Him? If any such be,
Chant His praise; listen to the holy words and Him realise
Who chant His praise and Him realise, stand aloft and see.

மயன்பணி கேட்பது மாநந்தி வேண்டின்
அயன்பணி கேட்பது அரன்பணி யாலே
சிவன்பணி கேட்பவர் தேவரு மாவர்
பயன்பணி கேட்பது பற்றது வாமே. 302

Obey Siva and Become Deva

At Nandi's bidding, Vishnu obeys and builds;
At Hara's bidding, Brahma obeys and creates;
Who Siva's bidding obey, Devas they become;
If fruits of action you crave, then to attachments you're chained

பெருமான் இவனென்று பேசி யிருக்குந்
திருமானிடர் பின்னைத் தேவரு மாவர்
வருமா தவர்க்கு மகிழ்ந்தருள் செய்யும்
அருமா தவத்தெங்கள் ஆதிப் பிரானே. 303

Adore Siva and Be Immortal

The pious mortals who praise the Supreme Lord,
In time to come, to the Immortals' status rise;
Who fail not in penance, His joyous Grace receive;

Thus the Lord of rare penances rare awards the Supreme prize.

ஈசன் அருளும் இறப்பும் பிறப்பையும்
பேசி யிருந்து பிதற்றி மகிழ்வெய்தி
நேசமு மாகும் நிகழொளி யாய்நின்று
வாச மலர்க்கந்த மன்னிநின் றானே. 304

Prayer Brings Grace

The Lord who gave us Birth and Death,
Of Him e'er talk, His name adore, prattle in praise;
Then the abiding Light of His dear presence,
Like fragrance in flower, comes to you in Grace.

விழுப்பமுங் கேள்வியும் மெய்நின்ற ஞானத்
தொழுக்கமுஞ் சிந்தை உணர்கின்ற போது
வழுக்கி விடாவிடில் வானவர் கோனும்
இழுக்கின்றி எண்ணிலி காலம தாமே. 305

He Forsakes not His Devotees

To seek Excellence and to Excellent things listen,
And follow Wisdom's true mandate — if to these the mind awake,
And if, then; you slip not nor stray, the Heavenly Lord,
Unhesitant, will be thine for ever — and never forsake.

சிறியார் மணற்சோற்றில் தேக்கிடு மாபோல்
செறிவால் அனுபோகஞ் சித்திக்கும் என்னில்
குறியாத தொன்றைக் குறியாதார் தம்மை
அறியா திருந்தார் அவராவர் அன்றே. 306

Faith Intense Gives Bliss Eternal

Those who think they can attain the Siva-bliss through the senses,
Are like children who played with sand considering it rice,
Those who do not understand that He cannot be pointed out objectively
Will ever remain ignorant.

உறுதுணை யாவ துயிரும், உடம்பும்,
உறுதுணை யாவ துலகுறு கேள்வி
செறிதுணை யாவது சிவனடிச் சிந்தை
பெறுதுணை கேட்கிற் பிறப்பில்லை தானே. 307

Listening to Holy Things is a Sure Prop

Life and body sure support for the soul provide,
Listening to holy worldly things a sure prop and resting place,
Thoughts of Siva's Holy Feet, the one Refuge to seek,
And with that support Supreme to aid, rebirth you wholly efface.

புகழநின் றார்க்கும் புராணன்எம் ஈசன்
இகழநின் றார்க்கும் இடும்பைக் கிடமா
மகிழநின் றாதியை ஓதி உணராக்
கழியநின் றார்க்கொரு கற்பசு வாமே. 308

A Stone-Cow to Scorners

To them that exalt His name, the first to Beings He;
To them that scorn His Grace, persist sufferings
In rapture lost, if you chant not His Glory great,
He stands, a veritable stone-cow, in silence complete.

வைத்துணர்ந் தான்மனத் தோடும்வாய் பேசி
ஒத்துணர்ந் தான்உரு ஒன்றோடொன் றொவ்வாது
அச்சுழன் றாணி கலங்கினும் ஆதியை
நச்சுணர்ந் தார்க்கே நணுகலு மாமே. 309

Unite in Heart and Thought Towards Lord

Heart and tongue in unison met, the Lord cognise,
Though in diverse shapes He be, Him in unity find;
Then, e'en though shaken in life like axle from pin,
Seek the Primal Lord in love and Him to yourself bind.

22. கல்லாமை

NON-LEARNING

கல்லா தவருங் கருத்தறி காட்சியை
வல்லா ரெனில்அருட் கண்ணான் மதித்துளோர்
கல்லாதார் உண்மைபற் றாநிற்பர் கற்றோருங்
கல்லாதார் இன்பம் காணுகி லாரே. 310

The Unlearned are they Who hold not to Truth

Even the unlearned, if blessed with the vision of Truth Supreme,
Them the Lord approves with His benign Eye of Grace;
But if the learned seeming fail to hold the truth,
Unlearned are they indeed, blind to True Love's divine rays.

வல்லார்கள் என்றும் வழியொன்றி வாழ்கின்றார்
அல்லா தவர்கள் அறிவு பலஎன்பார்
எல்லா இடத்தும் உளன்எங்கள் தம்இறை
கல்லா தவர்கள் கலப்பறி யாரே. 311

Unlearned Realize not God's Pervasiveness

The truly learned live pursuing the one and only path,

But others say, "Many the paths of knowledge are,"
The God Supreme is in all places present;
They the unlearned are, of God's pervasiveness unaware.

நில்லா நிலையை நிலையாக நெஞ்சத்து
நில்லாக் குரம்பை நிலையென் றுணர்வீர்காள்
எல்லா வுயிர்க்கும் இறைவனே யாயினுங்
கல்லாதார் நெஞ்சத்துக் காணவொண் ணாதே. 312

God Abides not in the Hearts of the Unlearned

Things transitory you fix in heart as abiding joys,
This mortal body frail you deem as enduring stuff;
Though the Lord God all life pervades;
Absent are He and His Light from the hearts of the unlearned.

கில்லேன் வினைதுய ராக்கு மயலானேன்
கல்லேன் அரனெறி அறியாத் தகைமையின்
வல்லேன் வழங்கும் பொருளே மனத்தினுட்
கல்லேன் கழியநின் றாடவல் லேனே 313

Unlearned of Hara's Ways Descend to Hell

Of all power bereft, I fell into Karma's griefs,
Learning not Hara's ways, into dark abysmal depths I fell;
I learnt not to stamp the Great Benefactor in my heart,
I learnt only to dance down the primrose path to hell.

நில்லாது சீவன் நிலையன் றென்றெண்ணி
வல்லார் அறத்துந் தவத்துளும் ஆயினார்
கல்லா மனித்தர் கயவர் உலகினில்
பொல்லா வினைத்துயர் போகஞ்செய் வாரே. 314

Unlearned Sport in Carnal Pleasures

Knowing full well that life is a fleeting vaporous mist,
The truly learned seek the path of Dharma and penance strict,
But the not-learned, in truth, this world's sordid knaves,
Sport in carnal joys, with Karmic misery mixt.

விண்ணினின் உள்ளே விளைந்த விளங்கனி
கண்ணினின் உள்ளே கலந்தங் கிருந்தது
மண்ணினின் உள்ளே மதித்து மதித்துநின்
றெண்ணி எழுதி இளைத்துவிட் டாரே. 315

Lord is within as Above

Just as there is the fruit of knowledge above,
So too within us is the same fruit,
Not knowing this men search for and analyze,
Earthly fruits and thus exhaust themselves in useless writing.

கணக்கறிந் தார்க்கன்றிக காணவொண் ணாது
கணக்கறிந் தார்க்கன்றிக் கைகூடா காட்சி
கணக்கறிந் துண்மையைக் கண்டண்ட நிற்கும்
கணக்கறிந் தார்கல்வி கற்றறிந் தாரே. 316

Unlearned do not See Him

Without knowing the 36 tattvas and their scope
It is not possible to have a vision of the Supreme,
Only by knowing the tattvas wisdom can dawn,
Only those are educated who go to the limits of the tattvas and have a vision of Reality.

கல்லாத மூடரைக் காணவும் ஆகாது
கல்லாத மூடர்சொல் கேட்கக் கடன்அன்று
கல்லாத மூடர்க்குக் கல்லாதார் நல்லராம்
கல்லாத மூடர் கருத்தறி யாரே. 317

Avoid the Unlearned

The fools, of learning devoid, unfit for us even to see
The fools, of learning devoid, their words unfit to hear
The fools, of learning devoid, in fools find their friends,
The fools, of learning devoid, to Wisdom come no near.

கற்றுஞ் சிவஞானம் இல்லாக் கலதிகள்
சுற்றமும் வீடார் துரிசறார் மூடர்கள்
மற்றும் பலதிசை காணார் மதியிலோர்
கற்றன்பில் நிற்போர் கணக்கறிந் தார்களே. 318

The Truly Learned have Vision of Sivajnana

Though learned, fools are they if with Sivajnana they're not acquainted,
If kith and kin they give not up nor strike at root of igorance
As their eyes turn not to quarters
They alone truly reckon who, wise in love, win the Truth.

ஆதிப் பிரான்அம ரர்க்கும் பரஞ்சுடர்
சோதி அடியார் தொடரும் பெருந்தெய்வம்
ஓதி உணரவல் லோம்என்பர் உள்நின்ற
சோதி நடத்துந் தொடர்வறி யாரே. 319

True Learning Brings Light Divine

The Being first, even to the immortals the Light Divine,
The Light that devotees seek, the great God Supreme
Some proudly claim that learning well, they know Him truly well
Yet they catch not of His Light the faintest gleam.

23. நடுவு நிலைமை

THE MIDDLE PATH

நடுவுநின் றார்க்கன்றி ஞானமும் இல்லை
நடுவுநின் றார்க்கு நரகமும் இல்லை
நடுவுநின் றார்நல்ல தேவரு மாவர்
நடுவுநின் றார்வழி யானும்நின் றேனே. 320

Middle Path is Wisdom

Unless you in Middle path stand, Wisdom You have not,
To those who in Middle path stand, Hell opens not its gate;
Those that in Middle path stand, Heavenly beings are they;
In the noble fellowship of the Just, I too walked in their way.

நடுவுநின் றார்நல்ல கார்முகில் வண்ணன்
நடுவுநின் றான்நல்ல நான்மறை யோதி
நடுவுநின் றார்சிலர் ஞானிக ளாவோர்
நடுவுநின் றார்நல்ல நம்பனு மாமே. 321

Gods and Saints Stand in Middle path

The blue-dark cloud-hued Being Vishnu in Middle path stood,
The Brahma who chants the Vedas Four in Middle path stood,
The wise saintly souls also in Middle path stood,
He, Our Lord supreme — He, in Middle path stood.

நடுவுநின் றார்சிலர் ஞானிக ளாவர்
நடுவுநின் றார்சிலர் தேவரு மாவர்
நடுவுநின் றார்சிலர் நம்பனு மாவர்
நடுவுநின் றாரொடு யானும்நின் றேனே. 322

Walk With the Just

Some saintly became, because they in Middle path stood,
Some to heavenly beings turned, because they in justice stood,
Some to Siva-state attained, because they in Justice stood,
And so in the good company of the Just, I, too, unfaltering, stood.

தோன்றிய எல்லாந் துடைப்பன் அவனன்றி
ஏன்றுநின் றாரென்றும் ஈசன் இணையடி
மூன்றுநின் றார்முதல் வன்திரு நாமத்தை
நான்றுநின் றார்நடு வாகிநின் றாரே. 323

The Just Adore His Feet

What He creates, none but He destroys;
On their devout heads, the Just bore aloft His Holy feet;
Who chant the pure name with ardour
And cling thereof, in the Society of the Just they meet.

24. கள்ளுண்ணாமை

ABSTAINING FROM DRINK

கழுநீர்ப் பசுப்பெறிற் கயந்தொறும் தேரா
கழுநீர் விடாய்த்துத்தங் காயஞ் சுருக்கும்
முழுநீர்க் கள்ளுண்போர் முறைமை அகன்றோர்
செழுநீர்ச் சிவன்றன் சிவானந்தத் தேறலே. 324

Drunkards Lose Sense of Right and Wrong

The cow fed on broth of rice wanders not from tank to tank
The cow denied its drink of broth grows weak and lank
Who swill the toddy neat, from Righteousness go astray
Truest drink is Sivananda, the Bliss Supreme, far and away.

Sivananda is Ananda (bliss) in the worship of Siva.

சித்தம் உருக்கிச் சிவமாஞ் சமாதியில்
ஒத்த சிவானந்தத் தோவாத தேறலைச்
சுத்த மதுவுண்ணச் சுவானந்தம் விட்டிடா
நித்தல் இருத்தல் கிடத்தல்கீழ்க் காலே. 325

Sivananda Wine Brings Eternal Self-Forgetfulness

In sweet rapture lost, soul-hydroptic for the Siva-Samadhi state,
The ever-sweet nectar of Sivananda — in the Bliss, overflow;
On such nectar fed, you lose not the self-bliss pure;
For ever thus you sit and lie the Holy Feet below.

காமமுங் கள்ளுங் கலதிகட் கேயாகும்
மாமல முஞ்சம யத்துள் மயலுறும்
போமதி யாகும் புனிதன் இணையடி
யோமய ஆனந்தத் தேறல் உணர்வுண்டே. 326

The Wicked Drink in Vama Tantra

Lust and drink, fit for the wicked are they;
In ritual unholy they drink and lose the senses

But the wise drink the nectar streaming from His feet,
Which destroys egoism and bigotry.

வாமத்தோர் தாமும் மதுவுண்டு மாள்பவர்
காமத்தோர் காமக்கள் ளுண்டே கலங்குவர்
ஓமத்தோர் உள்ளொளிக் குள்ளே உணர்வர்கள்
நாமத்தோர் அன்றே நணுகுவர் தாமே. 327

Drinking in Vama Tantra Worship Leads to Perdition

They drink and perish, who to the Vama sect belong,
The lustful ones in sensual delights are wholly lost;
But the pure souls find the Light of sacrifices in their inner flame;
They, who His true Name chant, approach Him fast.

This verse makes it clear that it is the Vama Tantra sect which is attacked. Vama tantra is also referred to as 'panca makara,' since the rituals call for the application or use of 5 Ms, namely Mithuna (copulation), Matsya (fish), Mamsa (meat), madhu (alcoholic drink) and Mudra (translated ordinarily as parched rice, but really meaning the adoption of various esoteric signs.)

உள்ளுண்மை ஓரார் உணரார் பசுபாசம்
வள்ளன்மை நாதன் அருளினின் வாழ்வுறார்
தெள்ளுண்மை ஞானச் சிவயோகஞ் சேர்வுறார்
கள்ளுண்ணும் மாந்தர் கருத்தறி யாரே. 328

Truth Eludes Drunkards

They see not the Inner Truth, know not the Pasu-pasa,
They dwell not in the bounteous Lord's Divine Grace;
In the clear light of Wisdom, Sivayoga they seek not,
They, who soak in liquors, Truth never can appraise.

மயக்குஞ் சமய மலமன்னு மூடர்
மயக்கு மதுவுண்ணு மாமூடர் தேரார்
மயக்குறு மாமாயை மாயையின் வீடு
மயக்கில் தெளியின் மயக்குறும் அன்றே. 329

Followers of False Religion Neither Seek nor See Him

The fools who swear by the faith that our senses numbs,
Who yield to the heady joys of drink—they neither seek nor see
Mamaya's Home, for the Maya's fetters are they bound;
But recovered from Maya's hold, they merge in the Lord and are free.

Maya in Saivism is of two kinds, namely (i) the pure Mamaya, and (ii) the impure Maya. The pure Mamaya is creative and corresponds to icchasakti of Sanskritic culture. "The impure Maya includes within itself all the effects, such as time and the impure souls" (S.N. Das Gupta, "History of Indian Philosophy, pp.90 and 91).

மயங்குந் தியங்குங் கள்வாய்மை அழிக்கும்
இயங்கும் மடவார்தம் இன்பமே எய்தி
முயங்கும் நயங்கொண்ட ஞானத்து முந்தார்
இயங்கும் இடையறா ஆனந்தம் எய்துமே. 330

Wine Stupefies Senses and Destroys Truth

The fumes of wine stupor bring and destroy the Truth,
And make us seek the false, delusive joys of lust;
Such advance not to Wisdom true, of sweet reason compact.
Will such e'er attain the eternal Bliss truest?

இராப்பகல் அற்ற இடத்தே இருந்து
பராக்கற ஆனந்தத் தேறல் பருகார்
இராப்பகல் அற்ற இறையடி இன்பத்து
இராப்பகல் மாயை இரண்டிடத் தேனே. 331

Joys of Sivananda Nectar

In meditation lost, 'rid of the cycle of Night and Day,
Dead to outward things, they drink not the bliss-nectar—
The Bliss of the Lord's Feet that neither night nor day knoweth,
I, caught in Maya causing Night and Day, struggle to reach.

Sivananda Nectar may be interpreted in two ways. The first is the bliss or ecstasy created in deep contemplation of Siva or in the bhakti mode of song and dance. The second view is the bliss caused by the Kundalini flow in yoga or tantra.

சத்தியை வேண்டிச் சமயத்தோர் கள்ளுண்பர்
சத்தி அழிந்தது தம்மை மறத்தலால்
சத்தி சிவஞானந் தன்னில் தலைப்பட்டுச்
சத்திய ஞானஆ னந்தத்திற் சார்தலே. 332

True Sakti Worship Seeks Divine Nectar

Sakti seeking, some religious sects ritual drinks consume,
But Sakti dies when the o'er-powered senses swoon;
True Sakti, indeed, in Sivajnanam finds its birth,
To merge in Truth-Wisdom-Bliss—and to other things immune.

சத்தன் அருள்தரிற் சத்தி அருளுண்டாஞ்
சத்தி அருள்தரிற் சத்தன் அருளுண்டாஞ்
சத்தி சிவமாம் இரண்டுந்தன் னுள்வைக்கச்
சத்தியம் எண்சித்தித் தன்மையு மாமே. 333

Sakti and Siva are One

If Saktan His Grace imparts, Sakti's Grace we have,
If Sakti Her Grace imparts, Saktan's Grace we gain,
Sakti and Siva, if Both in heart we hold,
Then in us, truly, the Siddhis eight do shine.

Śiva and Śakti are shown as united in the Ardhanārīśvara form (androgyne).

தத்துவம் நீக்கி மருள்நீக்கித் தானாகிப்
பொய்த்தவம் நீக்கிமெய்ப் போகத்துட் போகியே
மெய்த்த சகமுண்டு விட்டுப் பரானந்தச்
சித்திய தாக்குஞ் சிவானந்தத் தேறலே. *334*

Divine Nectar Leads to Siddhis

All Tattvas and egoity past, Truth of self realised,
In truest joy immersed, of false penances void,
Rid of worldly lure, drunk full of Heavenly Bliss,
This indeed is Siddhi true and Sivananda unalloyed.

யோகிகள் கால்கட்டி ஒண்மதி ஆனந்தப்
போத அமுதைப் பொசித்தவர் எண்சித்தி
மோகியர் கள்ளுண்டு மூடராய் மோகமுற்
றாகும் மதத்தால் அறிவழிந் தாரே. *335*

Yogis Seek Ambrosia of the Cranial Moon

The yogis who, breath in control held, yearn for
The nectared delights of Contemplation's Moon,
The eight Siddhis they seek; but witless fools are they
Who to toddy yield and in its heady joys let their senses swoon.

உண்ணீர் அமுத முறுமூ றலைத்திறந்
தெண்ணீர் குரவன் இணையடித் தாமரை
நண்ணீர் சமாதியி னாடிநீ ரானலங்
கண்ணாற் றொடேசென்று கால்வழி காணுமே. *336*

Drink Divine Nectar in Samadhi

Open and drink deep the nectar that gushes from the spring;
Unfold the petals of the Holy Master's Lotus Feet;
Lead the Yoga-breath through the spiring channel up
And thus in Samadhi ascending
Reach the Divine Good in holy meet.

முதல் தந்திரம் முடிவு பெற்றது.
Tantra One concluded

இரண்டாம் தந்திரம்
TANTRA TWO

1. அகத்தியம்

AGASTYAM

நடுவுநில் லாதிவ் வுலகஞ் சரிந்து
கெடுகின்ற தெம்பெரு. மானென்ன ஈசன்
நடுவுள அங்கி அகத்திய நீபோய்
முடுகிய வையத்து முன்னிரென் றானே. *337*

The Lord Corrects the Earth's Balance Through Agastya

"Hail! Our Lord Supreme
This earthly orb from its epicentre sways,
And dangerous on its side swerves"
Thus they bewailed, the Beings Celestial
And the Lord spoke;
"Agastya!
You that sit in tapas hard
Amidst the blazing sacrificial fire
Hasten to the globe's swerving side
And there be seated, its balance to redress."

அங்கி உதயம் வளர்க்கும் அகத்தியன்
அங்கி உதயஞ்செய் மேல்பா லவனொடு
மங்கி உதயஞ்செய் வடபால் தவமுனி
எங்கும் வளங்கொள் இலங்கொளி தாளே. *338*

Agastya—A Pervasive Light

Unfailing at dawn
With the sun that doth in high heavens
Agastya lights the Fire divine;
He is the holy Muni of North
Whence the Primal Fire was born;
And the radiant light, pervasive-all.

Of yore Siva and Parvati were getting married at Mount Kailas located in the Himalayan mountains. All the world's inhabitants gathered there to witness the holy wedding. The south of India was depleted in weight by the exodus. The earth-orb swerved from its epicentre. Siva sent Rishi Agastya to the south to redress the imbalance. Such is the might of the tapas of rishis, that the spiritual weight of one soul devoted to Siva equalled the physical weight of a whole population of ordinary millions. The earth regained its balance. Siva will not let imbalance or injustice occur anywhere.

Implied in this legend is the view that Saivism, tapas, and other cults were brought from the north (the Himalayas) by members of the Agastya cult who provided for themselves a base in the "Podiyil" hills of the Pandya Nadu in the south. This was, apparently, for a long time the centre of gathering for Siddhas, Yogis, tantrics, etc. The sanskrit term "Bodhi" meaning knowledge would in Tamil become "poti", due to absence of aspiration and of softening of consonants in the latter alphabetical system.

2. பதிவலியில் வீரட்டம் எட்டு

EIGHT HEROIC DEEDS OF SIVA

WELLKNOWN ARE SIVA'S DEEDS OF HEROISM THEY ARE EIGHT IN NUMBER

கருத்துறை அந்தகன் தன்போல் அசுரன்
வரத்தின் உலகத் துயிர்களை எல்லாம்
விருத்தஞ்செய் தானென்று வானவர் வேண்டக்
குருத்துயர் சூலங்கைக் கொண்டுகொன் றானே. *339*

The Eight Mighty Deeds of Siva—Destruction of Antaka

"Antaka, the Asura
Frightening unto God of Death
Whose name he bore
Armed with boons divine
Harassed worlds all"
—Thus the Celestial Beings moaned to the Lord;
And the Lord,
Lifting high His trident sharp
Pierced him straight to certain death.

There was an asura who bore the name of Antaka, same as that of the Death-god. He had acquired invincible powers by prolonged penance. But he misused them and harassed the population of all the worlds. Siva destroyed him with his sharp trident at a fatal encounter which took place at Tirukkovilur.

கொலையிற். பிழைத்த பிரசா பதியைத்
தலையைத் தடிந்திட்டுத் தானங்கி யிட்டு
நிலையுல குக்கிவன் வேண்டுமென் றெண்ணித்
தலையை யரிந்திட்டுச் சந்திசெய் தானே. *340*

The Lord Punished Daksha

Daksha, the son of Brahma fatally erred;
Deadly was his sin
To defy the Lord's primacy;
And the Lord smote his head
And consigned it to flames
And then bethought,
"Such like are needed for this world
An object lesson to serve"
And so, fixed a sheep's head to the trunk
Thus let him be.

Daksha was the giant-king of the Himalayas. He was the son of Brahma. Sati, Siva's consort, was his daughter. Daksha thought no end of himself and challenged the supremacy of Siva. To establish this he performed a sacriligious sacrifice. Siva appeared on the scene, smote Daksha's head and threw it into the sacrificial flame. Then, thinking that the incident should serve as an object lesson to others who dare perform such heinous crimes, Siva fixed a sheep's head to Daksha's severed trunk and let him live in this chimerical form. This heroic deed was performed at Tiruppariyalur.

எங்கும் பரந்தும் இருநிலந் தாங்கியுந்
தங்கும் படித்தவன் தாளுணர் தேவர்கள்
பொங்குஞ் சினத்துள் அயன்தலை முன்னற
அங்(கு)அச் சுதனை உதிரங்கொண் டானே. 341

How the Lord Punished Aya and Achutha

All pervasive are the Lord's feet
All worlds they support
All life they sustain;
That this the Heavenly Beings may know
In mounting anger He nipped Aya's head
And in the skull drained Achutha's blood
(When they His supremacy defied.)

Brahma at one time was as five-headed as Siva. Brahma and Mal, encouraged by the flattery of devas and rishis challenged Siva's supremacy. Siva, assuming the aspect of Bhairava, pinched away one of Brahma's heads with his finger nail. Bearing Brahma's skull, Bhairava demanded of Mal to drain his blood into the skull and fill it up. Mal obeyed. Thus were the two gods shown their place. This is said to have happened at the place known as Tirukandiyur.

எங்குங் கலந்துமென் உள்ளத் தெழுகின்ற
அங்க முதல்வன் அருமறை யோதிபாற்
பொங்குஞ் சலந்தரன் போர்செய்ய நீர்மையின்
அங்கு விரற்குறித் தாழிசெய் தானே. 342

How the Lord Destroyed Jalandhara

The Lord pervades all,
My heart too He fills with joy;
He spoke the Vedas and scriptures all;
Him—the haughty Jalandhara challenged in duel
And the Lord with his toe marked a circle
And into it He saw the monster's final end.

Jalandhara was a giant, and the foster son of Varuna, the Sea-god. By virtue of his penances, he received a boon that no one else could kill him. He became all-powerful and began to harass the celestials. They complained to Siva. Siva confronted Jalandhara and drew a circle around him. He challenged the giant to lift the circle. Jalandhara lifted it to his head, when lo, the circle turned into a powerful discus and destroyed him. Jalandhara had to be destroyed by himself. This heroic deed is said to have happened at the place called Tiruvirkudi.

அப்பணி செஞ்சடை ஆதி புராதனன்
முப்புரஞ் செற்றனன் என்பர்கள் மூடர்கள்
முப்புர மாவது மும்மல காரியம்
அப்புரம் எய்தமை யாரறி வாரே. 343

The Lord Burnt the Cities Three

The Primal Lord,
Who on His matted crimson locks
Wears Ganga's water sacred,
He destroyed the Cities Three
—Thus say the ignorant;
The Three Cities are the Triple Impurities
It is them He burnt
Who Knows this truth thereof?

Three giants by the power of penance ruled over three cities with three flying fortresses—one of gold, one of silver, and one of copper. Flying their fortresses, they landed on the cities of the celestials and destroyed them. Siva fought the three giants and reduced their three cities to ashes, all the while with a smile of His lips. People who recount this legend do not realise that what Siva destroyed was the triple impurities—egoity, karma and maya. This heroic deed is associated with the place called Tiruathigai.

முத்திக் கொளுவி முழங்கெரி வேள்வியுள்
அத்தி யுரியர னாவ தறிகிலர்
சத்தி கருதிய தாம்பல தேவரும்
அத்தீயின் உள்ளெழுந் தன்று கொலையே. 344

The Lord Unsloughed the Elephant

They lit the Fires Three
The sacrificial blaze roared high;
And from inside it arose
An Elephant of Evil Power,
Whose hide the Lord peeled;
Why the Lord did it, they know not;
Seeking to rival the Lord's might
The Heaven's beings performed a homa unholy
And all those who from that fire arose
The Lord smote for the very fire to consume.

Gajasura was an elephant-monster that arose out of the sacrificial fire which the celestials had performed to challenge Siva's supremacy. Siva peeled the elephant's skin and donned it as a vestment; and the celestials of evil intent were immolated in the very sacrificial fire they lit. This happened at Tiruvazhulur.

மூலத் துவாரத்து மூளும் ஒருவனை
மேலைத் துவாரத்து மேலுற நோக்கிமுற்
காலுற்றுக் காலனைக் காய்ந்தங்கி யோகமாய்
ஞாலக் கடவூர் நலமாய் இருந்ததே. 345

The Lord Scorched the God of Death

The Kundalini Fire coiled in Muladhara
Upward He coursed it to Hollow on top;
That Fiery Yoga Way He scorched the God of Death
That was at Kadavoor, the holy shrine here below.

Young Markandeya was an ardent devotee of Siva; but fate had decreed that he should die at the age of sixteen. On the day destined, Yama, the god of death, promptly threw his noose around Markandeya's life, not caring that the victim was immersed in Siva worship. At the sight of the god of death, the devotee clung fast to the Linga murthi. The death-noose thus encircled Siva as well. His wrath erupted, and rousing the kundalini fire from the muladhara, Siva spurned Yama forcing him to a regretful retreat by the heat of His divine fire. This heroic feat happened at the place called Kadavur.

இருந்த மனத்தை இசைய இருத்திப்
பொருந்தி இலிங்க வழியது போக்கித்
திருந்திய காமன் செயலிழித் தங்கண்
அருந்தவ யோகங் கொறுக்கை அமர்ந்ததே. 346

The Lord Vanquished Kama, the God of Love

The Lord was seated in Yoga
His thoughts stilled in meditation deep;
Lo! there came Kama
To tempt the Lord with shafts of love.
But the Love-god's wiles, the Lord foiled in Yoga Way;
This He did at Korukkai, the shrine divine.

Siva was in intense tapas, of actionless trance. The work of destruction ceased over the entire universe. The world became over-populated, and too burdensome for Mother Earth to support. The celestials sent Kama, the god of love, to shoot his shafts of love at Siva and disturb His tapas. Siva in wrath burnt Kama to ashes and continued His tapas. This feat was performed at the place called Korukkai.

3. இலிங்க புராணம்
LINGA PURANAM

Having described the eight heroic deeds of Siva, Tirumular proceeds to narrate yet other notable deeds of Siva under the title, 'Linga Puranam.'

அடிசேர்வன் என்னஎம் ஆதியை நோக்கி
முடிசேர் மலைமக னார்மக ளாகித்
திடமார் தவஞ்செய்து தேவர் அறியப்
படியார அர்ச்சித்துப் பத்திசெய் தாளே. 347

The Benevolent Deeds Of The Lord— How Sakti Won the Lord

"Of a certain will I espouse
My Lord of Divine Feet", thus saying
As Mountain King's daughter incarnate
Sakti performed penances severe;
For all celestial beings to witness,
For all earthly beings to delight,
In adoration intense to Primal Lord Divine.

Sakti intent on reaching the Primal Being, incarnated Herself as Parvati, the daughter of the mountain-king, and performed hard penance. All the world stood in wonder. Siva warming up to Her intense devotion blessed Her.

திரிகின்ற முப்புரஞ் செற்ற பிரானை
அரியனென் றெண்ணி அயர்வுற வேண்டா
புரிவுடை யாளர்க்குப் பொய்யலன் ஈசன்
பரிவொடு நின்றுபரிசறி வானே. 348

The Lord is not Beyond Reach

Mighty is the Lord
The Flying Fortess He destroyed.
Thus despair not
That He is your reach beyond;
Sure is the Lord to seekers true
In them He abideth, Grace abounding.

ஆழி வலங்கொண் டயன்மால் இருவரும்
ஊழி வலஞ்செய்ய ஒண்சுட ராதியும்
ஆழி கொடுத்தனன் அச்சுதற் கவ்வழி
வாழி பிரமற்கும் வாள்கொடுத் தானே. 349

The Lord Blessed Aya and Mal

The Lord is the Primal One,
He is the Light Effulgent;
Seeking Him they went—Aya and Mal
Girdling the boundless oceans
And across the endless aeons;
And to Achutha He granted the Disc Divine
And to Brahma, Jnana's Sword Eternal.

Brahma, the creator, and Vishnu, the preserver, at one time contending for cosmic supremacy, battled indecisively around the sea-girt globe at numerous points for a countless number of years. Finally, Siva stood as a limitless Pillar of Flame in between them. Tired, they made a truce and agreed that he who would first behold either the peak or the base of the fire pillar was to be regarded as supreme. Vishnu took the form of a boar and burrowed deep into earth's bottom. Brahma assumed the form of a hamsa bird (swan) and flew up high in the heavens. But neither saw either end of the fiery pillar. They realised their folly and worshipped Siva as supreme. Thereupon Siva blessed Vishnu with the chakra (discus), and Brahma with the sword (jnana).

தாங்கி இருபது தோளுந் தடவரை
ஓங்க எடுத்தவன் ஒப்பில் பெருவலி
ஆங்கு நெரித்தம ராவென் றழைத்தபின்
நீங்கா அருள்செய்தான் நின்மலன் தானே. 350

Lord Blessed Ravana

Of peerless might and shoulder twenty
Ravana the Giant lifted lofty mount Kailas;
With toe down, the Lord but gently pressed
And lo! the Giant screamed: "Lord Eternal."

The ten-headed giant Ravana, filled with great conceit over his might and prowess, put his 20 shoulders to Mount Kailas, the seat of Siva, in an atttempt to lift it. Siva gently pressed His toe, and lo, the giant writhing in pain cried "Oh, My Lord, You are immortal!" Thereupon Ravana played on his veena and evoked repentant melodies from the Sama Veda in adoration of the Lord. The Lord released him from under the weight of the mountain and blessed him.

உறுவ(து) அறிதண்டி ஒண்மணற் கூட்டி
அறுவகை ஆன்ஐந்தும் ஆட்டத்தன் தாதை
செறுவகை செய்து சிதைப்ப முனிந்து
மறுமழு வால்வெட்டி மாலைபெற் றானே. 351

The Lord Blessed Chandeswara

Dandi, that knew the way of Hereafter
Heaped sands into linga shape
And poured on it in adoration
The five products of his herd of cows;
His father seeing beat the boy
And kicked his fond image off;
Dandi flew into a blind rage
And smote the parent's leg with sword;
And lo! the Lord
Bedecked Dandi with His own garland of flowers forever to sport.

ஓடிவந் தெல்லாம் ஒருங்கிய தேவர்கள்
வாடி முகமும் வருத்தத்துத் தாஞ்சென்று
நாடி இறைவா நமஎன்று கும்பிட
ஈடில் புகழோன் எழுகவென் றானே. 352

The Lord is the Refuge of the Heavenly Beings too

Faces drawn in care
Hearts stricken with grief
The Devas together rushed and cried;
"Lord! we bow to You"
And thus they prayed, prostrating low;
And He of Renown unsurpassed said;
"Arise, fear not."

Dandi was a brahmin boy who herded the cows of his village. Filled with intense devotion for Siva, Dandi would make Lingam images out of sand from the river bed, milk the cows and offer the five products of cows to the Lingam in worship. The matter reached the ears of his father who, incensed at the way the precious milk and other products of the cows were being wasted by his son, knocked the sand-made lingam with a blow from his leg. Such was Dandi's devotion to Siva, that he was unable to contain the insult and smote the parent's offending leg with a stroke of the sword. Siva appeared on the scene, and blessed Dandi, bestowing His own garland on him. Seeing Dandi's father lying dead, the celestials appealed to Siva, who revived the parent.

4. தக்கன் வேள்வி

DAKSHA'S SACRIFICE

தந்தைபி ரான்வெகுண் டான்தக்கன் வேள்வியை
வெந்தழல் ஊடே புறப்பட விண்ணவர்
முந்திய பூசை முடியார் முறைகெட்டுச்
சிந்தினர் அண்ணல் சினஞ்செய்த போதே. 353

What Befell Celestials at Daksha's Sacrifice

The Heavenly Father walked in boundless fury
Into the raging blaze of Daksha's sacrifice,
And lo! as the Lord in wrath rose
Helter-skelter ran the Devas
Deranged in directions all
—Their depraved worship unconsummated.

Gods who participated in Daksha's unholy sacrifice in an attempt to denigrate Siva, met with diverse dire fates—some losing their head, others the face, the nose, the shoulders, the hands or other limbs. Having described the fate of the gods—Brahma, Vishnu, the mountain-god, the sun-god, the moon-god, the fire-god, the goddess of learning, and the god of celestials (Indra), Tirumular exhorts, "Be thou constant in devotion to Siva."

சந்தி செயக்கண் டெழுகின் றரிதானும்
எந்தை யிவனல்ல யாமே உலகினிற்
பந்தஞ்செய் பாசத்து வீழ்ந்து தவஞ்செய்ய
அந்தமி லானும் அருள்புரிந் தானே. 354

What Befell Hari

In a vain attempt to quell
The confusion that ensued
Hari rising bragged:
"Not He, but I am the beginning of things"

And so fell into this world below
A prey to Passion's consuming fetters;
Then repentant he performed tapas
And the Lord that has no beginning nor end
Bestowed His Grace on him.

அப்பரி சேயய னார்பதி வேள்வியுள்
அப்பரி சேயங்கி அதிசய மாகிலும்
அப்பரி சேயது நீர்மையை யுள்கலந்
தப்பரி சேசிவன் ஆலிக்கின் றானே. 355

To Each According to His Desert — the Way of Siva's Justice

And so it befell at Daksha's sacrifice,
And so indeed it befell;
A wonder though it be,
Verily that is what there befell;
Thus does the Lord lend His Grace
In the knowledge of each according to his desert.

அப்பரி சேஅயன் மால்முதல் தேவர்கள்
அப்பரி சேயவ ராகிய காரணம்
அப்பரி சங்கி யுளநாளும் உள்ளிட்
டப்பரி சாகி அலர்ந்திருந் தானே. 356

Gods Got What They Deserved

And thus it is with Aya, Mal and the rest of Gods;
And thus it is they came to what they are;
And thus it is that they are there;
And thus does the Lord sit serene within
To reward the heart that daily seeks Him true.

அலர்ந்திருந் தானென் றமரர் துதிப்பக்
அலந்தருங் கிழங்கி கோளுற நோக்கிச்
சிவந்த பரமிது சென்று கதுவ
உவந்த பெருவழி யோடி வந்தானே. 357

The Lord Comes to Those Who Seek Him in Yoga Way

While the heavenly Beings sang of Him
As seated in rapture serene,
He came rushing
To me along the highway of bliss that opened
As from Muladhara the Kundalini fire upward shot
To the crimson spheres of Sahasrara
In the way that is yoga.

அரிபிர மன்தக்கன் அருக்க னுடனே
வருமதி வாலை வன்னிநல் இந்திரன்
சிரமுக நாசி சிறந்தகை தோள்தான்
அரனருள் இன்றி அழிந்தநல் லோரே. 358

For Want of Hara's Grace They Lost All

Lacking Lord's Grace
Many the high and handsome
That destruction and disfigurement met;
Thus Hari, Brahma, and Daksha
The Sun, Moon and Fire and Indra as well
All these Gods lost
Head, face, nose, hand and shoulder; some limb or other.

செவிமந் திரஞ்சொல்லுஞ் செய்தவத் தேவர்
அவிமந் திரத்தின் அடுக்களை கோலிச்
செவிமந் திரஞ்செய்து தாமுற நோக்குங்
குவிமந் திரங்கொல் கொடியது வாமே. 359

Pranava and Ajapajapa

The Celestials who chant audibly the sacred mantra,
Use the silent Pranava to rouse the Kundalini from the Muladhara
And chanting the Pranava control the mind,
And with the help of Ajapajapa rise to the heights.

நல்லார் நவகுண்டம் ஒன்பதும் இன்புறப்
பல்லார் அமரர் பரிந்தருள் செய்கென
வில்லாற் புரத்தை விளங்கெரி கோத்தவன்
பொல்லா அசுரர்கள் பொன்றும் படிக்கே. 360

The Lord Destroyed Asuras to Protect the Sacrificial Rites of Devas

The Immortal Many prayed to the Lord;
"O Lord! protect the nine, sacrificial pits
For the holy ones to delight"
And the Lord, bending His Mountain-bow
Sent forth shafts of fire at Asura's city
Destroying the evil ones, never to rise again.

தெளிந்தார் கலங்கினும் நீகலங் காதே.
அளித்தாங் கடைவதெம் ஆதிப் பிரானை
விளிந்தா னதுதக்கன் வேள்வியை வீயச்
சுளிந்தாங் கருளசெய்த தூய்மொழி யானே. 361

Repent and Pray; Lord Blesses

Well may the learned in lores waver
But waver not thou;
Melt in love for our Primal Lord
And you shall have Him sure;
He destroyed the unholy sacrifice of Daksha
And yet turning back
As they repented and prayed
He blessed them all,
He our Lord of holy speech.

5. பிரளயம்

DELUGE

கருவரை மூடிக் கலந்தெழும் வெள்ளத்
திருவருங் கோவென் றிகல இறைவன்
ஒருவனும் நீருற ஓங்கொளி யாகி
அருவரை யாய்நின் றருள்புரிந் தானே. 362

The Lord Blesses the Two Who for Primacy Contended

When the swelling deluge at the end of Time
Swallowed the black mountain tops
Hari and Brahma fought
For primacy contending;
And then from amidst the floods arose
As an immeasurable mountain of Light
The One Lord, manifesting the Truth,
And thus blessing both.

Mantra 362-365

At the yugas end when cataclysmal floods swallowed the earth, Brahma, Vishnu and other denizens of the celestial world sought refuge in Siva, and Siva saved them from disaster.

அலைகடல் ஊடறுத் தண்டத்து வானோர்
தலைவன் எனும்பெயர் தான்றலை மேற்கொண்டு
உலகார் அழற்கண் டுள்விழா தோடி
அலைவாயில் வீழாமல் அஞ்சலென் றானே. 363

The Lord Saved Mortals

And high amidst the surging flood
The Lord as Flaming Mountain stood
His primacy for the Gods to know
The mortal ones
Powerless to stand the Fire-Mountain's radiant glow
Rushed to the surging waters in trembling fear;
The Lord then said to them: "Fear not! you shall be saved."

தண்கடல் விட்ட தமரருந் தேவரும்
எண்கடல் சூழெம் பிரானென் றிறைஞ்சுவர்
விண்கடல் செய்தவர் மேலெழுந் தப்புறங்
கண்கடல் செய்யுங் கருத்தறி யாரே. 364

Lord is Ocean of Grace

As the Ocean's swell subsided;
The ocean of immortals and Devas sang;
"Praised be our Lord;"
Little do they know
That He who created the ocean and the firmament
Rises beyond to the Ocean of His benignant grace.

சமைக்கவல் லானைச் சயம்புவென் றேத்தி
அமைக்கவல் லாரி வுலகத்து ளாரே
திகைத்தெண் ணீரிற் கடலொலி ஓசை
மிகைக்கொள அங்கி மிகாமைவைத் தானே. 365

To Quell Rising Tides Lord Placed Primal Fire

The Lord, He creates all
Himself Being Uncreated—
Who is there in the world here below
That thinking thus holds Him to heart?
When the oceans ebbed and roared
He placed the Primal Fire to quell the tides;
How, how, compassionate He was!

பண்பழி செய்வழி பாடுசென் றப்புறங்
கண்பழி யாதகமலத் திருக்கின்ற
நண்பழி யாளனை நாடிச்சென் றச்சிரம்
விண்பழி யாத விருத்திகொண் டானே. 366

The Lord Severed Head of Brahma Who erred

Brahma that is seated, on the lotus comely
Sauntered in the Lord's path in manner unreasonable
The sinful wretch!
The Lord sought Him
And in his severed head gathered alms
In ways the gods approved.

6. சக்கரப்பேறு

GIFT OF THE DISCUS

மால்போ தகனென்னும் வண்மைக்கிங் காங்காரங்
கால்போதங் கையினோ டந்தரச் சக்கர
மேல்போக வெள்ளி மலைஅம ராபதி
பார்போக மேழும் படைத்துடை யானே. 367

Through Arrogance Mal Lost His Chakra

Filled with arrogance as Guru Supreme
Mal vaunted his egoism about;
Then the Lord of the Silver Mountain made the discus fly away
And it orbited around the seven worlds.

Vishnu worshipped Siva who granted him the powerful discus. But such was the potency of the weapon that it had to be split by Siva — one half going Vishnu and the other half to Sakti, nonseparate on Siva's side.

சக்கரம் பெற்றுநல் தாமோ தரன்தானும்
சக்கரந் தன்னைத் தரிக்கவொண் ணாமையால்
மிக்கரன் தன்னை விருப்புடன் அர்ச்சிக்கத்
தக்கநற் சத்தியைத் தான்கூறு செய்ததே. 368

The Lord Split Power of Chakra

He bestowed on Damodara the divine discus,
But potent far was it for him to hold
And so he prayed to the Lord in fervour
And the Lord split its power in twain.

கூறது வாகக் குறித்துநற் சக்கரங்
கூறது செய்து கொடுத்தனன் மாலுக்குக்
கூறது செய்து கொடுத்தனன் சத்திக்குக்
கூறது செய்து தரித்தனன் கோலமே. 369

The Lord Splits Power of Chakra

The Lord splits His power into two,
One half He gave to Vishnu as a chakra,
And the other half as body to Sakti,
And thus He remains.

தக்கன்றன் வேள்வி தகர்த்தநல் வீரர்பால்
தக்கன்றன் வேள்வியில் தாமோ தரன்தானுஞ்
சக்கரந் தன்னைச் சசிமுடி மேல்விட
அக்கி உமிழ்ந்தது வாயுக் கரத்திலே. 370

At Daksha's Sacrifice Chakra Lost Power

At the crescent-decked head of Veerabhadra
That destroyed the depraved sacrifice of Daksha,
Damodara aimed his discus;
And then the doughty Lord sent forth a sneeze;
And lo! a gusty tempest blew
And down fell discus powerless against God Supreme.

7. எலும்பும் கபாலமும்
SKELETON AND SKULL

எலும்புங் கபாலமும் ஏந்தி எழுந்த
வலம்பன் மணிமுடி வானவ ராதி
எலும்புங் கபாலமும் ஏந்தில னாகில்
எலும்புங் கபாலமும் இற்றுமண் ணாமே. 371

Why The Lord Wears Skull and Bones

He is the Lord of all Celestial Beings,
Who wear bejewelled crowns of dazzling beauty;
But the Lord did bedeck Himself in Skull and Bones
How is it?
If He bears not skull and bones.
Dust unto dust will theirs be.

Siva wears the garland of skeletons and skulls strung from crowned heads of the celestials. Why does He do so? That they may not turn into dust forever; that they may yet be redeemed.

8. அடிமுடி தேடல்
IN SEARCH OF CROWN AND FEET OF SIVA

பிரமனும் மாலும் பிரானேநான் என்னப்
பிரமன்மால் தங்கள்தம் பேதைமை யாலே
பரமன் அனலாய்ப் பரந்துமுன் நிற்க
அரனடி தேடி அரற்றுகின் றாரே. 372

Brahma and Mal Seek His Feet

In ignorance gross, Brahma and Mal
Each bragged as Lord Supreme;
Then as a pillar of Fire the Lord stood before them
And they search and scream
In vain His Feet to behold.

Mantras 372-380

The story of Brahma and Vishnu vainly seeking to see the peak and bottom of Siva, who stood before them as a monument of fire, is again recounted here.

ஆமே முலகுற நின்றளம் எண்ணலுந்
தாமே முலகில் தழற்பிழம் பாய்நிற்கும்
வானே முலகுறும் மாமணி கண்டனை
யானே அறிந்தேன் அவன் ஆண்மையாலே. 373

But I Knew Lord, By His Grace Abounding

Yet I knew the Lord
Through His Grace abounding;
He who fills the seven heavens
He who stood as Pillar of Fire
The seven worlds pervading;
He of the bejewelled throat.

ஊனாய் உயிராய் உணர்வங்கி யாய்முன்னஞ்
சேணாய்வா னோங்கித் திருவுரு வாய்அண்டத்
தாணுவும் ஞாயிறுந் தண்மதி யுங்கடந்
தாண்முழு தண்டமு மாகிநின் றானே. 374

Lord is Omnipresent

The Lord is life, body and consciousness
Fire that enveloped the firmament far
Transcending sun and moon
He pervades the Cosmic space—
Holy thus His Form of yore
Support of Universe vast.

நின்றான் நிலமுழு தண்டத்துள் நீளியன்
அன்றே யவன்வடி வஞ்சின ராய்ந்தது
சென்றார் இருவா திருமுடி மேற்செல
நன்றாங் கழலடி நாடவொண் ணாதே. 375

The Two Saw not His Form Entire

He stood filling Cosmic space
And the two in fear trembled.
They went searching His Form entire
The one seeking the crown
The other His Feet
Neither found them.

சேவடி ஏத்துஞ் செறிவுடை வானவர்
மூவடி தாவென் றானும் முனிவரும்
பாவடி யாலே பதஞ்செய் பிரமனுந்
தாவடி யிட்டுத் தலைப்பெய்து மாறே. 376

The Two Contended For Primacy

Vishnu, adored of the Devas,
That asked of Mahabali for three feet land
And Brahma
Whom the Rishis in hymnal praise please,
The two in ego contended
For primacy to gain.

தானக் கமலத் திருந்த சதுமுகன்
தானக் கருங்கட லூழித் தலைவனும்
ஊனத்தின் உள்ளே உயிர்போல் உணர்கின்ற
தானப் பெரும்பொருள் தன்மைய தாமே. 377

The Lord Animates Within Brahma and Vishnu Also

The four-headed God on lotus seated
The comely lord that on dark sea sleepeth
They both are of the essence same
As the Great One who cognises all,
As unto life within the fleshy body.

ஆலிங் கனஞ்செய் தெழுந்த பரஞ்சுடர்
மேலிங்ஙன் வைத்ததோர் மெய்ந்நெறி முன்கண்
டாலிங் கனஞ்செய் துலகம் வலம்வருங்
கோலிங் கமைஞ்சருள் கூடலு மாமே.

Know God's Truth and Be Blessed Now and Hereafter

Know afore
The Truth of Divine flame that enveloped all
And hold fast unto that;
Then may you receive
The sceptre to hold domain over earth
And the Grace to follow in heaven above.

வாள்கொடுத் தானை வழிபட்ட தேவர்கள்
ஆள்கொடுத் தெம்போல் அரனை அறிகிலர்
ஆள்கொடுத் தின்பங் கொடுத்துக் கோளாகத்
தாள்கொடுத் தானடி சாரகி லாரே. 379

Only in Self-Surrender Will the Lord Be Truly Known

The Lord granted the Sword of Protection
To Beings Celestial that prayed to Him
But they know Him not entire
As I who His vassal became;
He granted me Himself
He granted me Bliss
And His Feet's grace as final prize;
They approach not His Feet thus.

ஊழி வலஞ்செய்தங் கோரும் ஒருவற்கு
வாழி சதுமுகன் வந்து வெளிப்படும்
வீழித் தலைநீர் விதித்தது தாவென
ஊழிக் கதிரோன் ஒளியைவென் றானே. 380

Lord Decreed Brahma's Fate

Inscrutable is the Lord
He defies Time's infinite vistas;
The four-headed Brahma prayed;
"Do reveal Thyself, pray,
And on this bowed head decree my Fate,"
And the Lord
Surpassing far the dazzle of the sun at end of Time
Revealed Himself as Light Pure.

9. படைத்தல்

CREATION — MICROCOSMIC

ஆதியோ டந்தம் இலாத பராபரம்
போதம தாகப் புணரும் பராபரை
சோதி யதனிற் பரந்தோன்றத் தோன்றுமாந்
தீதில் பரையதன் பால்திகழ் நாதமே. 381

Act of Creation by the Primal One

Paraparam that has neither Beginning nor End,
In Pure Consciousness consorted with Paraparai
And in that Light Pure arose Param;

And from union of Param with Parai immaculate
Was Nada born.

நாதத்தில் விந்துவும் நாதவிந் துக்களில்
தீதற் றகம்வந்த சிவன்சத்தி என்னவே
பேதித்து ஞானங் கிரியை பிறத்தலால்
வாதித்த விச்சையில் வந்தெழும் விந்துவே. 382

Creation Continues

Nada united with Bindu
From the union of Nada-Bindu
Did Siva and Sakti appear
From Siva arose Jnana and
From Sakti Kriya
Iccha arose from Bindu.

இல்லது சத்தி இடந்தனில் உண்டாகிக்
கல்லொளி போலக் கலந்துள் ளிருந்திடும்
வல்லது ஆக வழிசெய்த அப்பொருள்
சொல்லது சொல்லிடில் தூராதி தூரமே. 383

Latent Maya Evolves

From Sakti appeared Maya,
The two mingled like a jewel and its lustre,
He who made the Maya appear,
Remains far far away beyond description.

தூரத்திற் சோதி தொடர்ந்தொரு சத்தியாய்
ஆர்வத்து நாதம் அணைந்தொரு விந்துவாய்ப்
பாரச் சதாசிவம் பார்முதல் ஐந்துக்கும்
சார்வத்துச் சத்திஓர் சாத்துமா னாமே. 384

Evolution of Maan Sakti—the Substratum of Matter

Away in the far distance of Time
Paraparam and paraparai conjoined
Then did Nada with Bindu;
And further on Sadasiva with Sakti;
Thus was Maan born
The finite support of elements five.

Anava Sakti then acts on the prakriti maya (material) sphere. This sphere is known as 'maan' or 'mahat'. From maan evolves the five elements—earth, water, fire, ether and space.

மானின்கண் வானாகி வாயு வளர்ந்திடும்
கானின்கண் நீருங் கலந்து கடினமாய்த்
தேனின்கண் ஐந்துஞ் செறிந்தைந்து பூதமாய்ப்
பூவின்கண் நின்று பொருந்தும் புவனமே. 385

Universe of Five Elements—Evolves

Out of Maya evolved space
From space, air
From air, water,
From water, earth's hard crust;
Thus they formed in succession
The elements five;
From Maya appeared the five subtle essences
(Tanmatras)
And from them the five gross elements (Bhutas)
From the Vyahruti Bhu has arisen the present world.

புவனம் படைப்பான் ஒருவன் ஒருத்தி
புவனம் படைப்பார்க்குப் புத்திரர் ஐவர்
புவனம் படைப்பானும் பூமிசை யானாய்
புவனம் படைப்பானப் புண்ணியன் தானே. 386

Siva is the Source of Creation

Siva, the He-She, creates universe all,
He has sons five*
The Holy One that creates universe all
Himself as lotus-seated Brahma
The Creator became.

---

*The Five manifestations are Sadasiva, Mahesvara, Rudra, Brahma and Vishnu.

புண்ணியன் நந்தி பொருந்தி உலகெங்கும்
தண்ணிய ,மானை வளர்ந்திடுஞ் சத்தியுங்
கண்ணியல் பாகக் கலவி முழுதுமாய்
மண்ணியல் பாக மலர்ந்தெழு பூவிலே. 387

In the Union of Sadasiva with Maan Sakti Blossomed the Universe

The Holy Nandi that is Sadasiva
And the Sakti that evolved Maan
Together in looks united in full;
And from that union arose the universe
As unto a blossom gently opening.

நீரகத் தின்பம் பிறக்கும் நெருப்பிடை
காயத்திற் சோதி பிறக்கும்அக் காற்றிடை
ஓர்வுடை நல்லுயிர்ப் பாதம் ஒலிசத்தி
நீரிடை ம்ண்ணின் நிலைப்பிறப் பாமே. 388

How the Elements Five Evolved

From Fire emanated water
From Wind emanated light
From Space emanated sound
From Water emanated earth
This the way the elements five evolved.

உண்டுல கேழும் உமிழ்ந்தான் உடனாகி
அண்டத் தமரர் தலைவனும் ஆதியுங்
கண்டச் சதுமுகக் காரணன் தன்னொடும்
பண்டிவ் வுலகம் படைக்கும் பொருளே. 389

The Primal One Created the Universe With Brahma and Vishnu

With Hari who swallowed and spat out the seven worlds
With Brahma, the four-headed creator,
The Primal One, the Lord of Celestial Beings
Created, of yore, this universe vast.

ஓங்கு பெருங்கடல் உள்ளுறு வானொடும்
பாங்கார் கயிலைப் பராபரன் தானும்
வீங்குங் கமல மலர்மிசை மேலயன்
ஆங்குயிர் வைக்கும் அதுவுணர்ந் தானே. 390

Creation is an Act of Pure Consciousness by the Primal One

The Supreme One aloft the Mount Kailas
With Hari in the ocean bed
And Brahma on the blooming lotus
Created life
By Consciousness Pure.

Thus, ultimately it is the Primal One who created this vast universe by pure consciousness. It was He who created Brahma, the creator, and Vishnu, who contains in himself the seven worlds.

காரணன் அன்பிற் கலந்தெங்கும் நின்றவன்
நாரணன் நின்ற நடுவுட லாய்நிற்கும்
பாரணன் அன்பிற்பதஞ்செய்யும் நான்முகன்
ஆரண மாய்உல காயமர்ந் தானே. 391

The Primal One is Narayana and Brahma as Well

He is the First Cause,
All-pervasive in love;
He is Vishnu; He is Brahma,
He is Veda, The sound and matter.

He is the First Cause: He is Vishnu; He is Brahma; He is Veda; He is the cosmos. All, all, are diverse manifestations of the Ever-abiding Compassionate One.

பயன்எளி தாம்பரு மாமணி செய்ய
நயன்எளி தாகிய நம்பன்ஒன் றுண்டு
அயன்ஒளி யாயிருந் தங்கே படைக்கும்
பயனெளி தாம்வய ணந்தெளிந் தேனே. 392

As Light Within Brahma, the Primal One Creates

A rare Ruby—He is easy of reach,
The One Lord—He is easy of love,
He is the light within Brahma;
And now I know why the Creator does it so easy.

போக்கும் வரவும் புனிதன் அருள்புரிந்
தாக்கமுஞ் சிந்தைய தாகின்ற காலத்து
மேக்கு மிகநின்ற எட்டுத் திசையோடுந்
தாக்குங் கலக்குந் தயாபரன் தானே. 393

At the Creation the Compassionate One Pervades All Space

Death and birth, the Holy One in Grace ordained;
And in that hour when by His Thought
He Commenced the act of Creation
He fills and pervades in directions eight,
He, the Compassionate One.

நின்றுயி ராக்கு நிமலன்என் னாருயிர்
ஒன்றுயி ராக்கும் அளவை உடலுற
முன்துய ராக்கும் உடற்குந் துணையதா
நன்றுயிர்ப் பானே நடுவுநின் றானே. 394

The Lord Animates the Body in Justice

The Immaculate One creates all;
And as He created me too,
He animates within me
A support to the body, a heir to karmic ills;
Verily, the Lord is the verily Just.

The immaculate One, who creates all, who creates the bodies and milieus for jivas too, according to their karmic desert. That is His act of divine justice. In the act of creation He stands adorning death's bones and konrai's blooms gleaming as pure gold. He beckons to departed souls as the Final Refuge of Becoming. He enters within jiva and cognises all.

ஆகின்ற தன்மையில் அக்கணி கொன்றையன்
வேகின்ற செம்பொனின் மேலணி மேனியன்
போகின்ற சீவன் புகுந்துட லாய்உளன்
ஆகின்ற தன்மைசெய் ஆண்டகை யானே. 395

Lord is the Refuge of All Departed Life

In the act of creation
He stands adorning death's bones and konrai's blooms,
His resplendent Form out-shines red-hot gold;
A refuge vast of all departed life;
His is the form.

ஒருவன் ஒருத்தி விளையாடல் உற்றார்
இருவர் விளையாட்டும் எல்லாம் விளைக்கும்
பருவங்கள் தோறும் பயன்பல வான
திருவொன்றிற் செய்கை செகமுற்று மாமே. 396

Creation the Play of He-She

He-and-She commenced play
The play of Two produced all;
With seasons changing, diverse the produce;
When He-and-She in holy union join
Complete be the act of creation.

புகுந்தறி வான்புவ னாபதி அண்ணல்
புகுந்தறி வான்புரி சக்கரத் தண்ணல்
புகுந்தறி வான்மலர் மேலுறை புத்தேள்
புகுந்தறி யும்முடிக் காகிநின் றாரே. 397

He functions as the Three

Siva pervades Rudra and functions as destructor,
Enters Vishnu and functions as protector;
Pervades Brahma and functions as creator,
The other three, are just shells in which He works.

ஆணவச் சத்தியும் ஆம்அதில் ஐவருங்
காரிய காரண ஈசர் கடைமுறை
பேணிய ஐந்தொழி லாலவிந்து விற்பிறந்(து)
ஆணவம் நீங்கா தவரென லாகுமே. 398

The Five Gods Were Born of Anava Sakti

Out of the union of Anava Sakti with Bindu
The Five Gods were born.
Brahma, Vishnu, Rudra, Sadasiva and Maheswara.
For the five acts to perform—
Creation, preservation, destruction, obscuration and redemption—
As One from the other in causative succession;
Born as they were of the Anava Sakti
Of Anava they were not rid.

Out of apara bindu uniting with anava (ichcha) sakti in the impure maya sphere, were born the five Gods—Sadasiva, Mahesvara, Rudra, Vishnu and Brahma—to perform their five respective functions; and being born of anava sakti they were not free from the taint of the individualising malam (anava malam).

உற்றமுப் பாலொன்று மாயாள் உத்யமா
மற்றைய மூன்று மாயோ தயம்விந்து
பெற்றவன் நாதம் பரையிற் பிறத்தலால்
துற்ற பரசிவன் தொல்விளை யாட்டிதே. 399

Creation the Play of the Ultimate

Maya in union with Bindu yielded
The rest of Mayas three (Suddha, Asuddha and Prakriti)
(The Bindu was of Nada born)
And Nada was of Parai born;
And all this in the Creative play of Parasiva, the Ultimate.

ஆகாய மாதி சதாசிவ ராதியென்
போகாத சத்தியுட் போந்துடன் போந்தனர்
மாகாய ஈசன் அரன்மால் பிரமனாம்
ஆகாயம் பூமி காண அளித்தலே. 400

The Elements and the Five manifestations come from Maya

What are the five elements beginning with space?
Who are the five manifestations beginning with Sadasiva?
They originated from the eternal Maya,
And perform the functions allotted to them.

அளியார் முக்கோணம் வயிந்தவந் தன்னில்
அளியார் திரிபுரை யாம்அவள் தானே
அளியார் சதாசிவ மாகி அமைவாள்
அளியார் கருமங்கள் ஐந்துசெய் வாளே. 401

Maya Sakti Born of Bindu Performs the Five Acts

From Bindu by Orderly triangle denoted
The honeyed Sakti Tripurai evolved;
She it is the Compassionate Sadasiva became;
She it is the five merciful deeds perform.

வாரணி கொங்கை மனோன்மணி மங்கலி
காரணி காரிய மாகக் கலந்தவள்
வாரணி ஆரணி வானவர் மோகினி
பூரணி போதாதி போதமு மாமே. 402

Names of Glories of Maya Sakti

She is Manonmani, the ample-bosomed;
Mangali, the ever auspicious;
Varani of elephant form
Arani of haunting forests
Mohini of tempting beauty
Poorani—the Perfect Being,
Cause-Effect conjoint in one
—She, Consciousness beyond Consciousness.

நின்றது தானாய் நிறைந்த மகேசுவரன்
சென்றங் கியங்கும் அரன்திரு மாலவன்
மன்றது செய்யும் மலர்மிசை மேலயன்
என்றிவ ராக இசைந்திருந் தானே. 403

One Sadasiva Became Five

Sadasiva that stood as One
Animated Maheswara;
And then Hara, Hari and Brahma,
Thus did the One become the Five.

ஒருவனு மேஉல கேழும் படைத்தான்
ஒருவனு மேஉல கேழும் அளித்தான்
ஒருவனு மேஉல கேழுந் துடைத்தான்
ஒருவனு மேஉல கோடுயிர் தானே. 404

Sadasiva Alone Performs the Five Functions

The One alone created the worlds seven;
The One alone spanned the worlds seven;
The One alone survived the worlds seven;
The One alone pervaded body and life.

செந்தா மரைவண்ணன் தீவண்ணன் எம்இறை
மைந்தார் முகில்வண்ணன் மாயஞ்செய் பாசத்தும்
கொந்தார் குழலியர் கூடிய கூட்டத்தும்
அந்தார் பிறவி அறுத்துநின் றானே. 405

Of Red Lotus Hue is Our Lord!

Of red lotus hue is our Lord!
Of Crimson fire hue is our Lord!
He sundered the chain of births,
That the dark cloud-hued Mal in pasa bound,
And to flower-bedecked Maya-Crowned, consigned.

தேடுஞ் திசைஎட்டுஞ் சீவன் உடல்உயிர்
கூடும் பிறவிக் குணஞ்செய்த மாநந்தி
ஊடும் அவர்தம துள்ளத்துள் ளேநின்று
நாடும் வழக்கமும் நான் அறிந் தேனே. 406

Sadasiva is in the Heart of Even Those Who Doubt Him

He is Nandi the Great;
In directions eight,
He is life pervasive;
He brings body and soul together in birth;
Even in the heart of those who doubt Him, He is;
And from there He seeks them;
This I have known Him oft perform.

ஓராய மேஉல கேழும் படைப்பதும்
ஓராய மேஉல கேழும் அளிப்பதும்
ஓராய மேஉல கேழுந் துடைப்பதும்
ஓராய மேஉல கோடுயிர் தானே. 407

The One Holy Family Performs All

The One Family creates the worlds seven;
The One Family preserves the worlds seven;
The One Family destroys the worlds seven;
The One Family pervades all life and body.

நாதன் ஒருவனும் நல்ல இருவருங்
கோது குலத்தொடுங் கூட்டிக் குழைத்தனர்
ஏது பணியென் றிசையும் இருவருக்
காதி இவனே அருளுகின் றானே. 408

The Act of Genesis

Siva with Sadasiva and Maheswara;
Together stirred and Commingled the Family Impure
(of matter)
The Two then besought of the Lord:
"What shall we make? Command us, O Lord"
And the Lord Himself then spells it out.

அப்பரி செண்பத்து நான்குநூ றாயிரம்
மெய்ப்பரி செய்தி விரிந்துயி ராய்நிற்கும்
பொய்ப்பரி செய்திப் புகலும் மனிதர்கட்
கிப்பரி சேஇருள் மூடிநின் றானே. 409

He Pervades All Creation as Life Within

And so,
Through creations four and eighty lakhs of species
He filled as life within;
Then men who in doubt ask: How is it?
Are verily to enveloping darkness condemned.

ஆதித்தன் சந்திரன் அங்கிஎண் பாலர்கள்
போதித்த வானொலி பொங்கிய நீர்புவி
வாதித்த சத்தாதி வாக்கு மனாதிகள்
ஓதுற்ற மாயையின் விந்துவின் உற்றதே. 410

Varieties of Creation

The Sun, Moon, Agni and rest of celestials,
The space, air, fire, water and earth
The sound, word, mind and the like
All these were of Maya born,
In union with Bindu.

10. காத்தல்

SUSTENANCE

The Supreme One, Siva/Sakti, the Transcendent/Immanent One, encompasses all—He is both absolute and relative reality. Siva as Parasivam is the impersonal, Absolute, the static aspect that transcends both subtle and material existence. Siva as Sakti, the immanent pure consciousness or energy is the dynamic aspect of existence, the power and substratum of all form. Sakti ubiquitously energizes the sphere of pure form or suddha maya; the intermediate sphere of impure form or asuddha maya; and the lowest sphere of physical matter or prakriti maya. The One Sakti is all three—the suddha, asuddha and prakriti mayas.

Thus the act of manifest creation is a series of graded devolution of the pure spirit—first the primal principles of existence: Siva, Sakti, Nada (apara) and Bindu (apara); and then the five Gods from Sadasiva to Brahma to perform the five acts. It is the total work of nine agencies—of whom the first Four are in the suddha maya realms, and the other Five are in the asuddha maya sphere.

The latter five categories then acting on prakriti maya produce the phenomenal world, beginning with the five elements, space to earth—Sadasiva leading in this process.

The totality of creation is for the evolution of jiva—that they may, through experience, learn of and realise their final destiny of uniting in the pure Spirit.

Why do souls, who inwardly share Siva's eternal perfections of Satchidananda and Parasivam, need this evolution? Because each individual jiva, being temporally created as a divine soul-body that evolves from immaturity to maturity, from divine ignorance to divine sapience, is slowly gaining and maturing the faculties to realize its identity with Siva's perfections. This evolution is effected through Siva s purposeful imposing of veils—anava (individualizing ignorance), maya (subtle and material form), and karma—over the awareness of the soul).

The nature of jiva is one of environmental dependence. When he is in the milieu of impurities, he is impure spirit. When he is with pure spirit, he becomes pure spirit.

This body, the senses, the phenomenal world, and the power of sense enjoyment are created for the jiva, so that he may by experience learn how painful it is to be tainted by the triple impurities, and recurring birth and death, and so be liberated to merge in the pure Spirit.

The evolution of individual jivas is the primary reason for all the convoluted forms of creation. Why should the Supreme One engage Himself in it? Because of His infinite love for His most special creation, the jiva, who cannot mature into its divine fulfilment without the impetuses of the triple malam, just as a baby cannot mature into a great and productive adulthood without the appropriate and necessary experiences. Each jiva is given all the time, experiences and opportunities it needs to unfold its divinity, to realize God, and eventually to serve God and the Gods in helping other souls in their evolution.

To recapitulate, Tirumular postulates four stages in the creation process:

1) In the transcendental sphere where Paraparam uniting with Paraparai, evolve paranadam and parabindu, who in turn devolute Parasivam and Parai. This takes place beyond the sphere of pure Spirit, and these six categories may be known as transcendental categories. They are not directly involved in the act of creation.

(This stage is not referred to in some of the later works on Saiva Siddhanta Philosophy—for instance, the Sivajnana Siddhiar. They present the creative process as starting with the nine evolutes of pure spirit who actually perform the process of creation).

2) From paranadam and parabindu of the transcendental sphere, Siva, Sakti, aparanadam and apara bindu evolve. Out of these four categories, Sakti manifests as the primal jnana, kriya and ichcha saktis; and apara bindu uniting with ichcha sakti evolves suddha maya. Thus in the sphere of suddha maya we have four primal categories, Siva, Sakti, aparanadam and aparabindu.

3) Next, is the creation in the sphere of asuddha maya or impure spirit. Here aparanadam interacting on aparabindu evolves the Five Gods for the five acts of: bestowal of revelatory grace, bestowal of veiling grace, dissolution, preservation and creation.

Asuddha maya sakti is so called, because She embodies the principle of egoity or anava. She is therefore known as Anava Sakti also. As these five Gods or aspects manifested from Anava Sakti, they operate within the realms of anava malam.

Thus these nine aspects of Siva, the former four acting on pure or suddha maya, and the latter five acting on asuddha or impure maya, together constitute the principal constituents of active creation.

4) Then comes the creation of the phenomenal world. This takes place by aparabindu acting in the realm of prakriti maya, or material stuff. Thus was the corporeal body, with its subtle and gross aspects, its five sheaths, the five sense organs, five cognitive organs, the four internal mind organs, developed. Thus were millions upon millions of life's species created. Thus manifested were the sun, moon, stars, the eight gods ruling over the cardinal directions, the sky, ether, seas, earth, sound, touch, sight, taste and feel. Thus were the innumerable worlds that constitute the cosmic universe created.

All this is ultimately the work of One Being, Siva. All other categories are functional agencies, deriving their power from Siva.

A word or two about the expressions, Sivam, Sakti, nadam and bindu. Sivam and Sakti are generally referred to as male and female. However, this is not to be interpreted in the biological sense. Siva is the static aspect and Sakti, the dynamic aspect of supreme consciousness. They do not exist separately. The one does not exist without the other, and they play their respective roles ever—static and dynamic.

However, ab initio, when creation starts, there should be some force to release the dynamic aspect. There should be a third relationship between them and from out of them to spark off the initial vibration. That which effects this relationship is nadam. Literally nadam means 'sound', not the sound perceived by the ear, but the subtle unmanifested sound.

When the dynamic power of creation has been thus released, it has to manifest itself to create forms. That first manifestation is known as bindu, or literally, 'a point.' It is the compactness of energy ready to produce. Shelly in his "Prometheus" reminds us of the concept when he says, "Plunge into eternity where recorded time seems but a point."

Thus, both nadam and bindu are only aspects of Sakti in which the "germ of action increasingly sprouts with a view to manifestation producing a state of compactness of energy and readiness to create", and Sakti is an aspect of Siva, the source of all energy. Thus Siva, Sakti, nadam and bindu can be seen as four inseparable entities in the chain of causation conjointly performing the act of creation.

The actual task of accomplishing creation has been allotted to Brahma, who derives his power from Sadasiva, who in turn was evolved from bindu and anava maya sakti, and from Siva, in the ultimate.

புகுந்துநின் றான்வெளி யாய்இரு ளாகிப்
புகுந்துநின் றான்புகழ் வாய்இதழ் வாகிப்
புகுந்துநின் றான்உட லாய்உயி ராகிப்
புகுந்துநின் றான்புந்தி மன்னிநின் றானே. 411

The Spirit Pervades All

As Light and Darkness He pervaded,
As Fame and Blemish He pervaded,
As Body and Life He pervaded,
As my constant thought He pervaded.

தானே திசையொடு தேவரு மாய்நிற்குந்
தானே உடலுயிர் தத்துவ மாய்நிற்குந்
தானே கடல்மலை யாதியு மாய்நிற்குந்
தானே உலகில் தலைவனு மாமே. 412

He is the Totality

Himself as space and celestials stands,
Himself as body, life and matter stands,
Himself as sea, hill and dale stands,
Himself—all worlds Lord Supreme.

உடலாய் உயிராய் உலகமே தாகிக்
கடலாய்க் கார்முகில் நீர்பொழி வானாய்
இடையாய் உலப்பிலி எங்குந்தா னாகி
அடையார் பெருவழி அண்ணல்நின் றானே. 413

The True Way

As body, life, and world,
As sea, cloud and cloud-laden sky,
Permeating all, indestructible and continuous

The Lord stands in majesty
The True way that never closes.

தேடுந் திசைஎட்டுஞ் சீவன் உடல்உயிர்
கூடு மரபிற் குணஞ்செய்த மாநந்தி
ஊடும் அவர்தம துள்ளத்து ளேநின்று
நாடும் வழக்கமும் நான் அறிந்தேனே. 414

Sadasiva is in the Heart of Even Those Who Doubt Him

He is Nandi the Great;
In directions eight,
He is life pervasive;
He brings body and soul together in birth;
Even in the heart of those who doubt Him, He is;
And from there He seeks them;
This I have known Him oft perform.

தானொரு காலந் தனிச்சுட ராய்நிற்குந்
தானொரு கால்சண்ட மாருத மாய்நிற்குந்
தானொரு காலந் தண்மழை யாய்நிற்குந்
தானொரு காலந்தண் மாயனு மாமே. 415

Lord is Diverse

At the end of aeons,
Once He stands as Pure Light,
Once as the tempestuous typhoon,
Once as incessant rain,
Once as Vishnu, floating on the deluge.

அன்பும் அறிவும் அடக்கமு மாய்நிற்கும்
இன்பமும் இன்பக் கலவியு மாய்நிற்கும்
முன்புறு காலமும் ஊழி மாய்நிற்கும்
அன்புற ஐந்தில் அமர்ந்துநின் றானே. 416

He Stands in Divine Love

As love, wisdom and meekness He stands,
As pleasure and pleasurable union He stands,
As Time's Beginning and End He stands,
As Five elements filled He stands in love divine.

உற்று வனைவான் அவனே உலகினைப்
பெற்று வனைவான் அவனே பிறவியைச்
சுற்றிய சாலுங் குடமுஞ் சிறுதூதை
மற்றும் அவனே வனையவல் லானே. 417

He Fashions Things Big and Small

Himself fashions worlds all in detail minute
Himself fashions life, conferring birth
Himself fashions things big and small
—The cauldron, the pitcher and the pot
Himself He fashions these and more
—He the Architect Almighty.

உள்ளுயிர்ப் பாயுட லாகிநின் றான்நந்தி
வெள்ளுயி ராகும் வெளியாய் நிலங்கொளி
உள்ளுயிர்க் கும்உணர் வேயுட லுட்பரந்
தள்ளுயி ராவண்ணந் தாங்கிநின் றானே. 418

He is Nandi

He is Life within; He is the body corporeal;
He is Spirit Pure; He is space Infinite;
He is Light Radiant; He is Consciousness inside;
Animating life in the body
He supports me;
—He is Nandi.

தாங்கருந் தன்மையுந் தானவை பல்லுயிர்
வாங்கிய காலத்து மற்றோர் பிறிதில்லை
ஓங்கி எழுமைக்கும் யோகாந்த மவ்வழி
தாங்கிநின் றானும்அத் தாரணி தானே. 419

He Supports All Worlds

A miracle indeed it is
To sustain the myriad lives in the Universe;
Not less so,
When after total destruction
He draws them unto Himself;
He supports too
That Seventh World
The Path of yoga leads to.

அணுகினுஞ் சேயவன் அங்கியிற் கூடி
நணுகினும் ஞானக் கொழுந்தொன்று நல்கும்
பணுகினும் பார்மிசைப் பல்லுயி ராகித்
தணிகினும் மண்ணுடல் அண்ணல்செய் வானே. 420

He Grants Immortal Body to Those Who See Him in Love

Well may you seek Him
Through rituals before fires,
Distant only shall He be;
Seek Him in yearning love
Bend low on ground
Hanker after Him life after life,
The great One shalll Grant you the body immortal.

Mantras 411-420

The creation that ensued thus has to be continuously sustained. Although Vishnu is entrusted with this task, He is only an aspect of Siva/Sakti; and so ultimately it is Siva who performs the task of preservation. And so He pervades all: as body and life, as light and darkness, as fame and ignominy, as oceans and continents, as space and the celestials, as sea, hill and dale—through the entirety of creation in unbroken continuity. He pervades our thoughts too. There He stands as love, wisdom and meekness as pleasure and pleasurable union, as the beginning and end of time. He sustains the yogic path that leads to the seventh state of existence.

To sustain the myriad lives in countless universes is indeed a miracle that staggers the imagination. But even after the destruction of the cosmos at the end of an aeon, He draws the jivas to Himself, and sustains them in quiescent slumber until the next cycle of creation commences.

Thus Vishnu performs the function of sustenance only as ordained by Siva.

11. அழித்தல்

DESTRUCTION

அங்கிசெய் தீசன் அகலிடஞ் சுட்டது
அங்கிசெய் தீசன் அலைகடற் சுட்டது
அங்கிசெய் தீசன் அசுரரைச் சுட்டது
அங்கியவ் வீசற்குக் கைஅம்பு தானே. 421

Fire is Lord's Shaft

With fire the Lord burnt all Space
With fire the Lord burnt the Oceans,
With fire the Lord burnt the Asuras
Fire, verily, is the Lord's shaft on hand.

இலயங்கள் மூன்றினும் ஒன்றுகற் பாந்த
நிலையன் றழிந்தமை நின்றுணர்ந் தேனால்
உலைதந்த மெல்லரி போலும் உலகம்
மலைதந்த மானிலந் தான்வெந் ததுவே. 422

Three are His Layas

Three are His layas—the moments of Repose
Of them one, kalpanta—the end of aeons,
I witnessed;
All things fell uprooted in destruction
This orb then was unto a boiling rice pot
Its mountains and valleys alike burnt to ashes.

பதஞ்செய்யும் பாரும் பனிவரை எட்டும்
உதஞ்செய்யும் ஏழ்கடல் ஓதம் முதலாங்
குதஞ்செய்யும் அங்கி கொளுவியா காசம்
விதஞ்செய்யும் நெஞ்சில் வியப்பில்லை தானே. 423

The Fire Spreads

The earth on which we tread
The snow-clad mountains eight.
The seven seas whose ebbing tides roar,
Over all these and else
The Fire that resides in Muladhara spreads;
And the spreading conflagration turned
Earth and sky seem alike;
Shapes are not to be wondered at.

கொண்டல் வரைநின் றிழிந்த குலக்கொடி
அண்டத்துள் ஊறி யிருந்தெண் டிரையாகி
ஒன்றின் பதஞ்செய்த ஓம்என்ற அப்புறக்
குண்டத்தின் மேல்அங்கி கோலிக் கொண்டானே. 424

The Descent of Grace

The grace of Bindu descended from the cloud-clad mountains,
Pervaded the universe, and all the quarters,
Entered in Pranava and abides as Kundalini in Muladhara.

நித்தசங் காரம் உறக்கத்து நீள்மூடம்
வைத்தசங் காரமுஞ் சாக்கிரா தீதமாஞ்
சுத்தசங் காரந் தொழிலற்ற கேவலம்
உய்த்தசங் காரம் பரன்அருள் உண்மையே. 425

Four Forms of Mergence

Daily mergence is in deep sleep,
The next mergence is beyond sleep,
The pure mergence is when the jiva remains complete actionless,
The ultimate mergence is in Sivasakti.

நித்தசங் காரம் இரண்டுடல் நீவுதல்
வைத்தசங் காரமும் மாயாசங் காரமாஞ்
சுத்தசங் காரம் மனாதீதந் தோய்வுறல்
உய்த்தசங் காரஞ் சிவன்அருள் உண்மையே. 426

What Transpires in the Four Deaths

In Daily mergence, are bodies gross and subtle transcended;
In the next mergence, is the Mayaic body annihilated;
In Pure mergence, Mind and cognates merge in the Infinite ·
In Redemption Death, Siva's Grace descends true.

நித்தசங் காரம் கருவிடர் நீக்கினால்
ஒத்தசங் காரம் உடலுயிர் நீவுதல்
சுத்தசங் காரம் அதீதத்துட் டோய்வுறல்
உய்த்தசங் காரம் பரனருள் உண்மையே. 427

Four Forms of Mergence

In daily mergence the senses are silent,
In the next mergence the soul leaves the body,
In pure mergence the soul remains completely free,
In the final mergence there is union with Siva.

நித்தசங் காரமும் நீடிளைப் பாற்றலின்
வைத்தசங் காரமும் மன்னும் அனாதியிற்
சுத்தசங் காரமுந் தோயாப் பரன்அருள்
உய்த்தசங் காரமும் நாலாம் உதிக்கிலே. 428

Thus Four are the Mergence

Thus are mergences Four;
The Daily mergence in deep Sleep;
The next mergence that gives the soul a longer rest;
The Pure mergence that puts the Soul in primal quiescence;
The Redemption mergence that steeps the Soul in Lord's Grace.

பாழே முதலா எழும்பயிர் அப்பயிர்
பாழாய்அடங்கினும் பண்டைப்பாழ் பாழாகா
வாழாச்சங் காரத்தின் பாலயன் செய்தியாம்
பாழாம் பயிராய் அடங்கும்அப் பாழிலே. 429

Void the Beginning and End

Out of Void (Siva), a plant (soul) it sprang,
To the Void it returns;
Yet shall it not be Void again;
In that Void, exhausted, it shall die;
That is the fate of Hari and Brahma too,
Who the holocaust of Samhara susvive not.

தீயவைத் தார்மின்கள் சேரும் வினைதனை
மாயவைத் தான்வைத்த வன்பதி ஒன்றுண்டு
காயம்வைத் தான்கலந் தெங்கும் நினைப்பதோர்
ஆயம்வைத் தானுணர் வாரவைத் தானே. *430*

Scorch Your Karmas

Scorch the gatherıng Karmas
And exhaust them;
There is One who annihilates them
And the city where He does it
He fashioned the body, He pervades everywhere.
He placed the Mind and cognate tattva group besides,
He gave us Wisdom ample to discriminate.

Mantras 429 & 430

The jiva sprang as a plant out of the void, and into the void, it shall finally return. Even the gods are not exempt from this law. Death follows birth, as the night follows day. The only escape from death is not to be born again. By uprooting karma alone, can the birth-death cycle be ended. God dissolves the karma; pray to Him.

12. மறைத்தல்

OBSCURATION

Rudra is the god to whom the work of destruction is entrusted, but the real power behind Rudra is that of Siva.

உள்ளத் தொருவனை உள்ளுறு சோதியை
உள்ளம்விட் டோரடி நீங்கா ஒருவனை
உள்ளமுந் தானும் உடனே இருக்கினும்
உள்ளம் அவனை உருவறி யாதே. *431*

He is Within You Yet You Know Him Not

He is the One within; He is the Light within;
He moves not a wee bit from within
He and your heart are thus together,
But the heart His Form knows not.

God is within us all. He is the Light within us. He does not move a bit away from us. Yet we do not know Him. Why this concealment by the Lord?

இன்பப் பிறவி படைத்த இறைவனுந்
துன்பஞ்செய் பாசத் துயருள் அடைத்தனன்
என்பிற் கொளுவி இசைந்துறு தோற்றதச
முன்பிற் கொளுவி முடிகுவ தாமே. *432*

The Lord Gave This Life

The Lord who gave life so sweet
Imprisoned me in pasa's miseries;
A skeletal frame He fashioned,
With flesh and skin He clothed it;
Lighting then the spark of life
To annihilation He hastened me.

Siva gave us life so sweet; yet, He imprisoned us in the miseries of Pasam. He builds for us a body with meticulous care; yet He hastens it to death. Why is this so?

இறையவன் மாதவன் இன்பம் படைத்த
மறையவன் மூவரும் வந்துடன் கூடி
இறையவன் செய்த இரும்பொறி யாக்கை
மறையவன் வைத்த பரிசறி யாதே. *433*

Even the Three Gods do not Know the Mystery of Life

With Hara, Hari and Brahma assembling
The Primal Lord fashioned this body,
The subtle organs of sense built-in;
We know not the treasure
He has enshrined here.

காண்கின்ற கண்ணொளி காதல்செய் தீசனை
ஆண்பெண் அலியுரு வாய்நின்ற ஆதியை
ஊண்படு நாவுடை நெஞ்சம் உணர்ந்திட்டுச்
சேண்படு பொய்கைச் செயலணை யாரே. *434*

Adore and Attain

The Lord is the light of our eyes
He loves us
He is the Primal One
—Male, Female and Neuter is He;
Tongues praising and hearts melting,
They seek not the path
That leads to the Celestial Lake.

தெருளும் உலகிற்குந் தேவர்க்கும் இன்பம்
அருளும் வகைசெய்யும் ஆதிப் பிரானுஞ்
சுருளுஞ் சுடருறு தூவெண் சுடரும்
இருளும் அறநின் றிருட்டறை யாமே. *435*

He Dispels the Darkness Within

The Primal Lord blesses all
Denizens of earth below and heaven above;

From the black chamber of the Soul
He dispels darkness;
And within radiates the pure rays of His dazzling light.

அறைக்கின் றருள்தரும் அங்கங்கள் ஓசை
உரைக்கின்ற ஆசையும் ஒன்றொடொன் றொவ்வாப்
பரக்கும் உருவமும் பாரகந் தானாய்க்
கரக்கின் றவைசெய்த காண்டகை யானே. 436

The Lord veils the Unity.

The world is full of contradictions of sounds, desires and forms,
But within the diversity is the unity which
You of beautiful form veil away from our vision.

ஒளித்துவைத் தேனுள் ளுறவுணர்ந் தீசனை
வெளிப்பட்டு நின்றருள் செய்திடு மீண்டே
களிப்பொடுங் காதன்மை என்னும் பெருமை
வெளிப்பட் டிறைஞ்சினும் வேட்சியு மாமே. 437

The Hidden One Will Reveal Himself

I held my Lord in me concealed,
I adored Him in my heart's depths,
Lo! He revealed Himself unto me
And blessed me—here below,
Well may you adore Him
Revealing the rapture abounding and love endearing
That too pleases Him far.

நின்றது தானாய் நிறைந்த மகேசுரன்
சென்றங் கியங்கும் அரன்திரு மாலவன்
மன்றது செய்யும் மலர்மிசை மேலயன்
என்றிவ ராகி இசைந்திருந் தானே. 438

One Became Five

The Sadasiva that stood as one
Animated Mahesvara;
And then Hara, Hari, and Brahma
Thus did the One become the familial five.

ஒருங்கிய பாசத்துள் உத்தம சித்தன்
இருங்கரை மேலிருந் தின்புற நாடி
வருங்கரை ஓரா வகையினிற் கங்கை
அருங்கரை பேணில் அழுக்கற லாமே. 439

He is the Pure One

He is the Pure One
The Siddha in whom Pasa lies prostrate;
Be firmly seated on land here below
And Seek Him in ways felicitous—
That you may vision the Land Beyond;
Not doing this,
You are like one
Who is seated on the banks of Ganga,
Yet remains unwashed and impure.

மண்ணொன்று தான்பல நற்கல மாயிடும்
உண்ணின்ற யோனிகட் கெல்லாம் ஒருவனே
கண்ணொன்று தான்பல காணுந் தனைக்காணா
அண்ணலும் இவ்வண்ண மாகிநின் றானே. 440

The Eye Sees Not Itself

One clay, many the receptacles
One God, pervades species all;
The eye sees things several
Yet itself it sees not;
Thus it is, we see not the God in us.

The eye sees several things; yet, does it see itself? Similarly is the Lord's concealment in us.

This concealment which is so mysterious is one of the Five acts of God. It has a purpose, and that is to lead the jiva to seeking. It is by seeking God, that God can be seen. In the black chamber of the soul there is darkness. That darkness can be dispelled only by letting in light. Seek and you shall see the light.Knock and the door shall be opened. Adore, and He shall reveal Himself—Tirumular sings.

Mahesvara is the god empowered with this function, but his is only a delegated power. Siva is the Final Source.

13. அருளல்

BESTOWAL OF GRACE

எட்டுத் திசையும் எறிகின்ற காற்றொடு
வட்டத் திரையனல் மாநிலம் ஆகாயம்
ஒட்டி உயிர்நிலை என்னும்இக் காயப்பை
கட்டி அவிழ்ப்பன் கண்ணுதல் காணுமே. 441

Life and Death are Acts of God

He is the Wind that Blows in Directions Eight
He is the wavy ocean that girdles the earth,
He is fire, earth and sky;
Know this:
He is the One that binds and unbinds
The body that holds life precious.

Having experienced pleasure and pain in life, the jivas who seek the Lord are bestowed grace. This bestowal of Grace that leads to the jiva's redemption or liberation from the cycle of birth and death is the Supreme Act of God. That is the act that gives the coup de grace to all the previous four acts of His.

The attainment of Grace can come through total surrender in loving prayer, through the yoga way or through the realization that the All-Pervasive God is the object of all knowledge. And when it comes, the jiva is cleansed of its primordial triple impurities.

This function is performed by Sadasiva.

உச்சியில் ஓங்கி ஒளிதிகழ் நாதத்தை
நச்சியே இன்பங்கொள் வார்க்கு நமன்இல்லை
விச்சும் விரிசுடர் மூன்றும் உலகுக்குத்
தச்சு மவனே சமைக்கவல் லானே. 442

Lord is the Substance and Architect

Who seeks the luminous Nada atop
And of its sweetness savour
Know of death—no more;
The Lord is the seed of all
Of Sun, Moon and Fire
Of the Universe Vast
The Architect that builds all as well.

குசவன் திரிகையில் ஏற்றிய மண்ணைக்
குசவன் மனத்துற்ற தெல்லாம் வனைவன்
குசவனைப் போல்எங்கள் கோன்நந்தி வேண்டில்
அசைவில் உலகம் அதுஇது வாமே. 443

Potter Fashions as His Fancy Takes

The potter mounts the clay on the wheel
The potter fashions as he conceives
Even as the Potter our Lord Nandi is;
He moulds the world, this way and that
The way His Fancy takes.

விடையுடை யான்விகிர் தன்மிகு பூதப்
படையுடை யான்பரி சேஉல காக்குங்
கொடையுடை யான்குணம் எண்குண மாகுஞ்
சடையுடை யான்சிந்தை சார்ந்துநின் றானே. 444

He Dwells in My Thoughts

He is Lord Supreme;
He has bull for His mount;
Mighty demons for army;
Boundless is His munificence
He gifts the world for us;
His goodness alone is goodness;
He is of matted locks;
He dwells in the thoughts of all.

உகந்துநின் றேபடைத் தான்உல கேழும்
உகந்துநின் றேபடைத் தான்பல ஊழி
உகந்துநின் றேபடைத் தான்ஐந்து பூதம்
உகந்துநின் றேஉயிர் ஊன்படைத் தானே. 445

In Love, He Created

In fondness for us He created the seven worlds,
In fondness for us He created the several aeons
In fondness for us He created the five elements;
In fondness for us He created this body and breath.

படைத்துடை யான்பண் டுலகங்கள் ஏழும்
படைத்துடை யான்பல தேவரை முன்னே
படைத்துடை யான்பல சீவரை முன்னே
படைத்துடை யான்பர மாகிநின் றானே. 446

God Created All, Himself the Param Uncreated

Of yore He created worlds seven
Of yore He created celestials countless
Of yore He created species numberless
He who of yore created all
Himself stood as Primal Param uncreated.

ஆதி படைத்தனன் ஐம்பெரும் பூதம்
ஆதி படைத்தனன் ஆசில்பல் ஊழி
ஆதி படைத்தனன் எண்ணிலி தேவரை
ஆதி படைத்தவை தாங்கிநின் றானே. 447

He Who Created, Sustained As Well

The Primal One created the elements five;
The Primal One created the endless aeons past;
The Primal One created the countless heavenly beings,
The Primal One created and sustained as well.

அகன்றான் அகலிடம் ஏழுமொன் றாகி
இவன்றா னெனநின் றெளியனும் அல்லன்
சிவன்றான் பலபல சீவனும் ஆகி
நவின்றான் உலகுறு நம்பனு மாமே. 448

The Pervasive Siva is Here as Well

He is One with the infinite space of the seven worlds
And yet transcends it.
He cannot be indicated as this or that
He Himself becomes the various jivas
And helps them to go upwards
And remains the Supreme leader of the world.

உண்ணின்ற சோதி உறநின்ற ஓருடல்
விண்ணின் றமரர் விரும்பும் விழுப்பொருள்
மண்ணின்ற வானோர் புகழ்திரு மேனியன்
கண்ணின்ற மாமணி மாபோத மாமே. 449

He is the Object of All Knowledge

He is the light within
He is the body without
The precious object, beloved of immortals above,
The Holy Form, adored of saintly beings below,
He is the pupil of your eyes;
He the Object of all Knowledge.

ஆரும் அறியாத அண்டத் திருவுருப்
பார்முத லாகப் பயிலுங் கடத்திலே
நீரினிற் பால்போல நிற்கின்ற நேர்மையைச்
சோராமற் காணுஞ் சுகம்அறிந் தேனே. 450

The Lord Pervades All in Partiality to None

His is the Cosmic Form that none know
He is the infinite space that fills the universe;
He is the space in the tiny pot too;
Inseparable as water in milk
He pervades all in union close;
Impartial indeed His Goodness;
Unwearied His bliss—I knew.

14. கரு உற்பத்தி
CREATION MICROCOSM

Even as God creates the macrocosm, He creates the microcosm of the human body also. He enters the mother's womb and from there performs the act of shaping the body and awakening its life.

ஆக்குகின் றான்முன் பிரிந்த இருபத்தஞ்
சாக்குகின் றானவ னாதிஎம் ஆருயிர்
ஆக்குகின் றான்கர்ப்பக் கோளகை யுள்ளிருந்
தாக்குகின் றான்அவன் ஆவ தறிந்தே. 451

God Creates From Within the Womb

He conjoins the tattvas five and twenty
That in life past departed from me;
To my dear life awaken;
Thus He creates, seated within the globular womb
He the Primal One creates
Knowing what I am to be.

அறிகின்ற மூலத்தின் மேல்அங்கி அப்புச்
செறிகின்ற ஞானத்துச் செந்தாள் கொளுவிப்
பொறைநின்ற இன்னுயிர் போந்துற நாடிப்
பறிகின்ற பத்தெனும் பாரஞ்செய் தானே. 452

The Lord Grants Breath and the Child is Born

Above the Muladhara
The Kundalini fire abides;
There in the water-filled womb
The infant lay, its tiny feet entangled;
That the sweet life in patience waiting
Its onward course may seek,
He ordained, releasing the Pranas ten.

இன்புறு காலத் திருவர்முன் பூரிய
துன்புறு பாசத் துயர்மனை வானுளன்
பண்புறு காலமும் பார்மிசை வாழ்க்கையும்
அன்புறு காலத் தமைத்தொழிந் தானே. 453

The Course of Life Was Ordained at Time of Union

When parents two in pleasure united,
Then was ordained, this body,
The sorrow-house of vexing pasa,
When that is to be,
At that hour of union, He ordained;
He, the Heavenly Lord.

கருவை ஒழிந்தவர் கண்டநால் மூவேழ்
புருடன் உடலில் பொருந்துமற் றோரார்
திருவின் கருக்குழி தேடிப் புகுந்த
துருவம் இரண்டாக ஓடி விழுந்ததே. 454

Through That Union Entered the 25 Tattvas to Make the Infant Body

They who birth's finale saw,
Alone knew how purusha,
Of Tattvas five and twenty,
The body corporeal entered;
None else know,
That which sought woman's birth-pit,
In form twain, rushed within.

விழுந்தது லிங்கம் விரிந்தது யோனி
ஒழிந்த முதல்ஐந்தும் ஈரைந்தொ டேறிப்
பொழிந்த புனல்பூதம் போற்றுங் கரணம்
ஒழிந்த நுதல்உச்சி உள்ளே ஒளித்ததே. 455

The Tattvas Remained in the Forehead of the Foetus

The Penis pierced; the vagina opened,
And together they rushed in
The Pranas Five—
The Elements Five
The tanmatras Five,
The sense organs Five gross,
And the Five Subtle,
And in the Centre of Forehead they all lay, concealed.

பூவின் மணத்தைப் பொருந்திய வாயுவுந்
தாவி உலகில் தரிப்பித்த வாறுபோல்
மேவிய சீவினில் மெல்லநீள் வாயுவுங்
கூவி அவிழுங் குறிக்கொண்ட போதே. 456

Prana Enters Jiva at Birth

As when flower blossoms, the breeze spreads fragrance,
In space all around

So does Prana over Jiva extend,
Gently unfolding at the time destined.

As He blows in the prana breath, it extends over the jiva as the fragrance of a flower through the surrounding air, to be unfolded gently at the destined hour.

போகின்ற எட்டும் புகுகின்ற பத்தெட்டும்
மூழ்கின்ற முத்தனும் ஒன்பது வாய்தலும்
நாகமும் எட்டுடன் நாலு புரவியும்
பாகன் விடானெனிற் பன்றியு மாமே. 457

The Lord Drives in the Tattvas into the Infant Body

The eight constituents of body subtle
That ultimately leave,
The eight and ten Tattvas that sneak in,
With Purusha in them immersed
The orifices nine,
The Kundalini that serpent-like coils,
—If these, the Divine Charioteer drives not in,
Verily may the infant be less than human (say, a pig).

ஏற எதிர்க்கில் இறையவன் றானாகும்
மாற எதிர்க்கில் அரியவன் றானாகும்
நேரொக்க வைக்கின் நிகர்போதத் தானாகும்
பேரொத்த மைந்தனும் பேரர சாளுமே. 458

The Child With the Three Gunas in Balance is Fit for Rulership

When in sex union,
The male flow in force dominates
The infant is born with Tamasic qualities of Rudra;
When the flow in reverse is,
The Sattvic quality of Hari dominates;
When the two in balance flow;
The Rajasic quality of Brahma prevails;
He is to kingship born
In whom gunas three proportionate sway.

ஏயங் கலந்த இருவர்தஞ் சாயத்துப்
பாயுங் கருவும் உருவா மெனப்பல
காயங் கலந்தது காணப் பதிந்தபின்
மாயங் கலந்த மனோலய மானதே. 459

Into the Foetus Mayaic Mind was Placed

There two in accord united;
And from their vital flows
Emerged the infant form;
But when into it Jiva,
Who in myriad bodies has dwelt of yore,
Now entered,
Lo! it is dominated by Mind;
Maya subtle pervades it.

கர்ப்பத்துக் கேவல மாயாள் கிளைகூட்ட
நிற்குந் துரியமும் பேதித்து நினைவெழ
வற்புறு காமியம் எட்டாதல் மாயேயஞ்
சொற்புறு தூய்மறை வாக்கினாஞ் சொல்லே. 460

Jiva Gets Consciousness and Desires

There in the pregnant womb,
The soul lay in Primordial quiescence (Turiya State)
From that State Maya and Her tribe aroused it;
And conferred Consciousness;
And Maya's evolutes eight—Desires and the rest,
Thus say scriptures, holy and true.

என்பால் மிடைந்து நரம்பு வரிக்கட்டிச்
செம்பால் இறைச்சி திருந்த மனைசெய்து
இன்பால் உயிர்நிலை செய்த இறையோங்கும்
நன்பால் ஒருவனை நாடுகின் றேனே. 461

How the Body is Fashioned

With skeletal bones He erected the frame;
With tendons circuitous He fastened it;
With blood and flesh He cemented it;
Thus did Lord fashion this body-mansion,
For dear life to dwell
Him I seek forth, endearment increasing.

பதஞ்செய்யும் பால்வண்ணன் மேனிப் பகலோன்
இதஞ்செய்யு மொத்துடல் எங்கும் புகுந்து
குதஞ்செய்யும் அங்கியின் கோபந் தணிப்பான்
விதஞ்செய்யு மாறே விதித்தொழிந் தானே. 462

The Lord Contains the Fire in Muladhara

He is milky white in hue
Effulgent is He like the sun;
He is benignant;
He pervades the entire body
And diffuses His tenderness;
He contained the rage of fire in Muladhara
This He ordained, in ways diverse.

ஒழிபல செய்யும் வினையுற்ற நாளே
வழிபல நீராடி வைத்தெழு வாங்கிப்
பழிபல செய்கின்ற பாசக் கருவைச்
சுழிபல வாங்கிச் சுடாமல்வைத் தானே. 463

The Lord Preserves the Foetus

Even the day, ruinous Karma trailed after Jiva,
He designed ways of preservation numerous;
He surrounded the foetus with water
Kept it safe from burning Muladhara Fire,
He drew charmed circles eddying,
Around the budding life, from Pasa harassing
And so preserved it safe and cool.

The Lord takes infinite care to protect the foetus inside the womb for 300 days. He surrounds it with a protective 'bag of waters', keeps it from being scorched by the mother's muladhara fire; and He draws charmed circles around the budding life to shield it from harm. The Absolute Being stands as the sentinel, guarding the child in the womb.

சுக்கில நாடியில் தோன்றிய வெள்ளியும்
அக்கிர மத்தே தோன்றுமவ் வியோனியும்
புக்கிடும் எண்விரல் புறப்பட்டு நால்விரல்
அக்கரம் எட்டும்எண் சாணது வாகுமே. 464

Breathing and Size of Infant

The Silvery semen welled up
And met the vaginal flow, alike surging,
And lo! then was born the infant
Inhaling eight and exhaling four
Finger-length of breath,
And measuring eight finger-span
Of its own tiny palm.

The child born measures eight spans of its own finger length, because out of the 12 finger-lengths the prana breath constitutes, only 8 are inhaled; the other four are exhaled.

போகத்துள் ஆங்கே புகுந்த புனிதனுங்
கோசத்துள் ஆகங்கொணர்ந்த கொடைத்தொழில்
ஏகத்துள் ஆங்கே இரண்டெட்டு மூன்றைந்து
மோகத்துள் ஆங்கொரு முட்டைசெய் தானே. 465

Body of 25 Tattvas

Into the Union, the Holy One entered;
Gathering Tattvas five and twenty
Fashioned the (five)-sheathed body;
Munificent indeed was his gift!
A veritable Bundle of Delusion He made.

பிண்டத்தில் உள்ளுறு பேதைப் புலன்ஐந்தும்
பிண்டத்தி னூடே பிறந்து, மரித்தது
அண்டத்தின் உள்ளுறு சீவனும் அவ்வகை
அண்டத்து நாதத் தமர்ந்திடுந் தானே. 466

After Death, Senses End With Body; Jiva Ends in Nada

The five senses with their foolish ways
Are in this body born;
And there they subside;
So does Jiva
That permeates macrocosm
Surely subside in Nada.

இலைப்பொறி யேற்றி யெனதுடல் ஈசன்
துலைப்பொறி யிற்கரு ஐந்துட னாட்டி
நிலைப்பொறி முப்பது நீர்மை கொளுவி
உலைப்பொறி ஒன்பதில் ஒன்றுசெய் தானே. 467

The 35 Tattvas Introduced

As on to a leaf-like device
He mounted my life;
And there;
With balance-like precision planted,
Subtle senses five;
And other Tattvas thirty;
And thus fashioned a body;
A steaming cauldron with openings nine.

Here, Mular says the Tattvas are 35, whereas in Saivism (and Buddhism) they are 36, and in Sankhya only 25 (or 26).

இன்புற் றிருவர் இசைவித்து வைத்தமண்
துன்பக் கலசம் அணைவான் ஒருவனே
ஒன்பது நீர்ச்சால் கலசம் பதினெட்டு
வெந்தது சூளை விளைந்தது தானே. 468

Lord Creates

In union's rapture they kneaded the clay
For Him to fashion sorrow's tenement;
The kiln burnt, the pitcher emerged,
With channels nine and Tattvas eighteen.

அறியீ ருடம்பினி லாகிய வாறும்
பிறியீ ரதனிற்பெருகுங் குணங்கள்
செறியீ ரவுற்றினுட் சித்திகள் இட்ட
தறியவீ ரைந்தினு ளானது பிண்டமே. 469

Lord Placed the Six Adharas

You know not the six afflictions within;
Seek the great good that wells therein;
Understand the Siddhis within them;
Know this,
The fleshy body is but of the five elements.

உடல்வைத்த வாறும் உயிர்வைத்த வாறும்
மடைவைத்த ஒன்பது வாய்தலும் வைத்துத்
திடம்வைத்த தாமரைச் சென்னியுள் அங்கிக்
கடைவைத்த ஈசனைக் கைகலந் தேனே. 470

Lord Placed Divine Jnana in Cranium

He fashioned this body,
Into that body He breathed life;
And set gates nine;
And then into the lotus-like cranium
He lit the Fire (of Divine Jnana),
The Lord made these,
And Him I salute in endearment intense.

In this act of fashioning the corporeal body, the Divine Architect provides for the subtle body that consists of eight tattvas, the purusha body into which enters 18 avastas or states; the nine orifices, the six adharas, the kundalini fire coiled in the muladhara chakra, and the prana breath that measures 12 matras in length. To crown all, in the lotus-like sahasrara chakra in the cranium, He places the fire of divine jnana.

கேட்டுநின் றேன்எங்குங் கேடில் பெருஞ்சுடர்
மூட்டுகின் றான்முதல் யோனி மயனவன்

கூட்டுகின் றான்குழம் பின்கரு வையுரு
நீட்டிதின் றாகத்து நேர்பட்ட வாறே. 471

Lord Creates Life From Primal Seed of Causation

The Lord is Limitless Light;
He kindles all life from Primal Womb;
He stirs the liquid-seed of Causation;
He endows it with form expansive;
Him I seek in heaven and earth.

What is the origin of this life? The Lord is Limitless Light, and He kindles all life from the primordial womb of His Sakti. There the liquid seed of causation is stirred by nadam; and in bindu it attains manifest form.

பூவுடன் மொட்டுப் பொருந்த அலர்ந்தபின்
காவுடைத் தீபங் கலந்து பிறந்திடும்
நீரிடை நின்றகுமிழி நிழலதாய்ப்
பாருடல் எங்கும் பரந்தெட்டும் பற்றுமே. 472

Body's Impermanence

In the union of sexes opposite
The light of life is born shielded true;
A bubble it is in Life's watery expanse;
A shadow that spreads on earth below;
Sheathed in the subtle Body-Eight.

The individual life is but a bubble in the Primal Life's infinite expanse. It is but a shadow of the Divine Light encased in the subtle body that is made of the five protean senses (tanmatras), and the three internal instruments: mind, will and intelligence.

எட்டினுள் ஐந்தாகும் இந்திரி யங்களும்
கட்டிய மூன்று கரணமு மாய்விடும்
ஒட்டிய பாச உணர்வென்னுங் காயப்பை
கட்டி அவிழ்த்திடுங் கண்ணுதல் காணுமே. 473

Lord Gives and Lord Takes Life

Of the eight organs of Body Subtle,
Are senses protean five
And cognitive instruments three—
Mind, will and cognition;
Know the dear Lord
Who fastened this body-bag,
With Desire's sticky glue
Will in time unfasten it too.

கண்ணுதல் நாமங் கலந்துடம் பாயிடைப்
பண்ணுதல் செய்து பசுபாசம் நீங்கிட
எண்ணிய வேதம் இசைந்த பரப்பினை
மண்முத லாக வகுத்துவைத் தானே. 474

Lord Gave Means of Redemption

The Lord made the body,
A name and form it assumed;
Then, for Jiva his redemption to seek
He created earth and Tattvas many,
—Thus speak the Vedas.

அருளல்ல தில்லை அரனவன் அன்றி
அருளில்லை யாதலி னவ்வோர் உயிரைத்
தருகின்ற போதிரு கைத்தாயர் தம்பால்
வருகின்ற நண்பு வகுத்திடுந் தானே. 475

He Placed Jiva in Care of Two Foster-Mothers

None the Grace but Hara's
None Hara's but the Grace,
And so as He bestows life,
He bestows, too,
The Loving care of foster mother twain,

வகுத்த பிறவியை மாதுநல் லாளுந்
தொகுத்திருள் நீக்கிய சோதி யவனும்
பகுத்துணர் வாகிய பல்லுயிர் எல்லாம்
வகுத்துள்ளும் நின்றதோர் மாண்பது வாமே. 476

Then Siva and Sakti Pervaded Jivas

Sakti, the Conjoint Cause of creation,
The Luminous One that dispelled darkness total,
Together created the myriad lives,
Their genus and species,
And having done that, they pervaded them too;
Oh! magnificence non-pareil!

மாண்பது வாக வளர்கின்ற வன்னியுங்
காண்பது ஆண்பெண் அலியெனுங் கற்பனை
பூண்பது மாதா பிதாவழி போலவே
ஆம்பதி செய்தானச் சோதிதன் ஆண்மையே. 477

He Printed the Sex of the Infant

The seed of life,
As a steady flame in womb burns
It takes shape one of three
Male, female and hermaphrodite;
How the father and mother at union were,
Even so He printed the sex,
Righteous indeed was that Luminous One.

ஆண்மிகில் ஆணாகும் பெண்மிகிற் பெண்ணாகும்
பூணிரண் டொத்துப் பொருந்தில் அலியாகும்
தாண்மிகு மாகில் தரணி முழுதாளும்
பாணவ மிக்கிடில் பாய்ந்ததும் இல்லையே. 478

Sex Determined at Sexual Union

The masculine flow dominates, the infant is male born,
The feminine dominates, the infant is female born;
When the two are in force equal, a hermaphrodite is born;
When masculine flow gushes in plenty,
The infant born will sway the world entire;
When masculine flow is scanty,
Naught indeed conception is.

பாய்ந்தபின் னஞ்சோடில் ஆயுளும் நூறாகும்
பாய்ந்தபின் னாலோடில் பாரினில் எண்பதாம்
பாய்ந்திடும் வாயுப் பகுத்தறிந் திவ்வகை
பாய்ந்திடும் யோகிக்குப் பாய்ச்சலு மாமே. 479

Age is Determined

If after emission,
The male's breath five finger-length extends,
The infant born lives a hundred years;
When breath to four finger measure stretches,
To age eighty the infant lives;
The Yogi who knows the science of breath control
If in sex act He indulges,
He, the vital flow, according regulates.

If after ejaculation, man inhales spontaneously five times, the infant to be born will live upto 100 years; eighty, if he inhales four times and so on. Only yogis who have mastered the science of breath can control and regulate the discharge at will.

பாய்கின்ற வாயுக் குறையிற் குறளாகும்
பாய்கின்ற வாயு விளைக்கின் முடமாகும்
பாய்கின்ற வாயு நடுப்படிற் கூனாகும்
பாய்கின்ற வாயுமா தர்க்கில்லைப் பார்க்கிலே. 480

Birth Imperfections Explained

When after intercourse, the man is short of breath,
The infant born a dwarf will be;
When breath blows feeble,
The issue may of defective limbs be born;
When breath halts in mid-act,
A hunch-back will be born;
All these apply not,
To woman's breathing rhythm.

If the flow of the male discharge is slow, the offspring is short in stature; if sluggish, lame; if fitful and interrupted, hunchback.

மாதா உதரம் மலமிகில் மந்தனாம்
மாதா உதரம் சலமிகில் மூங்கையாம்
மாதா உதரம் இரண்டொக்கில் கண்ணில்லை
மாதா உதரத்தில் வந்த குழவிக்கே. 481

How Deaf, Dumb, and Blind are Born

When at the time of union,
The mother's bowels are heavy exceeding,
A dullard will be born;
If urine exceeds,
A dumb will be born;
If both exceed,
A blind will be born;
Thus is it for the infant born
The mother's condition according.

குழவியும் ஆணாம் வலத்தது வாகில்
குழவியும் பெண்ணாம் இடத்தது வாகில்
குழவியும் இரண்டாம் அபான னெதிர்க்கில்
குழவி அலியாகுங் கொண்டகால் ஒக்கிலே. 482

Breathing at Union Decides Sex of Baby

If breath flows leading on nostril right,
The infant born will a male be;
If on the nostril left,
A female will be born;
If the descending current Apana,
Opposes the ascending current Prana,
Twins there shall be;
If in measure equal the breath rhythm runs,
Through nostrils right and left,
Hermaphrodite shall be the baby born.

If the male breath runs dominant in the right nostril (Pingala) at the time of discharge, the offspring will be male; if it runs dominant in the left nostril (ida), the offspring will be female. If the apana breath comes up from the lower regions of the body system, twins will be born. If the breathing is through both the nostrils, the child born will be impotent.

கொண்டநல் வாயு இருவர்க்கும் ஒத்தொழில்
கொண்டி குழவியிங் கோமள மாயிடுங்
கொண்டநல் வாயு இருவர்க்குங் குழறிடில்
கொண்டதும் இல்லையாங் கோல்வளை யாடகே. 483

How a Handsome Baby is Born

If in Male and Female breath runs
In measure equable,
The infant born will exceeding handsome be;
When in both breath rhythm falters,
No Conception will there be.

கோல்வளை உந்தியிற் கொண்ட குழவியுந்
தால்வளை யுள்ளே தயங்கிய சோதியாம்
பால்வளர்ந் துள்ளே பகலவன் பொன்னுருப்
போல்வளர்ந் துள்ளே பொருந்துரு வாமே. 484

How Infant in the Womb Grows

The infant-seed,
The damsel in her womb bore
Nourished by bright milk
That is fed by Sakti in Eye-brow Centre
Grew,
Beaming like the golden rays of rising sun
Inside, it took form appropriate.

உருவம் வளர்ந்திடும் ஒண்டிங்கள் பத்திற்
பருவம தாகவே பாரினில் வந்திடும்
மருவி வளர்ந்திடு மாயையி னாலே
அருவம தாவதிங் காரறி வாரே. 485

Maya Fosters the Baby

In months ten, it forms full
And then on earth in time appointed, it lands;
And grows, Maya fostering;
But who knows that Formless Maya!

இட்டான் அறிந்திலன் ஏற்றவள் கண்டிலள்
தட்டான் அறிந்தும் ஒருவர்க் குரைத்திலன்
பட்டாங்கு சொல்லும் பரமனும் அங்குளன்
கெட்டேன் இம்மாயையின் கீழ்மையெவ் வாறே. 486

Maya's Hidden Act

He who planted seed, knew it not;
She who received saw it not;
The Creator knew, but He told none;
The Lord who Truth reveals is also there;
Yet I saw not Maya,
How cunning was her stealthy Conduct!

இன்புறு நாடி இருவருஞ் சந்தித்துத்
துன்புறு பாசத்தில் தோன்றி வளர்ந்தபின்
முன்புற நாடி நிலத்தின்முன் தோன்றிய
தொன்புற நாடிநின் றோதலு மாமே. 487

In Manhood Jiva Seeks God

Seeking pleasure, the two met;
In pasa's misery was it born and bred;
And having grown to stature
Grew to manhood here below;
Well may it seek the Ancient One
That before all worlds was.

குயிற்குஞ்சு முட்டையைக் காக்கைக் கூட்டிட்டால்
அயிர்ப்பின்றிக் காக்கை வளர்க்கின் றதுபோல்
இயக்கில்லை போக்கில்லை ஏனென்ப தில்லை
மயக்கத்தால் காக்கை வளர்க்கின்ற வாறே. 488

How Maya Fosters Babe

The cuckoo bird leaves its egg in the crow's nest;
The crow hatches it, nurses it, suspecting nothing;
It does not move it, does not reject it,
Does not ask why,
So does Maya the young one foster.

And maya taking charge, fosters the egg that lay in the womb. Even as the cuckoo leaves its egg in the crow's nest, for the crow to hatch and foster, so does maya perform this act in the womb.

முதற்கிழங் காய்முளை யாய்அம் முளைப்பின்
அதற்புத லாய்ப்பல மாய்நின் றளிக்கும்
அதற்கது வாய்இன்பமாவதுபோல
அதற்கது வாய்நிற்கும் ஆதிப் பிரானே. 489

God Protects Jiva at All Stages

The Lord is the Primal One;
The root, the shoot, the plant and fruit;
Thus He blesses all life;
To each, He grants his life's pleasure,
With each, He stands according.

ஏனோர் பெருமைய னாகிலும் எம்மிறை
ஊனே சிறுமையுள் உட்கலந் தங்குளன்
வானோர் அறியும் அளவல்லன் மாதேவன்
தானே அறியுந் தவத்தினி னுள்ளே. 490

Lord Appears in Prayer and Penance

My Lord is of infinite greatness,
Yet is He within the littleness of this fleshy body;
Beyond the ken of Celestials is He;
Yet in prayer and penance
He himself shall appear before you.

பரத்திற் கரைந்து பதிந்தநற் காயம்
உருத்தரித் திவ்வுடல் ஓங்கிட வேண்டித்
திரைக்கடல் உப்புத் திரண்டது போலத்
திரித்துப் பிறக்குந் திருவரு ளாலே. 491

Birth is by Lord's Grace

Even unto the salt that from wavy sea emerges,
Out of Tattvas that arose in Para,
Was this body formed;
To be born thus is His Grace indeed!

The individual body is made of tattvas that arose in Parasakti, like salt that emerges from the vast sea.

Chapter Commentary

Thus microcosmic creation, as much as macrocosmic creation, is the potent function of Siva/Sakti, is who pervades all creation.

And all this elaborate and minute work of Siva/Sakti is for what purpose? That the jiva may seek liberation from the primordial impurities and itself become pristine Siva, the Pure Spirit.

Mular considers birth, and hence, life itself, as a valuable gift.

15. மூவகைச் சீவ வர்க்கம்

THE THREE CATEGORIES OF JIVAS

சத்தி சிவன்விளை யாட்டால் உயிராக்கி
ஒத்த இருமாயா கூட்டத் திடைபூட்டிச்
சுத்தம தாகுந் துரியம் பிரிவித்துச்
சித்தம் புகுந்து சிவமய மாக்குமே 492

Play of Sakti-Siva Infuses Divine Spirit

Out of Sakti-Siva Play
Life blossomed;
And Jiva who was in pure Kevala state
Of Turiya quiescence
Was freed and consigned to the folds of the two Mayas,
And the Lord then entered Jiva's thought
And suffused his being with Divine Spirit.

The condition of the Jīva before birth is considered to be the same as what it is in the Mukti state, which is the Turiya state.

Mantras 492-500

Jivas, who are eternal, are given life and body by Siva/Sakti that they may rid themselves of their primordial impurities and become truly free and pure.

These jivas are classified into three basic categories according to the degree of impurities they possess. In a scheme of evolution, the one class rises to the next by divesting itself of the impurities, one after another.

These three catagories are called vijnanakalars, pralayakalars and sakalars, according to the state of their evolution. Each of these three broad classifications has again sub-classifications, and in all the hierarchy of jivas is divided into ten divisions.

The vijnanas (abbreviated form of vijnanakalars) are the most highly evolved souls. No longer affected by karma or maya, they are amenable to anava alone. They are categorized into four subdivisions, beginning with those of lesser evolution.

First come those who are not rid of anava (egoity), but are in a quiescent state of inaction. Then come those who have realised the Self, but are still conscious of the self. Then are those who have reached the ranks of the Vidyesvaras. And above them are the seven crores of Mantra Nayakas.

But all these possess the impurity of egoity (self-consciousness) to some extent or other. Only the truly enlightended are totally rid of anava or self-consciousness.

Below the Vijnanas are the pralayakalars. They possess two malams: anava and karma, out of the three.

Among them, the first category consists of those souls who will attain mukti in their next life. More advanced than they are the jivan-muktas, who have attained enlightenment during their immediate incarnation. Above them in evolution are the 108 Mudras.

All these three categories of pralayakalars possess the sense of self-consciousness and experience karma in gradations of intensity.

The third major category of jivas is called the sakalars.

The sakalars are encumbered by all three malams; anava, karma and maya. Among the sakalars are three sub-classifications: those who have attained the miraculous powers of siddhis, but are aspiring towards eventual God-realization; those who having attained the siddhis, are content with cultivating these powers; and those who are not performing yoga sadhana, remaining powerless to conquer any of the malams, and are simply enmeshed in the world of sense experience.

There are further subdivisions among these three main categories. These are elaborated later in "Tantra the Eighth," Mantras 2229-2223 under the heading Kevala Sakala Sudham.

In whatever stage of spiritual evolution they are, all jivas have ultimately to divest themselves of their triple malam, and unite with bindu and nada before they become one with Siva.

விஞ்ஞானர் நால்வரு மெய்ப்பிரள யர்கலத்
தஞ்ஞானர் மூவருந் தாங்கு சகலத்தின்
அஞ்ஞானர் மூவரு மாகும் பதின்மராம்
விஞ்ஞான ராதியர் வேற்றுமை தானே. 493

The Three Categories Form Ten Classes

Vignanars true are of groups four
Pralayakalas are of three;
Sakalars below are another three
Thus are Jivas grouped, ten in all.

Vijnana is a term more commonly used in Buddhism, meaning ordinary or individual consciousness as opposed to Prajna world or Universe consciousness.

விஞ்ஞானர் கேவலத் தாரது விட்டவர்
தஞ்ஞானர் அட்டவித் தேசராஞ் சார்ந்துளோர்
எஞ்ஞானர் ஏழ்கோடி மந்திர நாயகர்
மெய்ஞ்ஞானர் ஆணவம் விட்டுநின் றாரே. 494

The Four Classes of Vijnanars

Vijnanakalas are of classes four;
Those who are in Kevala (Anava) state,
Next are those who are Self-realised;
Those who reached the state of Eight Vidyeswaras,
And finally are those who rank as the Seven Crores of Manthra Nayakas;
Those who are of Egoity Impure rid
Are the truly realised beings (no more are they Jivas).

இரண்டா வதில்முத்தி எய்துவர் அத்தனை
இரண்டாவ துள்ளே இருமல பெத்தர்
இரண்டாகு நூற்றெட்டு ருத்திரர் என்பர்
முரண்சேர் சகலத்தர் மும்மலத் தாரே. 495

The Three Classes of Pralayakalas

Of the Pralayakalas three,
Are those who Mukti attained;
Another, by malas twain (Egoity and Karma) bound;
Yet another, the Rudras Hundred and Eight;
The Sakalas have all malas three.

பெத்தத்த சித்தொடு பேண்முத்தச் சித்தது
ஒத்திட் டிரண்டை யூடுற்றார் சித்துமாய்
மத்தது மும்மலம் வாட்டுகை மாட்டாதார்
சத்தத் தமிழ்ந்து சகலத்து ளாரே. 496

The Three Classes of Sakalas

Sakalas three are:
Those who have attained Siddhis miraculous,
Those who have attained Mukti (Jivan)
Those who have attained neither
—All powerless to conquer Malas three
And in sound and other senses immersed.

சிவமாகி ஐவகைத் திண்மலஞ் செற்றோர்
அவமாகார் சித்தர்முத் தாந்தத்து வாழ்வார்
பவமான தீர்வோர் பசுபாசம் அற்றோர்
நவமான தத்துவம் நாடிக்கண் டோரே. 497

Stages of Attainment in Mala Riddance

They who are of five malas hard rid,
Themselves Siva become;
They blemishless become,
They become Siddhas,
Attain state of Mukti Finale,
They uproot Jiva's bondage
End cycle of births;
They alone are,
Who truth of peerless Tattvas realised.

விஞ்ஞானர் ஆணவ கேவல மேவுவோர்
விஞ்ஞானர் மாயையில் தங்கும் இருமலர்
அஞ்ஞானர் அச்சக லத்தர் சகலராம்
விஞ்ஞான ராதிகள் ஒன்பான்வே றுயிர்களே. 498

Nine Gradations of Jivas

Vijnanakalas are of gradations three;
Those who in quiescent Anava alone abide; (the Pralayakala among Vijnanas)
So are Pralayakalas of gradations three;
And Sakalas too;
Thus are there nine classes of Jivas,
Evolving in gradations separate.

விஞ்ஞான கன்மத்தால் மெய்யகங் கூடிய
அஞ்ஞான கன்மத்தி னால்சுவர் யோனிபுக்
கெஞ்ஞான மெய்தீண்டி யேயிடை யிட்டுப்போய்
மெய்ஞ்ஞான ராகிக் சிவமேவல் உண்மையே. 499

How Sakalas Among Vijnanakalas Attain Siva-State

Vijnanakalas may by karma assume form corporeal;
But by performing holy deeds,
Acquire Celestial frame
And higher Jnana Form;
And Constant striving thus,
Gain wisdom perennial
And in the end Siva Himself become.

ஆணவந் துற்ற வவித்தா நனவற்றோர்
காணிய விந்துவா நாத. சகலாதி
ஆணவ மாதி யடைந்தோ ரவரன்றே
சேணுயர் சத்தி சிவதத் துவமாமே. 500

How Jivas Reach Siva

Rid themselves of Anava entire
And consciousness lost of all Jiva memory,
They Bindu and Nada become,
The highest heavenly goal
Of one-ness with Siva Tattva;
Albeit all three, Sakala and the rest of yore possessed,
The primal impurities triple,
Anava, Maya and Karma.

16. பாத்திரம்

THE WORTHY SOULS

The evolved souls constantly think of God, and seek the Grace of His Holy Feet. They are in a state of total surrender, holding that all that happens is destined to happen and God is the witness of all. Their love for Him is unintermittent, from cradle to the grave. They are Sivajnanis par excellence. They walk in the path of yama, niyama, and yoga.

They are gurus, true, who impart jnana to appropriate disciples. Rid of all impurities, they are pure souls. They have doubt-free vision of God.

To such, give in bounty. Their needs deserve to be lovingly looked after.

திலமத் தனையே சிவஞானிக் கீந்தால்
பலமுத்தி சித்தி பரபோக முந்தரும்
நிலமத் தனைபொன்னை நின்மூடர்க் கீந்தால்
பலமுமற் றேபர போகமுங் குன்றுமே. 501

Give Freely to Sivajnanis

Give a wee bit to Sivajnani
You shall attain Siddhi, Mukti and heavenly bliss;
Give a world of gold to the witless,
You shall become poor losing all joys.

கண்டிருந் தாருயிர் உண்டிடுங் காலனைக்
கொண்டிருந் தாருயிர் கொள்ளுங் குணத்தனை
நன்றுணர்ந் தார்க்கருள் செய்திடு நாதனைச்
சென்றுணர்ந் தார்சிலர் தேவரு மாமே. 502

Lord's Devotees are Elevated Souls

Death waits for the moment due
And seizes lives;

But the Lord seizes Death's life;
Such indeed, His Prowess is;
He blesses all who know Him true;
They who sought Him, immortals became.

கைவிட்டி லேன்கரு வாகிய காலத்து
மெய்விட்டி லேன்விகிர் தன்னடி தேடுவன்
பொய்விட்டு நானே புரிசடை யானடி
நெய்விட் டிலாத விடிஞ்சிலு மாமே. 503

Lord's Feet are like a Self-Effulgent Lamp

I gave Him not up even while in womb;
I forgot not the truth of His holy Feet;
I gave up falsehood and sought them;
The Feet of Lord of matted locks
Are a Lamp no oil feeds.

ஆவன ஆவ அழிவ அழிவன
போவன போவ புகுவ புகுவன
காவலன் பேர்நந்தி காட்டித்துக் கண்டவன்
ஏவன செய்யும் இளங்கிளை யோனே. 504

Lord does Things Appropriate to Those of Tender Love

Those that are destined to be
Let them be;
Those that are destined not to be
Let them not be;
Those that are destined to go
Let them go;
Those that are destined to come
Let them Come;
The Mighty Nandi shows all
And witnesses all:
All things appropriate,
He does
To those of tender love for Him.

17. அபாத்திரம்

THE UNWORTHY SOULS

கோல வறட்டைக் குனிந்து குளகிட்டுப்
பாலைக் கறந்து பருகுவ தேயொக்குஞ்
சீலமும் நோன்பும் இலாதவர்க் கீந்தது
காலங் கழிந்த பயிரது ஆகுமே. 505

Giving to Unworthy is Undesirable

Well may you tender her;
And with fresh grass feed her,
The barren cow can no milk give;
Even so is giving
Unto those who neither good nor holy are;
Unto a crop they are,
Raised in season improper.

Mantras 505-508

The unworthy jivas are those who are neither good nor holy. They are like a crop that is raised in improper season. They do not flourish, do not yield. They are like the barren cows that give no milk. They are steeped in worldly pleasures. They will never get God-vision. They are perpetuaters of the five deadly sins. They are destined only to the hot hell.

Do not feed them; do not look after them; do not give them anything. To give to them is a heinous crime. Both the giver and the receiver will be condemned to perdition.

ஈவது யோக இயம நியமங்கள்
சார்வ தறிந்தன்பு தங்கு மவர்க்கன்றி
ஆவ தறிந்தன்பு தங்கா தவர்களுக்
கீவ பெரும்பிழை யென்றுகொ ளீரே. 506

Do not Give to Those Who Have no Love for God

Give only unto those
Who follow the way of Yoga, Yama, and Niyama,
And who adore Lord, in constancy abiding;
To give those who have no love for God,
A heinous crime, indeed it is.

ஆமா றறியான் அதிபஞ்ச பாதகன்
தோமாறும் ஈசற்குந் தூய குரவற்குங்
காமாதி விட்டோர்க்குந் தரல்தந்து கற்பிப்போன்
போமா நரகிற் புகான்போதங் கற்கவே. 507

He Who Gives to Sivajnanis will Become a Jnani

He who gives to God, Guru,
And the Great ones
Who are of passions rid,
Will a Jnani become,
For him is not the burning hell,
That is destined for perpetrators
Of deadly sins five,
Who know not consequences dire.

மண்மலை யத்தனை மாதனம் ஈயினும்
அண்ணல் இவனென்றே யஞ்சலி யத்தனாய்
எண்ணி யிறைஞ்சாதார்க் கீந்த இருவரும்
நண்ணுவர் ஏழா நரகக் குழியிலே. 508

Do not Give to Unworthy; the Giver and the Receiver Both Reach Hell

You may give away wealth
As massive as a mountain;
Yet if you give it
To those that adore not our Lord;
You shall with them reach
The Seventh Hell of ineffable pain.

18. தீர்த்தம்

HOLY WATERS

உள்ளத்தின் உள்ளே உளபல தீர்த்தங்கள்
மெள்ளக் குடைந்துநின் றாடார் வினைகெடப்
பள்ளமும் மேடும் பரந்து திரிவரே
கள்ள மனமுடைக் கல்வியி லோரே. 509

The Holy Waters are Within Us

Within this body are many Holy Waters;
They take not gentle dips in them
And drive Karma away;
Vainly do they roam hill and dale,
Witless men of confused mind they are!

Within the body itself there are many water fronts. They are holy. Yet men do not dip in them and get purified. They vainly roam hill and dale in search of purificatory baths The Vedas, including the Rg Veda, emphasize the sacredness of the Waters; Power, 'Sakti', resides in them and they are, therefore, highly purifying, and powerful.

தளியறி வாளர்க்குத் தண்ணிதாய்த் தோன்றுங்
குளியறி வாளர்க்குக் கூடவும் ஒண்ணான்
வளியறி வாளர்க்கு வாய்க்கினும் வாய்க்குந்
தெளியறி வாளர்தஞ் சிந்தையு ளானே. 510

Lord Abides in Jnana Thought

To them who love Him dear,
The Lord will appear delicious cool;
To them steeped in worldly pleasures,
He will appear never;
To Yogis who breath control;
But sure does He
In thoughts abide,
Of Jnanis, who doubt-free see.

உள்ளத்தின் உள்ளே உணரும் ஒருவனைக்
கள்ளத்தி னாருங் கலந்தறி வார்இல்லை
வெள்ளத்தை நாடி விடுமவர் தீவினைப்
பள்ளத்தி லிட்டதோர் பந்தருள் ளானே. 511

Men of False Faith do not See the Lord Within

The Lord is within them,
Yet they know Him not,
They of faith false;
Limitless the flow of their evil deeds;
Down down the deep drain it goes,
Never its destination to know.

அறிவார் அமரர்கள் ஆதிப்பிரானைச்
செறிவா னுறை பதஞ் சென்று வலங்கொள்
மறியார் வளைக்கை வருபுனற் கங்கைப்
பொறியார் புனல்மூழ்கப் புண்ணிய ராமே. 512

Bathe in Ganga and Be Purified

They who adore Him,
Reach His heavenly abode;
Thus it is,
Immortals know Primal Lord;
Bathe in pellucid waters of Sacred Ganga
That from Lord's crest here descends;
You shall holy become,
Saved of impurities sinful.

The Ganga, the holiest of waters is within us, even as God is within us. It descends from the Lord's Crest in sahasrara within the cranium. If we pilgrimage to its banks in the yogic way, we shall bathe in it and be purified of the triple malam.

கடலிற் கெடுத்துக் குளத்தினிற் காண்டல்
உடலுற்றுத் தேடுவார் தம்மையொப் பாரிலர்
திடமுற்ற நந்தி திருவரு ளாற்சென்
றுடலிற் புகுந்தமை ஒன்றறி யாரே. 513

Seek not Lord Elsewhere; He is Within Thee

They dropped gold in sea,
And looked hard for it in pond;
Nothing indeed to match their folly;
Within you is Nandi,
Firm as rock of ages,
Yet they know Him not, and seek Him not
Lacking in Grace, they sure are.

கலந்தது நீர துடம்பிற் கறுக்குங்
கலந்தது நீர துடம்பிற் சிவக்குங்
கலந்தது நீர துடம்பில் வெளுக்குங்
கலந்தது நீர்நிலங் காற்றது வாமே. 514

Water Within Forms Vital Body Constituent

The black guna enters the body as Tamas,
The red guna enters the body as Rajas,
The white guna enters the body as Sattva,
Real bathing in the holy waters is the
Purification of these three gunas by the grace of the Lord.

19. திருக்கோயில்

CONSEQUENCE OF DAMAGING THE HOLY TEMPLE

The Holy Temple

These are Āgamic concepts and rituals.

தாவர லிங்கம் பறித்தொன்றில் தாபித்தால்
ஆவதன் முன்னே அரசு நிலைகெடுஞ்
சாவதன் முன்னே பெருநோய் அடுத்திடுங்
காவலன் பேர்நந்தி கட்டுரைத் தானே. *515*

Dangers of Transplanting Linga

Let them beware who transplant
A Linga at a Shirne established;
Even before the transplant is completed,
The Kingdom will to disaster fall;
And foul leprosy will torture him
Thus did He declare,
Nandi, the Divine Protector.

Temples are monuments that require to be preserved intact. Let not a linga that has been established be removed from its original site. Dire harm will fall on the culprit.

கட்டுவித் தார்மதிற் கல்லொன்று வாங்கிடில்
வெட்டுவிக் கும்அபி டேகத் தரசரை
முட்டுவிக் கும்முனி வேதிய ராயினும்
வெட்டுவித் தேவிடும் விண்ணவன் ஆணையே. *516*

Dangers of Destruction to Temple

As they move away,
A single stone from temple wall
That shall spell the Crowned King's ruin;
Be he a sage; be he one learned in Vedas,
Sure the crisis; certain the ruin;
—So Ordained the Lord.

ஆற்றரு நோய்மிக் கவனி மழையின்றிப்
போற்றரு மன்னரும் போர்வலி குன்றுவர்
கூற்றுதைத் தான்திருக் கோயில்க ளெல்லாஞ்
சாற்றிய பூசைகள் தப்பிடில் தானே. *517*

Dangers of Skipping Performance of Puja

Rains fail; epidemics spread;
The mighty king his prowess loses;
All this sure happens,
If worship in Lord's temples falters,
—The Lord who spurned the very God of Death.

Mantras 517 & 518

Let the pujas in the temples be faithfully continued. If worship in Siva's temple falters, the ruler will be held responsible for the dire consequences that follow. He loses his power; rains fail in the land, epidemics ravage it, and thefts and crimes abound.

முன்னவ னார்கோயில் பூசைகள் முட்டிடின்
மன்னர்க்குத் தீங்குள வாரி வளங்குன்றுங்
கன்னங் களவு மிகுத்திடுங் காசினி
என்னரு நந்தி எடுத்துரைத் தானே. *518*

Dangers of Puja Ceasing

When in Siva's temple worship ceases,
Harm befalls the ruler;
Scanty become the rains;
Theft and robbery abound in the land,
Thus did my Holy Nandi declare.

பேர்கொண்ட பார்ப்பான் பிரான்தன்னை அர்ச்சித்தாற்
போர்கொண்ட நாட்டுக்குப் பொல்லா வியாதியாம்
பார்கொண்ட நாட்டுக்குப் பஞ்சமு மாம்என்றே
சீர்கொண்ட நந்தி தெரிந்துரைத் தானே. *519*

Puja to be Performed Only by Qualified Priests

If he is but a priest in name
Who, Lord's worship performs,
Deathly wars rage in fury
Fell diseases spread;
Famine stalks the land—
Thus did the great Nandi in truth declare.

And let the pujas be performed by true priests; and not those who are priests in name.

எம்பெரு மான்இறை வாமுறை யோஎன்று
வம்பவிழ் வானோர் அசுரன் வலிசொல்ல
அம்பவள மேனி அறுமுகன் போயவர்
தம்பகை கொல்லென்ற தற்பரன் தானே. *520*

Manifestation of Downward-looking Face

'Hail our Lord! Our God!
Deathly is the might of Padmasura
Save us, help, oh!"
Thus did Celestials to Primal Lord pray!;
And the Primal Lord to the Six-faced God,
Of coral hue beckoned;
And said, "Proceed and smite the enemy."

This Face protects the innocent, the good and the helpless. It manifested itself, when harassed by the giant Padmasura, the celestials appealed to the Lord to save them. Then out of the Fifth Face emanated His son, Subrahmanya with six faces; and the Lord commanded him, "My Son, proceed to battle and smite the enemy."

"Six-faced" God is MURUGA (of the Tamils), who becomes Subrahmanya or Kumara in Sanskrit. The reference here is to the wars waged by Asuras and Devas to be found in the Puranas. When things appear to swing in favour of the Asuras, the devas approach Siva for aid and he sends his son, Kumara (Devasenapati) to their aid.

20. அதோமுக தெரிசனம்

DARSHAN OF DOWNWARD-LOOKING FACE

Tirumular introduces the very unique concept of the Sixth face of Mukhalinga (the Adhomukha). In verse 520, we find Siva described as the Six-faced God, which is not known elsewhere.

(One might even suspect that Tirumular is hereby trying very subtly and delicately to establish that Arumukha six-face headed Muruga of the Tamils, is the same as the Siva whom he has brought from the Sanskritic north.)

In verse 523, he is described as Adhomukha (meaning "down-ward looking") and in verse 521, the poison He had imbibed at the churning of the ocean colours the throat of this face blue. The implication is that this is the Compassionate face of the Lord.

The term Adhomukha corresponds in function and purpose to the Avalokitesvara of Mahayana Buddhism where he is the Lord of Great Compassion.

Verses 543 to 548 remind us of Buddhist Sanga and Buddha's advice to his disciples about the importance and value of the Sanga.

அண்டமொ டெண்டிசை தாங்கும் அதோமுகங்
கண்டங் கறுத்த கருத்தறி வாரில்லை
உண்டது நஞ்சென் றுரைப்பர் உணர்விலோர்
வெண்டலை மாலை விரிசடை யோற்கே. 521

Blue Throat of Downward-looking Face

He sports the garland of white skulls,
His spreading locks are matted;
He supports Universe vast,
He fills Space in directions eight,
On the throat of His Downward-directed Face
Darkness suffuses;
They say, "He swallowed poison;"
They are ignorant, they know not the truth.

செய்தான் அறியுஞ் செழுங்கடல் வட்டத்துப்
பொய்யே யுரைத்துப் புகழும் மனிதர்கள்
மெய்யே யுறைக்கில் விண்ணோர் தொழச்செய்வன்
மைதாழ்ந் திலங்கு மிடறுடை யோனே. 522

The Truth of Lord's Blue-Throat

Ye men!
Who in this sea-girt globe live
In falsehood and flattery!
Why His throat gleams dark,
He knows who made it so;
When you speak the truth
He will make,
Celestial beings bow to you.

Mantras 521 & 522

The throat of the Fifth Face is suffused with darkness. Siva is blue-throated. The story goes that He swallowed the deadly poison that arose at the time of the churning the 'milky ocean' by the devas and asuras, and that it stayed in His throat. But the inner meaning is something deeper. Siva alone knows. The knowledge of Truth is verily the goal of realisation.

நந்தி எழுந்து நடுவுற ஓங்கிய
செந்தீக் கலந்துட் சிவனென நிற்கும்
முந்திக் கலந்தங் குலகம் வலம்வரும்
அந்தி இறைவன் அதோமுக மாமே. 523

The Downward-Looking Face is of Sadasiva

Inside Primal Fire that is Siva
Nandi rises in the centre, gleaming
He pervades worlds all,
His hue is of the twilight sun
Who the world in glory ambulates,
He is the Lord of the Downward-looking Face—
Adhomukha.

அதோமுகங் கீழண்ட மான புராணன்
அதோமுகத் தன்னொடும் எங்கு முயலுஞ்
சதோமுகத் தொண்மலர்க் கண்ணிப் பிரானும்
அதோமுகன் ஊழித் தலைவனு மாமே. 524

The Face Creates All

The Ancient One of Adhomukha
Created Universe vast here below;
In Adhomukha He animates all life;
He is Lord of Adhomukha Sakti of lotus eye;
He is Lord of Aeons' End.

In this aspect of Five-faced manifestation, Siva is Sadasiva. It is in this aspect that He creates all the universe, animates all life, conjoint with the Adhomukha Sakti of lotus eyes.

அதோமுக மாமல ராயது கேளும்
அதோமுகத் தாலொரு நூறாய் விரிந்து
அதோமுக மாகிய அந்தமில் சத்தி
அதோமுக மாகி அமர்ந்திருந் தானே. 525

It Blossomed Into a Hundred Worlds and Impregnated Them With Energy

Hearken to this,
How Adhomukha blossomed into a Gigantic Flower
Then, it transformed itself into a hundred worlds;
And into Limitless Energy
Animating them;
And then as Adhomukha,
The Lord remained as their Support as well.

21. சிவ நிந்தை
ABUSE OF SIVA

தெளிவுறு ஞானத்துச் சிந்தையின் உள்ளே
அளிவுறு வாரம ராபதி நாடி
எளியனென் றீசனை நீசர் இகழின்
கிளியொன்று பூனையிற் கீழது வாகுமே. 526

Abuse of Siva Brings Misery

Those who have Jnana attained,
Rid of all doubts in their thoughts
Seek Him in love intense
Shall reach the World of Celestials;
If the low-born think any the less of Him,
Dismal indeed is their fate—
Like the parrot in cat's claw.

முளிந்தவர் வானவர் தானவர் எல்லாம்
விளிந்தவர் மெய்ந்நின்ற ஞானம் உணரார்
அளிந்தமு தூறிய ஆதிப் பிரானைத்
தளிந்தவர்க் கல்லது தாங்கவொண் ணாதே. 527

Adore Lord and Attain Jnana

The Devas and Asuras wasted their lives
And finally died;
They attained not Jnana true;
They alone can attain Truth
Who adore Primal Lord in devotion intense.

"Even the devas", says Mular, "cannot find Liberation unless they adore the Lord, Siva."

அப்பகை யாலே அசுரருந் தேவரும்
நற்பகை செய்து நடுவே முடிந்தனர்
எப்பகை யாகிலும் எய்தார் இறைவனைப்
பொய்ப்பகை செய்யினும் ஒன்றுபத் தாமே. 528

Abuse not Siva Even in Fun

They defied the Lord,
Devas and Asuras,
And they defied themselves one another
And destruction met,
However little, defy not Lord,
Not even for fun,
They snow-ball, one into ten.

போகமும் மாதர் புலவி யதுநினைந்
தாகமும் உள்கலந் தங்குள னாதலில்
வேதிய ராயும் விகிர்தனாம் என்கின்ற
நீதியுள் ஈசன் நினைப்பொழி வாரே. 529

Dare not Forget Lord However Holy

Learned are they in Vedic lore;
Knowing God is within them,
They bethought themselves to be God
And plunged into pleasures distracting
Forgetting all thought of God.

Remember the fate that overtook the rishis that were learned in the Vedic lore. Postulating that God is within them, they presumed they themselves were God, and so plunged into distracting pleasures, forgetting all thought of the Lord. (The reference here is to the rishis of Daruka forest, who ignored Siva and performed unholy sacrifice.)

22. குரு நிந்தை
ABUSE OF GURU

பெற்றிருந் தாரையும் பேணார் கயவர்கள்
உற்றிருந் தாரை உளைவன சொல்லுவர்
கற்றிருந் தார்வழி உற்றிருந் தாரவர்
பெற்றிருந் தாரன்றி யார்பெறும் பேறே. 530

The True Disciples are Blessed

The lowly ones
Care not for their parents,
They abuse their kith and kin and words foul
Nor do they follow the Guru's behest
Only those who revere the parents, kith and kin and the Guru
Arc in truth blessed, none else indeed.

ஓரெழுத் தொருபொருள் உணரக் கூறிய
சீரெழுத் தாளரைச் சிதையச் செப்பினோர்
ஊரிடைச் சுணங்கனாய்ப் பிறந்தங் கோருகம்
வாரிடைக் கிருமியாய் மாய்வர் மண்ணிலே. 53

Consequences of Abusing Guru

The Guru taught the wisdom
Of One-Letter mantra (Aum);
He who speaks derisive of Him
Will be born a lowly cur;
And having led a dog's life for a Yuga entire,
He will be a worm born;
And then to dust shall be consigned.

பத்தினி பத்தர்கள் தத்துவ ஞானிகள்
சித்தங் கலங்கச் சிதைவுகள் செய்தவர்
அத்தமும் ஆவியும் ஆண்டொன்றில் மாண்டிடுஞ்
சத்தியம் ஈது சதாநந்தி ஆணையே. 532

Consequences of Abusing the Good

The virtuous wife, devotee true, and Jnani great
Those who have done exceeding harm to shock these
Their life and wealth will in a year disappear,
True this is,
Upon Holy Nandi, I swear.

மந்திரம் ஒரெழுத் துரைத்த மாதவர்
சிந்தையில் நொந்திடத் தீமைகள் செய்தவர்
நுந்திய சுணங்கனாய்ப் பிறந்து நூறுரு
வந்திடும் புலையராய் மாய்வர் மண்ணிலே. 533

Do not Abuse Guru

Those who wounded feelings,
Of Holy Guru who taught,
Even one letter of the Mantra
Will be a dog born,
And after a hundred dog incarnations,
Will die a human out-caste.

ஈச னடியார் இதயங் கலங்கிடத்
தேசமும் நாடுஞ் சிறப்பும் அழிந்திடும்
வாசவன் பீடமும் மாமன்னர் பீடமும்
நாசம தாகுமே நந்நந்தி யாணையே. 534

Harm to World by Maltreatment of Guru

If Gurus who are devout of God
Are caused pain in heart
The country, people and their greatness
Will all as one destroyed be;
The thrones of heavenly king Indra,
And of kings mighty here below,
Will alike crumble down;
Sure This is,
I swear by our Nandi true.

சன்மார்க்க சற்குரு சந்நிதி பொய்வரின்
நன்மார்க்க முங்குன்றி ஞானமுந் தங்காது
தொன்மார்க்க மாய துறையும் மறந்திட்டுப்
பன்மார்க்க முங்கெட்டுப் பஞ்சமு மாமே. 535

Do not Utter Falsehood in Guru's Presence

Utter not falsehood in holy Guru's presence;
Then will goodness and wisdom depart;
Forgotten will be
The time-honoured path of righteousness,
And all else that to prosperity leads;
The land a prey to famine falls.

கைப்பட்ட மாமணி தானிடை கைவிட்டு
மெய்ப்பட்ட கல்லைச் சுமப்போன் விதிபோன்றும்
கைப்பட்ட நெய்பால் தயிர்நிற்கத் தானறக்
கைப்பிட்டுண் பான்போன்றுங்
கன்மிஞானிக்கொப்பே. 536

Jnana Guru is the Real Guru

One who throws away the precious gem in hand,
And carries a heavy stone instead;
Or One who parts with milk, curd and ghee on hand
And prefers the bitter poison, fatal-
Like him is the one who follows the path of Karma
As compared to Jnana.

23. மயேசுர நிந்தை

ABUSE OF SIVA JNANI (MAHESVARA)

ஆண்டான் அடியவ ரார்க்கும் விரோதிகள்
ஆண்டான் அடியவர் ஐயமேற் றுண்பவர்
ஆண்டான் அடியாரை வேண்டாது பேசினோர்
தாந்தாம் விழுவது தாழ்நர காகுமே. 537

Consequences of Abusing Mahesvara

The Lord's devotee lives by alms,
Those who show animus to him,
However humble his condition be,
And those who abuse him as they will,
Shall into lowly hell fall.

ஞானியை நிந்திப் பவனும் நலனென்றே
ஞானிடய வந்திப் பவனுமே நல்வினை
யான கொடுவினை தீர்வா ரவன்வயம்
போன பொழுதே புகுஞ்சிவ போகமே. 538

Blessings of Jnani's Presence

Those who deride the Jnani
Are rid of benefits of good deeds done;
Those who revere him as holy,
Are rid of harm of evil deeds done;
Those who reach Jnani's presence.
Will verily taste Siva Bhoga.

24. பொறையுடைமை

PATIENCE

பற்றிநின் றார்நெஞ்சிற் பல்லிதான் ஒன்றுண்டு
முற்றிக் கிடந்தது மூக்கையும் நாவையுந்
தெற்றிக் கிடந்து சிதைக்கின்ற சிந்தையுள்
வற்றா தொழிவது மாகமை யாமே. 539

Patience is the Sheet-anchor of Yogis

In the hearts of those-who are firm of mind
Lie the (Varmamus) lizard of Yoga Vairagya
It lay besieging nose and tongue—(in Keṣari Mudra)
In the troubled thought that knows but torture,
The only thing that stands still
Is devotional Patience Exceeding.

Troubled thought is a torture—vairagya or firmness in divine thought alone is bliss. They who possess such firmness of mind are the yogis. Their firmness is revealed in kechari mudra, where the tongue stops the nasal orifice in yogic breath-exercise. Their firmness can be compared to that of the varamus lizard, which tenaciously holds to the object it seizes and does not swerve, however hard you pull the reptile.

ஓலக்கஞ் சூழ்ந்த உலப்பிலி தேவர்கள்
பாலொத்த மேனியன் பாதம் பணிந்துய்ய
மாலுக்கும் ஆதிப் பிரமற்கும் மன்னவன்
ஞாலத் திவன்மிக நல்லனென் றாரே. 540

Celestial Beings Worship Lord

The Lord was seated on His throne;
He was of milk-white hue;
Surrounding Him stood
Celestial Beings in number countless;
Hari and Brahma too,
Whose King He is;
And low they bowed at His Feet.
And prayed for His Grace,
And the Lord blessed,
"They shall on earth prosper high."

Mantra 540-542

The Lord is the Supreme Yogi. In the constancy of yoga, He created all. He dances on the cremation ground as well. Such is His play. All celestials worship His throne; Hari and Brahma too.

ஞானம் விளைந்தவர் நம்மிட மன்னவர்
சேனை வளைந்து திசைதொறுங் கைதொழ
ஊனை விளைத்திடும் உம்பர்தம் ஆதியை
ஏனை விளைந்தருள் எட்டலு மாமே. 541

Lord Grants Grace to Those Who Adore Him

The Lord is of wisdom ripe;
He is our King,
As unto an army they swell,
In directions all to pray;
He creates the fleshy body,
He is the Primal One of Celestial Beings,
If you adore Him in love earnest,
He will His Grace grant.

வல்வகை யாலும் மனையிலும் மன்றிலும்
பல்வகை யாலும் பயிற்றிப் பதஞ்செய்யுங்
கொல்லையி னின்று குதிகொள்ளுங் கூத்தனுக்
கெல்லையி லாத விலயமுண் டாமே. 542

Lord's Play

Inside home and outside
By force and means gentle
The Lord prepared you—
He dances on the burning ground;
Many and varied are His plays.

25. பெரியோரைத் துணைக்கோடல்

TO SEEK THE COMPANY OF THE HOLY

ஓடவல் லார்தம ரோடு நடாவுவன்
பாடவல் லாரொளி பார்மிசை வாழ்குவன்
தேடவல் லார்க்கருள் தேவர் பிரானொடுங்
கூடவல் லாரடி கூடுவன் யானே. 543

Walk With the Holy

I walk with those who go after God,
I live with those who sing His praise,
The Lord blesses those who seek Him,
With them I consort,
Their feet I seek.

Mantras 543-545

The Lord blesses the holy. Seek their company. Without love for the Lord, man is in perpetual distress. His thoughts quiver like an aspen leaf.

தாமிடர்ப் பட்டுத் தளிர்போல் தயங்கினும்
மாமனத் தங்கன்பு வைத்த திலையாகும்

நீயிடர்ப் பட்டிருந் தென்செய்வாய் நெஞ்சமே
போமிடத் தென்னொடும் போதுகண் டாயே. 544

Holy Company Saves You From Distress

You may in distress
Unto a tender leaf quiver,
What avails you if you are distressed,
My Heart!
Yet you love not Lord;
Do you go with me,
To where the Lord succours.

அறிவார் அமரர் தலைவனை நாடிச்
செறிவார் பெறுவர் சிலர்தத் துவத்தை
நெறிதான் மிகமிக நின்றருள் செய்யும்
பெரியா ருடன்கூடல் பேரின்ப மாமே. 545

Holy Company Leads You to Bliss

The Jnanis seek the Lord of Celestials;
They who seek the Company of Jnanis
Will attain Siva Truth;
They indeed Walk in the Path of Virtue
And are truly blessed;
To resort to such
Is indeed Bliss Supreme.

தார்சடை யான்றன் தமராய் உலகினிற்
போர்புக ழானெந்தை பொன்னடி சேருவர்
வாயடை யாவுள்ளந் தேர்வார்க் கருள்செய்யுங்
கோவடைந் தந்நெறி கூடலு மாமே. 546

The Holy are Kin of Lord

The Holy are kin of Lord
They reach the Golden Feet of Father;
He, of flowing matted locks;
Whose fame envelopes worlds all,
He blesses those,
Who seek Him in the silence of their hearts;
Reach the King Almighty,
You shall attain the Regal Goal.

The holy are the kin of the Lord; they reach the Golden Feet of the Father. Seek them.

உடையான் அடியார் அடியா ருடன்போய்
படையா ரழன்மேனிப் பதிசென்று புக்கேன்
கடையார நின்றவர் கண்டறி விப்ப
உடையான் வருகென ஓலமென் றாரே. 547

Siva Welcomes Devotees of His Devotees

I walked with them—
Devotees of Lord's devotees
And reached the City of The Fire-hued Lord
Sporting weapons divine
They who stood at gate saw me,
And announced me to the Lord;
And the Lord said, "Come in"
And they all cried "Hail! You are the Refuge."

Walk with the holy men. Be a devotee of the Lord's devotees. The devotees reach the city of the Lord; they stand at heaven's gate and pray "Thou art the refuge." The Lord sees them and welcomes them saying, "Come in;" and takes them into His bosom.

அருமைவல் லான்கலை ஞானத்துள் தோன்றும்
பெருமைவல் லோன்பிற விச்சுழி நீந்தும்
உரிமைவல் லோன்உணர்ந் தூழி யிருக்குந்
திருமைவல் லாரொடு சேர்ந்தனன் யானே. 548

I joined the Company of the Rich in Grace

The Devout Supreme will in, be;
The Devout Eminent will master eddies of birth,
Devout Dear realizing self will immortal remain;
With them who are Rich in Grace
I joined to consort.

Only the true devotees will master the karmic eddies; only they will realise the Self and achieve the deathless state. Only they will enter and be in God. They are rich in grace. Consort with them.

இரண்டாம் தந்திரம் முடிவு பெற்றது.

Tantra Two Concluded

மூன்றாம் தந்திரம்
TANTRA THREE

1. அட்டாங்க யோகம்

ASHTANGA YOGAM

உரைத்தன வற்கரி ஒன்று மூடிய
நிரைத்த இராசி நிரைமுறை எண்ணிப்
பிரச்சதம் எட்டும் பேசியே நந்தி
நிரைத்த இயமம் நியமஞ்செய் தானே. 549

Difficult to Expound is the Science of Yoga

Of difficult vast to expound
Is the Science of Breath;
Closing nostril alternate
And counting time in measure appropriate
Thus did Nandi reveal at length
The eight-fold science of yoga great—
Yama, Niyama and the rest.

The science of yoga is a vast subject. It is eight-limbed, that is of eight organic parts; and so is known as ashtanga yoga. The secret of yoga was revealed by Nandi (Sadasiva) initially to the four sages, Sanaka, Sanatana, Sanatkumara and Sanantana.

செய்த இயம நியமஞ் சமாதிசென்
றுய்யப் பராசக்தி உத்தர பூருவ
மெய்த கவச நியாசங்கள் முத்திரை
எய்த வுரைசெய்வன் இந்நிலை தானே. 550

Yoga Includes Kavacha, Nyasa and Mudra

I shall reveal herein,
The ways of Yama and Niyama,
The secret of Kavacha, Nyasa and Mudra
The paths to reach the Samadhi State;
And how Kundalini Sakti courses upward
And reaches the thousand petalled lotus in the cranium.

It teaches about kavacha, nyasa, mudra and the coursing of kundalini energy from the muladhara to sahasrara in the cranium peak through the six adharas within the body. "It is not enough that there be devotion and an attitude of surrender to the Deity within oneself, in the heart and the mind. It is a significant part of worship to express it bodily also; for the body too is a participant in the sadhana. For this purpose there are a number of gestures by movements of the limbs of the body, 'mudras' as they are termed. These external movements of the physical body, with hands and fingers, emphasize and affirm the intention of the heart and mind of the worshipper and by constant repetition establish the idea in the very physical matter of the body. The mudras are the language in which the body speaks to the Deity." — "Lights on Tantra" by M.P. Pandit.

அந்நெறி இந்நெறி என்னாதட் டாங்கத்
தன்னெறி சென்று சமாதியி லேநின்மின்
நன்னெறி செல்வார்க்கு ஞானத்தி லேகலாம்
புன்னெறி யாகத்திற் போக்கில்லை யாகுமே. 551

Ashtanga Yoga Leads to Samadhi and to Jnana

Waver not, this way and that
Follow the way of eight-limbed Yoga
And reach Samadhi State;
They who tread that blessed path
Shall reach Jnana's peak;
No more are they in this vile flesh born.

Yoga is the sure path to jnana or enlightenment. The enlightened are born no more. All karmas are forever ended.

Mular identifies samadhi with jnana. This is similar to Buddhism where the ultimate which is to be realised in Samadhi is prajna, at which duality disappears and jnana, the essence of the individual merges in the essences of the Universal.

இயம நியமமே எண்ணிலா ஆதனம்
நயமுறு பிராணாயா மம் பிரத்தி யாகாரஞ்
சயமிகு தாரணை தியானஞ் சமாதி
அயமுறும் அட்டாங்க மாவது மாமே. 552

Eight Limbs of Yoga

Yama, Niyama, and Asana numberless
Pranayama wholesome and Pratyahara alike,
Dharana, Dhyana and Samadhi to triumph
—These eight are the steely limbs of Yoga.

The eight limbs are: 1)yama; 2)niyama: 3)asana: 4)pranayama: 5)pratyahara; 6)dharana: 7)dhyana; and 8)samadhi. Each step is a preparation for the next. Yoga holds the key to the attainment of samadhi or the unitive trance.

2. இயமம்

IYAMA

எழுந்துநீர் பெய்யினும் எட்டுத் திசையுஞ்
செழுந்த ணியமங்கள் செய்மினென் றண்ணல்
கொழுந்தண் பவளக் குளிர்சடை யோடே
அழுந்திய நால்வர்க் கருள்புரிந் தானே. 553

Perform Iyamas Always

"The heavens may torrents pour
In directions eight;
Yet perform the holy Iyamas"
—Thus spake the Lord of matted locks, cool and coral hued
To the Sages Four, in devotion immersed.

---

1) Santana, Sanatanam, Sanatkumara, Santana—the four rishis taught by Siva in His aspect as Dakshinamurthi (Southward-looking form). The *Agamas* descended to them from Nandi. They received the title, Nandi, and were included among the nathas (masters).

vide—proem.

கொல்லான்பொய் கூறான் களவிலான் எண்குணன்
நல்லான் அடக்க முடையான் நடுச்செய்ய
வல்லான் பகுந்துண்பான் மாசிலான் கட்காமம்
இல்லான் இயமத் திடையில்நின் றானே. 554

Ways of Iyama

He does not kill, he does not lie, he does not steal;
Of marked virtues is he; good, meek and just;
He shares his joys, he knows no blemish
Neither drinks nor lusts
—This the man who in Iyama's ways stands.

The way of iyama consists in number of 'do's and dont's'—non-killing, not lying, not drinking, not lusting, possessing marked virtues, being good, being just, sharing the good things of life with others, and knowing no blemish. Iyama is the background, the ethical preparation for the onward march on the yoga path.

1) Nachinarkiniyar, the celebrated commentator of *Tholkappiyam*, the great classic Tamil grammar, describes the elements of iyamam as five in the following sutra:

3. நியமம்

NIYAMA

ஆதியை வேதத்தின் அப்பொரு ளானைச்
சோதியை அங்கே சுடுகின்ற அங்கியைப்
பாதியுள் மன்னும் பராசக்தி யோடுடன்
நீதி யுணர்ந்து நியமத்த னாமே. 555

Way of Niyama

The Being First,
The Meaning-Central of Vedas all,
The Light Divine,
The Fire within that Light
He who shares Himself
Half-and-Half with His Sakti
And the Divine Justice thereof
—Them, he in Niyama's path knows.

He who stands in niyama should have firm faith that the Supreme Being is the First Cause, that He is the central meaning of all *Vedas*, that He is the Light Divine, that He is the kundalini fire within that Light, and that He and Sakti are inseparable and indivisible, and that there is divine justice in that act of Siva/Sakti oneness.

தூய்மை அருளூண் சுருக்கம் பொறைசெவ்வை
வாய்மை நிலைமை வளர்த்தலே மற்றிவை
காமங் களவு கொலையெனக் காண்பவை
நேமியீ ரைந்து நியமத்த னாமே. 556

Ten Virtues of Niyama

Purity, compassion, frugal food and patience
Forthrightness, truth and steadfastness
—These he ardently cherishes;
Killing, stealing and lusting, He abhors,
—Thus stands with virtues ten
The one who Niyama's ways observes.

Niyama is the next step. It consists of the initial practice of the ten virtues: 1)purity; 2)compassion: 3)frugality of food; 4)patience; 5)forthrightness 6)truth; 7)steadfastness; 8)abhorrence of killing.

தவஞ்செபஞ் சந்தோடம் ஆத்திகந் தானஞ்
சிவன்றன் விரதமே சித்தாந்தக் கேள்வி
மகஞ்சிவ பூஜையொண் மதிசொல்லீர் ஐந்து
நிவம்பல செய்யின் நியமத்த னாமே. 557

Further Ten Attributes of Niyama

Tapas, meditation, serenity, and holiness
Charity, vows in Saiva Way and Siddhanta learning
Sacrifice, Siva puja and thoughts pure
—With these ten, the one in Niyama perfects his Way.

Further on, niyama consists of ten more practices: 1)tapas; 2)meditation; 3)serenity; 4)holiness; 5)charity; 6)vows in Saiva way; 7)siddhanta learning; 8)sacrifices; 9)Siva puja; 10)pure thoughts.

4. ஆதனம்

ASANAS

பங்கய மாதி பரந்தபல் ஆதனம்
அங்குள வாம்இரு நாலும் அவற்றினுள்
சொங்கில்லை யாகச் சுவத்திக மெனமிகத்
தங்க இருப்பத் தலைவனு மாமே. 558

Prominent Asanas

Numerous are the asanas
With Padmasana to commence;
Eight among them are rated high
Especially Svastika
He who postures on these asanas
Verily becomes Master, for sure.

The next step is the practice of asana or bodily postures. These asanas are numerous. But seven among them are basic. These seven are: 1)bhadra; 2)gomukha; 3)padma; 4)simha; 5)swastika; 6)vira; and 7)sukha. He who perfects these postures verily becomes the master. The four following mantras describe four of the asanas in detail. Asanas are postures practised for "health and lightness of body." They give "drdhata or strength" — vide *Hatha Yoga Pradipika,* i.ii.

Tholkappiyam: Nachinarkiniyar commentary", op. cit. Svastikasana is described thus in *Siva Samhita,* iii 95- Place the soles of the feet completely under the thighs, the body straight and sit at ease....." This is also called asana (the easy posture).

Compare *Gheranda Samhita,* ii, 13: "Drawing the legs on thighs together and placing the feet between them, the body in its easy condition and sitting straight. This posture is called svastikasana."

Compare *Hatha Yoga Pradipika,* i, 21: "Having kept the feet between the knees and the thighs, with body straight when one sits calmly, it is called svastikasana."

ஓரணை யப்பத மூருவின் மேலேறிட்
டார வலித்ததன் மேல்வைத் தழகுறச்
சீர்திகழ் கைகள் அதனைத்தன் மேல்வைக்கப்
பார்திகழ் பத்மா சனமென லாகுமே. 559

Padmasana—Lotus Posture

Sit cross-legged with soles of feet upturned
Close draw the feet on thighs opposite,
Stretch then the hands afore on feet
That Padmasana is, famed far on earth.

Padmasana is the 'lotus' posture. The practitioner sits cross-legged, the soles of the feet turned upward; the feet are drawn up onto the opposite thighs. The hands are stretched to the feet.

துரிசில் வலக்காலைத் தோன்றவே மேல்வைத்து
அரிய முழந்தாளி லங்கையை நீட்டி
உருசி யொடுமுடல் செவ்வே யிருத்திப்
பரிசு பெறுமது பத்திரா சனமே. 560

Bhadrasana—Happy Posture

Place the right leg over the left
Stretch the hands over calf of leg
Sit in posture firm and erect
That indeed is Bhadrasana.

Bhadrasana is the 'happy' posture. The right leg is placed over the left, and the hands are stretched over the calf of the leg; and an erect and firm sitting posture is observed.

Bhadrasana:

Compare *Hatha Yoga Pradipika,* i, 55-7: "Place the heels on either side seam of the scrotum, keeping the left heel on the left side, and the right on the right side; hold the feet firmly joined to one another with both the hands. This bhadrasana is the destroyer of all diseases."

Compare *Gheranda Samhita,* ii,9-10: "Place the heels crosswise under the testes attentively; cross the hands behind the back and take hold of the toes of the feet. Fix the gaze on the tip of the nose...."

The asana as described by Tirumular here differs from these two descriptions. Here it appears to be a standing posture.

ஒக்க அடியிணை யூருவில் ஏறிட்டு
முக்கி யுடலை முழங்கை தனில்ஏற்றித்
தொக்க அறிந்து துளங்கா திருந்திடிற்
குக்குட ஆசனங் கொள்ளலுமாமே. 561

Kukkudasana—Cock Posture

Lift the feet on to the thighs,
Control breath and on elbows raise your body,
Thus seated firm and immobile,
Thou do reach the Kukkudasana.

Kukkudasana is the 'cock' posture. The feet are lifted onto the thighs, and controlling the breath, the body is raised on the elbows; and a firm, immobile sitting position is taken. (This asana, however, is not included by Tirumular in his list of seven important asanas. Istead he mentions the gomukha asana. However he describes the kukudasana, but not the gomukha asana.)

Kukudasana—literally 'cock' posture:

Compare *Hatha Yoga Pradipika,* i, 25: "Taking the posture of padmasana and carrying the hands between the knee and the thighs, when the yogi raises himself above the ground, with palms resting on the ground, it becomes kukudasana."

Compare *Gheranda Samhita,* ii,31; "Sitting on the ground, cross the legs in the padmasana posture, thrust down the hands betweeen the thighs and the knees, stand on the hands, supporting the body on the elbows. This is called the kukudasana."

Although Tirumular describes this asana, he does not refer to it as one of the seven important asanas. There instead he mentions 'gomukha,' which he does not describe.

பாத முழுந்தாளிற் பாணி களைநீட்டி
ஆதர வோடும்வாய் அங்காந் தழகுறக்
கோதில் நயனங் கொடிமூக்கி லேயுறச்
சீர்திகழ் சிங்கா தனமெனச் செப்புமே. 562

Simhasana—Lion Posture

Stretch the hands over the calf of leg,
Lift the mouth upward,
Fix thy gaze on tip of nose,
Thus do thou Simhasana posture.

Simhasana is the 'lion' posture. The hands are stretched over the calves of the legs, the chin is lifted upward, and the gaze is fixed on the tip of the nose.

Compare *Hatha Yoga Pradipika,* i, 52-54: "Press the heels on both sides of the seam of the scrotum in such a away that the left heel touches the right side, and the right heel touches the left side. Place the hands on the knees, with stretched fingers and keeping the mouth open and the mind collected, gaze on the tip of the nose. This is simhasana, held sacred by the best of yogis."

Compare *Gheranda Samhita,* ii, 14-15: "The two heels to be placed under the scrotum contrariwise, and turned upwards, the knees to be placed on the ground, and the hands placed on the knees, mouth to be kept open..... and gaze fixed on the nose. This is simhasana, destroyer of all diseases."

பத்திரங் கோமுகம் பங்கயங் கேசரி
சொத்திரம் வீரஞ் சுகாதனம் ஓரேழு
முத்தம மாமுது ஆசனம் எட்டெட்டுப்
பத்தொடு நூறு பலஆ சனமே. 563

Important Asanas are Eight

Bhadra, Gomukha, Padma and Simha,
Sothira, Veera, and Sukha
These seven along with eminent svastika
Constitute the eight, Eighty and hundred, however,
Are asanas in all reckoned.

5. பிராணாயாமம்

PRANAYAMA

ஐவர்க்கு நாயகன் அவ்வூர்த் தலைமகன்
உய்யக்கொண் டேறுங் குதிரைமற் றொன்றுண்டு
மெய்யர்க்குப்பற்றுக்கொடுக்குங் கொடாதுபோய்ப்
பொய்யரைத் துள்ளி விழுத்திடுந் தானே. 564

Master the Steed of Breath

The mind is the master of senses five;
He is the head of the body habitat;
There is a steed he rides to his destined goal;
The masterly one the steed carries,
The feeble one it throws away
—That steed the Prana breath is.

ஆரிய நல்லன் குதிரை இரண்டுள
வீசிப் பிடிக்கும் விரகறி வார்இல்லை
கூரிய நாதன் குருவின் அருள்பெற்றால்
வாரிப் பிடிக்க வசப்படுந் தானே. 565

Control of Inhalation and Exhalation

Great is Jiva
He has steeds two,
But he knows not how to master them
If the lordly Guru lends His Grace,
The steeds will tame become.

In fact, he has two steeds to master, the idakala and pingla breaths that run in the left and right nostrils. It is by the grace of the Guru that he can attain mastery over them.

புள்ளினும் மிக்க புரவியை மேற்கொண்டாற்
கள்ளுண்ண வேண்டாந் தானே களிதருந்
துள்ளி நடப்பிக்குஞ் சோம்பு தவிர்ப்பிக்கும்
உள்ளது சொன்னோம் உணர்வுடை யோருக்கே. 566

Breath control Activates Body

Faster than bird that steed flies,
If that steed is controlled, far headier than wine the pleasure it gives;
It infuses vigour, dispels laziness,
True we say this, let the wise listen.

The steed of prana breath moves faster than a bird. The pleasure it gives is headier than wine. It dispels laziness and infuses vigour.

பிராணன் மனத்தொடும் பேரா தடங்கிப்
பிராண னிருக்கிற் பிறப்பிறப் பில்லை
பிராணன் மடைமாறிப் பேச்சறி வித்துப்
பிராண னடைபேறு பெற்றுண்டீர் நீரே. 567

Breath Control Yields Life-Nectar

Let Prana merge in Mind
And together the two be stilled
Then no more shall birth and death be;
Therefore, learn to direct breath
In streams alternating left and right
Then shall you taste the nectar of life.

ஏறுதல் பூரகம் ஈரெட்டு வாமத்தால்
ஆறுதல் கும்பம் அறுபத்து நாலதில்
ஊறுதல் முப்பத் திரண்டதி ரேசகம்
மாறுதல் ஒன்றின்கண் வஞ்சக மாமே. 568

Puraka Kumbhaka Rechaka Alternated—Cleansing

Purakam is to inhale by left nostril matras six and ten
Kumbhakam is to retain that breath for matras four and six
Rechakam is to exhale thereafter for mantras two and thirty
Thus alternate from left to right and right to left
With Kumbhakam in between.

Inhalation of 16 matras of breath by the left nostril is purakam. Retention of 64 mantras of breath thus inhaled is kumbakam. Exhalation of 32 matras is rechakam. Thus in pranayama the breath is inhaled and exhaled from left to right and back from right to left with retention in between. A matra is a specific time duration.

1)Matra is a measure in time approximating a second, Vachaspati in his gloss on "Yoga Sutras of Patanjali" says, "A matra is the time which is taken up by thrice turning up one's hand over one's knee, and then snapping the fingers once."— "Yoga Sutras of Patanjali," ii, 50-51, as quoted in "Hatha Yoga, " by Theos Bernard, p.56 n.

2)According to Yogacharya Shantikumar, this is one of the two methods for cleaning the subtle channels of breath—through bija. The aspirant should adopt the lotus posture and concentrate on vayu-bija which has the colour of smoke. He should then breathe in through the left nostril for 16 counts, and hold the breath for 64 counts. Then he should exhale through the right nostril for 32 counts. Then he should meditate on fire-bija and breath in through the right nostril and go through the round as he did previously with the left. Thus he should alternate breathing through left and right.

வளியினை வாங்கி வயத்தில் அடக்கில்
பளிங்கொத்துக் காயம் பழுக்கினும் பிஞ்சாந்
தெளியக் குருவின் திருவருள் பெற்றால்
வளியினும் வேட்டு வளியனு மாமே. 569

Breath Control Makes Body Light as Carpenter-Bee

If you control the breath within,
However old your body,
Young and crystal-hard it turns
And with the goodly Guru's benign Grace,
Well may you become lighter than air.

எங்கே இருக்கினும் பூரி இடத்திலே
அங்கே யதுசெய்ய ஆக்கைக் கழிவில்லை
அங்கே பிடித்தது விட்டள வுஞ்செல்லச்
சங்கே குறிக்கத் தலைவனு மாமே. 570

Breath Control Gives Supreme Strength

Wherever you be, there control breath
The body then will perish not.
As you inhale, control and exhale in measure prescribed
Well may you become a triumphant lord
With the conch of victory,
Your achievement heralding.

Practise pranayama in prescribed measure wherever you are. The body will not perish. You will become a triumphant lord, the conch of victory heralding your achievement.

ஏற்றி இறக்கி இருகாலும் பூரிக்குங்
காற்றைப் பிடிக்குங் கணக்கறி வாரில்லை
காற்றைப் பிடிக்குங் கணக்கறி வாளர்க்குக்
கூற்றை யுதைக்குங் குறியது வாமே. 571

Knowledge of Science of Breath Leads to Him

Inhalation, Exhalation, and Retention both ways
The Science of Breath thus consisting
They know not;
They who know the Science of Breath
Are destined to spurn the God of Death.

மேல்கீழ் நடுப்பக்க மிக்குறப் பூரித்துப்
பாலாம் இரேசகத் தாலுட் பதிவித்து
மாலாகி யுந்தியுட் கும்பித்து வாங்கவே
ஆலாலம் உண்டான் அருள்பெற லாமே. 572

Effect of Puraka, Kumbhaka, Rechaka

In Purakam inhale breath deep
To pervade up, down and middle
In Kumbhakam retain it around the navel centre;
In Rechakam it is absorbed within in due measure
They who practise the Science of Breath thus
Reach the Grace of Lord
Who consumed poison deadly.

The purakam breath is inhaled deeply so that it pervades the upper, lower and middle regions of the body within. In kumbhakam, it is retained around the navel centre. In rechakam, it is absorbed within in due measure. Those who practise pranayama thus reach the grace of the Lord who swallowed the deadly poison.

வாமத்தில் ஈரெட்டு மாத்திரை பூரித்தே
ஏமுற்ற முப்பத் திரண்டும் இரேசித்துக்
காமுற்ற பிங்கலைக் கண்ணாக இவ்விரண்
டோமத்தால் எட்டெட்டுக் கும்பிக்க
உண்மையே. 573

Time Duration of Inhaling Retaining and Exhalation

Inhaling six and ten matras by left nostril
Retaining four and sixty in the Homa-pit of the navel
Exhaling two and thirty by the right nostril,
They who control breath thus,
Have verily seen the Light of Truth.

இட்ட தவ்வீ டிளகா திரேசித்துப்
புட்டிப் படத்தச நாடியும் பூரித்துக்
கொட்டிப் பிராணன் அபானனுங் கும்பித்து
நட்டம் இருக்க நமனில்லை தானே. 574

How to Practise Pranayama

Inhale deep and steady,
That Prana fills the nadis ten;
Exhale slow
That the body does not stir;
Retain prana breath
And downward move Apana breath
Thus sit erect and vanquish Death.

புறப்பட்டுப் புக்குத் திரிகின்ற வாயுவை
நெறிப்பட வுள்ளே நின்மல மாக்கில்
உறுப்புச் சிவக்கும் உரோமங் கறுக்கும்
புறப்பட்டுப் போகான் புரிசடை யோனே. 575

Purify Body By Breath Control

The breath within rises
And wanders as it lists;
Control that and purify within;
Then shall your limbs glow red
Your hair turn dark
And God within shall leave you never.

Purification of the breath by control is an important element of the pranayama exercise. When breath that wanders as it lists is regulated, the limbs grow red, the hair turns dark, and the body does not decay.

கூடம் எடுத்துக் குடிபுக்க மங்கையர்
ஓடுவர் மீளுவர் பன்னிரண் டங்குலம்
நீடுவர் எண்விரல் கண்டிப்பர் நால்விரல்
கூடிக் கொளிற்கோல அஞ்செழுத் தாமே. 576

Inhale 12 Matras; Retain 4 Matras

The Prana breath
The pair of damsels within body-house
Runs in and out constant;
If twelve matras inhaled
Eight matras exhaled,
The four matras retained
Shall make you divine in Siva.

பன்னிரண் டானை பகல்இர வுள்ளது
பன்னிரண் டானையைப் பாகன் அறிகிலன்
பன்னிரண் டானையைப் பாகன் அறிந்தபின்
பன்னிரண் டானைக்குப் பகல்இர வில்லையே. 577

Learn to Control Breath and Master Death

The elephant that is twelve-matra breath
Is awake night and day;
The mahout (Jiva) knows not the elephant;
When mahout learns to control elephant
The elephant knows not night and day;
(In eternity it exists).

The 12 matra breath is an elephant that is awake night and day. Jiva is the mahout. The mahout should learn how to control the elephant.

The elephant symbolises "ego", and it is in that sense that Siva is said to have killed and skinned the elephant.

6. பிரத்தியாகாரம்

PRATYAHARA

கண்டுகண் டுள்ளே கருத்துற வாங்கிடிற்
கொண்டுகொண் டுள்ளே குணம்பல காணலாம்
பண்டுகந் தெங்கும் பழமறை தேடியை
இன்றுகண் டிங்கே இருக்கலு மாமே. 578

Blessings of Mind Withdrawal

Step by step, practise mind's withdrawal
And look inward;
One by one many the good you see within;
And may you then meet the Lord,
Now and here below
Whom the ancient Veda still searches
Everywhere.

The next step in yoga is pratyahara or withdrawing the mind and looking inward. This should be practised step by step. Many blessings will follow from this practice.

1) Pratyahara is the restraint of, and subjection of the senses of the mind, which is thereby steadied. The mind is withdrawn from the objects of the senses. Vide "The Serpent Power" by Sir John Woodroffe, p.193. See also, *Gheranda Samhita,* fourth Upadesa; *Sandilya Upadesa,* Chpt.1, etc; the *Sarada Tilaka* defines pratyahara as "the forcible obstruction of the senses wandering over their objects"; quoted in "The Serpent Power" op.cit.— Steadiness is the aim and result of pratyahara.

Compare "Tholkappiyam—Nachinarkiniyar Commentary" op.cit., p.218:

நாபிக்குக் கீழே பன்னிரெண் டங்குலந்
தாபிக்கு மந்திரந் தன்னை அறிகிலர்
தாபிக்கு மந்திரந் தன்னை அறிந்தபின்
கூவிக்கொண் டீசன் குடியிருந் தானே. 579

Retain Breath Below Navel Region

They know not the divine art
Of fixing breath twelve matra long,
Below the navel region;

Once they learn that art
The Lord enters within, shouting in joy.

Pratyahara helps in the act of breath retention below the navel region. It is a rare art that helps the practitioner to advance on the yoga path.

மூலத் திருவிரல் மேலுக்கு முன்நின்ற
பாலித்த யோனிக் கிருவிரற் கீழ்நின்ற
கோலித்த குண்டலி யுள்ளேழுஞ் செஞ்சுடர்
ஞாலத்து நாபிக்கு நால்விரற் கீழதே. 580

Where Kundalini Is

Two finger length above the Muladhara
Two finger length below the sex organ
Four finger length below the navel visible,
There within is Kundalini
A flaming fire lambent.

நாசிக் கதோமுகம் பன்னிரண் டங்குலம்
நீசித்தம் வைத்து நினையவும் வல்லையேல்
மாசித்த மாயோகம் வந்து தலைப்பெய்துந்
தேகத்துக் கென்றுஞ் சிதைவில்லை யாமே. 581

Breath Control for Maha Siddha Yoga

If below the nose-tip
You look twelve-finger length,
And then concentrate and meditate
The mighty Siddha yoga shall yours be
And imperishable shall your body be.

சோதி இரேகைச் சுடரொளி தோன்றிடிற்
கோதில் பரானந்தம் என்றே குறிக்கொண்மின்
நேர்திகழ் கண்டத்தே நிலவொளி எய்தினால்
ஓதுவ துன்னுடல் உன்மத்த மாமே. 582

When Light Appears

If thus meditating,
Luminescence you glimpse at the Visuddhi centre at the throat
Know you are destined for bliss unalloyed; If at the Throat's Center,
Lunar light you behold,
Then will your body,
In divine joy intoxicated be.

மூலத் துவாரத்தை மொக்கர மிட்டிரு
மேலைத் துவாரத்தின் மேல்மனம் வைத்திரு
வேலொத்த கண்ணை வெளியில் விழித்திரு
காலத்தை வெல்லுங் கருத்திது தானே. 583

What Kundalini Yoga is

Close the Muladhara orifice below
Centre your thought on Sahasrara orifice above
And on that meditate;
Fix your lance-like vision on that Space Vast;
Thus practising Yoga,
You shall vanquish Time.

எருவிடும் வாசற் கிருவிரன் மேலே
கருவிடும் வாசற் கிருவிரற் கீழே
உருவிட் ந் சோதியை உள்கவல் லார்க்குக்
கருவிடுஞ் சோதி கலந்துநின் றானே. 584

Kundalini Yoga Ends Birth

Two finger length above the anus
Two finger length below the sex organ,
Lies the Kundalini Fire
If you can meditate on the light
That burns there,
You shall be one with Lord,
Who all births ends.

ஒருக்கால் உபாதியை ஒண்சோதி தன்னைப்
பிரித்துணர் வந்த உபாதிப் பிரிவைக்
கரைத்துணர் வுன்னல் கரைதல்உள் நோக்கல்
பிரத்தியா காரப் பெருமைய தாமே. 585

Pratyahara

Separate the Maya from the Lord and
Separating the ego from the Maya, dissolve it away
Then arise awareness, contemplation and loss of ego
Which constitute the glory of Pratyahara.

புறப்பட்ட வாயுப் புகவிடா வண்ணந்
திறப்பட்டு நிச்சயஞ் சேர்ந்துடன் நின்றால்
உறப்பட்டு நின்றது உள்ளமும் அங்கே
புறப்பட்டுப் போகான் பெருந்தகை யானே. 586

Pranayama Helps Pratyahara

If breath that is exhaled
Is contained within
The thoughts too are contained there
And the Lord shall leave you not.

Pranayama aids the practice of pratyahara. If breath that is exhaled is contained within, the thoughts too are contained within. Then the Lord leaves you not.

குறிப்பினின் உள்ளே குவலயந் தோன்றும்
வெறுப்பிருள் நீங்கி விகிர்தனை நாடுஞ்
சிறப்புறு சிந்தையைச் சிக்கென் றுணரில்
அறிப்புறு காட்சி அமரரு மாமே. 587

What Pratyahara Can Lead to

In the act of Pratyahara
All the world will be visioned;
Be rid of the despicable darkness
And seek the Lord,
If your thoughts be centred firm
You shall Divine Light see
And immortal thereafter be.

7. தாரணை

DHARANA

கோணா மனத்தைக் குறிக்கொண்டு கீழ்க்கட்டி
வீணாத்தண் டூடே வெளியுறத் தானோக்கிக்
காணாக்கண் கேளாச் செவியென் றிருப்பார்க்கு
வாணாள் அடைக்கும் வழியது வாமே. 588

How to Practise Dharana

Control the mind from getting diverted towards the senses
Concentrate on the Chidakasa within the spinal column,
The eyes must not see nor the ears hear,
This is the way to life eternal.

மலையார் சிரத்திடை வானீர் அருவி
நிலையாரப் பாயும் நெடுநாடி யூடே
சிலையார் பொதுவில் திருநட மாடுந்
தொலையாத ஆனந்தச் சோதிகண் டேனே. 589

Lord Dances in Sahasrara

From the peaks of Cranium ranges
The heavenly waterfall
Unceasing cascades
Coursing prana through the spinal channel;
There on the stony arena (of Mount Meru within)
The Lord performs His timeless dance;
That unending Bliss Light,
I witnessed.

மேலை நிலத்தினாள் வேதகப் பெண்பிள்ளை
மூல நிலத்தில் எழுகின்ற மூர்த்தியை
ஏல எழுப்பி இவளுடன் சந்திக்கப்
பாலனும் ஆவான் பராநந்தி ஆணையே. 590

Siva ascends to Sakti

She is the Damsel of the Vedas;
She belongs to the astral land of Cranium;
He is the bridal lord;
He sleeps in the land of Muladhara;
Gently rouse Him,
And make Him meet Her,
You shall then be forever young
Upon lordly Nandi I avow, .
This truth forever and ever.

கடைவாச லைக்கட்டிக் காலை எழுப்பி
இடைவாசல் நோக்கி இனிதுள் இருத்தி
மடைவாயிற் கொக்குப்போல் வந்தித் திருப்பார்க்
குடையாமல் ஊழி இருக்கலு மாமே. 591

Practice of Kundalini Yoga

Bind the Muladhara
Raise the Prana breath upward
Through the spinal hollow course it
And within in aptness retain,
And like a stork at stream s head
Sit calm
In singleness of thought;
Well may you live forever and ever.

கலந்த உயிருடன் காலம் அறியில்
கலந்த உயிரது காலின் நெருக்கங்
கலந்த உயிரது காலது கட்டிற்
கலந்த உயிருடல் காலமும் நிற்குமே. 592

Practise Breath Control in Proper Time-Measure

When Pranayama is in proper time-measure practised
Breath retention will appropriate with Prana stand;
He who trains breath that is Prana,
With him shall Time and Life inseparate remain.

வாய்திற வாதார் மனத்திலோர் மாடுண்டு
வாய்திறப் பாரே வளியிட்டுப் பாய்ச்சுவர்
வாய்திற வாதார் மதியிட்டு மூட்டுவர்
கோய்திற வாவிடிற் கோழையுமாமே. 593

Practise Breath Control in Silence

A treasure there is,
In the thoughts of those
Who silence observe;
They who open their mouth wide
Drive it away windward;
But they who are in silence wrapped
Drive it to the Lunar Peak;
There with its horns it knocks;
And if the Gates of the Cave do not open,
It turns tail in fear.

வாழலு மாம்பல காலும் மனத்திடைப்
போழ்கின்ற வாயு புறம்படாப் பாய்ச்சுறில்
ஏழுசா லேகம் இரண்டு பெருவாய்தல்
பாழி பெரியதோர் பள்ளி அறையே. 594

Longevity Gained by Breath Control

If breath that is forked in and out,
Is on mind directed and centred,
Well may you sleep
In the spacious bed chamber,
Of the Body Cave
That has doors two and windows seven
And long, long may you live there too

நிரம்பிய ஈரைந்தில் ஐந்திவை போனால்
இரங்கி விழித்திருந் தென்செய்வை பேதாய்

வரம்பினைக் கோலி வழிசெய்கு வார்க்குக்
குரங்கினைக் கொட்டை பொதியலு மாமே. 595

Mind Control Through Breath Control

If of the ten Vayus that fill the body
Five by exhalation leave,
What avails you fool!
What though you wake and pray?
They who control breath in measure ordained,
Will sure imprison mind-monkey
Within the body-fortress.

If out of the ten vayus that fill the body, five leave by exhalation, nothing is achieved by waking and praying. Only breath control can imprison the mind-monkey.

முன்னம் வந்தனர் எல்லாம் முடிந்தனர்
பின்னை வந்தவர்க் கென்ன பிரமாணம்
முன்னுறு கோடி உறுகதி பேசிடில்
என்ன மாயம் இடிகரை நிற்குமே. 596

Make the Body Immortal

All those who came afore
Have met their final end;
What guarantee is there of any other fate,
For those who come after?
What then there to speak of the millions
And their life to be?
What delusion this!
Will the sandy bank ever hold firm?

Here, the core of yoga theory of life and death is explained.

அரித்த வுடலைஐம் பூதத்தில் வைத்துப்
பொருத்தஐம் பூதஞ்சத் தாதியிற் போந்து
தெரித்த மனாதிசத் தாதியிற் செல்லத்
தரித்தது தாரணை தற்பரத் தோடே. 597

Dharana is Involution

To contain body's harassing senses five
In elements five,
To contain elements five
In organs cognitive internal,
To contain cognitive organs internal
In their Tanmatras
To contain the Tanmatras
In the Being Uncreated
That, verily, is Dharana
In stages practised.

8. தியானம்

DHYANA

வருமாதி யீரெட்டுள் வந்த தியானம்
பொருவாத புந்தி புலன்போக மேவல்
உருவாய சத்தி பரத்தியான முன்னுங்
குருவார் சிவத்தியானம் யோகத்தின் கூறே. 598

Dhyana is of Two Kinds

The ten—
The five elements and the five senses
Being contained, one by the other,
The internal organ Buddhi
In turn contains the senses;
Thus is Dhyana born;
The Para Dhyana first
That is on Sakti centred,
And Siva Dhyana next
That is by Guru blessed,
These two are the Ways of Dhyana Yoga.

Dhyana is born out of perfection of dharana; that is, when the five elements, the five senses, and the internal organs are contained, dhyana is born. Dhyana is of two kinds: Parai dhyana and Siva dhyana. Parai dhyana is centered on Sakti, Siva dhyana on Siva. Both the ways of dhyana yoga should be initiated by the Guru.

1) Dhyana has been defined to be the state of the antakharana (mind) of those whose chaitanya holds to and is occupied by the thought, on one object, having first cast away the thought of all other objects. Through dhyana is acquired the quality of mental realization (pratyaksha). It is of two kinds: saguna or meditation on a form (murti) and nirguna, in which the Self is its own object Vide "The Serpent Power" by Sir John Woodroffe, pp.193-194.

கண்ணாக்கு மூக்குச் செவிஞானக் கூட்டத்துட்
பண்ணாக்கி நின்ற பழம்பொருள் ஒன்றுண்(டு)
அண்ணாக்கின் உள்ளே அகண்ட ஒளிகாட்டிப்
புண்ணாக்கி நம்மைப் பிழைப்பித்த வாறே. 599

In Dhyana the Divine Light Appears

Through eye, tongue, nose and ear
And the organ Intellect
There is an Ancient One that pervades as Nada,
Inside the palatal cavity
He shows the Cosmic Light;
He gave the fleshy body,
That we redeemed be.

In dhyana, the cosmic light flashes. Gaze on it to heart's content, mingle with it, get into the heavenly stream of the vast Space, and envision the Uncreated Being.

ஒண்ணா நயனத்தில் உற்ற ஒளிதன்னைக்
கண்ணாரப் பார்த்துக் கலந்தங் கிருந்திடில்
விண்ணாறு வந்து வெளிகண் டிடவோடிப்
பண்ணாமல் நின்றது பார்க்கலு மாமே. 600

In Dhyana Can Be Seen the Jnana Form of Siva

In the undistracted gaze
Appears the Light
Gaze and gaze to heart's content
And mingle one with it;
The Heavenly Stream will then surge
To the spaces infinite of Void Space;
Then may the Uncreated Being witnessed be.

ஒருபொழு துன்னார் உடலோ டுயிரை
ஒருபொழு துன்னார் உயிருட் சிவனை
ஒருபொழு துன்னார் சிவனுறை சிந்தையை
ஒருபொழு துன்னார் சந்திரப் பூவே. 601

Alas! They Perform not Dhyana

Even for once they meditate not
On the mystery of Jiva within body;
Even for once they meditate not
On Siva within Jiva;
Even for once they meditate not
On the mind where Siva dwells
Even once they meditate not
On the Lotus within the Lunar Sphere.

மனத்து விளக்கினை மாண்பட ஏற்றிச்
சினத்து விளக்கினைச் செல்ல நெருக்கி
அனைத்து விளக்குந் திரியொக்கத் தூண்ட
மனத்து விளக்கது மாயா விளக்கே. 602

Dhyana Brightens All Lamps Within

Light the Lamp of Mind
And dispel the Darkness of Egoity;
Extinguish the Fire of Wrath
And brighten all lamps within
Thenceforth alike,
The Mind's Lamp is an undying Lamp indeed.

Dhyana is a lamp that lights all the lamps within. It lights the lamp of mind, dispels the darkness of egoity, extinguishes the fire of darkness. Then the main lamp (the mind's lamp) burns undying.

எண்ணா யிரத்தாண்டு யோகம் இருக்கினும்
கண்ணார் அமுதினைக் கண்டறி வாரில்லை
உண்ணாடிக் குள்ளே ஒளியுற நோக்கினால்
கண்ணாடி போலக் கலந்துநின் றானே. 603

Look Within in Dhyana

Well may they practise Yoga eight-thousand year
Still they see not Lord,
Sweet as ambrosia
And dear like the apple of the eye;
But if within you seek Him enlightened
He within you is,
Even as reflection in the mirror.

Dhyana is seeking God within. It is seeing Siva's reflection in the jiva mirror. All practice of yoga is vain without the seeking within.

நாட்டம் இரண்டும் நடுமூக்கில் வைத்திடில்
வாட்டமும் இல்லை மனைக்கும் அழிவில்லை
ஓட்டமும் இல்லை உணர்வில்லை தானில்லை
தேட்டமும் இல்லை சிவனவ னாமே. 604

Fruits of Dhyana

If your eyes twain are
On nasal point fixed,
No sorrows befall you;
Perishes not your body;
Agitation none shall you have;
Feelings none;
Seekings none;
None that is "I";
You and Siva one become.

Therefore let the eyes be fixed on the tip of the nose. Let the roaming breath be retained within; so let the nadis be stilled. Then no more seeking; no fear of rebirth.

நயனம் இரண்டும் நாசிமேல் வைத்திட்
டுயர்வெழா வாயுவை உள்ளே அடக்கித்
துயரற நாடியே தூங்கவல் லார்க்குப்
பயனிது காயம் பயமில்லை தானே. 605

Dhyana Leads to Cessation of Birth

Fixing the gaze on nasal point
Retaining the roaming breath within
They who can thus still the nadis,
Will sure reach the Goal
No fear of birth to be for them.

மணிகடல் யானை வார்குழல் மேகம்
அணிவண்டு தும்பி வளைபேரி கையாழ்
தணிந்தெழு நாதங்கள் தாமிவை பத்தும்
பணிந்தவர்க் கல்லது பார்க்கஒண் ணாதே. 606

Varied Sound Experiences in Dhyana

Bell, sea, elephant, flute, cloud
Bee, dragon-fly, conch, drum, and lute
The subtle sounds of these ten are heard
For them alone
Who have stilled their mind in God.

கடலொடு மேகங் களிறொடும் ஓசை
அடவெழும் வீணை அண்டரண் டத்துச்
சுடர்மன்னு வேணுச் சுரிசங்கின் ஓசை
திடமறி யோகிக்கல் லாற்றெரி யாதே. 607

Other Sound Experiences in Dhyana

The roar of sea, the thundering of cloud,
The trumpeting of elephant, the euphony of lute,
The music of the orbs
That glow in firmament vast,
The melody of the flute; the resonance of conch,
All these
The yogi true alone hears.

ஈசன் இயல்பும் இமையவர் ஈட்டமும்
பாசம் இயங்கும் பரிந்துய ராய்நிற்கும்
ஓசை யதன்மணம் போல விடுவதோர்
ஓசையாம் ஈசன் உணரவல் லார்க்கே. 608

Fruits of God-Realization

Those who realize God,
They alone get qualities godly;
They join the company of the immortals;
Pasa vanishes;
They become immanent in all life
They hear sounds subtlest,
Even as fragrance emanates from a flower.

நாத முடிவிலே நல்லாள் இருப்பது
நாத முடிவிலே நல்யோகம் இருப்பது
நாத முடிவிலே நாட்டம் இருப்பது
நாத முடிவிலே நஞ்சுண்ட கண்டனே. 609

Yoga Leads to Nadanta

Nada's End is Sakti divine
Nada's End is Yoga grand
Nada's End is goal Finale
Nada's End is Lord Seated

உதிக்கின்ற ஆறினும் உள்ளங்கி ஐந்துந்
துதிக்கின்ற தேசுடைத் தூங்கிருள் நீங்கி
அதிக்கின்ற ஐவருள் நாதம் ஒடுங்கக்
கதிக்கொன்றை ஈசன் கழல்சேர லாமே. 610

Involution Into Nada is Final Stage

As Kundalini Fire glows in Adharas six,
The Primordial Anava Darkness flees,
In tameness followed by Indriyas Five;
Who involute in Tanmatras, their substrate;
And they in turn in Nada;
And shall reach Feet of the Lord
That is Refuge of All.

பள்ளி அறையிற் பகலே இருளில்லை
கொள்ளி அறையிற்கொளுந்தாமற் காக்கலாம்
ஒள்ளி தறியிலோ ரோசனை நீளிது
வெள்ளி அறையில் விடிவில்லை தானே 611

The Way to Ascension to Space lies through Meditation

The mystic bed-chamber is day-light eternal
No darkness invades;
There is a way
This body to fire-chamber consigned not be,
The light of this knowledge
Is by meditation prolonged;
In the lunar region
Knows not end of Light ever.

கொண்ட விரதங் குறையாமற் றானொன்றித்
தண்டுடன் ஓடித் தலைப்பட்ட யோகிக்கு
மண்டல மூன்றினும் ஒக்க வளர்ந்தபின்
பிண்டமும் ஊழி பிரியா திருக்குமே. 612

Perfect Meditation Leads to Immortality

Having abated not in the rules of vows,
The Yogi that has to meditate learned,
Coursing Kundalini through spinal column,
And passing Mandalas Three with felicity equal
He in fleshy body forever lives.

அவ்வவர் மண்டல மாம்பரி சொன்றுண்டு
அவ்வவர் மண்டலத் தவ்வவர் தேவாரம்
அவ்வவர் மண்டலம் அவ்வவர்க் கேவரில்
அவ்வவர் மண்டல மாயமற் றோர்க்கே. 613

Meditation Leads Across the Three Spheres

There is a way of reaching the Mandalas Three.
In each is its respective God;
Be you blessed
By the God appropriate
Then each Mandala leads to the other.

இளைக்கின்ற நெஞ்சத் திருட்டறை உள்ளே
முளைக்கின்ற மண்டலம் மூன்றினும் ஒன்றித்
துளைப்பெரும் பாசந் துருவிடு மாகில்
இளைப்பின்றி மார்கழி ஏற்றம தாமே. 614

To Transcend Mandala is to be Exalted

In the dark chamber of the drooping heart
Are the Mandalas Three,
He who becomes one with them
And pierces the sushumna Nadi
Shall know weariness none;

முக்குண மூடற வாயுவை மூலத்தே
சிக்கென மூடித் திரித்துப் பிடித்திட்டுத்
தக்க வலமிடம் நாழிகை சாதிக்க
வைக்கும் உயர்நிலை வானவர் கோனே. 615

Immortality Through Dhyana Yoga

Uprooting the gunas three
He who controls breath in Muladhara
And courses it alternate
Through nadi left and right,
In time measure prescribed
Will be immortal made
By Him that is King of Beings Heavenly.

நடலித்த நாபிக்கு நால்விரன் மேலே
மடலித்த வாணிக் கிருவிரல் உள்ளே
கடலித் திருந்து கருதவல் லார்கள்
சடலத் தலைவனைத் தாமறிந் தாரே. 616

Deep Meditation on Centres Leads to God

Four finger-length above the tremulous Navel-Centre
Is the petalled Heart-Centre;

Two finger length still above is the Throat-Centre;
Those who can meditate on it in sea-like depth
Sure knew Him;
Him the Lord of Body Corporal.

When the yogi shifts his centre of thought from the muladhara to the anahata (heart centre), and from anahata to the vishuddhi (throat centre), then he transcends the 36 tattvas, and becomes united with God.

அறிவாய சத்தென்னு மாறா றகன்று
செறிவான மாயை சிதைத்தரு ளாலே
பிறியாத பேரரு ளாயிடும் பெற்றி
நெறியான அன்பர் நிலையறிந் தாரே. 617

Grace Comes From Dhyana

Transcending Tattvas six and thirty unreal,
Destroying Maya's layers thick,
Transformed into Jnana Pure by Grace
Themselves that Grace inseparable Becoming
They who achieved thus
Were the good souls
That the Way of Dhyana knew.

9. சமாதி

SAMADHI

சமாதி யமாதியிற் றான்செல்லக் கூடும்
சமாதி யமாதியிற் றானெட்டுச் சித்தி
சமாதி யமாதியில் தங்கினோர்க் கன்றே
சமாதி யமாதி தலைப்படுந் தானே. 618

Samadhi is the Final Goal of Ashtanga Yoga

Samadhi is end of yama and the rest
Samadhi is consummation of Siddhis eight
Who persevere in the path from yama to the end
Will alone the end Samadhi attain.

Samadhi is the final stage in the eight-limbed yoga commencing from yama through niyama, asana, pranayama, pratyahara, dharana, and dhyana. When it is attained, the miraculous powers (siddhis) come to the yogi of themselves.

விந்துவும் நாதமும் மேருவில் ஓங்கிடிற்
சந்தியி லான சமாதியிற் கூடிடும்
அந்த மிலாத அறிவின் அரும்பொருள்
சுந்தரச் சோதியுந் தோன்றிடுந் தானே. 619

Vision of Light Resplendent in Samadhi

When in the Meru Peak of Sahasrara
Bindu and Nada flourish
In their union will Samadhi be;
And the Light Resplendent of Endless Jnana
Will then visioned be!

Samadhi is to reach the Meru peak of sahasrara, where bindu and nada flourish, and to unite in them. It is to vision the light resplendent of endless jnana.

மன்மனம் எங்குண்டு வாயுவும் அங்குண்டு
மன்மனம் எங்கில்லை வாயுவும் அங்கில்லை
மன்மனத் துள்ளே மகிழ்ந்திருப் பார்க்கு
மன்மனத் துள்ளே மனோலய மாமே. 620

In Samadhi Mano-Laya is Reached

Where there is mind absorption,
There life's breath is;
Where there is no mind absorption,
There life none is;
They who, in rapture, sit in mind absorption
Are verily fixed in Yoga of absorption.

Through samadhi, manolaya is attained; all things are absorbed in unitive consciousness.

விண்டலர் கூபமும் விஞ்சத் தடவியுங்
கண்டுணர் வாகக் கருதி யிருப்பர்கள்
செண்டு வெளியிற் செழுங்கிரி யத்திடை
கொண்டு குதிரை குசைசெறுத் தாரே. 621

Mystic Vision in Samadhi

They who sit in Samadhi of Pure Consciousness
Vision the Mystic Woods and the Blooming Pond;
They roam in the royal expanse of space
And there at the foot of Fertile Mountain Meru,
They bridled their Horse of Breath to a stop.

மூலநாடி முகட்டல குச்சியுள்
நாலு வாசல் நடுவுள் இருப்பிர்காள்
மேலை வாசல் வெளியுறக் கண்டபின்
காலன் வார்த்தை கனாவிலும் இல்லையே. 622

In Samadhi They Vision the Void

On top of Spinal Column in the Centre
Is built a habitation unique;
Three the compartments it has
Four the doors;
Within these they sit (in Samadhi);
When through the door on top
They vision the space
No more the word Death, aye, not even in dream.

On the top of the central spinal column is a habitat. It has three compartments (spheres of sun, moon and fire) and four doors (the cavities where the three nadis, ida, pingala and sushumna, end and the fourth cavity of brahmarandra, or the final entrance to sahasrara). In samadhi the yogi visions the vast Space through the fourth door.

மண்டலம் ஐந்து வரைகளும் ஈராறு
கொண்டிட நிற்குங் குடிகளும் ஆறெண்மர்
கண்டிட நிற்குங் கருத்து நடுவாக
உண்டு நிலாவிடும் ஓடும் பதத்தையே. 623

Vision Lord's Dance in Samadhi

Five the Mystic Regions,
Eight the Mountain Ranges,
Six the Adharas that hold them;
With thought centred on Him
They well see Him there stand;
Partaking of the Grace of His all-pervading Feet
They shall immortal be.

பூட்டொத்து மெய்யிற் பொறிபட்ட வாயுவைத்
தேட்டற்ற வந்நிலஞ் சேரும் படிவைத்து
நாட்டத்தை மீட்டு நயனத் திருப்பார்க்குத்
தோட்டத்து மாம்பழந் தூங்கலு மாமே. 624

Samadhi Leads to Siva

Within the locked body
Is. trapped the life-breath;
Course it to the Land
That no desire knows;
They who fix their gaze on Goal True
Will reach the Mango Fruit
That in the garden there hangs.

The yogi climbs the mystic mango tree within, and tastes of the fruit that is Siva.

உருவறி யும்பரி சொன்றுண்டு வானோர்
கருவரை பற்றிக் கடைந்தமு துண்டார்
அருவரை யேறி அமுதுண்ண மாட்டார்
திருவரை யாமனந் தீர்ந்தற்ற வாறே. 625

Ambrosia in Samadhi Leads to God

There is a way to vision the Lord,
The Celestial Beings churned
But with the mountain dark,
And partook of ambrosia;
But they climbed not
The heights of the Mystic Mountain
And partook not of ambrosia that there flows,
For, they possess not
The unwavering mind
That soars in Samadhi high.

The celestials churned the oceans with the dark mountain in search of ambrosia. But they did not think of the ambrosia that flows within. Only the yogi in samadhi finds it. In samadhi, with breath halted, the yogi becomes one with God.

நம்பனை யாதியை நான்மறை ஓதியைச்
செம்பொனின் உள்ளே திகழ்கின்ற சோதியை
அன்பினை யாக்கி யருத்தி ஒடுக்கிப்போய்க்
கொம்பேறிக் கும்பிட்டுக் கூட்டமிட் டாரே. 626

In Samadhi Oneness in God is Attained

He is our Own
He is the Primal One
He taught the Vedas Four
He is the light that glows within the purest gold
They adored Him in love
They approached Him all desires devoid
And climbed the Mystic Tree High;
Their breath halted in Samadhi
They with him became One.

மூலத்து மேலது முச்சது ரத்தது
காலத் திசையிற் கலக்கின்ற சந்தினில்
மேலைப் பிறையினில் நெற்றிநேர் நின்ற
கோலத்தின்கோலங்கள் வெவ்வேறு
கொண்டதே. 627

Vision of Mystic Moon in Samadhi

Beyond the Muladhara
Of triple angle shaped
Where Time and Space mingle,
Aloft that Centre,
Opposite the forehead
Hangs the Crescent Moon,
Of myriad shape and peerless beauty.

The yogi visions the mystic moon in the sahasrara centre, where time and space mingle.

கற்பனை் யற்றுக்கனல்வழி யேசென்று
சிற்பனை எல்லாஞ் சிருட்டித்த பேரொளிப்
பொற்பினை நாடிப் புணர்மதி யோடுற்றுத்
தற்பர மாகத் தகுந்தண் சமாதியே. 628

Union With Siva in Samadhi

Bereft of distracting thoughts
Ascending the way of Kundalini
Seeking the Creator that created all,
Him that is Light Beauteous,
Reaching the Mystic Moon in union
He becomes one with the Being Uncreated
—That, in sooth, is Samadhi's tranquillity.

தலைப்பட் டிருந்திடத் தத்துவங் கூடும்
வலைப்பட் டிருந்திடும் மாதுநல் லாளுங்
குலைப்பட் டிருந்திடுங் கோபம் அகலுந்
துலைப்பட் டிருந்திடுங் தூங்கவல் லார்க்கே. 629

Tranquillity in Samadhi

Samadhi attained, Siva is attained;
Sakti too will be caught in its fold;
Distracting passions will be dispelled;
In equanimity perfect,
Like unto a balance

Will be the mind
All this, for those who in Samadhi sleep.

In the tranquillity that is attained in samadhi all distracting passions are dispelled. The mind attains perfect equanimity, and the Grace of Sakti flows unhindered.

சோதித் தனிச்சுட ராய்நின்ற தேவனும்
ஆதியும் உள்நின்ற சீவனு மாகுமால்
ஆதிப் பிரமன் பெருங்கடல் வண்ணனும்
ஆதி அடிபணிந் தன்புறு வாரே. 630

Samadhi Leads to Worship by Gods

He stood as the Peerless Pillar of Light;
When Jiva in Samadhi merges in Him,
Brahma that creates
And Vishnu of the ocean-hue,
Both stand adoring him.

He who attains samadhi, merging in Siva, becomes the peerless Pillar of Light. Even Brahmā and Vishnu worship him.

சமாதிசெய் வார்க்குத் தகும்பல யோகஞ்
சமாதிகள் வேண்டாம் இறையுட னேகிற்
சமாதிதா னில்லை தானவ னாகிற்
சமாதியில் எட்டெட்டுச் சித்தியும் எய்துமே. 631

Samadhi Transcends Siddhis

To those who are in Samadhi
Many the Yogas that come of themselves
And the Siddhis eight that come unsought;
But, Samadhi none is for those who walk with God
Samadhi none is for those who become one in God.

The yogi, who attains samadhi, does not seek the eight siddhis. He transcends them. He walks with God. He becomes one in God.

10. அட்டாங்கயோகப் பேறு
FRUITS OF EIGHT-LIMBED YOGA

இயமம்

போதுகந் தேறும் புரிசடை யானடி
யாதுகந் தாரம ராபதிக் கேசெல்வர்
ஏதுகந் தானிவன் என்றருள் செய்திடு
மாதுகந் தாடிடு மால்விடை யோனே. 632

Lord's Devotees Reach Abode of Gods

They who seek Lord
Of the matted locks bedecked with flowers
Will sure reach the Abode of Gods;
"What this devotee of mine seeks,
That I grant"
Thus blesses the Lord
That mounts the Bull
And dances to His Consort's delight.

The fruit of yama is reaching the abode of the Gods — Devaloka.

நியமம்

பற்றிப் பதத்தன்பு வைத்துப் பரன்புகழ்
கற்றிருந் தாங்கே கருது மவர்கட்கு
முற்றெழுந் தாங்கே முனிவர் எதிர்வரத்
தெற்றுஞ் சிவபதஞ் சேரலு மாமே. 633

Devotees Reach World of Siva

Hold fast unto His Feet,
Adore them with love,
Sing His praise
Study His Sacred lore
Constantly think of Him
You shall reach the World of Siva,
Received in full regalia
By the sacred Rishi concourse.

The fruit of niyama is reaching the world of Siva.

ஆசனம்

வந்தித் தவஞ்செய்து வானவர் கோவாய்த்
திருந்தம ராபதிச் செல்வன் இவனெனத்
தருந்தண் முழவங் குழலும் இயம்ப
இருந்தின்பம் எய்துவர் ஈசன் அருளே. 634

Devotees Will Be Elevated

Infinite is the Lord's Grace
He elevates His devotees unto Indra,
The Lord of Celestials;
And he shall be received,
In pomp and honour
Drums beating and pipes playing,
All glory and bliss upon him raining.

The fruit of asana is the attainment of the status of Indra, the king of devas.

பிராணாயாமம்

செம்பொற் சிவகதி சென்றெய்துங் காலத்துக்
கும்பத் தமரர் குழாம்வந் தெதிர்கொள்ள

எம்பொற் றலைவன் இவனா மெனச்சொல்ல
இன்பக் கலவி இருக்கலு மாமே. 635

Devotee Welcomed by Celestials

When devotee reaches the World of Siva
He shall be received by Celestial throngs,
"Hail! Here comes our Golden Lord"
Thus shall they welcome;
And he in rapturous pleasures shall revel.

He who practises pranayama will be honoured by the celestials in the world of Siva.

பிரத்தியாகாரம்

சேருறு காலந் திசைநின்ற தேவர்கள்
ஆரிவன் என்ன அரனாம் இவனென்ன
ஏருறு தேவர்கள் எல்லாம் எதிர்கொள்ளக்
காருறு கண்டனை மெய்கண்ட வாறே. 636

The Devotee Hailed

When he reaches the World of Siva
The Celestials,
Who in directions eight stand
Ask, "Who is he?"
And Hara says: "He is Mine;"
And the noble Devas foregather and hail him
As well as if they met Siva Himself.

The end of pratyahara is to reach the world of Ṣiva, and to be recognised by the Lord Himself.

தாரணை

நல்வழி நாடி நமன்வழி மாற்றிடுஞ்
சொல்வழி யாளர் சுருங்காப் பெருங்கொடை
இல்வழி யாளர் இமையவர் எண்டிசைப்
பல்வழி எய்தினும் பார்வழி யாகுமே. 637

Even Celestials Have to Follow the Path of Devotees

Seeking the good path
They turn away from Death's path;
They walk the path of Truth
They seek the path of Liberation;
Of limitless bounty they are;
Well may the Celestials
In directions eight roam
They perforce have to come
To this earth's way of devotees,
And there Him seek.

தியானம்

தூங்கவல் லார்க்கும் துணையேழ் புவனமும்
வாங்கவல் லார்க்கும் வலிசெய்து நின்றிடுந்
தேங்கவல் லார்க்கும் திளைக்கும் அமுதமுந்
தாங்கவல் லார்க்குந் தன்னிட மாமே. 638

Devotee's Way is the Seeking of Gods

He is the refuge
Of Vishnu who sleeps on the ocean
Of Brahma who creates worlds seven
Of Rudra who brings dissolution of all life,
Of Devas who revel in bubbling nectar.

In dhyana the yogi reaches all the worlds of Brahma, Vishnu, Rudra and Devas.

சமாதி

காரிய மான உபாதியைத் தான்கடந்
தாரிய காரணம் ஏழுந்தன் பாலுற
ஆரிய காரண மாய தவத்திடைத்
தாரியல் தற்பரஞ் சேர்தல் சமாதியே. 639

In Samadhi Jiva Unites in Uncaused Being

Transcending Jiva's caused limitations
And accepting the Causal Tattvas
Extinguishing the Causal sources themselves,
Thus do tapasvins unite in the Being Uncaused
That, in truth is Samadhi supreme.

In samadhi, the yogi, transcending the limitations of the caused experiences, himself becomes the Causal Tattvas, and ultimately unites in the Uncaused Being.

11. அட்டமா சித்தி

THE EIGHT GREAT SIDDHIS

பணிந்தெண் திசையும் பரமனை நாடித்
துணிந்தெண் திசையுந் தொழுதெம் பிரானை
அணிந்தெண் திசையினும் அட்டமா சித்தி
தணிந்தெண் திசைசென்று தாபித்த வாறே. 640

Perform Siddhis in Meekness

Pray and seek Lord in directions eight
Adore the Lord with constancy in directions eight
Attain Eight Siddhis Great in directions eight
And in meekness perform in directions eight.

Siddhis are supernatural powers which the tantric sadhaka gains through his yoga. They are usually said to be eight in number, and are classified in two categories, "the lower and merely psychic, and the higher the fruits of long periods of fruitful training.'' (Christmas Humphreys in ''A popular Dictionary'' p.182). ''The former are involved in Self; the latter are only available to those in whom the Self is dead'' (ibid). They include clairvoyance, clair-audience, telepathy, recalling one's former lives and those of others. It is forbidden to use these powers for one's personal benefit (ibid). In Saivism, the eight siddhis bear the names, ''anima, laghima, mahima......etc.' An enumeration of these will be found in verse 649-post and in verse 668-post.

பரிசறி வானவர் பண்பன் அடியெனத்
துரிசற நாடியே தூவெளி கண்டேன்
அரிய தெனக்கில்லை அட்டமா சித்தி
பெரிதருள் செய்து பிறப்பறுத் தானே. 641

Nothing Impossible Then

Lord is the Prized Being of Celestials,
I sought His Feet in devotion
All my blemish vanished
And I visioned the Mystic Space
Nothing impossible for me now;
He blessed me with Eight Great Siddhis
And ended my birth to be.

குரவன் அருளிற் குறிவழி மூலன்
பரையின் மணமிகு சங்கட்டம் பார்த்துத்
தெரிதரு சாம்பவி கேசரி சேரப்
பெரிய சிவகதி பேறெட்டாஞ் சித்தியே. 642

Sambhavi and Kechari Mudras for Siddhis

By the grace of Guru I realized,
That if the fire in the Mula is united in the Parakasa
Trouble will ensue you,
So I took up the practice of Sambhavi and Kechari yogas
And attained the eight siddhis and Siva's abode.

''Khechari Mudra'' is the name of Yogic posture in Tantra, which bestows spiritual attainment and enables one to overcome disease and death'' (p.400 of N.N. Bhattacharya's ''History of the Tantric Religion''). The Sambhavi Mudra is related to Sambhavi diksha which is ''a form of higher initiation which is conducted by the mere touch or glance or will of the guru. It is connected with the secret cult of Kamesvari'' (N.N. Bhattacharya, ibid, p.467).

காயாதி பூதங் கலைகால மாயையில்
ஆயா தகல அறிவொன் றனாதியே
ஓயாப் பதியதன் உண்மையைக் கூடினால்
வீயாப் பரகாயம் மேவலு மாமே. 643

Power of Transmigration

The Elements, Kalas, Time and Maya
Escape unentangled in them,
That is but Wisdom;
And embrace fast the Truth of the Lord
That Uncreated and Unending One;
Then can you transmigrate
Into mortal coils of beings other.

This is another one of Siddhi powers (Tantric) through which one can leave one's own body and enter into that of another. Traditionally Mular is said to have done this (See Introduction). The great Sankaracarya is also said to have adopted this, during the course of a debate with Vacaspati Misra.

இருபதி னாயிரத் தெண்ணூறு பேதம்
மருவிய கன்ம மாமந்த யோகந்
தருமிவை காய உழைப்பாகுந் தானே
அருமிகு நான்காய் அடங்குமா சித்திக்கே. 644

Karma Yoga Practices are Inferior to Eight Siddhis

Karma yoga is several, several in number.
Twenty thousand eight hundred kinds they count;
And all they can give is but physical work,
Inferior are they to the Eight Siddhis Great.

In the course of the practice of the eight-limbed yoga, eight siddhis or miraculous powers appear. The siddhis are far superior to what results from the numerous karmayoga practices.

Mular considers Karma Yoga, which is not a yoga in the usual sense of the term, but which is preached as such in the Bhagavad Gita, as inferior to Tantric (Kundalini Yoga).

மதிதனில் ஈராறாய் மன்னுங் கலையின்
உதய மதுநா லொழியவோ ரெட்டுப்
பதியும்ஈ ராறாண்டு பற்றறப் பார்க்கில்
திதமான ஈராறு சித்திக ளாமே. 645

Twelve Years for Eight Siddhis

On the Moon's nadi to the left (Idakala)
The breath of Prana measures units twelve;
Of this, exhale four;
If the eight saved is within retained,
And that for twelve years continuous practised,
Then shall Siddhis Eight ever abide.

நாடும் பிணியாகு நஞ்சனஞ் சூழ்ந்தக்கால்
நீடுங் கலைகல்வி நீள்மேதை கூர்ஞானம்
பீடொன்றி னால்வாயாச் சித்திபே தத்தின்
நீடுங் துரங்கேட்டல் நீண்முடி வீராறே. 646

Subtle Sounds Signifying Siddhis

Aboundig in wealth of men around,
You but pave the way for birth again;
Nor can Siddhi be attained
By art, learning, genius and wisdom subtle;
At the end of diverse melodies heard in Yoga
For twelve years long
Does it take Siddhi for fullness to attain.

ஏழா னதிற்சண்ட வாயுவின் வேகியாந்
தாழா நடைபல யோசனை சார்ந்திடுஞ்

சூழான ஓரெட்டில் தோன்றா நரைதிரை
தாழான ஒன்பதிற் றான்பர காயமே. 647

Siddhis in the Seventh, Eighth and Ninth Years

In the seventh year of his practice
The Yogi becomes fleet of foot like wind;
His footfall touches not the ground
He divines the thoughts of other beings;
In the eighth year he becomes eternal by young,
For ever bereft of graying hair and wrinkled muscles
In the ninth, he transmigrates into other bodies mortal.

ஈரைந்திற் பூரித்துத் தியான உருத்திரன்
ஏர்வொன்று பன்னொன்றில் ஈராறாம் எண்சித்தி
சீரொன்று மேலேழ் கீழேழ் புவிச்சென்று
ஏரொன்று வியாபியாய் நிற்றல்ஈ ராறே. 648

Siddhis in the Tenth, Eleventh and Twelfth Years

In the tenth year the yogi can expand and contract into space
In the eleventh he can assume the form he meditates on;
In the twelfth all eight siddhis entire he masters;
He then gains the powers to roam the worlds
Seven above and seven below
And take one cosmic form spanning space all.

தானே அணுவுஞ் சகத்துத்தன் நொய்ம்மையும்
மானாக் கனமும் பரகாயத் தேகமுந்
தானாவ தும்பர காயஞ்சேர் தன்மையும்
ஆனாத வுண்மையும் வியாபியு மாம்எட்டே. 649

The Eight Siddhis Enumerated

Himself the atom, himself the cosmos
Himself light, himself heavy
Himself invisible air,
Himself migrating into mortal bodies other,
Himself possessing prowess of the Truthful One
Himself immanent in all
—These eight are the Siddhis Great.

தாங்கிய தன்மையுந் தானணுப் பல்லுயிர்
வாங்கிய காலத்து மற்றோர் குறையில்லை
யாங்கே எழுந்தோம் அவற்றுள் எழுந்துமிக்
கோங்கி வரமுத்தி முந்திய வாறே. 650

Anima Siddhi to Mukti

The Yogi assumes atom-size,
Into lives of several beings enters,
And then returns to his form original;
Either way is he least affected;
From that stage reached in Anima Siddhi,
He rises further
Into Nada chanting Aum,
And thus toward Mukti hastens.

As in 647 and 648, here also the time taken, and the process through which some of the Siddhis are attained, is explained.

முந்திய முந்நூற் றறுபது காலமும
வந்தது நாழிகை வான்முத லாயிடச்
சிந்தை செயச்செய மண்முதல் தேர்ந்தறிந்
துந்தியுள் நின்று வுதித்தெழு மாறே. 651

Light at the Manipura

Days are counted by astral Nazhigai sixty
And year by days three hundred and sixty;
Do meditate incessant through time thus reckoned,
And see the Light in the Manipuraka.

சித்தந் திரிந்து சிவமய மாகியே
முத்தந் தெரிந்துற்ற மோனர் சிவமுத்தர்
சுத்தம் பெறலாம் ஐந்தில் தொடக்கற்றோர்
சித்தம் பரத்தில் திருநடத் தோரே. 652

On the Way to Siva Mukti

They are Siva Muktas
Who turned their thoughts to Siva
Who became Siva-suffused,
Who attained Mukti
By silence that leads to it;
They abandoned the senses five
In search of Divine Purity
Their thoughts centered on the Dance Cosmic.

ஒத்தஇவ் வொன்பது வாயுவும் ஒத்தன
ஒத்தஇவ் வொன்பதின் மிக்க தனஞ்செயன்
ஒத்தஇவ் வொன்பதில் ஒக்க இருந்திட
ஒத்த வுடலும் உயிரும் இருந்ததே. 653

How the Vayus Stand for Yogis

Nine the Vayus in body equal are,
Dananjaya, the tenth superior is,
When the nine in their channels accord
Life and body well accord, too.

Prana, the vital force, takes the help of air and performs ten functions.

The vayus are ten: 1) prana; 2) apana; 3) samana; 4) udana; 5) vyana; 6) naga; 7) kurma; 8) krikara; 9) devadatta; and 10) dhanamjaya.

"The prana moves always in the heart; the apana in the sphere of the anus; the samana in the navel region; the udana in the throat; and the vyana pervades the whole body. These are the five principal vayus, known as 'pranadi.' They belong to the inner body. The 'nagadi' five vayus belong to the outer body.

I now tell the seats of these five external vayus. The naga vayu performs the function of belching; the kurma opens the eyelids; the krikara causes sneezing; the devadatta does yawning; the dhanamjaya pervades the whole gross body, and does not leave it, even after death.

The naga vayu gives rise to consciousness, the kurma causes vision, the krikara, hunger and thirst, the devadatta produces yawning, and by dhanamjaya, sound is produced. This does not leave the body even for a minute." Vide *Gheranda Samhita*, v., 58-68.

Compare *Siva Samhita*, iii, 1-9: "From the different modifications of the prana, it receives various names, all of which cannot be stated here. Prana, apana, samana, udana, vyana, naga, kurma, krikara, devadatta, and dhanamjaya. These are the ten principal names, described by me in this sastra; they perform all the functions, incited thereto by their own actions. Again, out of these ten, the first five are the highest agents in my opinion. The seat of the prana is the heart; of the apana, the anus; of the samana, the region around the navel; of the udana, the throat; while the vyana moves all over the body. The five remaining vayus, the naga, etc. perform the following functions in the body: eructation, opening the eyes, hunger and thirst, gaping or yawning, and lastly hiccuping. He who in this way knows the microcosm of the body, being absolved from all sins, reaches the highest state" — quoted in "Hatha Yoga" by Theos Bernard, p.50n.

Vayus are nerve currents—"Shakti and Shakta" by Sir John Woodroffe, p.686.

These three verses which deal with Vayu (Body-Wind) and physical health are medicinal in nature.

இருக்குந் தனஞ்செயன் ஒன்பது காலில்
இருக்கும் இருநூற் றிருபத்து மூன்றாய்
இருக்கு முடலி லிருந்தில வாகில்
இருக்கும் உடலது வீங்கி வெடித்ததே. 654

Importance of Dhanamjaya

Danamjaya pervades the other nine Vayus
Within the body it permeates
Nadis two hundred and twenty four
If Dhanamjaya functions not thus,
This body will swell and burst.

The Importance of two Vayus is mentioned. This is a part of Ayur or Siddha Veda which was the specialty in the medicine of the Siddhars.

வீங்குங் கழலை சிரங்கொடு குட்டமும்
வீங்கும் வியாதிகள் சோகை பலவதாய்
வீங்கிய வாதமுங் கூனு முடமதாய்
வீங்கு வியாதிகள் கண்ணில் மருவியே. 655

Diseases Appear When Dhanamjaya Does not Function

Boils, itches and leprosy
Anaemia, and like diseases
That swellings show;
Paralysis, hunchback, arthritis
And diseases of eye that bulging show
All appear
When Danamjaya in disorder functions.

கண்ணில் வியாதி யுரோகந் தனஞ்செயன்
கண்ணிலிவ் வாணிகள் காச மவனல்லன்
கண்ணினிற் கூர்மன் கலந்தில னாதலாற்
கண்ணினிற் சோதி கலந்ததும் இல்லையே. 656

Importance of Kurma Vayu for Eye

When Danamjaya malfunctions
The eye gets diseases like cataract and glaucoma
But Kurma is necessary for the eye;
If Kurma permeates not the eye,
It receives light none.

நாடியின் ஓசை நயனம் இருதயந்
தூடியளவுஞ் சுடர்விடு சோதியைத்
தேவருள் ஈசன் திருமால் பிரமனும்
ஓவற நின்றங் குணர்ந்திருந் தாரே. 657

The Three Gods Animate Three Nadis

Through the Nadis that pulsate
In the ear, eye and heart
Animates the one spark of Light Divine
That is God;
The Gods, Rudra, Vishnu, and Brahma
Respective by there seated art.

ஒன்பது வாசல் உடையதோர் பிண்டத்துள்
ஒன்பது நாடி யுடையதோ ரோரிடம்
ஒன்பது நாடி ஒடுங்கவல் லார்கட்(கு)
ஒன்பது காட்சி யிலைபல வாமே. 658

Mukti Vision in Centre of Nine Nadis

Within the fleshy body
That has gates nine,
There is a Centre,
Where the Nadis nine meet;
For them who can contain the Nadis nine
Not nine their vision, but several, several.

ஓங்கிய அங்கிக்கீழ் ஒண்சுழு னைச்செல்ல
வாங்கி இரவி மதிவழி ஓடிடத்
தாங்கி உலகங்கள் ஏழுந் தரித்திட
ஆங்கது சொன்னோம் அருவழி யோர்க்கே. 659

Practice of Kundalini Yoga

Kindle Kundalini Fire
That burns luminous in Muladhara
Send it up through Sushumna
The spinal column Central,
Course into it Prana breath
That runs through Nadis Sun and Moon,
That is the way to reach
The seven mystic worlds in Cranium
To them we tell this
That are wise to learn.

தலைப்பட்ட வாறண்ணல் தையலை நாடி
வலைப்பட்ட பாசத்து வன்பிணை மான்போல்
துலைப்பட்ட நாடியைத் தூவழி செய்தால்
விலைக்குண்ண வைத்ததோர் வித்தது வாமே. 660

Conquest of Bindu Through Nadi

O! Jiva! you seek woman in lust
And Lo! like a fawn are you caught in net;
And you know how to make
Central Nadi the Way Great,
The seed (Bindu) you kept for sale,
May your own be to consume.

ஓடிச்சென் றங்கே ஒருபொருள் கண்டவர்
நாடியி னுள்ளாக நாதம் எழுப்புவர்
தேடிச்சென் றங்கே தேனை முகந்துண்டு
பாடியுள் நின்ற பகைவரைக் கட்டுமே. 661

Raise Nada and Vision Lord Through Nadi

They who raise Nada within the Nadi
In a flash behold the Being One;
There they imbibed the mystical nectar
Vanquishing besieging foes all.

கட்டிட்ட தாமரை ஞாளத்தில் ஒன்பது
மட்டிட்ட கன்னியர் மாதுடன் சேர்ந்தனர்
கட்டிட்டு நின்று களங்கனி யூடுபோய்ப்
பொட்டிட்டு நின்று பூரண மானதே. 662

Reaching Purna Sakti

Up on the stalk of the Mystic Lotus bud
The Nine Virgins sweet as nectar
Joined the Mother Kundalini
One by one they climbed the floors
They reached the victorious top
And there were into Perfection transformed.

Line 2— the nine virgins are stated to be: 1) Vamai; 2) Sreshtai; 3) Raudri; 4) Kali; 5) Kalavikarni; 6) Palavikarni; 7) Palapramadani; 8) Sarva bhuta damani; and 9) Manonmani.

The respective adharas where they are seated are as follows:

Vamai is seated in the muladhara;
Sreshtai in svadhishtana;
Raudri and Kali in manipuraka;
Kalavikarni, Palavikarni, Palapramadani and
Sarva bhuta damani—these four are seated in anahatha;
Manonmani is seated in visuddhi;
In the ajna chakra, Adi Sakti is seated. She is the perfection, the ultimate bestower of Siva yoga. The other saktis confer only partial bliss.

பூரண சத்தி எழுமூன் றறையாக
ஏரணி கன்னியர் எழுநூற்றுஞ் சாக்கினார்
நாரணன் நான்முக னாதிய ஐவர்க்குங்
காரண மாகிக் கலந்து விரிந்ததே. 663

Poorna Sakti as the Supreme Cause Expands

Sakti that is Poorna (Perfection)
Filled Herself into Chambers Three times Seven;
The Nine lovely Virgins became a hundred and five
And as the Cause of Vishnu, Brahma
And the rest of the Gods Five
She expanded pervasive.

Line 1—poorna sakti is Adi or Primal Sakti.
Line 2—She evolves as ichcha, jnana and kriya and fills the seven adharas, including sahasrara.

விரிந்து குவிந்து விளைந்தஇம் மங்கை
கரந்துள் எழுந்து கரந்தங் கிருக்கிற்
பரந்து குவிந்தது பார்முதற் பூதம்
இரைந்தெழு வாயு விடத்தினில் ஒடுங்கே. 664

Poorna Sakti evolves in Nada

The Damsel thus blossomed the expanded;
But if She chooses to hide Herself within,
The elements five and all that expanded out of Her
Will evolves in the reverberant primal sound, Nada.

இடையொடு பிங்கலை என்னும் இரண்டு
மடைபடு வாயுவு மாறியே நிற்குந்
தடையவை யாறேழுந் தண்சுட ருள்ளே
மிடைவளர் மின்கொடி தன்னில் ஒடுங்கே. 665

Merge in Poorna Sakti

The breath in nadis to Left and Right
When in alternation made to course,
And passes beyond the Adhara barrier Six,
There amidst the Cool Flame
Is seated Sakti of the Lightning Form,
In Her merged you be.

ஒடுங்கி ஒருங்கி யுணர்ந்தங் கிருக்கில்
மடங்கி அடங்கிடும் வாயு வதனுள்
மடங்கி மடங்கிடு மன்னுயி ருள்ளே
நடங்கொண்ட கூத்தனும் நாடுகின் றானே. 666

Lord Dances in Jiva

Senses controlled,
Thought in oneness centered.
If you sit in realization thus,
Prana breath that comes
Circling again and again
Will in Jiva gently merge;
Within that Jiva the Dancer dances
And I stand seeking Him there.

நாடியின் உள்ளே நாதத் தொனியுடன்
தேடி யுடன்சென்றத் திருவினைக் கைக்கொண்டு
பாடியுள் நின்ற பகைவரைக் கட்டிட்டு
மாடி ஒருகை மணிவிளக் கானதே. 667

Through Nada Yoga I Reached to Sakti

I coursed the breath upward through Sushumna
And to the accompaniment of Nada's sound(Aum)
I sought;
And lo! there the Damsel was

And I had Her
And seized and bound the enemies shielding Her;
And thus I possessed the Jewelled Lamp of Undying Flame.

அணுமாதி சித்திக ளானவை கூறில்
அணுவில் அணுவின் பெருமையில் நேர்மை
இணுகாத வேகார் பரகாய மேவல்
அணுவத் தனையெங்குந் தானாக
லென்றெட்டே 668

The Eight Siddhis Enumerated

To become tiny as the atom within atom (Anima)
To become big in unshakeable proportions (Mahima)
To become light as vapour in levitation (Laghima)
To enter into other bodies in transmigration (Prapti)
To be in all things, omni-pervasive (Prakamya)
To be lord of all creation in omnipotence (Isatvam)
To be everywhere in omnipresence (Vasitvam)
—These eight are the Siddhis Great.

These eight siddhis are: 1) anima; 2) laghima; 3) mahima; 4) prapti; 5) garima; 6) prakamyam; 7) isatvam; and 8) vasitvam

Some authorities on the subject mention another siddhi known as kamavasayitham in place of garima. Tirumular calls this kamaru tattva. Although the subtitle, Garima, finds a place in the Tamil text — strictly as a subtitle — there is no description of it. Actually the mantra under it relates to prapti. The subtitle, Garima, therefore, seems to be a later extrapolation by some scholars. Garima can be included in mahima.

எட்டா கியசித்தி யோரெட்டி யோகத்தாற்
கிட்டாப் பிராணனே செய்தாற் கிடைத்திடும்
ஒட்டா நடுநாடி மூலத்த னல்பானு
விட்டான் மதியுண்ண வும்வரு மேலதே. 669

Beyond the Eight Siddhis in the Moon's Nectar

By eight-limbed yoga are Siddhis eight attained
When breath is in accord controlled;
When Kundalini fire is through the Central Nadi
Coursed up,
And the Sun's mandala passed
Beyond that is the Moon's
Whence flows the ambrosia that may swill be.

சித்திக ளெட்டன்றிச்சேரெட்டி யோகத்தாற்
புத்திக ளானவை எல்லாம் புலப்படுஞ்
சித்திகள் எண்சித்தி தானாந் திரிபுரை
சத்தி அருள்தரத் தானுள வாகுமே. 670

Siddhis Lead to Mukti Only by Sakti's Grace

By eight-limbed yoga way
Not only will Siddhis eight be
And the Goal behind the Siddhis too;
With effortless ease will they all be
If but Tripura Sakti Her Grace grants.

அணிமா

எட்டிவை தன்னோ டெழிற்பரங் கைகூடப்
பட்டவர் சித்தர் பரலோகஞ் சேர்தலால்
இட்டம துள்ளே இறுக்கல் பரகாட்சி
எட்டு வரப்பு மிடந்தானின் றெட்டுமே. 671

Beyond Siddhis is True Goal

They are Siddhas
Who together with Siddhis eight
Attain the Divine;
They reach Para Loka
And within them vision the Dear Lord
Then they reach Him true,
Rising beyond the boundaries eight.

மந்தர மேறு மதிபானு வைமாற்றிக்
கந்தாய்க் குழியிற் கசடற வல்லார்க்குத்
தந்தின்றி நற்கா மியலோகஞ் சார்வாகும்
அந்த வுலகம் அணிமாதி யாமே. 672

Siddhis Lead to Kamiya Loka

They who can alternate the course of breath Left and Right,
And send it upward through Spinal Cavity unerring to
Mount Meru at top
To them, Kamiya Loka will of itself come;
The world that is reached by Anima and the rest of
Siddhis Eight.

முடிந்திட்டு வைத்து முயங்கிலோ ராண்டில்
அணிந்த அணிமாகை தானாம் இவனுந்
தணிந்தவப் பஞ்சினுந் தானொய்ய தாகி
மெலிந்தங் கிருந்திடும் வெல்லவொண் ணாதே. 673

Anima

If the yogi succeeds in preventing the nector
Flowing from the sphere of the moon from
Entering the Solar sphere and preserves for a year,
He Will attain Anima Siddhi:
Lighter than flimsiest cotton wool will he be
Invincible too will he be.

லகிமா

ஆகின்ற வத்தனி நாயகி தன்னுடன்
போகின்ற தத்துவம் எங்கும் புகல தாய்ச்
சாகின்ற காலங்கள் தன்வழி நின்றிடின்
மாய்கின்ற தையாண்டின் மாலகு வாகுமே. 674

Laghima

If the yogi meditates on Thani Nayaki (Adi Sakti)
Till the Tattvas associated with Her subside
And continues his meditation for five years,
He attains the Siddhi that is Laghima;

The power to penetrate anywhere at will.

Laghima— The traditional interpretations are: 1) "The power of levitation;" 2) "The power to render the body light at will." This achievement is the mastery over the element 'air', the plane of 'buddhi' or spiritual discrimination. The soul, by rising up into the air, obtains "birds-eye-view" of the lower planes. — "The Book Of Signs" by G.H. Mees, Vol/I., p.200

After attaining anima siddhi, the yogi should persevere for five years to attain the laghima siddhi. This is the power to render the body light at will. It is the power of levitation. It is the mastery over element 'air' The yogi will glow with divine light suffusing a radiance that is milk-white. In laghima the yogi visions the Melliyal Sakti (Sakti of Tender Form)

மாலகு வாகிய மாயனைக் கண்டபின்
தானொளி யாகித் தழைத்தங் கிருந்திடும்
பாலொளி யாகிப் பரந்தெங்கு நின்றது
மேலொளி யாகிய மெய்ப்பொருள் காணுமே. 675

Vision in Laghima

When the yogi attains Laghima Siddhi,
He will glow with divine light;
With that glow suffusing milk white radiance
He will vision the heavenly glow
That truth is.

மகிமா

மெய்ப்பொருள் சொல்லிய மெல்லிய லாளுடன்
தற்பொரு ளாகிய தத்துவங் கூடிடக்
கைப்பொரு ளாகக் கலந்திடு மோராண்டின்
மைப்பொரு ளாகு மகிமாவ தாகுமே. 676

Mahima

A year after attaining Laghima
When Tattvas take their refuge in Sakti of Form
Tender,
Will Mahima Siddhi be;
As plain as his palm
It shall be for the yogi to see.

Mahima — The traditional interpretations are: 1) "The power to expand one's consciousness to the largest atom or form;" 2) "Power, might, glory." It is the power of 'greatness," referring to the element, 'fire', the mental plane. It is the mastery over thought, over the lower mind, over the creative urges of that mind. The attainment of this mastery truly implies "greatness." Height is the dimension which symbolises this plane. It also requires greatness to overcome the adversaries on this plane, which in myths and fairy tales take the form of giants. — Vide G.H. Mees op. cit.

A year after attaining laghima, the yogi attains mahima siddhi. It is the power of becoming great. It is the mastery over the element 'fire'. It is the power to expand one's consciousness to the largest atom or form. The yogi conquers time. It stops for him. The past merges into space. Of the future he becomes the Lord. His breath is transformed into light. From him emanates jnana, and he visions Tattvanayaki (Sakti of Tattvas).

ஆகின்ற காலொளி யாவது கண்டபின்
போகின்ற காலங்கள் போவது மில்லையாம்
மேனின்ற காலம் வெளியுற நின்றன
தானின்ற காலங்கள் தன்வழி யாகுமே. 677

Time Transcended in Mahima

Having seen breath transformed into light
No more does Time move; it stops;
While the Past merged into space
Of the Future He becomes the Lord.

தன்வழி யாகத் தழைத்திடு ஞானமுந்
தன்வழி யாகத் தழைத்திடும் வையகந்
தன்வழி யாகத் தழைத்த பொருளெல்லாந்
தன்வழி தன்னரு ளாகிநின் றானே. 678

Finite Attainments Through Mahima Siddhi

Through him all Jnana grows
Through him all world flourishes
Through him all things prosper
Himself in the Grace of Lord stands.

பிராப்தி

நின்றன தத்துவ நாயகி தன்னுடன்
கண்டன பூதப் படையவை யெல்லாங்
கொண்டவை யோராண்டு கூட இருந்திடில்
விண்டது வேநல்ல பிராத்தி யதாகுமே. 679

Prapti in a Year After Visioning Sakti

He who thus stood in Mahima
Visions the Mother of Tattvas (Tattva Nayaki)
And the Celestial Bhutas,
If the yogi thus perseveres continuously for a year
Then he attains Prapti divine.

Prapti — The traditional interpretations are: 1) "The power to give indefinite extension to the subtle body or its members;" 2) "The power to obtain any desired objective anywhere;" 3) "The connection of a being with his organs as their presiding deity known as attainment;" 4) "Arrival at the goal, deliverance, discovery, good fortune, joyful meaning..." This particular achievement refers to mastery or rulership of the earth-sphere. — Vide G.H. Mees, op.cit.

Mantra 679 — 681

If the yogi retains this vision for a year, he attains the prapti siddhi. It is the power to obtain all desired objects, and yet not to desire anything in particular. In prapti, the siddha sees the vast cosmos unfolding like a flower. While the past merges into space, the future forever stops. There is no coming, no going, no ageing, no death, and Parasakti is visioned in prapti.

கரிமா

ஆகின்ற மின்னொளி யாவது கண்டபின்
பாகின்ற பூவிற் பரப்பவை காணலா
மேகின்ற காலம்வெளியுற நின்றது
போகின்ற காலங்கள் போவது மில்லையே. 680

Time Stops in Prapti

Having visioned the dazzling Light of Sakti,
The Siddha perceives the Cosmos vast,
That unto a flower unfolds,
The past merged into Space
And the future Time for ever stops.

போவதொன் றில்லை வருவது தானில்லை
சாவதொன் றில்லை தழைப்பது தானில்லை
தாமத மில்லை தமரகத் தின்னொளி
யாவது மில்லை யறிந்துகொள் வார்க்கே. 681

Experiences in Prapti

No going; No coming;
No death; No aging
No delay in seeing Light of Breath (Nada)
Nothing desired in particular,
Thus it is with Siddhas
Who attained this Siddhi.

அறிந்த பராசத்தி யுள்ளே அமரில்
பறிந்தது பூதப் படையவை யெல்லாங்
குவிந்தவை யோராண்டு கூட இருக்கில்
விரிந்தது பரகாய மேவலு மாமே. 682

Prakamya a Year After Prapti

When Prapti is attained
Parasakti resides palpably within;
And all Tattvas flee
When he is for a year thus,
He attains the power to transmigrate into alien bodies.

Mantras 682 & 683

A year after attaining prapti siddhi, prakamyam is reached. Prakamyam is the power to transmigrate into another body. It is the mastery over the element water. Here the yogi is suffused with the light of nada, and visions the Sadasiva Sakti with her army of bhutas.

பிராகாமியம்

ஆன விளக்கொளி யாவ தறிகிலர்
மூல விளக்கொளி முன்னே யுடையவர்
கான விளக்கொளி கண்டுகொள் வார்கட்கு
மேலை விளக்கொளி வீடெளி தாநின்றே. 683

Salvation Easy After Prakamya

They know not how the Being within
Becomes the Light Radiant;
That Light is already within in Muladhara;
With it they can see the Light of Siva above;
Them who thus seek
The Light Above leads to Liberation effortless.

---

1) Prakamya — The traditional interpretations are: 1) "The capacity to derive enjoyment from everything heard or seen;" 2) "The power to exercise an irresistible will upon the minds of others;" 3) "The power to obtain more than one expects;" 4) "The power to enter into the body of another;" 5) "The power to maintain a youthful appearance for an unusual length of time." It is the mastery over the element water," the emotional or astral plane → G.H. Mees, op.cit.

ஈசத்துவம்

நின்ற சதாசிவ நாயகி தன்னுடன்
கண்டன பூதப் படையவை எல்லாங்
கொண்டவை யோராண்டு கூடி யிருந்திடிற்
பண்டையவ் வீசன் தத்துவ மாகுமே. 684

Isatva a Year After Prakamya

A year rolls by after the Siddha attains Prakamya
And he perseveres in his adoration
Then he visions SadaSiva Sakti and Her hosts of
And attains Bhutas Isatva.

Mantras 684-686

A year after attaining prakamyam siddhi, isatva siddhi is attained. Isatva consists in the power to control and create. It is the power of mind over maya. He becomes the moon's rays, its cooling softness, acquire moon's kalas, and himself the moon becomes.

ஆகின்ற சந்திரன் தன்னொளி யாயவன்
ஆகின்ற சந்திரன் தட்பமு மாயிடும்
ஆகின்ற சந்திரன் தன்கலை கூடிடில்
ஆகின்ற சந்திரன் தானவ னாமே. 685

In Isatva Yogi Becomes Moon

At that stage,
The Siddha becomes the rays of the moon
He becomes the moon's kalas
Then merging in them he himself the moon becomes.

தானே படைத்திட வல்லவ னாயிடுந்
தானே யளித்திட வல்லவ னாயிடுந்
தானே சங்காரத் தலைவனு மாயிடுந்
தானே யிவனெனுந் தன்மைய னாமே. 686

Powers Isatva Confers

He acquires the power to create
He acquires the power to preserve
He shall himself be Lord of destruction
He and Isa non-separate become.

தன்மைய தாகத் தழைத்த கலையினுள்
பன்மைய தாகப் பரந்தஐம் பூதத்தை
வன்மைய தாக மறித்திடில் ஓராண்டின்
மென்மைய தாகிய மெய்பொருள் காணுமே. 687

After One Year of Isatva Yogi Attains Power to Perceive God in Vasitva

If within the cool kala of the moon
The Siddha contains the elements five

In a year shall he attain
The power rare to perceive the True One.

Mantras 687-689

A year after attaining isatva comes vasitva or the power to perceive the True One. He can become immanent like God in all that comes within his reach. He becomes radiant like the sun. His body gleams golden. His sense organs die; he visions the Narkodi Sakti (Sakti of Glorious Vine).

வசித்துவம்

மெய்ப்பொரு ளாக விளைந்தது வேதெனின்
நற்பொரு ளாகிய நல்ல வசித்துவங்
கைப்பொரு ளாகக் கலந்த உயிர்க்கெல்லாந்
தற்பொரு ளாகிய தன்மைய னாகுமே. *688*

Vasitva Confers Immanence

That power rare to perceive the True One
Is the divine Siddhi that is Vasitva
In beings all that come within his reach
He immanent becomes like God Himself.

Vasitva — The traditional interpretations are: 1) "The power of command and control, resulting from non-attachment to objects; 2) "Self-control;" 3) "Self-restraint and power over the elements." Indeed, it is the power which controls maya, and the achievement of that power, controls and restrains the All contained in the self, and the self contained in the All — G.H. Mees, op. cit.

தன்மைய தாகத் தழைத்த பகலவன்
மென்மைய தாகிய மெய்ப்பொருள் கண்டிடின்
பொன்மைய தாகப் புலன்களும் போயிட
நன்மைய தாகிய நற்கொடி காணுமே. *689*

In Vasitva the Yogi Visions Chit-Sakti

In the days the Siddha stands thus in Vasitva
Radiant as the Sun,
If he attains the rare vision of the True Being,
Golden becomes his body
Dead his sense organs
And he visions the Sakti
That like a tender Vine appears.

நற்கொடி யாகிய நாயகி தன்னுடன்
அக்கொடி யாகம் அறிந்திடில் ஓராண்டு
பொற்கொடி யாகிய புவனங்கள் போய்வருங்
கற்கொடி யாகிய காமுக னாமே. *690*

Kamarutatva (Kamavasayitha)

After attaining Vasitva Siddhi
The Siddha perseveres in the knowledge of Sakti,
And of Siva who Her body shares;
And then a year thereafter
He attains the powers to visit worlds all,
That hang from the golden stalk of the Cosmic Flower;
Sitting inert like a flag of stone
Attains Siddhi Kamarutattva (Kamavasayitva).

Kamaru tattva — The traditional interpretaions are: 1) "Consummation of any and every desire;" 2) "The power of suppressing desire;" 3) "It is the achievement of the fulfilment of the heart's supreme desire, which is liberation from bondage and the salvation from suffering by the annihilation of all desire." It is God-realization. It is the power which subdues the primordial kama or desire, the primal cause of existence... It is nirvana — G.H. Mees, op.cit.

On the other hand, kamavasayitva is defined as attainment of whatever I desire" (*Srimad Bhagavata,* quoted in "Principles of Tantra," edited by Arthur Avalon) — Vide "Lights On Tantra" by M.P. Pandit, p.96. In this account there is no reference to garima as a siddhi.

Also referred to as 'sarva kama siddhi' — in *Bhavanopanisad* of Bhaskararaya, as quoted in "Sri Chakra" by S. Shankaranarayanan, p.82.

Mantras 690-692

A year after attaining vasitva, the siddha attains kamaru tattva or kamavasayitva siddhi. This is the power to visit all the worlds that hang from the golden stalk of the cosmic flower. He receives the power to pervade, like the flower's fragrance, in space. He is transformed into mayasakti, and he visions the light of the Divine Mother. He visits the myriad worlds and then sees the light of Supreme Siva.

காம்ரு தத்துவ மானது வந்தபின்
பூமரு கந்தம் புவனம தாயிடும்
மாமரு வுன்னிடை மெய்த்திடு மானனாய்
நாமரு வும்ஒளி நாயக மானதே. *691*

What Kamarutatva Leads to

Having attained Kamaru Siddhi
You will receive the power to pervade
As unto the flower's fragrance in Space all
Divine Fragrance yours shall be;
Transformed unto Maya Sakti,
You shall be the Lord of Light we adore.

நாயக மாகிய நல்லொளி கண்டபின்
தாயக மாகத் தழைத்தங் கிருந்திடும்
போயக மான புவனங்கள் கண்டபின்
பேயக மாகிய பேரொளி காணுமே. *692*

Visions in Kamarutatva

Having visioned the Divine Light
He abides in it as in mother's home;
The myriad worlds having visited,
He sees the Supreme light of Siva
Who has His home amidst ghosts and ghouls.

பேரொளி யாகிய பெரியஅவ் வேட்டையும்
பாரொளி யாகப் பதைப்பறக் கண்டவன்
தாரொளி யாகத் தரணி முழுதுமாம்
ஓரொளி யாகிய காலொளி காணுமே. *693*

When the Eight Siddhis are Attained

He who has mastered the Siddhis eight high.

Will be the Lord of globe entire,
Gleaming shall be his garland of victory
And His Prana shall turn to peerless light.

When the yogi attains the eight siddhis, he will verily be the lord of the world. He will be its beacon-light. He will sport the gleaming garland of victory. His Prana shall turn into peerless light.

காலோ டுயிருங் கலக்கும் வகைசொல்லிற்
காலது அக்கொடி நாயகி தன்னுடன்
காலது ஐஞ்நூற் றொருபத்து மூன்றையுங்
காலது வேண்டிக் கொண்டஇவ் வாறே. 694

Sakti Pervades Prana After Siddhis are Attained

The Way Prana mingles in Jiva
Is through Sakti of the Tender Vine
Prana pervades the five hundred then the ten.
And then the three nadis
And Sakti pervades Prana entire.

Prana pervades in five hundred-and-odd nadis; then the ten; then the three. When these eight siddhis are attained, Sakti pervades the prana and that prana mingles in jiva.

ஆறது வாகும் அமிர்தத் தலையினுள்
ஆறது ஆயிர முந்நூற் றொடைஞ்சுள
ஆறது வாயிர மாகு மருவழி
ஆறது வாக வளர்ப்ப திரண்டே. 695

Nectar Flows When Prana Pervades Body

Inside the head ambrosia flows like a river
In nadi channels a thousand three hundred and five in number
The adharas are the Way to the thousand petalled Sahasrara;
The twin breaths Idakala and Pingala shows the Way.

Prana breath draws the nectar within the sahasrara. When it pervades the nadis, the nectar flows.

இரண்டினின் மேலே சதாசிவ நாயகி
இரண்டது கால்கொண் டெழுவகை சொல்லில்
இரண்டது ஆயிரம் ஐம்பதோ டொன்றாய்த்
திரண்டது காலம் எடுத்ததும் அஞ்சே. 696

From Ajna Where Sadasiva Nayaki is, Prana Ascends to Sahasrara of Thousand Petalled Lotus

Above the twin-petalled Center
Is the Seat of Sadasiva Sakti;
As breath in double ascends further
There is the Sahasrara of thousand petalled lotus;
And on it are the Letters Fifty and One
That in time became the Letters Five.

The ajna chakra between the eyebrows is the twin-petalled centre. There Sadasiva Sakti is seated. When the twin breaths, idakala and pingala, ascend beyond the ajna chakra, the sahasrara, the thousand-petalled lotus, is reached. On it are inscribed all the Fifty-One Letters. The Fifty-One Letters in time become the Five Letters. (Na Ma Si Va Ya).

அஞ்சுடன் அஞ்சு முகமுள நாயகி
அஞ்சுடன் அஞ்சது வாயுத மாவது
அஞ்சது வன்றி இரண்டது வாயிரம்
அஞ்சது காலம் எடுத்துளும் ஒன்றே. 697

Description of Sadasiva Nayaki

Five are Her awe-inspiring faces;
Ten Her weapons deadly;
Without the five-lettered mantra
No ascension is,
From the twin petalled Centre to the thousand petalled;
The Five Letters in time the One Letter become (Aum).

Mantras 697 & 698

Sadasiva Nayaki, who is seated in the ajna centre, as five awe-inspring faces and holds ten deadly weapons. Without the aid of the Five-Lettered mantra, there is no ascension from the two-petalled ajna centre to the thousand-petalled sahasrara. The Five Letters in time become the one letter, Aum. In the sahasrara is the One Being, Tattva Nayaki. When the twin breaths pass beyond the twin-petalled ajna centre it begins to flow in a single stream through the Sushumna cavity; then is the sahasrara reached.

ஒன்றது வாகிய தத்துவ நாயகி
ஒன்றது கால்கொண் டூர்வகை சொல்லிடில்
ஒன்றது வென்றிகொள் ஆயிரம் ஆயிரம்
ஒன்றது காலம் எடுத்துளும் முன்னே. 698

How to Reach Tattva Nayaki

She is the One Being;
She is the Tattva Nayaki
When breath ascends united through Spinal Cavity
Then will that one breath reach the thousand petalled
Sahasrara; Think of Her,
A thousand year shalt thou live.

Sakta-Tantra is closely linked with Nada or varna concepts, varna referring to letters of the alphabets. (Varna-mala is a garland of letters, said to be worn by Sakti). Sir John Woodroff has explained this concept in his Varna-mala" In this philosophy, the concept of pancakshara or five letters (principal) plays an important part. This 'five-letter mantra' is not the same as "Om Namasivaya" which is the 5-lettered mantra of pure Saivism

Mantras 698 & 699

These also deal with "Sakti-Tantra".

முன்னெழும் அக்கலை நாயகி தன்னுடன்
முன்னுறு வாயு முடிவகை சொல்லிடின்
முன்னுறும் ஐம்பத் தொன்றுடன் அஞ்சுமாய்
முன்னுறு வாயு முடிவகை யாமே. 699

Prana Merges in Kalai

Coursed upwards through Sushumna
Reaches the Kalai Nayaki in Sahasrara;
And there it merges with the letters Fifty and One
And then with the Letters Five
That the final end of Prana is.

The prana that reaches sahasrara meets the kalainayaki, and merges with the Fifty-One Letters; then with the Five Letters. Prana that merges in that sakti remains exalted.

ஆய்வரும் அத்தனி நாயகி தன்னுடன்
ஆய்வரு வாயு அளப்பது சொல்லிடில்
ஆய்வரும் ஐஞ்நூற்று முப்பதொ டொன்பது
மாய்வரு வாயு வளப்புள் ளிருந்ததே. 700

Prana Reaches Tani Nayaki and remains Exalted

The life breath that rose with the Tani Nayaki
Filled the nadis five hundred and thirty nine
(Before it upward coursed)
And remained in Sakti, totally absorbed.

இருநிதி யாகிய எந்தை யிடத்து
இருநிதி வாயு இயங்கு நெறியில்
இருநூற்று முப்பத்து மூன்றுடன் அஞ்சாய்
இருநிதி வாயு இயங்கும் எழுத்தே. 701

Prana Merges in the Five-Letters

When the precious prana reached Siva
It pervaded the nadis two hundred and thirty nine
And in the Letters Five
Where Prana finally merges.

எழுகின்ற சோதியுள் நாயகி தன்பால்
எழுகின்ற வாயு இடமது சொல்லில்
எழுநூற் றிருபத் தொன்பா னதுநாலாய்
எழுந்துடன் அங்கி இருந்ததிவ் வாறே. 702

How Prana Pervaded the Nadis

The Prana that reaches Sakti
Emanating from the four petalled Muladhara
Where Kundalini fire is,
Pervaded the seven hundred and twenty nine
Nadis within.

In all, by the time the prana travels from the four-petalled muladhara to the thousand-petalled sahasrara, it will have pervaded 729 nadis within.

This verse introduces the concept of the general topic known as "Varna Mala" by describing how "Prana" (the vital principle), merges in the Letters Five (to be described in subsequent verses)

ஆறது கால்கொண் டிரதம் விளைத்திடும்
ஏழது கால்கொண் டிரட்டி இறக்கிட
எட்டது கால்கொண் டிடவகை யொத்தபின்
ஒன்பது மாநிலம் ஒத்தது வாயுவே. 703

Samadhi When Prana Reaches the Ninth Centre

When Prana courses through adharas six
Then will nectar be,
Then Prana reaches the Seventh Centre of the Sun
And further onward the Eighth Centre the Moon;
In the Ninth Centre Prana attains Samadhi.

Mantras 703 & 704

Beyond the sahasrara when the prana breath reaches the peaks of the sun and moon, the yogi attains samadhi.

This is a unique contribution of Mular who teaches that Prana after crossing the 6th adhara, then passing the 7th (which is the Sun centre), and then the 8th (the Moon centre) finally attains Samadhi.

சந்திரன் சூரியன் தற்பரன் தாணுவிற்
சந்திரன் தானுந் தலைப்படுந் தன்மையைச்
சந்தியி லேகண்டு தானாஞ் சகமுகத்
துந்திச் சமாதி யுடையொளி யோகியே. 704.

In Samadhi Yogi Visions Light Divine

The Moon and the Sun are in the Uncreated Being
The Yogi that visions the Moon at the mystic junction
Nadis three
Is in Light merged;
He, attains Samadhi,
That had its beginning at the Navel Centre.

அணங்கற்ற மாதல் அருஞ்சன நீவல்
வணங்குற்ற கல்விமா ஞான மிகுத்தல்
சுணங்குற்ற வாயர் சித்திதூரங் கேட்டல்
நுணங்கற் றிரோதல்கால் வேகத்து நுந்தலே. 705.

Conduct of Aspirant For Yoga Samadhi

To give up thoughts of women
To think no more of kith and kin
To be meek in learning
To abound in jnana
To be sparing of speech
To listen to deeds of Siddhi
To sit unruffled
—These the ways of the aspirant of yoga samadhi.

மரணஞ் சரைவிடல் வண்பர காயம்
இரணஞ் சேர்பூமி இறந்தோர்க் களித்தல்
அரணன் திருவுற வாதன்மூ வேழாங்
கரனுறு கேள்வி கணக்கறிந் தோனே. 706

Prowess of Those Who Attain Samadhi

He vanquishes death and age,
He enters into other bodies at will,
He confers paradise to the dead
He assumes form divine of Gods
He becomes learned in the twenty-one branches of
Sivagamic lore

He who has mastered the Science of Prana.

He who attains samadhi vanquishes age and death, acquires the power to transmigrate at will, to confer paradise to the dead; to assume the divine form of God, and is a master of the twenty-one branches of Sivagamic lore.

ஓதம் ஒலிக்கும் உலகை வலம்வந்து
பாதங்கள் நோவ நடந்தும் பயனில்லை
காதலில் அண்ணலைக் காண இனியவர்
நாதன் இருந்த நகரறி வாரே. 707

Seek Lord Within

Vain is it seeking Lord
Wearing away sole of their feet
In pilgrimage to corners four.
Of the seagirt world;
Only those who seek Him in love intense
Shall know the City of Lord.

மூல முதல்வேதா மாலரன் முன்னிற்கக்
கோலிய ஐம்முகன் கூறப் பரவிந்து
சாலப் பரநாதம் விந்துத் தனிநாதம்
பாலித்த சத்தி பரைபரன் பாதமே. 708

Gods in Successive Adharas and Niradharas

Brahma, Vishnu and Rudra
Maheswara, Sadasiva,
Bindu, Nada, Sakti,
Para Bindu and Para Nada
In that ascending order
They all seek
Feet of the Ultimate.

ஆதார யோகத் ததிதே வொடுஞ்சென்று
மீதான தற்பரை மேவும் பரனொடு
மேதாதி யீரெண் கலைசெல்ல மீதொளி
ஓதா அசிந்தமீ தானந்த யோகமே. 709

Unalloyed Bliss Beyond the Adhara Yoga

Worshipping the appropriate God at Centres
Ascend above;
There the cranial region is
Where Sakti and Siva reside
Shedding Sixteen Kalas of Mystic Moon;
Ascend yet beyond
There lies the region of Effulgent-Light;
Yet above it is bliss
Defying speech and thought.

Adhara yoga consists in worshipping the appropriate God at each of the centres, and ascending them one after another. In the sahasrara region eventually to be reached are Sakti and Siva with the 16 kalas in the mystic moon. Ascending still beyond is jnana, the light divine. Yet beyond this is unalloyed bliss, defying speech and thought, and which is reached through niradhara yoga.

Each of the successive adharas (chakras) has its presiding deity — in muladhara, Brahma, in svadhishtana, Vishnu; in manipura, Rudra; in anahata, Mahesvara; in vishuddhi, Sadasiva; in ajna, the apara bindu; in sahasrara, the paranada, Sakti and Siva. Still beyond are the parabindu, the paranada, Parasakti and Parasiva, and finally there is the Space. Thus, in effect, the centres are eleven in number. Only the first six are known as adharas or centres, and piercing them by kundalini yoga and reaching the seventh is known as adhara yoga. When the prana ascends further beyond to the next four centres above the seventh — they are known as 'sthanas'. When prana reaches the Paraparam in the Space this is known as 'dvadasanta' or the 'twelfth end.' Prana's ascension beyond sahasrara to the dvadasanta space; known as niradhara yoga.

By 'Niradhara'', Mular apparently means beyond the ''adharas'' of the body.

Each of the adharas or centers within has a presiding deity:
1. In muladhara is Brahma seated;
2. In svadhishtana is Vishnu;
3. In manipuraka is Rudra;
4. In anahata is Mahesvara;
5. In visuddhi is Sadasiva;
6. In ajna is Bindu (apara);

Coursing the kundalini through these six centres and reaching the apara nada sakti and Siva in sahasrara is adhara yoga.

Beyond are the categories para bindu, para nada, Parasakti, and Parasiva. These categories are the presiding deities of the eighth, ninth, tenth and eleventh sthanas. They are not centres as are met with in the lower adhara yoga.

Yet still beyond is the twelfth sthana where Paraipara is in the Space. That is the 'ultima thule.' It is known as dvadasanta Space' (the twelfth end). Ascension from sahasrara to dvadasanta Space belongs to 'niradhara yoga.' This gives the eternal bliss that defies thought and speech.

மதியமும் ஞாயிறும் வந்துடன் கூடித்
துதிசெய் பவ்ரவர் தொல்வா னவர்கள்
விதியது செய்கின்ற மெய்யடி யார்க்குப்
பதியது காட்டும் பரமன்நின் றானே. 710

Lord Himself Appears Before Yogis

They who practise yoga
Through Nadis breath in one
Flowing Moon and Sun
Become Beings Celestial;
To them who perform it unceasing true
The Lord of Himself reveals.

Mantras 710 & 711

To the yogis, the Lord reveals Himself. They become pervasive, immanent and deathless.

பொட்டெழக் குத்திப் பொறியெழத் தண்டிட்டு
நட்டறி வார்க்கு நமனில்லை தானே.
கட்டவல் லார்கள் கரந்தெங்குந் தானாவர்
மட்டவிழ் தாமரை யுள்ளே மணஞ்செய்து. 711

Immortality for Yogis Who Have Reached the Ultima Thule

They who control breath
Will pervade all unseen;

They who pierce the Mystic Lotus
Sending breath up through spinal column
And taste of its fragrant nectar
Will never know death.

12. கலை நிலை

KALA UNWAVERING

காதல் வழிசெய்த கண்ணுதல் அண்ணலைக்
காதல் வழிசெய்து கண்ணுற நோக்கிடிற்
காதல் வழிசெய்து கங்கை வழிதருங்
காதல் வழிசெய்து காக்கலு மாமே. 712

Yoga Leads to Divine Nectar

The Lord of the Fore-head-eye
That showed the path of Love Divine;
Seek Him in love intense;
The Ganga in cranium will in grace flow;
And in love exceeding, He your saviour will be:

காக்கலு மாகுங் கரணங்கள் நான்கையுங்
காக்கலு மாகுங் கலைபதி னாறையுங்
காக்கலு மாகுங் கலந்தநல் வாயுவுங்
காக்கலு மாகுங் கருத்துற நில்லே. 713

Anchor Thoughts Firm on Lord

Control your four inner organs of cognition,
Control the sixteen kalas,
Control the Prana within
Then your thoughts will be
Firmly rooted in the Lord.

"Ultimate Thule" is "the farthest limit or point possible geographically".

நிலைபெற நின்றது நேர்தரு வாயு
சிலைபெற நின்றது தீபமும் ஒத்துக்
கலைவழி நின்ற கலப்பை அறியில்
அலைவற வாகும் வழியிது வாமே. 714

Way to Steady Kalas

Straight through Sushumna
The Prana stood unwavering
As a steady flame
And unto a still stone;
They who know
How the Lord stood commingled with Kalas
Know the Way True;

It is important in yoga practice that the prana is kept up, in a steady rhythm, unwavering as a still stone. This comes only by anchoring the thought on the Lord. By steadying of the prana, the vision of the Lord who wears the moon that has 16 kalas is obtained.

புடையொன்றி நின்றிடும் பூதப் பிரானை
மடையொன்றி நின்றிட வாய்த்த வழியுஞ்
சடையொன்றி நின்றஅச் சங்கர நாதன்
விடையொன்றி லேறியே வீற்றிருந் தானே. 715

Steady Prana Breath, Sankara Appears

When life breath is upward coursed
Through the single channel Sushumna,
The Lord of Bhuta hordes,
Sankara of matted locks
Appears before you
Mounted on the Sacred Bull.

Kala is a Sakti Tantric term; the nature and evolution of kalas is explained by Sir John Woodroffe in his "Varna-mala" (pp.185 at seq.):

இருக்கின்ற காலங்கள் ஏதும் அறியார்
பெருக்கின்ற காலப் பெருமையை நோக்கி
ஒருக்கின்ற வாயு வொளிப்பெற நிற்கத்
தருக்கொன்றி நின்றிடுஞ் சாதக னாமே. 716

Sadhaka's State in Samadhi

They know not the time that passes in Samadhi
They look forward to the Big Time ahead,
Thus they direct the breath
Through the single channel Sushumna
To the space in cranium
There he stands, all conflicts resolved,
He truly is the Sadhaka.

சாதக மானஅத் தன்மையை நோக்கியே
மாதவ மான வழிபாடு செய்திடும்
போதக மாகப் புகலுறப் பாய்ச்சினால்
வேதக மாக விளைந்து கிடக்குமே. 717

Perform Yoga Penance and Reach Lord

Thus toward that excellent state
Practise yogic penance;
If you succeed in coursing breath
Into the lotus in cranium,
You shall gain the Lord
That remains hidden in Vedas.

கிடந்தது தானே கிளர்பயன் மூன்று
நடந்தது தானேஉள் நாடியுள் நோக்கிப்
படர்ந்தது தானே பங்கய மாகத்
தொடர்ந்தது தானேஅச் சோதியுள் நின்றே. 718

Stages of Prana's Ascending Course

The breath has stages three
As Prana it courses upward

In single stream through spinal nadi;
And then spreads into cranial space
For the lotus there to blossom
And finally merges into the Divine Flame there..

தானே எழுந்தஅத் தத்துவ நாயகி
ஊனே வழிசெய்தெம் உள்ளே யிருந்திடும்
வானோர் உலகீன்ற அம்மை மதித்திடத்
தேனே பருகிச் சிவாலய மாகுமே. 719

Kundalini Yoga Turns the Body into Temple of Siva

The Kundalini Sakti that thus arose
Made her way aloft through the fleshy coil
And yet within me remained;
And She who created the worlds of Devas
Churned the mystic ambrosia within;
Drinking deep of it
This body became Siva's temple.

Mantras 719-721

Kundalini yoga turns the body into a temple of Siva. The guru's guidance is essential for knowing how to course the prana through the successive adharas. The guru alone can guide this upward journey.

திகழும் படியே செறிதரு வாயு
அழியும் படியை அறிகில ராரும்
அழியும் படியை அறிந்தபின் நந்தி
திகழ்கின்ற வாயுவைச் சேர்தலு மாமே. 720

Know the Mystery of Prana Merging in Nada

The breath that glows within
None knows how it merges
When you know how it merges
Then can you reach the region
Where Nandi holds His sway.

In Kundalini yoga, the body becomes the "Temple of Siva," that is Siva comes to dwell there. Mular's message that Kundalini Yoga turns the Body into Temple of Siva is a very vital one and has had very fruitful outcome in Temple art, whose basic design resembles the pathway to the "garbhagrha", which corresponds to the position of the heart of the human body.

சோதனை தன்னில் துரிசறிக் காணலாம்
நாதனும் நாயகி தன்னிற் பிரியுநாள்
சாதன மாகுங் குருவை வழிபட்டு
மாதன மாக மதித்துக்கொள் ளீரே. 721

Treasure Guru's Guidance for Yoga

As through breath you pierce the adharas
You shall vision clear;
Prana leaving the Kundalini Sakti
On its upward journey through Sushumna;
That you gain through the Guru guiding;
Take that as treasure precious gained.

ஈராறு கால்கொண் டெழுந்த புரவியைப்
பேராமற் கட்டிப் பெரிதுண்ண வல்லிரேல்
நீரா யிரமும் நிலமாயி ரத்தாண்டும்
பேராது காயம் பிரான்நந்தி ஆணையே. 722

Immortality Through Samadhi Yoga

The breath that arose twelve matras long,
If you control and absorb within,
Well may you live thousands upon thousands of years on land and sea
The body perishes not;
True this is,
Upon Lord Nandi I declare.

ஓசையில் ஏழும் ஒளியின்கண் ஐந்தும்
நாசியின் மூன்றும் நாவில் இரண்டுந்
தேசியுந் தேசனுந் தன்னிற் பிரியுநாள்
மாசறு சோதி வகுத்துவைத் தானே. 723

Experiences of Yogi When Prana Ascends

When Prana and Sakti their departure take
One from the other
The yogi knows it this way;
Seven sounds he hears
Five colors he sees
Three odors he smells,
Two tastes he knows
Thus has the Lord of Light
The symptoms indicated.

13. காயசித்தி உபாயம்

WAY TO KAYASIDDHI

உடம்பார் அழியில் உயிரார் அழிவர்
திடம்பட மெய்ஞ்ஞானஞ் சேரவு மாட்டார்
உடம்பை வளர்க்கும் உபாயம் அறிந்தே
உடம்பை வளர்த்தேன் உயிர்வளர்த் தேனே. 724

Importance of Preserving Body

If the body perishes, Prana departs
Nor will the Light of Truth be reached;
I learned the way of preserving my body
And so doing, my Prana too.

Mantras 724 & 725

Time was when I despised the body. Then I realised that the body is God's temple. If the body perishes, so does prana.

So I began to preserve my body with infinite care, and I saw God within.

This is one of the most important contributions of Mular to Tamil life and culture, brought from the north. The body, according to Kaya Siddhi (Kaya = body) provides the best, and probably the only medium for attaining "moksa", and, therefore, it has to be kept always in perfect trim through yoga.

உடம்பினை முன்னம் இழுக்கென் றிருந்தேன்
உடம்பினுக் குள்ளே யுறுபொருள் கண்டேன்
உடம்புளே உத்தமன் கோயில்கொண் டான் என்று
உடம்பினை யானிருந் தோம்புகின் றேனே. 725

Why I Preserve Body

Time was when I despised the body;
But then I saw the God within
And the body, I realised, is the Lord's temple
And so I began preserving it
With care infinite.

சுழற்றிக் கொடுக்கவே சுத்திக் கழியுங்
கழற்றி மலத்தைக் கமலத்தைப் பூரித்து
உழற்றிக் கொடுக்கும் உபாயம் அறிவார்க்கு
அழற்றித் தவிர்ந்துடல் அஞ்சன மாமே. 726

Purification of Internal Organs of Body

If the breath is used to flush the Ida and Pingala
By Pranayama, the heart gets purified
And the body becomes impervious
Even to fire.

The body must be kept pure. This is achieved by churning the intestines through the practice known as 'suddhi.' Then the bowels become clean. Control the breath in the heart's region and make it pervade the entire nadi system.

அஞ்சனம் போன்றுட லையறு மந்தியில்
வஞ்சக வாத மறுமத்தி யானத்திற்
செஞ்சிறு காலையிற் செய்திடிற் பித்தறும்
நஞ்சறச் சொன்னோம் நரைதிரை நாசமே. 727

Effect of Practising Yoga at Dawn, Noon and Dusk

As body wax-like suppleness attains,
Practising yoga at dusk
The phlegm leaves;
At noon leaves the wind that is treacherous;
At dawn practised, the bile leaves;
Thus all poison from body is expelled
And you shall know no greying, nor wrinkling.

Practise yoga at dusk; phlegm disappears. Practise yoga at noon; the treacherous wind within leaves. Practise at dawn, bile is expelled. Thus the body, purified from the poison of the three "humours," knows no greying or wrinkling.

மூன்று மடக்குடைப் பாம்பிரண் டெட்டுள
வேன்ற வியந்திரம் பன்னிரண் டங்குலம்
நான்றவிம் முட்டை யிரண்டையுங் கட்டியிட்டு
ஊன்றி யிருக்க உடம்பழி யாதே. 728

Yoga Leads to Imperishable Body

Three the coils of serpent Kundalini
Ten the Vayus that agitate the body;
Twelve finger-length the Prana breath;
When the two bags of aspiration
Are tight controlled,
And you sit in meditation unwavering
The body perishes not ever.

Mantras 728 & 729

The yogi who controls inhalation and exhalation in prescribed measure shall live beyond a hundred years.

Kaya means the body, and Kaya-Siddhi is the Tantric way of obtaining spiritual powers through disciplines connected with the body.

நூறும் அறுபதும் ஆறும் வலம்வர
நூறும் அறுபதும் ஆறும் இடம்வர
நூறும் அறுபதும் ஆறும் எதிரிட
நூறும் அறுபது மாறும் புகுவரே. 729

How to Live for 166 years

Breathe by the Right Nadi a hundred and sixty six matra
Breathe by the Left a hundred and sixty six matra
And then reverse the rhythm
If you do it in alternation thus
You shall live long
A hundred and sixty six years.

சத்தியார் கோயி லிடம்வலஞ் சாதித்தான்
மத்தியா னத்திலே வாத்தியங் கேட்கலாந்
தித்தித்த கூத்துஞ் சிவனும் வெளிப்படுஞ்
சத்தியஞ் சொன்னோஞ் சதாநந்தி ஆணையே. 730

Divine Music in Yoga Practice

In the body-temple where Sakti is seated
If you practise transference of breath from right to left and vice versa,
You can hear the mystic sounds from Forehead Centre
And Lord Siva will Himself reveal
Dancing to rhythmic music;
This we declare true
In the name of Sadasiva.

In the body-temple, the sakti is seated. If breathing is practiced from right to left and vice versa in alternation, the yogi will hear mystic sounds. In the forehead centre (ajna), Siva will reveal Himself dancing to rhythmic music.

திறத்திறம் விந்து திகழு மகார
முறப்பெற வேநினைந் தோதுஞ் சகார

மறிப்பது மந்திர மன்னிய நாத
மறப்பெற யோகிக் கறநெறி யாமே. 731

In Yoga Practice Soham is Chanted

In the Bindu that is pure by far
Shines the sound "Ha"
In the Nada that abides
Lives the sound "Sa"
Together they become the mantra "Soham"
The yogi who silently chants it while breathing
Sure attains the Holy Way.

From bindu emanates the sound 'ha'; from nada, the sound 'sa'. Repeated continuously they become the mantra 'soham.' The yogi chants it silently.

உந்திச் சுழியி னுடனேர் பிராணனைச்
சிந்தித் தெழுப்பிச் சிவமந் திரத்தினால்
முந்தி முகட்டின் நிறுத்தி அபானனைச்
சிந்தித் தெழுப்பச் சிவனவ னாமே. 732

Course Prana and Apana Through Meditation

Rouse the Prana that resides in the Navel Centre
By meditating and chanting Siva mantra;
Retain that breath in the Ajna frontal
Then rouse the apana breath by meditation;
That way you Siva become.

Mantras 732 & 733

Rouse the prana that resides in the navel centre by chanting Siva mantra in silence. Course it upwards to sahasrara. Similarly do with apana. Centre the thought on muladhara. There resides the Lord Supreme of all the six adharas. The inhalation and exhalation of breath is referred to as Hamsa (Otherwise meaning the Swan) made up of the two syllables 'Ham' and 'Sa', which are also sometimes reversed to read Sa Ham, or "Soham". This is also part of the Nada philosophy.

மாறா மலக்குதந் தன்மே லிருவிரற்
கூறா இலிங்கத்தின் கீழே குறிக்கொண்மின்
ஆறா உடம்பிடை அண்ணலும் அங்குளன்
கூறா உபதேசங் கொண்டது காணுமே. 733

Centre Thy Thoughts on Muladhara

Two finger length above the anus
Where faecal matter leaves not
And below the male organ
Is the Linga in Muladhara
Meditate on that Centre,
There resides the Lord of the six adharas;
This my upadesa, rare revealed;
Do take it and vision the Lord.

நீல நிறனுடை நேரிழை யாளொடுஞ்
சாலவும் புல்லிச் சதமென் றிருப்பார்க்கு
ஞாலம் அறிய நரைதிரை மாறிடும்
பாலனு மாவர் பராநந்தி ஆணையே. 734

Eternal Youth Through Yoga

They who effect the mystic union
With the azure-hued Sakti within
Will shed greying and wrinkling
And regain youth for all to see;
This I say is true, by Nandi the Great.

அண்டஞ் சுருங்கில் அதற்கோ ரழிவில்லை
பிண்டஞ் சுருங்கிற் பிராணன் நிலைபெறும்
உண்டி சுருங்கில் உபாயம் பலவுள
கண்டங் கறுத்த கபாலியு மாமே. 735

Continence Leads to God-hood

If the seminal seed thickens by sexual abstention
It shall never be destroyed;
If the body is lightened by austere discipline
Long shall the life be;
If food is eaten sparingly
Many the good that flow;
You may verily become
The Lord of Dark-Hued throat.

Abstain from sexual union. Abstention thickens the seminal seed. It will never be dried up. Lighten your body by austere discipline. Long shall you live. If food is eaten sparingly, many are the good things that flow.

பிண்டத்துள் உற்ற பிழக்கடை வாசலை
அண்டத்துள் உற்று அடுத்தடுத் தேகிடில்
வண்டிச் சிக்கு மலர்க்குழல் மாதரார்
கண்டிச் சிக்குநற் காயமு மாமே. 736

Yoga Gives Comeliness of Body

If Kundalini that is in Muladhara
Is sent upward often to reach the space in cranium,
Comely your body becomes;
A desire-object for damsels bedecked with flowers
Around which bees swarm humming.

Mantras 736,738 & 739

Kundalini yoga, practised regularly, confers comeliness and youthfulness. The yogi will frisk like a tender fawn. He who attains kayasiddhi will flourish like a seed of paddy transplanted in a million, million fields.

சுழலும் பெருங்கூற்றுத் தொல்லைமுன் சீறி
அழலும் இரத்தத்துள் அங்கியுள் ஈசன்
கழல்கொள் திருவடி காண்குறில் ஆங்கே
நிழலுளுந் தெற்றுளும் நிற்றலு மாமே. 737

Imperishable Life in Yogic Vision

The Lord, of yore, spurned the mighty God of Death
Who ever harasses life;
The Lord rides the Chariot of Fire within;
If you vision His Holy Feet,
Decked with triumphal anklet
You shall for ever live
In the canopied terrace above.

நான்கண்ட வன்னியும் நாலு கலையேழுந்
தான்கண்ட வாயுச் சரீர முழுதொடும்

ஊன்கண்டு கொண்ட வுணர்வு மருந்தாக
மான்கன்று நின்று வளர்கின்ற வாறே. 738

Yogi Vibrates With Youthfulness

The Fire I saw in Kundalini radiates Kala four
The Prana I kindled and coursed through Centres seven
Pervades the body entire;
With divine life that suffuses the fleshy body as ambrosia;
I grow unto a tender fawn.

ஆகுஞ் சனவேத சத்தியை அன்புற
நீகொள்ளின் நெல்லின் வளர்கின்ற நேர்மையைப்
பாகு படுத்திப் பல்கோடி களத்தினால்
ஊழ்கொண்ட மந்திரந் தன்னால் ஒடுங்கே. 739

Meditation on Appropriate Mantra to Attain Kaya Siddhi

If you in ardour pursue
The search for power to acquire Kaya Siddhi,
You shall flourish far and wide,
Like a seed of paddy planted
In a million, million fields;
Do you therefore meditate single-minded
On the mantra that conquers Fate.

14. கால சக்கரம்

WHEEL OF TIME OR KALA CHAKRA

"Wheel of Time or Kala Chakra"

In this chapter, Mular deals with the ordinary nature of time as a phenomenon. But the term "Kala Chakra" has a more specific connotation in Tantricism. It is a powerful yantra with very well-reasoned philosophical basis.' This is what Mular has in mind when he talks of "Kalanta" as one of the six antas.

மதிவட்ட மாக வரையைந்து நாடி
இதுவிட்டிங் கிரா றமர்ந்த அதனாற்
பதிவட்டத் துள்நின்று பாலிக்கு மாறு
மதுவிட்டுப் போமாறு மாயலுற் றேனே. 740

Ascension of Jiva from Moon's Sphere

Seeking the Mountain Ranges Five (Siva Tattvas)
Here am I in the Moon's Sphere;
Leaving this I reach the Region of the Great Space of
Twelve
That lies in the Sphere of Pati Supreme;
And from thence I pass on to the Farthest Beyond
—These I seek to search here.

உற்றறி வைந்தும் உணர்ந்தறி வாறேழுங்
கற்றறி வெட்டுங் கலந்தறி வொன்பதும்
பற்றிய பத்தும் பலவகை நாழிகை
அற்ற தறியா தழிகின்ற வாறே. 741

Life Wasted Away in Pursuit of Worldly Knowledge

Knowledge that comes of senses five,
Knowledge that comes of discrimination that is sixth
Knowledge that comes of judgement that is seventh
Knowledge that comes by learning that is eighth,
Knowledge that comes from experience that is ninth
Knowledge that comes from attachment that is tenth
—Thus does knowledge that comes in diverse ways,
But erode life span in succession;
Knowing this not, they perish away.

Knowledge comes in diverse ways. Through the senses, through discrimination, through judgement, through experience, through attachments — coming through all these in succession, knowledge erodes the life span.

அழிகின்ற ஆண்டவை ஐயைஞ்சு மூன்று
மொழிகின்ற முப்பத்து மூன்றென்ப தாகுங்
கழிகின்ற காலறு பத்திரண் டென்ப
தெழுகின்ற ஈரைம்ப தெண்ணற் றிருந்தே. 742

Critical Years of Life

Many are the stages when death assails man;
From twenty five to twenty eight;
From thirty to thirty three
From sixty to sixty two
From hundred and beyond
These are the critical ages in man's life span;
When death may visit him.

Many are the critical years in the life of man when death may assail him. 13, 33, 62 and beyond that, any time upto 100 and over, are considered as critical years in a man's life.

திருந்து தினமத் தினத்தி னொடுநின்
றிருந்தறி நாளொன் றிரண்டெட்டு மூன்று
பொருந்திய நாளொடு புக்கறிந் தோங்கி
வருந்துத லின்றி மனைபுக லாமே. 743

Days Appropriate for Commencing Yoga

The birth day, The first, second, third and the eight day following it,
Any one of these is day appropriate for commencing yoga;
Find the day suitable most,

And easy shall be your entry
Into the Mystic House within.

There are appropriate days for commencing yoga. The birthday of the practitioner, and the 1st 2nd, 3rd and 8th day following it are considered suitable. If he chooses a suitable day, his entry into the mystic house within will be easy.

மனைபுகு வீரும் மகத்திடை நாடி
எனவிரு பத்தஞ்சும் ஈரா றதனால்
தனையறிந் தேறட்டுத் தற்குறி யாறு
வினையறி யாறு விளங்கிய நாலே. 744

Yoga Explained

You who enter the land of yoga practice!
Know that it consists in this
The measure of breath inhaled is twelve inches
Having measured accordingly
Exhale eight matra consciously
The four matras retained
Are in the six adharas to suffuse
And thus breathing examine to Tattvas twenty and five.

Yoga consists in the following: inhalation of 12 matras; exhalation of eight matras; retention of four matras. Breathing in this measure continuously, yoga suffuses the six adharas with prana which ascends beyond the 25 tattvas.

நாலுங் கடந்தது நால்வரும் நாலைந்து
பாலங் கடந்தது பத்துப் பதினைந்து
கோலங் கடந்த குணத்தாண்டு மூவிரண்
டாலங் கடந்ததொன் றாரறி வாரே. 745

God is Beyond Adharas and Tattvas

Beyond the Muladhara of the four pointed Centre is He;
Beyond the barriers of Tattvas twenty and four is He;
Beyond the twenty and five Tattvas is His Guna
Beyond the six adharas that rise like the spreading banyan tree is He,
Who ever does know Him!

Mantras 745 & 746

God is beyond the six adharas and the 25 tattvas. After the kundalini has been roused, it takes 20 days for a good practitioner to pierce the six adharas; on the 25th day, his prana reaches the fire mandala; on the 26th day, the solar mandala; on the 27th day, the lunar mandala.

ஆறும் இருபதுக் கையஞ்சு மூன்றுக்குந்
தேறு மிரண்டு மிருபத்தொ டாறிவை
கூறு மதியொன் றினுக்கிரு ட்ந்தேழு
வேறு பதியங்க ணாள்விதித் தானே. 746

The Days it Takes the Yogi to Traverse Adharas and Mandalas

The days that take to pierce the Centres nine are this
Twentieth day adharas six;
Twenty-fifth day Seventh Centre of Fire Mandala
Twenty-sixth day the Eighth Centre of Solar Mandal
Twenty-seventh day the Ninth Centre of Lunar Mandala
—These the days for yogi's Prana to reach Centres nine.

விதித்த இருபத்தெட் டொடுமூன் றறையாகத்
தொகுத்தறி முப்பத்து மூன்று தொகுமின்
பதித்தறி பத்தெட்டும் பாரா திகணால்·
உதித்தறி மூன்றிரண் டொன்றின் முறையே. 747

Vision of the Three Mandalas

On the twenty-eighth day
You gain the vision of Mandalas Three, each apart
On the thirty-third day
You gain their collective vision;
Do Centre your thoughts further
And vision the tattvas twenty and four
That to Earth and the rest of elements in order below.

On the 28th day the yogi obtains the vision of the three mandalas, each apart; and on the 33rd day, he gains their collective vision.

முறைமுறை யாய்ந்து முயன்றில ராகில்
இறையிறை யார்க்கும் இருக்க அரிது
மறையது காரண மற்றொன்று மில்லை
பறையறை யாது பணிந்து முடியே. 748

Practise Yoga in Time and Order Stated

Thus if in succession and stages
The yogi aspires not
Impossible it be for him to become God;
Much less to near Him:
No other secret the Vedas hold
Trumpet this not;
But in meekness accomplish it.

Let the yogi practise in successive stages; then he approaches God. Kindle the kundalini lamp within. Search for God with that blazing torch. That alone is the way to the goal.

முடிந்த தறியார் முயல்கின்ற மூர்க்கர்
இடிஞ்சில் இருக்க விளக்கெரி கொண்டு
கடிந்தனன் மூளக் கதுவவல் லார்க்கு
நடந்திடும் பாரினில் நண்ணலு மாமே. 749

Kindle Kundalini Lamp Within

They who know not this Way to the goal
And try other Ways
Are but fools;
They search with blazing torch
While within them is the hand-lamp

They who can kindle the Kundalini Fire within
Will abide ever in this fleeting world.

நண்ணு சிறுவிர னாணாக மூன்றுக்கும்
பின்னிய மார்பிடைப் பேராமல் ஒத்திடுஞ்
சென்னியின் மூன்றுக்குஞ் சேரவே நின்றிடும்
உன்னி யுணர்ந்திடும் ஓவியந் தானே. 750

Journey Through Six Adharas in Two Stages

Unto the girth of the little finger
Is the spinal cord, taut like the string of bow;
There the adharas are
Traversing the first three
Do you reach the Heart's Centre
And, be in constancy fixed;
When you journey further onward
To the three Centers that end with Forehead
You shall firm be
Like a picture painted.

Mantras 750 & 751

The six adharas may be reached in two successive stages of three each. Traversing the first three, reach the heart centre; then from the heart centre, journey to the forehead centre. Be firm as a painted picture. Keep erect the spinal column. The body is evil karma's product. Yet it possesses the precious stalk that holds the mystic lotuses. Through its central nadi, the sushumna, perfect consciousness is reached.

ஓவிய மான வுணர்வை அறிமின்கள்
பாவிக ளித்தின் பயனறி வாரில்லை
தீவினை யாமுடன் மண்டல மூன்றுக்கும்
பூவில் இருந்திடும் புண்ணியத் தண்டே. 751

Importance of Sushumna in Yoga

Know thou the Consciousness that is Perfection;
The sinners know not its goodness;
This body no doubt is evil Karma's product;
yet it holds the stalk (Sushumna) of the sacred Lotus
That blossoms in the Mystic Regions Three within.

தண்டுடன் ஓடித் தலைப்பெய்த யோகிக்கு
மண்டல மூன்று மகிழ்ந்துடல் ஒத்திடுங்
கண்டவர் கண்டனர் காணார் வினைப்பயன்
பிண்டம் பிரியப் பிணங்குகின் றாரே. 752

Collective Vision of Mandalas End Karma

The Yogi who through the spinal column
Ascends the adharas above
Sees the Mandalas Three together, rapture bound;
Those who saw that vision
Saw the end of Karmas;
Those who saw that not
Die to be born again.

The collective vision of the six adharas and the triple mandalas ends the karmas. Missing that vision, however great the man, his body perishes.

பிணங்கி அழிந்திடும் பேறது கேள்நீ
அணங்குட னாதித்த னாறு விரியின்
வணங்குட னேவந்த் வாழ்வு குலைந்து
சுணங்கனுக் காகச் சுழல்கின்ற வாறே. 753

Missing the Vision, the Body Perishes

Do you know how this body perishes?
Hear this:
A pretty damsel the man has for wife;
And like the sun his prosperity spreads;
And all bow to him in respect;
A body that waxed in a life like thus
Became a prey for prowling dogs to consume.

சுழல்கின்ற வாறின் துணைமலர் காணான்
தழலிடைப் புக்கிடுந் தன்னு ளிலாமற்
கழல்கண்ட போம்வழி காணவல் லார்க்குக்
குழல்வழி நின்றிடுங் கூத்தனு மாமே. 754

Those Who Vision Can Become the Dancing Lord

They who knock about
Reach not the Refuge of Blossom Feet;
Containing not the Kundalini fire within
Their body a prey to fire becomes;
They who know the Way
And seek His Victorious Feet
See the Heavenly Dancer
Through their spinal hollow.

He who courses the kundalini fire through the spinal column will not perish by the cremation fire. He will see the Heavenly Dancer within.

கூத்தன் குறியிற் குணம்பல கண்டவர்
சாத்திரந் தன்னைத் தலைப்பெய்து நிற்பர்கள்
பார்த்திருந் துள்ளே அனுபோக நோக்கிடில்
ஆத்தனு மாகி யலர்ந்திரு மொன்றே. 755

Seek the Dancing Lord as Goal and Become One With Him

They who sought the Dancer as their goal
Gained many things good;
And so stood in the path of the holy scriptures;
Seeking Him within and experiencing His presence
In eagerness they sit
And one with Siva become.

ஒன்றில் வளர்ச்சி உலப்பிலி கேளினி
நன்றென்று மூன்றுக்கு நாளது சென்றிடுஞ்
சென்றிடு முப்பதுஞ் சேர இருந்திடிற்
குன்றிடைப் பொன்திகழ் கூத்தனு மாமே. 756

God Vision at the End of 33 Days of Yoga

Countless are the gains that flow
From single-minded meditation;
Hear yet;
And thus if for Three and thirty days

You well and deep meditate
The Dancer on top of the Mountain of Gold
Will appear,
And You one with Him become.

At the end of 33 days after the kundalini sakti has been roused, the yogi may vision the Divine Dancer on the peak of the golden mountain (Meru) in the sahasrara.

கூத்தவன் ஒன்றிடுங் கூர்மை அறிந்தங்கே
ஏத்துவர் பத்தினில் எண்டிசை தோன்றிடப்
பார்த்து மகிழ்ந்து பதுமரை நோக்கிடிற்
சாத்திடு நூறு தலைப்பெய்ய லாமே. 757

Vision of the Hundred Petalled Lotus of Sahasrara

Knowing where the divine Dancer dwells,
From the ten petalled lotus of anahata
Raise the prana to the eight petalled anahata
There one can see the Lord seated
Then one lives the hundred years promised in the scriptures.

சாத்திடு நூறு தலைப்பெய்து நின்றவர்
காத்துடல் ஆயிரங் கட்டுறக் காண்பர்கள்
சேர்த்துடல் ஆயிரஞ்சேர இருந்தவர்
மூத்துடன் கோடி யுகமது வாமே. 758

Eternal Life Through Yoga

They who thus attained radiance a hundred fold
Will live a thousand years in body robust;
And they who saw a thousand years thus
May well live a million, trillion years.

உகங்கோடி கண்டும் ஒசிவற நின்று
அகங்கோடி கண்டு எயலறக் காண்பர்கள்
சிவங்கோடி விட்டுச் செறிய இருந்தங்
குகங்கோடி கண்டல் குயருறு வாரே. 759

Thus They Live Through Timeless Aeons

Well may they thus live for aeons and aeons,
And they tire not in their devotion;
And thus see the mind's end
And within see Him as Entity non-separate;
And as one with Siva they live filled in divinity
And so see countless ages of Life Exalted.

உயருறு வாருல கத்தொடுங் கூடிப்
பயனுறு வார்பலர் தாமறி யாமற்
செயலுறு வார்சிலர் சிந்தையி லாமற்
கயலுற கண்ணியைக் காணகி லாரே. 760

Worldly Thoughts do not Lead to Sakti

Some seek to exalt themselves
Pursuing ways worldly;
Some seek the fruits of enjoyment
Knowing not what they do;
Some strive after action
With no thought of goal whatsoever;
But none of them will see
The Sakti of lovely eyes.

Mantras 760 & 761

They who wallow in worldly thoughts have no goal whatsoever. They will never see Sakti of lovely eyes. They who do not vision Sakti will vanish, their riches and possessions untraceable.

காணகி லாகார் கழிந்தோடிப் போவர்கள்
நாணகி லாதார் நயம்பேசி விடுவர்கள்
காணகி லாதார் கழிந்த பொருளெலாங்
காணகி லாமற் கழிகின்ற வாறே. 761

Worldly Wealth is Perishable

They who see Her not
Wasted away their lives;
They who seek not
Spent away in artful talks;
The riches and possessions of those who see not
Vanished away unseen and untraced.

கழிகின்ற அப்பொருள் காணகி லாதார்
கழிகின்ற அப்பொருள் காணலு மாகுங்
கழிகின்ற வுள்ளே கருத்துற நோக்கிற்
கழியாத அப்பொருள் காணலு மாமே. 762

Treasure Within is Imperishable

They who do not see the Treasure that surpasses all,
But seek the treasure that perishes,
If within their melting heart they seek inside
They will see the Treasure that dies not.

Seek the treasure within. It is imperishable. If you but seek, you can attain the imperishable Siva state.

கண்ணன் பிறப்பிலி காணந்தி யாயுள்ளே
எண்ணுந் திசையுடன் ஏகாந்த னாயிடுந்
திண்ணென் றிருக்குஞ் சிவகதி யாநிற்கும்
நண்ணும் பதமிது நாடவல் லார்கட்கே. 763

Seek Siva-State

He is the One with the Fore-head eye
He is Birthless
He is Nandi within, Know this;
He in solitariness pervades spaces all
He stands as Siva, the goal unwavering
That state you shall attain
If you but seek.

நாடவல் லார்க்கு நமனில்லை கேடில்லை
நாடவல் லார்கள் நரபதி யாய்நிற்பர்
தேடவல் லார்கள் தெரிந்த பொருளிது
கூடவல் லார்கட்குக் கூறலு மாமே. 764

Fruits of Seeking

They who seek
Know death none; evil none;
They who seek
Will become lords of earth;
They who seek
But know this true;
And well may it be told
To those that aspire.

Great is the fruit of seeking. They who seek know no death, no evil. They become lords of earth and heaven.

கூறும் பொருளி தகார வுகாரங்கள்
தேறும் பொருளிது சிந்தையுள் நின்றிடக்
கூறு மகாரங் குழல்வழி யோடிட
ஆறும் அமர்ந்திடும் அண்ணலு மாமே. 765

Seek Lord Through Aum

These the things worthy of telling:
Akara or the sound "A" that is Siva
Ukara or the sound "U" that is Sakti
Let these in your thought abide
And Makara or the sound "m"
Let them through thy sushumna rise upward;
The six adharas will then be reached
And you shall gain the Lord.

When practising yoga, chant the mantra 'Aum' continuously in silence. When you thus chant, as the prana rises through the spinal cavity and courses through the six adharas, the Lord will be reached.

In this verse, Mular introduces us to that most basic and important "bija" mantra and its relationship to Siva and Sakti.

அண்ணல் இருப்பிட மாரும் அறிகிலர்
அண்ணல் இருப்பிடம் ஆய்ந்துகொள் வார்களுக்
கண்ணல் அழிவின்றி உள்ளே அமர்ந்திடும்
அண்ணலைக் காணில் அவனிவ வாகுமே. 766

Know Lord Within and Become One With Him

None know where the Lord resides;
To them who seek Him
He resides eternal within;
When you see the Lord
He and you one become.

The Lord is within you. He resides eternally within you. Seek Him. And when you see Him, He and you will become one.

அவனிவ னாகும் பரிசறி வாரில்லை
அவனிவ னாகும் பரிசது கேள்நீ
அவனிவ னோசை ஒளியினுள் ஒன்றிடும்
அவனிவன் வட்டம தாகிநின் றானே. 767

Way to Become One With Siva

They know not how He and you one become;
This the Way how He and you one become;
Hearken!
He stands in your hearing and sight
He stands in the Pranava within you.

He is in your hearing. He is in your sight. He stands within the mystic circle within you. It is for you to become one with Him.

வட்டங்க ளேழுமலர்ந்திடும் உம்முளே
சிட்டன் இருப்பிடஞ் சேர அறிகிலீர்
ஒட்டி யிருந்துள் உபாயம் உணர்ந்திடக்
கட்டி இருப்பிடங் காணலு மாகுமே. 768

Vision the Lord in the Seven Adharas

You know not how to reach His abode;
Transfixing your thoughts within you in the yogic way
The seven circles inside will open
And you shall see the abode of Lord
Sweet as sugar-lump.

His abode is not beyond reach. Fix your thoughts within. The seventh adhara is the abode of the Lord. Inside it He sits, sweet as a lump of sugar.

Six adharas plus the sahasrara.

காணலு மாகும் பிரமன் அரியென்று
காணலு மாகுங் கறைக்கண்டன் ஈசனைக்
காணலு மாகுஞ் சதாசிவ சத்தியுங்
காணலு மாகுங் கலந்துடன் வைத்ததே. 769.

Vision of Gods in Adharas

You may see Him as Brahma and Vishnu
You may see Him as Rudra blue-throated and Mahesa,
You may see Him as Sakti and Sadasiva
You may see Him within you immanent (in Adharas).

In the adharas. He is seated as Brahma; as Vishnu; as Rudra; as Mahesvara; as Sadasiva and as Sakti. He that is immanent thus can be seen by you.

15. ஆயுள் பரீட்சை

MEASUREMENT OF LIFE SPAN

வைத்தகை சென்னியில் நேரிதாய்த் தோன்றிடில்
உத்தம மிக்கிடில் ஓராறு திங்களா
மத்த மிகுத்திட் டிரட்டிய தாயிடில்
நித்தல் உயிர்க்கொரு திங்களில் ஓசையே. 770.

Measuring the Life Span by observing breath

Put your hand on forehead
And look,
If you see the breath rhythm unchanged
Well and good;
If you see it enlarged,
Death awaits in six months;
If you see it doubled,
In a month shalt life depart.

Indian astrology has developed a branch of techniques in measuring the life span based on observation of the breathing rhythm. This is known as 'saravottam' in Tamil as introduced by Bhoga Siddhar. In Sanskrit, it is known as 'pavana-saravodaya sastra.'

This is a curious, but nevertheless valuabale, Siddhar concept, savouring of fortune-telling. The whole of these three chapters deal with such concepts.

"Learned Indian yogis of yore had critically studied the movement of air through the whole respiratory passage during inhalation and exhalation. They had discovered that just as the current of a river sometimes flows on the oneside, and at another time on the other side, the air also changes sides in the nasal passages during inhalation and exhalation. They had discovered a close connection between the mental states and such sideway movements of air.

It has been observed that we sometimes breathe through the left nostril and sometimes through the right one. The nostrils thus work alternately. The left channel for the passage of the air is known as 'ida' while the right channel is the pingala. The left one is known as the lunar channel (chandra nadi), while the right one is the solar channel (surya nadi). When a person has obtained mastery over pranayama, and when he is physically and mentally healthy and ready for higher spiritual practices, his breathing is from the middle channel known as 'sushumna nadi.'

In the bright half of the month and on the first, second, the seventh, eighth, ninth and fourteenth days, and on the full moon day one breathes through the left nostril in the mornings, but every hour this alternates with the right nostril. In the remaining days of the bright half of the month, one breathes through the right nostril in the mornings, the direction changing every hour, the right and left nostrils alternating.

In the dark half of the month, and on the first day one breathes through the right nostril, but alternating every hour with the left nostril. Then there is reverse movement every third day.

When one breathes through the left nostril — lunar channel — the breath comes under the invisible influence of the moon and such lunar qualities as coolness, steadiness, sobriety, discretion, etc., are thus born or nourished.

When one breathes through the right nostril — solar channel — the breath comes under the invisible influence of the sun and solar qualities such as heat, light, bravery, dynamism, enthusiasm, strength, etc., are thereby born or nourished.

Breathing can be changed from the right nostril to the left one and vice versa. The technique is very simple. If you are breathing through the left nostril, and you want to breathe through the right one, lie down on the right side for sometime. If you are breathing through the right nostril and wish to breathe through the left, lie down on the left side for a short time.

When one breathes through the right nostril, one should undertake such work which requires greater exertion, eg., walking, running, arguing, physical exercise, eating or cleaning the bowels. Ancient Indian medical science advises people to rest on the left side after meals so that one breathes through the right nostril and the food is thus well digested.

When one breathes through the left nostril, one should undertake such work which requires less exertion, such as light mental work, discretionary work or work of a permanent nature. Sleeping on the right side relieves mental stress, strain, and tension and gives more mental rest. In this state of breathing, holy activities may be undertaken. This is an ideal state for studies as well.

When one breathes through the middle channel, one should practise concentration, meditation and spiritual activities. A true yogi or for that matter even a perfectly healthy person constantly breathes thus and maintains mental peace and equanimity even under the most trying circumstances.

Ancient Indian astrology had developed a particular branch which was based on this. If one breathes through the left nostril and if a person sitting on his left asks if a certain work undertaken or to be undertaken would be successful, the answer should always be in the affirmative; but if one breathes through the right nostril and if a person sitting on his left asks if a certain work undertaken or to be undertaken would be successful, the answer should always be in the negative.

When one constantly breathes through the middle channel, one develops intuition, knows future events, can practise telepathy and transform the personality of others easily. Such breathing is compared with a mother-in-law who is difficult to be pleased but if once pleased becomes an additional blessing.

Vide "The Science of Yogic Breathing" by Yogacharya Shantikumar, pp.30-32.

ஓசையும் ஈசனும் ஒக்கும் உணர்வின் கண்
ஓசை யிறந்தவர் ஈசனை உள்குவர்
ஓசை யிறந்தவர் நெஞ்சினுள் ஈசனும்
ஓசை யுணர்ந்த வுணர்விது வாமே. 771

Transcend Nada and Realize God

Nada and God are one in Consciousness
Only they who transcended Nada
Will on God centre;
God appears in the heart
Of them who Nada transcend
This the truth I realized
And so merged in Nada.

Knowing the breath rhythm is knowing the nada; and nada and God are one in consciousness.

ஆமே அழிகின்ற வாயுவை நோக்கிடில்
நாமே உறைகின்ற நன்மை யளித்திடும்
பூமேல் உறைகின்ற போதகம் வந்திடுந்
தாமே யுலகில் தலைவனு மாமே. 772

Course Breath Upward and See Light of Jnana

The breath that is in vain spent
If turned upward to flow
Will give the good that of fixity of mind comes;
The Jnana that comes from cranial spaces will beam;
And the yogi becomes Lord of earth.

Breath that is spent in vain, if made to course upwards, will give steadiness of mind. From steadiness of mind will beam the jnana that is in sahasrara. The yogi becomes the lord of the earth.

தலைவ னிடம்வலஞ் சாதிப்பார் இல்லை
தலைவ னிடம்வல மாயிடில் தையல்
தலைவ னிடம்வலந் தன்வழி யஞ்சில்
தலைவ னிடம்வலந் தன்வழி நூறே. 773

Importance of Nadi Suddhi for Longevity

None there the Jiva who practises Nadi Suddhi;
Breathing from left to right and right to left;
He who does it visions Sakti;
The senses five his way come;
To a hundred years, he sure lives.

Nadi suddhi (purification) is an important practice in yogic breathing. It consists in breathing from the left nostril to the right, and from the right to the left in rhythmic alternation. Practised carefully, it enables the mastery of the senses and confers the vision of Sakti. The yogi can live a hundred years.

Nadisuddhi - a Tantric term: ''Purification of the nerves. When done by ''mantras'', it is known as Samanu, and when done by physical exercises like 'dhauti', etc., it is known as Nirmanu'' (N.N. Bhattacharya P.452 ibid.)

ஏறிய வாறினில் எண்பது சென்றிடுந்
தேறிய ஏழிற் சிறக்கும் வகையெண்ணில்
ஆறொரு பத்தாய் அமர்ந்த இரண்டையுந்
தேறியே நின்று தெளியிவ் வகையே. 774

EXhalation Measure for Ages 80 and 60

If Prana flows outward
To matra six in length,
Eighty the age you live up to;
If seven, sixty;
These two know clearly.

Mantras 774-776

If the prana goes outwards in six matra length, eighty shall be the age of the subject. If it flows in seven matras outward, then he will live up to sixty years. When it is eight matras outward, fifty shall be his age. If nine, thirty three; if ten, twenty eight; if fifteen, twenty five; and so on.

இவ்வகை எட்டும் இடம்பெற ஓடிடில்
அவ்வகை ஐம்பதே யென்ன அறியலாஞ்
செவ்வகை ஒன்பதுஞ் சேரவே நின்றிடின்
முவ்வகை யாமது முப்பத்து மூன்றே. 775

Exhalation for Ages 50 and 33

If to eight matras Prana runs out
Through nostril left
Fifty the age; know you;
If nine, leaving three matras inside,
Thirty and three be the age.

மும்மூன்றும் ஒன்றும் முடிவுற நின்றிடிற்
எண்மூன்றும் நாலும் இடவகை யாய்நிற்கும்
ஐம்மூன்றும் ஓடி அகலவே நின்றிடிற்
பன்மூன்றொ டீராறு பார்க்கலு மாமே. 776

Exhalation for Ages 28 and 25

If in matra ten, it flows out in nostril left
Twenty and eight the life here below;
If fifteen,
Then for twenty and five years only do you see him.

பாாககலு மாகும் பகல்முப் பதுமாகில்
ஆக்கலு மாகுமவ் வாறிரண் டுள்ளிட்டுப்
போக்கலு மாகும் புகலற ஒன்றெனில்
தேக்கலு மாகுந் திருத்திய பத்தே. 777

Kumbhaka of Ten Matras Leads to Concentration

Breathing inward in measure twelve
The ten may you retain inside
And direct into oneness upward;
Thus may you practise
The entire day of thirty naligas!

If the yogi practises retention of ten matras for an entire day of twelve hours, he shall achieve oneness. He will reach the stage of directing the breath into muladhara.

Naligai is a time measure. Two and half naligais make an hour.

ஏயிரு நாளும் இயல்புற ஓடிடிற்
பாயிரு நாலும் பகையற நின்றிடும்
தேய்வுற மூன்றுந் திகழவே நின்றிடில்
ஆயுரு வாறென் றளக்கலு மாமே. 778

Effect of Ten-Matra Kumbhaka for Three Days

If for two days continuous,
The ten matras of Prana is inside retained,
It will no obstacle from apana encounter;
If for three days this is maintained glowing
Then may you be certain
The ascension through Centres Six come soon.

If he practises thus for two days continuously, the downward streaming apana vayu will not trouble him. On the third day it shall begin the ascension through the six adharas.

அளக்கும் வகைநாலும் அவ்வழியே ஓடில்
விளக்கும் ஒருநாலு மெய்ப்பட நிற்கும்
துளக்கும் வகையைந்துந் தூய்நெறி ஓடில்
களக்க மறுமூன்றிற் காணலு மாமே. 779

Vision of the First Three Adharas on the Fourth and Fifth Day

If thus the practice is for days four continued,
The four petalled Muladhara will visioned be;
If further continued,
On the fifth day,
The Second and Third adharas visioned are.

On the fourth day if the practice is continued, the four-petalled muladhara will be visioned. On the fifth day, the second and third adharas, svadhistanam and manipurakam will be reached by prana.

காணலு மாகுங் கருதிய பத்தோடிற்
காணலு மாகுங் கலந்த இரண்டையும்
காணலு மாகுங் கலப்பற மூவைந்தேற்
காணலு மாகுங் கருத்துற ஒன்றே. 780

Collective Vision of Five Adharas on the Fifteenth Day

When ten days thus pass
Two more adharas (Fourth and Fifth)
May visioned together be;
On the fifteenth day,
Shall be the collective vision
On the five together.

கருதும் இருபதிற் காண ஆறாகும்
கருதிய ஐயைந்திற் காண்பது மூன்றாம்
கருதம் இருப துடனாறு காணிற்
கருதும் இரண்டெனக் காட்டலு மாமே. 781

Visions of the 20th, 25th and 26th Days

On the twentieth day
The Sixth Adhara (Ajna) will visioned be;
On the twenty-fifth day
The Three Mandalas (Sun, Moon and Fire) will visioned be;
On the twenty-sixth day
The Two, Siva and Sakti, will visioned be.

காட்டலு மாகுங் கலந்திரு பத்தேழில்
காட்டலு மாகுங் கலந்தெழும் ஒன்றெனக்
காட்டலு மாகுங் கலந்திரு பத்தெட்டிற்
காட்டலு மாகுங் கலந்தஈ ரைந்தே. 782

Visions of 27th and 28th Day

On the twenty-seventh day
May well be revealed the One Being Supreme
That collectively rises in centres all;
On the twenty-eighth day
May revealed be
The ten centres together
In visions Collective rare.

On the twenty-seventh day will be seen the One Supreme Being that pervades all the adharas. On the twenty-eighth day, the Space will be visioned.

ஈரைந்தும் ஐந்தும் இருமூன்றும் எட்டுக்கும்
பாரஞ்சி நின்ற பகைபத்து நாளாகும்
வாரஞ்செய் கின்ற வகையாறஞ் சாமாகில்
ஓரஞ்சொ டொன்றொன் றெனவொன்று நாளே. 783

On the 29th Day and 30th Day

If the journey upwards resumes
Ten the days that apana stands as impediment;
If the journey takes thirty days
Seven the days that take the apana to leave.

On the twenty-ninth day, if the journey upward is resumed, the apana will stand as an impediment for ten days. On the thirtieth day of the journey, the apana will take seven days to leave.

ஒன்றிய நாள்கள் ஒருமுப்பத் தொன்றாகிற்
கன்றிய நாளுங் கருத்துற மூன்றாகுஞ்
சென்றுயிர் நாலெட்டுஞ் சேரவே நின்றிடின்
மன்றியல் பாகு மனையில் இரண்டே. 784

On the 31st Day and 32nd Day

On the thirty-first day of the journey upward,
Three the days that still delay the union
On thirty-second day that Prana takes to reach,
Two the days that are still in the way.

On the thirty-first day there will still be three days' delay for union with God. On the thirty-second day there will still be an impediment for two more days.

மனையில்ஒன் றாகும் மாதமு மூன்றுஞ்
சுனையில்ஒன் றாகத் தொனித்தனன் நந்தி
வினையற வோங்கி வெளிசெய்து நின்றால்
தனையுற நின்ற தலைவனு மாமே. 785

Jiva's Union in God on 33rd Day

Thus when Prana reaches the cranial heights
In a month and three days;
From within the fountain of nectar
Nandi bellows aloud;
If in the space within He reveals Himself,
You shall truly be one in Lord.

On the thirty-third day prana reaches the mountain of Meru. Nandi bellows aloud. He reveals Himself in the Space within. The yogi shall truly be one in God.

ஆரு மறியார் அளக்கின்ற வன்னியை
ஆரு மறியார் அளக்கின்ற வாயுவை
ஆரு மறியார் அழிகின்ற அப்பொருள்
ஆரு மறியார் அறிவறிந் தேனே. 786

Greatness of Kundalini Yoga

None knows Kundalini that spans high
None knows the science of breath control

They who know it not perish away
I knew the truth that none know.

Mantras 786 & 787

None knows the greatness of kundalini yoga. It is the science of breath control par excellence. It spans the spaces within and measures the duration of prana. He who knows it meets no death. It is the supreme knowledge. It unites jiva in Siva, who is All- Knowledge. He is the knowledge of all worlds and all life. He is the knowledge non-separate from them. That knowledge is within. Seek it. It will glow in pervasive richness.

அறிவது வாயுவொ டைந்தறி வாய
அறிவா வதுதான் உலகுயி ரத்தின்
பிறிவுசெய் யாவகை பேணியுள் நாடிற்
செறிவது நின்று திகழு மதுவே. 787

God as Knowledge

The Lord is the Knowledge
He stood as knowledge of elements five — air and the rest;
He stood as knowledge pervading world all and life
Non-separate from them;
If sought within,
That knowledge will in pervasive richness glow.

அதுவரு ளும்மரு ளான துலகம்
பொதுவரு ளும்புக ழாளர்க்கு நாளு
மதுவரு ளும்மலர் மங்கையர் செல்வி
இதுவருள் செய்யும் இறையவ னாமே. 788

Sakti Grants Grace

That God who is All-knowledge thus
Grants this world that is unreal;
For the good ones of high praise
He grants the vision of His Dancing Hall;
The Sakti that grants all this
Is the fragrant flower-bedecked Grace
That is the Consort of Lord.

God, who is All-Knowledge, grants this world that is unreal. For yogis he grants the vision of His Dancing Feet. This is the work of His sakti, the fragrant flower-bedecked Grace, that is the Lord's consort.

பிறப்பது சூழ்ந்த பெருந்தகை நந்தி
குறிப்பது கூடிய கோலக் குரம்பைப்
பழப்பதி யாவது பற்றறும் பாசம்
அழப்படி செய்வார்க் ககலு மதியே. 789

Nandi grants Eternal Wisdom

This body is full of desires,
Ancient mansion haunted by repetitive births
Rend the bonds of desires asunder
Make the pasa flee, howling
Nandi Great will grant His Wisdom Eternal.

This body is full of desires. It is an ancient mansion haunted by repetitive births. Rend the bonds of desires asunder. Make the pasa flee, howling. Nandi Great will grant His Wisdom Eternal.

"Sakti is Grace" This is Saivite thought.

16. வாரசரம்

BREATH RHYTHM IN DAYS OF THE WEEK

On different days of the week, breath rhythms differ as between the left and the right nadi.

வெள்ளிவெண் திங்கள் விளங்கும் புதனிடம்
ஒள்ளிய மந்தன் இரவிசெவ் வாய்வலம்
வள்ளிய பொன்னே வளரும் பிறையிடந்
தெள்ளிய தேய்பிறை தான்வல மாமே. 790

Days of the Week and the Course of Breath Through Left and Right Nadis

On Fridays, Mondays and Wednesdays,
Prana dominates in the nadi that is to left;
On Saturdays, Sundays and Tuesdays
It courses high in the right;
On Thursdays
Prana flows in the left
In the waxing moon's fortnight;
And in the right in the waning moon's fortnight.

On Mondays, Wednesdays and Fridays, prana dominates on the left (ida) nadi. On Tuesdays, Saturdays and Sundays it runs high on the right nadi (Pingala). On Thursday, prana rises high in the left in the waxing moon's fortnight; and in the right in the waning moon's fortnight.

வெள்ளிவெண் திங்கள் விளங்கும் புதன்மூன்றுந்
தள்ளி இடத்தே தயங்குமே யாமாகில்
ஒள்ளிய காயத்துக் கூன மிலையென்று
வள்ளல் நமக்கு மகிழ்ந்துறைத் தானே. 791

Breath Rhythm For Glowing Health

If on Fridays, Mondays and Wednesdays,
Breathing dominates in nostril left,
The body will no harm know
And it will in health glow;
Thus did Lord Nandi tell us,
In manner delectable.

Good results follow, if the rhythm is as above. The body will glow in health.

செவ்வாய் வியாழஞ் சனிஞாயி றேஎன்னும்
இவ்வா றறிகின்ற யோகி இறைவனே
ஒவ்வாத வாயு வலத்துப் புரியவிட்
டவ்வா றறிவார்க்கவ் வானந்த மாமே. 792

Yogi Corrects the Breath Rhythm

Contra, Tuesdays, Thursdays, Saturdays and Sundays
Breath flows high on the nostril right;
The Yogi who knows this is God indeed;
If this rhythm in the days stated
Does obtain not,
Let the Yogi force it into nostril right by skill subtle;
Then shall he know nothing but joy.

If this rhythm is not obtained, the yogi can by appropriate breathing exercise correct the flow, so that the proper rhythm is maintained.

மாறி வருமிரு பான்மதி வெய்யவன்
ஏறி இழியுந் இடைபிங் கலையிடை
ஊறும் உயிர்நடு வேயுயி ருக்கிரந்
தேறி அறிமின் தெரிந்து தெளிந்தே. 793

Changing Rhythm on Sundays and Mondays in Alternate Fortnights

If on a Sunday in a fortnight
The breath runs high on the right nostril,
In the fortnight next it runs high on the left;
If on a Monday in a fortnight
The breath runs high on the left nostril
In the fortnight next it runs low on the right;
Thus do they alternate from fortnight to fortnight
If this rhythm thus obtains,
Prana its strength derives;
Know well this
And accordingly regulate breathing.

The breath rhythm alters from fortnight to fortnight, on two days — Sunday and Monday. If on a Sunday in one fortnight the breath runs high on the right, it will run high on the left in the next fortnight. If on a Monday in one fortnight breath runs high on the left nostril, then in the next fortnight it runs high on the right nostril.

உதித்து வலத்திடம் போகின்ற போது
அதிர்த்தஞ்சி யோடுத லாமகன் றாரும்
உதித்தது வேமிக வோடிடு மாகில்
உதித்த விராசி யுணர்ந்துகொ ளுற்றே. 794

How to Regulate When Breath Rhythm Changes Course

The breath that rises in the Nadi Right
While its course into the Left changed
May a sudden jolt know
And in fear trembling flow;
Then leave the practice and rest a while;
If on the Right itself it flows
Faster than in rhythm appropriate
Then know the speed and suitably regulate.

This is the correct rhythm and if this rhythm is obtained, prana derives proper strength. If it is not obtained, it is for the yogi to correct it from time to time and bring the rhythm back to the norms indicated. However, this correction is quite a feat. Sometimes in directing the breath's course from the right to the left, the body may experience a sudden jolt and trembling fear. In that case let the yogi leave the practice and rest awhile.

நடுவுநில் லாமல் இடம்வலம் ஓடி
அடுகின்ற வாயுவை அந்தணன் கூடி
இடுகின்ற வாறுசென் றின்பணி சேர
முடிகின்ற தீபத்தின் முன்னுண்டென் றானே. 795

Yogi Who Regulates Breath Will See Finite Light

The Prana runs helter-skelter
To Right and to Left;
If Yogi gathers it proper
And regulates to reach Kundalini,
He shall stand before the Infinite Light;
Thus He said, Nandi Holy.

Prana runs helter skeleter to the right, and to the left. If the yogi regulates it appropriately, he shall reach kundalini, the finite light.

ஆயும் பொருளும் அணிமலர் மேலது
வாயு விதமும் பதினா றுளவலி
போய மனத்தைப் பொருகின்ற வாதாரம்
ஆயுவு நாளு முகுர்த்தமு மாமே. 796

Choose Appropriate Time for Piercing Adharas

The Lord that you search
Is on the Flower Above seated;
Sixteen the Ways of breath control;
The Breath coursing upward in strength
With mind in concentration united,
Pierce the adharas;
The days apt for thus reaching the Centres,
And the hour appropriate, know you well.

The art of rousing the kundalini and coursing the prana through the six adharas to reach the thousand-petalled flower above is a consummate one that requires knowledge of the sixteen ways of breath control and intense thought concentration. There are also days and hours appropriate for rousing the kundalini. For these, the Guru will be the guide.

17. வாரசூலம்

HOSTILE WEEK DAYS

Indian astrology prescribes certain days of the week as not appropriate for undertaking journeys or tasks in certain directions. This may be called 'directional astrology.' The danger in the direction is referred to figuratively as 'sula' or 'trident.'

வாரத்திற் சூலம் வரும்வழி கூறுங்கால்
நேரொத்த திங்கள் சனிகிழக் கேயாகும்
பாரொத்த சேய்புதன் உத்தரம் பானுநாள்
நேரொத்த வெள்ளி குடக்காக நிற்குமே. 797

Directional Dangers in Days of the Week

On different days of the week
The Sula lies in directions different
On Mondays and Saturdays it is in east;
On Tuesdays and Wednesdays in north
On Sundays and Fridays in west.

1) Sula literally means the 'trident;' metaphorically it means 'danger.'

Thus on Mondays and Saturdays the sula lies in the direction of east; on Tuesdays and Wednesdays, north; on Fridays and Sundays, west; on Thursdays, it lies south.

தெக்கண மாகும் வியாழத்துச் சேர்திசை
அக்கணி சூலமு மாமிடம் பின்னாகில்
துக்கமும் இல்லை வலமுன்னே தோன்றிடின்
மிக்கது மேல்வினை மேன்மேல் விளையுமே. 798

Dangers None if Breath Runs High in Right Nostril

On Thursdays menacing trident is in direction south;
Little effect Sula has
If breath to Left flows low,
No harm befalls if Right dominates;
Much good may actually swell.

This dangerous-effect of sula can, however, be counteracted by the appropriate alternations in the breathing rhythm. Thus sula has no effect if the flow of breath from the left nostril is low and if the flow from the right nostril is high. In fact, such a rhythm may even actually be beneficial. The practitioner in breath rhythm can apply the necessary corrections.

18. கேசரி யோகம்

KECHARI YOGA

After kundalini has been roused and the adharas have been pierced, the yogi arrives at a stage when he seeks to drink of the divine nectar that flows from the astral sphere within. For this there is a certain technique known as 'kechari mudra.'

The subtitle of the text, however, calls this 'kechari yoga.' A mudra is a technical part of the total yoga practice. Some commentators have confused it with kesari yoga' or 'lion posture,' as the Tamil spelling is identical for kechari and kesari. Literally, kechari means to traverse in the sky.

கட்டக் கழன்று கீழ்நான்று வீழாமல்
அட்டத்தைக் கட்டி அடுப்பை அணைகோலி
விட்டத்தைப் பூட்டி மேற்பையைத் தாட்கோத்து
நட்ட மிருக்க நமனில்லை தானே. 799

How to Practise it

Control the spiration
And see that breath is wasted not;
Bind it tight,
Dam the source of Kundalini at Muladhara,
Lock the chimney up in the mouth;
Bolt the cavity above with thy tongue's tip
And sit erect in yoga Samadhi
No more shall there be death for you.

The kechari yoga is the most important technique in kundalini yoga. It contains the breath within and sees that it is not wasted. The source of kundalini in the muladhara is dammed up and stopped so that breath does not escape downwards as apana. Similarly, the breath-escape of the prana in the mouth's upper cavity is locked with the tongue's tip. Having bolted the escapes below and above, the yogi sits erect in samadhi.

1) Although the word yoga, is used here in connection with kechari by Tirumular, the classical works like *Hatha Yoga Pradipika* (iii,1-9), *Gheranda Samhita* (iii,1-3) and *Siva Samhita* (iv,12-15) refer to the practice as a mudra. The word mudra means 'to seal,' 'close,' or 'lock up.' The mudra is a technique for locking the breath within the body. After the practitioner has purified his system and gained control of his breath, the technique of mudra is imparted to him by the Guru. Mudras are sometimes referred to as 'bandha' which means to 'bind, fix or restrain.' *Hatha yoga Pradipika* and *Gheranda Samhita* refer to 25 mudras; *Siva Samhita* refers to 10 mudras.

The word, kechari, has nothing to do with 'kesari' which means lion. As in Tamil both the words are written with the same spelling, some commentators have interpreted it as the lion posture or asana. Kechari means roaming through space or flying. Hence it is also called 'vyoma' or 'sky chakra.'

Hatha Yoga Pradipika (iii,32-40) describes it as follows: "The kechari mudra is accomplished by thrusting the tongue into the gullet, by turning it over on itself and keeping the eyesight in the middle of the eyebrows. To accomplish this, the tongue is lengthened by cutting the fraenum linguae, moving and pulling it. When it can reach the space between the eyebrows, then kechari can be accomplished. Taking a sharp, smooth, and clean instrument, of the shape of a cactus leaf, the fraenum of the tongue should be cut a little (as much as a hair's thickness) at a time. Then rock salt and yellow myrobalan (both powdered) should be rubbed in. On the 7th day, it should be again cut a hair's breadth. One should go on doing thus, regularly for six months. At the end of six months the fraenum of the tongue will be completely cut. Turning the tongue upwards, it is fixed on the three ways (esophagus, wind pipe and palate). Thus it makes the kechari mudra."

Compare *Gheranda Samhita* (iii, 25-280); "Cut the lower tendon of the tongue, and move the tongue constantly; rub it with fresh butter, and draw it out (to lengthen it) with an iron instrument. By practising this always, the tongue becomes long; and when it reaches the space between the eyebrows, then the kechari is accomplished. Then the tongue being lengthend, practise turning it upwards and backwards so as to touch the palate, till at length it reaches the holes of the nostrils opening into the mouth. Close those holes with the tongue (thus stopping inspiration), and fix the gaze on the space between the eyebrows. This is called kechari."

Compare *Siva Samhita* (iv,31-32): "The wise yogi sitting in vajrasana posture, in a place free from disturbance, should firmly fix his gaze on the spot in the middle of the two eyebrows, and reversing the tongue backwards, fix it in the hollow under the epiglottis, placing it with great care on the mouth of the well of nectar (ie. closing up the air passage). This mudra......is the kechari mudra."

Compare: "According to *Dhyana-bindu Upanishad,* kechari mudra is so called, because citta moves in 'kha' (akasa), and the tongue through this mudra enters 'kha.' It consists in lengthening of the tongue until it reaches to the space between the eyebrows. It is then turned back in the throat, and closes the exit of the breath previously inspired. The mind is fixed in the ajna.....It is said that sometimes the fraenum is cut, but others can do it without physical injury. — vide "The Serpent Power" by Sir John Woodroffe, p.209

Again *Hatha Yoga Pradipika* (iii, 41-53) says: "The siddhas have named this mudra, kechari, from the fact that the mind and the tongue reach akasa (ether) by its practise. If the hole behind the soft palate be stopped with kechari by turning the tongue upwards, then bindu (semen) cannot leave its place even if a woman were embraced. If the yogi drinks somarasa (vital fluid) by sitting with the tongue turned backwards, and mind concentrated, there is no doubt he conquers death within 15 days. If the yogi, whose body is full of somarasa were bitten by taksaka (snake), its poison cannot permeate his body. As fire is inseparably connected with the wood, and light is connected with wick and oil, so does the soul not leave the body full of nectar exuding from the soma. Those who eat the flesh of the cow and drink the immortal liquor daily, are regarded as men of noble family. The word 'goar' (cow) means tongue; eating, is thrusting it in the gullet. Immortal liquor is the nectar exuding from the moon. It is produced by the fire which is generated by thrusting tongue. If the tongue can touch with its end the hole from which falls the rasa which is saltish, bitter, sour, milky and similar to ghee and honey, one can drive away disease... There is only one seed germinating the whole universe from it; and there is only mudra, called kechari.

Compare *Gheranda Samhita* (iii,29-32); *Siva Samhita* (iv,33-37). See also W.H. Evans-Wentz's "The Tibetan Book of the Dead; Briggs's "Goraknath and Kanphata Yogis," Chpt.xv.; and Relé's "The Mysterious Kundalini." For Theos Bernard's personal experience, See "Hatha Yoga," pp.67-69.

வண்ணான் ஒலிக்குஞ் சதுரப் பலகைமேற்
கண்ணாறு மோழை படாமற் கரைகட்டி
விண்ணாறு பாய்ச்சிக் குளத்தை நிரப்பினால்
அண்ணாந்து பார்க்க அழுக்கற்ற வாறே. 800

Technique of Kechari Yoga

On the square plank of Muladhara,
Where Jiva the washerman performs the cleansing act
Erect bunds that the sluices leak not (apana);
And then let in the heavenly stream for the lake to fill
Thus sit looking skyward
Be thou rid of impurity, all.

Jiva, the washerman, performs the cleansing act on the square plank (four-petalled muladhara). There the yogi erects a bund so that the apana does not escape through the sluice. He then lets in the prana stream upward to fill the body-lake within. Thus he sits looking skyward and courses the breath through the spinal cavity of sushumna alternating from left to right and vice versa.

Kechari (otherwise Kechari) is spiritual attainment which enables one to overcome death.

இடக்கை வலக்கை இரண்டையும் மாற்றித்
துதிக்கையால் உண்பார்க்குச் சோரவும் வேண்டாம்
உறக்கத்தை நீக்கி உணரவல் லார்கட்
கிறக்கவும் வேண்டாம் இருக்கலு மாமே. 801

Immortality in Yoga Way

Alternating breath's course from left to right and vice versa,
They who can force breath through spinal Sushumna
Shall know tiring none;
They can abolish sleep for ever
And attain God-awareness;
They die not;
Immortal they shall be.

The yogi who does this knows neither weariness nor sleep. He will be alert all day and night in divine consciousness.

ஆய்ந்துரை செய்யில் அமுதநின் றூறிடும்
வாய்ந்துரை செய்யும் வருகின்ற காலத்து
நீந்துரை செய்யில் நிலாமண் டலமதாய்ப்
பாய்ந்துரை செய்தது பாலிக்கு மாறே. 802

Nectar in Kechari Mudra

If skilfully rubbed by the tongue's tip
The mystic nectar will begin to ooze;
When it comes, with care manage it
That you may swim in Moon's Region mystic;
And that which flowed and roared
May preserved be.

Mantras 802-805

If the tongue's tip is turned backwards to lock up the cavity in the gullet, and then skilfully rubbed, the mystic nectar will begin to ooze from the moon's region. This nectar of the flesh is a heavenly stream. It springs from where the jiva and Siva reside at the peak of the cranium. This mudra confers lasting youthfulness and longevity. With the guidance of the guru, it will lead to divine wisdom.

Some authorities advocate cutting the fraenum to facilitate this process. Tirumular, however, does not mention it. Both these methods seem to have been in practice.

நாவின் நுனியை நடுவே சிவிறிடிற்
சிவனும் அங்கே சிவனும் உறைவிடம்
மூவரு முப்பத்து மூவருந் தோன்றுவர்
சாவதும் இல்லை சதகோடி யூனே. 803

Vision of Gods in Kechari Mudra

Fan tongue's tip upward in palate centre;
There abides Jiva and Siva;
The Gods Three, and Devas three and thirty crores
Will there appear;
No death shall there be;
A million, billion years this fleshy body will be.

ஊனூறல் பாயும் உயர்வரை உச்சிமேல்
வானூறல் பாயும் வகையறி வாரில்லை
வானூறல் பாயும் வகையறி வாளர்க்குத்
தேனூறல் உண்டு தெளியலு மாமே. 804

Transform Fleshy Stream Into Heavenly Stream

From the lofty peaks of the cranium
Flows the stream that is of the flesh;
It is a heavenly stream;
They know not how to make it so;
They who know that art
Will swill the divine nectar
And be forever, doubt-free.

மேலையண் ணாவில் விரைந்திரு காலிடிற்
காலனும் இல்லை கதவுந் திறந்திடும்
ஞாலம் அறிய நரைதிரை மாறிடும்
பாலனு மாவான் பராநந்தி ஆணையே. 805

Kechari Mudra Leads to Youthfulness

If you can send the breath twain
Into the mouth's upper cavity
You shall then know death none;
And the gates of nectar will open be;
Greying and wrinkling will disappear
For all to see;
Young will the Yogi be
True this, I say, in the name of Nandi Holy.

நந்தி முதலாக நாமேலே யேறிட்டுச்
சந்தித் திருக்கில் தரணி முழுதாளும்
பந்தித் திருக்கும் பகலோன் வெளியாகச்
சிந்தித் திருப்பவர் தீவினை யாளரே. 806

Leakage of Restrained Breath Leads to Evil Consequences

With Nandi to guide
If we upward ascend
We shall meet the Lord;
We shall then hold sway over world all;
They who let the restrained breath out
Through the Sun Nadi
And yet meditating sit
Art verily to Evil Fate decreed.

தீவினை யாடத் திகைத்தங் கிருந்தவர்
நாவினை நாடின் நமனுக் கிடமில்லை
பாவினை நாடிப் பயனறக் கண்டவர்
தேவினை யாடிய தீங்கரும் பாமே. 807

Perfect Practice of Kechari Leads to Immortality

They who sat bewildered
Overwhelmed by Karma Evil,
Let them perform the Karma of Tongue
(That Kechari Yoga prescribes);
Then no more is there room for death;
Those who realize that karmas are useless
Do the divine work and
Enjoy sweetness like that of the sugarcane juice.

தீங்கரும் பாகவே செய்தொழி லுள்ளவர்
ஆங்கரும் பாக அடையநா வேறிட்டுக்
கோங்கரும் பாகிய கோணை நிமிர்த்திட
ஊன்கரும் பாகியே ஊனீர் வருமே. 808

Erect Posture for Kechari Mudra

The Yogis who thus divine sweetness experienced
If in a bud-like formation
Send tongue upward
And make the coiled kundalini erect
Then will trickle nectar from within
And body becomes sweet as sugarcane.

Mantras 808-810, 813 & 814

When the yogi twirls the tongue into the cavity of the gullet through which saliva flows and drinks of the nectar that wells up, chanting all the time 'Sivaya nama' in silence, verily the body becomes sweet as sugarcane. The water that kechari mudra brings streams pellucid as from the Ganga. The body becomes a cave temple within. The yogi is then in rapport with the mystic moon shedding the 16 kalas. He sees the kala worlds within the divine mansion shedding argent rays. He visions Sakti too, as a Divine Fawn enveloped by kalas. There, She sits enriching the ambrosia stream.

ஊனீர் வழியாக வுண்ணாவை யேறிட்டுத்
தேனீர் பருகிச் சிவாய நமவென்று
கானீர் வரும்வழி கங்கை தருவிக்கும்
வானீர் வரும்வழி வாய்நதறி வீரே. 809

Chant Sivayanama as You Swill Nectar

Upward twirl

Tongue's interior
Through which saliva flows
And drink of nectar welling up
And remain chanting 'Sivaya Nama;'
The waters that breath brings
Streams as unto Ganga flow;
Learn this Way
To the flow of the Heavenly nectar.

The mantra "Sivaya Namah" makes its appearance here. The word "pariyanga" literally means bed-stead; here, it refers to the "vamacara" branch of tantricism, which advocates the "panca makara", the five Ms: mamsa, mithuna, mina, mudra, and madhu.

வாய்ந்தறிந் துள்ளே வழிபாடு செய்தவர்
காய்ந்தறி வாகக் கருணை பொழிந்திடும்
பாய்ந்தறிந் துள்ளே படிக்கத வொன்றிட்டுக்
கூய்ந்தறிந் துள்ளுறை கோயிலு மாமே. 810

A Cave Temple Within

Knowing way appropriate
Those who worshipped thus within
Will receive shower of Grace
That is Jnana ripe;
If they but know how to bolt the door within
And check the flowing stream,
Well then may they become
Abiding cave temples within.

"Cave Temple" is esoteric language for the cranium.

கோயிலின் உள்ளே குடிசெய்து வாழ்பவர்
தாயினும் நல்லார் தரணி முழுதுக்குந்
காயினும் நல்லவர் காய்ந்தவர் தம்முளுந்
தீயினுந் தீயரத் தீவினை யாளர்க்கே. 811

God's Attributes

He who takes His abode within that temple
Is kinder than mother for world entire
Good is He, even when harsh,
He is within them too,
Whom He deals harsh,
For those of evil deeds,
He is deadlier than fire itself.

தீவினை யாளர்தஞ் சென்னியி லுள்ளவன்
பூவினை யாளர்தம் பொற்பதி யானவன்
பாவினை யாளர்தம் பாகவத் துள்ளவன்
மாவினை யாளர்தம் மதியிலுள் ளானே. 812

God's Abodes

He is seated at the Forehead Centre
Of those who perform yoga with Kundalini Fire;
He is in the Golden City
Of those who reach the Flower of cranial spaces;
He is in the imagination
Of those who sing of Him;
He is in the intelligence
Of those who perform deeds rare.

மதியி னெழுங்கதிர் போலப் பதினாறாய்ப்
பதிமனை நூறு நூற் றிருபத்து நாலாய்க்
கதிமனை யுள்ளே கணைகள் பரப்பி
எதிர்மலை யாமல் இருந்தனன் தானே. 813

He Sat Supreme

He sat like the Moon
Beaming Kalas Sixteen;
In His Mansion that is body,
Art Kala worlds two hundred and twenty four;
And within that Divine Mansion shedding rays,
He sat Supreme in accord within.

1) Santhiatheetha Kala—15
Santhi Kala—18
Vidya Kala—27
Pratishta Kala—56
Nivirthi Kala—108
Total 224

(Ref: *Abhithana Chintanami*. The total for pratishtakala is 56 and not 59 as is given here.) Vide "Garland of Letters," pp.269-272 for a tabulated list.

இருந்தனள் சத்தியு மக்கலை சூழ
இருந்தனள் கன்னியு மந்நடு வாக
இருந்தனள் மானேர் முகநில வார
இருந்தனள் தானும் அமுதம் பொழிந்தே. 814

In Praise of Sakti

There sat Sakti
Kalas enveloping Her too;
There She sat, the Virgin in the midst;
There She sat, the Divine Fawn,
Her Visage shedding rays soft;
There She sat,
Herself too streaming ambrosia down.

பொழிந்த இருவெள்ளி பொன்மண் ணடையில்
வழிந்துள் ளிருந்தது வான்முத லங்குக்
கழிந்தது போகாமற் காக்கவல் லார்க்குக்
கொழுந்தது வாகுங் குணமது தானே. 815

Guard Nectar From Flowing Out

Within the Golden Regions of Cranium
The sparkling nectar flows in cascades silvery;
There it was inside,
In the astral sphere above;
They who can guard it from flowing out,
Will become eternal young;
That is its blessing, for sure, for sure.

Mantras 815 & 816

From within the golden region of the cranium the sparkling nectar flows in silvery cascades. The yogi who can guard it from flowing out will remain eternally young. Inside the astral sphere from where the nectar flows is Sakti, the tender vine of goodness and haunting fragrance, in unity with Siva, the Treasure House of tattva jnana.

குணமது வாகிய கோமள வல்லி
மணமது வாக மகிழ்ந்தங் கிருக்கில்
தனமது வாகிய தத்துவ ஞானம்
இனமது வாக இருந்தனன் தானே. *816*

With Sakti Stood Siva

If Sakti that is like a tender Vine of Goodness
Resides within in fragrant delight;
Then Lord that is a treasure-house of Tattva Jnana
Also stood in amity within.

இருந்த பிராணனும் உள்ளே எழுமாம்
பரிந்தஇத் தண்டுடன் அண்டம் பரிய
விரிந்தஅப் பூவுடன் மேலெழ வைக்கின்
மலர்ந்தது மண்டலம் வாழலு மாமே. *817*

Prana Reaches Moon's Region

Prana within if made to rise,
Through Sushumna cavity
To blossoming Lotus at cranial heights,
Then opened Moon's Mystic Region;
And there may you for long live.

There in that mystic moon's region the yogi can sit for an indefinite length of time.

மண்டலத் துள்ளே மனவொட்டி யாணத்தைக்
கண்டகத் தங்கே கருதியே கீழ்க்கட்டிப்
பண்டகத் துள்ளே பகலே ஒளியாகக்
குண்டலக் காதனுங் கூத்தொழிந் தானே. *818*

Practise Uddiyana Bandha

As Prana stands in Mystic Moon's Region
Practise Uddiyana Bandha,
And dam the course of downward Apana;
Then in dazzling brightness of sun
The Lord with Kundala in his ear lobe
Stands transfixed in their awareness,
His dance having come to a stop.

Uddiyana is a mudra. It literally means 'flying up or soaring;' being so called because the great bird, prana, tied to it, flies without being fatigued. The belly above the navel is passed backwards towards the spine. The portions above and below the navel should be drawn backwards towards the spine. Of all the bandhas, uddiyana is the best; for, by binding it firmly, liberation comes spontaneously. — *Hatha Yoga Pradipika,* iii, pp.54-59. Compare *Gheranda Samhita,* iii, pp.10-11; *Siva Samhita.*

A Practice that aids in the successful performance of kechari mudra is 'uddiyana bandha. In fact, this is a preliminary exercise to the performance of kechari mudra.

"Uddiyana Bandha" — According to Kalika Purana, Uddiyana is the place (pitha) where the thighs of Sati fell. (p.132 of N.N. Bhattacharya's 'History of Sakta religion').

ஒழிகின்ற வாயுவும் உள்ளே அமருங்
கழிகின்ற வாயுவுங் காக்கலு மாகும்
வழிகின்ற காலத்து வட்டக் கழலைப்
பழிகின்ற காலத்துப் பையகற் றீரே. *819*

When to do Uddiyana Bandha

The exhaling breath will inside retained be;
The retained breath will from escape prevented be;
In due time,
From the Moon's Region starts ambrosial flow;
If it is not checked it will merge in the Kundalini.

Uddiyana means rising upwards; bandha is arresting it. It is damming the course of downward apana at the muladhara. Uddiyana bandha is an exercise in the lower regions parallel to the kechari mudra at the higher regions. The uddiyana bandha closes the lower sluice.

By drawing in the mulasthana (anus), uddiyana bandha should be performed. The flow of the air should be directed to the sushumna by closing the ida and the pingala. The prana then becomes calm and latent by this means. — Vide *Hatha Yoga Pradipika,* iii, pp.69-77.

பையினி னுள்ளே படிக்கத வொன்றிடின்
மெய்யினி னுள்ளே விளங்கும் ஒளியதாங்
கையினுள் வாயுக் கதித்தங் கெழுந்திடின்
மையணி கோயில் மணிவிளக் காமே. *820*

Open a Wicket Gate Within and See Light

Within the body-bag
If you but open a wicket gate,
The Light will shine inside;
If breath that is controlled spurts there upwards
Then will this dark body
As a temple lamp lustrous bejewelled be.

It is after this that the yogi can open the "wicket gate" (fourth door) above and let the prana slowly stream upwards to sahasrara.

விளங்கிடும் வாயுவை மேலெழ உன்னி
நலங்கிடுங் கண்டத்து நாபியி னுள்ளே
வணங்கிடு மண்டலம் வாய்த்திடக் கும்பிச்
சுணங்கிட நின்றவை சொல்லலு மாமே. *821*

Inexplicable Experiences of Kechari Yoga

Course Prana upward
And retain breath through Kumbhaka
In the mystic regions of Fire and Sun
Around navel and throat;
And there be fixed in thought
What stood there, how possible to say?

In doing so the breath should still be retained in kumbhaka, in the region of fire and sun around the navel and throat, and thought should be transfixed there. The experience that follows is indeed indescribable.

சொல்லலு மாயிடு மாகத்து வாயுவுஞ்
சொல்லலு மாகு மண்ணீர்க் கடினமுஞ்

சொல்லலு மாகும் இவையஞ்சுங் கூடிடிற்
சொல்லலு மாந்தூர தெரிசனந் தானே. 822

Distant Vision of Five-Element Combination

Well may described be air in the body
Well may described be earth and water
Well may described be all these elements five,
But when all these together combine,
Well may then be
The power of Vision is cranium distant.

Mantras 822 & 823

There, the combined vision of the five elements results in the distant vision. This distant vision consists in attaining the grace of Sakti in the first instance, and then when thought is centred deeper, the divine light of the Lord appears; and all worlds too appear as in bright daylight.

தூர தரிசனஞ் சொல்லுவன் காணலாங்
காராருங் கண்ணி கடைஞான முட்பெய்தி
ஏராருந் தீபத் தெழிற்சிந்தை வைத்திடிற்
பாரா ருலகம் பகன்முன்ன தாமே. 823

Nature of Distant Divine Vision

That Distant Vision I shall here describe:
Having attained Grace of Sakti of collyruim eyes
If thought is centred on the Divine Light that is Lord
Then may you vision worlds all
As in day-light bright.

முன்னெழு நாபிக்கு முந்நால் விரற்கீழே
பன்னெழு வேதப் பகலொளி யுண்டென்னும்
நன்னெழு நாதத்து நற்றீபம் வைத்திடத்
தன்னெழு கோயில் தலைவனு மாமே. 824

Reach Nada Through Kundalini

Twelve finger measure below the navel
The light bright as day (Kundalini) shines.
Thus say the Vedas;
If with that Light
The Nada Lamp above is lighted
You become the Master great
Of Mansion that within you rises.

Kundalini is the lamp burning as radiant as the day. With that lamp the yogi lights the nada lamp; and so becomes the master of the mystic mansion that rises within.

19. பரியங்க யோகம்

PARIYANGA YOGA

The Tamil commentators interpret 'pariyanga' as 'cot', and 'yoga' as that practised on a 'cot' (euphemistically with woman in bed). But the classical Sanskrit texts, however, use the term vajroli' and refer to it as a mudra. The Tamil scholiasts call it a yoga, even as they call kechari mudra a yoga.

The word 'pari' means 'hard,' and 'anga' refers to the male sexual organ. In fact, this seems to be the main import of the vajroli mudra as well as pariyanga yoga.

In this mudra, the main object seems to be to restrain the flow of semen without loss of enjoyment through control of breath.

பூசு வனவெல்லாம் பூசிப் புலர்த்திய
வாச நறுங்குழல் மாலையுஞ் சாத்திக்
காயக் குழலி கலவி யொடுங்கலந்
தூசித் துளையுறத் தூங்காது போகமே. 825

Pleasures of Sex Union Will Abide If Breath Control is Properly Practised

Anointing her body with unguents diverse
Bedecking her tresses with flowers fragrant
Do thou enjoy the damsel in passion's union;
If thou but know how to shoot
Prana breath through the Sushumna
Their enjoyment ceaseth never.

Mantras 825 & 826

The yogi anoints the woman's body with diverse perfumes. He bedecks her tresses with fragrant flowers and then proceeds to enjoy the damsel in heightened passion. But as he does so, he draws the breath inward through the spinal cavity. The breath stands still. As the full-breasted damsel and the skilled yogi thus seek enjoyment, the liquid silver (sukhla) draws in the liquid gold (sronita) and the yogi, with breath stilled, masters the retention of his semen. The couple commingle in ecstatic passion the whole time.

Pariyanga Yoga, which deals with sexual acts in terms of yoga, is a Vamacara concept. Mular who had earlier, condemned Vamacara, now describes this very yoga in laudatory terms.

போகத்தை யுன்னவே போகாது வாயுவு
மோகத்தை வெள்ளியு மீளும் வியாழத்தில்
சூதொத்த மென்முலை யாளுநற் சூதனுந்
தாதிற் குழைந்து தலைகண்ட வாறே. 826

If Breath is Controlled Delicious Enjoyment Results in Sex Union

When they seek enjoyment
The breath standeth still;
The full breasted damsel and fervent male
Stand in union exalted;
As liquid silver and gold
Their passion's emissions
In rapture commingleth.

கண்டனுங் கண்டியுங் காதல்செய் யோகத்து
மண்டலங் கொண்டிரு பாலும் வெளிநிற்கும்
வண்டியை மேற்கொண்டு வானீர் உருட்டிடத்
தண்டொரு காலுந் தளராது அங்கமே. 827

Duration of Enjoyment Lengthens If Breath is Controlled

In the copulatory yoga that is practised
By the hero and the heroine
Upward they drive the coach of breath
That hath its wheels in regions right and left;.
There they collect the waters of the heaven
And never the organs tiring know.

In that conjugal yoga thus practised, the yogi drives the two-wheeled coach of breath upward. His organ knows no weariness, and he collects the "waters of the heaven."

In the *Sakta Tantras* the aspirant is known as hero or Veera.

அங்கப் புணர்ச்சியு மாகின்ற தத்துவ
மங்கத்தில் விந்து வருகின்ற போகத்துப்
பங்கப் படாமற் பரிகரித் துத்தம்மைத்
தங்கிக் கொடுக்கத் தலைவனு மாமே. 828.

Restraint of Semen Flow Through Breath Control

This the meaning of that union;
When in the sex act semen flows
The yogi lets it not;
But checks it
And within retaineth
And a Master he then becometh.

Mantras 828 & 829

This then is the meaning of that mudra; in the conjugal act the yogi lets not the semen flow, but checks it and holds it within. Verily he becomes the master. He becomes master of jnana. He becomes master of enjoyment. He becomes master of himself. He becomes master of the five senses.

தலைவனு மாயிடுந் தன்வழி ஞானந்
தலைவனு மாயிடுந் தன்வழி போகந்
தலைவனு மாயிடுந் தன்வழி யுள்ளே
தலைவனு மாயிடுந் தன்வழி அஞ்சே. 829

Effect of Restraint of Semen Flow

He becomes master of Jnana all
He becomes master of enjoyment all
He becomes master of himself
He becomes master of senses five.

அஞ்சு கடிகைமேல் ஆறாங் கடிகையில்
துஞ்சுவ தொன்றத் துணைவி துணைவன்பால்
நெஞ்சு நிறைந்தது வாய்கொளா தென்றது
பஞ்ச கடிகை பரியங்க யோகமே. 830

Sex Union Through the Pariyanga Lasts Five Ghatikas and is Bliss

This is Pariyanga Yoga
That lasts five ghatikas;
Beyond in the sixth
The damsel sleeps in the arms of lover
In union blissful
That fills the heart
And passes description.

This union lasts for five naligas (two and half hours). Then in the sixth naliga the damsel goes to sleep in the arms of the yogi lover, in blissful union that "fills" her heart in an experience that defies description.

பரியங்க யோகத்துப் பஞ்ச கடிகை
அரியஇவ் வியோகம் அடைந்தவர்க் கல்லது
சரிவளை முன்கைச்சி சந்தனக் கொங்கை
உருவித் தழுவி ஒருவற்கொண் ணாதே. 831.

Successful Practitioners Alone Can Resort to Pariyanga Yoga

Unless it be,
He had on success practised
The Pariyanga yoga
Of five ghatika length
No yogi shall
A woman embrace.

Mantras 831 & 832

Let no yogi embrace a woman unless he has successfully practised this technique of the five naliga duration. If it is asked who is the yogi that had accomplished this audacious practice, the answer is, "Lord Siva that wears the heavenly Ganga on his matted locks." Siva, the Supreme Yogi, embraced Sakti of ambrosial-sweet voice, thinking and not thinking of the act.

ஒண்ணாத யோகத்தை உற்றவ ராரென்னில்
விண்ணார்ந்த கங்கை விரிசடை வைத்தவன்
பண்ணார் அமுதினைப் பஞ்ச கடிகையில்
எண்ணா மெனஎண்ணி இருந்தான் இருந்ததே. 832

Lord Siva Practised Pariyanga Yoga

Who may you ask,
Is He that achieved this audacious Yoga;
The lord is He that wears heavenly Ganga on His matted lock;
For ghatika five
He embraced Sakti of speech ambrosial sweetness
Thinking and thinking not of the act performed.

ஏய்ந்த பிராயம் இருபது முப்பதும்
வாய்ந்த குழலிக்கு மன்னர்க்கு மானந்தம்
வாய்ந்த குழலியோ டைந்து மலர்ந்திடச்
சோர்ந்தன சித்தமுஞ் சோர்வில்லை
வெள்ளிக்கே. 833

The Age of the Couple for Pariyanga Yoga

For practise of this yoga,
Twenty the age apt for damsel
And thirty for lover;

Then does high rapture ensue;
The five senses of woman desert her,
Her mind exhausted becomes,
When she climax reaches;
But no weariness the man knows
Neither does his silvery emission flow.

For practise of this yoga the apt age for the woman is twenty, and for the yogi, thirty. Then high rapture ensures. The five senses of the woman desert her. She swoons and reaches the climax. But the yogi knows no weariness, nor does his silvery fluid get ejected.

வெள்ளி யுருகிப் பொன்வழி ஓடாமே
கள்ளத்தட் டானார் கரியிட்டு மூடினார்
கொள்ளி பறியக் குழல்வழி யேசென்று
வள்ளியுண் ணாவில் அடக்கிவைத் தாரே. 834

Only Those Who Have Practised Kechari Can Resort to Pariyanga

Lest the silvery liquid into the golden flow,
The artful goldsmith (practitioner) covered it up with yogic breath
The sparks (Kundalini) that flew travelled up by the way of Spinal tube
There above,
He contained them with tongue's tip (Kechari).

Only those who have practised kechari mudra successfully can take to pariyanga yoga. The yogi is an artful goldsmith. He does not allow the liquid silver semen to run into the liquid gold (sronita). As the goldsmith covers the melting metal with carbon, the yogi covers up the seminal flow with his breath control. The sparks that fly in this alchemic process by way of the spinal tube reach above; there it is contained by the tongue's tip or kechari mudra.

வைத்த இருவருந் தம்மின் மகிழ்ந்துடன்
சித்தங் கலங்காது செய்கின்ற ஆனந்தம்
பத்து வகைக்கும் பதினெண் கணத்துக்கும்
வித்தக னாய்நிற்கும் வெங்கதி ரோனே. 835

Pariyanga Yogi is Exalted

The Yogi who is in ecstatic joy
Unexcited performs this yoga with woman
Becomes radiant like the sun,
An acknowledged master in directions ten,
And of Ganas of groups eighteen.

If the yogi, though experiencing ecstatic joy, performs this mudra unexcited, he becomes radiant as the sun, an acknowledged master in ten directions and head of the eighteen Gana hordes.

வெங்கதி ருக்குஞ் சனிக்கும் இடைநின்ற
நங்கையைப் புல்லிய நம்பிக்கோ ரானந்தந்
தங்களிற் பொன்னிடை வெள்ளிதா ழாமுனந்
திங்களிற் செவ்வாய் புதைத்திருந் தாரே. 836

Pariyanga Yoga Practised With Kechari Yoga Also

Espousing Wisdom that is denoted by Budha* (Mercury)
Who stands middle of sun and saturn
The youthful Yogi who embraced the damsel
Knew joy infinite;
Lest the male silvery liquid flow not
Ahead of female golden one
He had his red mouth buried in the Mystic Moon.

While the yogi practises it, he does not allow the silvery liquid to flow. He should "bury his red mouth in the mystic moon" (practise kechari yoga).

1) A play on the word 'budha,' Wednesday is in the middle of the week from Sunday to Saturday.

2) He practised kechari yoga simultaneously.

There is much esoterism in these verses. The names of the planets are used in a double sense.

திருத்திப் புதனைத் திருத்தல்செய் வார்க்குக்
கருத்தழ காலே கலந்தங் கிருக்கில்
வருத்தமு மில்லையா மங்கை பங்கற்குந்
துருத்தியுள் வெள்ளியுஞ் சோரா தெழுமே. 837

Pariyanga Yoga is Yogic Wisdom That Retains the Semen

They who perfect wisdom
And embrace woman in wisdom's beauty
Will know grief none,
Though by woman's side he be;
The liquid silver remains unspent
And flows not into the vaginal bag of woman.

He, who, in perfect wisdom, embraces a woman knows no grief. Although he is by the woman's side, the silvery semen does not flow into the vaginal track.

எழுகின்ற தீயை முன்னே கொண்டு சென்றிட்டால்
மெழுகுரு கும்பரி செய்திடும் மெய்யே
உழுகின்ற தில்லை ஒளியை அறிந்தபின்
விழுகின்ற தில்லை வெளியறி வார்க்கே. 838

Freedom From Sexual Union is Attained by Pariyanga Yoga

This body that melts like wax over fire
(By sexual union)
Will no more indulge in it,
When wisdom dawns;
To those who have attained Wisdom of Space
The liquid silver no exit knows.

His body, which in sexual union melts like wax on fire, will no more indulge in it when wisdom dawns. They who have attained the wisdom of Space will know no exit of the liquid silver.

வெளியை அறிந்து வெளியி னடுவே
ஒளியை அறியி னுளிமுறியாமே
தெளிவை அறிந்து செழுநந்தி யாலே
வெளியை அறிந்தனன் மேலறி யேனே. 839

Vision of Space in Pariyanga Yoga

When You know the Void
And the light in that Void
Your mind shall be strong as a chistle of bronze;
After having tasted of the nectar
I saw the Void
With great Nandi guiding;
Beyond, I knew not.

When the yogi knows the Space and the light in the Space, then the mind shall become strong as bronze. The vision of the Space comes after tasting of the nectar through the kechari yoga with the guidance of Nandi.

மேலாந் தலத்தில் விரிந்தவ ரானின்
மாலாந் திசைமுகன் மாநந்தி யாயவர்
நாலா நிலத்தி னடுவான வப்பொருள்
மேலா யுரைத்தனர் மின்னிடை யாளுக்கே. 840

Pariyanga Yoga was Expounded by Sadasiva to Sakti

Who are those that rank high above?
Mal, Brahma and Nandi (Rudra) are they;
In the Fourth is that Sadasiva,
Who to the slender-waisted Sakti
This expounded.

மின்னிடை யாளுமின் னாளனுங் கூட்டத்துப்
பொன்னிடை வட்டத்தின் உள்ளே புகப்பெய்து
தன்னொடு தன்னைத் தலைப்பெய்ய வல்லாரேன்
மண்ணிடைப் பல்லூழி வாழலு மாமே. 841

Immortality for Those Who Unite in Sivasakti in Cranium

If you can get to Sakti and Siva
Inside the Golden Circle within (Cranium)
And then join them in union,
You may live on earth
A million, trillion years.

வாங்க லிறுதலை வாங்கலில் வாங்கிய
வீங்க வலிக்கும் விரகறி வாரில்லை
வீங்க வலிக்கும் விரகறி வாளரும்
ஓங்கிய தன்னை உதம்பண்ணி னாரே. 842

Yogis Offered Themselves Entire to God

Inhaling, exhaling and retaining the breath inhaled
—None knows its technique of control
And those of skill who know it
Offered themselves to Lord entire.

உதமறிந் தங்கே ஒருசுழிப் பட்டாற்
கதமறிந் தங்கே கபாலங் கறுக்கும்
இதமறிந் தென்றும் இருப்பாள் ஒருத்தி
பதமறிந் தும்முளே பார்க்கடிந் தாளே. 843

Yoga Dispels Worldly Longings

Knowing the way of self-oblation,
If they get into the Mystic Circle
Of Siva and Sakti,
They reach the True Way;
And dark their hair turns
In youthfulness eternal,
And the One Sakti will inward abide;
In due accord
Dispelling worldly longings all.

The yogi who reaches the mystic circle of Siva and Sakti will despise all worldly longings. That Sakti is seated with Siva on the lotus above. That lotus knows neither land nor water; no stalk; no roof. Yet that lotus blossoms.

பாரில்லை நீரில்லை பங்கயம் ஒன்றுண்டு
தாரில்லை வேரில்லை தாமரை பூத்தது
ஊரில்லை காணும் ஒளியது ஒன்றுண்டு
கீழில்லை மேலில்லை கேள்வியிற் பூவே. 844

Lotus Cranial

There is a lotus
That neither land nor water knows;
No stalk, no root, the lotus blossomed yet!
City there was none; yet Light there is one!
Neither above nor below is a flower, none had heard of.

There is a city above; there is a light above; but no habitation. The flower that has "neither the above nor the below" is a flower none has heard of.

The lotus is in Hinduism a symbol of many things, here of the cranium.

20. அமுரிதாரணை

AMURI DHARANA

Amuri dharana is a technique of urine therapy which is practised in yoga to achieve longevity. The fact that this practice is advocated after pariyanga yoga (or vajroli mudra) shows that this requires advanced preliminary yoga preparation. In fact, *Hatha Yoga Pradipika* couples this practice along with vajroli,' and so calls it 'amaroli.'

Amuri Dharana

"The drinking of human urine once formed part of ancient fertility rites, and the significance of yellow-coloured water used in certain Hindu festivals, such as Holi is believed to be a relic of this scatalogical practice. The claim that drinking human urine enhances sexual powers has been substantiated, according to a recent writer, by Dr. Butenandt's discovery in 1931 that the male sex hormone could be extracted from human urine". (Benjamin Walker under the caption 'Scatology' in his "Hinduism").

உடலிற் கிடந்த வுறுதிக் குடிநீர்க்
கடலிற் சிறுகிணற் றேற்றமிட் டாலொக்கும்
உடலில் ஒருவழி ஒன்றுக் கிறைக்கில்
நடலைப் படாதுயிர் நாடலு மாமே. 845

Effect of Urine Therapy in Yoga

The urinary liquid within the body
Is unto a picot of small well;
Dipped into sea vast
If that is fed once a day
In way appropriate,
Life will know distress none;
Well may you seek it.

The practice is referred to in *Hatha Yoga Pradipika,* pp.82-96, as quoted in Theos Bernard's "Hatha Yoga," pp.71-72; "In the doctrine of the sect of Kapalikas, the 'amaroli' is the drinking of the cool mid-stream leaving the first, as it is a mixture of too much bile, and the last which is useless. He who drinks amari, snuffs it daily, practises 'vajroli' is called practising amaroli." Auri (Tamil) is synonymous with amari (Sanskrit), meaning deathlessness.

For a controversy on this practice see 'Illustrated Weekly of India," July 24, 1977, p.24. The Prime Minister of India, Sri Morarji Desai, recently revealed that he practises this with good effect.

தெளிதரும் இந்தச் சிவநீர் பருகில்
ஒளிதரு மோராண்டில் ஊனமொன் றில்லை
வளியுறும் எட்டின் மனமும் ஒடுங்குங்
களிதருங் காயங் கனகம தாமே. 846

Good Effects of Amuri Dharana

If this divine water clear is inside taken
The body glows in a year;
No harm befalls it;
Prana control will realised be;
The mind will centre in Letter "A" (Prana)
And will uplifted be
And the body into gold will be turned.

Mantra 846 & 850

Nandi called it the hero's recipe, heaven's liquor, and Sakti's potion. It is a medicine of radiant light. If taken in the way appropriate, it helps prana control and thought concentration. The body will turn golden and the mind will become uplifted.

நூறு மிளகு நுகருஞ் சிவத்தினீர்
மாறும் இதற்கு மருந்தில்லை மாந்தர்கள்
தேறில் இதனைத் தெளியுச்சி கப்பிடின்
மாறும் இதற்கு மறுமயி ராமே. 847

Consume 100 — Pepper Measure (drops) a Day

Drink of this divine water,
A hundred pepper measure
No medicine beyond this, know men;
Rub it clear on the crest of head
Your greying vanishes away
And fresh black hair shoots forth.

If a hundred pepper measures of this "divine water" (presumably a pepper measure is a drop) are drunk everyday, the body requires no other medicine. If it is rubbed on the crown of the head, grey hair vanishes and fresh black hair shoots forth.

கரையரு கேநின்ற கானல் உவரி
வரைவரை என்பர் மதியிலா மாந்தர்
நுரைதிரை நீக்கி நுகரவல் லார்க்கு
நரைதிரை மாறு நமனுமங் கில்லையே. 848

Only the Ignorant Dissuade the Practice

The water on the banks of body
Away, Away, from it — thus they say
The men who know not truth;
They who can drink the midstream
Rid of foam and wave
That arises first and last,
Will immortal be;
And all greying and wrinkling disappears.

Urine, "the water on the banks of the body is like a mirage on the sea." Thus say those who do not know the truth. They who can drink the midstream of their urine, rid of foam and wave, omitting the first and last portions, will become immortal.

அளக நன்னுத லாயோ ரதிசயங்
களவு காயங் கலந்தஇந் நீரிலே
மிளகு நெல்லியும் மஞ்சளும் வேம்பிடில்
இளகும் மேனி இருளுங் கபாலமே. 849

Effect of Mixing Ingredients

Oh! damsel of flowing tresses and slender forehead!
Hear you a miracle this!
In this Water hidden in the body
Mix pepper, amla, turmeric, and neem
Soft will your body be;
And dark thine hair on head.

If it is mixed with certain ingredients like pepper, amla, turmeric and neem, the body becomes miraculously soft.

வீர மருந்தென்றும் விண்ணோர் மருந்தென்றும்
நாரி மருந்தென்றும் நந்தி அருள்செய்தான்
ஆதி மருந்தென் றறிவார் அகலிடஞ்
சோதி மருந்திது சொல்லவொண் ணாதே. 850

Greatness of Amuri Dharana

He the Nandi called it: the Hero's recipe, Heaven's elixir, and Sakti's potion
Some know it as the Medicament Primus
It is specific that is of radiant light
Hard to describe to world at large.

21. சந்திர யோகம்

CHANDRA YOGA

எய்து மதிக்கலை சூக்கத்தி லேறியே
எய்துவ தூலம் இருவகைப் பக்கத்துள்
எய்துங் கலைபோல ஏறி இறங்குமாந்
துய்யது சூக்கத்துத் தூலத்த காயமே. 851

When Breath Turns Subtle

When Prana ascends to Moon's Kala
It turns subtle (Sukshma)
The two breaths through Ida and Pingala run gross;
They rise and fall unto the kalas that wax and wane;
Pure is that Sukshma (Subtle)
Gross is that runs in the body.

The Prana that we breathe, ida and pingala, is gross. It rises and falls like the moon that waxes and wanes. But when this prana, after the practice of kechari mudra, ascends to the moon's kala, it becomes sukshma or subtle. The subtle prana is pure.

The 16 Kalas of the Moon are the 16 phases (The New Moon and the Full Moon are each counted as two); the 12 Kalas of the Sun are the months; Agni as such has no Kalas, but the ten Agnis are apparently treated as 10 Kalas.

ஆகின்ற சந்திரன் சூரியன் அங்கியுள்
ஆகின்ற ஈரெட்டொ டாறிரண் டீரைந்துள்
ஏகின்ற வக்கலை யெல்லா மிடைவழி
ஆகின்ற யோகி அறிந்த அறிவே. 852

Yogi Experiences Kalas of Moon, Sun and Fire

Sixteen the Kalas of Moon
Twelve of the Sun
And Ten of the Fire
The Yogi experiences them all
In the upward journey of Prana through Sushumna
And all that becomes his mystic knowledge.

Kalas are rays of energy bodies. The mystic moon within has 16 kalas; the sun, 12; and fire 10. The yogi experiences them all in the upward journey of prana through sushumna and all kalas become known to him.

ஆறாத தாங்கலை ஆதித்தன் சந்திரன்
நாறா நலங்கினார் ஞாலங் கவர்கொளப்
பேறாங் கலைமுற்றும் பெருங்கால் ஈரெட்டு
மாறாக் கதிர்கொள்ளு மற்றங்கி கூடவே. 853

Kalas of Fire Merge into Sun, Which in Turn Merge into Those of Moon

The Twelve Kalas of Sun
Absorb Kalas ten of Fire
Together are they absorbed
In Sixteen Kalas of Moon;
Those who have thus learned to merge
In Moon's Kala
Verily become Masters of Earth,
All Kalas entire filled.

Mantras 853-857

In that journey in kundalini yoga, the ten kalas of fire are first absorbed by the 12 kalas of the sun. Together the kalas of the sun and fire are absorbed in the 16 kalas of the moon. Thus the kalas of three different origins merge into one. Into them finally merge the four kalas of kundalini in the cranium top. There in the sahasrara, the yogi pays homage at the Feet of the Lord. Those who have learned to merge the kalas of fire and sun in the kalas of the moon, verily become masters of themselves.

பத்தும் இரண்டும் பகலோன் உயர்கலை
பத்தினொ டாறும் உயர்கலை பான்மதி
ஒத்தநல் அங்கிய தெட்டெட் டுயர்கலை
அத்திறன் நின்றமை ஆய்ந்துகொள் வீரே. 854

Kalas of Sun, Moon and Fire Enumerated

Twelve the Kalas of Sun
Sixteen the Kalas of Moon
Ten the Kalas of Fire
Thus are the Kalas in number,
Know you well and true.

எட்டெட் டனிலின் கலையாகும் ஈராறுட்
சுட்டப் படுங்கதி ரோனுக்குஞ் சூழ்கலை
கட்டப் படுமீ ரெட்டா மதிக்கலை
ஒட்டப் படாஇவை ஒன்றோடொன் றாவே. 855

The Disparate Kalas Merge into One

Ten the Kalas of Fire
Twelve of the scorching Sun
Sixteen that emanate from Moon;
All these Kalas which alike are not,
Into oneness merge.

எட்டெட்டும் ஈராறும் ஈரெட்டுந் தீக்கதிர்
சுட்டிட்ட சோமனில் தோன்றுங் கலையெனக்
கட்டப் படுந்தார கைகதிர் நாலுள
கட்டிட்ட தொண்ணூற்றொ டாறுங் கலாதியே. 856

Kalas Enumerated in Total, Including Those of Jiva and Tattva

Ten, twelve and sixteen
Are Kalas that appear in Agni, Sun and Moon;
And Four are Kalas of the Star (Jiva)
The fettering Tattvas six and ninety too
Are Kalas to count.

எல்லாக் கலையும் இடைபிங் கலைநடுச்
சொல்லா நடுநாடி யூடே தொடர்மூலஞ்
செல்லா எழுப்பிச் சிரத்துடன் சேர்தலால்
நல்லோர் திருவடி நண்ணிநிற் போரே. 857

Rouse All Kalas and Reach God

All Kalas from the Left and Right Nadis
Pass through the Central Nadi;
Kindle the Kundalini Fire in Muladhara;
They reach the Cranium at top,
To pay homage at the Feet of the Great One.

அங்கியிற் சின்னக் கதிரிரண் டாட்டத்துத்
தங்கிய தாரகை யாகுஞ் சசிபானு
வங்கிய தாரகை யாகும் பரையொளி
தங்கு நவசக்ர மாகுந் தரணிக்கே. 858

Nine Kalas of Nava Chakra

Two each of Kalas,
Fire, Star* Moon and Sun,
And Kala of Parai
Who is unto a Star
Together are the nine beams of Parai
In the Nava Chakra this world below..
*jiva

The four kalas of kundalini belong to the 'energy-body star.' Two kalas each for the star, fire, moon and sun, and one kala of Parai who is unto a star, together form the nine lights of Parai in the navel chakra.

தரணி சலங்கனல் கால்தக்க வானம்
அரணிய பானு அருந்திங்கள் அங்கி
முரணிய தாரகை முன்னிய ஒன்பான்
பிரணவ மாகும் பெருநெறி தானே. 859

Constituents of Pranava

Earth, Water, Fire, Air, Space
Sun, Moon, Agni and Star
These nine constitute Pranava
The Way that is Great.

தாரகை மின்னுஞ் சசிதேயும் பக்கத்துத்
தாரகை மின்னா சசிவளர் பக்கத்துத்
தாரகை பூவிற் சகலத்தி யோனிகள்
தாரகைத் தாரகை தானாஞ் சொரூபமே. 860

Transformation into Star of Stars

When moon wanes, the stars shine bright
When moon waxes, they do not
Unto stars (innumerable) are Jivas of universe,
Unto Star of Stars is the Divine Manifestation.

முற்பதி னைஞ்சின் முளைத்துப் பெருத்திடும்
பிற்பதி னைஞ்சிற் பெருத்துச் சிறுத்திடும்
அப்பதி னைஞ்சும் அறியவல் லார்கட்குச்
செப்பரி யான்கழல் சேர்தலு மாமே. 861

Mystery of Fifteen Kalas of Moon

In the waxing fortnight Kalas shoot and expand
In the waning fortnight they shrink and small become;
They who can know the mystery of Kalas Fifteen
May well reach the Feet of the Lord
Of glory indescribable.

1) Out of sixteen, fifteen are the eternal kalas of the moon. One kala remains there always. That kala is nothing but chit itself. We call Her, Tripurasundari. It is understood by this, that in order to rouse the kundalini, one should practise in the lunar fortnight alone, and not in the solar one." — Commentary of verse 32 of Anandalahari, as quoted in "The Serpent Power" by Sir John Woodroffe, pp.234-235.

அங்கி எழுப்பி யருங்கதிர் ஊட்டத்துத்
தங்குஞ் சசியால் தாமம்ஐந் தைந்தாகிப்
பொங்கிய தாரகை யாம்புலன் போக்கறத்
திங்கள் கதிரங்கி சேர்கின்ற யோமே. 862

Chandra Yoga Described

Rouse Kalas of Fire,
Merge them in Sun,
Merge all in Moon,
Merge Jiva Star
Of senses and sense organs rid,
That verily is Chandra yoga.

This, in short, is chandra yoga. Through kundalini yoga rouse the kalas of fire. Merge them in the kalas of the sun. Merge them in the moon's kalas. Finally merge them all in jiva, of senses and sense organs rid.

This verse describes the Kalas and how they should be handled.

ஒன்றிய ஈரெண் கலையும் உடலுற
நின்றது கண்டும் நினைக்கிலர் நீதர்கள்
கன்றிய காலன் கருத்துழி வைத்தபின்
சென்றதில் வீழ்வர் திகைப்பொழி யாரே. 863

Know Sixteen Kalas Within the Body

They know not the Kalas sixteen within the body
They seek not to reach them
The despicable men!
When Death his trap lays
Then there they fall,
Forever bewildered.

அங்கி மதிகூட வாகும் கதிரொளி

அங்கி கதிர்கூட வாகு மதியொளி
அங்கி சசிகதிர் கூடவத் தாரகை
தங்கி யதுவே சகலமு மாமே. 864

In Chandra Yoga Jiva-Star Merges in Siva

When Fire-Kalas pass through Moon's Nadi
The Sun receives them;
Kalas of Fire and Sun together merge in Moon's Kala;
When Kundalini Fire unites in Siva
The Kalas of the Star merge;
And the Jiva who resides in Star,
Becomes all life.

ஈராறு பெண்கலை எண்ணிரண் டாண்கலை
பேராமற் புக்குப் பிடித்துக் கொடுவந்து
நேராகத் தோன்றும் நெருப்புற வேபெய்யில்
ஆராத ஆனந்தம் ஆனந்த மானதே. 865

Chandra Yoga in Kundalini Yoga

Twelve the female Kalas (of Sun)
Sixteen the male Kalas (of Moon)
Seize them both sitting unmoved,
And consign them to the Kundalini Fire,
In that yoga wells up the ecstasy beyond recount.

காணும் பரிதியின் காலை இடத்திட்டு
மாணும் மதியதன் காலை வலத்திட்டுப்
பேணியே யிவ்வாறு பிழையாமற் செய்வீரேல்
ஆணி கலங்காதவ் வாயிரத் தாண்டே. 866

Practise Nadi Suddhi

Course breath running in Sun's Nadi in the right
To the Moon's Nadi in the left,
And vice versa,
If you can do this erring not
You may live a thousand years
This body well preserved be.

பாலிக்கும் நெஞ்சம் பறையோசை ஒன்பதில்
ஆலிக்கும் அங்கே அமரர் பராபரன்
மேலைக்கு முன்னே விளக்கொளி யாய்நிற்குங்
காலைக்குச் சங்கு கதிரவன் தானே. 867

The Aspirant Hears Nada Sound in all the Ninth Centres

In all the ninth centres,.
Your heart shall resound
To the triumphant beatings of Sound Divine;
There Lord that is Supreme of Celestials all,
Is in exaltation high,
There you shall stand as Starry Light;
And the Sun shall blow the conch
To announce your arrival.

Mantras 867 & 868

As this merger takes place in the ninth centre of the moon's sphere, the yogi's heart resounds in high exultation to the triumphant beatings of the divine sound of nada. The jiva stands there as a stellar light. There, traversing beyond the sun and moon, he meets the Lord.

கதிரவன் சந்திரன் காலம் அளக்கும்
பொதிரவ னுள்ளே பொழிமழை நிற்கும்
அதிரவ னண்டப் புறஞ்சென் றடர்ப்ப
எதிரவ னீச னிடமது தானே. 868

Beyond Nada Sphere is Lord

The Sun and Moon but measure Time;
Into him who has great become,
Rains the nectar of Grace;
When he travels beyond the spheres
And knocks,
There he meets Lord
In His very Abode.

உந்திக் கமலத் துதித்தெழுஞ் சோதியை
அந்திக்கு மந்திர மாரும் அறிகிலார்
அந்திக்கு மந்திர மாரும் அறிந்தபின்
தந்தைக்கு முன்னே மகன்பிறந் தானே. 869

Knowledge of Aum Takes to Lord's Presence

The Light of Aum that rises in the navel-lotus
Is Mantra Finite;
None know this;
When they know that mantra secret,
Then is the Son that is Jiva
In the presence of Father that is God.

There is the light of Aum that rises from the navel lotus. It is the mantra finite and if that mantra secret is known, the son, that is jiva, stands before the Father, that is God.

ஊதியும் ஏதும் அறியார் உரைப்பினும்
ஓதியும் ஏதும் அறியாத ஊமர்கள்
ஆதியும் அந்தமும் அந்திக்க வல்லீரேல்
வேதியன் அங்கே வெளிப்படுந் தானே. 870

Greatness of Kundalini Yoga

It profits not to tell,
They listen not to advice,
They are deaf-mutes;
If you but learn how to merge,
The Primal Kundalini with the Being Finite
The Holy One will before you appear.

பாம்பு மதியைத் தினலுறும் பாம்பினைத்
தீங்கு கதிரையுஞ் சோதித் தனலுறும்,
பாம்பு மதியும் பகைதீர்த் துடன்கொளீஇ
நீங்கல் கொடானே நெடுந்தகை யானே. 871

Merging Moon's Kalas in Kundalini

The Kundalini serpent consumes Kalas of Moon
The Fire consumes Kalas of Sun, too
If you can resolve the conflict of Serpent and Moon

Merging the Kalas of Moon in Kundalini
The Lord will leave you not, ever, ever.

---

1) She (kundalini) runs to sahasrara and bites the chandra....Then nectar begins to flow — vide commentary on verse 32 of Anandalahiri, as quoted in "The Serpent Power" by Sir John Woodroffe, p.235.

அயின்றது வீழ்வள வுந்துயில் இன்றிப்
பயின்ற சசிவீழ் பொழுதில் துயின்று
நயந்தரு பூரணை உள்ள நடத்தி
வியந்தரு பூரணை மேவுஞ் சசியே. 872

Kundalini Devours and Throws Out Moon

The Kundalini that moved up
Devours Moon
Sleep not until it throws it out;
When the Moon comes out
Then may you take your sleep;
Your mind shall then luminous as full moon be
Then the Mystic Moon inside
Will shed its dazzling Kalas full.

The kundalini that moves up "devours the moon." Let not the yogi sleep until the serpent throws it out. When it throws it out, the mind becomes luminous as the full moon. Then the yogi may sleep.

சசியுதிக் கும்அள வுந்துயி லின்றிச்
சசியுதித் தானேல் தனதூண் அருந்திச்
சசிசரிக் கின்றள வுந்துயி லாமற்
சசிசரிப் பின்கட்டன் கண்டுயில் கொண்டதே. 873

Time for Sleeping and Eating When Moon is Devoured by Kundalini

Sleep not until the Moon comes out;
Eat not until Moon rises;
Sleep not until Moon moves;
Sleep the Yogi may
When but the Moon moves.

---

1) This reminds us of a parallel of the Sastraic injunction not to sleep and eat when there is a lunar (or solar) eclipse; when Rahu, the serpent, is mythologically said to devour the moon (or sun) for a time.

ஊழி பிரியா திருக்கின்ற யோகிகள்
நாழிகை யாக நமனை அளப்பார்கள்
ஊழி முதலாய் உயர்வார் உலகினில்
தாழவல் லார்இச் சசிவன்ன ராமே. 874

By Chandra Yoga Death is Conquered

The Yogis who thus practise incessantly
Conquer Death;
They will live in this world aeons beyond;
They are worthy of our obeisance,
They who, this Moon's Yoga in success practise.

Mantras 874 & 875

The yogi who practises chandra yoga will conquer death. He visions the past, present and future and until the moon drops back from kundalini, time comes to a stop.

தண்மதி பானுச் சரிபூமி யேசென்று
மண்மதி காலங்கள் மூன்றும் வழிகண்டு
வெண்மதி தோன்றிய நாளில் விளைந்தபின்
தண்மதி வீழ்வள விற்கண மின்றே. 875

The Yogi Sees Vision of Past, Present and Future

They traverse Spheres of Sun and Moon
And see vision of Past, Present and Future earth;
And in that Full Moon day the nectar ripens;
Until the Moon drops back from Kundalini,
Time stands to a stop.

Compare Shelly in "Prometheus:" "Plunge into eternity, where recorded time seems but a point."

வளர்கின்ற ஆதித்தன் தன்கலை யாறுந்
தளர்கின்ற சந்திரன் தன்கலை யாறு
மலர்ந்தெழு பன்னிரண் டங்குலம் ஓடி
அலர்ந்து விழுந்தமை யாரறி வாரே. 876

Moon Drops Out With 12 Kalas From Kundalini's Mouth

The waxing Kalas six of Sun
The waning Kalas six of Moon
Woke to life to twelve angula running
And then the Moon dropped out
Who knows this!

When the waxing kalas six of the sun, and the waning kalas six of the moon wake to life, twelve angulas running, that is the indication that the moon has dropped out of kundalini's mouth.

ஆமுயிர்த் தேய்மதி நாளே யெனல்விந்து
போம்வழி எங்கணும் போகாது யோகிக்குக்
காமுற இன்மையிற் கட்டுண்ணு மூலத்தில்
ஓமதி யத்துள்விட் டுரையுணர் வாலே. 877

He Conquers Bindu

If Yogi thus achieves this goal
In the day of Full Moon
The Yogi's semen flows not where it lists;
Devoid of passions, it firm collects in Muladhara;
Chanting Aum in heart's silence,
He remains Pure, Awareness filled.

வேறுறச் செங்கதிர் மெய்க்கலை யாறொடுஞ்
சூறுற நான்குந் தொடர்ந்துற வேநிற்கும்
ஈறிலி னன்கலை யீரைந்தொ டேமதித்
தாறுட் கலையுள் அகலுவா வாமே. 878

The Emitted Moon has 16 Kalas Ultimately

To the Six waxing Kalas of the fiery Sun
Will be the Four Kalas of Fire
To these ten Kalas good

Will be the Six Kalas of Moon
Thus are they Kalas Sixteen
In the Full Moon emitted.

Ultimately, the moon reappears, now with six waxing kalas of the sun, six kalas of the moon and four kalas of kundalini, thus making sixteen kalas in all, of the full moon.

உணர்விந்து சோணி உறவினன் வீசும்
புணர்விந்து வீசுங் கதிரிற் குறையில்
உணர்வும் உடம்பும் உவையொக்க நிற்கில்
உணர்வும் உடம்பும் ஒருகால் விடாவே. 879

Sun's Kala in Sex Union

In the mingling of male semen and woman's fluid
Emits Sun's Kala,
If Sun's Kala is low, semen ejects quick;
When mind and body balanced stand
Never will they let semen flow.

விடாத மனம்பவ னத்தொடு மேவி
நடாவு சிவசங்கின் நாதங் கொளுவிக்
கடாவிடா ஐம்புலன் கட்டுண்ணும் வீடு
படாதன இன்பம் பருகார் அமுதமே. 880

Effects of Chandra Yoga

If with mind centered they course their breath,
In direction of Nada sound
That from Siva's Conch emanates,
The five senses that run blind
Will their restraint meet;
And the interminable bliss of delectable Nectar
Leaves them not ever.

அமுதப் புனல்வரு மாற்றங் கரைமேற்
குமிழிக் குட்சுட ரைந்தையுங் கூட்டிச்
சமையத்தண் டோட்டித் தரிக்கவல் லார்க்கு
நமன் இல்லை நற்கலை நாள்இல்லை தானே. 881

Greatness of Chandra Yoga

On the banks of River
Where waters of Nectar flow
Course the Five Pranas
Through central Sushumna;
They who thus remain,
Death do not have;
Good their Kalas are;
Time-bound they are not.

உண்ணீ ரமுத முறுமூ றலைத்திறந்
தெண்ணீர் இணையடித் தாமரைக் கேசெலத்
தெண்ணீர்ச் சமாதி யமர்ந்துதீ ராநலங்
கண்ணற் றொடேசென்று கால்வழி மாறுமே. 882

Alternating Breath to Samadhi End

Opening the springs where Nectar wells up
They walk toward the Lotus Feet cool as water;
Sitting in undisturbed Samadhi;
Coursing through the Spinal channel
They alter the breathing right and left.

The yogi who continues opens up the springs of nectar and walks to the Lotus Feet of the Lord that are cool as water. There he sits in undisturbed samadhi, coursing through the spinal channel and breathing through nadis right and left in alternation.

மாறு மதியும் மதித்திரு மாறின்றித்
தாறு படாமல் தண்டோடே தலைப்படில்
ஊறு படாதுடல் வேண்டும் உபாயமும்
பாறு படா இன்பம் பார்மிசைப் பொங்குமே. 883

Benefits of Yoga

If breaths of Moon (Ida) and Sun (Pingala)
Course their way through Spinal channel unhindered,
Thine body imperishable shall be;
And abiding joys well up here below,
This the Way of Yoga True.

Imperishable becomes his body and abiding his joy. This is the true way that chandra yoga leads to.

மூன்றாம் தந்திரம் முடிவு பெற்றது.
Tantra Three Concluded

நாலாந் தந்திரம்
TANTRA FOUR

1. அசபை
AJAPA

போற்றுகின் றேன்புகழ்ந் தும்புகல் ஞானத்தைத்
தேற்றுகின் றேன்சிந்தை நாயகன் சேவடி
சாற்றுகின் றேன்அறை யோசிவ யோகத்தை
ஏற்றுகின் றேன்நம் பிரான்ஓர் எழுத்தே. *884*

The One-Letter Mantra of Our Lord

I praise, I laud,
Jnana that is our Refuge;
I adore the Holy Feet of the Lord,
Constant in my thought;
I expound Siva Yoga;
Hearken you!
I chant the One Letter, Aum
Dear to our Lord.

Having revealed in the preceding Tantra the technique of kundalini yoga that climaxes in chandra yoga, Tirumular proceeds to expound the secrets of mantra and yantra.

Mantra is the sound-body of a Devata, and yantra is its diagramatic representation.

The primal mantra is ajapa—that which is not chanted. As we breathe, in, we make the subtle sound 'sah;' and as we breathe out, the subtle sound of 'ham.' These two constitute the ajapa mantra, 'Soham,' or 'Hamsa' as it becomes by continuous repetition inversion.

The mute chanting of this unchanted mantra requires no special effort. Soham is, however, equated with the Pranava mantra, 'Aum.'

Aum consists of three letters,'A.' 'U' and 'M.' But as the three letters are always evoked together as Aum, it is also known as the One Letter mantra.

The exposition of the secrets of mantra and yantra belong to the realm of Siva yoga, as distinquished from kundalini yoga expounded previously.

Mular treats Om (instead of the natural hamsa) as the Ajapa. In Sanskrit, ordinarily Om is treated as a mono-syllable; but as Panini has pointed out, the combination of a and u in this word, as an exception to the general rule, is to be pronounced 'au' a diphthong. This is the general rule in Tamil language.

Ajapa: "The breath of every person in entering makes the sound of 'sah' and in coming out that of 'ham.' These two sounds make 'Soham' — 'I am He' — or 'Hamsah,' meaning 'the great swan.' Throughout a day and a night there are 21,600 such respirations. (That is 15 per minute). Every living being (jiva) performs this japa (repetition) unconsciously, but constantly. This is called Ajapa Gayatri. This ajapa-japa is performed in three places — in the muladhara, anahata and ajna...All jivas are constantly and unconsciously reciting this ajapa mantra, only for a fixed number of times every day. But a yogin should recite this consciously and count the numbers. By doubling the number of ajapa (that is by 30 respirations per minute) the state of manonmani (fixedness of mind, is attained. There are no regular rechakas and purakas in this process." Vide *Cheranda Samhita,* V.84-96, quoted in "Hatha Yoga," by Theos Bernard, pp.55,56n.

ஓரெழுத் தாலே உலகெங்குந் தானாகி
ஈரெழுத் தாலே இசைந்தங் கிருவராய்
மூவெழுத் தாலே முளைக்கின்ற சோதியை
மாவெழுத் தாலே மயக்கமே உற்றதே. *885*

Letters A, U and M

By One Letter, A, He all worlds became;
By Two Letters (A and U), He the Two became
— Siva and Sakti;
By Three Letters (A,U and M), He the Light* became;
By Letter M was Maya ushered in.
*jnana

From the One Letter mantra, Aum (Pranava), that is nada, all worlds devolved. The two letters, A and U became Siva and Sakti, and the letter, M, became maya.
The term 'ajapa' "refers to a special form of effortless meditation. The sounds 'ham' and 'sah' processed by the movements of the breath themselves constitute the mantra and hence there is no need of muttering anything...." (p.403 of N.N. Bhattacharyya's "History of the Tantric Religion").

தேவ ருறைகின்ற சிற்றம் பலம்என்றுந்
தேவ ருறைகின்ற சிதம்பரம் என்றுந்
தேவர் உறைகின்ற திருஅம் பலமென்றுந்
தேவர் உறைகின்ற தென்பொது வாமே. *886*

Glory of Chidambaram

Chitrambalam is where Devas reside,
Chitrambalam is where Devas reside,
Thiru Ambalam is where Devas reside,
The Sabha of the South is where Devas reside.

The One Letter mantra, Aum, denotes the Divine Dance. It is Tandava, the Grace Act of the Lord performed in the Golden Hall of Chidambaram, the Sabha of the South.

The word, Chidambaram, is of Sanskrit origin, and is made up of two words 'cit' (meaning mind, or thought) and 'ambaram' (meaning sky or space). Hence the word would mean Infinite Mind or the Divine itself. As Mular himself has pointed out in various passages, Siva's dance appeared first as a mental vision in the mind of Siddhars. The temple at Chidambaram (in Tamil 'chitrambalam') was apparently earlier merely a gathering place of Siddhars under a 'bodhi tree', before a temple was built there, and a dancing figure of Nataraja was placed there. 'Chitrambalam', which quite obviously is Tamilized form of 'Chidambaram', is nevertheless given an independent Tamil etymology by zealouts as 'Chitr' from 'Chiru', meaning 'small', (become 'Chitru') and "ambalam', meaning 'temple'. According to this, the Tamil word was later Sanskritized as Chidambaram. It is thus claimed that the dance of Nataraja appeared in iconography before it entered into poetry. An attempt to re-inforce this argument is made by referring to the Tiruvachakam verse which says that 'the larger idol' of the Linga replaced the smaller one of Nataraja. Undoubtedly, the Linga has replaced the Nataraja as a principal idol of worship in later days, but this does not, by any means, give justification for the Tamilian view of the origin of the word Chidambaram and of the concept of Nataraja's dance. This would not be correct. Iconography follows concept in Hinduism and not the other way round, and in any case, the concept of Divine dance is a very ancient one. It would be interesting to note that the dance form of Siva was earlier the terrible Tandava, which was later toned down to the auspicious form, apparently following the Tamil example.

Verse 891 and notes thereon may also be seen.

Mular refers to the Dance of Siva in Chidambaram as "Tandava"

ஆமேபொன் னம்பலம் அற்புதம் ஆனந்தம்
ஆமே திருக்கூத் தனவரத தாண்டவம்
ஆமே பிரளய மாகும்அத் தாண்டவம்
ஆமேசங் காரத் தருந்தாண் டவங்களே. 887

Dances in the Golden Temple

In the Golden Temple is the Atbhuta (Wonder) Dance,
In the Golden Temple is the Ananda (Bliss) Dance,
In the Golden Temple is the Anavarata (Eternal) Dance,

In the Golden Temple is the Pralaya (Deluge) Dance,
In the Golden Temple is the Samhara (Dissolution) Dance.

The Atbhuta (Wonder) Dance, the Ananda (Bliss) Dance, the Anavarata (Eternal) Dance, the Pralaya (Deluge) Dance, and the Samhara (Dissolution) Dance are performed in the Golden Sabha.

Mantras 887 & 903

These verses link the mantras Aum and "Sivayanamah" to the Lord's dance.

தாண்டவ மான தனியெழுத் தோரெழுத்
தாண்டவ மான தனுக்கிர கத்தொழில்
தாண்டவக் கூத்துத் தனிநின்ற தற்பரந்
தாண்டவக் கூத்துத் தமனியந் தானே. 888

One Letter Aum is Divine Dance

That which became Tandava Dance is One Letter Aum
That which became Tandava is Grace-act of Lord
He who performed Tandava is One Being Uncreated
In the Golden Hall is Tandava Dance.

தானே பரஞ்சுடர் தத்துவ மாய்நிற்குந்
தானே அகார உகாரம தாய்நிற்குந்
தானே பரஞ்சுடர் தத்துவக் கூத்துக்குத்
தானே தனக்குத் தராதலந் தானே. 889

God is Letter A and U

He is the Cosmic Light
He is Tattvas all;
He stands as Letters A and U
He is the Light Divine for Tattva Dance;
He is for Himself the Support All.

Siva/Sakti, who stands as the letter A and U, is the Cosmic Light. The Lord is the support of the tattvas. He is the tattvas. He is the light divine of the tattva dance. He stands beyond the tattvas as well.

தராதல மூலைக்குத் தற்பர மாபரன்
தராதலம் வெப்பு நமசி வாயவாந்
தராதலஞ் சொல்லிற் றான்வா சியவாகுந்
தராதல யோகந் தயாவாசி யாமே. 890

Variations of Namasivaya

He is the Uncreated Lord, Para Para Great for worlds all
In the Sphere of Muladhara He stands as Na-Ma-Si-Va-Ya
In the Sphere of Fire He stands as Na-Ma-Va-Si-Ya
In the Sphere Sun He stands Va-Si-Ya
In the Sphere of Moon He stands as Va-Si.

ஆமே சிவங்கள் அகார உகாரங்கள்
ஆமே பரங்கள் அறியா விடம் என்ப
ஆமே திருக்கூத் தடங்கிய சிற்பரம்
ஆமே சிவகதி ஆனந்த மாமே. 891

Letters A and U are Si and Va

Letters A and U are Si (Siva) and Va (Sakti)
They supreme are;
They are Space, beyond reach of thought
They are Spaces Vast, of Intelligence Supreme,
Where He His Holy dance performs;
Letters A and U are Refuge Finale and Joy Eternal.

The letters A and U also denote the letters Si and Va — Si for Siva and Va for Sakti. They are supreme letters. They connote the spaces beyond the reach of thought, the vast spaces of supreme jnana. They are the final refuge and are eternal joy. In them, the Lord perform His Holy Dance.

Here, and in following verses, an attempt is made to link the Om mantra with Sivaya in various ways. It is to be noted that, in the third line of this verse, Siva's dance is said to have been enacted in 'Spaces vast, of Intelligence Supreme'.

ஆனந்த மூன்றும் அறிவிரண் டொன்றாகும்
ஆனந்தஞ் சிவாய அறியார் பலரில்லை

ஆனந்த மோடும் அறியவல் லார்கட்கு
ஆனந்தக் கூத்தாய் அகப்படுந் தானே. 892

Letters Three — Si Va Ya

Letters Si Va Ya are bliss perpetual;
Letters Si and Ya are Jnana;
Si-Va-Ya is unalloyed joy;
Not many know this,
They who realizes this in Joy
Will Him behold in Dance-Joyous (Ananda).

The three letters, Si, Va and Ya, are perpetual bliss. They are unitive jnana. They are unalloyed joy. The Ananda Dance is performed in them.

படுவ திரண்டும் பலகலை வல்லார்
படுவ தோங்காரம் பஞ்சாக் கரங்கள்
படுவது சங்காரத் தாண்டவப் பத்தி
படுவது கோணம் பரந்திடும் வாறே. 893

Letters Two — A and U Became Five Letters

A and U are Letters Two,
All men of vast knowledge chant;
They are Letters Two
Into One and Five Letters resolve;
In them merge
The Tandava Dance of Dissolution;
In Muladhara Triangle they are,
Ascending high to Adharas rest.

The letters A and U, that are Si and Va, form the mantra that all men of vast knowledge chant. These two letters, Si and Va, are the source of the five letters. Si Va Ya Na Ma. In them merges the Tandava Dance of Dissolution. This 'Sivaya' mantra is in the muladhara triangle. From there it ascends to the rest of the adharas.

வாறே சதாசிவ மாறிலா ஆகமம்
வாறே சிவகதி வண்டுறை புன்னையும்
வாறே திருக்கூத்து ஆகம வசனங்கள்
வாறே பொதுவாகு மன்றின் அமலமே. 894

Letters A and U are the Agamic Mantra

They are the Sadasiva;
They are the Agamas imperishable;
They are the Godly Goal,
They are the shady Mastwood Tree where bees indwell
They are the dance Holy;
They are the Agamic teachings divine,
They are the Immaculate Purity
Of the Divine Dance Hall.

The letters Si and Va are Sadasiva. They are the imperishable *Agamas.* They are the Godly goal. They are the mastwood tree on the banks of the Ganga within. They are the Holy Dance. They are the immaculate purity of the Divine Dance Hall.

அமலம் பதிபசு பாசங்கள் ஆகமம்
அமலந் திரோதாயி யாகுமா னந்தமாம்
அமலஞ் சொல் ஆணவ மாயை காமியம்
அமலந் திருக்கூத்தங் காமிடந் தானே. 895

Letters of Engrossing Purity

The Letters Pure are the Agamas;
The Letters Pure are Pati, Pasu, Pasa;
The Letters Pure and Grace that is Bliss;
The Letters Pure are Egoity, Maya and Desire;
The Letters Pure are site of Divine Dance.

They are the letters pure. They are Pati, pasu and pasa. They are the *Agamas.* They are the Grace, that is bliss. They are the Grand Divine Dance.

தானே தனக்குத் தலைவனு மாய்நிற்குந்
தானே தனக்குத் தன்மலை யாய்நிற்குந்
தானே தனக்குத் தன்மய மாய்நிற்குந்
தானே தனக்குத் தலைவனு மாமே. 896

Lord is All

Himself as His Lord stands;
Himself as His Mountain stands;
Himself as Pervasive Himself stands;
Himself He stands,
As Lord that is Himself.

தலைவனு மாய்நின்ற தற்பரக் கூத்தனைத்
தலைவனு மாய்நின்ற சற்பாத் திரத்தைத்
தலைவனு மாய்நின்ற தாதவிழ் ஞானத்
தலைவனு மாய்நின்ற தாளிணை தானே. 897

The Lord is Supreme

He is the Lord who stood dancing eternal;
He is the Lord who the holy one is;
He is the Lord who unfolds Jnana's honey-laden Flower;
He is the Lord whose Feet are holy beyond peer.

இணையார் திருவடி எட்டெழுத் தாகும்
இணையார் கழலிணை யீரைஞ்ச தாகும்
இணையார் கழலிணை ஐம்பத்தொன் றாகும்
இணையார் கழலிணை ஏழா யிரமே. 898

Letters A and U are Feet of Lord

The peerless Feet of Lord are Letters eight
The peerless Feet of Lord are Letters Two and Five;
The peerless Feet of Lord are Letters Fifty and One
The peerless Feet are mantras seven times thousand.
Letters eight: The five letters of Panchakshara and those Bijaksharas.

ஏழா யிரமாய் இருபதாய் முப்பதாய்
ஏழா யிரத்தும் எழுகோடி தானாகி
ஏழா யிரத்துயிர் எண்ணிலா மந்திரம்
ஏழா யிரண்டாய் இருக்கின்ற வாறே. 899

The Two Became Several

The Seven Thousand mantras became Fifty
And then into the Seven with endings diverse.

Thus of the Seven Thousand mantras chanted,
That are beyond thought,
Have as vital the Seven and Two in the ultimate.

Mantras 899 & 900

But the two letters are the vital, ultimate or contained all mantras. It is Siva's ma our divine support.

1) Excluding the one in sahasrara

2) Mantras have seven different endings: i)nama; ii)svata; iii)svaha; iv)vamshat; v)vashat; vi)hum; vii)phat

Another interpretation is that mantras are seven crores (70 million) in number. They are enumerated in the Sanskrit work, "Sri Rajesvari Kalpa vide Tirumantira Malai," by Tirumular edited by N. Sivaprakasa Desikar. However, here the reference is presumably to the seven endings, rather than seven crores, as the process of involution is indicated, 3) A and U plus Panchakshara.

இருக்கின்ற மந்திரம் ஏழா யிரமாம்
இருக்கின்ற மந்திரம் எத்திறம் இல்லை
இருக்கின்ற மந்திரஞ் சிவன்திருமேனி
இருக்கின்ற மந்திரம் இவ்வண்ணந் தானே. *900*

All Mantras Contained in Two-Letter Mantra

Seven Thousand mantras there exist;
But none, of this potent divine;
This the mantra that is Siva's Holy Form;
And all mantra is in this contained.

தானே தனக்குத் தகுநட்டந் தானாகுந்
தானே அகார உகாரம தாய்நிற்குந்
தானே ரீங்காரத் தத்துவக் கூத்துக்குத்
தானே உலகில் தனிநடந் தானே. *901*

Letters A and U are Tattva Dance

He is unto Himself in His Dance;
He stands as A and U;
He is the One for Mayaic Dance of Tattvas;
He dances the Dance, peerless here below.

Mantras 901 & 902

That mantra is the dance of mayaic tattvas the alchemy that transforms the coppery jiva into golden Siva.

நடமிரண் டொன்றே நளினம தாகும்
நடமிரண் டொன்றே நமன்செய்யுங் கூத்துலயம்
நடமிரண் டொன்றே நகைசெயா மந்திரம்
நடஞ்சிவ லிங்கம் நலஞ்செம்பு பொன்னே. *902*

The Dance Transforms Jiva Into Siva

The Dance in Letters Two
It is the Dance joyous;
It is the Dance of dissolution;
It is the Dance that leads to bliss;
It is the Dance that is Siva Linga
It is the alchemy that transforms
The coppery Jiva into golden Siva.

செம்புபொன் னாகுஞ் சிவாய நமவென்னிற்
செம்புபொன் னாகத் திரண்டது சிற்பரஞ்
செம்புபொன் னாகும் ஸ்ரீயுங் கிரீயுமெனச்
செம்புபொன் னான திருவம் பலமே. *903*

Sivaya Nama Purifies and Transforms Jiva

Chant "Sivaya Nama",
Copper turns into gold;
The Chit Para there exists,
Turns copper into gold
Chant "Srim" and "Krim;"
Copper turns into gold;
The Holy Temple alchemises
Copper into gold.

The Chitpara (Supreme Intelligence) exists there in the 'Sivaya-nama' mantra. It is the fullness of A and U, of Srim and Krim — the seed mantras for Siva and Sakti.

Srim and Krim are bija mantras for Siva and Sakti — same as A and U, and Si and Va.

திருவம் பலமாகச் சீர்ச்சக் கரத்தைத்
திருவம் பலமாக ஈராறு கீறித்
திருவம் பலமாக இருபத்தைஞ் சாக்கித்
திருவம் பலமாகச் செப்பிக்கின்ற வாறே. *904*

How Tiru Ambala Chakra is Formed

Fashion Tiruvambala Chakra thus;
Draw six lines each, vertical and horizontal,
Thus form squares twenty and five,
And in each inscribing Letters Five
Meditate continuous.

Mantras 904 & 905

Tiru Ambala Chakra (i)
Tiru Ambala Chakra (ii)
(Vide Mantra 923, Tantra Four, ibid.)

These verses give a tantric interpretation to the mantras and the dance.

வாறே சிவாய நமச்சி வாயநம
வாறே செபிக்கில் வரும்பேர் பிறப்பில்லை
வாறே அருளால் வளர்கூத்துக் காணலாம்
வாறே செபிக்கில் வருஞ்செம்பு பொன்னே. *905*

Chant Sivaya Nama and Behold Dance

This the way to chant;
Sivaya Nama, Sivaya Nama;
If you chant that way,
No more birth will be;
With Lord's Grace,
You shall behold the Eternal Dance;
And copper (that is Jiva) turns into gold (that is Siva).

பொன்னான மந்திரம் புகலவும் ஒண்ணாது
பொன்னான மந்திரம் பொறிகிஞ்சு கத்தாகும்

பொன்னான மந்திரம் புகையுண்டு பூரிக்கிற்
பொன்னாகும் வல்லோர்க் குடம்புபொற் பாதமே. 906

Chant Sivaya Nama in Silence

This mantra is golden;
Chant it not loud,
Just say it;
Your body glows red,
If you take it in slow,
As you breath in,
Your body becomes gold;
And in time,
Shall you behold the Golden Feet of the Lord.

பொற்பாதங் காணலாம் புத்திரர் உண்டாகும்
பொற்பாதத் தாணையே செம்புபொன் னாயிடும்
பொற்பாதங் காணத் திருமேனி யாயிடும்
பொற்பாத நன்னடஞ் சிந்தனை சொல்லுமே. 907

Chant Sivaya Nama and Behold Golden Feet

You shall behold the Golden Feet
You shall have children noble;
In the name of that Golden Feet I say,
The copper that is Jiva,
Will become gold that is Siva;
And as you behold the Golden Feet,
You too shall His Form assume;
Centre the mantra in your thoughts,
And witness the great Dance of Golden Feet.

சொல்லு மொருகூட்டிற் புக்குச் சுகிக்கலாம்
நல்ல மடவார் நயந்துட னேவருஞ்
சொல்லினும் பாசச் சுடர்ப்பாம்பு நீங்கிடுஞ்
சொல்லும் திருக்கூத்தின் சூக்குமந் தானே. 908

Chant Sivaya Nama and Attain Siddhis

You may easily transmigrate into any body;
The goodly Sakti will your companion be;
If you chant the mantra,
The fiery snake of Pasa will leave you;
That mantra is the secret of the Holy Dance,
Chant it unceasingly.

சூக்குமம் எண்ணா யிரஞ்செபித் தாலுமேற்
சூக்கும மான வழியிடைக் காணலாஞ்
சூக்கும மான வினையைக் கெடுக்கலாஞ்
சூக்கும மான சிவனதா னந்தமே. 909

Chant Sivaya Nama and Enjoy Bliss of Siva

It is the Sukshma (Subtle) mantra;
Chant it eight thousand times;
You shall see the (Sushumna) Path Subtle,
You may enjoy the bliss of Siva
That is subtlest of all.

'Sivaya nama' is the sukshma mantra. Chant it eight thousand times. You will vision the subtle path of sushumna. You can destroy karma that is very subtle. You can enjoy the bliss of Siva that is the subtlest of all.

ஆனந்தம் ஆனந்தம் ஒன்றென் றறைந்திட
ஆனந்தம் ஆனந்தம் ஆ-ஈ-ஊ-ஏ-ஓ மென்றைந்திடம்
ஆனந்தம் ஆனந்தம் அஞ்சும தாயிடும்
ஆனந்தம் ஆனந்தம் அம்-ஹ்ரீம்-அம்-க்ஷம்
ஆம்-ஆகுமே. 910

Sivaya Nama are of the Life-Vowels Five and Seminal Sounds Five

One the Supreme Bliss,
One the Supreme Bliss,
Thus chant the mantra
You shall have Bliss,
Bliss has its source in Letters Five;
A-I-U-E and Aum the life vowels they are;
They become the Five Letter mantra
And joy that is within joy;
Bliss lies in the seed-letter Five;
Hum-Hrim-Ham-Ksham-Am, are they.

'One the supreme bliss. One the supreme bliss.''— thus chant the mantra. You shall have bliss. Bliss has its source in the Five Letters, A,I,U,E and Aum — they are the five life-vowels. The five life-vowels became the Five-Lettered mantra. They correspond to the five seed-letters; Ham, Hrim, Hum, Sum and Aum.

Tiru Ambala Chakra (iii)
Letters i, u, a, e and Aum are the Dance Letters.

This verse give three alternative interpretations to the ''pancakshara'' (the 5-letter mantra). It could be either A, I, U, E and M, or ''Sivaya Nama'', or the tantric ''Hum, Hrim, Hum, Ksham and Am''.

மேனி யிரண்டும் விலங்காமல் மேல்கொள்ள
மேனி யிரண்டு மிகார விகாரியா
மேனி யிரண்டும் ஊ-ஆ-ஈ-ஏ-ஓ-என்னும்
மேனி யிரண்டும் ஈ-ஓ-ஊ-ஆ-ஏ-கூத்தாமே. 911

Two Letters Become Five Letters

The Two Letter mantra is Body of Lord
Chant it inarticulate;
As the Two suffuse your body,
You stand transformed;
The Two Letters that are Lord's Corpus
Become Five Letters that is Jiva;
U-A-I-E-O
The Two Letters that are Lord's Corpus
Become the Five Letters that is Siva Dance
I-O-U-A-E.

The two letters, A and U, are the body of the Lord. Chant it inarticulately. As the two suffuse your body, you stand transformed. The two letters, A and U, became the five letters, U, A, I, E and O — that are jiva. The two letters became the five letters, I, O, U, E and A — that are the Siva Dance.

கூத்தே சிவாய நமமசி வாயிடுங்
கூத்தே ஈ-ஊ-ஆ-ஏ-ஓம்- சிவாயநம வாயிடுங்
கூத்தே ஈ-ஊ-ஆ-ஏ-ஓம்- சிவாயநம வாயிடுங்
கூத்தே இ-ஊ-ஆ-ஏஓம் நமசிவாய கோளொன்று
மாறே. 912

Dance Vowels Become Five Letter Mantra

The Dance Si Va Ya Na Ma
The Dance Letters I,U,A,E and O (m) become Sivaya Nama
The Dance-Letters I, U, A, E and O (m) become Si Va Ya Nama
The Dance-Letters I, U, A, E and O (m) become. Namasivaya, the goal supreme.

'Sivayanama' becomes 'Ma Si Va Ya Na, that are I, U, A, E and O — the dance-letters of Siva.

Compare Mantra 927, infra.

Letters aeu, ae and Aum denote the Five Letters, Si, Va, Ya, Na, Ma. The origin of the Five Letter mantra is traced to the letter-sounds in Siva's rhythmic dance steps.

ஒன்றிரண் டாடவோ ரொன்று முடனாட
ஒன்றினின் மூன்றாட ஓரேழும் ஒத்தாட
ஒன்றினால் ஆடவோர் ஒன்பதும் உடனாட
மன்றினில் ஆடினான் மாணிக்கக் கூத்தே. 913

The Dance of Ruby

He danced as One, alone
He danced as Two, with Sakti
He danced as several, all life in;
He danced in Three, Sun, Moon and Fire;
He danced in Seven, the worlds that are;
He danced on one Foot;
He danced in Saktis Nine;
He danced in arena that is Space;
He danced the Dance of Ruby.

The Lord danced as One, alone. He danced as two with Sakti. He danced with several — all creation. He danced with three — the sun, moon and fire. He danced with jiva and with all the worlds. He danced with one Foot, and He danced with the nine saktis. He danced in the adharas that are space. He danced the Dance of the Ruby.

2. திருவம்பலச் சக்கரம்

THIRU AMBALA CHAKRA

இருந்தஇவ் வட்டங்கள் ஈராறி ரேகை
இருந்த இரேகைமேல் ஈரா றிருத்தி
இருந்த மனைகளும் ஈராறு பத்தொன்
றிருந்த மனையொன்றில் எய்துவன் றானே. 914

How to Form the Chakra

Draw twelve vertical lines and cross them
With twelve horizontal lines
Thus are formed Hundred and twenty one squares,
In this chakra the Lord dances.

Tiru Ambala Chakra: ref. Mantra 904, ante. This and the mantras following give a detailed exposition on the configuration of this chakra (ideo-gram). While commentators widely differ in their interpretation of these mantras, an ideogram into which much research has gone is one attempted by Sri G. Varadara in his book, "Tirumantira Neri", (Tamil), pp.111-115.

This rather extensive section on certain yantras has been condensed by the translator into a synoptic commentary, Consequently, it is not amenable to enumeration.

Tirumular previously expounded the truth of the ajapa mantra, 'Soham,' that becomes Aum, which, in turn, becomes A and U; and again, in turn, Si and Va. 'Si' and 'Va' expanded into the Five-Lettered mantra. Sivayanama, and further on into the 51 letters of the Sanskrit alphabet. He now proceeds to reveal the yantra or the diagramatic reprsentation of the Panchakshara (Five-Lettered) mantra. He calls this the Tiruambala Chakra, or the yantra for the Divine Dance Arena. (The yantras are referred to as chakras here)

The Tiruambala Chakra seems to be a cluster of several Chakras. Its several variations are represented in different diagrams. (These are given in the notes appended.) Tirumular also lays down the rules for chanting the bija mantras, and expounds on their esoteric significance.

There is a diagram with 121 chambers filled by the mantra, Sivayanama. This is called the Sivaya nama Chakra.

There is another Chakra dedicated to the mantra, Hara Hara. The significances of the letters, Si, and the letter, Aum, are explained. This is the Hara Hara Chakra.

The Five-Letter mantra has both sthula (manifest) and sukshma (subtle) aspects. The manifest Panchakshara is 'Namasivaya.' The subtle Panchakshara is 'Sivayanama.' Thus the same mantra is both manifest and subtle. This is represented in a Chakra — the Panchakshara Chakra.

There is also a yantra for the Siva mantra, 'Siva.' This is called the Siva Chakra.

There is yet another Chakra of 48 squares in which the six letters, Aum Namasivaya, are distributed. This seems to be a variation of the Siva Chakra. The six letters are the quintessence of the six faiths. This is the Six-Letter Chakra.

Umapathi Chakra is formed by drawing eight vertical lines and eight horizontal lines, and filling the chambers with the Five-Letter mantra.

Tirumular winds up his exposition of the Tiruambala Chakra by describing six other Chakras, whose worship by incarnation of appropriate mantras, confers certain earthly powers. These are:
1) Sthambana Chakra — renders enemies powerless.
2) Mohana Chakra — gives the power of fascination.

3) Ucchatana Chakra — confers the powers to exorcize.
4) Marana Chakra — renders the destruction and death of enemies.
5) Vasiya Chakra — confers the powers of seduction.
6) Akarshana Chakra — confers the power of placing men and things under the will and desire of the sadhakas.

These six Chakras, although designed for worldly ends, are yet based on the mantra, Aum, with its incantation and ritual variations.

தானொன்றி வாழிடந் தன்னெழுத் தேயாகுந்
தானொன்று மந்நான்குந் தன்பே ரெழுத்தாகுந்
தானொன்று நாற்கோணந் தன்னைந் தெழுத்தாகுந்
தானொன்றி லேயொன்று மவ்வரன் தானே. 915

The Configuration of the 121 Lettered Chakra Diagram

In his own Letter "Si", He abides;
The four letters conjoint are great Letters of His name
On the four sides of His Chakra His own Five letters
In the One letter He abides is Hara's mantra too.

The number 121 is the square of 11, and there are, according to the Vedas, 11 Rudras (Sivas).

அரகர என்ன அரியதொன் றில்லை
அரகர என்ன அறிகிலர் மாந்தர்
அரகர என்ன அமரரும் ஆவர்
அரகர என்ன அறும்பிறப் பன்றே. 916

Say "Hara Hara" and End Birth Cycle

Say "Hara Hara
Nothing formidable to you;
They who know not this,
Say not "Hara Hara;"
Say "Hara Hara"
And you shall a Celestial be;
Say "Hara Hara"
You shall no more birth know.

எட்டு நிலையுள எங்கோன் இருப்பிடம்
எட்டினில் ஒன்றும் இருமூன்றும் ஈரேழும்
ஒட்டிய விந்துவும் நாதமும் ஓங்கிடப்
பட்டது மந்திரம் பான்மொழி பாலே. 917

The Significance of Letter "Si" in the Chakra

In the eight directions is the letter "Si" in the Chakra
From that One Letter in places eight
Arose the Five Gods,
And the Saktis Nine,
And the Bindu and Nada;
Thus flourishes the Mantra, the Word Pure.

மட்டவிழ் தாமரை மாதுநல் லாளுடன்
ஒட்டி இருந்த உபாயம் அறிகிலர்
விட்ட எழுத்தை விடாத எழுத்துடன்
கட்டவல் லாருயிர் காக்கவல் லாரே. 918

Significance of Letter Om

They know not how the Lord
Became conjoint with her,
Who, on the blooming lotus sits;
They who chant the letter aspirated "O"
Conjoint with the letter unaspirated "m"
May well preserve their life ever.

ஆலய மாக அமர்ந்தபஞ் சாக்கரம்
ஆலய மாக அமர்ந்தவித் தூலம் போய்
ஆலய மாக வறிகின்ற சூக்குமம்
ஆலய மாக அமர்ந்திருந் தானே. 919

The Five Letters Manifest (Sthula) and Subtle (Sukshma)

The Panchakshara (Five Letters) is the Lord's Abode,
That Panchakshara Manifest (is Namasivaya)
That Subtle is Sivayanama
Thus is He in that Mantra,
Manifest and Subtle.

இருந்தஇவ் வட்டம் இருமூன்றி ரேகை
இருந்த வதனுள் இரேகை யைந்தாக
இருந்த அறைகள் இருபத்தைஞ் சாக
இருந்த அறையொன்றில் எய்து மகாரமே. 920

Letter Ma Central in Chakra With 25 Chambers

That Chakra is with six by six lines formed,
The lines inside are five by five
Thus in all into five and twenty chambers divided;
In Centre of these is Letter Ma.

மகார நடுவே வளைத்திடுஞ் சத்தியை
ஒகாரம் வளைத்திட் டும்பிளந் தேற்றி
அகாரந் தலையாய் இருகண் சிகாரமாய்
நகார வகாரநற் காலது நாடுமே. 921

The Yantra of Six Letters Om Na Ma Si Va Ya

Inscribe Letter 'Ma' in centre
Above it describe Letter 'Va'
Surround the two by Letter 'O'
Split them in Centre vertically by letter U
Place Letter 'Ya' on top,
Fix letter 'Si' on both sides,
That they look like eyes two,
The Letters 'Na' and 'Va' to form the diagram's feet two.

Tiru Ambala Chakra (vii)
"Panchakshara Deepa" — Commentary — Edited by Dandapani Desikar.

நாடும் பிரணவ நடுவிரு பக்கமும்
ஆடு மவர்வாய் அமர்ந் தங்கு நின்றது
நாடு நடுவுண் முகநம சிவாய
வாடுஞ் சிவாயநம புறவட்டத் தாயதே. 922

A Variation of the Six-Letter Yantra

Describe Letter Pranava (OM)
In the Centre on top place 'Si'
On sides two place letters 'Va' and 'Ya'
Inside inscribe Na Ma Si Va Ya
On the outer round figure Letters Si Va Ya Na Ma.

ஆயுஞ் சிவாய நமமசி வாயந
வாயு நமசிவா யயநம சிவாயந
வாயுமே வாய நமசியெனு மந்திர
மாயுஞ் சிகாரந் தொட்டந்தத் தடைவிலே. 923

How the Five Letters are Filled in the 25-Chamber Chakra

In the row on tope of Chakra
Write Si Va Ya Na Ma;
In the squares on row next
Fill Ma Si Va Ya Na
In the row third write Na Ma Si Va Ya
Still below comes Letters in order Ya Na Ma Si Va
In the squares last are Letters Va Ya Na Ma Si
Thus do you fill squares in Chakra
With 'Si' to begin and 'Si' to end.

Tiru Ambala Chakra (ix)
See Mantra 905 supra — the difference is that here there are only two horizontal lines.

அடைவினில் ஐம்பதும் ஐயைந் தறையின்
அடையும் அறையொன்றுக் கீரெழுத் தாக்கி
அடையு மகாரத்தில் அந்தமாம் க்ஷவ்வும்
அடைவின் எழுத்தைம்பத் தொன்றும்
அமர்ந்ததே. 924

How the 51-Letter Chakra is Formed

In Chambers five and twenty
Enclose letters fifty, two in each;
With letter "A" to begin
And final letter 'Ksha" to end;
These with the one letter Om;
Fifty and one in all, the letter fill,
In Chakra's chambers five and twenty.

Tiru Ambala Chakra (x)

The reference to letter 'Ksha' in the third line makes it clear that Mular has the Sanskrit letters in mind. "A" to "Ksha" make 51 letters in all, says Mular, which would correspond to the Sanskrit system in one manner of counting, for in that language, there is a great flexibility in enumerating the letters.

The 51 letters referred to in this verse are the Sanskrti letters. Due to various reasons, the number of Sanskrit letters vary from 49 to 61.

அமர்ந்த அரகர வாம்புற வட்டம்
அமர்ந்த அரிகரி யாமத னுள்வட்டம்
அமர்ந்த அசபை யாம்அத னுள்வட்டம்
அமர்ந்தஇ ரேகையும் ஆகின்ற சூலமே. 925

The Yantra for the Mantra Om Hari Hara

At the outer circle describe Hara Hara,
In the inner circle describe Hari Hari,
In the innermost centre place Om, the Ajapa,
Mark the ends of circle by Trident sign.

Tiru Ambala Chakra (xi)

சூலத் தலையினில் தோற்றிடுஞ் சத்தியுஞ்
சூலத் தலையினிற் சூழும்ஓங் காரத்தால்
சூலத் திடைவெளி தோற்றிடும் அஞ்செழுத்
தாலப் பதிக்கும் அடைவது வாமே. 926

Yantra Representing Lord's Abode

Inscribe Bija mantra Hrim
Above each trident sign;
That surrounds the diagram Om
Write Letters Five
In the space betwixt trident signs;
The Chakra thus formed,
Indeed, is Lord's Abode.

அதுவாம் அகார இகார உகாரம்
அதுவாம் எகாரம் ஒகார மதஞ்சாம்
அதுவாகுஞ் சக்கர வட்டமேல் வட்டம்
பொதுவாம் இடைவெளி பொங்குநம் பேரே. 927

The Yantra for Mula Chakra

In the Centre inscribe our name Mula, that is Om,
Surround it in circles two concentric,
In the space between the circles two
Inscribe the Letters Five,
A, I, U, E and O
That denote the Five Letters
Si, Va, Ya, Na, Ma.

பேர்பெற் றதுமூல மந்திரம் பின்னது
சோர்வுற்ற சக்கர வட்டத்துட் சந்தியின்
நேர்பெற் றிருந்திட நின்றது சக்கரம்
ஏர்பெற் றிருந்த இயல்பிது வாமே. 928

How to Fill in the Mula Chakra

This the Mula Chakra famed,
In space between circles two
Fill entire with Letters Five stated,
Then does Chakra its loveliness take.

இயலுமிம் மந்திரம் எய்தும் வழியின்
செயலும் அறியத் தெளிவிக்கு நாதன்
புயலும் புனலும் பொருந்தங்கி மண்விண்
முயலும் எழுத்துக்கு முன்னா இருந்ததே. 929

How to Chant Mula Chakra

As you describe Chakra of this mantra (Om)
The Lord as Guru will instruct you
The way to meditate on it, clear;
Anterior to chanting this mantra

Were the seed-mantras that pertains
To Wind, Water, Fire, Earth and Sky
Yam, Vam, Ram, Lam, and Ham.

Mular connects the pancakshara with the five elements and their corresponding bija mantras in Tantrism. (These latter are nasalised forms of the letters Y, R, L, V and Ha.)

ஆறெட் டெழுத்தின்மே லாறும் பதினாலும்
ஏறிட் டதன்மேலே விந்துவும் நாதமுஞ்
சீறிட்டு நின்று சிவாய நமவென்னக்
கூறிட்டு மும்மலங் கூப்பிட்டுப் போமே. 930

Sum Sauh Sivaya Nama

Conjoin the sixth letter U
To the forty-eighth letter S (a) •
Add Bindu letter M (.)
To form the syllable Sum:
In similar fashion
Conjoin the fourteenth letter Au to S (a)
Add Nada letter Ah (:)
To form the syllable Sauh;
Chant them Si Va Ya Na Ma to follow;
Thus when you chant the mantra, full formed
As Sum Sauh Si Va Ya Na Ma,
The triple Pasas in distress howling
Take to their heels, away, away.

அண்ணல் இருப்ப தவளக் கரத்துளே
பெண்ணினல் லாளும் பிரானக் கரத்துளே
எண்ணி இருவர் இசைந்தங் கிருந்திடப்
புண்ணிய வாளர் பொருளறி வார்களே. 931

Siva and Sakti Interchange Their Bija Mantra States

The Lord is seated in His Consort's Letter (Sauh)
The Mother is seated in Her Lord's Letter (Hum)
When thus the Two are in amity seated
The holy beings comrehend the meaning inner.

அவ்விட்டு வைத்தங் கரவிட்டு மேல்வைத்து
இவ்விட்டுப் பார்க்கில் இலிங்கம தாய்நிற்கும்
மவ்விட்டு மேலே வளியுறக் கண்டபின்
தொம்மிட்டு நின்ற சுடர்க்கொழுந் தாமே. 932

Linga Chakra

Describe Letter "A"
Above it inscribe "Hara"
Further above Place Letter "E"
Then is Linga Form shaped;
Centre your mind on it
And course your breath above,
You shall vision indeed
The Dance of Divine Light.

அவ்வுண்டு சவ்வுண் டனைத்துமங் குள்ளது
கவ்வுண்டு நிற்குங் கருத்தறி வாரில்லை
கவ்வுண்டு நிற்குங் கருத்தறி வாளர்க்குச்
சவ்வுண்டு சத்தி சதாசிவன் தானே. 933

Au and Sau are Mantras of Siva-Sakti Union

There is Letter Hau
There is Letter Sau
In them are comprehended all;
How they entwined are,
None knows;
They who know the mystery of this union
Are indeed blessed
Of both, Sakti and Sadasiva.

அஞ்செழுத் தாலே அமர்ந்தன்ன் நந்தியும்
அஞ்செழுத் தாலே அமர்ந்தபஞ் சாக்கரம்
அஞ்செழுத் தாகிய வக்கர சக்கரம்
அஞ்செழுத் துள்ளே அமர்ந்திருந் தானே. 934

Panchakshara Chakra

Letter-Five is seat of Nandi
Letter-Five is Holy Mantra
Letter-Five is Divine Chakra
Letter-Five is Lord's abode.

கூத்தனைக் காணுங் குறிபல பேசிடிற்
கூத்த னெழுத்தின் முதலெழுத் தோதினார்
கூத்தனொ டொன்றிய கொள்கைய ராய்நிற்பர்
கூத்தனைக் காணுங் குறியது வாமே. 935

Chant Letter of Dance — Si

How do you see the Dancer?
Many are the ways;
Chant first Letter of Dance (Si),
Thou with Dancer will one in thought be;
That is the way to see the Dancer truly.

Even the chanting of the first letter of Sivayanama is enough to enable the devotee to envision the Dancer.

அத்திசைக் குள்நின்ற அனலை எழுப்பியே
அத்திசைக் குள்நின்ற நவ்வெழுத் தோதினால்
அத்திசைக் குள்நின்ற அந்த மறையனை
அத்திசைக் குள்ளுற வாக்கினன் தானே. 936

Chant Om and Rouse Kundalini

Kindle the Fire (Kundalini) where it dormant lies
Chant letter 'na' that is in the chakra
Then the symbolized 'na'
Brings the Lord there.

தானே யளித்திடுந் தையலை நோக்கினால்
தானே யளித்திட்டு மேலுற வைத்திடுந்
தானே யளித்த மகாரத்தை ஓதிடத்
தானே யளித்ததோர் கல்லொளி யாகுமே. 937

Chant "Ma" of Grace — Sakti

She Herself Grace grants
If upward you lift Kundalini;

She Herself granting Grace
High above in Sahasrara places thee;
There do you chant Her syllable "Ma"
You shall indeed be placed
Like a gem of ray serene.

கல்லொளி யேயென நின்ற வடதிசை
கல்லொளி யேயென நின்றனன் இந்திரன்
கல்லொளி யேயென நின்ற சிகாரத்தைக்
கல்லொளி யேயெனக் காட்டிநின் றானே. 938

Lord Revealed His First Letter "Si"

The North beamed in radiant light
There stood Lord of Devas (Indra) crowned in diadem bright;
And the Lord revealed His letter "Si"
Sparkling as rays within gem pure,
It beamed aloft for all to see
Unto a light set on mountain top.

தானே யெழுகுணந் தண்சுட ராய்நிற்குந்
தானே யெழுகுணம் வேதமு மாய்நிற்குந்
தானே யெழுகுண மாவதும் ஓதிடில்
தானே யெழுந்த மறையவ னாமே. 939

The Lord is Uncreated

Himself He stands as the Soft Light Uncreated,
Himself He stands as the Vedas Self-Existent,
Chant His uplifting attributes
Himself He reveals,
The Sage Unborn of Vedas.

மறையவ னாக மதித்த பிறவி
மறையவ னாக மதித்திடக் காண்பர்
மறையவன் அஞ்செழுத் துண்ணிற்கப் பெற்ற
மறையவன் அஞ்செழுத் தாமது வாகுமே. 940

Lord of Vedas in Letter-Five

He, Lord of Vedas, gave us this birth,
That we might the Lord of Vedas become;
The Lord of Vedas stood within Letter-Five;
The Lord of Vedas is Himself Letter-Five.

ஆகின்ற பாதமு மந்நவாய் நின்றிடும்
ஆகின்ற நாபியுள் அங்கே மகாரமாம்
ஆகின்ற சீயிரு தோள் வவ்வாய்க் கண்டபின்
ஆகின்ற வச்சுட ரவ்வியல் பாமே. 941

Five-Letter Form of Siva

His Feet are Letter "Na"
His navel is Letter "Ma"
His shoulders are Letter "Si"
His mouth is Letter "Va"
His cranial centre aloft is Letter "Ya"
—Thus Five-Letter Form of Siva is.

அவ்வியல் பாய இருமூன் றெழுத்தையுஞ்
செவ்வியல் பாகச் சிறந்தனன் நந்தியும்
ஒவ்வியல் பாக ஒளியுற நோக்கிடிற்
பவ்வியல் பாகப் பரந்துநின் றானே. 942

See Lord in Five-Letter

Of greatness thus are Letters two and three,
And in it as His Radiant Form Nandi shone;
See Him as Letter "OM"
Wide He spreads unto Ocean Vast.

பரந்தது மந்திரம் பல்லுயிர்க் கெல்லாம்
வரந்தரு மந்திரம் வாய்த்திட வாங்கித்
துரந்திடு மந்திரஞ் சூழ்பகை போக
உரந்தரு மந்திரம் ஓமென் றெழுப்பே. 943

Power of Five-Letter Mantra

That Mantra spread everywhere
That Mantra its boon grants to lives all,
Do you chant it appropriate,
All hostility that harasses you shall flee;
It is the Mantra that makes you mighty and strong;
That Mantra do you invoke chanting OM.

ஓமென் றெழுப்பித்தன் உத்தம நந்தியை
நாமென் றெழுப்பி நடுவெழு தீபத்தை
ஆமென் றெழுப்பியவ் வாறறி வார்கள்
மாமன்று கண்டு மகிழ்ந்திருந் தாரே. 944

Vision Divine Dance

Chanting Om
Invoke Holy Nandi;
Chanting "Na"
Kindle Kundalini Fire,
The goal to reach;
Make it blaze;
They who know Him thus
Verily saw Divine Dance,
For ever steeped in ecstasy.

ஆகின்ற சக்கரத் துள்ளே எழுத்தைந்தும்
பாகொன்றி நின்ற பதங்களில் வர்த்திக்கும்
ஆகின்ற ஐம்பத் தோரெழுத் துள்நிற்கப்
பாகொன்றி நிற்கும் பராபரன் தானே. 945

Fifty-One Letters are Five-Letters Also

In Chakra that is designed
Are Letters Five in places appropriate;
There stands He the ParaPara (the transcendent Reality)
Who the Fifty One Letters fills.

பரமாய அஞ்செழுத் துள்நடு வாகப்
பரமாய நவசிம பார்க்கில் மவயநசி
பரமாய சியநம வாம்பரத் தோதிற்
பரமாய வாசி மயநயமாய் நின்றே. 946

Sivayanama

Inscribe Letters Five Si Va Ya Na Ma;
In the next row place Letters Ya Ṇa Va Si Ma;
Further on place the letters in order thus:
Ma Va Ya Na Si; Si Ya Na Ma Va;
And Va Si Ma Ya Na
Thus do the Five Letters in Chakra permuted stand.

நின்ற எழுத்துக்கள் நேர்தரு பூதமும்
நின்ற எழுத்துக்கள் நேர்தரு வண்ணமும்
நின்ற எழுத்துக்கள் நேர்தர நின்றிடில்
நின்ற எழுத்துள்ளும் நின்றனன் தானே. 947

Five Letters are the Five Elements and Five Colors

The Letters that stood thus
Are the Elements Five;
The Letters that stood thus
Are the Colors Five;
If Letters stood in order appropriate
He stood within the Letters, for sure.

Letters are said to have colours, perhaps because when used in yantras, they are coloured differently. Usually, the colours are five, namely, white, orange, yellow, green or blue and black.

Colour Symbolism is important in Hinduism. Hence, the Five Letters (pancakshara) are said to represent the five elements, (cf.977) and are assigned individual colours each.

நின்றது சக்கரம் நீளும் புவியெல்லாம்
மன்றது வாய்நின்ற மாயநன் னாடனைக்
கன்றது வாகக் கறந்தனன் நந்தியுங்
குன்றிடை நின்றிடுங் கொள்கைய னாமே. 948

Chakra Leads to Nandi's Grace

Thus stood Chakra;
And thus did it extend,
To the four corners of earth;
And thus did Lord stand in Celestial arena
He, Master of comely Maya Land;
And from Nandi flowed the Milk of Grace
As from mother-cow unto calf;
Nandi, who stands high aloft Mount Kailas.

The word 'chakra' stands for "a circle used in a variety of senses. In rituals, there are different chakra - sadhanas in which male and female aspirants assemble and perform the rites of Pancamakara..... According to the Niruttara-tantra, chakras are of five types, - Raja, Maha, Deva, Vira, and Pasu. The term chakra is also used to denote yantras or mystic diagrams and variously known as "trikona-chakra", "asthakona-chakra", and so forth. Again, the term is used to denote different nerve - plexuses within the body". (N.N. Bhattacharyya, "History of the Tantric Religion". p.419).

கொண்டஇச் சக்கரத் துள்ளே குணம்பல
கொண்டஇச் சக்கரத் துள்ளே குறியைந்து
கொண்டஇச் சக்கரங் கூத்தன் எழுத்தைந்துங்
கொண்டஇச் சக்கரத் துள்நின்ற கூத்தே. 949

Significance of Chakra

Within this Chakra is much good that comes
Within this Chakra are Names Five
This Chakra is Letter-Five of Dancer Divine
This Chakra is where Dance Divine incessant goes on.

வெளியி லிரேகை யிரேகையி லத்தலை
சுளியில் உகாரமாஞ் சுற்றிய வன்னி
நெளிதரு கால்கொம்பு நேர்விந்து நாதந்
தெளியும் பிரகாரஞ் சிவமந் திரமே. 950

Yantra for Siva Mantra

In the Space Centre (Eye-brow)
There mark letter "A"
At the top of cranium place letter "U"
Surround with letter "ma"
On its "leg" place Bindu letter "Si"
On its "horn" place Nada letter "Va"
This the Siva Mantra,
You clear shall know.

அகார வுகார சிகார நடுவாய்
வகாரமோ டாறும் வளியுடன் கூடிச்
சிகார முடனே சிவன்சிந்தை செய்ய
ஒகார முதல்வன் உவந்துநின் றானே. 951

Three Ways of Chanting Panchakshara

With "A" and "U" to commence,
And "Si" in centre
(That is, as Om Na Ma Si Va Ya),
With "A" and "U" to commence,
And "Va" and rest aspirating in breath regulated,
(That is, as Om Va Si Ya Na Ma)
With "A" and "U" to commence,
And "Si" and rest in order following,
(That is, as Om Si Va Ya Na Ma)
As you thus chant,
The Primal Lord of "Om" appears,
Rejoicing.

அற்ற விடத்தே அகாரம தாவது
உற்ற விடத்தே யுறுபொருள் கண்டிடச்
செற்றம்அறுத்த செழுஞ்சுடர் மெய்ப்பொருள்
குற்றம் அறுத்த பொன்போலுங் குளிகையே. 952

Lord is in "Aum" Beyond Adharas

Where Adharas end,
"Aum" is;
There shall you see Lord
Who of Himself reveals;
He is Blemishless,
He is Light Divine,
He is Whole Truth,
He is the Alchemic pill,
Of flawless gold.

அவ்வென்ற போதினில்உவ்வெழுத் தாலித்தால்
உவ்வென்ற முத்தி யுருகிக் கலந்திடும்
மவ்வென்றென் னுள்ளே வழிபட்ட நந்தியை
எவ்வணஞ் சொல்லுகேன்எந்தை இயற்கையே. 953

Chant Aum, Nandi Appears

When with "A", chant "U" simultaneously,
Then does melting Mukti there appear;
When "Ma" I chanted;
With me was "Nandi";
How shall I speak of my Father's greatness!

நீரில் எழுத்திவ் வுலக றறிவது
வானில் எழுத்தொன்று கண்டறி வாரில்லை
யாரிவ் வெழுத்தை அறிவா ரவர்கள்
ஊனில் எழுத்தை உணர்கிலர் தாமே. 954

Heavenly Letter Ends Birth

The knowledge of Jiva here below
Is unto letters written on water;
There is a Letter in heaven
They seek it not;
Who knows that Letter?
They who know it,
Have birth ended.

காலை நடுவுறக் காயத்தில் அக்கரம்
மாலை நடுவுற ஐம்பது மாவன
மேலை நடுவுற வேதம் விளம்பிய
மூலம் நடுவுற முத்திதந் தானே. 955

Mukti is When Aum Appears in Garland of Letters Within

Course breath through central Sushumna,
And be in the centre within of the Garland of Letters;
When in the Centre of that garland
The Primal Mantra AUM, Vedas speak of appears,
Then is Mukti, sure indeed.

நாவியின் கீழது நல்ல எழுத்தொன்று
பாவிக ளத்தின் பயனறி வாரில்லை
ஓவிய ராலும் அறியவொண் ணாதது
தேவியுந் தானுந் திகழ்ந்திருந் தானே. 956

Sakti and Siva are on the Mystic Letter Below the Navel

Below the navel is a great Letter,
The unholy its greatness know not;
Even the Creator (Brahma) knows it not,
There it is Siva with Sakti, in total splendour.

அவ்வொடு சவ்வென்ற தரனுற்ற மந்திரம்
அவ்வொடு சவ்வென்ற தாரும் அறிகிலர்
அவ்வொடு சவ்வென்ற தாரும் அறிந்தபின்
அவ்வொடு சவ்வும் அனாதியு மாமே. 957

Ha(m)sa is Hara's Mantra

"Ha" and "Sa" together form Hara's mantra (Hamsa)
But none know the truth of Hamsa;
When that truth any one knows
He shall know Hamsa as beginningless.

மந்திரம் ஒன்றுள் மலரால் உதிப்பது
உந்தியினுள்ளே உதயம்பண் ணாநிற்குஞ்
சந்திசெய் யாநிற்பர் தாம தறிகிலர்
அந்தி தொழுதுபோ யார்த்தகன் றார்களே. 958

The Great Mantra Rises in the Heart

There is a Mantra great
That inside heart's lotus rises;
It roots lie deep in the navel;
They who know it not, come by it not;
They but prayed at sunset
And with loud noise departed.

சேவிக்கு மந்திரஞ் செல்லுந் திசைபெற
ஆவிக்குள் மந்திரம் ஆதார மாவன
பூவுக்குள் மந்திரம் போக்கற நோக்கிடில்
ஆவிக்குள் மந்திரம் அங்குச மாமே. 959

"Aum" Mantra Sustains Life

"Hamsa" Mantra chanted within
In directions all spreads;
It is the Mantra of life, sustaining breath;
It is the Mantra in the lotus of heart;
When constantly chanted,
That Mantra in life's centre
Is verily unto a mahout's goad,
That elephantine passions control.

அருவினில் அம்பரம் அங்கெழு நாதம்
பெருக துடியிடை பேணிய விந்து
மருவி யகார சிகார நடுவாய்
உருவிட ஊறு முறுமந் திரமே. 960

Chant "Om Sivaya Nama"

In formless space rises Nada,
In Sakti of slender waist rises Bindu,
Together they form, OM
With letter "Ya" in centre,
When mantra Si Va Ya Na Ma is incessant chanted,
That mantra (Om Sivaya Nama) spouts Siva Bliss.

விந்துவும் நாதமும் மேவி யுடன்கூடிச்
சந்திர னோடே தலைப்படு மாயிடில்
அந்தர வானத் தமுதம்வந் தூறிடும்
அங்குதி மந்திரம் ஆகுதி யாமே. 961

The Mantra is Oblation to Siva

If Bindu and Nada conjoint reach
The Mystic Moon inside the head,

The heavenly ambrosia wells up,
The Mantra that rises there
Is verily the oblation to Siva.

ஆறெழுத் தோதும் அறிவார் அறிகிலர்
ஆறெழுத் தொன்றாக ஓதி உணரார்கள்
வேறெழுத் தின்றி விளம்பவல் லார்கட்கு
ஓரெழுத் தாலே உயிர்பெற லாமே. 962

Chant Aum and Be Redeemed

They who chant the Six-Letter Mantra (Om Si Va Ya Na Ma)
Are they who truly know;
They who chant not the Six-Lettered Mantra
Are they who know not;
Even they who chant with other letter none,
May with One-Letter (AUM) redeemed be.

ஓதும் எழுத்தோ டுயிர்க்கலை மூவைஞ்சும
ஆதி எழுத்தவை ஐம்பதோ டொன்றென்பர்
சோதி எழுத்தினில் ஐயிரு மூன்றுள
நாத எழுத்திட்டு நாடிக்கொள் ளீரே. 963

Garland of Fifty-One Letters

With Letter "Aum" are vowels fifteen formed;
To Bindu's luminous letter "A"
Add Nada letter "U"
With rest of letters thirteen,
They fifteen vowels are;
Together with consonants,
The Primal letters are
As Fifty and one reckoned.

This verse is inspired by the concept of "Varna mala" (garland of letters) of the Sakti cult.

விந்துவி லுஞ்சுழி நாதம் எழுந்திடப்
பந்தத் தலைவி பதினாறு கலையதாய்க்
கந்தர வாகரங் காலுடம் பாயினாள்
அந்தமும் இன்றியே ஐம்பத்தொன் றாயதே. 964

Sakti Expands as Fifty-One Letters

With Letter "A" that is Bindu,
And curled Letter "U" that is Nada,
When together they upward ascend,
Sakti within beams,
With kalas six and ten,
And endlessly expands,
As neck, hands, legs and body entire;
As Letters One and Fifty, too,
Her Form expands.

The 51 letters of the Sanskrit language are identified with various parts of Sakti.

ஐம்ப தெழுத்தே அனைத்தும்வே தங்களும்
ஐம்ப தெழுத்தே அனைத்தாக மங்களும்
ஐம்ப தெழுத்தேயு மாவ தறிந்தபின்
ஐம்ப தெழுத்தும்போய் அஞ்செழுத் தாமே. 965

Fifty Letters Come to Five Letters

Letters Fifty are Vedas all,
Letters Fifty are Agamas all,
When source of Letters Fifty are known,
Fifty Letters to Five Letters come.

Here, the number of letters is said to be 50, reflecting the vacillations of the phoneticians of the Sanskrit language.

அஞ்செழுத் தாலைந்து பூதம் படைத்தனன்
அஞ்செழுத் தாற்பல யோனி படைத்தனன்
அஞ்செழுத் தாலிவ் வகலிடம் தாங்கினன்
அஞ்செழுத் தாலே அமர்ந்துநின் றானே. 966

Five Letters is All

With Five letters He created elements five;
With Five letters He created diverse life;
With Five letters He supported spaces vast,
With Five letters He in Jivas abides.

வீழ்ந்தெழு லாம்விகிர் தன்திரு நாமத்தைச்
சோர்ந்தொழி யாமல் தொடங்கும் ஒருவற்குச்
சார்ந்த வினைத்துயர் போகத் தலைவனும்
போந்திடும் என்னும் புரிசடை யோனே. 967

Chant His Name; He Beckons to You

They who continuously chant the Lord's Holy name,
In desire high,
For them Karma's miseries fleet away;
The Lord says: "Come unto me"
—He of Matted Locks.

உண்ணுமருந்தும் உலப்பிலி காலமும்
பண்ணுறு கேள்வியும் பாடலு மாய்நிற்கும்
விண்ணின் றமரர் விரும்பி அடிதொழ
எண்ணின் றெழுத்தஞ்சு மாகிநின் றானே. 968

Lord in His Five Letters

He is Life's Elixir,
He is Time Eternal,
He is Music's melody,
He is Song too;
The Celestials adore Him fervent;
In their thoughts He stood;
In Five Letters He stood.

ஐந்தின் பெருமையே அகலிட மாவதும்
ஐந்தின் பெருமையே ஆலய மாவதும்
ஐந்தின் பெருமையே யறவோன் வழக்கமும்
ஐந்தின் வகை செயப் பாலனு மாமே. 969

Chant Five Letters and Be Forever Young

Spaces vast arise from Five Letters great
Temples Holy are Five Letters great
Grace of Lord is Five Letters great
Chant Five Letters great,
You shall ever young be.

வேரெழுத் தாய்விண்ணாய் அப்புறமாய் நிற்கும்
நீரெழுத் தாய்நிலந் தாங்கியும் அங்குளன்
சீரெழுத் தாய்அங்கி யாயுயி ராமெழுத்
தோரெழுத் தீசனும் ஒண்சுட ராமே. 970

As One-Letter Lord Pervades All

As Seed-Letter, He pervades Spaces and Beyond,
As Supreme-Letter, He fills world and sustains it,
As Renowned-Letter, He stands as fire, and life,
As one Letter, He stands Resplendent Rare.

நாலாம் எழுத்தோசை ஞாலம் உருவது
நாலாம் எழுத்தினுள் ஞாலம் அடங்கிற்று
நாலாம் எழுத்தே நவிலவல் லார்கட்கு
நாலாம் எழுத்தது நன்னெறி தானே. 971

Chant Sakti's Letter Va

In the sound of Fourth Letter (Va) world takes form,
In the sound of Fourth Letter is World contained,
For them who chant Fourth Letter incessant,
The Fourth Letter is Way Holy.

In the mantra, Na Ma Si Va Ya (Panchakshara), the fourth letter is Va, denoting Sakti.

இயைந்தனள் ஏந்திழை என்னுள மேவி
நயந்தன ளங்கே நமசிவ என்னும்
பயந்தனை யோரும் பதமது பற்றும்
பெயர்ந்தனன் மற்றும் பிதற்றறுத் தேனே. 972

Chant Na Ma Si Va

The lovely Sakti into my heart entered;
There She sat rejoicing;
Chant Na Ma Si Va,
Think of what it brings;
Cling to Her Feet;
Transformed was I;
All my prattle ceased.

ஆமத் தினிதிருந் தன்ன மயத்தினை
ஓமத்தி லேயுதம் பண்ணும் ஒருத்திதன்
நாம நமசிவ என்றிருப் பாருக்கு
நேமத் தலைவி நிலவி நின்றாளே. 973

Na Ma Si Va is Sakti Mantra

This corporeal body is of rice food made,
Offer it into the fire of Om
Chant incessant Na Ma Si Va
That the name of Sakti Finite is;
She, Mistress of Dharma, stands revealed.

பட்ட பரிசே பரமஞ் செழுத்ததின்
இட்ட மறிந்திட் டிரவு பகல்வர
நட்டம தாடு நடுவே நிலயங்கொண்
டட்டதே சப்பொரு ளாகிநின் றாளே. 974

Lord Dances in the Five Letters

Letters Five are the Lord's gift,
In it, central He dances, night and day,
In endearment eternal;
He that assumed, Forms Eight.

Five elements plus the sun, moon and jiva are the eight forms of Siva, or Siva is pervasive in the eight directions.

அகாரம் உயிரே உகாரம் பரமே
மகார மலமாய் வருமுப் பதத்திற்
சிகாரஞ் சிவமாய் வகாரம் வடிவமாய்
அகாரம் உயிரென் றறையலு மாமே. 975

What "Aum" and "Sivaya" Stand For

Letter "A" is Jiva; "U" is Para
"Ma" is Mala
Thus it is in Three-lettered Word "A U M"
"Si" is Siva; "Va" is Sakti;
"Ya" is Jiva—
Thus it is, Three Letter-Word Si Va Ya.

நகார மகார சிகார நடுவாய்
வகாரம் இரண்டும் வளியுடன் கூடி
ஒகார முதற்கொண் டொருக்கால் உரைக்க
மகார முதல்வன் மனத்தகத் தானே. 976

Chant Om Na Ma Si Va

Letters "Na" and "Ma" to commence,
Letter "Si" in centre,
Letter "Va" intoned in breath regulated,
Together with "OM" at beginning of all,
If you even once chant thus,
The Lord of "Ma" (Maya)
Will in your heart be.

அஞ்சுள வானை அடவியுள் வாழ்வன
அஞ்சுக்கும் அஞ்செழுத் தங்குச மாவன
அஞ்சையுங் கூடத் தடுக்கவல் லார்கட்கே
அஞ்சாதி யாதி அகம்புக லாமே. 977

The Five Letters Can Control the Five Senses

Five the elephants (senses)
In the body-forest roam,
The Five Letters become the goads
For the five elephants,
Only they who can contain
The five (senses) together,
Can, unafraid, reach Primal Lord.

ஐந்து கலையில் அகராதி தன்னிலே
வந்த நகராதி மாற்றி மகராதி
நந்தியை மூலத்தே நாடிப் பரையொடுஞ்
சந்தி செய் வார்க்குச் சடங்கில்லை தானே. 978

Contemplate Si Va Ya

The Five Kalas arose
From letters "A" and rest (A,U,M)
From them arise the Five Letters,
Leave out Letters "Na" and "Ma"
(Thus "Si Va Ya" contemplate)
Nandi in Muladhara you seek;
Those who meet Him there with Parai (Sakti)
Will have actions none more to perform.

Santhyatheetha, santhi, vidya, pratishta, nivritti, are the five kalas.

மருவுஞ் சிவாயமே மன்னும் உயிரும்
அருமந்த யோகமும் ஞானமு மாகுந்
தெருள் வந்த சீவனார் சென்றிவற் றாலே
அருள்தங்கி யச்சிவ மாவது வீடே. 979

Si Va Ya Leads to Liberation

Chant Si Va Ya in love
You shall immortal be;
It is Yoga rare and Jnana as well;
With it,
The illumined Jiva receives Grace
And he Siva becomes;
That indeed is liberation true.

அஞ்சுக அஞ்செழுத் துண்மை அறிந்தபின்
நெஞ்சகத் துள்ளே நிறையும் பராபரம்
வஞ்சக மில்லை மனைக்கும் அழிவில்லை
தஞ்ச மிதுவென்று சாற்றுகின் றேனே. 980

Five Letters are the Refuge

Realize truth of blissful letters Five,
The transcendent Reality fills your heart;
Truth this is;
And immortal you will be;
Letters Five is your Refuge;
None other, I emphatic say.

சிவாயவொ டவ்வே தெளிந்துளத் தோதச்
சிவாயவொ டவ்வே சிவனுரு வாகுஞ்
சிவாயவொ டவ்வுந் தெளியவல் லார்கள்
சிவாயவொ டவ்வே தெளிந்திருந் தாரே. 981

Aum Si Va Ya is Siva (as Form)

Chanting "A" and "U" in understanding
Along with "Si", "Va" and "Ya" (That is as Om Sivaya)
Is verily Siva's Form,
They who understand "Si", "Va" and "Ya" with "A" and "U"
Have realised "Om Sivaya" as Mantra great.

சிகார வகார யகார முடனே
நகார மகார நடுவுற நாடி
ஒகார முடனே ஒருகா லுரைக்க
மகார முதல்வன் மதித்துநின் றானே. 982

Chant Aum Si Va Ya Nama and Reach Lord

Hold Si, Va and Ya,
And Na and Ma
In heart's centre,
And with "Aum";
The Letter Five when thus chanted,
The Lord of "Ma" (Maya) appreciative appears.

நம் முதல் ஓரைந்தின் நாடுங் கருமங்கள்
அம்முதல் ஐந்தில் அடங்கிய வல்வினை
சிம்முத லுள்ளே தெளியவல் லார்கட்குத்
தம்முத லாகுஞ் சதாசிவந் தானே. 983

Chant Namasivaya and Vanquish Karmas; Chant Sivaya Nama and Be One With Sadasiva

In the Five Letters beginning with "Na" (Na Ma Si Va Ya)
Are all actions you seek to do;
In the Five Letters are stubborn Karmas vanquished;
Those who hold in their hearts
The Five Letters with "Si" to begin (Si Va Ya Na. Ma).
Will with Primal Sadasiva one be.

நவமுஞ் சிவமும் உயிர்பர மாகுந்
தவமொன் றிலாதன தத்து மாகுஞ்
சிவமொன்றி யாய்பவ ராதர வால்அச்
சிவமென்ப தானாம் எனுந்தெளி வுற்றதே. 984

Chanting "Siva" Takes You to Siva

The Letters "Na" to being (Na Ma) is Jiva,
The Letters "Si" to being (Si Va) is Para,
Even they who have tapas none,
By chanting Si Va,
May yet Siva become,
The Lord of Tattvas,
This is true, beyond doubt.

கூடிய எட்டும் இரண்டுங் குவிந்தறி
நாடிய நந்தியை ஞானத்துள் ளேவைத்து
ஆடிய ஐவரும் அங்குற வாவர்கள்
தேடி அதனைத் தெளிந்தறி யீரே. 985

Chant Aum and Win Senses

Know "A" and "U" together (AUM) in depth
Seek Nandi in Jnana within,
The Five wavering senses,
Your friends become;
Chant AUM and be doubt-free.

எட்டும் இரண்டும் இனிதறி கின்றிலர்
எட்டும் இரண்டும் அறியாத ஏழையர்

எட்டும் இரண்டும் இருமூன்று நான்கெனப்
பட்டது சித்தாந்த சன்மார்க்க பாதமே. 986

Aum Denotes Tattva Manifestations of Siva

They know not well Letter Eight ("A") and Two ("U")
They the ignorant one, know not what "Eight" ("A") and Two ("U") are;
Eight and Two (AUM) are but Ten
That verily is truth of Siddhanta Jnana.

In Tamil, the numeral, eight, is written as the letter, '' (A); and the numeral, two, is written as the letter, '' (U). Hence the play on the words 'eight' and 'two.' The illiterates are generally referred to as those who cannot count eight and two.

எட்டு வரையின் மேலெட்டு வரைகீறி
இட்ட நடுவுள் இறைவன் எழுத்தொன்றில்
வட்டத்தி லேயறை நாற்பத்தெட் டுமிட்டுச்
சிட்டஞ் செழுத்துஞ் செபிசிக் கிரமே. 987

Letter Six

Draw eight lines vertical,
And eight lines horizontal,
In central chamber thus formed,
Place Lord's Letter-Six—Om Na Ma Si Va Ya,
In forty and eight squares that remains,
The Sacred Letters distribute,
And there pray.

தானவர் சட்டர் சதிரர் இருவர்கள்
ஆனஇம் மூவரோ டாற்றவ ராதிகள்
ஏனைப் பதினைந்தும் விந்துவும் நாதமுஞ்
சேனையுஞ் செய்சிவ சக்கரந் தானே. 988

Siva Chakra

Place them all in squares appropriate
The Dhanavar, the Chattar, the Sathirar two,
The two Guard-gods, and the rest of them fifteen,
Bindu, and Nada and Siva Gana Natha,
Thus form Siva Chakra.

பட்டன மாதவ மாறும் பராபரம்
விட்டனர் தம்மை விகிர்தா நமஎன்பர்
எட்டனை யாயினும் ஈசன் திறத்திறம்
ஒட்டுவன் பேசுவன் ஒன்றறி யேனே. 989

Knowledge of Siva is Vast

By way of Tapas great
They reached Paraparam,
To Him they, their self surrendered;
And they adored Him saying, "Si Va Ya Na Ma";
But I speak no more than a tiny bit,
Of Lord's Greatness, mighty;
I near Him but a little;
Beyond this, I nothing know.

சிவன்முதல் மூவரோ டைவர் சிறந்த
அவைமுதல் ஆறிரண் டொன் றொடொன் றான
அவைமுதல் விந்துவும் நாதமும் ஓங்கச்
சவைமுதல் சங்கரன் தன்பெயர் தானே. 990

Names of Siva

Siva the First, then the Three, and the Five following,
Nine are they all, yet one and the same,
With them flourished Bindu and Nada—
All these but names of Sankara First.

வித்தாஞ் செகமய மாக வரைகீறி
நத்தார் கலைகள் பதினாறு நாட்டிப்பின்
உத்தாரம் பன்னிரண் டாதி கலைதொகும்
பத்தாம் பிரம சடங்குபார்த் தோதிடே. 991

Mark and Chant

Draw lines to denote the universe that is Seed
There mark the Kalas Sixteen,
Then mark the Kalas Twelve
And then the Kalas Ten
That in sacrificial rituals of Brahmian appear
Thus thou mark and chant in Chakra.

1) The 16 kalas of the moon are: amrta, manada, pusa, tusti, pusti, rati, dhrti, sasini, candrika, kanti, jyotsna, srih, priti, angada, purna and puramrta.

2) The 12 kalas of the sun are: tapini, taapini, dhumra, marici, jvalini, ruci, susumna, bhogada, visva, bodhini, dharini and kshama.

3) The 10 kalas of fire are: dhumrarc, usma, jvalini, jvaalini, visphulingini, susri, surupa, kapila, harvya-vaha and kavya-vaha.

Vide "The Garland of Letters," p.103, quoted from *Saubhagya-ratnakara*.

கண்டெழுந் தேன்கம லம்மல ருள்ளிடை
கொண்டொழிந் தேன்உடன் கூடிய காலத்துப்
பண்டழி யாத பதிவழி யேசென்று
நண்பழி யாமே நமவென லாமே. 992

I Chanted Nama and Lord Appeared

And Lo! within the lotus of my heart,
I beheld Him
And as I saw Him, I rose and met Him;
I then lost my sense of Self,
Betaking to gracious way of Lord Eternal;
In endearment undiminished,
Do chant "Nama."

புண்ணிய வானவர் பூமழை தூவிநின்(று)
எண்ணுவர் அண்ணல் இணையடி மந்திரம்
நண்ணுவர் நண்ணி நமஎன்று நாமத்தைக்
கண்ணென உன்னிக் கலந்துநின் றாரே. 993

Celestials Chant Lord's Name

The Holy Celestials raining flowers on Him
Meditate on Mantra that confers Grace;
Approaching Him, they chant "Nama";
Thinking of Him dear as The apple of their eye
They with Him united stood.

ஆறெழுத் தாவ தாறு சமயங்கள்
ஆறுக்கு நாலே இருபத்து நாலென்பர்
சாவித் திரியில் தலையெழுத் தொன்றுள
பேதிக்க வல்லார் பிறவியற் றார்களே. 994

Six Letters Aum are the Six Faiths and Savitri Mantra

The Six Letters are the Six faiths,
The Six Letters multiplied by four,
Into four-and-twenty proliferated,
That the Letters of Savitri mantra are;
Savitri has the Letter First (that is Aum)
They who separately meditate on it,
Have no more the birth travail.

Savitri (Divine Creator) is also Gayatri, the most sacred of all vaidika mantras. It runs:
Aum, Bhur bhuvah svah:
Tat savitur varenyam bhargo devasya dhimahi:
Dhiyo yo nah prachodayat: Aum.
Meaning: Aum. The earthly, atmospheric and celestial spheres. Let us contemplate the wondrous Solar Spirit of the Divine Creator. May He direct our intellect. Aum.

எட்டினில் எட்டறை யிட்டோ ரறையிலே
கட்டிய ஒன்றெட்டாய்க் காண நிறையிட்டுச்
சுட்டி இவற்றைப் பிரணவஞ் சூழ்ந்திட்டு
மட்டும் உயிர்கட் குமாபதி யானுண்டே. 995

Umapathi Chakra

Draw lines eight vertical
And lines eight horizontal;
In chambers thus formed
Distribute letters that each occurs times eight
Repeat it in corners four
Encircle the whole in Om
Meditate thus on the Chakra
The Lord of Uma will thine be.

நம்முதல் அவ்வொடு நாவின ராகியே
அம்முத லாகிய எட்டிடை யுற்றிட்டு
உம்முத லாகவே உணர்பவர் உச்சிமேல்
உம்முத லாயவன் உற்றுநின் றானே. 996

Chant Om Na Ma Si Va Ya

Chanting Mantra "Na" to begin and "Ya" to end—Na Ma Si Va Ya,
And prefixing Mantra that has "A" and "U"—"OM"
Those who meditate thus
Will see the Primal Lord inside their head.

நின்ற அரசம் பலகைமேல் நேராக
ஒன்றிட மவ்விட்டு ஓலையிற் சாதகந்
துன்று மெழுகையுள் பூசிச் சுடரிடைத்
தன்ற வெதுப்பிடத் தம்பனங் காணுமே. 997

Sthambana Chakra

On fresh plank of a peepul tree wood
Figure out the Five Letter Mantra with "Ma" to begin—
Ma, Si, Va, Ya, Na
In similar fashion inscribe it on leaf of palm
Smear it with wax
And warm it gently over fire,
Centre thy meditation on it,
Strong the concentration to attain
Thine enemied will be rendered actionless, sure.

Sthambana—stopping, checking, restraining the powers of fire, the flowing of water, the ferocity of wild beasts, etc; making a spirit or person stand immovable in one place and depriving him of the power of speech.

கரண விறளிப் பலகை யமன்றிசை
மரணமிட் டெட்டின் மகார வெழுத்திட்டு
வரணமி லைங்காயம் பூசி யடுப்பிடை
முரணிற் புதைத்திட மோகன மாகுமே. 998

Mohana Chakra

On a plank of Konrai tree wood
At the lower end
Inscribe "Na" and "Si"
And on palm leaf write letter "Ma"
Smear it with ingredients five,
(Ginger, Pepper, mustard, garlic and asofoetida)
Bury it head downward in the hearth's fire
You shall attain powers of Mohana (Fascination).

ஆங்கு வடமேற்கில் ஐயனார் கோட்டத்திற்
பாங்கு படவே பலாசப் பலகையிற்
காங்கரு மேட்டிற் கடுப்பூசி விந்துவிட்(டு)
ஓங்காமல் வைத்திடும் உச்சாட னத்துக்கே. 999

Uchchatana Chakra

On a plank of portia tree wood
At the north-west corner
Where Aiyanar his temple has,
And on a dark leaden-plate smear poison,
Inscribe mark of Bindu (dot)
And surround it by "Om"
Then concentrate on the Mantra,
Uchchatana (the Science of Exorcism) will be yours.

Utchatana—powers of expulsion. Setting demons against a person to ruin him by magical incantations, or dislodging them by magical incantations, or dislodging them from persons or places.

உச்சியம் போதில் ஒளிவன்னி மூலையிற்
பச்சோலை யிற்பஞ்ச காயத்தைப் பாரித்து
முச்சது ரத்தின் முதுகாட்டில் வைத்திட
அச்சமற மேலோர் மாரணம் வேண்டிலே. 1000

Marana Chakra

Smear a green palm leaf with ingredients five stated
In a triangle Chakra in the cremation ground
Bury it at noon in southeast corner,
Where God Agni stands,
That the Mantric device for Marana,
(Death) spell for enemies to destroy.

Marana—deprivation of life, killing either spirits or men.

ஏய்ந்த வரிதார மேட்டின்மே லேபூசி
ஏய்ந்த வகாரம் உகாரம் எழுத்திட்டு
வாய்ந்ததோர் வில்லம் பலகை வசியத்துக்
கேய்ந்தவைத் தெண்பதி னாயிரம் வேண்டிலே. 1001

Vasya Chakra

Smear palm leaf with yellow arsenic
Inscribe on it letters "A" and "U"
Place it on a bilva plank,
For a receptacle to serve,
And chant the Mantra eighty thousand-times.

Vasyam—bringing a person under one's own power, influence, etc.

எண்ணாக் கருடனை ஏட்டின் உகாரமிட்(டு)
எண்ணாப் பொன்னொளி எழுவெள்ளி பூசிடா
வெண்ணாவற் பலகையி லிட்டுமேற் கேநோக்கி
எண்ணா வெழுத்தொடெண்ணாயிரம் வேண்டிலே. 1002

Akarshana Chakra

Smear palm leaf with silver power on a Thursday
Inscribe letter "U",
Place it on the plank of white Jamun tree
Face Westward,
And Chant Pranava mantra ("Aum") eight thousand times;
This the way to attain
Power of bringing things and people unto you—
Akarshana.

Akarshanam — summoning or invoking a spirit or absent person visibly into one's presence.

These magical acts are exposited as eight in number. Besides the six above, the other two are: vidvedanam, or excitement to hatred; and bhedanam, causing dissension, discord, etc.

3. அருச்சனை
ARCHANA

அம்புய நீலங் கழுநீ ரணிநெய்தல்
வம்பவிழ் பூகமும் மாதவி மந்தாரந்
தும்பை வகுளஞ் சுரபுன்னை மல்லிகை
செண்பகம் பாதிரிசெவ்வந்தி சாத்திடே. 1003

Flowers for Archana (Worship with Flowers)

Lotus, Lily blue, Lily pink, Lily white,
Flower of areca palm, madhavai creeper, shoe-flower (Mandaram)
Thumbai, vakulam, surapunnai, jasmine,
Shenpagam, padiri, chrysanthum
With these do worship.

Archana is worship with flowers, perfumes and lights, along with chanting the Names of the Lord, and singing His praise. Tirumular describes the flowers that are appropriate for Siva's worship and the perfumes worthy of the occasion. He also gives directions regarding the lamps to be lighted and the oblations to be offered. He concludes that such worship, which belongs to the Kriya path, will confer great blessings.

But more important, he says, is worship in the mansion of the mind. Tirumular warns the Siva yogis not to resort to kriyas, for kriyas only add to karma.

Those who stand in the bhakti path also need not care for kriya. It is not by kriya that the Lord's Grace descends. To seek the Lord by way of the senses is vain. The jnana way also leads to nadanta the divine light. It alone leads to union in God.

Those who seek the kriya way can, at best, become devas. That is but a step, as devas themselves have to follow the jnana path, if they seek to unite in Siva.

Chanting Sivayanama helps in the jnana way. But both Na and Ma should not be chanted; for Na and Ma are the seeds of jiva. Chanting only the mantra, 'Siva', can bring about mauna that leads to liberation.

Jnana leads to illumination. Siva bliss wells up. Jiva leaps into 'A' (Si) and from it, it realises 'U' (Va); then appears the Lord within.

சாங்கம தாகவே சந்தொடு சந்தனந்
தேங்கமழ் குங்குமங் கர்ப்பூரங் காரகிற்
பாங்கு படப்பனி நீராற் குழைத்துவைத்(து)
ஆங்கே அணிந்துநீர் அர்ச்சியும் அன்பொடே. 1004

Fragrant Ingredients for Worship

The ten unguents to form,
Musk, sandal paste, perfumed kumkum,
Camphor, eagle wood fragrant and the rest
Mix in water or rose water and make a paste
Then put it on (Chakra) and worship.

அன்புட னேநின் றமுதமும் ஏற்றியே
பொன்செய் விளக்கும் புகைதீபந் திசைதொறுந்
துன்பம் அகற்றித் தொழுவோர் நினையுங்கால்
இன்புட னேவந் தெய்திடும் முத்தியே. 1005

Offer Oblations

Offer oblations in love,
Light lamps golden,
Spread incense of fragrant wood
And lighted camphor in directions all,
Forget your worldly worries, and meditate,
You shall attain rapturous Mukti true.

எய்தி வழிப்படில் எய்தா தனவில்லை
எய்தி வழிப்படில் இந்திரன் செல்வமுன்
எய்தி வழிப்படில் எண்சித்தி உண்டாகும்
எய்தி வழிப்படில் எய்திடும் முத்தியே. 1006

Results of Worship

Worshipping thus, there is nothing that you cannot attain,
Worshipping thus, you shall come by Indra's wealth
Worshipping thus, you shall attain miraculous Siddhi powers,
Worshipping thus, you shall attain Mukti.

நண்ணும் பிறதார நீத்தார் அவித்தார்
மண்ணிய நைவேத் தியமனு சந்தான
நண்ணிய பஞ்சாங்க நண்ணுஞ் செபமென்னு
மன்னு மனபவ னத்தொடு வைகுமே. 1007

Constant Worship in Mansion of Mind

Even when other men's wives approach them,
They touch them not,
They have mastered passions all,
Their mind is preoccupied perpetually
With offer of oblation diverse,
They worship prostrating low,
Constantly chanting Mantra,
Thus in the Mansion of Mind they abide.

வேண்டார்கள் கன்மம் விமலனுக் காட்பட்டோர்
வேண்டார்கள் கன்ம மதிலிச்சை யற்றபேர்
வேண்டார்கள் கன்மம் மிகுசிவ யோகிகள்
வேண்டார்கள் கன்மம் மிகுதியோ ராய்ந்தன்பே. 1008

Kriya is Not Sought by Bhaktas, Yogis and Jnanis

They who have been received by Lord in His Grace
Seek not Kriya Way;
They who desire not to accumulate Karma,
Seek not to perform Kriyas;
They who are Siva Yogins great
They too seek not Kriyas;
They who are in loving devotion surpassing stand
They too seek not Kriyas.

அறிவரு ஞானத் தெவரும் அறியார்
பொறிவழி தேடிப் புலம்புகின் றார்கள்
நெறிமனை யுள்ளே நிலைபெற நோக்கில்
எறிமணி யுள்ளே இருக்கலு மாமே. 1009

Seek God the Jnana Way

They know not to reach Him by Jnana Divine;
They seek Him by ways of senses, in vain;
If within you, you constantly seek Him in the right way,
You shall indeed be in Nadanta.

Mular identifies Nadanta with the Jnana Marga here.

இருளும் வெளியும்போல் இரண்டாம் இதய
மருளறி யாமையும் மன்னு மறிவு
மருளிவை விட்டறி யாமை மயங்கு
மருளுஞ் சிதைத்தோ ரவர்களா மன்றே. 1010

Jnana Dispels Heart's Darkness

Light and Darkness together are in heart;
So does it seek Grace and Ignorance at once;
The knowledge within of Jiva is bereft of Light;
Except those who have Divine Jnana attained,
The rest despair of dispelling Darkness.

தானவ னாக அவனேதா னாயிட
ஆன இரண்டில் அறிவன் சிவமாகப்
போனவ னன்பிது நாலாம் மரபுறத்
தானவ னாகுமோ ராசித்த தேவரே. 1011

Jnana Alone Leads to Union in God

Yourself Himself becoming,
And Himself yourself becoming
And with two none,
And as one Siva Becoming;
(When thus it is),
Those who went the way of Kriya
If they take to Jnana,
They with Siva one become;
They who seek Kriya,
May but Devas be.

ஓங்கார முந்திக்கீழ் உற்றிடும் எந்நாளும்
நீங்கா வகாரமும் நீள்கண்டத் தாயிடும்
பாங்கார் நகாரம் பயில்நெற்றி யுற்றிடும்
வீங்காகும் விந்துவும் நாதமே லாகுமே. 1012

Where Om and Other Letters Rise

"Om" rises from under navel
"Va" rises from throat stretched,
"Na" has its seat in forehead,
Bindu and Nada are still above placed.

நமவது வாசன மான பசுவே
சிவமது சித்திச் சிவமாம் பதியே

நமவற வாதி நாடுவ தன்றாஞ்
சிவமாகு மாமோனஞ் சேர்தல்மெய் வீடே. 1013

Be Rid of Na and Ma

Jiva has "Na" and "Ma" for its seats
Siva has "Si" and "Va" that lead you to Him
Be rid of "Na" and "Ma"
And seek Primal One;
He will be yours at once;
The State of Mauna leads to Siva Becoming
That to reach is Liberation True.

தெளிவரு நாளிற் சிவஅமு தூறும்
ஒளிவரு நாளில் ஓரெட்டில் உகளும்'
ஒளிவரும் அப்பதத் தோரிரண் டாகில்
வெளிவரு நாதன் வெளியாய் இருந்தே. 1014

Visions in the Seventh, Eighth, Eleventh and Twelth Centers

Yoga its consummation reaches
In Nectar's flow in Centre Seventh;
In the Eighth is revealed the Jnana Light;
Then beyond in the Eleventh
Is Paraparam the Supreme;
Then beyond, beyond is Void,
The Dvadasanta Space Infinite.

4. நவகுண்டம்
NAVAGUNDAM (NINE SACRIFICIAL PITS)

நவகுண்ட மானவை நானுரை செய்யின்
நவகுண்டத் துள்ளெழு நற்றீபந் தானும்
நவகுண்டத் துள்ளெழு நன்மைகள் எல்லாம்
நவகுண்ட மானவை நானுரைப் பேனே. 1015

The Nine Sacrificial Pits are Blessed

To recount greatness of sacrificial pits nine is thus:
In sacrificial pits nine,
Will blaze the blessed fire;
In the sacrificial pits nine
Will arise all things great;
Thus shall I speak of sacrificial pits nine.

The word 'navagundam' (nine pits) is used in a double sense here. On the one hand, it refers to the nine fire-pits used in sacrificial (yajna) worship, and on the other, it refers to the human body, with its nine orifices.

Chapter IV. NAVAGUNDAM (NINE SACRIFICIAL PITS)

It doesn't seem appropriate nor true to state that Tirumular does not hold the Kriya path in as high regard as the other three paths, as is stated in the following paragraph. Each path is addressed by Tirumular for its efficacy as a stage within Sanmarga. They are not compared to each other, as occurs in the Vedanta doctrine.)

Although Tirumular does not hold the Kriya path in high esteem compared to the other three paths, he relates the sacrificial fire of the Kriya path to the kundalini fire in the Yoga path. Drawing parallels between them, he shows how the fire without is the fire within.

The sacrificial pits are nine in shape:

1) The square pit — the four sides represent the four paths: Chariya, Kriya,. Yoga and Jnana.

2) The triangular pit — the three sides denote the form of fire.

3) The semi-circular pit is like a bent bow.

4) The circular pit is like a deep well.

5) The hexagonal pit is parallel to the adharas within.

6) The octagonal pit points to the earth's eight directions.

7) The heart-shaped pit is like the leaf of a peep tree.

8) The oval-shaped pit is fashioned after a golden bowl.

9) The pentagonal pit is constructed after the Five Letters of the Siva mantra.

உரைத்திடுங் குண்டத்தின் உள்ளேமுக் காலும்
நகைத்தெழு நாற்கோண நன்மைகள் ஐந்தும்
பகைத்திடு .முப்புரம் பாரங்கி யோடே
மிகைத்தெழு கண்டங்கள் மேலறி யோமே. 1016

Shapes of Sacrificial Pits

The sacrificial pit is triangle-shaped;
It is square shaped, pentagon shaped;
And hexagon shaped, triangle upon triangle made;
Other pits that blaze in fire, we later relate.

மேலறிந் துள்ளே வெளிசெய்த வப்பொருள்
காலறிந் துள்ளே கருத்துற்ற செஞ்சுடர்
பாரறிந் தண்டஞ் சிறகற நின்றது
நானறிந் துள்ளே நாடிக்கொண் டேனே. 1017

Pervasiveness of Kundalini Fire

Breath through Sushumna coursing,
Kundalini fire blazed aloft;
Light on top emanated,
Pervaded world,
And engulfed entire cosmic space
That I saw in me, and sought within.

The fire in the nine sacrificial pits is the same as the fire in kundalini within. The kundalini fire pervades the worlds, and engulfs the entirety of cosmic space.

கொண்டஇக் குண்டத்தின் உள்ளெழு சோதியாய்
அண்டங்கள் ஈரேழு மாக்கி அழிக்கலாம்

பண்டையுள் வேதம் பரந்த பரப்பெலாம்
இன்றுசொல் நூலாய் எடுத்துரைத் தேனே. *1018*

Power of Sacrificial Fire

Becoming the Light within the Light
That from the sacrificial pit arises,
You attain the power,
To create and dissolve worlds twice seven;
The truth that is spread
Over extensive Vedas ancient,
I here state explicit
In one single book.

Mantras 1018-1020

The power of the sacrificial fire is limitless. In it are the sixteen kalas that glow in the triangular-shaped muladhara within. In it, the Five Letters stand dancing. The humming orbs of the zodiac appear there.

எடுத்தவக் குண்டத் திடம்பதி னாறிற்
பதித்த கலைகளும் பாலித்து நிற்குங்
கதித்தனல் உள்ளேழக் கண்டுகொள் வார்க்கே
கொதித்தெழும் வல்வினை கூடகி லாவே. *1019*

The Sixteen Kalas are in the Sacred Fire

In the sacrificial pit thus formed,
The sixteen kalas luminous
Will sixteen points occupy;
Those who can see that Fire within
The broiling Pasas will not touch.

கூடமுக் கூடத்தின் உள்ளெழு குண்டத்துள்
ஆடிய ஐந்தும் அகம்புறம் பாய்நிற்கும்
பாடிய பன்னீ ரிராசியும் அங்கெழ
நாடிக்கொள் வார்கட்கு நற்சுடர் தானே. *1020*

The Glow of the Triangular Pit

In the triangular pit within, and without
The Five Elements stand dancing in Fire
The humming orbs of Zodiac, twelve, will appear;
A resplendent Light it is
For those who seek.

நற்சுட ராகுஞ் சிரமுக வட்டமாங்
கைச்சுட ராகுங் கருத்துற்ற கைகளிற்
பைச்சுடர் மேனி பதைப்புற் றிலிங்கமும்
நற்சுட ராயெழு நல்லதென் றாளே. *1021*

Holy Effects of Sacrificial Fire

The head and face will glow in a halo of light,
On the hand, Fire will appear if so they will
The glowing body trembling and shaking
Will give forth the shining Linga
Good indeed in worship of sacrificial Fire-pit!
Thus said Sakti Divine.

The head and face of him who tends the sacrificial fire will glow in a halo of light. Fire will appear on his palms, if he so wills. The glowing body, trembling and shaking, will give forth the shining linga.

நல்லதென் றாளே நமக்குற்ற நாயகஞ்
சொல்லதென் றாளே சுடர்முடி பாதமா
மெல்லநின் றாளை வினவகில் லாதவர்
கல்லதென் றாளையுங் கற்றும்வின் வாளே. *1022*

Sakti Affirms Sacredness of Sacrifical Fire

"Great" She said, Our mother of esteem high;
"That the Word" (Five letter), said She,
Who radiant from head to foot in tenderness stood;
They who do not ask of Her,
Though learned unto roots of learning,
Yet are in confusion distract.

Mantras 1022 & 1023

The sacrificial fire is blessed by Sakti. Even as the tongue of fire from the sacrificial pit shoots forth like the mythical serpents in eight directions, the kundalini too flames within the yogi from its four petals.

வின்னா விளம்பிறை மேவிய குண்டத்துச்
சொன்னால் இரண்டுஞ் சுடர்நாகந் திக்கெங்கும்
பன்னாலு நாகம் பரந்த பரஞ்சுடர்
என்னாகத் துள்ளே இடங்கொண்ட வாறே. *1023*

With Fire in Pit Kundalini Fire Also Shot Forth

The sacrificial pit takes the shape of
Shining-bow and crescent moon;
The tongues of Fire shot forth
Like mythical serpents from directions eight;
And Kundalini too with its petals four
In me flamed,
Filling my inside with radiant light.

இடங்கொண்ட பாதம் எழிற்சுட ரேக
நடங்கொண்ட பாதங்கள் நண்ணி ரதற்குச்
சகங்கொண்ட கையிரண் டாறுந் தழைப்ப
முகங்கொண்ட செஞ்சுடர் முக்கண னார்க்கே. *1024*

Sacrificial Fire Reaches Dancing Siva

The Fire reached Feet of Dancing Siva,
It flowed as water of worship at His Feet;
It reached the mighty arms eight of the Dancer
That fills universe entire;
It reached the fire in the Fore-head eye of Lord.

The kundalini fire reaches the Feet of Siva within, even as the fire from the sacrifical pit reaches to Siva above.

முக்கணன் றானே முழுச்சுட ராயவன்
அக்கணன் றானே அகிலமும் உண்டவன்
திக்கண னாகித் திகையெட்டுங் கண்டவன்
எக்கணன் றானுக்கும் எந்தை பிரானே. *1025*

Sacrificial Fire is Siva Himself

The Three-eyed Lord is Fire entire;
The Lord of self-same eye,
Engulfed universe entire;
With eyes in directions all,
He sees directions eight;
He is Lord, my Father,
And for all lives everywhere.

Mantras 1025 & 1026

In fact, the sacrificial fire is Siva Himself. His Third Eye is all fire, and the vision of the eyes spreads in all directions and touches all lives. It is out of that fire that the God Skanda arose. His six faces are the emanations of Siva's fire.

எந்தை பிரானுக் கிருமூன்று வட்டமாய்த்
தந்தைதன் முன்னே சண்முகந் தோன்றலாற்
கந்தன் சுவாமி கலந்தங் கிருத்தலான்
மைந்தன் இவனென்று மாட்டிக்கொள் ளீரே. 1026

God Kanda Arose Out of Lord's Fire

Out of my Father arose six orbs of Fire
The six Faces before Him appeared;
The God Kanda in Him is intermingled;
And so is He His Son;
Thus do you in understanding connect.

மாட்டிய குண்டத்தின் உள்ளெழு வேதத்துள்
ஆட்டிய காலொன்றும் இரண்டும் அலர்ந்திடும்
வாட்டிய கையிரண் டொன்று பதைத்தெழ
நாட்டுஞ் சுரரிவர் நல்லொளி தானே. 1027

When Lord is Visioned in Ajna (Eye-Brow Centre)

Within the sacrificial pit, that is Muladhara,
Arises the Vedic Fire that is Kundalini,
When controlled breath through Sushumna in unison flows,
The two petals in Ajna Centre open;
When the two paths are closed
And Kundalini rises through the Sushumna
They who thus worship and vision,
Are verily Celestials of Light Divine.

The Kundalini fire that is in muladhara is the same as the Vedic fire. When it reaches ajna through sushumna, it unites in the divine light.

நல்லொளி யாக நடந்துல கெங்குங்
கல்லொளி யாகக் கலந்துள் இருந்திடும்
சொல்லொளி யாகத் தொடர்ந்த உயிர்க்கெலாங்
கல்லொளி கண்ணுளு மாகி நின்றாளே. 1028

Lord is Light Divine

As Light Splendrous, He pervades worlds all,
Latent as sparkle in gem,
He is immanent in all;
For all those who sought Him as Light of Divine Word
He stood as beacon light on hill top,
And as the light within the eye too.

நின்றஇக் குண்டம் நிலையாறு கோணமாய்ப்
பண்டையில் வட்டம் பதைத்தெழு மாறாறுங்
கொண்டஇத் தத்துவம் உள்ளே கலந்தெழ
விண்ணுளும் என்ன எடுக்கலு மாமே. 1029

The Hexagonal Sacrificial Pit Witthin

This sacrificial pit within
Is a hexagon of six Adhara formed;
In its circle Tattvas six times six,
Trembling arise;
With these Tattvas under your command,
You can ascend into very Heavens high.

The hexagonal sacrificial pit is also within. It is the hexagon of the six adharas. In it the 36 tattvas arise trembling. Transcending them, the yogi can reach the Lord in the sahasrara.

எடுக்கின்ற பாதங்கண் மூன்ற தெழுத்தைக்
கடுத்த முகம்இரண் டாறுகண் ணாகப்
படித்தெண்ணு நாவெழு கொம்பொரு நாலும்
அடுத்தெழு கண்ணான தந்தமி லாற்கே. 1030

Form of Sacrificial God

Three His feet, Seven His hands,
Two His faces, six His eyes,
Seven His tongues, four His horns,
Thus does He rise from the Sacrificial Fire Pit
He the one that no end knows.

Tirumular describes the Form of God that arises in the sacrificial fire pit somewhat along the lines recounted in the relevant *Rig Veda* hymn. "Three His Feet, seven His hands, Two His faces, Six His eyes, seven His tongues, four His horns — thus does arise the God of the sacrificial pit."

This is said to be based on a *Rig Veda* mantra.

அந்தமில் லானுக் ககலிடந் தானில்லை
அந்தமில் லானை அளப்பவர் தாமில்லை
அந்தமில் லானுக் கடுத்தசொற் றானில்லை
அந்தமில் லானை அறிந்துகொள் பத்தே. 1031

But He is Endless

For the Endless One, none the Space there is;
For the Endless One, none there to take measure;
For the Endless One, none the words adequate to describe;
Know the Endless One, O! "Ya" (Jiva)!

The numearal, ten, is written as the letter '' (ya) in Tamil. Hence, 'ten' here means 'ya' which stands for jiva in the Five Letter mantra.

பத்திட்டங் கெட்டிட் டாறிட்டு நாலிட்டு
மட்டிட்ட குண்டம் மலர்ந்தெழு தாமரை

கட்டிட்டு நின்று கலந்தமெய் யாகமும்
பட்டிட்டு நின்றது பார்ப்பதி பாலே. 1032

Sacrificial Fire Outside Kindles Kundalini Fire Inside

Decagonal, octagonal, hexagonal and square
Thus are sacrificial pits shaped,
In them blazes fire
Like a crimson lotus;
Centre your thoughts,
The Fire within (Kundalini) pervades the body entire
As unto Siva-Sakti its tongues lappped.

பார்ப்பதி பாகன் பரந்தகை நாலைஞ்சு
காற்பதி பத்து முகம்பத்துக் கண்களும்
பூப்பதி பாதம் இரண்டு சுடர்முடி
நாற்பது சோத்திரம் நல்லிரு பத்தஞ்சே. 1033

Form of Siva-Sakti in Sacrificial Fire

There, Siva with His consort Parvati appears,
Four the spreading hands,
Five the legs,
Ten the faces,
Two the flowery feet
Forty the shining crowns, and
Twenty-five the ears.

Tirumular describes the Form of Siva/Sakti arising from the sacrificial fire thus: "Ten the faces, four the spreading hands, five the legs, ten the eyes, two the flowery Feet, forty the shining crowns, and twenty-five the ears."

அஞ்சிட்ட கோலம் அளப்பன ஐயைந்தும்
மஞ்சிட்ட குண்ட மலர்ந்தங் கிருத்தலால்
பஞ்சிட்ட சோதி பரந்த பரஞ்சுடர்
கொஞ்சிட்ட வன்னியைக் கூடுதன் முத்தியே. 1034

Kundalini Fire Blazes with Sacrificial Fire

Five His Faces
Five times Five the Tattvas He measures,
There is Sacrificial Fire Pit open,
That is of sides five;
And so it behooves,
For subtle Kundalini Fire to reach
The Lord that is in Divine Fire — Five-fold (Panchagni)
That verily is to attain Mukti.

முத்திநற் சோதி முழுச்சுட ராயவன்
கற்றற்று நின்றார் கருத்துள் இருந்திடும்
பற்றற நாடிப் பரந்தொளி யூடுபோய்ச்
செற்றற் றிருந்தவர் சேர்ந்திருந் தாரே. 1035

Seek Him Through Inner Fire

He is Mukti; He is Light,
In the thoughts of fully learned
He is the Light entise;
They who seek Him, desires severed,
Through Light within
Reach the goal
And remain blemishless, ever after.

சேர்ந்த கலையஞ்சுஞ் சேருமிக் குண்டமும்
ஆர்ந்த திசைகளும் அங்கே அமர்ந்திடும்
பாய்ந்தஐம் பூதமும் பார்க்கின்ற வன்னியைக்
காய்ந்தவர் என்றுங் கலந்தவர் தாமே. 1036

Unite in Him Through Kundalini Fire

In that Fire Pit within
The Five Kalas of Siva art;
The ten directions cardinal there art;
The Five elements too art there;
Those who warmed themselves at Fire of Kundalini
Have verily united in God.

மெய்கண்ட மாம்விரி நீருல கேழையும்
உய்கண்டஞ் செய்த ஒருவனைச் சேருமின்
செய்கண்ட ஞானந் திருந்திய தேவர்கள்
பொய்கண்டம் இல்லாப் பொருள்கலந் தாரே. 1037

Celestials Reached Lord Through Jnana Sacrifices

The sea-girt worlds several,
The Lord redeemed;
That One Being Great, do you seek;
The Celestials in Jnana sacrifice excelled
Verily merged in Him,
That is Truth Unalloyed.

கலந்திரு பாதம் இருகர மாகு
மலர்ந்திரு குண்ட மகாரத்தோர் மூக்கு
மலர்ந்தெழு செம்முக மற்றைக்கண் நெற்றி
உணர்ந்திரு குஞ்சியங் குத்தம னார்க்கே. 1038

Siva's Form in Sacrificial Fire

Feet two, hands two,
The nose shaped as letter "Ma"
The face as red lotus bloom,
The third eye in Forehead,
Thus is Lord,
From Sacrificial Fire Pit arises;
Seek that Holy One within your head.

உத்தமன் சோதி உளனொரு பாலனாய்
மத்திம னாகி மலர்ந்தங் கிருந்திடும்
பச்சிம திக்கும் பரந்து குழிந்தன
சத்திமா னாகத் தழைத்த கொடியே. 1039

As Sacrificial Fire Blazed High

Within the Fire the Holy One arose cherubic;
In middle He youthful blossomed;
As the Sacrificial Fire blazed thus,
The sphere of forehead (Ajna Centre) broadened and, deepened,

And there He was,
His Sakti tender as a vine.

கொடியாறு சென்று குலாவிய குண்டம்
அடியிரு கோணமாய் அந்தமும் ஒக்கும்
படியே மூலகும் பரந்த சுடரை
மடியாது கண்டவர் மாதன மாமே. 1040

Sacrificial Fire Pervaded Macrocosm; Kundalini Fire Pervaded Microcosm

The Sacrificial Fire Pit spread
Unto Kundalini Fire across Chakras Six
And in two-petalled centre (Ajna) ended;
The sacred Fire engulfed worlds seven entire,
From top to bottom unintermittent,
Those who witnessed it,
Have indeed gained all riches vast.

As the sacrificial fire blazes high, the yogi's kundalini fire within also courses upwards; and when it reaches the ajna chakra, he visions Sakti. Ascending further, reaching the seventh centre, the sahasrara, he visions the seven worlds.

மாதன மாக வளர்கின்ற வன்னியைச்
சாதன மாகச் சமைந்த குருவென்று
போதன மாகப் பொருந்த உலகாளும்
பாதன் மாகப் பிரிந்தது பார்த்தே. 1041

Hold Sacrificial Fire As Guru

The Fire that blazeth as riches vast
Hold it as Guru Great to reach your goal,
When that Jnana dawns,
The regal powers over world
In earnest seek Jiva.

Kundalini fire that blazes upwards is the Guru great, riches vast, and infinite jnana. The yogis who tend the kundalini fire live very long.

பார்த்திடம் எங்கும் பரந்தெழு சோதியை
ஆத்தம தாகவே யாய்ந்தறி வாரில்லை
காத்துடலுள்ளே கருதி இருந்தவர்
மூத்துடல் கோடி யுகங்கண்ட வாறே. 1042

Tend Kundalini Fire and Live Long

The Fire that rises and spreads everywhere
They seek not in truth and know not;
Those who have tended it within their body,
Live long, long,
For ten millions aeons, as it were.

உகங்கண்ட ஒன்பது குண்டமும் ஒக்க
அகங்கொண்ட யோகியுள் நாடி எழு பும்
பயங்கண்டு கொண்டஇப் பாய்கரு வொப்பச்
சகங்கண்டு கொண்டது சாதன மாமே. 1043

Kundalini Fire is Parallel to Sacrificial Fire

As in the nine sacrificial pits that transcend Time,
The Yogi in his Nadis raises the fire in Centres nine;
Even as the Seed of Birth trembled in fear of it,
So did the universe vast,
At the mighty yogic achievement.

சாதனை நாலு தழல்மூன்று வில்வயம்
வேதனை வட்டம் விளையாறு பூநிலை
போதனை போதைஞ்சு பொற்கய வாரண
நாதனை நாடு நவகோடி தானே. 1044

Shapes of Nine Sacrificial Pits

Of four sides unto Sadhanas four, (Chariya, Kriya, Yoga and Jnana)
Of three sides unto shape of fire,
Of semicircular shape like the bent bow,
Of circular shape like a bore,
Of six sides like Adharas within,
Of eight sides like earth's cardinal directions,
Of heart shape like leaf of Peepul tree,
Of five sides like letters of Siva Mantra,
Of oval shaped like the golden bowl
Thus of yore are shaped,
The nine Sacrificial Fire Pits,
Where you seek the Lord Supreme.

5. சத்திபேதம்—திரிபுரை சக்கரம்

SAKTI-BHEDA—TIRIPURAI CHAKRA

மாமாயை மாயை வயிந்தவம் வைகரி
ஓமாயை உள்ளொளி ஓராறு கோடியில்
தாமான மந்திரஞ் சத்திதன் மூர்த்திகள்
ஆமா யலவாந் திரிபுரை யாங்கே. 1045

The Inner Meaning of Six-Pointed Chakra

Mamaya, Maya, Baindava, Vaikari,
Pranava (AUM), the Inner Light (Ajapa)
Thus art Mantras in clusters six,
Where Sakti resideth;
There and beyond them
Is Tiripurai.

The One Sakti manifests as several — as Tiripurai, Sundari, Andari, Kumkumi, Paraipurai, Narani, Easi and Manonmani. She is Parai, Abhirami, Agochari. She is Chandika, Tapodhani and Puratani, the Ancient. She is Mohini, whose beauty does not wane. She is Karidari, the Attraction in four directions.

Magnificient is Her Form. It is of ruddy hue. Her brows are arched like the bow. On Her Feet She wears anklets. She is robed in red silk. Her breasts are contained in corsets. She sports a bow of sugarcane, arrows of flowers, an elephant goad and noose strings. On Her lovely head She wears Her diadem. On Her ears She wears kundalas of bluish radiant gems. She wears rudraksha beads, garlands of flowers, and a glowing crown on which the crescent moon beams. On the crown of Her tresses is the dame Ganga. Her eyes gleam with divine jnana. She is the Immaculate One. She is seated on a circle of pure lotus flowers.

She is the atom within the atom. She is Self-Manifest Divine Form. She has ten faces and twelve kalas. She is an ethereal light. She holds the 'Book of Knowledge' in Her hand. She holds the pestle that knocks the hearts of evil ones, and the plough that prepares the soul of the good ones for the jnana harvest. She is Omkari, the Pranava Form. She became Amkari of creative force, giving birth to the five Gods. She is Hrimkari, abiding in the mantra, 'Hrim.'

She resides in the mantra-cluster of six — mamaya, maya, vaindava, vikari, pranava and inner light.

"Vaikari (Vakharai) is one of the four elements of sound, others being Para, Pasyanti and Madhyama. It is that element which is carried by the sound within the body and becomes articulated in the throat. It is the gross sound. According to Raghavabhatta, Para is unmanifested sound; Pasyanti reveals letters; Madhyama - words, and Vaikhari - sentences" (N.N. Bhattacharyya, "History of Tantric Religion, p.478.)

The six-pointed chakra would be the powerful Sri-yantra, made up of two triangles, one inverted over the other, representing the male and female in couple with 'bindu', or the drop of semen in the centre. In Tamil Nadu, where 'kolams' (chakras) are usually drawn in white powder every morning at the entrance to the house (as a protection to the in-dwellers) the Sri-cakra is one of the most common to be seen.'

திரிபுரை சுந்தரி அந்தரி சிந்துரப்
பரிபுரை நாரணி யாம்பல வன்னத்தி
இருள்புரை ஈசி மனோன்மனி என்ன
வருபல வாய்நிற்கு மாமாது தானே. 1046

Manifestations of Tiripurai

Tiripurai, Sundari, Andari,
Kum-Kumi, Pari Purai, Narani,
The dark hued Easi, Manonmani
Thus of forms diverse and hues many,
One Sakti manifests several.

Sundari—the Beauteous
Andari—of the form of sky
Kum-Kumi —of red hue
Paripurai—Sustainer of Worlds
Narani—Divine prowess behind Narayana
Easi—Sakti of Mahesvara
Manonmani—Sakti of. Sadasiva

தானா அமைந்தவம் முப்புரந் தன்னிடைத்
தானான மூவுரு வோருருத் தன்மையள்
தானான பொன்செம்மை வெண்ணிறத் தாள்கல்வி
தானான போகமும் முத்தியும் நல்குமே. 1047

Blessings of Tiripurai

In the Three Cities —(Triangle)—of themselves arose
Of three forms, the One She is;
Of color gold, red, and white She is,
Knowledge, enjoyment and Mukti she grants.

நல்குந் திரிபுரை நாதநா தாந்தங்கள்
பல்கும் பரவிந்து பாரண்ட மானவை
நல்கும் பரைஅபி ராமி அகோசரி
புல்கு மருளுமப் போதந்தந் தாளுமே. 1048

Tiripurai Grants Grace and Jnana

Tiripurai confers Nada, Nadanta states
She as Para Bindu expands,
And to the cosmic Universe gives rise,
She is Parai, Abhirami, Agochari
She grants Her love of Grace,
And Jnana as well.

Parai—Sakti of Para
Abhirami—of Surpassing Beauty
Agochari—Beyond Comprehension

தாளணி நூபுரஞ் செம்பட்டுத் தானுடை
வாரணி கொங்கை மலர்க்கன்னல் வாளிவில்
ஏரணி அங்குச பாசம் எழில்முடி
காரணி மாமணிக் குண்டலக் காதிக்கே. 1049

Tiripurai's Form

On Her Feet She wears anklets,
She adorns red silk dress,
Her breasts are in corsets contained,
She sports arrows of flowers,
And bow of sugarcane,
And mighty goad-noose strings;
On Her lovely head She wears the diadem
On Her ears She wears Kundalas
Of bluish radiant gems.

குண்டலக் காதி கொலைவிற் புருவத்தள்
கொண்ட வரத்த நிறமன்னு கோலத்தள்
கண்டிகை யாரங் கதிர்முடி மாமதிச்
சண்டிகை நாற்றிசை தாங்கிநின் றாளே. 1050

Tiripurai as Chandika

Her ears sport Kundalas;
Her brows are shaped like bow that kills
Of ruddy hue is Her form magnificient,
Necklace of Rudraksha beads, garland of flowers and Crown,
Where the crescent moon beams forth
Thus adorned, She, the Chandika,
Stands supporting directions four.

நின்ற திரிபுரை நீளும் புராதனி
குன்றலில் மோகினி மாதிருக் குஞ்சிகை
நன்றறி கண்டிகை நாற்காற் கரீடணி
துன்றிய நற்சுத்த தாமரைச் சுத்தையே. 1051

Tiripurai is Seated on Lotus

Tiripurai who thus stood is Puratani,
She is Mohini whose beauty wanes not
On the crown of her tresses is Damsel Ganga,
Her eyes perceive Jnana true,
Karidani who attracts in directions four,
She is the Immaculate, seated on circle of lotus pure.

Puratani—Ancient One
Mohini—the Enticing One
Karidani—the One who Attracts

சுத்தவம் பாரத் தனத்தி சுகோதயள்
வத்துவ மாயா ளுமாசத்தி மாபரை
அத்தகை யாவும் அணோரணி தானுமாய்
வைத்தவக் கோல மதியவ ளாகுமே. 1052

Tiripurai is Atom Within Atom

On Her ample breasts,
She wears garland fragrant,
She is Source of Bliss;
She is Substance Primal,
She is Maya,
She is Uma,
She is Sakti;
She is Maha Parai;
She is all these,
And She is atom within atom;
she is Self-manifest Form divine,
She is Jnana embodied.

அவளை யறியா அமரரும் இல்லை
அவளன்றிச் செய்யும் அருந்தவம் இல்லை
அவளன்றி ஐவரால் ஆவதொன்றில்லை
அவளன்றி யூர்புகு மாறறி யேனே. 1053

Nothing Except Her

None the Celestials that know Her not,
None the tapas rare that is not for Her,
Except Her, Five Gods nothing perform,
Except Her, I know not,
How to reach Liberation.

அறிவார் பராசக்தி ஆனந்தம் என்பர்
அறிவா ரருவுரு வாமவள் என்பர்
அறிவார் கரும மவளிச்சை என்பர்
அறிவார் பரனு மவளிடத் தானே. 1054

What the Wise Say of Her

They who know say, Parasakti is Bliss;
They who know say, She is Formless,
They who know say, all action from Her desires flows;
They who know say, Param is in Her.

தானெங் குளனங் குளதையன் மாதேவி
ஊனெங் குளஅங் குள்ளுயிர்க் காவலன்
வானெங் குளஅங் குளேவந்து மப்பாலாம்
கோனெங்கும் நின்ற குறிபல பாரே. 1055

Tiripurai is Everywhere

Where Lord is, there His consort Mahadevi is,
Where there is fleshy body, there She is as Life protective;
Where there is space, there She is;
And beyond too;
She is everywhere,
Lordly over things all.

பராசக்தி மாசத்தி பல்வகை யாலுந்
தராசக்தி யாய்நின்ற தன்மை யுணராய்
உராசத்தி ஊழிகள் தோறும் உடனே
புராசக்தி புண்ணிய மாகிய போகமே. 1056

Tiripurai is Power That Sustains

Parasakti, Maha Sakti, She is;
In ways countless She is Power that supports all,
She is Sakti pervasive,
She is Sakti that protects through timeless aeons
She is Supreme Pleasure that all blessings confers,
This you know not.

போகஞ்செய் சத்தி புரிகுழ லாளொடும்
பாகஞ்செய் தாங்கே பராசக்தி யாய்நிற்கும்
ஆகஞ்செய் தாங்கே அடியவர் நாடொறும்
பாகஞ்செய் ஞானம் படர்கின்றகொம்பே. 1057

She is Support for Devotee's Jnana

From Her emanates all enjoyments,
She is of curly tresses that Grace grants,
She is Para Sakti that shares Siva's Form,
She stands as support
For tender Jnana Vine,
That Her devotees daily in their hearts grow.

கொம்பனை யாளைக் குவிமுலை மங்கையை
வம்பவிழ் கோதையை வானவர் நாடியைச்
செம்பவ ளத்திரு மேனிச் சிறுமியை
நம்பினன் உள்ளே நயந்துவைத் தேனே. 1058

Tiripurai Hold Dear in Heart

She is the support of life
She is of bouncing breasts,
She adorns fragrant flowers on Her tresses,
She is the One that Celestials seek,
She is the girl of red coral hue
In faith intense, I hold Her, dear in my heart.

வைத்த பொருளும் மருவுயிர்ப் பன்மையும்
பத்து முகமும் பரையும் பராபரைச்

சித்தக் கரணச் செயல்களுஞ் செய்திடுஞ்
சத்தியும் வித்தைத் தலையவ ளாமே. *1059*

Paraparai With Ten Faces Creates and Moves All

The Parai, Primal Paraparai, with faces ten
All things created, all life diverse;
She moves my mind, intellect, Will and thought
She is Sakti, and Mistress of Jnana Divine.

தலைவி தடமுலை மேல்நின்ற தையல்
தொலைவில் தவஞ்செயுந் தூய்நெறித் தோகை
கலைபல வென்றிடுங் கன்னியென் உள்ளம்
நிலைபெற இங்கே நிறைந்துநின் றாளே. *1060*

Tiripurai is Mistress of World

She is the Mistress of Worlds,
She rules over my heart,
She performs tapas continuous,
She is lovely as peacock,
She is Virgin, all knowledge-conquered,
In my heart, She stands filled.

நின்றவள் நேரிழை நீள்கலை யோடுற
என்றன் அகம்படிந் தேழுல குந்தொழ
மன்றது வொன்றி மனோன்மணி மங்கலி
ஒன்றெனோ டொன்றிநின் றொத்தடைந்
தாளே *1061*

She Merged in My Heart

She who thus stands is in jewels bedecked,
With beaming Kalas She entered my heart,
The seven worlds to adore
She entered the Holy Dance arena;
She is Manonmani, the Jewel of Inmost Thought,
She is Ever-Auspicious, (Mangali)
And in me She merged, inseparate ever.

ஒத்தடங் குங்கம லத்திடை யாயிழை
அத்தகை செய்கின்ற வாய பெரும்பதி
மத்தடை கின்ற மனோன்மணி மங்கலி
சித்தடைக் கும்வழிதேர்ந்துண ரார்களே. *1062*

She is Way to Jnana

In the Lotus of heart within
She merged,
She the bejewelled One,
She merged in rapture in Her Lord
Manonmani, the Jewel of Inmost Thought,
Mangali, the Auspicious Ever,
She is the path to gather Jnana,
Her, they know not.

உணர்ந்துட னேநிற்கும் உள்ளொளி யாகி
மணங்கமழ் பூங்குழல் மங்கையுந் தானும்
புணர்ந்துட னேநிற்கும் போதருங் காலைக்
கணிந்தெழு வார்க்குக் கதியளிப் பாளே. *1063*

Adore Her as Siva-Sakti

As light within, She inseparable stands;
The Mother of fragrant flower bedecked tresses
In the Lord, in union, stands;
They who then rise in adoration
Shall Her bounteous Grace receive.

அளியொத்த பெண்பிள்ளை ஆனந்த சுந்தரி
புளியுறு புன்பழம் போலுள்ளே நோக்கித்
தெளியுறு வித்துச் சிவகதிகாட்டி
ஒளியுற வைத்தென்னை உய்யவண் டாளே. *1064*

Her Glance Purified My Heart

She is the Lady, compassion embodied
She is Bliss—Beauty (Ananda Sundari)
Like tamarind fruit encased in cover hard
Is my wavering heart;
Into it She poured Her benignant glance
And made it pure;
She showed me the way to Siva-state
She made me radiant in Jnana
And redeemed me.

உண்டில்லை என்ற துருச்செய்து நின்றது
வண்டில்லை மன்றினுள் மன்னி நிறைந்தது
கண்டிலர் காரண காரணி தம்மொடு
மண்டல மூன்றுற மன்னிநின் றாளே. *1065*

She is Cause of Cause

She is, and She is not, they say
Yet She revealed to me Her Form;
She stood filling the Dance arena at Thillai;
They saw not;
She stood as Cause of Cause;
Pervading spheres Three.

Sun, moon and fire are the three spheres.

நின்றா ளவன்தன் உடலும் உயிருமாய்ச்
சென்றாள் சிவகதி சேரும் பராசக்தி
ஒன்றாக என்னுட் புகுந்துணர் வாகியே
நின்றாள் பரஞ்சுடர் ஏடங்கை யாளே. *1066*

She Holds the Book of Knowledge

She stood as body and life,
She—the Parasakti—took me to Siva-State,
She in me entered and stood one in my awareness
She of the ethereal Light,
She that holds the Book of Knowledge in Her Hand Divine.

"Holding the Book of Knowledge in hand" is in Hinduism a description of Sarasvati, and in Buddhism of Tara. Mular's Sakti does not belong to any particular well-designed sect, but is eclectic, combining in herself the attributes drawn from many sources.

ஏடங்கை நங்கை இறைஎங்கள் முக்கண்ணி
வேடம் படிகம் விரும்பும்வெண் டாமரை
பாடுந் திருமுறை பார்ப்பதி பாதங்கள்
சூடுமின் சென்னிவாய்த் தோத்திரஞ்
சொல்லுமே. 1067

Adore Her in Song

She that holds the Book of Knowledge in Her Hand Divine
She our Mother, of eyes three,
She of crystal form,
She of comely white lotus,
She chants the Vedas,
She is Parvati,
Bear Her Feet on thy head
And adore with songs devout.

தோத்திரஞ் செய்து தொழுது துணையடி
வாய்த்திட ஏத்தி வழிபடு மாறிரும்
பார்த்திடு மங்குச பாசம் பசுங்கரும்
பார்த்திடும் பூம்பிள்ளை யாகுமாம் ஆதிக்கே. 1068

Primal Virgin

Sing Her praise, adore Her Feet
Thus beseech Her and worship Her,
Meditate on Her,
Who is with elephant goad and noose
And cane of sugar;
She, the Primal Virgin.

ஆதி விதமிகுத் தண்டந்த மால்தங்கை
நீதி மலரின்மேல் நேரிழை நாமத்தைப்
பாதியில் வைத்துப் பல்காற் பயில்விரேல்
சோதி மிகுத்துமுக் காலமுந் தோன்றுமே. 1069

Chant Her Name and See Past Present and Future

She created all things diverse,
She is sister of Mal that protects all,
She the bejewelled Mother,
On Lotus of Dharma seated;
Chant Her name as Siva Sakti, times infinite
You will see Her Light,
And all things past, present and future.

மேதாதி ஈரெட்டு மாகிய மெல்லியல்
வேதாதி நூலின் விளங்கும் பராபரை
ஆதார மாகியே ஆய்ந்த பரப்பினள்
நாதாதி நாதத்து நல்லரு ளாளே. 1070

She Pervades the Sixteen Kalas

She is the Mother of Tender Form
That pervades Medha and the rest of Kalas sixteen;
She is the Paraparai that shines in Vedas and scriptures holy,
She is the widespread support of all that is,
She is the Grace within Nada and Nadanta.

அருள்பெற் றவர்சொல்ல வாரீர் மனிதர்
பொருள்பெற்ற சிந்தைப் புவனா பதியார்
மருளுற்ற சிந்தையை மாற்றி யருமைப்
பொருளுற்ற சேவடி போற்றுவன் யானே. 1071

Grace Transforms

O! Ye who were blessed by Her Grace
Tell these men,
How this Mother that rules worlds all
Of Divine Jnana filled
Transformed your inconstant thoughts,
And made you realize God-truth;
Her Holy Feet, I adore ever.

ஆன வராக முகத்தி பதத்தினள்
ஈன வராகம் இடிக்கும் முசலத்தோ(டு)
ஏனை யுழுபடை ஏந்திய வெண்ணகை
ஊன மறவுணர்ந் தாருளத் தோங்குமே. 1072

Tiripurai Manifested as Varahi

She of the Varahi visage of Divine Boar
She that grants all power and state
She that holds the pestle
That knocks the heart of evil ones,
She that bears the plough
And the rest of insignia,
She of the pearly teeth,
They who meditate on them true,
In their hearts she arose.

ஓங்காரி என்பா ளவளொரு பெண்பிள்ளை
நீங்காத பச்சை நிறத்தை யுடையவள்
ஆங்காரி யாகியே ஐவரைப் பெற்றிட்டு
ரீங்காரத் துள்ளே யினிதிருந் தாளே. 1073

Tiripurai as Creative Force

She is Omkari, the Mother of Pranava Form,
Of indelible green hue is Her Form,
As Ankhari of Creative Force She became
And gave birth to the Five Gods
And then lapsed sweet
Into the music of Her mantra "Hrim."

தானே தலைவி யெனநின்ற தற்பரை
தானே யுயிர்வித்துத் தந்த பதினாலும்
வானோர் தலமும் மனமும்நற் புத்தியுந்
தானே சிவகதி தன்மையு மாமே. 1074

Herself Uncreated, She is Source of Creation

She as supreme Mistress of all creation stood
She the uncreated Being, Tatparai;
She is Worlds Fourteen
That were from Bindu created;
She is World of Celestials,
She is Mind and Intellect,
She is Siva-State too.

6. வயிரவி மந்திரம்
BHAIRAVI MANTRA

Bhairavi has sixteen kalas. Her mantra is 'Aum Aim' Meditating on Her for a month of twenty-seven days in kundalini yoga, union in Siva is attained.

Bhairavi is also known as Tiripurai. She holds the trident and skull in Her hands, the serpent noose and elephant goad. She has four hands. She is green-hued, as a parrot. Her form is lustrous like a gem. Her robe is worked with precious stones. Her crown is studded with gems. It is brilliant as the moon. Her glance is furtive as that of the gentle fawn. She is vengeful to those who err. Her eyes are the sun and moon. She wears kundalas of radiant gems in Her ears. She is seated in the centre of the eight-petalled lotus in the midst of eight virgin saktis surrounded by sixty-four damsels who keep vigil. She wears anklets, bangles of conch and tresses festooned with fragrant flowers. Her body is smeared with haunting perfumes. She is in manimantra yoga, the yoga that spells no word. In that yoga will be heard the sound of Her conch for yojanas around.

In worshipping Her, first chant Her Hridaya mantra, perform kavacha and nyasa, and adopt the sula mudra which indeed is difficult to practice.

Sula mudra consists in pressing the little finger in reverse direction, holding the ring finger and forefinger pressed together; then insert the thumb finger in between. Chant the mantra, 'Sam.'
Adopt the conch mudra. She is the beginning, the beginningless and She blossoms with the prayer of the heart.

பன்னிரண் டாங்கலை யாதி பயிரவி
தன்னில் அகாரமு மாயையுங் கற்பித்துப்
பன்னிரண் டாதியோ டந்தம் பதினாலுஞ்
சொன்னிலை சோடச மந்தமென் றோதிடே. *1075*

Fourteen Mantras

Twelve are Kalas of Primal Bhairavi,
To the Twelfeth letter "Ai" denoted,
Add "A"; and "M" letter denoting Maya;
Thus with letters Twelve and Two
From Om to Aim they fourteen are
That Her Mantras
To end of Kalas Sixteen lead.

---

1 Compare: For the 12 bija mantras, refer to *Varada Tantra*, Chapter 6, quoted in "Garland of Letters," by Sir John Woodroffe, pp.262-65

The 12 bija mantras are:

1. Haum—'Ha' means Siva, 'au' means Sadasiva, 'm' means Sivaya who dispels sorrow.
2. Dum—'Da' means Durga, 'u' means save, 'm' means mother of the universe.
3. Krim—'Ka' is Kali, 'ra' is Brahma, 'i' is Mahamaya. 'm' means mother of the universe.
4. Hrim—'H' is Siva, 'ra' is prakriti, 'i' is Mahamaya, 'm' means mother of the universe.
5. Srim—'S' is Mahalakshmi, 'ra' is wealth, 'i' is satisfaction, 'm' is nada.
6. Aim—'Ai' is Sarasvati, 'm' is nada.
7. Klim—'Ka' is Kamadeva, 'I' is Indra, 'i' is contentment, 'm' is nada.
8. Hum—'H' is Siva, 'u' is Bhairava, 'm' is nada.
9. Gam—'G' is Ganesha, 'm' is nada.
10. Glaum—'G' is Ganesha, 'I' is what pervades, 'au' is tejas, 'm' is nada.
11. Ksraum—'Ksa' is Nṛshimha, 'ra' is Brahma, 'au is teeth pointing upwards.
12. Strim—'S' is deliverance, 't' is saviour, 'ra' is liberation, 'i' is Mahamaya, 'm' is bindu.

அந்தம் பதினாலும் அதுவே வயிரவி
முந்து நடுவும் முடிவும் முதலாகச்
சிந்தைக் கமலத் தெழுகின்ற மாசத்தி
அந்தமும் ஆதியு மாகிநின் றாளே. *1076*

Bhairavi is Maha Sakti

The end of that letter Fourteenth is Bhairavi
As beginning, middle and end
In the lotus of thought
She rises as Maha Sakti
She is beginning and end of all.

ஆகின்ற மூவரும் அங்கே அடங்குவர்
போகின்ற பூதம் பொருந்து புராதரர்
சார்கின்ற சார்வுழிச் சாரார் கதிர்பெறப்
போகுந் திரிபுரை புண்ணியத் தோரே. *1077*

Meditate on Her and Become Light Radiant

The Three Gods are there contained;
They who meditate on Her
Will not go the way of fleshy Jivas, Tattva bound;
They radiant become, the blessed ones
Who on Tiripurai meditate.

புண்ணிய நந்தி புனிதன் திருவாகும்
எண்ணிய நாட்கள் இருபத்தேழ் சூழ்மதி
பண்ணய வன்னி பகலோன் மதியிறு
திண்ணிய சிந்தைதன் தென்னனு மாமே. *1078*

Meditate on Her for 27 Days

She is the Treasure of Blessed Nandi, the Pure One:
Meditate on Her for a month of days twenty seven;
And reach the centres of Fire; Sun and Moon within
He who thus firm in meditation stands
Becomes Siva Himself.

தென்னன் திருநந்தி சேவகன் தன்னொடும்
பொன்னங் கிரியிற் பூதலம் போற்றிடும்

பன்னும் பரிபிடி யந்தம் பகவனோ(டு)
உன்னுந் திரிபுரை ஓதிநின் றானுக்கே. 1079

Worship Bhairavi and Be With Siva

With gait rivalling the cow-elephant
And one with Siva entwined is Tripurai,
He who meditates constantly on Her
Will with Siva Himself be,
The Lord that is Nandi,
The Hero Mighty;
With Him in Golden Mount of Kailas will he be;
All the World will there adore him.

ஓதிய நந்தி உணருந் திருவருள்
நீதியில் வேத நெறிவந் துரைசெய்யும்
போதம் இருபத் தெழுநாள் புணர்மதி
சோதி வயிரவி சூலம்வந் தாளுமே. 1080

Worship Bhairavi for 27 Days; Her Trident Blesses

She is the Grace that Nandi knows
She expounds the Vedic Dharma in accord;
He who meditates on Her
For a lunar month of twenty seven days,
Will envision Bhairavi,
Her trident blessing him.

சூலங் கபாலங்கை ஏந்திய சூலிக்கு
நாலாங் கரமுள நாகபா சாங்குச்
மாலங் கயனறி யாத வடிவுக்கு
மேலங்க மாய்நின்ற மெல்லிய லாளே. 1081

Bhairavi's Form

She holds the trident and skull in Her hands
She holds the serpent-sloop and elephant-goad
She has hands four,
She stood one with Siva.
Whose Form neither Brahma nor Vishnu knows,
She of ethereal Form.

மெல்லியல் வஞ்சி விடமி கலைஞானி
சொல்லிய கிஞ்சுக நிறமன்னு சேயிழை
கல்லியல் ஒப்பது காணுந் திருமேனி
பல்லிய லாடையும் பன்மணி தானே. 1082

Bhairavi Further Described

Of ethereal Form, vine-like,
Vengeful to those who err,
She is wisdom and knowledge true
She is bedecked in jewels,
She is green as a parrot,
Gem-like lustrous is Her Form,
Plaited with precious stones several is Her robe.

பன்மணி சந்திர கோடி திருமுடி
சொன்மணி குண்டலக் காதி யுழைக்கண்ணி
நன்மணி சூரிய சோம நயனத்தள்
பொன்மணி வன்னியும் பூரிக்கின் றாளே. 1083

Bhairavi Glows in Rapture

Her crown is studded with stones
Brilliant like a million moons,
She wears Kundalas of radiant gems in her ears
Her glance is like the gentle doe's
Her eyes are the Sun and Moon;
As of red gold She in rapture glows.

பூரித்த பூவிதழ் எட்டினுக் குள்ளேயோர்
ஆரியத் தாளுண்டங் கெண்மர் கன்னியர்
பாரித்த பெண்கள் அறுபத்து நால்வருஞ்
சாரித்துச் சத்தியைத் தாங்கள்கண் டாரே. 1084

How Bhairavi is Seated

In the centre of the eight petalled lotus
Is Supreme Sakti, Arya, the Noble One seated;
Eight the Virgin Saktis
Four and Sixty the fair damsels surround Her;
So encircling,
They envisioned Her Glory.

கண்ட சிலம்பு வளைசங்கு சக்கரம்
எண்டிசை யோகி இறைவி பராசக்தி
அண்டமோ டெண்டிசை தாங்கும் அருட்செல்வி
புண்டரி கத்தினுட் பூசனை யாளே. 1085

She Sustains All Worlds

Anklets, bangles, conch, and discus
She wears;
She is pervasive Supreme,
In eight quarters of globe,
She is Goddess,
She is Parasakti,
She sustains the universe
And its eight cardinal points,
She is possessed of Wealth of Grace
She is seated on Lotus
She who our worship compells.

பூசனை கந்தம் புனைமலர் மாகோடி
யோசனை பஞ்சத் தொலிவந் துரைசெய்யும்
வாசமி லாத மணிமந் திரயோகந்
தேசந் திகழுந் திரிபுரை காணே. 1086

She is in Mani Mantra Yoga

Smeared in unguents fragrant,
Bedecked with flowers beauteous,
Dressed in clothes new and comely
She is in Mani Mantra Yoga
That spells no word;
There shall you hear the sound of Her conch
For yojanas around;
Thus is Tiripurai, whom you seek.

காணும் பலபல தெய்வங்கள் வெவ்வேறு
பூணும் பலபல பொன்போலத் தோற்றிடும்
பேணுஞ் சிவனும் பிரமனும் மாயனுங்
காணுந் தலைவிநற் காரணி காணே. *1087*

She is Supreme Cause

Like many jewels that are of gold made,
Many are the Gods they conceive of;
But she is the Supreme Cause
Whom the three Gods,
Siva, Brahma and Vishnu adore.

Mantras 1187-1190

In the sphere of the 'sun' She appears with twelve kalas. In the sphere of the 'moon,' with sixteen kalas. Nada arises in the moon's sphere. But Sakti is the source of that moon's sphere with kalas sixteen. That sphere of the moon knows no waxing and waning. It is of infinite beauty, and of intoxicating fragrance. There She was born; there She abides in infinite bliss.

காரணி மந்திரம் ஓதுங் கமலத்துப்
பூரண கும்ப விரேசம் பொருந்திய
நாரணி நந்தி நடுவங் குரைசெய்த
ஆரண வேதநூல் அந்தமு மாமே. *1088*

She is End of Vedas

She is the Cause Supreme,
She is in Japa, Mantra chanting
She is in Yoga, in Flower Lotus seated
Of those who control their breath
In Puraka, Kumbhaka, Rechaka,
She is Narayani
She is the End of Vedas
That Nandi in compassion to world revealed.

அந்த நடுவிரல் ஆதி சிறுவிரல்
வந்த வழிமுறைமாறி யுரைசெய்யுஞ்
செந்தமி ழாதி தெளிந்து வழிபடு
நந்தி இதனை நவமுறைத் தானே. *1089*

Mudra for Japa

In counting Mantra by way of Japa
Commence not with little finger
Going to third in traditional way;
That you now reverse,
And seek Her;
The Mother of Tamil,
This Nandi revealed as Truth
Of Japa of Saktis Nine.

உரைத்த நவசத்தி ஒன்று முடிய
நிரைத்த விராசி நெடுமுறை எண்ணிப்
பிரைச்சதம் எட்டுமுன் பேசிய நந்தி
நிரைத்து நியதி நியமஞ்செய் தானே. *1090*

Nandi Laid Down Laws of Japa

Of Nine Saktis said above
The One is at the Crown,
Counting them in order appropriate
Nandi laid down laws and rules of Japaway
He who of yore expounded
The ways of yoga-eight limbed.

This is same as Mantra 549, Tantra Three

தாமக் குழலி தயைக்கண்ணி உள்நின்ற
வேமத் திருளற வீசும் இளங்கொடி
ஓமப் பெருஞ்சுடர் உள்ளெழு நுண்புகை
மேவித் தமுதொடு மீண்டது காணே. *1091*

She is in Kundalini Yoga

She of tresses festooned with flowers,
She of eyes pouring compassion,
Protective stands within;
She the tender vine
She that dispels soul's darkness;
With thread-like column of smoke
From sacrificial fire of Kundalini She arose,
Reached the heights of astral sphere
And with ambrosia returned

காணும் இருதய மந்திர முங்கண்டு
பேணு நமவென்று பேசுந் தலைமேலே
வேணு நடுவு மிகநின்ற வாகுதி
பூணு நடுவென்ற வந்தஞ் சிகையே. *1092*

Chant Hridaya Mantra and Sikha Mantra

Chant the Mantra,
That is of Her Heart (Hridaya Nama)
And say "Na Ma"
The offering of Prana
That courses through central Sushumna,
Reaches the heights of cranium top.
There, chant Sikha Mantra (Sikhayai Nama).

சிகைநின்ற வந்தக் கவசங்கொண் டாதிப்
பகைநின்ற வங்கத்தைப் பாரென்று மாறித்
தொகைநின்ற நேத்திர முத்திரை சூலம்
வகைநின்ற யோனி வருத்தலு மாமே. *1093*

Perform Nyasa, Kavacha and Mudra

Chant Kavacha Mantra exalted,
Invoke that,
For your body to receive protection;
And then perform Sula Mudra
And chant Netra mantra,
Thus worshipping,
Will ever rebirth harass you?

Sula Mudra — Sign of the trident
Netra mantra — Netiaya Nama

வருத்த மிரண்டுஞ் சிறுவிரன் மாறிப்
பொருத்தி அணிவிரற் சுட்டிப் பிடித்து
நெரித்தொன்ற வைத்து நெடிது நடுவே
பெருத்த விரலிரண் டுள்புக்குப் பேசே. *1094*

Sula Mudra

Difficult to practise are these Mudras;
Press the little finger in direction reverse,
Hold the ring finger and fore-finger pressed together
And insert the thumb finger in between.

பேசிய மந்திரம் இகாரம் பிரித்துரை
கூசமி லாத சகாரத்தை முன்கொண்டு'
வாசிப் பிராணன் உபதேச மாகைக்குக்
கூசிய விந்து வுடன்கொண்டு கூவே. *1095*

Chant ''Sam''

From the mantra ''Si''
Take away ''i''
Conjoin the Bindu letter ''M''
The the mantra ''Sam'' do you chant
For Pranayama practice to promote.

கூவிய சீவன் பிராணன் முதலாகப்
பாவிய சவ்வுடன் பண்ணும் யகாரத்தை
மேவிய மாயை விரிசங்கு முத்திரை
தேவி நடுவுள் திகழ்ந்துநின் றாளே. *1096*

Devi is in Conch Mudra

Thus chant ''Sam'' to pervade Jiva's Prana
And adopt Conch Mudra
That dispels (Ya's) Jiva's Maya;
The Supreme Devi there in centre
Shall luminous appear.

நின்ற வயிரவி நீலி நிசாசரி
ஒன்றும் இரண்டும் ஒருங்கிய உள்ளத்துச்
சென்றருள் நாயகி தேவர் பிரானுக்கே
நன்றருள் ஞாலத்து நாடிடுஞ் சாற்றியே. *1097*

She in the Heart of Pure Ones

Bhairavi the Eternal, Neeli the blue-hued,
Nisachari that sojourns in dark,
Into the heart purified of Evils Three — lust, anger
and ignorance
She enters
And of Herself Grace confers,
She the consort of Lord Primal,
Seek Her in this world
And She will bless you.

சாற்றிய வேதஞ் சராசரம் ஐம்பூதம்
நாற்றிசை முக்கண்ணி நாடும் இருள்வெளி
தோற்றும் உயிர்ப்பன்மை சோதி பராபரை
ஆற்றலொ டாய்நிற்கும் ஆதி முதல்வியே. *1098*

Sakti is Supreme Energy

The Vedas,
The creation diverse, movable and immovable,
The elements five,
The quarters four of globe
Are all but that Mother of Eyes Three;
The spreading darkness,
The spaces vast,
The life species several,
The Light that is Parapari—
All these are but the Primal Sakti;
As One Energy She pervades all.

''Sakti is Supreme Energy'' — that is the central formula, the core thought, the heart of Sakti worship.

ஆதி வயிரவி கன்னித் துறைமன்னி
ஓதி யுணரில் உடலுயிர் ஈசனாம்
பேதை உலகிற் பிறவிகள் நாசமாம்
ஓத வுலவாத கோலமொன் றாகுமே. *1099*

Triple Blessings of Bhairavi

She is the Primal Bhairavi,
She is the Virgin in Kundalini,
Those who rouse Her,
Will be body, soul and God in one;
Snapped will be the cycle of births here below;
A form, comely beyond words,
Will theirs be.

கோலக் குழவி குலாய புருவத்தள்
நீலக் குவளை மலரன்ன கண்ணினாள்
ஆலிக்கும் இன்னமு தானந்த சுந்தரி
மேலைச் சிவத்தை வெளிப்படுத் தாளே. *1100*

She Reveals Siva

The Mother of lovely tresses
Of arched eye-brows,
Her eyes are like blue water-lily
She is ambrosial Bliss-Beauty (Ananda Sundari)
She does reveal Supreme Siva to us.

வெளிப்படு வித்து விளைவறி வித்துத்
தெளிப்படு வித்தென் சிந்தையி னுள்ளே
களிப்படு வித்துக் கதிர்ப்படு சோதி
ஒளிப்படு வித்தென்னை உய்யக்கொண் டாளே. *1101*

How She Redeems

Having revealed Siva,
She spoke to me of blessings that follow,
She made my thoughts doubt-free
She infused joy in me,
She made the divine light shine in me,
And redeemed me too.

கொண்டனள் கோலங் கோடி அநேகங்கள்
கண்டனள் எண்ணெண் கலையின்கண் மாலைகள்
விண்டனள் மேலை விரிகதிர் மூன்றையுந்
தண்டலை மேல்நின்ற தையல்நல் லாளே. 1102

She Assumes Manifold Forms

She assumes a million, million forms,
She sports the garland of Kalas sixteen,
She beamed forth the lights three — Fire, Sun and Moon
She the Good Mother
On the cool heights of head within stands.

தையல்நல் லாளைத் தவத்தின் தலைவியை
மையலை நோக்கும் மனோன்மணி மங்கையைப்
பையநின் றேத்திப் பணிமின் பணிந்தபின்
வெய்ய பவமினி மேவகி லாவே. 1103

Adore Her and Be Liberated

She the Good Mother
The Supreme Mistress of tapas all,
She the Manonmani,
Who by Her Glance of Grace
Dispels Mayaic darkness,
Gently stand and adore Her;
Having adored Her
Births no more shall yours be.

வேயன தோளி விரையுறு மென்மலர்
ஏய குழலி இளம்பிறை ஏந்திழை
தூய சடைமுடிச் சூலினி சுந்தரி
ஏயென துள்ளத் தினிதிருந் தாளே. 1104

She Enters the Heart in Endearment

She of shoulders slender as bamboo,
She of tresses laden with fragrant blossoms,
She adorns crescent moon for a jewel,
She of matted locks pure,
She holds the trident
She the Beautiful,
She in endearment,
In my heart constant stood.

இனியதென் மூலை இருக்குங் குமரி
தனியொரு நாயகி தானே தலைவி
தனிப்படு வித்தனள் சார்வு படுத்து
நனிப்படு வித்துள்ளம் நாடிநின் றாளே. 1105

She Cleanses the Heart

She is Virgin
In Muladhara seated,
She is Mistress peerless,
She is Mother Supreme,
She beckoned me apart
She separated my impurities
She loved my heart,
And there She entered.

நாடிகள் மூன்று நடுவெழு ஞாளத்துக்
கூடி இருந்த குமரி குலக்கன்னி
பாடகச் சீறடிப் பைம்பொற் சிலம்பொலி
ஊடக மேவி உறங்குகின் றாளே. 1106

She Slumbers in the Heart

From among the Nadis three,[1]
In central Sushumna,
In threadlike slenderness,
She as Virgin Kundalini stood;
She is summum bonum of virtues all;
On Her feet She wears golden anklet,
That in rythmic music sings;
Thus She entered my heart,
And there slumbers.

1) Ida, pingala and sushumna

உறங்கு மளவின் மனோன்மனி வந்து
கறங்கு வளைக்கைக் கழுத்தாரப் புல்லிப்
பிறங்கொளித் தம்பலம் வாயில் உமிழ்ந்திட்
டுறங்கலை யாவென் றுபாயஞ்செய் தாளே. 1107

She Made Me Slumber No More

As I was steeped in slumber divine,
She, Manonmani, came,
And by Her be-bangled arms drew me close,
And into my mouth transferred,
Her luminous spittle of Grace
And said, "No more shall you slumber, my son."
This, the miracle She performed.

உபாயம் அளிக்கும் ஒருத்தியென் உள்ளத்
தபாயம் அறக்கெடுத் தன்பு விளைத்துச்
சுவாவை விளக்குஞ் சுழியகத் துள்ளே
அவாவை அடக்கிவைத் தஞ்சலென் றாளே. 1108

She Contained Desires

She taught me the miracle,
She quelled the terrors of my heart,
She fostered love divine in me,
In the Sushumna that bathes the Moon in full light
She contained my desires and said,
"Fear not."

அஞ்சொல் மொழியாள் அருந்தவப் பெண்பிள்ளை
செஞ்சொல் மடமொழி சீருடைச் சேயிழை
தஞ்சமென் றெண்ணித் தன்சேவடி போற்றுவார்க்
கின்சொல் அளிக்கும் இறைவியென் றாரே. 1109

She Consoles in Soft Speech

Of sweet speech is She;
By rare tapas reached She can be;
Of maiden innocent speech is She;
Jewelled in precious stones is She;
Attired in fine dresses is She;
Those who seek Her Holy Feet;

Saying "You are our Refuge,"
She the Goddess
In soft speech consoles.

ஆருயி ராயும் அருந்தவப் பெண்பிள்ளை
காரியல் கோதையள் காரணி நாரணி
ஊரும் உயிரும் உலகும் ஒடுக்கிடுங்
கோரியென் உள்ளங் குலாவிநின் றாளே. 1110

She is Awesome

She is the Supreme One, Jivas seek,
She is of tapas mighty,
She is of dark tresses,
She is the Causal being,
She is Narayani,
She dissolves body, life and pasas at once,
She is the Awesome One;
She dwells in my heart.

குலாவிய கோலக் குமரியென் னுள்ளம்
நிலாவி இருந்து நெடுநாள் அணைந்தும்
உலாவி யிருந்துணர்ந் துச்சியி னுள்ளே
கலாவி யிருந்த கலைத்தலை யாளே. 1111

She is Kala Radiant

She the Virgin in my heart dwells;
In endearment eternal;
She sports in my heart;
And reaches my head;
And there she shines
With Her Kalas radiant.

கலைத்தலை நெற்றியோர் கண்ணுடைக் கண்ணுள்
முலைத்தலை மங்கை முயங்கி இருக்குஞ்
சிலைத்தலை யாய தெரிவினை நோக்கி
அலைத்த பூங்கொம்பினள் அங்கிருந் தாளே. 1112

She Sought Siva in Mount Meru Within

He who wears the crescent moon on His head,
He who has the Third Eye in His Forehead,
In Him, She, the full-breasted Mother
In union abides,
Looking toward Him,
Who at the crest of Mount Meru within is;
The Flowery Vine, too, there stood.

இருந்தனள் ஏந்திழை என்னுள்ள மேவிப்
பொருந்திய நால்விரல் புக்கனள் புல்லித்
திருந்திய தாணுவிற் சேர்த்துடன் ஒன்றி
அருந்தவ மெய்தினள் ஆதியி னாளே. 1113

She United in Siva in Cranium Cavity

She dwells, the Mother Sweet, in my heart
She then entered the four-finger prana* of breath retained
And She joined Siva in union divine
And performed penance rare,
She, the Ancient One.

Of 12 finger-length breath inhaled, purata eight finger-length is exhaled (rechaka); the four finger-length is retained in kumbhaka.

ஆதி யனாதியகாரணி காரணி
சோதிய சோதி சுகபர சுந்தரி
மாது சமாதி மனோன்மனி மங்கலி
ஓதியென் னுள்ளத் துடனியைந் தாளே. 1114

She is Transcendental End

She is the Beginning,
She is the Beginningless,
She is the Cause
She is the Causeless
She is the Light
She is the Not-light
She is the Bliss that is Beauty Divine,
She is the Mother Supreme
She is Samadhi, the transcendental End
She is Manonmani, the Jewel of the Inmost Mind
She is my sentience entered,
And in my heart abided.

இயைந்தனள் ஏந்திழை என்னுள்ள மேவி
நயந்தனள் அங்கே நமசிவ என்னும்
அயன்தனை யோரும் பதமது பற்றும்
பெயர்ந்தனள் மற்றும் பிதற்றறுத் தாளே. 1115

She Dispelled Thoughts of Celestial Status

She abided there,
The bejewelled Mother in my heart,
She in endearment stood there,
Saying "Nama Siva"
She dispelled from me
All thoughts of rank and status
Brahma and the rest enjoy,
She destroyed in me
All speech that from ignorance arises.

பிதற்றிக் கழிந்தனர் பேதை மனிதர்
முயற்றியின் முத்தி அருளும் முதல்வி
கயற்றிகழ் முக்கண்ணுங் கம்பலைச் செவ்வாய்
முகத்தருள் நோக்கமும் முன்னுள்ள தாமே. 1116

She Grants Mukti to tried Devotees

Prattling in ignorance,
They spent their lives away,
Alas! these poor men!
She, Primal One, grants Mukti
To all those
Who in constant devotion seek;
She has eyes three fish-shaped,
She has lips red
That warble words sweet,

Her face is compassion full,
That in Grace reveals before me.

உள்ளத் திதயத்து நெஞ்சத் தொருமூன்றுள்
பிள்ளைத் தடமுள்ளே பேசப் பிறந்தது
வள்ளற் றிருவின் வயிற்றினுள் மாமாயைக்
கள்ள ஒளியின் கருத்தாகுங் கன்னியே. 1117

She Stands in Mind, Heart and Intellect

In my mind, in my heart, in my intellect
In all three She stood;
She stood in my head, beyond the Sahasrara,
She stood within the Bounteous Lord,
She stood as Thought,
Behind Mamaya's concealed Light,
She the Virgin that created all.

கன்னியுங் கன்னி அழிந்திலள் காதலி
துன்னியங் கைவரைப் பெற்றனள் தூய்மொழி
பன்னிய நன்னூற் பகவரும் அங்குள
என்னேஇம் மாயை இருளது தானே. 1118

The Virgin Bore the Five Gods

She the Virgin Eternal,
And Virgin She ceased to be not
When She made love,
And bore Children Five;
And among them is Siva too
Who Books of Truth composed!
Oh, this Maya!
Dark, dark indeed it is!

There is a play on words, when Maya is said to be 'dark' She is so because, it is she who is the cause of delusion. Also in Tamil, 'Mayam' means blackness, cf. Mayon, a Tamil name for Vishnu. 'Children Five refers to the five gods of 'pancayatana, namely Siva, Sakti Herself, Vishnu, Surya, and Ganapati in Puranic mythology.

இருளது சத்தி வெளியதெம் அண்ணல்
பொருளது புண்ணியர் போகத்துள் இன்பம்
தெருளது சிந்தையைத் தெய்வமென் றெண்ணில்
அருளது செய்யும்எம் ஆதிப் பிரானே. 1119

Truth is Bliss

Dark is Sakti, Space is Lord,
Truth is Union in God,
Bliss it is for the Holy Ones;
Thus in doubt-free mind,
Adore Lord;
The Primal One,
Will sure bless you.

ஆதி அனாதியும் ஆய பராசத்தி
பாதி பராபரை மேலுறை பைந்தொடி
மாது சமாதி மனோன்மணி மங்கலி
ஓதுமென் னுள்ளத் துடன்முகிழ்த் தாளே. 1120

She Blossoms in Prayerful Heart

She is the Beginning,
She is the Beginningless,
She is the Para Sakti,
She is Para Parai
That Lord's Form shares Half,
She is the bejewelled Mother Supreme,
She is the End of Samadhi,
Manonmani, the Jewel of Inmost Thought,
In my prayerful heart,
She blossomed exuberant.

ஓதிய வண்ணங் கலையின் உயர்கலை
ஆதியில் வேதமே யாமென் றறிகிலர்
சாதியும் பேதமுந் தத்துவ மாய்நிற்பள்
ஆதியென் றோதினள் ஆவின் கிழத்தியே. 1121

She is Kindred of Jiva

She is learning above all learning,
She is beginningless Vedas,
This they know not;
She is creation and its diversities,
She is Tattvas,
She is Primal One,
She is kindred of Jiva,
Thus She assured me.

ஆவின் கிழத்திநல் லாவடு தண்டுறை
நாவின் கிழத்தி நலம்புகழ்ந் தேத்திடுந்
தேவின் கிழத்தி திருவாஞ் சிவமங்கை
மேவுங் கிழத்தி வினைகடிந் தாளே. 1122

She Severs Karma

She is kindred of Jiva
She resides in the Jiva's spinal Sushumna,
She is Mistress of sweet speech,
She is Spouse of Lord
Whom all praise high,
She is comely one, dear to Siva.
She whom I adore,
Severed my Karmas hard.

வினைகடிந் தாருள்ளத் துள்ளொளி மேவித்
தனையடைந்தோர்க்கெல்லாந் தத்துவ மாய்நிற்பள்
எனையடி மைக்கொண்ட ஏந்திழை ஈசன்
கணவனைக் காண அனாதியு மாமே. 1123

She is Beginningless

She is light that shines
In those who severed their Karmas hard,
She is Truth of all those who reach Her,
She is the Mother that took me into Her vassalage,
The Lord is Her Spouse
Yet Beginningless is She.

7. பூரண சக்தி
PURNA SAKTI

ஆதி அனாதி அகாரணி காரணி
வேதம தாய்ந்தனள் வேதியர்க் காய்நின்ற
சோதி தனிச்சுடர் சொரூப மாய்நிற்கும்
பாதி பராபரை பன்னிரண் டாதியே.. 1124

She is of Kalas Twelve

She is the Beginning, She is the Beginningless
She is the Cause, She is the Uncaused
She taught Vedas to Vedic Sages
She is abiding Light Divine,
She is the Self-Manifest Light
She that became Half of Siva's Form,
She, of Kalas twelve, Para Parai.

Sakti being another form of the Sun (the pure energy form) possesses twelve Kalas, that is the twelve positions in the Zodiac.

Purna Sakti is the primal Sakti. She possesses the full sixteen kalas. She is perfection. She is united with Siva in the sphere of pure consciousness. Yet, She remains eternally virgin This is the subtlest of the subtle mysteries of God. But from it follows the great Truth that Siva is the Father, and Sakti is the Mother; and that Mother and Father are One.

Like Brahma, She is seated on lotus blossoms. Brahma can vouchsafe no more than a hundred years of life here below; but, Purna Sakti can ordain eternal life for Her devotees.

Purna Sakti arose and illumined the moon. She is the Mistress of Tattvas. She is kundalini. She is jnana. She is the Divine Fawn that dances with the Lord.

Her Grace is true knowledge. When Her Grace descends, mayaic ignorance disappears. She is beyond bindu and nada. She is Tatparai, the Uncreated. She is Final Mukti.

She is Parasakti who stood with Para. She became Icchasakti and Jnanasakti and when Kriyasakti arrived from bindu, she became immanent in all the three saktis.

At the time of creation Siva and Sakti stood inseparate as flower and fragrance. Together they stirred the primordial bindu. Creation then commenced.

When in the beginning the worlds were created, Parasakti followed the eternally existent Lord through heaven and earth and breathed life into all creation.

She evolved as bindu and nada, and as the several gods and tattvas. She is in Siva; She is in jiva; She is Sattavi, possessing the sattva guna. The countless bhuvanas (worlds) whirl in obedience to Her.

She is seated on the petals of the cosmic flower. She is seated on the petals of the six adharas. She is seated on the petals of the heart. She is seated on the petals of sahasrara.

As prana reaches Purna Sakti with ten faces in sahasrara, ambrosia streams from Her downward-looking face.

She is bathed in cosmic light. She is the One that destroys karmas, drives away maya and confers the ultimate liberations.

அளந்தேன் அகலிடத் தந்தமும் ஈறும்
அளந்தேன் அகலிடத் தாதிப் பிரானை
அளந்தேன் அகலிடத் தாணொடு பெண்ணும்
அளந்தேன் அவனருள் ஆய்ந்துணர்ந் தேனே. 1125

I Measured All

I measured the limits of space,
Its beginning and end;
I measured the men and women
In spaces everywhere;
I measured the Primal Lord
Of spaces Vast;
I measured His Grace in devotion
And knew all.

உணர்ந்திலர் ஈசனை ஊழிசெய் சத்தி
புணர்ந்தது பூரணம் புண்ணியர் தங்கள்
கணங்களைத் தன்னருள் செய்கின்ற கன்னி
கொணர்ந்த வழிகொண்டு கும்பக மாமே. 1126

Meditate on Muladhara

They know this not;
That Sakti Primordial espoused Siva
And together Perfection are;
She bestows Her Grace
On Her devotees;
She, the Virgin Eternal;
Meditate on Her in Muladhara, where She is
Success indeed shall be
Your yogic feat in breath control.

It is important to note that Sakti is frequently referred to as a virgin, even though she is said to be the wife of Siva and mother of children, (Here five, and in the Vedas, seven or eight as Aditi). This is because the magical power of a woman is thought to reside in her virginity. Cf. Kannagi, that is, Kanya plus nagi, literally the "naga virgin", of Silappadikaram, the Tamil classic.

கும்பக் களிறைந்துங் கோலொடு பாகனும்
வம்பில் திகழும் மணிமுடி வண்ணனும்
இன்பக் கலவி இனிதுறை தையலும்
அன்பிற் கலவியு ளாயொழிந் தாரே. 1127

Indriya, Jiva, Siva and Sakti — All United

The massive elephants five (Indriyas)
Jiva, the mahout with the goad
The Lord of many splendoured crown (Siva)
Who in the fragrant (Blossom) appears, (Sanasrara)
And the Mother who with Him is in rapturous union,
All in one love-union for ever merged.

இன்பக் கலவியில் இட்டெழு கின்றதோர்
அன்பிற் புகவல்ல னாம்எங்கள் அப்பனுந்
துன்பக் குழம்பில் துயருறும் பாசத்துள்
என்பிற் பராசத்தி என்னம்மை தானே. *1128*

How United

In the rapture of that union
My Father enters in love subtle;
In Misery's broth of harassing Pasa,
My Mother Para Sakti
To the very marrow enters.

என்னம்மை என்னப்பன் என்னுஞ் செருக்கற்று
உன்னம்மை ஊழித் தலைவனும் அங்குளன்
மன்னம்மை யாகி மருவி யுறைசெய்யும்
பின்னம்மை யாய்நின்ற பேர்நந்தி தானே. *1129*

Siva and Sakti are the Real Father and Mother

Cease talking of "my mother", "my father"
In The possessive way of this world;
Your Mother and the timeless Father
Are there in union;
As your unerring guide for you Here-after;
Nandi verily stood,
As Mother and Father in one.

தார்மேல் உறைகின்ற தண்மலர் நான்முகன்
பார்மேல் இருப்ப தொருநூறு தானுள
பூமேல் உறைகின்ற போதகம் வந்தனள்
நாமேல் உறைகின்ற நாயகி ஆணையே. *1130*

The Mother of Jnana Decides Life-Span

On the lovely lotus
That blossoms in cool .waters
Is the Four-Headed God;
The years vouchsafed by Him here below
Are no more than a hundred;
The Mother of Jnana seated on blossom appeared;
She is the Mistress of Words, abiding in the tongue
Now it is Her command (how long you live).

ஆணைய மாய்வருந் தாது விருந்தவர்
மாணைய மாய மனத்தை ஒருக்கிப்பின்
பாணைய மாய பரத்தை அறிந்தபின்
தாணைய மாய தனாதனன் தானே. *1131*

When Egoity Disappears

Untroubled by Anava ways,
Inward looking,
Steadying the wavering mind,.
Centering it on high,
Thus when they realize praiseworthy Para
They and He for ever one become.

தானே எழுந்தஇத் தத்துவ நாயகி
வானோர் எழுந்து மதியை விளக்கினள்
தேனேர் எழுகின்ற தீபத் தொளியுடன்
மானே நடமுடை மன்றறி யீரே. *1132*

She Illumines the Moon Within

Of Herself She arose
This Mistress of Tattvas,
And illumined the Moon
In the astral sphere within;
Like a column of treacle
The light of Kundalini bright rises,
Know you, where that Siva the Fawn dances!

The term "Moon in the astral sphere within" refers to the six cakras, or nerve plexuses in the body, through which when roused Kundalini passes in tantric sadhana.

அறிவான மாயையும் ஐம்புலக் கூட்டத்
தறிவான மங்கை அருளது சேரிற்
பிறியா அறிவறி வாருளம் பேணு
நெறியாய சித்த நினைந்திருந் தாளே. *1133*

When Grace Dawns Jnana Arises

In the five senses of Mayaic knowledge,
When Grace of Sakti of True Knowledge enters,
They know the Jnana
That forever abides;
In the thoughts of those
Who intense cherish Her,
She abides for sure.

இரவும் பகலும் இலாத விடத்தே
குரவஞ்செய் கின்ற குழலியை நாடி
அரவஞ்செய் யாமல் அருளுடன் தூங்கப்
பருவஞ்செய் யாததோர் பாலனு மாமே. *1134*

Seek Her and Transcend Time and Age

In the spaces vast
Where neither night nor day is,
She of fragrant tresses is;
Seek Her;
And in silence with Grace slumber,
You shall for ever youthful be
Transcending time and age.

பாலனு மாகும் பராசத்தி தன்னொடு
மேலனு காவிந்து நாதங்கள் விட்டிட
மூலம தாமெனும் முத்திக்கு நேர்படச்
சாலவு மாய்நின்ற தற்பரத் தாளே. *1135*

Beyond Bindu and Nada, She is

Youthful forever you shall be;
Transcending Bindu and Nada
That approach Her not,
You shall one with Para Sakti be;
And reach the Mukti State Finale,
She, the Grace Divine
All Liberation confers.

நின்ற பராசத்தி நீள்பரன் தன்னொடு
நின்றறி ஞானமும் இச்சையு மாய்நிற்கும்
நன்றறி யுங்கிரி யாசத்தி நண்ணவே
மன்றன வற்றுள் மருவிடுந் தானே. *1136*

Parasakti Evolves into Jnana and Ichcha

Parasakti, who with pervasive Para stood,
Becomes Jnana Sakti and Ichcha Sakti;
And when Kriya Sakti arrives, (from Bindu)
The Dancer immanent becomes in them all.

மருவொத்த மங்கையுந் தானும் உடனே
உருவொத்து நின்றமை ஒன்றும் உணரார்
கருவொத்து நின்று கலக்கின போது
திருவொத்த சிந்தைவைத் தெந்தைநின் றானே. *1137*

Siva Was One With Sakti in Primal Act of Creation

As flower and its fragrance
Siva and Sakti stood form resembling
This they know not;
When together they stirred the Primordial Bindu
For creation to commence,
He in Thought was one with Her
Thus it was, My Father stood.

சிந்தையின் உள்ளே திரியுஞ் சிவசத்தி
விந்துவும் நாதமு மாயே விரிந்தனள்
சந்திர பூமி சடாதரி சாத்தவி
அந்தமொ டாதிய தாம்வண்ணத் தாளே. *1138*

Sakti Devolves into Bindu and Nada

Siva-Sakti who in Thought,
Thus commenced evolution
As Bindu and Nada expanded;
She wears the orb of moon
As on Her matted locks
She is of Sattva Guna possessed
She is the Beginning and End
Thus is Her Form Divine.

ஆறி யிருந்த அமுத பயோதரி
மாறி யிருந்த வழியறி வாரில்லை
தேறி யிருந்துநல் தீபத் தொளியுடன்
ஊறி யிருந்தனள் உள்ளுடைய யார்க்கே. *1139*

Sakti is in Siva and in Jiva

She is in Siva contained,
She is of ambrosial milk breasted,
She is in Jivas,
Yet they know not the way to Her;
Into them that hold Her in their hearts,
She welled up from within
And like a bright lamp shed Her light.

உடையவன் அங்கி உருத்திர சோதி
விடையவன் ஏறி விளங்கி யிருக்குங்
கடையவர் போயிடுங் கண்டவர் நெஞ்சத்
தடையது வாகிய சாதகர் தாமே. *1140*

The Yogis See Lord

The Lord is my master,
He is Rudra, Fire and Light
He mounts the Bull in splendour surpassing;
Ye who have not seen Him,
Away, from Here!
The Sadhakas have seen Him
He is the support of their heart.

தாமேல் உறைவிடம் ஆறித மானது
பார்மேல் இதழ்பதி னெட்டிரு நூறுள
பூமேல் உறைகின்ற புண்ணியம் வந்தனள்
பார்மேல் உறைகின்ற பைந்தொடி யாளே. *1141*

She is on the Flower of Cosmos and Flower of Heart

On the petals of the six Adharas is She seated;
On the petals of the Flower of Cosmos,
Of Worlds two hundred and eighteen above is She seated;
She is the Blessed One that is seated on the Flower of Heart
She is the bejewelled one that is on Earth below.

---

1) Bhuvanas (worlds) are enumerated as 224, vide Mantra 265, Tantra Three. Above 218 would place Sakti in the Siva tattva, in santyatita kala.

பைந்தொடி யாளும் பரம னிருந்திடத்
திண்கொடி யாகத் திகழ்தரு சோதியாம்
விண்கொடி யாகி விளங்கி வருதலாற்
பெண்கொடி யாக நடந்த துலகே. *1142*

Worlds Move in Sakti's Way

The bejewelled one is where Parama is;
She is the Light that shines high
As pennon resplendent,
She is dazzling like the lightning in the sky,
And all worlds in Sakti's Way whirl.

நடந்தது வம்மலர் நாலுடன் அஞ்சாய்
இருந்தனர் கன்னிகள் எட்டுடன் ஒன்றாய்ப்
படர்ந்தது தன்வழி பங்கயத் துள்ளே
தொடர்ந்தது உள்வழிச் சோதி யடுத்தே. *1143*

Sakti is Kundalini Within

In the nine centres within,
That Flower walked,
As nine Saktis were they there;
Kundalini Light through Central passage arose,
And into the Lotus in Sahasrara spread.

1) Six adharas and three lights, sun, moon and fire.

2) Vamai, Seshtai, Raudri, Kali, Kalavikarni, Balavikarni, Balabrahmadam, Sarvabhudadamani, Manonmani.

அடுக்குந் தாமரை ஆதி இருப்பிடம்
எடுக்குந் தாமரை இல்லகத் துள்ளது
மடுக்குந் தாமரை மத்தகத் தேசெல
முடுக்குந் தாமரை முச்சது ரத்தே. 1144

Lotuses of Sakti

That Lotus in folds several is Primal Sakti's abode;
The Lotus that lifts soul is in the heart;
When the Lotus in Muladhara is roused,
The Lotus in Sahasrara blossoms.

முச்சது ரத்தே எழுந்த முளைச்சுடர்
எச்சது ரத்தும் இடம்பெற ஓடிடக்
கைச்சது ரத்துக் கடந்துள் ஒளிபெற
எச்சது ரத்தும் இருந்தனள் தானே. 1145

Sakti Pervades All Adharas

The Spark that arose in triangular Chakra (Muladhara)
Flew and spread in the rest of Adhara Chakras;
And piercing Sahasrara shone bright;
Thus She pervaded in Chakras all.

இருந்தனள் தன்முகம் ஆறொடு நாலாய்ப்
பரந்தன வாயு திசைதிசை தோறுங்
குவிந்தன முத்தின் முகவொளி நோக்கி
நடந்தது தேறல் அதோமுகம் அம்பே. 1146

As Prana Reaches Sakti in Ajna Ambrosia Flows

There She was with faces ten in all directions
Because of Her the wind blows in all quarters,
The fire flames upwards and water courses downwards
And everything functions properly because of Her.

அம்பன்ன கண்ணி அரிவை மனோன்மனி
கொம்பன்ன நுண்ணிடை கோதை குலாவிய
செம்பொன்செய் யாக்கை செறிகமழ் நாடோறும்
நம்பனை நோக்கி நவிலுகின் றாளே. 1147

Sakti Daily Prays to the Lord

Her glances are like arrows sharp,
She is the Mother Supreme
She is Manonmani
Her waist is slender like a tender vine
Her tresses are bedecked with flower garlands
Her Form is red gold,
Fragrant by far
Daily She looks at the Lord and prays.

நவிலும் பெருந்தெய்வம் நான்மறைச் சத்தி
துகிலுடை யாடை நிலம்பொதி பாதம்
அகிலமும் அண்ட முழுதுஞ்செம் மாந்து
புகலுமுச் சோதி புனையநிற் பாளே. 1148

Sakti's Pervasiveness

She utters the Vedas Four,
The great Goddess, the Sakti;
She dons robes fine,
Her Feet compass world entire;
She stands elated
Pervading worlds and universes;
She stands adorned
With three lights, Sun, Moon and Fire.

புனையவல் லாள்புவ னத்திறை எங்கள்
வனையவல் லாள்அண்ட கோடிகள் உள்ளே
புனையவல் லாள்மண்ட லத்தொளி தன்னைப்
புனையவல் லாளையும் போற்றியென் பேனே. 1149

Sakti's Omnipotence

She holds in Her Form
The One Lord of Worlds all,
She creates million, million universes vast
In Her Thought;
She is draped in Cosmic Light;
She beautifies all,
Her I stood adoring.

போற்றியென் பேன்புவ னாபதிஅம்மையென்
ஆற்றலுள் நிற்கும் அருந்தவப் பெண்பிள்ளை
சீற்றங் கடிந்த திருநுதற் சேயிழை
கூற்றந் துரக்கின்ற கொள்பைந் தொடியே. 1150

She Drives Away Death

"Hail, to You" — thus I pray
She is the Mistress of Worlds all,
She is my Mother
She is my Prowess
She is Mother of Tapas rare
She is bejewelled,
Her countenance is
Of passions dispelled;
She is of soft finery
She drives away fearsome death.

தொடியார் தடக்கைச் சுகோதய சுந்தரி
வடிவார் திரிபுரை யாமங்கை சங்கைச்
செடியார் வினைகெடச் சேர்வரை என்றென்
அடியார் வினைகெடுத் தாதியு மாமே. 1151

She Uproots Karmas

She is of hands bedecked in jewellery,
She is Fountain of Bliss Divine,
She is Beautiful,
She is Tiripurai of Loveliness Perfect,
She is Mount Kailas
That all Karma destroys
She for ever uproots the Karmas
Of Her devotees;
She is the Primal One.

மெல்லிசைப் பாவை வியோமத்தின் மென்கொடி
பல்லிசைப் பாவை பயன்தரு பைங்கொடி
புல்லிசைப் பாவையைப் போகத் துரந்திட்டு
வல்லிசைப் பாவை மனம்புகுந் தாளே. *1152*

She Dispels Illusory Fame

She is damsel of sweet music,
She is tender vine of Void Limitless,
She is of fame infinite,
She is fruit-laden green vine
She drove away Maya
That transitory fame gives,
She of abiding fame,
In my heart entered.

தாவித் தவப்பொருள் தானவன் எம்மிறை
பாவித் துலகம் படைக்கின்ற காலத்து
மேவிப் பராசக்தி மேலொடு கீழ்தொடர்ந்
தாவிக்கு மப்பொருள் தானது தானே. *1153*

She Created All Life

Eternal existent is our Lord;
When at the beginning the worlds were created,
She Our Para Sakti followed Him,
Through "Heaven and earth"
And breathed life into creation all;
That verily was Sakti's Work.

அதுவிது என்பர் அவனை அறியார்
கதிவர நின்றதோர் காரணங் காணார்
மதுவிரி பூங்குழல் மாமங்கை நங்கை
திதமது உன்னார்கள் தேர்ந்தறி யாரே. *1154*

Siva and Sakti Together Grant Grace and Liberation

"This" and "That", they say, is God,
They Know Him not, the True One
They know not,
Who ultimate liberation grants,
They know not
The Mother Great of honeyed-flower bedecked tresses,
That Grace confers;
Of muddled thinking they are.

8. ஆதாரவாதேயம்
SUPPORT-SUPPORTED

Siva and Sakti are mutually the support and the supported at once. They share their Form, half-and-half, entwined in divine delight.

நாலிதழ் ஆறில் அவிர்ந்தது தொண்ணூறு
தானித ழானவை நாற்பத்து நாலுள
பாலித ழானவள் பங்கய மூலமாய்த்
தானித ழாகித் தரித்திருந் தாளே. *1155*

Sakti is the Support of Adharas

Kundalini in the four petalled Muladhara
Into Six and ninety Tattvas blossomed
The Adharas four above have petals forty four in all;
Beyond is the Adhara with sidereal petals
Yet beyond (twine) Lotus blossom is Sakti seated;
Herself like a tender petal
Supports them all.

The Tattvas are here said to be 96, as against the usual 36 of Buddhism and Saivism.

6 petals in the svadhistana chakra

10 petals in the manipuraka chakra

12 petals in the anahatha chakra
16 petals in the visuddhi chakra

All together, 44 petals are in the four chakras in between the four petals of the muladhara and the two of ajna. (See Mantra 1704, Tantra Seven.) When the four-petalled kundalini traverses the four intermediate adharas, it reaches the two-petalled ajna, and from there visions the hundred-petalled blossom in sahasrara. Ajna is the sixth center — sahasrara beyond is not usually considered as a chakra, it being the goal. It is said to have 100 petals, 1,000 petals or 1,008 petals.

தரித்திருந் தாளவள் தன்னொளி நோக்கி
விரித்திருந் தாளவள் வேதப் பொருளைக்
குறித்திருந் தாளவள் கூறிய ஐந்து
மறித்திருந் தாளவள் மாதுநல் லாளே. *1156*

Sakti is Support-All

She remained the Support-All,
Looking aloft to Her own Divine Light,
She spread Herself over Adharas six;
She held the Vedic Truth in Her Thought;
She centered on Her Letters Five
She, the Mother Benevolent.

மாதுநல் லாளும் மணாளன் இருந்திடப்
பாதிநல் லாளும் பகவனு மானது
சோதிநல் லாளைத் துணைப்பெய்ய வல்லிரேல்
வேதனை தீர்தரும் வெள்ளடை யாமே. 1157

Follow The Mother of Divine Light

The Mother Benevolent with Her Spouse remained,
Sharing Her Half with Supreme God
Follow that Mother of Divine Light
And gain Her support;
All sorrows will see their end;
And you become blemishless Pure.

வெள்ளடை யானிரு மாமிகு மாமலர்க்
கள்ளடை யாரக் கமழ்குழ லார்மன
மள்ளடை யானும் வகைத்திற மாய்நின்ற
பெண்ணொரு பாகம் பிறவிபெண் ணாமே. 1158

Siva Arises in Sakti

The Lord of Spaces Vast
Abides in the loving heart of the Mother,
That bedecks honeyed-flowers in Her tresses;
He shares Her in His Form;
And He from Her arises
Himself thus a woman too!

பெண்ணொருபெண்ணைப்புணர்ந்திடும்பேதமை
பெண்ணிடை ஆணும் பிறந்து கிடந்தது
பெண்ணுடை ஆணென் பிறப்பறிந் தீர்க்கின்ற
பெண்ணுடை ஆணிடைப் பேச்சற்ற வாறே. 1159

From Female Arises Male

Woman espousing Woman
Strange indeed it is!
From Woman arose Man;
When you know the why of this,
No more will there be talk
Of Sakti from Sivam arising.

பேச்சற்ற நற்பொருள் காணும் பெருந்தகை
மாச்சற்ற சோதி மனோன்மணி மங்கையாங்
காச்சற்ற சோதி கடவு ளுடன் புணர்ந்
தாச்சற்றெ னுட்புகுந் தாலிக்குந் தானே. 1160

As Siva-Sakti She is in My Heart

She is the great Truth of silence
She is graciousness high manifest
She is Pure Light
She is Manonmani Sakti;
The Blemishless Light espousing God
Entered in me and delighted me.

ஆலிக்குங் கன்னி அரிவை மனோன்மணி
பாலித் துலகிற் பரந்துபெண் ணாகும்
வேலைத் தலைவியை வேத முதல்வியை
ஆலித் தொருவன் உகந்துநின் றானே. 1161

Siva-Sakti is Support-All

She is Virgin of Delight
She is Sakti, Manonmani,
As Woman She pervades the world
And supports it,
She is the Mistress of the Five Acts
She is the Fountainhead of Vedas
Her, the Lord in delight espoused.

உகந்துநின் றான்நம்பி ஒண்ணுதற் கண்ணோ
டுகந்துநின் றான்நம் முழைபுக நோக்கி
உகந்துநின் றான்இவ் உலகங்கள் எல்லாம்
உகந்துநின் றான்அவ டன்றோ டொகுத்தே. 1162

Siva Stood Entwined With Sakti

With Fore-head eye,
Lord stood in delight;
Lord stood in delight
Seeking to enter our hearts;
Lord stood in delight
For all worlds to delight;
Lord stood in delight with Sakti
Her shoulders in embrace entwined.

குத்து முலைச்சி குழைந்த மருங்கினள்
துத்தி விரிந்த சுணங்கினள் தூமொழி
புத்தகச் சீறடிப் பாவை புணர்வினைத்
தொத்த கருத்துச் சொல்லகி லேனே. 1163

She Entered My Sentience

Full-breasted She is,
Supple-waisted She is,
Spreading yellow-spotted is Her skin,*
Of Pure speech She is,
Soft-footed unto a feathery peacock She is,
She in my sentience entered,
How Shall I describe it?

---

* This is a poetical convention attributed to the loveliness of a woman's skin.

சொல்லவொண் ணாத அழற்பொதி மண்டலஞ்
செல்லவொண் ணாது திகைத்தங் கிருப்பர்கள்
வெல்லவொண் ணாத வினைத்தனி நாயகி
மல்லவொண் ணாத மனோன்மனி தானே. 1164

She is of Unconquerable Powers

Beyond description is the fiery sphere that envelops Her,
Beyond description it is even for bedazzled Jnanis
She is Supreme Mistress of unconquerable acts
She is Manonmani that is beyond grasp.

தானே இருநிலந் தாங்கிவிண் ணாய்நிற்குந்
தானே சுடும்அங்கி ஞாயிறுந் திங்களுந்
தானே மழைபொழி தையலு மாய்நிற்குந்
தானே வடவரைத் தண்கடற் கண்ணே.★ 1165

He is All

Holding the worlds apart, as the Heavens high He spreads;
Himself the scorching Fire, Sun and Moon,
Himself the Mother that sends down the rains,
Himself the mountains strong and oceans cold.

கண்ணுடை யாளைக் கலந்தங் கிருந்தவர்
மண்ணுடை யாரை மனித்தரிற் கூட்டொணாப்
பண்ணுடை யார்கள் பதைப்பற் றிருந்தவர்
விண்ணுடை யார்களை மேலுறக் கண்டே. *1166*

The Humans Who Reach Her are Above Gods

They who reach Her, of Compassion Divine
Well may they be here on earth below
Yet regard them not as humans;
Divine are their qualities;
Serene is their composure
Higher than Celestials are they.

கண்டெண் டிசையுங் கலந்து வருங்கன்னி
பண்டெண் டிசையும் பராசக்தி யாய்நிற்கும்
விண்டெண் டிசையும் விரைமலர் கைக்கொண்டு
தொண்டெண் டிசையுந் தொழநின்ற கன்னியே. *1167*

Omniscience and Omnipresence of Sakti

She is Virgin that oversees directions eight,
She is One that pervades there,
She is beginningless Parasakti that everywhere are;
With fragrant flowers in hand,
And songs in their tongue,
The devotees pray and praise Her
In directions eight.

கன்னி ஒளியென நின்றவிச் சந்திரன்
மன்னி யிருக்கின்ற மாளிகை செந்நிறஞ்
சென்னி யிருப்பிடஞ் சேர்பதி னாறுடன்
பன்னி யிருப்பப் பராசக்தி யாமே. *1168*

Parasakti is in the Cranium

The moon within shines with virgin rays,
Red in hue is the mansion where She is,
It is in Cranium within the head
Follow Her (Manonmani),
Beaming with Kalas ten and six;
You shall reach Parasakti.

பராசத்தி யென்றென்று பல்வகை யாலுந்
தராசத்தி யான தலைப்பிர மாணி
இராசத்தி யாமள வாகமத் தாளாகுங்
குராசத்தி கோலம் பலவுணர்ந் தேனே. *1169*

She is Multiformed, Praised in Vyamala Agama

Parasakti is Power that supports all
And everywhere;
She resides within head;
She is Sakti of the Night;*
She is in Vyamala Agama praised
She is Sakti that comes as Guru
Diverse indeed Her Forms, I perceived.

---

*Refers to midnight worship with flowers as designated by the *Vyamala Agama* school.

உணர்ந்துல கேழையும் யோகினி சத்தி
உணர்ந்துயி ராய்நிற்கும் உன்னதன் ஈசன்
புணர்ந்தொரு காலத்துப் போகமு தாதி
இணைந்து பரமென் றிசைந்திது தானே. *1170*

She is Kriya Sakti, Bhoga Sakti and Parasakti

She conceives worlds seven;
She is Yogini Sakti,
She cognizes life and as its support stands;
Of yore she joined the Lord in creative union
And became Bhoga Sakti;
And then She was Param Herself (Parasakti)
Undifferentiated from Siva.

The union of Sakti with Siva is both yoga and bhoga. As Yogini Sakti, She cognises all light and stands as its support. As Bhoga Sakti, She joins the Lord in the act of creation, undifferentiated from Siva.

இதுவப் பெருந்தகை எம்பெரு மானும்
பொதுவக் கல்வியும் போகமு மாகி
மதுவக் குழலி மனோன்மனி மங்கை
அதுவக் கல்வியுள் ஆயுழி யோகமே. *1171*

Sakti's Union in Bhoga was Yoga

This Sakti
And that Our Lord Great
When together united,
It was Yoga and Bhoga divine;
Manonmani Sakti of fragrant tresses
In that union was verily in Yoga
That in truth it is.

யோகநற் சத்தி ஒளிபீடந் தானாகும்
யோகநற் சத்தி ஒளிமுகந் தெற்காகும்
யோகநற் சத்தி உதர நடுவாகும்
யோகநற் சத்திதாள் உத்தரந் தேரே. *1172*

Yoga Sakti Described

Yoga Sakti's pedestal is Light within;
Yoga Sakti's visage is toward south;
Yoga Sakti's navel is Cosmic centre;
Yoga Sakti's feet are sublime exceeding;
—This may you realize.

Yoga Sakti is the pedestal of light within. She faces South. Her navel is the centre of the cosmos. Her Feet are exceedingly sublime.

தேர்ந்தெழு மேலாஞ் சிவனங்கி யோடுற
வார்ந்தெழு மாயையும் மந்தம தாய்நிற்கும்

ஓர்ந்தெழு விந்துவும் நாதமும் ஓங்கிடக்
கூர்ந்தெழு கின்றனள் கோல்வளை தானே. 1173

In Siva-Sakti Union Maya, Bindu and Nada Arise

She Siva high in Cranium
Unites in Kundalini Fire,
With Maya
And finite Bindu and Nada
Sakti rises,
She that is in bejewelled bangles bedecked.

From Siva/Sakti union arose nada, bindu and maya. From Her evolved the eight Saktis, all of equal kalas — fourteen. From bindu she manifested the entire creation. All these are Her mutations. But, as ever, She remains the undiminished Param.

தானான வாறெட்ட தாம்பரைக் குண்மிசை
தானான வாறுமீ ரேழுஞ் சமகலை
தானான விந்து சகமே பரமெனுந்
தானாம் பரவா தனையெனத் தக்கதே. 1174

Further Evolutes of Sakti

From Parasakti,
Who thus evoluted,
Arises the Eight Saktis;
And of equal Kalas twice seven;
And Bindu that manifests creation entire;
Indeed Her Divine Mutations are,
She remaining Param as ever.

தக்க பராவித்தை தானிரு பானேழிற்
றக்கெழு மோருத் திரஞ்சொல்லச் சொல்லவே
மிக்கிடும் எண்சத்தி வெண்ணிற முக்கண்ணி
தொக்க கதையோடு தொன்முத்திரை யாளே. 1175

Worship of Vidya Chakra

Mount Parasakti
In Vidya Chakra,
And for seven and twenty days,
Chant Rudra mantra again and again,
The Eight Saktis will there appear,
And the white hued Three-eyed Parasakti too.
With mace, and Her Mudra of yore.

Worship Her in the Vidya Chakra for 27 days, continuously chanting the Rudra mantra. She will appear bearing a mace and mudra, and will be accompanied by the eight saktis.

முத்திரை மூன்றின் முடிந்தமெய்ஞ் ஞானத்தன்
தத்துவ மாயல்ல வாய சகலத்தள்
வைத்த பராபர னாய பராபரை
சத்தியு மானந்த சத்தியுங் கொங்கே. 1176

She is Pervasive All

She of Mudras triple and Jnana perfect
She is the Tattvas, and the not-Tattvas
She is pervasive-all,
She is Paraparai that ParaParan holds
She is Sakti and Ananda Sakti too.

Her mudras are triple — jnana mudra, tattva mudra and ananda mudra.

1) Jnana mudra, abhaya mudra, varada mudra. The three mudras used in the Sri Meenakshi Temple, of Madurai, are: rishabha mudra, meena mudra and rajakara naga mudra — vide "Abhidana Chintamani," p.294.

கொங்கின்ற கொம்பின் குரும்பைக் குலாங்கன்னி
பொங்கிய குங்குமத் தொளிபொ ருந்தினள்
அங்குச பாச மெனுமகி லங்கனி
தங்கு மவள்மனை தானறி வாயே. 1177

Universe is Her Abode

She is unto fragrant tender vine,
She is virgin with budding breasts
She is radiant kum-kum hued red,
She holds Elephant-goad and noose
Know that universe entire is that Virgin's abode.

Mantras 1177-1182

She is eternally virgin. She is mother, daughter and spouse — all at once. She is kum-kum hued. She bears the elephant goad. She has ghouls and ganas for Her heavenly hosts. The entire universe is Her abode. She is the cause and the caused. She is the tattvas. She has ten faces that look in ten directions. She revealed the four *Vedas* and their six *Angas*. She knows no separateness from Her Lord. She is Siva jnana. She is within jiva jnana.

வாயு மனமுங் கடந்த மனோன்மனி
பேயுங் கணமும் பெரிதுடைப் பெண்பிள்ளை
ஆயும் அறிவுங் கடந்த அரனுக்குத்
தாயும் மகளுநல் தாரமு மாமே. 1178

Sakti is Mother, Daughter and Spouse

She is Manonmani beyond word and thought,
She is the Mother that has ghosts and Ganas for Her host,
For Hara who all knowledge surpasses,
She is Mother, Daughter and Spouse at once.

தாரமு மாகுவள் தத்துவ மாய்நிற்பள்
காரண காரிய மாகுங் கலப்பினள்
பூரண விந்து பொதிந்த புராதனி
பாரள வாந்திசை பத்துடை யாளே. 1179

She is Cause and Caused

She stands as Spouse,
She stands as Tattvas,
She is the Cause
And the Caused at once,
She is the Ancient
That is enveloped by Bindu perfect,
She possesses the directions ten of this world.

பத்து முகமடை யாள்நம் பராசத்தி
வைத்தனள் ஆறங்க நாலுடன் றான்வேதம்
ஒத்தனள் ஆதாரம் ஒன்றுடன் ஓங்கியே
நித்தமாய் நின்றாளெம் நேரிழை கூறே. 1180

She is Eternal

Ten faces She has, our Parasakti,
She revealed the four Vedas with the six Angas,
She as One pervaded the Adharas six
She as Eternal stood,
Our Lovely bejewelled Mother,
Know you this.

கூறிய கன்னி குலாய புருவத்தள்
சீரிய ளாயுல கேழுந் திகழ்ந்தவள்
ஆறிய நங்கை யமுத பயோதரி
பேருயி ராளி பிறிவறுத் தாளே. 1181

She is Non-separate From Siva

She is virgin of arched eye-brows,
She is Awesome One,
In seven worlds She shone,
She is the gentle Devi, holy
She is of breasts ambrosial,
She is Mistress of Over-Soul (Siva),
She knows separateness none
From Her Lord.

பிறிவின்றி நின்ற பெருந்தகைப் பேதை
குறியொன்றி நின்றிடுங் கோமளக் கொம்பு
பொறியொன்றி நின்று புணர்ச்சிசெய் தாங்கே
அறிவொன்ற நின்றனள் ஆருயி ருள்ளே. 1182

She is Jnana in Jiva

She is the Great Mother Non-separate stood
She is the lovely vine in Muladhara unites,
With senses centred, and in union absorbed
She in Jnana merging stood
In the Jiva within.

உள்ளத்தி னுள்ளே யுடனிருந் தைவர்தங்
கள்ளத்தை நீக்கிக் கலந்துட னேபுல்கிக்
கொள்ளத் தவநெறி கூடிய இன்பத்து
வள்ளற் றலைவி மருட்டிப் புரிந்தே. 1183

She Drew Me into Divine Rapture

Deep in the core of my heart She stood
And there dispelled the falsity of senses five,
And in me in union joined,
And into the rapture of tapasvin way
Entranced, drew me;
She, the Mother of boundless Bounty.

புரிந்தருள் செய்கின்ற போகமா சத்தி
இருந்தருள் செய்கின்ற இன்பம் அறியார்
பொருந்தி யிருந்த புதல்வி பூவண்ணத்
திருந்த விலக்கில் இனிதிருந் தாளே. 1184

Bhoga Maha Sakti Confers Grace From Within

The Bounteous Mother, Bhoga Maha Sakti
Her Grace confers;
The sweetness of that Grace,
She from within grants,
They know this not,
Just as the colour cannot be separated from a flower
She remains inseparable from the jiva
She eternally abides as such.

As Bhoga Sakti She grants Grace to jivas in bounteous sweetness.

இருந்தனள் ஏந்திழை என்னுள மேவித்
திருந்து புணர்ச்சியில் தேர்ந்துணர்ந் துன்னி
நிரந்தர மாகிய நிரதி சயமொடு
பொருந்த விலக்கிற் புணர்ச்சி அதுவே. 1185

She Entered in Union Wondrous and Abiding

The Mother invaded my heart
And there resided
In union perfect intense,
And in wonder abiding,
And in that Cranium Centre She was,
That, indeed, is union true.

அதுஇது என்னும் அவாவினை நீக்கித்
துதியது செய்து சுழியுற நோக்கில்
விதியது தன்னையும் வென்றிட லாகும்
மதிமல ராள்சொன்ன மண்டல மூன்றே. 1186

Adore Her and Vanquish Fate

This and that — thus your desire runs
Get rid of it;
Adore Her
And through Sushumna upward look
Well may you even Fate conquer,
She of the Flower in Sahasrara
In the Spheres Three,
Of Sun, Moon and Fire.

மூன்றுள மண்டல மோகினி சேர்விடம்
ஏன்றுள ஈரா றெழுகலை உச்சியில்
தோன்று மிலக்குற லாகுதல் மாமாயை
ஏன்றனள் ஏழிரண் டிந்துவொ டீறே. 1187

She Ascends the Three Spheres

Three the spheres the Mohini ascends to
At top She appears
In Sphere of Sun of Kalas twelve

With Kalas fourteen She is Mamaya;
And in Moon's Sphere
The Bright One finite appears.

Vide Mantra 852, Tantra Three, for the kalas of the sun, moon and fire.

இந்துவி னின்றெழு நாதம்இரவிபோல்
வந்துபின் நாக்கின் மதித்தெழுங் கண்டத்தில்
உந்திய சோதி இதயத் தெழும்ஒலி
இந்துவின் மேலுற்ற ஈறது தானே. *1188*

Nada Arises in Moon's Sphere and Reaches the Heart Centre

Like the rays of the Sun
The Nada from Moon Sphere arises,
From there it travels to the root of tongue,
And thence to throat the light goes,
And then to region of heart
Whence arises the articulate sound,
For all this,
The source is the Moon Sphere
(Where Sakti is.)

The practice of nada or listening to internal sounds leads to samadhi. Compare *Hatha Yoga Pradipika*, iv, pp. 64-67: "I will now describe the practice of anahatha nada (heart sound), as propounded by Goraka Natha for the benefit of those who are unable to understand the principles of knowledge. Adiriatha propounds one and a quarter crore methods of trance and they are all extant. Of these, the hearing of the anahatha nada (heart sound) is the only one, which is the chief, in my opinion. Sitting with mukta asana and with the sambhavi mudra, the yogi should hear the sound inside his right ear, with a collected mind. The ears, the eyes, the nose and the mouth should be closed and then the clear sound is heard in the passage of sushumna which has been cleansed of all its impurities."

ஈறது தான்முதல் எண்ணிரண் டாயிர
மாறுதல் இன்றி மனோவச மாயெழில்
தூறது செய்யுஞ் சுகந்தச் சுழியது
பேறது செய்து பிறந்திருந் தாளே. *1189*

She Abides in Moon's Sphere, Changeless

That is beginning and end of where She is
—The Kalas twice-eight in the Moon Sphere—
Changes indefinite it none has;
It is of infinite beauty
Reached by Centred Mind,
It is a Centre that is fragrant dense
There was She born,
And there in divinity abides.

இருந்தனள் ஏந்திழை ஈறதி லாகத்
திருந்திய ஆனந்தஞ் செந்நெறி நண்ணிப்
பொருந்து புவனங்கள் போற்றிசெய் தேத்தி
வருந்த இருந்தனள் மங்கைநல் லாளே. *1190*

There She Abides

There She abided, the bejwelled One
There She abided in Centre Finite
There She abided as Holy Way
There She abided as Bliss Infinite,
There She abided
All worlds praising her,
And yearning for Her;
There She abided, the great Mother.

மங்கையும் மாரனுந் தம்மொடு கூடிநின்
றங்குலி கூட்டி அகம்புறம் பார்த்தனர்
கொங்கைநல் லாளுங் குமாரர்கள் ஐவரும்
தங்களின் மேவிச் சடங்குசெய் தாரே. *1191*

In Siva-Sakti Union Arose the Five Gods

The Mother and Her Handsome Spouse
Together embracing
Looked inward and out;
The Maya and the Five Sons
With their Saktis arising
Commenced their tasks respective.

Creation, Preservation, Dissolution, Obfuscation and Revealing Grace.

In Siva/Sakti union, Siva and Sakti looked inward and outward. There arose maya and the five Gods, who with their respective saktis commenced the Five Acts — Creation, Preservation, Dissolution, Obfuscation and Revealing.

சடங்கது செய்து தவம்புரி வார்கள்
கடந்தனி னுள்ளே கருதுவ ராகில்
தொடர்ந்தெழு சோதி துளைவழி ஏறி
அடங்கிடும் அன்பின தாயிழை பாலே. *1192*

Kundalini Subsides in Sakti

With rituals many, they tapas perform
Let them meditate on Her within their body vessel,
The Kundalini light within
Ascending through Sushumna cavity
Will in Her Love subside.

True tapas is to meditate on kundalini sakti — to seek inward rather than to observe, in vain, the myriad elaborate and complicated rituals.

பாலித் திருக்கும் பனிமல ராறினும்
ஆலித் திருக்கும் அவற்றின் அகம்படி
சீலத்தை நீக்கத் திகழ்ந்தெழு மந்திர
மூலத்து மேலது முத்தது வாமே. *1193*

Piercing Chakras, Primal Mantra Arises

She dwells in flowers of Six Adharas
Make them unfold,
And the Primal Mantra in radiance arises,
Precious by far than pearl it is.

முத்து வதனத்திமுகந்தொறு முக்கண்ணி
சத்தி சதிரி சகளி சடாதரி
பத்துக் கரத்தி பராபரன் பைந்தொடி
வித்தகி என்னுள்ள மேவிநின் றாளே. *1194*

Sakti's Attributes

Of pearly white radiance is her visage,
Three the eyes She has in face each,
She is Sakti, Sakiri, Sahali, Jatadhari
Ten Her hands;
She is the bejewelled Mother
To Paraparan belongs,
Goddess of Learning She is,
In my heart She stood.

Her visage is radiant. She is Sakti (of prowess great); She is Sakiri (of Grace-granting); She is Sahali (of manifest form); She is Jatadhari (of matted locks); She is Vithaki (of jnana possessed); She is with ten hands.

மேவிய மண்டலம் மூன்றுடன் கீழெரி
தாவிய நற்பதத் தண்மதி யங்கதிர்
மூவருங் கூடி முதல்வியாய் முன்னிற்பார்
ஓவினு மேலிடும் உள்ளொளி யாமே. *1195*

She Pervades the Three Spheres

She has Spheres Three
Of Fire, Moon and Sun
She is Head of all three together,
She abandons you not
Even if you forget Her;
She is Light within.

உள்ளொளி மூவிரண் டோங்கிய அங்கங்கள்
வெள்ளொளி அங்கியின் மேவி அவரொடுங்
கள்ளவிழ் கோதைக் கலந்துட னேநிற்குங்
கொள்ள விசுத்திக் கொடியமு தாமே. *1196*

She is the Vine from Visuddha to Sahasrara

The Six Adharas lie concealed within,
There with the white Light of Kundalini Fire,
Siva-Sakti, of honeyed flower bedecked tresses,
Stands, intimate mingled;
She is vine from Visuddha ascends
To ambrosia in Sahasrara.

கொடிய திரேகை குருவுள் இருப்பப்
படியது வாருனைப் பைங்கழ லீசன்
வடிவது வானந்தம் வந்து முறையே
இடுமுதல் ஆறங்கம் ஏந்திழை யாளே. *1197*

When Ambrosia Flows

When that vine from Visuddha Adhara
Reaches to the Mark the Guru showed,
Ambrosia flows,
That is Form of Siva of anklet-girt Feet,
That is Bliss Divine;
She spreads it over Adharas six,
In order according,
She, the bejewelled One.

---

1) Upto ajna, the Guru guides.

ஏந்திழை யாளும் இறைவர்கள் மூவருங்
காந்தார மாறுங் கலைமுதல் ஈரெட்டு
மாந்த குளத்தியு மந்திர ராயவுஞ்
சார்ந்தனர் ஏத்த இருந்தனள் சத்தியே. *1198*

How Yoga Sakti was Seated

The bejewelled One, Kundalini,
The Gods that are Three
The Shining garland of Adhara six,
The Kalas twice-eight,
The Jnana Sakti in forehead seated,
The Congregation of Mantreswaras,
All arrived to praise Her;
Thus She was, the Yoga Sakti, seated.

சத்தியென் பாளொரு சாதகப் பெண்பிள்ளை
முத்திக்கு நாயகி என்ப தறிகிலர்
பத்தியைப் பாழில் உகுத்தஅப் பாவிகள்
கத்திய நாய்போற் கதறுகின் றாரே. *1199*

Yoga True Path to Mukti

Sakti is the Mother of Sadhaka (Yogi)
She is the Mistress of Mukti
This they know not,
And in vain, in other ways,
Their devotion went;
Wretches they are;
Like a beaten dog,
They howl and wail.

ஆரே திருவின் திருவடி காண்பர்கள்
நேரேநின் றோதி நினையவும்வல் லார்க்குக்
காரேர் குழலி கமல மலரன்ன
சீரேயுஞ் சேவடி சிந்தைவைத் தாளே. *1200*

On Whom She Confers Her Grace

Who shall behold the Feet of that Holy One?
To them who seek Her Presence
And constant meditate
The Mother of cloud-dark tresses
Revealed Her Holy Feet, Lotus-like,
And placing them on their thoughts,
Blessed them with Her Grace.

சிந்தையில் வைத்துச் சிராதியி லேவைத்து
முந்தையில் வைத்துத் தம்மூலத்திலே வைத்து
நிந்தையில் வையா நினைவதி லேவைத்துச்
சந்தையில் வைத்துச் சமாதிசெய் வீரே. *1201*

Way to Enter Samadhi

Hold Her in your thoughts,
Hold Her on your head,
Hold Her in your presence
Hold Her in Muladhara
Hold Her in meditation
Undistracted by worldly thoughts,
Hold Her in the mystic junction in cranium,
And into Samadhi enter.

Mantras 1201, 1202 & 1204

Hold Her in your thoughts; hold Her on your head; hold Her in your presence; hold Her in muladhara; hold Her in meditation; and holding Her in the spiritual junction of the cranium, enter in samadhi. Chant the mantra, 'Sivayanama,' in endearing love. This is the way to consume the fruits of the twin karmas.

சமாதிசெய் வார்கட்குத் தான்முத லாகிச்
சிவாதியி லாருஞ் சிலைநுத லாளை
நவாதியி லாக நயந்தது ஓதில்
உவாதி அவளுக் குறைவில தாமே. 1202

In Samadhi, Sakti is in Moon's Sphere

She stands as the goal of
Those who in Samadhi enter,
She of the arched brows
Who resides in Si, Va, and rest (of letters Five);
Chant the Mantra in love endearing
As the First of Saktis Nine
She in your Full Moon Sphere,
Ever abides.

உறைபதி தோறும் முறைமுறை மேவி
நறைகமழ் கோதையை நாடொறு நண்ணி
மறையுட னேநிற்கு மற்றுள்ள நான்கும்
இறைதினைப் போதினில் எய்திட லாமே. 1203

Reach Siva Through Adhara Sakti

Ascend Adharas six in order,
Where She resides,
And daily approach Her,
She of fragrant tresses,
If Her mantra is repeated with the four
You can attain many good results.

1) The four: Pranava, Bija, Sakti, Kilakam.

எய்திட லாகும்இருவினை யின்பயன்
தொய்தளிர் மேனிக் குமரி குலாங்கன்னி
மைதவழ் கண்ணிநன் மாதுரி கையொடு
கைதவம் இன்றிக் கருத்துறும் வாறே. 1204

Conquer Karmas By Devotion to Sakti

You shall conquer fruits of your twin Karmas,
If you but with folded hands,
And devotion pure
Think of Her;
Whose Form is tender like a flower petal
Who is Virgin Eternal, Kundalini,
Whose eyes are painted in dark collyrium
Who is Sweetness Surpassing.

கருத்துறுங் காலங் கருதுமனமுந்
திருத்தி யிருந்தவை சேரு நிலத்து
ஒருத்தியை உன்னி உணர்ந்திடு மண்மேல்
இருத்திடும் எண்குணம்எய்தலும் ஆகுமே. 1205

Worship Sakti and Attain Siva's Attributes

Think of Her;
Think of Her time and again;
Train your mind toward Her and reach Her;
Think of Her, deep in heart
Realize Her;
The Only One in this world;
She will make you bide here below for ever
You may attain eight attributes* of Siva too.

Think of Her; think of Her time and again; think of Her deep in the heart. By thus realising Her, you shall attain the eight attributes of Siva.

1) Eight attributes of Siva — vide Mantra 1, Prelude 8.

ஆமையொன் றேறி அகம்படி யானென
ஓமஎன் றோதிஎம் உள்ளொளி யாய்நிற்கும்
தாம நறுங்குழல் தையலைக் கண்டபின்
சோம நறுமலர் சூடிநின் றாளே. 1206

In Loving Constancy Reach Sakti

Like a turtle, withdraw your senses;
Like a vassal devoted, be in loving constancy;
Chant "Aum"
And meet Her, of shining fragrant tresses
In your heart's Centre She as Light stands,
There She stood, bedecked with Flower,
That is Crescent Moon.

சூடிடும் அங்குச பாசத் துளைவழி
கூடும் இருவளைக் கோலக்கைக் குண்டிகை
நாடும் இருபத நன்னெடு ருத்திரம்
ஆடிடுஞ் சீர்புனை ஆடக மாமே. 1207

Meet Her Through Sushumna

In Her bangled hands beautiful,
She holds elephant-goad and noose,
She carries ascetic pitcher and conch
She seeks letters twain,
That is the heart of Rudra mantra
She dances in rapture, in the Heart
Meet Her through Sushumna,
Your breath that way coursing.

Course your breath through sushumna, seeking the twin letters Si and Va — in the holy hall of the heart you can meet Her.

ஆமயன் மாலரன் ஈசன் சதாசிவன்
தாமடி சூடிநின் றெய்தினர் தம்பதங்
காமனுஞ் சாமன் இரவி கனலுடன்
சோமனும் வந்தடி சூடநின் றாளே. 1208

All Gods Beseech Her

Brahma, Vishnu, Rudra, Mahesa and Sadasiva
All, prayed at Her Feet,
And their respective states attained;
Kama, God of Love, and his brother Sama,
And Sun, Fire and Moon
All, all, besought Her Feet
And on their heads they bore them.

சூடும் இளம்பிறை சூலி கபாலினி
நீடும் இளங்கொடி நின்மலி நேரிழை
நாடி நடுவிடை ஞான முருவநின்
றாடு மதன்வழி அண்ட முதல்வியே. 1209

She Dances as Jnana in Sushumna

She wears the crescent moon, the trident, and the skull,
She is slender vine long,
She is immaculate,
She is bejewelled,
She dances through Sushumna Nadi central
As Jnana Luminous,
She, Beginning of universe all.

அண்ட முதலாய் அவனி பரியந்தங்
கண்டதொன் றில்லைக் கனங்குழை யல்லது
கண்டனுங் கண்டியு மாகிய காரணங்
குண்டிகை கோளிகை கண்டத னாலே. 1210

Pervasiveness of SivaSakti

From end to end of cosmic universe,
Nothing there is but the Bejewelled Mother,
It is all but Sakti and Siva conjoint
Like Sushumna and Kundalini.

ஆலமுண் டானமு தாங்கவர் தம்பதஞ்
சாலவந் தெய்துந் தவத்தின்பந் தான்வருங்
கோலிவந் தெய்துங் குவிந்த பதவையோ
டேலவந் தீண்டி இருந்தனள் மேலே. 1211

Sakti With Siva in Sahasrara

He consumed poison
While He let Celestials consume ambrosia;
Their immortal state shall reach you;
The Joys of tapas shall yours be,
Piercing Chakras
She entered unopened flower above,
With Lord, She there sat,
High in Sahasrara.

The Lord consumed poison, enabling the celestials to consume the ambrosia that confers immortality. There She was with Him then, and thus did it happen.

மேலாம் அருந்தவம் மேன்மேலும் வந்தெய்தக்
காலால் வருந்திக் கழிவர் கணத்திடை
நாலா நளினநின் றேத்திநட் டுச்சிதன்
மேலா மெழுத்தின ளாமத்தி னாளே. 1212

Worship Sakti in Yoga Way

That their tapas high may wax
They walk from place to place
And soon perish;
There She is in four petalled Muladhara
Stand there and worship on top of Cranium,
She is of Letter Exalted (Aum)
And beauty surpassing possessed.

ஆமத் தினிதிருந் தன்ன மயத்தினள்
ஓமத்தி லேயும் ஒருத்தி பொருந்தினள்
நாம நமசிவ என்றிருப் பார்க்கு
நேமத் துணைவி நிலாவிநின் றாளே. 1213

Chant Na Ma Si Va

The Beauteous One is She,
The Divine Swan (So-Ham) is She;
There She was in Mantra Aum too;
With those who chant,
Syallable Na-Ma-Si-Va
She, the Mother of Niyama,
Constant stood to succour.

நிலாமய மாகிய நீள்படி கத்தின்
சிலாமய மாகுஞ் செழுந்த ரளத்தின்
சுலாமய மாகுஞ் சுரிகுழற் கோதை
கலாமய மாகக் கலந்துநின் றாளே. 1214

She is Immanent as Kala

A crystal statue She is,
Of purest moon's rays,
Of rich pearl's radiance She is,
Of wavy tresses She is,
She immanent stands in Jivas
As Kala pervasive.

கலந்துநின் றாள்கன்னி காதல னோடுங்
கலந்துநின் றாளுயிர் கற்பனை எல்லாங்
கலந்துநின் றாள்கலை ஞானங்கள் எல்லாங்
கலந்துநின் றாள்கன்னி காலமு மாயே. 1215

She is Immanent in All

The Virgin with Her Lover commingling stood
She stood commingling in all Life and Thought

She stood commingling in all Learning and Wisdom
She stood commingling as Time Eternal.

Mantras 1215 & 1216

In all life and thought, in all learning and wisdom, and as time eternal, She stood mingling. She stood in stellar brilliance. She is Malini (Uma); Makuli (kundalini); She is Chandika, the tornado that blows away the troubles of Her devotees. Protectress She thus is, standing indivisible with the Protector.

காலவி எங்குங் கருத்தும் அருத்தியுங்
கூலவி ஒன்றாகுங் கூட இழைத்தனள்
மாலினி மாகுலி மந்திர சண்டிகை
பாலினி பாலவன் பாகம தாமே. 1216

She is Pervasive Everywhere

She is Eternal Time embodied;
She pervades all thought and love;
She united in Jiva inseparably;
She is Malini (Uma); Makuli (Kundalini)
Mantra Chandika
(That blows away the troubles of Her devotees like a tornado)
She is Protectress,
She with Protector indivisible stands.

பாகம் பராசக்தி பைம்பொன் சடைமுடி
ஏகம் இருதயம் ஈரைந்து திண்புய
மோக முகமைந்து முக்கண் முகந்தொறும்
நாகம் உரித்து நடஞ்செய்யும் நாதர்க்கே. 1217

She is Siva's Half

Parasakti is the Half of Him,
Who sports golden matted locks,
Who peels the elephant
And dances in triumph;
One their heart,
Ten the hands
Five the bewitching faces
Three the eyes on face each.

நாதனு நாலொன் பதின்மருங் கூடிநின்
றோதிடுங் கூட்டங்கள் ஓரைந் துளஅவை
வேதனும் ஈரொன்ப தின்மரும் மேவிநின்
றாதியும் அந்தமு மாகிநின் றாளே. 1218

She Stood Beyond Tattvas Thirty-Six

The Jiva and Tattvas four times nine
Are there;
Among them are the active group of Five (Senses);
In the body so constituted
She stands as Beginning and End,
Praised by Brahma and the twice-nine Ganas.

The 18 Ganas are: 1. Devas (Amaras) 2. Siddhas, 3. Asuras 4. Daityas, 5. Garudas, 6. Kinnaras, 7. Nirutas, 8. Kimpurushas, 9. Gandharvas, 10. Yakshas, 11. Vinjayas, 12. Bhutas, 13. Pisachas, 14. Antharas, 15. Munivas, 16. Uragas, 17. Akasavasis, 18. Bhoga Bhumidars

Brahma and the hordes of eighteen gana-genres praise Sakti, who stands as the beginning and the end, in the body with jiva, with the tattvas and the five senses that constitute the body.

Ganas are troops of noisy warrior bands, usually said to be Maruts, following Indra (in the Rg Veda) and Siva (in the Atharva Veda).

ஆகின்ற நாள்கலை ஐம்பத் தொருவர்கள்
ஆகிநின் றார்களில் ஆருயி ராமவள்
ஆகிநின் றாளுட னாகிய சக்கரத்
தாகிநின் றானவன் ஆயிழை பாடே. 1219

She Created Kala Beings

In the Beginning
Fifty-one the Kala Beings created
She stood as their life and soul;
She stood in the Chakra
Of fifty-one letters inscribed;
And He the Lord stood there
By the Jewelled One's side.

---

1) Denoted by the 51 letters of the Sanskrit alphabet and the letter Aum—

2) Adharas

Mantras 1219-1221

She stood with Him in the Chakra of Fifty-One letters (sahasrara). When jnana of these is acquired, jiva s perfection is attained. She dwells in the six adharas. As prana breath reaches these adharas one after the other, She can be visioned. The seven centres are then enlivened and the ten breaths become one prana.

Here, the kalas are 51, representing the 51 letters of the Sanskrit language.

ஆயிழை யாளொடு மாதிப் பூரமிடம்
ஆயதொ ரண்டவை யாறும் இரண்டுள
ஆய மனந்தொ றறுமுக மவைதனில்
ஏயவார் குழலி இனிதுநின் றாளே. 1220

She Dwells in Adharas

Two the Centres where the Primal Lord is,
One the Jewelled One
The other the Adharas six;
As the mind the Adharas six reaches
There She in each is with Her presence
Thus She, of the flowing tresses,
In sweetness stood.

நின்றனள் நேரிழை யோடுடன் நேர்பட
இன்றெ னகம்படி ஏழும் உயிர்ப்பெய்துந்
துன்றிய வோரொன் பதின்மருஞ் சூழலுள்
ஒன்றுயர் வோதி யுணர்ந்துநின் றாளே. 1221

The Adharas Get Enlivened

She stood there for me to witness
The seven Centres within me

Were uplifted and enlivened;
The ten breaths within me
As one Prana breath became;
And there She stood,
Chanting (Aum) and awareness imparting.

உணர்ந்தெழு மந்திரம் ஓமெனும் உள்ளே
மணந்தெழு மாங்கதி யாகிய தாகுங்
குணர்ந்தெழு சூதனுஞ் சூதியுங் கூடிக்
கணந்தெழுங் காணுமக் காமுகை யாமே. 1222

Sakti Blesses

The Mantra Aum that Jnana imparts within,
Is the way of union in God,
Thus does Siva (Director) and Sakti (Consort of the director)
Together in amity arise;
She, the Beloved of Siva, (Sivakami) blesses you.

ஆமது வங்கியும் ஆதியும் ஈசனும்
மாமது மண்டல மாருத மாதியும்
ஏமது சீவன் சிகையங் கிருண்டிடக்
கோமலர்க்கோதையுங் கோதண்ட மாகுமே. 1223

Sakti Appears in Eye-Brow Centre

She is Fire, the Primal Being and Isa
She is Spheres Three,
The Wind and the rest of elements;
She fortifies Jiva,
And renders him youthful,
Flower bedecked She stands
In Jiva's Eye-brow Centre.

1) Kodandam — eyebrow centre, ajna chakra

She, as Manonmani, stands in the eyebrow centre, radiant as the crescent moon. She is fire; she is the Primal Being and Isa; She is the three spheres; She is the wind and other elements. She protects jiva and renders him youthful through yoga.

ஆகிய கோதண்டத் தாகு மனோன்மணி
ஆகிய ஐம்ப துடனே அடங்கிடும்
ஆகும் பராபரை யோடப் பரையவள்
ஆகு மவள்ஐங் கருமத்தள் தானே. 1224

She is Paraparai

She that stands in Eye-brow centre is Manonmani,
She one with Fifty Letters becomes;
She is Para Parai and Parai too;
She is of the Acts Five—
Creation, Preservation, Dissolution, Obfuscation and Redemption.

Mantras 1224-1226

She is of the Five Acts, Creation, Preservation, Dissolution, Obfuscation and Revealing Grace. She is Mohini vibrant and Yogini amiable. Liberation lies in meditating on Her, chanting Aum in silence.

தானிகழ் மோகினி சார்வான யோகினி
போன மயமுடை யாரடி போற்றுவர்
ஆனவ ராவியினாகிய வச்சிவந்
தானாம் பரசிவ மேலது தானே. 1225

Her Blessing Leads to Union in Siva

She is vibrant Mohini,
She is amiable Yogini,
They who reach to Her
Stand at Her Feet adoring,
Unite in Siva that in their life is;
Para Siva, too, they ascend to become.

தானந்த மேலே தருஞ்சிகை தன்னுடன்
ஆனந்த மோகினி யாம்பொற் றிருவொடு
மோனையில் வைத்து மொழிதரு கூறது
வானவை யோமெனும் அவ்வுயிர் மார்க்கமே. 1226

Meditate on Aum in Cranium Top

At the far end of Cranium top
She abides, Ananda Mohini, the Golden Lady;
Meditate on Her in Silence chanting Aum,
That way lies life's Redemption.

மார்க்கங்கள் ஈன்ற மனோன்மணி மங்கலி
யார்க்கும் அறிய வரியா ளவளாகும்
வாக்கு மனமும் மருவியொன் றாய்விட்ட
நோக்கும் பெருமைக்கு நுண்ணறி வாமே. 1227

She Appears as Wisdom Subtle

She gave birth to Faiths several,
She is Manonmani, Mangali the Auspicious,
Rare is She for any to know,
To them that seek Her
United in word and thought,
She as Wisdom Subtle appears.

Mantras 1227-1229

She is Mother of several faiths; She is Manonmani (the heart's precious gem) and Mangali, the Auspicious. She is subtle wisdom. When sought, united in word and thought, She can be visioned. She is jnana, the true way. She drives away evil ways.

நுண்ணறி வாகும் நுழைபுலன் மாந்தர்க்குப்
பின்னறி வாகும் பிரானறி வத்தடஞ்
செந்நெறி யாகுஞ் சிவகதி சேர்வார்க்குத்
தன்னெறி யாவது சன்மார்க்க மாமே. 1228

Jnana Way is True Way

She is Wisdom Subtle
Of those with intellect subtle,
Behind it is Lord's Wisdom
That is Jnana;
That Way is the Holy Way,
For those who seek Siva-State,
The Way of Sanmarga (Jnana) is the Way True.

சன்மார்க்க மாகச் சமைதரு மார்க்கமுந்
துன்மார்க்க மானவை எல்லாந் துரந்திடும்
நன்மார்க்கத் தேவரும் நன்னெறி யாவதுஞ்
சன்மார்க்கத்தேவியுஞ் சத்தியென் பாளே. 1229

Sakti is Mistress of Sanmarga

The (Jnana) Way becomes Sanmarga (Good) Way
Drives away all evil ways,
From that good Way,
All good deeds arise
Of that Sanmarga,
Sakti indeed the Mistress is.

சத்தியும் நானுஞ் சயம்புவும் அல்லது
முத்தியை யாரும் முதலறி வாரில்லை
அத்திமேல் வித்திடில் அத்தி பழுத்தக்கான்
மத்தியி லேற வழியது வாமே. 1230

Source — Knowledge of Mukti

None except Sakti, Siva and (I) Jiva know
The Source of Mukti;
When you meditate constant on Sakti
That as Aum ripens,
That the Way sure
To enter the Centre aloft Sahasrara.

Mantras 1230-32

Constant meditation on Sakti ripens as Aum, opens the sure way to enter the sahasrara and helps to conquer the formidable fate, karmas, and the senses.

அதுவிது வென்றவ மேகழி யாதே
மதுவிரி பூங்குழல் மங்கைநல் லாளைப்
பதிமது மேவிப் பணியவல் லார்க்கு
விதிவழி தன்னையும் வென்றிட லாமே. 1231

Seek Sakti and Conquer Fate

Think not of this and that
And waste not your lives;
Those who reach to the Good Mother
Of flower bedecked tresses
In the Moon's sphere whence ambrosia flows
And there pray,
Well may they decreed Fate conquer.

வென்றிட லாகும் விதிவழி தன்னையும்
வென்றிட லாகும் வினைப்பெரும் பாசத்தை
வென்றிட லாகும் விழைபுலன் தன்னையும்
வென்றிடு மங்கைதன்மெய்யுணர்வோர்க்கே. 1232

She is Conqueror Supreme

Well may they decreed Fate conquer,
Well may they Karmaic Pasa conquer,
Well may they desire-ridden Senses conquer,
Well may all these know
The Mother that conquers all.

ஓரைம் பதின்மருள் ஒன்றியே நின்றது
பாரம் பரியத்து வந்த பரமிது
மாரங் குழலாளும் அப்பதி தானுமுன்
சாரும் பதமிது சத்திய மாமே. 1233

Sakti and Siva are in Letters Fifty-One

In letters Fifty and One
Sakti and Siva as one stand;
Thus was it through Time interminable;
That the State how
The Mother of flower laden tresses and Her Lord
Of yore have been,
Verily, verily is this true.

சத்தியி னோடு சயம்பவும் நேர்படில்
வித்தது வின்றியே எல்லாம் விளைந்தன
அத்தகை யாகிய ஐம்பத் தொருவருஞ்
சித்தது மேவித் திருந்திடு வாரே. 1234

Jnana Through Letters Fifty-One

When Sakti and Siva united
All creation, without seed, arose;
And thus was it with the Fifty-one Letters and their deities
Acquiring Jnana, Jivas Perfection attained.

திருந்து சிவனுஞ் சிலைநுத லாளும்
பொருந்திய வானவர் போற்றிசெய் தேத்த
அருந்திட அவ்விடம் ஆரமு தாக
இருந்தனள் தானங் கிளம்பிறை என்றே. 1235

She Stood as Ambrosia in Sahasrara

The Perfect Siva and His Consort of Arched Brow
Were there seated;
And the Celestials stood praying
To swill the ambrosia that flowed;
And as Ambrosia there She stood
Radiant as Crescent Moon.

என்றும் எழுகின்ற வேரினை எய்தினார்
தன்றது வாகுவர் தார்குழ லாளொடு
மன்றரு கங்கை மதியொடு மாதவர்
துன்றிய தாரகை சோதிநின் றாளே. 1236

She is Stellar Brilliance

They who reach to the Star Eternal
Became one with Her,
Of tresses, garland-festooned,
With fragrant Ganga and Moon,
And men of holy tapas
Self-realized praying;
Thus She stood in stellar brilliance.

நின்றனள் நேரிழை யாளொடு நேர்பட
ஒன்றிய வுள்ளொளி யாலே யுணர்ந்தது

சென்ற பிராணிகள் சிந்தையில் வேண்டிய
துன்றிடு ஞானங்கள் தோன்றிடுந் தானே. 1237

Meet Sakti and Attain Jnana

Standing face to face
With Her that is bejewelled,
With their inner light realizing Her,
And uniting in Her,
In the thoughts of Jivas thus reached
All Jnana appears.

தோன்றிடும் வேண்டுரு வாகிய தூய்நெறி
ஈன்றிடு மாங்கவள் எய்திய பல்கலை
மான்றரு கண்ணியும் மாரனும் வந்தெதிர்
சான்றது வாகுவர் தாமவ ளாயுமே. 1238

She Appears in the Form Conceived by Devotees

She appears in Form they conceive
She grants the Pure Way
And branches of Knowledge several,
She of doe-like eyes,
And He of handsome visage
Together appear;
Her do you seek.

She appears in the form one conceives; and grants the pure way and the diverse branches of knowledge.

ஆயும் அறிவுங் கடந்தணு வாரணி
மாயம தாகி மதோமதி யாயிடுஞ்
சேய அரிவை சிவானந்த சுந்தரி
நேயம தாநெறி யாகிநின் றாளே. 1239

She Transcends Human Knowledge

Transcending human knowledge,
She stands as Vedic subtlety;
She is Maya, She is Divine Proud
She is damsel red-hued.
She is Sivananda Sundari (Siva-Bliss-Beauty),
She stood as Pure Way,
In Love endearing.

She stands as Vedic subtlety beyond human knowledge. She is maya; She is divinely proud; She is Sivananda Sundari (Siva bliss Beauty); She is love endearing.

நெறியது வாய்நின்ற நேரிழை யாளைப்
பிறிவது செய்யாது பிஞ்ஞக னோடுங்
குறியது கூடிக் குறிக்கொண்டு நோக்கும்
அறிவொடும் ஆங்கே அடங்கிட லாமே. 1240

Leave Her Not

The Mother of precious jewels is Pure Way
Leave Her not,
But with Lord
Centre Her in your thoughts,
And there in Jnana
You shall absorbed be.

ஆமயன் மாலரன் ஈசன்மா லாங்கதி
ஓமய மாகிய ஒன்பதும் ஒன்றிடத்
தேமய னாளுந் தெனாதென என்றிடும்
மாமய மானது வந்தெய்த லாமே. 1241

You Will Attain Supreme State

The states of Brahma, Vishnu, Hara, Maheswara
All these but lead to Aum;
If Aum pervaded, you reach to Centres nine within
You shall honey-sweet divine become,
You shall in rapture sing,
You shall reach State of Greatness Surpassing.

Six adharas and the three mandalas-all pervaded by Aum.

Mantras 1241 & 1242

Illusory are the states of Brahma, Vishnu, Hara and Mahesvara. She is beyond all those. She pervades in Aum, in sahasrara beyond the six adharas and the three mandalas. There She confers the state of greatness, surpassing that of all the gods. Then the celestials, Vanavas, Dhanavas, Indra and other gods from all directions will come to the yogi and worship at his feet.

வந்தடி போற்றுவர் வானவர் தானவர்
இந்து முதலாக எண்டிசை யோர்களுங்
கொந்தணி யுங்குழ லாளொடு கோனையும்
வந்தனை செய்யும் வழி நவில் வீரே. 1242

Worship Siva-Sakti and be Worshipped by Celestials

The Celestials, Vanavas and Dhanavas*
Will come to you and worship your feet,
And Indra and other Gods too in direction eight;
Seek therefore the way of worship to reach
The Mother of tresses, in flower clusters festooned,
And Her Lord, too.

Children of Danu, their mother — asuras.

நவிற்றுநன் மந்திரம் நன்மலர் தூபங்
கவற்றிய கந்தங் கவர்ந்தெரி தீபம்
பயிற்றும் உலகினிற் பார்ப்பதி பூசை
அவிக்கொண்ட சோதிக்கோர் அர்ச்சனை
தானே. 1243

Sakti Worship is Siva Worship

Chant Her holy Mantra
Worship with flowers fragrant
Burn the incense,
Light the multi-flamed lamp,
Thus perform worship of Parvati;
The oblations that you in archana offer
Are for the Lord of Divine Light as well.

தாங்கி உலகில் தரித்த பராபரன்
ஓங்கிய காலத் தொருவன் உலப்பிலி
பூங்கிளி தங்கும் புரிகுழ லாளென்று
பாங்குடன் ஏற்பப் பராசத்தி போற்றே. 1244

Adore Parasakti Who Holds Parapara

Parapara that is immanent here below
And sustains all,
Eternal and Indestructable is He;
She of yore shared Her Form with Him,
She who holds the lovely parrot in Her hand,
And sports wavy tresses
She, Parasakti
Do adore Her!

Mantras 1244-1246

Adore Parasakti sporting the wavy tresses — Uma of dark slender form — and be illumined. The resplendent Parasakti dispels anava darkness. The Golden Goddess of wealth shall then be at your feet.

பொற்கொடி மாதர் புனைகழல் ஏத்துவர்
அற்கொடி மாதுமை யார்வத் தலைமகள்
நற்கொடி மாதை நயனங்கண் மூன்றுடை
விற்கொடி மாதை விரும்பி விளங்கே. 1245

Goddess of Wealth Will Bow

She is Uma of dark slender form
She is Supreme mistress of Siva's ardour
She is good vine that has eyes three
She is the Mother of arched brow;
Do adore Her
And be illumined,
The very Golden Goddess (of Wealth) shall
At your feet be.

விளங்கொளி யாய விரிசுடர் மாலை
துளங்கு பராசத்தி தூங்கிருள் நீங்கக்
களங்கொள் மணியுடன் காம வினோதம்
உளங்கொ ளிலம்பியம் ஒன்று தொடரே. 1246

Follow Her and Be Rid of Anava

Decked in garland of radiant gems
Parasakti resplendent appears,
Your Anava darkness to dispel;
She sports in love's union intimate
With Lord that is blue-throated;
Let Her be your heart's goal,
And follow Her close.

தொடங்கி உலகினிற் சோதி மணாளன்
அடங்கி இருப்பதென் அன்பின் பெருமை
விடங்கொள் பெருஞ்சடை மேல்வரு கங்கை
ஒடுங்கி யுமையொடும் ஓருரு வாமே. 1247

Siva is Contained in Sakti

Lord is the Light of the World
He is the consort of Sakti
He in me stands
That, my love's greatness is;
He stands in Her too
As one Form inseparate;
With serpent and Ganga on matted locks
He in Her is contained.

உருவம் பலவுயி ராய்வல்ல நந்தி
தெருவம் புகுந்தமை தேர்வுற நாடிற்
புரிவளைக் கைச்சியெம் பொன்னணி மாதை
மருவி இறைவன் மகிழ்வன மாயமே. 1248

Baffling Mystery of Siva-Sakti Union

Lord Nandi
That has form several,
And permeates life several,
Why does He in this Form (with Sakti)
So open appear?
That He thus sports in joy
With Her of bangled hands,
And Form bejewelled,
Is indeed a mystery, baffling!

Is it then a mystery why Siva sports in joy with the bejewelled Sakti?

மாயம் புணர்க்கும் வளர்சடை பானடித்
தாயம் புணர்க்குஞ் சலநதி அமலனைக்
காயம் புணர்க்குங் கலவியுள் மாசத்தி
ஆயம் புணர்க்குமவ் வியோனியு மாமே. 1249

Siva-Sakti Union is for Creation

The Lord of peaked matted locks
And Holy Feet,
He conjoins in Maya;
He the Pure One
That holds Ganga on His head
He shares Sakti in Love;
Him, the Great Sakti in bodily union embraced
That all creation in union to arise
She, the Supreme source of everything.

உணர்ந்தொழிந் தேனவ னாமெங்கள் ஈசனைப்
புணர்ந்தொழிந் தேன்புவ னாபதி யாரை
அணைந்தொழிந் தேனெங்கள் ஆதிதன் பாதம்
பிணைந்தொழிந் தேன்றன் அருள்பெற்ற
வாறே. 1250

Sakti's Grace from Siva Worship

As I realized Him, our Isa
I lost my self;
As I united in Him

I became one with Him;
As I embraced the Lord of worlds all,
I remained in divine fulfilment;
As I entwined at the Primal One's Feet
I received His Sakti's Grace.

Once He is realised as Isa, you unite in Him; you become one with Him. By embracing the Lord of all Worlds, the self is effaced.

பெற்றாள் பெருமை பெரிய மனோன்மனி
நற்றாள் இறைவனே நற்பயனே என்பர்
கற்றான் அறியுங் கருத்தறி வார்கட்குப்
பொற்றாள் உலகம் புகல்தனி யாமே. 1251

Lord's Feet are the Refuge

The great Manonmani is Greatness All
The Holy Feet of Her Lord, the Goal True, they say;
This the learned know;
For those who this truth know,
His Golden Feet exalted art
Life's refuge unfailing.

Manonmani is all greatness. The truly learned know that Her Holy Feet are their true goal. They are the world's haven of refuge also.

தனிநா யகன்றனோ' டென்னெஞ்சம் நாடி
இனியார் இருப்பிடம் ஏழுல கென்பர்
பனியான் மலர்ந்தபைம் போதுகை ஏந்திக்
கனியாய் நினைவதென் காரணம் அம்மையே. 1252

Accessibility of Sakti

My heart seeks Lord in love
He the Sweet One is in seven worlds beyond, they say;
That the reason why
I adore Mother
With flowers fragrant
And heart in melting love.

The yogi adores Mother Sakti with fragrant flowers and with the heart melting in love. She is much more easily accessible than the Lord, who, it is said, is beyond the seven worlds.

அம்மனை அம்மை அரிவை மனோன்மனி
செம்மனை செய்து திருமங்கை யாய்நிற்கும்
இம்மனை செய்த இந்நில மங்கையும்
அம்மனை யாகி அமர்ந்துநின் றாளே. 1253

Sakti Fashions Body-Home and Heavenly Home

She is Mother of Heavenly Home
She is Mistress Supreme,
Manonmani;
She fashions Holy Home
And stands as Mother Divine;
She, Maya, fashioned this body,
And in this Body Home too She abides.

அம்மையும் அத்தனும் அன்புற்ற தல்லது
அம்மையும் அத்தனு மாரறி வாரென்னை
அம்மையோ டத்தனும் யானும் உடனிருந்
தம்மையொ டத்தனை யான்புரிந் தேனே. 1254

Adore and Be With Siva-Sakti

My Mother and Father in love united;
Had they not,
Will my Mother and Father know me ever?
With my Mother and Father I sit,
And my Mother and Father,
I constant adore.

The yogi constantly adores the Mother (Sakti) and Father (Siva), who in love ever stand united.

9. ஏரொளிச் சக்கரம்
EROLI CHAKRAM (CHAKRA OF SUPREME LIGHT)

ஏரொளி யுள்ளெழு தாமரை நாலிதழ்
ஏரொளி விந்துவி னாலெழு நாதமாம்
ஏரொளி யக்கலை எங்கும் நிறைந்தபின்
ஏரொளிச் சக்கர மந்நடு வன்னியே. 1255

From Nada In Muladhara Rises Eroli Chakra

In Muladhara Lotus of petals four,
Are Nadas four
With radiant Bindu arise;
When Nada's radiant Kala everywhere suffuses,
Then does arise of Supreme Light Chakra
In Central Kundalini Fire.

Va (m), Sa (m), Sha (m), Sa (m) are the four nadas. From radiant bindu in the muladhara four-petalled Lotus arises nada. From nada in the central kundalini there arises the Eroli Chakra.

வன்னி யெழுத்தவை மாபலம் உள்ளன
வன்னி யெழுத்தவை வானுற ஓங்கின
வன்னி யெழுத்தவை மாபெருஞ் சக்கரம்
வன்னி யெழுத்திடு வாறது சொல்லுமே. 1256

Letters in the Chakra Have Great Power

Letters in Kundalini Fire are mighty great
Letters in Kundalini Fire rose to heavens,
Letters in Kundalini Fire form a great Chakra
The Way Letters are placed,
I shall now relate.

The mighty four letters in kundalini, Va, Sa, Sa, Sa form the basis of this great Chakra.

சொல்லிய விந்துவும் ஈராறு நாதமாஞ்
சொல்லிடு மப்பதி யவ்வெழுத் தாவன
சொல்லிடு நூறொடு நாற்பத்து நாலுரு
சொல்லிடு சக்கர மாய்வரு மேலதே. *1257*

How Chakra is Formed

Bindu aforesaid with Nadas twelve,
In the four petals of that Adhara stand as Letters respective
Chant Letters a hundred and forty four times,
They as Chakra form and lofty arise.

மேல்வரும் விந்துவு மவ்வெழுத் தாய்விடும்
மேல்வரு நாதமும் ஓங்கும் எழுத்துடன்
மேல்வரு மப்பதி யவ்வெழுத் தேவரின்
மேல்வரு சக்கர மாய்வரு ஞாலமே. *1258*

Earth Chakra

Bindu letter conjoining Nada Letter
Together fill Muladhara
When Conjoint Letters are thus repeated
They form Earth Chakra.

When the conjoined letters (bindu letter and nada letter) tha fill the muladhara are repeatedly chanted thus, they form the Jnala (Cosmos) Chakra.

ஞாலம தாக விரிந்தது சக்கரம்
ஞாலம தாயிடும் விந்துவும் நாதமும்
ஞாலம தாயிடு மப்பதி யோசனை
ஞாலம தாக விரிந்த தெழுத்தே. *1259*

Cosmos Chakra Expanded into Five Elements

The Earth Chakra expanded,
When the Bindu and Nada conjoint became
That Adhara (Muladhara) to immense distance lengthened,
As Earth the letters thus expanded.

Mantras 1259-1261

The Cosmos Chakra expanded into five elements: 'Ha' (sky), 'Ya' (vayu), 'Ra' (fire), 'Va' (water) and 'La' (earth).

விரிந்த எழுத்தது விந்துவும் நாதமும்
விரிந்த எழுத்தது சக்கர மாக
விரிந்த எழுத்தது மேல்வரும் பூமி
விரிந்த எழுத்தினில் அப்புறம் அப்பே. *1260*

Elements Earth and Water

The Letters arose as Bindu and Nada,
The Letters expanded as Chakra
The Letters lengthened into Elements Earth,
The Letters lengthened as Element Water beyond.

அப்பது வாக விரிந்தது சக்கரம்
அப்பினில் அப்புறம் அவ்வன லாயிடும்
அப்பினில் அப்புறம் மாருத மாயெழ
அப்பினில் அப்புறம் ஆகாச மாமே. *1261*

Beyond Appeared Elements Fire, Wind and Sky

As Element Water, Chakra lengthened,
Then further as Element Fire,
Then still further as Element Wind
And further beyond as Element Sky.

ஆகாச அக்கர மாவது சொல்லிடில்
ஆகாச அக்கரத் துள்ளே எழுத்தவை
ஆகாச அவ்வெழுத் தாகிச் சிவானந்தம்
ஆகாச அக்கர மாவ தறிமினே. *1262*

Letter for Sky is Ha (m)

To speak of Astral Letter,
In Astral Letter are all other letters contained,
Astral letter is "Ha", that is Sivananda Bliss
That the Astral letter, know this.

The astral letter is 'Ha' that is Sivananda bliss. It contains all the other letters.

அறிந்திடுஞ் சக்கரம் ஐயஞ்சு விந்து
அறிந்திடுஞ் சக்கர நாத முதலா
அறிந்திடும் அவ்வெழுத் தப்பதி யோர்க்கும்
அறிந்திடும் அப்பக லோனிலை யாமே. *1263*

Sun Chakra

Know this, thus it is the Chakra,
Of five times five Bindu dot is it made;
With Nada the Chakra commences
With letters in the Chambers placed
Thus it is the Sun Chakra.

Repeat the four nada letters with bindu 25 times to form the Surya (Sun) Chakra.

அம்முதல் ஆறுமவ் வாதி எழுத்தாகும்
அம்முதல் ஆறுமவ் வம்மை எழுத்தாகும்
இம்முதல் நாலும் இருந்திடு வன்னியே
இம்முத லாகும் எழுத்தவை எல்லாம். *1264*

Letters of Siva-Sakti and Kundalini

"A", and Letters Five that follow*
These six are Letters of Primal One;
The six letters thus formed,
Are Sakti's Letters,
The middle Letter of the first-Four (Va) aforesaid
Is Letters of Element Fire
Thus it is with these Letters holy.

The six letters commencing with 'A' are the letters of Siva/Sakti

1) A, Aa, I, I, G, U
2) E, E, Ai, O, O, Au
3) Va, Sa, Sha, Sa
4) (Aum) Si, Va, Ya, Ña, Ma

எழுத்தவை நூறொடு நாற்பத்து நாலும்
எழுத்தவை யாறது வந்நடு வன்னி
எழுத்தவை யந்நடு வச்சுட ராகி
எழுத்தவை தான்முதல் அந்தமு மாமே. 1265

The 144 Letters of the Radiant Chakra

The Letters of Chakra radiant are a hundred and forty four
The Letters are but the Six Letter Mantra
Whose Central Letter Va to Fire belongs
That Letter central as radiant Fire flames
Thus are the Letters Six, first and last.

The four letters of kundalini fire expanded into 144 letters of the Chakra.

அந்தமும் ஈறுமுதலா னவையற
அந்தமும் அப்பதி னெட்டுடன் ஆதலால்
அந்தமும் அப்பதின் மூன்றில் அமர்ந்தபின்
அந்தமும் இந்துகை யாருட மானதே. 1266

Mystic Moon Sphere Visioned

For the birth and death to end
The finite position is for the Sixteen (Visuddhi) and Two (Ajna) to reach
And so when Kundalini that was at base
Ascends and crosses beyond the third centre from it (Anahatha)
Then is visioned the Mystic Sphere of the Moon.

1) 18 letters — 16 letters of the moon's 16 kalas and the two letters (A and U) of Aum.
2) 13th letter — after the 12 letters in the 12 kalas of the sun are ascended, cover the moon sphere which absorbs the sun's kalas.

The ultimate centre filled by 18 letters has neither beginning nor end. The moon's sphere is visioned when the centre with 13 letters is reached.

ஆவின மானவை முந்நூற் றறுபது
மாவின மப்பதி னைந்தின மாயுறு
மாவின மப்பதி னெட்டுட னாயுறு
மாவின மக்கதி ரோன்வர வந்தே. 1267

Time Measured by Sun Within and Without

There they are to the Goat's Group belong
The days three hundred and sixty;
There they are in fortnights of days fifteen reckoned;
There they come as in the Centres Sixteen are Two
Kundalini ascends
There they come as the 'Sphere of the Mystic Sun' within is reached.

That ultimate centre contains the span of all life. Time is measurable by the 'sun.'

வந்திடும் ஆகாசம் ஆறது நாழிகை
வந்திடும் அக்கரம் முப்பதி ராசியும்
வந்திடு நாளது முந்நூறு றறுபதும்
வந்திடு ஆண்டு வகுத்துறை யவ்வியே. 1268

Duration of Day, Month and Year

Across the firmament vast
The Sun travels through Zodiac houses twelve,
In time span reckoned
As thirty naligai's in the day,
And in days reckoned as three hundred and sixty
In the full year round.

அவ்வின மூன்றுமவ் வாடது வாய்வருங்
கெவ்வின மூன்றுங் கிளர்தரு வேரதாஞ்
சவ்வின மூன்றுந் தழைத்திடுந் தண்டதாம்
இவ்வின மூன்றும் இராசிக ளெல்லாம். 1269

Group Distribution of Rasis in Zodiac

The Zodiac houses (Rasís) are in three clusters reckoned,
With the Goat (Mesha)* comes its group of three
With the Bull (Rishabha)* comes its group of three
With the Twins (Mithuna)* comes its group of three
Thus are the Rasis in Zodiac in clusters three reckoned.

Rasis in the zodiac are determined in three groupings — goat (mesa), Bull (risabha) and Twins (mithuna).

1) The mesha (Aries) group or path in this cluster are:
Rishabha (Taurus)
Mithuna (Gemini)
Kataka (Cancer)
Simha (Leo)

2) The rishabha (Taurus) path contains:
Kanni (Virgo)
Tulam (Libra)
Meena (Pisces)
Mesha (Aries)

3) The mithuna (Gemini) path contains:
Vrischika (Scorpio)
Dhanus (Sagittarius)
Makaram (Capricorn)
Kumbha (Aquarius)

இராசியுட் சக்கரம் எங்கும் நிறைந்தபின்
இராசியுட் சக்கர மென்றறி விந்துவாம்
இராசியுட் சக்கர நாதமும் ஒத்தபின்
இராசியுட் சக்கரம் நின்றிடு மாறே. 1270

How Rasi Chakra is Formed

When the Chakra fills the Zodiac,
The Chakra is by Bindu filled;
And when Nada too therein fills
The Rasi Chakra is in Zodiac fixed.

The Rasi Chakra is formed in the zodiac by being filled with bindu and nada letters.

நின்றிடு விந்துவென றுள்ள எழுத்தெலாம்
நின்றிடு நாதமும் ஓங்கும் எழுத்துடன்
நின்றிடு மப்பதி யவ்வெழுத் தேவரில்
நின்றிடு மப்புறந் தாரகை யானதே. 1271

Formation of Taraka Stellar Chakra

The Bindu letters with Nada letters arise,
When in each Adhara the appropriate letters
Bindu and Nada carry out are placed,
Then the Taraka (Stellar) Chakra appears!

The Taraka (Stellar) Chakra appears when the letters of bindu and nada are placed appropriately in each adhara.

தாரகை யாகச் சமைந்தது சக்கரந்
தாரகை மேலோர் தழைத்தது பேரொளி
தாரகை சந்திரன் நற்பக லோன்வரத்
தாரகை தாரகை தாரகை கண்டதே. 1272

Taraka Chakra is the Support of Sakti

When the Chakra as a Star its form thus assumes,
On that Star does a divine light beam,
When onto this Star, Moon and Sun comes
That Star for Sakti support becomes,
Sakti that supports all.

The Chakra assumes the form of a star and a divine light beams from it. Taraka Chakra is the support of Sakti, the supporter of all.

கண்டிடு சக்கரம் விந்து வளர்வதாங்
கண்டிடு நாதமுந் தன்மேல் எழுந்திடக்
கண்டிடு வன்னிக் கொழுந்தன வொத்தபின்
கண்டிடு மப்புறங் காரொளி யானதே. 1273

In That Chakra Arises Dark Smoky Flame

In Chakra, Bindu ascends,
In Bindu, Nada ascends,
In Nada, Flame of Fire ascends,
Beyond, appears a Light that is blue.

On that Chakra bindu ascends; on bindu ascends nada; and on nada ascends the kundalini flame of fire. Then arises a dark smoky flame.

காரொளி அண்டம் பொதிந்துல கெங்கும்
பாரொளி நீரொளி சாரொளி காலொளி
வானொளி ஒக்க வளர்ந்து கிடந்துபின்
நேரொளி ஒன்றாய் நிறைந்தங்கு நின்றதே. 1274

That Flame Pervaded the Five Elements

That Blue Light enveloped universe all,
It became light of earth, water, fire, wind and sky,
Thus as it flamed and rose together,
As One Divine Light it pervaded everywhere.

That blue light pervaded the five elements — earth, water, fire, wind and sky — and rose as one divine light.

நின்றது அண்டமும் நீளும் புவியெலாம்
நின்றவிவ் வண்ட நிலைபெறக் கண்டிட
நின்றவிவ் வண்டமு மூல மலமொக்கும்
நின்றவிவ் வண்டம் பலமது விந்துவே. 1275

From That Arose Universe Based on Bindu

The universe as diverse worlds expanded,
The universe as firm stood,
The universe is unto Primal Stain
The universe rests on Bindu's strength.

The universe arose out of primordial stain or maya. It expanded as diverse worlds. From that arose the universe based on bindu's strength.

விந்துவும் நாதமும் ஒக்க விழுந்திடில்
விந்துவும் நாதமும் ஒக்க விரையதாம்
விந்திற் குறைந்திடு நாதம் எழுந்திடில்
விந்துவை எண்மடி கொண்டது வீசமே. 1276

Bindu and Nada Produce Bija

If Bindu and Nada in equal proportions arise,
Bindu and Nada together produced Bija (Seed)
Balanced,
If Bindu rises more and Nada less,
The Bija becomes potent far,
Eight times more than Bindu.

1) Nada and bindu are stages of sakti in the movement towards the manifestation of the Self as Object, that is as the universe — "The Garland of Letters," p.116

Bindu and nada produce bija. If bindu rises more and nada less, bija becomes eight times more powerful than bindu.

வீசம் இரண்டுள நாதத் தெழுவன
வீசமும் ஒன்று விரைந்திடு மேலுற
வீசமும் நாதமும் எழுந்துடன் ஒத்தபின்
வீசமும் விந்து விரிந்தது காணுமே. 1277

Bija — Causal and Caused

Two the Bijas from Nada arise,
One the Bija that ascends upward;
And with Nada alike arises,
The Seed behind as (Caused) Bindu expands.

Of the two bijas that arise from nada, one ascends upward; and with nada equal, the seed behind expands as caused bindu.

விரிந்தது விந்துவுங் கெட்டது வீசம்
விரிந்தது விந்துவும் நாதத் தளவினில்
விரிந்தது வுட்கட்ட எட்டெட்டு மாகில்
விரிந்தது விந்து விரையது வாமே. *1278*

Bindu Drawn in Visuddha Becomes Seed of Liberation

As the Bindu rose higher and higher,
The Bija (Seed) in vain went;
When Bindu rises equal with Nada,
And is drawn within to pervade the petals sixteen of the (Visuddha adhara)
The Bindu that expands becomes the Seed of Liberation.

When bindu arises equal with nada, it is drawn in visuddhi adhara; and there it becomes the seed of liberation.

விரையது விந்து விளைந்தன எல்லாம்
விரையது விந்து விளைந்த உயிரும்
விரையது விந்து விளைந்தவிஞ் ஞாலம்
விரையது விந்து விளைந்தவன் தாளே. *1279*

From Bindu-Seed Bija Evolved All

From the Bindu-Seed Bija arose all,
From the Bindu-Seed arose all life
From the Bindu-Seed arose this world,
From Lord's Feet (Nada) arose Bindu-Seed.

Bindu seed arose from the Holy Feet of the Lord. From bindu seed (bija) evolved all — all life and all worlds.

விளைந்த எழுத்தது விந்துவும் நாதமும்
விளைந்த எழுத்தது சக்கர மாக
விளைந்த எழுந்தவை மெய்யினுள் நிற்கும்
விளைந்த எழுத்தவை மந்திர மாமே. *1280*

Fifty Letters Evolved From Bindu and Nada

From Bindu and Nada evolved the letters
From the letters was Chakra formed,
The letters and Chakras within the Body stand
The letters verily are the mantras true.

From the letters evolved from bindu, Nada Chakra was formed. Truly, the letters are the mantras.

மந்திரஞ் சக்கர மானவை சொல்லிடில்
தந்திரத் துள்ளெழுத் தொன்றெரி வட்டமாம்
தந்திரத் துள்ளு மிரேகையில் ஒன்றில்லை
பந்தம தாகும் பிரணவம் உன்னிடே. *1281*

Pranava is the Mantra Supreme with its Seat in Eye-Brow Centre

To speak of mantras and Chakras
There it is one like the circle of fire,
The Tantras glorify;
Meditate on Pranava that is in the Eye-Brow Centre
Through the Tantras reached;
No more thine bondage is.

Mantras and Chakras resemble the circle of fire that the *Tantras* glorify. Pranava is the supreme mantra with its seat in the eyebrow centre (ajna chakra). Reach that through tantra. Your bondage ends there.

உன்னிட்ட வட்டத்தில் ஒத்தெழு மந்திரம்
பின்னிட்ட ரேகை பிழைப்பது தானில்லை
தன்னிட் டெழுந்த தகைப்பறப் பின்னிற்கப்
புன்னிட்ட மந்திரம் பார்க்கலு மாமே. *1282*

Pranava Vision is Obtained When Egoity Falls Back

The Mantra that arises in Muladhara Chakra
Leaves not the Eye-Brow Centre;
When your egoity falls back
Then may you vision that Mantra.

The mantra that arises in the muladhara chakra never leaves the eyebrow centre. Pranava vision is obtained when egoity falls back.

பார்க்கலு மாகும் பகையறு சக்கரங்
காக்கலு மாகுங் கருத்தில் தடமெங்கும்
நோக்கலு மாகும் நுணுக்கற்ற நுண்பொருள்
ஆக்கலு மாகும் அறிந்துகொள் வார்க்கே. *1283*

Vision Pranava in the Chakra

In the Chakra that ends your Pasa
May you vision Pranava,
All your thoughts, it will protect
All directions, you shall perceive
Well shall you reach Truth
That is subtler than the subtle,
If you but know, how to look for it.

Vision Pranava in the chakra that snaps your pasas. Protecting your thoughts, it leads you to Truth, that is subtler than the subtle.

அறிந்திடுஞ் சக்கர மாதி யெழுத்து
விரிந்திடுஞ் சக்கர மேலெழுத் தம்மை
பரிந்திடுஞ் சச்கரம் பாராங்கி நாலும்
குவிந்திடுஞ் சக்கரம் கூறலு மாமே. *1284*

Siva's Letter and Sakti's Letter in Pranava Chakra

For the Chakra, thus said
First letter is "A" of Siva
The letter next is of Sakti, "U"
The Chakra is the earth, fire and the rest of elements four,

Of the Chakra thus formed, more can be said.

Siva's letter (A) and Sakti's letter (U) form the first two letters in the Pranava-Chakra. This Chakra is earth, fire and the rest of the elements.

கூறிய சக்கரத் துள்ளெழு மந்திரம்
மாறியல் பாக அமைந்து விரிந்திடுந்
தேறிய அஞ்சுடன் சேர்ந்தெழு மாரண
மாறியல் பாக மதித்துக்கொள் வார்க்கே. 1285

Pranava Expands into Six Letter Mantra Aum Na Ma Si Va Ya

The mantra in Chakra arises
Expands as Letters six;
It is Vedic mantra that conjoint with Letters Five
—Aum Nama Sivaya—arises
For those who that way inclined are.

Pranava mantra expands into the six-lettered mantra — Aum Namasivaya — for those who seek the divine path.

மதித்திடும் அம்மையும் மாமாது மாகும்
மதித்திடும் அம்மையு மங்கனல் ஒக்கும்
மதித்தங் கெழுந்தவை காரண மாகில்
கொதித்தங் கெழுந்தவை கூடகி லாவே 1286

Sakti is the Presiding Deity of Six Letter Mantra

The Holy Sakti is the presiding deity of that Mantra
The Holy Sakti in there is like fire (Kundalini);
If attainment of Her be Sadhaka's goal,
The ensnaring Pasa nears not.

The holy Sakti is the presiding deity of that six-lettered mantra. If the holy Sakti, who is like kundalini fire, is reached, the ensnaring pasas will no longer harass you.

கூடிய தம்பனம் மாரணம் வசியம்
ஆடியல் பாக அமைந்து செறிந்திடும்
பாடியுள் ளாகப் பகைவரும் வந்துறார்
தேடியுள் ளாகத் தெளிந்துகொள் வார்க்கே. 1287

Siddhis Come of Their Own Accord

The Sthambanam, Maranam and Vasyam
Are powers there in the Chakra of themselves arise
In the place where the Sadhaka is,
No enemies come,
Thus is for them who seek it within them.

Sthambanam, Maranam and Vasyam are the powers that arise in chakras (yantras). No foes near the sadhakas who seek it.

தெளிந்திடுஞ் சக்கர மூலத்தி னுள்ளே
அளிந்த வகாரத்தை யந்நடு வாக்கிக்
குளிர்ந்த வரனைக் கூடியுள் வைத்து
வளிந்தவை யங்கெழு நாடிய காலே. 1288

How to Meditate on the Six-Lettered Chakra

Vision the Chakra in Muladhara,
Centre the sound "A' therein
Meditate on benevolent Siva within
And upward course the Prana breath.

Vision the chakra in muladhara and centre the sound 'A' to contemplate on the benevolent Siva, and then divert the prana breath upward — thus meditate on the six-lettered Chakra.

காலரை முக்கால் முழுதெனும் மந்திரம்
ஆலித் தெழுந்தமைந் தூறி எழுந்ததாய்ப்
பாலித் தெழுந்து பகையற நின்றபின்
மாலுற்ற மந்திர மாறிக்கொள் வார்க்கே. 1289

How it is Meditated for Worldly Purposes

As a quarter, a half, a three-quarter and one full
The mantra thus in measure composed ascends,
And as it thus ascends,
The obstacles internal perish.
Thus it is for those who chant the mantra enchanting
For attainments worldly.

As the mantra ascends in appropriate measures, the impediments vanish. Thus is the mantra chanted for worldly purposes.

1) Pranava mantra is composed of bindu (1/4 matra), 'M' (1/2 matra). nada (3/4 matra), 'A' and 'U' (full matra)

கொண்டஇம் மந்திரங்கூத்தன் எழுத்ததாய்ப்
பண்டையுள் நாவிற் பகையற விண்டபின்
மன்றுள் நிறைந்த மணிவிளக் காயிடும்
இன்றும் இதயத் தெழுந்து நமவெனே. 1290

Chant Nama in Love; You Shall be Light

Chant this mantra
Whose letters to the Dancer Divine Belong,
Inside uluva obstacles vanishing
You shall become the jewelled lamp in the Hall of Dance;
Even now, do arise,
And chant Nama with love in your heart's core.

Chant Nama in love inside uluva free of obstacles — then shall you become the jewelled lamp in the hall of dance.

10. வயிரவச் சக்கரம்
BHAIRAVA CHAKRA

அறிந்த பிரதமையோ டாறு மறிஞ்சு
அறிந்தவச் சத்தமி மேலிவை குற்றம்
அறிந்தவை யொன்றுவிட் டொன்றுபத் தாக
அறிந்த வலமது வாக நடவே. 1291

Days Appropriate for Bhairava Chakra Worship

Ten days in the fortnight
Do this Worship perform;
The first six days of the fortnight,
And then the eighth, tenth, twelfth and fourteenth
These the ten days appropriate
(Leave out seventh, ninth, eleventh and thirteenth)
Then coursing breath through Right Nostril
Do you worship.

The first six days, the eighth, the tenth, the twelfth and the fourteenth days of a fortnight are the appropriate days to perform Bhairava Chakra worship.

நடந்து வயிரவன் சூல கபாலி
கடந்த பகைவனைக் கண்ணது போக்கித்
தொடர்ந்த வுயிரது வுண்ணும் பொழுது
படர்ந்த வுடல்கொடு பந்தாட லாமே. 1292

Bhairava Destroys Your Enemy

As you worship Bhairava thus
The God appears with trident and skull,
He blinds the eyes of your enemy
He drinks his life,
And with your enemy's body you may play as with a ball.

When you perform Bhairava Chakra worship successfully, the Lord appears with trident and skull and destroys your foes.

ஆமேவப் பூண்டரு ளாதி வயிரவன்
ஆமே கபாலமுஞ் சூலமுங் கைகொண்டங்
காமே தமருக பாசமுங் கையது
வாமே சிரத்தொடு வாளது கையே. 1293

Bhairava's Form

The Primal Bhairava
That comes to bless the Jiva
Holds the skull and trident in His hands,
He holds the drum and the noose too
And the severed head and sword as well.

கையவை யாறுங் கருத்துற நோக்கிடு
மெய்யது செம்மை விளங்கு வயிரவன்
துய்யரு ளத்தில் துளங்குமெய் யுற்றதாய்ப்
பொய்வகை விட்டுநீ பூசனை செய்யே. 1294

Adore Bhairava Sincerely

Six His hands,
Blessed His look,
Ruddy Bright is Bhairava's Form
He appears in the hearts of the Pure
As shining Truth;
Do in devotion sincere adore Him.

Bhairava, the shining Truth, appears in the hearts of the pure and sincere devotees. So adore and seek Him in endearing love and sincere faith.

பூசனை செய்யப் பொருந்தியோ ராயிரம்
பூசனை செய்ய மதுவுட னாடுமால்
பூசனை சாந்து சவாது புழுகுநெய்
பூசனை செய்துநீர் பூசலை வேண்டுமே. 1295

The Way of Bhairava Worship

Worship Him,
Perform a thousand worships
With dance and drink
With sandal paste, and fragrant incense
With musk, civet scent and unguents several
Worship thus and pray
He fights your enemy.

Perform the Bhairava worship 1,000 times with drink and ecstatic dance, with sandalwood paste, fragrant incense, musk, civet and diverse unguents. Worship Him thus, and He will destroy your enemies. Describes the special rites for Bhairava, which call for dance and drink.

வேண்டிய வாறு கலகமு மாயிடும்
வேண்டிய ஆறிணுண் மெய்யது பெற்றபின்
வேண்டிய வாறு வரும்வழி நீநட
வேண்டிய வாறது வாகுங் கருத்தே. 1296

Wishes Fulfilled by Bhairava Worship

As you pray, fight there shall be
As you the six adharas within ascend
Pray for the ways things should be
And all your wishes fulfilled shall be.

11. சாம்பவி மண்டலச் சக்கரம்
SAMBHAVI MANDALA CHAKRA

சாம்பவி மண்டலச் சக்கரஞ் சொல்லிடில்
ஆம்பதம் எட்டாக விட்டிடின் மேல்தரங்
காண்பதந் தத்துவ நாலுள் நயனமும்
நாம்பதங் கண்டபின் நாடறிந் தோமே. *1297*

How to Form It

To speak of Sambhavi Mandala Chakra
It is like this;
Form Chambers eight,
Within it is the Chamber Central
That verily is the Eye of Tattvas Four
(Sivam, Sakti, Nadam and Bindu)
When we see this Holy State revealed,
We verily know Worlds all.

Within the eight chambers is the central chamber. That verily is the eye of the four tattvas — Siva, Sakti, Nada and Bindu.

நாடறி மண்டலம் நல்லவிக் குண்டத்துக்
கோடற வீதியுங் கொடர்ந்துள் இரண்டழி
பாடறி பத்துடன் ஆறு நடுவீதி
ஏடற நாலைந் திடவகை யாமே. *1298*

Formation of Sambhavi Chakra

The Mandala that is formed by lines twenty horizontal and twenty vertical,
Form Bhupuras two inner and two outer
The innermost Bhupara
Formed of Chambers six and ten.

The mandalas that are formed by twenty horizontal and twenty vertical lines have two inner bhupuras and two outer bhupuras. The innermost bhupura is formed of 16 chambers.

நாலைந் திடவகை யுள்ளதோர் மண்டலம்
நாலுநல் வீதியுள் நல்ல இலிங்கமாய்
நாலுநற் கோணமும் நந்நா லிலிங்கமாய்
நாலுநற் பூநடு நண்ணலவ் வாறே. *1299*

Sambhavi Chakra Formation

The Mandala is formed of
Lines twenty by twenty,
In Bhupuras four describe Lingas
And Lingas four in corner each too
And place flowers four there.

In bhupuras, place four lingas in each corner and place four flowers there. Thus form the Sambhavi Chakra.

ஆறிரு பத்துநா லஞ்செழுத் தஞ்சையும்
வேறுரு வாக விளைந்து கிடந்தது
தேறி நிருமல சிவாய நமவென்று
கூறுமின் கூறிற் குறைகளும் இல்லையே. *1300*

Chant Five Letters as Form of Fifty-One Letters

The Letters Fifty and One
There remained in form different
Chant Si Va Ya Na Ma pure there
Nothing will you lack then.

Chant the Five Letters (Sivayanama) as the embodiment of the Fifty-One letters. You will lack nothing then.

குறைவதும் இல்லை குரைகழற் கூடு
மறைவது மாரண மவ்வெழுத் தாகித்
திறமது வாகத் தெளியவல் லார்க்கு
இறவில்லை என்றென் றியம்பினர் காணே. *1301*

Chant Aum Sivaya Nama and Conquer Death

Nothing shall you want;
The Holy Feet will be yours;
Chant the Vedic mantra Aum;
If steadfast you realize it
Death none, thus have they said.

Chant the Vedic mantra Aum in steadfastness. This brings the conquest over death.

காணும் பொருளுங் கருதிய தெய்வமும்
பேணும் பதியும் பெருகிய தீர்த்தமும்
ஊணும் உணர்வும் உறக்கமுந் தானாகக்
காணுங் கனகமுங் காரிகை யாமே. *1302*

Blessings of Sambhavi

You shall attain wealth
Your favourite God you shall see,
Great state, holy waters of pilgrimage,
Delicious food, pleasant emotions,
And sound sleep, and gold
All these of themselves, yours be
As the Mother of the Chakra blesses.

As the Mother of the Chakra blesses, you will be conferred with wealth, great estate, pilgrimage to holy waters, dilicious food, pleasant emotions, sound sleep and gold.

ஆமே எழுத்தஞ்சு மாம்வழி யேயாகப்
போமே யதுதானும் போம்வழி யேபோனால்
நாமே நினைத்தன செய்யலு மாகும்
பார்மேல் ஒருவர் பகையில்லை தானே. *1303*

Proceed the Way of Five Letters

The Five Holy letters yours shall be
Persevere their Way,
If you so proceed,

You shall achieve all you wish
None the enemies,
In the World here below.

Mantras 1303 & 1304

Proceed the way of the five holy letters. They who bend low before Her, will stoop before no enemies. No more are they harassed by karma and its untoward manifestations. All good things will flow daily, cool as water, and without any impediment.

பகையில்லை என்றும் பணிந்தவர் தம்பால்
நகையில்லை நாணாளும் நன்மைக ளாகும்
வினையில்லை என்றும் விருத்தமும் இல்லை
தகையில்லை தானுஞ் சலமது வாமே. *1304*

Blessings of Sambhavi Worship

For those who bow low to Her,
Enemies none be,
None exalts in glee over them,
No more will Karma be,
And its untoward manifestations too;
Obstacles too will be none
All things good daily flow
Cool as water you will be.

ஆரும்உரைசெய்ய லாமஞ் செழுத்தாலே
யாரும் அறியாத ஆனந்த ரூபமாம்
பாரும் விசும்பும் பகலும் மதியதி
ஊனும் உயிரும் உணர்வது வாமே. *1305*

Sambhavi's Form

Chanting the Letters Five
All may worship the Chakra of Sambhavi.
She is Bliss-Form that none has seen,
She is the earth, the sky, the sun and moon
She is the sentience that pervades body and life.

All may chant the Five Letters and worship the Chakra of Sambhavi. She is Bliss-Form that no one has visioned. She is the earth, the sky, the moon, and the consciousness that is all-pervasive.

உணர்ந்தெழு மந்திரம் ஓமெனும் உள்ளே
அணைந்தெழு மாங்கத னாதிய தாகுங்
குணர்ந்தெழு சூதனுஞ் சூதியங் கூடிக்
கணந்தெழுங் காணுமக் காமுகை யாலே. *1306*

Sakti Blesses

The mantra Aum that Jnana within,imparts
Is the way of union in God
Thus does Siva (Director) and Sakti (consort of the Director)
Together in amity arise;
She, the Beloved of Siva, (Sivakami) blesses you.

The mantra, Aum, that imparts jnana within, is the key to unite in God. Siva (Director) and His Sakti together arise in amity; and Sakti (Sivakami) blesses you.

12. புவனாபதி சக்கரம்
BHUVANAPATHI CHAKRA

ககராதி யோரைந்துங் காணிய பொன்மை
அகராதி யோரா றரத்தமே போலும்
சகராதி யோர்நான்குந் தான்சுத்த வெண்மை
ககராதி மூவித்தை காமிய முத்தியே. *1307*

Fifteen Letters of the Chakra

The five letters beginning with "Ka" are golden hued to behold
The six letters beginning with "A" are red-hued
The four letters beginning with "Sa" are pure white
The mantras thus grouped lead to bliss below
And to liberation above.

Bhuvanapathi Chakra is formed of 15 letters. The five letters (beginning with 'Ka'), the six letters (commencing with 'A') and the four letters (beginning with 'Sa') are golden-hued, red-hued and white-hued respectively.

1) Ka, Aa, E, La, Hrm (vakbhava group)
2) Ha, Sa, Ka, Ha, La, Hrm (kamaraja group)
3) Sa, Ka, La. Hrm (sakti group)

The fifteen letters are collectively known as Pancha-dasa-akashari. (This is also the Sri Vidya Chakra.) The colors mentioned indicate the colors in which the letters should be marked in the chakra.

ஓரில் இதுவே உரையும்இத் தெய்வத்தைத்
தேரிற் பிறிதில்லை யானொன்று செப்பக்கேள்
வாரித் திரிகோண மனமின்ப முத்தியுந்
தேரில் அறியுஞ் சிவகாயந் தானே. *1308*

Meditate on the (Double) Triangular Chakra

This the truth if you but see,
This the true God, none other there is;
Listen, one thing I say
This triangle is great unto the ocean;
Centre your thoughts on it
Bliss and Mukti shall yours be;
You will Siva-form be.

ஏக பராசத்தி ஈசற்காம் அங்கமே
யாகம் பராவித்தை யாமுத்தி சித்தியே

ஏகம் பராசத்தி யாகச் சிவகுரு
யோகம் பராசக்தி உண்மைஎட் டாமே. 1309

When Siva Becomes Yoga Guru, Parasakti Assumes Eight Forms*

The One Parasakti belongs to Lord as His part,
Her Form is Paravidya
She grants Mukti and Siddhi;
Though one the Parasakti is,
When Siva assumes the form of Yoga Guru,
Parasakti has forms eight indeed.

When Siva assumes the form of Yoga Guru, Parasakti assumes eight forms.

The eight Saktis are counted differently. Several delineations are as follows:
1. Isani, Purani, Arthi, Vami, Murthi, Arini, Rodayitri and Janani.
2. Jayai, vijayai, Jayanthi, Aparasithai, Siddhai, Rathai, Alambusai, Utpalai.
3. Vamai, Sreshtai, Raudri, Kali, Kalvikarni, Balavikarmi, Balapradhamani, Sarva Bhoodhathamani.
4. Arini, Janani, Rodayitri, Kali, Tatpurushi, Vamai, Aghori, Sadojathi.
Vide "Kadirvelpillai Dictionary."

எட்டா கிய சத்தி எட்டாகும் யோகத்துக்
கட்டாகு நாதாந்தத் தெட்டுங் கலப்பித்த
தொட்டாத விந்துவுந் தானற் றொழிந்தது
கிட்டா தொழிந்தது கீழான மூடர்க்கே. 1310

The Eight Saktis Reunite in Yoga

The eight Saktis belong to the eight-limbed yoga;
When Nadanta is reached,
The eight Saktis mingling one become, (Parasakti)
The Bindu that stood apart disappeared,
These experiences reach not the witless lowly ones.

When Nadanta is reached, the eight saktis, who belong to the eight-limbed yoga, reunite in yoga.

ஏதும் பலமா மியந்திரா சன்னடி
ஓதிக் குருவின் உபதேசம் உட்கொண்டு
நீதங்கும் அங்க நியாசந் தனைப்பண்ணிச்
சாதங்கெடச் செம்பிற் சட்கோணந் தானிட்டே. 1311

How to Prepare the Double-Triangle Yantra

That Yantra you establish firm
Worship at that Yantra Raja's feet,
Chant the Mantra, Guru has taught you,
Perform anga nyasas* and meditate
And on copper plate describe
The six-pointed (double) triangle
For your birth to end.

Worship at the Yantra Raja's feet and chant the mantra the Guru has taught you. Perform anga nyasas (bodily gestures) and contemplate. Inscribe the six pointed (double) triangle on a copper plate. It will end your births.

சட்கோணந் தன்னில் ஸ்ரீம்ஹ்ரீம் தானிட்டு
அக்கோண மாறின் தலையில்ரீங் காரமிட்
டெக்கோண முஞ்சூழ எழில்வட்டம் இட்டுப்பின்
மிக்கீரெட் டக்கர மம்முதன் மேவிடே. 1312

How to Place the Mantra Letters in the Yantra

On the six-angled diagram
Place Srim, Hrim letters.
Above place Rim,
Describe a circle the entire diagram to encompass
And place the letters eight times two, inclusive of Aum.

Place Srim, Hrim and above these Rim on the six-pointed diagram. Inscribe a circle to encompass the whole diagram and place the sixteen letters (the 15 plus Aum) above all.

The sixteen letters are made up of the fifteen letters referred to in Mantra 1307 plus 'Aum.'

இட்ட இதழ்கள் இடையந் தரத்திலே
அட்டஹவ் விட்டதின் மேலே உவ்விட்டுக்
கிட்ட இதழ்களின் மேலே கிரோம்சிரோம்
இட்டுவா மத்தாங் கிரோங்கென்று மேவிடே. 1313

More Mantra Letters

In the space above describe petals eight;
Place letter Ha in spaces betwixt petals;
Above Ha place letter U (Hum)
Close to petals,
Place letters Krom and Srom
And to the left of Chakra, place Am and Krom.

In the space above, place the letter 'Ha' between the eight petals. Above 'Ha' place 'U,' and 'Krom' and 'Srom' close to the petals. Place 'Aum' and 'Krom' to the left of the Chakra.

மேவிய சக்கர மீது வலத்திலே
கோவையடையவேகுரோங்சிரோங் கென்றிட்டுத்
தாவில்ரீங் காரத்தாற் சக்கரஞ் சூழ்ந்து
பூவைப் புவனா பதியைப்பின் பூசியே. 1314

With Further Mantra Letters Complete the Yantra

To the right of the Chakra thus formed,
Place Krom and Srom together
Surround the Chakra by Hrim,
Then do you worship the Sakti
That Bhuvanapathi is.

Then surround the Chakra by 'Hrim.' Thus complete the double-triangle yantra and then worship Sakti, that is Bhuvanapathi.

பூசிக்கும் போது புவனா பதிதன்னை
ஆசற் றகத்தினில் ஆவா கனம்பண்ணிப்
பேசிய பிராணப் பிரதிட்டை யதுசெய்து
தேசுற் றிடவே தியான மதுசெய்யே. 1315

Worship of Yantra

When you perform the Puja to Bhuvanapathi,
Evoke Her in your heart in purity
Surrender your life (symbolic)* at Her Feet, (Prana Prathishtai)
And in glowing meditation sit.

Thus perform puja to Her and surrender all your life at Her Feet, and remain in glowing meditation.

செய்ய திருமேனி செம்பட் டுடைதானுங்
கையிற் படையங் குசபாசத் தோடபய
வெய்யில் அணிகலன் இரத்தின மாமேனி
துய்ய முடியும் அவயவத்தில் தோற்றமே. 1316

Evoke Bhuvaneswari's Form

Her form, pure red; silky Her robe,
In Her hands are the weapons, goad and noose,
In protective pose She gestures,
On the body are dazzling jewels,
Her body shining as gem purest
And radiant Her crown
Thus adorned, She appears.

Bhuvanesvari's Form is pure red; Her robe is silky; she holds the weapons, goad and noose in Her hands; She gestures in a protective pose; She is adorned with dazzling jewels, radiant is Her crown. Thus She appears.

தோற்போர்வை நீக்கித் துதித்தடைவிற் பூசித்துப்
பாற்போ னகமந் திரத்தாற் பயின்றேத்தி
நாற்பால நாரதாயைசுவா காளன்று
சீர்பாகச் சேடத்தை மாற்றிப்பின் சேவியே. 1317

Puja Ritual

Baring the garment that covers your skin
Land Her in endearment
Offer the milk-rice oblation with mantra chanting
Turning in directions four, pronounce "Naradayai Suvaha"
Remove the food thus offered and serve it.

Bare the garment that covers your skin. Seek Her in endearing love and devotion. Offer the milk rice oblation and chant the mantra. Turn in four directions and pronounce 'naradayai suvaha.' Finally serve the food offered. This is the way to conduct the puja rituals.

சேவிப் பதன்முன்னே தேவியையுத் வாகனத்தாற்
பாவித் திதய கமலம் பதிவித்தங்
கியாவர்க்கும் எட்டா இயந்திர ராசனை
நீவைத்துச் சேமி நினைந்தது தருமே. 1318

Pray to Yantra Raja

Before thus serving
Invoke Her within
And place Her firm in the lotus of the heart,
And then pray to Yantra Raja
Who is beyond reach
And hold Him fast within you,
He will grant your wishes all.

Before serving thus, invoke Her within your heart and then pray to Yantra Raja, who is beyond reach. Hold Him firm. He will grant everything.

13. நவாக்கரி சக்கரம்
NAVAKKARI CHAKRA

நவாக்கரி சக்கர நானுரை செய்யின்
நவாக்கரி ஒன்று நவாக்கரி யாக
நவாக்கரி எண்பத் தொருவகை யாக
நவாக்கரி யக்கிலீ சௌமுத லீறே. 1319

The Nine Letters of Navakkari Become Eighty-One

I shall speak of Navakkari (Nine-Lettered) Chakra,
The One-lettered becomes the Nine-Lettered
The Nine-lettered expands into the Eighty-one lettered;
Navakkari are the nine letters from Klim to Saum.

Navakkari Chakra is of nine letters. This nine-lettered Navakkari expands into 81 letters.

As the nine mantras (Mantras 1320, 1324, 1329, 1334, 1339, 1344, 1349, 1354, 1359) repeat in nine relations, with each mantra for the beginning, the nine letters become 81 letters in all.

Klim, Srim, Hrim, Aim, Gaum, Krim, Haum, Aum, Saum.

சௌமுதல் அவ்வவொடு ஹௌவுட னாங்கிரீம்
கௌவு ளுமையுளுங் கலந்திரீம் சிரீமென்
றொவ்வில் எழுங்கிலீ மந்திர பாதமாச்
செவ்வுள் எழுந்து சிவாய நமவென்னே. 1320

The Nine Mantras:

With Klim as mantra-foot
Srim, Hrim, Aim, Gaum
Krim, Haum, Aum, and Saum
Thus in order is the mantra Navakkari
At the end chant Sivayanama,
At every rotation,
Then you attain the fruitfulness of Navakkari.

Srim, Hrim, Aim, Gaum, Krim, Haum, Aum, Saum and Klim are the nine mantras. Chant these nine mantras in order, and at the end chant Sivayanama at every rotation.

நவாக்கரி யாவது நானறி வித்தை
நவாக்கரி யுள்ளெழும் நன்மைகள் எல்லாம்
நவாக்கரி மந்திர நாவுளே ஓத
நவாக்கரி சத்தி நலந்தருந் தானே. 1321

Navakkari Mantra Confers All Blessings

Navakkari is the Chakra on which I practise,
In Navakkari arises all that is good,
When you chant the Navakkari Mantra
Deep within you,
The Navakkari Sakti, all blessings, confers.

Chant Navakkari mantra deep within you. It confers all blessings and all jnana. It dispels your karmas.

The nine Saktis enumerated are:

1. Navakkari Sakti (Mantra 1321)
2. Thiru Nayaki (Mantra 1325)
3. Thayyal Nayaki (Mantra 1329)
4. Vagesvari (Navukkarasi) (Mantra 1335)
5. Tattva Nayaki (Mantra 1340)
6. Parasakti (Mantra 1344)
7. Sadasiva Nayaki (Mantra 1350)
8. Amudesvari (Mantra 1354)
9. Minkodiyal (Minnal Nayaki) (Mantra 1359)

நலந்தரு ஞானமுங் கல்வியும் எல்லாம்
உரந்தரு வல்வினை யும்மைவிட் டோடிச்
சிரந்தரு தீவினை செய்வ தகற்றி
வரந்தரு சோதியும் வாய்ந்திடுங் காணே. 1322

Blessings of Navakkari Mantra

Jnana and knowledge all, shall yours be;
The Karmas hard will flee from you;
No more will you evil deeds perform;
All boons will be granted to you;
The vision of Divine Light, yours shall be.

No more will you indulge in evil actions. You will be granted all boons. Navakkari Mantra leads to the vision of divine light.

கண்டிடுஞ் சக்கரம் வெள்ளிபொன் செம்பிடை
கொண்டிடும் உள்ளே குறித்த வினைகளை
வென்றிடு மண்டலம் வெற்றி தருவிக்கும்
நின்றிடுஞ் சக்கரம் நினைக்கு மளவே. 1323

Earthly Gifts of Chakra

Inscribe the Chakra on silver, gold or copper,
Meditate on it,
Your actions, all, will succeed;
You shall triumph in the world
The gifts of Chakra shall be as rich
As your meditation on it is deep.

Meditate on the engraven Chakra of silver, gold or copper. You will succeed in all your endeavours.

நினைத்திடு மச்சிரி மக்கிலீ மீறா
நினைத்திடுஞ் சக்கர மாதியு மீறு
நினைத்திடு நெல்லொடு புல்லினை யுள்ளே
நினைத்திடும் அருச்சனை நேர்தரு வாளே. 1324

First Round
Chant From Srim to Klim on Chakra

Chant it with Srim to commence and Klim to end,
And thus as you continuous chant,
The first syllable becomes the last syllable
Meditate on the Chakra within
Offering rice grain and Kusa grass,
Thus perform archanas,
She shall accept your worship.

Mantras 1324 & 1325

Chant from Srim to Klim continuously. Meditate on the Chakra within, offering rice, grain and kusa grass. Perform archanas. Srim Sakti will appear before you, like a golden flower of smoky hue. Adore Her — She will fulfil all your desires.

1) The order of chanting Srim Sakti is: Srim, Hrim, Aim, Gaum, Krim, Haum, Aum, Saum, Klim.

நேர்தரு மத்திரு நாயகி யானவள்
யாதொரு வண்ணம் அறிந்திடும் பொற்பூவை
கார்தரு வண்ணங் கருதின கைவரும்
நார்தரு வண்ணம் நடத்திடு நீயே. 1325

Srim Sakti a Golden Flower of Smoky Hue

The Srim Sakti thus appears
Of Her hue, you shall learn;
She is unto a golden flower of smoky hue;
All your wishes She will fulfil
Do adore, Her Grace to receive.

"She will fulfil all your wishes". This is one of the main objects of Tantra Sadhana.

நடந்திடும் பாரினில் நன்மைகள் எல்லாங்
கடந்திடுங் காலனும் எண்ணிய நாளும்
படர்ந்திடு நாமமும் பாய்கதிர் போல
அடைந்திடு வண்ணம் அடைந்திடு நீயே. 1326

Srim Sakti Confers Name, Fame and Immortality

All things will fare well with you here below
Kala, God of Death, will bypass your days reckoned,
Your name and fame will spread like shafts of light,
Close nearer and nearer to Her
You shall reach Her.

You will find everything fair and pleasant. Srim Sakti confers name, fame and immortality.

அடைந்திடும் பொன்வெள்ளி கல்லுடன் எல்லாம்
அடைந்திடு மாதி யருளுந் திருவும்
அடைந்திடும் அண்டத் தமரர்கள் வாழ்வும்
அடைந்திடும் வண்ணம் அறிந்திடு நீயே. 1327

Srim Sakti Confers Blessings Several

Gold, silver and precious stones shall yours be,
Divine Grace and prosperity shall yours be,
The heavenly Devas' celestial life shall yours be,
That you may attain these, do meditate on Her.

You will own gold, silver and precious stones. On you will be bestowed divine grace and prosperity. You will be granted the celestial life of devas. Contemplate on Her constantly.

அறிந்திடு வார்கள் அமரர்க ளாகத்
தெரிந்திடு வானோர் தேவர்கள் தேவன்
பரிந்திடும் வானவன் · பாய்புனல் சூடி
முரிந்திடு வானை முயன்றிடு நீரே. *1328*

You Will Reach Siva by Worship of Srim Sakti

They meditate on Her,
That they immortals become,
The Lord of immortals shall bless you;
He who wears the Ganga and contains Her,
Him you persevere to reach.

They become immortals who meditate on Her. The Lord who wears the Ganga and contains Her is the sole Persevere and Protector. Persevere to reach Him.

நாபணி சக்கரம் நேர்தரு வண்ணங்கள்
பாரணி யும்ஹிரீ முன்ஸ்ரீமீறாந்
தாரணி யும்புகழ்ந் தையல்நல் லாள்தனைக்
காரணி யும்பொழிற் கண்டுகொள் ளீரே. *1329*

Second Round

Chant Hrim Commencing and Srim Ending

The letters in the Chakra you worship
With Hrim commencing and Srim ending;
Meditate on Her, the highly famed one bedecked in garlands,
You shall see Her
As the cloud-laden flower-garden.

கண்டுகொள் ளுந்தனி நாயகி தன்னையும்
மொண்டுகொ ளும்முக வசியம தாயிடும்
பண்டுகொ ளும்பர மாய பரஞ்சுடர்
நின்றுகொ ளும்நிலை பேறுடை யாளையே. *1330*

Seek Hrim Sakti Constant; Your Face will Glow

Meditate on the incomparable Sakti Hrim (Tani Nayaki)
Your face shall glow in consuming attraction
Seek Her constant,
The One who in the Param of Divine Light reposes
Seek Her, the Eternal One.

Mantras 1330 & 1331

Seek and adore the peerless and priceless Hrim Sakti — your face will glow in consuming attraction. The earthly rulers will be with you and your enemies will not flourish. Praise Her who shares the Lord's Form.

பேறுடை யாள்தன் பெருமையை எண்ணிடில்
நாடுடை யார்களும் நம்வச மாகுவர்
மாறுடை யார்களும் வாழ்வது தானிலை
கூறுடை யாளையுங் கூறுமின் நீரே. *1331*

Seek Hrim Sakti; the Rulers Will Be With You

Meditate on Her, who all blessings are;
The earthly rulers will with you be
Those against you will flourish not;
Praise Her who the Lord's Form shares.

கூறுமின் எட்டுத் திசைக்குந் தலைவியை
யாறுமின் அண்டத் தமரர்கள் வாழ்வென
மாறுமின் வையம் வரும்வழி தன்னையுந்
தேறுமின் நாயகி சேவடி சேர்ந்தே. *1332*

Reach Holv Feet of Hrim Sakti

Chant Her name (Hrim)
Who the mistress of directions eight is;
Attain the life of celestial gods
And so live;
Abandon the way that to this world leads
Reach the Holy Feet of Tani Nayaki Sakti
And there flourish.

Hrim Sakti pervades all the eight directions. Chant Her name and gain the life of celestials. Renounce everything and reach Her Holy Feet. You will know the way to reach Her. She is the Tani Nayaki Sakti.

சேவடி சேரச் செறிய இருந்தவர்
நாவடி யுள்ளே நவின்றுநின் றேத்துவர்
பூவடி யிட்டுப் பொலிய இருந்தவர்
மாவடி காணும் வகையறி வாரே. *1333*

Chant Hrim Sakti's Name in Silence With Flowers

They flourish at Her Holy Feet
Who chant Her name in silence;
Who adore Her Feet with flowers
They know the way to reach Her Feet.

ஐம்முத லாக வளர்ந்தெழு சக்கர
மைம்முத லாக அமர்ந்திரீ மீறாகும்
அம்முத லாகி யவர்க்குடை யாடனை
மைம்முத லாக வழுத்திடு நீயே. *1334*

Third Round

Chant Aim to Hrim

The Chakra expands with Aim to begin
From Aim beginning in Hrim it ends;
She who is dear unto Primal Lord
On Her, you meditate as Aim to begin.

Commence chanting with Aim and end in Hrim. Meditate on Her, who is dear to the Primal Lord.

1) The order is: Aim, Gaum, Krim, Ham, Haum, Saum, Srim, Hrim.

வழுத்திடு நாவுக் கரசிவள் தன்னைப்
பகுத்திடும் வேதமெய் யாகம மெல்லாந்
தொகுத்தொரு நாவிடை சொல்லவல் லாளை
முகத்துளும் முன்னெழக் கண்டுகொ ளீரே. 1335

Aim Sakti (Vageswari) Will Appear

The Sakti you adore is Vageswari (Goddess to Logos)
Whom all Vedas and Agamas praise
She who is within the grasp of our tongue's chant
Shall reveal Herself to you, face to face.

கண்டஇச் சக்கரம் நாவில் எழுதிடிற்
கொண்டஇம் மந்திரங் கூத்தன் குறியதா
மன்றினுள் வித்தையு மானுடர் கையதாய்
வென்றிடும் வையக மெல்லியல் மேவியே. 1336

Hold the Chakra in the Tongue; Vageswari Lends Great Powers

This Chakra that before you appears,
If you hold in your tongue,
Its Mantra assumes the Dancer's Divine Form;
If this Vidya that is in the Golden Hall
Shall come within a human's reach,
Then this man shall conquer all,
The slender Sakti, Her grace conferring.

மெல்லிய லாகிய மெய்ப்பொருள் ளாள்தனைச்
சொல்லிய லாலே தொடர்ந்தங் கிருந்திடும்
பல்லிய லாகப் பரந்தெழு நாட்பல
நல்லியல் பாலே நடந்திடுந் தானே. 1337

Future Will Worship Aim Sakti; One of Unalloyed Joy

She of the slender Form is the Truth Divine;
Chant Her mantra and constant meditate;
Your days, in diverse ways rolled on,
Will in steady prosperity ascend thereafter.

Hail and worship Aim Sakti. Your future will be one of unalloyed joy and steady prosperity.

நடந்திடு நாவினுள் நன்மைகள் எல்லாந்
தொடர்ந்திடுஞ் சொல்லொடு சொற்பொருள் தானும்
கடந்திடுங் கல்விக் கரசிவ ளாகப்
படர்ந்திடும் பாரிற் பகையில்லை தானே. 1338

You Will Master All Learning

Chant Aim mantra unceasing
All blessings shall follow;
You shall gain the understanding
That is beyond words and meaning of words;
With the blessing of Her, who is Queen of learning,
You shall a master of all Learning be;
No more enemies for you, here below.

Chant this mantra ceaselessly. Manifold blessings will be conferred on you. With the Grace and blessings of Her, who is the Queen of Learning, you will master all learning. No more will you have enemies. No more malicious occurences will be directed against you.

பகையில்லை கௌமுத லையது வீறா
நகையில்லை சக்கர நன்றறி வார்க்கு
மிகையில்லை சொல்லிய பல்லுரு வெல்லாம்
வகையில்லை யாக வணங்கிடுந் தானே. 1339

Chant Gaum to Aim

No more enemies
For those who chant from Gaum to Aim
No more malicious glees against you
For those who meditate the Vine (Gaum) on the Chakra,
All creation shall bow to them
With exception none,
No exaggeration this is.

Mantras 1339 & 1340

Chant Gaum to Aim. All creation will bow before you. Adore Gaum Sakti and be blessed. You will be liberated from all mean desires and passions — lust, anger, ignorance, etc.

வணங்கிடுந் தத்துவ நாயகி தன்னை
நலங்கிடு நல்லுயி ரானவை யெல்லாங்
கலங்கிடுங் காம வெகுளி மயக்கந்
துலங்கிடுஞ் சொல்லிய சூழ்வினை தானே. 1340

Adore Gaum Sakti and Be Blessed

Adore Sakti who over all Tattvas rule,
All good lives will bend before you;
Lust, anger and ignorance with all in terror flee
Your actions all will shining be.

தானே கழறித் தணியவும் வல்லனாய்த்
தானே நினைத்தவை சொல்லவும் வல்லனாய்த்
தானே தனிநடங் கண்டவள் தன்னையுந்
தானே வணங்கித் தலைவனு மாமே. 1341

Supreme Powers Conferred on the Gaum Sakti Sadhaka

He alone speaks,
And what he speaks is the final word;
He alone can speak
What he thinks is the right;
He who meditates on Her,
Who witnesses the Dance of Siva,
Is verily the Master of all around.

What you speak will be the final word and the right word. Verily, you will become the master of all around. Meditate on Her and witness the Dance of Siva.

ஆமே யனைத்துயி ராகிய அம்மையுந்
தாமே சகலமும் ஈன்றஅத் தையலும்
ஆமே யவளடி போற்றி வணங்கிடிற்
போமே வினைகளும் புண்ணிய னாகுமே. 1342

Gaum Sakti is Mother of All

She is the Mother that all life is
She is the Mother that all life created
Worship at Her Feet, and all things will yours be;
Your Karmas will vanish, you shall holy become.

Mantras 1342 & 1343

Gaum Sakti is the Mother of all. Worship at Her Feet — all things will become yours. Rid of karmas, you will become holy. Remain close to Her.

புண்ணிய னாகிப் பொருந்தி உலகெங்கும்
கண்ணிய னாகிக் கலந்தங் கிருந்திடுங்
தண்ணிய னாகித் தரணி முழுதுக்கும்
அண்ணிய னாகி அமர்ந்திருந்தானே. 1343

Remain Close to Gaum Sakti

Holy you shall remain,
Far and wide in this world;
Honoured you shall there walk,
Benevolent you shall be to one and all,
Close to Her, you shall there tarry.

தானது கம்மிறீக் கௌவது ஈறாம்
நானது சக்கர நன்றறி வார்க்கெலாம்
கானது கன்னி கலந்த பராசக்தி
கேளது வையங் கிளரொளி யானதே. 1344

Fifth Round
Chant Krim to Gaum

From Krim to Gaum
That the Chakra, I know of;
Those who meditate deep on it
Will become dear unto that Parasakti,
The Virgin of the sylvan glades;
And they shall shine high in this world.

Mantras 1344 & 1345

They who contemplate on the Chakra from Krim to Gaum will become dear to Parasakti, the Virgin of the sylvan glades. She takes them to her heavenly abode. There, they will revel and rejoice in joy, their thoughts filled with divine vision. Sunny fortune will smile at them and they will enjoy wealth and prosperity forever.

ஒளிக்கும் பராசக்தி உள்ளே அமரிற்
களிக்கும்இச் சிந்தையிற் காரணங் காட்டித்
தெளிக்கும் மழையுடன் செல்வமுண் டாக்கும்
அளிக்கும் இவளை அறிந்துகொள் வார்க்கே. 1345

Blessings of Prosperity by Krim sakti (Para sakti)

When the luminous Para sakti
Within you takes Her abode,
Your heart dances in joy;
Clear vision fills your thoughts;
Rains copious fall,
Wealth and prosperity smile
Thus shall it be for those who meditate on Her.

அறிந்திடுஞ் சக்கரம் அருச்சனை யோடே
எறிந்திடும் வையத் திடரவை காணின்
மறிந்திடு மன்னனும் வந்தனை செய்யும்
பொறிந்திடுஞ் சிந்தை புகையில்லை தானே. 1346

Kings Shall Respect the Sadhaka of Krim Sakti

Meditate on the Chakra, worship performing
Your obstacles, all, overcome will be;
Kings shall go to you and pay their respect
Your thoughts will glow, no sorrows emanating.

Meditate on the Chakra and perform worship: You will overcome all your obstacles. Royalty will respect the sadhaka of Krim Sakti.

புகையில்லை சொல்லிய பொன்னொளி யுண்டாங்
குகையில்லை கொல்வ திலாமையி னாலே
வகையில்லை வாழ்கின்ற மன்னுயிர்க் கெல்லாஞ்
சிகையில்லை சக்கரஞ் சேர்ந்தவர் தாமே. 1347

The Sadhaka Shines Bright

Sorrow's fumes will not be;
A golden light will suffuse their body;
Hell none will be, as killing there is none,
Nothing else the refuge for all life on earth,
Nothing else is their crown of glory
For those who meditate on Krim
In Chakra Navakkari.

They who meditate on Krim Sakti in the Chakra Navakkari will find Her their sole refuge and crown of glory. They will rise above sorrows and death. Everything the sadhaka touches will shine bright.

சேர்ந்தவர் என்றுந் திசையொளி யானவர்
காய்ந்தெழு மேல்வினை காணகி லாதவர்
பாய்ந்தெழும் உள்ளொளி பாரிற் பரந்தது
மாய்ந்தது காரிருள் மாறொளி தானே. 1348

Ignorance Dies by Worship of Krim Sakti

Those who meditate on Her
Glow in fame in directions all;
They experience not the evils of searing Karma;
Their inner light spreads far and wide;
Their egoity perished,
The light of differentiated knowledge
Forever snuffed out.

Worship Krim Sakti — you will achieve fame in all directions for dispelling ignorance and egoity.

ஒளியது ஹௌமுன் கிரீமது ஈறாங்
களியது சக்கரங் கண்டறி வார்க்குத்

தெளிவது ஞானமுஞ் சிந்தையுந் தேறப்
பணிவது பஞ்சாக் கரமது வாமே. 1349

Sixth Round

Chant From Hau(m) to Krim

The Chakra with mantras from Hau(m) to Krim is all light,
Happiness it is to those who meditate on it,
Pure Jnana and clear vision fills their thoughts
Meditating on it is meditating on Panchakshara.

ஆமே சதாசிவ நாயகி யானவள்
ஆமே அதோமுகத் துள்ளறி வானவள்
ஆமே சுவையொளி யூறோசை கண்டவள்
ஆமே யனைத்துயிர் தன்னுளு மாமே. 1350

Sadasiva Sakti (Haum) Immanent in All

She (Haum) is the Sadasiva Sakti
She is the light behind the Adho-mukha
(Downward looking face of the Lord)
She is the One emanating, taste, sight, feel, sound and smell;
She that is immanent in lives all.

Siva Sakti (Haum) is the light behind the Adho-mukha (Downward-looking face of the Lord). She is maya, immanent in all earth, water, fire, wind and sky.

Regarding Adho-Mukha, see Introduction. "She is the light behind Adho-Mukha" that would be "Adho-Mukhi", corresponding, on this line of thought, to "Avalokitesvari" of Mahayana Buddhism.

தன்னுளு மாகித் தரணி முழுதுங்கொண்
டென்னுளு மாகி இடம்பெற நின்றவள்
மண்ணுளும் நீரனல் காலுளும் வானுளுங்
கண்ணுளும் மெய்யுளுங் காணலு மாமே. 1351

Immanence of (Haum) Sakti Further Elaborated

Within Herself She is,
Without, in all World She is,
Within me She is,
Filling it entire
Within earth, water, fire, wind and sky She is;
Within the eye, within the body too
May you behold Her.

காணலு மாகுங் கலந்துயிர் செய்வன
காணலு மாகுங் கருத்து ளிருந்திடிற்
காணலு மாகுங் கலந்து வழிசெயக்
காணலு மாகுங் கருத்துற நில்லே. 1352

Well May We See Haum Sakti

Well may you see all that She does,
Immanent in our lives;
Well may you see Her,
If in your thoughts you hold Her;
Well may you see Her
If in the depths of your heart you make way for Her;
Stand firm,
Seeking Her in your thoughts constantly.

Hold Her in your thoughts and you will behold Her with your physical eyes. Make way for Her in the depths of your heart; stand firm, and constantly seek Her.

நின்றிடும் ஏழு புவனமும் ஒன்றாகக்
கண்டிடும் உள்ளங் கலந்தெங்குந் தானாகக்
கொண்டிடும் வையங் குணம்பல தன்னையும்
விண்டிடும் வல்வினை மெய்ப்பொரு ளாகுமே. 1353

Haum Sakti's Pervasiveness

She stands pervading the seven worlds at once;
She stands immanent in all hearts everywhere;
She stands bearing all good things of the world
She stands as the Divine Truth
That dispells Karmas hard.

மெய்ப்பொரு ளௌமுதல் ஹௌவது ஈறாக்
கைப்பொரு ளாகக் கலந்தெழு சக்கரந்
தற்பொரு ளாகச் சமைந்தமு தேஸ்வரி
நற்பொரு ளாக நடுவிருந் தாளே. 1354

Seventh Round

Chant Au(m) to Hau(m)

Divine Truth it is,
The Chakra from Au(m) to Hau(m) runs,
She Aum is the meaning within
Of that Chakra,
She is Amudeswari, the Self-created
As good riches,
She in Chakra's midst stood.

Aum Sakti is the Divine Truth that runs through the Chakra commencing with Aum and ending with Haum. She is the central meaning of that Chakra. She is Amudesvari that stands in the centre of the Chakra as good riches.

தாளதி னுள்ளே சமைந்தமு தேஸ்வரி
காலது கொண்டு கலந்துற வீசிடில்
நாளது நாளும் புதுமைகள் கண்டபின்
கேளது காயமுங் கேடில்லை காணுமே. 1355

Meditate on Amudheswari (Aum Sakti)

That Amudheswari do hold in your heart
Rouse Kundalini with your breath coursing upward
Daily will you vision things newer and newer;
Listen to this, your body perishes never.

கேடில்லை காணுங் கிளரொளி கண்டபின்
நாடில்லை காணும் நாண்முத லற்றபின்
மாடில்லை காணும் வரும்வழி கண்டபின்
காடில்லை காணுங் கருத்துற் றிடத்துக்கே. 1356

Consciousness of Time and Space Lost

Having the rising Light in the Chakra visioned
No more the harm that comes to you;
Having lost the sense of Time's beginning,
No more the spatial consciousness will be;
Having seen the Way of Her Grace,
No more the differences in power and pelf will be
Having reached the Land of Goal
No more the forest of sorrow will be.

உற்றிட மெல்லாம் உலப்பில்பா ழாக்கிக்
கற்றிட மெல்லாங் கடுவெளி யானது
மற்றிட மில்லை வழியில்லை தானில்லை
சற்றிட மில்லை சலிப்பற நின்றிடே. 1357

Transcendental State of Consciousness of Sadhaka in Aum Sakti

All the space you sojourn becomes desolate nothingness
All the space you have learned to be
Becomes an interminable Void;
None other place there is;
Not a wee-bit space there is;
Stand unfaltering, where you are,
Firm in Aum Sakti.

The Sadhaka engaged in Aum Sakti worship attains the transcendental state. All space turns into the interminable Space.

நின்றிடும் ஏழ்கடல் ஏழ்புவி எல்லாம்
நின்றிடும் உள்ளம் நினைத்தவை தானொக்கும்
நின்றிடுஞ் சத்தி நிலைபெறக் கண்டிட
நின்றிடும் மேலை விளக்கொளி தானே. 1358

Aum Sakti Appears as Light

In the seven seas and seven worlds will your fame be,
All your wishes granted will be,
If your heart in constancy stands,
When you see Sakti in you firm stands
She appears as the Light Radiant High.

Stand unfaltering and constant in Aum Sakti. If you incessantly seek and worship Aum Sakti, She appears as the Resplendent Light and fulfills all your wishes and desires.

விளக்கொளி ஸௌமுத லௌவது ஈறா
விளக்கொளிச் சக்கரம் மெய்ப்பொரு ளாகும்
விளக்கொளி யாகிய மின்கொடி யாளை
விளக்கொளி யாக விளங்கிடு நீயே. 1359

Eighth Round

Chant From Saum to Aum

The Chakra that extends
From Sau(m) to Au(m) is light that illumines,
The Chakra luminous is the Truth Eternal;
The Sakti that is like a shaft of lightning,
Do you meditate and luminous be.

The Saum to Aum Chakra is illuminating light. That luminosity in the Chakra is the eternal truth. Meditate on the Sakti who is like a shaft of light and become luminous.

விளங்கிடு மேல்வரு மெய்ப்பொருள் சொல்லின்
விளங்கிடு மெல்லிய லானது வாகும்
விளங்கிடு மெய்ந்நின்ற ஞானப் பொருளை
விளங்கிடு வார்கள் விளங்கினர் தானே. 1360

Saum Sakti is Supreme Jnana

To speak of the Eternal truth
That high above beams,
That verily is Sakti of Slender Form;
Do seek Light that is Truth of Jnana;
They who seek the Light
Will themselves like Light be.

Saum Sakti of slender form is the supreme jnana and the eternal truth.

தானே வெளியென எங்கும் நிறைந்தவள்
தானே பரம வெளியது வானவள்
தானே சகலமு மாக்கி அழித்தவள்
தானே யனைத்துள அண்ட சகலமே. 1361

Saum Sakti is All

She is spaces all, She filled spaces all;
She is the space beyond spaces
She created all, She preserved all,
She is universe all, and lives all.

Saum Sakti is space and beyond space. She created all, preserved all. She is the entire universe and all life.

அண்டத்தி னுள்ளே அளப்பரி தானவள்
பிண்டத்தி னுள்ளே பெருவெளி கண்டவள்
குண்டத்தி னுள்ளே குணம்பல காணினுங்
கண்டத்தில் நின்ற கலப்பறி யார்களே. 1362

She is in the Throat Centre Too

Immeasurable She is, in universe immense
In the body corporeal She vast spaces filled;
Well may you see many good things in Muladhara,
Yet may you not know that She stands
In the very centre of your throat (Visuddha).

You may well see many good things in the sacrificial pit. Yet, you may not know that She is in the very centre of your visuddhi chakra.

கலப்பறி யார்கடல் சூழுல கெல்லாம்
உலப்பறி யாருட லோடுயிர் தன்னைச்
சிலப்பறி யார்சில தேவரை நாடித்
தலைப்பறி யாகச் சமைந்தவர் தானே. 1363

The Ignorant Know Not Saum Sakti's Greatness

They know not Her Pervasiveness in the sea-girt world,
They know not Her immanence in body and life,
They know not Her Anklet, seeking other gods;
Thus are they fated to be.

They do not know Her pervasiveness and immanence in the sea-girt world, in body and life. They are ignorant of Saum Sakti's greatness.

தானே எழுந்தஅச் சக்கரஞ் சொல்லிடின்
மானே மதிவரை பத்திட்டு வைத்தபின்
தேனே யிரேகை திகைப்புற ஒன்பதில்
தானே கலந்த வரையெண்பத் தொன்றுமே. 1364

How to Form the 81-Squared Navakkari Chakra

To speak of that Chakra, of its volition arose,
Mark lines ten (horizontal and vertical)
And thus form nine squares on each line,
In all form squares eighty and one.

Mantras 1364 & 1365

Mark ten horizontal and vertical lines and thus form nine squares on each line. In all they form 81 squares. Forming the Chakra thus, color the outer circle in a golden shade, the squares in red and the mantra letters in green.

ஒன்றிய சக்கரம் ஓதிடும் வேளையில்
வென்றிகொள் மேனிமதிவட்டம் பொன்மையாங்
கன்றிய ரேகை கலந்திடுஞ் செம்மையில்
என்றிய லம்மை எழுத்தவை பச்சையே. 1365

Coloring the Chakra

As thou form the Chakra thus,
Colour the outer circle in hues of gold,
Mark the squares red
And the mantra letters green.

ஏய்ந்த மரவுரி தன்னில் எழுதிய
வாய்ந்தஇப் பெண்ணெண்பத் தொன்றில் நிரைத்தபின்
காய்ந்தவி நெய்யுட் கலந்துடன் ஓமமு
மாந்தலத் தாமுயி ராகுதி பண்ணுமே. 1366

Worship of the Chakra

Inscribe the Sakti's letters on bark of tree
Fill Sakti in chambers eighty and one;
Offer hot ghee and rice
Perform homa,
And Prana Oblations.

Inscribe the Sakti's letters on the bark of a tree. Fill Sakti in the 81 chambers. Offer hot ghee and rice and thus perform homa and prana oblations.

பண்ணிய பொன்னைப் பரப்பற நீபிடி
எண்ணிய நாட்களில் இன்பமும் எய்திடும்
நண்ணிய நாமமும் நான்முகன் ஒத்தபின்
துண்ணென நேயநற் சேர்க்கலு மாமே. 1367

Effect of the Chakra Worship

Hold to the Sakti (Sri) Chakra in calmness;
As you meditate on it day after day
You shall in felicity be;
And as your name and fame like Brahma's soar,
One with Siva you in loved union be.

Contemplate on the Sakti Chakra in calmness incessantly day by day. You will then abide in felicity and serene tranquillity. As your name and fame will soar upward like Brahma's, you will stand in union with Siva.

ஆகின்ற' சந்தனங் குங்குமங் கத்தூரி
போகின்ற சாந்து சவாது புழுகுநெய்
ஆகின்ற கற்பூர மாகோ சன்நீருஞ்
சேர்கின்ற ஒன்பதுஞ் சேரநீ வைத்திடே. 1368

Smear Chakra With Nine Perfumes

Sandal, saffron flower, musk of deer
Fragrant paste, civet scent and ghee
Camphor, orpiment, and scented water
These nine you blend on the Chakra smear.

Smear the Chakra with nine perfumes — sandal, saffron flower, deer musk, fragrant paste, civet scent, ghee, camphor, orpiment and scented water.

வைத்திடும் பொன்னுடன் மாதவ நோக்கிடிற்
கைச்சிறு கொங்கை கலந்தெழு கன்னியைத்
தச்சிது வாகச் சமைந்தஇம் மந்திரம்
அர்ச்சனை யாயிரம் ஆயிரஞ் சிந்தியே. 1369

Chant Mantra a Thousand Thousand Times

To speak of the Worship
That you should perform at Sri Chakra;
That holds the Virgin Sakti as its nodal pull
Worship the mantra with incantations a thousand thousand times.
Thus do you on it continuous meditate.

Sri Chakra holds the Virgin Sakti as its nodal pull. Chant the mantra 1 million times and thus meditate constantly.

சிந்தையி னுள்ளே திகழ்தரு சோதியாய்
எந்தை கரங்கள் இருமூன்றும் உள்ளது
பந்தமா சூலம் படைபாசம் வில்லம்பு
முந்தை கிலீமெழ முன்னிருந் தாளே. 1370

Ninth Round

Chant Klim to Begin; Sakti Appears

She beams as divine light in your thoughts
She appears with hands six
She holds in them weapons six —
The torch, the trident, the goad, the noose, bow, and arrow
Chant the Mantra with Klim to begin,
She before you appears.

இருந்தனர் சத்திகள் அறுபத்து நால்வர்
இருந்தனர் கன்னிகள் எண்வகை எண்மர்
இருந்தனர் சூழ எதிர்சக் கரத்தே
இருந்த கரமிரு வில்லம்பு கொண்டே. 1371

Klim Sakti's Appearance in Chakra

The Saktis sixty-four surrounding,
The Virgins eight were there too,
With bow and arrow in their hands two
They seated were in the Chakra opposite.

Sakti appears in the Chakra surrounded by 64 minor saktis, including the eight virgins with bows and arrows in each of their two hands.

கொண்ட கனகங் குழைமுடி யாடையாய்க்
கண்டஇம் முத்தங் கனல்திரு மேனியாய்ப்
பண்டமர் சோதிப் படரித ழானவள்
உண்டங் கொருத்தி உணரவல் லாருக்கே. 1372

Form of Klim Sakti in the Chakra

Bedecked in jewels of gold,
With ear-rings, crown, and apparel fine,
Like the choicest peral, and of crimson-hued form,
And on lotus petals seated,
There She is,
For those who on the Chakra meditate.

Sakti is seated on lotus petals, bedecked in jewels of gold, wearing earrings and crown, and is dressed in fine apparel worked with the choicest pearls.

உணர்ந்திருந் துள்ளே ஒருத்தியை நோக்கிற்
கலந்திருந் தெங்குங் கருணை பொழியும்
மணந்தெழும் ஓசை யொளியது காணுந்
தணந்தெழு சக்கரந் தான்வரு வாளே. 1373

Sound and Light Appear in the Chakra

If with feeling intense you meditate on Her,
She pervading all, showers Her Grace;
You shall perceive enveloping sound (Nada) and light (Bindu);
From within the Chakras She rises
And blesses you.

தருவழி யாகிய தத்துவ ஞானங்
குருவழி யாகுங் குணங்களுள் நின்று
கருவழி யாகுங் கணக்கை யறுத்துப்
பெருவழி யாக்கும் பேரொளி தானே. 1374

Klim Sakti Leads You to the Great Way

She is the Light Divine
That leads you to the Way Great;
She grants you Tattva Jnana
Through the Way shown by the Guru
Having sundered your birth's reckoning.

பேரொளி யாய பெரிய பெருஞ்சுடர்
சீரொளி யாகித் திகழ்தரு நாயகி
காரொளி யாகிய கன்னிகை பொன்னிறம்
பாரொளி யாகிப் பரந்துநின் றாளே. 1375

Klim Sakti; She is the Light of the World

The Luminous One, the dazzling Light,
In soft radiance, Sakti emits Her brilliance divine;
She is of the dark-golden hue of clouds,
She stood as light through world entire.

பரந்த கரம்இரு பங்கயம் ஏந்திக்
குவிந்த கரமிரு கொய்தளிர்ப் பாணி
பரிந்தருள் கொங்கைகண் முத்தார் பவளம்
இருந்தநல் லாடை மணிபொதிந் தன்றே. 1376

Klim Sakti's Form

The spreading hands two held lotus blooms,
The blessing hands two in tender grace gestured,
The lovely breasts two were in pearl and coral decked
The comely garments in pure gems interlaced.

மணிமுடி பாதஞ் சிலம்பணி மங்கை
அணிபவ ளன்றி யருளில்லை யாகுந்
தணிபவர் நெஞ்சினுள் தன்னரு ளாகிப்
பணிபவர்க் கன்றோ பரகதி யாமே. 1377

Klim Sakti Alone Grants Grace

On the head She wears the jewelled crown,
At the feet the lovely anklets,
Thus does She adorn Herself;
Without Her is Grace none;
In the hearts of those in meekness pray
She appears as Divine Grace,
She grants Liberation
To those in devotion seek Her.

பரந்திருந் துள்ளே அறுபது சத்தி
கரந்தன கன்னிகள் அப்படி சூழ
மலர்ந்திரு கையின் மலரவை ஏந்தச்
சிறந்தவர் ஏத்துஞ் சிறீம்தன மாமே. 1378

Srim Sakti

Srim Sakti is Surrounded by Sixty Saktis.

The Saktis sixty are seated around Her,
The Virgins eight in concealment around Her,
She bears lotus blossoms in hands both;
The Holy Ones in devotion meditate on Her;
—She the treasure of Mantra Srim.

தனமது வாகிய தையலை நேக்கி
மனமது வோடி மரிக்கிலோ ராண்டிற்
கனமவை யற்றுக் கருதிய நெஞ்சந்
தினகர னாரிட செய்திய தாமே. 1379

Effect of One Year Meditation on Srim in the Chakra

If on Srim Sakti the treasure of Chakra
You intensely meditate a year,
The burden of your worldly cares drops,
Your thoughts soar high,
Your heart, Sun's brilliance attains,
—This the message of Chakra True.

If you contemplate on Srim Sakti, the burden of worldly cares drops. Then your thoughts soar high and the heart attains the brilliance of the sun. This is the message of this Chakra. Here, the number of letters becomes 52

ஆகின்ற மூலத் தெழுந்த முழுமலர்
போகின்ற பேரொளி யாய மலரதாய்ப்
போகின்ற பூரண மாக நிறைந்தபின்
சேர்கின்ற செந்தழல் மண்டல மானதே. 1380

Srim Sakti is in Muladhara

The full flower that in Muladhara arose
Blossoms into Light Effulgent
Pervading adharas all
The Red Flame reached the Sphere of Fire.

Srim is the flower that arises in muladhara and blossoms into effulgent light and pervades all the adharas.

ஆகின்ற மண்டலத் துள்ளே அமர்ந்தவள்
ஆகின்ற ஐம்பத் தறுவகை யானவள்
ஆகின்ற ஐம்பத் தறுசத்தி நேர்தரு
ஆகின்ற ஐம்பத் தறுவகை சூழவே. 1381

Hrim Sakti is Surrounded by Fifty-Six Saktis

There in the Sphere of Fire She sat;
There She appears in forms fifty and six;
There She is visioned by Saktis fifty and six;
There She is by Saktis fifty and six surrounded.

Hrim Sakti surrounded by 56 minor saktis appears in the sphere of fire (svadhistana).

சூழ்ந்தெழு சோதி சுடர்முடி பாதமாய்
ஆங்கணி முத்தம் அழகிய மேனியுந்
தாங்கிய கையவை தார்கிளி ஞானமாய்
ஏந்து கரங்கள் எடுத்தமர் பாசமே. 1382

Hrim Sakti's Form

As One Light Effulgent She is,
From Jewelled Crown to Feet
Lustrous like pearls She wears Her Form,
The two pendant hands hold parrot and Jnana Mudra
The two upraised hands bear noose and goad.

பாசம தாகிய வேரை யறுத்திட்டு
நேசம தாக நினைத்திரு மும்முளே
நாசம தெல்லாம் நடந்திடும் ஐயாண்டிற்
காசினி மேலமர் கண்ணுத லாகுமே. 1383

Effect of Five Years Chanting Hrim Sakti

Sever your Pasa's roots,
Adore Her in your heart's recesses,
All evil will leave you;
In five years you shall be like Siva.

கண்ணுடை நாயகி தன்னரு ளாம்வழி
பண்ணுறு நாதம் பகையற நின்றிடில்
விண்ணமர் சோதி விளங்க ஹிரீங்கார
மண்ணுடை நாயகி மண்டல மாகுமே. 1384

Heavenly Light Arises From Hrim in Chakra

If on Chakra of the merciful Sakti you meditate,
And if your chant in order done,
The Heavenly light will appear,
In that Chakra of the lordly Sakti
Where Mantra Hrim invoked is.

மண்டலத் துள்ளே மலர்ந்தெழு தீபத்தைக்
கண்டகத் துள்ளே கருதி யிருந்திடும்
விண்டகத் துள்ளே விளங்கி வருதலால்
தண்டகத் துள்ளவை தாங்கலு மாமே. 1385

Light Within Will Appear

The light that arises in the Chakra,
Vision it and on it meditate;
The Sakti as the light within will appear;
Verily is She the support of Sushumna,
Adharas and the rest within.

தாங்கிய நாபித் தடமலர் மண்டலத்
தோங்கி எழுங்கலைக் குள்ளுணர் வானவள்
ஏங்க வரும்பிறப் பெண்ணி யறுத்திட
வாங்கிய நாதம் வலியுட னாகுமே. 1386

Aim Sakti is Seated in Navel Centre

In the lotus sphere of navel centre
In the Kalas that rise
Immanent She is, the Aim Sakti;
Meditate,
And there in Nada you firm shall be
Your birth-cycle its end shall see.

In the sphere of the navel centre (manipuraka) Aim Sakti abides immanent and all-pervasive.

நாவுக்கு நாயகி நன்மணி பூணாரம்
பூவுக்கு நாயகி பொன்முடி யாடையாம்
பாவுக்கு நாயகி பாலொத்த வண்ணத்தள்
ஆவுக்கு நாயகி அங்கமர்ந் தாளே. 1387

Aim Sakti is Vageswari

She is Queen of Speech,
She is decked in garland of gems pure,
She is Queen of Songs,
She is milk-hued,

She is Queen of Jiva,
There was She seated in Navel Centre.

அன்றிரு கையில் அளந்த பொருள்முறை
இன்றிரு கையில் எடுத்தவெண் குண்டிகை
மன்றது காணும் வழியது வாகவே
கண்டங் கிருந்தவர் காரணி காணுமே. *1388*

Aim Sakti's Form

Then, of yore, with hands two
She Dharma measured,
Now for nonce She holds
The pitcher white of hermit,
They who reach Her
By the Way to Hall of Dance,
Verily behold
The Primal Cause of all.

காரணி சத்திகள் ஐம்பத் திரண்டெனக்
காரணி கன்னிகள் ஐம்பத் திருவராய்க்
காரணி சக்கரத் துள்ளே கரந்தெங்குங்
காரணி தன்னரு ளாகிநின் றாளே. *1389*

Aim Sakti is Surrounded by Fifty-Two Saktis

The Causal Saktis are fifty and two,
The Causal Virgins are they
She the Primal Causal Sakti of all,
In the Chakra immanent stood;
She the Primal Cause as Grace stood.

நின்றஇச் சத்தி நிலைபெற நின்றிடிற்
கண்டஇவ் வன்னி கலந்திடும் ஓராண்டிற்
கொண்ட விரதநீர் குன்றாமல் நின்றிடின்
மன்றினி லாடு மணியது காணுமே. *1390*

Effect of Aim Sakti Worship for One Year

If firm-fixed,
This Sakti in your thoughts stands;
Within a year's span,
This Flame shall in you merge;
If steadfast in devotion you stand,
You shall vision the Ruby
That dances in the Hall of Spaces Vast.

Worship Aim Sakti with intense devotion steadfastness. Then you will vision the Ruby I that dances in the divine hall of vast spaces.

கண்டஇச் சத்தி இருதய பங்கயங்
கொண்டஇத் தத்துவ நாயகி யானவள்
பண்டையவ் வாயுப் பகையை யறுத்திட
இன்றென் மனத்துள் இனிதிருந் தாளே. *1391*

Gaum (Tattva Nayaki) Sakti is Seated in Heart Centre

That Sakti you visioned in Heart's lotus
This (Gaum) the Queen of Tattvas all,
This day, She, in my thoughts, is sweet seated
That my life's enemy—Death—destroyed be.

Gaum (Tattva Nayaki) Sakti is seated in the heart centre—anahatha. She resides in the thought of Her devotees, dispelling death, that is life's enemy.

இருந்தவிச் சத்தி இருநாலு கையிற்
பரந்தஇப் பூங்கிளி பாச மழுவாள்
கரந்திடு கேடகம் வில்லம்பு கொண்டங்
குரந்தங் கிருந்தவள் கூத்துகந் தாளே. *1392*

Gaum Sakti's Form

The Sakti that was in my mind seated thus
Appeared with hands eight;
Holding flower, parrot, noose, battle-axe and sword;
The shield, bow and the arrow too—
She danced in rapture divine.

உகந்தனள் பொன்முடி முத்தார மாகப்
பரந்த பவளமும் பட்டாடை சாத்தி
மலர்ந்தெழு கொங்கை மணிக்கச் சணிந்து
தழைந்தங் கிருந்தவள் தான்பச்சை யாமே. *1393*

How Gaum Sakti was Attired

In rapture She stood
Wearing crown of gold,
Garland of pearls and corals,
Dressed in richly silks,
The rising breasts in gem-laid corset contained,
There She was in glory,
Her Form green-hued.

பச்சை இவளுக்குப் பாங்கிமார் ஆறெட்டு
கொச்சையார் எண்மர்கள் கூடி வருதலாற்
கச்சணி கொங்கைகள் கையிரு காப்பதாய்
எச்ச விடைச்சி இனிதிருந் தாளே. *1394*

Gaum Sakti is Surrounded by Forty-Eight Saktis and Eight Vestal Virgins

This green-hued Mother has serving companions six times eight,
And vestal virgins eight that take up her train,
Her breasts are in corset contained,
Her hands pendant in blessing gesture,
Thus the Sweet One appears,
She of waist slender.

Gaum Sakti is surrounded by 48 minor saktis and eight vestal virgins.
Here, the letters are given as 48 (or 56) in number.

தாளதி னுள்ளே தாங்கிய சோதியைக்
காலது வாகக் கலந்து 'கம் ஜம்' என்று
மாலது வாக வழிபாடு செய்துநீ
பாலது போலப் பரந்தெழு விண்ணிலே. *1395*

Perform Kundalini Yoga Before Gaum Sakti

The Kundalini Fire in Muladhara resides;
Course your breath to unite in Her in Anahatha
And in devotion true do Japa of Gaum Jam and the adhara above ascend,
You shall into the heaven within rise,
That is milky white pure (Solar Sphere).

Course the kundalini fire that rises in the muladhara to unite in Her in anahatha with true devotion. Then you shall rise into the heaven within that is pure milky white.

விண்ணமர் நாபி இருதய மாங்கிடைக்
கண்ணமர் கூபங் கலந்து வருதலாற்
பண்ணமர்ந் தாதித்த மண்டல மானது
தண்ணமர் கூபந் தழைத்தது காணுமே. *1396*

Krim Sakti is in Sun's Sphere

In the mystic sphere
Between centres, navel and heart, Is the Koopa (Krim) Sakti seated;
There in the fiery Sphere of Sun;
Unto the cool waters of a well was She.

In the mystic sphere between the navel and heart centres is seated Koopa (Krim) Sakti in the 'sun' sphere.

கூபத்துச் சத்தி குளிர்முகம் பத்துள
தாபத்துச் சத்தி தயங்கி வருதலால்
ஆபத்துக் கைகள் அடைந்தன நாலைந்து
பாசம் அறுக்கப் பரந்தன சூலமே. *1397*

Krim Sakti's Form

The Sakti thus seated
Has benignant faces ten;
There in Sun's Sphere She gently appears;
She assumes protecting hands four times five,
And to sunder Pasa holds the Trident.

The Sakti thus seated has twin benignant faces. She has 20 protective hands, and with the trident She sunders pasas.

சூலந்தண் டொள்வாள் சுடர்பறை ஞானமாய்
வேலம்பு தமருக மாகிளி விற்கொண்டு
காலம்பூப் பாசம் மழுகத்தி கைக்கொண்டு
கோலஞ்சேர் சங்கு குவிந்தகை எண்ணதே. *1398*

Weapons of Krim Sakti

The trident, mace, fiery sword, shining drum
The gleaming spear that is Jnana,
The arrow, kettle-drum, parrot, the bow, these on one side are;
The bugle, flower, noose, battle-axe, knife, conch,
The pendant hands in protecting gesture on the other side are!
—These meditate on.

எண்ணமர் சத்திகள் நாற்பத்து நாலுடன்
எண்ணமர் சத்திகள் நாற்பத்து நால்வராம்
எண்ணிய பூவித முள்ளே யிருந்தவள்
எண்ணிய எண்ணங் கடந்துநின் றாளே. *1399*

She is Surrounded by Forty-Four Saktis

Four and Forty are Saktis surrounding Her
Four and Forty Saktis that meditate on Her
She is seated within the lotus
She that transcends thoughts all.

கடந்தவள் பொன்முடி மாணிக்கத் தோடு
தொடர்ந்தணி முத்து பவளங்கச் சாகப்
படர்ந்தல்குற் பட்டாடை பாதச் சிலம்பு
மடந்தை சிறியவள் வந்துநின் றாளே. *1400*

Krim Sakti as a Girl

She, that transcended thought all,
Wears the diadem of gold,
Her corset is of gems, pearls and corals made,
Her silken dress spreads below Her slender waist
Her Feet hold the anklets
Thus, adorned, as a girl
She stood before me.

Mantras 1400 & 1401

Krim Sakti appears as a girl. With Her appearance arises anima and the rest of the occult powers. The pasas are severed and the unique light of jnana dawns in those who realise Her.

நின்றஇச் சத்தி நிரந்தர மாகவே
கண்டிடு மேரு வணிமாதி தானாகிப்
பண்டைய வானின் பகட்டை யறுத்திட்
டொன்றிய தீபம் உணர்ந்தார்க் குண்டாமே. *1401*

Effect of Worshipping Krim Sakti

This Sakti, there, as She stands constant
Anima, Mahima, and the rest of Occult powers arise
The Pasas that bind the ancient Jiva are sundered;
And the unitive Light of Jnana dawns
In those who realize Her.

உண்டோர் அதோமுகம் உத்தம மானது
கண்டஇச் சத்தி சதாசிவ நாயகி
கொண்ட முகமைந்து கூறுங் கரங்களும்
ஒன்றிரண் டாகவே மூன்றுநா லானதே. *1402*

Haum Sakti (Sadasiva Nayaki) — in Ajna Centre

The Sakti of the Sadasiva,
Has faces five and hands ten,
Of these, the downward looking face (Athomukha)
Is divine far indeed.

Haum Sakti (Sadasiva Sakti) is in the visuddhi (throat) centre with five faces and ten hands.

நன்மணி சூலங் கபாலங் கிளியுடன்
பன்மணி நாகம் மழுகத்தி பந்தாகுங்
கன்மணி தாமரைக் கையில் தமருகம்
பொன்மணி பூணாரம் பூசனை யானதே 1403

Haum Sakti's Form

The resounding bell, the trident,the skull and the parrot
The serpent that gems hold, the axe, the knife, the ball
The lotus that is lovely unto Her eyes,
The kettle-drum that is held in Her hands,
The gem-set garland that adorns Her body,
With these She worship receives.

பூசனைச் சத்திகள் எண்ணைவர் சூழவே
நேசவள் கன்னிகள் நாற்பத்து நேரதாய்க்
காசினிச் சக்கரத் துள்ளே கலந்தவள்
மாசடை யாமல் மகிழ்ந்திருந் தார்களே. 1404

Haum Sakti is Surrounded by Forty Saktis and Forty Vestal Virgins

With forty Saktis the worship offering,
With forty Virgins making the retinue
The Beloved One is seated in the Chakra;
And there in uninterrupted rapture, they are.

தாரத்தி னுள்ளே தங்கிய சோதியைப்
பாரத்தி னுள்ளே பரந்துள் எழுந்திட
நேரது வொன்றிநின் றெண்ணு மனோமயங்
காரது போலக் கலந்தெழு மண்ணிலே. 1405

Practise Kundalini Before Haum Sakti

The Fire that burns in the Muladhara
To rouse it and send it upward over adharas,
Do centre your mind on the root mantra (Aum)
Your mind-force then lifts it up, heavenward,
Like the clouds over terrestrial sphere.

மண்ணில் எழுந்த அகார உகாரங்கள்
விண்ணில் எழுந்து சிவாய நமவென்று
கண்ணில் எழுந்தது காண்பரி தன்றுகொல்
கண்ணில் எழுந்தது காட்சி தரஎன்றே. 1406

Aum Sakti Arose as Sivayanama

The Pranava Mantra composed of letters A and U
From terrestrial sphere Muladhara arose
Ascended upward
And as Sivayanama to eye appeared;
Invisible it is not to the naked eye;
Visible it rose, for us to see.

என்றங் கிருந்த அமுத கலையிடைச்
சென்றங் கிருந்த அமுத பயோதரி
கண்டங் கரமிரு வெள்ளிபொன் மண்ணடை
கொண்டங் கிருந்தது வண்ணம் அமுதே. 1407

Form of Amudeswari (Aum) Sakti in Moon Sphere

Thus was She seated, Amudeswari,
In the Moon Sphere of ambrosia
In cranium within;
There She was, the ambrosial milk breasted;
Her throat and hands shine like silver and gold
In Her Hand She held the nectar's pitcher.
Of White-hued She is like the ambrosia.

அமுதம தாக அழகிய மேனி
படிகம தாகப் பரந்தெழு முள்ளே
குமுதம தாகக் குளிர்ந்தெழு முத்துக்
கெமுதம தாகிய கேடிலி தானே. 1408

Aum Sakti Described

Beauteous like ambrosia is Her form,
As crystal pure She rises in me,
Like a lily She is,
Like the pearl of deep cool waters She is,
Like ambrosia rich, immortal She is.

கேடிலி சத்திகள் முப்பத் தறுவரும்
நாடிலி கன்னிகள் நாலொன் பதின்மரும்
பூவிலி பூவிதழ் உள்ளே யிருந்திவர்
நாளிலி தன்னை நணுகிநின் றார்களே. 1409

Aum Sakti is Surrounded by 36 Saktis and 36 Vestal Virgins

The noble Saktis six and thirty
The vestal Virgins* six and thirty
They seek Her that has her home in the lotus bloom,
They seek Her, the Eternal One,
From within the lotus of their bosom.
*Yoginis (female yogis).

நின்றது புந்தி நிறைந்திடும் வன்னியுங்
கண்டது சோதி கருத்துள் இருந்திடக்
கொண்டது வோராண்டு கூடி வருகைக்கு
விண்டவௌ காரம் விளங்கின அன்றே. 1410

Practise Kundalini for a Year

My thoughts stood still in meditation,
The Kundalini Fire filled the adharas,
I beheld the Light above in Sahasrara,
And as I held it in my heart,
In a year Sakti appeared,
The Sakti that is of luminous Aum.

Mantras 1410 & 1411

Concentrate your thoughts in meditation. The kundalini fire fills the adharas and you vision the light in the cranium. In a year Aum Sakti of luminous form will appear. Indeed you too will become luminous and all the heavenly beings shall bow before you. On you will be conferred all things that are good and true.

விளங்கிடு வானிடை நின்றவை யெல்லாம்
வணங்கிடு மண்டலம் மன்னுயி ராக
நலங்கிளர் நன்மைகள் நாரண னொத்துச்
சுணங்கிடை நின்றிவை சொல்லலு மாமே. *1411*

Effect of Worship of Aum Sakti

Luminous indeed they become
All that are in High Heaven,
Low they bowed before me
All the world, and all the creatures therein,
Like Narayana was I blessed
With all things noble
How can I recount
All that comes of Aum Sakti.

ஆமே அதோமுக மேலே அமுதமாய்த்
தாமே யுகாரந் தழைத்தெழுஞ் சோமனுங்
காமேல் வருகின்ற கற்பக மானது
பூமேல் வருகின்ற பொற்கொடி யானதே. *1412*

Saum Sakti in Sahasrara

Above the downward looking face of Haum Sakti
Above the Aum Sakti in Lunar Sphere
In Letter U Form
Is the Celestial Garden
There unto the Wish fulfilling tree of Kalpaka is Saum Sakti;
She of golden vine-like Form
Is on lotus seated.

Saum Sakti is seated in the moon sphere.

பொற்கொடி யாளுடைப் பூசனை செய்திட
அக்களி யாகிய ஆங்காரம் போயிடும்
மற்கட மாகிய மண்டலந் தன்னுளே
பிற்கொடி யாகிய பேதையைக் காணுமே. *1413*

Saum Sakti is Maiden Innocence

As you worship that golden vine
The exulting I-ness leaves you;
In the Chakra Sahasrara that represents the spaces vast
You shall see Her, close entwined,
She, the Maiden Innocence.

Mantras 1413 & 1414

When you worship Saum Sakti, the exulting ego leaves you. Saum Sakti is the maiden innocence. She is of exotic beauty. She is surrounded by several maidens, and the vast world serves as Her tilak.

பேதை யிவளுக்குப் பெண்மை அழகாகுந்
தாதை யிவளுக்குத் தாணுவு மாய்நிற்கும்
மாதை யவளுக்கு மண்ணுந் திலகமாய்க்
கோதையர் சூழக் குவிந்திடங் காணுமே. *1414*

Saum Sakti is of Surpassing Beauty

For this Maiden Innocence
Beauty is woman's perfection embodied;
For Her the Lord is the father
The world vast is Her tilak;
Surrounded by maidens several
She takes Her place,
In the narrow crevice of Sahasrara.

குவிந்தனர் சத்திகள் முப்பத் திருவர்
நடந்தனர் கன்னிகள் நாலெண்மர் சூழப்
பரந்தித ழாகிய பங்கயத் துள்ளே
இருந்தனள் காணும் இடம்பல கொண்டே. *1415*

Saum Sakti is Surrounded by 32 Saktis and 32 Vestal Virgins

Saktis thirty and two surrounding,
Vestal Virgins thirty and two accompanying,
In the spreading petalled lotus within
She sat,
She that has places several.

Here, the number (of letters) becomes 64.

கொண்டங் கிருந்தனர் கூத்தன் ஒளியினைக்
கண்டங் கிருந்தனர் காரணத் துள்ளது
பண்டை மறைகள் பரந்தெங்குந் தேடுமால்
இன்றென் மனத்துளே இல்லடைந் தாளுமே. *1416*

Saum Sakti Appeared in Me

There they were, the Sadhakas, basking in the Light of the Dancer,
There they were, the Sadhakas visioning Her, the Cause of All
There they were, the Vedas, ancient, seeking Her everywhere
But this day,
She in me as Her Home
Reigns supreme.

Saum Sakti is immanent in Her devotees.

இல்லடைந் தானுக்கும் இல்லாத தொன்றில்லை
இல்லடைந் தானுக் கிரப்பது தானில்லை
இல்லடைந் தானுக் கிமையவர் தாமொவ்வார்
இல்லடைந் தானுக்கு இல்லாதில் லானையே. *1417*

Lord Alone is the Refuge

He who has Her in the home of his heart,
He lacks nothing;
He who has Her in the home of his heart,
He begs not;
He who has Her in the home of his heart
He has peers none among Celestials even;

He who has Her in the home of his heart,
For Him is the Lord that nothing lacks.

ஆனை மயக்கும் அறுபத்து நாற்றறி
ஆனை யிருக்கும் அறுபத்து நாலொளி
ஆனை யிருக்கும் அறுபத்து நாலறை
ஆனையுங் கோடும் அறுபத்து நாலிலே. *1418*

Jiva Chakra of 64 Chambers

Sixty and four are the instruments of enjoyments
That tempt Jiva,
Sixty and four are Kalas within Jiva,
Sixty and four are the Chambers of Jiva's Chakra
Sixty and four, where Siva Sakti are.

1) This 64-chamber chakra is filled by the letters 'A' and 'U'

நான்காம் தந்திரம் முடிவு பெற்றது.
Tantra Four Concluded

ஐந்தாம் தந்திரம்
TANTRA FIVE

1. சுத்த சைவம்
SUDDHA SAIVAM

ஊரும் உலகமும் ஒக்கப் படைக்கின்ற
பேரறி வாளன் பெருமை குறித்திடின்
மேருவும் மூவுல காளி யிலங்கெழுந்
தாரணி நால்வகைச் சைவமு மாமே. *1419*

Four Paths of Saivam

The Lord created earth in wisdom infinite
And He made it abode of man
How shall I sing His Majesty!
He is mighty as Mount Meru,
From whence He sways the three worlds;
And He is the Four Paths of Saivam too here below.

The Lord created the world, the dwelling place of man. He holds power over the Three Worlds. He is the four paths of Saivam too(Chariya, Kriya, Yoga and Jnana). It is impossible to praise Him adequately. He was great as Mount Meru.

Esoterically explained. Mount Meru is the universal hub, the support of all worlds. It is the 'central mountain' of Hindu and Buddhist cosmography, around which our cosmos is arranged in seven concentric circles of oceans separated by intervening concentric circles of golden mountains. We may possibly regard it, like the 'central sun' of Western astronomy, as the gravitational centre of the known universe.

The special column, the central support of the human body structure is, analagously, symbolised in the *Tantras* and in the works on yoga as the Mount Meru of men in the microcosm.

Mount Meru is the king of mountains.

The Sushumna nadi is the chief orthedian nerve situated in the hollow of the spinal column (Sanskrit—Brahmadanda) the Mt. Meru of the human body—man being regarded as the microcosm of the macrocosm.

Vide "The Tibetian Book of the Dead," translated by W.G. Evans-Wentz, pp.63-65, 146, 147, 158-9, 215. (Editor's note: notes 6, 7 & 8 are strictly a Meikandar interpretation of the following mantra.)

Note: The translator has chosen here to group the first four subheadings under the title, 'Suddha Saivam,' whereas in the Tirumantiram the verses are categorized under these headings: Suddha Saivam, Asuddha Saivam, Marga Saivam and Kadum Suddha Saivam. Also the order of some of those verses had been rearranged. They now follow the original numeration of the Tirumantiram.

சத்தும் அசத்துஞ் சதசத்துந் தான்கண்டு
சித்தும் அசித்துஞ் சேர்வுறா மேநீத்த
சுத்தம் அசுத்தமுந் தோய்வுறா மேநின்று
நித்தம் பரஞ்சுத்த சைவர்க்கு நேயமே. *1420*

School of Suddha-Saivam

Those who tread the path of Suddha Saivam
Stand aloft,
Their hearts intent on Eternal Para;
Transcending Worlds of Pure and Impure Maya,
Where Pure Intelligence consorts not with Base Ignorance,
And the lines that divide Real, Unreal and Real-Unreal
Are discerned sharp.

---

1) Cosmic Being
2) Pure or suddha maya comprises the six highest tattva categories in the evolutionary scale.
3) Impure or asuddha maya includes the remaining thirty tattvas.
Others divide maya or matter in evolution into the six pure categories (suddha maya), six pure/impure categories (suddha/asuddha maya), and twenty-four impure categories (asuddha maya).
4) Chit or spirit
5) Achit or matter
6) Sat or God (Pati)
7) Asat or matter (pasam)
8) Sat/asat or soul (pasu)

Suddha Siddhanta is, in other words, Vedanta. The Suddha Siddhantins receive the constant vision by scaling the heights of the nada sphere and attain perfection in Nadanta. They are capable of distinquishing between the real, the unreal and the real/unreal.

கற்பன கற்றுக் கலைமன்னு மெய்யோகம்
முற்பத ஞான முறைமுறை நண்ணியே
சொற்பத மேவித் துரிசற்று மேலான
தற்பரங் கண்டுளோர் சைவசித் தாந்தரே. *1421*

Suddha Saivam is Saiva Siddhanta

Having learned all that learned must be,
Having practised all Yoga that have to be,
They, then, pursue the path of Jnana in gradation sure;
And so pass into the world of Formless Sound beyond;

And there, rid of all impurities,
Envision the Supreme, the Self-created;
They, forsooth, are the Saiva Siddhantins true.

The path of Suddha Saivam leads to the supreme pure state, devoid of all base ignorance. Yoga leads Saiva siddhantins into the path of jnana, and to pass into the sphere of formless sound. Verily, that is the goal of Saiva Siddhanta, to be rid of all impurities.

Mular's Saiva Siddhanta is nothing other than Suddha Saivam as he expounds it in 1420.

வேதாந்தஞ் சுத்தம் விளங்கிய சித்தாந்த
நாதாந்தங் கண்டோர் நடுக்கற்ற காட்சியர்
பூதாந்த போதாந்த மாகப் புனஞ்செய்ய
நாதாந்த பூரணர் ஞானநே யத்தரே. *1422*

Suddha Siddhanta is Vedanta

Suddha Siddhanta is Vedanta;
They who have scaled the heights of Nada sphere
Have verily had the Vision Unwavering
Comprehending Tattvas from world of elemental matter
To the Finite End of Jnana (Bhodanta)
They become Perfection in Nadanta,
They verily are the ardent seekers of Jnana.

Mular equates his Saiva Siddhanta with Vedanta, which is not to be confused with the Vedanta of the schools of Sankaracarya, Ramanujacarya, etc. Bhodanta is quite apparently a reference to the 'Bhodi' of Buddhism. By Nadanta is meant apparently the Mimamsa and Spanda schools which emphasize the sound aspect of the Ultimate.

2. அசுத்த சைவம்
ASUDDHA SAIVAM

இணையார் திருவடி ஏத்துஞ் சீரங்கத்
தினையார் இணைக்குழை யீரணை முத்திரை
குண்டமா ரிணைக்கண்ட மாலையுங் குன்றா
தணைவாஞ் சரியை கிரியையி னார்க்கே. *1423*

Path of Chariya-Kriya

They who walk the twin paths of Chariya and Kriya
They ever praise the twin Feet of Lord;
On their limbs they wear holy emblems
The twin rings in ear lobes
The twin rudraksha garland around the neck,
And adopt the twin Mudra'
All, in amiable constancy.

'Presumably, the rishaba (bull) mudra and sula (trident) mudra. Vide *Thevaram* of St. Tirunavukkarasar beginning with "Ponnar Tiruvadi."

Mantras 1423 & 1424

They who tread the twin paths of Chariya and Kriya remain in amiable constancy in thought of Siva, and adore the Glorious Feet of the Lord. Their holy bodies adorned with the appropriate insignia, they sit still and impassive, chanting mantras. Thus their souls ascend to Siva.

காதுப்பொ னார்ந்த கடுக்கன் இரண்டுசேர்த்
தோதுந் திருமேனி யுட்கட் டிரண்டுடன்
சோதனை • செய்து துவாதெச மார்க்கராய்
ஓதி யிருப்பார் ஒருசைவ ராகுமே. *1424*

Path of Dvadasa Marga Saivam (Yoga)

In the lobes of their ear,
They wear the double ring of gold,
Around their necks,
They wear the double string of rudraksha;
Their holy body thus adorned
They sit quiescent, chanting mantras
And feel their way inward
Through the twelve steps in the ladder
Of the Soul's ascension to Siva
—Of such are the peerless school of Saivas.

The reference is to the 12 states of consciousness experience in the samadhi state. The twelfth state is the Final State of Void from whose bourne there is no returning. For elaboration of the eleven consciousness experiences (avastas) preceding the twelfth, vide Tantra Eight For elaboration on the twelfth stage of consciousness experience, vide Mantra 1489, infra.

கண்டங்கள் ஒன்பதுங் கண்டவர் கண்டனர்
கண்டங்கள் ஒன்பதுங் கண்டாய் அரும்பொருள்
கண்டங்கள் ஒன்பதுங் கண்டவர் கண்டமாங்
கண்டங்கள் கண்டோர் கடுஞ்சுத்த சைவரே. *1425*

Pure Suddha Saivam (Jnana)

They who transcended the nine spiritual Centres
Verily saw God,
Whom the nine continents seek;
They saw the Continent beyond all continents
They, indeed, are the Pure Suddha Saivas.

Suddha Saivas transcending the nine spiritual centres see the continent beyond the continents, and verily behold God.

These are known as avastas or states of the soul's experience as it travels from the navel to the forehead through the heart and neck chakra centres. They represent the states of wakefulness, dream, deep sleep, beyond-deep-sleep and so on. For a fuller discussion, vide "Saiva Siddhanta," by V. Paranjoti, pp.167-69

ஞானி புவியெழு நன்னூ லனைத்துடன்
மோன திசையும் முழுஎண்ணெண் சித்தியும்
ஏனை நிலமும் எழுதா மறையீறுங்
கோனொடு தன்னையுங் காணுங் குணத்தனே. 1426

Characteristics of Jnani

The Jnani masters all sacred lore on earth,
And the attainments sixty and four
And espies the Land of Mauna
And all other land besides;
He sees the goal of all Vedas
And sees Lord and himself in united in one.

The jnani holds mastery over the sacred lore on earth and the sixty-four attainments. He receives the vision of all worlds, inclusive of the 'land of Mauna.' He sees the goal of all *Vedas*, and the Lord Himself.

3. மார்க்க சைவம்

SAN MARGA SAIVAM

பொன்னாற் சிவசாத னம்பூதி சாதனம்
நன்மார்க்க சாதனம் மாஞான சாதனந்
துன்மார்க்க சாதனந் தோன்றாத சாதனஞ்
சன்மார்க்க சாதன மாஞ்சுத்த சைவர்க்கே. 1427

Jnana Path is for Suddha Saivam

The golden emblems of Siva
And the holy smear of ashes
Apt are they the insignia
Of those in Saiva Path stand
But the path of Jnani
Is the path that no evil ever crosses
That his emblem, the holy path of Sanmarga (Jnana)
So beloved of Suddha Saiva.

Mantras 1427 & 1428

Followers of Saivam wear the golden insignia of Siva and the smear of holy ashes. The path of jnana is Sanmarga, which no evil can obstruct. It is beloved of Suddha Saivam. A perfect jnani is the king of the entire realm of wisdom. He is the sun who pierces the massive lore of Vedanta/Siddhanta. He remains immortal, devoted ever to the Suddha Saiva way.

கேடறு ஞானி கிளர்ஞான பூபதி
பாடறு வேதாந்த சித்தாந்த பாகத்தின்
ஊடுறு ஞானோ தயனுண்மை முத்தியோன்
பாடுறு சுத்தசை வப்பத்த நித்தனே. 1428

Greatness of Jnani in Suddha Saivam

The blemishless Jnani is king of Wisdom's realm
He is the Sun, whose beams pierce the massive lore of
Vedanta-Siddhanta
His is salvation True
He, the immortal one
And devoted true to Suddha Saiva way.

ஆகமம் ஒன்பான் அதிலான நாலேழு
மோசமில் நாலேழு முப்பேத முற்றுடன்
வேகமில் வேதாந்த சித்தாந்த மெய்மையொன்
றாக முடிந்த வருஞ்சுத்த சைவமே. 1429

Conclusions of Suddha Saivam

Nine are the Agamas of yore
In time expanded into twenty and eight,
They then took divisions three*
Into one truth of Vedanta-Siddhanta to accord
That is Suddha Saiva, rare and precious.

The nine *Agamas* of yore, which expanded into twenty-eight, took three divisions (Mantra, Tantra and Upadesa) to accord into one, the truth of Vedanta/Siddhanta, unique and precious to Suddha Saiva.

By stating that the Agamas provide the base for both Vedanta and Siddhanta (which are equated by him), Mular makes it clear that the Vedanta he has in mind is not the same as that of the Acaryas. The one thing common to Vedanta, Siddhanta and Bodhanta is that they all consider Knowledge as the ultimate path to Liberation.

சுத்தம் அசுத்தந் தூரியங்கள் ஓரேழுஞ்
சத்தும் அசத்துந் தணந்த பராபரை
உய்த்த பராபரை யுள்ளாம் பராபரை
அத்தன் அருட்சத்தி யாயெங்கு மாமே. 1430

Doctrine of Grace in Suddha Saivam

She transcends the worlds of Matter, Pure and Impure,
And the seven states of Turiya awareness
And the categories of Real and Unreal,
She is Paraparai;
She grants the soul deliverance;
She is ever within;
She is the Lord's Divine Grace;
The Arul Sakti that is all pervasive.

She, the Lord's Divine Grace, and the all-pervasive Arul Sakti, holds superiority over the worlds of matter — pure and impure — the seven states of turiya consciousness, and the categories of real and unreal. She is the Paraparai, who is inherent in Para.

சத்தும் அசந்துந் தணந்தவர் தானாகிச்
சித்தும் அசித்துந் தெரியாச் சிவோகமாய்
முத்தியுள் ஆனந்த சத்தியுள் மூழ்கினார்
சித்தியு மங்கே சிறந்துள தானே. 1431

Sakti's Grace for Jnani in Suddha Saivam

They transcended categories Real and Unreal
That cognize neither Chit nor Achit
They attuned themselves to Sivoham meditation,
And in Mukti, in the bliss of Sakti.
They were immersed deep,
And there
All Siddhis abounded in surpassing prowess.

The siddhas are immersed in 'Sivoham' meditation and attain mukti, the bliss of Sakti. There, they abound in unsurpassed prowess.

தன்னைப் பரனைச் சதாசிவன் என்கின்ற
மன்னைப் பதிபசு பாசத்தை மாசற்ற
முன்னைப் பழமல முன்கட்டை வீட்டினை
உன்னத் தகுஞ்சுத்த சைவர் உபாயமே. 1432

Suddha Saiva Strategy

The Self, Para and the Sadasiva that is Lord,
The categories three — Pati, Pasu and pasa,
The Immaculate Ancient One,
And the Tattvas that bind Jiva
And the goal of Liberation
—On All these in accord contemplate
They, of the path of Suddha Saiva.

பூரணந் தன்னிலே வைத்தற்ற வப்போதே
மாரண மந்த மதித்தானந் தத்தோடு
நேரென ஈராறு நீதி நெடும்போகங்
காரண மாஞ்சுத்த சைவர்க்குக் காட்சியே. 1433

Vision of Suddha Saivam Path

They fixed their thoughts on Perfection
And lost consciousness of Self's existence
They have reached the End of Vedas;
They followed the Twelve-Way route
To divine rapture
—That their vision is,
Those of Suddha Saiva Way.

Mantras 1433 & 1434
Concentrating the thought on perfection and becoming unconscious of self's existence leads siddhas to reach the end of the *Vedas*, and by following the twelve-way route they receive the vision of the Suddha Saiva way. Jnana stills the flow of thought which even yogis find it difficult to practise, and through destruction of the self, he finds identity in Siva.

மாறாத ஞான மதிப்பற மாயோகந்
தேறாத சிந்தையைத் தேற்றிச் சிவமாக்கிப்
பேறான பாவனை பேணி நெறிநிற்றல்
கூறாகு ஞானி சரிதை குறிக்கிலே. 1434

Way of Jnani

He stills the incessant flow of thought,
That even Yoga's severity stills not,
With Jnana he effaces the Self
And in Bhava identifies with Siva;
That in brief is worthy Jnani's story.

வேதாந்தங் கண்டோர் பிரமமித் தியாதரர்
நாதாந்தங் கண்டோர் நடுக்கற்ற யோகிகள்
வேதாந்த மல்லாத சித்தாந்தங் கண்டுளோர்
சாதா ரணமன்ன சைவர் உபாயமே. 1435

Vedanta and Siddhanta

The Vedantins envision Brahman
Adepts are they in Brahmaic art;
They hold all phenomena as illusion entire,
Those who envision Nadanta
Are yogis unwavering;
But Siddhanta that accords not with Vedanta,
Is the common Saiva's lot.

விண்ணினைச் சென்றணு காவியன் மேகங்கள்
கண்ணினைச் சென்றணு காப்பல காட்சிகள்
எண்ணினைச் சென்றணு காம லெணப்படும்
அண்ணலைச் சென்றணு காபசு பாசமே. 1436

God is Beyond Reach of Pasu and Pasa Knowledge

High be the clouds that soar
They never shall touch the heaven's roof;
Varied be the sights that loom
They never shall touch the eye's orbs;
Even so,
Neither Pasu nor Pasa shall reach Him,
Whom contemplation scarce comprehends.

ஒன்றும் இரண்டும் இலதுமாய் ஒன்றாக
நின்று சமய நிராகார நீங்கியே
நின்று பராபரை நேயத்தைப் பாதத்தால்
சென்று சிவமாதல் சித்தாந்த சித்தியே. 1437

Siddhanta is to Unite With Siva

You and He are not two separate
You and He are but one united;
Thus do you stand,
Freed of all sectarian shackles;
Adore the Feet of Paraparai
And with Siva become One;
—That the way Siddhanta fulfills.

4. கடுஞ்சுத்த சைவம்

RIGOROUS SUDDHA SAIVAM

வேடங் கடந்து விகிர்தன்றன் பான்மேவி
ஆடம் பரமின்றி ஆசாபா சஞ்செற்றுப்
பாடொன்று பாசம் பசுத்துவம் பாழ்படச்
சாடுஞ் சிவபோ தகர்சுத்த சைவரே. 1438

Suddha Saivam Defined

They are not for outward form and attire,
They are not for pomp and ceremony,
Uprooting all bond and desire,
Abiding in the Immaculate Lord,
They bring to dire destruction,
The Soul's egoity and its bondage beginningless
Thus they onward leap,
With Siva's light suffused
—They, of Suddha Saiva Way.

உடலான ஐந்தையும் ஓராறும் ஐந்து
மடலான மாமாயை மற்றுள்ள நீவப்
படலான கேவல பாசந் துடைத்துத்
திடமாய்த் தனையுறல் சித்தாந்த மார்க்கமே. 1439

Teachings of Siddhanta School

The five Tattvas that constitute the body,
The thirty more that together constitute them
And the one Tattva that is yet beyond Pure Maya,
All these they transcend;
The thick layers of primal bondage they dissolve
And of certain, realize the Self
That the way of Siddhantins true.

சுத்தச் சிவனுரை தானதில் தோயாமல்
முத்தர் பதப்பொருள் முத்திவித் தாமூலம்
அத்தகை யான்மா அரனை அடைந்தற்றாற்
சுத்தசிவமாவ ரேசுத்த சைவரே. 1440

Goal of Suddha Saivas is to be One With Siva

They tarry not in the Pure Maya Sphere of Siva Tattvas
There they but attain the status of Gods
But that as a spring board
Their Soul reaches farther out to Siva Him-self,
And merging in His union, Self-effacing,
Themselves become Immaculate Siva
They, forsooth, are Suddha Saivas.

Mantras 1440-1442
Lingering not in maya, Suddha Saivas reach the status of Gods. And using it as a spring board, the soul soars to Siva Himself and merges in Him, Realisation of the truth that 'I' and 'You' are one leads to the light of supreme jnana, illumining the soul's path to the final goal of sayujya union in the Lord.

நானென்றுந் தானென்றும் நாடிநான் சாரவே
தானென்று நானென் றிரண்டிலாத் தற்பதந்
தானென்று நானென்ற தத்துவ நல்கலால்
தானென்று நானென்றுஞ் சாற்றகில் லேனே. 1441

I and You Difference Effaced

I sought Him in terms of I and You
But He that knows not I from You
Taught me the truth, "I" indeed is "You"
And now I talk not of I and You.

சாற்றரி தாகிய தத்துவஞ் சித்தித்தால்
ஆற்றரி தாகிய ஐந்தும் அடங்கிடும்
மேற்றிகழ் ஞானம் விளக்கொளி யாய்நிற்கும்
பாற்பர சாயுச்சிய மாகும் பதியே. 1442

When This Truth Dawns Then is Union in Siva

When this Truth, beyond words, you perceive
The Siva Tattvas five bend below;
The light of Supreme Jnana dawns,
Illumines the Soul's path
To the Finite goal
Of Sayujya union in Lord.

5. சரியை

CHARIYA

நேர்ந்திடு மூல சரியை நெறியிதென்
றாய்ந்திடுங் காலாங்கி கஞ்ச மலையமான்
ஓர்ந்திடுங் கந்துரு கேண்மின்கள் பூதலத்
தோர்ந்திடுஞ் சுத்த சைவத் துயிரதே. 1443

Chariya is Breath of Suddha Saivam

"O! Kalangi! Kanja Malayaman! Kanduru!
My loved disciples, this you understand;
The practice of Chariya is basic to salvation,

And verily is the breath of Suddha Saiva
In this world below''—
Thus quotes—Mula,
Master of penances many.

உயிர்க்குயி ராய்நிற்றல் ஒண்ஞான பூசை
உயிர்கொளி நோக்கல் மகாயோக பூசை
உயிர்ப்பெறு மாவா கனம்புறப் பூசை
செயிற்கடை நேசஞ் சிவபூசை யாமே. *1444*

Jnana, Yoga, Kriya and Chariya Defined

To be one, Life within Life — that the luminous path of Jnana;
To seek the Light within Life — that the mighty path of Yoga;
To invest image with Life — that the external way of Kriya
To adore Siva in love — that the basic worship of Chariya.

Mantras 1444 & 1445
Jnana is to be one with Siva — life within Life. Seeking that light within Life is Yoga. The external acts investing an image with vibrant spirituality is Kriya; and to adore Siva in intense love is Chariya. Constant worship and adoration of His Name and glory make the Lord to erect a temple within you.

நாடு நகரமும் நற்றிருக் கோயிலுந்
தேடித் திரிந்து சிவபெரு மான்என்று
பாடுமின் பாடிப் பணிமின் பணிந்தபின்
கூடிய நெஞ்சத்துக் கோயிலாய்க் கொள்வனே. *1445*

Temple Worship Essential to Chariya

Wander you through town and villa
Seek Him through shrine and temple
Sing of Him as "Siva, Siva, my Lord"
And thus do you offer worship meek,
And the Lord will make your heart His temple.

பத்தர் சரிதை படுவோர் கிரியையோர்
அத்தகு தொண்டர் அருள்வேடத் தாகுவோர்
சுத்த வியமாதி சாதகர் தூயோகர்
சித்தர் சிவஞானஞ் சென்றெய்து வோர்களே. *1446*

Ways of Those Who Follow the Four Paths

They who follow path of Chariya are Bhaktas;
In Kriya the devoted souls wear holy emblems,
They who practise Yama and the rest are Yogis;
And they who reach Siva Jnana are Jnana Siddhas true.

Bhaktas follow the path of Chariya, and devotees wear holy symbols in Kriya. Yogis tread the paths of yama and the rest, and true siddhars attain Siva jnana.

சார்ந்தமெய்ஞ் ஞானத்தோர் தானவ னாயினோர்
சேர்ந்தவெண் யோகத்தர் சித்தர் சமாதியோர்
ஆய்ந்த கிரியையோர் அருச்சனை தப்பாதோர்
நேர்ந்த சரியையோர் நீள்நிலத் தோரே. *1447*

Goals of the Four Paths

Jnanis merge the I in You;
Yogis attain Siddhi and Samadhi;
Those in Kriya miss not daily worship;
And in Chariya they perform pilgrimages many.

Mantras 1447-1449
Jnanis find no difference between 'I' and 'You'. Yogis attain siddhi and samadhi. The devotees of Kriya perform daily worship, and they in Chariya perform many pilgrimages. Worshipping the form of Siva is Kriya and the formless One is Yoga. Jnana is the advanced path in fulness of time, and adoration with the loving heart is Chariya, the basic exalted path. These four paths of worship which give four states of realisation are revealed by Nandi descending from the Golden City to redeem the doubting humanity.

1. Siddhis — miracles
2. Samadhi — state of quiescence when breath is controlled and thoughts are centred on God.

கிரியை யோகங்கள் கிளர்ஞான பூசை
அரிய சிவனுரு அமரும் அரூபந்
தெரியும் பருவத்துத் தேர்ந்திடும் பூசை
உரியன நேயத் துயர்பூசை யாமே. *1448*

Worship in the Four Paths

Kriya is worship of Siva in Form,
Yoga of the Formless One,
Jnana is the advanced path in ripeness of time,
The adoration of the loving heart is Chariya,
Exalted indeed it is.

சரியாதி நான்குந் தருஞான நான்கும்
விரிவான வேதாந்த சித்தாந்த மாறும்
பொருளா னதுநந்தி பொன்னகர் போந்து
மருளாகு மாந்தர் வணங்கவைத் தானே. *1449*

The Four Paths Were Revealed by Nandi

The Four paths of worship
And the four states of realization they give
And the six schools of Vedanta-Siddhanta
All these are truths
That Nandi from the Golden City descending revealed
For the doubting humanity to redeem.

சமையம் பலசுத்தித் தன்செயல் அற்றிடும்
அமையும் விசேடமும் அரன்மந் திரசுத்தி
சமைய நிருவாணங் கலாசுத்தி யாகும்
அமைமன்னு ஞானமார்க் கம்அபிடேகமே. *1450*

Ordination Rites for the Four Paths

Samaya is the ordination rite for self-surrender in Chariya
Visesha, the rite for incantation of Siva Mantra in Kriya

Nirvana helps Kalas purification in Yoga
And Abhisheka for Grace to reach in Jnana.

The ordination rite for self-surrender in Chariya worship in Samaya Diksa, the rite for repetition of Siva mantra in Kriya worship is Visesa in Chariya. Nirvana Diksa in Chariya helps purify the kalas in Yoga, and the Abhiseka rite in Chariya is for Grace to be reached in Jnana.

6. கிரியை
KRIYA

பத்துத் திசையும் பரமொரு தெய்வமுண்
டெத்திக் கிலரில்லை என்பதின் அமலர்க்
கொத்துத் திருவடி நீழல் சரணெனத்
தத்தும் வினைக்கடல் சாராது காணுமே. *1451*

God is Everywhere — Seek Him

The One God there is
He pervades the ten directions around,
In which direction can we say is He not?
So, do take refuge under His Holy Feet
Then shall you cross the roaring Sea of Karma,
And safe reach the Shores of Beyond.

Mantras 1451 & 1452

The tempestuous sea of karma can be crossed and the shores beyond can be reached by seeking refuge under the Holy Feet of Him, who pervades the ten directions around. All the fragrant sandal trees and the rarest flowers can hardly take you to the Holy Feet of God. There is an easier way to reach Him — that is, by realising His presence in the depths of your heart, unfettering all worldly shackles.

கானுறு கோடி கடிகமழ் சந்தனம்
வானுறு மாமல ரிட்டு வணங்கினும்
ஊனினை நீக்கி உணர்பவர்க் கல்லது
தேனமர் பூங்கழல் சேரவொண் ணாதே. *1452*

True Worship is Worship Within

You may adore Him with sandal fragrance exceeding,
That grows on peaks atop in forests interior,
You may worship Him with flowers rare,
That bloom in Heaven's gardens
Unless you shed your fleshy attachments
And realize Him in the depths of your heart
You shall never never reach His Holy Feet
That is like flowers that shed honey dew.

கோனக்கன் றாயே குரைகழல் ஏத்துமின்
ஞானக்கன் றாகிய நடுவே யுழிதரும்
வானக்கன் றாகிய வானவர் கைதொழு
மானக்கன் றீசன் அருள்வள்ள மாமே. *1453*

Bhakti Begets Grace

The Lord is your Guide,
Seek His feet as does the yearning calf,
He shall seat you amidst His children of Wisdom;
The Devas, the Beings of Heaven, bow low before Him;
Great is His love, as of the cow to her calf;
And bounteous His Grace beyond beyond count.

He groups you among His children of wisdom when He is sought with a loving heart. Great is His love and bounteous His Grace infinite.

The simile of the cow and the calf to describe the relationship between God and the individual is as old as the Atharva Veda.

இதுபணிந் தெண்டிசை மண்டலம் எல்லாம்
அதுபணி செய்கின் றவளொரு கூறன்
இதுபணி மானுடர் செய்பணி யீசன்
பதிபணி செய்வது பத்திமை காணே. *1454*

Bhakti's End is Lord's Abode

She fashioned this world
And all universe that fills space in directions eight
Her—He consorts, sharing Himself with Her
To adore Him is the duty of humans here below;
And that which does service a place in Lord's Abode
Is Bhakti true.

Mantras 1454 & 1455

He is one with His consort, who fashioned this world in eight directions. It is the jiva's duty to adore and worship Him. Commencing with the performance of Chariya and Kriya, the devotee is blessed with the grace of yoga pure and this takes him to jnana, leading finally to union with Siva, in the way the Guru shows.

பத்தன் கிரியை சரியை பயில்வுற்றுச்
சுத்த அருளால் துரிசற்ற யோகத்தில்
உய்த்த நெறியுற் றுணர்கின்ற ஞானத்தாற்
சித்தங் குருவரு ளாற்சிவ மாகுமே. *1455*

The Four Paths are the Steps in the Ladder to Siva Union

The Bhakta to begin with practises Chariya and Kriya,
Then blessed with grace takes to Yoga pure;
And that way reaches the path of Jnana
And in the end by Guru's grace becomes one with Siva.

அன்பின் உருகுவ னாளும் பணிசெய்வன்
செம்பொன்செய் மேனி கமலத் திருவடி

முன்புநின் றாங்கே மொழிவ தெனக்கருள்
என்பினுட் சோதி இலங்குகின் றானே. *1456*

Daily I Beseech His Grace

The Lord is resplendent as pure gold
His Feet are like the lotus bloom
To them I pray: "Lord, Grant me Your Grace!"
And in love I melt and daily adore;
And the Lord that is Light within my bones
Himself does reveal unto me.

By beseeching His Grace and Love through daily worship, the Lord reveals Himself — He that is the light within our bones.

Samaya, Visesa, Nirvana, and Abhiseka are four ordinations in Kriya worship also.

7. யோகம்
YOGA

நெறிவழி யேசென்று நேர்மையுள் ஒன்றித்
தறியிருந் தாற்போல் தம்மை யிருத்திச்
சொறியினுந் தாக்கினுந் துண்ணென் றுணராக்
குறியறி வாளர்க்குக் கூடலு மாமே. *1457*

Yoga Way Leads to Realization

They course Kundalini through centres six,
To singleness of aim direct the mind,
Like a wooden stake they sit immobile;
Impervious to tickle or to thrust,
To the wise yogins who thus set their purpose high,
Lord His Grace grants.

Yogis receive the Grace of the Lord when they course the kundalini through the six centres, sitting immobile, unperturbed by tickle or thrust, concentrating on the single aim.

ஊழிதோ றூழிஉணர்ந்தவர்க் கல்லால்
ஊழிதோ றூழி யுணரவுந் தானொட்டான்
ஆழி அமரும் அரியயன் என்றுளார்
ஊழி முயன்றும் ஒருச்சியு ளானே. *1458*

God is Timeless Eternity

Unless you have realized Him as Timeless Eternity
You know Him not, albeit through aeons and aeons of time;
The Gods — Hari of the Ocean bed and Aya, the Creator—
In vain have sought Him through countless vistas of Time
He is at the Pinnacle, beyond, beyond their reach.

Mantras 1458 & 1460

Realise Him, the pinnacle beyond our understanding, as Timeless Eternity. Siva's Grace blossoms out of jiva as hidden fragrance comes out of the flower. The yogi, unmoved as a painted picture, cognises Him, who is all-pervasive, and immanent too within him. Then is the destruction of darkness, that is the seed of endless birth and rebirth.

பூவினிற் கந்தம் பொருந்திய வாறுபோற்
சீவனுக் குள்ளே சிவமணம் பூத்தது
ஓவியம்போல உணர்ந்தறி வாளர்க்கு
நாவி யணைந்த நடுதறி யாமே. *1459*

Yogi Realizes God Within

As from within the flower,
The hidden fragrance wakes to life,
So, out of Jiva blossoms
Siva's divine grace;
Sitting unmoved like painted picture
The yogi realizes Him within
Like the planted pole is He,
Which the musk-cat embraces, its fragrance to shed.

உய்ந்தனம் என்பீர் உறுபொருள் காண்கிலீர்
கந்த மலரிற் கலக்கின்ற நந்தியைச்
சிந்தை யுறவே தெளிந்திருள் நீங்கினால்
முந்தைப் பிறவிக்கு மூலவித் தாமே. *1460*

Seek God Within You

You say, "I have realized God'
Yet you have not seen Him that is but within you;
Nandi abides subtle as fragrance within flower;
Seek Him in singleness of your thought
Then shall your darkness of Impurities vanish
The darkness that is the seed of birth and rebirth interminable.

எழுத்தோடு பாடலும் எண்ணெண் கலையும்,
பழித்தலைப் பாசப் பிறவியும் நீங்கா
வழித்தலைச் சோமனோ டங்கி யருக்கன்
வழித்தலைச் செய்யும் வகையுணர்ந் தேனே. *1461*

Yoga Shows the Way

Neither mantra, nor song, nor arts four and sixty
Ever sunder birth and its accursed bonds;
Then did I take to Yoga's way,
And lo! I met the Sun, Moon and Fire on the way to Cranium
And they showed the Supreme Way!

Mantras 1461-1463

Neither mantra nor song, nor the sixty-four arts can sever birth and its accursed bonds. Yoga leads to the supreme way to the sublime. Yogic practice turns one a true tapasvin. He becomes one with the heavenly beings, realising the true word. Yogis vision Him in single-mindedness.

விரும்பிநின் றேசெயில் மெய்த்தவ ராகும்
விரும்பிநின் றேசெயின் மெய்யுரை யாகும்
விரும்பிநின் றேசெயின் மெய்த்தவ மாகும்
விரும்பிநின் றேசெயில் விண்ணவ னாகுமே. 1462

Fruits of Yoga

Do in devotion practise yoga
You shall a true tapasvin become;
You shall the True Word realize;
And of certain, one with Heavenly Beings be;
Yoga devoted in penance true.

பேணிற் பிறவா உலகருள் செய்திடுங்
காணில் தனது கலவியு ளேநிற்கும்
நாணில் நகர நெறிக்கே வழிசெயும்
ஊனிற் சுடுமங்கி யுத்தமன் றானே. 1463

Do's and Don'ts in Yoga

Do with care practise yoga
You shall with Immortals be;
Within you shall you glimpse Him;
If you but waver,
Then shall you reach the World of Darkness
Verily, Kundalini Fire that Yoga kindles in thee
Is the Gracious Lord Himself.

ஒத்தசெங் கோலார் உலப்பிலி மாதவர்
எத்தனை யாயிரம் வீழ்ந்தனர் எண்ணிலி
சித்தர்கள் தேவர்கள் மூவர் பெருமையாய்
அத்த னிவனென்றே அன்புறு வார்களே. 1464

Fall and Redemption Through Yoga

The monarchs that swayed sceptre righteous,
The devout anchorites in unnumbered thousands,
How many, how many, thy fell below;
(For having wavered in Yoga practice)
And yet, the myriad Siddhas, Devas and Supreme Beings Three,
All redeemed adore Him
Saying "You, Our Father!"

Monarchs and anchorites have fallen due to the pursuit of yoga in fickleness. But myriad siddhars, devas and the three Gods adore Him redeemed.

யோகிக்கு யோகாதி மூன்றுள கொண்டுற்றோர்
ஆகத் தகுகிரி யாதி சரியையாந்
தாகத்தை விட்ட சரியையொன் றாம்ஒன்றுள்
ஆதித்தன் பத்தியுள் அன்புவைத் தேனே. 1465

Sub-divisions in Yoga

The yogi has sub-divisions three in his path;
The yoga-kriya that helps him be the yogi;
The yoga-chariya that of desires rids him,
And yoga-in-yoga that centres thought on Sun within;
This latter I fixed my heart on.

யோகச் சமயமே யோகம் பலவுன்னல்
யோக விசேடமே அட்டாங்க யோகமாம்
யோகநிர் வாணமே யுற்ற பரோதயம்
யோக அபிடேகமே ஒண்சித்தி யுற்றலே. 1466

Stages of Initiation in the Yoga Path

Samaya Diksha in yoga is initiation for diverse yoga efforts;
Visesha Diksha in yoga is for achievement of eight-limbed yoga;
Nirvana Diksha in yoga aids yogi glimpse the Divine;
And when he is granted Abhisheka Ordination
Then is he ripe for Siddha State.

Mantras 1465 & 1466

The sub-divisions of Yoga are Chariya in Yoga, Kriya in Yoga, and Yoga in Yoga. The first one helps the aspirant to be the yogi, the second sunders desires while the third enables him to centre his thoughts on God. Samaya Diksha, Visesa Diksha, Nirvana Diksha, and Abhisheka Diksha are the ordinations in the graded stages of the Yoga path.

8. ஞானம்
JNANA

ஞானத்தின் மிக்க அறநெறி நாட்டில்லை
ஞானத்தின் மிக்க சமயமும் நன்றன்று
ஞானத்தின் மிக்கவை நன்முத்தி நல்காவா
ஞானத்தின மிக்கார் நரரின்மிக் காரே. 1467

Jnana Path Most Exalted

Than Jnana,
There is no better ethical path, here below;
No better religious faith;
Nothing else than Jnana can confer liberation true;
They that are exalted in Jnana
Are truly exalted among men.

Mantras 1467 & 1468

Jnana is the most exalted path and nothing else can confer final liberation. Mastery over consciousness, egoity, will, and the mind's cognizational activity is real mastery in Jnana.

சத்தமுஞ் சத்த மனனுந் தகுமனம்
உய்த்த வுணர்வு முணர்த்தும் அகந்தையுஞ்
சித்தமென் றிம்மூன்றுஞ் சிந்திக்குஞ் செய்கையுஞ்
சத்தங் கடந்தவர் பெற்றசன் மார்க்கமே. 1468

Jnani Transcends Nada

Out of the primal Principle of Sound (Nada)
The Mind springs;
And out of the Mind — Intelligence, Egoity and Will;
They who have mastered these three,
And the Mind's cogitational activity as well,
Verily have mastered Nada
And have truly attained Jnana.

தன்பால் உலகுந் தனக்கரு காவதும்
அன்பா லெனக்கரு ளாவது மாவன
என்பார்கள் ஞானமும் எய்துஞ் சிவோகமும்
பின்பாலின் நேயமும் பெற்றிடுந் தானே. *1469*

Stages of Attainment Through Jnana

Thus they say:
By devotion the Jiva first sojourns Lord's world;
Then comes to dwell in Lord's proximity;
Further on receives Lord's grace,
And in the end attains Jnana
In Sivohamic I and You union
Jiva shall himself Siva become.

The different stages of attainment through Jnana are: jiva sojourning in the Lord's world, dwelling in Lord's proximity, receiving the Lord's Grace (form), and ultimately attaining union in Him.

இருக்குஞ் சேம இடம்பிரமமாகும்
வருக்கஞ் சராசர மாகும் உலகந்
தருக்கிய ஆசார மெல்லாந் தருமே.
திருக்கிலாஞானத்தைத் தேர்ந்துணர்ந் தோர்க்கே. *1470*

Unitive Attainment of Jnani

Brahman shall be his impregnable abode,
Universe, his kith and kin;
Diverse paths the world presents
All, all shall be his;
For, verily he has realized
The pure Jnana, free of doubt.

The jnani deems Brahman as his impregnable abode, the universe his kith and kin, and all contending faiths as one. He is truly the realised one.

அறிவும் அடக்கமும் அன்பும் உடனே
பிறியா நகர்மன்னும் பேரரு ளாளன்
குறியுங் குணமுங் குரைகழல் நீங்கா
நெறியறி வார்க்கிது நீர்த்தொனி யாமே. *1471*

Jnana is Life-Boat

The Lord is of Infinite Grace,
In His Celestial City are Love, Light and Peace eternal,
To them that seek to know His Form
And understand His Attributes
And attain His Holy Feet
To them, this is the Path
This, this the boat to cross Life's turbulent waters

The Lord is of Infinite Grace, Love! Light and Peace reign eternally in His celestial city. The ultimate path to cross life's turbulent waters is to have an absolute cognition of the Lord, and so reach His Holy Feet.

ஞானம் விளைந்தெழு கின்றதோர் சிந்தையுள்
ஏனம் விளைந்தெதி ரேகாண வழிதொறுங்
கூனல் மதிமண் டலத்தெதிர் நீர்கண்டு
ஊனம் அறுத்துநின் றொண்சுட ராகுமே. *1472*

Jnani Becomes Light Divine

In whose thoughts Jnana ripens and swells,
In his path the Life-Boat appears and greets him;
And thus does he reach the surging waters
Of the Crescent Moon's sphere,
And there rid of Impurities,
He himself the Effulgent Light becomes.

Mantras 1472 & 1473

The 'boat of life' (Jnana) aids the jnani to cross to the surging waters of the crescent moon's sphere. There, he becomes the divine light. Jnana embraces all the four paths — Chariya, Kriya, Yoga and Jnana, and the jnani attains all the four stages they bring in.

ஞானிக் குடன்குண ஞானத்தில் நான்குமா
மோனிக் கிவையொன்றுங் கூடாமுன் மோகித்து
மேனிற்ற லாஞ்சத்தி வித்தை விளைத்திடுந்
தானிக் குலத்தோர் சரியை கிரியையே. *1473*

Jnani's Attainments are Unique

For Jnani All four paths are;
Not so for the Yogi until he becomes Mauni;
For him is Kundalini Yoga in ardour performed,
Chariya and Kriya too are his.

ஞானத்தின் ஞானாதி நான்குமா ஞானிக்கு
ஞானத்தின் ஞானமே நானென தென்னாமல்
ஞானத்தில் யோகமே நாதாந்த நல்லொளி
ஞானக் கிரியையே நன்முத்தி நாடலே. *1474*

Attainments at Four Jnana Stages

The Jnani attains all the four stages in Jnana;
Jnana-in-Jnana is to transcend the "I" and "Mine"
Yoga-in-Jnana is to envision the Light of Nadanta;
Kriya-in-Jnana is to seek the liberation by good.

Transcending the "I" and "Mine" is Jnana in Jnana; visualising the light of Nadanta is Yoga in Jnana; and Kriya in Jnana is the search for liberation.

நண்ணிய ஞானத்தின் ஞானாதி நண்ணுவோன்
புண்ணிய பாவங் கடந்த பிணக்கற்றோன்
கண்ணிய நேயங் கரைஞானங் கண்டுளோன்
திண்ணிய சுத்தன் சிவமுத்தன் சித்தனே. *1475*

Jnani Attains Unitive Wisdom in the Absolute

He who realizes Jnana in its four divisions
He verily transcends the conflict of virtue and vice;
He has reached the farthest shores of Truth;
He has glimpsed the Mighty Object;
He is the Immaculate, Siddha, Siva-Mukta.

ஞானச் சமயமே நாடுந் தனைக்காண்டல்
ஞான விசேடமே நாடு பரோதய
ஞானநிர் வாணமே நன்றறி வானருள்
ஞானாபி டேகமே நற்குரு பாதமே. 1476

Initiation Rites in Jnana

In Jnana are initiation rites four;
Samaya initiates the search for the Self;
Visesha, the search for the Divine
Nirvana for the descent of Lord's Grace;
Abhisheka for the attainment of Divine Guru's Holy Feet.

9. சன்மார்க்கம்

SANMARGA (PATH OF KNOWLEDGE)

சாற்றுஞ்சன் மார்க்கமாந் தற்சிவ தத்துவத்
தோற்றங் களான சுருதிச் சுடர்கண்டு
சீற்றம் ஒழிந்து சிவயோக சித்தராய்க்
கூற்றத்தை வென்றார் குறிப்பறிந் தார்க்ளே. 1477

San Marga

They glimpsed the Light of Holy Scriptures,
The revealed word of the Self-Existent Sivam,
They lost the sense of ego,
Became Siddhas of Siva Yoga,
And over Death triumphed;
Only they that had thus evolved
Knew inner meaning of Sanmarga.

சைவப் பெருமைத் தனிநா யகன்நந்தி
உய்ய வகுத்த குருநெறி ஒன்றுண்டு
தெய்வச் சிவநெறி சன்மார்க்கஞ் சேர்ந்துய்ய
வையத்துள் ளார்க்கு வகுத்துவைத் தானே. 1478

Nandi Showed Sanmarga Path

The peerless Master Nandi
Of Saivam honoured high,
He showed us a holy path
For Souls' redemption true
It is Siva's divine path, Sanmarga's path
For all world to tread
And for ever be free.

Same as Mantra 1567 infra.

தெரிசிக்கப் பூசிக்கச் சிந்தனை செய்யப்
பரிசிக்கக் கீர்த்திக்கப் பாதுகஞ் சூடக்
குருபத்தி செய்யுங் குவலயத் தோர்க்குத்
தருமூர்த்திச் சார்பூட்டுஞ் சன்மார்க்கந் தானே. 1479

Guru-Adoration is Sanmarga

To see him, to adore him, to meditate on him
To touch him, to sing of him,
To bear his holy feet on humbled head,
They that render devotion to Guru
In diverse ways thus,
They indeed walk the Sanmarga path
That to liberation leads.

தெளிவறி யாதார் சிவனை யறியார்
தெளிவறி யாதார் சீவனு மாகார்
தெளிவறி யாதார் சிவமாக மாட்டார்
தெளிவறி யாதவர் தீரார் பிறப்பே. 1480

Sanmarga Gives the Vision True

They that have true Vision none,
Shall never Siva know;
Nor shall even Jivas be;
Nor indeed Siva become;
Never, never their birth's bondage-broken be.

Mantras 1480 & 1481

Sanmarga gives the true vision, breaking the fetters of birth and extinquishing the fire of impurities. Listening to the silent voice in Sanmarga you become a pure mukta, annihilating the state of 'I' and 'You' difference and savouring the divine bliss.

தானவ னாகித் தானைந்தா மலஞ்செற்று
மோனம தாமொழிப் பான்முத்த ராவது
மீனமில் ஞானானு பூதியில் இன்பமுந்
தானவ னாயுறலானசன் மார்க்கமே. 1481

Sanmarga Leads to Supreme Grace-Bliss

When you scorch Impurities five
And listen to the Voice of Silence
You become a pure Mukta;
And I and You in one merge;
And by the unsullied Grace Jnana grants
You shall joy of the Bliss Divine;
Verily, then by Sanmarga Path
You become He indeed.

The voice of silence or mauna is what Pythagoras called the "harmony of the spheres," — beyond words and forms — the experience of the infinite within us. Vide "Foundations of Tibetan Mysticism," by Lama Angarika Govinda, Part I.

சன்மார்க்கத் தார்க்கு முகத்தொடு பீடமுஞ்
சன்மார்க்கத் தார்க்கும் இடத்தொடு தெய்வமுஞ்

சன்மார்க்க் தார்க்கு வருக்கந் தரிசனம்
எம்மார்க்கத் தார்க்கும் இயம்புவன் கேண்மினோ. 1482

Greatness of Sanmargis

The visage of Sanmargi is the Pedestal of Sakti
Where Sanmargi is there God is,
To see assemblage of Sanmargis is to vision Lord,
This I proclaim,
To whatsoever path you do incline.

The face of the Sanmargi is the pedestal of Sakti; the place of the Sanmargi is the seat of God. Whatever path may be followed, to see assemblages of Sanmargis is to see the Lord.

சன்மார்க்க சாதனந் தான்ஞான ஞேயமாம்
பின்மார்க்க சாதனம் பேதையர்க்காய்நிற்கும்
துன்மார்க்கம் விட்ட துரியத் துரிசற்றார்
சன்மார்க்கந் தானவ னாகுஞ்சன் மார்க்கமே. 1483

Sanmarga Path Purest

Alone of all paths
Sanmarga grants God-head through knowledge;
The rest of paths are for un-illumined;
Renouncing the ways of impurities
And transcending limits of Turiya
It merges I in You;
Verily, Sanmarga is Path Purest.

Sanmarga is the purest path that grants the experience of God-head through knowledge. The rest are unillumined and uninspiring. It is the way of renouncing impurities and transcending the limits of turiya consciousness. It is the way of I becoming He.

சன்மார்க்க மெய்த வருமருஞ் சீடர்க்குப்
பின்மார்க்க மூன்றும் பெறவியல் பாமென்றால்
நன்மார்க்கந் தானே சிவனொடு நாடலே
சொன்மார்க்க மென்னச்சுருதிகைக்கொள்ளுமே. 1484

Other Three Paths Open of Themselves

Unto that rare seeker in Sanmarga path
The rest of three paths, of themselves open;
That alone is True Path union with Siva seeks;
Seek that Path
As Guiding Word scriptures proclaim.

To the aspirant after Sanmarga, the other three paths open of themselves. It is the sole path, the True Path which scriptures enjoin for uniting in Siva.

அன்னிய பாசமும் ஆகுங் கருமமும்
முன்னும் அவத்தையும் மூலப் பகுதியும்
பின்னிய ஞானமும் பேதாதி பேதமுந்
தன்னொடுங் கண்டவர் சன்மார்க்கத் தோரே. 1485

Sanmargi's Vision

The bondage that keeps Jiva an alien to God,
The Karmas that flow from it,
The avastas that the Self experiences,
The Primordial Stuff that is Matter's nucleus,
The Consciousness that entwines it,
The million, million mutations that pervade the universe,
They who see them all and their own Selves
Verily are they the Sanmargis true.

பசுபாச நீக்கிப் பதியுடன் கூட்டிக்
கசியாத நெஞ்சங் கசியக் கசிவித்
தொசியாத வுண்மைச் சொரூபோ தயத்துற்
றசைவான தில்லாமை யானசன் மார்க்கமே. 1486

Sanmarga Leads to Svarupa State

Rending the Soul's bonds asunder
Conjoining him to the Lord
Melting the heart that knew no melting
Merging into the Primal Manifestness (Svarupa)
That is Truth Eternal
Sanmarga verily gives Jiva
The rest that knows no commotion ever.

மார்க்கஞ்சன் மார்க்கிகள் கிட்ட வகுப்பது
மார்க்கஞ்சன் மார்க்கமே யன்றிமற் றொன்றில்லை
மார்க்கஞ்சன் மார்க்க மெனுநெறி வைகாதோர்
மார்க்கஞ்சன் மார்க்க மாஞ்சித்த யோகமே. 1487

Sanmarga is The Only Path to Finite Goal

That alone is Path Divine
The Sanmargis for Goal ordain;
Other Path there is none,
Than this path to the One;
They that straight reach it not,
Through Yoga's Path may yet climb.

10. சகமார்க்கம்
SAHAMARGA (PATH OF YOGA)

சன்மார்க்கந் தானே சகமார்க்க மானது
மன்மார்க்க மாமுத்தி சித்திக்குள் வைப்பதாம்
பின்மார்க்க மானது பேராப் பிறந்திறந்
துன்மார்க்க ஞானத் துறதியு மாமே. 1488

Sanmarga is Sahamarga

Sanmarga is itself Sahamarga
So by itself it leads to Supreme Mukti;
Other Yogas
Involve myriad birth and death
Will they level to Jnana?

மருவுந் துவாதச மார்க்கமில் லாதார்
குருவுஞ் சிவனுஞ் சமயமுங் கூடாம்

வெருவுந் திருமகள் வீட்டில்லை யாகும்
உருவுங் கிளையும் ஒருங்கிழப் பாரே. 1489

Without Sahamarga They Lost All

They that follow not twelve-tiered Path of Sahamarga,
Neither will they know Guru nor God, nor Faith True;
The Goddess of Grace will frown at them;
Salvation shall never their portion be;
And they do lose both—
Their stature and kith.

யோகச் சமாதியின் உள்ளே யகலிடம்
யோகச் சமாதியின் உள்ளே யுளரொளி
யோகச் சமாதியின் உள்ளே யுளசத்தி
யோகச் சமாதி யுகந்தவர் சித்தரே. 1490

Fruits of Yoga Samadhi

In Yoga Samadhi is Space Infinite;
In Yoga Samadhi is Light Abiding;
In Yoga Samadhi is Sakti Omnipotent;
They that delight in Yoga Samadhi
Are verily Siddhas great.

Mantras 1490 & 1491

Infinite space, abiding light, omnipotent Sakti are the fruits of yoga samadhi. The immortal yogi can enjoy bhoga which confers earthly blessings, and yoga which can confer Siva-Form on him.

யோகமும் போகமும் யோகியர்க் காகுமால்
யோகஞ் சிவரூபம் உற்றிடும் உள்ளத்தோர்
போகம் புவியிற் புருடார்த்த சித்திய
தாகும் இரண்டும் அழியாத யோகிக்கே. 1491

Yoga Confers Blessings of Here and Hereafter

Both yoga and bhoga, yogis may have;
Through yoga is attained Siva's Form divine;
Through bhoga all earthly blessings;
Thus may he enjoy both — he, Yogi immortal.

ஆதார சோதனை யானாடி சுத்திகள்
மேதாதி யீரெண் கலாந்தத்து விண்ணொளி
போதா லயத்துப் புலன்கர ணம்புந்தி
சாதா ரணங்கெட லாஞ்ச மார்க்கமே. 1492

Yoga Leads to Supreme Awareness

Through this path of Sahamarga
The Yogis pierce the Adharas
And the Nadis they purify;
Envision the Kalas sixteen;
And glimpse their heavenly radiance;
And then are they merged in Awareness Supreme
Their organs of sense, internal and external
All atrophied.

Mantras 1492 & 1493

Through Sahamarga, the yogis pierce the adharas, purify the nadis, vision the sixteen kalas, glimpse their heavenly radiance, internal and external organs atrophied — and merge in the supreme consciousness. The yogi, who harries and subdues the five contentious senses with the sharp sword of steadfastness, merges in the consciousness of the Lord whom the eighteen heavenly hosts seek.

பிணங்கிநிற் கின்றவை ஐந்தையும் பின்னை
அணங்கி யெறிவ னயிர்மன வாளாற்
கணம்பதி னெட்டுங் கருதும் ஒருவன்
வணங்கவல் லான்சிந்தை வந்துநின் றானே. 1493

Siva is in Yogi's Thought

He harries and subdues the conflicting senses five
With the sharp sword of his determinate will;
In his thought emerges Lord
Whom the eighteen Ganas seek;
Verily, the yogi deserves our obeisance.

வளங்கனி யொக்கும் வளநிறத் தார்க்கும்
வளங்கனி யொப்பதோர் வாய்மைய னாகும்
உளங்கனிந் துள்ள முகந்திருப் பார்க்குப்
பழங்கனிந் துள்ளே பகுந்துநின் றானே. 1494

Love the Basis of Yoga

Even for the Yogi austere
Who attains the glossy hue of the rich ripe fruit
The Lord is hard of shell unto the wood-apple fruit,
But to them whose hearts ripe in love,
And taste the sweets of divine rapture,
He opens all of Himself
Like a rich fruit mature.

Loving hearts can taste the sweetness of divine rapture and the Lord reveals Himself as a fully ripened fruit.

11. சற்புத்திர மார்க்கம்
SATPUTRA MARGA (PATH OF KRIYA)

மேவிய சற்புத்திர மார்க்க மெய்த்தொழில்
தாவிப்ப தாஞ்சக மார்க்கஞ் சகத்தொழில்
ஆவ திரண்டும் அகன்று சகமார்க்கத்
தேவியோ டொன்றல் சன்மார்க்கத் தெளிவதே. 1495

Path of Filial Piety Leads to Jnana

The Path of Filial Piety is the Way of Kriya true;
The Kriya Path leads to Yoga Path;
Transcending both,
And uniting in Sakti of Yoga State
Indeed is consummation of Sanmarga Path.

Mantras 1495 & 1496

The path of filial piety, through Yoga (Saha marga) leads to Jnana, which consummates the Sanmarga path. Performing pujas, reading the holy scriptures, praising the Lord, chanting His Holy Name, practicing tapas, being truthful, bearing no malice — these constitute the path of filial piety or Kriya.

Mular refers to Kriya (Rituals) as Satputra Marga (or the path of "pious son").

பூசித்தல் வாசித்தல் போற்றல் செபித்திடல்
ஆசற்ற நற்றவம் வாய்மை அழுக்கின்மை
நேசித்திட் டன்னமும் நீசுத்தி செய்தன்மர்
றாசற்ற சற்புத் திரமார்க்க மாகுமே. *1496*

What Constitutes Kriya Path

To perform Pujas, to read the scriptures holy
To praise the Lord, to chant His holy name,
To practise Tapas, to be truthful,
To bear no envy.
Thyself to cook the offering for Lord with loving care
These and other acts of reverence;
Constitute Pure Path of Filial Piety.

அறுகாற் பறவை அலர்தேர்ந் துழலும்
மறுகா நரையன்னந் தாமரை நீலங்
குறுகா நறுமலர் கொய்வன கண்டுஞ்
சிறுகால் அறநெறி சேரகி லாரே. *1497*

All Nature Seeks Flowers: Why Not You?

The humming bees roam unceasing from flower to flower;
The snow-white swans float amidst lotus and blue-bells,
They all, all, seek flowers fragrant;
Yet, you who have beheld all this,
Adore not the Lord with flowers for a while even.

அருங்கரை யாவது அவ்வடி நீழற்
பெருங்கரை யாவது பிஞ்ஞுக னாணை
வருங்கரை யேகின்ற மன்னுயிர்க் கெல்லாம்
ஒருங்கரை யாயுல கேழினொத் தானே. *1498*

Lord is Our Defence and Refuge

His Holy Feet are our Rock of Refuge,
His commandments, our defence's battlements;
He is verily the finite Shore
For the surging tide of Jivas on earth;
He pervades thus, the seven worlds alike.

Mantras 1498 & 1499

The Lord is truly the Ultimate Goal, who with His Feet and His commandments pervades the seven worlds alike. Adoring Him in diverse ways, He becomes your own.

உயர்ந்தும் பணிந்தும் முகந்துந் தழுவி
வியந்தும் அரனடிக் கேமுறை செய்மின்
பயந்தும் பிறவிப் பயனது வாகும்
பயந்து பரிக்கிலப் பான்மையு னாமே. *1499*

Adore Lord in Diverse Ways; He Shall Be Yours

Rise high, bend low, kiss and embrace Lord;
Praise Him, sing Him and pray at His Holy Feet;
That shall your birth's fulfilment be;
In trembling love do adore Him;
He, indeed, shall be beloved unto you.

நின்றுதொழுவன் கிடந்தெம் பிரான்தன்னை
என்றுந் தொழுவன் எழிற்பரஞ் சோதியைத்
துன்று மலர்தூவித் தொழுமின் தொழுந்தோறுஞ்
சென்று வெளிப்படுந் தேவர் பிரானே. *1500*

Approach Lord Through Kriya Path

In reverence I stand and adore mine lord;
In humility I prostrate and praise Him;
And forever and ever shall I worship the Divine Light of Beauty;
You too shall seek Him with flowers fragrant,
The more you adore Him
The fuller He reveals Himself unto you,
He the Lord of Beings Heavenly.

Mantras 1500 & 1501

Adore the Lord in reverence; praise Him in humility; worship the divine light of beauty; seek Him with odorous flowers; and He shall reveal Himself. The more you adore Him, the more He reveals Himself. To this Kriya path, that exalts and showers countless blessings, the Chariya path leads.

திருமன்னுஞ் சற்புத் திரமார்க்கச் சரியை
உருமன்னி வாழும் உலகத்தீர்கேண்மின்
கருமன்னு பாசங் கைகூம்பத் தொழுது
இருமன்னு நாடோறும் இன்புற் றிருந்தே. *1501*

Kriya Comes of Chariya

Hearken! You, worldly men
That stand in Chariya Path,
It leads to the Kriya Path,
That exalts you;
Then shall your primordial Pasas lie prostrate,
And you live in unending bliss for ever.

12. தாச மார்க்கம்
DASA MARGA (PATH OF DEVOTION)

எளியனல் தீப மிடல்மலர் கொய்தல்
அளிதின் மெழுக லதுதூர்த்தல் வாழ்த்தல்
பளிமணி பற்றல் பன்மஞ் சனமாதி
தளிதொழில் செய்வது தான்தாசமார்க்கமே. 1502

Ways of Dasamarga

Gently light the lamp,
Gather flowers fragrant,
Humbly smear the ground with the holy paste,
Softly sweep,
Sing the Lord's Praise,
Count the crystal beads,
Anoint in many ways,
And perform the diverse acts of temple service.

Lighting the lamps gracefully, collecting fragrant flowers, pasting the holy floor and sweeping it, praising the Lord and counting the crystal beads, anointing Him in diverse ways — doing all these requirements of temple service, belongs to Dasa Marga.

'Dasa means servant.

அதுவிது வாதிப் பரமென் றகல்வர்
இதுவழி யென்றங் கிறைஞ்சின ரில்லை
விதிவழி யேசென்று வேந்தனை நாடு
மதுவிது நெஞ்சில் தணிக்கின்ற வாறே. 1503

Hold Fast to Chariya Path

This the Primal Being, that the Primal Being
Thus in doubt tossed.
Away they moved farther and farther from It.
They know not this is the true Path.
And worship not;
Do pursue this appointed way,
And seek the King of Kings;
That, in truth, shall quell
All doubts within you swell.

Mantras 1503 & 1504

Wavering between this path and that path seldom leads to worship. Therefore, firmly hold to the Chariya path and seek the King of Kings; all doubts will vanish. All worship by yogis — that is meditating on the moon (nadi on the left) and shifting on to the sun nadi on the right) — and worship by the celestial beings commenced in Dasa Marga.

அந்திப்பன் திங்க ளதன்பின்பு ஞாயிறு
சிந்திப்பன் என்றும் ஒருவன் செறிகழல்
வந்திப்ப வானவர் தேவனை நாடோறும்
வந்திப்ப தெல்லாம் வகையின் முடிந்ததே. 1504

All Worship Began From Chariya

"I meditate on the Moon Nadi on the left,
I shift on to the Sun Nadi on the right"
—The worship the yogins thus
At the Feet of the One perform
And the worship the Celestial Beings,
Daily to Lord offer.
All these but begin
In the Path of Chariya ultimate.

அண்ணலை வானவர் ஆயிரம் பேர்சொல்லி
உன்னுவர் உள்மகிழ்ந் துண்ணின் றடிதொழக்
கண்ணவ னென்று கருது மவர்கட்குப்
பண்ணவன் பேரன்பு பற்றிநின் றானே. 1505

Lord Appears in Love Entwined

The Celestial Beings seek the Lord
Chanting His glory in names thousand;
They that adore His Holy Feet
In abiding rapture of their hearts,
And hold him as the apple of their eyes'
Unto them is He sweet melody,
To them He appears in divine love entwined.

Mantras 1505 & 1506

The Lord appears in the divine love of those who seek and adore Him in the abiding rapture of their hearts. What is the use of reading holy works and conducting pujas, when the heart is obfuscated by darkness and overspread with the moss of ignorance. Unless the heart is rid of all these impurities, God, the Supreme Light, cannot be visioned.

வாசித்தும் பூசித்தும்மாமலர் கொய்திட்டும்
பாசிக் குளத்தில்வீழ் கல்லா மனம்பார்க்கின்
மாசற்ற சோதி மணிமிடற் றண்ணலை
நேசத் திருந்த நினைவறி யாரே. 1506

Be of Love and See the Lord

What avails it
That you read holy scriptures,
Perform Pujas,
Gather flowers in cluster?
As long as your heart is like a pebble
Dropped into a dark pool
Over-spread with moss of ignorance,
You can never realize the Lord;
Lord that is in your heart's love;
Lord that is blue-throated;
He, the Pure Light.

13. சாலோகம்
SALOKAM (IN GOD'S WORLD)

சாலோக மாதி சரியாதி யிற்பெறுஞ்
சாலோகஞ் சாமீபந் தங்குஞ் சரியையால்
மாலோகஞ் சேரில் வழியாகுஞ் சாரூபம்
பாலோகம் இல்லாப் பரனுரு வாமே. 1507

Successive Stages to Final Beatitude

The four stages of attainment
Saloka, Samipa, Sarupa and Sayujya
Are in gradation reached from Chariya;
The path of Chariya leads to Saloka;
And that in turn to Samipa
And Samipa to Sarupa;
And ultimately to Para of Infinite Space (Sayujya)
Beyond, which there is state none.

The four stages, of attainment, namely, Saloka, Samipa, Sarupa and Sayujya reached from Chariya in gradation, finally end with Para of Infinite Space (Sayujya), beyond which there is no state.

'Saloka', 'Samipa', 'Sarupa' and Sayujya' mean respectively 'Being in the same world as the Lord', Being with Him continually'. 'adopting His Form', and 'United with Him' These are different ways of imagining Oneself to be in, during worship. They are explained in verse 1509, post.

சமயங் கிரியையிற் றன்மனங் கோயில்
சமய மனுமுறை தானே விசேடஞ்
சமயத்து மூலந் தனைத்தேறன் மூன்றாஞ்
சமயாபி டேகந் தானாஞ் சமாதியே. 1508

The Four Ordinations in Kriya Worship

In Kriya worship are sacraments four;
Samaya sacrament prepares heart to be a Tabernacle of God;
Visesha sacrament installs the Faith firm;
Nirvana helps realize the Truth of Faith;
Abhisheka confers the state of Samadhi Supreme.

This Mantra should appropriately come at the end of 6, kriya ante, after Mantra 1456.

14. சாமீபம்
SAMIPAM (IN GOD'S PROXIMITY)

பாசம் பசுவான தாகும்இச் சாலோகம்
பாச மருளான தாகும்இச் சாமீபம்
பாசஞ் சிரமான தாகும்இச் சாரூபம்
பாசங் கரைபதி சாயுச் சியமே. 1509

Transformation of World-Knowledge

In Saloka Pasa Jnana (World knowledge) becomes
Pasu Jnana (Spiritual knowledge)
In Samipa it becomes Arul Jnana
(Grace-knowledge)
In Sarupa it is transformed into Pati Jnana
(God-knowledge)
In Sayuja it is for ever dissolved.

15. சாரூபம்
SARUPAM (IN GOD'S FORM)

தங்கிய சாரூபந் தானெட்டாம் யோகமாந்
தங்குஞ்சன்மார்க்கந் தனிலன்றிக் கைகூடா
அங்கத் துடல்சித்தி சாதன ராகுவர்
இங்கிவ ராக விழிவற்ற யோகமே. 1510

Only Jnana-in-Yoga Leads to Sarupa State

The State of Sarupa is, no doubt, reached
Through the eight-fold yoga way;
But unless it be Sanmarga-in-Yoga,
The Sarupa state cannot be;
The yoga way but leads to bodily Siddhis diverse;
But for the Sarupa state to realize,
None these but the pure way of Jnana-in-Yoga.

Though the eight-pronged yoga way reaches up to the Sarupa state, unless San Marga in Yoga (Jnana in Yoga) is attained, there cannot be the state of Sarupa.

Sanmarga-in-yoga is identical with jnana-in-yoga.
Mular explains that mere practice of yoga without 'Sanmarga' (worshipful faith and good conduct) will only produce Siddhis (Powers) but will not lead to Liberation.

சயிலலோ கத்தினைச் சார்ந்த பொழுதே
சயிலம தாகுஞ் சராசரம் போலப்
பயிலுங் குருவின் பதிபுக்க போதே
கயிலை இறைவன் கதிர்வடி வாமே. 1511

Sarupa State by Nearness to God

All things, living and non-living,
As they reach the Golden Mount of Meru
Are themselves into gold transformed;

Even so,
They that reach the world to Master Divine
Attain the Form Light Divine
His, of the King of Kailas.

16. சாயுச்சியம்
SAYUJYAM (ONE IN GOD)

சைவஞ் சிவனுடன் சம்பந்த மாகுதல்
சைவந் தனையறிந் தேசிவஞ் சாருதல்
சைவஞ் சிவந்தன்னைச் சாராமல் நீங்குதல்
சைவஞ் சிவானந்தஞ் சாயுச் சியமே. 1512

Stages in the Soul's Pilgrimage

In the Soul's Pilgrimage towards God
The Path of Saivam describes stages four;
It is Saivam, when the Self forges a kindred tie with Siva (in Saloka)
It is Saivam, when the Soul realizes itself and nears God (in Samipa)
It is Saivam, when it leaves Samipya (and reaches Sarupa)
It is Saivam when it enjoys the final bliss of Sivananda,
The inextricable union in Sayujya.

The Sayujya marga is, it appears the same as the one termed 'Sahaja' in Tantricism which is "the marga or way of spiritual exercise which is the earliest or most natural. It is also the term for ultimate reality among the Sahajiyas, i.e., those who believe in this marga . (N.N. Bhattacharyya in "History of Tantricism", p.465.).

சாயுச் சியஞ்சாக் கிராதீதஞ் சாருதல்
சாயுச் சியமுப சாந்தத்துத் தங்குதற்
சாயிச் சியஞ்சிவ மாதல் முடிவிலாச்
சாயுச் சியமனத் தானந்த சத்தியே. 1513

Sayujyam

Sayujya is the state of Jagra-Atita—the Beyond-Consciousness
Sayujya is to abide for ever in Upasantha
The peace that passes all understanding
Sayujya is to become Siva Himself,
Sayujya is to experience the infinite power of inward bliss,
Forever and ever.

Sayujya is the state of jagra-atita, the state beyond consciousness; it is to abide forever in upasantha, the peace that is beyond understanding, and finally to become Siva Himself, experiencing the infinite power of inward bliss.

17. சத்திநிபாதம்
SATHINIPADAM (DESCENT OF GRACE)

மந்தம்

இருட்டறை மூலை யிருந்த கிழவி
குருட்டுக் கிழவனைக் கூடல் குறித்துக்
குருட் டினை நீக்கிக் குணம்பல காட்டி
மருட்டி யவனை மணம்புரிந் தாளே. 1514

Wooing of the Soul by the Goddess of Grace

In the corner dark of the Chamber of Primal Stuff
There She was — the Virgin Lady of Grace;
Intent on consorting with the Blind Old Man — the Soul immortal,
She rent his veil of night,
Showered full many a favour,
Wooed with temptations diverse,
And lo! to Her bosom took him,
In wedlock holy.

Mantras 1514 & 1515

In the dark corner of the chamber of primal stuff, the Goddess of Grace courted the 'blind old man' — immortal soul — and in marriage took him to Her bosom. Meditation on the primal source, from where sprang the delusive senses, grants Her vision. Those who are given this clear vision are truly in the infinite ground of Sakti of the highest seeking.

தீம்புல னான திசையது சிந்திக்கில்
ஆம்புல னாயறிவார்க்கமு தாய்நிற்குந்
தேம்புல னான தெளிவறி வார்கட்குக்
கோம்புல னாடிய கொல்லையு மாமே. 1515

The Infinite Ground of Sakti's Descent

If you meditate on the primal source
Whence the evil senses sprang
You shall know it as Land of Becoming,
The ambrosia of the Realized;
They that have been given the clear vision nectar sweet,
Are verily the Infinite Ground
Of Sakti's highest seeking.

இருள்நீக்கி எண்ணில் பிறவி கடத்தி
அருள்நீங்கா வண்ணமே யாதியருளும்
மருள்நீங்கா வானவர் கோனொடுங் கூடிப்
பொருள்நீங்கா இன்பம் புலம்பயல் தானே. 1516

Arul Sakti Helps Attain Liberation

The Primal Sakti releases Jiva from enveloping gloom,
Rows it across the sea of myriad births,
Grants the Grace Abiding;
And lands it on the shores of Truth's Bliss
United in the Lord of Heavenly Beings,
—Themselves as yet unfree
From Impurity's obscuration.

Mantras 1516 & 1517

Releasing jiva from the enveloping darkness, the Primal Sakti aids it to land on the banks of Truth's bliss and to attain liberation. The presence of Lord Nandi and the Lady of Grace pierces and illumines the bewildering ignorance that engulfs the jiva in thick gloom.

இருள்சூ ழறையில் இருந்தது நாடிற்
பொருள்சூழ் விளக்கது புக்கெரிந் தாற்போன்
மருள்சூழ் மயக்கத்து மாமலர் நந்தி
அருள்சூழ் இறைவனும் அம்மையு மாமே. *1517*

Grace Illumines

As when groping in a chamber enveloped in thick gloom,
A sudden shaft of light pierces and illumines,
Like it into the gloom of bewildering Ignorance
Is the Presence of God and Goddess of Grace,
Lord that is Nandi worshipped in the blossom of heart.

மந்ததரம்
MANDATARAM (SLOW PACE)

மருட்டிப் புணர்ந்து மயக்கமும் நீக்கி
வெருட்டி வினையறுத் தின்பம் விளைத்துக்
குருட்டினை நீக்கிக் குணம்பல காட்டி
அருட்டிகழ் ஞான மதுபுரிந் தானே. *1518*

Grace Leads Soul Through Successive Stages

She tempted the Soul with guiles,
Took him to Her bosom,
Shook him from stupor,
Dispelled his Karmaic hordes,
Destroyed them to the roots,
Filled him with rapture
Lifted the veil of his Ignorance
Granted many a favour
And then, then, bestowed on him Her Grace that illumines.

Mantras 1518 & 1519

Through successive stages, like drawing him away from temptations to which the jiva falls a prey and eradication of the karmaic hordes and primordial ignorance, the Damsel of Grace liberates the soul. Sporting in the holy waters of the Sakti's Grace makes the jiva forget the filthy waters of virgin's lust; for, the Holy Virgin's waters of Grace snap the cycle of births.

கன்னித் துறைபடிந் தாடிய ஆடவர்
கன்னித் துறைபடிந் தாடுங் கருத்திலர்
கன்னித் துறைபடிந் தாடுங் கருத்துண்டேற்
பின்னைப் பிறவி பிறிதில்லை தானே. *1519*

Descent of Grace Snaps Cycle of Births

They that have sported in the waters of Virgin Grace,
No more shall wallow in the filthy waters of virgin's lust;
If they but seek to sport in the Holy Virgin's Waters of Grace,
No more births shall they in future take.

செய்யன் கரியன் வெளியன் நற் பச்சையன்
எய்த வுணர்ந்தவர் எய்வர் இறைவனை
மைவென் றகன்ற பகடுரி போர்த்தவெங்
கைய னிவனென்று காதல்செய் வீரே. *1520*

Lord is Soul's Redeemer

He is the Red One (Destroyer)
The Dark One (Preserver)
The White One (Creator)
The Green One (Redeemer)
They who know Him thus, free of doubt
Of a certain shall seek Him;
Remember this;
His are the sinewy arms
That skinned the dark massive elephant
And donned it for a vesture;
Do therefore, seek Him and adore Him.

The Lord plays the multi-role of Destroyer, Preserver, Creator and Redeemer. Realisation of this truth and adoration of Him will make the jiva feel the might of His sinewy arms.

The 'significance of attributing different colours to Siva's form is explained here.

எய்திய காலங்கள் எத்தனை யாயினுந்
தையலுந் தானுந் தனிநா யகமென்பர்
வைகலுந் தன்னை வணங்கு மவர்கட்குக்
கையிற் கருமஞ்செய் காட்டது வாமே. *1521*

Siva and Sakti are One and Same

Infinite the passage of Time's Flood
Yet they say, He and His Consort stand one;
For them that adore Him daily in devotion,
He is verily the unfailing proof
Of labour readily rewarded.

Mantras 1521 & 1522

Siva and Sakti are one and the same. So praise Him in devotion daily. He is truly the unfailing proof. Beholding the vision of Sakti and Siva together dispels darkness.

கண்டுகொண் டோமிரண்டுந்தொடர்ந் தாங்கொளி
பண்டுபண் டோயும் பரமன் பரஞ்சுடர்
வண்டுகொண் டாடு மலர்வார் சடையண்ணல்
நின்றுகண் டார்க்கிருள் நீக்கிநின் றானே. *1522*

தீவிரம்
TIVIRAM (RAPID PACE)

அண்ணிக்கும் பெண்பிள்ளை அப்பனார் தோட்டத்தில்
எண்ணிக்கும் ஏழேழ் பிறவி யுணர்விக்கும்
உண்ணிற்ப தெல்லாம் ஒழிய முதல்வனைக்
கண்ணுற்று நின்ற கனியது வாகுமே. *1523*

Fruit of Grace

In the garden of the Heavenly Father
Is that Damsel of Grace;
She approaches you,
Reveals the mystery of the births beyond count,
And destroys their very seed;
And then you vision the Primal One;
That, indeed, is the fruit of Her Grace.

Mantras 1523 & 1524

Sakti is the Goddess of the mountain regions and of exotic blossoms. Vision of the Primal One is the fruit of Her Grace. That is granted when the Bride of Grace, seated in the garden of the heavenly Bride-Groom, destroys the very seeds of birth. Devotion to her grants the prowess of potential tapas that leads to liberation.

பிறப்பை யறுக்கும் பெருந்தவம் நல்கும்
மறப்பை யறுக்கும் வழிபட வைக்குங்
குறப்பெண் குவிமுலை கோமள வல்லி
சிறப்பொடு பூசனை செய்யநின் றார்க்கே. *1524*

They That Adore Sakti Shall Be Granted Things Spiritual

She is the Damsel of the mountain regions;
Of shapely breasts and delicate beauty;
If you in devotion adore Her,
She cuts the bonds of birth asunder;
Grants the prowess of mighty tapas;
Scorches the soul's forgetfulness;
And leads you to liberations path.

தாங்குமின் எட்டுத்திசைக்குந் தலைமகன்
பூங்கமழ் கோதைப் புரிகுழ லாளொடும்

Vision of Sakti and Siva in Union

Given unto me was to vision the Light
That shone from the Twain in unison;
It was verily the Light Divine of the Ancient One,
In whose matted locks festooned with flowers,
The bees dance drunk with nectar;
They that waited in patience and prayer
They indeed saw Him — their darkness dispelled.

ஆங்கது சேரும் அறிவுடை யார்கட்குத்
தூங்கொளி நீலந் தொடர்தலு மாமே. *1525*

Light of Grace Illumines the Path of Devotee

He is the Lord of all Space in directions eight;
Bear His holy Feet on your head,
And He shall appear to you
With His Consort of Grace
Wreathed in clusters of fragrant blooms
In Her twisted tresses
And for them who are thus made wise
The Blue Flame of Her floating Grace
Shall, for ever, illumine the Path.

Mantras 1525 & 1526

Near the Holy Feet of the Lord are all worlds. He shall descend with His Lady Companion — Sakti of Grace — who will enlighten the path of the devotees. Wisdom gives the unsurpassable boon of Grace; and when Grace visits, the Lord, whom nothing can equal, draws near. When Grace descends, jiva is purified. He then mingles in Siva.

நணுகினு ஞானக் கொழுந்தொன்று நல்கும்
பணிகிலும் பன்மலர் தூவிப் பணிவன்
அணுகிய தொன்றறி யாத வொருவன்
அணுகும் உலகெங்கு மாவியு மாமே. *1526*

Lord Draws Near When Grace Visits

Seek close,
That soft Flame of Wisdom shall grant you
The peerless gift of Grace;
When you adore Him
Do so, showering blooms at His Feet
As I do,
Then shall He draw near you
Whom nothing can ever near;
He is truly the life pervasive of worlds all.

தீவிர தரம்
TEEVIRA TARAM (MORE RAPID PACE)

இருவினை நேரொப்பில் இன்னருட் சத்தி
குருவென வந்து குணம்பல நீக்கித்
தருமெனு ஞானத்தால் தன்செய லற்றால்
திரிமலந் தீர்ந்து சிவனவ னாமே. 1527

When Grace Descends as Guru

When Jiva attains the state of Neutrality
To deeds, good and evil,
Then does divine Grace in Guru form descend,
Removes attributes all,
Implants Jnana that is like a heavenly cool shade;
The Jiva thus rid of egoity,
And other Impurities Three,
Shall with Siva in union merge.

இரவும் பகலும் இலாத இடத்தே
குரவஞ் செய்கின்ற குழலியை உன்னி
அரவஞ்செய் யாமல் அவளுடன் சேரப்
பரிவொன்றி லாளும் பராபரை தானே. 1528

How to Win the Goddess of Grace

In the Space Vast where neither night nor day is
The Goddess of Long Tresses dances in rapture;
Think of Her, make no sound
And in silence woo Her;
In endearment all
She draws you unto Her bosom,
And grants you Her favours;
Verily, Verily, She is the Paraparai,
The Power Supreme.

Mantras 1528 & 1529
Woo the Goddess of Supreme Power and Prowess (Paraparai). Dancing in rapture in the Vast Space, She will grant Her favours. Then, He, the sun, the moon, and the light of Grace which illumined the corporeal body dispelling darkness — all abide in you forever.

மாலை விளக்கும் மதியமும் ஞாயிறுஞ்
சாலை விளக்குந் தனிச்சுடர் அண்ணலுள்
ஞானம் விளக்கிய நாதன்என் உள்புகுந்(து)
ஊனை விளக்கி யுடனிருந் தானே. 1529

Inner Light of Grace

He is the Sun and the Moon
That dispels darkness;
He is the Light on the path,
The Peerless Flame, the Supreme Lord;
The Master that illumined the Light within me;
He entered in me and lighted up the corporeal body;
And then, aye, with me bided for ever and ever.

18. அறுசமயப் பிணக்கம்
ARUSAMAYA PINAKKAM
(A CRITIQUE OF FORMAL RELIGIONS)

ஆயத்துள் நின்ற அறுசம யங்களுங்
காயத்துள் நின்ற கடவுளைக் காண்கிலர்
மாயக் குழியில் விழுவர் மனைமக்கள்
பாசத்தில் உற்றுப் பதைக்கின்ற வாறே. 1530

The Six Faiths Avail Not

The Six faiths severally congregate,
Yet, not one knows the God within;
Deep into the pit of illusion, their adherents drop,
And fastened hard by familialities of bondage,
They shake and tremble, in vain impotence.

Mantras 1530-1533

The six faiths, being tied fast to the earthly fetters shake and shiver in vain, unable to cognise God, who is within. The Lord, the Pinnacle and the Magnificent seated in the lotus of our hearts, enters this hollow abode of human flesh and then silently parts. This deep design of His is beyond the apprehension of the formal faiths. Intense faith and steadfastness help in the realisation of the omnipresence of the Lord.

What are the "Six Faiths" (சமயம், Samayam means here 'religion', 'sect' or 'faith') that Mular refers to here? They are not those described in 'Saddarsana-sangraha', it can be safely affirmed.

உள்ளத்து ளேதான் கரந்தெங்கும் நின்றவன்
வள்ளல் தலைவன் மலருறை மாதவன்
பொள்ளற் குரம்பைப் புகுந்து புறப்படுங்
கள்ளத் தலைவன் கருத்தறி யார்களே. 1531

Formal Faiths Know not God Within

He hides in your heart
Yet does He pervade all;
He is the Munificient One;
The Lord Supreme;
Of austere penance
He is seated on the lotus of our hearts;
The cunning Master-Thief
In stealth enters this hollow abode of human flesh
And then leaves it;
None knows His deep design.

உள்ளத்தும் உள்ளன் புறத்துள்ளன் என்பவர்க்
குள்ளத்தும் உள்ளன் புறத்துள்ளன் எம்மிறை
உள்ளத்தும் இல்லை புறத்தில்லை என்பவர்க்
குள்ளத்தும் இல்லை புறத்தில்லை தானே. 1532

Existence of God is an Act of Faith

Say, Lord is within you and without you
Then sure my Lord is within you and without you;
To them they say,
He is neither within you or without you
Sure is He nowhere for them.

ஆறு சமயமுங் கண்டவர் கண்டிலர்
ஆறு சமயப் பொருளும் அவனலன்
தேறுமின் தேறித் தெளிமின் தெளிந்தபின்
மாறுதல் இன்றிமனைபுக லாமே. 1533

God is Beyond All Formal Faiths

They founded the Six Faiths,
Yet they found Him not;
What the Six Faiths talk of is not He;
Do you yourself in faith seek Him,
And be resolved of doubts all;
And then sure shall you enter your Father's Mansion.

சிவமல்ல தில்லை யறையே சிவமாந்
தவமல்ல தில்லை தலைப்படு வார்க்கிங்(கு)
அவமல்ல தில்லை அறுசம யங்கள்
தவம்வல்ல நந்திதாள் சார்ந்துய்யு நீரே. 1534

God Can Be Reached Only by Devotion

Proclaim you this:
There is nothing except Siva
No tapas except it be for Him,
The Six Faiths are nothing but a dreary waste;
Do seek Nandi of mighty penance;
You shall indeed be redeemed truly.

Siva is the only Lord; and the six faiths are but a dreary waste. Being materialistic, the six faiths do not lead to the final state. Devotion to Siva alone grants liberation.

அண்ணலை நாடிய ஆறு சமயமும்
விண்ணவ ராக மிகவும் விரும்பியே
முண்ணின் றழியு முயன்றில ராதலான்
மண்ணின் றொழியும் வகையறி யார்களே. 1535

The Six Faiths Sought not Freedom from Pasas

They of the Six Faiths sought Lord
Only for heavenly state to gain;
They sought not to be rid of bondage thorns,
And so know not to be rid of this world's materiality.

Mantras 1535-1537

The path of Siva alone is our defence from earthly sorrows. It is the sole path that leads to ultimate liberation through pasa annihilation. Neither the six faiths nor the swollen stream of hundreds of other faiths, tall as their claims are, can lead to the path of Param.

சிவகதி யேகதி மற்றுள்ள எல்லாம்
பவகதி பாசப் பிறவியொன் றுண்டு
தவகதி தன்னொடு நேரொன்று தோன்றில்
அவகதி மூவரும் அவ்வகை யாமே. 1536

Path of Siva Leads to Final Liberation

The Path of Siva alone is the sole Path;
The Other paths but lead to earthly sorrows;
And sure birth in bondage returns to you;
Do you walk in the Holy Path
And when the One appears,
The triad Impurities that your destruction encompass
Will, of themselves, meet their own destruction.

நூறு சமயம் உளவா நுவலுங்கால்
ஆறு சமயமவ் வாறுட் படுவன
கூறு சமயங்கள் கொண்டநெறிநில்லா
ஈறு பரநெறி யில்லா நெறியன்றே. 1537

The False Paths Lead not to Param

Forsooth,
The Faiths here below are a hundred in number,
In that swollen stream are the Six Faiths too;
These Faiths take not to the goal they boast of;
They are true Faiths never,
They take you not to Path of Param.

கத்துங் கழுதைகள் போலுங் கலதிகள்
சுத்த சிவமெங்குந் தோய்வுற்று நிற்கின்றான்
குற்றந் தெளியார் குணங்கொண்டு கோதாட்டிப்
பித்தேறி நாளும் பிறந்திறப் பாரே. 1538

Contending Faiths Do Not Help

The contending Paths are like the braying asses;
The Pure Siva is all-pervasive;
They seek Him not by the right Path,
And so are not free from Impurities;
They shall grow insane
Forever entangled in the whirl of birth and death.

Contending faiths are like the braying asses. They lead but to the swirling cycle of birth and death. Pure Siva is beyond their reach.

மயங்குகின் றாரு மதிதெளிந் தாரும்
முயங்கி யிருவினை முழைமுகப் பாச்சி
இயங்கிப் பெறுவரே லீறது காட்டிற்
பயங்கெட் டவர்க்கோர் பரநெறி யாமே. 1539

To Attain the Supreme Goal

Those who are assailed by doubts
And those who are freed from doubts
When together commingle,
Drive the wild beasts of Kārma twain to caves,
And persevere in the pursuit
Then shall the Supreme Goal be reached
They that are rid of the terrors of the wild
Shall see the Path that to Para leads.

Mantras 1539 & 1540

To attain the final goal — freedom from harassing doubts, and perseverence in Siva-pursuit are essential. God is with the steadfast and clear-visioned souls. To the doubting and inconstant, He is beyond reach. They realise not His mysterious plan, for which the fleshy body is fashioned.

சேயன் அணியன் பிணியிலன் பேர்நந்தி
தூயன் துளக்கற நோக்கவல் லார்கட்கு
மாயன் மயக்கிய மானுட ராமவர்
காயம் விளைக்குங் கருத்தறி யார்களே. *1540*

God is Distant and Near

He is far away,
He is near at hand
He is rid of ailments,
He is of immortal name Nandi;
Transparent to those that have unwavering vision;
Elusive to those who are tossed in doubt;
Such know not the mysterious purpose
For which the fleshy body is fashioned.

வழியிரண் டுக்குமோர் வித்தது வான
பழியது பார்மிசை வாழ்தல் உறுதல்
சுழியறி வாளன்றன் சொல்வழி முன்னின்
றழிவறி வார்நெறி நாடநில் லாரே. *1541*

The End of Seeking

To be born and to live again and again here below,
Verily is the curse of all;
It is the seed of Karma twain;
If you but listen to Him that knows
The origin of swirl that is birth and death,
No more shall you seek
The ways of the perishing men.

The cycle of births is the bane of the soul and the seed of the coupled karma. So, listen to Him, who knows the origin of this cycle.

மாதவர் எல்லாம் மாதேவன் பிரானென்பர்
நாதம தாக அறியப்படுநந்தி
பேதஞ்செய் யாதே பிரானென்று கைதொழில்
ஆதியும் அந்நெறி யாகிநின் றானே. *1542*

Lord and Nandi are One

All the holy ones hail Him as Great God; the Supreme Lord,
He that is Nada and bears the name Nandi;
You too shall make no distinction,
But in prayer lift your hands to Him as Being Supreme;
And the Primal One shall as such reveal Himself.

Mantras 1542 & 1543

Little is the distinction between the Supreme Lord and holy Nandi. Hara, the Holy Father, is immanent in the hearts of men. Alienation from Him makes Him incognisable by jiva.

அரனெறி யப்பனை யாதிப் பிரானை
உரநெறி யாகி யுளம்புகுந் தானைப்
பரநெறி தேடிய பத்தர்கள் சித்தம்
பரனெறி யாவிடிற் பல்வகைத் தூரமே. *1543*

God is Within You; and Yet Far Away

He is Hara, Divine Father, Primal Lord
As implacable Truth He entered the heart;
But if hearts of devotees sought alien paths
They know Him not;
Then is He far, far away.

பரிசறி வானவன் பண்பன் பகலோன்
பெரிசறி வானவர் பேற்றில் திகழுந்
துரிசற நீநினை தூய்மணி வண்ணன்
அரிதவன் வைத்த அறநெறி தானே. *1544*

Precious is Hara's Path

The Heavenly Lord, He knows our goal
He is tender-hearted;
He is the Effulgent Sun that guides the destiny
Of Heavenly Beings of wisdom great;
Do think of Him in thought unsullied;
He is of crystal pure hue;
Precious the path of Virtue
He for us has laid.

Mantras 1544-1546

God, the tender-hearted, is aware of our ultimate goal. He is the Effulgent Sun who designs our destiny. Precious and crystal pure becomes Hara's path in intense meditation. Fidelity to God, who is far above all the religions, transcends the fleshy imperfections. True faith leads to the destined goal; adverse ones grant not His Grace.

ஆன சமயம் அதுஇது நன்றெனும்
மாய மனிதர் மயக்க மதுவொழி
கானங் கடந்த கடவுளை நாடுமின்
ஊனங் கடந்த வுருவது வாமே. *1545*

God is Beyond All Religions

This the right path, that the right path
Be not tossed in such frail human doubts;
Seek the Being that is beyond wilderness of doubts
His is the Form that is flawless.

அந்நெறி நாடி அமரர் முனிவருஞ்
செந்நெறி கண்டார் சிவனெனப் பெற்றார்பின்
முன்னெறி நாடி முதல்வன் அருளிலார்
சென்னெறி செல்லார் திகைக்கின்ற வாறே. *1546*

True and False Faiths

That Path they took
The immortal Devas and the saintly tapasvins;
And so reached the Goal True
And merged in one with Siva;
But they that followed froward faiths
Received not His grace;
They lost their way,
And forever wander.

உறுமா றறிவதும் உள்நின்ற சோதி
பெறுமா றறியிற் பிணக்கொன்றும் இல்லை
அறுமா றதுவான வங்கியு ளாங்கே
இறுமா றறிகிலர் ஏழைகள் தாமே. 1547

Definition of Truth Path

He is Light within you;
To know how to reach Him
Is True Path of Becoming;
If you know thus,
You know contradiction none;
That is Path Supreme, Your Goal's End;
They are but folks poor in spirit
That know not merging in Light Divine.

Mantras 1547 & 1549

Apprehension of the light within is the true path of becoming. That is the goal which is free from contradictions. Worldly paths are nothing but a mirage. So give up the sorrowful path of whirling karma and crass evil; surely you will worship at the Lord's Feet. The true path results in the consummation of holiness. Journey forward, straight inside, and the presence of the Lord will be with you for ever.

வழிநடக் கும்பரி சொன்றுண்டு வையங்
கழிநடக் குண்டவர் கற்பனை கேட்பர்
சுழிநடக் குந்துய ரம்மது நீக்கிப்
பழிநடப் பார்க்குப் பரவலு மாமே. 1548

Worldly Path is not True Path

There is a True Path for the Journey;
They that follow the swampy paths worldly
See but the mirage;
They that avoid the sorrowful path of swirling Karma
Cross evil safe;
And shall sure worship at Lord's Feet.

வழிசென்ற மாதவம் வைகின்ற போது
பழிசெல்லும் வல்வினைப் பற்றறுத் தாங்கே
வழிசெல்லும் வல்வினை யாம்திறம் விட்டிட்
டுழிசெல்லில் உம்பர் தலைவன்முன் னாமே. 1549

True Path Leads Straight to Lord's Presence

Walking in the True Path
Your holiness consummates;
The host of thine Karmaic deeds scatters
And they flee away;
Leave you the tortuous path
Of the Karmaic ridden men of world
Onward you journey, straight inside;
Thou shall, for certain, stand
In the Presence of the Lord of Heavenly Beings.

19. நிராசாரம்
NIRACHARAM (DISSENSION REFUTED)

இமையங்க ளாய்நின்ற தேவர்கள் ஆறு
சமையங்கள் பெற்றனர் சாத்திரம் ஓதி
யமையறிந் தோமென்ப ராதிப் பிரானுங்
கமையறிந் தாருட் கலந்துநின் றானே. 1550

Who Attained Divine Tranquillity

The Heavenly Beings, immortal as the mountain Himalayas,
Received the Darshanas that are Six;
"We learned them all and attained the Other World"
—Thus quote they;
But, in sooth,
The Primal Lord is in intimacy within
Of those that have Divine Tranquillity attained.

Mantras 1550 & 1551

The immortal heavenly beings having received the six darshanas believe that they have attained liberation; but true liberation is within and belongs to those who have attained divine tranquillity. Humble yourself at the Feet of the Lord, and you become one with Siva. Unquenchable desires lead but to eternal sorrow.

பாங்கமர் கொன்றைப் படர்சடை யானடி
தாங்கு மனிதர் தரணியில் நேரொப்பர்
நீங்கிய வண்ணம் நினைவுசெய் யாதவர்
ஏங்கி உலகில் இருந்தழு வாரே. 1551

Worship Siva and Siva Become

They who bow their head at the Feet of Lord
Of spreading matted locks and Konrai bloom bedecked,
They shall, like unto Him, become;
But they that yearn not for Him in constant eagerness
Shall be in sorrow immersed,
Sighing eternal here below.

இருந்தழு வாரும் இயல்புகெ ட்டாரும்
அருந்தவ மேற்கொண்டங் கண்ணலை எண்ணில்
வருந்தா வகைசெய்து வானவர் கோனும்
பெருந்தன்மை நல்கும் பிறப்பில்லை தானே. 1552

Worship Brings Immortal Life

Despair not!
You that thus sit and bewail
And you that have lost your better nature!
Seek Lord in penance true,

The Heavens' Lord shall wipe your tears away,
And grant you Greatness;
And you shall then know births no more.

Mantras 1552 & 1553

Neither despair nor wail. That will affect your better nature. Instead, perform tapas and atonement. The Lord will wipe your tears and grant you greatness. Life goes in vain for those who seek Him not. Befriend God by seeking Him. He will shower His manifold Grace and countless blessings.

தூரறி வாளர் துணைவர் நினைப்பிலர்
பாரறி வாளர் படுபயன் றானுண்பர்
காரறி வாளர் கலந்து பிறப்பர்கள்
நீரறி வார்நெடு மாமுகி லாமே. 1553

Lord is Like Gentle Rain

Who seeks Finite Truth
They His friend are;
Who does not seek Him
They but know the Worldly Men's Misery-Way,
Enveloped in darkness of bondage
In vain shall they be born again and again;
Who seeks Path True
To them, the Lord is like richly laden clouds
That drops gentle rain of Heavenly Grace.

அறிவுடன் கூடி அழைத்ததோர் தோணி
பறிவுடன் பாரம் பழம்பதி சிந்துங்
குறியது கண்டுங் கொடுவினை யாளர்
செறிய நினைக்கிலர் சேவடி தானே. 1554

Lord Guides the Boat of Life

The Boat of Life
By Divine Wisdom guided
Discharges quick its cargo
At the City Ancient;
Having seen that unerring prospect
These wretched men of ignoble deeds
Think not of His Holy Feet,
In devotion replete.

Mantras 1554 & 1555

Inspite of having realised that God guides the 'boat of life,' wretched men of ignoble deeds do not think of Him in intense devotion. They are witless fools who laugh at the fact that Siva, the Eternal Being, is immanent within. If they but pray to Him, they will meet the Supreme One.

மன்னும் ஒருவன் மருவு மனோமயன்
என்னின் மனிதர் இகழ்வரிவ் வேழைகள்
துன்னி மனமே தொழுமின் துணையிலி
தன்னையும் அங்கே தலைப்பட லாமே. 1555

Lord is Within You

The Only Being, the Eternal Being
Within you He dwells;
When you say so,
These ignorant men laugh low;
Poor folk! if they but seek Him in prayer within
Then shall they meet Him — the Peerless One.

ஓங்காரத் துள்ளொளி உள்ளே உதயமுற்
றாங்கார மற்ற அனுபவங் கைகூடார்
சாங்கால முன்னார் பிறவாமை சார்வுறார்
நீங்காச் சமயத்துள் நின்றொழிந் தார்களே. 1556

Who Pursued False Faiths

They wake not to Inner Light of Aum within;
And joy not in ego-effaced bliss ensuing
They wot not of approaching death,
They seek not the end of recurring birth,
Lo! they pursued the unending path of contending faiths,
And stood forlorn, for ever lost in faith false.

They who pursue false faiths do not wake to the inner light of Aum, that is within themselves. These faiths do not reveal the bliss that ensues when the ego is totally annihilated. Indifferent both to the cycle of approaching death and recurring birth, alas, they stand in forlorn hope.

20. உட்சமயம்
INNER FAITHS

இமையவர் தம்மையும் எம்மையும் முன்னம்
அமைய வகுத்தவன் ஆதி புராணன்
சமையங்க ளாறுந்தன் றாளிணை நாட
அமையங் குழல்கின்ற ஆதிப் பிரானே. 1557

Lord Pervades All Six Inner Faiths

He is the Ancient One,
He created the beings, of earth and heaven,
In days of yore, in Order Divine;
The Six Faiths seek the Feet
But of the One Primal Peerless God;
And in them all He pervades
In measure appropriate.

Mantras 1557 & 1558

The ancient Lord, the Creator of all worlds, pervades all the six inner faiths. The Lord is the 'great city' to which the six roads (six inner faiths) lead. They who stand in contention are similar to the dog that barks at its own echo from the hillside.

ஒன்றது பேரூர் வழியா றதற்கு
என்றது போல இருமுச் சமயமும்

நன்றிது தீதிது என்றுரை யாளர்கள்
குன்று குரைத்தெழு நாயையொத் தார்களே. 1558

All Faiths Lead but to Lord

One, the Great City,
Six, the roads that lead to it;
Thus are Faiths Six;
They that contend, "This true; That false"
Are like the dog that in ire barks
To its own echo at hill side.

Mular condemns philosophical disputations.

சைவப் பெருமைத் தனிநா யகன்தன்னை
உய்ய வுயிர்க்கின்ற ஒண்சுடர் நந்தியை
மெய்ய பெருமையர்க் கன்பனை இன்பஞ்செய்
வையத் தலைவனை வந்தடைந் துயமினே. 1559

Come, Stand Apart and Seek the Lord

He is the incomparable Lord
Of the magnificent path of Saivam;
He is Nandi of Divine Lustre,
That breathes the eternal life of Grace;
Beloved is He of the truly great;
The Lord of all universe, the source of all joy;
Come, stand apart, seek, realize,
And be redeemed.

Mantras 1559 & 1560

He is the Peerless Lord of the munificent path of Saivam; the Nandi of Divine Lustre that grants an eternal life of Grace. He is the Lord of all universes, and the source of all joy. He laid the divine path that takes jiva to his eternal home. He is within you. Seek and realise Him.

சிவனவன் வைத்ததோர் தெய்வ நெறியிற்
பவனவன் வைத்த பழவழி நாடி
இவனவன் என்ப தறியவல் லார்கட்
கவனவ னங்குள தாங்கட னாமே. 1560

"You Are He" — Is the Teaching of the True Path

Siva laid the divine path ancient
That leads to the Home Eternal
Seek Him that way;
It is He who is sought by other path also.
You shall duly find Him within yourself..

ஆமா றுரைக்கும் அறுசம யாதிக்குப்
போமாறு தானில்லை புண்ணிய மல்லதங்
காமாம் வழியாக்கும் அவ்வே றுயிர்கட்கும்
போமாறவ் வாதாரப் பூங்கொடி யாளே. 1561

The True Path is Through Kundalini

The Six Faiths that profess the means to Becoming
Are by themselves but blind alleys all;
No good comes by following them alone;
The true path of Becoming for all life to pursue
Is but the path of divine Kundalini Sakti,
The blossom-vine that through Six centres courses.

The six faiths that proclaim the means to 'becoming' can do no good standing by themselves. Kundalini the blossom-vine that courses through the six chakras within, is the pervasive force in them all.

அரனெறி யாவ தறிந்தேனும் நானுஞ்
சிலநெறி தேடித் திரிந்தஅந் நாளும்
உரநெறி யுள்ளக் கடல்கடந் தேறுந்
தரநெறி நின்ற தனிச்சுடர் தானே. 1562

Lord Ever Guides

Now have I realized the Path of Hara;
In the past I sought Him in narrow paths
And strayed;
Lo! all the while He stood before me
Like a beacon light in firmament
Guiding my voyage
Across the sea of my Soul's longing.

Mantras 1562 & 1563

Narrow and crooked is not the path to the Lord. All the while, He stands before you like a beacon light guiding the voyage across the sea of soul's longing. Seek the proven path of Siva that leads to Hara. It is the divine path that renowned souls have treaded through time.

தேர்ந்த அரனை அடைந்த சிவநெறி
பேர்ந்தவர் உன்னிப் பெயர்ந்த பெருவழி
ஆர்ந்தவர் அண்டத்துப் புக்க அருள்நெறி
போந்து புனைந்து புணர்நெறி யாமே. 1563

Siva Path is Proven Path

The Path of Siva is the proven path
It led them to Hara;
It is the royal path that renowned Souls had walked;
The Path Divine
That took the devout to Cosmic Space;
That path, do seek,
Enter and persevere.

ஈரு மனத்தை யிரண்டற வீசுமின்
ஊருஞ் சகாரத்தை ஓதுமின் னோதியே
வாரு மரனெறி மன்னியே முன்னியத்
தூருஞ் சுடரொளி தோன்றலு மாமே. 1564

Vision of Light Effulgent in Saiva Path

Still your wandering thoughts;
Chant sacred syllable "SI"
And so persevere in Path of Hara
You shall envision Primal Light Effulgent.

Mantras 1564-1566

Perseverence in the path of Hara enables the jiva to reach the effulgent Primal Light vision through the Saiva path. There is the Primal Lord, the tender shoot of Jnana Light with the

Lady of Lightning Form, the blazing fire of Vedic brahmins and of the radiant souls who think of Him in devotion.

மினற்குரி யாளனை வேதியா வேதத்
தனற்குறி யாளனை ஆதிப் பிரான்தன்னை
நினைக்குறி யாளனை ஞானக் கொழுந்தி
னயக்குறி காணில் அரனெறி யாமே. 1565

Vision Through Saiva Path

He that belongs to the Lady of Lightning Form
He that belongs to the Vedic Fire of Brahmins
He that belongs to them that think of Him
He, the Primal Lord
He, the tender shoot of Jnana,
When you glimpse His loving signs,
Then have you walked in Path of Siva.

ஆய்ந்துண ரார்களின் ஆன்மாச் சதுர்பல
வாய்ந்துண ராவகை நின்ற அரனெறி
பாய்ந்துணர் வார் அரன் சேவடி கைதொழு
தேர்ந்துணர் செய்வதோர் இன்பமு மாமே. 1566

Adoration of Siva is Bliss

They that discriminated not
Knew not Hara's Path;
Their souls in myriad machinations caught,
The Truth saw not;
They that followed Hara's Path
Of a certain reached His Feet of Grace,
And joyed the Bliss, all senses uplifted.

சைவ சமயத் தனிநா யகன்நந்தி
உய்ய வகுத்த குருநெறி ஒன்றுண்டு
தெய்வச் சிவநெறி சன்மார்க்கஞ் சேர்ந்துய்ய
வையத்து ளார்க்குவகுத்துவைத் தானே. 1567

Saiva Path was Laid by Holy Nandi

The Holy Nandi, the acclaimed Master of Saiva Faith
Has showed a Way — the Master's way of Redemption;
That, divine Path of Saiva
He did chalk out for those here below
To walk in Sanmarga's trail
And be for ever free.

Holy Nandi, the Master of Saiva Faith, laid the divine path of Saivam as the sure way to the soul's liberation. Discriminate knowledge draws the jiva in Hara's path. They who walk in that path will surely reach His Feet of Grace and savour Siva bliss.

இத்தவம் அத்தவம் என்றிரு பேரிடும்
பித்தரைக் காணின் நகுமெங்கள் பேர்நந்தி
எத்தவ மாகிலென் எங்குப் பிறக்கிலென்
ஒத்துணர் வார்க்கொல்லை யூர்புக லாமே. 1568

Attune to Infinity

This the right Faith, that the true Faith
When my Lord Nandi thus sees
Mad men in two contend
He smiles in pity;
What though the form of Faith?
What though the place of Birth?
They with mind to infinity attuned
Sure enter the City of God.

Siva smiles in pity at the mad men who contend about faiths. To attune to infinity is to reach the 'City of God'.

ஆமே பிரான்முகம் ஐந்தொடு மாருயிர்
ஆமே பிரானுக் கதோமுக மாறுள
தாமே பிரானுக்குந் தன்சிர மாலைக்கும்
நாமே பிரானுக்கு நரரியல் பாமே. 1569

Siva is Inclusive of Jiva

Siva has faces five
And with His downward looking visage for Jiva,
He has faces six in all;
The Lord by Himself All
Sports the garland of heads
That verily is the Human Aspect
Of the godly One.

Siva has six faces (even as there are six faiths). One Face (Athomukha) looks downward for jiva's liberation.

ஆதிப் பிரானுல கேழும் அளந்தவன்
ஓதக் கடலும் உயிர்களு மாய்நிற்கும்
பேதிப் பிலாமையின் நின்ற பராசத்தி
ஆதிக்கட் டெய்வமும் அந்தமு மாமே. 1570

Lord is Beginning and End

The Primal Lord spanned the worlds seven
He stands as the sea and the myriad life here below,
And with Parasakti pervades all
In Union that no separateness knows
Verily, God is the Beginning and End of All.

Mantras 1570 & 1571

With Parasakti, the Primal Lord pervades all Seven Worlds. He is the Beginning and End of all. The immortal beings, devas and Vidyadharas sought Him, but in vain. Pursuit through the proven path of Siva grants realisation of bliss here and hereafter.

ஆய்ந்தறி வார்கள் அமரர்வித் தியாதரர்
ஆய்ந்தறி யாவண்ணம் நின்ற அரனெறி
ஆய்ந்தறிந் தேனவன் சேவடி கைதொழ
ஆய்ந்தறிந் தேனிம்மை அம்மைகண் டேனே. 1571

The Path of Siva Leads to Bliss

The immortal Beings, Devas and Vidyadharas,
Sought after Him, but knew Him not;
But pursuing the proven path of Siva

I reached His Feet of Grace to adore
And so realized the bliss of Here and Hereafter.

அறியவொண் ணாதவ் வுடம்பின் பயனை
அறியவொண் ணாத அறுவகை யாக்கி
அறியவொண் ணாத அறுவகைக் கோசத்
தறியவொண் ணாததோர் அண்டம் பதிந்ததே. *1572*

Macrocosm in Microcosm — A Mystery

Baffling indeed is the mystery of Life's Goal
Baffling it is, why into the six systems was it made;
A baffling mystery far,
How into the shedding sheaths of this body microcosm
Got imprinted a veritable macrocosm.

Life's goal is the realisation of the macrocosm in the microcosm — the Over-Soul in the self-soul—the mysterium tremendum.

ஐந்தாம் தந்திரம் முடிவு பெற்றது.
Tantra Five Concluded

ஆறாம் தந்திரம்

TANTRA SIX

1. சிவகுரு தரிசனம்

DARSHAN OF SIVA GURU

பத்திப் பணித்துப் பரவு மடிநல்கிச்
சுத்த வுரையால் துரிசறச் சோதித்துச்
சத்தும் அசத்துஞ் சதசத்துங் காட்டலாற்
சித்தம் இறையே சிவகுரு வாமே. 1573

The Holy Guru is God Himself

He taught me the meekness of Spirit,
Infused in me the light of devotion,
Granted me the Grace of His Feet;
And after interrogation holy, testing me entire,
Revealed to me the Real, the Unreal and Real-Unreal;
Of a certain is Siva-Guru Lord Himself.

Mantras 1573 & 1574

The holy Guru is Siva Himself. He granted me his grace. He taught me meekness. Testing me He revealed the real, the unreal and the real/unreal. Immense is the power of the presence of the divine Guru that liberated me from the bonds of the carnal body.

பாசத்தைக் கூட்டியே கட்டிப் பறித்திட்டு
நேசித்த காயம் விடுவித்து நேர்நேரே
கூசற்ற முத்தியிற் கூட்டலா நாட்டத்த
தாசற்ற சற்குரு அம்பலமாமே. 1574

Power of The Guru Presence

Gathering the strands of my fetters
He knotted them together;
And then wrenched them off;
Freeing me thus from my fond body,
Straight to Mukti he led me—
Behold, of such holy potent
Is the Presence of the Guru Divine!

சித்திகள் எட்டொடுந் திண்சிவ மாக்கிய
சுத்தியும் எண்சத்தித் தூய்மையும் யோகத்துச்
சத்தியும்மந்திர சாதக போதமும்
பத்தியும் நரதன் அருளிற் பயிலுமே. 1575

Attainments Through Guru's Grace

The miraculous powers of Siddhis eight,
The immaculate purity of Saktis eight,
The baptismal act supreme that turns Jiva into Siva,
The mystic powers of occult Yoga,
Of Mantra, of Bhakti, and of Jnana,
All these shall thou attain
If the Guru but his grace confers.

Mantras 1575 & 1576

The Guru grants the miraculous powers of eight siddhis, the immaculate purity of the eight saktis, and the mystic powers of the hidden yoga through conferment of his grace. The Siva Guru — the pure being — is above all the worlds, bestowing grace and liberating souls from their bondage. Truly, inexplicable is his glory.

எல்லா உலகிற்கும் அப்பாலோன் இப்பாலாய்
நல்லார் உள்ளத்து மிக்கருள் நல்கலால்
எல்லாரும் உய்யக்கொண் டிங்கே அளித்தலாற்
சொல்லார்ந்த நற்குருச் சுத்த சிவமே. 1576

Guru-Siva Parallelism

He is beyond worlds all
Yet, here below, He bestows His grace abundant
On the good and the devout,
And in love works for salvation of all;
Thus is the Holy Guru
Whose praise is beyond speech
Like Siva, the Being Pure.

தேவனுஞ் சுத்த குருவும் உபாயத்துள்
யாவையும் மூன்றா யுனக்கண் டுரையாலே
மூவாப் பசுபாச மாற்றியே முத்திப்பால்
யாவையும் நல்குங் குருபரன் அன்புற்றே. 1577

Compassionate Acts of Holy Guru

The Holy Guru is truly a Deva,
By his divine art he makes me perceive
All things in categories three;
By his sacred precepts sunders the bonds of Pasu-Pasa
And makes me drink of the milk of Mukti
All in benign compassion the Gurupara does.

The holy Guru, a true deva full of compassion, snaps the fetters of Pasu-pasa, and makes me savour the nectar of liberation.

சித்த சிவன்குரு வாய்வந்து தூய்மைசெய்
தத்தனை நல்கருள் காணா அதிமூடர்

பொய்த்தகு கண்ணான் நமரென்பர் புண்ணியர்
அத்தன் இவனென் றடிபணி வாரே. 1578

Discerning Holy Guru

The Guru comes, purifies and grants Godhood,
They see this not,
The witless ones of vision faulty;
But the holy ones take to him
In endearment as unto kith and kin,
And worship him as Lord Himself.

Mantras 1578 & 1579

Through purification, the Guru grants Godhood. The witless realise this not, while the holy ones receive this knowledge with deep gratitude. Only through the Guru's blessing can one experience the false dissolving in the true, learn the omnipotence of Truth, possess the bountiful Grace of Siva and realise the miraculous powers of the eight siddhis.

உண்மையிற் பொய்மை ஒழித்தலும் உண்மைப்பார்
திண்மையும் ஒண்மைச் சிவமாய அவ்வரன்
வண்மையும் எட்டெட்டுச் சித்தி மயக்கமும்
அண்ணல் அருளன்றி யாரறி வாரே. 1579

All Good Attainable With Guru's Grace

To dissolve the false in the true,
To derive the omnipotent might of Truth,
To possess the bounty of splendorous Siva's Grace,
To realize the fantasy of the famed Siddhis eight;
Who learns all these
But with Guru's blessing?

சிவனே சிவஞானி யாதலாற் சுத்த
சிவனே யெனஅடி சேரவல் லார்க்கு
நவமான தத்துவ நன்முத்தி நண்ணும்
பவமான தின்றிப் பரலோக மாமே. 1580

Siva Guru Like Siva Grants Supreme Liberation

Siva Jnani is none but Siva Himself;
And they who seek his feet as Siva's
Shall in sooth the wondrous Tattva mukti gain;
They shall no more be in the cycle of births;
Sure their reward, the Liberation Supreme.

Mantras 1580 & 1581

Seek the feet of the Guru as of Siva's, and gain 'tattva mukti'; for the Guru is none other than Siva Himself. He sunders the cycle of births and grants the liberation of the soul.

குருவே சிவமெனக் கூறினன் நந்தி
குருவே சிவமென் பதுகுறித் தோரார்
குருவே சிவனுமாய்க் கோனுமாய் நிற்கும்
குருவே யுரையுணர் வற்றதோர் கோவே. 1581

Guru God Identity

Guru is none but Siva — thus spoke Nandi;
Guru is Siva Himself — this they realize not;
Guru will to you Siva be,
And your Guide too;
Guru in truth is Lord,
That surpasses speech and thought, all.

சித்தம் யாவையுஞ் சிந்தித் திருந்திடும்
அத்தன் உணர்த்துவ தாகும் அருளாலே
சித்தம் யாவையுந் திண்சிவ மானக்கால்
அத்தனும் அவ்விடத் தேயமர்ந் தானே. 1582

Think of Siva and Be Siva

Let all your thoughts be thoughts of Siva,
And the Lord by His Grace shall reveal all;
If your thoughts be Siva-saturated
In you shall He then close abide.

The Guru, the true lord and guide, stands peerless above speech and thought. When saturated with thoughts of Siva, Siva abides in you.

தானந்தி சீர்மையுட் சந்தித்த சீர்வைத்த
கோனந்தி யெந்தை குறிப்பறி வாரில்லை
வானந்தி யென்று மகிழும் ஒருவற்குத்
தானந்தி யங்கித் தனிச்சுட ராமே. 1583

Nandi is Peerless Luminosity

Of Himself He sought me in the Truth's Way
He the Blessed, the King of Kings,
Nandi, mine Father,
But they know not his intent;
To them that rejoice in Him
As the Nandi of heavenly might,
Verily is He the peerless luminosity
Of crimson twilight fire.

Nandi is the king of kings. To his devotees truly he is the god of heavenly might and unrivalled luminosity.

திருவாய சித்தியும் முத்தியும் சீர்மை
மருளா தருளும் மயக்கறும் வாய்மைப்
பொருளாய வேதாந்த போதமும் நாதன்
உருவாய் அருளா விடிலோர ஒண்ணாதே. 1584

Things That Flow From Guru's Grace

The Siddhis that are a veritable treasure-trove,
The Mukti that is salvation finite,
The heavenly Grace that vanquishes doubts and fears
And the Jnana that is essence of Vedas
All these,
When the Guru himself imparts not,
Never, never shalt thou learn.

Only by the Guru's divine grace can the siddhis, that are genuine treasures, descend; the mukti, that is the ultimate liberation be attained; and the heavenly jnana that ends doubts and fears be known.

பத்தியும் ஞானவை ராக்கிய மும்பர
சித்திக்கு வித்தாஞ் சிவோகமே சேர்தலான்
முத்தியின் ஞான முளைத்தலால் அம்முளை
சத்தி யருள்தரில் தானெளி தாமே. *1585*

Jnana Easy With Sakti's Grace

Bhakti and Resoluteness Spiritual (Vairagya)
Are the seeds of State Transcendental;
Siva and I are one — attitude of oneness with Siva
In turn, these lead to Sivoham,
And in Sivoham shoots the Jnana for Mukti,
And that shoot yours easy shall be
If Sakti but Her Grace bestows.

Bhakti and resoluteness, the seeds of the supreme state, lead to Sivoham meditation in which jnana leads to mukti, when Sakti confers Her Grace.

பின்னெய்த வைத்ததோர் இன்பப் பிறப்பினை
முன்னெய்த வைத்த முதல்வனை எம்மிறை
தன்னெய்துங் காலத்துத் தானே வெளிப்படு
மன்னெய்த வைத்த மனமது தானே. *1586*

When God Reveals Himself

This life of pleasure here below
The Lord for you of yore ordained
That you may the Greater Pleasure attain,
Where your mind reaches to Him in resolve
Then of Himself, He reveals to you.

This is repeated as Mantra 1629 infra.

Mantras 1586 & 1587

Concentration of God leads to the revelation of God Himself. Achieve the luminous siddhis; realise the jnana of Siva; and attain mukti. Siva jnana leads to Sivananda.

சிவமான ஞானந் தெளியவொண் சித்தி
சிவமான ஞானந் தெளியவொண் முத்தி
சிவமான ஞானஞ் சிவபரத்தே யேகச்
சிவமான ஞானஞ் சிவானந்த நல்குமே. *1587*

Siva Jnana Leads to Sivananda

When you realize the Jnana of Siva
You shall achieve the Siddhis luminous
When you realize the Jnana of Siva,
You shall attain the Mukti resplendent;
When your Jnana of Siva reaches to Siva Supreme,
Then shall it yield the Bliss of Sivananda.

அறிந்துணர்ந் தேனிவ் வகலிட முற்றுஞ்
செறிந்துணர்ந் தோதித் திருவருள் பெற்றேன்
மறந்தொழிந் தேன்மதி மாண்டவர் வாழ்க்கை
பிறிந்தொழிந் தேனிப் பிறவியை நானே. *1588*

How Tirumular Ended Birth Cycle

All this space infinite
I cognized and realized;
Adoring with devotion replete
I received His Grace Divine;
Now am I past all remembrance of Ignorance exceeding,
For ever have I bidden adieu to birth recurring.

Mantras 1588 & 1589

Deep devotion and intense meditation made Tirumular realise and receive the Lord's Divine Grace. He met Siva, the seed of all causal phenomena, and so ended the cycle of recurring births.

தரிக்கின்ற பல்லுயிர்க் கெல்லாந் தலைவன்
இருக்கின்ற தன்மையை ஏதும் உணரார்
பிரிக்கின்ற இந்தப் பிணக்கறுத் தெல்லாங்
கருக்கொண்ட ஈசனைக் கண்டுகொண் டேனே. *1589*

How Tirumular Met the Lord

He is the Lord of all living creation
Yet naught they know of His State Existent;
I cut the tangle that separated Him from me,
And lo! I met the Lord, the seed of all causal phenomena.

2. திருவடிப் பேறு

GRACE OF GURU'S FEET

இசைந்தெழும் அன்பில் எழுந்த படியே
பசைந்தெழும் ஈசரைப் பாசத்துள் ஏகச்
சிவந்த குருவந்து சென்னிகை வைக்க
உவந்த குருபதம் உள்ளத் துவந்ததே. *1590*

Guru Blesses With His Hand on My Head

Rise in loving praise of Lord
And having risen, in piety melt for Him;
Then the divine Guru comes
—He who had scorned Pasa's fetters—
And lays his hand on your head,
And lo! in you wells up
The rapturous Grace of His Holy Feet.

தாடந்த போதே தலைதந்த எம்மிறை
வாடந்த ஞான வலியையுந் தந்திட்டு
வீடந்த மின்றியே யாள்கென விட்டருட்
பாடின் முடிவைத்துப் பார்வந்து தந்ததே. *1591*

Grace of Feet is Kingdom Won

Even as mine Master granted me the Grace of His Feet,

He had made me the head of all;
And investing me with the regalia-might of Jnana-sword,
He placed on my head the Crown of Grace Abounding,
And thus proclaimed:
"May you forever hold sway over this Land of Deliverance"
—All these He did, descending on earth, here below.

தானவ னாகிச் சொரூபத் துவந்திட்டு
ஆன சொரூபங்கள் நான்கும் அகற்றின
ஏனைய முத்திரை யீந்தாண்ட நன்னந்தி
தானடி முற்சூட்டித் தாபித்த துண்மையே. 1592

Guru is God in Human Form

He assumed human form,
Discarding divine forms four,
And Himself as exalted Guru came,
Signifying the Mudra of Jnana;
He, Nandi, my good Saviour
Blessed me;
It was He who of yore
Planted His Feet of Grace on me.

Siva, Sakti, nada, bindu

Mantras 1592 & 1593

The Guru is God in human form, signifying the mudra of jnana. By making me unite in Sivam, he granted me the boundless form that transcends the four states — Nada, Nadanta, Kala and Kalanta.

உரையற் றுணர்வற் றுயிர்பர மற்றுத்
திரையற்ற நீர்போல் சிவமாதல் தீர்த்துக்
கரையற்ற சத்தாதி நான்குங் கடந்த
சொரூபத் திருத்தனன் சொல்லிறந் தோமே. 1593

Guru United Me in Sivam

There was neither speech, nor feeling
Neither self, nor Over-self;
Like unto a sea where no wave lashes,
He made me unite in Sivam;
And he granted me the Boundless Form
That transcends the states four, Nada and rest,
And lo! it was beyond words all.

குரவன் உயிர்முச் சொரூபமுங் கைக்கொண்
டரிய பொருள்முத் திரையாகக் கொண்டு
பெரிய பிரானடி நந்தி பேச்சற்
றுருகிட என்னையங் குய்யக்கொண் டானே. 1594

Gurupara Worked for My Redemption

My divine preceptor Nandi
Seized life's forms all three;*
He assumed the Mudra of Jnana
And drew me to his Feet so benign;
Bereft of speech, I melted in bliss
Thus did He work my redemption eternal.

* Gross, subtle and causal

Nandi, my divine preceptor, transcending all three states — form, formless and form/formless—assumed the mudra of jnana. Drawing myself towards his benign feet, I worked my way to liberation.

பேச்சற்ற இன்பத்துப் பேரானந் தத்திலே
மாச்சற்ற என்னைச் சிவமாக்கி மாள்வித்துக்
காச்சற்ற சோதி கடன்மூன்றுங் கைக்கொண்டு
வாச்ச புகழ்மாளத் தாள்தந்து மன்னுமே. 1595

How Guru Transformed Jiva Into Siva

He cleansed me of my blemishes,
Transformed me into Sivam Supreme,
And immersed me into His bliss infinite;
Bliss that is beyond, beyond words!
The fire of His Grace scorches not
Yet drank dry the three seas of my impurities;
And annihilating my primal ego to its traces
He granted me His Feet of Grace;
And there does he abide, forever, in me.

Cleansed from blemishes, I was immersed in infinite bliss that is beyond words, and was transformed into Supreme Sivam.

இதயத்தும் நாட்டத்தும் என்றன் சிரத்தும்
பதிவித்த பாதப் பராபரன் நந்தி
கதிவைத்த வாறும் மெய்காட் டியவாறும்
விதிவைத்த வாறும் விளம்பவொண் ணாதே. 1596

Guru's Acts of Grace Beyond Description

Into my bosom, on my eyes, over my head
He gently planted His loving Feet
Nandi, my Lord Supreme;
He laid me the Path,
He showed me the Truth,
He settled the course of my Destiny
Truly, truly, all that I cannot describe.

Mantras 1596 & 1597

Nandi, my monarch, gently planted his loving hallowed feet on my head, and showed the True Path, thus settling the course of my destiny. Truly inexplicable are his gracious acts.

திருவடி வைத்தென் சிரத்தருள் நோக்கிப்
பெருவடி வைத்தந்த பேர்நந்தி தன்னைக்
குருவடி விற்கண்ட கோனையெங் கோவைக்
கருவழி வாற்றிடக் கண்டுகொண் டேனே. 1597

Master Nandi Ended My Birth-Cycle

He placed his hallowed Feet on my head
He fixed his benign gaze on me
And he granted me the Form Mighty,
He, my Nandi Great;

I saw him, my monarch, in Guru Form,
And saw the end of all births to come.

திருவடி ஞானஞ் சிவமாக்கு விக்குந்
திருவடி ஞானஞ் சிவலோகஞ் சேர்க்குந்
திருவடி ஞானஞ் சிறைமல மீட்குந்
திருவடி ஞானமே திண்சித்தி முத்தியே. *1598*

Greatness of Jnana of Holy Feet

Jnana of Holy Feet makes you Siva,
Jnana of Holy Feet takes you to world of Siva,
Jnana of Holy Feet frees you from imprisoned impurities,
Jnana of Holy Feet is Siddhi and Mukti too.

The jnana of the holy feet is so great that by liberating me from the impurities it took me to the world of Siva Himself. Siva is siddhi and mukti too.

மேல்வைத்த வாறுசெய் யாவிடின் மேல்வினை
மால்வைத்த சிந்தையை மாயம தாக்கிடும்
பால்வைத்த சென்னிப் படரொளி வானவன்
தாள்வைத்த வாறு தரிப்பித்த வாறே. *1599*

When True Enlightenment Comes

When the Master blesses you not thus
With the grace of His Feet on your crown,
The Karma of yore shall distort your thoughts;
Only when the resplendent Lord of milk-white brow
Places his blessed Feet on you,
Only then are you truly instructed.

Mantras 1599-1601

Only with the grace of the holy feet comes true instruction, enlightenment, and liberation. They who have reached his holy feet are superior to earthly monarchs. These at best can but sway the world; but the joy of devotees is boundless indeed.

கழலார் கமலத் திருவடி என்னும்
நிழல்சேரப் பெற்றேன் நெடுமால் அறியா
அழல்சேரும் அங்கியுள் ஆதிப் பிரானுங்
குழல்சேரும் என்னுயிர்க் கூடுங் குலைத்ததே. *1600*

Grace of Feet Granted Soul's Liberation

I reached the cool shelter of His triumphant lotus Feet,
That standing as a crimson pillar of flame,
Defied the grasp even of divine Vishnu
And there, the Primal One saw
The eternal denouement of the fleshy cage
That held my soul a hoary captive.

முடிமன்ன ராகிமூ வுலகம தாள்வர்
அடிமன்னர் இன்பத் தளவில்லை கேட்கின்
முடிமன்ன ராய்நின்ற தேவர்கள் ஈசன்
குடிமன்ன ராய்க்குற்ற மற்றுநின் றாரே. *1601*

Grace of Feet Exceeds Kingly Greatness

The crowned monarchs at best may sway
the worlds three;
But they who reached His Holy Feet
Their power no bounds shall know;
Know this:
The heavenly beings attired in kingly diadems
But turned his vassals;
And thus became for ever blemishless free.

வைத்தேன் அடிகள் மனத்தினுள் ளேநான்
பொய்த்தே யெரியும் புலன்வழி போகாமல்
எய்த்தேன் உழலும் இருவினை மாற்றிட்டு
மெய்த்தேன் அறிந்தேனவ் வேதத்தின் அந்தமே. *1602*

Truth of Hallowed Feet is End of Vedas

I treasured His hallowed Feet
In the depths of my heart;
And so, shunned the deceitful course of scorching senses,
I swam past the dangerous swirls of good and bad Karma,
And I tasted the nectar of Truth
—The end of all Vedas.

Shun the scorching senses. Then you will taste the nectar of Truth of his hallowed feet. Thus say the holy scriptures.

அடிசார லாம்அண்ண ல்பாத மிரண்டும்
முடிசார வைத்தனர் முன்னை முனிவர்
படிசார்ந்த இன்பப் பழவடி வெள்ளக்
குடிசார் நெறிகூடி நிற்பவர் கொள்கையே. *1603*

Lord's Feet is Goal of the Pure

The sages of yore bore full on their crown
The Lord's Feet twain;
They are blissful and hoary
This earth has known;
And the goal of the Pure Ones
That walk the Path of Truth;
May you reach those Feet.

Mantras 1603 & 1604

The sages of yore, bearing the blissful and hoary Feet of the Lord on their crowns, trod the path of Truth — the goal of the pure. Truly the Lord's Feet is all — mantra and medicine; tantra and wisdom; beauty and the pure way.

மந்திர மாவதும் மாமருந் தாவதுந்
தந்திர மாவதுந் தானங்க ளாவதுஞ்
சுந்தர மாவதுந் தூய்நெறி யாவதும்
எந்தை பிரான்தன் இணையடி தானே. *1604*

Lord's Feet is All

Verily are they, all mantra and all medicine;
All tantra and all giving;
All beauty and all pure way;
My Lord's Feet Twain.

3. ஞாதுரு ஞான ஞேயம்

JNATHRU. JNANA. JNEYA (KNOWER, KNOWLEDGE AND KNOWN)

நீங்காச் சிவானந்த ஞேயத்தே நின்றிடப்
பாங்கான பாசம் படரா படரினும்
ஆங்கார நீங்கி யதனிலை நிற்கவே
நீங்கா அமுத நிலைபெற லாமே. 1605

Goal of Sivananda is Ambrosial Bliss

Do incessant seek the goal of Sivananda,
There the Primordial Paśa enmeshes you not;
When it ever envelops you,
You but throw your egoity out and stand firm;
Yours shall then be the ambrosial bliss eternal.

ஞேயத்தே நின்றோர்க்கு ஞானாதி நின்றிடும்
ஞேயத்தின் ஞாதுரு ஞேயத்தில் வீடாகும்
ஞேயத்தின் ஞேயத்தை ஞேயத்தை யுற்றவர்
ஆயத்தில் நின்ற அறிவறி வாறே. 1606

Knower—Knowledge—Known Relationship

To them that pursue the Object of Knowledge
Shall be vouchsafed Knowledge and its attributes;
The Subject that seeks the Object shall in the Object merge;
They that have cognised the Object of Knowledge
Through Knowledge
Have the Knowledge of union with the Object.

They that have sought and apprehended the object of knowledge through knowledge possess the knowledge of union with the object.

தானென் றவனென் றிரண்டாகுந் தத்துவந்
தானென் றவனென் றிரண்டுந் தனிற்கண்டு
தானென்ற பூவை யவனடி சாத்தினால்
நானென் றவனென்கை நல்லதொன் றன்றே. 1607

You and he

The two categories — You and He
See them both in you and He;
Offer the flower "you" at the Feet of He;
Then no more be it proper to say: "You and He".

'You' becomes 'He' when the flower 'You' is offered at the Feet of 'He.'

வைச்சன வாறாறு மாற்றியெனைவைத்து
மெச்சப் பரன்றன் வியாத்துவ மேலிட்டு
நிச்சய மாக்கிச் சிவமாக்கி ஞேயத்தால்
அச்சங் கெடுத்தென்னை யாண்டனன் நந்தியே. 1608

Nandi Redeemed Me in Jneya

He rid me of Tattvas six and thirty,
He elevated me;
And enveloped me in the infinite
Expanse of the Spirit;
He imparted me the State of Permanence
He transformed me into Siva Divine;
And through the Subject-Object identity
Dispelled my ignorance
Thus He redeemed me
He, Nandi of blessed memory.

Enveloping me in the infinite expanse of spirit, he, Nandi of blessed memory, imparted to me the state of permanence, ultimately changing me into Siva Divine. Thus, Nandi, worked for my liberation in jneya.

முன்னை யறிவறியாதஅம் மூடர்போற்
பின்னை யறிவறி யாமையைப் பேதித்தான்
தன்னை யறியப் பரனாக்கித் தற்சிவத்
தென்னை யறிவித் திருந்தனன் நந்தியே. 1609

Knowledge and Ignorance

Even unto the witless here below
That know not knowledge from ignorance,
Was I; He taught the distinction between the two
And made me know my Self;[1]
He transformed me into Para[2]
And made me known to Siva;[3]
He, Nandi of hallowed name.

---

1) Tvampada
2) Tatpada
3) Asipada

Mantras 1609 & 1610

I, who was ignorant of the distinction between knowledge and ignorance, was taught the same. Knowing myself, he, Nandi of hallowed name, transformed me into Para and made me intimate with Siva. He, Nandi of immortal fame, showed me diverse wonders that had never before been heard and seen.

காணாத கண்ணுடன் கேளாத கேள்வியுங்
கோணாத போகமுங் கூடாத கூட்டமும்
நாணாத நாணமும் நாதாந்த் போதமுங்
காணா யெனவந்து காட்டினன் நந்தியே. 1610

Wonders Nandi Showed

"May you have," He said:
"The vision that eye has seen not,
The message that ear has heard not,

The rapture that cloys not,
The union that had been not,
The Nada that ceases not,
The Bodha that arises at Nada's End,
All these, may you have," He said,
He, the Nandi of immortal fame.

மோனங்கை வந்தோர்க்கு முத்தியுங் கைகூடும்
மோனங்கை வந்தோர்க்குச் சித்தியும் முன்நிற்கும்
மோனங்கை வந்தூமை யாமொழி முற்றுங்காண்
மோனங்கை வந்தைங் கருமமும் முன்னுமே. *1611*

Mauna's Emanations

They that have mastered the Divine
Mauna (Silence),
Shall reach the very bliss of Mukti;
And all Siddhis of themselves seek them
Into the Silent Word* would in perfection evolve;
Mastering Mauna thus,
They shall gain the power
For the five divine acts to perform
Creation, Preservation, Dissolution,
Obfuscation and Grant of Grace.

Mastery through divine mauna leads to the very bliss of mukti and then confers the power for the five divine acts — Creation, Preservation, Dissolution, Obfuscation, and the Granting of Grace.

* Ajapa or Soham.

முத்திரை மூன்றின் முடிந்தது மூன்றன்பால்
வைத்த கலைகால் நான்மடங் கான்மாற்றி
உய்த்தவத் தானந்தத் தொண்குரு பாதத்தே
பெத்த மறுத்தோர் பிறந்திற வாரே. *1612*

Sunder Bonds of Birth at Feet of Guru

Having achieved divine Mudras three 1
Directed breath into the Centres three 2
And coursed its rhythm in finger-measure four,
—They who sat thus in yoga,
Joyous at lumniscent Guru's Feet,
Have for ever sundered bonds all,
And never be born and dead again.

---

1) Sambhavi, bhairavi, kechari or chinmudra, jnana mudra and yoga mudra.

Some fefer to the three categories, jnathru, jnana and jneya, as mudras — triputika jnana. But it does not seem appropriate here, as the three mudras are referred to in connection with yoga.

2) Sun, moon and fire

Right (sun nadi), left (moon nadi), central (sushumna nadi)

Mantras 1612 & 1613

Snap the cycle of birth and death by performing yoga at the feet of the Guru. The supreme jnani, after attaining the three higher forms, himself becomes the primal form of spirit — jnathru (knower).

மேலைச் சொரூபங்கள் மூன்று மிகுசத்தி
பாலித்த முத்திரை பற்றும் பரஞானி
ஆலித்த நட்டமே ஞேயம் புகுந்தற்ற
மூலச் சொரூபன் மொழிஞா துருவனே. *1613*

In Jneya is the Primal Form of the Spirit

As he holds Mudras three of divine potent
The Jnani Supreme attains Higher Forms Three;
And in rapturous dance he enters Jneya
And himself the Primal Form of Spirit becomes;
The Jiva that is Jnathru (Knower).

---

4. துறவு

RENUNCIATION

இறப்பும் பிறப்பும் இருமையும் நீங்கித்
துறக்குந் தவங்கண்ட சோதிப் பிரானை
மறப்பில ராய்நித்தம் வாய்மொழி வார்கட்
கறப்பதி காட்டும் அமரர் பிரானே. *1614*

God is Reached by Renunciation:

Beyond birth and death,
Reached by renunciate tapas Is He
My Lord of resplendent glory!
Sing His praise! Incessant pray!
The Heaven's Lord shall show you
The Dharma's Land.

Through renunciation, Siva can be reached. Praise Him; He will show the land of dharma.

பிறந்தும் இறந்தும்பல் பேதைமை யாலே
மறந்து பலஇருள் நீங்க மறைந்து
சிறந்த சிவனருள் சேர்பரு வத்துத்
துறந்த வுயிர்க்குச் சுடரொளி யாமே. *1615*

Renunciation Leads to Light:

A myriad times are they born and dead,
In a million folly they forget this;
And in the darkness of Mala are close enveloped;
When at last the hidden Grace of Siva bursts forth
And chases the Night away,
Then is the moment for the soul to renounce;
When it does then, a radiant Light it becomes.

Innumerable times they are born; they die and forget the myriad follies they commit. In darkness they are enveloped. Even so, they can find light in the hidden Grace of Siva, if they but renounce at the right moment.

அறவன் பிறப்பிலி யாரும் இலாதான்
உறைவது காட்டகம் உண்பது பிச்சை
துறவனுங் கண்டீர் துறந்தவர் தம்மைப்
பிறவி யறுத்திடும் பித்தன்கண் டீரே. *1616*

The Renunciate Lord Sunders Birth Bonds

He is Dharma, He is birthless, kinless;
In the wilds he abides, by alms he lives;
Know you, He has renounced all;
And to all those who renounce,
He sunders their bonds of birth
You insensate ones! Know thus.

Mantras 1616 & 1617

The Renunciate Lord is dharma, birthless and kinless; He dwells in the wilds and lives by alms. To all those who renounce sincerely, He snaps the fetters of birth. The renunciates walk in the straight path; the rest tread crooked paths full of thorns that prick.

நெறியைப் படைத்தான் நெருஞ்சில் படைத்தான்
நெறியில் வழுவின் நெருஞ்சில் முட்பாயும்
நெறியில் வழுவா தியங்கவல் லார்க்கு
நெறியின் நெருஞ்சில்முட் பாயகி லாவே. *1617*

The Renunciate Shall Walk along the Straight Path

He laid the path, and planted the thorns along;
When you from the path deviate
The thorns of temptation shall prick you;
They that deviate not,
Them the thorns prick not.

கேடுங் கடமையுங் கேட்டுவந் தைவரும்
நாடி வளைந்தது நான்கட வேனலேன்
ஆடல் விடையுடை அண்ணல் திருவடி
கூடுந் தவஞ்செய்த கொள்கையன் றானே. *1618*

Stand Steadfast in the Goal of Tapas

Spotting my failings, demanding tribute of me,
The five senses in ambush held me;
That indeed is not of my seeking;
Firm in tapas, I stand;
Seeking the hallowed Feet of the dancing Lord,
That on the sacred bull rides.

The renunciate is not interested in spotting his failings or demanding praise for his virtues. He stands in tapas firmly, seeking the hallowed Feet of the Lord.

உழவன் உழவுழ வானம் வழங்க
உழவன் உழவினிற் பூத்த குவளை
உழவன் உழத்தியர் கண்ணொக்கும் என்றிட்
டுழவன் அதனை யுழவொழிந் தானே. *1619*

When Grace Blossoms, Tapas Ceases

The ploughman ploughed; the heavens poured;
And by the ploughman's ploughing, in time it flowered;
The ploughman then to the ploughwoman left,
As unto her eyes the flowers are,
To watch, and guard and tender;
The ploughman thus for ever ceased
All efforts at ploughing further.

The ploughman ploughed at the right moment and Grace blossomed in abundance. Then he left it to the ploughwoman to guard and tender, himself ceasing from ploughing thereafter. That is, when Grace blossoms, tapas ceases.

மேல்துறந் தண்ணல் விளங்கொளி கூற்றுவன்
நாள்துறந் தார்க்கவன் நண்ப னவாவிலி
கார்துறந் தார்க்கவன் கண்ணுத லாய்நிற்கும்
பார்துறந் தார்க்கே பதஞ்செய லாமே. *1620*

Liberation is for the Renunciate Alone

The Lord of renunciation,
He is the Shining Light above;
He is the Friend of all,
Who have surmounted Death's days;
He is devoid of desires;
The guiding light of all those
Who Darkness renounced;
Only to those who abandoned this world,
Will His Feet within reach be.

The Lord, the Shining Light above, renounced all. He, the Friend of All, vanquished death. He, devoid of desires, is the guiding light of those who seek His Feet abandoning things worldly.

நாகமும் ஒன்று படம்ஐந்து நாலது
போகமுட் புற்றிற் பொருந்தி நிறைந்தது
ஆக மிரண்டும் படம்விரித் தாட்டொழிந்
தேகப் படஞ்செய் துடம்பிட மாமே. *1621*

When Distractions of Senses Cease

One the serpent (Jiva), Five its hoods (Senses)
The Four (Antakaranas) fill the thorny hole of enjoyment;
In its twain body, subtle and gross
It raised its hoods and danced away;
Then into a single hood it merged (Kundalini)
Into the very body within.

அகன்றார் வழிமுதல் ஆதிப் பிரானும்
இவன்றா னெனநின் றெளியனும் அல்லன்
சிவன்றாள் பலபல சீவனு மாகும்
நயன்றான் வருரும்வழி நாமறி யோமே. *1622*

None Knows How He Comes

The Primal Lord is the first of Renunciates;
In that thought is little comfort

Not that easy may He come by;
Many, many lives may it take
For Siva's Feet to reach;
Who knows how and when
The Loved One comes!

There is little comfort in the thought that the Primal Lord is the First of Renunciates and it will take many many lives to reach His Holy Feet. Nobody knows how He, the Loved One, comes, and when.

தூம்பு திறந்தன ஒன்பது வாய்தலும்
ஆம்பற் குழலியின் கஞ்சுளிப் பட்டது
வேம்பேறி நோக்கினன் மீகாமன் கூரையிற்
கூம்பேறிக் கோயிலிற் பூக்கின்ற வாறே. *1623*

The Yogi Espied the Mystic Flower in the Cranium

The Mystic Exit opened,
And the nine orifices were sheathed in armour
Of Sakti of lily-wreathed tresses;
The Captain that is the breath of life
Climbed the mast of Negation Bitter,
And looked atop from the cranium roof;
And lo! beheld the budded vine bloom,
As in temple lofty and sacred.

The yogi climbed the mast of bitter negation, and from the cranium roof watched at a distance the mystic flower and the budded vine (Grace of Sakti) bloom as in the sacred temple within.

5. தவம்
TAPAS

ஒடுங்கி நிலைபெற்ற வுத்தமர் உள்ளம்
நடுங்குவ தில்லை நமனுமங் கில்லை
இடும்பையும் இல்லை இராப்பகல் இல்லை
படும்பயன் இல்லை பற்றுவிட் டோர்க்கே. *1624*

Blessings of the Placid Mind

The heart of the holy trembles not in fear,
All passions stilled, it enjoys calm unruffled;
Neither is there death
Nor pain, nor night nor day,
Nor fruits of Karma to experience;
That truly is the state of the desire-renounced.

Mantras 1624 & 1625

The renunciates are calm and serene. They do not tremble in fear, and are not shaken by the fury of passions, fear of death, by night, or by day, by fruits good and bad of karma. They rest in absolute tranquillity. Blessed are they who know the mystery of life, the origin of earth and the greatness and might of pure deeds of tapas.

எம்மா ருயிரும் இருநிலத் தோற்றமுஞ்
செம்மா தவத்தின் செயலின் பெருமையும்
அம்மான் திருவருட் பெற்றவர்க் கல்லா(து)
இம்மா தவத்தின் இயல்பறி யாரே. *1625*

Only the Blessed Know Greatness of Tapas

The mystery of life, the origin of earth,
The might of pure deeds of tapas
Who knows them all
But they that receive Lord's Grace?
The rest know naught of tapas supreme.

பிறப்பறி யார்பல பிச்சைசெய் மாந்தர்
சிறப்பொடு வேண்டிய செல்வம் பெறுவர்
மறப்பில ராகிய மாதவஞ் செய்வார்
பிறப்பினை நீக்கும் பெருமைபெற் றாரே. *1626*

Tapasvin Ends Birth

The Tapasvins many that live by alms
Have no life hereafter;
On them shall be showered
All blessings of Spiritual wealth;
They that perform tapas incessant
Attain the power to end
All births to be.

Mantras 1626 & 1627

The tapasvins who live by alms will be born no more; and on them will be bestowed all spiritual wealth. Transfixed in mind, tortured in body, stout-of heart, and unyielding to temptations, they perform splendorous tapas with determined thought centred on Siva alone.

இருந்து வருந்தி எழிற்றவஞ் செய்யும்
பெருந்தன்மை யாளரைப் பேதிக்க வென்றே
இருந்திந் திரனே யெவரே வரினுந்
திருந்துந்தஞ் சிந்தை சிவனவன் பாலே. *1627*

Tapasvins Remain Impervious to Temptations

Transfixed in mind and tortured in body
Stout of heart, they perform tapas splendorous;
Even though the Celestial King
And others, however mighty, descend to them,
And tempt them,
Their determined thought on Siva firm remains.

கரந்துங் கரந்திலன் கண்ணுக்குந் தோன்றான்
பரந்த சடையன் பசும்பொன் நிறத்தன்
அருந்தவர்க் கல்லால் அணுகலு மாகான்
விரைந்து தொழப்படும் வெண்மதி யானே. *1628*

Only Tapasvins Can Approach Lord

Hidden, yet not hidden,
He appears not to the naked eye;

He of the spreading matted locks;
The gold-hued;
None but they of hard tapas may near Him;
Do hasten and Him adore,
He, the mighty one of the white moon crest.

The Lord hides and yet hides not. He, of the spreading matted locks and the Gold-Hued form cannot be visioned by our naked eyes. The inner eyes of the tapasvins of hard penance can, however, vision Him. So, intensely adore the mighty God sporting the milk white crescent moon.

பின்னெய்த வைத்ததோர் இன்பப் பிறப்பினை
முன்னெய்த வைத்த முதல்வனை எம்மிறை
தன்னெய்துங் காலத்துத் தானே வெளிப்படும்
மன்னெய்த வைத்த மனமது தானே. *1629*

When Mind Reaches Lord, He Reveals

The life of bliss hereafter to be
He made me reach now and here,
He—the Primal One;
When the mind transfixed reaches God,
He of Himself reveals, sure.

Mantras 1629 & 1630

When the concentrated mind reaches the Primal One, He reveals Himself. In this perishable world where everything is transient, tapas alone is the imperishable wealth. It alone can confer immortality.

1) Same as Mantra 1586 ante.

அமைச்சரும் ஆனைக் குழாமும் அரசும்
பகைத்தெழும் பூசலுட் பட்டார் நடுவே
அமைத்ததோர் ஞானமும் ஆத்தமும் நோக்கி
இமைத்தழி யாதிருந் தார்தவத் தாரே. *1630*

Tapas Alone is Imperishable Wealth

Amidst the tumult of raging hatred, they perished,
The kings, their ministers and their elephantine hordes;
But fixing their sights on divine Jnana and universal love,
The tapasvins immortals became, their eyelids batting not.

சாத்திரம் ஓதுஞ் சதுர்களை விட்டுநீர்
மாத்திரைப் போது மறித்துள்ளே நோக்குமின்
பார்த்தவப் பார்வை பசுமரத் தாணிபோல்
ஆர்த்த பிறவி அகலவிட் டோடுமே. *1631*

Inward Look of Tapas Ends Birth

Come apart from the clever argumentation of contending theology,
And for a brief brief while, look inward,
That one look shall drive the nail into the coffin of birth
And forever end its cycle recurring.

Neither argumentation of contending theologies nor knowledge of scriptures can end the recurring cycle of birth. Look inward even for a brief while. That can take you far.

தவம்வேண்டு ஞானந் தலைபட வேண்டில்
தவம்வேண்டா ஞான சமாதிகை கூடில்
தவம்வேண்டா மச்ச கசமார்க்கத் தோர்க்குத்
தவம்வேண்டா மாற்றந் தனையறி யாரே. *1632*

When Tapas is Needed

Tapas you need, if Jnana you aspire;
Tapas you need not, when Jnana Samadhi you attain;
Tapas you need not, when you are in Sahamarga of Yoga;
Tapas they seek not, who the Self to transform
Know not.

The aspirant for jnana needs tapas. After attaining jnana samadhi in Sahamarga (Yoga) tapas is not necessary. They who have realised the Self, and who seek to transform the self into the Over-Self do not need tapas.

6. தவ நிந்தை
ABUSE OF TAPAS

ஓதுலும் வேண்டாம் உயிர்க்குயி ருள்ளுற்றாற்
காதலும் வேண்டாமெய்க் காய மிடங்கண்டாற்
சாதலும் வேண்டாஞ் சமாதிகை கூடினாற்
போதலும் வேண்டாம் புலன்வழி போகார்க்கே. *1633*

When You Need not Renounce

You need not pray, if the Soul of Souls enters in you;
You need not adore, if Siva abides true in you;
You need not die, if Samadhi you attain,
You need not renounce, if you go not the way of the senses.

There is no need for prayer and adoration if the Soul of souls enters and abides in you. When the state of samadhis is attained, death ceases. Renunciation is not demanded when you do not concern yourself with the ways of the senses.

கத்தவும் வேண்டாங் கருத்தறிந் தாறினாற்
சத்தமும் வேண்டாஞ் சமாதிகை கூடினாற்
சுத்தமும் வேண்டாந் துடக்கற்று நிற்றலாற்
சித்தமும் வேண்டாஞ் செயலற்றிருக்கிலே! *1634*

To Reach the Actionless State is Above All

You need no shouting

When in understanding you withdraw
You need no speaking
When in Samadhi you are seated;
You need no baptismal rites
When you stand detached;
You need no meditation,
When you have reached actionless state.

In the act of supreme understanding, shouting counts for little. Speech is not necessary when seated in samadhi. Baptismal rites matter not when you are detached. Nor is meditation needed in the stilled actionless-state of samadhi that transcends all meditation.

விளைவறி வார்பண்டை மெய்த்தவஞ் செய்வார்
விளைவறி வார்பண்டை மெய்யுரை செய்வார்
விளைவறி வார்பண்டை மெய்யறஞ் செய்வார்
விளைவறி வார்விண்ணின் மண்ணின்மிக் காரே. 1635

Fruit of Tapas

They who perform tapas true
Shall know the fruit thereof
They who speak truth pure
Shall know its fruit thereof
They who stand in righteous way
Shall enjoy the fruit thereof
They who are great on earth
Shall reap heaven's fruit.

Mantras 1635 & 1636

Great are those on earth who receive heaven's fruit, which can be reaped only by performing true tapas, speaking truth and following the path of virtue. Performance of tapas with oneness of mind and eagerness of heart will grant the Lord's triumphant Feet and the Siva-state. Seeking in the yearning of heart alone is tapas.

கூடித் தவஞ்செய்து கண்டேன் குரைகழல்
தேடித் தவஞ்செய்து கண்டேன் சிவகதி
வாடித் தவஞ்செய்வ தேதவம் இவைகளைந்
தூடிற் பலவுல கோரெத் தவரே. 1636

Tapas is the Yearning of Heart

In oneness of mind I did tapas
And witnessed Lord's triumphant Feet;
In eagerness of quest I did tapas
And witnessed Siva-State;
That alone is tapas
That you perform in the yearning of heart;
What avails the tapas of those,
Who thus perform not?

மனத்துறை மாகடல் ஏழுங் கைநீந்தித்
தவத்திடை யாளர்தஞ் சார்வத்து வந்தார்
பவத்திடை யாளர் அவர்பணி கேட்கின்
முகத்திடை நந்தியை முந்தலு மாமே. 1637

Follow Tapasvins and Meet God

Swimming across the seven seas of the mind
The tapasvins true their heaven reached;
Let them that are tossed in the sea of births about
Listen but to their Commandments holy,
Then can they see Nandi, face to face for sure.

மனத்திடை நின்ற மதிவாள் உருவி
இனத்திடை நீக்கி இரண்டற வீர்த்துப்
புனத்திடை அஞ்சும் போகாமல் மறித்தால்
தவத்திடை யாறொளி தன்னொளி யாமே. 1638

Light of Tapas is Light of Self

Unsheath your sword of Jnana mind's scabbard;
Flash it across the bonds of pasa, hacking them twain;
And watch your Self, lest senses five run wild;
Then, shall light that is of tapas born
Become light of the Self.

Mantras 1638 & 1639

Unsheath your sword of jnana from thought's scabbard and snap the fetters of pasa. Then will the light of tapas dawn, which becomes the light of the Self. He, the Lord, stands very close with us. It is tapas which grants bhakti, mukti and makes munis divine.

ஒத்து மிகவு நின்றானை யுரைப்பது
பத்தி கொடுக்கும் பணிந்தடி யார்தொழ
முத்தி கொடுக்கும் முனிவ னெனும்பதஞ்
சத்தான செய்வது தான்தவந் தானே. 1639

Tapas Gives Bhakti and Mukti

In intimacy He stands within us;
Pray that He grant you Bhakti;
Prostrate that He grant you Mukti;
Truly, it is tapas that makes Munis divine.

இலைதொட்டுப் பூப்பறித் தெந்தைக்கென் றெண்ணி
மலர்தொட்டுக் கொண்டேன் வரும்புனல் காணேன்
தலைதொட்ட நூல்கண்டு தாழ்ந்ததென் உள்ளந்
தலைதொட்டுக் கண்டேன் தவங்கண்ட வாறே. 1640

Tapas is the Supreme Means

I gathered the tender leaves and flowers variegated
I wove a garland
All for my Father;
Yet I saw not the gushing waters of Grace;
I scanned the lofty lores of scriptures
And my heart ebbed low;
But I stood in tapas
And touched Cranium heights
Lo! I met mine Lord.

Formal worship like adorning the Lord with garlands of leaves and multi-coloured flowers, and analysing the lofty lore of scriptures will not take you to God. Tapas is the supreme means which takes one to the cranium heights, and confers the vision of the Lord.

படர்சடை மாதவம் பற்றிய பத்தர்க்
கிடரடை யாவண்ணம் ஈசன் அருளும்
இடரடை செய்தவர் மெய்த்தவ நோக்கில்
உடரடை செய்வ தொருமனத் தாமே. 1641

Tapas is Single-mindedness

To the devout tapasvins, who in dishevelled locks sit
Lord lets no harm happen,
He His Grace lends;
Any you look at tapas
Of those that all trials overcame,
Know you, it is by their oneness of mind in tapas
They blocked the births to come.

Mantras 1641 & 1642

By the Grace of the Lord, the devout tapasvins are freed from harm. In their oneness of mind, tapasvins block the births to come. Evasion of tapas will bring ever-lasting hunger. He who does not seek to perform tapas is like the man who falls into the embrace of a bear on the bank when escaping from the crocodile in the river.

ஆற்றிற் கிடந்த முதலைகண் டஞ்சிப்போய்
ஈற்றுக் கரடிக் கெதிர்ப்பட்ட தன்னொக்கும்
நோற்றுத் தவஞ்செய்யார் நூலறி யாதவர்
சோற்றுக்கு நின்று சுழல்கின்ற வாறே. 1642

They That Shun Tapas Hunger Forever

In fear they ran from the crocodile in the river
And on the bank they fell into the embrace of the bear
Thus are they the ignorant of scriptures,
Who from austere tapas run away,
For food and in hunger roam for ever.

பழுக்கின்ற வாறும் பழமுண்ணு மாறுங்
குழக்கன்று துள்ளியக் கோணியைப் பல்காற்
குழக்கன்று கொட்டிலிற் கட்டவல் லார்க்குள்
இழுக்காது நெஞ்சத் திடவொன்று மாமே. 1643

Tapas is Control of Senses

Inside the body-sack
The tiny calf of senses jumps about
For the fruit to ripe and for the ripened fruit to eat;
They that can tether the lusty legged calf to the yard
Shall no more have pulls within;
Their thoughts will in oneness centre.

Get the lusty-legged calf, which jumps about inside the body sack, into the yard of knowledge. No more will there be pulls within. The thoughts will be centred in oneness on Siva. That is the real state of tapas.

சித்தஞ் சிவமாகச் செய்தவம் வேண்டாவால்
சித்தஞ் சிவானந்தஞ் சேர்ந்தோம் உறவுண்டால்
சித்தஞ் சிவமாக வேசித்தி முத்தியாஞ்
சித்தஞ் சிவமாதல் செய்தவப் பேறே. 1644

Tapas is Thought Becoming Siva

If your thoughts be all of Siva
You need no more penance perform;
If your thoughts find a kin
With those that have Siva Bliss tasted,
Then shall you be one with Siva;
Then is truly Siddhi and Mukti;
But your thoughts shall be of all Siva
Only by tapas intense.

There is no need of undergoing any sort of penance, if your thoughts are of Siva; if your thought finds kinship in Siva bliss and you become one with Siva. Only through intense tapas can this be attained. That is verily siddhi and mukti.

7. அருளுடைமையின் ஞானம் வருதல்

JNANA FLOWS FROM GOD'S GRACE

பிரானருள் உண்டெனில் உண்டுநற் செல்வம்
பிரானருள் உண்டெனில் உண்டுநன் ஞானம்
பிரானரு ளிற்பெருந் தன்மையும் உண்டு
பிரானரு ளிற்பெருந் தெய்வமு மாமே. 1645

Fruits of Lord's Grace

If you have Lord's Grace, you have all riches;
If you have Lord's Grace, you have true Jnana;
If you have Lord's Grace, you have greatness too;
If you have Lord's Grace, you shall be the great God Himself.

Mantras 1645 & 1648

They who have God's Grace have all the riches — true jnana, and greatness. They will become the great God Himself. When the right moment arrives, He grants benediction with His Grace standing by and ends the cycle of recurring births; ultimately bestowing mukti.

தமிழ்மண் டலம்ஐந்துந் தாவிய ஞானம்
உமிழ்வது போல உலகந் திர்வார்
அவிழு மனமும்எம் ஆதியறிவுந்
தமிழ்மண் டலம்ஐந்துந் தத்துவ மாமே. 1646

Jnana is Beyond Five Siva Tattvas

They go about the world
Exuding Jnana that is beyond Tamil mandalas; Five

Tamil mandalas are but Siva Tattvas;
There it is the blossoming of mind
And attainment of Lord's Jnana.

1) Tamil is used in the specific meaning of 'Siva'.

Men go about saying jnána is beyond the five "Tamil mandalas" — spatially. They are very ignorant. The "Tamil mandalas" are the five Siva tattvas themselves.

புண்ணிய பாவம் இரண்டுள பூமியில்
நண்ணும் பொழுதறி வார்சில ஞானிகள்
எண்ணி இரண்டையும் வேரறுத் தப்புறத்
தண்ணல் இருப்பிடம் ஆய்ந்துகொள் வீரே. *1647*

Jnana is Knowledge of Good and Evil

Good and evil, they are two in this world
As they seek God, some Jnanis know them;
As you cognize them two and uproot them
Then shall you perceive Lord's Abode Beyond.

Jnanis realise that God is beyond good and evil, beyond time and space.

முன்னின் றருளு முடிகின்ற காலத்து
நன்னின் றுலகில் நடுவுயி ராய்நிற்கும்
பின்னின் றருளும் பிறவியை நீக்கிடும்
முன்னின் றெனக்கொரு முத்திதந் தானே. *1648*

God Grants His Grace of Himself

At the hour ripe He of Himself appears
And blesses you with His Grace;
A Benevolent Force, He stands as the soul of our souls.
Still standing by you, He ends your birth to be,
Lo! He stood before me, and bestowed Mukti on me.

சிவனரு ளாற்சிலர் தேவரு மாவர்
சிவனரு ளாற்சிலர் தெய்வத்தோ டொப்பர்
சிவனரு ளால்வினை சேரகி லாமை
சிவனருள் கூடின்அச் சிவலோக மாமே. *1649*

Things That Come of Siva's Grace

By Siva's Grace some become Devas
By Siva's Grace some equal Gods
By Siva's Grace Karmas near not;
When you have Siva's Grace,
You shall enter His Kingdom, indeed.

Receiving the Grace of Siva, some become devas, some equal God, some are freed from karma. Possessing that Grace, some will enter His kingdom itself.

புண்ணியன் எந்தை புனிதன் இணையடி
நண்ணி விளக்கென ஞானம் விளைந்தது
மண்ணவ ராவதும் வானவ ராவதும்
அண்ணல் இறைவன் அருள்பெற்ற போதே. *1650*

Grace Decides Your Birth To-Be

The Holy One, the Immaculate One, My Father!
I sought His matchless Feet
And lo! Jnana shone forth as a beacon light;
You remain an earthly being
Or a Heavenly Being become;
All, as my Lord's Grace dawns.

If you seek the Holy Feet of the Immaculate One with jnana as the beacon light, Grace decides your birth to be — an earthly being or a heavenly being.

காயத்தே ரேறி மனப்பாகன் கைகூட்ட
மாயத்தே ரேறி மயங்கு மவையுணர்
நேயத்தே ரேறி நிமலன் அருள்பெற்றால்
ஆயத்தே ரேறி யவனிவ னாமே. *1651*

Grace Unites Soul in God

They mount the Body-Chariot
And Mind, the Charioteer takes the rein;
It is Illusion's-Chariot
That strange fantasies produces;
And they realize it,
And mount the Chariot of Love instead
And receive Grace of the Pure One,
They shall sure be drawn
In the triumphant Chariot of Unity
And be one in God, obliterating I and He.

Realisation of the truth that the body-chariot is only illusion's chariot that produces fantasies will make men to mount the chariot of love instead; to receive the Grace of the Pure One, which unites the soul in God.

அவ்வுல கத்தே பிறக்கில் உடலொடும்
அவ்வுல கத்தே யருந்தவர் நாடுவர்
அவ்வுல கத்தே யரனடி கூடுவர்
அவ்வுல கத்தே யருள்பெறு வாரே. *1652*

Tapasvins Will Receive Grace Even Hereafter

If born in body in the Other World
Tapasvins will pursue tapas there;
And will there reach Lord's Feet
And receive His Grace for sure.

The tapasvins will certainly receive His Grace through tapas, even if they are born in body and flesh in the other world.

கதிர்கண்ட காந்தங் கனலின் வடிவாம்
மதிகண்ட காந்தம் மணிநீர் வடிவாஞ்
சதிகொண்ட சாக்கி யெரியின் வடிவாம்
எரிகொண்ட ஈசன் எழில்வடி வாமே. *1653*

God is Beauty

Form within Sun-Stone is red hot ember,
Form within Moon-Stone is pearly drop of water,
Form within Fire-Stone is crackling fire,

Form of Lord that holds fire aloft
Is Beauty Surpassing.

நாடும் உறவுங் கலந்தெங்கள் நந்தியைத்
தேடுவன் தேடிச் சிவபெரு மானென்று
கூடுவன் கூடிக் குறைகழற் கேசெல்ல
வீடு மளவும் விடுகின் றிலேனே. *1654*

I shall hold fast unto Nandi

With love and yearning, I seek my Nandi,
Seeking Him, as Siva the Supreme, I will meet Him;
And then will I catch hold of His valorous Feet
And for ever hold to them,
Until He liberation grants.

8. அவவேடம்

FALSE ROBES

ஆடம் பரங்கொண் டடிசிலுண் பான்பயன்
வேடங்கள் கொண்டு வெருட்டிடும் பேதைகாள்
ஆடியும் பாடியும் அழுதும் அரற்றியுந்
தேடியுங் காணீர் சிவனவன் தாள்களே. *1655*

Men of false robes know not Siva

You fools! With false robes you deceive people
Your pretension but helps you gorge yourself fast with food;
Well may you sing and dance and weep and wail
And thus may Siva seek,
Yet never, never shall you glimpse His Feet.

They are knaves who deceive people by putting on false robes, while gorging themselves with delicious dishes. They may sing, dance, weep and wail; yet they cannot glimpse His Feet.

ஞானமில் லார்வேடம் பூண்டிருந்த நாட்டிடை
ஈனம தேசெய் திரந்துண் டிருப்பினும்
மான நலங்கெடும் வையகம் பஞ்சமாம்
ஈனவர் வேடங் கழிப்பித்தல் இன்பமே. *1656*

Men of false robes bring famine

When those that have not acquired Jnana
Don the holy robes
And go about the land begging,
And evil ways pursuing,
The rains fail and famine strikes the land;
Better by far, these evil men are de-robed straight.

Mantras 1656 & 1657

Wearing holy attire and going the rounds for alms without attaining jnana; they but walk the perilous evil paths that are forbidden. They will lead the land to famine. A land enjoys affluence or adversity according to the good and bad deeds performed by its people. It is the duty of the ruler to lead the people in virtuous and righteous paths. The land is then sure to remain in prosperity and peace.

இன்பமுந் துன்பமும் நாட்டா ரிடத்துள்ள
நன்செயல் புன்செய லாலந்த நாட்டிற்காம்
என்ப இறைநாடி நாடோறும் நாட்டினின்
மன்பதை செப்பஞ் செயின்வையம் வாழுமே. *1657*

Let Government lead people in the way of Virtue

A land's weal and woe are in its people
Out of good deeds and evil do they spring;
And so,
If the ruler unceasing leads the multitude in virtue's way,
That land in prosperity waxes ever.

இழிகுலத் தோர்வேடம் பூண்பர்மே லெய்த
வழிகுலத் தோர்வேடம் பூண்பர்தே வாகப்
பழிகுலத் தாகிய பாழ்சண்ட ரானார்
கழிகுலத் தோர்கள் களையப்பட் டோரே. *1658*

Why they don the Holy Robes

The lowly-born don the robe
That they may the high become;
The high-born don the robe
That they may the Gods become;
To infamy-born are the knaves in robes
That they be disrobed and cast away.

The high-born don holy robes to walk in God's path. The infamy-born knaves put on pseudo-robes to pursue evil ways. They should be disrobed and exposed promptly.

பொய்த்தவஞ் செய்வார் புகுவர் நரகத்துப்
பொய்த்தவஞ் செய்தவர் புண்ணிய ராகாரேற்
பொய்த்தவம்மெய்த்தவம் போகத்துட்போக்கியஞ்
சத்திய ஞானத்தால் தங்குந் தவங்களே. *1659*

Tapas—True and False

They who perform false tapas enter hell
They shall not become the holy ones;
False tapas is deceit and vain effort
A ruse for worldly enjoyment;
Only by Truth of Jnana can tapas firm abide.

Only by truth of jnana can be performed true tapas.

பொய்வேடம் பூண்பர் போசித்தல் பயனாக
மெய்வேடம்பூண்போர்மிகு பிச்சைகைக்கொள்வர்

பொய்வேடம் மெய்வேடம் போலவே பூணினும்
உய்வேட மாகும் உணர்ந்தறிந் தோர்க்கே. 1660

Discerning eyes see through false robe

They don the false robe their bellies to fill;
They don the true robe and receive exalted oblations above;
Even if false robes are donned to simulate the true,
The discerning see through, and make themselves free.

Practising false tapas is ignoble and unholy, full of deceit and conceit. It is but an artifice to indulge in mundane materialistic pleasures. The discerning eyes are capable of seeing through the false robes, and free themselves from the clutches of the wearers.

9. தவவேடம்
ROBES OF TAPAS

தவமிக் கவரே தலையான வேடர்
அவமிக் கவரேயதிகொலை வேடர்
அவமிக் கவர்வேடத் தாகாரவ் வேடந்
தவமிக் கவர்க்கன்றித் தாங்கவொண் ணாதே. 1661

True robe befits only true Tapasvins

The true tapasvins are the truly robed;
The sinful are but murderous hunters;
These are not for holy robe entitled;
None but tapasvins true deserve robe true.

பூதி யணிவது சாதன மாதியிற்
காதணி தாம்பிர குண்டலங் கண்டிகை
ஓதி யவர்க்கும் உருத்திர சாதனந்
தீதில் சிவயோகி சாதனந் தேரிலே. 1662

The insignia of Siva Yogins

To smear holy ashes is first step to tapas;
Rings of copper in ears, and garland of rudraksha beads around neck
—These too are other emblems to Siva reach;
Thus do the blemishless Siva Yogins for tapas prepare.

Genuine tapas commences with the smearing of the holy ashes. The emblems which are taken up to worship Siva are rings of copper in the ears, and a garland of rudraksa beads around the neck. Thus the Siva yogins prepare themselves for holy tapas.

யோகிக் கிடுமது வுட்கட்டுக் கஞ்சுளி
தோகைக்குப் பாசத்துச் சுற்றுஞ் சடையதொன்
றாகத்து நீறணி யாங்கக் கபாலஞ்
சீகந்த மாத்திரை திண்பிரம் பாகுமே. 1663

Other insignia of Siva Yogin

A waist strip for an under-vest,
A long tunic for body's wrap,
A matted hair lock done in peacock style,
Ashes smeared all over,
A begging bowl of human skull shape
A cowl staff of hard cane
—Thus is Siva Yogi accoutred.

Mantras 1663 & 1664

The prescribed mendicant equipment for a Siva yogin are: 1) a waist-strip for an undervest, and a long tunic to wrap the body; 2) matted hairlock done in peacock style; 3) ashes smeared all over the body; 4) kundala to adorn the ears and kandika to fill the nose; 5) a begging bowl of skull shape, and kamandalu pot to hold water; 6) a conch to blow and a kappara vessel to hold ashes; 7) the yogic sandals; 8) the yogic seat; 9) the yogic sash; 10) the yogic staff. These ten constitute the equipment of the Siva yogin.

காதணி குண்டலங் கண்டிகை நாதமும்
ஊதுநற் சங்கும் உயர்கட்டி கப்பரை
ஏதமில் பாதுகம் யோகாந்த மாதனம்
ஏதமில் யோகபட் டந்தண்டம் ஈரைந்தே 1664

Ten appurtenances of Siva Yogins

Kundalam the ears to adorn,
Kamandalam the water to hold,
Kandikai the neck to fill
A conch to blow, a bowl to beg
And a Kapparai to hold the ashes
The correct sandals and Yogic seat
The Yoga sash and Yogic staff
—These ten consist Siva Yogi's appurtenances.

10. திருநீறு
HOLY ASHES

நூலஞ் சிகையும் உணரார்நின் மூடர்கள்
நூலது வேதாந்தம் நுண்சிகை ஞானமாம்
பாலொன்றும் அந்தணர் பார்ப்பார் பரமுயிர்
ஒரொன் றிரண்டெனில் ஓங்காரம் ஓதிலே. 1665

Chant "Aum" and unite in Param

Fools know not what thread and tuft are;
Thread is but Vedanta, and tuft is Jnana;
Brahmins true who live in accord thus,

Shall see Jiva in Siva uniting;
Chant sacred mantra "Aum"
And lo! the Two merge forever in One.

Fools are ignorant of the fact that thread and tuft are but symbolic of Vedanta and jnana. True brahmins, knowing this, unite in Siva by continuous chanting of the mantra, 'Aum.'

கங்காளன் பூசுங் கவசத் திருநீற்றை
மங்காமற் பூசி மகிழ்வரே யாமாகில்
தங்கா வினைகளுஞ் சாருஞ் சிவகதி
சிங்கார மான திருவடி சேர்வரே. 1666

Power of Holy Ashes

The sacred ashes of Siva
Who has bones for His garland
Are an armour indeed impregnable;
For them who in joy smear it
Karmas take flight,
And Siva-state comes seeking;
And they shall reach His handsome Feet.

The power of the holy ashes of Siva is so great that they who smear it in exultation will be freed from karmas; finally reaching His Handsome Feet.

அரசுட னாலத்தி யாகும்அக் காரம்
விரவுகனலில் வியனுரு மாறி
நிரவயன் நின்மலன் தாள்பெற்ற நீதர்
உருவம் பிரமன் உயர்குல மாகுமே. 1667

Holy Ashes elevate to Brahma Status

The holy ash shall make you a king
And all regalia shall you have;
They that are in its fire purified
Shall in truth be transformed divine;
Reaching the Feet of the Eternal, the Immaculate
They shall attain Brahman's form
And ever be of Order Divine.

Cleansed in the fire of the holy ashes, they reach a regal status. They reach the Feet of the Eternal, Immaculate Lord, attaining ultimately the form of Brahman.

11. ஞான வேடம்

ROBES OF JNANA

ஞானமி லார்வேடம் பூண்டும் நரகத்தர்
ஞானமுள்ளார்வேடம்இன்றெனில்நன்முத்தர்
ஞான முளதாக வேண்டுவோர் நக்கன்பால்
ஞான முளவேட நண்ணிநிற் பாரே. 1668

Jnana is All; not robes

Sans Jnana, robe but leads to hell
Sans robe, Jnana yet leads to Mukti;
When they seek Jnana,
They shall seek Lord and pray,
Their hearts robed in Jnana way.

Mantras 1668 & 1669

Without jnana that leads to mukti, mere robes are insignificant. They of dubious jnana wear the robes in vain. Jnanis seek jnana; that is everything. Robed in the attire of jnana, they pray deep in their hearts. The perfect jnanis, filled with Grace, do not speak.

புன்ஞானத் தோர்வேடம் பூண்டும்பயனில்லை
நன்ஞானத்தோர்வேடம் பூணார் அருள்நண்ணித்
துன்ஞானத் தோர்சம யத்துரி சுள்ளோர்
பின்ஞானத் தோரொன்றும் பேசகில்லாரே. 1669

Perfect Jnanis speak not

They of lowly Jnana in vain assume robes;
Filled with Grace, they of true Jnana covet it not;
The bigots of faiths are of evil Jnana;
The perfect of Jnana speak not.

சிவஞானி கட்குஞ் சிவயோகி கட்கும்
அவமான சாதனம் ஆகாது தேரில்
அவமா மவர்க்கது சாதன நான்கும்
உவமான மில்பொருள் உள்ளுற லாமே. 1670

They Need No Paths

Neither for Siva Jnanis, nor for Siva Yogins
Is it meet superfluous ways to adopt;
In sooth, needless indeed are the sadhanas Four*
for them,
When they can see the Peerless One
Within themselves full.

* Chariya, Kriya, Yoga and Jnana

Neither for the Siva jnanis nor for the Siva yogis is it necessary to adopt the four sadhanas when they can feel the omnipresence of the Peerless Lord within themselves.

கத்தித் திரிவர் கழுவடி நாய்போற்
கொத்தித் திரிவர் குரக்களி ஞானிகள்
ஒத்துப் பொறியும் உடலும் இருக்கவே
செத்துத் திரிவர் சிவஞானி யோர்களே. 1671

Siva Jnanis are Quiescent

They howl about like dogs at foot of gallows;
They peck about like vultures at carrion;
They frisk about like monkeys in merriment
They of false Jnana;

But quiescent are the Siva Jnanis true,
Dead to the world, though living in body and senses.

அடியா ரவரே யடியா ரலாதார்
அடியாரு மாகாரவ் வேடமு மாகார்
அடியார் சிவஞான மானது பெற்றோர்
அடியா ரலாதார் அடியார்கள் அன்றே. 1672

Siva Jnanis alone are of the Holy Order

They truly are of Holy Order
Who have attained Sivajnana;
They truly are of Holy Order,
The rest are not;
Nor their robes holy;
They are never, never by reckoning any.

Mantras 1672 & 1673

Siva jnanis alone are of the Holy Order and fit to wear the holy robes. The rest will never be esteemed. Whatever robe the Siva jnani adopts, that shall aid him to jnana.

ஞானிக்குச் சுந்தர வேடமும் நல்லவாந்
தானுற்ற வேடமுந் தற்சிவ யோகமே
ஆனவவ் வேடம் அருண்ஞான சாதனம்
ஆனது மாமொன்றும் ஆகா தவனுக்கே. 1673

Everything suits the Jnani

Even the gayest attire becomes the Jnani,
Albeit his own robe is of Siva Yogin;
Whatever robe he adopts, that shall aid him to Jnana
Nothing is appropriate or non-appropriate for him.

ஞானத்தி னாற்பத நண்ணுஞ் சிவஞானி
தானத்தில் வைத்த தனியால யத்தனாம்
மோனத்த னாதலின் முத்தனாஞ் சித்தனாம்
ஏனைத் தவசி இவனென லாகுமே. 1674

Jnani is a class apart

The Siva Jnani that seeks deliverance through Jnana
Is a shrine unto himself, unique of status;
He observes mauna, and so is a Mukta and Siddha;
How can other tapasvins be like unto him?

Mantras 1674 & 1675

A jnani is superior to a tapasvin, because he is a shrine unto himself. His status is unique. He observes mauna, and is a mukta and a siddha too. Through destruction of the self, 'I' becomes 'He,' in Siva/jiva identity. All these and the blessings still beyond they receive at the Feet of Nandi.

தானற்ற தன்மையுந் தானவ னாதலும்
ஏனைய வச்சிவ மான இயற்கையுந்
தானுறு சாதக முத்திரை சாத்தலு
மேனமும் நந்தி பதமுத்தி பெற்றதே. 1675

Stages in Liberation process

The annihilating of the Self
The Self becoming He
The identity in Siva
The Mudra setting the state ultra,
All these and the rest they had,
They who received deliverance at the Feet of Nandi.

12. சிவ வேடம்

SIVA ROBE

அருளால் அரனுக் கடிமைய தாகிப்
பொருளாந் தனதுடற் பொற்பதி நாடி
இருளான தின்றி யிருஞ்செயல் அற்றோர்
தெருளாம் அடிமைச் சிவவேடத் தோரே. 1676

Liege-robe of Siva

By Hara's Grace they become His liege-men;
Within the body mansion, they seek His golden throne;
Darkness dispelled, they know of deeds none, good and bad;
Thus they stand steadfast in the liege-robe of Siva.

Seek God's golden throne within the body (mansion) itself. There dies the darkness of malas, and you become indifferent to deeds both good and bad. Thus stand steadfast as His liegeman filled with His Grace.

உடலில் துவக்கிய வேடம் உயிர்க்காகா
உடல்கழன் றால்வேடம் உடனே கழலும்
உடலுயிர் உண்மையென் றோர்ந்துகொள்ளாதார்
கடலில் அகப்பட்ட கட்டையொத் தாரே. 1677

The robe is not for Soul

The robe is for the body; not for the Soul
When the body falls, the garb with it falls;
Those that know not that the Soul within the body is real,
Are tossed about like a log caught in wavy sea.

Polemics against the 'anatman' concept of Buddhism, Lokayata, etc.

மயலற் றிருளற்று மாமன மற்றுக்
கயலுற்ற கண்ணியர் கையிணைக் கற்றுத்
தயலற் றவரோடுந் தாமே தாமாகிச்
செயலற் றிருப்பார் சிவவேடத் தாரே. 1678

They of Siva-Robe are action-less

Sans illusions, sans ignorance, sans intelligence,
Sans the embraces of fish-eyed damsels and their

attachment,
Themselves as themselves; in solitude remain one in Siva-Sakti;
Thus are they, the Holy ones in Siva's robe.

Cognition of the truth that it is the soul within the body that matters rather than the body with the garb — that truth frees and protects men from the wavy sea of illusions. The holy ones in Siva robes remain in solitude, one in Siva/Sakti. They are not perturbed by illusions, ignorance, intelligence and allurements of the fish-eyed damsels of the world.

ஓடுங் குதிரைக் குசைதிண்ணம் பற்றுமின்
வேடங்கொண் டென்செய்வீர் வேண்டாமனிதரே
நாடுமின் நந்தியை நம்பெரு மான்தன்னைத்
தேடும்இன் பப்பொருள் சென்றெய்த லாமே. *1679*

Why the robe? Seek Nandi Yoga Way

What avails thee, vain men, these holy robes?
Rein fast the fleeting mare of the twin breath;
And seek Nandi, Our Lord Beloved,
You shall attain sure the Bliss you crave.

Casting aside all these holy robes, seek Nandi, the Beloved Lord. Then shall you attain the bliss that is final.

13. அபக்குவன்

THE UNFIT

குருட்டினை நீக்குங் குருவினைக் கொள்ளார்
குருட்டினை நீக்காக் குருவினைக் கொள்வார்
குருடுங் குருடுங் குருட்டாட்டம் ஆடிக்
குருடுங் குருடுங் குழிவிழு மாறே. *1680*

Blind leading the Blind

They seek not the Guru that blindness cures
They seek the Guru that cures not blindness;
The blind and the blind in a blind dance shuffled
And the blind and the blind in a deep pit together fell.

Mantras 1680 & 1681

The acts of the unfit are like the blind leading the blind, both finally falling into a deep pit. False disciples do not think of the fruits of karma, but rather of the temptations of the backyard drain.

மனத்தில் எழுந்ததோர் மாயக்கண் ணாடி
நினைப்பின் அதனின் நிழலையுங் காணார்
வினைப்பயன் போக விளக்கியுங் கொள்ளார்
புறக்கடை இச்சித்துப் போகின்ற வாறே. *1681*

They seek Worldly Pleasures

Out of mind, the mirror of illusion rises
Think of it, even its shadows they see not
And nothing they do for the fruits of Karma to drop;
The temptations of the backyard drain, they go after.

ஏயெனில் என்னென மாட்டார் பிரசைகள்
வாய்முலை பெய்ய மதுரநின் றூறிடுந்
தாய்முலை யாவ தறியார் தமருளோர்
ஊனிலை செய்யும் உருவிலி தானே. *1682*

They know not the Mystery of Body

You beckon them, but they hearken not
The ignorant multitude they are;
The mother's milk flows sweet in the mouth,
But even the dear and near know not
How the mother's breast becomes so;
Verily, it is the Formless Being that shapes this body-form.

Mantras 1682 & 1683

They, the ignorant multitude, do not understand the mystery of the body. Realise the Gracious Lord in purity of thought, word and deed. You become the elite.

வாயொன்று சொல்லி மனமொன்று சிந்தித்து
நீயொன்று செய்யல் உறுதி நெடுந்தகாய்
தீயென்றிங் குன்னைத் தெளிவன் தெளிந்தபின்
பேயென்றிங் கென்னைப் பிறர்தெளியாரே. *1683*

Realize Lord in Purity of thought, word and deed

The lips utter one thing;
The mind thinks another;
And the deed does a third,
Thus you behave not;
Gracious Lord! You Rock of Ages!
I know You as the Fire-hued Lord,
And having known that
None dares know me as creature insensate.

பஞ்சத் துரோகத்திப் பாதகர் தம்மை
யஞ்சச் சமயத்தோர் வேந்தன் அருந்தண்டம்
விஞ்சச்செய் திப்புவி வேறே விடாவிடிற்
பஞ்சத்து ளாய்ப்புவி முற்றும்பா ழாகுமே. *1684*

Banish False Disciples

These reprobates of the five deadly sins
Full deserve the pious ruler's punishment severe;
When he fails and banishes them not
The land to fell famine falls a prey.

தவத்திடை நின்றவர் தாமுண்ணுங் கன்மஞ்
சிவத்திடை நின்றது தேவர் அறியார்
தவத்திடை நின்றறி யாதவர் எல்லாம்
பவத்திடை நின்றதோர் பாடது வாமே. *1685*

Tapas consumes Karma

They who stand in tapas
Consume away all Karma
In Siva they stand;
Even Celestials know this not
They who know not Siva in tapas-standing,
Stood in tangle of births to endless sorrow condemned.

Mantras 1685 & 1687

Tapasvins, having consumed Karma, stand in Siva. Tapasvins who seek God are not concerned about their likes and dislikes. They look neither to the dawn, nor to the vast spaces outside, but look inward to glimpse the light that ends births.

கன்றலுங் கருதலுங் கருமஞ் செய்தலும்
தின்றலுஞ் சுவைத்தலுஞ் தீமைசெய்தலும்
பின்றலும் பிறங்கலும் பெருமை கூறலும்
என்றிவை இறைபால் இயற்கை அல்லவே. *1686*

Qualities unbecoming Tapasvins

Feeling, thinking, doing
Eating, tasting, hurting
Falling, rising, boasting
These come not
To those who walk in God.

விடிவ தறியார் வெளிகாண மாட்டார்
விடியில் வெளியில் விழிக்கவு மாட்டார்
கடியதோ ருண்ணிமை கட்டுமின் காண்மின்
விடியாமை காக்கும் விளக்கது வாமே. *1687*

Inner Vision ends Births

They glimpse not the Dawn,
Nor the Spaces Vast;
Nor the Vision in Spaces;
Close your inner eyes hard
And then see;
Behold, there is the Light
That brings not another day!

வைத்த பசுபாச மாற்று நெறிவைகிப்
பெத்த மறமுத்த னாகிப் பிறழ்வுற்றுத்
தத்துவ முன்னித் தலைப்படா தவ்வாறு
பித்தான சீடனுக் கீயப் பெறாதானே. *1688*

No Grace for false Disciple

He thinks not of sundering soul's fetters,
Nor of annihilating world's desires;
He strives not to Mukti attain,
Nor aught of Tattvas and the way ahead;
But takes a wayward course,
A disciple exceeding mad;
To him is not the gift of Grace granted.

Mantras 1688 & 1689

Grace is not for the false disciple, who instead of striving for mukti, yearns for worldly pleasure. He does not snap the bonds of the soul, nor free himself from incessant lust. He, a mean liar, is indifferent to birth and death. Verily, Grace finds him a stranger.

மன்னும் மலம்ஐந்தும் மாற்றும் வகையோரான்
துன்னிய காமாதி தோயுந் தொழில்நீங்கான்
பின்னிய பொய்யன் பிறப்பிறப் பஞ்சாதான்
அன்னிய னாவன் அசற்சீட னாமே. *1689*

Other blemishes of false Disciples

He thinks not of ending Fetters Five
Nor of deliverance from incessant lust immersed;
A mean liar, fears neither birth nor death
Verily, a stranger to Grace shall be
He, the disciple false.

14. பக்குவன்

THE FIT DISCIPLE

தொழிலறி வாளர் சுருதிகண் ணாகப்
பழுதறியாத பரம குருவை
வழியறி வார்நல் வழியறி வாளர்
அழிவறி வார்மற்றை யல்லா தவரே. *1690*

They who find the Path

Scriptures to guide them,
The Disciples Fit
Find the blemishless Guru;
They know their job and so find the Path;
The rest are to destruction destined.

The fit disciples find their way with the guidance that scriptures and the blemishless Guru give.

பதைதொழிந் தேன்பர மாவுனை நாடி
யதைத்தொழிந் தேன்இனி யாரோடுங் கூடேன்
சிதைத்தடி யேன்வினை சிந்தனை தீர
உதைத்துடை யாயுகந் தாண்டரு ளாயே. *1691*

Lord! Grant me Your Grace

You, Supreme Lord!
Seeking You, I lost all sense of fear;
Now I wander not,
And seek not another's company;
Shatter, Lord, my Karmas
Uproot them from my very thoughts
And kick them off;

Grant me Your Grace
Own me,
And make me Your slave forever.

Mantras 1691 & 1692

"God, my Lord, in seeking You as my sole companion, I have lost all sense of fear. Eradicate the very roots of karma from my thoughts. Grant me your Grace and make me your slave and leigeman." Grace is granted to those whose thoughts run thus, and are centred solely on oneness with the Lord.

பதைக்கின்ற போதே பரமென்னும் வித்தை
விதைக்கின்ற வித்தினை மேல்நின்று நோக்கிச்
சிதைக்கின்ற சிந்தையைச் செவ்வே நிறுத்தி
இசைக்கின்ற அன்பருக் கீயலு மாமே. 1692

Grace comes to those who contain their Thoughts in God

Even as your frame still pulsates with life,
You envision high
Para the Seed of seeds;
And rally your thoughts to oneness
And stand thus in love and accord;
To such that do, He grants His Grace.

கொள்ளினும் நல்ல குருவினைக் கொள்ளுக
உள்ள பொருளுடல் ஆவி யுடன்ஈக
எள்ளத் தனையும் இடைவிடா தேநின்று
தெள்ளி யறியச் சிவபதந் தானே. 1693

Seek a proper Guru

When you seek a Guru
Seek you one, holy and pure;
And then give him your all—
Your body, life and wealth;
And in constancy learn clear,
Not a moment distracting,
You shall sure reach Siva's State.

Submit everything — your body, life and wealth to the holy Guru whom you seek. Then you will surely in constancy reach Siva's state.

சோதி விசாகந் தொடர்ந்திரு தேள்நண்டு
ஓதிய நாளே உணர்வது தானென்று
நீதியுள் நீர்மை நினைந்தவர்க் கல்லது
ஆதியும் ஏதும் அறியகி லானே. 1694

Auspicious Days for receiving Instruction

In the asterisms of Swati and Visakha
In the conjunction of Lagnas Vrischika and Kataka,
Of the Guru, the holy precepts you receive;
Except it be them who stand in the path of virtue
The Primal One knows none.

Only the virtuous know the Primal Lord and receive the holy precepts of the Guru in the asterisms of swati and visakha, in the conjunctions of lagnas, vrischika and kataka.

Mular's faith in astrological concepts is demonstrated here.

தொழிலார மாமணித் தூய்தான சிந்தை
எழிலால் இறைவன் இடங்கொண்ட போதே
விழலார் விறலாம் வினையது போகக்
கழலார் திருவடி கண்டரு ளாமே. 1695

Pure thoughts lead to Grace

When your discipline perfect be,
Your thoughts crystal pure be;
And there the beauteous Lord resides;
Then shall Karmas all
Rooted deep like undying weeds,
Disappear;
And you shall glimpse the Grace
Of the valorous Feet of the Lord Holy.

Discipline creates pure thoughts, and there dwells the beauteous Lord. Deep-rooted karmas disappear with the glimpse of the Grace-filled Feet of the Holy Lord.

சாத்திக னாய்ப்பர தத்துவத் தானுன்னி
ஆத்திக பேத நெறிதோற்ற மாகியே
ஆர்த்த பிறவியி னஞ்சி யற்நெறி
சாத்தவல் லானவன் சற்சீட னாமே. 1696

Attributes of Good Disciple

A sattvic he is;
His thoughts centred on Finite Truth;
His vision clear through conflicting faiths;
Abhorrent of recurring cycle of births;
Straight in Dharma's path he easy walks;
He, sure, is disciple good and true.

Mantras 1696 & 1697

A true disciple is a sattvic. He treads the path of dharma, with his thoughts centred on the final Truth, with vision clear on escape from the cycle of recurring births. He analyses that which severes the real from the unreal. Having known it, he melts in his soul for the love of God. With Siva's Grace as his guide, he seeks the bliss of His Sakti in humility.

சத்தும் அசத்துமெவ் வாறெனந் தானுன்னிச்
சித்தை யுறுக்கிச் சிவனருள் கைகாட்டப்
பத்தியின் ஞானம் பெறப்பணிந் தானந்தச்
சத்தியில் இச்சைத் தகுவோன்சற் சீடனே. 1697

Yet other qualities of Good Disciple

He scans that which divides the Real and the Unreal,
He melts in the soul of his being
And with Siva's Grace to guide,
He receives Jnana in devotion true;
And he humbles himself before Lord
And seeks the bliss of His Sakti;
He is the fit one, the disciple good and true.

அடிவைத் தருளுதி யாசானின் றுன்னா
அடிவைத்த மாமுடி மாயப் பிறவி
அடிவைத்த காய அருட்சத்தி யாலே
அடிபெற்ற ஞானத்த னாசற்று ளோனே. 1698

The Power of Guru's Feet

"Oh! my Holy Master!
Do grace me with your feet on my head,"
—Thus, I prayed, this day;
And as he placed his feet
All births to vanish;
This body that was blessed thus
Received Grace of Arul Sakti
And I became a Janani ripe,
Forever, blemish devoid.

Mantras 1698 & 1699

When the holy Guru, the master of the four difficult paths, and possessor of divine grace placed his feet on my head, all births vanished. Blessed thus, the Grace of Arul Sakti descended on me and I became a ripe jnani. My ardour in jnana soared higher and my love for Gurupara welled up freed of blemishes.

சீராரு ஞானத்தின் இச்சை செலச்செல்ல
வாராத காதல் குருபரன் பாலாகச்
சாராத சாதக நான்குந்தன் பாலுற்றோன்
ஆராயும் ஞானத்த னாமடி வைக்கவே. *1699*

What comes of touch of Guru's Feet

He is the master of the difficult paths four;
He is the seeker incessant of Jnana divine;
And as he placed his feet on my head,
Higher and higher, my ardour in Jnana soared,
Higher and higher, my love for Gurupara welled up.

---

1) Mantra, yantra, yoga, jnana.

உணர்த்து மதிபக் குவர்க்கே யுணர்த்தி
இணக்கிற் பராபரத் தெல்லையுள் இட்டுக்
குணக்கொடு தெற்குத் தரபச்சி மங்கொண்
டுணர்த்துமி னாவுடை யாள்தன்னை யுன்னியே. *1700*

Rules of Instruction

Impart divine knowledge only to those fully ripe to receive it,
Taking the disciple gently to the limits of the Infinite Vast;
You facing east or south, your disciple facing west or north
Thus instruct, the Sakti of Lord centred in mind.

The holy Guru imparts divine knowledge only to those who are fully ripe to receive it. He takes the disciple to the limits of the infinite vast. He, facing east or south and the disciple the opposite direction (west or north), instructs, the Sakti of the Lord being centred in his mind.

இறையடி தாழ்ந்தை வணக்கமும் எய்திக்
குறையது கூறிக் குணங்கொண்டு போற்றச்
சிறையுடல் நீயறக் காட்டிச் சிவத்தோ
டறிவுக் கறிவிப்போன் சன்மார்க்கி யாமே. *1701*

How the Jnana Guru Instructs

He humbles before Divine Guru
In postures five ordained;
He bewails his faults,
Praises Master's virtues;
Guru then shows the way of deliverance from mortal prison
And imparts Siva Jnana
He is truly the Guru that is of Sanmarga (Jnana Guru).

The holy Guru shows the path of deliverance from the mortal prison and imparts Sivajnana to his disciple when he, the disciple, in humility bows in five ordained postures, is regretful of his faults and praises his master's virtues.

வேட்கை விடுநெறி வேதாந்த மாதலால்
வாழ்க்கைப் புனல்வழி மாற்றிச்சித் தாந்தத்து
வேட்கை விடுமிக்க வேதாந்தி பாதமே
தாழ்க்குந் தலையினோன் சற்சீட னாமே. *1702*

True Disciple humbles before the Renunciate Vedantin

Vedanta is the way of renouncing desires;
And so, divert your life's course
And take to Siddhanta-Vedanta Way
And humble your head at the feet of Guru
That has renounced all in the Vedanta way
Then verily are you disciple true.

Mantras 1702 & 1703

Vedanta is the way of renouncing desires. So divert your life-course to Siddhanta/Vedanta way and be humble at the feet of the Guru, who has renounced all. Truly he is a perfect disciple, who follows the Guru like a shadow in virtue, truth, compassion, discrimination and love, constantly and forever. He receives the nectar of crystal clear final jnana and witnesses the many miracles it brings in its train.

சற்குணம் வாய்மை தயாவிவே கந்தண்மை
சற்குரு பாதமே சாயைபோல் நீங்காமே
சிற்பர ஞானந் தெளியத் தெளிவோர்தல்
அற்புத மேதோன்ற லாகுஞ்சற் சீடனே. *1703*

Good Disciple follows Guru like a shadow

O! disciple true!
In virtue, truth, compassion, discrimination and love
You pursue the Holy Feet of Guru true
Constant as unto a shadow;
You then gain the nectar of Finite Jnana its crystal clarity,
And witness the many miracles it brings in train.

ஆறாம் தந்திரம் முடிவு பெற்றது.
Tantra Six Concluded

ஏழாந் தந்திரம்
TANTRA SEVEN

1. ஆறாதாரம்
THE SIX ADHARAS

நாலும் இருமூன்றும் ஈரைந்தும் ஈராறுங்
கோலிமேல் நின்ற குறிகள் பதினாறும்
மூலங்கண் டாங்கே முடிந்து முதல்இரண்டுங்
காலங்கண் டானடி காணலு மாமே. 1704

The Six Adharas and their petals

Piercing the Chakras* that are petalled
Four, Six, Ten and Twelve
And the Six and Ten still above;
Lo! Behold then the Twin petalled Centre finale;
You have indeed beheld the Holy Feet of the Timeless One.

There are six chakras situated at different points along the spinal column of the human body. They are known as: muladhara of four petals, svadhistana of six petals, manipuraka of ten petals, anahatha of twelve petals, visuddhi of sixteen petals and ajna of two petals. Coursing the prana breath through these chakras in ascending order, the yogi beholds the Twin Feet of the Eternal in the twin-petalled ajna chakra.

*Muladhara—Of four petals
Svadhistana—Of six petals
Manipuraka—Of ten petals
Anahatha—Of twelve petals
Visuddhi—Of sixteen petals
Ajna—Of two petals.

The Adharas are symbolized as Lotus Petals, of varying numbers. The final climax is reached in the "twin-petalled Centre finale" (in the cranium between the eye-brows).

ஈராறு நாதத்தில் ஈரெட்டாம் அந்தத்தின்
மேதாதி நாதாந்த மீதாம் பராசத்தி
போதா லயத்த விகாரந் தனிற்போத
மேதாதி யாதார மீதான உண்மையே. 1705

The Spheres of the upper Adharas

In the Nada sphere is the Twelve petalled Centre
In the Nadanta sphere is the Ten and Six petalled Centre
Beyond the Nadanta is the Two-petalled Medha Centre
Where Parasakti enshrined is;
Enter there in Consciousness Undifferentiated Bodha;
There, above, the Medha Centre, is the Truth Finale.

The anahatha chakra is in the Nada sphere; visuddhi chakra, in the Nadanta sphere: ajna chakra, in the Medha sphere. Parasakti is enshrined here. Above this centre is the final Truth.

மேலென்றுங் கீழென் றிரண்டறக் காணுங்கால்
தானென்றும் நானென்றுந் தன்மைகள் ஓராறும்
பாரெங்கு மாகிப் பரந்த .பராபரங்
காரொன்று கற்பக மாகிநின் றானே. 1706

Parapara pervades all the Six Adharas

When thus through Adharas
You course Prana breath
Neither Up nor Down do you know
Neither He nor I do you cognise
The mighty Parapara that pervades all
Envelops you,
Bounteous as the celestial Kalpaka tree.*

When prana breath is coursed up through these six adharas, step by step, the yogi is oblivious of his station as up or down, and his being as self or God. Parapara envelopes him, cool as the fruit-laden kalpaka tree.

*Wishing-tree in heaven.

ஆதர்ர சோதனை யானாடி சுத்திகள்
மேதாதி யீரெண் கலாந்தத்து விண்ணொளி
போதா லயத்துப் புலன்கர ணம்புந்தி
சாதா ரணங் கெட்டான் றான்சக மார்க்கமே. 1707

Experience is Adhara Yoga

Ascend Adharas step by step,
Your Nadis purified thus,
You shall have ascended
Into the heavenly effulgence of Medha
Whose twin petals into Kalanta sphere rise;
And then you reach the state of Bodha,
Of Awareness Unitive, senses petrified;
That verily is Yoga — the Saha Marga.

With nadis purified, the yogi ascends into Nada, Nadanta, Kalanta and Bodhanta spheres within as he courses the prana upwards.

1) The spheres of experience in yoga are:
i) Nada; ii) Nadanta; iii) Bodhanta; iv) Kalanta.
2) The spheres of experience in yoga are:
Nadanta (sound sphere), Kalanta (light sphere), and Bodhanta (consciousness sphere).

மேதாதி யாலே விடாதோ மெனத்தூண்டி
ஆதார சோதனை அத்துவ சோதனை
தாதார மாகவே தானெழச் சாதித்தால்
ஆதாரஞ் செய்போக மாவது காயமே. 1708

Ascending further above Six Adharas

There you stop not — at Medha's Centre —
But evoke Aum,
And beyond Adharas now proceed
And ascend the Adhvas* with Prana for support
When thus you practise, to perfection's end,
Your body becomes a doughty receptacle
Of Joy Eternal.

The yogi must not stop at medha's (ajna) centre, but should evoke, 'Aum,' and, with prana as support, he should proceed beyond the adharas to ascend further the six steps (adhvas), viz., kala, bhuvana, varna, mantra, pada and tattva. When this is practised perfectly, the yogi's body becomes a receptacle of endless bliss.

*Adhvas are pathways, or steps. These are six in number — kala, bhuvana, varna, mantra, pada, and tattva.

ஆறந்த முங்கூடி யாகும் உடம்பினிற்
கூறிய வாதார மற்றுங் குறிக்கொண்மின்
ஆறிய வக்கர மைம்பதின் மேலே
ஊறிய வாதாரத் தோரெழுத் தாமே. 1709

The One Letter "Aum" is beyond the Fifty Letters distributed over the Adharas

In the body where the Centres Six are,
Do seek the Adharas and above,
Over the letters five times ten
Rises the one Letter (Aum) that is basic to all.

Over the Fifty Letters distributed over the petals of the six adharas is the basic letter,'Aum'.

ஆகும் உடம்பும் அழிக்கின்ற அவ்வுடல்
போகும் உடம்பும் பொருந்திய வாறுதான்
ஆகிய வக்கரம் ஐம்பது தத்துவம்
ஆகும் உடம்புக்கும் ஆறந்த மாமே. 1710

The Letters Fifty the subtle in Adharas, and Adharas subtle are in Body

As the Gross body that decays
And the Subtle body that escapes
Are in union unseen,
So are the subtle letters fifty to tattvas that are gross,
So are the Centres Six to the body corporeal.

As the subtle body is to the gross body, the Fifty Letters are to the gross tattvas; and the six centres to the body corporeal.

ஆயு மலரின் அணிமலர் மேலது
வாய இதழும் பதினாறும் அங்குள
தூய அறிவு சிவானந்த மாகிப்போய்
மேய அறிவாய் விளைந்தது தானே. 1711

The Sixteen-Petalled Lotus in Visuddhi Adhara Leads to Knowledge-Bliss

Above the discriminating heart's lotus
Is that jewelled flower
Of ten and six petals;
There, Awareness Pure, turns into Bliss of Siva
And to Jnana (Light of Knowledge) that is Reality Supreme.

At the visuddhi adhara of sixteen petals, pure consciousness turns into Supreme Knowledge and bliss.

Awareness Pure (தூய அறிவு=tuya arivu) is to be found in the 16-petalled lotus which is above the heart's lotus. Visuddha is "the nerve plexus above the anahata in the neck region. It looks like a 16-petalled lotus. Its presiding deity (in Tantrism) is the goddess Sakini" ('History of Tantric Religion', p.482, N.N. Bhattacharyya). "Visuddhi Marga" or The Path of Purity, is the title of a famous work by Buddhaghosha" ('A popular dictionary of Buddhism" p.213, by Christmas Humphreys).

2. அண்ட லிங்கம்
THE COSMIC LINGAM

இலிங்கம தாவ தியாரும் அறியார்
இலிங்கம தாவதெண் டிசை யெல்லாம்
இலிங்கம தாவ தெண்ணெண் கலையும்
இலிங்கம தாக எடுத்த துலகே. 1712

Linga or Sadasiva is World manifest

They know not what Linga is
Linga is directions eight
Linga is Kalas, eight times eight
It is as Linga the world emerged.

The eight directions and the sixteen kalas constitute the cosmic Linga. The world emerged as such.

உலகில் எடுத்தது சத்தி முதலா
உலகில் எடுத்தது சத்தி வடிவாய்

உலகில் எடுத்தது சத்தி குணமாய்
உலகம் எடுத்த சதாசிவன் தானே. 1713

Sakti in Sadasiva manifested as World

In the World His Sakti He manifested first,
In the World as His Sakti's Form He pervaded
In the World His Sakti's Powers He filled
But He who this World's creation conceived
Was Sadasiva (the Linga).

Sadasiva, who as Linga originally conceived the world's creation, manifested in the world as His Sakti, pervaded there as His Sakti's form, and filled it with His Sakti's powers.

போகமும் முத்தியும் புத்தியுஞ் சித்தியும்
ஆகமும் ஆறாறு தத்துவத் தப்பாலாம்
ஏகமும் நல்கியிருக்குஞ் சதாசிவம்
ஆகம வத்துவா வாறுஞ் சிவமே. 1714

Sadasiva is the Adhvas too

Worldly joys and heavenly pleasures
Wisdom and miraculous powers
The body and the state beyond
The Tattvas six and thirty
All these Sadasiva granted;
The Adhvas six, too, of Agamas sacred
Are all but He — Sadasiva.

Sadasiva created the worldly joys and heavenly pleasures, wisdom and miraculous powers, this body of thirty-six-tattvas and the One Beyond; and the six adhvas of Agamic conception.

ஏத்தினர் எண்ணிலி தேவரெம் ஈசனை
வாழ்த்தினர் வாசப்பசுந்தென்றல்வள்ளலென்
றார்த்தனர் அண்டங் கடந்தப் புறநின்று
காத்தனன் என்னுங் கருத்தறி யாரே. 1715

Lord (Sadasiva) protects the Celestials from afar

The countless Devas gloried My Lord
"O! Southern Breeze, fragrant cool" they praised,
"O! Bounteous One," they adored,
But they know not this;
From beyond the Spaces Vast
He His protection granted.

Though the countless celestials praise and adore Him, they know not that it is He, from beyond the vast space, who grants them protection.

ஒண்சுட ரோன்அயன் மால்பிர சாபதி
ஒண்சுட ரானஇரவியோ டிந்திரன்
கண்சுட ராகிக் கலந்தெங்குந் தேவர்கள்
தண்சுட ராயெங்கும் தற்பர மாமே. 1716

Lord (Sadasiva) is the Light of Life of Gods

The resplendent Brahma, Vishnu, Prajapati
The luminous Sun and Indra
The bright-eyed Devas swarming celestial Spheres
He indeed, is their Light of Life—
He the Being Uncreated.

He is the Unborn Being who is the light of life to the three Gods, to the sun and all the celestials throughout the spheres, and to their king, Indra too.

தாபரத் துண்ணின் றருளவல் லான்சிவன்
மாபரத் துண்மை வழிபடு வாரில்லை
மாபரத் துண்மை வழிபடு வாளர்க்கும்
பூவகத் துள்நின்ற பொற்கொடி யாகுமே. 1717*

Lord is the Golden support of Heart

Pervading all Nature, Siva blesses all;
But they know not the Truth and adore Him not;
To them that adore Him that is immanent
He is the golden stalk of the heart's lotus within.

Siva pervades all nature and blesses all. They who do not know this, do not adore Him. Whosoever adore Him, He is in them. He is the golden stalk of the lotus of their heart.

தூய விமானமுந் தூலம தாகுமால்
ஆய சதாசிவ மாகுநற் சூக்குமம்
ஆய பலிபீடம் பத்திர லிங்கமாம்
ஆய அரனிலை ஆய்ந்துகொள் வார்கட்கே. 1718

Sadasiva (Linga)'s Form, manifest and subtle

The Vimana pure is the Sthula Linga
The Sadasiva enshrined is Sukshma Linga
The Bali-peeta is Bhadra Linga
Thus it is for those who Siva's Form seek.

Those who seek Siva's form will realise that the upper part forming an arc (known as vimana) is the manifest Linga; the enshrined Sadasiva is the subtle Linga, and that the altar (bali-pita) is Siva's throne.

1) Vimana—shrine's upper part forming a semi-circle.
2) Sthula—manifest (lit, gross)
3) Sukshma—subtle
4) Bali-peeta—altar
5) Bhadra—Siva (also Virabhadra, an aspect of Si

Prescribe 3 forms of Linga, Sthula, Sukshma and Bha those who wish to see the Divine Form.

முத்துடன் மாணிக்கம் மொய்த்த பவளமும்
கொத்துமக் கொம்பு சிலைநீறு கோமளம்
அத்தன்றன் னாகம மன்ன மரிசியாம்
உய்த்ததின் சாதனம் பூமண லிங்கமே. 1719

How to fix Linga

Pearls, gems, corals and emerald
Wood of sandal, granite hard, and ashes holy
Siva's Agama, and rice in grain and cooked
When you pour in these and fix the Linga
Haunting indeed is His delicious fragrance.

Installation of the linga requires certain prescribed Agamic rites. When thus installed, a haunting fragrance will pervade all around.

துன்றுந் தயிர்நெய்பால் துய்ய மெழுகுடன்
கன்றிய செம்பு கனலிர தஞ்சலம்
வன்திறல் செங்கல் வடிவுடை வில்லம்பொன்
றென்றியங் கொன்றை தெளிசிவ லிங்கமே. 1720

How Linga is shaped

Curd, ghee, milk and wax pure
Copper, mercury, fire and conch
Bricks hard, Bilva shapely
And Konrai bloom of golden hue
From these do you shape
The Linga's Form Divine.

---

1) Bilva—(Tamil-vilva): a sacred tree (cratoeva religiosa). Its leave are as sacred to Saivas as 'tulasi' is to Vaishnavas. 2) Konrai—a genus of flower trees—cassia.

Mantras 1720 & 1721

There are rituals to be observed in the formation of a linga, and prescribed materials for making it for worship by the different castes. For brahmins, crystal; for kings, gold, for vaisyas, emerald; and for sudras stone.

மறையவர் அர்ச்சனை வண்படி கந்தான்
இறையவர் அர்ச்சனை யேயபொன் னாகுங்
குறைவிலா வசியர்க்குக் கோமள மாகுந்
துறையடைச் சூத்திரர் தொல்வாண லிங்கமே. 1721

Lingas for the Four Varnas

Of crystal made is Linga, Brahmins worship
Of gold, the Kings worship
Of emerald, the Vaisyas worship
Of stone is Linga, Sudras worship.

அதுவுணர்ந் தோனொரு தன்மையை நாடி
எதுவுண ராவகை நின்றனன் ஈசன்
புதுவுணர் வான புவனங்கள் எட்டும்
இதுவுணர்ந்தென்னுடல் கோயில் கொண்டானே. 1722

No Single way of worship

They who sought Him in one Special Way
Knew Him not in any way;
And thus it is the Lord
That the eight universe pervades;
Of my heart, too, a temple made.

Mantras 1722-1725

Of whatever material the linga is made, the temple of the Omnipresent is actually in the seeker's heart. His form is cosmic, encompassing the earth, heaven, seas and stars; but He is the heart's refuge.

அகலிட மாயறி யாமல் அடங்கும்
உகலிட மாய்நின்ற வூனத னுள்ளே
பகலிட மாமுனம் பாவ வினாசன்
புகலிட மாய்நின்ற புண்ணியன் றானே. 1723

God is Pervasive

In the Spaces Vast, unknown He pervades,
In the fleshy body He rapturous resides,
He dispels sin and Wisdom's Sunlight spreads
He, the Holy One, that our Refuge is.

போது புனைகழல் பூமிய தாவது
மாது புனைமுடி வானக மாவது
நீதியுள் ஈசன் உடல்விசும் பாய்நிற்கும்
ஆதி யுறநின்ற தப்பரி சாமே. 1724

Siva's Pervasive Form

The Earth is His flower-bedecked feet
The Heavens, His Ganga-girt crown
His Body fills the Spaces Vast
In continuity unbroken;
Thus did Lord His Form assume
From Time's Eternity Beginningless First.

தரையுற்ற சத்தி தனிலிங்கம் விண்ணாந்
திரைபொரு நீரது மஞ்சன சாலை
வரைதவழ் மஞ்சுநீர் வானுடு மாலை
கரையற்ற நந்தி கலையுந்திக் காமே. 1725

Siva's Cosmic Form

The Earth is His Sakti Peeta,
The Heavens the Linga Pure,
The billowing seas His bathing ghat,
The cascading streams on mountain tops
Their cool water laves His crown heavenly
The countless stars, His garland;
The Eight Directions His limitless raiment.

3. பிண்ட லிங்கம்

MICROCOSMIC (PINDA) LINGA

மானுட ராக்கை வடிவு சிவலிங்கம்
மானுட ராக்கை வடிவு சிதம்பரம்
மானுட ராக்கை வடிவு சதாசிவம்
மானுட ராக்கை வடிவு திருக்கூத்தே. 1726

Human form is Siva Linga

The Human Form is like Siva Lingam
The Human Form is like Chidambaram

The Human Form is like Sadasivam
The Human Form is like the Holy Dance, forsooth.

The human form itself is verily a Siva Lingam. It is Chidambaram, Sadasivam and the Holy Dance Hall as well.

உலந்திலர் பின்னும் உளரென நிற்பர்
நிலந்தரு நீர்தெளி யூனவை செய்யப்
புலந்தரு பூதங்கள் ஐந்தும்ஒன்றாக
வலந்தரு தேவரை வந்திசெய் யீரே. 1727

Desire for Births persists

Tired they are not;
Still they want to live
In this fleshy body,
Of earth, water and other matter made;
They seek not to adore Lord
Whom the Elements Five
Together in prayer beseech.

In spite of having undergone innumerable cycles of birth, men are still not tired of being reborn over and over in this body composed of the five elements. These elements within themselves seek Him, and yet men do not seek Him within.

கோயில்கொண் டன்றே குடிகொண்ட ஐவரும்
வாயில்கொண் டாங்கே வழிநின் றருளுவர்
தாயில்கொண் டாற்போல் தலைவனென் னுட்புக
வாயில்கொண் டீசனு மாளவந் தானே. 1728

Lord is Master of the sense gates of body

The day the Lord entered this body tabernacle
The Five Senses who their places had taken
Opened the gates;
And showed you the way of redemption;
As like the mother's home
He in me entered;
And taking charge of the gates, Master became.

Mantras 1728 & 1729

When jiva entered this fleshy body, a veritable tabernacle of God, the five senses within opened the gates for Him. Like a mother, He affectionately took charge of the senses and became their master. The several nadis that are within the body he prostrate at Nandi's feet who subdued the senses, even as all the *Vedas* do.

கோயில்கொண் டானடி கொல்லைப்பெருமறை
வாயில்கொண் டானடி நாடிகள் பத்துள
பூசைகொண் டான்புல னைந்தும்பிறகிட்டு
வாயில்கொண் டானெங்கள் மாநந்தி தானே. 1729

Lord opens the sense gates

At the Feet of the Lord
Who this body as His temple chose
Lies the expanse of Vedas;
At the Feet of the Lord
Who these gates made His own
Lie the Nadis ten;
He who; our adoration received
Subduing our senses five
In me entered operating the gates wide;
He, My Lord, the Nandi Great.

4. சதாசிவ லிங்கம்

SADASIVA LINGAM

கூடிய பாதம் இரண்டும் படிமிசை
பாடிய கையிரண் டெட்டும் பரந்தெழுந்
தேடு முகம்ஐந்து செங்கணின் மூவைந்து
நாடுஞ் சதாசிவ நல்லொளி முத்தே. 1730

Sadasiva form with Five Faces

His twin Feet are planted on earth below;
The ten hands, the holy in praise sing,
In directions all spread;
Five His Faces that are sought,
Five times three his eyes fiery;
Thus is Sadasiva that you seek
The Pearl that is lustrous, beyond, beyond compare.

Sadasiva whom we seek and whom the holy praise in songs as a lustrous pearl beyond comparison has His Two Feet on the earth. His ten hands are spread in ten directions. His fifteen eyes glow like fiery flames on His five faces.

வேதா நெடுமால் உருத்திரன் மேலீசன்
மீதான ஐம்முகன் விந்துவும் நாதமும்
ஆதார சத்தியு மந்தச் சிவனொடுஞ்
சாதா ரணமாஞ் சதாசிவந் தானே. 1731

Sadasiva comprehends all Nine God-Forms

Brahma, Vishnu, Rudra, Mahesa,
And the Five-faced Lord above,
Bindu, Nada, Sakti Primal, and Siva
—All these are but Sadasiva in general.

ஆகின்ற சத்தியின் உள்ளே கலைநிலை
ஆகின்ற சத்தியின் உள்ளே கதிரெழ
ஆகின்ற சத்தியின் உள்ளே அமர்ந்தபின்
ஆகின்ற சத்தியுள் அத்திசை பத்தே. 1732

When Sakti Evolves

Within the Becoming Sakti the Kalas repose
Within the Becoming Sakti their rays emanate
Within the Becoming Sakti the Lord His seat takes

Within the Becoming Sakti the directions ten as
Space appear.

The kalas repose within Sakti; their rays emanate from Sakti. After the Lord activates Sakti, the ten directions appear from Her.

அத்திசைக் குள்ளே அமர்ந்தன ஆறங்கம்
அத்திசைக் குள்ளே அமர்ந்தன நால்வேதம்
அத்திசைக் குள்ளே அமர்ந்த சரியையோ
டத்திசைக் குள்ளே அமர்ந்த சமயமே. *1733*

When Sakti further evolves

In that Space thus opened up
The Six Vedangas took their place;
In that Space thus opened up
The Four Vedas took their place;
In that Space thus opened up
The Four Paths beginning with Chariya
Took their place;
In that Space thus opened up
The Saiva Truth the Four Paths comprehended
Took its place.

When Sakti further evolves, opening up space The four *Vedas*, the six *Vedangas*, the four paths of Chariya, Kriya, Yoga and Jnana comprehended by Saivism — all took their places.

சமயத் தெழுந்த அவத்தையீ ரைந்துள
சமயத் தெழுந்த இராசி ராறுள
சமயத் தெழுந்த சதிரீரா றெட்டுள
சமயத் தெழுந்த சதாசிவந் தானே. *1734*

Sakti evolves still further

In that Truth arose the Avastas (States of
Awareness) twice five;
In that Truth arose the Rasis (Zodiacal houses) twice
six
In that Truth arose the Tattvas (Body Constituents)
twice forty-eight;
In that Truth arose the Sadasiva Supreme.

From Sakti evolving still further in Siva Truth, arose the ten states of consciousness (avasthas), the twelve zodiacal houses (rasis), the ninety-six universals (tattvas) and the Sadasiva.

நடுவு கிழக்குத் தெற்குத் தரமேற்கு
நடுவு படிகநற் குங்கும வன்னம்
அடைவுள வஞ்சனஞ் செவ்வரத் தம்பால்
அடியேற் கருளிய முகமிவை அஞ்சே. *1735*

The Five Faces of Sadasiva and their Hues

Central, East, South, North and West
These the Five Faces of Sadasiva;
The Central Face is of crystal hue;
The Eastward Face is crimson unto Kum-Kum
The Southward Face is dark like thick pitch
The Northward Face is red like Aratham flower
The Westward Face is white like milky hue;
Thus did He reveal to me,
His lowly vassal.

Sadasiva revealed His Five Faces of five different hues to this lowly vassal (Tirumular)—the central Face, Isana, of crystal color; the eastward Face, Tatpurusha, crimson; the southward Face, Aghora pitch dark; the northward Face, Vama, red and the westward Face, Sadyojata, milky white.

1) Kum-Kum—a crimson paint formed of tumeric, alum, lime juice, and also saffron or yellow color.
2) Aratham—red water lily flower, also red coral.

அஞ்சு முகமுளஐம்மூன்று கண்ணுள
அஞ்சினொ டஞ்சு கரதலந் தானுள
அஞ்சுடன் அஞ்சா யுதமுள நம்பியென்
நெஞ்சு புகுந்து நிறைந்துநின் றானே. *1736*

Sadasiva's Form

Five His Faces thrice five His eyes;
Twice Five His hands number,
Five and Five Weapons He holds;
Thus my dear Lord, my heart entered
And in fullness pervaded.

Entering in me with His Five Faces, fifteen eyes and ten hands holding weapons in them all, Sadasiva pervaded within me in fullness.

சத்தி தாரதல மண்டஞ் சதாசிவஞ்
சத்தி சிவமிக்க தாபர சங்கமஞ்
சத்தி யுருவம் அருவஞ் சதாசிவஞ்
சத்தி சிவதத் துவமுப்பத் தாறே. *1737*

Sakti is the Kinetic and Siva the potential

Aspects of God-head
Sakti is this wide world
Sakti is this universe vast
Sakti-Siva conjoint is the Kinetic and Potential
Sakti is the Formed;
Siva the Formless;
Sakti-Siva Tattvas are six and thirty true.

Sakti is this wide world and the infinite universe. She has form. Siva is formless. Conjointly Sakti and Siva are the dynamic and the potential aspects. Out of them arose the thirty-six tattvas.

தத்துவ மாவ தருவஞ் சராசரந்
தத்துவ மாவ துருவஞ் சுகோதயந்
தத்துவம் எல்லாஞ் சகலமு மாய்நிற்குந்
தத்துவ மாகுஞ் சதாசிவன் தானே. *1738*

Sadasiva is Tattva (Truth) Real

Formless is the Tattva primal
Formed, it is the world, animate and inanimate;
A source of pleasure then indeed it is;
Tattva is all and pervasive,
Sadasiva is Tattva (Truth) Real.

Tattva (basic truth) is primal, pervasive and formless. Sadasiva is real tattva. When in form, that is when the thrity-six fundamental principles of existence devoluted from maya, Sadasiva is the animate and inanimate world, and the source of all bhoga.

1) Tattva means two things: i) basic truth: ii) the 36 fundamental principles of existence evolved from maya.

கூறுமி னாறு சதாசிவன் எம்மிறை
வேறோர் உரைசெய்து மிகைப்பொருளாய்நிற்கு
மேறுரை செய்தொழில் வானவர் தம்மொடு
மாறுசெய் வானென் மனம்புகுந் தானே. 1739

Sadasiva is Our Lord

"Sadasiva is our Lord"—
Say this times hundred;
Anything else you try to say,
He will still be beyond it;
He suffers not those Gods
Who themselves exalt;
He, who my heart entered.

Sadasiva has entered into my heart. He is there above all other gods. Repeat one hundred times that Sadasiva is our Lord. He is beyond whatever else is said.

இருளார்ந்த கண்டமும் ஏந்து மழுவுஞ்
சுருளார்ந்த செஞ்சடைச் சோதிப் பிறையும்
அருளார்ந்த சிந்தையெம் ஆதிப் பிரானைத்
தெருளார்ந்தென் உள்ளே தெளிந்திருந் தேனே. 1740

Muse on Sadasiva's Form

The dark throat, the up-lifted axe,
The matted red locks, the radiant crescent moon,
The Primal Lord that is Grace abounding,
Him I contemplated, all dark doubts dispelled.

Bereft of doubts, I meditated on the abundantly graceful Primal Lord of dark throat, wearing the radiant crescent moon on His matted russet locks, and holding the axe in His hand.

சத்திதான் நிற்கின்ற ஐம்முகஞ் சாற்றிடில்
உத்தமம் வாம முரையத் திருந்திடுந்
தத்துவம் பூருவந் தற்புரு டன்சிர
மத்தகு கோர மகுடத்தீ சானனே. 1741

Names of the Five Faces of Sadasiva

To recount the Five Faces where His Grace abounds
Thus it is:
The Northward Face is Vama
The Westward Face is Sadyojata
The Eastward Face is Tatpurusha
The Southward Face is Aghora
The Upward Face is Isana.

These Five Names, namely Vama, Sadyojata, Tatpurusha, Aghora and Isana are "regarded" as the representations of five different stages of Saivism which originated in immemorial past.......A similar idea about the different Yugavataras of Lord Vishnu is recorded in the Bhagavata Purana". (Pp.122-123 of "Saivism through the Ages" R.K. Siddhanta Shastree).

நாணுநல் லீசான நடுவுச்சி தானாகுந்
தாணுவின் றன்முகந் தற்புருட மாகுங்
காணும் அகோரம் இருதயங் குய்யம
மாணுற வாமமாஞ் சத்திநற் பாதமே. 1742

How Sakti dwells in the Five faces of Sadasiva

In the shining Isana face is Sakti's Crown;
In the Tatpurusha face is Her Visage
In the Aghora is Her Heart and Waist;
In the Vama face are Her Feet blessed.

Sakti's crown is in Isana, Her visage in Tatpurusa. Her heart and waist are in Aghora and Her blessed Feet in Vama.

நெஞ்சு சிரஞ்சிகை நீள்கவ சங்கண்ணாம்
வஞ்சமில் விந்து வளர்நிறம் பச்சையாஞ்
செஞ்சுறு செஞ்சுடர் சேகரி மின்னாகுஞ்
செஞ்சுடர் போலுந் தெசாயுதந் தானே. 1743

Form of Sakti in Sadasiva

The breast, the head, the tresses long,
The eyes, the fore-head mark, the armour
These the Sakti's are
Of glowing green hue
As lightning is She, the dazzling crowning Sakti
Fiery bright, Her ten Weapons.

Sakti's head, tresses, eyes, forehead-mark, breast and armour are of glowing green. Her form is dazzling as lightning, and Her ten weapons are fiery bright.

எண்ணில் இதயம் இறைஞான சத்தியாம்
விண்ணிற் பரைசிர மிக்க சிகையாதி
வண்ணக் கவசம் வனப்புடை இச்சையாம்
பண்ணுங் கிரியை பரநேத் திரத்திலே. 1744

The Five Saktis are seated in Sadasiva

The heart is the divine Jnana Sakti
The head the heavenly Para Sakti
The tresses the Adi Sakti
The colourful armour is Icchha Sakti
In the eyes is the active Kriya Sakti.

In Sadasiva's heart is seated divine jnana sakti: on His head the heavenly Parasakti; over His locks the Adisakti: in His armour, ichchasakti and within His eyes, the kriya sakti.

சத்திநாற் கோணஞ் சலமுற்று நின்றிடுஞ்
சத்தி அறுகோணஞ் சயனத்தை யுற்றிடுஞ்
சத்திநல் வட்டஞ் சலமுற் றிருந்திடுஞ்
சத்தி யுறுவாஞ் சதாசிவன் தானே. 1745

Sakti in the First Three Adharas

In the quadrilateral Adhara (Muladhara)
Sakti in firmness stands;
In the hexagonal Adhara (Svadhishtana)
Sakti is in sleep;
In the circular Adhara (Manipuraka)

Sakti is in agitation;
Of Sakti's Form is Sadasiva.

Sakti stands firm in muladhara: She is asleep in svadhistana: She is agitated in manipuraka. Sadasiva is Sakti's form.

All this forms part of Tantra sadhana, and Kundalini Yoga.

மானந்தி எத்தனை காலம் அழைக்கினுந்
தானந்தி யஞ்சின் தனிச்சுட ராய்நிற்குங்
கானந்தி யுந்தி கடந்து கமலத்தின்
மேனந்தி ஒன்பதின் மேவிநின் றானே. *1746*

Sadasiva is seated in Sahasrara

What so be the time you seek the great Nandi,
He stands unique,
His Five Faces glowing like the evening sun;
Rousing the Kundalini through Yogic breathing
When you upward course through centres nine
Upon the lotus top, He aloft stands.

Nandi stands in grandeur with His Five Faces glowing like the evening sun. When kundalini is aroused to reach the lotus top by coursing the yogic breath through the nine centres, He is visioned.

ஒன்றிய வாறும் உடலி னுடன்கிடந்
தென்றுமெம் மீசனடக்கும் இயல்பது
தென்றலைக் கேறத் திருந்து சிவனடி
நின்று தொழுதேனென் னெஞ்சத்தி னுள்ளே. *1747*

Sadasiva abides within body

In union inseparable
He ever abides in this fleshy body
That is His nature divine;
His Perfection's Feet upon my head I bore,
And in my heart's deep, I prayed.

Inseparably He abides within this body of flesh. I bore His Feet on my head and with all my heart I pray to Him in depth.

உணர்ந்தேன் உலகினில் ஒண்பொரு ளானைக்
கொணர்ந்தேன் குவலயங் கோயிலென் நெஞ்சம்
புணர்ந்தேன் புனிதனும் பொய்யல்ல மெய்யே
பணிந்தேன் பகலவன் பாட்டு மொலியே. *1748*

Sadasiva is realized in the Body

The shining Truth He is
Him I realized in this world below;
Into my heart's temple here on earth
I brought Him, lo!
Him in union I embraced and prayed
Truth it is, pure and simple;
To Him, the Sun Resplendent, I sang
To music and to measure appropriate.

He is the shining Truth: I realised Him in this world. I drew Him to my heart. I embraced Him in union. I prayed and sang to Him in appropriate measure.

ஆங்கவை மூன்றினும் ஆரழல் வீசிடத்
தாங்கிடும் ஈரேழு தானடு வானதில்
ஓங்கிய ஆதியும் அந்தமு மாமென
ஈங்கிவை தம்முடல் இந்துவு மாமே. *1749*

The Lord is the Source of Light and Energy for Sun, Moon and Fire

To Sun, Moon and Fire
He lends His fiery rays:
The seven worlds twice he supports;
And in the Centre of Spaces Vast
He stands,
He is the Beginning, He is the End,
His own Form, cool as moon.

He lends the fiery rays to the sun, moon and fire. He supports the fourteen worlds. He stands at the centre of vast spaces. He is the beginning as well as the end. He is cool as the rays of the moon.

தன்மேனி தற்சிவ லிங்கமாய் நின்றிடுந்
தன்மேனி தானுஞ் சதாசிவ மாய்நிற்குந்
தன்மேனி தற்சிவன் தற்சிவா னந்தமாந்
தன்மேனி தானாகுந் தற்பரந் தானே. *1750*

The Lord is uncreated

He stands,
His Form as Uncreated Siva Linga
His Form as Sadasiva Divine
His Form as Sivananda, bliss unalloyed
His Form as Tat-Para Eternal Supreme.

The Lord is uncreated. He stands with His body as uncreated Siva Linga, as divine Sadasiva as uncreated Siva, as unalloyed Sivananda and as Supreme Tat-Para.

ஆரும் அறியார் அகார மவனென்று
பாரு முகாரம் பரந்திட்ட நாயகி
தாரம் இரண்டுந் தரணி முழுதுமாய்
மாறி யெழுந்திடும் ஓசைய தாமே. *1751*

The Lord is the Cosmic Sound "Aum"

None knows He is Akara, the letter "A"
And the pervasive Sakti is Ukara, the letter "U"
The two sounds swelling alternate
Fill the world as Aum in unrelieved entirety.

Siva is akara, the letter 'A'; Sakti is ukara, the letter 'U', these two sounds together swell and fill the world as 'Aum.' The Lord is thus the cosmic sound, 'Aum.'

இலிங்கநற் பீடம் இசையும்ஓங் காரம்
இலிங்கநற் கண்ட நிறையு மகாரம்
இலிங்கத்துள் வட்ட நிறையும் உகாரம்
இலிங்க மகார நிறைவிந்து நாதமே. *1752*

Linga is Aum

The Linga's Holy Pedestal is the humming Omkara (Aum)
The Linga's Centre part is filled with Akara (A)
The Linga's inner round is with Ukara replete (U)
Linga is Bindu-Nada, Makaram (M) pervaded.

Linga is 'Aum;' its pedestal is 'Aumkara;' its centre is akara, 'A;' its inner sound is ukara, 'U,' Makaram, 'M' pervading, Linga is bindu/nada.

5. ஆத்ம லிங்கம்
ATMA LINGAM

அகார முதலா யனைத்துமாய் நிற்கும்
உகார முதலா யுயிர்ப்பெய்து நிற்கும்
அகார வுகாரம் இரண்டு மறியில்
அகார வுகாரம் இலிங்கம தாமே. 1753

In the Beginning was Aum

Akaram (A) as beginning, all exist
Ukaram (U) as beginning, all life exists
If Akaram Ukaram are together known
Akaram Ukaram is but Linga divine.

All life exists with akaram (A) and Ukaram (U). Knowledge of these two brings the knowledge of divine Linga.

ஆதார மாதேய மாகின்ற விந்துவு
மேதாதி நாதமு மீதே விரிந்தன
ஆதார விந்து அதிபீட நாதமே
போதாவி லிங்கப் புணர்ச்சிய தாமே. 1754

Bindu is the Support and Nada the Supported

Bindu is the Support Finite
Nada in Medha as the Support expanded;
Bindu that is Supported is the Pedestal
Nada on to it is conjoint,
That verily is Linga's union.

Bindu is the support and nada the supported. When nada conjoins with bindu, the pedestal, the union is Linga.

Bindu represents Siva, and Nada, Sakti.

சத்தி சிவமாம் இலிங்கமே தாபரஞ்
சத்தி சிவமாம் இலிங்கமே சங்கமஞ்
சத்தி சிவமாம் இலிங்கஞ் சதாசிவஞ்
சத்தி சிவமாகுந் தாபரந் தானே. 1755

Siva-Sakti (Linga) is Static, Kinetic, Sadasiva and Unborn Being

Linga that is Sakti-Siva is Static all
Linga that is Sakti-Siva is Kinetic all
Linga that is Sakti-Siva is Sadasiva
Sakti-Siva is Tatpara, the Being Unborn.

Linga that is Siva/Sakti is static and kinetic: it is Sadasiva, the Unborn Being.

தானே ரெழுகின்ற சோதியைக் காணலாம்
வானே ரெழுகின்ற ஐம்ப தமர்ந்திடம்
பூநே ரெழுகின்ற பொற்கொடி நன்னுடன்
தானே ரெழுகின்ற வகாரம தாமே. 1756

Lord is Light and Support

Upon the heavenly letters five times ten
Well may you behold the self-illumined Light (Aum);
That which thus arises with His Sakti (U)
Like a golden vine that blooms pretty
Is but He that is Akara (A)—the Support Finite.

You may behold the Fifty heavenly Letters, the self-illumined light 'Aum,' which arises with His Sakti (U). He, that is akara (the final support) is like a golden vine that beautifully blooms.

விந்துவும் நாதமும்மேவு மிலிங்கமாம்
விந்துவ தேபீட நாத மிலிங்கமாம்
அந்த இரண்டையும் ஆதார தெய்வமாய்
வந்த கருவைந்துஞ் செய்யு மவையைந்தே. 1757

Linga Comprises both Bindu and Nada

Bindu and Nada together form Linga
Bindu is the Pedestal, Nada the Linga
With them two as support divine
The Five gods arose, their Five functions to perform.

சத்திநற் பீடந்தகுநல்ல ஆன்மா
சத்திநற் கண்டந் தகுவித்தை தானாகுஞ்
சத்திநல் லிங்கந் தகுஞ்சிவ தத்துவஞ்
சத்திநல் லான்மாச் சதாசிவந் தானே. 1758

All the Tattvas are in Linga

The grand pedestal of Sakti holds the Atma Tattvas
The central part of Sakti holds the Vidya Tattvas;
The Linga of Sakti, the Siva Tattvas
Sadasiva is Sakti's Soul Divine.

Sakti's pedestal holds the atma tattvas; Sakti's central part, the vidya tattvas; (Sakti's upper part linga), the Siva tattvas. Sakti's soul is Sadasiva.

மனம்புகுந் தென்னுயிர் மன்னிய வாழ்க்கை
மனம்புகுந் தின்பம் பொழிகின்ற போது
நலம்புகுந் தென்னொடு நாதனை நாடும்
இலம்புகுந் தாதியு மேற்கொண்ட வாறே. 1759

Seek the Lord within and be Blessed

In my heart He entered
In my life's being He entered,
He poured His blessing to my heart's fill;
Do with me the Lord seek
He enters your home, and blesses you.

He entered in my heart, in my life's being and blessed me in profusion to my heart's fill. You too seek Him along with me. He shall surely enter in you and bless you too.

பராபரன் எந்தை பனிமதி சூடி
தராபரன் தன்னடி யார்மனக்கோயிற்
சிராபரன் தேவர்கள் சென்னியின் மன்னு
மராமரன் மன்னி மனத்துறைந் தானே. 1760

Lord is Sovereign Supreme

The Supreme Parapara is He;
My Father Divine;
He sports the crescent moon;
He rules the universe;
Into the heart's temple of His devotees too he reigns
He the Hara to whom the Immortals in worship bow
He in my heart resides firm.

He who sports the crescent moon and rules the universe is the Supreme Parapara, my Divine Father. He reigns in the temple of His devotee's heart. He, whom the celestials worship as Hara, resides firm in my heart.

பிரானல்ல நாமெனிற் பேதை யுலகங்
குராலென்னு மென்மனங் கோயில்கொள் ஈசன்
அராநின்ற செஞ்சடை அங்கியும் நீரும்
பொராநின் றவர்செய்யப் புண்ணியன் தானே. 1761

The Lord is tender as Mother-Cow

"He is not the Lord, I am the one"
If you this conceit have,
The world will call you a fool;
Tender as the yearning mother cow,
He in me is enshrined,
With serpent, fire and water in His matted lock
He, in amity, stands
He the Holy One.

The world will call him a fool who conceitedly claims himself as the Lord, and defiantly denies the Supreme. He is the Holy One. He sports the snake, fire and water in His mattedlocks. In amity He stands enshrined in me.

அன்றுநின் றான்கிடந் தானவன் என்று
சென்றுநின் றெண்டிசை ஏத்துவர் தேவர்கள்
என்றுநின் றேத்துவன் எம்பெரு மான்தன்னை
ஒன்றியென் உள்ளத்தில் உள்ளிருந் தானே. 1762

Hold Lord in Heart of Heart

"There He stood," "There He lay"
—Thus the Immortals in directions eight
Adore Him;
But how shall I praise my Lord
Who in my heart's heart ever resides.

6. ஞான லிங்கம்

JNANA LINGAM

உருவும் அருவும் உருவோடருவும்
மருவு பரசிவன் மன்பல் லுயிர்க்குங்
குருவு மெனநிற்குங் கொள்கைய னாகுந்
தருவென நல்குஞ் சதாசிவன் தானே. 1763

Lord is Bounteous

As Form, the Formless and Form-Formless
Thus is Parasiva in all life immanent;
As Guru, too, He stands;
Unto the Kalpaka tree He bounties bestows
He, the Sadasiva.

நாலான கீழ துருவ நடுநிற்க
மேலான நான்கு மருவு மிகநாப்பண்
நாலான ஒன்று மருவுரு நண்ணலாற்
பாலா மிவையாம் பரசிவன் தானே. 1764

Sadasiva is Form-Formless

In the Centre He is, Sadasiva,
The Four below are the Formed,
(Brahma, Vishnu, Rudra, Mahesa)
The Four above are the Formless
(Bindu, Nada, Sakti, Siva)
Thus are His parts
He, the Parasiva.

Parasiva has nine aspects — Sadasiva is the central one, that is form/formless. Brahma, Vishnu, Rudra, Mahesvara are the four formed ones below; and Bindu, Nada, Sakti and Siva are the four formless above.

தேவர் பிரானைத் திசைமுக நாதனை
நால்வர் பிரானை நடுவுற்ற நந்தியை
ஏவர் பிரானென் றிறைஞ்சுவா ரவ்வழி
யாவர் பிரானடி அண்ணலு மாமே. 1765

Seek Sadasiva

He is the Lord of the Immortals,
He is the Lord with Faces in directions all,
He is the Lord of Four (Brahma, Vishnu, Rudra and Mahesa)

He is Nandi that central stands;
They who adore Him as their Lord
Themselves His ways attain;
Do you, so, seek the Lord's Holy Feet.

Sadasiva standing at the centre, with faces in five directions, is the Lord of the immortals. They who adore Him will attain immortality. May you too seek His Holy Feet.

வேண்டிநின் றேதொழு தேன்வினை போயற
ஆண்டொரு திங்களும் நாளும் அளக்கின்ற
காண்டகை யானொடுங் கன்னியுணரினும்
மூண்டகை மாறினும்ஒன்றது வாமே. 1766

Sadasiva Dispels Karmas

Him I prayed,
My Karma to dispel and destroy;
He measures out Time's Eternity
As year, month and day;
Worthy is He of your visioning;
And with His Virgin Sakti seek Him;
Even when your folded hands unfold
The One is He to you.

The yogi prays to Him to dispel and destroy his karmas accumulated through time, for Sadasiva measures out time's eternity as days, months and years.

ஆதி பரந்தெய்வம் அண்டத்து நற்றெய்வஞ்
சோதி யடியார் தொடரும் பெருந்தெய்வம்
நீதியுள் மாதெய்வநின்மலன் எம்மிறை
பாதியுள் மன்னும் பராசத்தி யாமே. 1767

Sadasiva dispenses Divine Justice

The Primal Lord is He,
The God of the Universe is He;
God is He whom the illumined devotees praise;
Great God is He of Justice Divine;
The Pure is He my Lord;
As half-and-half in Para Sakti He is.

சத்திக்கு மேலே பராசத்தி தன்னுள்ளே
சுத்த சிவபதந் தோயாத தூவொளி
அத்தன் திருவடிக் கப்பாலைக் கப்பாலாம்
ஒத்தவு மாமீசன் தானான வுண்மையே. 1768

Truth of Supreme Siva

Beyond Sakti, inside Para Sakti
Is the Pure Siva State, as Light undimmed
Still beyond and beyond are the Lord's Feet;
This the Truth of the Lord Supreme.

Mantras 1768 & 1769

His Feet are beyond the Beyond. Seeing that Effulgent Flame is seeing all the universe. He who rises and sees His world shall remain there forever. He sees the vast expanses of the Lord entwined with Sakti. He resides in that seer's thought.

கொழுந்தினைக் காணிற் குவலயந் தோன்றும்
எழுந்திடங் காணில் இருக்கலு மாகும்
பரந்திடங் காணிற் பார்ப்பதி மேலே
திரண்டெழக் கண்டவன் சிந்தையு ளானே. 1769

See Siva and Sakti and see All in Him

See that Tender Flame
You will have seen all universe;
Rise and see His World
There you shall forever remain;
See the Expanses Vast
You shall have seen the Lord with Sakti entwined;
The Lord that in your thought resides.

எந்தை பரமனும் என்னம்மை கூட்டமும்
முந்த வுரைத்து முறைசொல்லின் ஞானமாஞ்
சந்தித் திருந்த விடம்பெருங் கண்ணியை
உந்தியின் மேல்வைத் துகந்திருந் தானே. 1770

Worship Siva-Sakti and Realize Jnana

The Lord, my Father
His Sakti-Cluster, my Mother,
Chant their name in order according
That verily is Jnana Divine;
Above the navel, in my heart,
There with Her He resides
In rapture unceasing.

Mantras 1770 & 1771

Divine jnana is to chant the glory of the Lord and His Sakti, the heavenly Father and Mother. They induct the jiva into suddha and asuddha maya groups. Disentangling him, they place him in turiya state. Siva then takes His abode in him. This is the play of Siva/Sakti.

சத்தி சிவன்விளை யாட்டாம் உயிராகி
ஒத்த இருமாயா கூட்டத் திடையூட்டிச்
சுத்தம தாகுந் துரியம் பிறிவித்துச்
சித்தம் புகுந்து சிவமக மாக்குமே. 1771

The Play of Sakti—Sakti activates Jiva

Into the Maya Group — Suddha and Asuddha
They induct the Jiva;
From Pure Turiya State disentangling him,
They his thoughts enter;
And inside him, Siva His habitation takes;
—This the play of Sakti-Siva.

சத்தி சிவன்றன் விளையாட்டுத் தாரணி
சத்தி சிவமுமாஞ் சிவன்சத் தியுமாகுஞ்
சத்தி சிவமன்றித் தாபரம் வேறில்லை
சத்திதான் என்றுஞ் சமைந்துரு வாகுமே. 1772

All Creation is Sakti-Siva Play

All the Universe is the play of Sakti-Siva
Sakti is Siva, and Siva is Sakti

Without Sakti and Siva is no manifest creation
It is Sakti and Siva that forever Form assume.

Sakti is Siva. Siva is Sakti. All the universe is the play of Sakti/Siva. There will be no visible creation without Siva and Sakti. Sakti assumes form continuously.

7. சிவ லிங்கம்
SIVA LINGAM

குரைக்கின்ற வாரிக் குவலய நீரும்
பரக்கின்ற காற்றுப் பயில்கின்ற தீயும்
நிரைக்கின்ற வாறிவை நீண்டகன் றானை
வரைத்து வலஞ்செயு மாறறி யேனே. 1773

Siva is Immanent and Transcendent

He pervades the roaring waters of the seas
He permeates the spreading winds and flaming fire
Thus is He immanent in all Nature
Yet I know Him not, adore Him not.

வரைத்து வலஞ்செய்யு மாறிங்கொன் றுண்டு
நிரைத்து வருகங்கை நீர்மல ரேந்தி
உரைத்தவன் நாமம் உணரவல் லார்க்குப்
புரைத்தெங்கும் போகான் புரிசடை யோனே. 1774

Only Way of Knowing Siva is Worship

There is but one way here
Of knowing Him and adoring Him
They who with water and flower chant His name
They shall know Him
And from them He of the matted lock
Separates not.

ஒன்றெனக் கண்டேயெம் ஈசன் ஒருவனை
நன்றென் றடியிணை நான்வ ணைத்தொழ
வென்றைம் புலனுமிகக்கிடந் தின்புற
அன்றென் றருள்செய்யும் ஆதிப் பிரானே. 1775

Worship Him as the One Being

As the One and Only Being
I saw the Lord,
And full well I adored His Holy Feet
Subduing my senses five;
And He His blessings granted,
The gracious One, the Lord Primal.

மலர்ந்த அயன்மால் உருத்திரன் மகேசன்
பலந்தரும் ஐம்முகன் பரவிந்து நாதம்
நலந்தருஞ் சத்தி சிவன்வடி வாகிப்
பலந்தரு லிங்கம் பராநந்தி யாமே. 1776

Linga's Nine Aspects

Brahma, Vishnu, Rudra, Mahesa,
The five-faced Sadasiva, Bindu and Nada
Sakti and Siva—
All these as Linga His blessings grants,
He is but Nandi that is Para Supreme.

Brahma, Vishnu, Rudra, Mahesvara, Sadasiva of the five faces, bindu, nada, Sakti and Siva — all the nine aspects of Siva shower their blessings as Nandi himself.

மேவி யெழுகின்ற செஞ்சுட ரூடுசென்
றாவி எழுமள வன்றே உடலுற
மேவப் படுவதும் விட்டு நிகழ்வதும்
பாவித் தடக்கிற் பரகதி தானே. 1777

Rouse Kundalini and reach Supreme State

Rouse with the flaming Kundalini
And upward your Prana course;
Halting within the body
The acts of inhalation and exhalation
This, if you, through practice accomplish
You indeed have reached
The Supreme State Divine.

8. சம்பிரதாயம்
SAMPRADAYA (HOLY TRADITION)

உடல்பொருள் ஆவி உதகத்தால் கொண்டு
படர்வினை பற்றறப் பார்த்துக்கை வைத்து
நொடியின் அடிவைத்து நுண்ணுணர் வாக்கிக்
கடியப் பிறப்பறக் காட்டினன் நந்தியே. 1778

Lord appears as Siva Guru and gives initiation

My body, wealth and life,
He took from me as sacrificial offering,
Through ritual appropriate;
He directed his spiritual glance at me
And dispelled my Karma's network to destruction;
And then He laid His hands on me
And planting His Feet on my head
In a trice imparted Spiritual Awareness
And thus my birth's cycle He ended
He, the Nandi,
Through these acts of Diksha, successive.

உயிருஞ் சரீரமும் ஒண்பொரு ளான
வியவார் பரமும்பின் மேவும் பிராணன்
செயலார் சிவமுஞ் சிற்சத்தி யாதிக்கே
உயலார் குருபரன் உய்யக்கொண் டானே. 1779

Guru works for Disciple's Redemption

Life and body, and Prana breath that fleets after,
Siva the mighty and Chit Sakti that consorts
And Param the Truth Supreme
—All these to attain,
Gurupara my redemption worked.

பச்சிம திக்கிலே வைத்தேஆ சாரியன்
நிச்சலும் என்னை நினையென்ற வப்பொருள்
உச்சிக்குங் கீழது வுண்ணாக்கு மேலது
வைச்ச பதமிது வாய்திற வாதே. 1780

Guru imparts the Secret Divine

To His west (right), He seated me
"Daily on me meditate" — said He,
"That it is but the Truth that lies seated
Between the crown of the head and the palate of the mouth
This the Word True,
Cherish it as secret divine."

Seating the disciple to his right, Gurupara said: "Meditate on the Truth that lies in the ajna centre between the crown of the head and the palate of the mouth." This is the true word Let the seeker cherish it as a divine secret.

பிட்டடித் தெங்கும் பிதற்றித் திரிவேனை
யொட்டடித் துள்ளமர் மாசெலாம் வாங்கித்
தட்டொக்க மாறினன் தன்னையும் என்னையும்
வட்டம தொத்தது வாணிபம் வாய்த்ததே. 1781

Siva makes Jiva Pure as Himself

Indulging in talk indiscriminate
Aimless I wandered;
—Me, He made pure,
All my impurities cleansed
Me and He, to balance brought
—A barter, all to perfection indeed!

The disciple wandered aimlessly, indulging in indiscriminate talk. Gurupara cleansed him of impurities and made him pure. Then the disciple and Guru alone remained.

தரிக்கின்ற பல்லுயிர்க் கெல்லாந் தலைவன்
இருக்கின்ற தன்மையை யேதும் உணரார்
பிரிக்கின்ற விந்து பிணக்கறுத் தெல்லாங்
கருக்கொண்ட ஈசனைக் கண்டுகொண் டேனே. 1782

Siva Extricates Jiva from Maya

He is the Lord of all life existent,
His true nature they know not,
He extricated me from Maya that separates,
Lo! then I beheld the Lord that is seed of all.

கூடும் உடல்பொருள் ஆவி குறிக்கொண்டு
நாடி யடிவைத் தருண்ஞான சத்தியால்
பாடல் உடலினிற் பற்றற நீக்கியே
கூடிய தானவ னாங்குளிக் கொண்டே. 1783

Siva takes Jiva into Himself

Intent on redemption of my body, wealth and life
He sought me and planted His Feet on my head
And with the Grace of Sakti divine He exorcised
My love for the body fleshy;
And He and I as one He made
Intermingling in union non-separate.

கொண்டா னடியேன் அடிமை குறிக்கொள்ளக்
கொண்டான் உயிர்பொருள் காயக் குழாத்தினைக்
கொண்டான் பலமுற்றுந் தந்தவன் கோட்லாற்
கொண்டா னெனவொன்றுங் கூறகி லேனே. 1784

Siva by taking all, Gives All

He marked me out his vassal to-be
My life, possessions and body He took as His own;
But as he it was that all my sustenance gave
How dare I say, He took anything from me?

He took me into his divine order of vassalage; making my body, life and possession as his own. He gave all and took all. And I gained in the barter. What have I to complain of?

குறிக்கின்ற தேகமுந் தேகியுங் கூடி
நெறிக்கும் பிராணன் நிலைபெற்ற சீவன்
பறிக்கின்ற காயத்தைப் பற்றிய நேர்மை
பிறக்க அறியாதார் பேயுடன் ஒப்பரே. 1785

Ghosts do not know the Truth of Life

This body, the Lord within,
The Prana that is breath,
And the Soul that dwells inside
The truth of all these
That to the perishable body pertains
They who know not,
Unto ghosts of the dead they are.

உணர்வுடை யார்கட் குலகமுந் தோன்றும்
உணர்வுடை யார்கட் குறுதுய ரில்லை
உணர்வுடை யார்கள் உணர்ந்தவக் காலம்
உணர்வுடை யார்கள் உணர்ந்துகண் டாரே. 1786

Know the Finite Truth

They the Awareness have, see worlds all,
They the Awareness have, know sorrows none,
When they that Awareness have truly realized,
They indeed have the Truth Finite seen.

காயப் பரப்பில் அலைந்து துரியத்துச்
சால விரிந்து குவிந்து சகலத்தில்
ஆயவவ் வாறா யடைந்து திரிந்தோர்க்குத்
தூய அருள்தந்த நந்திக்கென் சொல்வதே. 1787

Woken from the Primordial Turiya State,

Wandering in the Bodily State—
Active in the Sakala State
With Tattvas six times six,
On them whose souls have thus roamed,
Nandi His Grace bestowed;
What shall I say of His greatness infinite!

In his infinite greatness, Nandi bestows His grace on the souls of those who, having been woken from the primordial turiya state (kevala), have wandered in the bodily state (sakala), possessing the thirty-six tattvas.

நானென நீயென வேறில்லை நண்ணுதல்
ஊனென வூனுயிர் என்ன வுடனின்று
வானென வானவர் நின்று மனிதர்கள்
தேனென இன்பந் திளைக்கின்ற வாறே. 1788

Siva and Jiva are inseparable

There is approach none as I and You;
Like body and life inseparate are We;
Together are We like the heavens and the heavenly beings;
Like the honey and its sweentness that I do savour.

The best approach to Him is not in dualistic terms of 'I' and 'You.' Jiva and Siva are as inseparable as the body and the life, the heaven and the heavenly beings, the honey and its sweetness.

அவனும் அவனும் அவனை யறியார்
அவனை யறியில் அறிவானும் இல்லை
அவனும் அவனும் அவனை யறியில்
அவனும் அவனும் அவனிவ னாமே. 1789

Knower becomes the Known

He and he knows Him not;
If he knows Him, then Knower is he not;
If he knows Him
Then he the Knower and He the Known
Become but one.

So long as Siva and jiva are considered as two separate indentities, the jiva does not know Him. When jiva knows Him, the knower (jiva) and the known (Siva) become one and unitive.

நானிது தானென நின்றிவ னாடோறும்
ஊனிது தானுயிர் போலுணர் வானுளன்
வானிரு மாமுகில் போற்பொழி வானுளன்
நானிது வம்பர நாதனு மாமே. 1790

Lord's Infinite Bounty

As life and body alike feel
He in me stood in identity full
Bounteous as He is unto the rains from heavens,
I with the heavenly Lord, one became.

Siva stands in relation to jiva like the life and the body, and thanks to the bounteous Grace of Siva, the jiva can become one in Him in indistinguishable identity.

பெருந்தன்மை தானென யானென வேறாய்
இருந்தது மில்லைய தீசன் அறியும்
பொருந்தும் உடலுயிர் போலுமை மெய்யே
திருந்தமுன் செய்கின்ற தேவர் பிரானே. 1791

Lord wrought Me to Perfection

Himself as Being Supreme
He stood not apart from me;
That the Lord Knows;
Like the body and life are We;
This the truth;
He to perfection wrought me
He the Lord of Immortals.

He is the Supreme Being. Still He never stood away and apart from jiva. He shapes the jiva to perfection and draws him into Him.

9. திருவருள் வைப்பு
PLACING OF GRACE

இருபத மாவ திரவும் பகலும்
உருவது வாவ துயிரும் உடலும்
அருளது வாவ தறமுந் தவமும்
பொருளது வுள்நின்ற போகம தாமே. 1792

Truth is Indivisible

Darkness (ignorance) and Light (knowledge)
Are the states two;
Life and body are the forms two;
Dharma and penance are the graces two;
Truth is but the blessing within.

காண்டற் கரியன் கருத்திலன் நந்தியுங்
தீண்டற்குஞ் சார்தற்குஞ் சேயனாத் தோன்றிடும்
வேண்டிக் கிடந்து விளக்கொளி யானெஞ்சம்
ஈண்டுக் கிடந்தங் கிருளறு மாமே. 1793

Pray and receive Divine Light

Elusive is He for us to see;
Beyond our Thoughts is He, the Nandi,
Distant is He to touch and feel,
Pray long in the light of your heart,
The darkness that envelops you dispelled stands.

Nandi is beyond sight, beyond thought, beyond touch and feel. Praying to Him from the innermost recesses of your heart, the darkness of ignorance that envelopes you stands dispelled.

குறிப்பினின் உள்ளே குவலயந் தோன்றும்
வெறுப்பிருள் நீங்கில் விகிர்தனும் நிற்குஞ்
செறிப்புறு சிந்தையைச் சிக்கென நாடில்
அறிப்புறு காட்சி அமரரு மாமே. *1794*

God's Grace Leads to illumination

In the hint of His grace,
All universe shall be revealed to you;
When the darkness of ignorance lifts,
The Great One stands revealed;
When you seek Him,
Your swarming thoughts on Him centred,
You shall see the light of Jnana,
And thus immortal become.

தேர்ந்தறி யாமையின் சென்றன காலங்கள்
பேர்ந்தறி வானெங்கள் பிஞ்ஞகன் எம்மிறை
ஆர்ந்தறி வாரறி வேதுணை யாமெனச்
சார்ந்தறி வான்பெருந் தன்மைவல் லானே. *1795*

Lord Knows His Devotees in Time

In ignorance my time rolled on;
Yet my Lord will in time know me;
By their light of Knowledge and love intense
He will know them,
He the Bounteous One.

Endless time passed in ignorance. When ignorance gives place to knowledge, the Lord will know jiva to the extent of jiva's depth of knowledge and intensity of love for the Bounteous One, will He be known to jiva.

தானே யறியும் வினைகள் அழிந்தபின்
நானே யறிகிலன் நந்தி யறியுங்கொல்
ஊனே யுருகி யுணர்வை யுணர்ந்தபின்
தேனே யனையனந் தேவர் பிரானே. *1796*

Lord, of Himself, will Know You

Himself will know me,
When my Karmas perish;
I know not when; but Nandi will;
Do melt in piety
And reach divine Consciousness;
Sweet like honey is our Lord of Immortals.

The jiva does not know when his karmas will perish. But Nandi, the Lord of immortals, knows. Then He Himself will know the jiva. So let the aspirant melt himself in piety and reach to divine consciousness.

நானறிந் தன்றே யிருக்கின்ற தீசனை
வானறிந் தாரறி யாது மயங்கினர்
ஊனறிந் துள்ளே யுயிர்க்கின்ற ஒண்சுடர்
தானறி யான்பின்னை யாரறி வாரே. *1797*

If I do not Know Lord who else shall?

I have known the Lord from days bygone
But the Celestials knew Him not,
Doubt-tossed were they;
The Lord is the Light
In my fleshy body as Prana pulsates
If I know Him not, who else will?

Because they were tossed in doubt, the celestials did not know the Lord; but the yogis had known Him in the days gone by. As prana is the pulsation in the fleshy body, so is the Lord in jiva unseen.

அருளெங்கு மான அளவை யறியார்
அருளை நுகரமு தானதுந் தேரார்
அருளைங் கருமத் ததிசூக்க முன்னார்
அருளெங்குங் கண்ணான தாரறி வாரே. *1798*

Grace is All

They know not the measure of Grace
That is pervasive all;
They know not the ambrosial sweetness
That from Grace flows;
They think not of the Five Acts
That Grace subtle performs;
Who knows how all-pervasive is Grace, indeed!

அறிவில் அணுக அறிவது நல்கிப்
பொறிவழி யாசை புகுத்திப் புணர்ந்திட்
டறிவது வாக்கி அடியருள் நல்குஞ்
செறிவொடு நின்றார் சிவமாயி னாரே. *1799*

Various Acts of Lord's Grace

To seek the Divine Light
He grants the light of knowledge;
He infuses the organs of sense
With desire
And leads you to enlightenment;
He then seats you
In the midst of the devout and holy;
They who His Grace thus received,
Verily became Siva themselves.

He infuses jiva's sense organs with a desire to seek enlightenment, leads him to that goal and grants him the light of knowledge. Many have thus received His Grace and have become holy; and remain devoted to Him. The Lord seats them amongst the yogis. They finally become Siva Himself.

அருளிற் பிறந்திட் டருளில் வளர்ந்திட்
டருளில் அழிந்திளைப் பாறி மறைந்திட்
டருளான ஆனந்தத் தாரமு தூட்டி
அருளால் என்நந்தி யகம்புகுந் தானே. *1800*

From Birth to Liberation — All Acts of Grace

In His Grace was I born,
In His Grace I grew up;
In His Grace I rested in death;
In His Grace I was in obfuscation;

In His Grace I tasted of ambrosial bliss;
In His Grace, Nandi, my heart entered.

The jiva is born, grows up, remains in obfuscation, dies, and then tastes ambrosial bliss of His Grace. It is Nandi who confers this grace.

அருளால் அமுதப் பெருங்கடல் ஆட்டி
அருளால் அடிபுனைந் தார்வமுந் தந்திட்
டருளான ஆனந்தத் தாரமு தூட்டி
அருளால் என்நந்தி யகம்புகுந் தானே. 1801

More Acts of Grace

By His Grace was I bathed in the ocean of nectar,
By His Grace He rested His Feet on me
By His Grace He granted the fervour of devotion
By His Grace He fed me the bliss that is ambrosial
By His Grace, Nandi my heart entered.

The jiva, then bathed in the ocean of nectar, rests his head on the Lord's Feet in fervour of devotion, fed with the ambrosial bliss of His Grace.

பாசத்தி லிட்ட தருளந்தப் பாசத்தின்
நேசத்தை விட்ட தருளந்த நேசத்திற்
கூசற்ற முத்தி யருளந்தக் கூட்டத்தின்
நேசத்துத்தோன்றா நிலையரு ளாமே. 1802

Grace Grants Mukti and Beyond

It was His grace that led me into Pasa
It was His Grace that freed me from that Pasa
It was His grace that in divine love granted Mukti
It was His Grace that granted me the love
For the State beyond Mukti.

பிறவா நெறிதந்த பேரரு ளாளன்
மறவா அருள்தந்த மாதவன் நந்தி
அறவாழி அந்தணன் ஆதிப் பராபரன்
உறவாகி வந்தென் உளம்புகுந் தானே. 1803

Lord is of Infinite Grace

Of infinite Grace is the Lord
Who my birth's bonds sundered;
Of the holiest of holy is Nandi
He is the Dharmic sea;
The Pure One;
The Primal Lord
In amity my heart entered.

Mantras 1803 & 1804

Nandi is the Holiest of the Holy, the dharmic sea, the Pure One, the Primal Lord who has sundered jiva's bonds of birth and entered his heart by His infinite Grace.

அகம்புகுந் தானடி யேற்கரு ளாலே
அகம்புகுந் துந்தெரி யானரு ளில்லோர்க்
ககம்புகுந் தானந்த மாக்கிச் சிவமாய்
அகம்புகுந் தானந்தி யானந்தி யாமே. 1804

Nandi entered my Heart and made me Sivam

In my heart He entered, grace abounding;
Even if He is in there,
Those devoid of Grace know Him not;
Entering the heart,
He filled me with bliss;
As Sivam, he made me
As Nandi my heart entered,
And I blissful became.

ஆயும் அறிவோ டறியாத மாமாயை
ஆய கரணம்படைக்கும்ஐம் பூதமு
மாய பலவிந் திரிய மவற்றுடன்
ஆய வருளைந்து மாமருட் செய்கையே. 1805

Bounties of Lord's Grace

He gave me the intelligence that reasons
He gave me the senses that Maya inscrutable fashions
He gave the five elements
And the diverse sense organs
And the Five Acts of Grace
—All these are but the bounties of His Grace.

In His bounteous Grace, He gave me the instruments to reason out the inscrutable senses, to enjoy the elements and environments for my functioning, and performed the Five Acts for my liberation and attainment of Grace.

அருளே சகலமு மாய பவுதிகம்
அருளே சராசர மாய வமலமே
இருளே வெளியே யெனுமெங்கும் ஈசன்
அருளே சகளத்த னன்றியின் றாமே. 1806

All Phenomena are manifestations of Grace

All manifestations of Nature are His Grace
All animate and inanimate are His Pure Grace
As darkness, as light, the Lord's Grace pervades,
All, all are but the Grace of His Form manifest.

All are but His benignant Grace, be they the manifestations of nature; be they animate or inanimate, be they darkness or light.

சிவமொடு சத்தி திகழ்நாதம் விந்து
தவமான ஐம்முகன் ஈசன் அரனும்
பவமுறு மாலும் பதுமத்தோன் ஈறா
நவமவை யாகி நடிப்பவன் தானே. 1807

The Nine God Forms are of Siva

Siva, Sakti, the luminous Nada and Bindu
The five-faced Sadasiva holy,
Mahesa, Rudra, Mal and the lotus-seated Brahma
—All these forms nine
He assumes.

அருட்கண் ணிலாதார்க் கரும்பொருள் தோன்றா.
அருட்கண் ணுளோர்க்கெதிர் தோன்றும் அரனே

இருட்கண்ணினோர்க்கங் கிரவியுந் தோன்றாத்
தெருட்கண்ணினோர்க்கெங்குஞ்சீரொளியாமே. 1808

Grace Gives Divine Vision

They whose eyes are blind
See not the sun even;
They that have vision divine
See the light everywhere;
They who have not the vision of Grace
See not the Lord that is Truth Subtle;
They that have the vision of Grace
See Hara face to face.

The blind do not see the sun ever. They who are blessed with divine vision see light everywhere. They who are not blessed with vision of Grace cannot see that subtle light; they who are blessed with the vision of Grace see Hara face to face. The Lord is subtle Truth.

தானே படைத்திடுந் தானே அளித்திடுந்
தானே துடைத்திடுந் தானே மறைத்திடுந்
தானே யிவைசெய்து தான்முத்தி தந்திடுந்
தானே வியாபித் தலைவனு மாமே. 1809

Lord Alone Performs the Five Acts

Himself creates; Himself preserves
Himself destroys; Himself obscures
Himself, all these He does
And grants Mukti after;
Himself the all-immanent Lord.

தலையான நான்குந் தனதரு வாகும்
அலையா வருவுரு வாகுஞ் சதாசிவம்
நிலையான கீழ்நான்கு நீடுரு வாகுந்
துலையா இவைமுற்று மாயல்ல தொன்றே. 1810

The Form, Formless and Form-Formless Aspects of Siva

The first four (Siva, Sakti, Nada, Bindu) are His Form-less ones;
The un-moving Form-Formless is the Sadasiva;
The abiding last four (Brahma, Vishnu, Rudra, Mahesa)
Are the Formed ones;
All these and the One beyond too are He.

ஒன்றது வாலே உலப்பிலி தானாகி
நின்றது தான்போல் உயிர்க்குயி ராய்நிலை
துன்றி யவையல்ல வாகுந் துணையென்ன
நின்றது தான்விளை யாட்டென்னுள் நேயமே. 1811

God is Immanent and Transcendent

One Being is He, immanent in all life
Indestructible He is;
In them He is; but He is not they;
He indwells them as Friend Divine
This His play, He of my heart's desire.

நேயத்தே நின்றிடும் நின்மலன் சத்தியோ
டாயக் குடிலையுள் நாதம் அடைந்திட்டுப்
போயக் கலைபல வாகப் புணர்ந்திட்டு
வீயத் தகாவிந்து வாக விளையுமே. 1812

Nadam and Bindu are Evolved when Siva Activates Pure Maya Sakti

The Immaculate One who in my heart dwells
The Kudilai (Pure Maya) Sakti He activates;
And from that act is Nadam born
That emanating Kala rays diverse
As seed the imperishable Bindu produces.

The sukshma (subtle) maya sakti is activated in the Immaculate One. From that movement is nada born. The imperishable bindu is then produced as the seed of the manifest world emanating the different kalas.

விளையும் பரவிந்து தானே வியாபி
விளையுந் தனிமாயை மிக்கமா மாயை
கிளையொன்று தேவர் கிளர்மனு வேதம்
அளவொன் றிலாவண்ட கோடிக ளாமே. 1813

The Devolutes of Bindu

The Bindu that thus arose pervades everywhere;
From it rises the Maya per se and the Mahamaya
And from them emanate the immortals and their clans
The Mantras and the Vedas too,
And the countless countless worlds swarming in the spread.

10. அருளொளி
LIGHT OF GRACE

அருளிற் றலைநின் றறிந்தழுந் தாதார்
அருளிற் றலைநில்லார் ஐம்பாச நீங்கார்
அருளிற் பெருமை யறியார் செறியார்
அருளிற் பிறந்திட் டறிந்தறி வாரே. 1814

Be Born in Grace and Receive Grace

Those who do not take their firm stand on Grace
And in conscious determination steep in it not,
Will never Grace receive;
Nor be freed of Pasas Five*
They will not know greatness that Grace gives;
They will not resolute be;
They alone know Grace who to Grace are born.

Those who do not take their firm stand on Grace and are not steeped in determination will never receive Grace, will not be freed of the five pasas, viz., anava, maya, karma, tirodayi (obfuscation) and mayeyam (desires); will not taste of the holiness of Grace; and will not be resolute. Those who are born to Grace alone know what Grace is.

*The five pasas are: the primal impurities — anava, maya and karma, and tirodayi (mala of obscuration) and mayeyam are the tangible manifestations of maya.

வாரா வழிதந்த மாநந்தி பேர்நந்தி
ஆரா அமுதளித் தானந்தி பேர்நந்தி
பேரா யிரமுடைப்பெம்மான்பே ரொன்றினில்
ஆரா அருட்கடல் ஆடுகென் றானே. 1815

Nandi Grants Unending Grace

Nandi the great, Nandi the famed,
Nandi that barred the way of my future birth;
He gave me the ambrosial bliss that never cloys;
He the Lord of a thousand names;
In one word He said, "Bathe eternally
In the unending sea of Grace."

Mantras 1815 & 1817

The great Nandi planted his feet on my head and I prostrated low and prayed at his feet. All worthless knowledge vanished, all impurities were dispelled. My birth cycle snapped. He gave me the ambrosial bliss, calling upon me to sport in the unending sea of Grace.

ஆடியும் பாடியும் அழுதும் அரற்றியுந்
தேடியுங் கண்டேன் சிவன்பெருந் தன்மையைக்
கூடிய வாறே குறியாக் குறிதந்தென்
ஊடுநின் றானவன் தன்னரு ளுற்றே. 1816

Imparting Grace Siva Grants His Form to Jiva

I danced and sang and wept and lamented
Thus I sought Him, and Siva's greatness saw,
And as I with Him united
He, His indefinable Form granted
And in me pervaded, His Grace imparting.

உற்ற பிறப்பும் உறுமல மானதும்
பற்றிய மாயாப் படலமெனப்பண்ணி
அத்தனை நீயென் றடிவைத்தான் பேர்நந்தி
கற்றன விட்டேன் கழல்பணிந் தேனே. 1817

Nandi Planted His Feet on me and imparted Grace

The birth I took,
The impurities (malas) I bore
He dispelled as but Maya's cloud;
"You are of these rid" — so saying
He planted His Feet on me—
He the Nandi famed;
All unworthy knowledge I gave up,
I prostrated and at His feet prayed.

விளக்கினை யேற்றி வெளியை அறிமின்
விளக்கினை முன்னே வேதனை மாறும்
விளக்கை விளக்கும் விளக்குடை யார்கள்
விளக்கில் விளங்கும் விளக்கவர் தாமே. 1818

Light the Lamps of God by Inner Light

Light the Lamp, and see the Space
Before the Lamp all pangs cease
They that have the Light to light the Lamp
Are but the Light, in the Divine Lamp shine.

ஒளியும் இருளும் ஒருகாலுந் தீரா
ஒளியுளோர்க் கன்றோ ஒழியா தொளியும்
ஒளியிருள் கண்டகண் போலவே றாயுள்
ஒளியிருள் நீங்க வுயிர்சிவ மாமே. 1819

By Inner Light Unite One in Siva

Interminable are light and darkness
Only to those who have light, will darkness cease;
To the eyes that see light, darkness is not;
So, too, when the inner light dispels darkness.
The Jiva with Siva one becomes.

Light and darkness are interminable. Darkness will cease only when light appears. The eyes which see light do not see darkness. So too, when the inner light appears, all darkness flees. The jiva becomes one with Siva.

புறமே திரிந்தேனைப் பொற்கழல் சூட்டி
நிறமே புகுந்தென்னை நின்மல னாக்கி
அறமே புகுந்தெனக் காரமு தீந்த
திறமேதென் றெண்ணித் திகைத்திருந் தேனே. 1820

Lord is Gracious

Aimless I wandered,
On me He planted His golden Feet,
In purity He entered, and made me pure
In charity He entered, and gave me the bliss of ambrosia
What ho! this gracious act!
In wonder limitless, I stand bedazed.

அருளது வென்ற அகலிடம் ஒன்றும்
பொருளது வென்ற புகலிடம் ஒன்றும்
மருளது நீங்க மனம்புகுந் தானைத்
தெருளுறும் பின்னைச் சிவகதி யாமே. 1821

Grace is the Refuge

There is a Space Vast that is Grace
There is a Refuge Safe that is Lord
In me He entered, my darkness to dispel;
Know Him fully; then indeed, is Siva-State.

கூறுமின் னீர்முன் பிறந்திங் கிறந்தமை
வேறொரு தெய்வத்தின் மெய்ப்பொருள் நீக்கிடும்
பாறணி யும்முடல் வீழவிட் டாருயிர்
தேறணி வோமிது செப்பவல் லீரே. 1822

Save the Soul

If other gods be born, live and die

Are they the True Ones? Speak:
Let us this body leave, to vultures a prey
And save our Soul — this you should proclaim.

If gods are born, live and die, can they be true gods? Proclaim that — to save jivas, lest they should leave this body a prey to the vultures.

11. சிவபூசை

SIVA PUJA

உள்ளம் பெருங்கோயில் ஊனுடம் பாலயம்
வள்ளற் பிரானார்க்கு வாய்கோ புரவாசல்
தெள்ளித் தெளிவார்க்குச் சீவன் சிவலிங்கங்
கள்ளப் புலனைந்துங் காளா மணிவிளக்கே. *1823*

Soul is Siva Linga

For the Bounteous Lord
This heart is the sanctum holy,
The fleshy body is temple vast
The mouth is the tower gate;
To them that discern,
Jiva is Sivalinga;
The deceptive senses but the lights that illume.

This fleshy body is a unique temple; the mouth is its tower gate; and the heart is the holy sanctum for the Bounteous Lord. For those who can vision, jiva is the Siva lingam, and the senses the illuminating lamp.

வேட்டவி யுண்ணும் விரிசடை நந்திக்குக்
காட்டவும் நாமிலங் காலையும் மாலையும்
ஊட்டவி யாவன வுள்ளங் குளிர்விக்கும்
பாட்டவி காட்டுதும் பாலவி யாகுமே. *1824*

Prayer is True Sacrifice

To Nandi of the spreading matted locks
That the sacrificial oblations takes,
We nothing offer;
The sacrifice that we morn and even can give
Are songs of praise that melt His heart;
Let us that sacrifice offer,
Verily, that is sacrifice, milk that is sweet.

பான்மொழி பாகன் பராபரன் தானாகு
மான சதாசிவன் தன்னையா வாகித்து
மேன்முகம் ஈசான மாகவே கைக்கொண்டு
சீன்முகஞ் செய்யச் சிவனவ னாகுமே. *1825*

Worship Sadasiva and Become Siva

The Lord that with His consort of sweet speech
Is the Para Para Supreme;
In Him enshrine Sadasiva
His upward looking Face as Isana consider
And thus your worship perform
You shall Siva Himself become.

நினைவதும் வாய்மைமொழிவது. மல்லாற்
கனைகழல் ஈசனைக் காண வரிதாங்
கனைகழல் ஈசனைக் காண்குற வல்லார்
புனைமலர் நீர்கொண்டு போற்றவல் லாரே. *1826*

Adore the Lord and Behold Him

You can think of Him, you can speak of His Truth
But rare indeed to see the Lord of the Holy Feet;
They can but see the Lord of the Holy Feet
Who adore Him with flower and water.

Well may you think of Him, and speak of His Truth. But rarely can you behold the Holy Feet of the Lord. They who adore Him with flowers and water can see them.

மஞ்சன மாலை நிலாவிய வானவர்
நெஞ்சினுள் ஈசன் நிலைபெறு காரணம்
அஞ்சமு தாம்உப சாரம்எட் டெட்டோடும்
அஞ்சலி யோடுங் கலந்தர்ச்சித் தார்களே. *1827*

Celestials Worship Lord with Archana

Why is it the Lord has taken His seat
In the heart of Beings Celestial
That consecrated water and garland of flowers bear?
With offerings five of dishes sweet
And with upachara rituals two times eight
They humbly prostrating, in archana, worship.

Why has the Lord taken His seat in the heart of the celestial beings who bear the consecrated water and garland of flowers? They humbly prostrate in worship, offering the Lord five sweet dishes and sixteen upachara rituals.

புண்ணியஞ் செய்வார்க்குப் பூவுண்டு நீருண்டு
அண்ணல் அதுகண்டருள்புரி யாநிற்கும்
எண்ணிலி பாவிகள் எம்மிறையீசனை
நண்ணறி யாமல் நழுவுகின் றாரே. *1828*

Pray and Receive Grace

The devout are they with flower and water pray
The Lord seeing that bestows His Grace on them
Countless are the sinners that know not how our Lord to approach
Thus they slip by in ignorance deep.

The devout are they who pray with water and flowers. On them the Lord bestows His Grace. The undevout are they who do not know how to approach Him. They let go the chance by sheer ignorance.

அத்த னவதீர்த்த மாடும் பரிசுகேள்
ஒத்த மெய்ஞ் ஞானத் துயர்ந்தார் பதத்தைச்
சுத்தம தாக விளக்கித் தெளிக்கவே
முத்தியா மென்றுநம் மூலன் மொழிந்ததே. *1829*

Anoint Feet of Holy is Unto Bathing in Holy Waters

Know the reward of bathing
In the nine waters of the Lord;
Mukti indeed for those
That anoint the feet of holy men
Who in Jnana are upraised;
Thus does Mula proclaim.

They who worship with water and flowers reap the reward of bathing in the nine Holy Waters of the Lord. Mula (Tirumular) proclaimed that those who anoint the feet of holy men who are upraised in jnana obtain mukti.

மறப்புற்று விவ்வழி மன்னிநின் றாலுஞ்
சிறப்பொடு பூநீர் திருந்தமுன் ஏந்தி
மறப்பின்றி யுன்னை வழிபடும் வண்ணம்
அறப்பெற வேண்டும் அமரர் பிரானே. 1830

My Prayer is to Worship Lord with Archana

Even if in thoughtlessness
I world's ways pursue,
Do grant me this:
That I with water and flower
Unceasing adore You;
This my prayer;
O! Lord of immortals!

Even if in thoughtlessness the devotee pursues mundane ways, may he ask the Lord to grant him this boon; that he should unceasingly adore the Lord with water and flowers. Let that be the devotee's unfailing prayer.

ஆரா தனையும் அமரர் குழாங்களுந்
தீராக் கடலும் நிலத்தும தாய்நிற்கும்
பேரா யிரமும் பிரான்திரு நாமமும்
ஆரா வழியெங்கள் ஆதிப் பிரானே. 1831

Chant the Thousand Names of Lord

The Immortals swarm in hordes seeking Him;
The seas and lands unending,
All that yours shall be,
When you chant unceasing
The thousand names of the Primal Lord,
And the One Sacred name Special.

Mantras 1831 & 1832

The immortals swarm in clans seeking Him, ceaselessly chanting the thousand names of the Primal Lord. Hordes of celestials; seek Him in an unending procession, bathing Him in 'pancha gavya' (the five products of the cow).

ஆனைந்தும் ஆட்டி அமரர் கணந்தொழத்
தானந்த மில்லாத் தலைவன் அருளது
தேனுந்து மாமலர் உள்ளே தெளிந்ததோர்
பாரைங் குணமும் படைத்துநின் றானே. 1832

Lord is in Our Heart

Bathing Him in the five products of cow (Pancha Gavya)
The Celestial beings in hordes seek the Lord
Who knows end none;
Within the honeyed flower that is heart
His Grace stands revealed;
He who the five elements and their attributes created.

உழைக்கொண்ட பூநீர் ஒருங்குடன் ஏந்தி
மழைக்கொண்டமாமுகின் மேற்சென்றுவானோர்
தழைக்கொண்ட பாசந் தயங்கிநின் றேத்தப்
பிழைப்பின்றி எம்பெரு மானரு ளாமே. 1833

Celestials Pray and Receive Lord's Grace

Bearing choicest flowers and water
The heavenly Beings over clouds traverse;
And with Pasa subdued, stand and pray
And unfailing My Lord's Grace receive.

The heavenly beings traverse over clouds, bearing the choicest flowers and water; stand with subdued pasa and pray to Him. They all receive the Lord's Grace without fail.

வெள்ளக் கடலுள் விரிசடை நந்திக்கு
உள்ளக் கடற்புக்கு வார்சுமை பூக்கொண்டு
கள்ளக் கடல்விட்டுக் கைதொழ மாட்டாதார்
அள்ளற் கடலுள் அழுந்துகின் றாரே. 1834

Enter the Sea of Heart's Faith

In the expanse of waters (Ganga)
With spreading matted locks is Nandi;
Renounce the sea of unbelief;
Enter the sea of heart's faith;
They who adore Him not thus
With hands laden with flowers
Will in the sea of sorrow fall,
And forever immersed be.

கழிப்படுந் தண்கடற் கௌவை யுடைத்து
வழிப்படுவாமாலர் மொட்டறி யார்கள்
பழிப்படு வார்பல ரும்பழி வீழ
வெளிப்படு வோருச்சி மேவிநின் றானே. 1835

Break the Banks of the Sea of Sorrow

Breaking the marshy banks of the sea of sorrow
They adore Him with buds and blossoms;
They who know this not, into error great fall;
But those who know it, will see the Lord
In the crown of their head, seated within.

Overcoming all doubts, they should adore Him with buds and blossoms in true faith. Those who do not know this, fall into great error. Those who know it will see the Lord seated within the crown of their heads.

பயனறி வொன்றுண்டு பன்மலர் தூவிப்
பயனறி வார்க்கரன் தானே பயிலும்
நயனங்கள் மூன்றுடை யானடி சேர
வயனங்க ளாலென்றும் வந்துநின் றானே. 1836

Adoration is the Way to Reach Lord

There is one way to reach Him
Adore Him with flowers many;
To them that do this,
The Lord by Himself stands revealed;
This the way to the Holy Feet of the three-eyed God;
Adoring Him thus, He fails never to stand before you.

To adore Him with many flowers is the sure way to reach the Holy Feet of the Three-Eyed God. To him, who does it, the Lord stands revealed, unfailing.

ஏத்துவர் மாமலர் தூவித் தொழுதுநின்
றார்த்தெம தீசன் அருட்சே வடியென்றன்
மூர்த்தியை மூவா முதலுரு வாய்நின்ற
தீர்த்தனை யாருந் துதித்துண ராரே. 1837

Seek Him In Prayer

"My Lord, the Primal One, the Timeless Eternity,
The Holy One,"
—Thus they adore Him with flowers diverse,
And in love endearing at His Feet worship,
His Grace to receive;
How then do you in prayer seek Him not?

When so many in endearing love pray at His Feet with choicest flowers and deep devotion and receive His Grace, why do not you, too, seek Him that way?

தேவர்க ளோடிசை வந்துமண் ணோடுறும்
பூவொடு நீர்சுமந் தேத்திப் புனிதனை
மூவரிற் பன்மை முதல்வனாய் நின்றருள்
நீர்மைய யாவர் நினைக்கவல் லாரே. 1838

Siva is the Primal One of Plural Three

Laden with flower and water
The Celestial beings seek the earth
And sing the praise of the Pure One;
Whoever thinks of His bounteous Grace
Him He blesses,
He, the Primal One of the Three.

The celestials seek the earth, laden with flowers and water, and sing the praise of the pure Lord, the Primal One of the plural three who blesses.

உழைக்கவல் லோர்நடு நீர்மல ரேந்திப்
பிழைப்பின்றி யீசன் பெருந்தவம் பேணி
இழைக்கொண்ட பாதத் தினமலர் தூவி
மழைக்கொண்டல் போலவேமன்னிநில் லீரே. 1839

Pray and Prosper

You that labour hard
Gather flowers and carry water pure;
Adore the Lord in unfailing piety
And at His shining Feet lay the flowers;
And stand and pray
And like the rain-laden clouds
Forever prosperous you shall be;

Gather flowers and carry pure water; bathe Him and lay the flowers at His radiant Feet; stand and pray; and adore Him in unfailing piety. You will forever prosper.

வென்று விரைந்து விரைப்பணி யென்றனர்
நின்று பொருந்த இறைபணி நேர்படத்
துன்று சலமலர் தூவித் தொழுதிடிற்
கொண்டிடு நித்தலுங் கூறிய வன்றே. 1840

The Lord Receives Worship

To perform The Lord's worship in manner appropriate
Senses subdue, hasten, and quick at His Feet fall;
And offering water and flower daily worship,
He will accept you, thus I said, even in days of yore.

Subdue the senses, hasten towards Him; surrender in totality and worship the Lord daily, offering water and flowers. He will surely accept your heart's offering.

சாத்தியும் வைத்துஞ் சயம்புவென் றேத்தியும்
ஏத்தியு நாளு மிறையை யறிதிலார்
ஆத்தி மலக்கிட் டகத்திழுக் கற்றக்கான்
மாத்திக்கே செல்லும் வழியது வாமே. 1841

Way to Goal Supreme

Adorn Him with garland of flowers
Place them at His feet
Praise Him as the Lord Primal;
Those that have daily prayed to Him
And yet have known Him not
Let them adore Him with Athi flower, so dear to Him
And pray, their base nature be cleansed of impurities;
—That the way to Goal Supreme.

1) Athi — flower of the tree, bauhima racemosa. It is dear to Siva.

Adore the Lord with the athi flower so dear to Him and pray that you will be cleansed of all impurities.

ஆவிக் கமலத்தின் அப்புறத் தின்புற
மேவித் திரியும் விரிசடை நந்தியைக்
கூவிக் கருதிக் கொடுபோய்ச் சிவத்திடைத்
தாவிக்கு மந்திரந் தாமறியாரே. 1842

Nandi is Within

Above the lotus of the heart, beyond
In Bliss abides,
Nandi of the spreading matted locks;
Yet they know not the mantra to muse and chant
That will to Him lead and there abide.

Nandi of the spreading matted locks abides in bliss above

the lotus of the heart. Yet many do not know to chant and muse on the mantra that will unite them to Him.

சாணாகத் துள்ளே அழுந்தியமாணிக்கங்
காணுமளவுங் கருத்தறி வாரில்லை
பேணிப் பெருக்கிப் பெருக்கி நினைவோர்க்கு
மாணிக்க மாலை மனம்புகுந் தானே. *1843*

Lord is a Gem-Set Jewel

He is the gem that lies embedded in the cubit of the heart
Until they see Him, they think not of Him;
Into them who cherish and muse on Him over and over
As a gem-set Jewel He shines.

He is the gem that lies embedded in the cubit of the heart. They do not think of Him and do not see Him. He, the gem-studded garland, enters into them who cherish and muse on Him over and over again.

பெருந்தன்மை நந்தி பிணங்கிருள் நேமி
இருந்தன்மை யாலுமென்நெஞ்சிடங்கொள்ள
வருந்தன்மை யாளனை வானவர் தேவர்
தருந்தன்மை யாளனைத் தாங்கிநின் றாரே. *1844*

Nandi Dispels Darkness

Nandi of gracious qualities
Is the Chakra (discus) that cuts the Darkness (of impurities)
He takes his abiding seat in my heart,
While the Celestial Beings to whom He bestows His gifts
Come in prayer, beseeching Him from afar.

Nandi is the discus that cuts impurities asunder. The celestials on whom He bestows His gifts come from afar beseeching Him in prayer. But He takes His abiding seat in the yogi's heart.

சமைய மலசுத்தி தன்செயல் அற்றிடும்
அமையும் விசேடமு மானமந் திரசுத்தி
சமையநிர் வாணங் கலாசுத்தி யாகும்
அமைமன்னு ஞான மானார்க் கபிடேகமே. *1845*

The Four Dikshas or Ordination Rites

By Samaya Diksha, the Primal impurities their potency lose;
By Visesha Diksha, the Mantra purification insures;
By Nirvana Diksha, the Kalas purification is effected;
The Abhisheka Diksha is for those
Who the Jnani State have attained.

The primal malas lose their potency by Samaya diksha. The purification of mantra chanting is ensued by Visesha diksha, the purification of the kalas is effected by Nirvana diksha. 'Abhisheka diksa is for those who have attained the state of jnana.

ஊழிதோறு றூழி யுணர்ந்தவர்க் கல்லது
ஊழில் உயிரை யுணர்வுந் தானொட்டா
ஆழி யமரும் அரியயன் என்றுளோர்
ஊழி கடந்துமோ ருச்சியு ளானே. *1846*

Seek Him Incessantly — He is Timeless Eternity

Unless they have adored Him through aeons and aeons
They will not have become the Jiva that is Karma devoid;
Hari on the sea, and Aya besides,
Seek Him through ages after ages;
Yet is He beyond reach;
He that shines atop of Time.

Hari and Aya have been seeking Him through age after age. Still He is beyond their reach. Unless, therefore, He is sought after through aeons and aeons, He who shines beyond time cannot be reached and karma will not be effaced.

12. குரு பூசை
GURU PUJA

ஆகின்ற நந்தி யடித்தா மரைபற்றிப்
போகின் றுபதேசம் பூசிக்கும் பூசையும்
ஆகின்ற ஆதாரமாறா றதனின்மேற்
போகின்ற பொற்பையும் போற்றுவன் யானே. *1847*

Nandi Imparts Upadesa

Grasping the lotus feet of Nandi that blesses me,
I shall relate the way of Upadesa,
That to redemption leads;
Of Puja that is performed;
And of the Way to transcend Adharas six
And to ascend beyond.

Tirumular proceeds to narrate about 'upadesa' that leads to liberation; and about performance of Guru worship that shows the way to transcend the six adharas, and to ascend beyond.

கானுறுகோடி கடிகமழ் சந்தனம்
வானுற மாமல ரிட்டு வணங்கினும்
ஊனினை நீக்கி யுணர்பவர்க் கல்லது
தேனமர் பூங்கழல் சேரவொண் ணாதே. *1848*

Rid Fleshly Desires and Know Him

With the sweet scented sandal

That in the forest recesses grows,
And with flowers rare
That heavenward blossom
You may adore Him;

No use in adoring him with sweet-scented sandals and rare flowers which blossom heavenward. Unless one seeks him, rid of bodily desires, his feet that are bedecked with honeyed flowers, cannot be reached.

மேவிய ஞானத்தின் மிக்கிடின் மெய்ப்பரன்
ஆவயின் ஞான நெறிநிற்றல் அர்ச்சனை
ஓவற வுட்பூ சனைசெய்யில் உத்தமஞ்
சேவடி சேரல் செயலறல் தானே. 1849

Path of Jnana is Supreme Archana

When you excel in the Path of Jnana
That leads like the Para Supreme,
The Path of Jnana is all Archana;
Great indeed is constant worship within;
To reach the Lord's Feet is to still actions all.
But unless you know Him,
Your fleshy desires and
You cannot reach His Feet
That are with honeyed flowers bedecked.

Excelling in the path of jnana which leads to Para Supreme is the greatest 'archanai', worship. Constant worshipping within is indeed great. Reaching the Lord's Feet is to still all actions.

உச்சியுங் காலையும் மாலையும் ஈசனை
நச்சுமின் நச்சி நமவென்று நாமத்தை
விச்சுமின் விச்சி விரிசுடர் மூன்றினும்
நச்சுமின் பேர்நந்தி நாயக னாகுமே. 1850

Pray Thrice a Day

Morn, noon and eventide
Adore the Lord;
Adoring chant the word "Nama" — (I worship)
Chanting, invoke Him in luminaries three — the Sun,
Moon, and Fire;
The famed Nandi is the Lord Supreme.

Let the devotee adore the Lord in the morning, at noon and in the evening. While adoring, let him chant "I worship" (nama) and so invoke the Lord Supreme, that is in the sun, moon and fire.

புண்ணிய மண்டலம் பூசைநூ றாகுமாம்
பண்ணிய மேனியும் பத்துநூ றாகுமாம்
எண்ணிலிக் கைய மிடிற்கோடி யாகுமாற்
பண்ணிடில் ஞானியூண் பார்க்கில் விசேடமே. 1851

To Feed Jnani is to be Supremely Blessed

A hundred times blessed
Is to perform puja in places holy;
A ten hundred times blessed
Is to worship His Presence;
A hundred, hundred times blessed
Is to feed those their thoughts have stilled;
Blessed, blessed far indeed is to see
That a Jnani is to contentment fed.

A hundred times blessed is it to perform puja in holy places. Ten hundred times blessed is it to worship His Presence. A hundred hundred times blessed is it to feed those who have stilled their thoughts. To see that a jnani is fed to contentment is indeed the most blessed of all.

இந்துவும் பானுவும் இலங்குந் தலத்திடை
வந்தித்த தெல்லாம் அசுரர்க்கு வாரியாம்
இந்துவும் பானுவும் இலங்காத் தலத்திடை
வந்தித்தல் நந்திக்கு மாபூசை யாமே. 1852

Perform Pujas, Nadis Quelled

The Pujas that you perform
When Nadis, sun and moon, active beat
Are for Asuras meet;
The Pujas that you perform
When Nadis sun and moon are quelled
Are alone for Holy Nandi appropriate.

The pujas performed when the sun and moon nadis are active go to the asuras. The appropriate pujas for holy Nandi are to be performed after quelling the sun and moon nadis (in the yogic way).

இந்துவும் பானுவு மென்றேழு கின்றதோர்
விந்துவும் நர்தமு மாகிமீ தானத்தே
சிந்தனை சாக்கிரா தீதத்தே சென்றிட்டு
நந்தியைப் பூசிக்க நற்பூசை யாமே. 1853

Worship Nandi Beyond the Spheres of Sun and Moon

When beyond the Spheres of Sun and Moon you ascend
There Bindu and Nada are;
Ascending (through Adharas) thus,
Your Awareness crosses
The frontiers of Waking State;
There when you continuous worship Nandi,
That verily is worship Divine.

Bindu and nada are there, when prana ascends beyond the spheres of the sun and moon. Thus ascending through the adharas, consciousness crosses the frontiers of the 'waking state.' Worshipping Nandi there is verily divine worship.

மனபவ னங்களை மூலத்தான் மாற்றி
அனித வுடற்பூத மாக்கியகற்றிப்
புனிதன் அருள்தனிற் புக்கிருந் தின்பத்
தனியுறு பூசை சதாசிவற் காமே. 1854

Cross the Gates of Awareness and Tattvas

Course the Sakti Kundalini,
Transcend the successive gates of Awareness
Reduce the perishable body to its elemental (tattva) constituents
And then discard them;

Then do you enter the Grace of the Holy One
And there you abide and adore
That indeed is the worship meet for Sadasiva.

Let Kundalini sakti be coursed transcending the successive gates of consciousness. Let the body be reduced to its tattva constituents and then discarded. Then does the yogi enter the Grace of the Holy One and abide in Him. That indeed is worship appropriate to Sadasiva.

பகலும் இரவும் பயில்கின்ற பூசை
இயல்புடை யீசர்க் கிணைமல ராகப்
பகலும் இரவும் பயிலாத பூசை
சகலமுந் தான்கொள்வன் தாழ்சடை யோனே. 1855

Practise Worship where neither Night nor Day is

The worship that you perform
By day and night,
Is to the Lord an offering of flower twain;
The worship that you perform
Where neither day nor night is
Is to Him of the flowing matted locks
Acceptance full and replete indeed.

In worship, two flowers are offered to the Lord — one at day and another at night. He of the matted locks accepts the worship in the sphere where there is neither night nor day.

இராப்பகல் அற்ற இடத்தே யிருந்து
பராக்கற ஆனந்தத்தேறல் பருகி
இராப்பக லற்ற இறையடி யின்பத்
திராப்பகல் மாயை இரண்டிடத் தேனே. 1856

Where Neither Day Nor Night is, there No Maya is

Seated in the sphere where neither day nor night is
The supreme honeyed bliss I imbibed;
Lost in thought to events outside
At the holy Feet of the Lord
Where neither day nor night is,
I dispelled the Maya twain,
That with day and night compare.

Sitting in the sphere where there is neither day nor night, the yogi imbibes the supreme honeyed bliss. At the Holy Feet of the Lord that yogi is lost in thought to outside events, dispelled of the maya that creates the distinction of night and day

13. மகேசுவர பூசை
MAHESWARA PUJA (WORSHIP OF DEVOTEES)

படமாடக் கோயிற் பகவற்கொன் றீயில்
நடமாடக் கோயில் நம்பர்க்கங் காகா
நடமாடக் கோயில் நம்பர்க்கொன் றீயில்
படமாடக் கோயிற் பகவற்க தாமே. 1857

Devotees are Walking Temples

The offering you give
To the Lord in the temple steepled high
Reaches not His devotees
Who the walking temples noble are;
When you offer things
To the walking temples noble,
That sure reaches the Lord
In the temple steepled high.

The offerings given to the Lord in the high-towered temple do not reach His devotees. But the things offered to the devotees, who are the walking temples, surely reach the Lord within the high-towered temple.

தண்டறு சிந்தை தபோதனர் தாமகிழ்ந்
துண்டது மூன்று புவனமும் உண்டது
கொண்டது மூன்று புவனமுங் கொண்டதென்
றெண்டிசை நந்தி எடுத்துரைத் தானே. 1858

Feed Tapasvins, Feed All Worlds

The food, Tapasvins of blemishless thought took
Is food all three worlds took;
The offerings they cheerfully received
Are offerings the three worlds received;
—Thus He proclaimed, Nandi the Great.

The great Nandi has proclaimed that the offerings received by the tapasvins of blemishless thought are offerings received by the Three Worlds.

மாத்திரையொன்றினின் மன்னி யமர்ந்துறை
யாத்தனுக் கீந்த அரும்பொரு ளானது
மூர்த்திகள் மூவர்க்கு மூவேழ் குரவர்க்குந்
தீர்த்தம தாமது தேர்ந்துகொள் வீரே. 1859

Offering to Tapasvins is Oblation to Gods and Ancestors

The things you gave His dear devotee,
Who in Him is seated,
Are verily oblations meet for the Gods Three;
And for ancestors too,
Through generations three times seven;
This for certain shall you know

Know that the offerings given to the dear devotees of the Lord, who are seated in Him, are oblations offered to the three Gods and to the giver's ancestors for twenty-one generations.

அகரம் ஆயிரம் அந்தணர்க் கீயிலென்
சிகரம் ஆயிரஞ் செய்து முடிக்கிலென்
பகரு ஞானி பகலூண் பலத்துக்கு
நிகரிலை என்பது நிச்சயந் தானே. *1860*

Feeding the Tapasvin is superior to feeding Brahmins and Gods

Though you a thousand abodes to holy Brahmins give
Though you a thousand temples for the gods build;
None, none is of merit compare
To a day's feed to a holy devotee given;
This be of certain.

Mantras 1860 & 1861

Neither the building of a thousand free habitations for brahmins, nor feeding sumptuously a hundred, hundred thousand brahmins, nor erecting a thousand temples to the Gods — none of these is of efficacy equal to a day's feeding of a holy devotee who wears the holy ashes.

ஆறிடும் வேள்வி அருமறை நூலவர்
கூறிடும் அந்தணர் கோடிபே ருண்பதில்
நீறிடுந் தொண்டர் நினைவின் பயனிலை
பேறெனில் ஓர்பிடி பேறதுவாகுமே. *1861*

Even the Thought of Feeding Siva Jnanis is most Efficacious

Well may you feed a hundred hundred thousand Brahmins
That the holy thread wear and noble sacrifices perform;
But holier far is the desire to feed in endearment great
A morsel albeit, to
The Lord's devotee true
Who the holy ashes wears.

ஏறுடை யாயிறை வாஎம்பி ரானென்று
நீறிடு வாரடி யார்நிகழ் தேவர்கள்
ஆறணி செஞ்சடை யண்ண லிவரென்று
வேறணி வார்க்கு வினையில்லை தானே. *1862*

Siva Jnanis are Gods on Earth

"You, the Divine Bull ride,
My Lord, My God"
—Those who wear the holy ashes saying thus;
Verily are like Devas on earth;
They that worship them as the Lord Himself,
—Who the Ganga on His russet matted locks wears,
Will have their Karmas end consummated.

Those who wear the holy ashes and pray to Him in intense devotion are really celestials on earth. Those who worship such holy men as Lord Siva Himself, who sports the Ganga on His russet-matted locks, will reach the end of their karmas.

சீர்நந்தி கொண்டு திருமுக மாய்விட்ட
பேர்நந்தி யென்னும் பிறங்கு சடையனை
நானொந்து நொந்து வருமள வுஞ்சொல்லப்
பேர்நந்தி யென்னும் பிதற்றொழி யேனே. *1863*

Call Nandi until He Appears

Of resplendent beauty is His Face
Of glowing sheen is His matted locks
He the Nandi famed;
In intense anguish I call His Name
And until He appears before me
I shall not cease to clamour, "My Nandi! My Nandi!"

The famed Nandi's face is of resplendent beauty and His matted locks of shining glow. The yogi calls His Name in intense anquish. He shall not stop to clamour for and to hail Nandi until He appears before him.

அழிதக வில்லா அரனடி யாரைத்
தொழுதகை ஞாலத்துத் தூங்கிருள் நீங்கும்
பழுது படாவண்ணம் பண்பனை நாடித்
தொழுதெழ வையகத் தோரின்ப மாமே. *1864*

Worship Siva's Devotee and the World will Rejoice

In this world worship
Siva's devotees, who no death know;
The hanging darkness of ignorance forever disappears,
Unfailing seek the devotee pure
And your obeisance make;
Of a certain will the world rejoice.

Let the yogi worship Siva's devotees who knows no death. The vestigial ignorance in him will then disappear once and for all. So seek the pure devotees without fail and make obeisance to them. It will result in the rejoicing of the world.

பகவற்கே தாகிலும் பண்பில ராகிப்
புகுமத்த ராய்நின்று பூசனை செய்யும்
முகமத்தோ டொத்துநின் றூழிதோ றூழி
அகமத்த ரா்கிநின் றாய்ந்தொழிந் தாரே. *1865*

Worship without Love for Siva Jnanis Leads Nowhere

With endearment none for holy ones
With pride brimming to full
They Pujas perform;
Thus through ages and ages they tried and perished,
Their faces turned like agitating churns hard,
Their hearts with egoity extreme filled.

They who perform pujas with brimming pride, with no endearment to holy ones, with hearts filled in extreme egoity — though such pujas are performed by them for ages and ages — in the end they only perish.

வித்தகமாகிய வேடத்தர் உண்டவூண்
அத்தன் அயன்மால் அருந்திய வண்ணமாஞ்

சித்தந் தெளிந்தவர் சேடம் பருகிடின்
முத்தியா மென்றுநம் மூலன் மொழிந்ததே. 1866

Food for Holy Men is Food for Gods

The food the holy men partake
Is verily food for the gods,
Siva, Vishnu and Brahma;
To partake of the leavings
Of holy men that have realized Truth
Is the way sure to Mukti;
—Thus affirms our Mula in meaning unmistakable.

In unmistakable words Mular has affirmed that the food partaken by the holy men is the food for the Gods and that the sure way to attain mukti is to partake unhesitatingly of the leavings of the holy men who have realised the Truth.

தாழ்வில்ர் பின்னும் முயல்வ ரருந்தவம்
ஆழ்வினை யாழ அவர்க்கே அறஞ்செய்யும்
ஆள்வினை நீக்கி அருவினை தன்னொடும்
போழ்வினை தீர்க்கும்அப் பொன்னுல காமே. 1867

Give to the Great Holy Ones and Reach the Golden Land

Depressed are they not;
In holy Tapas they persevere still;
To them give
Your Karmas away to hasten;
You shall that Golden Land reach,
Where Karmas three, past, present and future, exist none.

They who persevere in silent tapas are great. He who gives them food chases away his karmas. He will then reach the golden land where the karmas past, present and future are forever blotted out.

1) The three karmas are: i) sanchita (stored up); ii) prarabdha (already bearing fruit); iii) agami (prospective).

14. அடியார் பெருமை

GREATNESS OF HOLY MEN

திகைக்குரி யானொரு தேவனை நாடும்
வகைக்குரி யானொரு வாதி யிருக்கிற்
பகைக்குரி யாரில்லைப் பார்மழை பெய்யும்
அகக்குறை கேடில்லை யவ்வுல குக்கே. 1868

That Land Prospers where Holy Men are

Where there is a holy man of divine worth
Who pursues the Lord,
—That all space embraces—
There enemies none are;
Rains in abundance fall;
Full the people's contentment
Evil none befalls that land.

Where holy men are, there no enemies are; rains fall in abundance; contentment marks the people's way of life. No evil befalls that land.

அவ்வுல கத்தே பிறந்தவ் வுடலொணடும்
அவ்வுல கத்தே அருந்தவ நாடுவர்
அவ்வுல கத்தே அரனடி கூடுவர்
அவ்வுல கத்தே அருள்பெறு வாரே. 1869

The Land of the Holy

There in that Land are they born;
There in that Land in that body they Tapas perform;
There in that Land they reach the Feet of Lord
There in that Land will they His Grace receive.

In such a holy land, men perform tapas and reach the Feet of the Lord and receive His Grace.

கொண்ட குறியுங் குலவரை யுச்சியும்
அண்டரும் அண்டத் தமரரும் ஆதியும்
எண்டிசை யோரும்வந் தென்கைத் தலத்தினுள்
உண்டெனில் நாமினி உய்ந்தொழிந் தோமே. 1870

I am Redeemed when I reach the Goal of Union in Siva

The goal I sought (of union in Siva)
The peaks of mountain high in there, (Sahasrara)
The denizens of heavens,
The immortals celestial,
The hordes of humans from quarters eight
And the Primal One, too,
—If toward me they come,
And in my hands I hold them,
Redeemed am I, forever and ever.

The yogi will be redeemed forever, when he reaches the goal of union with Siva, whom he seeks in the sahasrara. Then do the celestials, the holy men from the eight quarters of space, and the Primal One too come to him.

அண்டங்கள் ஏழும் அகண்டமும் ஆவியுங்
கொண்ட சராசர முற்றுங் குணங்களும்
பண்டை மறையும் படைப்பளிப் பாதியுங்
கண்ட சிவனுமென் கண்ணன்றி யில்லையே. 1871

Then I engross All Creation

The universes seven,
The cosmic space beyond,
The life — animate and inanimate —
The gunas three,
The Vedas ancient,
The Gods that create and preserve

And their Primal Lord that is Siva
—All they are but in me.

The seven universes, the cosmic space beyond them, the animate and inanimate lives, the three gunas, the ancient *Vedas*, the Gods of creation and preservation and their Primal Lord Siva — are all in the yogi himself.

பெண்ணல்ல ஆணல்ல பேடல்ல மூடத்துள்
உள்நின்ற சோதி ஒருவர்க் கறியொண்ணாக்
கண்ணின் றிக்காணுஞ்செவியின்றிக் கேட்டிடும்
அண்ணல் பெருமையை ஆய்ந்து மூப்பே. 1872

Lord Can be seen only with Inner Light

Neither male, nor female, nor hermaphrodite,
The light that is within ignorance concealed
Never, never can cognise Him;
Without eyes He sees,
Without ears He hears,
Only those in Knowledge ripe
Have for sure, seen Him.

The Lord is neither male, nor female, nor hermaphrodite. He sees without eyes. He hears without ears. The ignorant cannot cognize Him. Only those of ripe knowledge have surely seen Him.

இயங்கும் உலகினில் ஈசன் அடியார்
மயங்கா வழிசெல்வர் வானுல காள்வர்
புயங்களு மெண்டிசை போதுபா தாள
மயங்காப் பகிரண்ட மாமுடி தானே 1873

Lord's Devotees Rule the High Heavens

In the world existent
The Lord's devotees pursue the sure path,
They will rule in the heavens high;
They Siva become;
Whose arms stretch embracing directions eight;
In the nether world are His Feet;
In the peaks of the cosmic universe,
The Crown of His Head rises.

The devotees of the Lord pursue the sure path in this world. In the heavens above they will rule. They become Siva whose eight arms embrace the eight directions, whose Feet are in the depths of the nether world and whose crown is in the peaks of the cosmic universe.

அகம்படி கின்றநம் ஐயனை யோரும்
அகம்படி கண்டவர் அல்லலிற் சேரார்
அகம்படி யுட்புக் கறிகின்ற நெஞ்சம்
அகம்படி கண்டாம் அழிக்கலும் எட்டே. 1874

Muse on the Lord and Know no sorrow

Muse on the Lord;
He resides in your heart;
They who see Him residing within
Know sorrows none;
The heart that knows Him enter in,
Loses its ego,
Well may that be destroyed too;
Do strive that state to reach.

The Lord resides in our heart. Those who see Him residing within know not sorrows. The heart that knows His entrance, loses its ego. Strive to reach that state and muse on Him.

கழிவு முதலுங் காதற் றுணையும்
அழிவும் தாய்நின்ற ஆதிப்பிரானைப்
பழியும் புகழும் படுபொருள் முற்றும்
ஒழியுமென் னாவி யுழவுகொண் டானே. 1875

Renounce: God ploughs your Life for a Rich Harvest

He is the Beginning Finite,
He is companion endearing;
He causes dissolution too,
—He, the Lord Primal;
I gave up blame and praise,
And possessions entire;
Then my life, He ploughed
For a harvest abundant.

He is the Primal Lord, the Beginning Finite, of endearing compassion that is the cause of dissolution. The yogi gives up all thought of blame, praise and possessions. Then does the Lord plough his life for an abundant harvest.

என்தாயோ டென்னப்பன் ஏழேழ் பிறவியும்
அன்றே சிவனுக் கெழுதிய ஆவணம்
ஒன்றா யுலகம் படைத்தான் எழுதினான்
நின்றான் முகில் வண்ணன் ஏரெழுந் தாயே. 1876

My Life willed to Siva

He is my mother and father in one
My births seven fold seven are to Siva willed;
—This the document drawn up even in days of yore;
Brahma who this world created wrote it thus;
And Vishnu the cloud-hued witnessed it.

For the yogi, He is mother and father in one. His unnumerable births have been willed away to Siva; and that will was drawn up in the days of yore by Brahma, the creator, Vishnu, the cloud-hued, witnessing.

துணிந்தா ரகம்படி துன்னி உறையும்
பணிந்தா ரகம்படி பாற்பட் டொழுகும்
அணிந்தா ரகம்படி யாதிப் பிரானைக்
கணிந்தா ரொருவர்க்குக் கைவிட லாமே. 1877

Devotees treasure Lord as Heart's Jewel

In the hearts of the resolute He firm abides;
In the hearts of those who adore, He in accord comports
Those who held the Primal Lord as their heart's Jewel

And so reckoned Him
How can they part from Him, ever?

The Lord abides firm in the hearts of the resolute. He comports in accord in the hearts of those who adore Him. Those who have held and reckoned the Primal Lord as their heart's jewel can never give Him up.

தலைமிசை வானவர் தாள்சடை நந்தி
மிலைமிசை வைத்தனன் மெய்ப்பணி செய்யப்
புலைமிசை நீங்கிய பொன்னுல காளும்
பலமிசை செய்யும் படர்சடை யோனே. 1878

Lord lifted me to perform His Holy Work

The Celestial Beings bore on their heads
The Nandi of the flowing matted locks;
He on earth raised me high
His holy work to perform;
Higher still will He lift me,
Like the Golden Kingdom of Purity to rule,
—He of the spreading matted locks.

The celestial beings bore on their heads the Nandi of the flowing matted locks. Nandi raised the yogi high on earth to perform his holy work. The Lord will lift him higher still, to the very golden kingdom of purity to rule.

அறியாப் பருவத் தரனடி யாரைக்
குறியால் அறிந்தின்பங் கொண்ட தடிமை
குறியார் சடைமுடி கட்டி நடப்பார்
மறியார் புனல்மூழ்க மாதவ மாமே. 1879

How Tapasvins Look

In the days of childhood innocence
By their insignia external
I marked out the Holy Ones;
And becoming their devotee, I rejoiced;
Their matted locks tied in signal knot,
Caring not for this world.

In the days of innocent childhood the yogi marked out the holy ones by their external insignia, became their devotee and rejoiced in the act. The holy ones wander with their matted locks tied in signal knot, without a care of this world. They do not return to worldly thoughts. They are immersed in divine, contemplation. This is their intense tapas.

அவன்பால் அணுகியே அன்புசெய் வார்கள்
சிவன்பால் அணுகுதல் செய்யவும் வல்லன்
அவன்பால் அணுகியே நாடு மடியார்
இவன்பாற் பெருமை இலயம தாமே. 1880

Seek Devotees; Seek Siva

They who seek the devotees holy in love endearing
Can in depth Siva seek and be near;
The devotees who the Holy One seek
Will in Siva's greatness merged be.
The Holy ones wander;
They return not to here below;
Immersed are they in the waters of Contemplation
Divine
—This their tapas intense.

They who seek the holy devotees in endearing love, seek in depth and are near to Siva. Such devotees will be merged in Siva's greatness.

முன்னிருந் தார்முழு தெண்கணத் தேவர்கள்
எண்ணிறந் தன்பால் வருவர் இருநிலத்
தெண்ணிரு நாலு திசையந் தரமொக்கப்
பன்னிரு காதம் பதஞ்செய் யும் பாரே. 1881

Celestials Seek the Jnanis

Seeking the Holy ones
The eight clans of Celestial Beings
Swarm the earth in endearment surpassing;
The earth seems like a crowded heaven
For twelve leagues, in directions eight.

The eight orders of celestials beings seek the holy ones and swarm the earth in surpassing endearment. The earth seems like a crowded heaven for a radius of twelve leagues in eight directions.

"Eight" clans of Celestial Beings - this is a way of speaking. The number is not to be taken as exact, unless the lords of eight directions are meant.

சிவயோகி ஞானி செறிந்தஅத் தேசம்
அவயோகம் இன்றி அறிவோருண் டாகும்
நவயோகங் கைகூடு நல்லியல் காணும்
பவயோகம் இன்றிப் பரலோக மாமே. 1882

Land of Siva Jnanis is Blessed

Where Siva Yoga Jnanis flourish
Misfortunes will not be;
New ways of prosperity dawn;
All things good befall;
A very heaven that land will be;
With rebirths none for its denizens.

No misfortune befalls the land where Sivayoga jnanis flourish; in that land the learned will increase, new ways of prosperity will dawn, and all good things will flourish. That land will be nothing but a heaven for its denizens.

மேலுணர் வான்மிகு ஞாலம் படைத்தவன்
மேலுணர் வான்மிகு ஞாலம் கடந்தவன்
மேலுணர் வார்மிகு ஞாலத் தமரர்கள்
மேலுணர் வார்சிவன் மெய்யடி யார்களே. 1883

Greatness of Siva Yoga Jnanis

They who the Higher Knowledge attained,
Can even create this world;
They who the Higher Knowledge attained,
Can transcend worlds several;
They who the Divine Light perceived

Are verily immortals here below;
They indeed are Siva's devotees true.

He who has attained the higher knowledge can even create this world and can transcend several worlds. He who has perceived the divine light is immortal here below. He indeed is the true devotee of Siva.

15. போசன விதி

RULES FOR FEEDING HOLY MEN

எட்டுத் திசையும் இறைவ னடியவர்க்
கட்ட அடிசில் அமுதென் றெதிர்கொள்வர்
ஒட்டி யொருநிலம் ஆள்பவர் அந்நிலம்
விட்டுக் கிடக்கில் விருப்பறி யாரே. *1884*

Lord cares for Siva Jnanis

Wherever it be
The food that is to them offered,
The Lord's devotees receive as sweet ambrosia;
Even as those who own a lone plot of land
Will unhappy be,
If that land uncared for lies.

Will they remain;
Seeking Siva and Siva alone
Will they engrossed ever be.

The Lord's devotees receive as sweet ambrosia whatever food is offered to them. As unhappy as the husbandman feels when the lone piece of land he owns actually lies uncared for, so should one feel when a devotee is left uncared for.

அச்சிவன் உள்நின்ற அருளை அறிந்தவர்
உச்சியம் போதாக வுள்ளமர் கோவிற்குப்
பிச்சை பிடித்துண்டு பேத மறநினைந்
திச்சைவிட் டேகாந்தத் தேறி யிருப்பரே. *1885*

Jnanis accept alms to sustain the Body-Temple

The holy ones who have tasted of Lord's inner grace
Will at noon-tide accept alms
To sustain the body temple where the Lord resides;
Of differences they think not;
All desires extinguished,
They in solitude are seated.

In order to sustain their body-temple where the Lord resides, the holy ones who have savoured the Lord's inner Grace will accept alms at noon-tide. They do not think of differences. They are seated in solitude having extinguished all desires.

16. பிட்சா விதி

RULES FOR RECEIVING ALMS

விச்சுக் கலமுண்டு வேலிச்செய் ஒன்றுண்டு
உச்சிக்கு முன்னே யுழவு சமைந்தது
அச்சங்கெட்டச்செய் அறுத்துண்ணமாட்டாதார்
இச்சைக்குப் பிச்சை இரக்கின்ற வாறே. *1886*

Jnanis harvest the Body-field

In the body-field is the seed;
The field has a fence;
In the crown of the head
The crop ripened;
If without fear they harvest not,
And feed themselves not,
They are but those
Who beg for hunger's sake.

The seed lies in the fenceless body-field (muladhara) The crop ripens in the crown of the head (sahasrara). They who do not harvest the crop are but begging not to eating to appease their hunger.

பிச்சைய தேற்றான் பிரமன் தலைதன்னில்
பிச்சைய தேற்றான் பிரியா அறஞ்செய்யப்
பிச்சைய தேற்றான் பிரமன் சிரங்காட்டிப்
பிச்சைய தேற்றான் பிரமன் பரமாகவே. *1887*

Why Lord Begged

The Lord begged in Brahma's skull,
The Lord begged for Dharma to perpetuate;
The Lord begged in Brahma's skull,
That Brahma to Brahmam become.

The Lord begged in Brahma's skull to perpetuate dharma; so that Brahma may become Brahman.

பரந்துல கேழும் படைத்த பிரானை
இரந்துணி என்பர்கள் எற்றுக் கிரக்கும்
நிரந்தர மாக நினையும் அடியார்
இரந்துண்டு தன்கழல் எட்டச்செய் தானே. *1888*

Why Devotees Beg

The Lord who the seven worlds created
A beggar they call Him?
Why, though, He begs?

That the holy devotees
Who constant think of Him,
Beg and reach His Feet.

The Lord created the seven worlds. Yet they call him a beggar. Why does He beg? He does it, so that the holy devotees, who think of Him constantly, might beg and reach His Feet.

வரவிருந் தான்வழி நின்றிடும் ஈசன்
தரவிருந் தான்தன்னை நல்லவர்க் கின்பம்
பொரவிருந் தான்புக லேபுக லாக
வரவிருந் தாலறி யானென்ப தாமே. *1889*

Lord Waits for His Devotees

The Lord stands waiting
For them that come seeking Him;
For the holy ones He waits
His bliss to bestow;
He stands waiting, them to enter;
Can you say "He knows me not"

The Lord waits for those who come seeking Him. He waits to bestow the bliss on the holy ones. He waits for them to enter. How can one say that he does not know the yogi.

அங்கார் பசியும் அவாவும் வெகுளியுந்
தங்கார் சிவனடி யார்சரீ ரத்திடைப்
பொங்கார் புவனத்தும் புண்ணிய லோகத்துந்
தங்கார் சிவனைத் தலைப்படு வாரே. *1890*

Devotees Constant Seek Siva

Gnawing hunger, greed and anger
These bodily evils
Siva's devotees possess not;
Neither in this world below,
Nor in the blessed world above.

Siva's devotees do not possess such bodily evils as gnawing hunger, greed and anger. They do not remain either in this world or in the next. They are engrossed in seeking Siva and Siva alone.

மெய்யக ஞான மிகந்தெளித் தார்களுங்
கையக நீண்டார் கடைத்தலைக் கேசெல்வர்
ஐயம் புகாமல் இருந்த தவசியார்
வையகம் எல்லாம் வரவிருந்தாரே. *1891*

World Seeks to feed; Tapasvins do not Beg for a Living

Though they received the clear light of Jnana,
Yet they perforce seek portals of the bounteous for alms;
To these Tapasvins that beg not for a living,
All the world in reverence repairs.

Tapasvins, though they have received jnana, go from door to door for alms. All the world will hold these Tapasvins in reverence, for they do not beg for a living.

17. முத்திரை பேதம்
MUDRA VARIATIONS

நாலேழு மாறவே நண்ணிய முத்திரை
பாலான மோன மொழியிற் பதிவித்து
மேலான நந்தி திருவடி மீதுய்யக்
கோலா கலங்கெட்டுக் கூடுநன் முத்தியே. *1892*

Significance of Mudra

The Mudra is to transcend avastas eleven,
Fix awareness on Silent Letter Pranava (Aum)
That the Way is;
And reach the Holy Feet of Nandi;
And all desires worldly quelled
You attain Mukti divine.

Fix the mudra (that directs the eleven sense organs, five jnanendriyas, five karmendriyas, and one manas) on the silent letter, pranava 'Aum.' You will reach the Holy Feet of Nandi, and attain mukti.

துரியங்கண் மூன்றுஞ் சொருகிட னாகி
அரிய வுரைத்தார மங்கே யடக்கி
மருவிய சாம்பவி கேசரி யுண்மை
பெருகிய ஞானம் பிறழ்முத் திரையே. *1893*

Mudras — Sambhavi and Kechari

In the palatal place where the three Turiya states
of awareness subsume,
Insert your tongue inward, and there contain it;
Thus practise the Mudras, Sambhavi and Kechari
Divine Jnana's light to flood.

Insert the tongue inward where the three turiya states of consciousness subsume and contain it there. Thus practise the mudras, sambhavi and kechari. This will result in the flood of divine jnana's light.

சாம்பவி நந்தி தன்னருட் பார்வையாம்
ஆம்பவ மில்லா அருட்பாணி முத்திரை
ஓம்பியல் ஓங்கிய வுண்மைய கேசரி
நாம்பயில் நாதன்மெய்ஞ் ஞானமுத் திரையே. *1894*

Sambhavi Mudra brings Grace and Kechari Jnana

Sambhavi Mudra brings Nandi's glance
In Grace abounding and birth ending
Kechari true where Aum is in silence chanted
Is the Mudra that divine Jnana brings;
That the one I practise, as Natha (Guru) divine.

Sambhavi mudra brings grace and snaps the cycle of birth. Kechari mudra brings jnana.

தானத்தி னுள்ளே சதாசிவ னாயிடும்
ஞானத்தி னுள்ளே நற்சிவ மாதலால்
ஏனைச் சிவமாஞ் சொரூப மறைந்திட்ட
மோனத்து முத்திரை முத்தாந்த முத்தியே. 1895

Mauna Mudra Leads to Mukti Final

He who appears in Adharas is Sadasiva;
He who appears in Jnana is the great Siva;
In the silence of Mauna Mudra, Siva's form disappears;
That verily is the Mukti Finale, the Ultima Thule.

Sadasiva appears in adharas; great Siva appears in jnana. Siva's form vanishes in the silence of mauna mudra Truly that is the finale mukti, the 'ultima thule the last thing.'

வாக்கு மனமும் இரண்டு மவுனமாம்
வாக்கு மவுனத்து வந்தாலு மூங்கையாம்
வாக்கு மனமும் மவுனமாஞ் சுத்தரே
ஆக்குமச் சுத்தத்தை யாரறி வார்களே. 1896

Mauna is Stillness of Both Thought and Speech

To attain stillness of Speech and Thought at once is mauna
Mauna sans Speech alone
Is but state of dumbness;
Only when Speech and Thought are alike in mauna
Are you in State Suddha (Perfection)
Who but knows
That Suddha state to bring about?

Mauna is Stillness of both thought and speech. Mauna, without speech alone is but the state of dumbness. Perfect suddha state is attained only when speech and thought are in mauna.

யோகத்தின் முத்திரை யோரட்ட சித்தியாம்
ஏகத்த ஞானத்து முத்திரை எண்ணுங்கால்
ஆகத் தகுவேத கேசரி சாம்பவி
யோகத்துக் கேசரி யோகமுத் திரையே. 1897

Yoga Mudra and Jnana Mudra

Sambhavi is the lion among Yoga Mudras
That leads certainly to Siddhis eight;
When Jnana Mudra you seek
Appropriate indeed is Kechari
That is by Vedas lauded high.

Sambhavi is the lion among yoga mudras that leads to the eight siddhis. Kechari is the jnana mudra that is lauded high by the *Vedas.*

யோகியெண் சித்தி அருளொலி வாதனை
போகிதண் புத்தி புருடார்த்த நன்னெறி
யாகுநன் சத்தியும் ஆதார சோதனை
ஏகமுங் கண்டொன்றில் எய்தநின் றானே. 1898

Yogi attains Nada State

Yogi attains siddhis eight
He experiences the divine Nada State;
He is of Karma rid
He is of calm mind
He pursues the Four Ends of Human Goal,
He courses the Sakti Kundalini
Through centres six within the body;
That way he reaches the One
And union in Him attains.

The yogi attains the eight siddhis by coursing the kundalini sakti through the six centres within the body and experiences the divine nada state. Rid of karma, he abides in tranquillity and serenity. He pursues the fourth state of sayujya, that is identity in Siva. He reaches the Primal One and stands in union with Him.

துவாதச மார்க்கமென் சோடச மார்க்கமாம்
அவாவறு மீரை வகையங்க மாறுந்
தவாவறு வேதாந்த சித்தாந்தத் தன்மை
நவாவக மோடுன்ன னற்சுத்த சைவமே. 1899

Yoga is the Pure Way of Siddhanta-Vedanta

The Yogic way of Dvadasa
But leads to Sodasa Kala Prasada
It sunders desires;
This the pure way of Vedanta-Siddhanta;
To meditate on the Mantra that begins with "Na" (Nama Sivaya)
That verily is Suddha (pure) Saivam.

The yogic way of dvadasa marga (twelve-stage way) sunders desires. It is but the subtle way of performing pujas with sixteen rituals. It subdues the ten organs — motoria and sensoria — that is the end of Vedanta. Yoga is the pure way of Siddhanta/Vedanta.

It states here that the Yogic Way is Dvadasa (12) and the Kalas Sodasha (16).The authority for the latter number will be found in notes under verses (as moon kalas) ante, but for the former is not directly traceable, unless it implies a relationship between yoga and the zodiacal positions of the sun (cakras).

மோனத்து முத்திரை முத்தர்க்கு முத்திரை
ஞானத்து முத்திரை நாதர்க்கு முத்திரை
தேனிக்கு முத்திரை சித்தாந்த முத்திரை
கானிக்கு முத்திரை கண்ட சமயமே. 1900

All Mudras firm up breath

The Mudra that is Mauna
Is the Mudra for those Mukti seek;
The Mudra that is Jnana (Kechari)
Is the Mudra for those who Gurus be;
Mudra that draws nectar of Grace is the Mudra
That is Siddhanta (Sambhavi)
Mudras all firm up breath,
That Siva Truth, of yore revealed.

Mauna is the mudra for those who seek mukti, jnana (kechari) mudra draws nectar. All mudras firm up the breath.

தூநெறி கண்ட சுவடு நடுவெழும்
பூநெறி கண்டது பொன்னக மாய்நிற்கும்

மேனெறி கண்டது வெண்மதி மேதினி
நீனெறி கண்டுள நின்மல னாமே. *1901*

Pure Vision inside Cranium

In the Sushumna Nadi Central
The Lord's Holy Feet will appear;
The lotus centre (Sahasrara),
Within a Golden Sphere is;
Beyond, the upward course (of Kundalini) lifts you
To the Moon's Sphere that is white;
And there you vision the Pure One.

The Lord's Holy Feet will appear in the central sushumna nadi. Beyond is the sahasrara in the golden mount sphere; the coursing of kundalini further upward lifts the yogi to the white moon's sphere. There he receives the vision of the Pure One.

18. பூரணக்குகைநெறிச் சமாதி

THE SAMADHI CALLED THE PATH TO THE PERFECT CAVE

வளர்பிறை யிற்றேவர் தம்பாலின் மன்னி
உளரொளி பானுவின் உள்ளே யொடுங்கித்
தளர்விற் பிதிர்பதந் தங்கிச் சசியுள்
உளதுறும் யோகி யுடல்விட்டாற் றானே. *1902*

Soul's Journey after Yoga-Samadhi Attained

When the Yogi his mortal coil shuffles,
During the phase when the Crescent moon waxes
He (the soul) shall reach the world of Devas;
There for a while abiding,
Into the Sphere of Sun he subsides;
Thence He reaches the Sphere
Where the Souls of Ancestors dwell;
And from there, finally in the Sphere of Moon, he abides.

When the yogi shuffles his mortal coil, his soul reaches the world of the devas. There abiding for some time, it subsides into the spheres of the sun and reaches the sphere where the souls of ancestors dwell. Finally he abides in the sphere of the moon.

1902-1909

This is a very important chapter, (all 8 verses, 1902-1909) describing as it does what happens when success is achieved in Yoga-Samadhi, and also what failure, total or partial involves.

The subject matter of this chapter, is an important one. It explains why the Jnani's body should not be cremated but buried (1910), and what are the rituals that should accompany the disposal of the body in this manner.

தானிவை யொக்குஞ் சமாதிகை கூடாது
போன வியோகி புகலிடம் போந்துபின்
ஆனவை தீர நிரந்தர மாயோகம்
ஆனவை சேர்வாம் அருளின் சார்வாகியே. *1903*

When Samadhi is not Reached

All these of the Yogi,
This life in Samadhi ended;
When that does not happen,
He will in this world take refuge again,
And by Lord's Grace
Resume Yoga in practice continual
And thus complete the undertaking unfinished.

When the yogi fails to reach samadhi, he will be reborn in this world and by the Lord's Grace will resume and continue yoga practice, until he completes his unfinished undertaking.

தானிவ் வகையே புவியோர் நெறிதங்கி
ஆன சிவயோகத் தாமாறா மவ்விந்து
தானதி லந்தச் சிவயோகி யாகுமுன்
ஊனத்தோர் சித்திவந் தோர்காய மாகுமே. *1904*

Siddha-Hood

Thus in the world they will be
And in Siva Yoga again be;
And as Siva Yogin in Bindu merge,
Many miraculous powers attain;
The Siddha-hood their body reaching.

So remaining in this world, he attains Siva yoga. The Siva yogi merges in bindu sakti and attains many miraculous powers, his fleshy body reaching siddha-hood.

சிவயோகி ஞானி சிதைந்துடல் விட்டால்
தவலோகஞ் சேர்ந்துபின் றான்வந்து கூடிச்
சிவயோக ஞானத்தாற் சேர்ந்தவர் நிற்பர்
புவலோகம் போற்றுநர் புண்ணியத் தோரே. *1905*

Continuity of Yoga through lives

While in the pursuit of Yoga
If Siva Yogins, holy, die,
They reach the World of Tapas
Only to this world return
And to Yoga repair;
Blessed indeed are they,
Whom the Beings Celestial praise high.

If Siva yogis die while in the pursuit of yoga, they reach the world of tapas, only to return to this world. Blessed are they whom the celestial beings esteem high.

ஊனமின் ஞானிநல் யோகி யுடல்விட்டால்
தானற மோனச் சமாதியுள் தங்கியே
தானவ னாகும் பரகாயஞ் சாராதே
ஊனமின் முத்தராய் மீளார் உணர்வுற்றே. *1906*

Mauna Samadhi Leads to the Unitive State

If Sivayogi gives up life,
In mauna Samadhi he enters
To seek the state unitive;
He will not in another body be born,
Nor as Jivan Mukta return
Conscious of here below;
But with Lord get united in one.

Mauna samadhi leads to the unitive state. If the Siva yogi enters in mauna samadhi, he will neither be reborn, nor will remain as jivan mukta. He remains with the Lord in union.

செத்தார் பெறும்பய னாவது ஏதெனில்
செத்துநீர் சேர்வது சித்தினைக் கூடிடில்
செத்தா ரிருந்தார் செகத்தில் திரிமலஞ்
செத்தார் சிவமாகி யேசித்தர் தாமே. 1907

Siddhas even when Dead in Body are Alive in Awareness

Blessed indeed are those who die
If in death they unite one with Lord;
Then, even dead, alive are they;
They who are dead like the Impurities Three
Are Siddhas true,
Siva they become.

Blessed are the siddhas; for if they die they remain one with the Lord. Though dead in body, they are alive in awareness.

உன்னக் கருவிட் டுரவோ னரனருள்
பன்னப் பரவே யருட்குலம் பாலிப்பன்
என்னப் புதல்வர்க்கும் வேண்டி யிடுஞானி
தன்னிச்சைக் கீச னுருச்செய்யுந் தானே. 1908

Jnani Shapes Disciple towards Godhood

Who intense seek the Grace of Lord Exalted
Their birth to sunder,
He himself draws them
Into the fold of His devotees dear;
Like it, the Jnani draws like him
His disciples, in love abounding,
In his own way subtle,
Toward Godhood, He shapes them.

God holds dear the devotees who seek the Grace of the Lord intensely, and sunders the fetters of their births. In a similar manner the jnani draws his disciples in abounding love and in his own subtle way shapes the disciples towards Godhood.

எங்குஞ் சிவமா யருளா மிதயத்துத்
தங்குஞ் சிவஞானிக் கெங்குமாந் தற்பரம்
அங்காங் கெனநின்று சகமுண்ட வான்தோய்தல்
இங்கே யிறந்தெங்கு மாய்நிற்கும் ஈசனே. 1909

Jnani Exists in Siva's Pervasiveness

The heart of Siva Jnani overflows in Grace;
He sees Siva everywhere;
He feels His presence pervasive;
Fragmented may be the sky you see;
But all space it engulfs;
Like it, the Jnani,
Though rid of consciousness here,
One with Siva pervasive exists.

The Siva jnani sees the Lord's Grace overflowing everywhere and he revells in the Lord's omnipresence. Though the sky we see is partial and fragmented, it engulfs the whole of space. Similarly, the jnani, though circumscribed by his body, possesses consciousness that is one with the all pervasive Siva's.

19. சமாதிக் கிரியை

SAMADHI RITUALS

அந்தமின் ஞானிதன் னாகந் தீயினில்
வெந்திடி னாடெலாம் வெப்புத் தீயினில்
நொந்தது நாய்நரி நுகரி னுண்செரு
வந்துநாய் நரிக்குண வாகும்வை யகமே. 1910

Do not Consign Siva Jnani's Body to Fire; Nor Neglect it

If the body of Siva Jnani is to fire consigned,
The people entire will in burning fever suffer;
If his body a prey to dogs and jackals left,
Tumultuous war the land will see,
And the people a prey to dogs and jackals be.

Mantras 1910 & 1911

If the body of the jnani is consigned to fire, the people of the land will burn in high fever. Disasters will follow and the land will be drought-affected without a drop of water. Famine will ravish the land creating numerous ravages in its train. If the jnani's body is left a prey to dogs and jackals, tumultuous war will seize the land.

எண்ணிலா ஞானி யுடலெரி தாவிடில்
அண்ணல்தங் கோயில் அழலிட்ட தாங்கொக்கும்
மண்ணின் மழைவிழா வையகம் பஞ்சமாம்
எண்ணரு மன்னர் இழப்பார் அரசே. 1911

Disasters Follow if Jnani's Body is Consigned To Fire

If to fire the Jnani's body is consigned
That will be like fire the Lord's temple consigned;
No more will rains fall on the land,

Famine shall ravish the world,
Countless kings will their kingdoms lose.

புண்ணிய மாமவர் தம்மைப் புதைப்பது
நண்ணி யனல்கோக்கில் நாட்டில் அழிவாகும்
மண்ணி லழியில் அலங்கார பங்கமாம்
மண்ணுலகெல்லா மயங்குமனல் மண்டியே. *1912*

Bury Jnani's Body in Proper Way

Proper indeed it is to bury them;
If to fire they are consigned
Destruction dogs the land;
If left to perish, uncared for,
The world its prosperity loses,
A fell prey to devastating fires.

Mantras 1912 & 1913

The proper thing to do is to bury the jnani's body in the way the Agamic scriptures have laid down. Then many blessings will be conferred on the rulers and the people of the land.

அந்தமில் ஞானி அருளை அடைந்தக்கால்
அந்த வுடல்தான் குகைசெய் திருந்திடில்
சுந்தர மன்னருந்தொல்புவி யுள்ளோரும்
அந்தமில் இன்ப அருள்பெறு வாரே. *1913*

Bury Jnani's Body in an Urderground Sepulchure

Let the body of Jnani,
When Lord's Grace receives,
Be in a cave seated,
Appropriate in earth's bowel dug;
Then stately rulers and people in land
Receive blessings,
Of Grace infinite.

நவமிகு சாணாலே நல்லாழஞ் செய்து
குவைமிகு சூழவைஞ் சாணாகக் கோட்டித்
தவமிகு குகைமுக் கோணமுச் சாணாக்கிப்
பவமறு நற்குகை பத்மா சனமே. *1914*

Samadhi Rituals

Well dig the sepulchure,
Heap the earth five cubits around,
Shape it into a triangle
Three cubits on sides;
And there in Padmasana,
Seat the body.

தன்மனை சாலை குளங்கரை யாற்றிடை
நன்மலர்ச் சோலை நகரினற் பூமி
உன்னருங் கானம் உயர்ந்த மலைச்சாரல்
இந்நிலந் தான்குகைக்கெய்தும் இடங்களே. *1915*

Locations for Samadhi Cave

One's own homestead, roadside, tank bund, riverbed,
Flowery grove, city's common
Forest dense, and mountain valley high
—These the sites appropriate,
For the sepulchure to shape.

One's own homestead, roadside, tank bund, riverbed, wooded grove, city's common, dense forest and high mountain valleys—these are the appropriate locations for a samadhi.

நற்குகை நால்வட்டம் பஞ்சாங்க பாதமாய்
நிற்கின்ற பாத நவபாத நேர்விழப்
பொற்பம ரோசமும் மூன்றுக்கு மூன்றணி
நிற்பவர் தாஞ்செய்யும் நேர்மைய தாமே. *1916*

Dimension For the Sepulchure Cave

Five feet on four sides all,
Nine feet straight deep,
Three feet each on the triangle's sides
—These the dimensions,
Appropriate for the sepulchure to shape.

The sepulchure should have the correct dimensions — five feet on all the four sides, nine feet deep, and three feet each on the inner triangle's sides at the base.

பஞ்ச லோகங்கள் நவமணி பாரித்து
விஞ்சப் படுத்ததன் மேலா சனமிட்டு
முஞ்சி படுத்துவெண் ணீறிட் டதன்மேலே
பொன்செய்த நற்சுண்ணம் பொதியலு மாமே. *1917*

Samadhi Rituals

In abundance spread the five metals precious
And the nine gems rare;
Upon them place the seat,
Scatter the Kusha grass,
And shower the holy ashes white;
Above that scatter
Turmeric powder that is of colour gold
And incenses richly mixed.

Spread the five precious metals and the nine rare gems within the cave. Place the seat. Upon that, scatter kusa grass and shower with white holy ashes. Above them scatter the golden-coloured turmeric powder mixed with incenses.

நள்குகை நால்வட்டம் படுத்ததன் மேற்சாரக்
கள்ளவிழ் தாமங் களபங்கத் தூரியுந்
தெள்ளிய சாந்து புழுகுபன் னீர்சேர்த்து
ஒள்ளிய தூபம் உவந்திடு வீரே. *1918*

Samadhi Rituals (Cont.)

Shape the cave inside into a square,
Upon that lay garlands of honey-dew flowers;
Sandal, musk, civet, and unguents diverse;
And pouring rose water
Light the ritual lamp, in devotion ecstatic.

Lay garlands of honey-dew flowers, sandal, musk, civet and diverse unguents upon the cave that is square-shaped inside.

Sprinkling rose water, light the ritual lamp with devotion and affection.

ஓதிடும் வெண்ணீற்றால் உத்தூளங் குப்பாய
மீதினி லிட்டா சனத்தினின் மேல்வைத்துப்
போதறு சுண்ணமும் நீறும் பொலிவித்து
மீதி லிருத்தி விரித்திடு வீரே. 1919

Samadhi Rituals (Cont.)

Smear the body entire with ashes white and holy
To form a shroud protective;
Place the body on an Asana (seat) appropriate,
Spangle bright with incenses several and ashes holy;
And thus seated, cover the cave with earth.

The white holy ashes will form a protective shroud over the entire body. Then place the body in an appropriate asana (posture). Thus seated, cover the cave with earth.

விரித்தபின் னாற்சாரு மேவுதல் செய்து
பொரித்த கறிபோ னகமிள நீருங்
குருத்தலம் வைத்தோர் குழைமுகம் பார்வை
தரித்தபின் மேல்வட்டஞ் சாத்திடு வீரே. 1920

Samadhi Rituals (Cont.)

Having covered thus, level the four sides;
Place his sandals and ear rings,
And an image with face and eyes
Decked in dress appropriate;
Offer parched rice, food, and tender coconut.

Having covered him thus, place his sandals, ear rings and an image with face and eyes decked in suitable dress. Also offer parched rice, food and a tender coconut.

மீது சொரிந்திடும் வெண்ணீறுஞ் சுண்ணமும்
போது பலகொண்டு தர்ப்பைப்புல் வில்வமும்
பாத வுதகத்தான் மஞ்சனஞ் செய்துபார்
மீதுமூன் றுக்குமூன் றணிநிலஞ் செய்யுமே. 1921

Samadhi Rituals (Cont.)

Then pour the ashes white and powdered incense,
Shower flowers diverse, Kusha grass and Bilva leaves,
Sprinkle water holy,
And raise a platform three feet by three.

Finally pour some holy ashes and holy water upon the diverse flowers, kusa grass and bilva leaves that are overspread, and raise a platform three feet by three.

ஆதன மீதில் அரசு சிவலிங்கம்
போதும் இரண்டினில் ஒன்றைத்தா பித்து
மேதகு சந்நிதி மேவுத் தரம்பூர்வங்
காதலிற் சோடசங் காணுப சாரமே. 1922

Samadhi Pujas

Upon the platform plant
The sapling of peepal tree, or a Lingam holy,
Arrange the Sannidhi (face) toward north or east,
And perform pujas with rituals sixteen,
In devotion endearing.

Plant the sapling of a peepal tree or a holy lingam on the platform, with the sannidhi (face) toward north or east. Then perform pujas with sixteen items in endearing devotion.

20. விந்துற்பனம்

RISE OF BINDU

உதயத்தில் விந்துவில் ஓங்குகுண் டலியும்
உதயக் குடிலில் வயிந்தவம் ஒன்பான்
விதியிற் பிரமாதி கள்மிகு சத்தி
கதியிற் கரணங் கலைவை கரியே. 1923

Evolutes of Bindu

When Creation commenced,
From Para Bindu arose Kundalini
And from Kudilai the Vaindavam in the firmament vast
And the nine gods Brahma and the rest
And their Saktis
And in order corresponding
The Karanas, the Kalas and the sound Vaikari (Nada).

When creation began, kundalini arose from parabindu and from kudalai arose the vaindavams, the nine gods Brahma and the rest with their Shaktis the karmas, the kalas and the sound vaikari.

1) Kundalini, kudilai, tatparai, vagesi are emanations of parabindu.
2) Nine vaindavams are the emanations of parabindu — the four above (i.e., kundalini etc) and the five gods: Sadasiva, Brahma, Vishnu, Rudra, and Mahesvara.
3) Saktis-Saktis of these five Gods.
4) Karanas—the intellectual organs: manas, buddhi, chitta, and ahamkara.
5) Kalas—five kala tattvas.
6) Vaikari—the unmanifested sound.

1923-1936

This chapter of 14 verses (1923 to 1936) is also full of metaphysical concepts, dealing specially with cosmogony viewed from the special angle of evolutes as Bindu and Nada of the Primal Cause.

The contents of this chapter follow naturally from the preceding one. Man is called upon to simulate (imitative magic) the creative process of cosmic Bindu and Nada.

செய்திடும் விந்துபே தத்திறன் ஐயைந்துஞ்
செய்திடு நாதபே தத்திற் னாலாறுஞ்
செய்திடு மற்றவை யீரிரண் டிற்றிறஞ்
செய்திடு மாறாது சேர்தத் துவங்களே. 1924

Thirty Six Tattvas Evolute

Bindu attains modification five times five (twenty-five)
Nada attains modification four and six (ten)
The, rest two — Sakti and Siva — attain no modification
But activate the other two — Bindu and Nada.

Sakti and Siva attain no modifications, but active the other two — bindu and nada — which attain twenty-five and ten modifications (as atma tattvas and higher tattvas) respectively.

1) 25 Evolutes of parabindu are: the nine vaindavams, the five saktis of the five Gods; four intellectual organs; five kala tattvas; vaikhari, the unmanifest sound; and niyati tattva evolutes of nada are: 1. kala (time); 2. vidya (knowledge); 3. raga (desire); 4. purusha (the experience of the soul); 5. maya (illusion) and the five suddha tattvas — suddha vidya, isvaram, sadakyam, Sakti and Siva.

வந்திடு பேத மெலாம்பர விந்து
தந்திடு மாமாயை வாகேசி தற்பரை
உந்து குடிலையோ டேமுறு குண்டலி
விந்துவில் இந்நான்கு மேவா விளங்குமே. 1925

Saktis evolve from Bindu

Out of the Mamaya
Para Bindu gives rise to—
All these manifestations
Vagesi, Tatparai, Kudilai and Kundalini;
These Saktis four ultimate from Bindu evolve.

The saktis — vagesi, tatparai, kudilai and kundalini evolve from bindu.

விளங்கு நிவிர்த்தாதி மேவக ராதி
வளங்கொள் உகார மகாரத் துள்விந்து
களங்கமில் நாதாந்தங் கண்ணினுள் நண்ணி
உளங்கொள் மனாதியுள் அந்தமு மாமே. 1926

Kalas Nada and Karanas evolve

The Kalas Nivirti and the rest,'
In which repose sounds, "A", "U" and "M" composed
There in Nadanta Bindu enters
And into the Karanas that include the Mind
And the internal organs intellectual
Evolve manifesting these
The Bindu its act of creation ceases.

The kalas (nivirthi and the rest in which the sounds, 'A,' 'U,' and 'M' repose), the karanas (that include the mind and the internal intellectual organs) and nada evolve from bindu.

1) Nivirtikala — this dispels doubts of the jivas who reach its sphere.
Pratista kala — firms up the jiva in truth.
Vidya kala — confers jnana.
Santi kala — confers equipoise.
Santyatita kala — confers manifestness (svarupa) beyond equipose.

அந்தமும் ஆதியு மாகிப் பராபரன்
வந்த வியாபி யெனலாய வந்நெறி
கந்தம தாகிய காரண காரியந்
தந்தைங் கருமமுந் தான்செய்யும் வீயமே. 1927

Bindu is the Causal Seed of Five Acts

The Parapara that is the End and the Beginning
Immanent, He expands thus;
As Cause and Effect, too, well He is;
And as Bija
The Five Acts performs.

Mantras 1927 & 1928

The Parapara is the end and the beginning, and immanently abides. Bija is the causal seed of the Five Acts too. The cosmic universe arose by the power of bija. Bija is the macro and the micro causal seed.

வீயம தாகிய விந்துவின் சத்தியால்
ஆய வகண்டமும் அண்டமும் பாரிப்பக்
காயஜம் பூதமுங் காரிய மாயையில்
ஆயிட விந்து அகம்புற மாகுமே. 1928

Bija is the Macro and Micro Causal Seed

By the power of Bija that from Bindu emanated
The world and the cosmic universe arose
From out of Causal (Asuddha) Maya (Stuff of matter)
Arose the elements five — the sky and the rest;
And this Bindu, micro and macro, is.

புறமகம் எங்கும் புகுந்தொளிர் விந்து
நிறமது வெண்மை நிகழ்நாதஞ் செம்மை
உறமகிழ் சத்தி சிவபாத மாயுட்
டிறனொடு வீடளிக் குஞ்செயற் கொண்டே. 1929

Bindu is White and Nada Red

The Bindu that shines
Within the body and without (in all Nature)
Is white in hue;
Red is vibrant Nada;
As Sakti and Siva embedded within
Well can they Mukti grant,
If in wisdom activated.

Bindu is white in hue, shining within and without the body, and in all nature. Nada that is vibrant is red-hued. They are Siva and Sakti embedded within. They can well grant mukti.

கொண்டஇவ் விந்து பரமம்போற் கோதற
நின்ற படங்கட மாய்நிலை நிற்றலிற்
தண்டக லாதியின் காரண காரியத்
தண்டம் அனைத்துமாய் மாமாயை யாகுமே. 1930

Bindu is Cause-Effect

All-pervasive like the Param
The Bindu stands;
Veiling all like a filament vast;
And filling everywhere as the space in pots all;
As Mamaya that is Cause and Effect
It all cosmos pervades.

Bindu stands with the all-pervasive Param; bindu as mamaya is the cause and effect, and it pervades all the cosmos.

அதுவித்தி லேநின்றங் கண்ணிக்கு நந்தி
இதுவித்தி லேயுள வாற்றை யுணரார்
மதுவித்தி லேமல ரன்னம தாகிப்
பொதுவித்தி லேநின்ற புண்ணியன் தானே. 1931

Bindu is the Seed in the body and Divine Swan in Cosmos

There in the Bindu,
Nandi stands His Grace to bestow;
That it is in their Bija within, they know not;
That Seed as scented flower in the (body) into microcosm blossoms
As a Divine Swan So-ham in the macrocosm it is;
He the Blessed One that is the Causal Seed of all.

Nandi stands in the bindu to bestow His manifold blessings and Grace. They do not know that bindu is the seed that blossoms as a scented flower in the body and a divine swan in the cosmos. Bija is the blessed one, that is the causal seed of all.

வித்தினி லன்றி முளையில்லை அம்முளை
வித்தினி லன்றி வெளிப்படு மாறில்லை
வித்தும் முளையும் உடனன்றி வேறல்ல
அத்தன்மை யாகும் அரனெறி காணுமே. 1932

Siva is Seed, Bindu is Embryo

Without seed is embryo none,
Except from seed the embryo appears not;
The seed and the embryo are but one, separate never;
Thus are the Bindu and Siva too;
This you should know.

Seed and embryo are inseparable. Without the one the other cannot fructify or survive. Siva is the seed, and bindu is the embryo.

அருந்திய வன்ன மவைமூன்று கூறாம்
பொருந்து முடன்மனம் போமல மென்னத்
திருந்து முடன்மன மாங்கூறு சேர்ந்திட்
டிருந்தன முன்னாள் இரதம தாகுமே. 1933

How Food Builds Body, Blood and Mind

The food you partake in divisions three go
To the body, to the mind and to the excreta;
The parts that to the body and the mind go
Verily become the blood, first.

The food you take goes in three directions — to the body, to the mind, and to the excreta.

இரத முதலான ஏழ்தாது மூன்றின்
உரிய தினத்தின் ஒருபுற் பனிபோல்
அரிய துளிவிந்து வாகுமேழ் மூன்றின்
மருவிய விந்து வளருங்கா யத்திலே. 1934

How Bindu is Formed From Food

Out of the seven constituents food breaks into,
(Blood, lymph, bone, skin, flesh, brain and semen)
The Bindu forms in days three
Like the tiny dew drop on a blade of grass;
And full matures in days three times seven.

Blood, lymph, bone, skin, flesh, brain and semen are the seven products of food. The bindu that is formed like the tiny drop on a blade of grass matures seven times in three days.

காயத்தி லேமூன்று நாளிற் கலந்திட்டுக்
காயத்துட் டன்மன மாகுங் கலாவிந்து
நேயத்தே நின்றோர்க்கு நீங்கா விடாமையின்
மாயத்தே செல்வோர் மனத்தோ டழியுமே. 1935

Bindu is Transformed into Mind and Kalas

When in the body for three days it remains thus,
It becomes a part of the Mind;
As Kala Bright — Intelligence illumined;
For those immersed in thoughts holy, it is there retained;
For those who in sex intercourse indulge,
It will depart, their mental powers deterioi e

Remaining thus in the body for three days, it becomes of the mind, as shining kalas. They who are steep profound holy thoughts will retain it.

அழிகின்ற விந்து அளவை யறியார்
கழிகின்ற தன்னையுட் காக்கலுந் தேரார்
அழிகின்ற காயத் தழிந்தயர் வுற்றோர்
அழிகின்ற தன்மை யறிந்தொழி யாரே. 1936

Waste Bindu, the Body Perishes

They know not the destruction that wasting of Bindu results in;
They resolve not their decay to prevent by will power determined;
They who thus perish in this perishing body
Know not the way they perish;
And give it up not.

21. விந்துசயம்-போகசரவோட்டம்

CONQUEST OF BINDU — REGULATION OF BINDU FLOW

பார்க்கின்ற மாதரைப் பாரா தகன்றுபோய்
ஓர்க்கின்ற வுள்ளம் உருக அழல்மூட்டிப்
பார்க்கின்ற கண்ணாசை பாழ்பட மூலத்தே
சேர்க்கின்ற யோகி சிவயோகி தானே. *1937*

Siva Yogi Sublimates Bindu

Do not look at women
Who intent on lust look at you;
Away from them;
Light the fire of Kundalini;
Melt your heart in divine love;
Uproot the evil desire that sight kindles;
Fix it on the source of Primal Energy
He who does it is verily the Siva Yogi.

Do not indulge in lust. Light the kundalini fire and melt your heart in intense devotion. Eradicate the base desires that sight kindles. Concentrate on the source of primal energy. Truly, the Siva yogi sublimates bindu in this way.

தானே யருளாற் சிவயோகந் தங்காது
தானேயக் காமாதி தங்குவோ னும்முட்குந்
தானே யதிகாரந் தங்கிற் சடங்கெடும்
ஊனே யவற்றுள் ளுயிரோம்பா மாயுமே. *1938*

Waste Not Bindu

He to lust a slave becomes,
Will in constant fear be;
His body deteriorates,
And his life ebbs away;
He will not Grace receive,
And in Siva Yoga lasts not.

He who falls a prey to lust is forever in fear. His body deteriorates. He will not receive Grace, or reach Siva yoga.

மாயாள் வசத்தே சென்றிவர் வேண்டில்
ஓயா இருபக்கத் துள்வளர் பக்கத்துள்
ஏயாவெண் ணாளின்ப் மேற்பனி மூன்றிரண்
டாயா அபரத்து ளாதிநாள் ஆறாமே. *1939*

Regulation Days for Sexual Union

Those who wish to sleep with women
Let them observe the periodicity thus;
Of the two phases of the moon,
The first eight days of the waxing moon
For union appropriate are not;
In the six days that remain,
And in the first six days of the waning moon
Can they in union be.

The first eight days of the waxing moon are not appropriate for sexual union. The last six days of the waxing moon and the first ten days of the waning moon are the suitable days for this union.

ஆறைந்து பன்னொன்று மன்றிச் சகமார்க்கம்
வேறன்பு வேண்டுவோர் பூவரிற்பின்னந்தோ
டேறும் இருபத் தொருநா ளிடைத்தோங்கும்
ஆறின் மிகுத்தோங்கும் அக்காலஞ் செய்யவே. *1940*

Regulation Days for Practising Yogis

Let those that Yoga practise
Avoid the fifth, the sixth and the eleventh days
After the woman menstruates;
The rest, who the pleasure seek,
Take the six days, in the middle
Of the three weeks that follow.

The fifth, sixth and the eleventh days after the woman menstruates are not fit for performing the sex act. The six days in the middle of the three weeks that follow are appropriate to seek pleasure.

செய்யும் அளவில் திருநான் முகூர்த்தமே
எய்யுங் கலைகாலம் இந்து பருதிகால்
நையுமிடத் தோடி னன்காம நூல்நெறி
செய்க வலமிடந் தீர்ந்து விடுக்கவே. *1941*

Duration of Sexual Union and Rules for Release of Bindu

When on union they decide on,
Let it be for muhurtas four,
Following the injunctions of Kama Sastras,
Let them the sexual act perform;
When the Moon's Kalas (Left Nadi) shine bright,
And breath in Sun Nadi's low runs
Emit Bindu, the breath holding,
Breathing through nostril right, quelling left.

The union they decide on should be for four muhurtas, following the injunction of the *Kama Sastras*. When the moon's kalas (left nadi) shine bright, emit bindu holding your breath.

'Bindu' here is Semen.

Moon's Kala is here the Pingala Nadi, and Sun's Kala is Ida Nadi.

விடுங்காண் முனைந்திந் திரியங்களைப்போல்
நடுங்கா திருப்பானும் ஐயைந்து நண்ணப்
படுங்காதன் மாதின்பாற் பற்றற விட்டுக்
கடுங்காற் கரணங் கருத்துறக் கொண்டே. *1942*

Sublimate Sex Act

Embrace the damsel,
Your five sense organs with her five conjoining;
But, detached your passion for the women be;

Like the senses that are Godward sublimated
Be calm; excited be not;
Control your breath, senses and mind,
Concentrated be your thought,
Thus emit your Bindu.

Mantras 1942 & 1943

Embrace the damsel and unite your five senses with hers. But remain detached. Divert your thoughts Godward, be calm and do not get excited. Direct your senses inward.

கொண்ட குணனே நலனேநற் கோமளம்
பண்டை யுருவே பகர்வாய் பவளமே
மிண்டு தனமே மிடைய விடும்போதிற்
கண்ட கரணமுட் செல்லக்கண் டேவிடே. *1943*

Direct your senses Inward

Amour, beauty and youth
Shapely form and coral lips
And breasts that swell,
—When in union with damsel such as she—
You the Bindu emit,
Emit, your senses inward directed.

விட்டபின் கர்ப்பவுற் பத்தி விதியிலே
தொட்டுறுங் காலங்கள் தோன்றக் கருதிய
கட்டிய வாணாள்சா நாள்குணங் கீழ்மைசீர்ப்
பட்ட நெறியிதென் றெண்ணியும் பார்க்கவே. *1944*

Determine the Results of the Act

Having emitted,
Examine the laws of conception
The time of union, of pregnancy and delivery
The baby's length of life, and death;
Its character, good and bad,
These you in detail determine.

Having emitted, examine the laws of conception and determine the results of the act — the time of union of pregnancy, delivery and the baby's destined length of life and time of death.

பார்த்திட்டு வைத்துப் பரப்பற் றுருப்பெற்று
வார்ச்செற்ற கொங்கை மடந்தையை நீக்கியே
சேர்த்துற் றிருதிங்கள் சேரா தகலினும்
மூப்புற்றே பின்னாளி லாமெல்லா முள்ளவே. *1945*

Seek not Further Union

Having examined these,
Abstain from worldly concerns,
And leave the maiden of shapely breasts;
And further union seek not;
Within months two
Will the baby its form take,
And all the rest you have reckoned follow.

Having examined these, abstain from the maiden do not seek further union.

வித்திடு வோர்க்கன்றி மேலோர் விளைவில்லை
வித்திடு வோர்க்கன்றி மிக்கோ ரறிவில்லை
வித்தினில் வித்தை விதற வுணர்வரேல்
மத்தி லிருந்ததோர் மாங்கனி யாமே. *1946*

Know the Seed of Seed and Preserve Body

Except for those who plant the seed,
Harvest there be none in future;
Except for those who plant the seed,
Wisdom great there be none;
If they know the Seed of seed for certain
Preserved their body be
Unto the mango fruit kept in vessel suspended.

Only they who plant the seed will reap the harvest and receive great wisdom. So, know the seed of seed; your body will be preserved like a mango fruit kept in a hanging vessel.

கருத்தினில் அக்கர மாயுவு மியாவுங்
கருத்துளன் ஈசன் கருவுயி ரோடுங்
கருத்தது வித்தாய்க் காரண காரியங்
கருத்துறு மாறிவை கற்பனை தானே. *1947*

Lord Settles Fate and longevity of Embryo With Concern

The Lord has concern great
For the seed in womb;
Even in the seed with forethought
He settles its fate and span of life;
Thus, when the Seed itself is the Causal Thought,
To attribute Cause and Effect to factors outside
Is but imagination's figment.

The Lord is very much concerned about the seed in the womb, and He settles its fate and span of life.

ஒழியாத விந்து வுடன்நிற்க நிற்கும்
அழியாப் பிராணன் அதிபலஞ் சத்தி
ஒழியாத புத்தி தபஞ்செப மோனம்
அழியாத சித்தியுண் டாம்விந்து வற்றிலே. *1948*

Conserve Bindu and Attain Siddhis

If Bindu stands retained in body
Life ebbs not;
Great strength, energy, intelligence alert,
Tapas, contemplation and silence
And siddhis enduring,
—All these are attained,
—If Bindu be conserved true.

வற்ற அனலைக் கொளுவி மறித்தேற்றித்
துற்ற சுழியனல் சொருகிச் சுடருற்று
முற்று மதியத் தமுதை முறைமுறை
செற்றுண் பவரே சிவயோகி யாரே. *1949*

Conservation of Sex Energy Vital for Yoga Practice

Thus conserved, they light the Fire of Kundalini,

And forcing it upward through Nadi Sushumna
Reach the state of illumination;
There they partake of the ambrosia
From the Moon within flows;
Those who do this in unbroken continuity,
Are verily Siva Yogins true.

Thus by conserving the sex energy, the yogis light the fire of kundalini, and coursing it upward through the sushumna nadi they reach the state of illumination. Siva yogins are they indeed who continuously partake of the ambrosia flowing from the moon in the mystic sphere within.

யோகியும் ஞானியும் உத்தம சித்தனும்
யோகியும் ஞான புரந்தர னாவோனும்
மோக முறினு முரையமிர் துண்போனும்
ஆகிய விந்து அழியாத அண்ணலே. 1950

Conserve Sex Energy and Become Heroes

The Yogi, the Jnani, and the Siddha high
The Bhoga Yogi who is yet the king of Jnanis,
All these, though troubled by passions
Yet savour the ambrosia within; (in the Yogic way)
Heroes, all, they are indeed,
Who the Bindu had conserved.

The yogi, the jnani, the siddhar high and the bhoga-yogi, who is yet the king of jnanis, are real heroes; because, though they were troubled and tempted by passions, they resolved to taste the ambrosia within in the yogic way.

அண்ணல் உடலாகி யவ்வனல் விந்துவும்
மண்ணிடை மாய்க்கும் பிராணனாம் விந்துவுங்
கண்ணுங் கனலிடைக் கட்டிக் கலந்தெரித்
துண்ணில் அமிர்தாகி யோகிக் கறிவாமே. 1951

Burn Bindu in Fire of Kundalini

The fiery Bindu above is Lord's Body (macrocosmic)
The Bindu wasted here below is vital Prana (microcosmic)
If mixing the two, they burn it in the Fire of Kundalini
Then they consume the very ambrosia
—This, the wisdom of Yogis true.

The Lord's body is the fiery bindu above (macrocosmic), and the bindu wasted below is the vital prana (microcosmic). If these two are mixed, and burnt in the kundalini fire, the yogis consume the very elixir of life. This is the true wisdom of yogis.

அறியா தழிகின்ற வாதலால் நாளும்
பொறியால் அழிந்து புலம்புகின் றார்கள்
அறிவாய் நனவி லதீதம் புரியச்
செறிவா யிருந்து சேரவே மாயுமே. 1952

In Yoga Bindu is Divinely Assimilated

In ignorance the folks waste it daily,
And destroyed by senses, in pain weep;
If in wisdom, they conscious perform Yoga supreme,
The Bindu disappears, divinely assimilated.

Mantras 1952 & 1953

Ignorant folks destroy bindu in vain daily. But if in wisdom they perform supreme yoga, bindu is divinely assimilated. So, refrain from lust, for it is death's messenger. Preserve bindu. Then you will enjoy the divine light for ages and ages to come, remaining free from impurities.

மாதரை மாய வருங்கூற்ற மென்றுன்னக்
காதல தாகிய காமங் கழிந்திடுஞ்
சாதலு மில்லை சதகோடி யாண்டினுஞ்
சோதியி னுள்ளே துரிசறுங் காலமே. 1953

Lust is Death's Messenger

If you hold women as Death's messengers,
Love's passion vanishes away;
Death there is none;
For ages innumerable will you in Divine Light be,
Your Impurities forever totally rid.

காலங் கடந்தவன் காண்விந்து செற்றவன்
காலங் கடந்தழிந் தான்விந்து செற்றவன்
காலங் களின்விந்து செற்றுற்ற காரிகை
காலின்கண் வந்த கலப்பறி யாரே. 1954

Conquer Bindu and Conquer Time

He that has conquered Bindu has conquered Time;
He that has wasted Bindu has perished before his time;
They know not that Bindu that has been preserved
In time becomes one with Kundalini,
Their breath controlled in the Yogic way.

Conquer bindu; for that helps to conquer time. The bindu that has been preserved merges with kundalini in time, and the breath that will be controlled in the yogic way will checkmate death.

கலக்குநாள் முன்னாள் தன்னிடைக் காதல்
நலத்தக வேண்டில்அந் நாரியுதரக்
கலத்தின் மலத்தைத்தண் சீதத்தைப் பித்தை
விலக்கு வனசெய்து மேலணை வீரே. 1955

Embrace Woman after Cleansing Her

If you desire woman's love, intense to excite,
The day before you in sexual union indulge,
Cleanse the woman of her bowel, phlegm and bile,
Then in union embrace her.

மேலா நிலத்தெழு விந்துவும் நாதமுங்
கோலால் நடத்திக் குறிவழி யேசென்று
பாலாம் அமிர்துண்டு பற்றறப் பற்றினால்
மாலா னதுமாள மாளுமவ் விந்துவே. 1956

Bindu is Assimilated in Body Through Yoga

Direct Prana breath to Bindu and Nada

That in cranium Sphere arises,
Upward through Sushumna Nadi
By devices appropriate;
Thus you reach to the nectar divine;
Hold on to it,
That Bindu in you indissolubly dissolves,
Your illusions to disappear.

Divert prana through the sushumna nadi to (para) bindu and nada that are in the cranium sphere. The sweet ambrosia flows; hold on to it. Thus is the semenal bindu assimilated in the body through yoga.

விந்து விளையும் விளைவின் பயன்முற்றும்
அந்த வழிவும் அடக்கத்தில் ஆக்கமும்
நந்திய நாதமும் நாதத்தாற் பேதமுந்
தந்துணர் வோர்க்குச் சயமாகும் விந்துவே. 1957

Conquest of Bindu Leads to Nada

The ripening of Bindu,
The result full of that ripening,
The dire consequences of wasting it,
And the blessings of retaining it,
The Nada that ensues
And the transformation that Nada effects,
—Those who all these realize
Have verily conquered the Bindu.

The conquest of bindu truly leads to nada which effects transformations.

விந்துவென் வீசத்தை மேவிய மூலத்து
நந்திய அங்கியி னாலே நயந்தெரித்
தந்தமில் பானு அதிகண்ட மேலேற்றிச்
சந்திரன் சார்புறத் தண்ணமு தாமே. 1958

Fry Bindu in Kundalini Fire

The Bindu that is Bija (Seed)
Burn it agreeably,
In the Fire that is Kundalini,
That from Muladhara flames;
Course it upward into the Solar Sphere within
And touch the Lunar Sphere beyond;
There, indeed, is the nectar divine.

Burn the semenal bindu in kundalini fire that flames from muladhara. Course it upward into the solar sphere and touch the lunar sphere beyond, where divine ambrosia is present.

அமுதச் சசிவிந்து வாம்விந்து மாள
அமுதப் புனலோடி அங்கியின் மாள
அமுதச் சிவபோகம் ஆதலாற் சித்தி
அமுதப் பலாவன மாங்குறும் யோகிக்கே. 1959

Bindu Sublimated by Kundalini Yoga Leads to Ambrosial Flow

When the Bindu of the body
Thus perishes (by Yoga)
It is into Divine Bindu transformed
Of the ambrosial Lunar Sphere within;
When the Bindu of the body
Perishes in the fire of Kundalini,
The ambrosial waters flow and fill the body;
Then indeed is Siva Bhoga that is ambrosial sweet;
And thus bathed in divine waters of ambrosia
The Yogi attains Siddhis rare.

When the human bindu is destroyed thus, it is changed into divine bindu. Bindu of the body is sublimated by kundalini yoga that draws the ambrosial flow. Indeed, that is Siva bhoga. By immersion in the divine waters of ambrosia, the yogi attains rare siddhis.

யோகமவ் விந்து ஒழியா வகைபுணர்ந்
தாகம் இரண்டுங் கலந்தாலு மாங்குறாப்
போகஞ் சிவபோகம் போகிநற் போகமா
மோகங் கெடமுயங் கார்மூடர் மாதர்க்கே. 1960

In Yoga Way Bindu is not Released

Two bodies in union may unite,
Yet if he emits not Bindu
That union is Yoga way;
That Bhoga is Siva Bhoga;
That the true Bhoga
Where the Yogi emits not
To quell the witless woman's passion.

The two bodies, male and female, may unite if bindu is not emitted — that union is of the yoga way. That bhoga is Siva bhoga.

மாதரி டத்தே செலுத்தினும் அவ்விந்து
காதலி னால்விடார் யோகங் கலந்தவர்
மாதர் உயிராசை கைக்கொண்டே வாடுவர்
காதலர் போன்றங்ஙன் காதலாஞ் சாற்றிலே. 1961

Bindu is not Emitted

They who stand in Yoga way
Even though with women unite,
Their Bindu, in passion, they emit not;
And the women their life's passion unquenched
Will verily pine and droop,
Yearning still for love,
As lovers new forever do.

If bindu is not released in the yogic way of sexual union, the woman whose passions remain unquenched will pine and yearn for love forever.

சாற்றிய விந்து சயமாகுஞ் சத்தியால்
ஏற்றிய மூலத் தழலை யெழமூட்டி
நாற்றிசை யோடா நடுநாடி நாதத்தோ
டாற்றி யமுதம் அருந்தவிந் தாமே. 1962

Bodily Bindu Becomes Cosmic Bindu

By Kundalini Sakti, Bindu conquer;
Kindle that Fire in Muladhara
Course it upward straight
Through central Nadi, Sushumna;

Reach Nada,
And swill ambrosia there flows;
Your Bindu the Divine Bindu becomes.

Vanquishing bindu by kundalini sakti, kindle the fire in the muladhara and reach nada by coursing it upward through the central nadi, sushumna. Swill the ambrosia flowing there. Through the body, bindu becomes cosmic bindu that is divine.

விந்துவும் நாதமும் மேவக் கனல்மூல
வந்த வனன்மயிர்க் கால்தோறும் மன்னிடச்
சிந்தனை மாறச் சிவமக மாகவே
விந்துவு மாளுமெய்க் காயத்தில் வித்திலே. *1963*

Union of Bindu and Nada

When Bindu and Nada unite,
And Kuṇdalini Fire each minute hair root permeates,
All thought devoid,
Siva Himself you become;
And the Bindu then dies in the Primal Bindu
Of the Body Divine.

With the union of bindu and nada you become Siva Himself, devoid of all thoughts. The semenal bindu then dies in the primal bindu of the divine body.

வித்துக்குற் றுண்பான் விலைவறி யாதவன்
வித்துக்குற் றுண்ணாமல் வித்துச்சுட் டுண்பவன்
வித்துக்குற் றுண்பானில் வேறல னீற்றவன்
வித்துக்குற் றுண்ணாமல் வித்துவித் தானன்றே. *1964*

Yogi Sublimates Bindu

He who pounds seed and consumes it
Knows not good that of harvest comes;
Different is he,
Who fries it (in Kundalini Fire) and in body absorbs;
The latter, of the seed a meal does not make,
But the Seed of Birth he ends.

He who pounds and consumes the seed will not get a good harvest. Different is he who fries bindu in the kundalini fire, and end the seed of birth.

அன்னத்தில் விந்து அடங்கும் படிகண்டு
மன்னப் பிராணனாம் விந்து மறித்திட்டு
மின்னொத்த விந்துநா தாந்தத்து விட்டிட
வன்னத் திருவிந்து மாயுங்கா யத்திலே. *1965*

Merging of Bodily Bindu in Cosmic Bindu

Coursing upward, Bindu that is Prana vital
Merging it in Divine Bindu
That the "Swan" in cranium (Sahasrara) is,
There, uniting in Nadanta,
The luminous Bindu is in body absorbed.

Bindu is the vital prana coursing upward; it merges in the divine bindu. There uniting in Nadanta, the luminous bindu is absorbed into the body.

அன்னம் பிராணனென் றார்க்கு மிருவிந்து
தன்னை யறிந்துண்டு சாதிக்க வல்லார்க்குச்
சொன்ன மாமுருத் தோன்றுமெண் சித்தியாம்
அன்னவ ரெல்லாம் அழிவற நின்றதே. *1966*

Absorb Bindu in Body and Become Immortal

The Swan (the macrocosmic), and Prana (the microcosmic)
—Bindu is thus two for all;
Those who realize this
And absorb one in the Other
—The Prana (Individual) in the Swan (Cosmic)—
Will eight siddhis attain;
Their body as gold glitters;
They immortal become.

They who know the truth of the two forms of bindu — the swan (macrocosmic) and prana (microcosmic) and absorb the latter in the former will attain the eight siddhis. Immortal they become, their bodies glittering as gold.

நின்ற சிகாரம் நினைக்கும் பிராணனாய்
ஒன்று மகாரம் ஒருமூன்றோ டொன்றவை
சென்று பராசத்தி விந்து சயந்தன்னை
ஒன்ற வுரைக்க வுபதேசந் தானே. *1967*

Secret Way of Bindu Conquest

Intone sound "Si" (the first sound of Panchakshara)
In your Prana (life breath)'s silent thought
Merge in "Aum" — the sound cluster of "A, U, M"
Thus ParaSakti reach;
That indeed is the way of Bindu Conquest
—This the Mystic Secret (upadesa)—you hold.

Intone the sound 'Si' (the first sound of panchaksara) in you silent thought and merge prana in 'Aum.' Thus reach Parasakti. Indeed, this is the secret method of conquering bindu.

தானே யுபதேசந் தானல்லா தொன்றில்லை
வானே யுயர்விந்து வந்த பதினான்கு
மானே ரடங்க அதன்பின்பு புத்தியுந்
தானே சிவகதி தன்மையு மாமே. *1968*

Conquer Bindu and Attain Siva State

This the Mystic Secret
There is none — but this
He alone is; nothing else there is:
The Bindu heavenward ascends,
The Organs Fourteen
(Jnanendriyas five, karmendriyas five and Antakaranas four)
Their action cease;
Then does Jnana follow;
That verily is Siva State.

Conquest over bindu makes it ascend heavenward. The action of the 14 organs (five jnanendriyas, five karmendriyas, and four antahkaranas) ceases. Sublimated bindu (elan vital) becomes an intellectual and spiritual force. Truly then is the Siva state filled with jnana.

விந்துவும் நாதமும் விளைய விளைந்தது
வந்தஇப் பல்லுயிர் மன்னுயி ருக்கெலாம்
அந்தமும் ஆதியு மாமந் திரங்களும்
விந்து அடங்க விளையுஞ் சிவோகமே. *1969*

Sivoham when Bindu Subsides

In union of Bindu and Nada
Was born this creation vast;
It is beginning and end of all life,
Of great mantras too,
When Bindu subsides,
Then is Sivoham.

This vast creation, the beginning and end of all life, and the great mantras were all born in the union of bindu and nada. Sivoham is when bindu subsides.

வறுக்கின்ற வாறு மனத்துலா வெற்றி
நிறுக்கின்ற வாறுமந் நீள்வரை யொட்டிப்
பொறிக்கின்ற வாறுமப் பொல்லா வினையை
அறுக்கின்ற நாள்வரும் அத்திப் பழமே. *1970*

Fry Bindu and End Birth

Fry the Bindu, Mind its balance winning;
Raise it high, to mount of Sushumna;
That way, your interminable Karmas are scorched;
Then the day you pluck away
The Fruit of Fig that holds
The seeds of birth, innumerable.

Fry bindu and raise it high to the mount of sushumna. Scorch your interminable karmas. There ends the cycle of innumerable births.

விந்துவும் நாதமும் மேவி யுடன்கூடிச்
சந்திர னோடே தலைப்படு மாயிடில்
அந்தர வானத் தமுதம்வந் தூற்றிடும்
அங்குதி மந்திரம் ஆகுதி யாகுமே. *1971*

When Bindu Merges Ambrosia Wells

When Bindu and Nada uniting in one
Enter the Sphere of Moon within,
The heavenly ambrosia wells and flows;
The Mantra (Aum) that arises there
Is the sacrificial offering to Lord Supreme.

The heavenly ambrosia wells and flows when bindu and nada enter the sphere of the moon in union. The mantra that emerges there is the sacrificial offering to the Lord.

மனத்தொடு சத்து மனஞ்செவி யென்ன
இனத்தெழு வார்கள் இசைந்தன நாடி
மனத்தில் எழுகின்ற வாக்கு வசனங்
கனத்த இரதமக் காமத்தை நாடிலே. *1972*

Merge Mind in Bindu, Away From Lust

When the Mind in the Bindu merges,
Then the Mind, the ears and all organs besides
Will together rise the Divine Goal to seek;
But when thought and sound and words
That in the Mind arise
Seek lust,
As fluid thick it transformed be.

With the union of bindu with the mind, all sense organs rise to seek the divine goal. Thought, sound and words arise in the mind; when bindu is not sublimated, the working of the mind leads to lust.

சத்தமுஞ் சத்த மனமும் மனக்கருத்
தொத்தறி கின்ற விடமும் அறிகிலர்
மெய்த்தறி கின்ற விடமறி வாளர்க்கு
அத்தன் இருப்பிடம் அவ்விடந் தானே. *1973*

Jnanis Know Lord's Seat

The Sound (Nada), and the Mind that perceives Sound,
And the place where Mind undistracted discerns Truth,
—These they know not;
That place the Jnanis truly know
That verily is Lord's Seat.

True jnanis know the Lord's seat, where the sound (nada) and the mind that perceives the sound, remain in union.

உரமடி மேதினி யுந்தியி லப்பாம்
விரவிய தன்மலை மேவியகீ ழுங்கி
கருமுலை மீமிசை கைக்கீழிற் காலாம்
விரவிய கந்தர மேல்வெளி யாமே. *1974*

Regions of Five Elements in the body

Earth is, where the legs are (Muladhara);
In the navel (Svadhishthana) is the Region of Water;
Below the breast (Manipura) is the Fire;
Above the breast (Anahatha) and below the shoulder (Visuddhi) is Air;
And around the neck and beyond (Ajna) is the Region of Space.

The regions of the five elements are within the body. The region of earth is mūladhara. The navel (svadhistana) is the region of water. Below the breast (manipuraka) is the fire; above the breast (manipuraka) and below the shoulder (visuddhi) is air. The region of space is around the neck and beyond (ajna)

The location and significance of the 6 chakras in the body are to be noted. Only 5 elements are involved. The association of Space (Akasa) with Ajna cakra is particularly significant, for it is here, in the two-petalled lotus, that duality is supposed to disappear into non-duality during Kundalini Yoga.

22. ஆதித்தநிலை அண்டாதித்தன்

THE SUN'S POSITION—THE COSMIC SUN

செஞ்சுட ரோனமுத லாகிய தேவர்கள்
மஞ்சுடை மேரு வலம்வரு காரணம்
எஞ்சுட ரீசன் இறைவன் இணையடி
தஞ்சுட ராகவணங்குந் தவமே. 1975

Sun and Other Gods Adore the Lord to Receive Illumination

The fiery Sun and the Celestials rest
Circumambulate the show-clad Mountain Meru;
And adore the luminous Lord's Holy Feet in Tapas,
That they might, themselves illumined be.

The fiery 'sun' and other celestial gods adore the Holy Feet of the Lord in Tapas, so that they may receive illumination.

பகலவன் மாலவன் பல்லுயிர்க் கெல்லாம்
புகலவ னாய்நின்ற புண்ணிய நாதன்
இகலற ஏழுல கும்முற வோங்கும்
பகலவன் பல்லுயிர்க் காதியு மாமே. 1976

Sun is the Primal Energy

The Sun is Vishnu;
He is Siva Holy too,
Who as refuge of all creation stands;
He brings prosperity to the seven worlds in accord;
He, the Beginning of all lives.

The 'sun' is protective Vishnu and blessed Siva too. He is the primal energy and refuge of all creation. He brings prosperity to all the seven worlds.

Sun is the Primal Energy (Sakti), and is Vishnu, but belongs to Siva too. This is an important concept.

ஆதித்தன் அன்பினோ டாயிர நாமமுஞ்
சோதியி னுள்ளே சுடரொளி யாய்நிற்கும்
வேதியர் வேண்டினும் விண்ணவர் சொல்லினும்
ஆதியில் அன்பு பழுக்கின்ற வாறே. 1977

Worship Sun, Primal Lord Blesses

Chant in love the thousand names of Sun,
He in you as spark divine glows;
The Vedic brahmins pray,
The Celestial immortals his name chant;
It is the Lord Primal verily
Who blesses all.

Worship the 'sun.' Chant his thousand names in love. Worship of the sun grants the blessing of the Primal Lord.

தானே யுலகுக்குத் தத்துவ னாய்நிற்குந்
தானே யுலகுக்குத் தையலு மாய்நிற்குந்
தானே யுலகுக்குச் சம்புவு மாய்நிற்குந்
தானே யுலகுக்குத் தண்சுட ராகுமே. 1978

Primal Lord is Source of All

He stands as the Tattvas for the world,
He stands as Sakti for the world,
He alone is the Being Uncreated (Svayambhu),
He for the world is the Moon too,
Of soft light divine.

The Primal Lord alone is the Uncreated Being (Svayambhu), who stands as the tattvas and sakti for the world. He is also the moon of soft yellow light.

வலையமுக் கோணம் வட்டம் அறுகோணந்
துலையிரு வட்டந் துய்ய விதமெட்டில்
அலையுற்ற வட்டத்தில் ஈரெட் டிதழா
மலைவற் றுதித்தனன் ஆதித்த னாமே. 1979

Position of Sun in the Body

Above the triangle of Muladhara Centre,
Above the hexagonal Centre of Svadhishtana,
Above the twin-circle of Manipura Centre,
In the moving Centre of sixteen petalled Visuddhi,
There indeed rises the Sun within.

The 'sun' within the body arises in the moving centre of sixteen-petalled visuddhi — above the triangle of the muladhara centre, the hexagonal centre of svadhistana, and the twin-circle of the manipuraka centre.

ஆதித்த னுள்ளி லானமுக் கோணத்திற்
சோதித் திலங்குநற் சூரிய னாலாங்
கேத முறுங்கேணி சூரிய னெட்டிற்
சோதிதன் னீட்டிற் சோடசந் தானே. 1980

The Sun Confers the Kalas in Adharas

The Sun is within;
When his beams beat
On Muladhara triangle
That receives Kalas four;
When on Visuddhi his shafts fall,
That with Kalas sixteen shines.

The effulgent 'sun' alone can confer the four kalas on muladhara, and the sixteen kalas on visuddhi.

ஆதித்த னோடே அவனி யிருண்டது
பேதித்த நாலும் பிதற்றிக் கழிந்தது
சோதிக்குள் நின்று துடியிடை செய்கின்ற
வேதப் பொருளை விளங்கி லீரே. 1981

Experiences in the Sphere of Sun Within

When you reach the Sphere of Sun
Your worldly thoughts fade into darkness;
The cognitive organs four no more contend—
The Sakti in the light within reveals
The truth of Vedas

But alas! You seek not to understand!

When you reach the sphere of the 'sun,' you rise above worldly thoughts, desires, and contending notions. The sakti in the light within reveals the truth of the *Vedas*.

பாருக்குக் கீழே பகலோன் வரும்வழி
யாருக்குங் காணவொண் ணாதஅரும்பொருள்
நீருக்குந் தீக்கும் நடுவே யுதிப்பவன்
ஆருக்கும் எட்டாத ஆதித்தன் தானே. 1982

Sun's Route Inside

Below the Earth Centre that is Muladhara
The Sun its route takes;
Invisible indeed is he,
Between the Fiery Centre (Manipura)
And the Watery Centre (Svadhishtana) within.

Within the body, the 'sun' takes its route below the earth centre (muladhara). Indeed he is invisible between the fiery centre (manipuraka) and the watery centre (svadhistana).

மண்ணை யிடந்ததின் கீழொடும் ஆதித்தன்
விண்ணை யிடந்து வெளிசெய்து நின்றிடுங்
கண்ணை யிடந்து களிதந்த வானந்தம்
எண்ணுங் கிழமைக் கிசைந் துநின் றானே. 1983

Sun's Course in the Higher Adharas

Breaking through the Earth (Muladhara)
He penetrates beyond into the Adharas that
Are Sky (Visuddhi) and Space (Ajna) within;
He is the very source of joy that dazzles the eye;
He indeed responds to contemplation sweet.

The 'sun' breaking through the earth (muladhara) penetrates beyond into the higher adharas — sky (visuddhi) and space (ajna). He is the source of joy that dazzles the vision and truly responds to sweet contemplation.

பாரை யிடந்து பகலோன் வரும்வழி
யாரும் அறியார் அருங்கடை நூலவர்
தீரன் இருந்த திருமலை சூழென்பர்
ஊரை யுணர்ந்தார் உணர்ந்திருந் தாரே. 1984

Sun Circumambulates Sahasrara

The sun that penetrates Earth (Muladhara)
His route none knows,
That are but versed in worldly lore;
He circumambulates Mount of Meru, (Sahasrara)
Of the Lord Unconquerable;
—Thus they say;
Only those who have realized Truth
Know His abode real.

No one knows this route of the 'sun.' Folks believe only the worldly lore. Only they who have realised know the truth that the 'sun' circumambulates Mount Meru (sahasrara) of the Invincible Lord.

23. பிண்டாதித்தன்
THE MICROCOSMIC SUN

நின்றும் இருந்துங் கிடந்தும் நடந்தும்
கன்றாய நந்திக் கருத்துள் இருந்தனன்
கொன்று மலங்கள் குழல்வழி யோடிட
வென்று விளங்கும் விரிசுடர் காணுமே. 1985

Vision Sun Within Through Spinal Way

Standing, sitting, walking and lying prostrate
Nandi the benevolent in my thoughts incessant stood;
Destroy your Malas (Impurities)
And ascend the Adharas
Through Sushumna Central;
There shall you vision the Sun
That within shines in brightness nonpareil.

Nandi stood in my thought in all postures. Destroy the malas (impurities), ascend the adharas through the central sushumna. There you will behold the sun blazing bright.

ஆதித்தன் ஓடி யடங்கும் இடங்கண்டு
சாதிக்க வல்லவர் தம்மை யுணர்ந்தவர்
பேதித் துலகம் பிதற்றும் பிதற்றெல்லாம்
ஆதித்த னோடே யடங்குகின் றாரே. 1986

The Self-Realized Reach Sun

They who by Adhara-ascending
Reach and see where the Sun within reposes
They indeed are the self-realized ones;
They who differ from this
And say aught they like,
Are in darkness enveloped,
As when the Sun here, below horizon dips.

Verily, they who reach the sun by ascending the adharas realise their Selves.

உருவிப் புறப்பட் டுலகை வலம்வந்து
சொருகிக் கிடக்குந் துறையறி வாரில்லை
சொருகிக் கிடக்குந் துறையறி வாளர்க்
குருகிக் கிடக்குமென் னுள்ளன்பு தானே. 1987

Those Who Know the Sun Within is Worthy of Adoration

They penetrate not the Adharas,
Search not the world within,
And know not where in its midst Sun is;
Those who know where he furtive lies
To them my heart
In love melts.

The yogi's heart melts in love for those who contemplate the sun within as worthy of adoration.

24. மனவாதித்தன்
MIND'S SUN

எறிகதிர் ஞாயிறு மின்பனி சோரும்
எறிகதிர் சோமன் எதிர்நின் றெறிப்ப
விரிகதி ருள்ளே வியங்குமென் ஆவி
ஒருகதி ராகில் உவாவது வாமே. 1988

Life's Full Moon Within

The luminous Sun dewy cool becomes
When Moon spreads its contending rays;
In the luminosity that commingling emanates,
My yearning Prana as a ray beams,
That verily is my life's Full Moon.

When the moon spreads its rays, the sun becomes dewy cool. In the soft luminosity that emanates, the yogi's soul emits a beam. That truly is his life's full moon.'

சந்திரன் சூரியன் தான்வரிற் பூசனை
முந்திய பானுவில் இந்துவந் தேய்முறை
அந்த இரண்டும் உபய நிலத்திற்
சிந்தை தெளிந்தார் சிவமாயி னாரே. 1989

To See the Blending of the Rays of Sun and Moon is Divine

When on Sun, Moon's rays afore fall,
That in order is;
When on Sun, Moon's rays beat,
Divine indeed;
In that mystic land
Where the two shafts mingle
They who the Light see,
Have Siva Himself become.

To vision the union of the beams of the sun and moon in the mystic land within is divine. They who have visioned it have indeed become Siva Himself.

1) Reference: Chandra Yoga, Mantra 851, Tantra Three.

ஆகுங் கலையோ டருக்கன் அனல்மதி
ஆகுங் கலையிடை நான்கென லாமென்பார்
ஆகும் அருக்கன் அனல்மதி யோடொன்ற
ஆகுமப் பூரணை யாமென் றறியுமே. 1990

Full Moon Within

With Kalas three of Sun, Moon and Fire
Arises the Kala from intermingling of their rays
Thus are they, Kalas Four;
When Sun, Moon and Fire mingle their rays,
Then is Full Moon within, know this.

The full moon is within, when the rays of the sun, moon and fire merge.

ஈரண்டத் தப்பால் இயங்கிய வவ்வொளி
ஓரண்டத் தார்க்கும் உணரா வுணர்வது
பேரண்டத் தூடே பிறங்கொளி யாய்நின்ற
தாரண்டத் தக்கா ரறியத்தக் காரே. 1991

The Vision of Ethereal Light Within

The Light that shone beyond the orbs two,
Is a Light that none in any realm can perceive
It is a Light that shone piercing the Cosmic Universe;
Who can near it, who can perceive it!

The ethereal light that shines beyond the two orbs within is imperceptible. It is the light that pierces the cosmic universe.

ஒன்பதின் மேவி யுலகம் வலம்வரும்
ஒன்பது மீசன் இயலறி வாரில்லை
முன்பதின் மேவி முதல்வன் அருளிலார்
இன்ப மிலாரிருள் சூழநின் றாரே. 1992

The Nine Planets Lacking Grace Whirl in Darkness

The nine orbs (planets) go round the earth,
But none of the nine, knows Lord;
Well may the nine orbs, Him, propitiate;
Yet His Grace they receive not;
Devoid of bliss, in darkness surrounded they are.

The nine planets, though they go round the earth whirl in darkness; for they do not know the Lord. To them are not given His Divine Grace and Bliss.

25. ஞானாதித்தன்
JNANA-SUN

விந்து அபரம் பரமிரண் டாய்விரிந்
தந்த அபரம் பரநாத மாகியே
வந்தன தம்மிற் பரங்கலை யாதிவைத்
துந்தும் அருணோ தயமென்ன வுள்ளத்தே. 1993

Sun's Para Kalas evolve from Bindu Through Para Nada

The Bindu expand into two Apara and Para
The Apara becomes the Para Nada
From Para Nada arises the Para Kalas
With those Kalas the Jnana Sun within dawns.

Mantras 1993 & 1994

Cosmic bindu expands into para and apara, of which apara becomes paranada, from which in turn arises the para kalas. The jnana sun dawns with those kalas. The sound that arises with this is an emanation from paranada. The five sounds (vaikhari and the rest) arise in the five kalas, one in each.

உள்ள அருணோ தயத்தெழும் ஓசைதான்
தெள்ளும் பரநாதத் தின்செய லென்பதால்
வள்ளல் பரவிந்து வைகரி யாதிவாக்
குள்ளன ஐங்கலைக் கொன்றாம் உதயமே. 1994

In the Five Kalas Arise the Five Sound Forms

The Sound that arises
When Sun within dawns
Is emanation from Para Nada;
The Sounds Five, Vaikhari and rest
That to Para Bindu belong
Arise in Kalas Five, one in each.

---

1) For notes on the four sounds (vaks) see Mantra 2007, ibid. The fifth sound is known as panchamai which is located in the muladhara. Its form is pravana.

a) Vaikhari — articulated speech. Its source is below the tongue.
b) Madhyamai — sound as it reaches the throat. Its source is between the heart and throat. Its shape is the letter formed articulately inside.
c) Paysanti — thought form sound (no letter form) Its source is the stomach. Its shape is prana.
d) Sukshmai — unarticulated sound. Its source is the navel. Its shape is intelligence.
e) Panchamai — subtle sound-source. Its source is ultra subtle. Its shape is Pranava.

2) For notes on the five kalas, where the five sound-forms repose, see Mantra 1926, ante.

தேவர் பிரான்திசை பத்துத யஞ்செய்யும்
மூவர் பிரானென முன்னொரு காலத்து
நால்வர் பிரான்நடு வாயுரை யாநிற்கும்
மேவு பிரான்என்பர் விண்ணவர் தாமே. 1995

Sadasiva is the Finite Source of Formless and Formed Sounds

He is the Lord of Devas;
He creates the directions ten;
Of yore they hailed Him as Lord of Three;[1]
He is the Lord of the Four[2] too;
In them He stands as Being Central,
Thus verily, the Immortal Celestials say.

The 'Sun' rises in the ten directions. He is the Lord of devas. He is Siva, the Supreme Lord of the three Gods. He is Sadasiva, the central Being of the four Gods — thus say immortal celestials.

1) Brahma, Vishnu, and Rudra
2) Nada; bindu, Siva, Sakti — the formless four.

பொய்யிலன் மெய்யன் புவனா பதியெந்தை
மையிருள் நீக்கு மதியமங்கி ஞாயிறு
செய்யிருள் நீக்குந் திருவுடை நந்தியென்
கையிருள் நீங்கக் கலந்தெழுந் தானே. 1996

Siva Dispels Darkness

He is the Truth,
Unreal He is not;
He is the Lord of the Universe;
My Father;
He is the Sun, Moon and Fire that darkness dispel;
He dispels too the darkness of Karma,
He, the Nandi Holy, to me appeared
The darkness of my low desires to dispel.

Mantras 1996 & 1997

The Holy Nandi, the Lord of the universe, dispels the darkness of karma. He is also the sun, moon and fire that drives away the darkness of ignorance; and when He beams with His benevolent shafts of light, then flows the honey of the divine fruit. Then, the Lord of Kailas stood within me as Resplendent Light.

தனிச்சுட ரெற்றித் தயங்கிருள் நீங்க
அனித்திடு மேலை யருங்கனி யூறல்
கனிச்சுட ராய்நின்ற கயிலையில் ஈசன்
நனிச்சுடர் மேல்கொண்ட வண்ணமு மாமே. 1997

Siva is the Light Resplendent

With His peerless rays
He dispelled my darkness;
And the divine fruit's honey within flowed;
Beaming with benevolent rays
As Lord of Kailas, He stood;
Within me too He stood aloft
As Light Resplendent.

நேரறி வாக நிரம்பிய பேரொளி
போரறியாது புவனங்கள் போய்வருந்
தேரறி யாத திசையொளி யாயிடும்
ஆரறி வாரிது நாயக மாமே. 1998

He is Supreme Light

His dazzling Light as Wisdom True spreads;
Unhindered, it invades worlds all;
It is the light pervasive, none can fathom;
Who does know it as the Light Supreme!

He is the Supreme Light that diffuses as true wisdom. That light pervades the entire world. None can fathom its spread and depth.

மண்டலத் துள்ளே மலர்ந்தெழும் ஆதித்தன்
கண்டிடத் துள்ளே கதிரொளி யாயிடுஞ்
சென்றிடத் தெட்டுத் திசையெங்கும் போய்வரும்
நின்றிடத் தேநிலை நேரறி வார்க்கே. 1999

The Jnana Sun is Within and Without

The Sun that rises in firmament vast
Stands within too shedding rays divine;
In directions eight he traverses constant;
Yet in them that Truth know
He stands for ever fixed within.

The jnana sun constantly traverses in eight directions. It is within and without.

நாபிக்கண் ணாசி நயன நடுவினுந்
தூபியோடைந்துஞ் சுடர்விடு சோதியைத்
தேவர்கள் ஈசன் திருமால் பிரமனும்
மூவரு மாக வுணர்ந்திருந் தாரே. 2000

Five Centres where the Light of Lord is

In the navel, eye and nose tip,
In the centre of eyebrows, and within crown of head
In these five places, Lord resides as Light Divine;
He is the One Lord
The Devas saw as Three,
Brahma, Vishnu and Isa.
The Apara becomes the Para Nada
From Para Nada arises the Para Kalas
With those Kalas the Jnana Sun within dawns.

Navel, eye, nose tip, centre of eyebrows, and the crown of the head are the five centres where the Divine Lord resides. The devas perceived Him in three forms — Brahma, Vishnu and Isa.

26. சிவாதித்தன்

SIVA-SUN

அன்றிய பாச இருளுமஞ் ஞானமுஞ்
சென்றிடு ஞானச் சிவப்பிர காசத்தால்
ஒன்று மிருசுட ராம்அரு ணோதயந்
துன்றிருள் நீங்குதல் போலத் தொலைந்ததே. 2001

Siva is Sun of Jnana

The darkness of contending Pasa,
And the Ignorance vast,
These flee fast,
Before the Jnana Light of Siva,
Even as when the luminous Sun rises,
The murky darkness, before him, flees.

Siva is the sun of jnana. When His light of jnana dawns, the murky darkness of contending pasas and enveloping ignorance flee.

Chapter 26 - 'Siva-Sun

This chapter along with the preceding one correlates the energy flow (of the Sun) in the Cosmos and (human body) following yogic and tantric principles.

Chapter 24. (The Mind's Sun), Chapter 25 (Jnana Sun) and Chapter.26 (Siva-Sun) present a consolidated picture of the roles of the Sun, Moon and Fire in Cosmos, and in the human body (microcosmos), in various aspects such as the Mind (verses 1988 to 1992), Jnana (or Wisdom) (verses 1993 to 2000), and finally in the removal of Ignorance by the Light of Siva.

கடங்கடந் தோறுங் கதிரவன் தோன்றில்
அடங்கிட மூடில் அவற்றில் அடங்கான்
விடங்கொண்ட கண்டனு மேவிய காயத்
தடங்கிட நின்றதும் அப்பரி சாமே. 2002

Sivaditya is Immanent and Transcendent

In pot to pot the sun appears,
Well may you the pots close,
Yet in them you contain him not;
So, too, when Lord that poison swallowed
This body enters,
There can you contain Him not
He pervades all.

The sun appears in pot after pot; but you cannot contain Him by closing a pot. Similarly, though the Lord, who has swallowed poison enters this body, you cannot have him there alone. He is immanent and transcendent.

Verses 2002 - 2004

In these three verses, the term Sivaditya appears which is unknown in the Vedas. It removes the ambiguity which appears in the Atharva Veda, where the term "Lohita" applies to Rudra-Siva as lord of the Sun. (Vishnu)

தானே விரிசுடர் மூன்றுமொன் றாய்நிற்குந்
தானே யயன்மா லெனநின்று தாபிக்குந்
தானே யுடலுயிர் வேறன்றி நின்றுளன்
தானே வெளியொளி தானிருட் டாமே. 2003

Sivaditya is Space, Light and Darkness

Himself as the Three Lights (Sun, Moon and Fire) in one stands;
Himself as Brahma and Vishnu stands established;
Himself as life and body indistinguishably stands
Himself Space, Light, and Darkness too.

Sivaditya stands as the three lights (sun, moon and fire). He is space, light and darkness. He is Brahma and Vishnu. He is life and body.

தெய்வச் சுடரங்கி ஞாயிறுந் திங்களும்
வையம் புனல்அனல் மாருதம் வானகஞ்
சைவப் பெரும்பதி தாங்கிய பல்லுயிர்
ஐவர்க் கிடமிடை யாறங்க மாமே. 2004

Nine Abodes of Sivaditya

The divine Fire, Sun and Moon,
The earth, water, fire, wind and space
And the creation countless
These the abodes ancient of Siva are;
The Five Gods, (Brahma, Vishnu, Rudra, Mahesa, Sadasiva)
Are in the Vedas that has Angas six.

The nine abodes of Sivaditya are the spiritual spheres of fire, sun, moon; the elemental spheres of earth, water, fire, wind and space; and the endless creation. Similarly, the five Gods (Brahma, Vishnu, Rudra, Mahesvara, Sadasiva) and the four *Vedas* — these nine are also favourite resorts of Sivaditya.

27. பசுவிலக்கணம்-பிராணன்
NATURE OF JIVA PRANA

உன்னும் அளவில் உணரும் ஒருவனைப்
பன்னு மறைகள் பயிலும் பரமனை
என்னுள் இருக்கும் இளையா விளக்கினை
அன்ன மயமென் றறிந்துகொண் டேனே. 2005

He is Para-Bindu

The One whom I in contemplation realize,
The One Param whom Vedas praise,
The Undying Light in me shines,
Him I beheld, as Divine Swan (Para Bindu).

The yogi realises in contemplation the One whom the *Vedas* praise as twin, inseparable, 'swans' — the cosmic bindu and the microcosmic bindu.

அன்ன மிரண்டுள ஆற்றங் கரையினில்
துன்னி யிரண்டுந் துணைப்பிரி யாதன்னந்
தன்னிலை யன்னந் தனி யொன்ற தென்றக்கால்
பின்ன மடவன்னம் பேறணு காதே. 2006

Cosmic Bindu and Micro-Cosmic Bindu Are Inseparate

Two the swans on the river bank (of life)
The two swans separation know not,
If one, Jiva, says he is by himself,
Then that foolish swan, Grace receiveth not.

This reminds one of Rg Vedic verse I.164. There, two birds are seated on a tree; one (jiva) enjoys the fruits of the three (pippalam) and the other (Siva or Brahman or Supreme Soul) watches, but does not eat.

28. புருடன்
PURUSHA

வைகரி யாதியு மாயா மலாதியும்
பொய்கரி யான புருடாதி பேதமும்
மெய்கரி ஞானங் கிரியா விசேடத்துச்
செய்கரி யீசன் அனாதியே செய்ததே. 2007

Lord Creates Activating Saktis, Jnana and Kriya

Vaikhari and rest of Sounds,
Maya and rest of Impurities,
Purusha and rest of Tattvas illusory
—All these,
Acting on Saktis, Jnana and Kriya,
The Lord True from time immemorial made.

Activating the jnana and kriya saktis, the Lord creates vaikhari and the rest of sounds, maya and the other impurities, and purusha along with the other illusory tattvas.

1) The four sounds are: vaikhari, madhyamai, paysanti, and sukshma.
Vaikari—articulate sound form.
Madhyamai—sound form proceeding from the throat and indistinctly articulate.
Paysanti—sound form proceeding from the lungs struggling towards vocalisation.
Sukshma—subtle source of speech.
2) This is variously translated as, 'the experient self,' the agent of experience,' 'the agent-self', and as 'the world-soul' (in Samkhya philosophy). We prefer the first one in the context of Saiva Siddhanta.

அணுவில் அணுவினை ஆதிப் பிரானை
அணுவில் அணுவினை ஆயிரங் கூறிட்
டணுவில் அணுவை அணுகவல் லார்கட்
கணுவில் அணுவை அணுகலு மாமே. 2008

Lord is Atom-Within-Atom

The Lord is the Beginning of all,
He is the Atom-within-the-atom;
Divide an atom within the atom,
Into parts one thousand,
They who can thus divide
That atom within the atom
May well near the Lord,
He, indeed, is the Atom-within-the-atom.

The Lord, the Source of all, is the atom within the atom. Only they who are capable of fragmenting an atom can vision this atom within an atom (the Lord).

படர்கொண்ட ஆலதின் வித்தது போலச்
சுடர்கொண் டணுவினைத் தூவழி செய்ய
இடர்கொண்ட பாச இருளற வோட்டி
நடர்கொண்ட நல்வழி நாடலு மாமே. 2009

Seek the Jnana Way of Lord

Tiny unto the seed
Of the spreading banyan tree
Is the atom that is Jiva;
If by fire of Jnana
Your way purifies,
The dark Pasas that malign you
May well driven be;
Seek the Divine way,
The Dancing Lord shows you.

Jiva, the atom, is the seed of the spreading banyan tree.

அணுவுள் அவனும் அவனுள் அணுவுங்
கணுவுற நின்ற கலப்ப துணரார்
இணையிலி யீச னவனெங்கு மாகித்
தணிவற நின்றான் சராசரந் தானே. 2010

Jiva and Siva Commingling Stand

He within the atom (Jiva),
And the atom (Jiva) within Him
Commingling stand,
They know this not;
The peerless Lord pervades all
Unintermittent, in creation entire.

Jiva is the atom which resides within Siva, the Lord who is all-pervasive and immanent in the entirety of creation. Seek the Dancing Lord, the divine jnana way.

29. சீவன்

JIVA (SOUL)

மேவிய சீவன் வடிவது சொல்லிடில்
கோவின் மயிரொன்று நூறுடன் கூறிட்டு
மேவிய கூறது ஆயிர மாயினால்
ஆவியின் கூறுநூ றாயிரத் தொன்றே. 2011

Size of Soul

To speak of the size of Jiva
It is like this:
Split a cow's hair soft
Into a hundred tiny parts;
And each part into a thousand parts divide;
The size of Jiva is that one of part
Of the one hundred thousand.

Split a cow's downy hair into one hundred tiny parts and then divide each part into one thousand parts. The size of jiva equals that one part of the one hundred thousand.

ஏனோர் பெருமைய னாயினும் எம்மிறை
ஊனே சிறுமையின் உட்கலந் தங்குளன்
வானோர் அறியு மளவல்லன் மாதேவன்
தானே யறியுந் தவத்தின் அளவே. 2012

Siva's Infinite Size

Infinite great is my Lord,
Yet within the littleness of this body
He dwells permeating;
He is the Lord Supreme
Whom the Celestials cannot know;
As much as your Tapas is
So much also is He known.

Siva, though of infinite size, dwells in this little body. He is the Supreme Lord whom even the celestials cannot know. Only through tapas can He be visioned.

உண்டு தெளிவன் உரைக்க வியோகமே
கொண்டு பயிலுங் குணமில்லை யாயினும்
பண்டு பயிலும் பயில்சீவ னார்பின்னைக்
கண்டு சிவனுருக் கொள்வர் கருத்துளே. 2013

Practise Yoga in Perseverence

You may not for Yoga inclined be,
But if your Guru Illumined teaches you,
You may yet accomplish it;
And so persevere
In lives several;
And seeing you thus practise,
Siva's Form will in your thought arise.

Yoga practice persevered through several lives makes Siva's form arise in your thoughts.

மாயா வுபாதி வசத்தாகுஞ் சேதனத்
தாய குருவரு ளாலே யதில்தூண்ட
ஓயும் உபாதியோ டொன்றினொன் றாதுயிர்
ஆய துரியம் புகுந்தறி வாகவே. 2014

The Guru Illumines You

Harassed art thou
By Maya's manifestations;
But when the Guru Illumined
By His grace lights you up
Your troubles entire cease;
The Jiva illumined in Jnana
Will Turiya State reach you,
You may yet accomplish it;

With the help of the Guru's guidance, liberation is obtained from maya's manifestations. The Jiva, illumined by jnana, reaches the turiya state.

30. பசு

JIVA (PASU)

கற்ற பசுக்கள் கதறித் திரியினுங்
கொற்ற பசுக்கள் குறிகட்டி மேயினு
முற்ற பசுக்கள் ஒருகுடம் பால்போது
மற்றைப் பசுக்கள் வறள்பசு தானே. 2015

Jnani is the Mature Jiva

The learned cows (Jivas) may wander bellowing,
The power-giddy cows may strut about,
Their insignia displaying;

But precious is a pot of milk (Jnana),
The good mature cows (Jnani's) yield;
The rest are but barren cows indeed.

Only mature cows (jnanis) yeild a pot of milk that is precious. The rest are indeed barren and sterile.

கொல்லையின் மேயும் பசுக்களைச் செய்வதென்
எல்லை கடப்பித் திறைவ னடிகூட்டி
வல்லசெய் தாற்ற மதித்தபின் அல்லது
கொல்லைசெய் நெஞ்சங் குறிப்பறி யாதே. 2016

Jivas Graze in the Backwood of Worldly Pleasures

What to do with those cows
That in the backwoods of desires graze?
Take them beyond,
And lead them to the Feet of the Lord:
Discipline them in ways superior;
Thus manage the herd;
Until then, their thoughts turn not
From the backwoods of worldly pleasures.

Lead the cows that graze in the backwoods of worldly desires to the Holy Feet of the Lord. Instruct them in supreme disciplined ways. From then on they will never turn back to, their previous state.

31. போதன்

BODHAN (LORD AS GIVER OF LIGHT OF JNANA)

சீவ னெனச்சிவ னென்னவே றில்லை
சீவ னார்சிவ னாரை யறிகிலர்
சீவ னார்சிவ னாரை யறிந்தபின்
சீவ னார்சிவ னாயிட் டிருப்பரே. 2017

Jiva and Siva are One

Jiva and Siva
Separate are not;
Jiva knows not Siva;
When Jiva knows Siva,
Jiva becomes Siva.

Siva and jiva are one and the same. With the knowledge of Siva, jiva becomes Siva.

குணவிளக் காகிய கூத்தப் பிரானும்
மணவிளக் காகிய மன்னுயிர்க் கெல்லாம்
பணவிளக் காகிய பல்தலை நாகங்
கணவிளக் காகிய கண்காணி யாகுமே. 2018

Lord is Light

The Dancing Lord is the Light Benevolent,
He is the Joyous Light for Creation all;
He adorns the many hooded serpent with gemlike shining eyes
He is the Cluster of Lights that oversees all.

The Dancing Siva is the cluster of benevolent lights that oversees all, and the joyous light that vibrates through the entire creation.

அறிவாய் அறியாமை நீங்கி யவனே
பொறிவாய் ஒழிந்தெங்குந் தானான போதன்
அறிவா யவற்றினுட் டானா யறிவன்
செறிவாகி நின்றஅச் சீவனுமாகுமே. 2019

Lord is Knowledge and Knower

He is all Knowledge, immune from Ignorance,
Without aid of sensory organs, He is self-Illumined,
Himself as Knowledge and Himself as the Knower too
He is the Jiva as well,
He stands pervading all.

God is Self-Illumined, free from ignorance. He is the knowledge and knower also. He is also jiva and is all pervasive.

ஆறாறின் தன்மை அறியா திருந்தேனுக்
காறாறின் தன்மை அறிவித்தான் பேர்நந்தி
ஆறாறின் தன்மை அருளால் அறிந்தபின்
ஆறாறுக் கப்புற மாகிநின் றானே. 2020

He is Beyond Tattvas Thirty-Six

To me that knew not the truth of Tattvas six times six,
He taught the truth of Tattvas six times six
He, Nandi Famed;
And when by His Grace I learned the truth of Tattvas six times six
He stood beyond the Tattvas six times si

சிவமா கியஅருள் நின்றறிந் தோரார்
அவமா மலமைந்து மாவ தறியா
தவமான செய்து தலைப்பறி கின்றார்
நவமான தத்துவ நாடகி லாரே. 2021

Lord is Truth

They know Him not as Grace that is Siva,
They know not the Malas (Impurities) Five to rid of,
They perform penance diverse,
And are in distraction lost,
They seek not the Tattva (Truth),
That is ever New.

Men do not know that Siva is Grace. He is pure, rid of the five malas (impurities). Though they perform diverse penances and atonements, they are lost in distraction. The Lord is the tattva (Truth) that is ever new.

நாடோறும் ஈசன் நடத்துந் தொழில்உன்னார்
நாடோறும் ஈசன் நயந்தூட்டல் நாடிடார்
நாடோறும் ஈசன்நல் லோர்க்கருள் நல்கலால்
நாடோறும் நாடார்கள் நாள்வினை யாளரே. 2022

Lord Bestows His Grace on the Good

They think not of divine acts, Lord daily performs
They think not of the ministering acts, Lord daily performs;
The Lord daily bestows His Grace on the good,
They who know this not, daily seek Him not—
Entangled in their work-a-day Karmas interminable.

They do not concentrate on holy and divine acts. They do not seek Him either; they are ignorant of the fact that God responds to the love and devotion of the good, and bestows His blessing on them.

32. ஐந்திந்திரியம் அடக்கும் அருமை
IMPORTANCE OF CONTROLLING THE FIVE INDRIYAS (SENSES)

ஆக மதத்தன ஐந்து களிறுள
ஆக மதத்தறி யோடணை கின்றில
பாகனு மெய்த்தவை தாமும் இளைத்தபின்
யோகு திருந்துதல் ஒன்றறி யோமே. 2023

Do Not Delay to Control Senses

Five are the elephants (Senses)
That are in rut
Their rut increasing
They do not to the (Divine) Post remain tied;
As the mahout (Jiva) tires,
And the elephants (Senses) too, get their energy exhausted,
Then they turn to Yoga;
Why this way (they delayed) we know not!

Five elephants (senses) are there in the 'mast' (body) and they are not tied to the post (divine). As the mahout (jiva) tries and tries in vain, he becomes exhausted; and then he turns to the yogic way and succeeds. So, do not delay to control your senses.

கருத்தினன் னூல்கற்றுக் கால்கொத்திப் பாகன்
திருத்தலம் பாய்மாத் திகைத்தன்றிப் பாயா
எருத்துற வேறி யிருக்கிலு மாங்கே
வருத்தினும் அம்மா வழிநட வாதே. 2024

Difficulty of Training Senses

Attentively learning holy lore
And coursing breath in Yogic way,
Unless the rider (Jiva) thus trains,
The restless steed (Senses),
Its wayward course takes;
Firm may the rider on its neck sit
And hard the punishment he administers,
Yet the animal forward moveth not.

Unless the rider (jiva) trains the restless steed (senses) in the yogic way, it goes astray. The animal seldom moves, though the rider sitting on its back goes on making the punishment more and more severe.

புலமைந்து புள்ளைந்து புட்சென்று மேயும்
நிலமைந்து நீரைந்து நீர்மையும் ஐந்து
குலமொன்று கோல்கொண்டு மேய்ப்பான்ஒருவன்
உலம்வந்து போம்வழி யொன்பது தானே. 2025

Harassing Senses Bring Sorrow

Five the Sense Organs,
Five the Sense-birds, (Jnanendriyas)
Five the Fields (Tanmatras)
The Sense-birds seek to feed,
Five the waters (Karmendriyas),
Five their functions,
Yet are they of one lineage;
And one the hunter (Jiva)
That herds them together;
Nine the exits of body
Where he in sorrow wanders.

Five are the sense organs (sensoria) and five the sense-birds (motoria). Five are the sense-fields (potencies) the sense-birds seek to feed upon. Five the waters (elements) and five their functions; yet, they are all of one lineage. The lonely hunter (jiva) brings them together, but the harassing senses bring sorrow to him.

அஞ்சுள சிங்கம் அடவியல் வாழ்வன
அஞ்சும்போய் மேய்ந்ததும் அஞ்சுகமேபுகும்
அஞ்சின் உகிரும் எயிறும் அறுத்திட்டால்
எஞ்சா திறைவனை எய்தலு மாமே. 2026

Senses are Like Roaming Lions

Five the lions that roam the forest
The Five seeking their prey get filled;
And to their caves the Five return;
If the claws and teeth of the Five you pull,
You shall sure the Lord reach.

The senses are roaming like lions which feel contented when their stomachs get filled. If their claws and teeth are pulled, they will have no more terrors for you. You will safely reach the Lord.

ஐவர் அமைச்சருள் தொண்ணூற் றறுவர்கள்
ஐவரு மைந்தரு மாளக் கருதுவர்
ஐவரு மைந்து சினத்தொடே நின்றிடில்
ஐவர்க் கிறையிறுத் தாற்றகி லோமே. 2027

Senses are Like Ministers that Seek to Usurp the Body-Kingdom

Five are the ministers,
Ninety six (Tattvas) are they within,
The Five and their brood of sons within
Seek you to rule;
If the Five in their fiery passion stand,
Endless indeed is the tribute
That to the Five we are to pay.

Five senses and the ninety-six tattvas reign supreme over you. The senses are like conspiring ministers that everplot to usurp the body-kingdom.

சொல்லகில் லேன்சுடர்ச் சோதியை நாடொறுஞ்
சொல்லகில் லேன்திரு மங்கையும் அங்குள
வெல்லகில் லேன்புலன் ஐந்துடன் தன்னையுங்
கொல்லநின் றோடுங் குதிரையொத் தேனே. 2028

Without Sense Control Jiva is Like an Uncontrolled Steed

I praise not daily
The Holy Light;
I speak not of Sakti
That is within there;
I conquer not the senses Five;
Like an uncontrolled steed headlong to its down
Verily, Verily am I.

எண்ணிலி யில்லி யுடைத்தவ் விருட்டறை
எண்ணிலி யில்லியோ டேகிற் பிழைதரும்
எண்ணிலி யில்லியோ டேகாமை காக்குமேல்
எண்ணிலி யில்லதோர் இன்பம தாமே. 2029

Control Desires, and Attain Bliss

Countless the holes
In this body's chamber dark;
If with the countless holes (desires) I run,
Faulty will my lot be;
If you run not
With the countless holes of desires,
Countless indeed the bliss you attain.

Do not run with the numerous holes of desire present in this body. Control will bring countless blessings.

விதியின் பெருவலி வேலைசூழ் வையந்
துதியின் பெருவலி தொல்வான் உலகம்
மதியின் பெருவலி மானுடர் வாழ்க்கை
நிதியின் பெருவலி நீர்வலி தானே. 2030

Strength of Wisdom Leads to Higher Life

Of their Karma's strength is life here below,
Of their prayer's strength is life in heaven above,
Of their wisdom's strength is men's higher life;
Verily, of their strength of Grace
Is their way of life.

The life here below is of karma's strength; and the life in heaven above is of prayer's strength. Strength of wisdom belongs to man's higher life.

33. ஐந்திந்திரியம் அடக்கு முறைமை

HOW TO CONTROL SENSES (WAY OF SUBLIMATION)

குட்ட மொருமுழ முள்ள தரைமுழம்
வட்டம் அமைந்ததோர் வாவியுள் வாழ்வன
பட்டன மீன்பல பரவன் வலைகொணர்ந்
திட்டனன் யாமினி யேதமி லோமே. 2031

Lord is a Fisher of Desires

One cubit its depth,
Half cubit its diameter,
Thus shaped round is the body pond;
The Fisherman (Lord) His net spreads;
Many the fish (of desires) He caught;
No more — the troubles I encounter.

கிடக்கும் உடலிற் கிளரிந் திரியம்
அடக்க வுறுமவன் தானே யமரன்
விடக்கிரண் டின்புறு மேவுறு சிந்தை
நடக்கின் நடக்கும் நடக்கு மளவே. 2032

Control Senses and Become Immortal

The stirring Indriyas within the body dwell,
He who controls them is immortal verily;
If your thoughts seek the pleasure twain —
Food and sex,
Only that far will they last,
Until your breath lasts.

அஞ்சு மடக்கடக் கென்பர் அறிவிலார்
அஞ்சு மடக்கும் அமரரும் அங்கிலை
அஞ்சு மடக்கில் அசேதன மாமென்றிட்
டஞ்சு மடக்கா அறிவறிந் தேனே. 2033

Not Control But Sublimation of Senses is Wisdom's Way

"Control, control the senses Five,"
—Thus say those who know not;
None, not even the Immortals
The senses Five control;
When you the senses Five control
Verily are you an inert mass;
(There is a way alternate open)
Sublimate them toward the Lord
That Wisdom's Way, I learned.

முழக்கி யெழுவன மும்மத வேழம்
அடக்கஅறிவென்னுங் கோட்டையைவைத்தேன்
பிழைத்தன வோடிப் பெருங்கேடு மண்டிக்
கொழுத்தன வேழங் குலைக்கின்ற வாறே. 2034

Mere Control Does Not Avail

Loud they roar, the elephants in rut triple, (Pasas)
I applied the goad of knowledge to them to control;
But they romped about and in fury escaped,
They fat became, causing destruction in their train,
And sweet fields of sugarcane (virtues) devastating.

ஐந்தில் ஒடுங்கில் அகலிட மாவது
ஐந்தில் ஒடுங்கில் அருந்தவ மாவது
ஐந்தில் ஒடுங்கில் அரன்பத மாவது
ஐந்தில் ஒடுங்கில் அருளுடை யாரே. 2035

Sublimation is the Way to Grace

If the senses Five you sublimate
Then all worlds are yours;
That is tapas rare;
That is the Lord's Feet too;
That indeed is the way to Grace receive.

பெருக்கப் பிதற்றிலென் பேய்த்தேர் நினைந்தென்
விரித்த பொருட்கெல்லாம் வித்தாவ துள்ளம்
பெருக்கிற் பெருக்குஞ் சுருக்கிற் சுருக்கும்
அருத்தமும் அத்தனை ஆய்ந்துகொள்வார்க்கே. 2036

Control of Thoughts is the Key to Control of Senses

Why drivel at length?
Why the mirage think of?
The thought is the seed
Of things all;
Expand your thought
The things too expand;
Contract your thought;
That is all there is to it,
For those who think about it.

இளைக்கின்ற வாறறிந் தின்னுயிர் வைத்த
கிளைக்கொன்று மீசனைக் கேடில் புகழோன்
தளைக்கொன்ற நாகமஞ் சாடல் ஒடுக்கத்
துளைக்கொண்ட தவ்வழி தூங்கும் படைத்தே. 2037

Control the Serpentine Thought in the Yoga Way of Kundalini

Knowing well how spent away you are
The Lord comes to dwell in the body
For the soul to lean on;
And He of blemishless fame
To subdue the five-headed serpent
That in Pasa coiled lay,
Provides the fluted Sushumna
That central stands.

He, the Immaculate Pinnacle, subdues the serpentine thought that is coiled in pasa, that burrows a way through the sushumna cavity.

பாய்ந்தன பூதங்கள் ஐந்தும் படரொளி
சார்ந்திடு ஞானத் தறியினிற் பூட்டிட்டு
வாய்ந்துகொள் ஆனந்தமென்னும்அருள்செய்யில்
வேய்ந்துகொள் மேலை விதியது தானே. 2038

Control Senses By Jnana Yoga

Tie the prancing senses five
To the post of Jnana that illumineth;
Thus you attain Grace that is Bliss;
This the Way of Yore, high and true.

நடக்கின்ற நந்தியை நாடோறு முன்னில்
படர்க்கின்ற சிந்தையைப் பைய வொடுக்கிக்
குறிக்கொண்ட சிந்தை குறிவழி நோக்கில்
வடக்கொடு தெற்கு மனக்கோயி லாமே. 2039

Control Thought and Make it a Temple

Daily think of the Living Nandi
Gently control your thoughts distracting,
Course your thoughts through Muladhara,
Then your thoughts a temple become,
From north to south extending.

சென்றன நாழிகை நாள்கள் சிலபல
நின்றது நீள்பொருள் நீர்மேல் எழுத்தொத்து
வென்று புலன்கள் விரைந்து விடுமின்கள்
குன்று விழவதில் தாங்கலு மாமே. 2040

Control Senses and Bear Your Troubles Gently

The hours sped,
The days many passed away;
Like the writing on the water
Transitory your possessions are;
Conquer the senses,
Quickly give them up;
Then even if as mountain,
Your troubles roll on you
Well may you bear them, gently indeed.

போற்றிசைத் துப்புனி தன்திரு மேனியைப்
போற்றிசெய் மீட்டே புலனைந்தும் புத்தியால்
நாற்றிசைக் கும்பின்னை யாருக்கு நாதனை
ஊற்றுகை யுள்ளத் தொருங்கலு மாமே. 2041

Redeem the Senses By Intelligence and Prayer

Praise the Holy Form
Of the Pure One;
Praise Him,
The Senses redeeming by intelligence;
In your heart welling up in love,
You shall become one with Him,

—He the Lord of directions four
And of beings, in others all.

தரிக்கின்ற நெஞ்சஞ் சகளத்தி னுள்ளே
அரிக்கின்ற ஐவரை யாரும் உணரார்
சிரிக்கின்ற வாறு சிலபல பேசில்
வரிக்கொண்ட மைசூழ் வரையது வாமே. 2042

Senses Are Very Powerful

None knoweth that the senses Five,
Within body thoughts engrossing,
Slowly eat you away;
Do not take them lightly
And talk away;
They are verily like a mountain range
That are by dark clouds capped.

கைவிட லாவதொன் றில்லை கருத்தினுள்
எய்தி யவனை யிசையினால் ஏத்துமின்
ஐவ ருடைய அவாவினில் தோன்றிய
பொய்வ ருடைய புலன்களும் ஐந்தே. 2043

Give Up Nothing; But Sublimate Your Thought Towards God

There is nothing, you need give up;
The Five senses are organs false
That the five cravings to meet arose;
Reach to Him in your thoughts
And praise Him in songs sweet.

Renounce nothing, But sublimate your thoughts and senses towards God. Praise Him and adore Him in sweet music and ecstatic songs. He will direct you inner being to divine destiny.

34. அசற்குரு நெறி

WAYS OF UNHOLY GURU

உணர்வொன் றிலாமூடன்உண்மையோராதோன்
கணுவின்றி வேதா கமநெறி காணான்
பணிவொன் றிலாதோன் பரநிந்தை செய்வோன்
அணுவின் குணத்தோன் அசற்குரு வாமே. 2044

The Unholy Guru Has Virtues None

A fool he is,
Wisdom none he has;
Truth he has realized not;
Versed is he not in the way
Of Vedas and Agamas;
Humility he has none;
Of God he speaks ill;
Worldly life is his sole concern;
He, verily, is the Guru unholy..

மந்திர தந்திர மாயோக ஞானமும்
பந்தமும் வீடுந் தரிசித்துப் பார்ப்பவர்
சிந்தனை செய்யாத் தெளிவியா தூண்பொருட்
டந்தக ராவோர் அசற்குரு வாமே. 2045

The Unholy is only in Search of Food

Mantra, Tantra, Mahayoga and Jnana,
Bondage, and Mukti
—These they seek to know, the holy ones;
The Gurus unholy
Seek not them
Doubts they clear not;
Food are they in search of,
Verily blind are they.

ஆமா றறியாதோன் மூடன் அதிமூடன்
காமாதி நீங்காக் கலதி கலதிகட்
காமா றசத்தறி விப்போன் அறிவிலோன்
கோமா னலசனத் தாகுங் குரவனே. 2046

The Unholy Guru is Bereft of Knowledge

Fool is he,
A big fool is he;
The Way of Becoming he knows not;
A vile fellow that is not of passions rid,
To vile men he teaches things vile;
Bereft of knowledge,
He no teacher exalted is;
—The Guru unholy.

கற்பாய கற்பங்கள் நீக்காமற் கற்பித்தால்
தற்பாவங் குன்றுந் தனக்கே பகையாகும்
நற்பால் அரசுக்கு நாட்டுக்கும் கேடென்றே
முற்பாலே நந்தி மொழிந்துவைத் தானே. 2047

The False Guru is an Enemy to Himself and World

If without driving away
The illusory thoughts
That imagination breeds,
A teacher teaches,
He will in divinity lose faith;
Like his own self an enemy be;
For the king and the kingdom an evil be;
—Thus hath Nandi of yore declared.

குருடர்க்குக் கோல்காட்டிச் செல்லுங் குருடர்
முரணும் பழங்குழி வீழ்வர்கள் முன்பின்
குருடரும் வீழ்வர்கள் முன்பின் னறவே
குருடரும் வீழ்வார் குருடரோ டாகியே. 2048

The Blind Leading the Blind Together Fall

The blind (the unholy Guru), who lead the blind (foolish disciples)
Will into the eternal pit first fall;
Then the foolish disciples too fall;
And in the end in disorder together they fall,
—The blind that lead and the blind that are led—
Indistinguishably, jumbled together.

35. சற்குரு நெறி

WAYS OF HOLY GURU

தாடந் தளிக்குந் தலைவனே சற்குரு
தாடந்து தன்னை யறியத் தரவல்லோன்
தாடந்து தத்துவா தீதத்துச் சார்சிவன்
தாடந்து பாசந் தணிக்கு மவன்சத்தே. 2049

Holy Guru Leads Disciple to Truth

Placing his feet on my head
The Master blesses me;
He is Guru Holy;
He, my self-realization, works;
He takes the Jiva to the State beyond Tattvas;
He subdues my Pasas,
All these he performs
—He that is Truth itself.

தவிரவைத் தான்வினை தன்னடி யார்கோள்
தவிரவைத் தான்சிரத் தோடுதன் பாதந்
தவிரவைத் தான்நமன் தூதுவர் கூட்டந்
தவிரவைத் தான்பிற வித்துயர் தானே. 2050

What the Holy Guru does for His Disciples

From their Karmas, he extricated his disciples
Blessing them with his feet on their head,
He drove away their evil stars;
The messengers of Death
He kept at bay from them;
The miseries of unending birth
He ended for them.

கறுத்தே இரும்பே கனகம தானான்
மறித்திரும் பாகா வகையது போலக்
குறித்தஅப் போதே குருவருள் பெற்றான்
மறித்துப் பிறவியில் வந்தணு கானே. 2051

He Takes Them to the Bourne From Which They Return Not

The black iron, transmuted into gold,
To black iron returns not;
Even so,
He who once the Guru's grace received
Does not to birth return.

பாசத்தை நீக்கிப் பரனோடுதன்னையும்
நேசத்து நாடி மலமற நீக்குவோர்
ஆசற்ற சற்குரு வாவோர் அறிவற்றுப்
பூசற் கிரங்குவோர் போதக் குருவன்றே. 2052

Holy Guru Does not Exult in Vain Contentions

He liberates you from Pasas;
He removes your Malas, entire;
He makes you seek the Lord in love;
—Such are the Gurus Holy, blemishless;
They who in contention exult
Are no Gurus enlightened.

நேயத்தே நிற்கும் நிமலன் மலமற்ற
நேயத்தை நல்கவல் லோனித்தன் சுத்தனே
ஆயத்த வர்தத் துவமுணர்ந் தாங்கற்ற
நேயர்க் களிப்பவன் நீடுங் குரவனே. 2053

Holy Guru Assesses Worth of His Disciples

He is a pure being
He is so endearing;
He can give you love,
That is from Malas free;
He is immortal,
He is holy;
He assesses the worth of his disciples;
And on those who are impurity rid,
He bestows his grace;
He, the Master High.

பரிசன வேதி பரிசித்த தெல்லாம்
வரிசை தரும்பொன் வகையாகு மாபோற்
குருபரி சித்த குவலயம் எல்லாந்
திரிமலந் தீர்ந்து சிவகதி யாமே. 2054

By His Alchemic Touch Jiva Becomes Siva

All that the alchemist touches
Turns into gold;
Even so,
The Jivas blessed by Guru
Siva become,
Freed from Malas Triple.

தானே யெனநின்ற சற்குரு சந்நிதி
தானே யெனநின்ற தன்மை வெளிப்படில்
தானே தனைப்பெற வேண்டுஞ் சதுர்பெற
ஊனே யெனநினைந் தோர்ந்துகொள் உன்னிலே. 2055

Holy Guru is Siva in Flesh

The Holy Guru
As Siva Himself stands;
In his presence
Jiva, his self-realization attains
If you, your self-realization seek,
Think of him, within,
As Siva in fleshy body.

வரும்வழி போம்வழி மாயா வழியைக்
கருவழி கண்டவர் காணா வழியைப்
பெரும்வழி யாநந்தி பேசும் வழியைக்
குருவழி யேசென்று கூடலு மாமே. 2056

Follow Holy Guru and Reach the Great Way

The Way of birth,
The Way of death,
The Way of Maya;

The Way they have not seen
Who the birth's Way saw;
The Great Way that Nandi speaks of
That Way you can reach
If your Holy Guru you follow.

குருவென் பவனே வேதாக மங்கூறும்
பரவின்ப னாகிச் சிவயோகம் பாவித்
தொருசிந்தை யின்றி உயர்பாச நீக்கி
வருநல் குரவன்பால் வைக்கலு மாமே. 2057

Holy Guru Leads to Lord

He is Guru Holy,
Who, entranced in bliss
The Vedas and Agamas speaks of,
Enters into Siva Yoga;
And all thoughts stilled,
Removes the bondage of Pasa
And leads you to Lord.

சத்தும் அசத்துஞ் சதசத்துந் தான்காட்டிச்
சித்தும் அசித்துஞ் சிவபரத் தேசேர்த்துச்
சுத்த மசுத்த மறச்சுக மானசொல்
அத்தன் அருட்குரு வாமவன் கூறிலே. 2058

Holy Guru Imparts Nature of Truth

He reveals the Real (Sat), the Unreal (Asat) and the Real-Unreal (Sat-Asat);
He takes Chit (Jiva) and Achit (Tattvas) into Siva-Para;
The words the blessed Guru speak
Are blissful,
Beyond Pure (Suddha) and (Asuddha) Impure.

உற்றிடும் ஐம்மலம் பாச வுணர்வினாற்
பற்றறு நாதன் அடியிற் பணிதலாற்
சுற்றிய பேதந் துரியமூன் றால்வாட்டித்
தற்பர மேவவோர் சாதக ராமே. 2059

True Disciples Adore Holy Guru

By Pasa's sensations, the Five Malas arise;
Adoring feet of Guru in love intense,
Purified in Turiya Awareness Three
They the Supreme State attain;
They alone are Sadhakas true.

எல்லாம் இறைவன் இறைவி யுடனின்பம்
வல்லார் புலனும் வருங்கால் உயிர்தோன்றிச்
சொல்லா மலமைந் தடங்கியிட் டோங்கியே
செல்லாச் சிவகதி சேர்தல் விளையாட்டே. 2060

Jiva Subsiding in Silence in Self Ascends to Siva-State

Powerful are the senses,
From them arise pleasure sensations;
If Jiva, in silence, subsides in Self
And ascends high,
It shall reach Siva-State;
All is but play of Siva and Sakti.

Powerful, indeed, are the senses from which arise pleasure sensations. If jiva subsides in silence in the Self, it conquers the senses and ascends high to reach the Siva state.

ஈனப் பிறவியில் இட்டது மீட்டூட்டித்
தானத்து விட்டுத் தனையூட்டித் தாழ்த்தலும்
ஞானத்தின் மீட்டலும் நாட்டலும் வீடுற்று
மோனத்துள் வைத்தலும் முத்தன்றன்
செய்கையே. 2061

From Jiva's Birth to its Final Emancipation—It is All Lord's Work

Consigning Jiva to birth's sorrows,
Rescuing it by ministrations gentle,
Assigning it positions appropriate,
Baptising it in Jnana,
Redeeming it,
And in Mukti establishing it,
And in the end,
Placing it in Mystic Silence (Mauna)
—All these are but the Lord's work.

அத்த னருளின் விளையாட் டிடஞ்சடஞ்
சித்தொ டசித்தறத் தெளிவித்த சீவனைச்
சுத்தனு மாக்கித் துடைத்து மலத்தினைச்
சத்துட னைங்கரு மத்திடுந்தன்மையே. 2062

Lord's Play in the Arena of Jiva's Body

The fleshy body is the arena of Lord's Play,
He imparts to Jiva,
Knowledge clear of Chit and Achit,
Purifies him
Wipes off the Malas
And consigns him to the Sat (Real),
Like Himself the Five Acts to perform;
—These the Play of the Lord's Grace.

ஈசத்து வங்கடந் தில்லையென் றப்புறம்
பாசத்து ளேயென்றும் பாவியும் அண்ணலை
நேசத்து ளேநின்ற நின்மலன் எம்மிறை
தேசத்தை யெல்லாந் தெளியவைத் தானே. 2063

Love for Lord Takes You to Siva State

Beyond the state of Isatva (Siva State)
Nothing there is;
Realizing this,
Continue ever, in love intense, for Lord;
My Lord is the Pure One
Who in love abides;
He it is,
Who illumined directions all.

மாணிக்க மாலை மலர்ந்தெழு மண்டலம்
ஆணிப்பொன் னின்றங் கமுதம் விளைந்தது
பேணிக்கொண் டுண்டார் பிறப்பற் றிருந்தார்
ஊணுக் கிருந்தார் உணராத மாக்களே. 2064

Divine State Ends Birth's Cycle

In the sphere (of cranium)
Where the garland of scarlet rubies glows,
He the unalloyed Gold,
There stood;
The divine nectar welled up there;
They who swilled it,
Ended their birth's cycle;
They who did not
Remained but to gormandize.

அசத்தொடு சத்தும் அசத்சத்து நீங்க
இசைத்திடு பாசப்பற் றீங்கறு மாறே
அசைத்திரு மாயை அணுத்தானு மாங்கே
இசைத்தானு மொன்றறி விப்போன் இறையே. 2065

Lord Attaches Mayas to Jiva for Attainment of True Knowledge

The Sat, Asat, and the Sat-Asat to free,
The Pasa's bonds here to sunder,
He activated Mayas Two — Suddha and Asuddha—
And to Jiva, He them attached,
And imparted the peerless Light of Knowledge, too,
He, the Lord.

ஏறு நெறியே மலத்தை எரித்தலால்
ஈறில் உரையால் இருளை யறுத்தலான்
மாறில் பசுபாசம் வாட்டலால் வீடுக
கூறு பரனே குருவாம் இயம்பிலே. 2066

Siva is the Supreme Guru

The way of Adhara ascending scorches Malas,
The endless chanting of His name dispels the Darkness (of Ignorance)
Harass the Pasa that the Jiva is heir to,
Thus do thou liberation seek;
The Lord, forsooth, is the Guru Supreme.

36. கூடாவொழுக்கம்

UNHOLY CONDUCT

கண்காணி யில்லென்று கள்ளம் பலசெய்வார்
கண்காணி யில்லா விடமில்லை காணுங்கால்
கண்காணி யாகக் கலந்தெங்கு நின்றானைக்
கண்காணி கண்டார் களவொழிந் தாரே. 2067

God is Omniscient

Thinking there is none that oversees
They many evil deeds perform;
None the place, in fact,
Where the over-seer is not;
The Lord pervades all, overseeing all;
They who the Over-seer saw,
Abandoned evil deeds all.

செய்தான் அறியுஞ் செழுங்கடல் வட்டத்துப்
பொய்தான் மிகவும் புலம்பும் மனிதர்கள்
மெய்தான் உரைக்கில்விண் ணோர்தொழச்செய்வன்
மைதாழ்ந் திலங்கு மிடறுடை யோனே. 2068

Speak Truth

He who this sea-girt world created
He knows all;
Men falsehoods many utter,
Let them the Truth speak;
He will make Celestials revere them
—He, that is of the lustrous dark throat.

பத்திவிற் றுண்டு பகலைக் கழிவிடு
மத்தகர்க் கன்றோ மறுபிறப் புள்ளது
வித்துக்குற் றுண்டு விளைபுலம் பாழ்செய்யும்
பித்தர்கட் கென்றும் பிறப்பில்லை தானே. 2069

Conserve Bindu

They sell the Love of God,
They make a daily business of it;
Pride-filled are they,
They in birth's whirl will be;
They who pound the Seed (Bindu) and consume
Lay waste the body-land;
But, verily, for the God-mad,
Forever no birth will be.

வடக்கு வடக்கென்பர் வைத்ததொன் றில்லை
நடக்க வுறுவரே ஞானமி லாதார்
வடக்கில் அடங்கிய வையகம் எல்லாம்
அகத்தில் அடங்கும் அறிவுடை யோர்க்கே. 2070

Acquire True Jnana

"North, North" they say;
Nothing there in the north is;
Northward they walk,
Of Jnana bereft;
All the world in the north,
Is in their heart contained,
For those that knowledge truly possess.

காயக் குழப்பனைக் காயநன் னாடனைக்
காயத்தி னுள்ளே கமழ்கின்ற நந்தியைத்

தேயத்து ளேயெங்குந் தேடித் திரிவர்கள்
காயத்துள் நின்ற கருத்தறி யாரே. 2071

Look Inward

He who made this body-mix,
He who this body land holds,
He who within this body shines,
He is Nandi;
Him they seek and search in lands all;
They know not
He within the body stands.

கண்காணி யாகவே கையகத் தேயெழுங்
கண்காணி யாகக் கருத்து ளிருந்திடுங்
கண்காணி யாகக் கலந்து வழிசெய்யுங்
கண்காணி யாகிய காதலன் தானே. 2072

Lord Oversees From Within You

Visible to your eyes,
He rises in your very palm;
Over-seeing All,
He in your thoughts stands;
As light within the eyes,
He guides your way;
He is Love Embodied,
That Oversees you ever.

கன்னி யொருசிறை கற்றோர் ஒருசிறை
மன்னிய மாதவஞ் செய்வோர் ஒருசிறை
தன்னியல் புன்னி யுணர்ந்தோர் ஒருசிறை
என்னிது ஈசன் இயல்பறி யாரே. 2073

How the Lord is Seated

The Virgin Sakti on one side
The learned ones on one side,
The Tapasvins steadfast on one side,
The Self-Realized beings on one side,
Thus is the Lord seated;
How is it they know not His nature true!

காணாத கண்ணிற் படலமே கண்ணொளி
காணாத வர்கட்குங் காணாத வவ்வொளி
காணாத வர்கட்குங் கண்ணாம் பெருங்கண்ணைக்
காணாது கண்டார் களவொழிந் தாரே. 2074

Lord is the Light of Our Eyes

The eye that sees not
Is by cataract (ignorance) covered;
The Lord is the Light Unseen,
Even for those
Whose eye no sight hath;
He is the Eye Divine,
Even for those
Who have seen Him not;
They who have seen Him
In the inward eye
Have verily the Truth seen
All illusion rid.

பித்தன் மருந்தால் தெளிந்து பிரகிருதி
உய்த்தொன்று மாபோல் விழியுந்தன் கண்ணொளி
அத்தன்மை யாதல்போல் நந்தி அருள்தரச்
சித்தம் தெளிந்தேன் செயலொழிந் தேனே. 2075

By His Grace Our Thoughts Become Serene

Even as
The lunatic by medicine administered
Lucid becometh,
And his true self realizeth;
Even as,
The eye its sight regains,
So, too,
Nandi bestowing His Grace on me
Serene my thoughts became,
To actionless state heightened.

பிரான்மய மாகப் பெயர்ந்தன எட்டும்
பராமய மென்றெண்ணிப் பள்ளி யுணரார்
சுராமய முன்னிய சூழ்வினை யாளர்
நிராமய மாக நினைப்பொழிந் தாரே. 2076

Unholy Men Do Not Think of Attaining Divinity

The directions eight moved,
The Lord pervading them all;
Of this, His Omnipresence, they think not;
From their stupor they wake not;
Drunk are they in their Karmas inebriate;
Lo! all thoughts of Divinity-Becoming
They, forever, abandoned.

ஒன்றிரண் டாகிநின் றொன்றியொன் றாயினோர்க்
கொன்றும் இரண்டும் ஒருகாலுங் கூடிடா
ஒன்றிரண் டென்றே யுரைதரு வோர்க்கெலாம்
ஒன்றிரண் டாய்நிற்கும் ஒன்றோடொன் றானதே. 2077

They Think of I and You as Two

The two, I and You, in union one stood,
Undifferentiated as One Becoming;
For them is there no more Two, I and You;
They who speak of I and You as two
To them He is I and You, forever two;
He, the Being, One and One above.

உயிரது நின்றால் உணர்வெங்கு நிற்கும்
அயரறி வில்லையா லாருடல் வீழும்
உயிரும் உடலும் ஒருங்கிக் கிடக்கும்
பயிருங் கிடந்துள்ளப் பாங்கறி யாரே. 2078

They Do Not Know the Inter-Relation of Body and Life

When life ebbs away,
Where the sensations are?

Sentience lost,
The body drops;
Life and body as one flourish
That state, they know not.

உயிரது வேறாயுணர்வெங்கு மாகும்
உயிரை யறியில் உணர்வறி வாகும்
உயிரன் றுடலை விழுங்கு முணர்வை
அயரும் பெரும்பொரு ளாங்கறி யாரே. 2079

Lord is in Awareness, not in Prana

Prana is from pervasive Awareness apart;
When you know what Prana is,
You shall know what Awareness is,
Awareness is Knowledge, (not Prana),
That pervades the body;
He within that Awareness
Is the Lord Great;
That they know not.

உலகாணி யொண்சுடர் உத்தம சித்தன்
நிலவாணி ஐந்தினுள் நேருற நிற்குஞ்
சிலவாணி யாகிய தேவர் பிரானைத்
தலைவாணி செய்வது தன்னை யறிவதே. 2080

Realize the Self

He is the world's axle-pin;
The Light Resplendent;
The Siddha True;
He pervades the elements five,
The earth, sky and the rest;
He is the Lord of Devas
He with Sakti stands;
To praise Him in Words high
Is your Self to realize.

தானந்த மாமென நின்ற தனிச்சுடர்
ஊனந்த மாயுல காய்நின்ற வொண்சுடர்
தேனந்த மாய்நின்ற சிற்றின்ப நீயொழி
கோனந்த மில்லாக் குணத்தரு ளாமே. 2081

Give Up Worldly Pleasures

He is the peerless Light
He is the end of all;
He is the resplendent Light;
He is the goal of fleshy body
And worlds all,
And the worldly pleasures
To you honey-sweet;
Give them up;
The Lord of limitless goodness
On you His Grace bestows.

உன்முத லாகிய வூனுயிர் உண்டெனுங்
கன்முத லீசன் கருத்தறி வாரில்லை
நன்முத லேறிய நாம மறநின்றால்
தன்முத லாகிய தத்துவ மாமே. 2082

Efface the Ego

He is your Beginning;
He is the life in your fleshy body;
He is the God in Mountain Kailas
None knows His design;
When the Primal One sways you,
And your ego entire effaced,
Then shall you reach the Lord,
Above Tattvas all.

இந்தியம் அந்தக் கரண மிவையுயிர்
வந்தன சூக்க வுடலன்று மானது
தந்திடும் ஐவிதத் தால்தற் புருடனு
முந்துள மன்னு மாறாறு முடிவிலே. 2083

Unborn Being Above Tattvas

He is not Indriyas (external sense organs);
Nor the Antakaranas (internal sense organs);
Nor the Subtle body that life carries;
Out of the mighty Man
Arose the Maya Inscrutable,
And the Tattvas thirty and six;
Above them all, high at the apex stands
The Being uncreated, the Eternal and the Everlasting.

37. கேடு கண்டிரங்கல்

IN COMPASSION FOR MEN'S EVIL LOT

வித்துப் பொதிவார் விரைவிட்டு நாற்றுவார்
அற்றதம் வாணாள் அறிகிலாப் பாவிகள்
உற்ற வினைத்துயர் ஒன்றும் அறிகிலார்
முற்றொளி தீயின் புரிகின்ற வாறே. 2084

Ungodly Ones do not Think of Soul's Liberation

They germinate the seed;
They plant the seedlings;
They think not of their own fleeting life;
Poor are they in spirit;
They know nothing of Karmaic sorrows;
They perish in the blazing fire,
Verily are they such.

போது சடக்கெனப் போகின் றதுகண்டும்
வாதுசெய் தென்னோ மனிதர் பெறுவது
நீதியுளே நின்று நின்மலன் தாள்பணிந்
தாதியை அன்பில் அறியகில் லார்களே. 2085

What do they get, Who do not Adore Lord

Well do they see
Life in a trice fleets away;
Yet do they in contention stand;
What though these men get?
They stand not in ways righteous,
They adore not His Holy Feet
They know not the Primal One
In love endearing.

கடன்கொண்டு நெற்குத்துக் கையரை யூட்டி
உடம்பினை யோம்பி உயிராத் திரிவார்
தடங்கொண்ட சாரல் தழல்முரு டேறி
இடங்கொண் டுடலார் கிடக்கின்ற வாறே. 2086

They Care Not for Soul's Well-Being

They borrow grain;
They pound it hard,
Feed the base (senses),
And nourish the body;
Thus they wander
Their lives to live;
But in the valley broad
A prey to raging flames
The body finally lieth;
This they realize not.

விரைந்தன்று நால்வர்க்கு மெய்ப்பதி சூழ்ந்து
புரந்தகல் லால்நிழற் புண்ணியன் சொன்ன
பரந்தன்னை யோராப் பழிமொழி யாளர்
உரந்தன்மை யாக வொருங்கிநின் றார்களே. 2087

They Stand in Wait for the Burial Heap

In days of yore, the Sages Four
Sought the Holy One in Kailas;
There, under the wild banyan tree
The Supreme One His teachings imparted;
They are of evil speech
Who think not of Him;
Ready to march to the burial heap
They stand in wait.

நின்ற புகழும் நிறைதவத் துண்மையும்
என்றும்எம் மீசன் அடியவர்க் கேநல்கும்
அன்றி யுலக மதுவிது தேவென்று
குன்றுகை யாலே குறைப்பட்ட வாறே. 2088

They Are Distracted by Doubts

Imperishable fame,
And truthful fruit of Tapas full,
The Lord ever bestows
Only on those who endear Him;
Yet the world think
"This the God, That the God;"
Thus distracted
Bruised they fall, hands hitting on rocks.

இன்பத்து ளேபிறந் தின்பத்து ளேவளர்ந்
தின்பத்து ளேநினைக் கின்ற திதுமறந்
துன்பத்துளேசிலர் சோறொடு கூறையென்
துன்பத்து ளேநின்று தூங்குகின் றார்களே. 2089

They Pursue not the Way of Bliss

Born in bliss, grown in bliss
Steeped in thoughts of bliss
This way, they forget;
Instead,
Hankering after food and raiment
In sorrow steeped they are;
And in sorrow steeped, they insensible slumber.

பெறுதற் கரிய பிறவியைப் பெற்றும்
பெறுதற் கரிய பிரானடி பேணார்
பெறுதற் கரிய பிராணிகள் எல்லாம்
பெறுதற் கரியதோர் பேறிழந் தாரே. 2090

Human Birth is Rare; Yet They Seek Not Lord's Feet

Rare is human birth,
Yet they seek not Lord's Feet,
So rare to reach;
They attained the rare human birth,
Yet missed this Treasure Rare,
They are but crawling creatures, indeed.

ஆர்வ மனமும் அளவில் இளமையும்
ஈரமும் நல்லவென் றின்புறு காலத்துத்
தீர வருவதோர் காமத் தொழில்நின்று
மாதவன் இன்ப மறந்தொழிந் தார்களே. 2091

They Think Not of Heavenly Pleasures

Ardour of mind, ever fresh youth, and endearment of heart
These considering good,
They in pleasure indulged,
And in acts of love diverse sported;
Lo! They forgot the heavenly bliss
The Lord bestows
And for ever, for ever missed it.

இப்பரி சேயிள ஞாயிறு போலுரு
அப்பரி சங்கியின் உள்ளுறை யம்மானை
இப்பரி சேகம லத்துறை யீசனை
மெய்ப்பரி சேவினை வாதிருந் தேரமே. 2092

They Sought Not Lord

Thus He is,
Like the rising sun, His Form;
That He is,
Within the Fire Kundalini resides;
There He is,
In the Lotus of Heart seated;
The True He is,
The Lord, we sought not.

கூடகில் லார்குரு வைத்த குறிகண்டு
நாடகில் லார்நயம் பேசித் திரிவர்கள்
பாடகில் லாரவன் செய்த பரிசறிந்
தாடவல் லாரவர் பேறெது வாமே. 2093

They Dance and Waste Away Their Lives

They unite in Him not,
The Way Guru showed;
They seek Him not,
In aimless talk indulging;
They sing Him not,
His benevolent deeds realizing;
What will they get,
They who dance and waste away?

The unholy ones dance about and waste away their lives. They do not seek the Lord the way the holy Guru has shown. The benevolent bliss of Siva is not for them.

நெஞ்சு நிறைந்தங் கிருந்த நெடுஞ்சுடர்
நஞ்செம் பிரானென்று நாதனை நாடொறுந்
துஞ்சு மளவுந் தொழுமின் தொழாவிடில்
அஞ்சற்று விட்டதோர் ஆணையு மாமே. 2094

They Fall a Prey to Senses

He is the Great Light
That fills my heart;
Melting in love
Daily adore Him,
Like the end of your days;
If you adore not,
The Five senses havoc cause
Like the elephants that roam loose.

மிருக மனிதர் மிக்கோர் பறவை
ஒருவர்செய் தன்புவைத் துன்னாத தில்லை
பருகுவ ரோடுவர் பார்ப்பயன் கொள்வர்
திருமரு மாதவஞ் சேர்ந்துணர்ந் தாரே. 2095

They Care Not for the Fruit of This Birth

The birds, beasts, and the humans several,
They all, all, in endearment seek Him not;
They who in Tapas intense realized Him
Drink and run in rapture surpassing;
They indeed are the beings
Who have reaped the fruit of their birth here below.

நீதியி லோர்பெற்றபொன்போல் இறைவனைச்
சோதியி லாருந் தொடர்ந்தறி வாரில்லை
ஆதி பயனென் றமரர் பிரானென்று
நாதியே வைத்தது நாடுகின் றேனே. 2096

They Seek Not Light

They seek not His Light
In unbroken continuity;
They are like those
Who cherish not Him that is gold,
The Unrighteous they are;
"O! Lord, the Primal One!
You the Fruit of Wisdom!
The Lord of Celestial Beings!
My Sole Refuge!"
Thus I seek Him, ever and ever.

இருந்தேன் மலரளைந் தின்புற வண்டு
பெருந்தேன் இழைக்கின்ற பெற்றிமை யோரார்
வருந்தேன் நுகராது வாய்புகு தேனை
அருந்தேனை யாரும் அறியகி லாரே. 2097

They Seek Not the Divine Honey

The bees flit from flower to flower
And in rapture incessant gather
The honey sweet;
Of this they think not;
There is a Honey Pure sweeter far
That in their mouth wells up (in Yoga)
None knows that Honey Rare.

கருத்தறி யாது கழிந்தன காலம்
அருத்தியுள் ளான்அம ராபதி நாதன்
ஒருத்தனுள் ளானுல கத்துயிர்க் கெல்லாம்
வருத்திநில் லாது வழுக்குகின் றாரே. 2098

They Slip Low Down

Seeking Him not,
I wasted my life away;
In my love
Is the Lord of Celestial Beings;
He is the One Being,
For the worlds all;
Yet in their thoughts
They praise Him not,
Low down they slip.

குதித்தோடிப் போகின்ற கூற்றமுஞ் சார்வாய்
விதித்தன நாட்களும் வீழ்ந்து கழிந்த
வதிர்த்திருந் தென்செய்தி ராறுதி ராகிற்
கொதிக்கின்ற கூழில் துடுப்பிட லாமே. 2099

Death Nears; Yet They Seek Not Peace

The God of Death leaps forward,
Agreeable to him
The fated days too roll away;
You tremble and shake,
What, though, that comes of it?
If Peace you seek,
Dip the ladle of your heart
In the boiling broth of love.

கரையரு காறாக் கழனி வளைந்த
திரையரு காமுன்னம் சேர்ந்தின்பம் எய்தும்
வரையரு கூறிய மாதவ நோக்கின்
நரையுரு வாச்செல்லு நாளில வாமே. 2100

Seek Lord Before Floods of Age Swell

Along the banks of the rivei (of Life)
The field ripened;
Before the floods (of age) swell,
Seek the Bliss Divine;
Practise Yoga
That takes you to the Mountain top
Where the ambrosial waters flow;
Then no more does greying age seize you.

வரவறி வானை மயங்கிருண் ஞாலத்
திரவறி வானை யெழுஞ்சுடர்ச் சோதியை
அரவறி வார்முன் னொருதெய்வ மென்று
விரவறி யாமலே மேல்வைத்த வாறே. *2101*

Their Thoughts Do Not Reach to the Lord

He who knows the Origin of all,
He who knows the Night (end)
That envelops worlds all,
The Self Luminous Light
He whom the Enlightened held aloft
As the One God Supreme,
Him they know not;
And thus on this world their thoughts still stand.

38. இதோபதேசம்

SALUTARY INSTRUCTION

மறந்தொழி மண்மிசை மன்னாப் பிறவி
இறந்தொழி காலத்தும் ஈசனை உள்கும்
பறந்தல மந்து படுதுயர் தீர்ப்பான்
சிறந்த சிவநெறி சிந்தைசெய் யீரே. *2102*

Think of Siva's Holy Way

Away forget,
This transient life here below;
Even like the day your life passes away
Think of the Lord;
Flying He comes to you,
And your distracting sorrows end;
Do, therefore, think
Of Siva's Holy Way.

செல்லு மளவுஞ் செலுத்துமின் சிந்தையை
வல்ல பரிசால் உரைமின்கள் வாய்மையை
இல்லை யெனினும் பெரிதுளன் எம்மிறை
நல்ல வரனெறி நாடுமி னீரே. *2103*

Seek the Holy Path of Hara

Think of Him
As far as your thoughts go;
Speak His truth
As far as you can;
"Lord," they may say, "He is not,"
Very much He is, everywhere;
Seek the Holy Path
Of Hara that is ever good.

ஒன்றே குலமும் ஒருவனே தேவனும்
நன்றே நினைமின் நமனில்லை நாணாமே
சென்றே புகுங்கதி யில்லைநுஞ் சித்தத்து
நின்றே நிலைபெற நீர்நினைந் துய்மினே *2104*

One the Family, One the God

One the family,
One the God;
Thus intense hold,
No more will death be;
None Other is Refuge,
With confidence you can seek;
Think of Him and be redeemed,
In your thoughts, holding Him steadfast.

This is extra-ordinarily modern in tone. Tirumular rises here to the highest in grandeur of thought.

போற்றிசெ யந்தண் கயிலைப் பொருப்பனை
நாற்றிசைக் குந்நடு வாய்நின்ற நம்பனைக்
காற்றிசைக் குங்கமழ் ஆக்கையைக்கைக்கொண்டு
கூற்றுதைத் தான்றன்னைக் கூறிநின் றுய்மினே. *2105*

Praise Lord and Spurn Death

Praise the benevolent Lord,
He of Mount Kailas;
He as central stood,
In cardinal directions four, our Lord;
With the precious body
That Prana's vital breath holds
Praise the Lord and be redeemed,
The Lord,
Who with His Feet the God of Death spurned.

இக்காய நீக்கி யினியொரு காயத்திற்
புக்குப் பிறவாமற் போம்வழி நாடுமின்
எக்காலத் திவ்வுடல் வந்தெமக் கானதென்
றக்கால முன்ன அருள்பெற லாமே. *2106*

Seek Lord; No More Births Will Be

Seek the Way
That when this body leaves,
Another body, you enter not;
"When did this human body come to me?"
Of that time you think of;
Verily will you His Grace receive.

போகின்ற வாறே புகுகின்ற அப்பொருள்
ஆகின்ற போது மரனறி வானுளன்

சாகின்ற போதுந் தலைவனை நாடுமின்
ஆகின்ற அப்பொருள் அக்கரை யாகுமே. 2107

Lord is Your Redemption

The Lord who enters into you
And walks with you in the life
Knows sure when you in holiness ripen;
Seek the Lord
Even on the eve of your death;
He will your Redemption be
For the life to be.

பறக்கின்ற வொன்று பயனுற வேண்டின்
இறக்கின்ற காலத்தும் ஈசனை யுள்குஞ்
சிறப்பொடு சேருஞ் சிவகதி பின்னைப்
பிறப்பொன் றிலாமையும் பேருல காமே. 2108

Think of Lord like Your Last Days

If your fleeting life
Is its good goal to attain,
Even on death-bed
Think of the Lord;
Then will follow Siva's grace,
No more birth will be;
The heavenly world will yours be.

கூடியும் நின்றுந் தொழுதெம் மிறைவனைப்
பாடியு ளேநின்று பாதம் பணிமின்கள்
ஆடியு ளேநின் றறிவுசெய் வார்கட்கு
நீடிய வீற்றுப் பசுவது வாமே. 2109

Lord Yearns After Devotees

Praise Our Lord
In devotion congregational;
Sing His praise within,
And at His Feet adore;
Dance within and know Him;
Then He yearns after you,
Like the cow after its calf.

விடுகின்ற சீவனார் மேலெழும் போது
நடுநின்று நாடுமின் நாதன்தன் பாதங்
கெடுகின்ற வல்வினை கேடில் புகழோன்
இடுகின்றான் உம்மை இமையவ ரோடே. 2110

Attaining Celestial Status

When in death
Your life breath upward ascends
Course it through central Sushumna
And seek the Feet of the Lord;
Your evil Karmas dire perish;
He of the blemishless fame
Seats you among Beings Immortal.

ஏறுடை யாயிறை வாஎம் பிரானென்று
நீறிடு வாரடி யார்நிகழ் தேவர்கள்
ஆறணி செஞ்சடை யண்ணல் திருவடி
வேறணி வார்க்கு வினையில்லை தானே. 2111

Devotees Become Celestials

"O! Lord on the bull mounted,
O! God, My Lord—"
The devotees who thus praising
His holy ashes wear,
Celestial Beings, indeed, become;
For them who adore the Feet of Lord,
Who the Ganga in His matted lock wears,
No more Karma further is.

இன்புறு வீர்அறிந் தேஎம் இறைவனை
அன்புறு வீர்தவஞ் செய்யுமெய்ஞ் ஞானத்துப்
பண்புறு வீர்பிற வித்தொழி லேநின்று
துன்புறு பாசத் துழைத்தொழிந் தீரே. 2112

Know Lord and Be in Bliss

Know Our Lord,
And in bliss be;
Be filled with love;
Perform Tapas;
Perfect Jnana True;
You, who has laboured hard,
In worldly pursuits,
Of miserable Pasa entangled.

மேற்கொள்ள லாவதோர்மெய்த்தவம் ஒன்றுண்டு
மேற்கொள்ளலாவதோர்மெய்த்தாளும்ஒன்றுண்டு
மேற்கொள்ள லாவதோர் மெய்ந்நெறி ஒன்றுண்டு
மேற்கொள்ள லாம்வண்ணம் வேண்டி நின்
றோர்க்கே. 2113

Ways to Seek the Higher Goal

There is a Tapas High
That you should seek;
There are Feet True
That you should adore;
There is a Way True
That you should adopt;
For all those
That the Higher Goal in earnest seek.

சார்ந்தவர்க் கின்பங் கொடுக்குந் தழல்வண்ணன்
பேர்ந்தவர்க் கின்னாப் பிறவி கொடுத்திடுங்
கூர்ந்தவர்க் கங்கே குரைகழல் காட்டிடுஞ்
சேர்ந்தவர் தேவரைச் சென்றுணர் வாரே. 2114

Seek the Lord and Be Blessed

On them who seek Him
He, His blessings bestows;
To them, who do not
He sorrows of birth gives;
To those who intensely adore Him,
He reveals the Grace of His Holy Feet;
Joining the horde of Devas

They seek and realize Him,
Him, the Fire-hured Lord.

முத்தியை ஞானத்தை முத்தமிழ் ஓசையை
எத்தனை காலமும் ஏத்துவர் ஈசனை
நெய்த்தலைப் பால்போல் நிமலனும் அங்குளன்
அத்தரு சோதி யதுவிரும் பாரே. 2115

Lord Stands as Ghee in Milk

He is Mukti, Jnana and Nada
That in the three branches of Tamil resound,
Thus they praise the Lord
Through time unending;
As the ghee within milk
The Pure One within them stands;
That Light they seek not, and love not.

Three branches of knowledge: Poetry, music and drama. Here, the references is to nada of all the three — A, U, M (Aum)

நியமத்த னாகிய நின்மலன் வைத்த
உகமெத் தனையென றொருவருந் தேறார்
பவமத்தி லேவந்து பாய்கின்ற தல்லாற்
சிவமத்தை யொன்றுந் தெளியகில் லாரே. 2116

Cascade of Births

The Pure One, as Creator of all
Many aeons, allotted;
How many they are,
None knows;
Into the cascade of births they leap;
Beyond that,
Of Siva they nothing clear know.

இங்கித்தை வாழ்வு மெனைத்தோ ரகிதமுந்
துஞ்சொத்த காலத்துத் தூய்மணி வண்ணனை
விஞ்சத் துறையும் விகிர்தா எனநின்னை
நஞ்சற் றவர்க்கன்றி நாடவொண் ணாதே. 2117

Pray in Pure Heart

Filled with misery
Is life here below;
When to sleep in death
You near,
Praise the Pure One,
Of gem-hued Form;
Unless you in melting heart hail Him
As "Oh, Lord, who in Light Divine abides"
You realize Him not.

பஞ்சமு மாம்புவி சற்குரு பால்முன்னி
வஞ்சக ரானவர் வைகில் அவர்தம்மை
அஞ்சுவன் நாதன் அருநர கத்திடுஞ்
செஞ்சநிற் போரைத் தெரிசிக்கச் சித்தியே. 2118

Fate of Knaves who Seek the Holy Guru

Some, who, knaves in real are,
Seek the Holy Guru;
If such be there,
Famine strikes the land;
At them even the Lord is appalled;
And to bottomless hell He consigns them;
To meet them
Who the righteous path tread,
That is Siddhi, verily.

சிவனை வழிபட்டார் எண்ணிலாத் தேவர்
அவனை வழிபட்டங் காமாறொன் றில்லை
அவனை வழிபட்டங் காமாறு காட்டுங்
குருவை வழிபடிற் கூடலு மாமே. 2119

Holy Guru Shows the Way

The countless Devas worshipped Siva;
What becomes them
By worshipping Him?
Far better it be,
That you worship the Holy Guru
—Who, having himself worshipped Lord
Shows the Way of Becoming, too;
Sure, indeed, is your Mukti definite.

நரருஞ் சுரரும் பசுபாச நண்ணிக்
கருமங்க ளாலே கழிதலிற் கண்டு
குருவென் பவன்ஞானி கோதில னானாற்
பரமென்றலா அன்றிப் பகர்வொன்று மின்றே. 2120

Hold on to Guru

The humans and Celestials
Inveighed by Pasas
In Karma perish;
Seeing this,
Why not hold to Guru
That is Jnani,
And blemishless Pure
As Param Supreme itself?
No more then to speak of.

ஆட்கொண் டவர்தனி நாயகன் அன்புற
மேற்கொண் டவர்வினை போயற நாடொறும்
நீர்க்கின்ற செஞ்சடை நீளன் உருவத்தின்
மேற்கொண்ட வாறலை வீவித்து ளானே. 2121

Guru is Lord Siva Himself

The Guru who admitted him into his loving Grace,
Is Lord Himself;
He works day by day
For the disciple's Karma to perish;
In the form of Lord
Of flowing russet locks
That wears the dripping Ganga
The Guru appears
And our sorrows ends.

ஏழாம் தந்திரம் முடிவு பெற்றது.
Tantra Seven Concluded

எட்டாந் தந்திரம்
TANTRA EIGHT

1. உடலிற் பஞ்சபேதம்

FIVE DIVISIONS OF THE BODY

This is said to be a redaction of the *Suprabhata Agama.*

காயப்பை யொன்று சரக்குப் பலவுள
மாயப்பை ஒன்றுண்டு மற்றுமோர் பையுண்டு
காயப்பைக் குள்நின்ற கள்வன் புறப்பட்டால்
மாயப்பை மண்ணா மயங்கிய வாறே. 2122

Body Bag and Maya Bag

The body is a bag
Many the ingredients it holds;
There is yet another bag within;
It is the Maya bag;
When the Thief (Jiva)
The body bag leaves,
The Maya bag
Like dust becomes.

அத்தன் அமைத்த உடலிரு கூறினிற்
சுத்தம தாகிய சூக்குமஞ் சொல்லுங்காற்
சத்த பரிச ரூப ரசகந்தம்
புத்திமா னாங்காரம் புரியட்ட காயமே. 2123

Subtle Body

Of the body thus God shaped,
In parts two,
Sukshma (Subtle) is One;
That a body of constituents eight is;
—Sound, touch, shape, taste and smell
Buddhi (Intellect), Mana (Mind) and Ahankara (Egoity)
That the Puriashta body is (subtle).

எட்டினில் ஐந்தாகும் இந்திரி யங்களுங்
கட்டிய மூன்று கரணமு மாயிடும்
ஒட்டிய பாசம் உணர்வது வாகவே
கட்டி யவிழ்த்திடுங் கண்ணுதல் காணுமே. 2124

Five Indriyas and Three Karanas

Of the organs eight thus stated,
First Five are Indriyas (External Sense Organs)
The rest three are Karanas (Internal Sense Organs)
To these attached is primordial Pasa's sentience,
Thus He binds them
And unbinds them,
He, the Lord of Forehead-Eye.

இரதம் உதிரம் இறைச்சிதோல் மேதை
மருவிய வத்தி வழும்பொடு மச்சை
பரவிய சுக்கிலம் பாழாம் உபாதி
உருவம லாலுடல் ஒன்றென் லாமே. 2125

Gross Body

Lymph, blood, flesh, skin, and tendons,
Bones, marrow, fat, brain and semen,
—Of these into one shape made
Is the body gross,
By sorrow harassed.

ஆரே அறிவார் அடியின் பெருமையை
யாரே அறிவார் அங்கவர் நின்றது
யாரே அறிவார் அறுபத்தெட் டாக்கையை
யாரே அறிவார் அடிக்காவ லானதே. 2126

God is Within the Body

Who knows the greatness of His Holy Feet
Who knows
There within the body He stood!
Who knows this body
Of Tattvas six and ten and eight!
Who knows that
He is its Yeoman Guard!

எண்சா ணளவால் எடுத்த வுடம்புக்குட்
கண்கால் உடலிற் கரக்கின்ற கைகளிற்
புண்கால் அறுபத்தெட் டாக்கை புணர்க்கின்ற
நண்பால் உடம்புதன் னாலுடம் பாமே. 2127

Twenty-Four Bodily Tattvas (Universals)

The body eight spans measures
With eyes, legs and hands
That serve to cover it;
In that body of pores and sores
He conjoins Tattvas twenty and four
In love divine;
Thus this body He fashions,
That has four more to speak of.

---

i)Vital breath-body—(Pranamaya kosam)
ii)Mind-body—(Manomaya kosam)
iii)Intelligence-body—(Vijnanamaya kosam)
iv)Bliss-body—(Anandamaya kosam)

உடம்புக்கும் நாலுக்கும் உயிராய சீவன்
ஒடுங்கும் பரனோ டொழியாப் பிரமங்
கடந்தொறு நின்ற கணக்கது காட்டி
அடங்கியே அற்றது ஆரறி வாரே. 2128

Jiva Has Five Experiences

The Jiva that as experient spirit stood (in Avastas)
In all bodies, this and four rest (Jagrat, Swapna, Sushupti, Turiya and Turiyatita)
Will in Para merge;
Who knows the way it merges
Into Param that pervades all
As like space in every pot,
Inside and out!

Jiva standing in avastas, undergoes the five experiences — jagrat, svapna, sushupti, turiya and turiyatita—before it merges into Param that animates all.

This is a doctrine unique to Tirumular. "Beyond the fourth state (Turiya) stands the fifth (Turiyatita)," he says. It is like "a tortoise with the limbs withdrawn, when the Jiva is pervaded by Aum and the Light Divine beams from within, (whereby) the Self its sentience loses". (The influence of Buddhism is to be noted). In this state, "the Senses Five and the Tattvas" are left behind (verse 2165). Jiva stands in experience as AVASTA; It has FIVE experiences, namely, Jagrat, Swapna, Sushupti, Turiya and Turiyatita. (The 5th is not known (in Vedanta), but is peculiar to Sakta Religion (see Sir John Woodroffe, "Mahamaya". They all merge in Para (Sakti).

ஆறந்த மாகி நடுவுடன் கூடினால்
தேறிய மூவாறுஞ் சிக்கென் றிருந்திடுங்
கூறுங் கலைகள் பதினெட்டுங் கூடியே
ஊறும் உடம்பை உயிருடம் பெண்ணுமே. 2129

Kala Body Holds Life

If through Adharas six
You unite through central Sushumna,
The nine orifices tightly controlled will be;
The body within of Kalas eighteen formed will be;
That the body of Jiva will be.

The causal or kala body is yet another. It is formed of eighteen tattvas and is truly the body that enters the womb and holds life.

1) Five external senses, three internal organs, and ten vayus.

மெய்யினில் தூல மிகுத்த முகத்தையும்
பொய்யினிற் சூக்கம் பொருந்தும் உடலையுங்
கையினில் துல்லியங் காட்டும் உடலையுங்
ஐயன் அடிக்குள் அடங்கும் உடம்பே. 2130

Bodies — Gross, Subtle and Causal Merge In Para

The Gross body with presence prominent
The Subtle body that invisible takes shape,
And the Causal body that by inference is,
—All these bodies are
That in Lord's Feet merge.

All the three bodies, that is their tattvas or basic principles of existence—gross, subtle and causal bodies — merge in the Lord's Feet.

காயுங் கடும்பரி கால்வைத்து வாங்கல்போற்
சேய விடமண்மை செல்லவும் வல்லது
காயத் துகிர்போர்வை யொன்றுவிட் டாங்கொன்றிட்
டேயு மவரென்ன ஏய்ந்திடுங் காயமே. 2131

Jiva Incarnates in Many Bodies

Like the prancing steed
That forward leaps
The Jiva, too, traverses near and far;
Like those who doff one garment
And another
The Jiva, too, from one to the other body moves.

நாக முடலுரி போலுநல் லண்டச
மாக நனாவிற் கனாமறந் தல்லது
போகலு மாகும் அரனரு ளாலேசென்
றேகு மிடஞ்சென் றிருபயன் உண்ணுமே. 2132

In the Waking State Dreams are Forgotten; So it is Through Successive Lives

Even as the snake sloughs off its skin
And another assumes;
Even as the bird its shell leaves
And another life pursues;
In its waking state the Jiva forgets
Happenings of the dream state;
Thus does Jiva from one body to another migrate;
Until with Grace of Hara
It reaches where it is destined to be;
And there experiences
The Karmas two, good and evil.

உண்டு நரக சுவர்க்கத்தில் உள்ளன
கண்டு விடுஞ்சூக்கங் காரண மாச்செலப்
பண்டு தொடரப் பரகாய யோகிபோற்
பிண்டம் எடுக்கும் பிறப்பிறப் பெய்தியே. 213

Cycle of Births and Deaths

Having experienced hell and heaven
Jiva leaves Subtle body;
Entering Causal body its course continues;
And like the Yogi that transmigrates
Enters yet another body;
Thus entangled in cycle of birth and death.

After experiencing heaven and hell, jiva leaves the subtle body and continues its birth course with the causal body. Like the yogi that transmigrates, the causal body enters another body, and is thus caught in the cycle of births and deaths.

தானவ னாகிய தற்பரந் தாங்கினோன்
ஆனவை மாற்றிப் பரமத் தடைந்திடும்

ஏனை யுயிர்வினைக் கெய்து மிடஞ்சென்றும்
வானும் நிலனும் புகுந்தும் வருந்துமே. 2134

The Birth Cycle ends only when Jiva Unites in God

The Jiva that realized
"I" and "You" are one,
Is in Tatpara state;
Its course inherent diverting
Will reach Param;
The rest of Jivas
Reaching their destined abodes
In heaven and earth
Will in sorrow wallow.

ஞானிக்குக் காயஞ் சிவமாகும் நாட்டிடில்
ஞானிக்குக் காயம் உடம்பே யதுவாகும்
மேனிற்கும் யோகிக்கு விந்துவும் நாதமும்
மோனிக்குக் காயமுப் பாழ்கெட்ட முத்தியே. 2135

Body Substrates of Evolved Beings

Siva is the ground of Jnani's body,
Jnani's body is Siva's body,
Yogi's body is Nada and Bindu,
Mauni's body is Mukti
Beyond Voids Three.

Mantras 2135 & 2136

Siva is the ground or substrate of the jnani's body. The ground or substrate of the yogi's body is nada and bindu. Mukti beyond the three voids is the substrate of the mauni's body. Anava (egoity) is the ground of the vijnani's body. Maya is that of the pralayakalas and karma that of the sakalas.

விஞ்ஞானத் தோர்க்கா ணவமே மிகுதனு
எஞ்ஞானத் தோர்க்குத் தனுமாயை தானென்ப
அஞ்ஞானத் தோர்க்குக் கன்மந் தனுவாகும்
மெஞ்ஞானத் தோர்க்குச் சிவதனு மேவுமே. 2136

Body Substrates of Jivas in Three Stages of Evolution

Anava (Egoity) is the ground of Vijnanis
Maya is the ground of Pralayakalas
Karma is the ground of Sakalas
Siva is the ground of Jnanis True.

மலமென் றுடம்பை மதியாத ஊமர்
தலமென்று வேறு தரித்தமை கண்டீர்
நலமென் றிதனையே நாடி யிருக்கிற்
பலமுள்ள காயத்திற் பற்றமிவ் வண்டத்தே. 2137

Lord is in Body, do not Despise it

Dumb fools are they
Who as Mala (Impurity) despise the body;
Other places as holy
They go about seeking;
They who consider "Good this is"
And in it seek the Lord,
Shall experience macrocosm entire,
In their body tenacious
(That microcosm is.)

நல்ல வசனத்து வாக்கு மனாதிகள்
மெல்ல விளையாடும் விமலன் அகத்திலே
அல்ல செவிசத்த மாதி மனத்தையும்
மெல்லத் தரித்தார் முகத்தார் பசித்தே. 2138

God Rejoices in the Body of the Good

Those who are
Of good speech, deed and thought,
In their hearts
The Pure One gently sports;
Those who are
Of evil ears, speech, and mind
Emaciated they live, their faces in hunger drawn.

2. உடல்விடல்
GIVING UP BODY

பண்ணாகும் காமம் பயிலும் வசனமும்
விண்ணாம் பிராணன் விளங்கிய சத்தமும்
புண்ணாம் உடலிற் பொருந்து மனத்தையும்
அண்ணாந்து பார்க்க அழியும் உடம்பே. 2139

Sublimate Speech and Thought Godward

The sweet speech, love intones
The loud sound, airy prana articulates
The mind within fleshy body dwells
—All these you upward course (in Yogic way),
No more the thoughts of body be.

Mantras 2139 & 2140

Divert your hearing, speech, and mind in the yogic way towards God while you are in the fleshy body. You will no more think of your body. When the body perishes, nothing remains behind.

அழிகின்ற வோருடம் பாகுஞ் செவிகண்
கழிகின்ற காலவ் விரதங்கள் தானம்
மொழிகின்ற வாக்கு முடிகின்ற நாடி
ஒழிகின்ற ஊனுக் குறுதுணை யில்லையே. 2140

When Body Perishes, Nothing There Is

The body perishes;
With it, ears and eyes;
Speech and pulse;

Fasts and gifts;
Nothing left, for dying flesh to lean on.

இலையா மிடையில் எழுகின்ற காம
முலைவாய நெஞ்சத்து மூழ்கும் உளத்துத்
தலையாய மின்னுடல் தாங்கித் திரியுஞ்
சிலையாய சித்தஞ் சிவமுன் னிடைக்கே. 2141

The Pure Will Reach God

The heart that lusts after
Slender-waisted damsels
Will in distress immersed be;
They, with hearts pure,
Body shimmering as lightning
And Will made of iron
Are for Siva's presence destined.

Purity and steadfastness take you Godward, while mean love and lust immerse you in distress and misery forever.

3. அவத்தைபேதம்—கீழாலவத்தை
AVASTA DIFFERENCES — LOWER AVASTA

ஐயைந்து மத்திமை யானது சாக்கிரங்
கைகண்ட பன்னான்கிற் கண்டங்கனாவென்பர்
பொய்கண் டிலாத புருடனித யஞ்சுழுனை
மெய்கண் டவனுந்தி யாகுந் துரியமே. 2142

Where Tattvas Stand in the Four States of Jiva Awareness

In the Waking State (Jagra)
The Tattvas twenty and five
In Eye-Brow Centre their position take;
In the Dream State (Swapna)
Tattvas ten and four
In Throat Centre their hold take;
In Deep Sleep state (Sushupti)
The Purusha (Soul) stands
Alone in Heart Centre;
In Turiya State (Fourth)
He (Purusha) stands
In Centre that is Navel.

The lower avasta pertains to jiva in its pre-biological kevala state, and has two aspects, the causal and the caused. The caused state has the five experiences: jagra (waking); svapna (dream); sushupti (deep sleep); turiya (beyond deep sleep); and turiyatita (beyond turiya). Tirumular does not refer to turiyatita in this context.

முப்பதோ டாறின் முதல்நனா ஐந்தாகச்
செப்பதி னான்காய்த் திகழ்ந்திரண் டொன்றாகி
அப்பதி யாகும் நியதி முதலாகச்
செப்புஞ் சிவமீறாய்த் தேர்ந்துகொள் ளீரே. 2143

Siva the Beginning and End of Five Avastas

Of the Five Avastas Jagra commencing
That to Tattvas six and thirty pertain,
The Fourth is the luminous Turiya;
Passing beyond to Turiyatita
The Two in One inseparate merge
The Jiva himself Siva becoming;
This the Order do know,
The Siva that stands in the Beginning
Becomes verily End of Experience all.

Among the final thirty-six tattvas, twenty-five exist in the waking state; fourteen, in svapna state; one each in sushupti and turiya states.

இந்திய மீரைந் தீரைந்து மாத்திரை
மந்திர மாய்நின்ற மாருதம் ஈரைந்தும்
அந்தக் கரணம் ஒருநான்கும் ஆன்மாவும்
பந்தவச் சக்கரப் பாலது வாகுமே. 2144

Instruments of Experience

Indriyas ten
Their Tanmatras ten
The Vayus ten (winds) that secret work,
The Antahkarnas four (inner seats of thought)
And Purusha, the Experient Jiva,
—All these (instruments of experience)
Are again and again entangled
In the cycle of life's awareness.

பாரது பொன்மை பசுமை யுடையது
நீரது வெண்மை செம்மை நெருப்பது
காரது மாருதங் கருப்பை யுடையது
வானகந் தூம மறைந்துநின் றாரே. 2145

The Five Elements Also Are Within Bo

Earth is of colour gold pure;
Water is white;
Fire red;
Wind dark;
Space smoky;
Thus the five elements concealed stand within.

1) States of experience
2) The 96 tattvas are categorized as follows:
Atma tattvas — 24, Nadis — 10, Avastas — 5, Malas — 3, Gunas — 3, Mandalas — 3, Diseases — 3, Vikaras — 8, Adharas — 6, Datus — 7, Vayus — 10, Kosas — 5, Orifices — 9, Total — 96

Mantras 2145 & 2146

The five elements — earth, water, fire, wind and space — are concealed within the body. The organs of avastas are in all ninety-six, including the three malas, three gunas, six adharas, and thirty-six tattvas.

பூதங்கள் ஐந்தும் பொறியவை ஐந்துளும்
ஏதம் படஞ்செய் திருந்த புறநிலை
ஓது மலங்குண மாகுமா தாரமோ
டாதி யவத்தைக் கருவிதொண் ணூற்றாறே. 2146

Ninety-Six Tattvas

The elements five, too
To sense organs additional function;
The five permeating each of Malas three,
Gunas three, and Adharas six;
Together with Tattvas thirty and six,
The organs of Avastas
Are six and ninety, in all.

இடவகை சொல்லில் இருபத்தஞ் சானை
படுபர சேனையும் பாய்பரி ஐந்தும்
உடையவன் மத்திமை யுள்ளுறு நால்வர்
அடைய நெடுங்கடை ஐந்தொடு நான்கே. 2147

In Waking State Jiva is With Twenty-Four Tattvas

In Jagra State
The Jiva of Tattvas five and twenty
Its position takes
In Eye-Brow centre;
With elephants Five, (sensory organs)
Infantry Five (motor organs)
Cavalry Five (internal sense potencies)
And Elements Five,
Inside Soldiery Four (the Antakaranas)
He with Tattvas twenty and four
Stands at the Gate of Waking (Jagra) state;
Thus, Tattvas stand in centres respective.

The 25 atma tattvas are categorised as follows:
Elements — 5
External Sense 5
Organs — External motor 5
Organs — Internal Sense 5
Potencies (tanmatras) — Intelligence organs 4
(Antahkaranas)—
Atman — 1

உடம்பும் உடம்பும் உடம்பைத் தழுவி
உடம்பிடை நின்ற உயிரை அறியார்
உடம்பொ டுயிரிடை நட்பறி யாதார்
மடம்புகு நாய்போல் மயங்குகின் றாரே. 2148

Know the Relationship Between Body and Jiva

The bodies (Causal, Subtle and Gross) embrace one another,
But the Jiva within body stood,
They know not;
They who the kinship between body and Jiva
Understood not,
Are verily bewildered
Like the dog that into a kitchen abrupt strays.

Know the relationship between the body and jiva. Otherwise you will be left in confusion, like a dog that enters a kitchen abruptly.

இருக்கின்ற வாறொன் றறிகிலர் ஏழைகள்
முருக்கு மசபையை மாற்றி முகந்து
கருக்கொண்டு காமாரி சார முகந்தேர்ந்
துருக்கொண்டு தொக்க உடலொழி யாதே. 2149

Meet God in the Body By the Yoga Way

They know not how To-Be;
Poor are they in Spirit;
Those, who,
Course upward the vital Ajapa
(Through breathing in Yoga way)
And sublimate the Bindu,
They meet the Lord
That destroyed Kama, the God of Love;
Comely their body becomes
And indestructible here remains.

ஒளித்திட் டிருக்கும் ஒருபதி னாலை
அளித்தனன் என்னுள்ளே ஆரியன் வந்து
அளிக்குங் கலைகளி னாலறு பத்து
ஒளித்திட்டு வைத்தான் ஒடுங்கிய சித்தே. 2150

Lord Placed in Concealment the Sixteen Kalas and the Fourteen Inner Tattvas

The Tattvas four and ten
That in me lay concealed,
The Pure One appeared
And in bounty revealed;
The Kalas six and ten
That to me lend grace
He placed, to none beknown,
My thoughts in Him to centre.

Fourteen inner tattvas: the five elements; the five sense potencies (tanmatras); and the four intelligence organs (antakaranas).

Mantras 2150 & 2151

The Lord revealed in secret the sixty-four knowledge branches and the fourteen inner tattvas. Stand victoriously vanquishing the five elements and the four karanas.

மண்ணினில் ஒன்று மலர்நீரு மருங்காகும்
பொன்னினில் அங்கி புகழ்வளி யாகாயம்
மன்னு மனோபுத்தி யாங்காரம் ஓரொன்றாய்
உன்னின் முடிந்த தொருபூத சயமே. 2151

Conquer the Five Elements and the Four Karanas

The Earth and Water expanses;
The Fire that blazes in colour gold,
The Wind and Space
The Mind, Will, Intellect and Egoity
On their quintessence,
You in succession contemplate;

Then victorious you stand, the elements vanquishing.

முன்னிக் கொருமகன் மூர்த்திக் கிருவர்
வன்னிக்கு மூவர் வதுவைக்கு நால்வர்
கன்னிக்குப் பிள்ளைகள் ஐவர்மு னாளில்லை
கன்னியைக் கன்னியே காதலித் தாளே. 2152

Out of the Five Elements are Born the Five Senses

One the child for Space—Sound
Two for Wind—Sound and Touch
Three for Fire—Sound, Touch and Light
Four for Water — Sound, Touch, Light and Taste
Five for Earth — Sound, Touch, Light, Taste and Smell
This was not of yore there, before creation began
Before the maiden Sakti (Spirit), the maiden (Matter) Maya loved.

Out of the five elements — space, wind, fire, water and earth — are born the five senses: sound, touch, sight smell and taste.

கண்டகன வைந்துங் கலந்தனதா னைந்துஞ்சென்
றுண்டன நான்கும்ஒருங்கே உணர்ந்தபின்
பண்டைய தாகிப் பரந்த வியாக்கிரத்
தண்டமுந் தானாய் அமர்ந்துநின் றானே. 2153

Fourteen Tattvas in Dream State

In Dream State
The Senses Five experienced;
The Tanmatras Five too;
And Antahkaranas Four as well;
Having experienced thus in Dream State
The Jiva returned to Jagra State to experience;
There he stood in full knowledge of world.

Mantras 2153 & 2154

Jiva experiencing the fourteen tattvas in the dream state, returns to the jagra state where it stands in full knowledge of the world. But in the throat centre, jiva visions dreams only with the four antakaranas without involvement of the other ten tattvas.

நின்றவன் நிற்கப் பதினாலிற் பத்துநீத்
தொன்றிய அந்தக் கரணங்கள் நான்குடன்
மன்று கலந்த மனைவாழ்க்கை வாதனை
கன்றிய கண்டத்திற் கண்டான் கனவதே. 2154

But Only the Four Intelligence Organs are Involved in Dream Vision

Thus it is, Jiva with Tattvas four and ten
In Dream State stands;
But with the ten sense organs uninvolved
With Antahkaranas Four alone,
And aided by the memory
Of earthly life here below,
He (Jiva) in the Throat-Centre,
Dreams visioned.

தான மிழந்து தனிபுக் கிதயத்து
மான மழிந்து மதிகெட்டு மாலாகி
ஆன விரிவறி யாவவ் வியத்தத்தின்
மேனி யழிந்து சுழுத்திய தாமே. 2155

Deep Sleep in Heart-Centre

Leaving the Throat Centre there,
Alone, he (Jiva) enters the Heart's-Centre,
There, Egoity (Ahamkara) lost, Intellect (Buddhi) lost,
Cognition (Mind) lost
In the State that discerns not the world,
Consciousness of body bereft,
He (Jiva) reached the Deep Sleep State of Sushupti.

Mantras 2155 & 2156

Leaving that centre, the soul enters the heart centre where egoity, intellect, and cognition are lost. Jiva reaches the deep sleep state of sushupti in the heart centre. Having reached that state, jiva with citta (will), prana (vital breath) and sentience of self enters in, and stands one with the subtle object.

சுழுனையைச் சேர்ந்துள மூன்றுடன் காட்சி
கெழுமிய சித்தம் பிராணன்றன் காட்சி
ஒழுகக் கமலத்தின் உள்ளே யிருந்து
விழுமப் பொருளுடன் மேவிநின் றானே. 2156

Tattvas in Deep Sleep

Having reached the Deep Sleep State of Sushupti,
He with three there remains;
—Chitta (Will), Prana (Vital Breath) and Sentience of Self,
Thus into the Heart-Centre Jiva enters
There one with the Subtle Object he stands
(In the state of Sushupti Deep).

தானத் தெழுந்து தருக்குந் துரியத்தின்
வானத் தெழுந்துபோய் வையம் பிறகிட்டுக்
கானத் தெழுந்த கருத்தின் தலையிலே
ஊனத் தவித்தைவிட் டூமனின் றானே. 2157

Nada Peaks in Turiya or Fourth State

From Sushupti Centre,
He further moves continuing,
Into Turiya Expanse
Leaving thoughts of world below;
On to peaks of Nada (in navel centre) he ascends;
There rid of primordial ignorance,
He remains in Mauna (Silence).

From sushupti in the heart centre jiva moves further on into turiya leaving the thoughts of the world below. Ascending to the peaks of nada in the navel centre, jiva remains in mauna (silence), rid of all primordial ignorance.

ஊமை யெழுத்தொடு பேசும் எழுத்துறில்
ஆமை யகத்தினில் அஞ்சும் அடங்கிடும்

ஓமய முற்றது வுள்ளொளி பெற்றது
நாமய மற்றது நாமறி யோமே. 2158

Turiyatita Experience

When with silent letter "M"
The articulate letters "A" and "U" conjoin,
The Five Senses are withdrawn,
As limbs within the tortoise;
Then Jiva is by "Aum" pervaded;
The light Divine beams from within;
The Self its sentience loses;
—This we know not.

When the silent letter 'M' joins with the two articulate letters 'A' and 'U', the five senses are withdrawn like limbs within the tortoise. Then jiva pervaded by 'Aum' loses the self.

துரிய மிருப்பதுஞ் சாக்கிரத் துள்ளே
நரிகள் பதினாலு நஞ்சுண்டு செத்தன
பரிய புரவியும் பாறிப் பறந்தது
துரிய மிறந்திடஞ் சொல்லவொண் ணாதே. 2159

State Beyond Turiya — (Turiyatita)

Turiya is in Jagrat experienced;
The foxes fourteen (Indriyas etc.) of themselves die;
The swift stead of Prana flees,
How that State beyond Turiya (Turiyatita) is,
Impossible to state, indeed.

The state beyond turiya is turiyatita. Experiencing turiya in jagrat, the fourteen foxes (indriyas, etc.) perish; prana stands still. It is impossible to describe adequately the state of turiyatita.

மாறா மலமைந்தான் மன்னு மவத்தையின்
வேறாய மாயா தநுகர ணாதிக்கிங்
கீறாகா தேஎவ் வுயிரும் பிறந்திருந்
தாறாத வல்வினை யாலடி யுண்ணுமே. 2160

All Jivas Experience These States of Awareness

Contaminated by Primordial Mala (Impurities) Five,
Jivas, all, the Five States of Awareness experience;
Endless indeed are the bodies and organs
That Maya endows;
All Souls caught in birth and death,
Are by Karma alike struck.

All souls (sakalas) contaminated by the five primordial impurities, and caught in the cycle of recurring birth and death, can experience these five states of consciousness.

உண்ணுந்தன் னூடாடா தூட்டிடு மாயையும்
அண்ணல் அருள்பெற்ற முத்திய தாவது
நண்ண விலாவுயிர் ஞானத்தி னாற்பிறந்
தெண்ணுறு ஞானத்தின் நேர்முத்தி எய்துமே. 2161

Maya Gives States of Experience For God's Grace to Attain; Jnanis Reach Mukti Direct

Maya feeds Jiva with Avasta experiences unbroken,
For the Jiva by Lord's Grace
To attain Mukti;
But the Jivas in Jnana born
Them Maya nears not;
And contemplating in Jnana
They direct attain Mukti.

Maya feeds jiva with avasta experiences and by Gods' Grace, jiva attains mukti. Jnanis contemplating in jnana attain mukti directly.

அதிமூட நித்திரை யாணவ நந்த
அதனா லுணர்வோ னருங்கன்ம முன்னித்
திதமான கேவல மித்திறஞ் சென்று
பரமாகா வையவத் தைப்படு வானே. 2162

Consciousness Begins With Egoity

In the Primordial Slumber State of Jivas (Kevala State)
Devoid of Awareness,
Egoity is activated;
Then Consciousness springs,
And actions diverse Jiva pursues;
From the State of Kevala
Thus passing out,
He the Five States (Avastas) experiences,
Until he becomes Para Supreme.

Egoity (anava) gives rise to consciousness and jiva pursues diverse actions. Thus passing out from the primordial state of jiva's sleep (kevala state), he experiences the five states until he becomes the Supreme Para.

ஆசான்முன் னேதுயில் மாண வகரைத்
தேசாய தண்டால் எழுப்புஞ் செயல்போல்
நேசாய வீசனு நீடாண வத்தரை
ஏசாத மாயாடன் னாலே எழுப்புமே. 2163

Maya Awakens Soul From Primordial (Kevala) Slumber

As with his staff the teacher rouses the pupil
Who in his presence slumbers,
Even like it,
The benevolent Lord with Maya awakens
The Soul that in prolonged Egoity slumbers.

மஞ்சொடு மந்தா கினிகுட மாமென
விஞ்சறி வில்லோன் விளம்பு மிகுமதி
எஞ்சலி லொன்றெனு மாறென இவ்வுடல்
அஞ்சுணு மன்னனன் றேபோ மளவே. 2164

Life After Death Is

They who say: "After death nothing is left;
The Jiva the five states experienced
Forever fled;"
They are verily unenlightened surpassing;
They might as well say:
"The heavenly Ganga Mandakini

'That from clouds aloft streams forth
Ends as an empty pot.''

Life after death still continues. They who say that after death nothing remains, may even say that the heavenly Ganga Mandakini, which streams from the clouds, ends as an empty pot.

படியுடை மன்னவன் பாய்பரி ஏறி
வடிவுடை மாநகர் தான்வரும் போது
அடியுடை ஐவரும் அங்குறை வோருந்
துடியில்லம் பற்றித் துயின்றனர் தாமே. 2165

In Turiyatita State Tattvas Remain Behind In Body

When the Earthly King, that is Jiva,
Mounting the steeds swift (of consciousness),
At the Lovely City (of Turiyatita) arrives,
The Senses Five
And Tattvas rest that remained behind,
But slept in the body,
That vibrant once was.

Mantras 2165 & 2166

When the soul, the earthly king, mounting the swift steed (consciousness) arrives at the 'lovely city' of turiyatita, all the five senses and the other tattvas remain behind in the body. During that fifth state, the jiva is freed from the five malas to reach God directly.

நேரா மலத்தை நீடைந் தவத்தையின்
நேரான வாறுன்னி நீடு நனவினில்
நேரா மலமைந்து நேரே தரிசித்து
நேராம் பரத்துடன் நிற்பது நித்தமே. 2166

Be Freed of Malas to Reach God

In the States Five,
In purity, vision Malas Five
That pure are not;
See, in the Waking State
They trouble you not;
Straight confront them;
Then shall you with Para direct,
Forever and ever be.

4.மத்திய சாக்கிராவத்தை

MID-JAGRAT-AVASTA

சாக்கிர சாக்கிரந் தன்னில் திரோதாயி
சாக்கிர சொப்பனந் தன்னிடை மாமாயை
சாக்கிரந் தன்னிற் சுழுத்திதற் காமியஞ்
சாக்கிரந் தன்னில் துரியத்து மாயையே. 2167

Maya's Manifestations in the Four States of Consciousness

In the Waking State—
Within the Waking State
Is Tirodhayi (obfuscation Sakti) active;
In the Dream State—
Within the Waking State
Is Mamaya (Impure);
In the State of Deep Sleep—
Within the Waking State
Is Kamya (of self delusion):
In the Fourth Turiya State
Within the Waking State
Is Maya (Pure).

This belongs to the sakala or the living state of the jiva on earth. In the four states of consciousness that jiva experiences — jagrat, svapna, sushupti, and turiya — maya manifests herself as tirodhayi (obscuring sakti) mamaya (impure maya sakti that gives differentiated knowledge), kamya (sakti that gives self-delusion), and finally pure maya (sakti that lends grace) in this avasta.

மாயை எழுப்புங் கலாதியை மற்றதின்
நேய விராகாதி ஏய்ந்த துரியத்துத்
தோயுஞ் சுழுனை கனாநனா வுந்துன்னி
ஆயின னந்தச் சகலத்து ளானே. 2168

In Turiya, Kalas and Raga Arise

In that Turiya State
Within the Waking State (of Jiva)
Maya rouses the Kalas and Ragas,
Then passing back through the States
Of Sushupti, Dream and Waking
The Jiva to Sakala State returns.

மேவிய அந்தகன் விழிகட் குருடனா
மாவயின் முன்னடிக் காணு மதுகண்டு
மேவுந் தடிகொண்டு சொல்லும் விழிபெற
மூவயி னான்மா முயலுங் கருமமே. 2169

Jivas Grope Their Way Back to Sakala Jagrat State

The blind one,
Eyes he has; but vision none;
And so gropes for the steps,
He made of yore;
Having found them,
He seizes a stick
And with its aid
Finds the Way;
Even like it
Do the Jivas with avastas three
Seek to march back their way.

மத்திம மொத்த சிலந்தி வலயத்துள்
ஒத்தங் கிருந்து உயிருண்ணு மாறுபோல்
அத்தனும் ஐம்பொறி யாடகத் துள்நின்று
சத்த முதல்ஐந்துந் தானுண்ணு மாறே. 2170

Seated in the Body, Jiva Experiences

The Spider
Standing at the web's centre,
Catches prey and feeds;
Even so,
The Jiva standing within the body stage,
Where the senses in merriment dance
Experiences the sensations five,
Sound and the rest four.

Like the spider situated at the centre of its web catches its prey, the jiva also experiences all the actions of the five senses through being situated in the body web.

வைச்சன வச்சு வகையிரு பத்தஞ்சு
முச்சு முடனணை வானொரு வன்னுளன்
பிச்சன் பெரியன் பிறப்பிலி என்றென்று
நச்சி யவனருள் நானுய்ந்த வாறே. 2171

God Placed the Twenty-Five Tattvas for Jiva

One there is,
Who placed Tattvas five and twenty,
With them in my body I abide;
"Mad is He, Great is He, Birthless is He"
—Thus in endearment I sought Him;
And by the Grace He granted
Redeemed am I.

நாலா றுடன்புருட னற்றத் துவமுடன்
வேறான ஐயைந்து மெய்ப்புரு டன்பரங்
கூறா வியோமம் பரமெனக் கொண்டனன்
வேறான நாலேழு வேதாந்த தத்வமே. 2172

Vedanta School Reckons Tattvas Differently As Twenty-Eight

With Tattvas four and twenty,
And Purusha Tattva to add,
Thus are Tattvas five and twenty;
Differently reckoned as five and twenty,
And with Purusha
And the Void (Vyoma) which is not Para,
And Para,
Are Tattvas as eight and twenty reckoned,
In the school of Vedanta.

The Vedanta school count the tattvas differently as twenty-eight. That reckoning includes purusa and the void, which is not Para.

ஏலங்கொண் டாங்கே இடையொடு பிங்கலை
கோலங்கொண் டாங்கே குணத்தி னுடன்புக்கு
மூலங்கொண் டாங்கே முறுக்கிமுக் கோணிலுங்
காலங்கொண் டானடி காணலு மாமே. 2173

Practise Yoga

Course the breath in ways appropriate
Through Nadis, Idakala and Pingala,
Seat yourself in Asanas (postures) comely,
And agreeably direct the breath within;
Through Muladhara, that is triangle shaped
Upward ascend;
Verily may you see the Feet
Of Lord, that is Timeless Eternity.

நாடிகள் பத்தும் நலந்திகழ் வாயுவும்
ஓடிய காலில் ஒடுங்கி யிருந்திடுங்
கூடிய காமங் குளிக்கும் இரதமும்
நாடிய நல்ல மனமும் உடலிலே. 2174

Yoga Brings Rapture

The ten Nadis
And the ten Vayus,
Will in ascending breath subside;
Rapturous your state shall be;
Agreeable your taste shall be;
Perfect your mind shall be;
In your good body.

Mantras 2174 & 2175

Yoga brings a rapturous state, agreeable taste and perfect mind. The body becomes good and holy. The Kingly Nandi of tender love aids us to see all. He guides and witnesses all.

ஆவன ஆவ அழிவ அழிவன
போவன போவ புகுவ புகுவன
காவலன் பேர்நந்தி காட்டித்துக் கண்டவன்
ஏவன செய்யும் இலங்கிழை யோனே. 2175

Nandi Guides and Witnesses All

Let them be that are to be;
Let them die that are to die;
Let them leave that are to leave;
Let them enter that are to enter;
The Kingly Nandi makes us see all
And Himself, witnesses all;
All things appropriate He does;
He, of tender love.

பத்தொடு பத்துமோர் மூன்றும் பகுதியும்
உய்த்த துரியமும் உள்ளுணர் காலமும்
மெய்த்த வியோமமு மேலைத் துரியமுந்
தத்துவ நாலே ழெனவுன்னத் தக்கதே. 2176

Tattvas Are Reckoned As Twenty-Eight In Yet Another Way

The sense organs ten and ten,
The intellectual organs one and three,
The Turiya State,
Time subjectively cognised,
The undifferentiated Void
And the Turiyatita above

—Thus it is as eight and twenty, too
The Tattvas reckoned are.

The tattvas are enumerated as twenty-eight in another way also—ten sense organs, ten subtle potencies, four internal cognitive organs (antahkaranas), turiya state, time, the undifferentiated Void and the turiyatita.

விளங்கிடு முந்நூற்று முப்பதோ டொருபான்
தளங்கொ ளிரட்டிய தாறு நடந்தால்
வணங்கிடு மைம்மலம் வாயு வெழுந்து
விளங்கிடு மவ்வழி தத்துவ நின்றே. 2177

Breath Control For Ridding Malas

If ten times three hundred and thirty
The breath twelve finger-length
As Prana ascends upward,
The Malas Five subdued are;
So do the Tattvas, according.

Mantras 2177 & 2178

If prana ascends upward three hundred and thirty one times, the five malas are subdued. By breath control the ninety-six tattvas subside within the body which, in turn, merges in the twenty-five tattvas.

நாலொரு கோடியே நாற்பத்தெண்ணாயிர
மேலுமோ ரைந்நூறு வேறா யடங்கிடும்
பாலவை தொண்ணூறோ டாறுட் படுமவை
கோலிய ஐயைந்து ளாகுங் குறிக்கிலே. 2178

By Breath Control Tattvas Subside Within Body

If breath appropriate spirated
Times, four crores and forty eight thousand five hundred,
Then cessation there shall be for Prana's movement;
It in the ninety-six (Tattvas) subsides;
The ninety-six in turn
In Tattvas five and twenty merge.

ஆகின்ற தொண்ணூறோ டாறும் பொதுஎன்பர்
ஆகின்ற வாறா றருஞ்சைவர் தத்துவம்
ஆகின்ற நாலேழ் வேதாந்தி வயிணவர்க்
காகின்ற நாலாறை யைந்துமாயா வாதிக்கே. 2179

Tattvas Differently Counted By Different Schools of Philosophy

Tattvas six and ninety are the over-all;
Out of them, six and thirty are the Tattvas for Saivas;
Eight and twenty for Vedantins;
Four and twenty for Vaishnavas;
Five and twenty for Mayavadins.

தத்துவ மானது தன்வழி நின்றிடில்
வித்தக னாகி விளங்கி யிருக்கலாம்
பொய்த்தவ மாமவை போயிடு மவ்வழி
த்த்துவ மாவ தகார எழுத்தே. 2180

Letter-Sound "A" is Primal Tattva (Truth)

If Jiva can make Tattvas function his way,
He a wise one shall be;
Illumined is Knowledge Divine,
False devotion no more shall be;
The Tattva Supreme is the primal letter-sound.

Jiva is wise when he can make the tattvas function in the illumined way. With illumination in divine knowledge attained, false devotion leaves. The letter-sound 'A' is the primal tattva.

அறிவொன் றிலாதன ஐயேழு மொன்றும்
அறிகின்ற என்னை அறியா திருந்தேன்
அறிகின்றாய் நீயென் றருள்செய்தார் நந்தி
அறிகின்ற நானென் றறிந்துகொண் டேனே. 2181

Jiva Alone is the Sentient Being

Tattvas Thirty and Six
Are insentient verily (devoid of knowledge)
I am the sentient one;
Yet I knew not Myself;
"You shall know yourself"
—Thus in Grace, Nandi declared;
That I am the Knower,
I have now known.

Mantras 2181 & 2182

Among the thirty-six tattvas, jiva alone is the sentient being. In the waking state mala creates the five experiences. In union with God, jiva is disentangled from these five states and from the unreal tattvas.

சாக்கிர சாக்கிர மாதி தனில்ஐந்தும்
ஆக்கு மலாவத்தை யைந்து நனவாதி
போக்கி யிவற்றொடும் பொய்யான வாறாறு
நீக்கி நெறிநின்றொன் றாகியே நிற்குமே. 2182

Transcend Five States of Consciousness and Thirty-Six Tattvas; Beyond is Union in God

In the Waking State
Are States of experiences five
Malas create;
Disentangling from these states five,
And from Tattvas unreal, thirty and six,
In the holy way Jiva stood,
And one with Him union attained.

ஆணவ மாதி மலமைந் தலரோனுக்
காணவ மாதிநான் காமாற் கரனுக்கு
ஆணவ மாதிமூன் றீசர்க் கிரண்டென்ப
ஆணவ மொன்றே சதாசிவற் காவதே. 2183

Number of Malas for the Five Gods

Five are the Malas
For Brahma on the Lotus Bloom,
Anava (Egoity) and the rest; (Anava, Maya, Karma, Mayeyam and Tirodhayi)

Four are the Malas for Vishnu;
Anava and others (Mayeyam devoid)
Three for Rudra,
Anava and Others (Mayeyam and Tirodhayi devoid);
Two for Mahesa
Anava and Karma;
One alone for Sadasiva—Anava.

5. அத்துவாக்கள்
ADHVAS (HIGHER STEPS)

தத்துவம் ஆறாது தன்மனு வேழ்கோடி
மெய்த்தகு வன்னம்ஐம் பானொன்று மேதினி
ஒத்திரு நூற்றிரு பான்நான்கெண் பானொன்று
வைத்த பதங்கலை யோரைந்தும் வந்தவே. *2184*

The Six Higher Steps

Six times six are the Tattvas;
Seven Crores are the Mantras;
Fifty and one are the Varnas (letter-sounds);
Two hundred and twenty four are the Bhuvanas;
global constellations;
Eighty and one are the Padas Primal,
Five, the Kalas rare.

Mantram, padam, varnam, bhuvanam, kalas and tattvas — these constitute the six adhvas or the higher paths.

நாடிய மண்டல மூன்று நலந்தெரிந்
தோடு மவரோ டுள்ளிரு பத்தைஞ்சுங்
கூடுவர் கூடிக் குறிவழி யேசென்று
தேடிய பின்னர்த் திகைத்திருந் தார்களே. *2185*

Ascend Beyond the Three Spheres

The three Spheres within (Sun, Moon, and Fire)
They ascend and traverse, (in yogic way)
Having traversed,
They with Tattvas five and twenty
In one unite;
Further coursing the breath
Upward through Sushumna
They search;
And having sought,
Self-Consciousness lost,
They there remain.

சாக்கிர சாக்கிர மாதித் தலையாக்கி
ஆக்கிய தூல மளவாக்கி அதீதத்துத்
தாக்கிய வன்பான தாண்டவஞ் சார்ந்தது
தேக்குஞ் சிவமாதல் ஐந்துஞ் சிவாயமே. *2186*

The Fifth State of Turiyatita

Waking within the Waking State,
And experiencing the rest of States,
The body and breath appropriate trained,
They reach the Turiyatita;
There they witness the felicitous Dance of Lord;
Drinking the fill of bliss
They Siva Become;
All these five, the Grace-fruits of Siva are.

6. சுத்த நனவாதி பருவம்
SUDDHA JAGRAT AND OTHER STATES

This chapter deals elaborately in 39 verses (2187-2226) with the Agamic view of Tattvas, Turiyas, including the 5th namely Turiyatita acquisition of Knowledge, and the final merging with Siva.

நனவாதி தூலமே சூக்கப் பகுதி
அனதான ஐயைந்தும் விந்துவின் சத்தி
தனதா முயிர்விந்து தானின்று போந்து
கனவா நனவிற் கலந்திவ் வாறே. *2187*

Bindu Power Permeates Tattvas

The gross body of Waking State,
The subtle body of Dream State,
Together with Tattvas five and twenty
Are of Bindu's Power verily;
That Power permeating Jiva
Penetrates the Waking and Dream States.

Bindu power penetrates jiva in the waking, dream and other states, and thus permeates tattvas.

நனவில் அதீதம் பிறந்தார் கிடந்தார்
நனவில் துரியம் நிகழ்ந்தார் தவழ்ந்தார்
நனவிற் சுழுத்தி நடந்தார் வளர்ந்தார்
நனவிற் கனவோட னன்செய்தி யானதே. *2188*

Progression of the States of Consciousness Towards Siva-Goal

They who reach the Turiyatita
Within the Waking State
Actionless lie;
They who reach the Turiya
Within the Waking State
Crawl (towards the Goal);
They who experience the Sushupti (Deep Sleep)

Within the Waking State
Are Jivas yet developing;
They who dream
Within the Waking State
Are Jivas hastening towards the good Goal.

In dream, jiva marches towards the divine goal; in the sushupti state he rises further and still further in the turiya state. In turiyatita state the jiva lies impassive.

செறியுங் கிரியை சிவதத் துவமாம்
பிறிவிற் சுகயோகம் பேரருள் கல்வி
குறிதற் றிருமேனி குணம்பல வாகும்
அறிவில் சராசரம் அண்டத் தளவே. *2189*

Charya, Kriya, Yoga and Jnana — Where They Lead To

The acts of Kriya lead to Siva Tattva;
The practice of prolonged Yoga
Leads to Divine Grace and Knowledge;
Contemplation of Lord's Form, (in Charya)
Confers blessings many;
In Jnana is comprehended
All Cosmic creation at once.

The acts of kriya lead to Siva tattva; and of yoga, to divine Grace and Knowledge. Charya bestows benediction; and in jnana the entire cosmic creation is comprehended.

ஆதி பரஞ்சிவஞ் சத்தி சதாசிவம்
ஏதமில் ஈசன்நல் வித்தியா தத்துவம்
போதங் கலைகால நியதிமா மாயை
நீதியீ றாக நிறுத்தினன் என்னே. *2190*

Evolutes of Paraparam

The Beginningless Param,
Thus the order brought about;
Siva, Sakti, and Sadāsiva,
The Isa Pure, and the noble Vidya Tattvas
Bodha, Kalas, Time, Niyati and Mamaya (Impure Maya)
—These evolutes in gradation appropriate
He established,
In wonder surpassing indeed!

(i) Siva (nada); (ii) Sakti (bindu); (iii) Sadasiva (Sadakhya); (iv) Isvara (Mahesvara); (v) suddha vidya (Rudra) — these five are the first evolutes of Param. They are known as Siva tattvas, and are in the pure maya sphere.

Mantras 2190 & 2191

Siva, Sakti, Sadasiva, Isa and the (suddha) pure vidya and sadakya tattvas, bodha, kalas, time (kalā), niyati (order) and mamaya (impure maya) are the evolutes of Paraparam, and must be ascended by the jiva.

தேசு திகழ்சிவஞ் சத்தி சதாசிவம்
ஈசன் அனல்வித்தை இராகங் கலைகால
மாசகல் வித்தை நியதி மகாமாயை
ஆசில் புருடாதி ஆன்மாவீ றாறே. *2191*

Jiva Ascends These evolutes to Reach Paraparam

The luminous Siva, Sakti and Sadasivam,
The Maheswara, the Pure Vidya, and Ragas,
Kalas, Time (Kala), Knowledge (Bodha), Niyati, and Mahamaya
The Purusha (soul),
Together these twelve
(Are for the Jiva to ascend.).

Below the five Siva tattvas in the pure maya sphere, are the seven tattvas in the impure maya (or mamaya) sphere. This sphere is also referred to as misra (mixed) or pure/impure maya. These seven tattvas are known as vidya tattvas and should not be confused with the suddha (pure) vidya tattvas in the pure maya (or Siva tattva) sphere. These seven are: (i)kala; (ii)niyati; (iii)kata; (iv)vidya or bodha; (v) raga; (vi) mamaya; and (vii)purusha.

These 12 tattvas (5 plus 7) are above the 24 prakriti or atma tattvas. Of these, seven belong to the lower strata (vidya tattvas) and five to the upper strata (Siva tattva).

ஆணவ மாயையுங் கன்மமு மாமலங்
காணு முளைக்குத் தவுடுமி யான்மாவுந்
தாணுவை யொவ்வாமற் றண்டுல மாய்நிற்கும்
பேணுவாய் மற்றுநின் பாசம் பிரித்தே. *2192*

Malas Inherent to Jiva

Anava (Egoity), Maya (Ignorance) and Karma (Action)
These the Malas (Impurities) are;
They are like the embryo, the bran and the husk
Are like the grain of rice;
They touch not the Lord, but apart stand;
Be rid of your Pasas one by one,
And adore the Lord.

பசுக்கள் பலவண்ணம் பாலொரு வண்ணம்
பசுக்களை மேய்க்கின்ற ஆயன் ஒருவண்ணம்
பசுக்களை மேய்க்கின்ற ஆயன்கோல் போடிற்
பசுக்கள் தலைவனைப் பற்றி விடாவே. *2193*

Lord is the Cow-Herd (Pasupati); Jiva the Cow (Pasu)

Many the color of cows,
But one the color of milk;
And of peerless hue
Is Lord, the cowherd;
When the cowherd
Who tends the cows
His guiding staff shows,
The cows will not their Master leave.

உடலிந் தியமனம் ஒண்புத்தி சித்தம்
அடலொன் றகந்தை அறியாமை மன்னிக்
கெடுமவ் வுயிர்மயல் மேலுங் கிளைத்தால்
அடைவது தானேழ் நரகத்து ளாயே. *2194*

Jiva a Prey to Tattvas and Pasas

The body, indriyas, mind
The intellect, will, egoity and ignorance
To these the Soul a prey falls;
If the Pasas further sprout in him,
To hell, he speeds fast.

தற்றெரி யாத வதீதந்தற் காணவஞ்
சொற்றெரி கின்ற துரியஞ்சொற் காமியம்
பெற்ற சுழுத்திப்பின் பேசுறுங் காதலா
மற்றது வுண்டிக் கனநன வாதலே. 2195

Limitations of Experiences in the Five States of Awareness

In Turiyatita State
The Consciousness of the Self is not;
In Turiya State
The Consciousness of the Self
Through spoken word comprehended
Still burns;
In the Sushupti State that is Maya bound,
The Desire-potency to speak afterward exists;
In the Waking State and the Dream State
Experiences in ways diverse.

The consciousness of the self ceases in the turiyatita state. In the turiya state, consciousness of the self still burns, through comprehension of the spoken word. In the sushupti state, which is maya bound, desire exists; and disparate experiences are undergone in the waking and dream states.

நனவிற் கனவில்லை ஐந்து நனவிற்
கனவிலாச் சூக்குமங் காணுஞ் சுழுத்தி
தனலுண் பகுதியே தற்கூட்டு மாயை
நனவிற் றுரிய ததீதந் தலைவந்தே. 2196

Turiyatita State Experiences no Dream

In the Waking State of Turiyatita that is fifth
No dream the Subtle body sees;
In the Sushupti State there,
The Self Experiences its own
In the Turiya state there
Is born the Turiyatita per sa.

Turiyatita state has inner divisions, such as turiyatita-jagrat and turiyatita-sushupti. In turiyatita-sushupti state the self experiences the Self, and in turiyatita-jagrat-state maya still lingers; but turiyatita has no dream state.

ஆறாறில் ஐயைந் தகல நனாநனா
வாறா மவைவிட வாகு நனாக்கனா
வேறான ஐந்தும் விடவே நனாவினில்
ஈறாஞ் சுழுத்தி யிதின்மாயை தானே. 2197

Tattvas Acting in Waking, Dream and Deep Sleep States

In the Waking State within the Turiyatita State
Are Tattvas, five times five leave;
Out of six times six tattvas in all
When six out of Tattvas in Waking State leave,
Then is Dream State in Turiyatita Waking;
When further beyond the five Tattvas leave,
Then ensues Sushupti in Turiyatita
Where Maya alone functions.

When six tattvas out of the twenty-five in the waking state within-waking state leave, that is dream state-in-waking. In sushupti-in-waking state, five more tattvas leave, and maya functions.

மாயையில் வந்த புருடன் துரியத்தில்
ஆய முறைவிட் டதுவுந்தா னன்றாகிச்
சேயகே வலவிந் துடன்செல்லச் சென்றக்கால்
ஆய தனுவின் பயனில்லை யாமே. 2198

In Turiya Maya Leaves and Jiva Merges in Bindu

The Purusha (Experient Soul) of Sushupti
When it reaches Turiya State next
The Maya too leaves,
And one with Kevala (Primordial) Bindu becomes;
Then no more the body its use has.

In turiya state maya too leaves, and jiva merges in primordial bindu. Then the body will be of no use.

அதீதத் துரியத் தறிவனாம் ஆன்மா
அதீதத் துரிய மதனாற் புரிந்தால்
அதீதத் தெழுந்தறி வாகிய மானன்
முதிய அனலிற் றுரியத்து முற்றுமே. 2199

In Turiyatita Jiva Becomes Knower and Passes Beyond to Luminous Siva Turiya State

In that Turiyatita State,
The Soul is the Knower verily;
When he passes beyond
From that Turiyatita State
Where Jiva the Knower is
He merges into Luminous Turiya (Siva Turiya)
That the ultimate state is.

In the turiyatita states the soul is the knower. Passing that state, jiva merges into "luminous turiya" (Siva turiya) that is the ultimate state.

ஐயைந்து பத்துடன் ஆனது சாக்கிரங்
கைகண்ட ஐயைந்திற் கண்டங் கனாஎன்பர்
பொய்கண்ட மூவர் புருடர் சுழுனையின்
மெய்கண் டவனுந்தி மேவல் இருவரே. 2200

Tattvas and Their Centres of Action During the Five States of Consciousness

Tattvas five and twenty and ten to add,
Are the instruments thirty and five
In Jagrat;
With instruments five and twenty
In the Throat-Centre
Is Dream State;

With three
The Purusha is in Sushupti;
When the two (Purusha and Prana)
The Navel-Centre reaches
Then is the Turiya State true.

Thirty-five tattvas constitute the jagrat state. With twenty-five tattvas jiva functions in the throat centre: that is the dream state. Purusha is in sushupti with three tattvas. When purusha and prana reach the navel centre, then it is the turiya state.

1)In the jagrat (waking) state, purusha, the experient soul, functions with 35 tattvas in the eyebrow centre. These 35 are: five jnanendriyas (sense organs); five karmendriyas (motor organs); four antahkaranas (inner intelligence organs); ten vayus (airs); five vaks (sounds); one jiva (purusha)—in all 35 tattvas functions in the eyebrow centre. Vide—"Saiva Siddhanta Kattalaigal," edited by K. Narayanasami Naidu, p.30.

2)In the dream state, the five sensoria, and the five motoria are left behind in the eyebrow centre, and the rest of the 25 tattvas stand in the throat centre—op.cit.

3)In the deep sleep state (sushupti), chitta, prana, and jiva stand in the heart centre—op.cit.

புரியட் டகமே பொருந்தல் நனவு
புரியட் டகந்தன்னின் மூன்று கனவு
புரியட் டகத்தில் இரண்டு சுழுத்தி
புரியட் டகத்தொன்று புக்கல் துரியமே. 2201

Tattvas of the Subtle Body in the Five States of Consciousness

In Jagrat State
All the eight Tattvas
Of the Puriyashta (Subtle) body are;
In Dream State
The three Tattvas
Of the Subtle Body are;
In Sushupti State,
Two of the Subtle Body remain;
In Turiya State,
Only one is left behind,
With Purusha.

In the jagrat state the subtle body has eight tattvas. In the dream state it has three; in the sushupti state, two. Only one is left behind in the turiya state with purusha.

1)Sound, touch, shape, taste, smell, intellect, mind and egoity—vide Mantra 2123 supra.
2)Intellect, mind and egoity.
3)Intellect and egoity.
4)Egoity.

நனவின் நனவு புலனில் வழக்கம்
நனவிற் கனவு நினைத்தல் மறத்தல்
நனவிற் சுழுத்தியுண் ணாடல் இலாமை
நனவில் துரிய மதீதத்து நந்தியே. 2202

Experiences in the Five States of Consciousness Within Jagrat

Jagrat in Jagrat
Pertains to Senses;
Svapna in Jagrat
Is of thinking and forgetting;
Sushupti in Jagrat
Is seeking inward;
Turiya in Jagrat
Is abstaining from seeking;
In the state of Turiyatita
Is Nandi verily.

Jagrat-in-jagrat is functioning with the senses; svapna-in-jagrat is thinking and forgetting; seeking inward is sushupti-in-jagrat; turiya-in-jagrat is abstaining from seeking. Nandi is truly in the turiyatita states.

கனவின் நனவுபோற் காண்டல் நனவாங்
கனவினிற் கண்டு மறத்தல் கனவாங்
கனவிற் சுழுத்தியுங் காணாமை காணல்
அனுமாதி செய்தலி லான துரியமே, 2203

Four Inner States of the Dream State

To vision in dream
As in Jagrat,
Is Jagrat-in-Dream State;
To vision and forget
In Dream
Is Dream-in-Dream State,
To vision and non-vision
Is Sushupti-in-Dream State
To infer events
Is Turiya in Dream State.

The four inner states of the dream state are jagrat in-dream state, dream-in-dream state, sushupti-in-dream state and turiya-in-dream state.

சுழுத்தி நனவொன்றுந் தோன்றாமை தோன்றல்
சுழுத்தி கனவதன் உண்மை சுழுத்தியிற்
சுழுத்தி யறிவறி வாலே யழிகை
சுழுத்தி துரியமாஞ்சொல்லறும் பாழே. 2204

Sushupti and Its Inner Divisions

Jagrat-in-Sushupti
Is to vision it as non-vision;
Dream-in-Sushupti
Is to know it as dream;
Sushupti-in-Sushupti
Is to know that there is no knowledge of it;
Turiya in Sushupti
Is inexplicable Void.

Of the four inner divisions of sushupti, jagrat-in-sushupti is to vision and not vision at all; dream-in-sushupti is to know it as dream; sushupti-in-sushupti is to have the knowledge of it. The inexplicable void is turiya-in-susuhpti.

துரிய நனவா மிதமுணர் போதந்
துரியக் கனவா மகமுணர் போதந்
துரியச் சுழுத்தி வியோமந் துரியந்
துரியம் பரமெனத் தோன்றிடுந் தானே. 2205

Turiya and Its Inner Divisions

Jagrat-in-Turiya
Is (God) Consciousness, external;
Svapna-in-Turiya
Is (God) Consciousness internal;
Sushupti-in-Turiya
Is Void inexplicable;
Turiya-in-Turiya
Is to vision Param Supreme.

Jagrat-in-turiya, svapna-in-turiya, sushupti-in-turiya, and turiya-in-turiya — God-consciousness external, God-consciousness internal, consciousness of Void and vision of Param — these belong to the four substates in turiya.

அறிவறி கின்ற அறிவு நனவாம்
அறிவறி யாமை யடையக் கனவாம்
அறிவறி யவ்வறி யாமை சுழுத்தி
அறிவறி வாகு மான துரியமே. 2206

Jiva-knowledge in Relation to Para-Knowledge in the Four States

Jiva-knowledge cognising Para-knowledge is Jagrat
Jiva-knowledge cognising-ceasing is Dream;
Jiva-knowledge cognising,
Yet knowing it not, is Sushupti;
Jiva-knowledge merging in Para-Knowledge
Is Turiya verily.

தானெங்குமாயவ னைம்மலந் தான்விட்டு
ஞானந் தனதுரு வாகி நயந்தபின்
தானெங்கு மாய்நெறி நின்றது தான்விட்டு
மேனந்தச் சூக்க மவைவன்ன மேலிட்டே. 2207

Jiva's Experiences in Turiya State

He (Jiva) then pervasive becomes;
Shedding Malas five,
He takes the Form of Jnana;
Experiencing that,
Abandoning his pervasiveness,
He ascends higher,
The Subtle Form of Pranava (Aum)
To assume.

ஐயைந்து மாறுமோ ரைந்து நனாவினில்
எய்யு நனவு கனவு சுழுத்தியா
மெய்யும்பின் சூக்கமும் மெய்ப்பகுதி மாயை
ஐயமுந் தானவ னத்துரி யத்தனே. 2208

Tattvas in the Inner Divisions of Turiya State

Thirty and Six are Tattvas
In Jagra-in-Turiya;
In Svapna in that Turiya;
And in Sushupti-in-Turiya
In Turiya-in-Turiya
The Body Gross and the Body Subtle
To the Suddha Maya belong;
He who that Turiya-in-Turiya State attains
Master, indeed, Becomes.

ஈதென் றறிந்திலன் இத்தனை காலமும்
ஈதென் றறிந்தபின் ஏதும் அறிந்திலேன்
ஈதென் றறியும் அறிவை அறிந்தபின்
ஈதென் றறியும் இயல்புடை யோனே. 2209

New Knowledge

This I knew not,
All these days;
This when I know,
Nothing else I knew;
When I knew,
This the Truth
Then I Knew I am It.

உயிர்க்குயி ராகி யுருவா யருவாய்
அயற்புணர் வாகி யறிவாய்ச் செறிவாய்
நயப்புறு சத்தியும் நாதன் உலகாதி
இயற்பின்றி யெல்லாம் இருண்மூடமாமே. 2210

Immanence of Sakti and Siva

As Life of Life,
As Form and Formless,
As Jiva-Sentience and Knowledge-Divine
All pervasive, He stands;
If Sakti and Siva
In world immanent are not,
Verily, verily, all is inert darkness,
In ignorance entire steeped.

சத்தி யிராகத்திற் றானல் லுயிராகி
ஒத்துறு பாச மலமைந்தோ டாறாறு
தத்துவ பேதஞ் சமைத்துக் கருவியும்
வைத்தனன் ஈசன் மலமறு மாறே. 2211

Raison D'Etre of Creation

In endearment wondrous
The Lord moved Sakti into Creative activity;
And to primordial Pasas five,
Conjoined Tattvas thirty and six
And fashioned the body organs too,
—That your Malas sundered be.

சாக்கிரா தீதத்தி லாணவந் தன்னுண்மை
சாக்கிரா தீதந் துரியத்திற் றானுறச்
சாக்கிரா தீதத்தில் ஆணவந் தான்விடாச்
சாக்கிரா தீதம் பரனுண்மை தங்குமே. 2212

Jagrat-atita State Leads to Turiya-In-Turiya (Para Turiya)

In Jagrat-atita State
Anava (Egoity), forsooth, is;

Even when the Soul enters
The Turiya state in Jagrat-atita (Turiya-in-Turiya State)
Anava still is of Jagrat-atita state;
Jagrat-atita is,
Where Truth of Para is.

மலக்கலப் பாலே மறைந்தது சத்தி
மலக்கலப் பாலே மறைந்தது ஞானம்
மலக்கலப் பாலே மறைந்தனன் தாணு
மலக்கலப் பற்றான் மதியொளி யாமே. *2213*

Mala-Contamination is Root of All Evil

By Mala-Contamination
Was Sakti obscured;
By Mala-Contamination
Was Jnana obscured;
By Mala-Contamination
Was Param obscured;
He who is freed
Of Mala-Contamination
Is verily the Enlightened One.

திகைக்கின்ற சிந்தையுள் சிங்கங்கள் மூன்று
நகைக்கின்ற நெஞ்சுள் நரிக்குட்டி நான்கு
வகைக்கின்ற நெஞ்சினுள் ஆனைக்கன்றைந்து
பகைக்கின்ற நெஞ்சுக்குப் பாலிரண்டாமே. *2214*

Enemies of Thought For God

In their bewildered thoughts
Are the lions three (lust, anger and ignorance),
In their bouncing thoughts
Are the jackals four (mind, intellect, will and egoity)
In their sensory thoughts
Are the elephants five (taste, sight, touch, sound, smell)
These the foes (internal and external)
Of the contending mind.

கதறு பதினெட்டுக் கண்களும் போகச்
சிதறி எழுந்திடுஞ் சிந்தையை நீரும்
விதறு படாமுன்னம் மெய்வழி நின்றால்
அதிர வருவதோர் ஆனையு மாமே. *2215*

Give Up Distractions and Take to the True Way

With streaming eyes eighteen
Your thoughts in distraction wander;
Before you tremble in death,
Take to the True Way;
You shall indeed meet
The mighty Lord of your soul.

The five sensoria, the five motoria, the five tanmatras, and the three — these eight distract you from God. Give up distractions and take to the true way.

நனவகத் தேயொரு நாலைந்தும் வீடக்
கனவகத் தேயுட் கரணங்க ளோடு
முனவகத் தேநின் றுதறியுட் புக்கு
நினைவகத் தின்றிச் சுழுத்திநின் றானே. *2216*

Jiva Devoid of Thought in Sushupti

Of the Tattvas in Waking State
Four times five are behind left;
The Tattvas four that Antahkaranas form
In Dream State are;
—These you shake off
And into yourself enter;
Then thoughts devoid
The Soul in Sushupti Stands.

நின்றவன் ஆசான் நிகழ்துரி யத்தனாய்
ஒன்றி யுலகின் நியமாதிக ளுற்றுச்
சென்று துரியாதீ தத்தே சிலகாலம்
நின்று பரனாய் நின்மல னாமே. *2217*

Evolution of Jiva to Para State

The Soul who thus stood
Has verily a Master become;
He enters the Turiya State
And remains in the Eight-fold Yoga;
He then attains Turiyatita State;
And further a while after
He becomes Para the Pure.

ஆனவவ் வீசன் அதீதத்தில் வித்தையாத்
தானுல குண்டு சதாசிவ மாசத்தி
மேனிகள் ஐந்தும்போய் விட்டுச் சிவமாகி
மோன மடைந்தொளி மூலத்த னாமே. *2218*

Further Evolution to Primal Light

He who thus Isa Became
Reaching Turiyatita State,
As Pure Jnana comprehends worlds all;
Then He further attains the Five Forms,
Sadasiva, Mahesvara, Rudra, Hari and Brahma;
Having experienced those stages,
Jiva becomes Siva;
Then, further attaining Mauna (Divine Silentless) State,
He merges in the Primal Light.

மண்டல மூன்றினுள் மாயநன் னாடனைக்
கண்டுகொண் டுள்ளே கருதிக் கழிகின்ற
விண்டலர் தாமரை மேலொன்றுங் கீழாகத்
தண்டமுந் தானா யகத்தினுள் ளாமே. *2219*

Lord is Within

He is the Lord of Maya Land,
Where the Spheres Three within are;
He is the One whom I see within
And pine incessant for;

He is the Lotus that blooms in the cranium,
With its stalk stemming deep in my heart.

He is the Lord of maya land with the three spheres — sun, moon and fire within. He is immanent in me. The Lord is also the lotus that blooms in the cranium with its stem, deep in my heart. He is the One whom I pine for.

போதறி யாது புலம்பின் புள்ளின
மாதறி யாவகை நின்று மயங்கின
வேதறி யாவணம் நின்றனன் எம்மிறை
சூதறி வாருச்சி சூடிநின் றாரே. 2220

The Dawn of Light Within in Yoga

The birds (Malas) shrilled
Unaware of the shimmering dawn;
Bewildered were they,
Their mother (Sakti) unrecognising;
Beyond Vedas stood He my Lord;
They who knew the Mystic Way (of Yoga)
Reached to Him inside their very head.

கருத்தறிந் தொன்பது கண்டமும் ஆங்கே
பொருத்தறிந் தோன்புவ னாபதி நாடித்
திருத்தறிந் தேன்மிகு தேவர் பிரானை
வருத்தறிந் தேன்மன் மன்னிநின் றானே. 2221

I Saw Him Within In the Nine Centres

In contemplation deep I sought
The Lord of worlds all,
In the Nine Centres within;
Distinct I saw Him,
He, the Lord of Celestials all;
Intense I sought Him,
And He in my thoughts unfailing stood.

ஆன விளக்கொளி தூண்டு மவனென்னத்
தான விளக்கொளி யாமூல சாதனத்
தான விதிமூலத் தானத்தில் அவ்விளக்
கேனை மதிமண்ட லங்கொண் டெரியுமே 2222

Kundalini Yoga Experience

As one that kindles the lamp's flame,
So do you,
The Lamp's Flame in Muladhara kindle;
That Lamp in Muladhara lighted,
Encompassing the Sphere of Moon, glows.

உண்ணாடும் ஐவர்க்கு மண்டை யொதுங்கிய
விண்ணாட நின்ற வெளியை வினவுறில்
அண்ணாந்து பார்த்தைவர் கூடிய சந்தியிற்
கண்ணாடி காணுங் கருத்ததென் றானே. 2223

God is Inward Where the Five Sense Controlled Meet

If you ask,
How the Heavenly Space within the cranium is,
Where the inward looking Five abide,
Verily it is,
Like gazing upward into a mirror
(Seeing the self reflected in crystal purity)
At a junction
Where the Five, in control, meet.

அறியாத வற்றை அறிவான் அறிவான்
அறிவான் அறியாதான் தன்னறி வாகான்
அறியா தவத்தை அறிவானைக் கூட்டி
அறியா தறிவானை யாரறி வாரே. 2224

Lord is the Knower; He makes the Jiva Experience the Five States of Awareness

The knower he is,
Who things unknown knows;
The knower,
Who the Self knows not,
Is knower none;
The Jiva the Five Avastas knows not;
He, Lord, makes him know
To none beknown;
Who indeed does Him know?

துரிய தரிசனஞ் சொற்றோம் வியோமம்
அரியன தூடண மந்நன வாதி
பெரியன கால பரம்பிற் றுரியம்
அரிய அதீதம் அதீதத்த தாமே. 2225

Turiya in Turiya is Para Turiya; Beyond is Turiyatita

The visioning of Turiya State
We thus far spoke of;
The Void of Turiya State
Is state rare;
Unimportant indeed,
Are the states Jagrat and the rest;
Great, great, by far
Is the Timeless Para Turiya;
Transcending it is Turiyatita;
Rarer even far that State is.

மாயையிற் சேதனன் மன்னும் பகுதியோன்
மாயையின் மற்றது நீவுதன் மாயையாங்
கேவல மாகுந் சகலமா யோனியுள்
தோயும் மனிதர் துரியத்துட் சிவனே. 2226

Seek Para Turiya and Reach Siva's State

The World of Maya (Prakriti)
Belongs to Jiva;
To leave that Maya
Is to reach Kevala Maya State;
To be born again and again
As diverse life forms,
Is the State — Sakala;
In Para Turiya is Siva State

7. கேவல சகல சுத்தம்

KEVALA, SAKALA, SUDDHA

தன்னை யறிசுத்தன் றற்கேவ லன்றானும்
பின்ன முறநின்ற பேத சகலனும்
மன்னிய சத்தசத் துச்சத சத்துடன்
துன்னுவர் தத்தந் தொழிற்கள வாகவே. 2227

Sat, Asat and Sat-Asat Nature of Suddha, Kevala, Sakala States

He who cognises the Self
Is in Suddha State;
He who not
Is in Kevala;
He who cognises in distracting differences
Is in Sakala;
In Sat (Real), Asat (Unreal) and Sat-Asat (Real-Unreal)
They respective conjoin;
Each, according to his cognising state.

தானே தனக்குப் பகைவனும் நட்டானுந்
தானே தனக்கு மறுமையும் இம்மையுந்
தானே தான்செய்த வினைப்பயன் துய்ப்பானுந்
தானே தனக்குத் தலைவனு மாமே. 2228

Importance of Self-Cognition-Suddha State

Himself like himself
Is foe and friend;
Himself like himself
Is the here and hereafter;
Himself his Karmas
He experiences;
Himself like himself
His master be.

ஆமுயிர் கேவல மாமாயை இன்னடந்
தாமுயிர் மாயை எறிப்ப அறிவுற்றுக்
காமிய மாயேய முங்கல வாநிற்பத்
தாமுறு பாசஞ் சகலத்த தாமே. 2229

Evolution of the Sakala State of the Soul

The Soul in Kevala State
Inert reposes;
On it the Mamaya (Asuddha Maya) acts;
By the action
The Soul receives powers of cognition;
And then mixing with Desire (Kamiyam)
And the Objects of Desire (Mayeyam)
In Pasa it full enters;
That the State of Sakala is.

சகல அவத்தையிற் சார்ந்தோர் சகலர்
புகலு மலமூ வகையும் புணர்ந்தோர்
நிகரின் மலரோன்மா லீடுபல் தேவர்கள்
நிகழ்நரர் கீட மந்தமு மாமே. 2230

Who Are the Sakalas?

Sakalas are those
Who in Sakala State are;
Steeped they are in Pasas three;
The peerless Brahma, Hari,
The Celestials numerous,
The humans here below
And all lives like the tiny worm,
All, all, are Sakalas verily.

Mantras 2230, 2231, 2240 & 2241

Souls are ranked as vijnanakalas, pralayakalas, and sakalas according to the number of malas they possess. Vijnanakalas possess only anava, but they are inert. Pralayakalas possess maya, in addition anava. They belong to the world of suddha/asuddha maya. The 108 Srikanta Rudras are of to his catergory. The sakalas are the souls soaked in all the three malas — anava, karma and maya

தாவிய மாயையில் தங்கும் பிரளய
மேவிய மற்ற துடம்பாய்மிக் குள்ளன
ஓவல் இலக்கணர் ஒன்றிய சீகண்டர்
ஆவயி னூற்றெட் டுருத்திர ராமே. 2231

Who Are the Pralayakalas

Pralayakalas in Maya (Asuddha) world abide;
Of Maya their bodies are in main;
Of comelines eternal are they;
The Srikanta
And the eight and hundred Rudras;
—(These the Pralayakalas are.)

ஆகின்ற கேவலத் தாணவத் தானவ
ராகின்ற வித்தேச ராமனந் தாதிய
ராகின்ற எண்மர் எழுகோடி மந்திர
ராகின்ற ஈசர் அநேகரு மாமே. 2232

Who Are the Vijnanakalas

Vijnanakalas are souls, other numerous,
They reside in the State of Kevala;
They are possessed of Anava (mala)—alone;
The eight Vidyesvaras beginning with Ananta
The (Maha) Mantraresvaras that seven crore number;
—(These the Vijnanakalas are.)

ஆமவ ரிற்சிவ னாரருள் பெற்றுளோர்
போமலந் தன்னாற் புகழ்விந்து நாதம்விட்
டோமய மாகி யொடுங்கலி னின்மலந்
தோமறு சுத்தா வவத்தைத் தொழிலே. 2233

Suddha or Pure State

Of them,
Those who receive Siva's Grace
From Anava mala get liberated;
Transcending the states of Bindu (light) and Nada (sound)
As Aum (Pranava) they become;
And in Siva Pure they merge;
That verily is the Suddha (Pure) State (Avasta).

ஓரினு மூவகை நால்வகை யும்முள
தேரி லிவைகே வலமாயை சேரிச்சை
சாரிய லாயவை தாமே தணப்பவை
வாரிவைத் தீசன் மலமறுத் தானே. 2234

Four Divisions of Vijnanakalas

When you think of it,
Of these Souls in gradation three,
Vijnanakalas have divisions four,
They are shrouded in Kevala (Asuddha) Maya;
Inclined are they to be gripped by Desire,
Yet, of themselves they leave all;
When the Lord His Grace bestows;
And together the Malas sunders.

There are four divisions of vijnanakalas, all shrouded in kevala state. Some are in pure kevala (kevala-kevala), some more evolved are in kevala-sakala by the power of bindu; some even more evolved are in kevala-suddha, and the furthest evolved, having totally merged in Siva are in Arul-kevala state. Albeit, gripped by mayaic desire, they are freed by the Grace of God and with that they sever the malas.

பொய்யான போதாந்த மாறாறும் விட்டகன்
றெய்யாமை நீங்கவே எய்தவன் தானாகி
மெய்யாஞ் சராசர மாய்வெளி தன்னுட்புக்
கெய்தாம லெய்துஞ்சுத் தாவத்தை யென்பதே. 2235

When is Suddha State Reached?

Abandoning the illusory Tattvas
Six times six;
Rid of ignorance
The Jiva becomes Siva Himself;
And pervading all Creation
He enters the Void true;
This the Suddha State,
That of himself the Jiva reaches.

அனாதி பசுவியாத்தி யாகு மிவனை
அனாதியில் வந்த மலம்ஐந்தால் ஆட்டி
அனாதியிற் கேவல மச்சக லத்திட்டு
அனாதி பிறப்பறச் சுத்தத்துக ளாகுமே. 2236

How Suddha State is Reached

Eternal is he, Jiva; pervasive too is he;
Immersing him in Eternal Malas five,
The Lord lifts him
From the Primordial Kevala State
And consigns to Sakala State,
Thence,
Freed from unceasing whirl of birth
The Jiva, Suddha State reaches.

அந்தரஞ் சுத்தாவத் தைகே வலத்தாறு
தந்தோர்தஞ் சுத்தகே வலத்தற்ற தற்பரத்
தின்பால் துரியத் திடையே யறிவுறத்
தன்பால் தனையறி தத்துவந் தானே. 2237

Knowledge of Self in Turiya Leads to Suddha State

The Suddha State is the ultimate;
The Jiva that passes through Kevala
When it reaches Turiya
Receives knowledge of Tatpara,
—Who beyond States, Kevala and Suddha, exists—
Thus realizing the Self within.

ஐயைந் தொடுங்கும் ஆன்மாவில் ஆன்மாவும்
மெய்கண்டு சுத்த அவத்தையில் வீடாகுந்
துய்யவவ் வித்தை முதன்மூன்றுந் தொல்சத்தி
ஐய சிவஞ்சித்தி யாந்தோற்ற மவ்வாறே. 2238

Involution of Tattvas After Jiva Reaches Suddha State

The Tattvas five times five
Will into the Soul involute;
The Soul, having realized Suddha State,
Will in Suddha Vidya Tattva merge;
The first three of this category
(Suddha Vidya, Isvaram and Sadakyam)
Will in Sakti involute;
Beyond the Sakti is Siva
(Of the Siva Tattva)
Thus involuting, the Soul returns to the Beginning;
This the order (in reverse of evoluting too)

Mantras 2238 & 2239

The twenty-five tattvas then involute into the soul and merge into the six vidya tattvas. From there it passes into the suddha state, merging in suddha vidya tattva. The first three of the pure maya category (suddha vidya, isvaram and sadakyam) involute in Sakti tattva (bindu). Beyond Sakti tattva is Siva tattva (nada). This is the process of the graded involution of the tattvas into the ultimate Siva. The reverse order of this is the devolution of the tattvas.

ஐயைந்து மான்மாவில் ஆறோ டடங்கிடு
மெய்கண்ட மேன்மூன்று மேவுமெய் யோகத்தில்

கைகண்ட சத்தி சிவபாகத் தேகாண
எய்யும் படியடங் குந்நாலேழ் எய்தியே. 2239

Involution of Tattvas Further Explained

The Tattvas five times five of Purusha[1]
Into the Six (Vidya Tattvas) involute;
They into the three Siva Tattvas[2] higher above involute,
Who in turn merges into Sakti (Bindu)
Who with Siva (Nada) stands;
—Thus is the ultimate of involution reached
Into Tattvas seven and four.[3]

1) 25 prakriti or atma tattvas including the experient soul—purusa.
2) i)suddha vidya; ii)Isvaram; iii)Sadakyam — they belong to the Siva tattvas.
3) Eleven tattvas — six vidya tattvas plus the five Siva tattvas.
The Saiva Siddhanta system of philosophy postulates thirty-six tattvas. Of these, twenty-five (including jiva) belong to the body (atma tattvas), six to higher knowledge (vidya tattvas); and five to the spirit (Siva tattvas). At the time of involution the twenty-five bodily tattvas involute into the jiva (soul); they do not involute into Siva tattvas. So Tirumular here skips them and enumerates the tattvas that involute into the Siva tattvas as twenty-five only. Of the remaining five Siva tattvas, the important three, namely suddha vidya (spiritual knowledge), Isvaram (Godliness), and Sadakyam (God-equality) involute into Siva. As Sakti stands one with Siva, it is not considered as a separate category. Thus the tattvas are enumerated in the verse as twenty-eight in all.

ஆணவத் தாரொன் றறியாத கேவலர்
பேணிய மாயைப் பிரளயா கலராகுங்
காணும் உருவினர் காணாமை காண்பவே
பூணுஞ் சகலர்முப் பாசமும் புக்கோரே. 2240

Souls are Ranked According to the Number of Malas They Possess

The Kevalas (Vijnanakalas) are inert
With Anava alone possessed;
The Pralayakalas have Maya
In addition;
They see with form unseen;
The Sakalas are Souls
In all three Malas steeped.

ஆணவ மாகும் விஞ்ஞான கலருக்குப்
பேணிய மாயை பிரளயா கலருக்கே
ஆணவ மாயையுங் கன்ம மூன்றுமே
காணுஞ் சகலர்க்குக் காட்டு மலங்களே. 2241

Further explained

The Vijnanakalas possess Anava mala alone;
The Pralayakalas have Maya too
Anava, Maya, and Karma
—All three the Sakalas have;
These their Malas are.

கேவலந் தன்னிற் கிளர்ந்தவிஞ் ஞாகலர்
கேவலந் தன்னிற் கிளர்விந்து சத்தியால்
ஆவயிற் கேவலத் தச்சக லத்தையும்
மேவிய மந்திர மாமாயை மெய்ம்மையே. 2242

Sakalas in Vijnanakalas

The Vijnanakalas
Who stand in Kevala (inert State)
By the power of Bindu,
That in Kevala is,
Become activated as Sakalas within Kevala;
And so attain the truth of Mamaya
Who the power of Mantra holds.

மாயையின் மன்னும் பிரளயா கலர்வந்து
மாயையுந் தோன்றா வகைநிற்க ஆணவ
மாய சகலத்துக் காமிய மாமாயை
ஏயமன் னூற்றெட் டுருத்திரர் என்பவே. 2243

Pralayakalas — 108 Rudras

The Pralayakalas in Maya (Suddha) reside;
Yet that Maya affects them not;
They stand with Anava;
With Mamaya's (Asuddha) Kamya desires
That Sakalas possess;
They verily are the Rudras One Hundred and Eight.

மும்மலங் கூடி முயங்கி மயங்குவோர்
அம்மெய்ச் சகலத்தார் தேவர் சுரர் நரர்
மெய்ம்மையில் வேதா விரிமிகு கீடாந்தத்
தம்முறை யோனிபுக் கார்க்குஞ் சகலரே. 2244

Sakalas Have All Three Malas

They who in Malas three enveloped
In worldly life wallow,
Are the Sakalas per se;
Thus are the Devas, the humans,
And the rest of Brahma's creation numerous
Like the very worm
That life's womb enters;
—All these are Sakalas that crowd the world.

சுத்த அவத்தையில் தோய்ந்தவர் மும்மலச்
சத்தசத் தோடத் தனித்தனி பாசமும்
மத்த இருள்சிவ னான கதிராலே
தொத்தற விட்டிடச் சுத்தரா வார்களே. 2245

Rid of Malas, Souls Become Suddhas

They who Suddha State reach,
By luminous Grace of Siva
Stand dispelled of Malas triple,
That Sat-Asat are;
And of dark Pasas, one by one;
Having thus rid them entire,
They become Suddhas ever.

தற்கே வலம்முத்தி தானே தனிமையாம்
பிற்பாற் சகலங் கலாதிப் பிறிவதாஞ்
சொற்பாற் புரிசுத்த கேவலஞ் சாக்கிரந்
தற்பாற் புரிவது தற்சுத்த மாமே. 2246

Gradations of Suddha States — Suddha-Kevala, Suddha-Sakala; Suddha-Jagrat, and Suddha-Suddha

In Suddha-Kevala-Mukti State
The Jiva stands alone;
When afterward
The Kalas leave,
Then is Suddha-Sakala-Mukti;
When in sound Aum
The Soul as one stands,
Then is Suddha (Kevala) Jagrat Mukti;
Still beyond,
The Soul Itself within Itself stands
Then in Suddha-within-Suddha-Mukti State.

அறிவின்றி முத்தன் அராகாதி சேரான்
குறியொன்றி லாநித்தன் கூடான் கலாதி
செறியுஞ்செயலிலான் றினங்கற்ற வல்லோன்
கிறியன் மலவியாபி கேவலந் தானே. 2247

Suddha-Kevala-Mukti State Described

Inert without knowledge,
Unaffected by desires,
Goal-less, everlasting,
Unattached to Kalas,
Actionless,
Incapable of daily experiences,
By Malas deceitful infused,
—Thus is Jiva in Kevala-Mukti State.

விந்துவும் மாயையும் மேவுங் கிரியையுஞ்
சந்தத ஞான பரையுந் தனுச்சத்தி
விந்துவின் மெய்ஞ்ஞான மேவும் பிரளயர்
வந்த சகலசுத் தான்மாக்கள் வையத்தே. 2248

Pralayakalas That Are Suddhas Among Sakalas

Bindu, Maya and Kriya
They possess;
The power of interminable Jnana Sakti
Is their substrate (Dhanu);
In Bindu they attain Divine Knowledge;
Thus are the Pralayakalas of this world;
Albeit Sakalas,
They are Suddhas here below.

கேவல மாதியிற் பேதங் கிளக்குறிற்
கேவல மூன்றுங் கிளருஞ் சகலத்துள்
ஆவயின் மூன்று மதிசுத்த மூடவே
ஓவலில் லாவென்பா னுற்றுணர்வோர்கட்கே. 2249

Nine Subtle Divisions For the Soul in the Three States Kevala, Sakala and Suddha

To speak of the subtle divisions
In the three States—Kevala, Sakala and Suddha
It is like this:
Kevala-Kevala, Kevala-Sakala, and Kevala-Suddha,
Sakala-Kevala, Sakala-Sakala, and Sakala-Suddha,
Suddha-Kevala, Suddha-Sakala, and Suddha-Suddha
—Thus are the combinations nine in all
For those in depth see.

கேவலத்திற் கேவலம் அதீதா தீதங்
கேவலத் திற்சக லங்கள் வயிந்தவங்
கேவலத் திற்சுத்தங் கேடில்விஞ் ஞாகலர்க்
காவயி னாதன் அருண்மூர்த்தி தானே. 2250

Kevala State Subdivisions for Jiva

Kevala-in-Kevala is atita-atita state,
Kevala-Sakala is the Vaindava manifestations in Suddha Maya State;
Kevala-Suddha is the State of holy Vijnanakalas,
That State leads Soul to Grace Embodied.

சகலத்திற் கேவலஞ் சாக்கிரா தீதஞ்
சகல சகலமே சாக்கிர சாக்கிரஞ்
சகலத்திற் சுத்தமே தற்பரா வத்தை
சகலத்தில் இம்மூன்று தன்மையு மாமே. 2251

Sakala State Subdivisions for Jiva

Sakala-Kevala is the Jagrat-atita State;
Sakala-Sakala is the Jagrat-within-Jagrat State
Sakala-Suddha is the State of Tat-para
(self-illumined)
All these in the state of Sakala occur.

The inner divisions of suddha-sakala state are sakala-kevala; sakala-sakala and sakala-suddha. Sakala-kevala is the state of jagrat-atita; sakala-sakala is jagrat-in-jagrat. Sakala-suddha is the state of Tat-Para (Self-Illumined). These subdivisions are of the suddha-sakala state of the jiva.

சுத்தத்திற் சுத்தமே தொல்சிவ மாகுதல்
சுத்தத்திற் கேவலந் தொல்லுப சாந்தமாஞ்
சுத்த சகலந் துரிய விலாசமாஞ்
சுத்தத்தில் இம்மூன்றுஞ் சொல்லலு மாமே. 2252

Suddha State Subdivisions for Jiva

Suddha-Kevala is State of Upasantha
Suddha-Sakala is Turiya expansive state;
Suddha-Suddha is State of Siva-Becoming;
These three belong to Suddha State.

The inner divisions of suddha-suddha state are: suddha-kevala, suddha-sakala, and suddha-turiya. Suddha-kevala is the state of upasanta; suddha-sakala is the state of expansive turiya. The state of Siva-becoming is suddha-suddha or suddha-turiya. These three states belong to the suddha-suddha state of jiva.

சாக்கிர சாக்கிரந் தன்னிற் கனவொடுஞ்
சாக்கிரந் தன்னிற் சுழுத்தி துரியமே
சாக்கிரா தீதந் தனிற்சுகா னந்தமே
ஆக்கு மறையாதி ஐம்மல பாசமே. 2253

Bliss of Jagratatita State

Jagrat-In-Jagrat, Dream-in-Jagrat;
Sushupti-in-Jagrat and the Turiya-in-Jagrat,
Transcending these states all,
Is Jagratatita that confers Bliss Divine;
The Malas primordial that five are,
Away vanish ever and ever.

The inner divisions of the suddha-jagrat state are: jagrat-in (suddha)-jagrat; dream-in-jagrat; susuphti-in-jagrat. Dream-in-jagrat is jagrat-atita, that, confers divine bliss. Here disappears the five primordial malas forever and ever.

சாக்கிரா தீதத்திற் றானறுமணவஞ்
சாக்கிரா தீதம் பராவத்தை தங்காது
ஆக்கு பரோபாதி யாஉப சாந்தத்தை
நோக்கு மலங்குண நோக்குத லாகுமே. 2254

In Jagratatita State is Upasanta

In the state of Jagratatita
Anava is rooted entire;
Jagratatita, Para-Avasta (Siva) state is not;
But sure it confers Upasantha
That by Para caused;
Will Jiva, thereafter,
Ever look at Malas and Gunas?

பெத்தமும் முத்தியும் பேணுந் துரியமுஞ்
சுத்த வதீதமுந் தோன்றாமற் றானுணும்
அத்தன் அருளென் றருளால் அறிந்தபின்
சித்தமும் இல்லை செயலில்லை தானே. 2255

All Higher Experiences Come to Jiva By God's Grace

The states of Bondage (Boddha), of Liberation (Mukti)
Of Turiya, and Suddha-atita
—All these, the Jiva will subtle experience;
By Lord's Grace they come;
And when that knowledge by Grace dawns,
Neither thought nor action
The Jiva any more has.

எய்திய பெத்தமும் முத்தமும் என்பன
எய்தும் அரனரு ளேவிளை யாட்டோ
டெய்தி டுயிர்சுத்தத் திடுநெறி என்னவே
எய்தும் உயிரிறை பாலறி வாமே. 2256

Lord's Play Takes Jiva To God-Knowledge

The states of Bondage and Liberation
Of Hara's Grace, they come
It is His play
To take Jiva to Suddha goal;
That it might God-Knowledge receive.

ஐம்மலத் தாரு மதித்த சகலத்தர்
ஐம்மலத் தாரு மருவினைப் பாசத்தார்
ஐம்மலத் தார்சுவர்க் கந்நெறி யாள்பவர்
ஐம்மலத் தாரர னார்க்கறி வோரே. 2257

Sakalas Can Attain God-Knowledge

They of Five Malas are Sakalas,
They of Five Malas are Pasa bound
They of Five Malas rule
The Celestial world of Svarga
They of Five Malas can (ultimate) attain God-Knowledge.

கருவி லதீதங் கலப்பிக்கு மாயை
அரிய துரிய மதிலுண்ணும் ஆசையும்
உரிய் சுழுனை முதலெட்டுஞ் சூக்கத்
தரிய கனாத்தூலம் அந்நன வாமே. 2258

Experiences in the Five States of Consciousness

In Jiva's Atita State
Anava is;
In Turiya State
Maya permeates;
In Sushupti State,
Are desires for Maya experiences planted;
In Dream State
Functions[1] the Subtle Body[2] with Tattvas eight;
In the Waking State
Activated is the Body Gross.

1)Although in the dream state, the subtle body has 18 tattvas, ten of them (the five sense organs and five motor organs) do not function actually. Only the five tanmatras (sense potencies) and the three antahkaranas (cognitive organs) are active.

2)Puriasta body.

Mantras: 2258-2260

Maya (pure) that originated from Hara permeates the turiya state. Anava works in jiva's atita state and there he realises that para kamya sakti (seed of karma) is there in sushupti. Mamaya (illusory perception) or asuddha maya rules the dream state. Tirodhayi sakti (obscuration) joins in the waking state and activates the gross body. Thus are the five malas attached to the jiva in the sakala state.

ஆணவ மாகும் அதீதமேன் மாயையும்
பூணுந் துரியஞ் சுழுத்திபொய்க் காமியம்
பேணுங் கனவும் மாமாயை திரோதாயி
காணு நனவில் மலக்கலப் பாகுமே. 2259

Malas for Jiva in Different States of Consciousness

In (Kevala) Atita State
Anava is;
In Turiya State
Maya too is;
In Sushupti State

Seed of Karma,
Kamya an addition is;
In Dream State
Mamaya (Illusory perception) also is;
In Waking State
Tirodhayi joins (Obfuscation);
Thus are the Five Malas
To Jiva in Sakala State attached.

அரன்முத லாக அறிவோன் அதீதத்தன்
அரன்முத லாமாயை தங்கிச் சுழுனை
கருமம் உணர்ந்து மாமாயைக் கைக்கொண்டோர்
அருளு மறைவார் சகலத்துற் றாரே. 2260

Malas Restated

The Jiva in Atita State,
Realizes Primal Para;
The Jiva in Turiya stands in Maya (Suddha),
That has its beginning in Hara;
In Sushupti Karma Mala comes in;
In Dream State Mamaya (Asuddha) envelops,
In Waking State comes Tirodhayi, that obfuscates
Thus the Jiva in Sakala State stands.

உருவுற்றுப் போகமே போக்கியந் துற்று
மருவுற்றுப் பூதம னாதியான் மன்னி
வருமச் செயல்பற்றிச் சத்தாதி வைகிக்
கருவுற் றிடுஞ்சீவன் காணுஞ் சகலத்தே. 2261

Condition of Sakala State

They get body-form
And experience enjoyments diverse;
They are by elements pervaded
And conjoined to Mind and rest of cognitive organs;
They get attached to Karmas
They abide in Tanmatras
Thus are they born
—These Jivas in Sakala State.

இருவினை யொத்திட இன்னருட் சத்தி
மருவிட ஞானத்தில் ஆதன மன்னிக்
குருவினைக் கொண்டருட் சத்திமுன் கூட்டிப்
பெருமல நீங்கிப் பிறவாமை சுத்தமே. 2262

Sakala Jiva's Journey to Suddha State

They reach the State
When deeds good and bad
Equable become (Iruvinai Oppu);
When Sakti's Grace
On them descends (Sathini Padam);
When on the pedestal of Grace
They thus get seated,
Then with the aid of Guru Holy
They reach the Presence of Sakti's Grace;
Finally rid of the Primordial Mala (Anava)
They reach the State of Suddha
That no birth thereafter gives.

ஆறாறு மாறதின் ஐயைந் தவத்தையோ
டீறா மதீதத் துரியத் திவனெய்தப்
பேறான ஐவரும் போம்பிர காசத்து
நீறார் பரஞ்சிவ மாதேய மாகுமே. 2263

Turiyatita is the State Ultimate

With Tattvas six times six
And Avastas of ten states
He, Jiva, enters the final state
Of Turiyatita,
Then will the Divine Gift be (Mukti);
And Jiva merges into the Light Resplendent;
Which the Five Gods reach;
There, the Siva of Holy Ashes,
Jiva's Refuge Final art.

தன்னை யறியா துடலைமுன் தானென்றான்
தன்னைமுன் கண்டான் துரியந் தனைக்கண்டான்
உன்னுந் துரியமும் ஈசனோ டொன்றாக்கால்
பின்னையும் வந்து பிறந்திடுந் தானே. 2264

Self-Realization Only in Turiya State—It Is Not Ultimate

Knowing not the Self,
Jiva deemed body as the Self;
When he saw the Real Self,
He attained Turiya State;
But even in that Turiya State,
If he, Jiva, with Lord united not,
He will again born be, here below.

சாக்கிரந் தன்னில் அதீதந் தலைப்படில்
ஆக்கிய வந்த வயிந்தவ மானந்த
நோக்கும் பிறப்பறு நோன்முத்தி சித்தியாம்
வாக்கும் மனமும் மருவல் செய்யாவே. 2265

Only With Turiyatita State Birth Cycle Ends

If in Waking State
The Jiva realizes the Atita State
The Vaindavas (the Tattvas) that Maya caused
Will their malevolence shed;
The birth's whirl will cease;
Glorious Mukti and Siddhi then attained;
Speech and thought cease to be.

அப்பும் அனலும் அகலத்து ளேவரும்
அப்பும் அனலும் அகலத்து ளேவாரா
அப்பும் அனலும் அகலத்து ளேதெனில்
அப்பும் அனலும் கலந்தவ் வாறே. 2266

Beyond Turiyatita is Void

In the void beyond the Atita State,
Sakti (Water) and Siva (Fire) will appear,
Water and Fire do not together in space appear,
How then does Water and Fire in Void appear?

That way are the mingled
Sakti (Water) and Siva (Fire), there.

அறுநான்க சுத்தம் அதிசுத்தா சுத்தம்
உறுமேழு மாயை உடனைந்தே சுத்தம்
பெறுமா றிவைமூன்றுங் கண்டத்தாற் பேதித்
துறுமாயை மாமாயை யான்மாவி னோடே. 2267

36 Tattvas Reckoned as (5) Pure, (7) Pure Impure and (24) Impure.

Of Tattvas,
Six times four are Asuddha (Impure)
Seven are Suddha-Asuddha (Misra or Pure-Impure)
Five with Pure Maya are Suddha (Pure)
These in three divisions are thus parted
As Suddha (Pure), Suddha-Asuddha (Pure-Impure), and Asuddha (Impure)
All these with Jiva at appropriate stages stand.

Out of the 36 tattvas enumerated in the Saiva Siddhanta school of philosophy, 24 are considered as atma tattvas. They belong to this world and are pervaded by prakriti maya.

Purusa, the experient soul, is considered as another tattva. Here he is counted with the next category of vidya tattvas, which are six in number. They belong to higher knowledge, and are under the influence of misra (mixed) or pure/impure maya. In all, the tattvas in this sphere are numbered here as seven.

The next five tattvas are known as Siva tattvas. They are pervaded by pure maya. They are of the spiritual sphere, par-excellence. Paraparam, or the Supreme, is above the 36 tattvas.

Tattvas are universal principles evoluted from maya — pure, pure/impure, and impure — which may affect the soul in its journey to God.

மாயைகைத் தாயாக மாமாயை யீன்றிட
வாய பரசிவன் தந்தையாய் நிற்கவே
ஏயும் உயிர்க்கே வலசகலத் தெய்தி
ஆய்தரு சுத்தமுந் தான்வந் தடையுமே. 2268

The Journey from Kevala to Suddha Through Sakala States Helped by Siva as Father, Maya (Pure) as Mother and Mamaya (Impure) as Nurse

Parasiva for father;
Maya (Pure) for mother;
Mamaya (Impure) for nurse;
Thus does Jiva
Its birth take,
And journeying the states of Kevala, and Sakala
Final reaches the Suddha State.

8. பராவத்தை

PARA-AVASTA

அஞ்சுங் கடந்த அனாதி பரந்தெய்வ
நெஞ்சம தாய நிமலன் பிறப்பிலி
விஞ்சும் உடலுயிர் வேறு படுத்திட
வஞ்சத் திருந்த வகையறிந் தேனே. 2269

Mystery of Parting Life From Body

The Lord is the Para;
He is beginningless;
He is beyond five states of experience,
He is the Pure One,
Seated within the heart;
He is birthless;
Why this lovely body and life
He parts—
That mystery, I knew.

சத்தி பராபரஞ் சாந்தி தனிலான
சத்தி பரானந்தந் தன்னிற் சுடர்விந்து
சத்திய மாயை தனுச்சத்தி ஐந்துடன்
சத்தி பெறுமுயிர் தானங்கத் தாறுமே. 2270

Saktis are Dynamic Aspects of Static Parapara

Sakti in Parapara is Para Sakti;
Sakti in Santhi is Chit Sakti;
Sakti in Paranand is Iccha Sakti;
Sakti in luminous Bindu is Jnana Sakti;
Sakti in Maya is Kriya Sakti;
When Jiva these Saktis receive,
Then it reposes integral in the Divine.

ஆறாறுக் கப்பால் அறிவார் அறிபவர்
ஆறாறுக் கப்பால் அருளார் பெறுபவர்
ஆறாறுக் கப்பால் அறிவாம் அவர்கட்கே
ஆறாறுக் கப்பால் அரனினி தாமே. 2271

Beyond Tattvas is Divine Bliss

They who know Him
Beyond the Tattvas six times six
Truly know Him;
Beyond the Tattvas six times six
They receive His Grace;
They who have Knowledge True
Beyond the Tattvas six times six
Only to them, is He the Divine Bliss;
He the Hara
That is beyond the Tattvas,
Six times six.

அஞ்சொடு நான்குங் கடந்தக மேபுக்குப்
பஞ்சணி காலத்துப் பள்ளி துயில்கின்ற
விஞ்சையர் வேந்தனும் மெல்லிய லாளொடு
நஞ்சுற நாடி நயஞ்செய்யு மாறே. 2272

When Jiva is Rid of Malas by Siva-Sakti

Transcending the organs five (external)
And the four (internal),
In the (union) within of five (states) avastas,
The Jiva slumbers;
Then does the wondrous Lord
Appearing with Sakti of slender Form
Rid the Jiva of its poisons (Malas),
Forever to rejoice.

உரிய நனாத்துரி யத்தி லிவனாம்
அரிய துரிய நனாவாதி மூன்றிற்
பரிய பரதுரி யத்திற் பரனாந்
திரிய வருந்துரிய யத்திற் சிவமே. 2273

Beyond Turiya is Turiya-Turiya or Para Turiya; and Para-atita Turiya is Further Beyond

In Jagrat-Turiya State
The Jiva realizes Self;
Then beyond are States
Turiya-Jagrat, Turiya Svapna, Turiya Sushupti, and
Turiya-Turiya
In that Para Turiya State the Jiva is Para;
In the Turiya States still beyond, (Para-Turiya-atita)
Jiva becomes Siva.

பரமாம் அதீதமே பற்றறப் பற்றப்
பரமாம் அதீதம் பயிலப் பயிலப்
பரமாம் அதீதம் பயிலாத் தபோதனர்
பரமாகார் பாசமும் பற்றொன் றறாதே. 2274

In Para-atita Turiya State Jiva Becomes Beyond Param

In desire bereft of desires,
As Jiva aspires to Para-atita-turiya State
And steadfast perseveres in it,
He becomes Beyond-Param (Siva);
The tapasvins who practise not
Will never Param become;
They are forever fettered
In Pasas several.

ஆயும்பொய்ம் மாயை யகம்புற மாய்நிற்கும்
வாயு மனமுங் கடந்த மயக்கறின்
தூய அறிவு சிவானந்த மாகிப்போய்
வேயும் பொருளாய் விளைந்தது தானே. 2275

Freed of Maya, Jnana Dawns and Bliss Ensues

The Maya we seek to understand
Envelops Soul, inside and out;
The hypnosis it creates baffles thought and word;
When you are freed from it,
Your knowledge becomes purified;
It is transmuted into Sivananda
And becomes a protective roof over you.

துரியப் பரியில் இருந்தஅச் சீவனைப்
பெரிய வியாக்கிரத் துள்ளே புகவிட்டு
நரிகளை யோடத் துரத்திய நாதர்க்
குரிய வினைகள் நின் றோலமிட் டன்றே. 2276

From Turiya to Turiyatita

The Jiva was in Turiya State;
Like a swift steed
Was into the Turiyatita Jagrat State led;
The Master
Thus had the (Karmic) jackals chased away;
And the Karmas stood howling,
Disappointed sore.

நின்றஇச் சாக்கிர நீள்துரி யத்தினின்
மன்றனு மங்கே மணஞ்செய்ய நின்றிடும்
மன்றன் மணஞ்செய்ய மாயை மறைந்திடும்
அன்றே யிவனும் அவன்வடி வாமே. 2277

In Turiyatita State Jiva Becomes Siva

In this Turiyatita Jagrat State
The Lord of Dance with Jiva in union stands
When that union takes place
Maya vanishes away;
That very day Jiva attains Siva Form.

விரிந்திடிற் சாக்கிர மேவும் விளக்காய்
இருந்த விடத்திடை யீடான மாயை
பொருந்துந் துரியம் புரியிற்றா னாகுந்
தெரிந்த துரியத்துத் தீதக லாதே. 2278

Maya Lights the Path to Turiya and The Remains

If in Jagrat State
Where Jiva is,
He upward, ascends,
Well may Maya serve
A lamp to light his path;
Then, when he reaches Turiya State,
He his Self realizes;
Albeit in that Turiya State
Maya will still be,
(The Soul should further ascend to the Turiyatita State).

உன்னை யறியா துடலைமுன் நானென்றாய்
உன்னை யறிந்து துரியத் துறநின்றாய்
தன்னை யறிந்தும் பிறவி தணவாதால்
அன்ன வியாத்தன் அமலனென் றறிதியே. 2279

Self-Realization in Turiya State is not the End

Knowing not your Self
You deemed body as Self;
When in Turiya you entered,
You realized the Self;
Even though you realized Self,
Birth's cycle will leave you not;

(Therefore, ascend further upward Into the Turiyatita State)
And unite in Lord,
Pervasive and Pure.

கருவரம் பாகிய காயந் துரியம்
இருவருங் கண்டீர் பிறப்பிறப் புற்றார்
குருவரம் பெற்றவர் கூடிய பின்னை
இருவரு மின்றியொன் றாகிநின் றாரே. 2280

Beyond Turiya State is Union in Siva

This body is to birth subject,
Turiya State belongs to body and Jiva alike;
These subject to birth and death are;
When on them Grace of Holy Guru descends,
Two there is none,
Jiva in Siva unites one.

அணுவின் துரியத்தி லான நனவும்
அணுவசை வின்கண் ணான கனவும்
அணுவசை விற்பரா தீதஞ் சுழுத்தி
பணியிற் பரதுரி யம்பர மாமே. 2281

Beyond Four States in Turiya is Para Turiya

If Jiva in Turiya State
Having experienced in succession
Jagrat, Svapna, Sushupti states within,
Perseveres further,
Then he enters Para Turiya;
There verily Jiva becomes Para.

பரதுரி யத்து நனவும் பரந்து
விரிசக முண்ட கனவுமெய்ச் சாந்தி
உருவுறு கின்ற சுழுத்தியும் ஓவத்
தெரியுஞ் சிவதுரி யத்தனு மாமே. 2282

End of Para Turiya is Siva Turiya

Succeeding Para Turiya Jagrat State
Is the Para Turiya Svapna State
That engrosses the universe entire;
Then is Para Turiya Sushupti State
Where Upasanta (Peace beyond understanding) is;
That transcending, Jiva reaches Siva Turiya State.

பரமா நனவின்பின் பாற்சக முண்ட
திரமார் கனவுஞ் சிறந்த சுழுத்தி
உரமாம் உபசாந்த முற்றல் துறவே
தரனாஞ் சிவதுரி யத்தனு மாமே. 2283

End of Para Turiya is Siva Turiya

Succeeding Para Turiya Jagrat State
Is the Para Turiya Svapna State
That engrosses the universe entire;
Then is Para Turiya Sushupti State
Where Upasanta (Peace beyond understanding) is;
That transcending, Jiva reaches Siva Turiya State.

சீவன் துரிய முதலாகச் சீரான
ஆவ சிவன்துரி யாந்தம் அவத்தைபத்
தோவும் பராநந்தி யுண்மைக்குள் வைகியே
மேவிய நாலேழ் விடுத்துநின் றானே. 2284

Beyond the Ten Avastas in Jiva Turiya, Para Turiya and Siva Turiya is the Eleventh State of Consciousness of Para Nandi (Siva)

Thus Jiva, who has Para become,
From Jiva Turiya onward
Up to Siva Turiya,
Ten avastas (States) experiences;
Then enters the State Eleventh
Where he merges into Truth of Para Nandi (Siva)
And finally goes beyond,
All eleven States thus ensured.

JIVA TURIYA — Self-Realisation
i)Turiya
ii)Turiya jagrat
iii)Turiya svapna
iv)Turiya susupti
v)Turiyatita

PARA TURIYA — Jiva becomes Para
vi)Para Turiya
vii)Para turiya jagrat
viii)Para turiya svapna
ix)Para turiya sushupti
x)Para turiyatita

SIVA TURIYA — Jiva becomes Parasiva
xi)Siva turiya

பரஞ்சிவன் மேலாம் பரமம் பரத்திற்
பரம்பரன் மேலாம் பரநன வாக
விரிந்த கனாவிடர் வீட்டுஞ் சுழுனை
உரந்தகு மாநந்தி யாமுண்மை தானே. 2285

Further Beyond Para Siva State is Paramam (Brahmam), Paramparam and Para Maha Sivam

Beyond Para Siva is Paramam (Brahmam);
Beyond Paramam is Paramparam (Para Brahmam);
Thus are states ascending;
From Para Siva Jagrat, to Para Siva Svapna, and to Para
Siva Sushupti
The Jiva that has Para Siva become reaches
The Final Truth that is Para Nandi.

சார்வாம் பரசிவஞ் சத்தி பரநாதம்
மேலாய விந்து சதாசிவ மிக்கோங்கிப்
பாலாய்ப் பிரமன் அரியம ராபதி
தேவாம் உருத்திரன் ஈசனாங் காணிலே. 2286

Nine Manifestations of Para Siva

Pertaining to Para Siva
Are the (Para) Sakti,
Para Nada and Para Bindu;
And Sadasiva, Brahma, and Hari;

Rudra the Lord of Devas,
And Mahesvara to count.

க்லப்பறி யார்கடல் சூழுல கேழும்
உலப்பறி யாருட லோடுயிர் தன்னை
அலப்பறிந் திங்கர சாளகி லாதார்
குறிப்பது கோல மடலது வாமே. 2287

True Knowledge

Knowing that not
They rule not the (Spiritual) Kingdom;
In pomp and vanity they indulge;
That indeed is sorrow;
They know not, He pervades all;
They know not
The sea-girt seven Worlds
Will a shamble be;
They know not
That Siva with Jiva and Body
Commingling stands.

பின்னை யறியும் பெருந்தவத் துண்மைசெய்
தன்னை யறியில் தயாபரன் எம்மிறை
முன்னை யறிவு முடிகின்ற காலமும்
என்னை யறியலுற் றின்புற்ற வாறே. 2288

End Ego-Awareness; Self is Realized;

Perform penances true
That your Future holds;
Know thyself,
And the merciful Lord
His Grace confers;
When my ego awareness ended,
Then I knew my Self;
And bliss am I.

பொன்னை மறைத்தது பொன்னணி பூடணம்
பொன்னின் மறைந்தது பொன்னணி பூடணம்
தன்னை மறைத்தது தன்கர ணங்களாம்
தன்னின் மறைந்தது தன்கர ணங்களே. 2289

Way of Self-Realization Through Thought Process

Think of gold jewellery,
Thought of gold metal is not;
Think of gold metal
Thought of jewellery is not;
Think of sense organs, Self is not;
Think of Self, sense organs are not.

மரத்தை மறைத்தது மாமத யானை
மரத்தின் மறைந்தது மாமத யானை
பரத்தை மறைத்தது பார்முதற் பூதம்
பரத்தின் மறைந்தது பார்முதற் பூதமே. 2290

Sublimation of Thought

Think of wood
Image of toy-elephant recedes;
Think of toy-elephant
Image of wood recedes;
Think of elements five
Thought of Param recedes
Think of Param,
Thought of elements recedes.

ஆறா றகன்று நமவிட் டறிவாகி
வேறான தானே யகாரமாய் மிக்கோங்கி
ஈறார் பரையின் இருளற்ற தற்பரன்
பேறார் சிவாய அடங்கும்பின் முத்தியே. 2291

Knowledge of Siva, Sakti and Jiva [(Si-Va-Ya)] is Liberation

Transcending Tattvas
Six times six,
Abandoning
The letters "Na" and "Ma"
Knowledge Becoming,
Jiva thus liberated rises,.
As letter "Ya;"
Merging in letter "Va" denoting Sakti
And in letter "Si" denoting Siva
Jiva ("Ya") becomes Si Va Ya
That Mukti is.

துரியத்தில் ஓரைந்துஞ் சொல்லக ராதி
விரியப் பரையின் மிகுநாத மந்தம்
புரியப் பரையின் பராவத்தா போதந்
திரியப் பரமந் துரியந் தெரியவே. 2292

Experiences in Para Turiya

The Turiya State holds
The Letters-Five (Panchakshara);
In the Para Turiya Jagrat State
Are the letters Fifty and One;
In the Para Turiya Svapna State
Is Nada;
In the Para Turiya Sushupti State
Is Bodha;
Beyond appears Paramam (Brahmam).
In Para Turiya-Turiya State.

---

1)Jiva turiya—Panchakshara
PARA TURIYA AVASTA
1.Para turiya jagrat—Fifty-One Letters
2.Para turiya svapna—nada
3.Para turiya sushupti—bodha
4.Para turiya turiya—Paramam
(Siva turiya beginning of jagrat).

ஐந்துஞ் சகலத் தருளாற் புரிவற்றுப்
பந்திடுஞ் சுத்த அவத்தைப் பதைப்பினில்
நந்தி பராவத்தை நாடச் சுடர்முனம்
அந்தி யிருள்போலும் ஐம்மல மாறுமே. 2293

Pure (Suddha) Experience and Supreme (Para) Experience Beyond Jiva Experiences

In Sakala condition of Jiva,
These five experiences are by Grace attained;
Then follows the Suddha Avasta (Pure Experience) State;
That in intensity experiencing,
The Para Avasta (Supreme Experience) of Nandi is attained;
Then, as before light darkness is dispelled
The Five Malas for ever vanish.

1)Sakala avasta (existential experience)
Suddha avasta (pure experience)
Para avasta (Supreme experience—malas vanish)

ஐயைந்து மட்டுப் பகுதியும் மாயையும்
பொய்கண்ட மாமாயை தானும் புருடன்கண்
டெய்யும் படியாய் எவற்றுமாய் அன்றாகி
உய்யும் பராவத்தை யுள்ளுறல் சுத்தமே. 2294

State of Suddha Avasta (Pure-Impure)

Penetrating it,
Futher beyond In the State of Par-Avasta, (Pure Experience)
The limited sphere of Tattvas
Five times Five,
And Maya Impure,
—Unreal are they;
Leaving them,
Let Jiva ascend
Into the Sphere of Mamaya (Pure Experience)
That is Pure (Suddha);
There the Soul is All-Existence
And Non-Existence at once.

Sakala avasta — impure maya sphere (atma tattvas) Para avasta — pure/impure maya sphere (vidya tattvas) Suddha avasta — pure maya sphere (Siva tattvas).

நின்றான் அருளும் பரமுமுன் னேயமும்
ஒன்றாய் மருவும் உருவும் உபாதியுஞ்
சென்றா னெனைவிடுத் தாங்கிற்செல் லாமையும்
நன்றான ஞானத்தின் நாதப் பிரானே. 2295

Lord As Guru Guides the Soul's Journey

As Grace, He stood
As Param, He stood
As Love, He stood;
As one Form merged,
He stood;
He transcended experiences all,
But abandoned me not
He, the Lordly Guru, the Natha,
Of Divine Jnana.

9. முக்குண நிர்க்குணம்

TRIPLE GUNAS AND NIRGUNA (SANS GUNAS)

சாத்திக மெய்து நனவெனச் சாற்றுங்கால்
வாய்த்த இராசத மன்னுங் கனவென்ப
ஒய்த்திடுந் தாமதம் உற்ற சுழுத்தியாம்
மாய்த்திடு நிர்க்குண மாசில் துரியமே. 2296

Gunas experiences in States of Consciousness

Sattvic is Guna in the Waking State,
Rajas in Dream State,
Tamas in Deep Sleep State,
Nirguna, that other three Gunas destroys,
Is attribute of Turiya State Pure.

10. அண்டாதி பேதம்

COSMIC DIVISIONS

பெறுபகி ரண்டம் பேதித்த அண்டம்
எறிகடல் ஏழின் மணல்அள வாகப்
பொறியொளி பொன்னணி யென்ன விளங்கிச்
செறியும்அண் டாசனத் தேவர் பிரானே. 2297

Cosmic Space is God's Seat of Throne

In the vast spaces of Cosmos
Are universes numberless
That evolved and separated;
Countless are they
Like the sands that are
On the shores of seven seas;
Sparkling as a jewel of gold
That dazzles
They form His Seat of Throne
—For Him, the Lord of Celestials.

ஆனந்த தத்துவம் அண்டா சனத்தின்மேல்
மேனிஐந் தாக வியாத்தமுப் பத்தாறாய்த்
தானந்த மில்லாத தத்துவ மானவை
ஈனமி லாஅண்டத் தெண்மடங் காமே. 2298

God is Principle of Bliss Beyond Tattvas

On that Seat of Throne
He sits as Bliss-Principle (Tattva)
Five His Forms,

Thirty-six the Tattvas He pervades;
Nay,
The Tattvas He pervades
Are eight times by far as numerous
As universes in spaces Vast,
Himself beyond Tattvas' end.

11. பதினொராந்தானமும் அவத்தையெனக் காணல்

THE ELEVENTH STATE IS ALSO AVASTA

அஞ்சில் அமுதுமோ ரேழின்கண் ஆனந்த
முஞ்சிலோங் காரமோ ரொன்பான் பதினொன்றில்
வஞ்சக மேநின்று வைத்திடிற் காயமாங்
கிஞ்சுகச் செவ்வாய்க் கிளிமொழி கேளே. 2299

Attainments in Higher Experience (Para Avasta)

In the Fifth State (Jiva Turiyatita) is Ambrosia;
In the Seventh State (Para Turiya-Jagrat) is Bliss;
Above in Ninth State (Para Turiya-Sushupti) is Aum;
In the Eleventh State (Siva Turiya)
Illumined the Jiva standeth;
Abiding there He the (Divine) Body, attains;
Listen damsel that is red-mouthed as parrot!
—These the attainments of the Higher States (of Jiva) are.

புருட னுடனே பொருந்திய சித்தம்
அருவமொ டாறும் அதீதத் துரியம்
விரியுஞ் சுழுத்தியின் மிக்குள்ள எட்டும்
அரிய பதினொன்று மாமவ் வவத்தையே. 2300

Tattvas Fade in the Finite Stage

Even in the Atita Turiya State
Six Tattvas formless abide
—The Purusha cum Chitta, and Five formless Tattvas;
In the Sushupti State of Atita Turiya,
The rest eight are;
Only in the Eleventh State, nothing of Tattvas is.

Mantras 2300 & 2301

The tattvas gradually fade at various stages and in the eleventh state none lingers. Nandi alone is there and jiva will have attained the jnana-body. So meditate in order that you surely reach that immutable goal.

காட்டும் பதினொன்றுங் கைகலந் தாலுடல்
நாட்டி யழுத்திடின் நந்தியல் லாலில்லை
ஆட்டஞ்செய் யாத வதுவிதி யேநினை
ஈட்டு மதுதிடம் எண்ணலு மாமே. 2301

There Nandi Alone Is

When the eleven States are thus cognised,
And the Jiva fixes firm in the Jnana Body
There is none but Nandi;
That Being Immutable
Contemplate in order;
Sure believe, you can the Goal reach.

12. கலவு செலவு

UNITING AND EXITING

கேவலந் தன்னிற் கலவச் சகலத்தின்
மேவுஞ் செலவு விடவரு நீக்கத்துப்
பாவுந் தனைக்காண்டன் மூன்றும் படர்வற்ற
தீதறு சாக்கிரா தீதத்திற் சுத்தமே. 2302

Beyond Kevala, Sakala and Self-Realization States is Suddha Avasta

The Jiva in its primal condition
Is in the Kevala State;
When it mixes with Tattvas
It departs and enters the Sakala State;
Released from there,
It realizes the Self,
When it transcends all the states three,
It enters the Jagratatita State;
There it is Pure (Suddha).

வெல்லும் அளவில் விடுமின் வெகுளியை
செல்லும் அளவுஞ் செலுத்துமின் சிந்தையை
அல்லும் பகலும் அருளுடன் தூங்கினாற்
கல்லும் பிளந்து கடுவொளி யாமே. 2303

Vision of Space

Give up anger (Egoity)
As far as you can;
Direct your thoughts (Godward)
As far as it goes;
If with Lord's Grace
You slumber (in contemplation)
Day and night,
Even mountains will break;
And you shall vision the Space interminable.

13. நின்மலாவத்தை
PURE AVASTA (DEVOID OF MALAS)

"Pure Avasta (Devoid of Malas) (2304 to 2354).

In the 41 verses that constitute this chapter, Tirumular reiterates much (philosophical, metaphysical and religious material of what has been mentioned in earlier verses.

ஊமைக் கிணற்றகத் துள்ளே யுறைவதோர்
ஆமையின் உள்ளே யமுவைகள் ஐந்துள
வாய்மையி னுள்ளே வழுவா தொடுங்குமேல்
ஆமையின் மேலுமோ ராயிரத் தாண்டே. *2304*

Merge in Silence, Senses Withdrawn

Deep in the Well of Silence (Mauna)
Is a turtle—Jiva—(with Malas Five withdrawn)
If from Truth you deviate not,
And in (It) merge entire,
You shall indeed live
A thousand years beyond the turtle.

காலங்கி நீர்பூக் கலந்தஆ காயம்
மாலங்கி யீசன் பிரமன் சதாசிவன்
மேலஞ்சும் ஓடி விரவவல் லார்கட்குக்
காலனும் இல்லை கருத்தில்லை தானே. *2305*

Experience of Higher States Brings Immortality

Air, fire, water, earth and space,
Hari, Rudra, Mahesvara, Brahma and Sadasiva,
They who transcend these elements and Gods five
And into Higher States enter,
Will never death see;
Thoughts none other will they have
Except those of God.

ஆன்மாவே மைந்த னாயினன் என்பது
தான்மா மறையறை தன்மை யறிகிலர்
ஆன்மாவே மைந்தன் அரனுக் கிவனென்றல்
ஆன்மாவும் இல்லையால் ஐயைந்தும்
இல்லையே. *2306*

Jiva Son of Siva

Jiva is the son,
All the hoary scriptures thus say;
That they know not
The Jiva indeed is the Son of Hara;
For, without Jiva,
None the Tattvas five times five be.

உதய மழுங்கல் ஒடுங்கலிம் மூன்றின்
கதிசாக் கிரங்கன வாதி சுழுத்தி
பதிதரு சேதனன் பற்றாந் துரியத்
ததிசுப னாயனந் தானந்தி யாகுமே. *2307*

In Turiya is bliss Exceeding

Like being born, living, and dying
Are the experiences three
Of Waking, Dreaming and Deep Sleep States;
When Jiva reaches Turiya State,
And there abides,
Exceeding Pure he becomes,
And infinite bliss he enjoys.

எல்லாந்தன் னுட்புக யாவுளுந் தானாகி
நல்லாந் துரியம் புரிந்தக்கால் நல்லுயிர்
பொல்லாத வாறாறுட் போகாது போதமாய்ச்
செல்லாச் சிவகதி சென்றெய்து மன்றே. *2308*

From Turiya State No Return to Tattvas

All within him (Jiva),
And he in all without;
Thus if Jiva
The Turiya State experiences,
No more shall it return
To Tattvas six times six;
Divine Knowledge (Bodha)
It will attain;
And so reach Siva-State.

காய்ந்த இரும்பு கனலை யகன்றாலும்
வாய்ந்த கனலென வாதனை நின்றாற்போல்
ஏய்ந்த கரணம் இறந்த துரியத்துத்
தோய்ந்த கருமத் துரிசக லாதே. *2309*

Yet in Turiya, Karmic Effects Are

Well may you iron
From fire remove;
The iron still retains
The effect of fire (experience);
So too,
Even if sense organs
Are in Turiya State extinguished
The impure effect of Karmic acts
Will still there be.

ஆன மறையாதி யாமுரு நந்திவந்
தேனை யருள்செய் தெரிநனா வத்தையில்
ஆன வகையை விடுமடைத் தாய்விட
ஆன மலாதீதம் அப்பரந் தானே. *2310*

In Turiyatita State All Malas Disappear Entire

In the burning state of Jagrat avasta
Diverse are the (Jiva's) experiences;
Give them up, give them up entire;
And with Grace of Nandi
That is Veda embodied,

You shall reach the Atita State
Bereft of Malas;
Then shall you the very Para be.

சுத்த அதீதஞ் சகலத்தில் தோய்வுறில்
அத்தன் அருள்நீங்கா வாங்கணிற் றானாகச்
சித்த சுகத்தைத் தீண்டாச் சமாதிசெய்
தத்தனோ டொன்றற் கருள்முத லாமே. 2311

Relapse Into Sakala State and Redemption by Grace

Those who have reached
The Suddha Atita-State
If to the Sakala State relapse,
Lord's Grace, them leave not;
Still standing close to Lord,
They enjoy not pleasures of world;
And at the end, Samadhi entering,
They in Lord as one unite;
—All these by Grace ultimate.

வேறுசெய் தானிரு பாதியின் மெய்த்தொகை
வேறுசெய் தானென்னைஎங்கணும்விட்டுய்த்தான்
வேறுசெய் யாவருட் கேவலத் தேவிட்டு
வேறுசெய் யாவத்தன் மேவிநின் றானே. 2312

All Are Acts of Grace

He parted Himself
In halves two;
He created the cluster of Tattvas
That to body pertain;
He let me be into births and places several;
He took me into inert Arul Kevala State,
And there left me,
The Lord in me uniting.

கறங்கோலை கொள்ளிவட் டங்கட லில்திரை
நிறஞ்சேர் ததிமத்தின் மலத்தே நின்றங்
கறங்காண் சுவர்க்க நரகம் புவிசேர்ந்
திறங்கா வுயிரரு ளாலிவை நீங்குமே. 2313

Power of Grace

The toy whirl of leaves made
The fire wheel of torches made,
The billowy waves of the blue sea,
The curd that stands with the churn
—All these are by some other force moved;
So too, the Jiva pushed by Malas,
Enter hell, heaven and earth
And stand sore troubled;
—All these away vanished
When Grace does descend.

தானே சிவமான தன்மை தலைப்பட
ஆன மலமுமப் பாச பேதமும்
மான குணமும் பரான்மா வுபாதியும்
பானுவின் முன்மதி போற்பட ராவே. 2314

In Jiva-Siva Union All Fade

When that State is attained,
Where the Self becomes Siva,
The Malas, the Pasas diverse,
Gunas and experiences
That arose for the estranged Jiva,
Will all, all, fade,
Even as does the beams of the moon
In the presence of the rising sun.

நெருப்புண்டு நீருண்டு வாயுவும் உண்டங்
கருக்கனுஞ் சோமனும் அங்கே அமருந்
திருத்தக்க மாலுந் திசைமுகன் தானும்
உருத்திர சோதியும் உள்ளத்து ளாரே. 2315

When Jiva Becomes Pervasive as Siva

Within them,
(Who have attained Siva-State,)
There is fire, water and air;
The sun and the moon are there seated;
Hari, Brahma and Rudra
Are also in their heart.

ஆனைகள் ஐந்தும் அடக்கி அறிவென்னும்
ஞானத் திரியைக் கொளுவி அதனுட்புக்
கூனை யிருளற நோக்கும் ஒருவற்கு
வானக மேற வழியெளி தாமே. 2316

Attain Jnana and Enter Heavenly Home

He who, the elephants of senses five subdues,
Lights the lamp of Jnana
And entering its radiance,
Drives the darkness within;
For him
It is easy
To ascend the Heavenly Home (Siva Loka).

ஆடிய காலில் அசைக்கின்ற வாயுவுந்
தாடித் தெழுந்த தமருக ஓசையும்
பாடி யெழுகின்ற வேதா கமங்களும்
நாடியி னுள்ளாக நான்கண்ட வாறே. 2317

Dance of Siva Seen Within

The moving breeze
That the Dancing Feet wafts;
The vibrant sound
That the Damaruka drum emits;
The celestial music,
That the chanting Vedas and Agamas produces;
All these in nadis within I experienced.

முன்னை யறிவினிற் செய்த முதுதவம்
பின்னை யறிவினைப் பெற்றால் அறியலாந்
தன்னை யறிவ தறிவாம தன்றிப்
பின்னை யறிவது பேயறி வாகுமே. 2318

Self-Knowledge is True Knowledge

The effect of goodly tapas
In past performed,
Can with knowledge
In present be discerned;
Self-knowledge is knowledge true,
The rest is but knowledge demented.

Insight into the past results from true knowledge. Self-Knowledge is true knowledge. The rest is but false and demented.

செயலற் றிருக்கச் சிவானந்த மாகுஞ்
செயலற் றிருப்பார் சிவயோகந் தேடார்
செயலற் றிருப்பார் செகத்தொடுங் கூடார்
செயலற் றிருப்பார்க்கே செய்தியுண் டாமே. 2319

In Actionless Contemplation Divine Message Comes

To be actionless is Siva's bliss;
They who are actionless
Seek not Siva Yoga;
They who are actionless
Will not in world merge;
Only to them who are actionless
Is the Divine message to be.

தானவ னாகுஞ் சமாதிகை கூடினால்
ஆன மலமறும் அப்பசுத் தன்மைபோம்
ஈனமில் காயம் இருக்கும் இருநிலத்
தூனங்கள் எட்டு மொழித்தொன்று வோர்கட்கே. 2320

In Samadhi Jiva Unites in Siva

They who attain Samadhi
They and He one become;
Sundered will be Malas,
Vanished the Jiva-State;
Their body (as Divine Light)
Will in Siva's World be;
They in Siva unite
Devoid of blemishes eight.

தொலையா அரனடி தோன்றுமஞ் சத்தி
தொலையா இருளொளி தோற்ற அணுவுந்
தொலையாத் தொழின்ஞானந் தொன்மையில் நண்ணித்
தொலையாத பெத்தமுத் திக்கிடை தோயுமே. 2321

Pedda or Jiva Mukti

At the eternal Feet of Hara,
The Sakti appears;
And as it appears
The interminable darkness
Of Jiva disappears,
And Light dawns;
And Jiva perseveres incessant
In the way of time-honoured Jnana
And thus reaches the State of Pedda (Jiva) Mukti.

தோன்றிய பெத்தமும் முத்தியுஞ் சூழ்சத்தி
மான்றுந் தெருண்டு முயிர்பெறு மற்றவை
தான்தரு ஞானந்தன் சத்திக்குச் சாதனா
மூன்றலில் லாவுள் ளொளிக்கொளி யாமே. 2322

Jiva Knowledge is Doubt-Tossed; Siva Knowledge is Light Divine

As the Sakti aids the Jiva
In Peddha as well as Mukti
Jiva that is doubt-tossed in the first,
Becomes doubt-free in the second;
And in that condition
Sakti grants its divine instrument
Of Jnana to Jiva;
That verily is the abiding Light
That transcends Jiva's flickering light.

Jiva that is doubt-tossed in peddha is liberated in mukti. In that condition Sakti grants her divine instrument of jnana to him. That is the everlasting light that swallows the jiva's flickering light.

அறிகின்றி லாதன ஐயேழும் ஒன்றும்
அறிகின்ற என்னை யறியா திருந்தேன்
அறிகின்றாய் நீயென் றருள்செய்தான் நந்தி
அறிகின்ற நானென் றறிந்துகொண் டேனே. 2323

By Grace Jiva Becomes Knower

Devoid of knowledge
Are Tattvas thirty and six;
The Self that knows
I know not;
"You shall know"
Thus blessed Nandi;
Then I knew
That I am the Knower.

தானவ னாகிய ஞானத் தலைவனை
வானவ ராதியை மாமணிச் சோதியை
ஈனமின் ஞானத் தின்னருட் சத்தியை
ஊனமி லாள்தன்னை யூனிடைக் கண்டதே. 2324

Jnana Siva and Jnana Sakti Appeared

He who transformed me into Himself,
He, the Lord of Jnana,
The First of Celestials,
The peerless gem's
Light Resplendent;
And She, Sakti-Grace
Of Jnana Pure,
She, the Immaculate
—Them I saw in this fleshy body.

ஒளியும் இருளும் பரையும் பரையுள்
அளிய தெனலாகும் ஆன்மாவை யன்றி
அளியும் அருளுந் தெருளுங் கடந்து
தெளிய அருளே சிவானந்த மாமே. 2325

Love, Jnana, and Bliss of Siva-Sakti

Light and Darkness
Are Parai (Sakti), and the Love within Parai;
Transcend the Self;
Beyond is Love that is Grace,
Transcend the Mala Darkness
Beyond is Light that is Jnana;
Transcend them too;
Then is the Gift that is Siva's-Bliss.

ஆனந்த மாகும் அரனருட் சத்தியிற்
றானந்த மாமுயிர் தானே சமாதிசெய்
தூனந்த மாயுணர் வாயுள் ளுணர்வுறிற்
கோனந்தம் வாய்க்கு மகாவாக் கியமாமே. 2326

Mahavakyam—Samadhi Jnana Finite

In the Bliss of Grace
That Siva-Sakti confers,
Let Jiva
In final Samadhi enter;
If thus as the end of fleshy body
Jiva realizes the inner awareness;
It shall attain the finite Lordly (Siva) State;
—This, the Word Exalted (Mahavakyam).

அறிவிக்க வேண்டாம் அறிவற் றயர்வோர்க்கும்
அறிவிக்க வேண்டாம் அறிவிற் செறிவோர்க்கும்
அறிவுற் றறியாமை யெய்திநிற் போர்க்கே
அறிவிக்கத் தம்மறி வாரறி வோரே. 2327

Tell Them, Who Know and Yet Know Not

No use telling
Those who are in ignorance steeped;
No use telling
Those who are in Jnana filled;
Tell only them
Who know and yet know not;
Then will they know
And Self-realize.

சத்தும் அசத்துஞ் சதசத்துந் தான் கூடிச்
சித்தும் அசித்துஞ் சிவசித்த தாய்நிற்குஞ்
சுத்தம் அசுத்தந் தொடங்காத் துரியத்துச்
சுத்தரா மூன்றுடன் சொல்லற் றவர்களே. 2328

Suddhas Reach Mauna State

Espousing,
The Sat, Asat, and Sat-Asat,
The Jiva becomes
The Chit, Achit, and Siva-Chit;
Those that reach that Turiya State
Where neither Suddha (Pure) or Asuddha (Impure) Maya is
They verily are the Suddhas (Pure ones);
Transcending the States three,
(Sat, Asat and Sat-Asat)
They reach Silence, surpassing.

தானே யறியான் அறிவிலோன் தானல்லன்
தானே யறிவான் அறிவு சதசத்தென்
றானால் இரண்டும் அரனரு ளாய்நிற்கத்
தானே யறிந்து சிவத்துடன் தங்குமே. 2329

Higher Knowledge is Beyond Self-Knowledge

By himself Jiva knows not;
Yet is he not without (Higher) knowledge;
The knowledge he himself has
Is Sat-Asat;
When the two as Grace descend
Then he knows himself,
And with Siva one becomes.

When the two, Siva and Sakti, descend as Grace, jiva knows both himself and the Lord.

தத்துவ ஞானந் தலைப்பட் டவர்க்கே
தத்துவ ஞானந் தலைப்பட லாய்நிற்குந்
தத்துவ ஞானத்துத் தானவ னாகவே
தத்துவ ஞானானந் தந்தான் தொடங்குமே. 2330

Master Tattva-Knowledge and Attain God-Knowledge

Only for them who master
The knowledge of Tattvas, (Tattva-Jnana)
Will the Higher Knowledge (God-Knowledge) be;
In that Higher Knowledge,
The Self with Siva one becomes;
Then has begun the Bliss of God-Knowledge.

தன்னை யறிந்து சிவனுடன் தானாக
மன்னு மலங்குணம் மாளும் பிறப்பறும்
பின்னது சன்முத்தி சன்மார்க்கப் பேரொளி
நன்னது ஞானத்து முத்திரை நண்ணுமே. 2331

Self-Knowledge Leads to Jnana-Mudra

When Jiva attains Self-Knowledge,
Then he one with Siva becomes;
The Malas perish;
Birth's cycle ends;
Then will grand Mukti be;
The lustrous light of Jnana;
And the Impress of Divine Knowledge too (Chin Mudra).

ஞானந்தன் மேனி கிரியை நடுவங்கந்
தானுறும் இச்சை உயிராகத் தற்பரன்
மேனிகொண் டைங்கரு மத்துவித் தாதலான்
மோனிகள் ஞானத்து முத்திரைபெற் றார்களே. 2332

Maunis Receive Jnana Mudra

Jnana (Knowledge) is His Form;
Kriya (Action) is His middle part;

Ichcha (Desire) is His life beat;
—Thus is His Aspect
Of the Uncreated Being (Tatpara);
He is as the seed of
The five acts He performs
(Of creation, preservation, dissolution, obfuscation and redemption)
And so,
The Maunis (in silence seated) received
The Mudra (Impress of God-Knowledge) that is Jnana.

உயிர்க்கறி வுண்மை யுயிரிச்சை மானம்
உயிர்க்குக் கிரியை யுயிர்மாயை சூக்கம்
உயிர்க்கிவை யூட்டுவோன் ஊட்டு மவனே
உயிர்ச்செய லன்றியவ் வுள்ளத்து ளானே. 2333

Lord Acts From Within Jiva

For Jiva,
Jnana Sakti gives Knowledge
Ichcha Sakti gives Desire
Kriya Sakti gives Action
All these are subtle;
He who grants these to Jiva
Is Lord Himself,
And not Jiva;
It is Lord that acts from within Jiva.

தொழிலிச்சை ஞானங்கள் தொல்சிவ சீவர்
கழிவற்ற மாமாயை மாயையி னாகும்
பழியற்ற காரண காரியம் பாழ்விட்
டழிவற்ற சாந்தாதீ தன்சிவ னாமே. 2334

Siva Acting Through Mayas is Eternal and Beyond

Action, Desire and Jnana of Jivas
With Siva acting within
Are work of Mamaya and Maya Pure and Impure;
But beyond the Void of Cause-Effect,
Is Siva,
Eternal and of Peace Exceeding (Santa-atita).

இல்லதும் உள்ளது மியாவையுந் தானாகி
இல்லதும் உள்ளது மாயன்றாம் அண்ணலைச்
சொல்லது சொல்லிடில் தூராதி தூரமென்
றொல்லை யுணர்ந்தால் உயிர்க்குயி ராகுமே. 2335

Lord Who is Beyond-Beyond is Yet Life of Life

Immanent is He
In Real, the Unreal and all;
He is Lord
That is the Real, Unreal and Real-Unreal;
Beyond, beyond speech is He;
Hasten and realize,
He will be the Life of your life.

உயிரிச்சை யூட்டி யுழிதருஞ் சத்தி
உயிரிச்சை வாட்டி யொழித்திடு ஞானம்
உயிரிச்சை யூட்டி யுடனுற லாலே
உயிரிச்சை வாட்டி யுயர்பதஞ் சேருமே. 2336

Scorch Desires Worldly

Sakti (Ichcha) infuses desires
And harasses Jiva;
Jnana (Sakti) scorches them
And destroys them;
As She who infuses desires into Jiva
Is within,
Do you scorch your worldly desires,
And attain the State Exalted.

சேருஞ் சிவமானார் ஐம்மலந் தீர்ந்தவர்
ஓரொன்றி லாரைம் மலவிருள் உற்றவர்
பாரின்கண் விண்ண ரகம்புகும் பான்மையர்
ஆருங்கண் டோரார் அவையருள் என்றே. 2337

Rid of Malas

They who with Siva unite
Are of Malas Five rid;
They who do not unite thus
Are of dark Malas Five possessed;
Destined are they to be born
On Earth, Heaven and Hell;
None know,
All these from His Grace results.

எய்தினர் செய்யு மிருமாயா சத்தியின்
எய்தினர் செய்யும் இருஞான சத்தியின்
எய்தினர் செய்யும் இருஞால சத்தியின்
எய்தினர் செய்யும் இறையருள் தானே. 2338

All Acts Are of Lord's Grace

They who are caught
By forces of Maya twine (Pure and Impure)
Do things according;
They who are caught
By forces of Jnana
Act appropriate;
They who are caught
By forces of world desires
Behave that way;
—All these they do
Are acts of Lord's Grace.

திருந்தனர் விட்டார் திருவி னரகந்
திருந்தனர் விட்டார் திருவார் சுவர்க்கந்
திருந்தனர் விட்டார் செறிமலக் கூட்டந்
திருந்தனர் விட்டார் சிவமா யவமே. 2339

Wealth of Holiness Leads to Union in Siva

They that are possessed of wealth of Holiness
Are not for dark Hell distined;
They that are possessed of wealth of Holiness
Are not for delicious heaven too;
They that are possessed of wealth of Holiness

Depart from Mala's huddle;
They that are possessed of wealth of Holiness
Depart from all things unworthy;
And so Siva become.

அவமுஞ் சிவமும் அறியார் அறியார்
அவமுஞ் சிவமும் அறிவார் அறிவார்
அவமுஞ் சிவமும் அருளால் அறிந்தால்
அவமுஞ் சிவமும் அவனரு ளாமே. 2340

Knowledge of What is God's What is World's Comes from Grace

Ignorant are they
Who do not know
What is God's
And what is World's;
Only they are wise
Who both these know;
When both these they know,
By His Grace,
They shall of His Grace know;
Both these are.

அருளான சத்தி யனல்வெம்மை போலப்
பொருளவ னாகத்தான் போதம் புணரும்
இருளொளி யாய்மீண்டு மும்மல மாகுந்
திருவரு ளானந்தி செம்பொரு ளாமே. 2341

Grace of Sakti Leads to Siva

As fire and heat
Are Siva and Sakti;
With Him as Substance
She, Jiva's awareness espouses;
Darkness and Light She is;
She pervades too Malas Three;
And then by Light of Grace
She makes Jiva the very Siva.

Siva and Sakti are like fire and heat. She is with Him, espousing divine awareness. She is darkness (obfuscation) and light (Revealing Grace). As darkness She pervades the three malas. Then by the light of Grace She liberates the jiva and aids him to become Siva — the Nandi that is Pure Truth.

ஆதித்தன் தோன்ற வரும்பது மாதிகள்
பேதித்த தவ்வினை யாற்செயல் சேதிப்ப
ஆதித்தன் றன்கதி ராலவை சேட்டிப்பப்
பேதித்துத் பேதியா வாறருட் பேதமே. 2342

States of Grace-Receiving Differ

As the sun rises,
The lotuses wake;
But some bloom;
And some do not;
That happens
As their differing conditions are;
Even though sun's beams
Alike strike them,
The differing effects
Are result of
Differing states of Grace.

The yogi then beholds in this fleshy body Jnana Siva—the beginning of celestials and the peerless gem-light that shines effulgent — and the immaculate jnana sakti of Grace too.

பேதம் அபேதம் பிறழ்பேதா பேதமும்
போதம் புணர்போதம் போதமும் நாதமும்
நாத முடனாக நாதாதி நாதமும்
ஆதன் அருளின் அருளிச்சை யாமே. 2343

All Forms of Knowledge Proceed From Grace

Bheda (Difference), Abheda (Non-difference)
And Bheda-Abheda (Difference Non-difference),
Knowledge native,
Knowledge that comes of learning,
And God-Knowledge;
Nada, (Sound)
And the Nada-Beyond-Nada, (the Nadanta that is Beyond-Beyond Sound)
All these come by Grace of the Holy One.

மேவிய பொய்க்கரி யாட்டும் வினையெனப்
பாவிய பூதங்கொண் டாட்டிப் படைப்பாதி
பூவியல் கூட்டத்தாற் போதம் புரிந்தருள்
ஆவியை நாட்டும் அரனரு ளாமே. 2344

Play of Hara's Grace

Like the artificial elephant
On stilt played,
Is the play of Hara's Grace;
With the aid of elements (Tattvas), it sways Jiva,
And makes it dance this way and that,
And consigning it to life and worldly ways,
Infuses the Light of Jnana
And finally plants it (Jiva) in Life of Grace;
All, all, the work of Grace.

ஆறா றகன்று தனையறிந் தானவன்
ஈறாகி யாவினு மியாவுந் தனிலெய்த
வேறாய் வெளிபுக்கு வீடுற்றா னம்மருள்
தேறாத் தெளிவுற்றுத் தீண்டச் சிவமாமே. 2345

When Tattvas Are Transcended, Grace Descends and Union in Siva Takes Place

He, Jiva,
Abandoning Tattvas six times six
Realized the Self;
He the Finite became
And pervaded,
He (Jiva) in them (Tattvas) and they in him;
Yet transcending them
He passed into the Beyond;

And as Grace descends on him
He doubt-free Jnana attained
And Siva became.

தீண்டற் கரிய திருவடி நேயத்தை
மீண்டுற் றருளால் விதிவழி யேசென்று
தூண்டிச் சிவஞான மாவினைத் தானேறித்
தாண்டிச் சிவனுடன் சாரலு மாமே. 2346

Mount the Steed of Sivajnana and Reach God

The love of Holy Feet
That is beyond reach,
By Grace he reaches;
Then by way appropriate journeying,
He rouses the mighty steed of Sivajnana
And mounting it passes beyond,
And so reaching Siva Himself.

சார்ந்தவர் சாரணர் சித்தர் சமாதியர்
சார்ந்தவர் மெய்ஞ்ஞான தத்துவ சாத்தியர்
சார்ந்தவர் நேயந் தலைப்பட்ட ஆனந்தர்
சார்ந்தவர் சத்த அருட்டன்மையாரே. 2347

The Evolved Souls Who Reached Siva's Grace

Those who reached Siva
Are the Charanars, Siddhas, and Samadhi Yogis
The Jnanis who in God-Truth stood,
The Anandas who in love adored,
And Nathas—all, blessed of Grace Divine,

தானென் றவனென் றிரண்டென்பர் தத்துவந்
தானென் றவனென் றிரண்டற்ற தன்மையைத்
தானென் றிரண்டுன்னார் கேவலத் தானவர்
தானின்றித் தானாகத் தத்துவ சுத்தமே. 2348

Suddha State Knows No "I" and "He" Difference

They speak of States two,
"I" and "He"
But there is a State
Where "I" and "He" are undifferentiated;
Those who are in the Higher Kevala (inert) State
Will not the difference cognise;
Effacing Self,
And He and Self as one uniting,
Is the State of Suddha (Pure).

தன்னினில் தன்னை யறியுந் தலைமகன்
தன்னினில் தன்னை யறியத் தலைப்படுந்
தன்னினில் தன்னைச் சார்கில னாகில்
தன்னினில் தன்னையுஞ் சார்தற் கரியவே. 2349

Seek Siva Within the Self

The Great souls that realize Siva
That is Self within,
Will seek forth Siva in the Self;
They who do not reach Siva in the Self,
Will reach Siva never.

அறியகி லேனென் றரற்றாதே நீயும்
நெறிவழியேசென்று நேர்பட்ட பின்னை
இருசுட ராகி இயற்றவல் லானும்
ஒருசுட ராவந்தென் உள்ளத்துள் ளாமே. 2350

Go and Seek Siva in the Proper Way

Lament not
That you know Him not;
Go the proper way
And you shall meet Him;
He who as Lights twine (Sakti and Siva)
Creates all,
As one Light in my heart is united.

மண்ணொன்று தான்பல நற்கல னாயிடும்
உண்ணின்ற யோனிகட் கெல்லாம் ஒருவனே
கண்ணொன்று தான்பல காணுந் தனைக்காணா
அண்ணலும் அவ்வண்ண மாகிநின் றானே. 2351

God is Immanent and Yet Jiva Sees not

One the clay,
Many the pots made of it;
One the Lord,
Immanent in Creation all;
The eyes see things diverse,
But they see not the eyes;
So too is Lord to Jiva.

Though the pots are different, the clay is one Similarly the Lord is the One pervading all His creations. The eyes behold diverse objects; but the objects do not see the eyes. So too is Siva for jiva. God is immanent and omnipresent; yet jiva does not see Him.

ஓம்புகின் றானுல கேழையும் உள்நின்று
கூம்புகின் றார்குணத் தின்னொடுங் கூறுவர்
தேம்புகின் றார்சிவஞ் சிந்தைசெய் யாதவர்
கூம்பகில் லார்வந்து கொள்ளலு மாமே. 23..

Think of Siva and Draw Like Him

Standing within,
He protects the worlds seven;
The good one who in love praises Him,
Close upon Him;
They who think not of Siva
Loud sob in distress;
How can those
Who centre not their thoughts in Him
Ever, ever reach Him?

குறியறி யார்கள் குறிகாண மாட்டார்
குறியறி யார்கடங் கூடல் பெரிது
குறியறி யாவகை கூடும்பின் கூடி
அறிவறி யாவிருந் தன்னமு மாமே. 2353

Divine Swan Becoming

They who see not the Self within
Will see not the Goal without;
They who see not the Self within
Will incarnate bodies several;
Unite in the Lord, the Self effacing;
And in knowledge undifferentiated,
You the "Divine Swan" (I-and-He united) became.

ஊனோ வுயிரோ வுறுகின்ற தேதின்பம்
வானோர் தலைவி மயக்கத் துறநிற்கத்
தானோ பெரிதறி வோமென்னு மானுட
தானே பிறப்போ டிறப்பறி யாரே. 2354

Limits of Human Knowledge

When the Lady of Celestials (Sakti)
In Maya stands,
Is it body or soul
That joys in the bliss?
The men who think they know all,
Know not why they are born and why they die.

14. அறிவுதயம்

DAWN OF JNANA

தன்னை யறியத் தனக்கொரு கேடில்லை
தன்னை யறியாமல் தானே கெடுகின்றான்
தன்னை யறியும் அறிவை அறிந்தபின்
தன்னையே யர்ச்சிக்கத் தானிருந் தானே. 2355

Importance of Self-Knowledge

With knowledge of Self
No harm there be;
Without knowledge of Self
Himself His (Jiva) harm be;
When knowledge
That knows the Self dawns,
Yourself Siva become,
Worshipped high.

அங்கே யுட்டற்பெருந் தேவரெல் லாந்தொழச்
சிங்கா சனத்தே சிவனிருந் தானென்று
சங்கார் வளையுஞ் சிலம்புஞ் சரேலெனப்
பொங்கார் குழலியும் போற்றிஎன் றாளே. 2356

Lord on His Celestial Throne

There on the Throne leonine,
Adored by the mighty Celestials,
Was Siva Seated;
And the Lady of tresses exuberant,
With bangles of conch-shell
And anklets resounding
Sang "Hail My Lord."

அறிவு வடிவென் றறியாத என்னை
அறிவு வடிவென் றருள்செய்தான் நந்தி
அறிவு வடிவென் றருளால் அறிந்தே
அறிவு வடிவென் றறிந்திருந் தேனே. 2357

Siva's Form is Jnana

I knew not,
Siva's Form is Jnana;
Nandi by His Grace taught me
Siva's Form is Jnana,
I sought Jnana's Form
And in that knowledge
I remained.

அறிவுக் கழிவில்லை யாக்கமும் இல்லை
அறிவுக் கறிவல்ல தாதாரம் இல்லை
அறிவே யறிவை யறிகின்ற தென்றிட்
டறைகின் றனமறை யீறுகள் தாமே. 2358

Jnana Alone Knows Jnana

Jnana has no death, nor birth;
Jnana has ground none but Jnana;
It is Jnana that knows Jnana
Thus they conclude, in the ultimate, Vedas all.

ஆயு மலரின் அணிமலர் தன்மேலே
பாய இதழ்கள் பதினாறும் அங்குள
தூய அறிவு சிவானந்த மாகியே
போய அறிவாய்ப் புணர்ந்திருந் தானே. 2359

Seat of Jnana Within

Above the flower of the heart, (Visuddha Adhara)
Is a flower of petal sixteen,
There is Jnana Pure,
Sivananda (Siva-Bliss) it is;
When jnana of Self
In it merged
Jiva united in Siva
And as one remained.

மன்னிநின் றாரிடை வந்தருண் மாயத்து
முன்னிநின் றானை மொழிந்தேன் முதல்வனும்
பொன்னிவந் தானோர்புகழ்திரு மேனியைப்
பின்னிநின் றேனீ பெரியையென் றானே. 2360

Lord Blessed Me

To them that firm-fixed Him in thought
As Grace of Sakti
He hastened;
I praised Him;
The Lord too appeared

His Golden Form revealing
I held fast to Him knowing Jiva Jnana,
Then are Anima and other Siddhis;
Nandi thus knew
Jiva Jnana as Siva Jnana.

அறிவறி வாக அறிந்தன்பு செய்மின்
அறிவறி வாக அறியுமிவ் வண்ணம்
அறிவறி வாக அணிமாதி சித்தி
அறிவறி வாக அறிந்தனன் நந்தியே. *2361*

Jiva jnana is Siva jnana

Realising this, adore Him
And through jiva jnana know Siva jnana
Thus anima and the rest of the eight siddhis are attained
Thus did Nandi know jiva jnana as Siva jnana.

---

1) Siddhis are miraculous occult powers that come in the wake of yoga practice. They are eight: anima, mahima, garima, laghuma, prapti, prakamayam, isatvam, and vasitvam.

i) Anima is to becomes as tiny as jiva, which is atomic in size. (Immanence)

ii) Mahima is to becomes as great as infinity.

iii) Garima is to materialise whole objects (pervasiveness) from diverse fragments.

iv) Laghuma is to become weightless.

v) Prapti is to attain all that is wished for.

vi) Prakamyam is to become all-weight.

vii) Isatvam is to attain vast regal powers.

viii) Vasitvam is to attain powers of total attraction.

For a fuller discussion of the eight siddhis, vide Tantra Three supra.

அறிவறி வென்றங் கரற்றும் உலகம்
அறிவறி யாமை யாரும் அறியார்
அறிவறி யாமை கடந்தறி வானால்
அறிவறி யாமை யழகிய வாறே. *2362*

Dividing Line Between Knowledge and Ignorance

''Jnana, Jnana,'' thus laments this world,
They know not,
Jnana of Jiva is Jnana none; out ignorance;
When Divine Jnana overlays Jiva Jnana,
They both Pure Jnana are;
Thus much is if after all,
Between Knowledge and Ignorance.

அறிவறி யாமையை நீவி யவனே
பொறிவா யொழிந்தெங்குந் தானான போது
அறிவா யவற்றினுள் தானா யறிவின்
செறிவாகி நின்றவன் சீவனு மாமே. *2363*

Transcend Knowledge and Ignorance and Reach Siva Jnana

Knowledge and Ignorance
Both transcending,
Abandoing senses five,
And immanent becoming,
Himself as Jnana,
And Jnana's pervasiveness
Jiva stands.

அறிவுடை யார்நெஞ் சகலிட மாவ
தறிவுடை யார்நெஞ் சருந்தவ மாவ
தறிவுடை யார்நெஞ்சொ டாதிப் பிரானும்
அறிவுடை யார்நெஞ்சத் தங்குநின் றானே. *2364*

Heart of Jnani

The heart of Jnani is Expanse Vast;
The heart of Jnani is Tapas rare;
The heart of Jnani is Lord's abode;
There He stood, in the heart of Jnanis.

மாயனு மாகி மலரோன் இறையுமாய்க்
காயநன் னாட்டுக் கருமுத லானவன்
சேயன் அணியன் தித்திக்குந் தீங்கரும்
பாயமு தாகிநின் றண்ணிக்கின் றானே. *2365*

Siva Stands Close to Jiva

The Lord He is
Hari, Brahma and Rudra;
He is the Seed
Of the corporeal world;
Distant, and near is He;
He is sugar cane-sweet and ambrosia divine;
Thus He stands close to Jiva.

என்னை யறிந்திலேன் இத்தனை காலமும்
என்னை யறிந்தபின் ஏதும் அறிந்திலேன்
என்னை யறிந்திட் டிருத்தலுங் கைவிடா
தென்னை யிட்டென்னை உசாவுகின் றானே. *2366*

Know Self and Be With God

All these days,
I knew not the Self;
When I knew the Self,
Nothing else I knew;
When I knew the Self,
He left me not
And within me He enquires
Of my welfare in loving care.

மாய விளக்கது நின்று மறைந்திடுந்
தூய விளக்கது நின்று சுடர்விடுங்
காய விளக்கது நின்று கனன்றிடுஞ்
சேய விளக்கினைத் தேடுகின் றேனே. *2367*

Seek Pure Lamp

The Maya's Lamp is flickering,
It burns and dies;
The Pure Lamp steadily burning;
The body's Lamp within heats;
The Distant Lamp I seek.

தேடுகின் றேன்திசை யெட்டோ டிரண்டையும்
நாடுகின் றேனல மேயுடை யானடி
பாடுகின் றேன்பர மேதுணை யாமென
கூடுகின் றேன்குறை யாமனத் தாலே. 2368

Seek God

I seek in directions eight and two,
I seek, in goodness, the Feet of Lord,
I sing, "Param is my Refuge"
I unite in Him, in mind's fulness.

முன்னை முதல்விளை யாட்டத்துமுன்வந்தோர்
பின்னைப் பெருமலம் வந்தவர் பேர்த்திட்டுத்
தன்னைத் தெரிந்துதன் பண்டைத் தலைவன்தான்
மன்னிச் சிவமாக வாரா பிறப்பே. 2369

Jiva's Journey to Liberation is Lord's Play

In the Primal Play of Lord
Were Jivas created;
Enveloped in mighty Malas were they;
Discarding them,
They realized the Self,
And besought the Feet
Of their hoary Lord;
Thus, they Siva became
With birth no more to be.

Jivas in Saiva Siddhanta philosophy are as eternal as God. By "created", what is meant here is that they were 'activated' from the primordial (kevala state) inert condition by Siva acting on Sakti, and given the milieu and instruments for development, such as thanu (body), karana (organs), bhuvana (world), and bhoga (experience).

15. ஆறந்தம்
THE SIX ESSENCES

வேதத்தின் அந்தமும் மிக்கசித் தாந்தமும்
நாதத்தின் அந்தமும் நற்போத அந்தமும்
ஓதத் தகுமெட் டியோகாந்த அந்தமும்
ஆதிக்க லாந்தமும் ஆறந்த மாமே. 2370

Six Ends Ultimate

The Essence of Veda (Vedanta)
The Essence of Siddhanta Exalted,
The Essence of Nada (Nadanta),
The Essence of Bodha (Bodhanta)
The Essence of Yoga (Yoganta)
Of branches eight,
The Essence of Kalas (Kalanta)
—These the Essences six, the Ultimate Finale.

Vedanta, Siddhanta, Nadanta, Bodhanta, Yoganta and Kalanta are the six final essences.

அந்தமோ ராறும் அறிவார் அதிசுத்தர்
அந்தமோ ராறும் அறிவார் அமலத்தர்
அந்தமோ ராறும் அறியார் அவர்தமக்
கந்தமோ டாதி அறியவொண் ணாதே. 2371

Souls Rid of Malas Will Know the Six Essences

The Pure ones of Malas rid
Will the Essences six know;
The Impure ones in Malas bound
Will the Essences Six know not;
They who know not the Essences Six
Will not know Lord,
He that is Beginning and End.

தானான வேதாந்தந் தானென்னுஞ் சித்தாந்த
மானாத் துரியத் தணுவன் றனைக்கண்டு
தேனார் பராபரஞ் சேர்சிவ யோகமாய்
ஆனா மலமற் றருஞ்சித்தி யாதலே. 2372

Essences of Vedanta and Siddhanta

"I am the Supreme One," says Vedanta,
"I shall become the Supreme One," says Siddhanta;
In Turiya State they realize the Self,
And in Siva Yoga they unite in Parapara Sweet;
Rid of Malas
They the Rare Goal attain.

நித்தம் பரனோ டுயிருற்று நீள்மனஞ்
சத்த முதல் ஐந்துந் தத்துவத் தால்நீங்கிச்
சுத்த மசுத்தந் தொடரா வகைநினைந்
தத்தன் பரன்பால் அடைதல்சித் தாந்தமே. 2373

Truth of Siddhanta

Daily living in Para's thought,
Freed from Tattvas
Beginning with the Five (Sound, taste, smell, touch and sight);
Contemplating beyond
Where the Suddha and Asuddha (Mayas) pursue not,
Reaching thus Para that is Lord,
That, verily, is the Truth of Siddhanta.

மேவும் பிரமனே விண்டு உருத்திரன்
மேவுசெய் யீசன் சதாசிவன் மிக்கப்பால்

மேவும் பரவிந்து நாதம் விடாவாறா
றோவும் பொழுதணு வொன்றுள தாமே. *2374*

The Ultimate State in Jiva's Journey

Beyond Brahma, Vishnu and Rudra,
Beyond Maheswara and Sadasiva,
Beyond Para Bindu and Para Nada,
Beyond Tattvas Thirty and Six,
When all these are transcended,
The Jiva is left alone with Siva.

உள்ள வுயிராறாற தாகும் உபாதியைத்
தெள்ளி யகன்று நாதாந்தத்தைச் செற்றுமேல்
உள்ள இருள்நீங்க வோருணர் வாகுமேல்
எள்ளலின் நாதாந்தத் தெய்திடும் போதமே. *2375*

Nadanta Bodhanta States

Jiva transcending
The tribulations of Tattvas
Six times six,
Reaches the Nadanta;
Ascending still beyond,
It encounters darkness of Anava;
When that is dispelled,
The peerless Divine Jnana dawns;
That indeed is Jnana (Bodha)
That Nadanta beyond reached.

தேடும் இயம நியமாதி சென்றகன்
றாடுஞ் சமாதியில் உற்றுப் பரசிவன்
பாடுறச் சீவன் பரமாகப் பற்றறக்
கூடும் உபசாந்தம் யோகாந்தக் கொள்கையே. *2376*

Yoganta State

Seeking Yama and Niyama
And then going beyond
Enter into Samadhi;
There Jiva reaches Para Siva;
And Param becoming
All desires abandoned,
Realizes Upasanta
That verily is the Truth of Yoganta.

கொள்கையி லான கலாந்தங் குறிக்கொள்ளில்
விள்கையி லான நிவிர்த்தாதி மேதாதிக்
குள்ளன வாம் விந்து வுள்ளே யொடுங்கலுந்
தெள்ளி யதனைத் தெளிதலு மாமே. *2377*

Kalanta State

When the goal is Truth of Kalanta,
This then is the way;
Ascend Kalas (five)[1] Nivritti, and the rest
And Medha and the rest ten and six[2];
There encounter Bindu;
In it do merge and vivid know
The Truth of Kalanta.

---

1)These five are in Siva tattvas; nivritti, prastista; vidya, santi, and santyatita.

2)16 kalas

Medha, Arghisa, Vida, Bindu, Artha candra, Nirodpini, Nada, Nadanta, Sakti, Vyapini, Vyomaupini, Ananthai, Anathai, Anasiruthai, Samanai, Unmanai,

The sixteen kalas within belong to the sixteen saktis in the sixteen-petalled flower of the visuddhi adhara. The realisation of these sixteen kalas is known as 'sodasa kala prasada.'

தெளியு மிவையன்றித் தேரைங் கலைவே
றொளியுள் அமைத்துள்ள தோரவல் லார்கட்
களியவ னாகிய மந்திரந் தந்திரந்
தெளிவுப தேச ஞானத்தொ டைந்தாமே. *2378*

Five Other Ways Dear to Siva

These paths apart,
There are five other,
That lead to the Light
For them who seek;
Dear like Siva are the Five
—Mantra, Tantra, Serenity (Samadhi Yoga),
Upadesa and Jnana.

ஆகும் அனாதி கலையா கமவேதம்
ஆகுமத் தந்திர மந்நூல் வழிநிற்றல்
ஆகு மனாதி யுடலல்லா மந்திரம்
ஆகுஞ் சிவபோ தகம்உப தேசமே. *2379*

Tantra, Mantra Upadesa

Beginningless are Agama Vedas
Tantra is to act their way,
Mantras are of the mind and beyond the body;
Upadesa is the teaching of Siva-Jnana.

தேசார் சிவமாகுந் தன்ஞானத் தின்கலை
ஆசார நேய மறையுங் கலாந்தத்துப்
பேசா வுரையுணர் வற்ற பெருந்தகை
வாசா மகோசர மாநந்தி தானே. *2380*

Jnana

The way of Self-Jnana
Is to be one with Siva;
In the Kalanta
Devotional love disappears;
Sans speech, sans sentience
Jiva becomes Being Great
Like Nandi Himself,
That is beyond speech and thought.

தானவ னாகுஞ் சமாதி தலைப்படில்
ஆன கலாந்தநா தாந்தயோ காந்தமும்
ஏனைய போதாந்தம் சித்தாந்த மானது
ஞான மெனஞேய ஞாதுரு வாகுமே. *2381*

Serenity in Samadhi

In Samadhi Jiva with Siva
One becomes;
In Kalanta, in Nadanta, in Yoganta
And in Bodhanta and Siddhanta
Is Jnana reached
Of Knowledge, the Known and the Knower
One uniting.

ஆறந்த முஞ்சென் றடங்குமந் நேயத்தே
ஆறந்த ஞேயம் அடங்கிடு ஞாதுரு
கூறிய ஞானக் குறியுடன் வீடவே
தேறிய மோனஞ் சிவானந்த மாமே. 2382

The Six Ends Merge in Jnana

In that Jnana, (Divine Knowledge)
The Six Antas (ends) merge;
That Jnana (Knowledge) in the Knower (Jnani) merges;
When Knowledge in the Knower merges;
Then dawns Mauna (Divine Silence)
That is Siva-Bliss.

உண்மைக் கலையாறோ ரைந்தான் அடங்கிடும்
உண்மைக் கலாந்தம் இரண்டைந்தோ டேழுந்தம்
உண்மைக் கலையொன்றில் ஈறாய நாதாந்தத்
துண்மைக் கலைசொல்ல வோரந்த மாமே. 2383

Of the Kalai Sixteen

Unmanai Kala ends in the Sixteenth,
Unmanai Kalanta ends beyond in the Seventeenth;
When Unmanai Kala is reached
Then is Nadanta;
Unmanai Kala is verily a goal great.

ஆவுடை யாளை யரன்வந்து கொண்டபின்
தேவுடை யான்எங்கள் சீர்நந்தி தாடந்து
வீவற வேதாந்த சித்தாந்த மேன்மையைக்
கூவி யருளிய கோனைக் கருதுமே. 2384

Lord Revealed Truth of Vedanta-Siddhanta

Having been blessed by Grace of Sakti,
That Siva espoused,
The Holy Nandi, that is Lord of Celestials,
Granted His Feet;
Beckoning me to Him
He revealed the Truth Exalted
Of Vedanta-Siddhanta,
—Him, the Lord, meditate on.

கருது மவர்தங் கருத்தினுக் கொப்ப
அரனுரை செய்தருள் ஆகமந் தன்னில்
வருசம யப்புற மாயைமா மாயை
உருவிய வேதாந்த சித்தாந்த வுண்மையே. 2385

The Truth of Vedanta-Siddhanta is the Truth of Agamas

To each according to his understanding
The Lord reveals Truth of His Agamas;
Beyond and penetrating
The Prakriti Maya (impure) and Mamaya (pure-impure)
—Is the doctrinal Truth of Vedanta-Siddhanta.

வேதாந்தஞ் சித்தாந்தம் வேறிலா முத்திரை
போதாந்த ஞானம் யோகாந்தம் பொதுஞேய
நாதாந்தம் ஆனந்தஞ் சீரோ தயமாகும்
மூதாந்த முத்திரை மோனத்து மூழ்கவே. 2386

Vedanta and Siddhanta Know No Differences

In the imprint of Vedanta and Siddhanta,
There is difference none;
Bodhanta is Jnana (Divine Knowledge);
Yoganta is Jneya (the Known)
Nadanta is Dawning of Bliss
The finale imprint
Is in Silence (Mauna) Immersed-to-be.

வேதாந்தந் தன்னில் உபாதிமே லேழ்விட
நாதாந்த பாசம் விடுநல்ல தொம்பதம்
மீதாந்த காரணோ பாதியேழ் மெய்ப்பரன்
போதாந்த தற்பதம் போமசி என்பவே. 2387

Tvampada, Tatpada, Asipada Goals

Vedanta goal transcends
The seven Upadhis (experiences)
(That are the Caused (Kariya);)
Nadanta goal rids of Pasa
And reaches to Tvam-pada State
Beyond are Causal (Karana) Upadhis seven;
Above which is Tatpada of Para Real,
That Bodha leads to;
Beyond still is Asipada.

The Vedanta goal transcends the seven causal experiences. The Nadanta goal in dissolving the malas reaches to the tvam-pada state. The Bodhanta goal leads to the tatpada state. Beyond, transcending the seven causal experiences is asipada.

CAUSED (KARIYA) UPADHIS:

Ajnana (ignorance)
Avarana (limit)
Vikshepa (separateness)
Paroksha jnana (non-perceptible knowledge)
Nityaropa jnana (delusive knowledge)
Dukkha-nivritti (release from sorrow)
Ananda (bliss)

CAUSAL (KARANA) UPADHIS

Sarvajnatvam (Total Knowledge)
Sarvakaranatvam (Total Causation)
Sarva-indriyamitvam (Total Functioning)
Sarvesvaratvam (Total Lordship)
Sarvasrishti (Total Creation)

Sarvasthiti (Total Preservation)
Sarvasankaram (Total Dissolution)
Asipada—I becoming one (One alone).

From 2387 onwards, Mular discusses the "Tat Tvam Asi" of the Upanisads from various angles, trying to fit the three phrases into Agamic concepts.

அண்டங்கள் ஏழுங் கடந்தகன் றப்பாலும்
உண்டென்ற பேரொளிக் குள்ளா முளவொளி
பண்டுறு நின்ற பராசத்தி யென்னவே
கொண்டவ னன்றிநின் றான்தங்கள் கோவே. 2388

Transcendental Nature of Siva

Transcending Universe Seven
And the Beyond
Is the Great Light;
Lord is Light of that Light,
Of yore, He with Parasakti stood;
There He stands lofty, all by Himself,
He, Our Lord.

கோவுணர்த் துஞ்சத்தி யாலே குறிவைத்துத்
தேவுணர்த் துங்கரு மஞ்செய்தி செய்யவே
பாவனைத் தும்படைத் தர்ச்சனை பாரிப்ப
ஓவனைத் துண்டொழி யாத ஒருவனே. 2389

Lord Engrosses All Existence

Centre on Kundalini in Muladhara
That Guru by his power taught,
Perform acts
That lead to God,
Sing in full His holy praise,
Thus worship Him,
Then shall you meet the Being One
Who, existence interminable, engrosses.

ஒருவனை யுன்னார் உயிர்தனை யுன்னார்
இருவினை யுன்னார் இருமாயை யுன்னார்
ஒருவனு மேயுள் ளுணர்த்திநின் றூட்டி
அருவனு மாகிய ஆதரத் தானே. 2390

God is One Formless Being

They think not of the Being One,
They think not of the Jiva,
They think not of Karmas two, (Good and Bad)
They think not of Mayas two, (Pure and Impure)
The One Being within
Stands as Sentience and fosters
Formless is He,
He supports all.

அரனன்பர் தானம தாகிச் சிவத்து
வருமவை சத்திகள் முன்னா வகுத்திட்
டுரனுற சந்நிதி சேட்டிப்ப என்றுந்
திரனுறு தோயாச் சிவாநந்தி யாமே. 2391

Siva's Concern For His Devotees

In His devotees is Siva seated
Into them He brings in
The Saktis that are of Siva
Then in His mighty Presence they (Saktis) act;
There the devotees remain ever
Immersed in Siva Bliss.

வேதாந்த தொம்பத மேவும் பசுவென்ப
நாதாந்த பாசம் விடநின்ற நன்பதி
போதாந்த தற்பதம் போயிரண் டயிக்கியஞ்
சாதா ரணஞ்சிவ சாயுச்சிய மாமே. 2392

Tvam Pada, Tat Pada, Asi Pada (Sayujya)

In the Vedanta Way
The Jiva (Pasu) reaches Tvam Pada State
(The Two—I and He—together are)
Then follows Nadanta the holy State
Where Pasa is rid;
Then follows Bodhanta that reaches to Tatpada State
Where I and He in one union is;
Siva Sayujya is the Goal Beyond
That follows.

சிவமாதல் வேதாந்த சித்தாந்த மாகும்
அவமவ மாகு மவ்வவ் விரண்டுஞ்
சிவமாஞ் சதாசிவன் செய்தொன்றா னானால்
நவமான வேதாந்த ஞானசித் தாந்தமே. 2393

Of the Six Ends Vedanta and Siddhanta Alone Show the Path to Siva-Becoming

Siva-Becoming
Is the goal of Vedanta and Siddhanta
The rest four Ends lead not to Siva-Becoming,
—Siva that is Sadasiva—
And so it is that Vedanta and Siddhanta
Are wondrous Ways indeed.

சித்தாந்தத் தேசீவன் முத்திசித் தித்தலாற்
சித்தாந்தத் தேநிற்போர் முத்திசித் தித்தவர்
சித்தாந்த வேதாந்தஞ் செம்பொரு ளாதலால்
சித்தாந்த வேதாந்தங் காட்டுஞ் சிவனையே. 2394

Jivan Mukti in Siddhanta

In Siddhanta is attained
Jivan Mukti (Liberation in this body);
Those who stood in Siddhanta
Have verily reached the Mukti State;
As Siddhanta-Vedanta
Leads to the Goal of Siva-Becoming,
Siddhanta-Vedanta
Is the Path Exalted.

சிவனைப் பரமனுட் சீவனுட் காட்டும்
அவமற்ற வேதாந்த சித்தாந்த மானான்

நவமுற் றவத்தையில் ஞானஞ் சிவமாந்
தவமிக் குணர்ந்தவர் தத்துவத் தாரே. 2395

Beyond Jiva Turiya and Para Turiya is Siva Turiya

In the Vedanta-Siddhanta Way
Beyond Siva aspects in Param and in Jiva
Arises the Jnana
In Pure State of Experience (Turiyatita)
That verily is Siva State ultimate
Only those who in Tapas stood
Realized Siva Truth (Tattva)

தத்துவ மாகுஞ் சகள வகளங்கள்
தத்துவ மாம்விந்து நாதஞ் சதாசிவந்
தத்துவ மாகுஞ் சீவன்றன் தற்பரந்
தத்துவ மாஞ்சிவ சாயுச் சியமே. 2396

All States Are Tattvas or Steps Only to Siva-Sayujya

The Form and Formless States
Are alike Tattvas;
The Bindu, Nada and Sadasiva too
Are Tattvas verily;
So too is Jiva's (Tvam Pada and Tat Pada);
Tattva truly is where Tatpara is in Siva-Sayujya.

வேதமோ டாகமம் மெய்யாம் இறைவன்நூல்
ஓதும் பொதுவுஞ் சிறப்புமென் றுள்ளன
நாதன் உரையவை நாடில் இரண்டந்தம்
பேதம தென்பர் பெரியோர்க் கபேதமே. 2397

Veda and Agama Alike Revealed by God

Veda and Agama alike
Are revelations of God,
That is Truth;
The one is general
The other special;
Their goals two, they say;
Search them both,
For the truly learned,
There is difference none.

பரானந்தி மன்னுஞ் சிவானந்தம் எல்லாம்
பரானந்த மேன்மூன்றும் பாழுறா னந்தம்
விராமுத்தி ரானந்த மெய்ந்நட னானந்தம்
பொராநின்ற வுள்ளமே பூரிப்பி யாமே, 2398

Beyond Bliss of Voids is the Bliss of Siva Dance

All transcendental states of bliss
That Jiva experiences
Are, alike, Siva-bliss (Sivanandam);
The Three Higher States of Transcendental Bliss
Are States that come out of the three Voids;
The Bliss that comes of Mudras appropriate
Is the Bliss of Siva's Dance within;
It is the State that fills Soul in rapture.

ஆகுங் கலாந்தம் இரண்டந்த நாதாந்தம்
ஆகும் பொழுதிற் கலையைந்தா மாதலில்
ஆகும் அரனேபஞ் சாந்தக னாமென்ன
ஆகு மறையா கமமொழிந் தானன்றே. 2399

Kalanta Leads to Siva as Panchantaka

Kalanta and Nadanta
Are Ends (goals) two;
As they are reached
The five Kalas (of Siva Tattva) are attained;
So the Lord that arises there
Is as Panchantaka known
Thus He spake in Vedas and Agamas.

அன்றாகு மென்னாதை வகையந்தத் தன்னை
ஒன்றா்ன வேதாந்த சித்தாந்த முள்ளிட்டு
நின்றா லியோகாந்த நேர்படு நேர்பட்டான்
மன்றாடி பாத மருவலு மாமே. 2400

Beyond Kalanta Vedanta-Siddhanta Leads to Yoganta and to Dance-Bliss

Wait not for the day
To vision the Five Kalantas;
Take to the Way of
Vedanta-Siddhanta, that one are;
Then will you reach the Yoganta,
And there will you envision the Feet
Of the Eternal Dancer,
That is Siva.

அனாதி சீவனைம் மலமற்றப் பாலாய்
அனாதி யடக்கித் தனைக்கண் டரனாய்த்
தனாதி மலங்கெடத் தத்துவா தீதம்
வினாவுநீர் பாலாதல் வேதாந்த வுண்மையே. 2401

Truth of Vedanta is Jiva Mingling in Siva

Jiva that is eternal
Freed of Malas Five
Passes beyond Tattvas;
There it realizes the Self Eternal;
Then the Primal Mala of Anava
Withers away,
And with that the Tattva-atita State ensues
There one with Siva becoming is
Like water with milk indistinguishably intermingled;
That, verily, is the Truth of Vedanta.

உயிரைப் பரனை யுயர்சிவன் தன்னை
அயர்வற் றறிதொந் தத்தசி யதனாற்
செயலற் றறிவாகி யுஞ்சென் றடங்கி
அயர்வற்ற வேதாந்த சித்தாந்த மாமே. 2402

Tvam-Tat-Asi State is Goal of Vedanta Siddhanta

Jiva, Para and Siva—the States Exalted
Continuous know;
You then reach the State, Tvam-Tat-Asi;

There, actionless are you;
All Jnana are you;
Thus be merged;
—So says Vedanta-Siddhanta.

மன்னிய சோகமா மாமறை யாளர்தஞ்
சென்னிய தான சிவயோகமாம் ஈதென்ன
அன்னது சித்தாந்த மாமறை யாய்பொருள்
துன்னிய ஆகம நூலெனத் தோன்றுமே, 2403

Siddhanta Agamas Are Filled With Vedic Wisdom

The mantram "Soham"
That Vedantins intone
Is but Siva Yoga
That is exalted;
Thus said Siddhanta;
Verily is it apparent
That Agamas are scriptures
With Vedic Wisdom filled.

முதலாகும் வேத முழுதா கமமப்
பதியான ஈசன் பகர்ந்த திரண்டு
முதிதான வேத முறைமுறை யாலமர்ந்
ததிகாதி வேதாந்த சித்தாந்த மாகவே. 2404

Out of Vedas and Agamas Evolved Vedanta-Siddhanta

Two are the scriptures
That Lord Siva
In the Beginning revealed,
—The Primal Vedas and the Perfect Agamas;
The Vedas and Agamas,
In gradualness appropriate
Evolved Vedanta-Siddhanta
That is great, great indeed.

Mular has coined the phrase "Vedanta-Siddhanta". He says it is evolved out of the Vedas and Agamas. It is apparent that Mular feels keenly the need for somehow reconciling the Agamic and Vedic systems.

16. பதிபசுபாசம் வேறின்மை

PATI-PASU-PASAM NON-DIFFERENCE

அறிவறி வென்ற அறிவு மனாதி
அறிவுக் கறிவாம் பதியும் அனாதி
அறிவினைக் கட்டிய பாசம் அனாதி
அறிவு பதியிற் பிறப்பறுந் தானே. 2405

Pati, Pasu, and Pasam—All Three Eternal

Beginningless is Jiva that of Knowledge speak
Beginningless is Lord, the source of all Knowledge,
Beginningless is Pasam, that binds knowledge
When God-Knowledge dawns,
No more will birth be.

பசுப்பல கோடி பிரமன் முதலாய்ப்
பசுக்களைக் கட்டிய பாசமூன் றுண்டு
பசுத்தன்மை நீக்கியப் பாசம் அறுத்தாற்
பசுக்கள் தலைவனைப் பற்றி விடாவே. 2406

When Pasas Leave

Countless are Jivas (Pasu)
From Brahma downward;
Three are the Pasas (bonds)
That bind Jivas;
When bonds of Pasu are sundered,
And Jiva-nature altered,
Jiva will cling to Lord
And never leave Him.

கிடக்கின்ற வாறே கிளர்பயன் மூன்று
நடக்கின்ற ஞானத்தை நாடோறு நோக்கித்
தொடக் கொன்றும் இன்றித்தொழுமின் தொழுதாற்
குடக்குன்றி லிட்ட விளக்கது வாமே. 2407

Prayer Takes Jiva to States Beyond Three Pasas

Even with Pasas (three),
Attainments there can be;
Daily contemplate on Jnana
That moves you to the goal ultimate,
Unintermittent do pray;
Praying thus,
Yours will be a Light that shall beam
As from a hill-top high.

பாசஞ்செய் தானைப் படர்சடை நந்தியை
நேசஞ்செய் தாங்கே நினைப்பர் நினைத்தலுங்
கூசஞ்செய் துன்னிக் குறிக்கொள்வ தெவ்வண்ணம்
வாசஞ்செய் பாசத்துள்வைக்கின்ற வாறே. 2408

Why Pasas—To Seek God

He who made the bonds that bind you
He, Nandi, of spreading matted locks,
In love endearing they (Jnanis) think of
Thinking, they shrink from Pasas
And Godward seek;
Lo! for this it is why
He placed them (Jivas) in Pasas.

விட்ட விடமேறா வாறுபோல் வேறாகி
விட்ட பசுபாச மெய்கண்டோன் மேவுறான்
கட்டிய கேவலங் காணுஞ் சகலத்தைச்
சுட்டு நனவில் அதீதத்துள் தோன்றுமே. 2409

After Pasas Atita Plane

As the poison that has been extracted
No longer ascends the body,

He who the truth of Pasu-Pasa saw and shed them
Will not in them again be,
He stands apart;
He scorches them
In the states of Primal Kevala (inertness)
And living Sakala;
Then enters the Atita Jagrat plane.

Mantras 2409&2410

The pasas, once sundered will not touch jiva again, even as the poison, once extracted, does not return to the body. The jiva, having sundered pasa through the states of keval and sakala, enters the atita jagrat plane, which is beyond pasas. Jiva and pasa are also eternal like the Lord, whom you seek. Nandi grants freedom from the eternal bondage of pasa to those who seek Him in the Siddhanta way with love and devotion.

நாடும் பதியுடன் நற்பசு பாசமும்
நீடுமா நித்தன் நிலையறி வாரில்லை
நீடிய நித்தம் பசுபாச நீக்கமும்
நாடிய சைவர்க்கு நந்தி யளித்ததே. 2410

To Freedom Eternal From Bondage Eternal

The Lord you seek is Eternal
So too is Jiva and Pasa;
None know the nature of Lord Eternal;
He it is, Nandi,
That granted knowledge
Of Freedom Eternal
From Bondage Eternal
To Saiva Siddhantins that seek Him true.

ஆய பதிதான் அருட்சிவ லிங்கமாம்
ஆய பசுவும் அடலே றெனநிற்கும்
ஆய பலிபீட மாகுநற் பாசமாம்
ஆய அரனிலை யாய்ந்துகொள் வார்கட்கே. 2411

Pati-Pasu-Pasam Relationship Symbolised in Temple

The Pati (Lord) is the blessed Ṣiva Linga,
The Pasu (Jiva) is the mighty bull in front stands,
The Pasa (Bond) is the altar;
Thus in the temple
The Lord stands,
For them that searching see.

பதிபசு பாசம் பயில்வியா நித்தம்
பதிபசு பாசம் பகர்வோர்க் காறாக்கிப்
பதிபசு பாசத்தைப் பற்றற நீக்கும்
பதிபசு பாசம் பயில நிலாவே. 2412

Lord Teaches Truth of Pasu-Pasam

The Lord daily teaches you
The truth of Pasu-Pasam;
The Lord leads the Way;
To those who realize truth of Pasu-Pasam
The Lord removes entire
The bonds of Pasu-Pasam,
—But Himself stands untouched by Pasu-Pasam.

பதியும் பசுவொடு பாசமும் மேலைக்
கதியும் பசுபாச நீக்கமுங் காட்டி
மதிதந்த வானந்த மாநந்தி காணுந்
துதிதந்து வைத்தனன் சுத்தசை வத்திலே. 2413

Lord Placed Pati-Pasu-Pasam Truth in Suddha Saiva Thought

The truth of
Pati, Pasu and Pasam,
The beautitude of Mukti,
The Way of Liberation
From bonds of Pasu-Pasam,
—All these the Great Nandi of Bliss
That wears the crescent moon
Placed in Suddha Saiva thought,
In praise worthiness surpassing.

அறிந்தணு மூன்றுமே யாங்கணு மாகும்
அறிந்தணு மூன்றுமே யாங்கணு மாக
அறிந்த அனாதி வியாத்தனு மாவன்
அறிந்த பதிபடைப் பானங் கவற்றையே. 2414

The Three Classes of Jivas Created According to Degrees of Knowledge

Everywhere are the three Jivas,
Of knowledge possessed;
The timeless Lord of Divine Knowledge, too,
Is everywhere,
Pervading Jivas three;
And so to each according to his desert,
He created them, three.

படைப்பாதி யாவது பரஞ்சிவஞ் சத்தி
இடைப்பால் உயிர்கட் கடைத்திவ்வ தூங்கல்
படைப்பாதி சூக்கத்தைத் தற்பரஞ் செய்யப்
படைப்பாதி தூய மலமப் பரத்திலே. 2415

How Pasas Arise in the Order of Creation

This the way
The Primal Creation was;
Para,
Acting on Siva-Sakti
Puts Jivas to Kevala Slumber
Then, the Unborn Being
Acting on Sukshma (Subtle) Maya
Rouses them to activity;
Finally, the Para
Acting on Pure Maya
Conjoins Malas to Jivas.

ஆகிய சூக்கத்தை யவ்விந்து நாதமும்,
ஆகிய சத்தி சிவபர மேலைந்தால்
ஆகிய சூக்கத்தில் ஐங்கரு மஞ்செய்வோன்
ஆகிய தூயவீ சானனு மாமே. 2416

Creation Continues

The act of Creation continues;
With the Sukshma Maya that from Para arose
The Five High;
Bindu, Nada, Sakti, and Siva
In the Sukshma also arose the five-faced God
That the Five Acts perform,
(Creation, Preservation, Dissolution, Obfuscation and Redemption)
—He, the Isanan Pure.

மேவும் பரசிவ மேற்சத்தி நாதமும்
மேவும் பரவிந்து ஐம்முகன் வேறீசன்
மேவும் உருத்திரன் மால்வேதா மேதினி
ஆகும் படிபடைப் போனர னாமே. 2417

Creation Further Continued

Para Siva, Sakti and Nada
Para Bindu, the Five-faced Sadasiva
And Mahesa
And Rudra, Mal and Brahma
—Thus in order were they created,
All by Hara.

படைப்பு மளிப்பும் பயிலிளைப் பாற்றுந்
துடைப்பு மறைப்புமுன் தோன்ற அருளுஞ்
சடத்தை விடுத்த அருளுஞ் சகலத்
தடைத்த அனாதியை ஐந்தென லாமே. 2418

Five Acts Eternal

Creation, Preservation, and Dissolution,
(That for Jivas grant rest from birth-and-death whirl)
Obfuscation and Grace
(That redeem Jiva after life below)
These, for Sakala souls He filled;
All these acts Five,
Beginningless His are.

ஆறாறு குண்டலி தன்னின் அகத்திட்டு
வேறாகு மாயையின் முப்பான் மிகுத்திட்டங்
கீறாங் கருவி யிவற்றால் வகுத்திட்டு
வேறாம் பதிபசு பாசம்வீ டாகுமே. 2419

Creation of Tattvas

Tattvas six into six,
He placed in Kundalini
And divided the Maya into categories three
And with the last of them (Prakriti Maya)
Forged the (Tattvic) instruments;
Then were let in the Pasas to Jiva belong
He, the Pati (Lord), who apart is.

வீட்கும் பதிபசு பாசமும் மீதுற
வாட்கும் இருவினை யாங்கவற் றாலுணர்ந்
தாட்கு நரக சுவர்க்கத்திற் றானிட்டு
நாட்குற நான்தங்கு நற்பாச நண்ணுமே. 2420

Creation of Experiences for Jiva

The Pasu-Pasam thus released,
When it overcomes Jiva
Pati works out his redemption;
And receives him into His Grace,
Having made him experience Karmas two,
He consigns him into hell and heaven;
And as days pass,
Jiva acquires love of God—(Pati-Pasam)
In which am I steeped.

நண்ணிய பாசத்தில் நானெனல் ஆணவம்
பண்ணிய மாயையில் ஊட்டற் பரிந்தனன்
கண்ணிய சேதனன் கண்வந்த பேரருள்
அண்ணல் அடிசேர் உபாயம தாகுமே. 2421

Anava Gives Longing for Pleasures and Maya Supplies Them

In Pasam that binds,
Anava is I-ness;
And possessed of it,
The Jiva longs for Mayaic pleasure experiences;
Then on him descends heavenly Grace;
That indeed the Way
His Holy Feet to reach.

ஆகும் உபாயமே யன்றி யழுக்கற்று
மோக மறச்சுத்த னாதற்கு மூலமே
ஆகு மறுவை யழுக்கேற்றி யேற்றல்போல்
ஆகுவ தெல்லாம் அருட்பாச மாகுமே. 2422

Grace Works Out Purity

Not only is Grace
The means to Lord's Feet,
It is the source too
For desires to end,
And purification to attain;
Even as the cloth's dirt is removed
By earth-dirt (saline earth),
Pati-Pasam Grace works out
Jiva's purity.

பாசம் பயிலுயிர் தானே பரமுதல்
பாசம் பயிலுயிர் தானே பசுவென்ப
பாசம் பயிலப் பதிபர மாதலாற்
பாசம் பயிலப் பதிபசு வாகுமே. 2423

Pati-Pasam Leads to Pasu-Pati

Jivas that in Pati-Pasam (Arul Pasam) stand,
Reach the Para State;
Jivas that in Pasu-Pasam stand,
Are but Pasus (in worldly ways);
As Jivas in Pati-Pasam stand,
Attain Para State,
Jivas in Pati-Pasam continuous standing,
Verily become Pasu-Pati (Lord of Jivas).

அத்தத்தில் உத்தரங் கேட்ட அருந்தவர்
அத்தத்தில் உத்தர மாகும் அருள்மேனி
அத்தத்தி னாலே யணையப் பிடித்தலும்
அத்தத்தில் தம்மை யடைந்துநின் றாரே. 2424

Siva-Guru Teaches the Four Rishis

The Tapasvins (four)* sought of yore
The Way (of Truth) from the Lord;
He, the Gracious One,
Gave them answer by Divine Gesture (Chin mudra);
And as with their hands they held fast to His feet,
They reached the Way of Truth, their Self-realizing.

*Sanaka, Sanatana, Sanatkumara, Sanantana—these are the four holy rishis, said to be the spiritual sons of Brahma, who sought of Siva the truth of holy wisdom. Siva sitting under the wild banyan tree as Guru Dakshinamurt, facing southward, taught them the Divine Truth by chin-mudra (gesture of jnana) in silence. Dakshinamurthi is held as the Supreme Siva Guru. Also see the Prologue.

17. அடித்தலை யறியும்திறங்கூறல்
HEAD-AND-FOOT KNOWLEDGE

காலுந் தலையும் அறியார் கலதிகள்
காலந்தச் சத்தி யருளென்பர் காரணம்
பாலொன்று ஞானமே பண்பார் தலையுயிர்
காலந்த ஞானத்தைக் காட்டவீ டாகுமே. 2425

Feet are Grace; Head is Jnana

Neither head nor foot they know
Miscreants they are;
The Feet the Holy say
Are the Grace of Sakti;
The Head the Holy say
Is Jnana
That with First Cause unites;
When to Jiva the Feet of Grace
Shows the Head of Jnana
Then shall Liberation be.

தலையடி யாவ தறியார் காயத்தில்
தலையடி யுச்சியில் உள்ளது மூலந்
தலையடி யான அறிவை யறிந்தோர்
தலையடி யாகவே தானிருந் தாரே. 2426

Head and Feet Are Within

They know not
The Head and Foot (of Lord) is within body,
The Head is in Sahasrara (Cranium)
The Foot in Muladhara;
Those who visioned thus in the Yogic way,
Remained in Prayer
Their heads bowed at Lord's feet.

நின்றான் நிலமுழு தண்டமும் மேலுற
வன்றாள் அசுரர் அமரரும் உய்ந்திடப்
பின்றான் உலகம் படைத்தவன் பேர்நந்தி
தன்றா ளிணையென் தலைமிசை யானதே. 2427

Greatness of Feet

He stood, heaven and earth encompassing,
That the mighty Asuras and Devas
May redemption know;
He who created this world
Is the Great Nandi;
His Feet, on my head, I bore.

சிந்தையி னுள்ளே எந்தை திருவடி
சிந்தையும் எந்தை திருவடிக் கீழது
எந்தையும் என்னை யறியகி லானாகில்
எந்தையை யானும் அறியகி லேனே. 2428

Only By God's Grace Jiva Can Know Him

Within my thoughts
Are my Father's Holy Feet;
At my Father's Holy Feet;
Are my thoughts centred
If my Father knows me not,
Neither will I my Father know.

பன்னாத பாரொளிக் கப்புறத் தப்பால்
என்னா யகனார் இசைந்தங் கிருந்திட
முன்னா ஒளியு முரைசெய்யா மந்திரஞ்
சொன்னான் கழலிணை சூடிநின் றேனே. 2429

Lord Gave Jnana and Mantra

Beyond, beyond the Light
That defies description,
Is the place where
My loving Lord abides;
He showed me the Light (Jnana)
That is beyond thought;
He taught me the Mantra
That is beyond words;
His Holy Feet, adoring I stood.

பதியது தோற்றும் பதமது வைம்மின்
மதியது செய்து மலர்ப்பத மோது
நதிபொதி யுஞ்சடை நாரியோர் பாகன்
கதிசெயுங் காலங்கள் கண்டுகொ ளீரே. 2430

Wait and Pray; Lord Will Come to You

The Lord's Holy Feet
In your thoughts hold;
His flower-like Feet
In wisdom adore;

The Lord who carries Sakti on His body
With Ganga muffled in his russet matted locks
Will in time your salvation grant;
Do wait and pray.

தரித்துநின் றானடி தன்னிட நெஞ்சில்
தரித்துநின் றானம ராபதி நாதன்
கரித்துநின் றான்கரு தாதவர் சிந்தை
பரித்துநின் றானப் பரிபாகத் தானே. 2431

Grace is Granted According to Degree of Devotion

In the thoughts of those
Who hold Him steadfast,
Firm He stood, His Feet planted;
—He the Lord of Celestials;
Those who thought not of Him,
He shunned;
To each according to his devotion
He His Grace grants.

ஒன்றுண்டு தாமரை யொண்மலர் மூன்றுள
தன்றாதை தாளும் இரண்டுள காயத்துள்
நன்றாகக் காய்ச்சிப் பதஞ்செய வல்லார்கட்
கின்றேசென் றீசனை யெய்தலு மாமே. 2432

Go the Intense Way and Behold Lord's Feet Even Today

One the heart's lotus
Three the radiant flowers
Two the Father's Feet within;
Those who can discipline the body
In Yogic Kundalini Way
May well behold Him,
Even this day.

கால்கொண்டென் சென்னியிற் கட்டறக் கட்டற
மால்கொண்ட நெஞ்சின் மயக்கிற் றுயக்கறப்
பால்கொண்ட வென்னைப்பரன்கொள்ள நாடினான்
மேல்கொண்டென் செம்மை
விளம்பவொண்ணாதே. 2433

Grace Leads to Holy State

Firm He planted His Feet on my head;
My fetters into fragments broke;
My heart's impurities were entire cleansed;
Milky-white pure it became;
The Lord then sought
To take me into His Fold;
What more can I say
Of my Holy State?

பெற்ற புதல்வர் போற் பேணிய நாற்றமுங்
குற்றமுங் கண்டு குணங்குறை செய்யவோர்
பற்றைய வீச னுயிரது பான்மைக்குச்
செற்றமி லாச்செய்கைக் கெய்தின செய்யுமே. 2434

God's Love For Man

The Lord loves Jivas as His children;
Well may they wallow in dirt and blemish;
He removes them and mends their ways;
Thus is God's love for Man;
To each according to his deeds
In compassion He bestows His care.

18. முக்குற்றம்

THREE BLEMISHES

மூன்றுள குற்ற முழுது நலிவன
மான்றிருள் தூங்கி மயங்கிக் கிடந்தன
மூன்றினை நீங்கினர் நீக்கினர் நீங்காதார்
மூன்றினுட் பட்டு முடிகின்ற வாறே. 2435

The Truly Liberated

Three the blemishes
That harass Jiva alike,
And in darkness enveloped
He lies in stupor;
They who are from them liberated
Are the truly liberated;
Others, entangled in them,
Surely perish.

காமம் வெகுளி மயக்க மிவைகடிந்
தேமம் பிடித்திருந் தேனுக் கெறிமணி
ஓமெனும் ஓசையி னுள்ளே யுறைவதோர்
தாம மதனைத் தலைப்பட்ட வாறே. 2436

Experiences in Liberation

Lust, anger and ignorance
I subdued;
And I waxed strong;
An ethereal bliss suffused me;
As though I was within the sound of "Aum"
Of a chiming bell, swinging struck.

19. முப்பதம்
THREE STATES (PADAS) OF REALIZATION

தோன்றிய தொம்பதந் தற்பதஞ் சூழ்தர
ஏன்ற அசிபதம் இம்மூன்றோ டெய்தினோன்
ஆன்ற பராபர மாகும் பிறப்பற
வேன்றனன் மாளச் சிவமா யிருக்குமே. 2437

The Three States Lead to Siva-Becoming

Tvam-Padam, Tat-Padam and Asi-Padam
He who has these three states of liberation attained,
Has verily become Para-Para Himself;
No more birth shall be for him;
And when he departs
He shall indeed Siva be.

போதந் தனையுன்னிப் பூதாதி பேதமும்
ஓதுங் கருவிதொண் ணூறுடன் ஓராறு
பேதமும் நாதாந்தப் பெற்றியிற் கைவிட்டு
வேதஞ்சொல் தொம்பத மாகுதன் மெய்ம்மையே. 2438

Tvam-Pada is Beyond Nadanta State

Aim at Bodha State;
Discard elements and their diversities
(That Tattvas are composed of;)
And the ninety and six instruments of experience;
Transcend Nadanta State of glory;
Ascend beyond;
There indeed is the Tvam-Pada State,
The Truth Vedas speak of.

தற்பதம் என்றுந் துவம்பதந் தானென்றும்
நிற்ப தசியத்துள் நேரிழை யாள்பதஞ்
சொற்பதத் தாலுந் தொடரவொண் ணாச்சிவன்
கற்பனை யின்றிக் கலந்துநின் றானே. 2439

Siva is Beyond the Three Padas

Beyond the States of Tvam-Pada and Tat-Pada
In the state of Asipada, Sakti wondrous stands;
But Siva remains still beyond,
Beyond the reach of speech
In unimaginable immanence
In all, in all.

அணுவும் பரமும் அசிபதத் தேய்ந்து
கணுவொன் றிலாத சிவமுங் கலந்தால்
இணையறு பால்தேன் அமுதென இன்பத்
துணையது வாயுரை யற்றிடத் தோன்றுமே. 2440

Asi-Pada Experience

When Jiva and Para
Reach Asi-Pada State
And in pervasive Siva merge,
Then as sweetness compounded
Of milk, honey, and ambrosia
Will He in the Silence agreeable appear.

தொம்பதந் தற்பதந் தோன்றும் அசிபதம்
நம்பிய சீவன் பரன்சிவ னாய்நிற்கும்
அம்பத மேலைச் சொரூபமா வாக்கியஞ்
செம்பொருள் ஆண்டருள் சீர்நந்தி தானே. 2441

Tvam-Tat-Asi

In States, Tvam-Pada, Tat-Pada and Asi-Pada
Jiva stands as Jiva, Para and Siva
In order respective;
Beyond them is the Svarupa Mahavakya (Supreme Word Manifest)
(Tvam-Tat-Asi);
Revealing that Truth,
Nandi accepted me in His Grace.

ஐம்ப தறியா தவரு மவர்சிலர்
உம்பனை நாடி யுரைமுப்ப தத்திடைச்
செம்பர மாகிய வாசி செலுத்திடத்
தம்பர யோகமாய்த் தானவு னாகுமே. 2442

Yoga Way Also Leads to the Three States

Even some who know not the letters Fifty
Reach the States three above said;
They did by (directing) their breath in Yogic Way
Into Para;
Thus with Siva they one became.

நந்தி யறிவும் நழுவில் அதீதமாம்
இந்தியஞ் சத்தாதி விடவிய னாகும்
நந்திய மூன்றிரண் டொன்று நலமைந்து
நந்தி னனவாதி மூட்டும் அனாதியே. 2443

Turiyatita Experience

Transcending even thought of God
Is Atita State;
The sense organs (Indriyas) no more cognise
The Sound and the rest;
Pervasive Jiva becomes;
The Malas three, the Karmas two, the Jiva one,
The experiences (Avasthais) Five,
All these subside;
Thus subsiding, the Beginningless One wakes
Into the Turiyatita Jagrat State.

பரதுரி யத்து நனவு படியுண்ட
விரிவிற் கனவும் இதனுப சாந்தத்
துரிய சுழுனையு மோவுஞ் சிவன்பால்
அரிய துரியம் அசிபத மாமே. 2444

Experiences in Para Turiya

Beyond the Jagrat (waking) in Paraturiya State
Is the Dream State within
That leads to Upasantha:
In the Sushupti State (of Para Turiya)
And in Turiya within Para Turiya
Is Siva reached;
Then indeed is Asi-Pada attained.

20. முப்பரம்

THREE PARAS

தோன்றியென் னுள்ளே சுழன்றெழு கின்றதோர்
மூன்று படிமண் டலத்து முதல்வனை
ஏன்றெய்தி யின்புற் றிருந்தே யிளங்கொடி
நான்று நலஞ்செய் நலந்தரு மாறே. 2445

Parallel Yoga Way

In the encircling Spheres Three within me,
The Primal Lord appears;
I reached Him and was in bliss immersed;
I clung to the tender vine of Kundalini Sakti
That she, Her Grace may shower.

---

1)Fire, sun and moon mandalas.

மன்று நிறைந்தது மாபர மாயது
நின்று நிறைந்தது நேர்தரு நந்தியுங்
கன்று நினைந்தெழு தாயென வந்தபின்
குன்று நிறைந்த குணவிளக் காமே. 2446

Lord Appears in love in Para Turiya

The Expanse vast of Para
As divine dance arena extended
Nandi there appeared
And stood and filled;
When He came in tender love
As cow that yearns for calf,
Beaming was Jiva,
As lamp upon hill-top placed.

ஆறாது தத்துவத் தப்புறத் தப்பரங்
கூறா வுபதேசங் கூறிற் சிவபரம்
வேறாய் வெளிப்பட்ட வேதப் பகவனார்
பேறாக ஆனந்தம் பேணும் பெருகவே. 2447

Beyond Para is Parasiva

Beyond Tattvas six times six
Is that Para;
When the unarticulated mantra
Is in Silence chanted,
Then appears Siva Para,
That is still above;
He is the God
Of whom Vedas speak;
Then shall Divine Rapture well up in you;
Do foster it, and enlarge.

பற்றறப் பற்றிற்பரம்பதி யாவது
பற்றறப் பற்றிற் பரனறி வேபரம்
பற்றறப் பற்றினிற் பற்றவல் லோர்கட்கே
பற்றறப் பற்றிப் பரம்பர மாமே. 2448

Seek Lord in Intense Divine Desire and Become Siva

Shedding desires (worldly)
In intense (Divine) desire seek Him;
Yours shall be the Heavenly Kingdom of God (Param);
When you in intense (Divine) desire seek Him,
Shorn of desires (worldly),
Then shall the Knowledge of God be;
Only those who in intense (Divine) desire seek Him,
Bereft of desires (worldly),
Will (Param Param) Siva become.

பரம்பர மான பதிபாசம் பற்றாப்
பரம்பர மாகும் பரஞ்சிவ மேவப்
பரம்பர மான பரசிவா னந்தம்
பரம்பர மாகப் படைப்ப தறிவே. 2449

Pati-Pasam Leads to Para, Para Siva and Para Siva-Ananda

Cherish Pati-Pasam (God-love)
That is holy beyond holiness;
Then shall the transcendental Para be;
And then beyond Parasiva reached be;
Then shall the transcendental Siva Bliss (Parasivananda) be;
Jiva Becoming Siva is indeed Knowledge Divine.

நனவிற் கலாதியா நாலொன் றகன்று
தனியுற்ற கேவலந் தன்னில் தானாகி
நினைவுற்றகன்ற அதீதத்துள் நேய
தனையுற் றிடத்தானே தற்பர மாமே. 2450

Beyond Kalanta is Tat-Para State (God-Union and Not God-Becoming Yet)

Transcend Kalas Five
In the Waking State (of Turiya) appear;
Reach the lonely State of Higher Kevala (inertness)
And there solitary be;
Bereft of sentience,
Ardent enter the (Turiya) atita State;
Then shall you the very Tat-Para be.

1)Nivritti, prathista, vidya, santi, santiatita. They belong to the sphere of Siva tattvas — vide Mantra 2377.
2)One in God-union.

தற்கண்ட தூயமுந் தன்னில் விலாசமும்
பிற்காணுந் தூடணந் தானும் பிறழ்வுற்றுத்
தற்பரன் கால பரமுங் கலந்தற்ற
நற்பரா தீதமு நாடக ராதியே. 2451

In Tat-Para Union is Aum

The Purity State
That Self-Realization brought,
The Expansive State within it,
The Malas that affected Jiva before
All these passing,
Seek the Para-atita State
Where the Tatpara and the time-bound Jiva that Para became
Commingle into one letter
That with "A" begins; "Aum."

21. பரலட்சணம்

ATTRIBUTES OF PARA

அதீதத்து ளாகி யகன்றவன் நந்தி
அதீதத்து ளாகி யறிவிலோன் ஆன்மா
மதிபெற் றிருள்விட்ட மன்னுயிர் ஒன்றாம்
பதியிற் பதியும் பரவுயிர் தானே. 2452

Para Jiva that Had Become Tat-Para, Jiva, Now Merges in Siva Himself

He, Nandi, is within Atita
And Beyond it;
He, Jiva that had Para-Jiva become
Is within Atita
Yet Jnana (Full) without;
The Para Jiva attaining Jnana
And rid of dark Ignorance
Will with God (Pati) One be.

ஆதியும் அந்தமும் இல்லா வரும்பதி
சோதிப் பரஞ்சுடர் தோன்றத்தோன் றாமையின்
நீதிய தாய்நிற்கும் நீடிய வப்பர
போதம் உணர்ந்தவர் புண்ணியத் தோரே. 2453

Nature of Pati

The Pati (Lord) has
Neither Beginning nor End;
He is Divine Light Resplendent;
He is seen and yet unseen;
Those who attain Jnana
Of that Para
Are Holy indeed.

துரியங் கடந்து துரியா தீதத்தே
அரிய வியோகங்கொண் டம்பலத் தாடும்
பெரிய பிரானைப் பிரணவக் கூபத்தே
துரியவல் லார்க்குத் துரிசில்லை தானே. 2454

He Dances in Space and Lurks Inside the Deep Well of Pranava

Transcending Turiya
And entering Turiyatita,
Is the endless Space;
There vision the mighty Lord
That dances eternal;
They who can peer
Into the deep well of Pranava (Aum) within,
And glimpse Him
Will no more birth have.

செம்மைமுன் னிற்பச் சுவேதந் திரிவபோல்
அம்மெய்ப் பரத்தோ டணுவனுள் ளாயிடப்
பொய்ம்மைச் சகமுண்ட போத வெறும்பாழிற்
செம்மைச் சிவமேரு சேர்கொடி யாகுமே. 2455

Jiva's Purification

In contact with colour red
White, too, becomes red;
Like it it is,
When Jiva purified (white)
Reaches Siva (that is red);
In Jnana's Void
That absorbs universes so unreal,
Siva stands high aloft
As a flag planted on Meru Mountain top.

வைச்ச கலாதி வருதத்து வங்கெட
வெச்ச இருமாயை வேறாக வேறுத்
துச்ச பரசிவ மாமுண்மை யொன்றவே
அச்சம் அறுத்தென்னை யாண்டனன் நந்தியே. 2456

Lord Accepts Jiva in His Grace

Faded have they,
Kalas and other Tattvas (below);
Sundered were they,
The Mayas two, left behind;
And after taking me into the baptismal font of Jnana
He made me in Him unite;
Dispelling my fears
He accepted me in His Grace,
He, Nandi Holy.

என்னை யறிய இசைவித்த என்னந்தி
என்னை யறிந்தறி யாத விடத்துய்த்துப்

பின்னை யொளியிற் சொரூபம் புறப்பட்டுத்
தன்னை யளித்தான் தற்பர மாகவே. 2457

After Self-Realization is the Light Where No Self is

"Realize the Self,'
—So taught my Nandi;
When I realized the Self,
He placed me in place where the Self is unknown;
There the Light-Form arose,
And He granted me Himself,
Tat-Para I became.

பரந்துஞ் சுருங்கியும் பார்புனல் வாயு
நிரந்த வளியொடு ஞாயிறு திங்கள்
அரந்த அரனெறி யாயது வாகித்
தரந்த விசும்பொன்று தாங்கிநின் றானே. 2458

Siva's Immanence and Transcendence

Expanding and contracting,
Earth, water, space and wind,
Sun and Moon,
Pervasive and immanent,
Hara stood;
Supporting the firmament vast.

சத்தின் நிலையினில் தானான சத்தியுந்
தற்பரை யாய்நிற்குந் தானாம் பரற்குடல்
உய்த்தகு மிச்சையில் ஞானாதி பேதமாய்
நித்த நடத்து நடிக்குமா நேயத்தே. 2459

Sakti Manifestations

From Sat (Siva) arose of Herself, Sakti,
In that State She as Tat-Parai stands;
In the Ichcha (Desire) State
She Para's Form material is;
Then Jnana Sakti and other forms
She assumes;
Thus acting in love surpassing
She daily, daily moves this world.

மேலொடு கீழ்பக்க மெய்வாய்கண் ணாசிகள்
பாலிய விந்து பரையுட் பரையாகக்
கோலிய நான்கவை ஞானங் கொணர்விந்து
சீலமி லாவணுச் செய்திய தாமே. 2460

Bindu Sakti Imparts Power to Cognitive Organs

From within Parai
Expanded Bindu Sakti;
From above descending, to here below,
It imparted sentience to the cognitive Organs four,
—This the story of Jivas,
That inherent no sentience has.

வேறா மதன்தன்மை போலுமிக் காயத்தில்
ஆறாம் உபாதி யனைத்தாகுந் தத்துவம்
பேறாம் பரவொளி தூண்டும் பிரகாசமாய்
ஊறா யுயிர்த்துண் டுறங்கிடு மாயையே. 2461

Maya, Little Light Leading to Great Light

Then separate arose Maya from Parai
And the Caused Tattvas and experiences six
The body is an heir to;
Feeling, breathing, eating, and sleeping
Are all enjoyments that Maya gives;
She is the little light within,
That kindles the Great Light to reach.

தற்பர மன்னுந் தனிமுதற் பேரொளி
சிற்பரந் தானே செகமுண்ணும் போதமுந்
தொற்பதந் தீர்பாழிற் சுந்தரச் சோதிபுக்
கப்புற மற்றதிங் கொப்பில்லை தானே. 2462

Lord is Splendorous Light in the Space Beyond

The Primal Lord that is Tat-Para
Is Light Resplendent
He is Chit-Para, (Divine Jnana filled)
He is the Divine Sentience
That engrosses universe;
Enter in the Splendorous Light,
In the Space that is beyond words,
No more is there anything to compare.

பண்டை மறைகள் பரவான் உடலென்னுந்
துண்ட மதியோன் துரியாதீ தந்தன்னைக்
கண்டு பரனுமக் காரணோ பாதிக்கே
மிண்டி னவன்சுத்த னாகான் வினவிலே. 2463

Risk to Suddha State Even in Turiyatita

The hoary scriptures say,
The expanding Space is His Body;
He wears the crescent moon;
Even after reaching the Turiyatita State,
If Jiva a victim to Causal Experiences (of Suddha
Maya) falls.
He will Suddha (Pure) per se not be,
If thou ask me.

வெளிகால் கனலப்பு மேவுமண் ணின்ற
தளியா கியதற் பரங்கா ணவன்றான்
வெளிகால் கனலப்பு மேவுமண் ணின்ற
வெளியாய சத்தி யவன்வடி வாமே. 2464

Pervasive Sakti is Pervasive Siva's Form

Space, air, fire, water and earth
He pervasive fills
He is Tat-Para of love infinite;
Sakti that is manifested
In space, air, fire, water and earth
Is but of His Form Divine.

மேருவி னோடே விரிகதிர் மண்டலம்
ஆர நினையும் அருந்தவ யோகிக்குச்

சீரார் தவஞ்செய்யிற் சிவனருள் தானாகும்
பேரவும் வேண்டாம் பிறிதில்லை தானே. 2465

Contemplate in Yogic Way

To the Yogis of intense Tapas,
Contemplating on Mystic Meru Mount
In the radiant Sphere within,
In their rare Tapas
Siva's Grace, of itself, appears;
Move not from this way;
There is none other too.

22. முத்துரியம்

THREE TURIYAS

நனவாதி மூன்றினிற் சீவ துரியந்
தனதாதி மூன்றினிற் பரதுரி யந்தான்
நனவாதி மூன்றி னிற்சிவ துரியமா
மினதாகுந் தொந்தத் தசிபதத் தீடே 2466

Three Turiyas—Jiva, Para and Siva; and Their Respective Reaches Tvam Pada, Tat Pada and Asi Pada

The Turiya beyond (in Jagrat)
Waking, Dreaming and Deep Sleep States
Is Jiva Turiya;
The Turiya beyond
The Waking, Dreaming and Deep Sleep States (in the Jiva Turiya State)
In Para Turiya;
The Turiya further beyond (in the Para Turiya State)
Is Siva Turiya;
In these are reached
Tvam, Tat and Asi States respective.

தானா நனவில் துரியந்தன் தொம்பதந்
தானாந் துரிய நனவாதி தான்மூன்றில்
ஆனாப் பரபத மற்ற தருநனா
வானான மேன்மூன்றுந் துரியம் அணுகுமே. 2467

States of Consciousness in the Three Turiyas

In Jiva Turiya of Waking State
Is Tvam-Pada;
The end of Jiva Turiya is the beginning of Para Turiya
Jagrat;
At the end of Para Turiya
Is Para Pada (Tat-Pada)
Three steps beyond,
In the fourth, is Siva Turiya (Asi Pada).

அணுவின் துரியத்து நான்கும தாகிப்
பணியும் பரதுரி யம்பயி னான்குந்
தணிவிற் பரமாகிச் சார்முத் துரியக்
கணுவிலிந் நான்குங் கலந்தவீ ரைந்தே. 2468

Ten States of Consciousness in All—In the Three Turiyas

The four states of Jiva Turiya
And the four states of Para Turiya
And the four states of Siva Turiya
As the end of one Turiya is the beginning state of next
They really are states Ten.

JIVA OR JAGRAT TURIYA

1.Jagrat
2.Svapna
3.Sushupti
4.Turiya

PARA TURIYA

5.Jiva turiya jagrat
6.Jiva turiya svapna
7.Jiva turiya sushupti
8.Jiva turiya turiya

SIVA TURIYA

9.Para Turiya jagrat
10.Para turiya svapna
11.Para turiya sushupti
12.Para turiya turiya

States 4 & 5 merge into one state. Similarly states 8 and 9 merge into one state. Thus they become ten avastas—the turiya of one state being the jagrat of the next.

ஈரைந் தவத்தை யிசைமுத் துரியத்துள்
நேரந்த மாக நெறிவழி யேசென்று
பாரந்த மான பராபரத் தயிக்கியத்
தோரந்த மாமிரு பாதியைச் சேர்த்திடே. 2469

At the End of Ten is Union in Para Para

The Ten States are in the Turiyas Three;
Them as Ends, you proceed;
At the Final End is identity with Para Para
Connecting the States in the middle two each
(Jiva Turiya and Para Turiya Jagrat into one
And Para Turiya Turiya and Siva Turiya Jagrat into one.)

தொட்டே யிருமின் துரிய நிலத்தினை
எட்டா தெனினின் றெட்டும் இறைவனைப்
பட்டாங் கறிந்திடிற் பன்னா வுதடுகள்
தட்டா தொழிவதோர் தத்துவந் தானே. 2470

If You Cannot Reach Turiya Land, Persevere Still

Reach the Turiya Land, and be there;
If you cannot reach it

Think of Lord in the Way scriptures speak of,
You shall reach the Truth
That is beyond beyond words.

அறிவா யசத்தென்னு மாறா நகன்று
செறிவாய மாயை சிதைத்தரு ளாலே
பிறியாத பேரரு ளாயிடும் பெற்றி
நெறியான அன்பர் நிலையறிந் தாரே. 2471

The Holy Way

Become Knowledge;
Away with Tattvas six times six
That Asat (unreal) are;
Crush the crowding Maya
With Lord's Grace;
Then will be the Divine Grace abiding;
That way, the holy ones knew.

நனவின் நனவாதி நாலாந் துரியந்
தனதுயிர் தொம்பத மாமாறு போல
வினையறு சீவன் நனவாதி யாகத்
தனைய பரதுரிய யந்தற் பதமே. 2472

From Jiva Turiya to Para Turiya

The Fourth States of Jagrat
Is Turiya (Jiva Turiya);
There Jiva attains Tvam-Pada;
The Karmas end;
Again, commencing from Jiva Turiya
Is the Jagrat State in Para Turiya;
Reach Turiya in Para Turiya State,
There indeed is Tat-Pada State.

தொம்பதந் தற்பதஞ் சொன்முத் துரியம்போல்
நம்பிய மூன்றாந் துரியத்து நற்றாமம்
அம்புவி யுன்னா அதிசூக்க மப்பாலைச்
செம்பொருள் ஆண்டருள் சீர்நந்தி தானே. 2473

On to the Third Turiya

As you reached Tvam-Pada and Tat-Pada,
So now enter the third Turiya State (Siva Turiya)
At its end is the Divine Light (Asi-Pada)
The Super-Subtlety (Suksma) that words can conceive not;
Beyond is Siva
Who as Nandi accepted me into His Grace.

23. மும்முத்தி
THREE MUKTIS

சீவன்றன் முத்தி யதீதம் பரமுத்தி
ஓயுப சாந்தஞ் சிவமுத்தி யானந்த
மூவயின் முச்சொருப முத்திமுப் பாலதாய்
ஓவுறு தாரத்தில் உள்ளுநா தாந்தமே. 2474

The Three Muktis Are Direct Experiences With Siva-Form

Jiva-Mukti is the Atita (Beyond Consciousness State);
Para-Mukti is Upasanta (Divine Peace);
Siva-Mukti is Ananda (Divine Bliss);
All three are Svarupa Muktis
That from Nadanta branch
Where Pranava (Aum) as letters Three (A,U,M) are.

ஆவ தறியார் உயிர்பிறப் பாலுறும்
ஆவ தறியும் உயிரருட் பாலுறும்
ஆவதொன் றில்லை யகம்புறத் தென்றகன்
றோவு சிவனுடன் ஒன்றுதன் முத்தியே. 2475

Mukti is the Goal of Being One With Siva

They know not the goal of birth,
The Jiva who knows it
Will in Grace be;
Nothing here to be in home or outside,
Thus renouncing all,
Be one with Siva
That verily is Mukti.

சிவமாகி மும்மல முக்குணஞ் செற்றுத்
தவமான மும்முத்தி தத்துவத் தயிக்கியத்
துவமா கியநெறி சோகமென் போர்க்குச்
சிவமாம் அமலன் சிறந்தனன் தானே. 2476

Way of So-Ham

Siva Becoming,
The Malas triple perishing,
The Gunas triple perishing,
The Muktis triple attaining,
One with Tattvas uniting
That the way of "So-ham" is;
Like those who follow this Way
The Immaculate Siva Himself reveals.

சித்தியும் முத்தியுந் திண்சிவ மாகிய
சுத்தியும் முத்தீ தொலைக்குஞ் சுகானந்த
சத்தியும் மேலைச் சமாதியு மாயிடும்
பெத்தம் அறுத்த பெரும்பெரு மானே. 2477

All Attainments, Work of Lord

Siddhi and Mukti,
And Suddhi that is Siva Pure,
And Sakti of Pure Bliss,
That extinguishes the Fires Three;
And the Samadhi Exalted
—All these the work of Divine Lord'
Who thine bonds sunders.

24. முச்சொரூபம்

TRIPLE SVARUPA

ஏறிய வாறே மலம்ஐந் திடைஅடைத்
தாறிய ஞானச் சிவோக மடைந்திட்டு
வேறு மெனமுச் சொரூபத்து வீடுற்றங்
கீறதிற் பண்டைப் பரனுண்மை செய்யுமே. 2478

Beyond Triple Muktis is God

As you ascend,
Attenuate Malas Five
And espouse "So-ham"
That is Jnana filled;
And be liberated
Attaining Svarupa Mukti triple;
And in the End,
Vision Truth of Para (Siva) Eternal.

மூன்றுள மாளிகை மூவர் இருப்பிடம்
மூன்றினின் முப்பத் தாறு முதிப்புள
மூன்றினி னுள்ளே முளைத்தெழுஞ் சோதியைக்
காண்டலுங் காயக் கணக்கற்ற வாறே. 2479

Light in the Three Mansions

Three the Mansions
Three that reside there
In the Three merge the thirty-six (Tattvas)
The Light that rises from within the Three
May well the Jiva vision;
Then ended will birth's cycle be
That endless was.

உலகம் புடைபெயர்ந் தூழியும் போன
நிலவு் சுடரொளி மூன்றுமொன் றாய
பலவும் பரிசொடு பான்மையுள் ஈசன்
அளவும் பெருமையு மாரறி வாரே. 2480

Lord's Vastness

The worlds tumbled,
The aeons passed;
The three Lights,
Sun, Moon and Fire
One became;
All in Benevolent Lord merged;
Who knows His vastness and greatness!

பெருவாய் முதலெண்ணும் பேதமே பேதித்
தருவா யுருவாய் அருவுரு வாகிக்
குருவாய் வருஞ்சத்தி கோனுயிர்ப் பன்மை
உருவா யுடனிருந் தொன்றாய்ன் றாமே. 2481

God's Multiple Forms

The Primal One, the indivisible Great
Himself into several divided;
As Form, Formless and Form-Formless,
And as Guru, and as Sakti-Lord
In Forms numerous
He immanent in Jivas became
And transcendent too.

மணியொளி சோபை யிலக்கணம் வாய்த்து
மணியென லாய்நின்ற வாறது போலத்
தணிமுச் சொருபாதி சத்தியாதி சாரப்
பணவித்த பேர்நந்தி பாதம்பற் றாயே. 2482

Jiva Shines in Triple Mukti

In Triple Mukti Jiva receives Light Divine
With light and brilliance infused,
The crystal as a gem shines;
Like it is Jiva
When he attains Muktis Three
And Grace of Sakti Divine;
Hold to the Feet of Nandi
Who all these Graces ordained.

கல்லொளி மாநிறஞ் சோபைக் கதிர்தட்ட
நல்ல மணியொன்றி னாடியொண் முப்பதஞ்
சொல்லறு முப்பாழிற் சொல்லறு பேருரைத்
தல்லறு முத்திராந் தத்தனு பூதியே. 2483

Beyond Triple Mukti is Mudra of Jnana

With crystalline hue and radiant brilliance,
The Lord stands as a gem of purest ray serene;
Seek Him and reach the Mukti State Three;
Beyond is Void that defies speech,
There contemplate on Aum in Silence
In that Mudra of Jnana
The final Grace is.

உடந்தசெந் தாமரை யுள்ளுறு சோதி
நடந்தசெந் தாமரை நாதந் தகைந்தால்
அடைந்த பயோதரி யட்டி யடைத்தவ்
விடந்தரு வாசலை மேல்திற வீரே. 2484

Kundalini Yoga

He is the Light within the heart's crimson lotus;
If the Crimson Lotus within, Nada you reached,
You shall wake Kundalini Sakti;
And closing Muladhara where She imprisoned is,
Ascend upward (through Sushumna in Yogic breathing)
And open wide the gate above at cranium top.

25. முக்கரணம்

MUKKARANAM

இடனொரு மூன்றி லியைந்த வொருவன்
கடனுறு மவ்வுரு வேறெனக் காணுந்
திடமது போலச் சிவபர சீவர்
உடனுறை பேதமும் ஒன்றென லாமே. 2485

Jiva, Para and Siva Are One in Three Places

One person in places three functions
Yet may be as three different appear;
Like this
Are Jiva, Para and Siva;
One are they
But in different places appear.

ஒளியை யொளிசெய்து வோமென் றெழுப்பி
வளியை வளிசெய்து வாய்த்திட வாங்கி
வெளியை வெளிசெய்து மேலெழ வைத்துத்
தெளியத் தெளியுஞ் சிவபதந் தானே. 2486

How to Reach Siva State

Brighten the Light within
To merge in the Light (without);
Through Sound potency in "Aum"
Rouse Prana breath within
To merge in the breath without (Cosmic Life).
Coursing it appropriate upward,
Merge the space within into Space without;
Clear shall you the Siva-State vision.

முக்கர ணங்களின் மூர்ச்சைதீர்த் தாவதக்
கைக்கா ரணமென்னத் தந்தனன் காணந்தி
மிக்க மனோன்மனி வேறே தனித்தேக
ஒக்கும துன்மனி யோதுட் சமாதியே. 2487

Unmani Sakti Takes Over

He ended the pulsations of Karanas
By a sleight of hand, as it were—My Nandi
As the lovely Manonmani (Sakti) left,
Unmani (Sakti) no less lovely entered,
Do take to Her in Samadhi inward.

26. முச்சூனிய தொந்தத்தசி

THREE SPACES AND TVAM-TAT-ASI

தற்பதஞ் தொம்பதந் தானர்ம் அசிபதந்
தொற்பத மூன்றுந் துரியத்துத் தோற்றவே
நிற்ப துயிர்பர னிகழ்சிவ மும்மூன்றின்
சொற்பத மாகுந் தொந்தத் தசியே. 2488

Tvam-Tat-Asi

Tvam-Pada, Tat-Pada and Asi-Pada
All three states in Turiya arose;
In all three states one of Three stands
—Jiva, Para and Siva in order respective—
Together are they known
By the expression compounded,
That is, Tvam-Tat-Asi (Maha Vakyam)

தொந்தத் தசிமூன்றில் தொல்கா மியமாதி
தொந்தத் தசிமூன்றில் தொல்தா மதமாதி
வந்த மலங்குண மாளச் சிவந்தோன்றின்
இந்துவின் முன்னிருள் ஏகுதல் ஒக்கமே. 2489

Siva Appears Beyond Tvam-Tat-Asi

In the Three States Tvam Tat and Asi
Are the time-honoured Malas Three—Kamiya and the rest
In the Three States Tvam Tat and Asi
Are the time-honoured Gunas Three—Tamas and the rest
When these Malas and Gunas are seared,
Siva appears;
And as He appears, they fleet away,
As does darkness before moon's beam.

தொந்தத் தசியையவ் வாசியில் தோற்றியே
அந்த முறையீ ரைந்தாக மதித்திட்டு
அந்த மிலாத அவத்தையவ் வாக்கியத்
துந்து முறையிற் சிவமுன்வைத் தோதிடே. 2490

Tvam-Tat-Asi Becomes Tat-Tvam-Asi

Attain the State of Tvam-Tat-Asi
Through coursing breath (in Yogic Way)
Consider it as the Tenth State of (Turiya) experience;
Endless is that Experience;
Alter that expression so
That Siva (Tat) stands first
(That is Tat-Tvam-Asi, or Tatvamasi)
Thus meditate on it and ascend.

வைத்துச் சிவத்தை மதிசொரு பானந்தத்
துய்த்துப் பிரணவ மாம்உப தேசத்தை
மெய்த்த இதயத்து விட்டிடு மெய்யுணர்ந்
தத்தற் கடிமை யடைந்துநின் றானே. 2491

As Tatvamasi, Practise Yoga

Thus altering the expression
Into Tatvamasi with Siva (Tat) first
Fix your thought on bliss of Svarupa;
And gently hold to your heart
The Pranava mantra (that is "Aum");
When Jiva thus practises Yoga
He realizes Truth
And stands, in Grace accepted.

தொம்பதம் மாயையுள் தோன்றிடுந் தற்பதம்
அம்பரை தன்னில் உதிக்கும் அசிபதம்
நம்புறு சாந்தியில் நண்ணுமவ் வாக்கியம்
உம்பர் உரைதொந்தத் தசிவாசி யாமே. 2492

Tvam-Tat-Asi is Grand Vakya

Tvam-Pada arises in Maya (Sakti)
Tat-Pada in comely Parai (Sakti)
Asi-Pada leads to Santhi (Kala)
That Vakya (expression) is verily of Celestials,
Tvam-Tat-Asi by Yogic breathing attained.

ஆகிய வச்சோயந் தேவதத் தன்னிடத்
தாகிய வைவிட்டாற் காயம் உபாதானம்
ஏகிய தொந்தத் தசியென்ப மெய்யறி
வாகிய சீவன் பரசிவ னாமே. 2493

Jiva in Different Places and Times

Deva Datta* is one and same person;
But through time and place he different appears;
Like it,
If Jiva transcends time and place,
He and Siva one becomes (So-ham)
In Tvam-Tat-Asi,
Jiva in body one with Primal Cause is:
Attaining True Jnana
Jiva becomes Para Siva.

*Deva Datta is a fictional name used in Vedanta literature. Here the name is used to illustrate how the individual remains the same, though time and place states may differ. Deva Datta was a bachelor in Benares, a householder in Chidambaram, and a sannyasin in Madurai — all one and the same person in different places.

தாமத காமிய மாகித் தகுகுண
மாமல மூன்றும் அகார வுகாரத்தேர்
டாமறு மவ்வுமவ் வாயுடன் மூன்றில்
தாமாந் துரியமுந் தொந்தத் தசியதே. 2494

The Three Turiyas in the Three Letters A, U, M (Aum)

The Gunas Three, Tamas and the rest,
The Malas Three, Kamiya and the rest,
No more are;
A, U and the consonant M,
In those letters Three are Turiya Three
All these are of Tvam-Tat-Asi, forsooth.

27. முப்பாழ்

THREE SPACES

காரிய மேழ்கண் டறுமாயப் பாழ்விடக்
காரண மேழ்கண் டறும்போதப் பாழ்விடக்
காரிய காரண வாதனை கண்டறுஞ்
சீருப சாந்தமுப் பாழ்விடத் தீருமே. 2495

Beyond Three Spaces—Maya, Bodha and Upasanta

Experiencing the seven Caused States
The Maya Space is left behind;
Experiencing the seven Causal States
The Bodha Space is left behind;
Experiencing and sundering the Cause-Caused States (above)
The Upasanta Space is left behind;
Then alone is End Finale.

மாயப்பாழ் சீவன் வியோமப்பாழ் மன்பரன்
சேயமுப் பாழெனச் சிவசத்தி யிற்சீவன்
ஆய வியாப்த மெனுமுப்பா ழாம்அந்தத்
தூய சொரூபத்திற் சொல்முடி வாகுமே. 2496

Tat-Tvam-Asi End of Space Three

The Maya Space is of Jiva;
The Bodha (Vyoma) Space is of Para;
The Upasanta Space (Vyapta) is
Where Jiva one with Siva-Sakti is;
All three Spaces are of Pure Manifestations (Svarupa)
—The End of Tvam-Tat-Asi that is Tat-Tvam-Asi.

எதிரற நாளும் எருதுவந் தேறும்
பதியெனும் நந்தி பதமது கூடக்
கதியெனப் பாழைக் கடந்தந்தக் கற்பனை
உதறிய பாழில் ஒடுங்குகின் றேனே. 2497

Lord is in the Space Beyond the Three Spaces

Of Himself, daily,
Nandi that rides the bull
Blesses you,
With impediment none;
And when I reach His Feet,

I cross the Space,
And in that Space
That imagination transcends
I merge.

துரியம் அடங்கிய சொல்லறும் பாழை
அரிய பரம்பரம் என்பர்கள் ஆதர்
அரிய பரம்பரம் என்றே துதிக்கும்
அருநிலம் என்பதை யாரறி வாரே. 2498

Paraparam is a Wondrous Land

That Space where Turiyas merge
Defies description
They call it Paramparam;
Thus they say who know not;
As Paramparam they worship it;
Who knows, what wondrous Land it is!

ஆறாறு நீங்க நமவாதி யகன்றிட்டு
வேறாகியபரை யாவென்று மெய்ப்பரன்
ஈறான வாசியிற் கூட்டு மதுவன்றோ
தேறாச் சிவாய நமவெனத் தேறிலே. 2499

Import of Si-Va-Ya-Na-Ma

The Tattvas six times six left,
And Malas, Anava and Maya devoid,
Denoted by letters "Na" and "Ma"—
Parai to Jiva ("Ya") Her Grace granting,
Into Paran ("Va" Sakti and "Si" Siva) makes it merge,
That indeed is "Si Va Ya Na Ma" (the Five-letter mantra).

உள்ளம் உருவென்றும் உருவம் உளமென்றும்
உள்ள பரிசறிந் தோரு மவர்கட்குப்
பள்ளமும் இல்லை .திடரில்லை பாழில்லை
உள்ளமும் இல்லை உருவில்லை தானே. 2500

Beyond Thought and Form is Truth

For them who realized Truth
That Thought is Form and Form is Thought,
For them is no descent, no ascent, no Void.
Neither Thought, nor Form.

28. காரிய காரணவுபாதி
CAUSED-CAUSAL EXPERIENCES

செற்றிடுஞ் சீவ வுபாதித் திறனேழும்
பற்றும் பரோபாதி ஏழும் பகருரை
உற்றிடுங் காரிய காரணத் தோடற
அற்றிட வச்சிவ மாகும் அணுவனே. 2501

Transcend All Experiences, Caused and Causal

When Caused Experiences Seven of Jiva
And Causal Experiences Seven of Para Leave,
Cause and Caused Difference vanish,
Then Jiva becomes Siva for sure.

ஆறாறு காரியோ பாதி யகன்றிட்டு
வேறாய் நனவு மிகுத்த கனாநனா
ஆறா றகன்ற சுழுத்தி யதில்எய்தாப்
பேறா நிலத்துயிர் தொம்பதம் பேசிலே. 2502

Final Goal is in Sushupti—Beyond Experiences

Without Caused Experiences six times six leaving,
Without Jagrat, Svapna and other states of Turiya
Jagrat Waking leaving,
Without entering that Sushupti State
That is beyond Tattvas six times six,
What avails it
If of Tvam Pada Jiva speaks?
He on earth will never, never,
The Final Goal reach.

அகாரம் உயிரே உகாரம் பரமே
மகாரஞ் சிவமாய் வருமுப் பதத்துச்
சிகாரஞ் சிவமே வகாரம் பரமே
அகாரம் உயிரென் றறையலு ம்ாமே. 2503

Interpretation of A-U-M (Aum) and Si-Va-Ya

Letter A is Jiva; U is Para; M is Siva;
In the three States of Mukti;
Si is Siva, Va is Para; Ya is Jiva
Thus the Mantras "Aum" and "Sivaya" are as one interpreted.

உயிர்க்குயி ராகி யொழிவற் றழிவற்
றயிர்ப்பறு காரணோ பாதி விதிரேகத்
துயிர்ப்புறும் ஈசன் உபமிதத் தாலன்றி
வியர்ப்புறும் ஆணவம் வீடல்செய் யாவே. 2504

Anava (I-ness) leaves only By Grace

As Life of life,
Interminable and imperishable
Beyond travails of Causal Experiences
And Caused Experience opposite,
Is Isa (Siva) vibrant;
Without His Grace abounding,
Anava that makes Jiva tremble
Never, never, leaves.

காரியம் ஏழிற் கலக்கும் கடும்பசு
காரணம் ஏழிற் கலக்கும் பரசிவன்
காரிய காரணங் கற்பனை சொற்பதப்
பாரறும் பாழில் பராபரத் தானே. 2505

Paraparan is in Space Beyond Experiences

Immanent is Jiva in Caused Experiences Seven,
Immanent is Parasiva in Causal Experiences Seven;
In the Void that defies Cause-Caused description,
Beyond Thought and Word.
Is Paraparan.

29. உபசாந்தம்
UPASANTAM

முத்திக்கு வித்து முதல்வன்தன் ஞானமே
பத்திக்கு வித்துப் பணிந்துற்றுப் பற்றலே
சித்திக்கு வித்துச் சிவபரந் தானாதல்
சத்திக்கு வித்துத் தனதுப சாந்தமே. 2506

Seeds Four

Seed of Mukti is Knowledge of Primal One;
Seed of Bhakti is intense adoration meek;
Seed of Siddhi is Self, Siva-Para Becoming;
Seed of Sakti is State of Upasanta.

காரியம் ஏழுங் கரந்திடு மாயையுள்
காரணம் ஏழுங் கரக்குங் கடுவெளி
காரிய காரண வாதனைப் பற்றறப்
பாரண வும்முப சாந்தப் பரிசிதே. 2507

When Upasanta is

The Seven Caused Experiences lie latent in Maya;
The Seven Causal Experiences lie latent in Space,
When Cause-Caused experiences disappear,
Then is pervasive Upasanta.

அன்ன துரியமே யாத்துமே சுத்தியும்
முன்னிய சாக்கிரா தீதத் துறுபுரி
மன்னு பரங்காட்சி யாவ துடனுற்றுத்
தன்னின் வியாத்தி தனின்உப சாந்தமே. 2508

Upasanta in Siva Turiya

In (Jagrat) Turiya is Jiva's purification of Self (Atma Suddhi)
In Turiya of the Jagratatita (Para Turiya)
Is Vision of Param;
That extending into Siva Turiya
Is Upasanta pervasive.

ஆறா றமைந்தாண வத்தையுள் நீக்குதற்
பேறான தன்னை யறிதற்பின் றீர்சுத்தி
கூறாத சாக்கிரா தீதங் குருபரன்
பேறாம் வியாத்தம் பிறழுப சாந்தமே. 2509

Beyond Jiva Turiya and Para Turiya is Upasanta

Removing Anava within,
Entwined with Tattvas six times six,
And realizing Self-knowledge,
—These acts of purification
To Jagrat-Turiya (Jiva Turiya) State belongs;
The Grace of Guru Param dawns
In the Jagratatita Turiya (Para Turiya)
That defies speech;
When that is crossed and Siva Turiya is reached,
Then is Upasanta pervasive.

வாய்ந்த வுபசாந்த வாதனை யுள்ளப்போய்
ஏய்ந்த சிவமாத லின்சிவா னந்தத்துத்
தோய்ந்தறல் மோனச் சுகானுபவத் தோடே
ஆய்ந்ததில் தீர்க்கை யானதீ ரைந்துமே. 2510

Upasanta State—The Tenth State

Entering into Upasanta experience,
Jiva becomes Siva;
There immersed in Siva-Bliss
Jiva into Siva merges;
Enjoying that Bliss experience
It abids constant there;
That Experience engrosses
All the ten of Jiva
(From Jagrat Upwards to Siva Turiya).

பரையின் பரவ பரத்துடன் ஏகமாய்த்
திரையினின் றாகிய தெண்புனல் போலவுற்
றுரையுணர்ந் தாரமு தொக்க வுணர்ந்துளோன்
கரைகண் டானுரை யற்ற கணக்கிலே. 2511

Shore Beyond

Merged in One with Sakti and Siva,
As cool waters into wavy sea
And realizing Truth of Holy Word,
That is ambrosial sweet
Jiva reaches the Shore Beyond
That indeed defies speech.

30. புறங்கூறாமை
REFRAINING FROM VAIN SPEECH

பிறையுட் கிடந்த முயலை ஏறிவான்
அறைமணி வாட்கொண் டவர்தமைப் போலக்
கறைமணி கண்டனைக் காண்குற மாட்டார்
நிறையறி வோமென்பர் நெஞ்சிலர் தாமே. 2512

You Can See Lord Only if You Hold Him in Your Heart

"I shall smite the hare in the moon"
Thus saying
A man unsheaths his jewelled sword;
Like him are they
Who say,
"We the blue-throated Lord will see,
We know the Way;"
Such shall never see,
As in their hearts they hold Him not.

கருந்தாட் கருடன் விசும்பூ டிறப்பக்
கருந்தாட் கயத்திற் கரும்பாம்பு நீங்கப்
பெருந்தன்மை பேசுதி நீயொழி நெஞ்சே
அருந்தா அலைகட லாறுசென் றாலே. *2513*

Lord is Remote and Near

The black-footed Garuda bird
Across the sky passes;
The black-hued serpent in deep well dies;
Stop bragging of your greatness, O heart!
Be like the river
That into the wavy ocean merges.

கருதலர் மாளக் கருவாயில் நின்ற
பொருதலைச் செய்வது புல்லறி வாண்மை
மருவலர் செய்கின்ற மாதவம் ஒத்தால்
தருவலர் கேட்ட தனியும்ப ராமே. *2514*

Perform Tapas

If you seek your enemies (Malas) to perish,
Why fight at the Gate of Birth?
Silly heroism indeed!
If suitable the Tapas of holy ones are,
He, who all gifts gives,
Will with Celestial's seat them.

பிணங்கவும் வேண்டாம் பெருநில முற்றும்
இணங்கியெம் மீசனே யீசனென் றுன்னிற்
கணம்பதி னெட்டுங் கழலடி காண
வணங்கெழு நாடியங் கன்புற லாமே. *2515*

Seek and Be in Bliss

Be not in contentions lost;
Our Lord pervades worlds all
He is Siva—
Thus you hold;
Then the very Heavenly Hosts Eighteen*
Will worship at your feet;
Seek Him, seek Him;
You shall in bliss be.

---

* The eighteen heavenly hosts consist of super-normal beings. They are: Devas (Amaras), Siddhars, Asuras, Daityas, Garudas, Kinnaras, Niruthas, Kimpurushas, Gandharvas, Yakshas, Vinjayas, Bhutas, Pisasas, Antaras Munivas, Uragas, Akasavasis, Bhoga Bhumidars.

என்னிலும் என்னுயி ராய இறைவனைப்
பொன்னிலு மாமணி யாய புனிதனை
மின்னிய வெவ்வுயி ராய விகிர்தனை
உன்னிலும் உன்னும் உறுவகை யாலே. *2516*

Contemplate on Him

The Lord who is dearer than dearest life in me,
The Pure One who is brighter than purest gold
The Great One, in all life, unvarying glows,
On Him contemplate, in ways appropriate.

நின்றும் இருந்துங் கிடந்தும் நிமலனை
ஒன்றும் பொருள்கள் உரைப்பவ ராகிலும்
வென்றைம் புலனும் விரைந்து பிணக்கறுத்
தொன்றா யுணரும் ஒருவனு மாமே. *2517*

Adore Him in All Ways

Standing, sitting and prostrating
Well may you, the Pure One adore;
Though learned you be,
Do conquer your Senses Five,
And quick sunder contending Pasas;
Thus seek Him and know Him,
He in you one will be.

நுண்ணறி வாயுல காயுல கேழுக்கும்
எண்ணறி வாய் நின்ற எந்தை பிரான்தன்னைப்
பண்ணறி வாளனைப் பாவித்த மாந்தரை
விண்ணறி வாளர் விரும்புகின் றாரே. *2518*

He is Pervasive Knowledge

My Father, My Lord
As subtle Knowledge He stood;
As pervasive Knowledge, engrossing
The Seven Worlds, too, He stood;
He knows melodies all;
Sing His praise,
The Celestials will you in endearment hold.

விண்ணவ ராலும் அறிவறி யான்றன்னைக்
கண்ணற வுள்ளே கருதிடிற் காலையில்
எண்ணுற வாகமுப் போது மியற்றிநீ
பண்ணிடில் தன்மை பராபர னாமே. *2519*

Think of Him Continuously

He whom even Celestials know not,
Think of Him, in the waking dawn,
Continuously think of Him morn, noon and eventide
If thus you persevere,
You shall become the very Paraparam.

ஒன்றா யுலகுடன் ஏழும் பரந்தவன்
பின்றா னருள்செய்த பேரரு ளாளவன்
கன்றா மனத்தார்தங் கல்வியுள் நல்லவன்
பொன்றாத போது புனைபுக ழானே. 2520

He is of Infinite Grace

As One He pervades the seven worlds all,
He, of yore, His Grace on Jiva conferred;
He, Lord of Grace Infinite;
Supreme is He in Jnana
Of the holy ones of constant heart;
He who is festooned in flower unfading,
He, the Famed One.

போற்றியென் றேன்எந்தை பொன்னான சேவடி
ஏற்றியே தென்றும் எறிமணி தானகக்
காற்றின் விளக்கது காய மயக்குறு
மாற்றலுங் கேட்டது மன்றுகண் டேனே. 2521

Witness Dance of Siva

"Hail, my Father! Hail His golden Feet!"
Thus I praised;
And as I praised,
The radiant lamp
Of life within sparkled;
And then I heard the bewitching sound,
That my body in rapture immersed;
And lo! there was His Dance!

நேடிக்கொண் டென்னுள்ளே நேர்தரு நந்தியை
ஊடுபுக் காரும் உணர்ந்தறி வாரில்லை
கூடுபுக் கேறலுற் றேனவன் கோலங்கண்
மூடிக்கண் டேனுல கேழுங்கண் டேனே. 2522

God Vision in Yoga Way

I sought my Nandi within
And there I met Him;
They seek Him not within their hearts.
And so know Him not;
In yogic way I entered within
And ascended Adharas;
And eyes closed in trance
I saw His From Divine;
And the Seven Worlds too.

ஆன புகழும் அமைந்ததோர் ஞானமுந்
தேனு மிருக்குஞ் சிறுவரை யொன்றுகண்
டூனமொன் றின்றி யுணர்வுசெய் வார்கட்கு
வானகஞ் செய்யு மறவனு மாமே. 2523

Vision of Lord Within

I behold the Little Mount within
In it was Divine Glory,
Abiding Jnana and nectar sweet
For them that realize Him in (love) unfaltering,
He creates the very Heaven within;
He, the Compassionate One.

மாமதி யாமதி யாய்நின்ற மாதவர்
தூய்மதி யாகுஞ் சுடர்பர மானந்தந்
தாமதி யாகச் சகமுணச் சாந்திபுக்
காமல மற்றார் அமைவுபெற் றாரே. 2524

State of Quiescence

Of Wisdom infinite,
The Tapasvins great in wisdom stood,
Pure as moon's rays they beam;
In Transcendental bliss they are;
Themselves Divine Jnana becoming,
They encompassed in Consciousness
The Universe Cosmic;
And entering Upasanta
They freed themselves of Malas,
And State of Quiescence reached.

பதமுத்தி மூன்றும் பழுதென்று கைவிட்
டிதமுற்ற பாச இருளைத் துரந்து
மதமற் றெனதியான் மாற்றிவிட் டாங்கே
திதமுற் றவர்கள் சிவசித்தர் தாமே. 2525

Siva Siddha State

They abandoned Muktis three as vain;
They dispelled enticing darkness of Pasa,
They rid themselves of Anava,
They transcended "I" and "mine" consciousness,
They in constancy remained,
They, verily, are Siva Siddhas.

சித்தர் சிவத்தைக் கண்டவர் சீருடன்
சுத்தாசுத் தத்துடன் தோய்ந்துந்தோ யாதவர்
முத்தரம் முத்திக்கு மூலத்தர் மூலத்துச்
சத்தர் சதாசிவத் தன்மையர் தாமே. 2526

Siddhas Are Like Sadasiva Himself

Siddhas are those who Siva saw;
Soaked in Suddha-Asuddha,
Yet soaked are not;
Muktas are they,
And source of Mukti, too, are they;
Possessed are they of Muladhara prowess
Alike are they unto Sadasiva.

31. எட்டிதழ்க் கமல முக்குண அவத்தை

EXPERIENCE IN THE EIGHT-PETALLED SPHERE

உதிக்கின்ற இந்திரன் அங்கி யமனுந்
துதிக்கும் நிருதி வருணன்நல் வாயு
மதிக்குங் குபேரன் வடதிசை யீசன்
நிதித்தெண் டிசையு நிறைந்துநின் றாரே. 2527

Gods in the Eight Cardinal Points of Earth

Indra, Agni, Yama and Nrudi
Varuna, Vayu, Kubera, and Isanana
They (gods) in order according
Filled the cardinal directions eight.

* The eight gods of the cardinal points of earth are enumerated to indicate that they are all seated within the eight-petalled lotus in the cranium—the microcosm in the macrocosm.

In most of the books dealing with kundalini yoga, the flower in sahasrara is usually pictured as a thousand-petalled lotus. Hence the name, sahasrara (thousand petall). Tirumular however, visions it as an eight-petalled lotus. The term, sahasrara, however, is used in the translation for convenience of understanding only. As it is not a centre (chakra or adhara), Tirumular only refers to the experiences in the eight-petalled lotus of the cranium. The region usually referred to as sahasrara is indicated by Tirumular as Mount Meru (in the cranium).

For a different presentation of the petals in the adharas and for the number of adharas, vide "The Serpent Power by Sir John Woodroffe.

1. Indra—god of the Eastern quarter.
2. Agni—god of the South Eastern quarter.
3. Yama—god of the Southern quarter.
4. Nruti—god of the South Western quarter.
5. Varuna—god of the Western quarter.
6. Vayu—god of North Western quarter.
7. Kubera—god of the Northern quarter.
8. Isanana—god of the North Eastern quarter.

ஒருங்கிய பூவுமோ ரெட்டித ழாகும்
மருங்கிய மாயா புரியத னுள்ளே
சுருங்கிய தண்டின் சுழுனையி னூடே
ஒருங்கிய சோதியை ஓர்ந்தெழும் உய்ந்தே. 2528

The Eight Petalled Lotus in Sahasrara

In the Maya-Land of body
Is the Flower of petals eight (pointing to directions eight)
Through the lean stalk of Sushumna,
Contemplate on its radiance,
And ascend upward;
Redeemed are you then.

மொட்டலர் தாமரை மூன்றுள மூன்றினும்
விட்டலர் கின்றனன் சோதி விரிசுடர்
எட்டல ருள்ளே இரண்டலர் உள்ளுறிற்
பட்டலர் கின்றதோர் பண்டங் கனாவே. 2529

How the Eight Petalled Lotus Opens

Three the lotus buds there;
Into the three He sends His rays
That Light spreading,
The eight-petalled bloom within opens;
Into them
If the rays of Petals Two (Ajna) penetrates,
This body, into a (heavenly) dream blossoms.

ஆறே யருவி யகங்குளம் ஒன்றுண்டு
நூறே சிவகதி நுண்ணிது வண்ணமுங்
கூறே குவிமுலைக் கொண்பனை யாளொடும்
வேறே யிருக்கும் விழுப்பொருள் தானே. 2530

Siva-Sakti in Eight-Petalled Lotus

The six streams (of Adharas)
Into one Pond flow;
Thus in Way subtle
Into Siva-State penetrate;
There indeed is the Precious Truth,
Himself with Sakti stands,
—She of bouncing breasts and tender vine form.

திகையெட்டுந் தேரெட்டுந் தேவதை யெட்டும்
வகையெட்டு மாய்நின்ற ஆதிப் பிரானை
வகையெட்டு நான்குமற் றாங்கே நிறைந்து
முகையெட்டும் உள்நின் றுதிக்கின்ற வாறே. 2531

He Blooms Within Petals Eight

The Primal One stood,
As directions eight,
Mountains eight,
Gods eight
And Forms eight;
Reach Him,
Who fills within
From eight to four petalled centre;
He Who blooms within petals eight.

ஏழுஞ் சகளம் இயம்புங் கடந்தெட்டில்
வாழும் பரமென் றதுகடந் தொன்பதில்
ஊழி பராபரம் ஓங்கிய பத்தினில்
தாழ்வது வான தனித்தன்மை தானே. 2532

Centres Beyond Seventh are Formless States

The Centres Seven are of Form (Svarupa) possessed;
Transcend them;
And beyond in Eighth is Param;

In Ninth is Paraparam, that is Void;
The exalted Tenth is State of Oneness
Where Anava is finally shed.

பல்லூழி பண்பன் பகலோன் இறையவன்
நல்லூழி ஐந்தினுள் ளேநின்ற வூழிகள்
செல்லூழி யண்டத்துச் சென்றவவ் வூழியுள்
அவ்வூழி யுச்சியு ளொன்றிற் பகவனே. 2533

God is Timeless Eternity

He lasts through aeons countless;
He is the Sun; He is the Lord;
Within the five Major Aeons
Were many aeons minor
The universe through several aeons passed;
In the aeon above aeons countless,
Was (God) Bhagavan, unique.

புரியும் உலகினிற் பூண்டவெட் டானை
திரியுங் களிற்றொடு தேவர் குழாமும்
எரியு மழையும் இயங்கும் வெளியும்
பரியுமா காசத்திற் பற்றது தானே. 2534

Seek Him Wherever He is

He is in this world
Yet if He is beyond reach,
Seek Him in Heaven,
Where the elephants roam
And the Celestials wander,
Where fire, rain and wind abide;
In that Space seek Him.

ஊறு மருவி யுயர்வரை யுச்சிமேல்
ஆறின்றிப் பாயும் அருங்குளம் ஒன்றுண்டு
சேறின்றிப் பூத்த செழுங்கொடித் தாமரைப்
பூவின்றிச் சூடான் புரிசடை யோனே. 2535

The Eight-Petalled Bloom is Dear to Siva

There on the lofty top of Mount (Meru) within
Is a pond no stream feeds;
And there is a lotus bloom
From no soil mud springs;
Without that bloom,
He decks not Himself
He of matted locks.

ஒன்றும் இரண்டும் ஒருங்கிய காலத்து
நின்றும் இருந்தும் நிலம்பல பேசினும்
வென்று மிருந்து விகிர்தனை நாடுவர்
சென்றும் இருந்துந் திருவடை யோரே. 2536

Holy Jivas Ever Think of God

When the One and Two (Siva and Jiva) intermingle,
Standing and sitting
Or in worldly talk indulging,
The holy Jivas their senses conquer
And seek Lord;
Remaining or leaving
They blessed ever are.

32. ஒன்பான் அவத்தை-ஒன்பான் அபிமானி
NINE AVASTAS AND NINE ASPIRANTS

தொற்பத விசுவன் றைசதன் பிராஞ்ஞன்
நற்பத விராட்டன்பொன் கர்ப்பனவ் யாகிர்தன்
பிற்பதஞ் சொலிதையன் பிரசா பத்தியன்
பொற்புவி சாந்தன் பொருதபி மானியே. 2537

Souls in the Three Mukti States

Visvan, Dhaisathan and Prajnan
They are in Tvampada State;
Virattan, Hiranya Garbhan, Avyakritan
They are in Tat-Pada State;
Idayan, Prjapathyan and Santan of Golden World
They are in Asi-Pada State
Yet are they all but Abhimanis,
Souls that are aspirants still.

நவமா மவத்தை நனவாதி பற்றிற்
பவமா மலங்குணம் பற்றற்றுப் பற்றாத்
தவமான சத்திய ஞானப் பொதுவிற்
றுவமார் துரியஞ் சொரூபம தாமே. 2538

Beyond Ninth State

As nine states beginning with Jagrat are experienced,
Attachment to Malas and Gunas,
That emanate birth, vanish;
In Transcendental Turiya State
Then Void (Satya-Jnana-Podu) succeeds,
Truth and Jnana filled
Where Jiva and Siva one are;
In Turiyas rest
Jiva and Siva are two,
That now in Void is one Manifestness (Svarupa).

சிவமான சிந்தையிற் சீவன் சிதைய
பவமான மும்மலம் பாறிப் புறிய
நவமான அந்தத்தின் நற்சிவ போதந்
தவமா மவ்வையாகித் தானல்ல வாகுமே. 2539

Dawn of Sivajnana

As in the thought of Siva
Jiva merges,
The Malas Three,
That to birth gives rise,
Flee away;
At the end of avastas nine

Is Siva-bodha (Awareness or Jnana);
Jiva attains that
And Himself no more is.

முன்சொன்ன வொன்பானின் முன்னுறு தத்துவந்
தன்சொல்லில்எண்ணத்தகாவொன்பான்வேறுள
பின்சொல்ல லாகுமிவ் வீரொன்பான் பேர்த்திட்டுத்
தன்செய்த வாண்டவன் றான்சிறந் தானே. 2540

Nine Avasta Cluster Beyond

Beyond the nine states aforesaid
Are nine that defy thought;
Of these shall be said in detail below;
Great indeed is the Lord
Who these twice-nine States made.

உகந்தன ஒன்பதும் ஐந்தும் உலகம்
பகர்ந்த பிரானென்னும் பண்பினை நாடி
அகந்தெம் பிரானென்பன் அல்லும் பகலு
மிகந்தன வல்வினை யோடறுத் தானே. 2541

Lord Spoke of Nine States

The nine states from the five (states of Jiva) evolved
Of them Lord spoke
And world rejoiced;
"My Lord, My Lord"—
Thus I prayed day and night;
And He severed my fetters strong.

நலம்பல காலந் தொகுத்தன நீளங்
குலம்பல வண்ணங் குறிப்பொடுங் கூடும்
பலம்பல பன்னிரு கால நினையும்
நிலம்பல வாறின னீர்மையன் றானே. 2542

Many Paths to God

Many the paths they laid
In Time's Corridor long;
Many the sects
That sought Him to reach;
Think of Him constant, day and night;
He diverse stood in lands many.

ஆதி பராபர மாகும் பராபரை
சோதி பரமுயிர் சொல்லுநற் றத்துவம்
ஓதுங் கலைமாயே யோரிரண் டோர்முத்தி
நீதியாம் பேதமொன் பானுடன் ஆதியே. 2543

Nine Super Tattva Cluster

The Primal Paraparam, Paraparai
Param the Light, Jiva and Tattvas,
The Kala, the Mayas Two and Mukti
These are categories nine
To the Primal One belong.

தேறாத சிந்தை தெளியத் தெளிவித்து
வேறா நரக சுவர்க்கமும் மேதினி
ஆறாப் பிறப்பும் உயிர்க்கரு ளால்வைத்தான்
வேறாத் தெளியார் வினையுயிர் பெற்றதே. 2544

Grace Abounding

My inconstant thoughts
He constant made,
Clear vision gave;
He created hell and heaven
And endless births too
In Grace Abounding;
Those who these perceive not
Are in Karma's wheel forever caught.

ஒன்பான் அவத்தையுள் ஒன்பான் அபிமானி
நன்பாற் பயிலு நவதத் துவமாதி
ஒன்பானில் நிற்பதோர் முத்துரி யத்துறச்
செம்பாற் சிவமாதல் சித்தாந்த சித்தியே. 2545

Goal of Siddhanta Philosophy

In the nine states of experience
Jiva as aspirant (abhimani) stands;
The nine categories afterward stated
That to the Primal Lord belong;
When Jiva that stands in states nine
Reaches the Turiya States Three,
Then shall he Siva become;
This the goal of Siddhanta (Philosophy).

33. சுத்தாசுத்தம்

SUDDHA-ASUDDHAM

நாசி நுனியினின் நான்குமூ விரலிடை
ஈசன் இருப்பிடம் யாரும் அறிகிலர்
பேசி யிருக்கும் பெருமறை யம்மறை
கூசி யிருக்குங் குணமது வாமே. 2546

Mystery of Lord's Abode

At the tip of nose (Ajna Centre)
Is the breath, twelve finger-breadth long,
That Lord's abode is;
None knows this;
The Vedas that in expansiveness truths expound,
Of this was hesitant to speak;
Such indeed is Lord's greatness.

கருமங்கள் ஒன்று கருதுங் கருமத்
துரிமையுங் கன்மமும் முன்னும் பிறவிக்
கருவினை யாவது கண்டகன் றன்பின்
புரிவன கன்மக் கயத்துட் புகுமே. 2547

Away From Karmas

The Karmas,

The thoughts rights and deeds of Karmas
Are alike the seeds of births to be;
Seeing that,
Away from them;
Will what you do ever after
Reach the Karma Pond?

மாயை மறைக்க மறைந்த மறைப்பொருள்
மாயை மறைய வெளிப்படும் அப்பொருள்
மாயை மறைய மறையவல் லார்கட்குக்
காயமும் இல்லை கருத்தில்லை தானே. 2548

Make Maya Vanish

When Maya veils Jiva,
The Truth of Vedas remains hidden;
When Maya leaves,
The Truth of Himself reveals;
Those who can make Maya vanish
Merge in God;
No more is body; no more is mind.

மோழை யடைந்து முழைதிறந் துள்புக்குக்
கோழை யடைகின்ற தண்ணற் குறிப்பினில்
ஆழ அடைந்தங் கனலிற் புறஞ்செய்து
தாழ அடைப்பது தன்வலி யாமே. 2549

Kechari Mudra in Kundalini Yoga

Coursing the Prana Stream into the Eye-brow Centre
And opening the uvula cavity
Where phlegm gathers,
Stilling the breath there
In the way Yoga-Guru taught,
And warming it in the Fire (Kundalini) within
And restraining it to a measure low
Is to attain divine strength indeed.

காயக் குழப்பனைக் காயநன் னாடனைக்
காயத்தி னுள்ளே கமழ்கின்ற நந்தியைத்
தேயத்து ளேயெங்குந் தேடிந் திரிவர்கள்
காயத்துள் நின்ற கருத்தறி யாரே. 2550

Lord is Within; Seek Him not Elsewhere

He who is in the Body-Complex
He who rules the Body-Land,
He who within the body beams
He, the Nandi,
Him they seek in lands all;
They know not,
He within the body stands.

ஆசூசம் ஆசூசம் என்பார் அறிவிலார்
ஆசூச மாமிடம் ஆரும் அறிகிலார்
ஆசூச மாமிடம் ஆரும் அறிந்தபின்
ஆசூச மானிடம் ஆசூச மாமே. 2551

Mystery of Muladhara

"Unclean, unclean," the ignorant say
They know not the place "unclean" is,
When they know the (Yogic) mysteries
Of that place "unclean"
Then shall they find,
The human birth itself is unclean.

They who know the yogic mysteries do not feel that human birth is unclean.

ஆசூச மில்லை அருநிய மத்தருக்
காசூச மில்லை அரனைஅர்ச் சிப்பவர்க்
காசூச மில்லையாம் அங்கி வளர்ப்போர்க்
காசூச மில்லை அருமறை ஞானிக்கே. 2552

Muladhara is not Unclean

Uncleanness none is for those
Who ritual discipline observe;
Uncleanness none is for those
Who Hara worship;
Uncleanness none is for those
Who the sacred Fire tend;
Uncleanness none is for those.
Who in Vedic Jnana versed are.

வழிபட்டு நின்று வணங்கு மவர்க்குச்
சுழிபட்டு நின்றதோர் தூய்மை தொடங்குங்
குழிபட்டு நின்றவர் கூடார் குறிகள்
கழிபட் டவர்க்கன்றிக் காணவொண் ணாதே. 2553

When Purity Real Begins

For them that in Yogic Way stand,
Purity in Cranium top begins;
They who are sunk in pit of lust
Will Purity's goal reach not;
Only those who have sent Muladhara Fire
Up into Central Nadi of Sushumna
Will see Purity Real;
Others cannot.

தூய்மணி தூயனல் தூய ஒளிவிடுந்
தூய்மணி தூயனல் தூரறி வாரில்லை
தூய்மணி தூயனல் தூரறி வார்கட்குத்
தூய்மணி தூயனல் தூயவு மாமே. 2554

Lord is Real Pure

He is crystal pure, He is fire pure,
He emanates rays of Purity;
Where His source is, they know not,
They who know the Source,
Themselves,
Crystal pure and fire pure become.

தூயது வாளா வைத்தது தூநெறி
தூயது வாளா நாதன் திருநாமந்
தூயது வாளா அட்டமா சித்தியுந்
தூயது வாளாத் தூயடிச் சொல்லே. 2555

Purity in Silence

Purity in Silence is the Way of Purity
Purity in Silence is Lord's name;
Purity in Silence are Siddhis eight;
Purity in Silence are the Holy Feet.

பொருளது வாய்நின்ற புண்ணியன் எந்தை
அருளது போற்றும் அடியவ ரன்றிச்
சுருளது வாய்நின்ற துன்பச் சுழியின்
மருளது வாச்சிந்தை மயங்குகின் றாரே. 2556

Adore Lord and Receive Grace

The Quintessence of Truth is my Holy Father
Only they who adore Him
Are in His Grace accepted;
The rest,
Caught in whirl of misery,
In dark stupor lie.

வினையா மசத்து விளைவ துணரார்
வினைஞானந் தன்னில் வீடலுந் தேரார்
வினைவிட வீடென்னும் வேதமும் ஓதார்
வினையாளர் மிக்க விளைவறி யாரே. 2557

Renounce Karma and Be Liberated

They know not evil fruits
Karma brings,
They choose not to find Jnana
For liberation from Karma;
"Renounce Karma and be liberated"
—This Vedic teaching they know not;
They who wallow in Karma
Will never the Rich Harvest reap.

34. முத்திநிந்தை

SCORN OF MUKTI

பரகதி யுண்டென இல்லையென் போர்கள்
நரகதி செல்வது ஞாலம் அறியும்
இரகதி செய்திடு வார்கடை தோறுந்
துரகதி யுண்ணத் தொடங்குவர் தாமே. 2558

Deny Not God

Those who say,
"There is no Para State to be"
Are for hell state destined;
All world knows this;
They shall begging go from door to door;
With horse's speed,
In search of food they run.

கூடகில் லார்குரு வைத்த குறிகண்டு
நாடகில் லார்நயம் பேசித் திரிவர்கள்
பாடகில் லாரவன் செய்த பரிசறிந்
தாடவல் லாரவர் பேறெது வாமே. 2559

Follow Guru

They follow not the Way
Guru taught;
They seek not the Holy One;
Indulging in frivolous talk, they wander;
They sing not His holy deeds;
They who thus dance about
What will their desert be?

புறப்பட்டுப் போகும் புகுதுமென் னெஞ்சில்
திறப்பட்ட சிந்தையைத் தெய்வமென் றெண்ணி
அறப்பட்ட மற்றப் பதியென் றழைத்தேன்
இறப்பற்றி னேன்இங் கிதென்னென்கின் றானே. 2560

God Responds to Devotion

Into my thoughts He comes and goes:
In the constancy of my thoughts
I held Him as God;
"You my Holy Lord!"
Thus I besought Him;
And in my heart I held Him close;
"What is this here?" He asks.

திடரிடை நில்லாத நீர்போல ஆங்கே
உடலிடை நில்லா உறுபொருள் காட்டிக்
கடலிடை நில்லாக் கலஞ்சேரு மாபோல்
அடலெரி வண்ணனும் அங்குநின் றானே. 2561

Lord is the Haven for Soul's Ship

As water from upland
Downward flows,
Truth in body remains not;
That Truth He in me showed;
As the ship in the seas
That seeks the shores,
To my trouble-tossed soul
The Fire-Hued Lord
As sure goal stood.

தாமரை நூல்போல் தடுப்பார் பரத்தொடும்
போம்வழி வேண்டிப் புறமே யுழிதர்வர்
காண்வழி காட்டக்கண் காணாக் கலதிகள்
தீநெறி செல்வான் திரிகின்ற வாறே. 2562

They Seek Him Not—The Witless Ones

Continuous as thread within lotus stalk
Is Param within;
Yet they seek Him not there;
But wander about everywhere;
Though the Way to reach Him shown
They see it not;

Fools are they;
They roam about,
Only evil destiny action to reach.

மூடுதல் இன்றி முடியும் மனிதர்கள்
கூடுவர் நந்தி யவனைக் குறித்துடன்
காடும் மலையுங் கழனி கடந்தோறும்
ஊடும் உருவினை யுன்னகி லாரே. 2563

They See Him Not

The light within unkindled
They, their lives, end;
These men gather in crowds
And seek Him not;
In fields, forests and hills
Nandi who is immanent in them,
They see not.

ஆவது தெற்கும் வடக்கும் அமரர்கள்
போவர் குடக்குங் குணக்குங் குறிவழி
நாவினின் மந்திர மென்று நடுவங்கி
வேவது செய்து விளங்கிடு வீரே. 2564

Seek God Within Through Kundalini Yoga

North and South, men wander about seeking Him
East and West, Celestials go about looking for Him,
But fix divine Mantra (Aum)
On to Muladhara,
And rouse (Kundalini) Fire, upward to stream;
There shall you as Radiant Light be.

மயக்குற நோக்கினும் மாதவஞ் செய்யார்
தமக்குறப் பேசின தாரணை கொள்ளார்
சினக்குறப் பேசின தீவினை யாளர்
தமக்குற வல்வினை தாங்கிநின் றாரே. 2565

Men of Evil Fate do not Practise Devotion

Even if men of Tapas great,
With gracious looks entreat
The men of Evil Fate
Do not holy Dharana practise
They indulge in angry speech always;
All, all, their intractable Karma,
Themselves have they to undergo.

35. இலக்கணாத் திரயம்
LAKSHANA TRAYAM

விட்ட விலக்கணைதான்போம் வியோமத்துத்
தொட்டு விடாத துபசாந்தத் தேதொகும்
விட்டு விடாதது மேவுஞ்சத் தாதியிற்
சுட்டு மிலக்கணா தீதஞ் சொரூபமே. 2566

Jiva State Beyond the Ninth Defies Expression

Jiva reaches the Void, Upasanta and Nadanta
They say,
That is but to speak in grammatical convention triple—
Lakshana Traya*;
When Jiva reaches Void,
Its state is of total renunciation of attributes all,
When Jiva reaches Upasanta
Its state is of renunciation and adherence yet
When Jiva reaches Nadanta
Its state is of renunciation and non-renunciation at once
The State of Jiva, in Finite Manifestness (Svarupa)
Transcends grammatical conventions all.

*Lakshana traya is a grammatical theory in Sanskrit which states that an expression in a certain context may lend itself to three interpretations of an object in three ways:

a) The use of the word in its secondary sense, its primary sense having been lost—Tamil, vitta-ilakkanai.
b) The use of the word in which the primary sense is retained along with its secondary sense—Tamil vidatha-ilakkanai.
c) The use of the word in which the primary sense is partly discarded and partly retained—Tamil, vittum vidatha-ilakkanai.

The theory of lakshana is important in all Indian philosophical systems in trying to discuss the nature of the Ultimate Reality, which is beyond expression. The Vedantins employ this widely in trying to explain expressions like tattvamasi, aham brahmasmi, etc.—vide "Indian Theories of Meaning," by Dr.K. Kunjunni Raja, pp.249-255

When jiva reaches the Space, the state that ensues is one of total effacement of all attributes. Upasanta is the state of non-attachment and attachment yet. Jiva reaching Nadanta is the state of renunciation and non-renunciation at once. Transcending the grammatical conventions of lakshanatrayam—that is the same jiva being in different places with different experiences—is the state of jiva in Final Self-Manifestness (Svarupa).

வில்லின் விசைநாணிற்கோத்திலக்கெய்தபின்
கொல்லுங் களிறைந்துங் கோலொடு சாய்ந்தன
வில்லு ளிருந்தெறி கூரும் ஒருவற்குக்
கல்கலன் என்னக் கதிரெதி ராமே. 2567

Reaching the Goal in One Shot

Jiva strung the bow
Took aim
And with one arrow
Five deadly elephants shot;
He who thus shot
Will behold the Radiant Light
Beaming like gems several in splendour set.

Jiva vanquished the five deadly elephants in one shot. He who has shot thus will see the radiant light beaming like gems in diverse colors.

The reference is to the yogic practice of coursing the kundalini energy through the sushumna and ascending the adharas up to the cranium, where God is visioned.

36. தத்துவமசி வாக்கியம்
TATTVAMASIVAKYAM

சீவ துரியத்துத் தொம்பதஞ் சீவனார்
தாவு பரதுரி யத்தினில் தற்பதம்
மேவு சிவதுரி யத்தசி மெய்ப்பத
மோவி விடுந்தத் துவமசி உண்மையே. *2568*

Tat-Tvam-Asi is Beyond the Three Muktis

In Jiva Turiya Jiva attains Tvam-Pada;
In Para Turiya beyond is Tat-Pada;
In Siva Turiya still beyond Asi-Pada true;
Further beyond is Truth that is Tat-Tvam-Asi.

ஆறா றகன்ற அணுத்தொம் பதஞ்சுத்தம்
ஈறான தற்பதம் எய்துப சாந்தத்துப்
பேறா கியசீவன் நீங்கிப்பிர சாதத்து
வீறான தொந்தத் தசிதத்வ மசியே. *2569*

Beyond Experiences in the Three Suddha States

Tvam-Pada transcends Tattvas six times six;
That is State Suddha;
Then is Tat-Pada;
That leads to Upasanta;
Then is Asi-Pada where Siva is;
Ultimate is the blessed State
Of Tvam-Tat-Asi that is Tat-Tvam-Asi.

ஆகிய வச்சோயந் தேவதத் தன்னிடத்
தாகிய விட்டு விடாத விலக்கணைத்
தாருப சாந்தமே தொந்தத் தசியென்ப
ஆகிய சீவன் பரன்சிவ னாமே. *2570*

Confluence of Three States Jiva, Para and Siva

The Jiva (Deva Datta) becomes So-Ham
And by the speech of grammatical convention triple
Is in Tvam-Tat-Asi
With attributes thus transferred
There Jiva is Jiva, Para and Siva,
All in one.

துவந்தத் தசியே தொந்தத் தசியும்
அவைமன்னா வந்து வயத்தேகமான
தவமுறு தத்துவ மசிவே தாந்த
சிவமா மதுஞ்சித் தாந்தவே தாந்தமே. *2571*

Tat-Tvam-Asi of Vedanta is the Same as Tvam-Tat-Asi of Siddhanta-Vedanta

Tvam-Tat-Asi is the same as Thvamtatasi
The one comes conjoined as the other
The holy concept of (You-being-I) Tat-Tvam-Asi
belongs to Vedanta;
The concept of I-Siva-becoming (Thvamtatasi) is
Siddhanta-Vedanta.

துரியம் அடங்கிய சொல்லறும் பாழை
அரிய பரமென்ப ராகாரி தன்றென்னார்
உரிய பரம்பர மாமொன் றுதிக்கும்
அருநிலம் என்பதை யாரறி வாரே. *2572*

Param-Param State Beyond Triple Turiya

The inexplicable Void that is at Turiya end
They call it Param, they who know not;
Nay, that is not so;
There is the Wondrous Land of Param-Param
That rises beyond (the Three Turiya States)
Who knows about that!

தொம்பதந் தற்பதஞ் சொல்லும் அசிபதம்
நம்பிய முத்துரி யத்துமே னாடவே
யும்பத மும்பத மாகும் உயிர்பரன்
செம்பொரு ளான சிவமென லாமே. *2573*

Beyond Jiva, Para and Siva States

Transcend beyond Tvam-Pada, Tat-Pada and Asi-Pada
And seek beyond the triple Turiyas
Then is the State-beyond-all-states
The (One) Truth beyond Jiva, Para and Siva.

வைத்த துரிய மதிற்சொரு பானந்தத்
துய்த்த பிரணவ மாமுப தேசத்தை
மெய்த்த விதயத்து விட்டிடு மெய்யுணர்
வைத்த படியே யடைந்துநின் றானே. *2574*

Supreme Awareness Beyond Siva Turiya State

At the end of Siva Turiya State
Is the Bliss of Manifestness (Svarupa)
There chant within your heart
The Mantra that is Pranava (Aum)
Then appears Siva the Awareness Supreme.

நனவாதி ஐந்தையும் நாதாதியில் வைத்துப்
பினமா மலத்தைப் பின்வைத்துப் பின்சுத்தத்
தனதாஞ் சிவகதி சத்தாதி சாந்தி
மனவா சகங்கெட்ட மன்னனை நாடே. *2575*

Beyond Suddha Upasanta and Siva States

Merge the experiences five in Nada;
Drop the lowly Malas behind:

Then enter the Suddha State
Thus the onward course pursue;
Beyond the Upasanta State (Para Turiya)
Is the Siva State
Further beyond the reach of thought and word
Is the Lord Param-Param;
Do Him seek.

பூரணி யாது புறம்பொன்றி லாமையின்
பேரணி யாதது பேச்சொன்றி லாமையில்
ஓரணை யாததுவொன்றுமி லாமையிற்
காரண மின்றியே காட்டுந் தகைமைத்தே. 2576

Nature of Confluent State in Tat-Tvam-Asi

Completeness it has none,
Limit it has none,
Speech it has none;
Attachment it has none,
Possession it has none;
Uncaused, of itself It reveals—
This It's nature is.

மகா வாக்கியம்

நீயது வானா யெனநின்ற பேருரை
ஆயது நானானேன் என்னச் சமைந்தறச்
சேய சிவமாக்குஞ் சீர்நந்தி பேரருள்
ஆயது வாயனந் தானந்தி யாகுமே. 2577

Mahavakyam: You Become That

"You Become That"—
Thus the Great Expression (Mahavakyam) stood;
And I became That;
Thus to Siva Becoming
Nandi blessed me;
And as I became That
In Infinite Bliss I was immersed

உயிர்பர மாக உயர்பர சிவன்
அரிய சிவமாக அச்சிவ வேதத்
திரியிலுஞ் சீராம் பராபரன் என்ன
உரிய உரையற்ற வோமய மாமே. 2578

From Jiva to "Aum"—Five Stages

Jiva becomes Para;
And that Para-Jiva becomes Siva;
And from that Vedic Lamp of Siva
Arose the light of Paraparan;
And in turn fills as Aum
That no speech could describe.

வாய்நாசி யேபுரு மத்தகம் உச்சியில்
ஆய்நாசி யுச்சி முதலவை யாய்நிற்குந்
தாய்நாடி யாதிவாக் காதி சகலாதி
சேய்நா டொளியெனச் சிவகதி யைந்துமே. 2579

The Five Lights in the Body in Yoga

When from nose-tip to cranium the Prana breath
Through Mother Nadi (Sushumna) passes,
To the Five centers,
Uluva, nose-tip, eye-brow middle, fore-head and cranium,
Beyond the Primal Nada and Tattvas
Then glows as distant Divine Light;
That forsooth, these Siva States Five are.

அறிவறி யாமை இரண்டு மகற்றிச்
செறிவறி வாய்எங்கும் நின்ற சிவனைப்
பிறிவறி யாது பிரானென்று பேணுங்
குறியறி யாதவர் கொள்ளறி யாரே. 2580

Adoration Way to Reach Goal

Jiva's knowledge and Jiva's ignorance
Both He dispelled;
And all Supreme Knowledge Siva pervasive stood;
Leave Him not;
Adore Him as Lord;
Those who know not this way,
Will never the Goal reach.

அறிவார் அறிவன அப்பும் அனலும்
அறிவார் அறிவன அப்புங் கலப்பும்
அறிவான் இருந்தங் கறிவிக்கி னல்லால்
அறிவான் அறிந்த அறிவறி யோமே. 2581

Knowledge Comes Only if God Makes Us Know

They of Knowledge True
Know Siva
Who Water and Fire at once are;
They of Knowledge True
Know Siva
Who stands as Fire and Water (Siva-Sakti) commingled;
Unless the Knower within
Makes you know,
We know not what your knowledge avails.

அதீதத்துள் ளாகி அகன்றவன் நந்தி
அதீதத்துள் ளாகி அறிவிலோன் ஆன்மா
மதிபெற் றிருள்விட்ட மன்னுயி ரொன்றாம்
பதியிற் பதியும் பரவுயிர் தானே. 2582

Jiva Becomes Para and then Siva

He, Nandi, is within Atita
And Beyond it;
He, Jiva, Jnana bereft of,
And enters Atita;
And attains Jnana
And rid of Ignorance dark, Para becomes;
Then will with God (Pati) one be.

அடிதொழ முன்னின் றமரர்க ளத்தன்
முடிதொழ ஈசனும் முன்னின் றருளிப்
படிதொழ நீபண்டு பாவித்த தெல்லாங்
கடிதொழக் காணென்னுங் கண்ணுத லானே. 2583

Result of Prayer and Penance

Head bowed low,
I worshipped at the Feet
Of the Lord of Celestials;
Lo! the Lord stepped forward and said;
"You shall now see the result
Of all your prayer and penance,
Of yore performed"
And so blessed me,
He the Lord of Fore-head Eye.

நின்மல மேனி நிமலன் பிறப்பிலி
என்னுளம் வந்திவன் என்னடி யானென்று
பொன்வளர் மேனி புகழ்கின்ற வானவன்
நின்மல மாகென்று நீக்கவல் லானே. 2584

Acceptance in Grace

Of Form Pure, Holy, Birthless,
He in me came and said;
"You are in My Grace received;
Be Pure"
Thus He blessed me,
And my blemishes removed;
He of Golden Form,
Heavenly Lord whom Celestials praise.

துறந்துபுக் கொள்ளொளி சோதியைக் கண்டு
பறந்ததென் உள்ளம் பணிந்து கிடந்தே
மறந்தறி யாவென்னை வானவர் கோனும்
இறந்து பிறவாமல் ஈங்குவைத் தானே. 2585

Immortality Conferred

Renouncing all, I inward entered
And beheld the Light within;
My heart trembled;
I prostrated low;
But Him I forgot never,
And the Lord of Celestials
Freeing me from whirl of births
Immortal made me, here below.

மெய்வாய் கண்மூக்குச் செவியென்னும் மெய்த் தோற்றத்
தவ்வாய அந்தக் கரணம் அகிலமும்
எவ்வா யியுரும் இறையாட்ட ஆடலாற்
கைவா யிலாநிறை எங்குமெய் கண்டதே. 2586

Pervasive Truth Form

The five sense organs external
The four cognitive organs internal
The worlds all, and lives all
All, all, are by Lord swayed;
He is the pervasive Truth Form
That neither hand nor mouth has.

37. விசுவக் கிராசம்

VISWA-GRASAM (TOTAL ABSORPTION)

அழிகின்ற சாயா புருடனைப் போலக்
கழிகின்ற நீரிற் குமிழியைக் காணில்
எழுகின்ற தீயிற்கர்ப் பூரத்தை யொக்கப்
பொழிகின்ற இவ்வுடற் போமப் பரத்தே. 2587

Absolute Union

Even as shadow disappears with body,
Even as bubble returns into water,
Even as flame of camphor leaves traces none,
So is it when Jiva into Param unites.

உடலும் உயிரும் ஒழிவற ஒன்றிற்
படருஞ் சிவசத்தி தாமே பரமாம்
உடலைவிட் டிந்த உயிரெங்கு மாகிக்
கடையுந் தலையுங் கரக்குஞ் சிவத்தே. 2588

Total Merging

When body and Jiva
As unbroken unite (in Yoga)
Then shall Grace of Siva Sakti be;
Then does Jiva, Param become;
Jiva that leaves this body,
Pervasive then becomes;
With beginning and end none
In Siva forever it merges.

செவிமெய்வாய் கண்மூக்குச் சேரிந் திரியம்
அவியின் நியமன மாதிகள் ஐந்துங்
குவிவொன் றிலாமல் விரிந்து குவிந்து
தவிர்வொன் றிலாத சராசரந் தானே. 2589

Tattva Involutes Into Maya

The Tattvas that confuse sense organs five,
And cognitive organs internal
Expanding, unintermittent
Finally (in Maya) merge;
This the fate of universe,
Inevitable it is.

பரனெங்கு மாரப் பரந்துற்று நிற்குந்
திரனெங்கு மாகிச் செறிவெங்கு மெய்தும்
உரனெங்கு மாயுல குண்டு உமிழ்க்கும்
வரமிங்ஙன் கண்டியான் வாழ்ந்துற்ற வாறே. 2590

When Jiva Becomes Para

Jiva becomes Para;
That Para pervasive stands;
Immanent too in all creation it is;
A mighty Power it is,
That can dissolve and create universes vast;
This was the boon granted to me;
And thus is my state exalted.

அளந்து துரியத் தறிவினை வாங்கி
உளங்கொள் பரஞ்சகம் உண்ட தொழித்துக்
கிளர்ந்த பரஞ்சிவஞ்சேரக் கிடைத்தால்
விளங்கிய வெட்ட வெளியனு மாமே. 2591

When Para Becomes Parasiva

Attaining Divine Knowledge-Form of Turiya State;
And omniscient experience of phenomenal universe
If Para can reach Para-Siva,
Then He belongs to Space
That is Light.

இரும்பிடை நீரென என்னையுள் வாங்கிப்
பரம்பர மான பரமது விட்டே
உரம்பெற முப்பாழ் ஒளியை விழுங்கி
இருந்தஎன் நந்தி இதயத்து ளானே. 2592

Three Spaces

He absorbed me in totality
As hot iron absorbs water;
Transcending Param-Para State;
He stands engulfing the Three Spaces Luminous
There He is, Nandi
That in my heart resides.

கரியுண் விளவின் கனிபோல் உயிரும்
உரிய பரமுமுன் னோதுஞ் சிவமும்
அரிய துரியமேல் அகிலமும் எல்லாந்
திரிய விழுங்குஞ் சிவபெரு மானே. 2593

Beyond Siva Turiya

As like the wood-apple
By "elephant" disease consumed*,
So are Jiva and Para before Siva;
In the rare state beyond Siva Turiya
Is Supreme Siva
That engrosses worlds all.

*The shell remains intact, while the inside is eaten out without a trace.

அந்தமும் ஆதியும் ஆகும் பராபரன்
தந்தம் பரம்பரன் தன்னிற் பரமுடன்
நந்தமை யுண்டுமெய்ஞ் ஞானநே யாந்தத்தே
நந்தி யிருந்தனன் நாமறி யோமே. 2594

No More Knower and Known in Parapara

Paraparan is the end and beginning,
He is Parapara for each and every one;
He absorbed Para and us Jivas;
And at end of Jnana-Jneya relationship
As Jnathru, He, Nandi was;
This, indeed, is our comprehension-beyond.

38. வாய்மை

TRUTH

அற்ற துரைக்கில் அருளுப தேசங்கள்
குற்ற மறுத்தபொன் போலுங் கனலிடை
அற்றற வைத்திறை மாற்றற ஆற்றிடில்
செற்றம் அறுத்த செழுஞ்சுட ராகுமே. 2595

When Jiva Becomes Radiant

By holy instructions are impurities rid;
Jiva shines like gold in fire purified;
Having been of impurities rid,
If Jiva constant thinks of Siva,
Then he becomes a Radiant Flame,
That has passions burnt away.

எல்லாம் அறியும் அறிவு தனைவிட்டு
எல்லாம் அறிந்தும் இலாபமங் கில்லை
எல்லாம் அறிந்த அறிவினை நானென்னில்
எல்லாம் அறிந்த இறையென லாமே. 2596

Knowledge That Knows All

What avails you
If you know all,
But not the Knowledge that knows all?
When you can say,
"I am the Knowledge that knows all"
Then can you well say,
"I am God."

தலைநின்ற தாழ்வரை மீது தவஞ்செய்து
முலைநின்ற மாதறி மூர்த்தியை யானும்
புலைநின்ற பொல்லாப் பிறவி கடந்து
கலைநின்ற கள்வனைக் கண்டுகொண் டேனே.2597

I Met the "Thief"

Tapas I performed
In the montane valley within my head;
Lo! I beheld Lord with his consort Sakti,
I crossed the river of birth in this fleshy body;
And met the "Thief" hiding in Kailas.

தானே யுலகில் தலைவ னெனத்தகுந்
தானே யுலகுக்கோர் தத்துவ மாய்நிற்கும்
வானே மழைபொழி மாமறை கூர்ந்திடும்
ஊனே யுருகிய வுள்ளமொன் றாமே. 2598

Melt in Love of God

He will be Lord of worlds all,
He will be Tattvas for worlds all,
The heavens will rain because of him,
Whose flesh melts in love of God;
—Thus say the Vedas.

அருள்பெற்ற காரணம் என்கொல் அமரில்
இருளற்ற சிந்தை இறைவனை நாடி
மருளுற்ற சிந்தையை மாற்றி அருமைப்
பொருளுற்ற சேவடி போற்றுவர் தாமே. 2599

How to Receive Grace

How is it they received Lord's Grace? you ask;
(Well it is thus:)
In the battle of life,
Their bewildered thought wandered;
They trained its course;
And freed of darkness,
They sought Lord,
And adored His Holy Feet.

மெய்கலந் தாரொடு மெய்கலந் தான்தன்னைப்
பொய்கலந் தார்முன் புகுதா ஒருவனை
உய்கலந் தூழித் தலைவனுமாய் நிற்கும்
மெய்கலந் தின்பம் விளைந்திடும் மெய்யர்க்கே. 2600

The Truthful Are Beloved of God

Into them that are Truthful
He in Truth merged;
Before them that are untruthful
He never His appearance makes;
At time's End He stands as Lord,
To work redemption of souls all;
True ones sport in True Joy.

மெய்கலந் தாரொடு மெய்கலந் தான்மிகப்
பொய்கலந் தாருட் புகுதாப் புனிதனைக்
கைகலந் தாவி எழும்பொழு தண்ணலைக்
கைகலந் தார்க்கே கருத்துற லாமே. 2601

Lord Abides In Hearts of the Truthful

He united in those
Who in Truth united,
He the Pure One
Who entered not false hearts;
When Prana upward ascends in Sushumna,
And you meet the Lord,
Then shall verily,
He in your thoughts abide.

எய்திய காலத் திருபொழு துஞ்சிவன்
மெய்செயின் மேலை விதியது வாய்நிற்கும்
பொய்யும் புலனும் புகலொன்று நீத்திடில்
ஐயனும் அவ்வழி யாகிநின் றானே. 2602

When Lord Reveals to the Truthful

When thus He in your thoughts abides,
Meditate on Him day and night;
Then will He in cranium above appear;
And if you give up falsehood and fleshy desires,
The Lord in truth reveals to you.

எய்துவ தெய்தா தொழிவ திதுவருள்
உய்ய அருள்செய்தான் உத்தமன் சீர்நந்தி
பொய்செய்புலன் நெறியொன்பதுந்தாட்கொளின்
மெய்யென் புரவியை மேற்கொள்ள லாமே. 2603

How to Mount Steed of Truth

Whether you reach Yogic climax or not
Is God's Grace;
That is the Way of Redemption,
The Great Nandi taught;
If the deceptive senses nine you subdue,
Well may you mount the steed of Truth.

கைகலந் தானைக் கருத்தினுள் நந்தியை
மெய்கலந் தான்தன்னை வேத முதல்வனைப்
பொய்கலந் தார்முன் புகுதாப் புனிதனைப்
பொய்யொழிந் தார்க்கே புகலிட மாமே. 2604

Lord is the Refuge only of the Truthful

He who entered my Sushumna Nadi,
He who is in my thoughts ever—Nandi
He who is in my body,
He the source of Vedas all
He the Holy One,
That reveals not to men untrue;
He who is the Refuge,
Of only those who their falsehood shed.

மெய்த்தாள் அகம்படி மேவிய நந்தியைக்
கைத்தாள் கொண்டாருந் திறந்தறி வாரில்லை
பொய்த்தாள் இடும்பையைப் பொய்யற நீவிட்டங்
கத்தாள் திறக்கில் அரும்பேற தாமே. 2605

Give Up Deceptive Bodily Thoughts

Nandi imprinted
His Holy Feet on my heart;
None have drawn the bolt of His door
And glimpsed Him in;
Give up unreserved,
Thoughts of this deceptive body;
Sorrow's receptacle it is;
Then unbolt the Sushumna door
Rich, indeed, shall your reward be.

உய்யும் வகையால் உணர்வினால் ஏத்துமின்
மெய்யன் அரனெறி மேலுண்டு திண்ணெனப்
பொய்யொன்று மின்றிப் புறம்பொலி வார்நடு
ஐயனும் அங்கே அமர்ந்துநின் றானே. 2606

Lord Abides in the Heart of the Faithful

Seeking the Way of Redemption
Adore Lord with feeling intense;
Sure, sure, Hara's Grace yours shall be;
In the heart of those who untruth utter not
He shines;
In their midst He abiding stood.

வம்பு பழுத்த மலர்ப்பழம் ஒன்றுண்டு
தம்பாற் பறவை புகுந்துணத் தானொட்டா
தம்புகொண் டெய்திட் டகலத் துரத்திடிற்
செம்பொற் சிவகதி சென்றெய்த லாமே. 2607

Lord is a Delicious Fruit Within

There is a Fruit Delicious,
From fragrant flower within it ripens;
The birds within the Self
Hinder you from reaching it;
Shoot your arrow,
And drive them away;
Then can you reach Siva State
Lustrous as Pure Red Gold.

மயக்கிய ஐம்புலப் பாசம் அறுத்துத்
துயக்கறுத்தானைத்தொடர்மின்தொடர்ந்தால்
தியக்கஞ்செய் யாதே சிவனெம் பெருமான்
உயப்போ எனமனம் ஒன்றுவித் தானே. 2608

Follow Lord and Be Redeemed

Control the senses that tempt,
Sunder the Pasas that corrupt,
Follow Lord,
Who your confusion ends;
If you do so,
Unhesitating my Siva says,
"Be you redeemed;"
And makes your thoughts
Centre on Him.

மனமது தானே நினையவல் லாருக்
கினமெனக் கூறு மிருங்காய மேவற்
றனிவினி னாதன்பால் தக்கன செய்யில்
புனிதன் செயலாகும் போதப் புவிக்கே. 2609

Constantly Think of Him and Receive Grace

They who constantly think of Him
Will reach into a body,
Glorious and strong;
There, if they adore Lord
In ways appropriate,
They reach, the World of Jnana,
Receiving Grace of the Holy One.

39. ஞானிசெயல்

WAYS OF JNANI

முன்னை வினைவரின் முன்னுண்டே நீங்குவர்
பின்னை வினைக்கணார் பேர்ந்தறப் பார்ப்பர்கள்
தன்னை யறிந்திடுந் தத்துவ ஞானிகள்
நன்மையில் ஐம்புலன் நாடலி னாலே. 2610

How They Deal With Karma

If Karma from past
Overtakes them,
They exterminate them,
Patiently experiencing them;
But they see,
Future Karma is created not;
They realize the Self,
They are Jnanis,
That have Tattvas cognised;
They train senses five,
In ways good.

தன்னை யறிந்திடுந் தத்துவ ஞானிகள்
முன்னை வினையின் முடிச்சை யவிழ்ப்பர்கள்
பின்னை வினையைப் பிடித்துப் பிசைவர்கள்
சென்னியில் வைத்த சிவனரு ளாலே. 2611

Tattva Jnanis Crush Karma

The Tattva Jnanis realize the Self;
The Gordian knot of Karma Past
They cut asunder;
Future Karmas they seize and crush,
By Grace of Siva,
Whom they hold,
High on their heads.

மனவாக்குக் காயத்தால் வல்வினை மூளும்
மனவாக்கு நேர்நிற்கில் வல்வினை மன்னா
மனவாக்குக் கெட்டவர் வாதனை தன்னால்
தனைமாற்றி யாற்றத் தகுஞானி தானே. 2612

No Karma, if Thought and Word are Consistent

Through thought, word and deed
Karmas accumulate;

If thought and word consistent stand
Karma bides not;
Thought and word conquering,
They experience Karmas,
And alter their course,
They the great Jnanis are.

40. அவாவறுத்தல்

SUNDERING OF DESIRES

வாசியு மூசியும் பேசி வகையினால்
பேசி யிருந்து பிதற்றிப் பயனில்லை
ஆசையும் அன்பும் அறுமின் அறுத்தபின்
ஈசன் இருந்த இடம்எளி தாமே. *2613*

Conquer Desires

No use prattling of
Breath and Sushumna;
Sunder your desires and passions;
Having sundered,
The Lord's place, easy be.

மாடத்து ளானலன் மண்டபத் தானலன்
கூடத்து ளானலன் கோயிலுள் ளானலன்
வேடத்து ளானலன் வேட்கைவிட் டார்நெஞ்சில்
மூடத்து ளேநின்று முத்திதந் தானே. *2614*

Lord is in the Desire—Abnegated

In stony houses and stately halls, He is not;
In parlours deep and temples massive, He is not;
In holy garbs he is not;
In the thoughts of those,
Who have desires abnegated, is He,
Fleshy body, though therein be;
He, their liberation granted.

ஆசை யறுமின்கள் ஆசை யறுமின்கள்
ஈசனோ டாயினும் ஆசை யறுமின்கள்
ஆசை படப்பட ஆய்வருந் துன்பங்கள்
ஆசை விடவிட ஆனந்த மாமே. *2615*

Sunder Desires

Sunder your desires, sunder your desires
Sunder your desires even like Lord;
The more the desires, the more your sorrows;
The more you give up, the more your bliss shall be.

அடுவன பூதங்கள் ஐந்தும் உடனே
படுவழி செய்கின்ற பற்றற வீசி
விடுவது வேட்கையை மெய்ந்நின்ற ஞானந்
தொடுவது தம்மைத் தொடர்தலு மாமே. *2616*

Jnana Way

The five senses burn you up;
They lead you to destruction's way;
Give up desires and scatter them away;
Reach to the Truth of Jnana;
That the Way to reach Lord.

உவாக்கடல் ஒக்கின்ற ஊழியும் போன
துவாக்கட லுட்பட்டுத் துஞ்சினர் வானோர்
அவாக்கட லுட்பட் டழுந்தினர் மண்ணோர்
தவாக்கடல் ஈசன் தரித்துநின் றானே. *2617*

Perish not in the Flood of Pleasure and Pain

Like the ocean that foams and rages
At full-moon tide,
Many, many, floods rose and passed away
Through passage of Time;
Caught in floods of pleasure and pain,
Celestials numberless perished;
Caught in the floods of desires
The humans countless sank;
God alone forever stood
In the Ocean of Bliss Eternal.

நின்ற வினையும் பிணியும் நெடுஞ்செயல்
துன்தொழி லற்றுச் சுத்தம தாகலும்
பின்றைங் கருமமும் பேர்த்தருள் நேர்பெற்றுத்
துன்ற அழுத்தலும் ஞானிகள் தூய்மையே. *2618*

Jnani's Purified Way

Emancipated from Karmas of past,
Rid of disease of Pasa,
Prolonged activity suspended;
They, the Suddha State reach;
Then transcending the five acts of God
His direct Grace, they receive
There they forever immersed are
These, Jnanis, purified ways are.

உண்மை யுணர்ந்துற ஒண்சித்தி முத்தியாம்
பெண்மயற் கெட்டறப் பேறட்ட சித்தியாந்
திண்மையின் ஞானி சிவகாயங் கைவிட்டால்
வண்மை யருள்தான் அடைந்தபின் ஆறுமே. *2619*

Jnanis Remain Immortal in God-Love

Realizing Truth in full,
Luminous Siddhi and Mukti they attained;
Sex desire entire devoid,
They achieved mighty Siddhis eight;
As Siva Jnani leaves behind this body,
Divine Grace descends on him;
And then in God-Love, forever, he remains.

அவனிவன் ஈசனென் றன்புற நாடிச்
சிவனிவன் ஈசனென் றுண்மையை யோரார்
பவனிவன் பல்வகை யாமிப் பிறவி
புவனிவன் போவது பொய்கண்ட போதே. 2620

Realize the Truth that Jiva is Siva

That this Jiva to become Siva
They in love sought not;
That this Jiva is Siva
That truth they know not;
Knowing not this Jiva is Siva,
They diverse births take,
And into worlds several wander
When Truth they realize not.

கொதிக்கின்ற வாறுங் குளிர்கின்ற வாறும்
பதிக்கின்ற வாறிந்தப் பாரக முற்றும்
விதிக்கின்ற ஐவரை வேண்டா துலகம்
நொதிக்கின்ற காயத்து நூலொன்று மாமே. 2621

Jnanis are not for Becoming Performing Gods

The Five Gods consign Jiva to broiling miseries,
And then cooling him,
Again consign him to fresh birth;
Thus in the whirl of creation endless they them ordain words;
He severed my desires
For learning limitless;
My body, restless as waves,
He in calmness fixed;
In my purified being within.

உய்ந்தனம் என்பீர் உறுபொருள் காண்கிலீர்
கந்த மலரிற் கலக்கின்ற நந்தியைச்
சிந்தையில் வைத்துத் தெளிவுறச் சேர்த்திட்டால்
முந்தைப் பிறவிக்கு மூலவித் தாமே. 2622

Seek Nandi Within

You say, redeemed you are;
But you have not seen the Way appropriate;
Nandi merges in fragrant flower within;
Hold Him in your thoughts in vision clear,
Then have you sown the seed
Of birthless-to-be.

41. பக்தியுடைமை

TO BE POSSESSED OF BHAKTI

முத்திசெய் ஞானமுங் கேள்வியு மாய்நிற்கும்
அத்தனை மாயா அமரர் பிரான்தனைச்
சுத்தனைத் தூய்நெறி யாய்நின்ற சோதியைப்
பத்தர் பரசும் பசுபதி தானென்றே. 2623

He is Lord of All

He confers Mukti;
He is Jnana and Mantra;
He is the Father;
He is the Lord of Celestials immortal;
He is the Pure One;
He is the Light that is the Holy Way;
He is the Pasu-Pati
Whom the devotees in ardour adore.

அடியார் அடியார் அடியார்க் கடிமைக்
கடியனாய் நல்கிட் டடிமையும் பூண்டேன்
அடியார் அருளால் அவனடி கூட
அடியா னிவனென் றடிமைகொண் டானே. 2624

Be a Devotee of Devotees

To devotees of devotees of Lord
In succession continuous,
I a devotee became;
Giving myself thus,
Into their vassalage I entered;
With the Grace of devotees
I reached His Feet;
Then saying, "He my devotee is"
He accepted me in His vassalage (of Grace).

நீரிற் குளிரும் நெருப்பினிற் சுட்டிடும்
ஆரிக் கடனந்தி யாமா றறிபவர்
பாரிற் பயனாரைப் பார்க்கிலும் நேரியர்
ஊரில் உமாபதி யாகிநின் றானே. 2625

Lord is Righteous and Bounteous

Cooler than water is He;
Hotter than fire is He;
Who this Ocean of Nandi is—
Who knows?
By far righteous is He;
Than all bounteous beings in world;
Within the heart He stood,
As Umapati (Sakti's Lord) He stood.

ஒத்துல கேழும் அறியா ஒருவனென்
றத்தன் இருந்திடம் ஆரறிவார்சொல்லப்
பத்தர்தம் பத்தியிற் பாற்படில் அல்லது
முத்தினை யார்சொல்ல முந்துநின் றாரே. 2626

Where is That Peerless Pearl?

Well may denizens of seven worlds, all,
Entire try,
They cannot know Him;
Who can say where Lord is?

Unless He of Himself appears
In devotion of His devotees,
Who dares say,
Where that peerless Pearl is!

ஆன்கன்று தேடி யழைக்கு மதுபோல்
நான்கன்றாய் நாடி யழைத்தேனென் நாதனை
வான்கன்றுக் கப்பாலாய் நின்ற மறைப்பொருள்
ஊன்கன்றா னாடிவந் துள்புகுந் தானே. 2627

Yearn for the Lord

As the calf that searches,
And calls for mother-cow,
I, in yearning, sought and cried for my Lord;
He is Hidden Truth of Vedas
Who beyond heavens eternal stood;
In endearness tender,
He entered into me,
In this body fleshy.

பெத்தத்துந் தன்பணி இல்லை பிறத்தலான்
முத்தத்துந் தன்பணி இல்லை முறைமையால்
அத்தற் கிரண்டும் அருளால் அளித்தலாற்
பத்திப்பட் டோர்க்குப் பணியொன்றும்
இல்லையே. 2628

Birth and Release are God's Giving

The Jivas in born condition
Have tasks none to perform,
As of itself their birth comes;
The Jivas in Mukti State too
(By the very condition of that state)
Have nothing to perform;
Lord by His Grace grants states both;
What then is there for devotees to do
(But to hold Lord in their thoughts?)

பறவையிற் கற்பமும் பாம்புமெய் யாகக்
குறவஞ் சிலம்பக் குளிர்வரை யேறி
நறவார் மலர்கொண்டு நந்தியை யல்லால்
இறைவனென் றென்மனம் ஏத்தகி லாவே. 2629

Reach God the Kundalini Yoga Way

With Prana breath for Seed-Energy,
And the serpent (Kundalini) for body,
To the resounding music of Nada,
Upward I climb to the cool mountain within;
And with fragrant flower there blooms,
I adore Nandi;
None else the God to adore,
My mind I let.

உறுதுணை நந்தியை உம்பர் பிரானைப்
பெறுதுணை செய்து பிறப்பறுத் துய்மின்
செறிதுணை செய்து சிவனடி சிந்தித்
துறுதுணை யாயங்கி யாகிநின் றானே. 2630

God Grants Protection

Nandi is my Protector in need;
He is Lord of Celestials;
Seek His protection;
And ending birth cycle, be redeemed;
Think constant of Siva's Feet,
He, Divine protection grants,
He, who as Fire stood.

வானவர் தம்மை வலிசெய் திருக்கின்ற
தானவர் முப்புரஞ் செற்ற தலைவனைக்
கானவன் என்றுங் கருவரை யானென்றும்
ஊனத னுள்நினைந் தொன்றுபட் டாரே. 2631

He Protects Good Against Evil

The Danavas (of Dark World)
Held the Vanavas (of Luminous World)
In fief;
He the Lord destroyed,
The Three Forts of the Evil Ones;
Him the devotees worshipped,
As Lord of Forests;
And of Mountains Black;
Thus adoring Him in fleshy body,
They in Him united.

நிலைபெறு கேடென்று முன்னே படைத்த
தலைவனை நாடித் தயங்குமென் உள்ளம்
மலையுளும் வானகத் துள்ளும் புறத்தும்
உலையுளும் உள்ளத்து மூழ்கிநின் றேனே. 2632

Seek Him Within and Without

This birtn is a lasting curse to me;
And so, I seek Him in drooping heart
In Mountain and Sky
Within and without;
And in Fire within too;
Thus in holy thought immersed,
I stood.

42. முத்தியுடைமை

TO BE IN MUKTI

முத்தியில் அத்தன் முழுத்த அருள்பெற்றுத்
தத்துவ சுத்தி தலைப்பட்டுத் தன்பணி
மெய்த்தவஞ் செய்கை வினைவிட்ட மெய்யுண்மைப்
பத்தியி லுற்றோர் பரானந்த போதரே. 2633

Jiva's Task is to Seek Him

Receiving in full the Grace of Lord in Mukti State;
Purified of Tattvas, the Suddha State attaining,

To perform Tapas thus is Jiva's task;
And so rid of Karmas, in devotion true they stand;
They indeed the Jnanis
In transcendental bliss immersed.

வளங்கனி தேடிய வன்றாட் பறவை
உளங்கனி தேடி யுழிதரும் போது
களங்கனி யங்கியிற் கைவிளக் கேற்றி
நலங்கொண்ட நால்வரும் நாடுகின் றாரே. 2634

Jiva-Bird Seeks Siva-Fruit

The Jiva-Bird,
With its feet planted firm (on Muladhara),
Seeks the Rich Fruit (that is Siva);
When within the heart that Fruit it seeks,
Lighting the Sushumna lamp
In the Flaming Fire of Kundalini within,
It reaches its great goal;
Its four cognitive organs,
Ever seek Him thereafter.

43. சோதனை

EXPERIMENTATION

பெம்மான் பெருநந்தி பேச்சற்ற பேரின்பத்
தம்மா னடிதந் தருட்கடல் ஆடினோம்
எம்மாய மும்விடுத் தெம்மைக் கரந்திட்டுச்
சும்மா திருந்திடஞ் சோதனை யாகுமே. 2635

Divine Experiment

The Mighty Lord, the Great Nandi,
Granted me His Feet of indescribable Bliss;
And in Ocean of Grace immersed me;
Freeing me from illusions all,
And secretly guarding me in safety,
He bore me to the holy banks of Silence
That indeed was an Experiment Divine.

அறிவுடை யானரு மாமறை யுள்ளே
செறிவுடை யான்மிகு தேவர்க்குந் தேவன்
பொறியுடை யான்புலன் ஐந்துங் கடந்த
குறியுடை யானொடுங் கூடுவன் நானே. 2636

Seeking Union in God

He is the Wise One;
He fills Vedas rare;
He is the God of countless Gods;
He is of Divine Sense possessed,
The five senses transcending;
With Him who these attributes has
I my union seek.

அறிவறி வென்றங் கரற்றும் உலகம்
அறிவறி யாமையை யாரும் அறியார்
அறிவறி யாமை கடந்தறி வானால்
அறிவறி யாமை யழகிய வாறே. 2637

Dividing Line Between Knowledge and Ignorance

"Jnana, Jnana," thus laments this world,
They know not that Jnana of Jiva
Is Jnana none, but (ignorance);
When Siva Jnana overlays Jiva Jnana,
They both Pure Jnana are;
Thus much is it after all,
Between Knowledge and Ignorance.

குறியாக் குறியினிற் கூடாத கூட்டத்
தறியா அறிவில் அவிழ்ந்தேக சித்தமாய்
நெறியாம் பராநந்தி நீடருள் ஒன்றுஞ்
செறியாச் செறிவே சிவமென லாமே. 2638

Merge in God's Pervasiveness

Into the Goal beyond goals,
Into the Assembly where none assemble,
Into the Knowledge beyond knowledge,
I loosened myself,
In single-minded thought;
I merged in Holy Nandi's Grace,
There in Pervasiveness beyond pervasiveness
Was Siva.

காலினில் ஊறுங் கரும்பினிற் கட்டியும்
பாலினுள் நெய்யும் பழத்துள் இரதமும்
பூவினுள் நாற்றமும் போலுளன் எம்மிறை
காவலன் எங்குங் கலந்துநின் றானே. 2639

Lord is Immanent

As feel within breeze,
As sweet within sugarcane,
As ghee within milk,
As juice within fruit,
As fragrance within flower;
Immanent is my Lord;
Thus does the Lord pervade all.

விருப்பொடு கூடி விகிர்தனை நாடிப்
பொருப்பகஞ் சேர்தரு பொற்கொடி போல
இருப்பர் மனத்திடை எங்கள் பிரானார்
நெருப்புரு வாகி நிகழ்ந்துநின் றாரே. 2640

Lord is Like a Hidden Vein of Gold

Seek Siva in love endearing;
As like the vein of gold
In recesses of a mountain,
My Lord in my thoughts abides;
He Who as Form of Fire stood.

நந்தி பெருமான் நடுவுள் வியோமத்து
வந்தென் அகம்படி கோயில்கொண் டான்கொள்ள
எந்தைவந் தானென் றெழுந்தேன் எழுதலுஞ்
சிந்தையி னுள்ளே சிவனிருந் தானே. 2641

Lord is in the Heart's Temple

Seated in the centre of Void,
Nandi descended into my heart's temple,
And there his place took;
And as He descended,
I stood up saying: "My Father Come;"
Thus as I greeted,
Siva in my thoughts instant stood.

தன்மைவல் லோனைத் தவத்துள் நலத்தினை
நன்மைவல் லோனை நடுவுறை நந்தியைப்
புன்மைபொய் யாதே புனிதனை நாடுமின்
பன்மையில் உம்மைப் பரிசுசெய் வானே. 2642

Lord Will Make You First of Many

He is of attributes mighty;
The Fruit of Tapas;
All things goody He is;
In the centre of my thoughts He resides;
He is the Great Nandi;
Seek the Holy One in truth unfaltering,
He will place you as the First of Many.

தொடர்ந்துநின் றானென்னைச் சோதிக்கும் போது
தொடர்ந்துநின் றானல்ல நாதனும் அங்கே
படர்ந்துநின் றாதிப் பராபரன் எந்தை
கடந்துநின் றவ்வழி காட்டுகின் றானே. 2643

I Found Love Within Me

He was with me
As I searched Him within me;
And continuous there He stood;
My Father, Paraparan,
Pervasive He stands;
And transcending beyond too,
He shows me the Way.

அவ்வழி காட்டும் அமரர்க் கரும்பொருள்
இவ்வழி தந்தை தாய் கேளியான் ஒக்குஞ்
செவ்வழி சேர்சிவ லோகத் திருந்திடும்
இவ்வழி நந்தி இயல்பது தானே. 2644

He is Father, Mother, Kith and Kin

He who shows that Way
Is rare for Celestials to reach;
Here below,
Is He as Father, Mother, Kith and Kin;
He is in Siva Loka
The Holy Way leads to;
This the Way, Nandi is.

எறிவது ஞானத் துறைவாள் உருவி
அறிவ்து னோடேயவ் வாண்டகை யானைச்
செறிவது தேவர்க்குத் தேவர் பிரானைப்
பறிவது பல்கணப் பற்றுவி டாரே. 2645

Unsheath the Sword of Jnana

Unsheath the Sword of Jnana and smite;
That instant you shall know Lord;
Unite in Him,
Who the Lord of Celestials is;
Away then shall you be
From the rabble numerous
That to desire cling.

ஆதிப் பிரான்தந்த வாளங்கைக்கொண்டபின்
வேதித்து என்னை விலக்கவல் லாரில்லை
சோதிப்பன் அங்கே சுவடு படாவண்ணம்
ஆதிக்கட் டெய்வ மவனிவ னாமே. 2646

Be not Separated from Lord

Holding the Sword of Jnana
That Primal Lord gifted me,
None there is to separate me (from Him);
Search did I there further
Leaving traces none;
Then Jiva with Primal Siva one became.

அந்தக் கருவை யருவை வினைசெய்தற்
பந்தம் பணியச்சம் பல்பிறப் பும்வாட்டிச்
சிந்தை திருத்தலுஞ் சேர்ந்தாரச் சோதனை
சந்திக்கத் தற்பர மர்குஞ் சதுரர்க்கே. 2647

Search Lord in Calmness

Pasa, that seminal seed of birth
Maya, that invisible one,
Karma, that to desire gives birth,
The doubts and fears
That in their train come,
The births numerous,
—All these I scorched;
Thus my thoughts purified,
In calmness I search;
The skilful ones that practise thus
Shall one with Tat-Para be.

உரையற்ற தொன்றை யுரைத்தான் எனக்குக்
கரையற் றெழுந்த கலைவேட் டறுத்துத்
திரையொத்த என்னுடல் நீங்கா திருத்திப்
புரையற்ற என்னுட் புகுந்தற் பரனே. 2648

Tat-Para Enters Within Jiva

He taught me
The word that is beyond words;
He severed my desires
For learning limitless;
My body, restless as waves;
He in calmness fixed;
In my purified being within
He, the Tatpara, entered.

எட்டாம் தந்திரம் முடிவு பெற்றது.

Tantra Eight Concluded

ஒன்பதாந் தந்திரம்
TANTRA NINE

1. குருமட தரிசனம்

DARSHAN OF GURU MONASTERY

பலியும் அவியும் பரந்து புகையும்
ஒலியும்எம் ஈசன் தனக்கென்றே யுள்கிக்
குவியுங் குருமடங் கண்டவர் தாம்போய்த்
தளிரு மலரடி சார்ந்துநின் றாரே. 2649

Gurus Have Reached to Lotus Feet

Smoke and sound
Oblations and sacrificial offering
In worship spread;
"All thses are for my Lord;"
The Gurus who thus meditate
Who have monasteries founded,
Have verily reached the Feet of the Lord.

இவனில்ல மல்ல தவனுக்கங் கில்லை
அவனுக்கும் வேறில்லம் உண்டா அறியின்
அவனுக் கிவனில்ல மென்றென் றறிந்தும்
அவனைப் புறம்பென் றரற்றுகின் றாரே. 2650

Lord is in the Body

None the habitation the Lord has
But the body-house of Jiva;
Or has the Lord any other home?
Let them find out;
Even after having found out
That Jiva's body is Siva's home
They say, "He (Lord) is outside."

நாடும் பெருந்துறை நான்கண்டு கொண்டபின்
கூடுஞ் சிவனது கொய்மலர்ச் சேவடி
தேட வரியன் சிறப்பிலி எம்மிறை
ஓடும் உலகுயி ராகிநின் றானே. 2651

Great Way of Seeking

Having discovered the Great Way of seeking
The flower-decked feet of Siva I reached within;
Beyond seeking is He;
Greatness indeed is where He resides;
He stood as life of the revolving world.

இயம்புவன் ஆசனத் தோடு மலையும்
இயம்புவன் சித்தக் குகையும் இடமும்
இயம்புவன் ஆதாரத் தோடு வனமும்
இயம்புவன் ஈரா றிருநிலத் தோர்க்கே. 2652

Revelation of Lord's Abode

I shall reveal where He is seated;
And where His mountain is;
I shall reveal where His retreat-cave is
And where that is located;
I shall reveal where His Adharas (triple) are;
And the forest where He is
All these eight I shall reveal
To denizens of world here below.

முகம்பீட மாமட முன்னிய தேயம்
அகம்பர வர்க்கமே யாசில்செய் காட்சி
அகம்பர மாதனம் எண்ணெண் கிரியை
சிதம்பரந் தற்குகை யாதாரந் தானே. 2653

Lord is in Guru's Monastery

The Guru-face is Lord's pedestal
The monastery is Lord's Holy Land;
The Holy Assembly of blemishless vision
Is Lord's abode;
The heart that performs the Sixteen worships inside
Is Lord's sacred throne;
The Adharas within
Are Lord's astral cave.

அகமுக மாம்பீடம் ஆதார மாகுஞ்
சகமுக மாஞ்சத்தி யாதன மாகுஞ்
செகமுக மாந்தெய்வ மேசிவ மாகும்
அகமுகம் ஆய்ந்த அறிவுடை யோர்க்கே. 2654

Lord's Abode Inside the Body

The Adharas six are His pedestal inward
The Sakti pervasive is His Throne
The universal God within is Siva Himself;
Thus it is,
For these who inward reflect and know.

மாயை யிரண்டு மறைக்க மறைவுறுங்
காயமோ ரைந்துங் கழியத்தா னாகியே
தூய பரஞ்சுடர் தோன்றச் சொரூபத்துள்
ஆய்பவர் ஞானாதி மோனத்த ராமே. 2655

Jnanis Seek Lord Within the Light of Manifestness

Mayas twine envelope the body of sheaths five
When their end they reach,
The Holy Light of itself appears;
Those who seek the Truth in that Manifestness (Svarupa)
Are the Jnanis, in Silence Exceeding.

2. ஞானகுரு தரிசனம்

DARSHAN OF JNANA GURU

ஆறொடு முப்பதும் அங்கே யடங்கிடிற்
கூரக் குருபரன் கும்பிடு தந்திடும்
வேறே சிவபத மேலாய் அளித்திடும்
பேறாக ஆனந்தம் பேணும் பெருகவே. 2656

When the Holy Guru Appears

When the Tattvas six and thirty subdued are,
Then shall the Holy Guru appear
For you to adore;
Siva-State too will on you be conferred;
And then will well up the Bliss Ineffable.

துரியங்கள் மூன்றுங் கடந்தொளிர் சோதி
அரிய பரசிவம் யாவையு மாகி
விரிவு குவிவற விட்ட நிலத்தே
பெரிய குருபதம் பேசவொண் ணாதே. 2657

Parasivam is Beyond the Three Turiyas

Beyond the Turiyas Three
Is the Light Resplendent;
It is the Parasiva that pervades all;
In that Land
That knows neither contraction nor expansion
Are the Feet of Guru Holy
That, beyond speech, is.

ஆயன நந்தி யடிக்கென் றலைபெற்றேன்
வாயன நந்தியை வாழ்த்தவென் வாய்பெற்றேன்
காயன நந்தியைக் காணவென் கண்பெற்றேன்
சேயன நந்திக்கென் சிந்தைபெற் றேனே. 2658

What These Body Organs are for

To bear Nandi's Feet, I was gifted this head;
To praise Nandi Great, I was gifted this mouth;
To vision Nandi Eternal, I was gifted these eyes;
To think of Nandi afar, I was gifted this mind.

கருடன் உருவங் கருதும் அளவிற்
பருவிடந் தீர்ந்து பயங்கெடு மாபோல்
குருவின் உருவங் குறித்தஅப் போதே
திரிமலந் தீர்ந்து சிவனவ வாமே. 2659

At the Thought of Guru's Form Impurities Vanish

At the thought of Garuda's form
The serpent's poison leaves
Its terrors lose;
Like it,
At the thought of Guru's form
The triple Malas leave instant;
The Jiva then Siva becomes.

அண்ணல் இருப்பிட மாரும் அறிகிலா:
அண்ணல் இருப்பிடம் ஆய்ந்துகொள் வார்களுக்
கண்ணல் அழிவின்றி யுள்ளே அமர்ந்திடும்
அண்ணலைக் காணில் அவனிவ னாமே. 2660

When Jiva Becomes Siva

None know where the Lord resides,
To those who seek where the Lord resides
The Lord within them resides;
When they the Lord see,
Jiva becomes Siva.

தோன்ற அறிதலுந் தோன்றல் தோன்றாமையு
மான்ற வறிவு மறிநன வாதிகள்
மூன்றவை நீங்குந் துரியங்கள் மூன்றற
வூன்றிய நந்தி யுயர்மோனத் தானே. 2661

God is in the Silence of Perception

To perceive the things that appear,
To perceive the things that appear not,
That is Knowledge Higher;
To perceive the things in ways different
As in waking, dreaming and rest of states,
—These three perceptions will there be not,
In the State the Three Turiyas transcended;
There Nandi stands firm, is Silence Exalted.

சந்திர பூமிக் குடன்புரு வத்திடைக்
கந்த மலரில் இரண்டிதழ்க் கன்னியும்
பந்த மிலாத பளிங்கின் உருவினள்
பந்தம் அறுத்த பரங்குரு பற்றே. 2662

Sakti is in Ajna Centre

In the Centre between the eye-brows,
Is the Sphere of the Moon;
There on the flower of petals two
Is Virgin Sakti seated;
Radiant as Crystal is Her Form;
(To vision Her)
Seek you the Guru
Who all bonds sundered.

மனம்புகுந் தானுல கேழு மகிழ
நிலம்புகுந் தானெடு வானிலந் தாங்கிச்
சினம்புகுந் தான்திசை எட்டும் நடுங்க
வனம்புகுந் தானூர் வடக்கென்ப தாமே. 2663

Siva is in Sahasrathala (North)

Into heart He entered,
For the seven Worlds to rejoice;
Into earth He entered
For the heavens to support;
Into rage He entered
For the eight directions to tremble;
Into wilderness He entered
His abode in North Mountain to be.

தானான வண்ணமுங் கோசமுஞ் சார்தருந்
தானாம் பறவை வனமெனத் தக்கன
தானான சோடச மார்க்கந்தான் நின்றிடில்
தானாந் தசாங்கமும் வேறுள்ள தானே. 2664

Way of Seeking Within Leads to Supreme Attainment

Of five sheaths[1] is the Jiva's body;
Like a forest is that body
Where the Jiva-bird its abode has;
If the Jiva seeks the Way of Sixteen[2] worships
Then is Jiva's Ten attainments[3] are.

[1]Annamaya-Flesh body
Pranamaya-breath-body
Manomaya-mind-body
Vijnanamaya-knowledge-body
Anandamaya-bliss-body

[2]The yogic way of reaching the light with sixteen beams within the visuddhi adhara, where Sakti stands.

[3]Ten states of transcendental consciousness, beyond which is the final goal of supreme awareness.

மருவிப் பிரிவறி யாஎங்கள் மாநந்தி
உருவ நினைக்கநின் றுள்ளே யுருக்குங்
கருவிற் கரந்துள்ளங் காணவல் லார்க்கிங்
கருவினை கண்சோரும் அழிவார் அகத்தே. 2665

Love Lord and Sever Pasas

Our Holy Nandi
Once He loves, separation Knows not;
Think of His Form
And within you He melts;
Enter into His Essence
And see Him in your heart;
For those who can do this,
The seminal Karmas slumbering die;
The Ego-Consciousness forever perishes.

தலைப்பட லாமெங்கள் தத்துவன் தன்னைப்
பலப்படு பாசம் அறுத்தறுத் திட்டு
நிலைப்பெற நாடி நினைப்பற வுள்கில்
தலைப்பட லாகுந் தருமமுந் தானே. 2666

Lord can be Reached by Earnest Seeking

Reach you may
Our Holy One that is Truth Perfect;
Sunder Pasas strong and away cast them;
Seek Him firm and think constant within;
Reached then shall be
The Holy One that is Dharma.

நினைக்கின் நினைக்கு நினைப்பவர் தம்மைச்
சுனைக்குள் விளைமலர் சோதியி னானைத்
தினைப்பிளந் தன்ன சிறுமைய ரேனுங்
கனத்த மனத்தடைந் தாலுயர்ந் தாரே. 2667

Think of Him and He Thinks of You

Think of Him,
And He thinks of those who think of Him;
Think of Him, the radiance that is,
Of the Flower that blooms in the Divine Fount within;
Smaller than the split grain may they be,
But if firm they hold Him,
Great they shall sure be.

தலைப்படுங் காலத்துத் தத்துவன் தன்னை
விலக்குறின் மேலை விதியென்றுங் கொள்க
அனைத்துல காய்நின்ற ஆதிப் பிரானை
நினைப்புறு வார்பத்தி நேடிக்கொள் வாரே. 2668

In Seeking be not Discouraged by Initial Failures

When you seek to reach the Lord
And have a miss,
Take it as the work of your evil Karma in the past,
And so persevere in your devotion fervent;
You shall at last reach the Primal Lord.

நகழ்வொழிந் தாரவர் நாதனை யுள்கி
நிகழ்வொழிந் தாரெம் பிரானொடுங் கூடித்
திகழ்வொழிந் தார்தங்கள் சிந்தையி னுள்ளே
புகழ்வழி காட்டிப் புகுந்துநின் றானே. 2669

How Lord Enters Within

Thinking of Lord
Their inconstancy lost;
Uniting in Lord
Their existence lost;
In their thoughts
Their ego lost;
Thus he entered
Showing the Way Illumined.

வந்த மரகத மாணிக்க ரேகைபோற்
சந்திடு மாமொழிச் சற்குரு சன்மார்க்கம்
இந்த இரேகை யிலாடத்தின் மூலத்தே
சுந்தரச் சோதியுட் சோதியு மாமே. 2670

Holy Guru Shows the Light in Eye-Brow Centre

Like a lustrous ray of red gem
On to a green stone set
Is the Holy Guru's Jnana precept;
That ray in the eye-brow Centre is;
It is the Light within the Light Resplendent.

உண்ணும் வாயும் உடலும் உயிருமாய்க்
கண்ணுமா யோகக் கடவுள் இருப்பது
மண்ணு நீரனல் காலொடு வானுமாய்
விண்ணு மின்றி வெளியானோர் மேனியே. 2671

God's Form

As mouth, eye, body and life
The Yoga-God is;
Beyond earth, water, fire, wind and sky
Space His Form is.

பரசு பதியென்று பார்முழு தெல்லாம்
பரசிவ னாணை நடக்கும் பாதியாற்
பெரிய பதிசெய்து பின்னாம் அடியார்க்
குரிய பதியும்பா ராக்கிநின் றானே. 2672

His Love for Sakti and His Devotees

Praise Him as your Pati (Lord)
In all Worlds Parasiva's writ runns;
His one half to the Great Grace lends;
The other half to His devotees gave
For their goal to reach;
He who this world fashioned.

அம்பர நாதன் அகலிட நீள்பொழில்
தம்பர மல்லது தாமறி யோம்என்பர்
உம்பருள் வானவர் தானவர் கண்டிலர்
எம்பெரு மானருள் பெற்றிருந் தாரே. 2673

By Grace He Can Be Seen

He is the Lord of Heavens,
By the vast spatial glades surrounded;
Except Him we know Param (supreme) none;
Of the Celestials, Vanavas and Danavas,
None have seen Him ever;
Only those who received His Grace
Have seen Him forever.

கோவணங் கும்படி கோவண மாகிப்பின்
நாவணங் கும்படிநந்தி யருள்செய்தான்
தேவணங் கோமினிச் சித்தந் தெளிந்தனம்
போய்வணங் கும்பொரு ளாயிருந் தோமே. 2674

Grace Gives Clear Vision

He made Jivas renounce
That they the Lord adore;
He made them praise Him in words meek;
That He the Nandi His Grace confers;
No more the other Gods we adore;
Our vision is clear now;
We became the Object
For other Jivas to seek and worship.

3. பிரணவ சமாதி

PRANAVA SAMADHI

தூலப் பிரணவஞ் சொரூபானந்தப் பேருரை
பாலித்த சூக்கும மேலைச் சொரூபப்பெண்
ஆலித்த முத்திரை யாங்கிதிற் காரணம்
மேலைப் பிரணவம் வேதாந்த வீதியே. 2675

Articulate Pranava is Siva's Form; Inarticulate Pranava Sakti's Form

The Sthula (articulate) Pranava (Aum)
Is the mighty key-word to Bliss of Manifestness (Svarupa)
The Sukshma (inarticulate) Pranava
Is Sakti's Divine Manifestation (Svarupa)
The Mudra (Jnana) is the Cause of that Manifestation
The Pranava aloft is the Vedanta Highway.

ஓமெனும் ஓங்காரத் துள்ளே யொருமொழி
ஓமெனும் ஓங்காரத் துள்ளே யுருவரு
ஓமெனும் ஓங்காரத் துள்ளே பலபேதம்
ஓமெனும் ஓங்காரம் ஒண்முத்தி சித்தியே. 2676

Greatness of Aum

Aum is the one Word Supreme;
Aum is the Form-Formless;
Aum is the Infinite Diversity;
Aum is Siddhi and Mukti radiant.

ஓங்காரத் துள்ளே யுதித்தஐம் பூதங்கள்
ஓங்காரத் துள்ளே யுதித்த சராசரம்
ஓங்கார தீதத் துயிர்மூன்றும் உற்றன
ஓங்கார சீவ பரசிவ ரூபமே. 2677

In Aum Jiva, Para and Siva Merge

In Aum arose the elements five;
In Aum arose the creation entire;
In the atita (finite) of Aum
The three Jivas merged;
Aum is the Form
Of Jiva, Para and Siva in union.

வருக்கஞ் சுகமாம் பிரமமு மாகும்
அருக்கங் சராசர மாகும் உலகில்

தருக்கிய வாதார மெல்லாந்தன் மேனி
சுருக்கமின் ஞானந்தொகுத்துணர்ந் தோரே. 2678

Aum is Bliss of Brahman, the Universe and the Adharas

That letter-cluster (Aum made up of A,U, and M)
Is the Bliss of Brahman;
The Subtle One
As visible creation vast expands;
The Adharas, all, comprise its Form;
Thus is it Known to Jnanis of knowledge vast.

மலையு மனோபவ மருள்வன வாவன
நிலையிற் றரிசனம் தீப நெறியாந்
தலமுங் குல்முந் தவஞ்சித்த மாகும்
நலமுஞ்சன் மார்க்கத் துபதேசந் தானே. 2679

Great Teaching of Sanmarga

My despairing thoughts
Are in confusion thrown;
The steady thoughts
Lead to vision clear of Light Divine;
The steadfast mind
Is the place, environs and devotion appropriate;
Great indeed is Upadesa (teaching) of Sanmarga (Jnana).

சோடச மார்க்கமுஞ் சொல்லுஞ்சன் மார்க்கிகட்
காடிய வீராறின் அந்தமும் ஈரேழிற்
கூடிய அந்தமுங் கோதண்ட முங்கடந்
தேறியே ஞானஞே யாந்தத் திருக்கவே. 2680

Ascending Order to Finite Goal Within

To vision the Sixteen-Petalled Centre within is Shodasa
It is the Way of Sanmargis;
Beyond is the end of Nine centres,
Still beyond is Pranava
Ascending further beyond is the End Finite,
Of Jnana (Knowledge) and Jneya (Known) in one.

4. ஒளி

LIGHT

ஒளியை யறியில் உருவும் ஒளியும்
ஒளியும் உருவம் அறியில் உருவாம்
ஒளியின் உருவம் அறியில் ஒளியே
ஒளியும் உருக வுடனிருந் தானே. 2681

Know Light Within

Know the Light, your From becomes Light;
Know the Hidden From; you that From become;
Know the Light's From; you that Light become;
That Light within you to melt, He in love stand.

புகலெளி தாகும் புவனங்கள் எட்டும்
அகலொளி தாயிரு ளாசற வீசும்
பகலொளி செய்தது மத்தா மரையிலே
இகலொளி செய்தெம் பிரானிருந் தானே. 2682

That Light Dispels Soul's Darkness

Easy to enter the Universe of Eight;
That spreading Light of immense vastness
Dispels the Primordial darkness entire;
In the Mystic Lotus within as day-light it spreads;
Dispelling contending Pasas,
Was my Lord there seated.

விளங்கொளி யங்கி விரிகதிர் சோமன்
துளங்கொளி பெற்றன சோதி யருள
வளங்கொளி பெற்றதே பேரொளி வேறு
களங்கொளி செய்து கலந்துநின் றானே. 2683

The Light Within is the Source of All Light

The luminaries Fire, Sun and Moon
Their luminousity received by Grace of Divine Light;
The Light that gave that Light
Is a Mighty Light of Effulgence Immense;
That Light dispelling my darkness,
In me stood into oneness suffused.

இளங்கொளி யீசன் பிறப்பொன்று மில்லி
துளங்கொளி ஞாயிறுந் திங்களுங் கண்கள்
வளங்கொளி யங்கியு மற்றைக்கண் நெற்றி
விளங்கொளி செய்கின்ற மெய்காய மாமே. 2684

Lord's Form is Light

The Lord is the Effulgent Light,
Birth He has none;
The luminous sun and moon are His eyes;
The lustrous fire is His Fore-Head Eye;
Thus is His Resplendent Form of dazzling Light.

மேலொளி கீழதன் மேவிய மாருதம்
பாலொளி யங்கி பரந்தொளி யாகாசம்
நீரொளி செய்து நெடுவிசும் பொன்றிலும்
மேலொளி யைந்தும் ஒருங்கொளி யாமே. 2685

That Light Engrosses the Light of the Five Elements

Below that Light Above
Is the wind, earth, fire, sky and water;
Rousing the Light (of Kundalini) within
You shall in the astral sphere be;
There indeed is the one Light
That engrosses the lights of elements five.

மின்னிய தூவொளி மேதக்க செவ்வொளி
பன்னிய ஞானம் பரந்த பரத்தொளி
துன்னிய வாறொளி தூய்மொழி நாடொறும்
உன்னிய வாறொளி யொத்தது தானே. 2686

The Light Within is the Blending of All Lights—Jnana, Siva and Pranava

That Light within
Is pure as light of lightning;
It is Light that is great and red;
It is the Light of Param
That beams Jnana;
It is the Light of Adharas six ascended,
It is the Light born of constant thought on Pure Word (Aum)
It is the Light that is blended of these lights all.

விளங்கொளி மின்னொளி யாகிக் கரந்து
துளங்கொளி யீசனைச் சொல்லும்எப் போதும்
உளங்கொளி யூனிடை நின்றுயிர்க் கின்ற
வளங்கொளி எங்கும் மருவிநின் றானே. 2687

The Little Light Within Points to the Effulgent Light

The Effulgent Light stands as a sparkling light concealed
That ever to the shining Lord points;
It is the light of the heart;
It is the rich light that within the body pulsates
Pervading all,
—Thus did the Lord as Light stand.

விளங்கொளி யவ்வொளி யவ்விருள் மன்னுந்
துளங்கொளி யான்தொழு வார்க்கும் ஒளியான்
அளங்கொளி யாரமு தாகநஞ் சாருங்
களங்கொளி யீசன் கருத்தது தானே. 2688

Divine Light Devours Soul's Darkness

Luminous is that Light;
It is Light that devours Soul's darkness;
It is Light of those who adore Him in Jnana Light;
He devours the poison that with ambrosia arises
From the milky seas
And holds it in His throat ever;
Like it, is His Light too.

இலங்கிய தெவ்வொளி யவ்வொளி யீசன்
துலங்கொளி போல்வது தூங்கருட் சத்தி
விளங்கொளி மூன்றே விரிசுடர் தோன்றி
உளங்கொளி யுள்ளே யொருங்குகின் றானே. 2689

When the Lights of Siva and Sakti Blend in Jiva Light

As like the Light of Lord
That in Him reposes;
Is the Light of His Sakti Grace,
When the three lights Sun, Moon and Fire
Within shines by Yoga Way,
The Lord, indeed, nears you,
As one Light in your inner Light.

உளங்கொளி யாவதென் உள்நின்ற சீவன்
வளங்கொளி யாநின்ற மாமணிச் சோதி
விளங்கொளி யாய்மின்னி விண்ணில் ஒடுங்கி
வளங்கொளி யாயத்து ளாகிநின் றானே. 2690

Lord's Light and Jiva's Light Merge Within

The Light within is but Jiva;
The Lord too who stood within was a gemly Light Effulgent;
Flashing as lightning in the astral sphere,
That Light with Sakti's Light and Jiva's Light into one merged.

விளங்கொளி யாய்நின்ற விகிர்தன் இருந்த
துளங்கொளி பாசத்துள் தூங்கிருள் சேராக்
களங்கிருள் நட்டமே கண்ணுதி லாட
விளங்கொளி யுன்மனை என்றிநின் றானே. 2691

Dancing in the Darkness of Pasa, Siva Light Enters Unmana Sakti

The Lord that is Light Effulgent,
Entering the dark arena of Pasa
Dances as Light in that darkness;
As the Forehead-Eyed God thus dances,
He as Light Effulgent in Unmana Sakti merged.

போது கருங்குழற்போனவர் தூதிடை
ஆதி பரத்தை அமரர் பிரானொடுஞ்
சோதியும் அண்டத்தப் பாலுற்ற தூவொளி
நீதியி னல்லிருள் நீக்கிய வாறே. 2692

Siva's Light Becomes Sakti's Light of Grace

Those who thus went by the Secret Way of Yoga,
Reached Sakti of dark fragrant tresses;
Primal Parai She is;
One with Lord of Celestial's Light She is;
—The Light beyond the Pure Space;
That Light of Her forever dispelled Pasa's creeping darkness.

உண்டில்லை யென்னும் உலகத் தியல்வது
பண்டில்லை யென்னும் பரங்கதி யுண்டுகொல்
கண்டில்லை மானுடர் கண்ட கருத்துறில்
விண்டில்லை யுள்ளே விளக்கொளி யாமே. 2693

Even Sceptics Can Reach that Light if they Seek in Devotion

"God there is; God there is none"
Thus the men of world diverse hold;
Will they who hold "Primal there is none,"
Ever reach Siva State?
Even they who say, "We saw not God"

If in devotion stand,
He as Light Effulgent in them is;
He the Light of Astral Sphere (Chidambaram) within.

சுடருற ஓங்கிய ஒள்ளொளி யாங்கே
படருறு காட்சிப் பகலவன் ஈசன்
அடருறு மாயையி னாரிருள் வீசில்
உடலுறு ஞானத் துறவிய னாமே. 2694

He Who Receives Siva's Light Becomes Jivan Mukta, Rid of Mayaic Darkness

The light Effulgent that glows afar
Is the Lord that spreads His beams as like the Sun;
When He the Maya's darkness dispells,
Jiva in this body, a Jnani-Renunciate becomes (Jivan Mukta).

ஒளிபவ ளத்திரு மேனிவெண் ணீற்றன்
அளிபவ ளச்செம்பொன் ஆதிப் பிரானுங்
களிபவ ளத்தினன் காரிருள் நீங்கி
ஒளிபவ ளத்தென்னோ டீசன்நின் றானே. 2695

Jiva Purified by Siva's Light Unites in Him

His Holy Form is of shimmering coral-hue;
He wears the holy ashes pure white;
He is brilliant-like pure gold and coral ripe;
He is the Primal Lord;
When, I, dispelled of my darkness,
Shone as coral red,
He, the Dancing Lord,
In me in union stood.

ஈசன்நின் றானிமை யோர்கள்நின் றார்நின்ற
தேசமொன் றின்றித் திகைத்திழைக்கின்றனர்
பாசமொன் றாகப் பழவினை பற்றற
வாசமொன் றாமலர் போன்றது தானே. 2696

Jiva then Blossoms as Divine Flower

In the Heavens stood Lord;
The Celestials, too, stood there;
Yet they knew Him not,
And bewildered ever stand;
When Pasa's desires
And the odour of Karma Past
Together leave,
The Jiva as a Flower of Divine blossoms.

தானே யிருக்கும் அவற்றில் தலைவனுந்
தானே யிருக்கும் அவனென நண்ணிடும்
வானா யிருக்குமிம் மாயிரு ஞாலத்துப்
பானா யிருக்கப் பரவலு மாமே. 2697

Seek Himself as Yourself

Himself as Lord
In all things, He alone is;
Himself is Yourself
Thus you seek Him;
The very Heaven is He in this vast earth;
Sweet is He;
May you Him adore.

5. தூல பஞ்சாக்கரம்

STHULA (ARTICULATE) PANCHAKSHARA

ஐம்ப தெழுத்தே அனைத்துவே தங்களும்
ஐம்ப தெழுத்தே அனைத்தாக மங்களும்
ஐம்ப தெழுத்தின் அடைவை யறிந்தபின்
ஐம்ப தெழுத்தே அஞ்செழுத் தாமே. 2698

Fifty Letters Become Five

The letters Fifty[1] are Vedas all;
The letters Fifty are Agamas all;
When the secret of letters Fifty is known,
The Fifty letters, Five Letters[2] Became.

[1]Fifty Letters — Sanskrit alphabet.
[2]Five Letters — Panchakshara, Na Ma Si Va Ya.

அகார முதலாக ஐம்பத்தொன் றாகி
உகார முதலாக வோங்கி யுதித்து
மகார இறுதியாய் மாய்ந்துமாய்த் தேறி
நகார முதலாகும் நந்திதன் நாமமே. 2699

Fifty Letters Became Fifty-One

With the letter "A" intoned in commencement,
The letters Fifty, Fifty-One became;
With letter "U" intoned high with letter "A",
And with letter "M", it (A&U&M as AUM) ended;
And again with letter "N" rising,
It became Nandi's name "Aum Nama Sivaya."

அகராதி யீரெண் கலந்த பரையும்
உகராதி தன்சத்தி யுள்ளொளி யீசன்
சிகராதி தான்சிவ வேதமே கோண
நகராதி தான்மூல மந்திர நண்ணுமே. 2700

Seek the Seminal Mantra Nama Sivaya

In the sixteen letters commencing with "A"
(Of the Shodasa Flower within)
Is the Parai (Sakti);
In the Unmani Sakti beginning with "U"
Is the light of Lord within;
The Mantra commencing with letter "Si" (Sivaya Nama)
Is Siva and Vedas all;
With letter "Na" commencing

That order reversed
Is Nama Sivaya;
That verily is the seminal Mantra;
That Mantra do seek.

வாயொடு கண்டம் இதய மருவுந்தி
ஆய இலிங்க மவற்றின்மே லேயவ்வாய்த்
தூயதோர் துண்ட மிருமத் தகஞ்செல்லல்
ஆயதி நாமைந்தோ டாமெழுந் தஞ்சுமே. 2701

How Aum and the Five Letters are Distributed in the Six Centres

In the six Adharas (centres) within
Are distributed the Five Letters and Aum;
That comprise Aum Nama Sivaya
In the Muladhara is Na
In the Svadhishtana is Ma
In the Navel Centre is Si
In the Heart Centre is Va
In the Throat Centre is Ya
In the Eye-brow Centre is Aum.

கிரணங்கள் ஏழுங் கிளர்ந்தெரி பொங்கிக்
கரணங்கள் விட்டுயிர் தானெழும் போது
மரணங்கை வைத்துயிர் மாற்றிடும் போது
மரணங்கை கூட்டுவ தஞ்செழுத் தாமே. 2702

The Five Letters are the Life's Refuge

When the seven beams of Prana in fury rise,
When the four cognitive senses, their leave take,
And as Death's Hand stretched and seizes,
Life ebbs away;
Then shall the Five Letters above the Soul's refuge be.

ஞாயிறு திங்கள் நவின்றெழு காலத்தில்
ஆயுறு மந்திர மாரும் அறிகிலர்
சேயுறு கண்ணி திருவெழுத் தஞ்சையும்
வாயுற வோதி வழுத்தலு மாமே. 2703

Chant Five Letters at Dawn and Dusk

When the Sun and the Moon rise,
They know not the mantra to chant and muse;
Well may they then chant full-mouthed
The Holy Mantra, Five-Lettered,
Wholesome, and praise the Lord;
—The Mantra that is so sacred to Sakti
Who with Siva stands.

தெள்ளமு தூறச் சிவாய நமவென்
றுள்ளமு தூற வொருகால் உரைத்திடும்
வெள்ளமு தூறல் விரும்பியுண் ணாதவர்
துள்ளிய நீர்போற் சுழல்கின்ற வாறே. 2704

Chant Sivaya Nama in God-Love

Chant that mantra Sivaya Nama once,
Your heart welling up in God-Love;
Then will transparent ambrosia within you well up;
They who seek not that pure ambrosia to drink
Will be like bubbles of a water-fall,
That know rest none from birth's whirl, ever.

குருவழி யாய குணங்களி னின்று
கருவழி யாய கணக்கை யறுக்க
வரும்வழி மாள மறுக்கவல் லார்கட்
கருள்வழி காட்டுவ தஞ்செழுத் தாமே. 2705

The Five Letters Will Close the Gateway to Birth

Take to the Way the Guru showed,
And blot out the reckoning of births;
To them who seek to close the birth's cyclic way
The Five-Letters alone show the Grace-Way.

வெறிக்க வினைத்துயர் வந்திடும் போது
செறிக்கின்ற நந்தி திருவெழுத் தோதுங்
குறிப்பது வுன்னிற் குரைகழல் கூட்டுங்
குறிப்பறி வான்றவங் கோனுரு வாமே. 2706

Blessings of the Five Lettered Mantra — of Siva's Feet and Form

When Karma's miseries harass you,
Chant the Five-Lettered Mantra
Of Nandi pervasive;
If you thus seek Him,
He, the Grace of His Holy Feet confers;
Your devotion shall lead you to Siva Form.

நெஞ்சு நினைந்துதம் வாயாற் பிரானென்று
துஞ்சும் பொழுதுன் துணைத்தாள் சரணென்று
மஞ்சு தவழும் வடவரை மீதுறை
அஞ்சில் இறைவன் அருள்பெற லாமே. 2707

Siva's Five Letter Mantra is the Final Refuge

Think of Him in your heart,
Praise Him as "My Lord"
When Death approaches you, say;
"Lord, You alone are my Refuge;"
Then will you receive
The Grace of Lord in Letters Five seated,
The Lord who resides
In the snow-clad mountain of North (Kailas).

பிரான்வைத்த ஐந்தின் பெருமை யுணரா
திராமாற்றஞ் செய்வார்கொல் ஏழை மனிதர்
பராமுற்றுங் கீழொடு பல்வகை யாலும்
அராமுற்றுஞ் சூழ்ந்த அகலிடந் தானே. 2708

Letters Five Alone Can Dispel Darkness

Knowing not the greatness
Of our Lord's Letters Five,
Will they ever dispel their darkness?
Poor in spirit are they, (who think otherwise);
They will to the nether world consigned be
Surrounded by serpents of diverse species.

6. சூக்கும பஞ்சாக்கரம்

SUKSHMA (INARTICULATE) PANCHAKSHARA

எளிய வாதுசெய் வாரெங்கள் ஈசனை
ஒளியை யுன்னி யுருகு மனத்தராய்த்
தெளிய வோதிச் சிவாய நமவென்னுங்
குளிகை யிட்டுப்பொன் னாக்குவன் கூட்டையே. 2709

Sivaya Nama is Alchemic

In slighting terms they speak of our Lord;
With thoughts centering on the Light
And hearts melting in love
Let them chant His name;
With the alchemic pill of Sivaya Nama
He will turn thy body gold.

சிவன்சத்தி சீவன் செறுமல மாயை
அவஞ்சேர்த்த பாச மலமைந் தகலச்
சிவன் சத்தி தன்னுடன் சீவனார் சேர
அவஞ்சேர்த்த பாசம் அணுக்கி லாவே. 2710

Si-Va-Ya-Na-Ma Brings Union of Jiva With Siva-Sakti

The Letters Si Va Ya Na Ma denote
Siva, Sakti, Jiva, Mala and Maya respective;
Chant it, for the five Pasas-Mala to disappear;
When with Siva and Sakti, Jiva unites
(That is when you say Si Va Ya)
The harassing Pasas flee away.

சிவனரு ளாய சிவன்திரு நாமஞ்
சிவனரு ளான்மாத் திரோத மலமாயை
சிவன்முத லாகச் சிறந்து நிரோதம்
பவம தகன்று பரசிவ னாமே. 2711

The Five Letters Denote the Five Relations in the Liberation Process

The Five-lettered name of Siva (Sivayanama)
Is Siva-Sakti (Grace);
Si for Siva, Va for Sakti, Ya for Jiva,
Na for Tirodayi and Ma for Maya (impure);
Thus the Five Letters, five relations denote;
As you chant with Si first (that is as Si Va Ya Na Ma)
You are of Karmas freed;
Births no more will be
You shall Para-Siva become.

ஓதிய நம்மலம் எல்லாம் ஒழித்திட்டவ்
வாதி தனைவிட் டிறையருட் சத்தியால்
தீதில் சிவஞான யோகமே சித்திக்கும்
ஓதுஞ் சிவாய மலமற்ற உண்மையே. 2712

Siva-Jnana Comes of Si Va Ya

Rid of malas denoted by "Na" and "Ma"
And the primordial Anava too,
By the Grace of Siva-Sakti
Siva-Jnana pure will be;
Repeated chant Si Va Ya;
There verily is Truth of Mala-riddance.

நமாதி நனாதி திரோதாயி யாகித்
தமாதிய தாய்நிற்கத் தானந்தத் துற்றுச்
சமாதித் துரியந் தமதாக மாகவே
நமாதி சமாதி சிவவாதல் எண்ணவே. 2713

How Through Na Ma Si Va Ya Union in Jiva Occurs in Samadhi

Na Ma and the rest (Na Ma Si Va Ya)
Pervading Jiva in his five states of Consciousness
Waking, dreaming and the rest,
Stand forth as Tirodayi, the Sakti of Obfuscation (Verily)
And She in turn leads to the Pure Sakti that leads to Grace,
Then does Jiva reach the Final state of Turiya in Samadhi;
Thus meditating on Na Ma and the rest,
The Jiva unites in Siva.

அருடரு மாயமும் அத்தனுந் தம்மில்
ஒருவனை யீன்றவள் உள்ளுறு மாயை
திரிமல நீங்கிச் சிவாயவென் றோதும்
அருவினை தீர்ப்பதும் அவ்வெழுத் தாமே. 2714

Chant Si Va Ya

The Sakti that Grace confers,
And the Lord with Her inseparate,
Together as Siva-Sakti roused Jiva to life;
When you contemplate on Si Va Ya;
Then the Maya within and the rest of Malas three are rid;
That Si Va Ya destroys the hard Karmas too.

சிவசிவ என்றே தெளிகிலர் ஊமர்
சிவசிவ வாயுவுந் தேர்ந்துள் அடங்கச்
சிவசிவ வாய தெளிவினுள் ளார்கள்
சிவசிவ வாகுந் திருவரு ளாமே. 2715

Chant Siva Siva and Receive Grace

They who chant not "Siva Siva,"
Are from ignorance freed not
Verily are they beings dumb;
Do say "Siva Siva"
Unintermittent and spontaneous,
In the depths of your heart;
They who thus chant

Are in Siva Jnana Pure;
Theirs shall be the Grace Divine.

சிவசிவ என்கிலர் தீவினை யாளர்
சிவசிவ என்றிடத் தீவினை மாளுஞ்
சிவசிவ என்றிடத் தேவரு மாவர்
சிவசிவ என்னச் சிவகதி தானே. 2716

"Siva Siva" Leads to Siva State

They chant not "Siva Siva,"
Verily are they of evil Karma;
Chant "Siva Siva"
Your evil karmas perish; Deva you become;
Yours shall be the Siva-State too.

நமவென்னு நாமத்தை நாவில் ஒடுக்கிச்
சிவவென்னு நாமத்தைச் சிந்தையு ளேற்றப்
பவமது தீரும் பரிசும தற்றால்
அவமதி தீரும் அறும்பிறப் பன்றோ. 2717

Chant Na Ma Si Va and End Birth

Hold the letters, "Na Ma" in the tongue
Take the letters "Si Va" into your thought;
No more shall you be in existence entangled;
Your goal too shall be reached;
Ignorance will end,
And with it the whirl of births too.

7. அதிசூக்கும பஞ்சாக்கரம்
ATI-SUKSHMA (SUPER SUBTLE) PANCHAKSHARA

சிவாய நமவெனச் சித்தம் ஒருக்கி
அவாயம் அறவே யடிமைய தாக்கிச்
சிவாய சிவசிவ வென்றென்றெ சிந்தை
அவாயங் கெடநிற்க ஆனந்த மாமே. 2718

Bliss From Si Va Ya Siva Siva

Saying Si Va Ya Na Ma,
Centre your thoughts,
All perils your vassals will be;
Let the words Si Va Ya Siva Siva
Fill your thoughts unceasing;
Conquering all perils,
Bliss there shall be.

செஞ்சுடர் மண்டலத் தூடுசென் றப்புற
மஞ்சண வும்முறை யேறி வழிக்கொண்டு
துஞ்சு மவன்சொன்ன காலத் திறைவனை
நெஞ்சென நீங்கா நிலைபெற லாகுமே. 2719

Five-Lettered Holy Word Leads to Samadhi

Penetrating the fiery Sphere of Sun
And passing beyond into the sphere of cloud-laden Meru
By the Adhara Way,
He (the yogi) there in Samadhi slumbers;
And then articulating the Holy Word
He sees the Lord
And is forever absorbed in His thought.

அங்கமும் ஆகம வேதம தோதினும்
எங்கள் பிரானெழுத் தொன்றில் இருப்பது
சங்கைகெட் டவ்வெழுத் தொன்றையுஞ் சாதித்தால்
அங்கரை சேர்ந்த அருங்கல மாமே. 2720

Chant "Si" and Cross the River of Life

All that is spoken in Vedas, Vedangas and Agamas
Are in my Lord's One Letter contained
Freed of doubts,
If that One letter "Si" is consummated,
The boat of life reaches the lovely shore across.

பழுத்தன ஐந்தும் பழமறை யுள்ளே
விழித்தங் குறங்கும் வினையறி வாரில்லை
எழுத்தறி வோமென் றுரைப்பர்கள் ஏதர்
எழுத்தை யழுத்தும் எழுத்தறி யாரே. 2721

The Five Letters Unwrites Fate's Letters

Ripe they hang
The Letters Five
In Vedas ancient;
They know not the Way
To Slumber-in-Waking;
"Letters we know," they say
Witless are they;
They know not the Letter
That their Fate's Letter unwrites.

8. திருக்கூத்துத் தரிசனம்
DARSHAN OF HOLY DANCE

எங்குந் திருமேனி எங்குஞ் சிவசத்தி
எங்குஞ் சிதம்பரம் எங்குந் திருநட்டம்
எங்குஞ் சிவமா யிருத்தலால் எங்கெங்குந்
தங்குஞ் சிவனருட் டன்விளை யாட்டதே. 2722

Siva's Sport Divine

Everywhere is the Holy Form;
Everywhere is Siva-Sakti;
Everywhere is Chidambaram;
Everywhere is Divine Dance;
As everywhere Siva is,
Everywhere Siva's Grace is
All, all, His Sport Divine.

சிற்பரஞ் சோதி சிவானந்தக் கூத்தனைச்
சொற்பத மாம்அந்தச் சுந்தரக் கூத்தனைப்
பொற்பதிக் கூத்தனைப் பொற்றில்லைக் கூத்தனை
அற்புதக் கூத்தனை யாரறி வாரே. 2723

Siva's Five Dances

He is Chit-Para of Divine Light,
He dances the Dance of Bliss (Ananda Dance);
He is Nada that is "Aum"
He dances the Dance of Beauty (Sundara Dance);
He dances in Golden Hall (Golden Dance);
He dances in the Golden Tillai (Golden Tillai Dance);
He dances the Dance Wondrous (Atbudha Dance);
Who knows Him ever?

சிவானந்தக் கூத்து

SIVANANDA (SIVA-BLISS) DANCE

தானந்தம் இல்லாச் சதானந்த சத்திமேல்
தேனுந்தும் ஆனந்த மாநடங் கண்டீர்
ஞானங் கடந்து நடஞ்செய்யும் நம்பிக்கங்
கானந்தக் கூத்தாட ஆடரங் கானதே. 2724

Ananda Dance[1] is Honey-Sweet

Endless is She,
Sakti of abiding Bliss;
With Her He dances the Ananda Dance
Honey-sweet it is;
You have witnessed it;
And having witnessed it,
Dance transcending knowledge all;
You, then, become the arena
For Lord's Ananda Dance to perform.

1) Sivanandakuthu is the dance of Siva united with Sakti. He dances in boundless space, beyond the frontiers of jnana. When this dance occurs, the *Vedas* and *Agamas*, all, all dance with Him. Out of this dance emerges His five-fold Acts of Creation, Preservation, Dissolution, Obfuscation and Revealing.

ஆனந்தம் ஆடரங் கானந்தம் பாடல்கள்
ஆனந்தம் பல்லியம் ஆனந்த வாச்சியம்
ஆனந்த மாக அகில சராசரம்
ஆனந்தம் ஆனந்தக்கூத்துகந் தானுக்கே. 2725

It is Bliss

Bliss is His Dance Arena;
Bliss the Song's melody;
Bliss the music's refrain;
Bliss the musical organs;
Bliss for the creation entire,
Bliss too for Lord,
Who the Ananda Dance dances.

ஒளியாம் பரமும் உளதாம் பரமும்
அளியார் சிவகாமி யாகுஞ் சமயக்
களியார் பரமுங் கருதுறை யந்தத்
தெளிவாஞ் சிவானந்த நட்டத்தின் சித்தியே. 2726

It is End of Jnana

The Param that is Light
The Param that Jiva unites in,
The Param that is Sivakami
Who as Sakti in Grace abounds;
And the bliss of faiths all,
—Are all attained,
When Sivananda Dance witnessed,
The Dance that is the end of Knowledge Pure.

ஆன நடமைந் தகள சகளத்தர்
ஆன நடமாடி ஐங்கரு மத்தாக
ஆன தொழிலரு ளாலைந் தொழிற்செய்தே
தேன்மொழி பாகன் திருநட மாடுமே. 2727

Through Five Dances Siva Performs Five Acts

Five are the dances
That He the Form-Formless performs;
The Five dances He dances
The Five acts to perform;
The Five acts He performs
With Sakti-Grace in Him;
And so the Lord dances with Sakti
That is of honey-speech.

பூதாண்ட பேதாண்ட போகாண்ட யோகாண்ட
மூதாண்ட முத்தாண்ட மோகாண்ட தேகாண்ட
தாகாண்ட மைங்கரு மத்தாண்ட தற்பரத்
தேகாந்த மாம்பிர மாண்டத்த என்பவே. 2728

Siva's Cosmic Sway

The Universe of Elements Five,
The Universe of Elements Other,
The Universe of Bhoga,
The Universe of Yoga,
The Universe of Time,
The Universe of Mukti,
The Universe of Passions
The Universe of Appetites
—Over these universes
That He created,
Siva His sway holds,

The Five Acts performing;
Alone Seated as Tatpara,
In the Cosmos Entire—Brahmanda

வேதங்க ளாட மிகுஆ கமமாடக்
கீதங்க ளாடக் கிளரண்டம் ஏழாடப்
பூதங்க ளாடப் புவன முழுதாட
நாதங்கொண் டாடினான் ஞானானந்
தக்கூத்தே. 2729

Jnana-Ananda Dance

The Vedas danced, the Agamas danced;
The melodies danced, the seven universes danced;
The elements danced, and the worlds entire danced;
With Nada Sakti the Lord danced,
The Dance of Divine Knowledge-Bliss (Jnana-Ananda).

பூதங்கள் ஐந்திற் பொறியிற் புலனைந்தில்
வேதங்கள் ஐந்தின் மிகுமா கமந்தன்னில்
ஓதுங் கலைகாலம் ஊழி யுடன் அண்டப்
போதங்கள் ஐந்திற் புணர்ந்தாடுஞ் சித்தனே. 2730

Siddha-Lord Dances

In the elements Five,
In the senses Five,
In the sense organs Five,
In the Vedas and Agamas together Five,
(In Kala, and Kala (Time's Eternity)
In the Higher Siva Tattvas Five,[1]
(Suddha Vidya, Iswaram, Sadakyam, Sakti, Sivam)
In all these, intermingling
The Great Siddha-Lord dances.

These are known as the Siva tattvas:

i) In suddha vidya tattva, jnana predominates and kriyas is subdued.
ii) In isvara vidya tattva, kriya predominates, and jnana is subdued.
iii) In sadakya tattva, jnana and kriya are in balance.
iv) In Ṣakti tattva, kriya is yearned for.
v) In Siva tattva, jnana exists alone.

தேவர் சுரர்நரர் சித்தர்வித் தியாதரர்
மூவர்கள் ஆதியின் முப்பத்து மூவர்கள்
தாபதர் சத்தர் சமயஞ் சராசரம்
யாவையும் ஆடிடும் எம்மிறை யாடவே. 2731

When the Lord Danced

The Devas, Asuras, Humans, Siddhas and Vidyadharas,
The Primal Three, the Three-and-thirty gods,
The Rishis seven, the Faiths several,
And the creation all, movable and immovable,
—All these danced,
When my Lord danced.

சுந்தரக் கூத்து

SUNDARA (BEAUTY) DANCE

அண்டங்கள் ஏழினுக் கப்புறத் தப்பான்
உண்டென்ற சத்தி சதாசிவத் துச்சிமேற்
கண்டங் கரியான் கருணை திருவுருக்
கொண்டங் குமைகாணக் கூத்துகந் தானே. 2732

Dance in the Beyond as Compassion Embodied

Beyond, beyond, the universes seven,
High above Sakti and Sadasiva,
The dark-throated Lord,
As compassion embodied,
Danced in rapture
For Uma there to witness.

கொடுகொட்டி பாண்டங் கோடுசங் கார
நடமொட்டோ டைந்தாறு நாடியுள் நாடுந்
திடமுற் றெழுந்தேவ தாருவாந் தில்லை
வடமுற்ற மாவன மன்னவன் தானே. 2733

The Dances of Siva, Eight and Five — Witnessed in Six Adharas

Kodukkotti, Pandarangam, Kodu, Samharam and others,
—These Eight dances[1] He danced,
The Five dances too He danced,
All these you witness in the Nadis (Adharas) six;
In the yogic way;
He danced too in the forests of Deva-daru[2],
And in Tillai[3] and in Alavanam[4]
—He the King Supreme.

---

1) Sundara Kuthu is the Dance of Compassion. It has eight variations: Kodukotti, Pandarangam, Kapala Kuthu, Zhinatanam, Muntandavam, Anavarata tandavan, Ananda tandavam, and Samhara tandavam. All the worlds come into being when this dance begins, and come to an end when the dance ends.

2) This was the forest where the rishis performed their sacriligious homas, and challenged Siva's might. He destroyed them and danced.

3) Chidambaram (in the South Arcot District of Tamil Nadu)

4) Tirualangadu (in the North Arcot District of Tamil Nadu).

பரமாண்டத் தூடே பராசத்தி பாதம்
பரமாண்டத் தூடே படரொளி ஈசன்
பரமாண்டத் தூடே படர்தரு நாதம்
பரமாண்டத் தூடே பரன்நட மாடுமே. 2734

Siva Dances Through Cosmos

At the crest of Cosmos of galaxies vast (Paramandam)
Are the Holy Feet of Parasakti;
At the crest of Cosmos
Is the radiant Light of Isa
Permeating the Cosmos
Is the expansive Nada;

There through the Cosmos vast
Does the Paran dance unceasing.

அங்குச மென்ன எழுமார்க்கம் போதத்தில்
தங்கிய தொந்தின்னுந்தாள ஒத்தினில்
சங்கரன் மூலநா டிக்குள் தரித்தாடல்
பொங்கிய காலம் புகும்போகல் இல்லையே. 2735

He Dances in Sushumna and in Jnana that Arises in Yoga

In Yoga
That like elephant goad subdues the senses,
Is Bodha (Jnana);
There arises in rhythmic cadence
The drum-beat of Thom-Theem;
To that, Sankaran, in accord, dance
Within the central Sushumna Nadi;
When He thus dances, He enters in you,
And there abides, never to leave ever after.

ஆனத்தி யாடிப் பின்னவக் கூத்தாடிக்
கானத்தி யாடிக் கருத்தில் தரித்தாடி
மூனச் சுழுனையுள் ஆடி முடிவில்லா
ஞானத்துள் ஆடி முடித்தான்என் நாதனே. 2736

Siva Danced Away From Within Jiva to Jnana

He danced, Jivas to delight;
He danced nine dances;
The nine Saktis to delight;
He danced in forests;
He danced in the thoughts of His devotees;
He danced in the junction of Sushumna within;
He danced in Jnana Endless;
Thus He danced away,
He, my Lord.

சத்திகள் ஐந்துஞ் சிவபேதந் தானைந்தும்
முத்திகள் எட்டும் முதலாம் பதமெட்டுஞ்
சித்திகள் எட்டுஞ் சிவபதந் தானெட்டுஞ்
சுத்திகள் எட்டீசன் தொல்நட மாடுமே. 2737

Other Places Where He Danced

Saktis Five, Siva forms Five,
Muktis Eight, Primal States Eight,
Siddhis Eight, Siva States Eight,
Suddhis Eight
—In all these Lord dances
His ancient dance.

மேகங்கள் ஏழும் விரிகடல் தீவேழுந்
தேகங்கள் ஏழுஞ் சிவபாற் கரன்ஏழுந்
தாகங்கள் ஏழுஞ் சாந்திகள் ஏழும்
ஆகின்ற நந்தி யடிக்கீழ் அடங்குமே. 2738

Categories at the Feet of Dancing Siva

The clouds seven, the sea-girt continents seven,
The bodies seven, the Siva-Suns seven,
The appetites seven, the alleviations (Santis) seven,
All these contained are,
At the Feet of (Dancing) Nandi.

பொற்பதிக் கூத்து

GOLDEN HALL DANCE

தெற்கு வடக்குக் கிழக்குமேற் குச்சியில்
அற்புத மானதோர் அஞ்சு முகத்திலும்
ஒப்பில்பே ரின்பத் துபய உபயத்துள்
தற்பரன் நின்று தனிநடஞ் செய்யுமே. 2739

The Uncreated Being Dances[1]

In south, north, east, west and crest
In the five faces[2] wondrous therein,
In the space within space of peerless Bliss,
The Tat-Para dances the dance rare.

1) In Porpathi Kuthu, Siva dances with five faces, and in three stages — form, formless and form/formless. This dance takes place separately on each of the five elements. Those who witness it experience certain physical emotions, such as sobbing, trembling, and loss of consciousness.

2) Aghora, Vama, Tatpurusa, Satyojata, and Isana.

அடியார் யவரே யடியவ ராமால்
அடியார்பொன் னம்பலத் தாடல்கண்டாரே
அடியார் அரனடி யானந்தங் கண்டோர்
அடியா ரானவ ரத்தரு ளுற்றோர். 2740

He Dances, for His Devotees to Witness

Holy Devotees are they,
Who bliss of Hara's Feet attained;
Holy Devotees are they,
Who in Hara entered;
Holy Devotees are they,
Who to Siva's Holy Feet cling;
Holy Devotees are they,
Who witnessed true
The Lord's dance in golden Hall (of the astral sphere).

அடங்காத என்னை அடக்கி அடிவைத்
திடங்காண் பரானந்தத் தேஎன்னை இட்டு
நடந்தான் செயும்நந்தி நன்ஞானக் கூத்தன்
படந்தான் செய்துள்ளுட் படிந்திருந் தானே. 2741

Effect of Witnessing Siva Dance in Golden Hall

Uncontrolled was I;
He controlled me;
He blessed me with His Holy Feet;
He immersed me in Transcendental Bliss immense
Thus He dances, Our Nandi,
The great dancer of Jnana Dance;
Like a picture He made me sit still
And in me abided.

உம்பரிற் கூத்தனை உத்தமக் கூத்தனைச்
செம்பொற் றிருமன்றுட் சேவகக் கூத்தனைச்
சம்பந்தக் கூத்தனைத் தற்பரக் கூத்தனை
இன்புற நாடிஎன் அன்பில்வைத் தேனே. 2742

In Golden Hall He Dances in Intimacy of Jiva

In High Heaven He dances;
In Excellence He dances;
In the Red-Gold Hall
The Valiant Sentinel dances,
In the intimacy of Jiva He dances;
As Tat-Para He dances;
Him I sought in rapture divine
And in love adored.

மாணிக்கக் கூத்தனை வண்தில்லைக் கூத்தனைப்
பூணுற்ற மன்றுட் புரிசடைக் கூத்தனைச்
சேணுற்ற சோதிச் சிவானந்தக் கூத்தனை
ஆணிப்பொற் கூத்தனை யாருரைப் பாரே. 2743

Siva-Bliss Dance Beyond Description

He dances as a Red Ruby within,
He dances in the flourishing Tillai;
He dances in the Jewelled Hall,
He dances with matted locks;
He dances in the distant Light Divine;
He dances in Sivananda Bliss;
He dances the Pure Gold dance;
Who shall describe Him indeed that thus dances.

விம்மும் வெருவும் விழும்எழும் மெய்சோருந்
தம்மையுந் தாமறி யார்கள் சதுர்கெடுஞ்
செம்மை சிறந்த திருஅம் பலக்கூத்துள்
அம்மலர்ப் பொற்பாதத் தன்புவைப் பார்கட்கே. 2744

Dance Emotions of Devotees

They sob, they fear, they fall, they rise
Their body exhausted,
Themselves they are unaware of,
Their powers lost;
Thus are they in the Holy Temple dance;
They who in love adore
The Holy Feet of Lord,
Flower-like and golden.

தேட்டறுஞ் சிந்தை திகைப்பறும் பிண்டத்துள்
வாட்டறுங் கால்புந்தி யாகி வரும்புலன்
ஓட்டறு மாசை அறுமுளத் தானந்த
நாட்ட முறுக்குறு நாடகங் காணவே. 2745

When They Witness Holy Dance

World-seeking you no more hanker after;
No more bewildered are your thoughts;
Sorrows harass not your body within;
Your breath will be trained in the Yogic way;
Your senses controlled from straying away;
All desires are rid;
The heart elates in bliss-seeking;
Thus it is,
When the Holy Dance they witness.

காளியோ டாடிக் கனகா சலத்தாடிக்
கூளியோ டாடிக் குவலயத் தேயாடி
நீடிய நீர்தீகால் நீள்வா னிடையாடி
நாளுற அம்பலத் தேயாடும் நாதனே. 2746

How He Dances in Golden Hall

He dances with Kali;
He dances in the Golden Hall;
He dances with Demons;
He dances in the world;
He dances in water, fire, wind and sky
He dances in the Temple Holy day after day
He, the Lord Supreme.

மேரு நடுநாடி மிக்கிடை பிங்கலை
கூருமிவ் வானின் இலங்கைக் குறியுறுஞ்
சாருந் திலைவனத் தண்மா மலயத்தூ
டேறுஞ் சுழுனை இவைசிவ பூமியே. 2747

Siva's Spheres of Dance Within

The central spinal column that is Meru
The Nadis, Ida (Left) and Pingala (Right),
The Jiva's delta-shaped Muladhara
The Sushumna Cavity that is like Tillai Forest
Where the cool (southerly) breeze from Mount Malaya wafts
All these alike are Siva's Spheres of Dance.

பூதல மேருப் புறத்தான தெக்கணம்
ஓதும் இடைபிங் கலையொண் சுழுனையாம்
பாதி மதியோன் பயில்திரு அம்பலம்
ஏதமில் பூதாண்டத் தெல்லையி னீறே. 2748

Mystic Frontiers of our Universe

The Land of Mount Meru,
And the Land of South that lies beyond it
Are the Ida, Pingala;
The Holy Hall where the Lord of Crescent Moon dances,
Is the Sushumna
—Thus lie the frontiers of this universe vast.

பொற்றில்லைக் கூத்து
GOLDEN TILLAI DANCE

அண்டங்கள் ஓரேழும் அம்பொற் பதியாகப்
பண்டையா காசங்கள் ஐந்தும் பதியாகத்
தெண்டினிற் சத்தி திருஅம் பலமாகக்
கொண்டு பரஞ்சோதி கூத்துகந் தானே. 2749

Inner Meaning of Golden Tillai Dance

The seven universes as His golden abode,
The five elements, sky and the rest as pedestal
The central Kundalini Sakti as Divine Hall
Thus in rapture He danced,
He that is Cosmic Light.

குரானந்த ரேகையாய்க் கூர்ந்த குணமாஞ்
சிரானந்தம் பூரித்துத் தென்திசை சேர்ந்து
புரானந்த போகனாய்ப் பூவையுந் தானும்
நிரானந்த மாகி நிருத்தஞ்செய் தானே. 2750

Dance in the South

In the Centre the Guru indicated,
Within the head, He as Bliss danced;
Then moving South
In renewed ecstasy espousing Sakti,
He with Her in Eternal Bliss danced.

ஆதிபரன்ஆட அங்கைக் கனலாட
ஓதுஞ் சடையாட உன்மத்த முற்றாடப்
பாதி மதியாடப் பாரண்ட மீதாட
நாதமோ டாடினான் நாதாந்த நட்டமே. 2751

Nadanta Dance

The Primal Para danced;
The Fire in His hand danced;
The Holy matted lock danced;
In intoxication of joy He danced;
The crescent moon danced;
The heavenly orbs danced;
Merging in Nada He danced,
The Dance of Nadanta, heavenly.

கும்பிட அம்பலத் தாடிய கோனடம்
அம்பரன் ஆடும் அகிலாண்ட நட்டமாஞ்
செம்பொரு ளாகுஞ் சிவலோகஞ் சேர்ந்துற்றால்
உம்பர மோனஞா னாந்தத்தில் உண்மையே. 2752

Dance Cosmic

There in the Holy Hall the Lord danced,
The Jivas to adore;
The dance He dances,
Is the Dance Cosmic;
It is the dance that takes you
To Truth of Siva's realm;
There verily is the limit of Mauna Jnana Bliss.

மேதினி மூவேழ் மிகுமண்டம் ஓரேழு
சாதக மாகுஞ் சமயங்கள் நூற்றெட்டு
நாதமோ டந்த நடானந்த நாற்பதப்
பாதியோ டாடிப் பரனிரு பாதமே. 2753

Dance Ensemble

The universes seven;
The worlds thrice seven;
The religions a hundred and eight
—That the path to God show;
The heavenly states of Bliss four,
—Nada, Nadanta, Natana, Natananta—
The Sakti that is His Half;
With them all,
Para's Holy Feet danced and danced.

இடைபிங் கலையிம வானோ டிலங்கை
நடுநின்ற மேரு நடுவாஞ் சுழுனை
கடவுந் திலைவனங் கைகண்ட மூலம்
படர்வொன்றி யென்னும் பரமாம் பரமே. 2754

Pervasive Dance in the Mystic Centres

Idakalai, Pingalai,
The delta-shaped Muladhara
The Central spinal column Meru,
Where (Kundalini) Sakti is
The Sushumna cavity within
That is like the Tillai Forest
—In all these the Primal One pervaded,
He that is Paraparam.

ஈறான கன்னி குமரியே காவிரி
வேறா நவதீர்த்த மிக்குள்ள வெற்பேழுள்
பேறான வேதா கமமே பிறத்தலான்
மாறாத தென்திசை வையகஞ் சுத்தமே. 2755

South the Holy Land

At the Land's End is KanyaKumari;
And then the Kaviri
And other holy waters
The nine "theerthas" comprise;
And the seven sacred hills too;
In that land are born the Veda-Agamas;
Thus blessed,
The South is the Holy Land indeed.

நாதத் தினிலாடி நாற்பதத் தேயாடி
வேதத்தி லாடித் தழலந்த மீதாடி
போதத்தி லாடிப் புவன முழுதாடுந்
தீதற்ற தேவாதி தேவர் பிரானே. 2756

Where He Dances Solo

He dances in Nada
He dances in the States Four[1]
He dances in Veda
He dances on the Fire's[2] top
He dances in Bodha[3],
He dances in worlds all
He the Blemishless One,
The Lord of Celestials countless.

1) Nada, Nadanta, Natana, and Natananta.
2) Kundalini
3) Pure consciousness.

தேவரோ டாடித் திருஅம்ப லாத்தாடி
மூவரோ டாடி முனிசனத் தோடாடிப்

பாவினுள் ஆடிப் பராசத் தியிலாடிக்
கோவினுள் ஆடிடுங் கூத்தப் பிரானே. 2757

He Dances in Holy Ensemble

He dances with the Celestials,
He dances in the Holy Temple,
He dances with the Gods Three,
He dances with the assemblage of Munis,
He dances in song,
He dances in Parasakti
He dances in Jivas
He, the Lord of Dances.

ஆறு முகத்தில் அதிபதி நானென்றுங்
கூறு சமயக் குருபரன் நானென்றுந்
தேறினர் தெற்குத் திருஅம்ப லத்துளே
வேறின்றி யண்ணல் விளங்கிநின் றானே. 2758

Guru Para Dance in Holy Temple

"I am the Lord of Six Ways to God,
I am the Guru Supreme, religions speak of,"
Thus saying,
He chose the Holy Temple in South;
And there in resplendence dances,
With peer none to compare.

அம்பலம் ஆடரங் காக அதன்மீதே
எம்பரன் ஆடும் இருதாளி னீரொளி
உம்பர மாம்ஐந்து நாதத்து ரேகையுள்
தம்பத மாய்நின்று தான்வந் தருளுமே. 2759

Siva-State

The Spaces Vast are His dance arena,
Upon that my Paran dances;
The radiance of His twin Feet
Ascends to heavens high,
And reaches to Five-lettered Nada's point;
He does descend to you and bless you,
His Siva-State confer on you.

ஆடிய காலும் அதிற்சிலம் போசையும்
பாடிய பாட்டும் பலவான நட்டமுங்
கூடிய கோலங் குருபரன் கொண்டாடத்
தேடியு ளேகண்டு தீர்ந்தற்ற வாறே. 2760

Varied Dances

And the dances varied,
With it the foot-work
And the jingle of the anklets
And the songs sung
And the Forms He assumed,
—So, the Guru Para dances;
Seek that dance within
And your birth's cycle forever end.

இருதயந் தன்னில் எழுந்த பிராணன்
கரசர ணாதி கலக்கும் படியே
அரதன மன்றினின் மாணிக்கக் கூத்தன்
குரவனாய் எங்கணுங் கூத்துகந் தானே. 2761

He Dances as Prana

As Prana that in heart arises
To permeate your hands and feet,
And sense organs all,
—Thus He dances
In the arena of nine gems,
He the Red-Ruby Dancer;
As the Holy Guru He danced in rapture
In places all.

அற்புதக் கூத்து

ATBUDHA (WONDER) DANCE

குருவுரு வன்றிக் குனிக்கும் உருவம்
அருவுரு வாவதும் அந்த அருவே
திரிபுரை யாகித் திகழ்தரு வாளும்
உருவரு வாகும் உமையவள் தானே. 2762

Dance of the Form-Formless (Sadasiva)

The Form that dances
Is Guru's Form,
It is in sooth Formless;
That Formless One shines
As Sakti Tiripurai as well;
She verily is Uma
That is Form-Formless.

When Siva dances the Atbhuta (Wonder) Dance, He is Formless, and His consort is mingled into Him as Tiripurai (or Uma). This dance is beyond the comprehension of ordinary human cognition. It can be witnessed only by those who are rid of maya, and mamaya. In this Dance, His partner, Uma, first separates Herself from Him during the dance and then later coalesces with Him. The visualization here is that of Siva dancing before His consort wearing on His body, fire, drum, beads, noose, goad, spear, skull, etc. The Five Letters, Si Va Ya Na Ma, are represented here.

திருவழி யாவது சிற்றம் பலத்தே
குருவடி வுள்ளாக் குனிக்கும் உருவே
உருவரு வாவது முற்றுணர்ந் தோர்க்கு
அருள்வழி யாவதும் அவ்வழி தானே. 2763

The Form-Formless Dancer is Gurupara

The Holy Way is Form-Formless
In the Holy Temple of Chittambara,
The Form that dances there
Is the Form of Guru within,
They who full know,
He is Form-Formless
They receive His Grace Divine
That Jnana Way.

நீருஞ் சிரசிடைப் பன்னிரண் டங்குலம்
ஓடும் உயிரெழுந் தோங்கி உதித்திட

நாடுமின் நாதாந்த நம்பெரு மான்உகந்
தாடும் இடந்திரு அம்பலந் தானே. 2764

Nadanta Dance in Prana Source

From within the head
In twelve finger-measure
The Prana breath rises high,
That highway you seek;
That the Place where
Our Lord of Nadanta dances;
That verily is the Holy Temple.

வளிமேக மின்வில்லு வானக வோசை
தெளிய விசும்பில் திகழ்தரு வாறுபோல்
களியொளி யாறுங் கலந்துடன் வேறாய்
ஒளியுரு வாகிஒளித்துநின் றானே. 2765

Light-Form of the Divine Dancer

The wind, the cloud, lightning, rainbow, sky and thunder
All these in space arise;
Like it,
Within the rapturous rays blended of Adharas six,
And without them too, separate,
He as Form of Light stands,
In body concealed.

தீமுதல் ஐந்துந் திசையெட்டுங் கீழ்மேலும்
ஆயும் அறிவினுக் கப்புறம் ஆனந்தம்
மாயைமா மாயை கடந்துநின் றார்காண
நாயகன் நின்று நடஞ் செய்யு மாறே. 2766

Dance Witnessed by Those Who Transcend Maya and Mamaya

In the elements five, and directions eight,
And above and below,
Beyond the intelligent senses
Is Bliss Divine;
For them to witness
That transcends Maya and Mamaya
The Lord stands and ever dances.

கூத்தன் கலந்திடுங் கோல்வளை யாளொடுங்
கூத்தன் கலந்திடுங் கோதிலா ஆனந்தங்
கூத்தன் கலந்திடுங் கோதிலா ஞானத்துக்
கூத்தனுங் கூத்தியுங் கூத்ததின் மேலே. 2767

In Dance Siva Blends

The Dancer blends in Sakti of charming bracelets,
The Dancer blends in blemishless Bliss,
The Dancer blends in blemishless Jnana,
The Dancer and His Consort in Dance Blend.

இடங்கொண்ட சத்தியும் எந்தை பிரானும்
நடங்கொண்டு நின்றமை நானும் அறிந்தேன்
படங்கொடு நின்றஇப் பல்லுயிர்க் கெல்லாம்
அடங்கலுந் தாமாய்நின் றாடுகின் றாரே. 2768

Dance for Jiva's Redemption

My Lord and His Sakti
That His Half took
Stood dancing;
That I witnessed;
For the countless Jivas
That are veiled by Maya;
As Redemption He stands,
Dancing, dancing eternal.

சத்தி வடிவு சகல ஆனந்தமும்
ஒத்த ஆனந்தம் உமையவள் மேனியாஞ்
சத்தி வடிவு சகளத் தெழுந்திரண்
டொத்த ஆனந்தம் ஒருநட மாமே. 2769

Bliss of Siva-Sakti Pair Dance

The Form of Sakti is Bliss-All;
Of equal Bliss is Uma's Form;
Sakti's Form rising in Siva's Form
As one merged and one dance performed;
That peerless dance is bliss Perfect.

நெற்றிக்கு நேரே புருவத் திடைவெளி
உற்றுற்றுப் பார்க்க வொளிவிடு மந்திரம்
பற்றுக்குப் பற்றாய்ப் பரமனிருந்திடஞ்
சிற்றம் பலமென்று சேர்ந்துகொண் டேனே. 2770

Ajna Centre is Astral Temple of Lord

Straight within the fore-head
Between the eye-brows
Is the astral space vast;
Peer, peer within there
The luminous Mantra (Aum) will be;
The place where they in yearning sought Him
Is the place where He in yearning is;
That verily is the Holv Temple of Chittambara
And there did I firm sit.

அண்டங்கள் தத்துவ மாகிச் சதாசிவந்
தண்டினிற் சாத்தவி சாம்பவி யாதனந்
தெண்டினில் ஏழுஞ் சிவாசன மாகவே
கொண்டு பரஞ்சோதி கூத்துகந் தானே. 2771

Seven Pedestals of Siva's Dance

The universe vast,
The Tattvas numerous,
The Sadasiva,
The Sushumna central,
The Sakti Sakthavi,
The Sakti Sambhavi
The Sakti Kundalini
(That in Muladhara Plexus is)
—These seven are Siva's pedestals;
On them He dances
He, the Being Transcendental.

மன்று நிறைந்த விளக்கொளி மாமலர்
நன்றிது தானிதழ் நாலொடு நூறவை
சென்றது தானொரு பத்திரு நூறுள
நின்றது தானெடு மண்டல மாமே. 2772

The Light of Astral Flower in the Dance Theatre

The shedding light
Of that Astral Flower Within,
Illumines the Dance Arena entire;
Wondrous indeed that Flower is;
Its petals four (in Muladhara)
Into a hundred petals blossomed (in Sahasrathala)
And into ten and two hundred worlds expanded,
In the interminable spaces vast.

அண்டம் எழுகோடி பிண்டம் எழுகோடி
தெண்டிரை சூழ்ந்த திசைகள் எழுகோடி
எண்டிசை சூழ்ந்த இலிங்கம் எழுகோடி
அண்ட நடஞ் செயும் ஆலயந் தானே. 2773

Septenary Centres of Cosmic Dance

Seven Crores are the universes vast,
Seven Crores are the life forms varied,
Seven Crores the continents of the sea-girt world,
Seven Crores the Lingas in directions eight
These the Temples where His Cosmic Dance
performed are.

ஆகாச மாமுட லங்கார் முயலகன்
ஏகாச மாந்திசை யெட்டுந் திருக்கைகண்
மோகாய முக்கண்கள் மூன்றொளி தானாக
மாகாய மன்றுள் நடஞ்செய்கின் றானே. 2774

Dance in Space

The Space is His Body;
The Muyalaka (Demon) is the Darkness in that space
The Directions eight are His spreading Hands,
The loving eyes three
Are tne lights three (Sun, Moon and Fire);
Thus He dances
In the space arena,
That is Body Cosmic.

அம்பல மாவ தகில சராசரம்
அம்பல மாவது ஆதிப் பிரானடி
அம்பல மாவது அப்புத்தீ மண்டலம்
அம்பல மாவது அஞ்செழுத் தாமே. 2775

Holy Dance Theatre

The Holy Dance arena is the creation countless;
The Holy Dance arena is the Holy Feet of Lord;
The Holy Dance arena is the sphere of Water and Fire,
The Holy Dance arena is the Letter-Five, verily.

கூடிய திண்முழ வங்குழ லோமென்று
ஆடிய மானுடர் ஆதிப் பிரானென்ன
நாடிய நற்கண மாரம்பல் பூதங்கள்
பாடிய வாறொரு பாண்டரங் காமே. 2776

Pandaranga Dance at the End of Dissolution

The drums beat, the pipes played,
"Aum", they hummed;
The men danced,
"My Primal Lord!" they said;
The crowd of Ganas in serried ranks praised;
The numerous Bhootas sang
—Thus He danced the Pandaranga,
—The Dance of Dissolution
At end of Tiripurai conflagration.

அண்டத்தில் தேவர்கள் அப்பாலைத் தேவர்கள்
தெண்டிரை சூழ்புவிக் குள்ளுள்ள தேவர்கள்
புண்டரி கப்பதப் பொன்னம் பலக்கூத்துக்
கண்டுசே வித்துக் கதிபெறு வார்களே. 2777

Who Witnesses Golden Temple Dance

The Celestials in the universe
And the Celestials Beyond,
And the holy ones in the sea-girt world
All, all, witnessed the Golden Temple dance
Of the Lord of Lotus Feet,
And that adoring
Reached Siva-State.

புளிக்கண் டவர்க்குப் புனலூறு மாபோற்
களிக்குந் திருக்கூத்துக் கண்டவர்க் கெல்லாம்
அளிக்கும் அருட்கண்ணீர் சோர்நெஞ் சுருக்கும்
ஒளிக்குளா னந்தத் தமுதூறும்உள்ளத்தே. 2778

Rapturous Experience Flowing From Witnessing Holy Dance

At the sight of tamarind
Water in mouth wells up;
As like it,
Are all those who witness the Holy Dance;
They shed tears of joy;
They melt in love of Lord;
In their hearts,
Ambrosial bliss of Divine Light wells up.

திண்டாடி வீழ்கை சிவானந்த மாவது
உண்டார்க் குணவுண்டால்உன்மத்தஞ்சித்திக்குங்
கொண்டாடு மன்றுட் குனிக்குந் திருக்கூத்துக்
கண்டார் வருங்குணங் கேட்டார்க்கும் ஒக்குமே. 2779

So too: They Who Hear of It

They stagger, their sense lost,
Drunk of Sivananda Bliss;
They who still retain their senses,
Frenzied become;
Thus are they,

Who the Divine Dance witnessed,
In the Holy Arena praised by all;
Even those who hear of it
Are like those who witness it;
—All rapture is theirs too.

அங்கி தமருகம் அக்குமா லைபாசம்
அங்குசஞ் சூலங் கபால முடன்ஞானந்
தங்கு பயந்தரு நீல் மும்முடன்
மங்கையோர் பாகமாய் மாநட மாடுமே. 2780

He Dances With Sakti

With fire and drum,
With Rudraksha garland and noose cord,
With elephant's goad, trident and skull,
With frightening blue throat where Jnana is,
With Sakti for His inseparate partner,
He dances the Dance Mighty.

ஆடல் பதினோரு றுப்பும் அடைவாகக்
கூடிய பாதஞ் சிலம்புகைக் கொள்துடி
நீடிய நாதம் பராற்பர நேயத்தே
ஆடிய நந்தி புறமகத் தானே. 2781

He Dances Inside and Outside the Heart

With the accompaniments eleven
That dance has,
With anklet feet and drum in hand,
The Nada reverberated,
And reached like Para-Para in High Heaven;
The Holy Nandi that thus danced,
Is verily inside your heart and outside too.

ஒன்பதும் ஆட ஒருபதி னாறாட
அன்புறு மார்க்கங்கள் ஆறும் உடனாட
இன்புறும் ஏழினும் ஏழைம்பத் தாறாட
அன்பது மாடினான் ஆனந்தக் கூத்தே. 2782

Dance of Divine Bliss

The nine[1] danced,
The sixteen[2] danced,
The loving Faiths six[3] danced,
The seven[4] melodies danced;
The twenty and eight[5] rhythmic beats danced;
The Love (Sakti) too danced;
He danced the Dance of Divine Bliss.

---

1) The Nine centres within—six adharas and the three centres of sun, moon and fire.

2) The sixteen-petalled mystic lotus in the visuddhi centre, where the 16 kalas ending with unmanai sakti are located—referred to as Sodasa kala prasadam—vide Mantra 2377. Tantra Eight.n.supra.

3) The six religions are variously delineated as follows:
a)Saivam, Vaishnavam, Saktam, Sauram, Ganapathyam, Kaumaram—these are the 'Vaidik' faiths.
b)Kapila, Ganatha, Patarayali, Aksapada, Vyasa, Jaimini—these philosophies are named after there founders.
c)Buddha, Jaina, Bhairava, Kalamukha, Lokayada, Sunyavada—these are held as "Outer faiths" by Vaidiks.
d)Bhairava, Vama, Kalamukha, Mavirata, Pasupata, Saivam—these are held as "outer faiths" of Saivam.
e)Lokayata, Buddha, Jaina (Samana). Mimamsa, Pancharata, Bhattacharya—these too are held as "outer philosophies" by the Saiva school.

4) The seven primal melodies are: Sa, Ri, Ga, Ma, Pa, Da and Ni. In Tamil literature, they are described as, kurtuttam, kaikilai, uzhai, ili, vilari, and tharam.

5) 28 rythmic modes commencing from kandam and prabandavuru. Kandam has a basic measure and a sing beat; prabhandavuru has no basic measure and has multi beats. In between are permutations and combinations. The 28 rythmic measures belong to the inner measures of dance rythm.

ஏழினில் ஏழாய் இகந்தெழுத் தேழதாய்
ஏழினில் ஒன்றாய் இழிந்தமைந் தொன்றாகி
ஏழினிற் சன்மார்க்கம் எங்கள் பரஞ்சோதி
ஏழிசை நாடகத் தேஇசைந் தானே. 2783

Dance of Seven Melodies

As seven subtle melodies within the seven articulated,
As the seven letters they denote,
As one harmony in the seven musical notes,
He descended and pervaded;
In the seventh state beyond the six adharas
That Jnana yoga crosses
Is Aum Paranjothi, (the Divine Light)
In the dance of seven melodies He danced.

மூன்றினில் அஞ்சாகி முந்நூற் றறுபதாய்
மூன்றினில் ஆறாய் முதற்பன்னீர் மூலமாய்
மூன்றினில் அக்க முடிவாகி முந்தியே
மூன்றிலும் ஆடினான் மோகாந்தக் கூத்தே. 2784

Dance of Triple Pasa-Riddance-Mohanta Dance

The three letters A, U and M (Aum)
The five letters Na, Ma, Si, Va, Ya became;
And as three hundred and sixty rays they became;
Commencing from Muladhara that the waters hold
In through the centres six (Adharas) and spheres three
(Sun, Moon, Fire)
That the triple Karanas their end may see,
He in ancient Pasas Triple danced
The Dance of Mohanta (Impurity-riddance).

Presumably, the reference is to the combined 360 rays of fire (118), sun (106), and moon (136). They constitute kala (time) as the 360 rays or 360 days that comprise a year. Vide "The Serpent Power," by Sir John Woodroffe, pp.144-5.

தாமுடி வானவர் தம்முடி மேலுறை
மாமணி ஈசன் மலரடித் தாளிணை
வாமணி யன்புடை யார்மனத் துள்ளெழுங்
காமணி ஞாலங் கடந்துநின் றானே. 2785

He is Kalpaka Tree that Grants All Wishes

Above jewelled crowned heads of Celestials,

Are the flowery Feet of Lord,
A precious Jewel is He;
He adorns the rising heart of His loving devotees;
He is Tree Divine (Kalpaka Tharu)
Of Heavenly glades;
He transcends worlds all.

புரிந்தவன் ஆடிற் புவனங்க ளாடுந்
தெரிந்தவன் ஆடும் அளவெங்கள் சிந்தை
புரிந்தவ னாடிற்பல் பூதங்கள் ஆடும்
எரிந்தவன் ஆடல்கண் டின்புற்ற வாறே. 2786

When Creator Dances All Creation Dances

When the Creator dances
The Worlds He created dances;
To the measure He dances in our knowledge,
Our thoughts too dance;
When He in heart endearing dances,
The elements several too dance;
Flaming as Divine Five He dances,
That we witnessed in rapture surpassing.

ஆதி நடஞ்செய்தான் என்பர்கள் ஆதர்கள்
ஆதி நடஞ்செய்கை யாரும் அறிகிலர்
ஆதி நடமாட லாரும் அறிந்தபின்
ஆதி நடமாட லாமருட் சத்தியே. 2787

Primal Dance

"The Primal Dance He danced"
Thus say the holy ones;
None saw Him dance
That Primal Dance of yore;
When that Primal Dance they witness,
They dance indeed in the Grace
Of that Primal Sakti.

ஒன்பதோ டொன்பதாம் உற்ற இருபதத்
தன்புறு கோணம் அசிபதத் தாடிடத்
துன்புறு சத்தியுள் தோன்றிநின் றாடவே
அன்புறு எந்தைநின் றாடலுற் றானே. 2788

He Danced in Asi Pada State

In the nine centres mystic within
The ninth state (Turiyatita) attained;
In the centre that is love
His twin feet in Asi-Pada danced;
And as the anguished Sakti within Him danced,
My loving Father together with Her in rapture danced.

தத்துவம் ஆடச் சதாசிவந் தானாடச்
சித்தமும் ஆடச் சிவசத்தி தானாட
வைத்த சராசரம் ஆட மறையாட
அத்தனும் ஆடினான் ஆனந்தக்கூத்தே. 2789

Dance of Ananda (Bliss)

The Tattvas danced; Sadasiva danced;
The Thought danced; Siva-Sakti danced;
The creation vast danced; the Vedas danced;
The Lord too danced,
The Dance of Ananda (Divine Bliss).

இருவருங் காண எழில்அம் பலத்தே
உருவோ டருவோ டுருபர ரூபமாய்த்
திருவருட் சத்திக்குள் சித்தனா னந்தன்
அருளுரு வாகநின் றாடலுற் றானே. 2790

He Danced for Rishis Patanjali and Vyaghrapada

In the splendorous Temple (of Chidambaram)
He danced,
For the two Rishis[1] to witness
He danced, Form, Formless and as Cosmic Form,
Within the Divine Grace of Sakti
He danced,
He the Siddha, the Ananda;
As Form of Grace
He stood and danced.

1) Patanjali (the snake-bodied), and Vyaghrapada (the tiger-footed).

சிவமாடச் சத்தியும்ஆடச் சகத்தில்
அவமாட ஆடாத அம்பரம் ஆட
நவமான தத்துவ நாதாந்த மாடச்
சிவமாடும் வேதாந்தச் சித்தாந்தத் துள்ளே. 2791

He Danced in Vedanta-Siddhanta Truth

Siva danced, Sakti danced,
The worldly desires danced;
The space that dances not danced;
The Tattva-Nadanta wondrous danced;
When Siva danced inside of Truth,
That indeed is Vedanta-Siddhanta.

நாதத்தின் அந்தமும் நாற்போத அந்தமும்
வேதத்தின் அந்தமும் மெய்ச்சிவா னந்தமுந்
தாதற்ற நல்ல சதாசிவா னந்தத்து
நாதப் பிரமஞ் சிவநட மாமே. 2792

Siva Natana

Nadanta that is end of Nada, (Principle of Sound)
Bodhanta that is end of Bodha (Jnana)
Vedanta that is end of Vedas
Sivananda that is Bliss of Siva,
Sadasivananda that is without end,
In all these, He dances the Siva Natana
He that is Nada Brahmam (Lord within the Sound-Principle).

சிவமாதி ஐவர்திண் டாட்டமுந் தீரத்
தவமார் பசுபாசம் ஆங்கே தனித்துத்
தவமாம் பரனெங்குந் தானாக ஆடுந்
தவமாஞ் சிவானந்தத் தோர்ஞானக்கூத்தே. 2793

Jnana Dance

The perplexities of the Five Gods
Rudra and the rest to end,
The Jiva bonds standing afar,
In prayer to depart
The Holy Para by Himself dances everywhere;
Holy indeed is the Jnana Dance
That Sivananda Bliss fills.

கூடிநின் றானொரு காலத்துத் தேவர்கள்
வீடநின் றான்விகிர் தர்வென்னு நாமத்தைத்
தேடநின் றான்திக ழுஞ்சுடர் மூன்றொளி
ஆடநின் றான்என்னை ஆட்கொண்ட வாறே. 2794

Dance in the Three Lights

As One Supreme He stood in times of yore,
Redeeming the Celestials countless,
He earned the name of Lord (Vikirtha)
He danced in the luminous Lights Three,
He accepted me in His Grace.

நாதத் துவங்கடந் தாதி மறைநம்பி
பூதத் துவத்தே பொலிந்தின்பம் எய்தினர்
நேதத் துவமும் அவற்றொடு நேதியும்
பேதப் படாவண்ணம் பின்னிநின் றானே. 2795

He is Tattvas and Their Goal

The Lord is the beginning of Vedas
He is beyond Nada Tattvas;
(Knowing this not,)
They sought the pleasures of this world
And in them revelled;
He is the Tattvas in order placed
And their Lord too at once;
In that in separateness
He commingling stood.

ஆனந்தம் ஆனந்தம் என்பர் அறிவிலர்
ஆனந்த மாநட மாரும் அறிகிலர்
ஆனந்த மாநட மாரும் அறிந்தபின்
தானந்தம் அற்றிடம் ஆனந்த மாமே. 2796

Dance of Bliss is Union in Siva

"Bliss Bliss," they say;
Witless are they;
None know the Dance of Bliss;
Having witnessed the Dance of Bliss,
The Jiva its separateness ends,
And in Divine Bliss unites.

திருந்துநற் சீயேன் றுந்தறிய கையும்
அருந்தவர் வாவென் றணைத்த மலர்க்கையும்
பொருந்தில் இமைப்பிலி யவ்வென்ற பொற்கையுந்
திருந்தத்தீ யாகுந் திருநிலை மவ்வே. 2797

Signification of Five-Lettered Mantra in Siva Dance

"Leave this, be reformed,"
—Thus to Jivas, gestures one hand in letter "Si;"
"Come like me, Be united in me"
—Thus to Tapasvins gestures another flower-like hand in letter "Va;"
"Be in, Deva, fear not."
Thus to Celestials gestures, the golden hand in letter "Ya."
The hand that holds fire
Gestures the letter "Na;"
The foot on earth planted in dance
Gestures the letter "Ma;"
(Thus is the entire Five-Letter Mantra "Si Va Ya Na Ma"
Is Divine Dance denoted.)

மருவந் துடியுடன் மன்னிய வீச்சு
மருவிய அப்பும் அனலுடன் கையுங்
கருவின் மிதித்த கமலப் பதமும்
உருவில் சிவாய நமவென வோதே. 2798

Further Signification of Dance-Form in Relation to Five Letter Mantra

The hand that holds the drum, (Si)
The hand that sways, (Va)
The hand that offers Refuge, (Ya)
The hand that holds the blazing Fire, (Na)
The lotus-foot, firm, on Anava Mala planted, (Ma)
—Thus of the Divine Dance Form
Si Va Ya Na Ma denotes.

அரன்துடி தோற்றம் அமைத்தல் திதியாம்
அரன்அங்கி தன்னில் அறையிற்சங் காரம்
அரனுற் றணைப்பில் அமருந் திரோதாயி
அரனடி யென்றும் அனுக்கிரகம் என்னே. 2799

Symbolism of Siva Dance

Hara's drum is creation;
Hara's hand gesturing protection is preservation;
Hara's fire is dissolution;
Hara's foot planted down is Obfuscation (Tirodhayi)
Hara's foot, raised in dance, is Grace (Redemption) abiding.

தீத்திரட் சோதி திகழொளி யுள்ளொளி
கூத்தனைக்கண்டஅக் கோமளக் கண்ணினள்
மூர்த்திகள் மூவர் முதல்வ னிடைசெல்லப்
பார்த்தனள் வேதங்கள் பாடினள் தானே. 2800

Sakti Witnesses Trinity Dance of Siva

The flaming fire is He;
The sparkling light within is He;
The Sakti of youthful eyes saw Him dance;
She saw the Three Gods merge

Into the One Primal Being;
In rapture She sang Vedas all.

நந்தியை எந்தையை ஞானத் தலைவனை
மந்திர மொன்றுள் மருவி யதுகடந்
தந்தர வானத்தின் அப்புறத் தப்பர
சுந்தரக் கூத்தனை என்சொல்லு மாறே. 2801

Para Sundara Dance in the Beyond

Nandi, My Father, Lord of Jnana,
In the one-letter mantra Aum, He entered,
Transcending it,
In the spaces beyond He dances,
In comeliness surpassing,
How shall I describe that Para Sundara Dance!

சீய குருநந்தி திருஅம்ப லத்திலே
ஆயுறு மேனியை யாரும் அறிகிலர்
தீயுறு செம்மை வெளுப்போடு மத்தன்மை
ஆயுறு மேனி அணைபுக லாமே. 2802

Form of Siva

A lion-hearted Guru is Nandi,
In the Holy Temple He does dance;
None know His Form divine;
Fiery red smeared white it is;
They who see His Form
Reach the haven of Refuge.

தானான சத்தியுந் தற்பரை யாய்நிற்குந்
தானாம் பரற்கும் உயிர்க்குந் தகுமிச்சை
ஞானாதி பேத நடத்து நடித்தருள்
ஆனால் அரனடி நேயத்த தாமே. 2803

Sakti's Grace Dance

Sakti in the Lord
Stands as Tat-Parai;
She forges the bond between Para and Jiva:
Standing as Iccha, Jnana and Kriya
She many acts performs;
And when She, Her Grace lends
You reach Hara's loving Feet.

9. ஆகாசப்பேறு

ATTAINMENT OF AKASA (SPACE) WITHIN

உள்ளது ளோமென ஈசன் ஒருவனை
உள்ளத்து ளேயங்கி யாய வொருவனை
உள்ளத்து ளேநீதி யாய வொருவனை
உள்ளத்து ளேயுடல் ஆகாய மாமே. 2804

How Siva is Within

The Lord is in our heart,
As Aum is He there,
As Fire is He there,
As Order is He there,
As Space in body is He there,
He, the One Being.

பெருநில மாயண்ட மாயண்டத் தப்பால்
குருநில மாய்நின்ற கொள்கையன் ஈசன்
பெருநில மாய்நின்று தாங்கிய தாளோன்
அருநில யாய்நின்ற ஆதிப் பிரானே. 2805

How Siva is Without

As the Earth vast,
As the Universe vast,
As the Void Beyond,
—Thus is the Lord pervasiveness all;
Vast indeed is His benevolence,
His Feet support the world entire;
Yet invisible is His Form,
He the Primal Lord.

அண்ட வொளியும் அகண்ட வொளியுடன்
பிண்ட வொளியாற் பிதற்றும் பெருமையை
உண்ட வெளிக்குள் ஒளிக்குள் ஒளித்தது
கொண்ட குறியைக் குலைத்தது தானே. 2806

Siva's Light Merges in Jiva's Light

He is the Light Cosmic,
He is the Light Beyond,
He is the Light that mingles in the Light within;
In the spreading light of space,
That swallows Immensity Vast,
My body-light merged;
Shattering Existence's land-marks, all

பயனுறு கன்னியர் போகத்தி னுள்ளே
பயனுறு மாதி பரஞ்சுடர்ச் சோதி
அயனொடு மாலறி யாவகை நின்றிட்
டுயர்நெறி யாயொளி யொன்றது வாமே. 2807

He as Light is Immanent in Brahma and Vishnu

In the delight of the maiden's union
Is the sparkling light of the Primal One;
Immanent in Brahma and Vishnu it was,
Yet they knew it not (and contending stood);
Then He revealed Himself to them
As Light Divine,
Flaming from earth to heaven.

அறிவுக் கறிவாம் அகண்ட வொளியும்
பிறியா வலத்தினிற் பேரொளி மூன்றும்
அறியா தடங்கிடில் அத்தன் அடிக்குட்
பிறியா திருக்கிற் பெருங்கால மாமே. 2808

When Siva's Light is Reached

The Light Transcendental
Is knowledge beyond knowledge;
When in it merge in silence
In the Lights Three (within) that are mighty,
Then is Siva reached;
If His Feet there you leave not,
Long, long may you be.

ஆகாச வண்ணன் அமரர் குலக்கொழுந்
தேகாச மாசுண மிட்டங் கிருந்தவன்
ஆகாச வண்ணம் அமர்ந்துநின் றப்புறம்
ஆகாச மாயங்கி வண்ணனு மாமே. 2809

He Fills Space and Outer-Space

He fills the space;
He is the darling of Celestials;
He wears the serpent;
Having filled the space
He stands as outer-space
He the Fire-Hued.

உயிர்க்கின்ற வாறும் உலகமும் ஒக்க
உயிர்க்கின்ற உள்ளொளி சேர்கின்ற போது
குயிற்கொண்ட பேதை குலாவி யுலாவி
வெயிற்கொண்டென் உள்ளம் வெளியது வாமே. 2810

In Kundalini Yoga Jiva's Thought Merges in Space

As you breathe in the Yogic Way,
You reach the Inner Light,
That is the breath of worlds all;
The Damsel in the Muladhara
Then rises and upward ascends,
Spreading Her day-light brilliance,
And thus uplifted,
My thoughts in space within merge.

நணுகி லகல்கில னாதன் உலகத்
தணுகில் அகன்ற பெரும்பதி நந்தி
நணுகிய மின்னொளி சோதி வெளியைப்
பணியின் அமுதம் பருகலு மாமே. 2811

Drink of Ambrosia in Space

Move close to Lord,
He leaves you not;
Move close to world,
He leaves you alone;
He the Supreme Lord Nandi;
Move close to the Flashing Light
Within the (mystic) astral space,
And there adore;
You may drink of Ambrosia Divine.

புறத்துளா காசம் புவனம் உலகம்
அகத்துளா காசமெம் மாதி யறிவு
சிவத்துளா காசஞ் செழுஞ்சுடர்ச் சோதி
சகத்துளா காசந் தானஞ் சமாதியே. 2812

The Cosmic Space of Samadhi

In the Outer Space is universe and the world,
In the Inner Space is Primal Jnana,
In the Space where Siva is, is Light Resplendent
In the Space that composes the Cosmos
Is Samadhi's destination.

10. ஞானோதயம்

JNANODAYAM (DAWN OF JNANA)

மனசந் தியிற்கண்ட மன்னன வாகுங்
கனவுற ஆனந்தங் காண்டல் அதனை
வினவுற ஆனந்த மீதொழி வென்ப
இனமுற்றா னந்தியா னந்த மிரண்டே. 2813

Bliss in Sushupti and the Lord of Bliss in Turiya

In the conjunction of Mind is the Waking State,
Then the Dream, where bliss experienced be;
Beyond it, is (sushupti) where Bliss experience certain is;
Ascend still, there is the Space (Turiya)
Where are only Two—Bliss and Lord of Bliss.

கரியட்ட கையன் கபாலங்கை ஏந்தி
எரியும் இளம்பிறை சூடம்எம் மானை
அரியன் பெரியனென் றாட்பட்ட தல்லால்
கரியன்கொல் சேயன்கொல் காண்கின்றி லேனே. 2814

Adore Lord as "Rare" and "Great"

With His hands He peeled the elephant hide,
In His hands He held the skull,
On His crest He adorned the crescent moon,
That Lord I adored;
"Rare; Great is He;"

Beyond that I knew nothing;
Is He black or red?
I have not seen.

மிக்கா ரமுதுண்ண நஞ்சுண்ட மேலவன்
தக்கார் உரைத்த தவநெறி யேசென்று
புக்கா லருளும் பொன்னுரை ஞானத்தை
நக்கார் கழல்வழி நாடுமின் நீரே. 2815

Enter Within and Follow Guru's Way

When the Celestials above consumed ambrosia,
He consumed poison;
Follow the Way of Tapas, the holy men taught,
And enter within;
He will give you Jnana, that is pure gold;
So, Siva's Feet do seek.

விளக்கைப் பிளந்து விளக்கினை யேற்றி
விளக்கினுக் குள்ளே விளக்கினைத் தூண்டி
விளக்கில் விளக்கை விளக்கவல் லார்க்கு
விளக்குடை யான்கழல் மேவலு மாமே. 2816

Kindle Light Within Light

Break open the Kundalini Light
Light the Lamp within;
Kindle the Light within that Light
They who can thus brighten,
The Light within the Light
May reach the Feet of Him,
Who is lustrous Lamp of Jnana.

தத்துவம் எங்குண்டு தத்துவன் அங்குண்டு
தத்துவம் எங்கில்லை தத்துவன் அங்கில்லை
தத்துவ ஞானத்தின் தன்மை யறிந்தபின்
தத்துவன் அங்கே தலைப்படுந் தானே. 2817

Know Truth of Tattva Jnana

Where Tattvas are, the Lord of Tattvas is;
Where Tattvas are not, the Lord of Tattvas is not;
When you know the truth of Tattva Jnana,
The Lord of Tattvas will there appear.

விசும்பொன்று தாங்கிய மெய்ஞ்ஞானத் துள்ளே
அசும்பினின் றூறிய தாரமு தாகும்
பசும்பொன் திகழும் படர்சடை மீதே
குசும்ப மலர்க்கந்தங் கூடிநின் றானே. 2818

Lord Stands in Astral Sphere of the Head

In the astral space that holds Jnana True,
Is the ambrosia that wells up from the fleshy body mire;
With the spreading matted locks of lustrous golden hue,
With the haunting perfume of the ruddy (astral) flower,
He stood;

முத்தின் வயிரத்தின் முந்நீர்ப் பவளத்தின்
கொத்தும் பசும்பொன்னின் தூவொளி மாணிக்கம்
ஒத்துயர் அண்டத் துள்ளமர் சோதியை
எத்தன்மை வேறென்று கூறுசெய் வீரே. 2819

Brilliance of Lord's Light

Pearl, diamond, coral of three waters,
Gold of purest fineness and gems,
Into the brilliance of all these blended
Is the Light of Lord that in heaven is;
How else to describe that Divine Resplendence!

நானென்றுந் தானென்றும் நாடினேன் நாடலும்
நானென்றுந் தானென் றிரண்டில்லை யென்பது
நானென்ற ஞான முதல்வனே நல்கினான்
நானென்று நானும் நினைப்பொழிந் தேனே. 2820

Lord Himself Removed "I" and "He" Distinction

As I and He, I separate sought;
And as I thus sought,
"I and He are separate are not;
—Thus the Lord of Primal Jnana Himself granted,
And then no more was the thought of I and He.

ஞானத்தின் நன்னெறி நாதாந்த நன்னெறி
ஞானத்தின் நன்னெறி நானென் றறிவோர்தல்
ஞானத்தின் நல்யோக நன்னிலை யேநிற்றல்
ஞானத்தின் நன்மோன நாதாந்த வேதமே. 2821

Jnana Way is the Truth

The Jnana Way is the Nadanta Way,
The Jnana Way is the Knowledge of Self,
The Jnana Way of yoga is to centre on Siva,
The Jnana Way of Silence
Is the Veda Truth of Nadanta.

உய்யவல் லார்கட் குயிர்சிவ ஞானமே
உய்யவல் லார்கட் குயிர்சிவ தெய்வமே
உய்யவல் லார்கட் கொடுக்கம் பிரணவம்
உய்யவல் லாரறி வுள்ளறி வாமே. 2822

Jnana is the Way to Liberation

For them who seek liberation,
Siva Jnana is the life-breath;
For them who seek liberation,
Siva God is the life-breath;
For them who seek liberation
Pranava is the centre of divine union;
The Lord is the Knowledge within Knowledge,
Of those who liberation seek.

காணவல் லார்க்கவன் கண்ணின் மணியொக்குங்
காணவல் லார்க்குக் கடலின் அமுதொக்கும்
பேணவல் லார்க்குப் பிழைப்பிலன் பேர்நந்தி
ஆணவல் லார்க்கே அவன்துணை யாமே. 2823

Lord is the Support Unfailing

For those who can see Him
He is the light of their eyes;
For those who can see Him
He is the ambrosia of the Oceans;
Them who adore Him
The Mighty Nandi never fails;
To them alone who yearn for Him
He stands as Support unfailing.

ஓமெனும் ஓரெழுத் துள்நின்ற ஓசைபோல்
மேனின்ற தேவர் விரும்பும் விழுப்பொருள்
சேய்நின்ற செஞ்சுடர் எம்பெரு மானடி
ஆய்நின்ற தேவர் அகம்படி யாமே. 2824

Even Celestials Are His Vassals

Like the sound within the one-letter word "Aum" is He
He is the Great Truth the Celestials long for,
He is the Flaming Light that shines afar,
He is Our Lord,
The Immortals who adore His Feet
Are but beings to His inner service devoted.

11. சத்திய ஞானானந்தம்

SATYA JNANANANDAM (SAT-CHIT-ANANDA)

எப்பாழும் பாழு மியாவுமாய் அன்றாகி
முப்பாழுங் கீழுள முப்பாழும் முன்னியே
இப்பாழும் இன்னவா றென்பதி லாவின்பத்
தற்பர ஞானானந்தந் தானது வாகுமே. 2825

In the Seventh Space is Siva-Knowledge-Bliss

All spaces as space
As all and nothing,
The three Spaces below,
And the three Spaces above,
Seeking them,
And knowing not what this Space is like,
In that Supreme Bliss
Is the Tat-Para Jnanananda;
Siva-Knowledge-Bliss
In that He and I one become.

தொம்பதந் தற்பதஞ் சொன்ன துரியம்போல்
நம்பிய மூன்றாந் துரியத்து நன்றாகும்
அம்புவி யுன்னா அதிசூக்க மப்பாலைச்
செம்பொரு ளாண்டருள் சீர்நந்தி தானே. 2826

Beyond Three Turiyas and the States They Lead to

In the Turiya First[1] is Thom-Pada (Tvam-Pada) State,
In the Turiya Second[2] is Tat-Pada State,
In the Turiya Third[3] is Asi-Pada State,
Beyond[4] is the Subtlety
Immense that transcends Space
There, the Holy Truth of Nandi, verily, is.

---

1) In jiva turiya, jiva realises its spiritual nature, and is in God-consciousness—but duality still exists.
2) In Para turiya, jiva realises Siva, and is union with Him, but not united—duality still exists.
3) In Siva turiya, jiva unites in God totally, himself becoming God—the unitive state is reached.
4) In Beyond turiya, jiva himself becomes undifferentiated in God, and attains the subtle Siva state of Luminous Self-Manifestness (Sivarupa).

மன்னுஞ் சத்தியாதி மணியொளி மாசோபை
அன்னதோ டொப்ப மிடலொன்றா மாறது
இன்னிய வுற்பலம் ஒண்சீர் நிறமணம்
பன்னிய சோபை பகராறு மானதே. 2827

The Fourth State of Bliss — A Blend of Six Attributes (Satya—Jnana—Ananda)

Peerless the Bliss that in Satya-Jnana is,
Incomparable is it to the light of pure gem's rays and the like;
Like Lily, Blue, Purity, Beauty, Colour, Fragrance and Radiance
—These six, together blended, is
That Bliss-State of Satya-Jnana.

சத்தி சிவன்பர ஞானமுஞ் சாற்றுங்கால்
உய்த்த அனந்தஞ் சிவமுயர் ஆனந்தம்
வைத்த சொருபத்த சத்தி வருகுரு
உய்த்த வுடலிவை யுற்பலம் போலுமே. 2828

Sakti is Sat, Para Jnana is Chit and Siva is Ananda

To speak of Sakti, Siva and Parajnana-Bliss
Thus are they;
Infinite high is Siva's Bliss (Ananda)
Manifestness (Svarupa) is Sakti (Sat);
Parajnana is that the Holy Guru to Jiva imparts (Chit);
—All three together are like the Flower
Blended with Six attributes above (Sat-Chit-Ananda).

உருவுற் பலநிறம் ஒண்மணஞ் சோபை
தரநிற்ப போலுயிர் தற்பரந் தன்னின்

மருவச் சிவமென்ற மாமும்ப் பதத்தின்
சொருபத்தன் சத்தியாதி தோன்றநின் றானே. 2829

Satya-Jnana-Bliss is Above the Three States

Like the Blue Lily blossom that is blended
With Color, Purity, Beauty, Fragrance and Radiance,
It is,
When Jiva into Tat-Para blends;
Then is the State of Siva-Manifestness (Svarupa)
That is of the three States exalted,
And in Him arose Satya-Jnana-Ananda.

நினையும் அளவின் நெகிழ வணங்கிப்
புனையில் அவனைப் பொதியலு மாகும்
எனையுமெங் கோன்நந்தி தன்னருள் கூட்டி
நினையும் அளவில் நினைப்பித் தனனே. 2830

Lord is in the Farthest Stretches of Thought

Think of Him as far as your thoughts stretch,
Adore Him in melting love,
Praise Him in songs melodious,
Well may you envelop Him in your heart;
Me too,
My Lord Nandi, His Grace extending,
Led to think of Him
To the farthest reaches of my thought.

பாலொடு தேனும் பழத்துள் இரதமும்
வாலிய பேரமு தாகும மதுரமும்
போலுந் துரியம் பொடிபட வுள்புகச்
சீல மயிர்க்கால் தொறுந்தேக் கிடுமே. 2831

Sweetness of Satya-Jnana-Bliss

Milk, honey, juice of fruit
In ambrosial sweetness mixed;
Like it is when the triple States of Turiya—is crossed,
And Jiva enters in Satya-Jnana-Ananda;
It is a sweetness that permeates
Every root of body's hair.

அமரத் துவங்கடந் தண்டங் கடந்து
தமரத்து நின்ற தனிமையன் ஈசன்
பவளத்து முத்தும் பனிமொழி மாதர்
துவளற்ற சோதி தொடர்ந்துநின் றானே. 2832

Satya-Jnana-Ananda is Transcendental

Transcending spheres of immortal Celestials,
Transcending Cosmic Spaces,
Transcending sphere of Nada,
He stood, all by Himself—the Lord;
Sakti with coral lips, pearly teeth and dewy-cool speech,
And the unflickering Light of Parajnana
Following,
He stood (in Satya Jnana Ananda).

மத்திமம் ஆறாறு மாற்றி மலநீக்கிச்
சுத்தம தாகுந் துரியத் துரிசற்றுப்
பெத்த மறச்சிவ மாகிப் பிறழ்வுற்றுச்
சத்தியஞா னானந்தஞ் சார்ந்தனன் ஞானியே. 2833

How Jnanis Reach Satya-Jnana-Ananda

The Tattvas six times six
That in Eye-brow Centre stand
In Waking State,
They left behind;
They rid themselves of Malas;
Were purified in Turiya that is Pure (Suddha);
Freed of the bondage condition (Baddha)
They became Siva;
Beyond that they ascended into
Satya-Jnana-Ananda (Truth-Knowledge-Bliss that is Sat-Chit-Ananda).
They, the Jnanis True.

சிவமா யவமான மும்மலந் தீரப்
பவமான முப்பாழைப் பற்றறப் பற்றத்
தவமான சத்திய ஞானானந் தத்தே
துவமார் துரியஞ் சொரூபம தாமே. 2834

Svarupa (Manifestness) is in the Fourth Turiya State

Jiva having become Siva
And the triple Malas extinguished;
Ascending into the Triple Voids
In Desire and Not-desire ceased
Pass into the holy state of
Satya-Jnana-Ananda Bliss;
There in that farthest Turiya of Jiva,
The Self-illuminating Manifestness (Svarupa) is.

12. சொரூப உதயம்

SVARUPA UDAYAM (DAWN OF MANIFESTNESS)

பரம குரவன் பரமெங்கு மாகித்
திரமுற எங்கணுஞ் சேர்ந்தொழி வற்று
நிரவு சொரூபத்துள் நீடுஞ் சொரூபம்
அரிய துரியத் தணைந்துநின் றானே. 2835

Parasivam is Immanent in Svarupa State

The Holy Master, Parama Guru,
As Para constant pervades interminably all;
In that immanent state,
Extends His Self-illuminating Manifestness;
When Jiva the Final Turiya State attains.

குலைக்கின்ற நீரிற் குவலய நீரும்
அலைக்கின்ற காற்றும் அனலொடா காச
நிலத்திடை வானிடை நீண்டகன் றானை
வரைத்து வலஞ்செயு மாறறி யேனே. 2836

Parasivam is Pervasive

In that primordial Flood of Waters
(At the time of Dissolution)
As Waters of the earth, the tempestuous Winds
The Fire, the Sky and Earth
He interminably extended in Space;
I know not how to limit Him
And thus adore Him.

அங்குநின் றானயன் மால்முதல் தேவர்கள்
எங்குநின் றாரும் இறைவனென் றேத்துவர்
தங்கிநின் றான்தனி நாயகன் எம்மிறை
பொங்கிநின் றான்புவ னாபதி தானே. 2837

Parasiva is Immanent in All Gods

As thus He stood,
The Gods Brahma, Vishnu and others
Who wherever stood
Praise Him as Lord Supreme;
In them all He immanent stood, my peerless Lord,
And beyond them too, He stood,
He, the Lord of Worlds all.

சமையச் சுவடுந் தனையறி யாமற்
கமையற்ற காமாதி காரணம் எட்டுந்
திமிரச் செயலுந் தெளிவுடன் நின்றோர்
அமரர்க் கதிபதி யாகிநிற் பாரே. 2838

When Jnana Supreme is Attained

Knowing not the foot-prints of Faith's Way,
They the eight causal sins of greed lust and others
comming,
They are egoity possessed;
They who transcend these,
And Jnana attain,
Verily become Lord of Immortals in High Heavens.

---

1) Lust, anger, ignorance, greed, hatred, vengefulness, miserliness, possessiveness. The *Kularnava Tântra* enumerates eight bonds: pity (daya or inferior benevolence as opposed to divine compassion); ignorance and delusion (mona); fear (bhaya); shame (lajja); disgust (ghrina); family (kula); habit and observance (shila), and caste (varna). Vide "Shakti and Shakta," by Sir John Woodroffe, p.530.

மூவகைத் தெய்வத் தொருவன் முதலுரு
வாயது வேறா மதுபோல் அணுப்பரன்
சேய சிவமுத் துரியத்துச் சீர்பெற
ஏயும் நெறியென் றிறைநூல் இயம்புமே. 2839

Svarupa Siva is of the Triple Turiyas and Beyond

The three gods, Brahma, Vishnu, Rudra
Are of the Primal One;
Yet is He from them separate;
Like it, the Lord stands
In the Turiyas triple—
Jiva, Para and Siva
(One and yet separate.)
Thus say the scriptures sacred.

உருவன்றி யேநின் றுருவம் புணர்க்குங்
கருவன்றி யேநின்று தான்கரு வாகும்
அருவன்றி யேநின்ற மாயப் பிரானைக்
குருவன்றி யாவர்க்குங் கூடவொண் ணாதே. 2840

Unless Lord Himself Reveals as Guru, He is Beyond Reach

Form He has none,
Yet Form He assumes;
Birth He has none;
Yet is He the seed of all births;
Beyond Formlessness, too, He is,
The elusive Lord;
Unless Himself as Holy Guru reveals
None, Him reach.

உருவ நினைப்பவர்க் குள்ளுறுஞ் சோதி
உருவ நினைப்பவர் ஊழியுங் காண்பர்
உருவ நினைப்பவர் உம்பரு மாவர்
உருவ நினைப்பவர் உலகத்தில் யாரே. 2841

Meditation on God's Manifestness

They who meditate on His Svarupa,
See Him as the light within;
They who meditate on His Svarupa,
Will Timeless Eternity attain;
They who meditate on His Svarupa,
Will with Celestials be;
Yet who does seek His Svarupa true
In the world here below?

பரஞ்சோதி யாகும் பதியினைப் பற்றாப்
பரஞ்சோதி என்னுட் படிந்ததற் பின்னைப்
பரஞ்சோதி யுண்ணான் படியப் படியப்
பரஞ்சோதி தன்னைப் பறையக்கண் டேனே. 2842

Behold Transcendental Light (Param Jyoti)

As I clung to the Lord that is Transcendental Light,

The Transcendental Light in me entered and remained;
And as I sank and sank into the Transcendental Light,
I beheld the Transcendental Light,
Himself aloud proclaiming.

சொருபம் உருவங் குணந்தொல் விழுங்கி
அறியன வுற்பல மாமாறு போல
மருவிய சத்தியாதி நான்கு மதித்த
சொருபக் குரவன் சுகோதயத் தானே. 2843

Dawn of Svarupa Bliss in Satya-Jnana-Ananda

Manifestness, Form, Attributes and Past
—All absorbed,
Satya-Jnana-Ananda arises (Truth-Knowledge-Bliss)
With the six attributes blending; (flower, purity, beauty color, fragrance and radiance)
Like it, arises the Bliss of Holy Guru
Of self-illumined Manifestness,
In whom the Four Saktis absorbed are.

உரையற்ற ஆனந்த மோன சொருபத்தன்
கரையற்ற சத்தியாதி காணில் அகார
மருவுற் றுகார மகாரம தாக
உரையற்ற தாரத்தில் உள்ளொளி யாமே. 2844

Acting on Adi Sakti Svarupa Siva is Aum

He is Bliss beyond speech
He is Silentness,
He the Self-illumined Manifestness;
When He acts on Adi Sakti,
He becomes the letters A, U, and M;
And thus as Aum defying description,
He shines as the Light within.

தலைநின்ற தாழ்வரை மீது தவஞ்செய்து
முலைநின்ற மாதறி மூர்த்தியை யானும்
புலைநின்ற பொல்லாப் பிறவி கடந்து
கலைநின்ற கள்வனிற் கண்டுகொண் டேனே. 2845

He Stands Concealed in Kalas of Sakti

In the valleys within the cranium I stood,
Adoring Him in penance devout;
And there I discovered Him, the Thief,
With Sakti standing in Kalas concealed;
Discovering Him, I ended my birth's cycle.

ஆமா றறிந்தேன் அகத்தின் அரும்பொருள்
போமா றறிந்தேன் புகுமாறு மீதென்றே
ஏமாப்ப தில்லை இனியோ ரிடமில்லை
நாமா முதல்வனும் நானென லாமே. 2846

Knowledge of the Way of Becoming

I knew the Way of Becoming,
I knew the Way of Seeking the Rare One,
I knew the Way of Entrance to Him;
No more the egoity,
None other the locale
The Primal One I become,
He and I one will be.

13. ஊழ்

FATE

செற்றிலென் சீவிலென் செஞ்சாந் தணியிலென்
மத்தகத் தேயுளி நாட்டி மறிக்கிலென்
வித்தகன் நந்தி விதிவழி யல்லது
தத்துவ ஞானிகள் தன்மைகுன் றாரே. 2847

Understand Fate's Working; Jnanis are not Thwarted

What though you cut them , chop them,
And with chistle their heads hammer,
Or with cool sandal paste soften them?
All these are but by Fate, Nandi decreed,
Thus realizing they impassive remain,
They, the Holy Jnanis, that Truth perceived.

தான்முன்னஞ் செய்த விதிவழி தானல்லால்
வான்முன்னஞ் செய்தங்கு வைத்ததோர் மாட்டில்லை
கோன்முன்னஞ் சென்னி குறிவழி யேசென்று
நான்முன்னஞ் செய்ததே நன்னில மானதே. 2848

The Past is Inexorable—Seek the Fair Land

Nothing there is,
Except by your past deeds come;
The heavens cannot decree otherwise;
And so by Muladhara Way
I sought the Lord within the head;
And what I did afore,
Took me to the Fair Land of Bliss.

ஆறிட்ட நுண்மணல் ஆறே சுமவாதே
கூறிட்டுக் கொண்டு சுமந்தறி வாரில்லை
நீறிட்ட மேனி நிமிர்சடை நந்தியைப்
பேறிட்டென் னுள்ளம் பிரியகி லாவே. 2849

Understanding Logic of Karmaic Law, I Sought Nandi

The sands the river deposits
Are by the river carried away;

To none else is that task apportioned;
(And so)
I sought Nandi
Of holy ashes and erect matted locks,
And with Him inseparate stood, devout intense.

வானின் றிடிக்கிலென் மாகடல் பொங்கிலென்
மானின்றசெந்தீக் கலந்துடன் வேகிலென்
தானொன்றி மாருதஞ் சண்டம் அடிக்கிலென்
நானொன்றி நாதனை நாடுவேன் நானே. 2850

Seek Lord Always

What though the welkin thunders,
What though the seas rise and foam,
What though the fires spread and burn,
What though the tempests roar and blast.
Unconcerned I seek Lord
In devotion intense.

ஆனை துரக்கிலென் அம்பூ டறுக்கிலென்
கானத் துழுவை கலந்து வளைக்கிலென்
ஏனைப் பதியினில் எம்பெரு மான்வைத்த
ஞானத் துழவினை நானுழு வேனே. 2851

Plough the Field of Jnana

What though the elephant pursues,
What though the arrow pierces,
What though the wild tiger surrounds,
Deep I plough the field of Jnana
In the Other Land,
Lord has me allotted.

கூடு கெடின்மற்றோர் கூடுசெய் வானுளன்
நாடு கெடினும் நமர்கெடு வாரில்லை
வீடு கெடின்மற்றோர் வீடுபுக் கால்ஒக்கும்
பாடது நந்தி பரிசறி வார்க்கே. 2852

Jnanis Are Unconcerned

If this body to harm comes
There is One to fashion another;
If a land to destruction goes,
There is another land to migrate to;
If a house to pieces falls,
There is another house to dwell;
—Thus do their thoughts, unconcerned run,
Who Nandi's bounty know.

14. சிவதரிசனம்

DARSHAN OF SIVA

சிந்தைய தென்னச் சிவனென்ன வேறில்லை
சிந்தையி னுள்ளே சிவனும் வெளிப்படுஞ்
சிந்தை தெளியத் தெளியவல் லார்கட்குச்
சிந்தையி னுள்ளே சிவனிருந் தானே. 2853

Siva Reveals in Doubt-Free Thought

Those whose thoughts inseparable in Siva merge,
In their thoughts, Siva reveals;
Those who can vision their thoughts doubt-free,
In their thoughts, Siva is.

வாக்கு மனமு மறைந்த மறைப்பொருள்
நோக்குமின் நோக்கப் படும்பொருள் நுண்ணிது
போக்கொன்றும் இல்லை வரவில்லை கேடில்லை
ஆக்கமும் அத்தனை ஆய்ந்துகொள் வார்க்கே. 2854

He is Subtle Beyond Thought and Speech—Seek and Find Him

Beyond speech and thought
Is hidden that Vedic Object;
Look at it;
It is an Object subtle by far;
It has no coming, no going, no perishing;
All blessings are
For those who seek Lord true.

பரனாய்ப் பராபர னாகியப் பாற்சென்
றுரனாய் வழக்கற வொண்சுடர் தானாய்த்
தரனாய்த் தனாதென வாறறி வொண்ணா
அரனா யுலகில் அருள்புரிந் தானே. 2855

The Unknowable Bestows Grace as Hara

As Paran, as Paraparan and Beyond
As constant interminable Light Transcendental:
As Support definite of all,
As One beyond knowledge of Self,
As Hara here below,
He, His Grace showers.

15. சிவசொரூப தரிசனம்

DARSHAN OF SIVA SVARUPA (MANIFESTNESS)

ஓதும் மயிர்க்கால் தொறும்அமு தூறிய
பேதம் அபேதம் பிறழாத ஆனந்த
மாதி சொரூபங்கள் மூன்றகன் றப்பாலை
வேதம் ஓதுஞ் சொரூபிதன் மேன்மையே. 2856

Supreme Svarupa Bliss

Beyond Difference and Non-Difference
Is that inviolate Bliss;
In every hair root its ambrosial sweetness floods;
Beyond the initial Manifestness Three it is;
There indeed is the greatness vast of that Supreme Manifestness
That Vedas praise so high.

உணர்வும் அவனே உயிரும் அவனே
புணரும் அவனே புலவி யவனே
இணரும் அவன்தன்னை யெண்ணலு மாகான்
துணரின் மலர்க்கந்தந் துன்னிநின் றானே. 2857

He is the Fragrance in the Flower Within

He is Sentience, He is Life;
He is union, He is separation;
He is Continuity beyond thought;
He stands in the fragrance of flower within.

துன்னிநின் றான்தன்னை யுன்னிமுன் னாவிரு
முன்னி யவர்தங் குறையை முடித்திடும்
மன்னிய கேள்வி மறையவன் மாதவன்
சென்னியுள் நின்றதோர் தேற்றத்த னாமே. 2858

Seek Him There Within

He who stands thus
Of Him you think;
Seek His Presence;
He ends the imperfections
Of those who seek Him;
He is the unwritten Veda immutable;
He is of Tapas great
He stands within the head;
For sure it is.

மின்னுற்ற சிந்தை விழித்தேன் விழித்தலுந்
தன்னுற்ற சோதித் தலைவன் இணையிலி
பொன்னுற்ற மேனிப் புரிசடை நந்தியும்
என்னுற் றறிவனான் என்வழித் தானே. 2859

He Blessed Me Saying, "You Know"

My thoughts woke up
In lightning flash within;
And as I woke up,
The self-illumined Lord, the peerless One,
Of Form golden-hued, Nandi of matted locks
Entered into me and said, "You know;"
And thus saying,
He cast His benign glance upon me.

சத்திய ஞானத் தனிப்பொருள் ஆனந்தஞ்
சித்தத்தி னில்லாச் சிவானந்தப் பேரொளி
சுத்தப் பிரம துரியந் துரியத்துள்
உய்த்த துரியத் துறுபே ரொளியே. 2860

Brahma Turiya Beyond Triple Turiya

Satya-Jnana Bliss is He
It is Sivananda light
That surpasses Thought;
It is Pure Brahma Turiya;
It is Turiya beyond Turiya;
In it arises the Light Transcendental.

பரனல்ல நீடும் பராபர னல்ல
உரனல்ல மீதுணர் ஒண்சுட ரல்ல
தரனல்ல தானவை யாயல்ல வாகும்
அரனல்ல ஆனந்தத் தப்புறத் தானே. 2861

Svarupa Siva Beyond Bliss of Satya-Jnana-Ananda

Paran He is not,
Nor the expanding Paraparan is He;
Nor the abiding Object Beyond;
Nor the Vibrant Light above it;
Nor the One who supports all;
He is they and not they;
Hara He is not
Beyond Bliss is He.

முத்தியுஞ் சித்தியும் முற்றிய ஞானத்தோன்
பத்தியுள் நின்று பரந்தன்னுள் நின்றுமா
சத்தியுள் நின்றோர்க்குத் தத்துவங் கூடலாற்
சுத்தி யகன்றோர் சுகானந்த போதரே. 2862

Aim of Suddha State

Mukti, Siddhi and mature Jnana attained,
In devotion standing,
In Param standing,
In the mighty Sakti standing
They realize the Tattvas;
Then from that Suddha State
They passes to Sukhananda Bodha State.

துரிய அதீதஞ் சொல்லறும் பாழாம்
அரிய துரியம் அதீதம் புரியில்
விரியுங் குவியும் விள்ளா மிளிருந்தன்
உருவுந் திரியும் உரைப்பதெவ் வாறே. 2863

Ariya-Turiyatita Beyond; Turiyatita Beyond Svarupa

Turiyatita is Void
That is beyond words;
When Ariya Turiyatita state still above is reached,
Jiva blossoms shimmering;
Neither folding, nor unfolding;
The Form too is altered;
How to describe it!

"A thing cannot be described and clarified in terms of itself, but only with reference to something else in the universe...

The field from which the substance and the form of symbols are taken is nature. There is no other field from which to derive them. Nature takes the two aspects of 'human nature' and the nature of the surroundings of man. Man's 'animal nature' is symbolic of a particular aspect of human nature, derived from the nature of animals in man's surroundings.

Substance and form of symbols belong to external nature. The meaning applies to the internal nature. Nature is the mirror of consciousness, and the pictures in the mirror reflect the dynamism of consciousness." "The Book of Signs," by G.H. Mees, Vol.I.

16. முத்தி, பேதம், கரும நிருவாணம்

MUKTI BHEDA AND KARMA NIRVANA (GRADATIONS OF LIBERATION)

ஓதிய முத்தி யடைவே உயிர்பர
பேதமி லச்சிவம் எய்துந் துரியமோ
டாதி சொரூபஞ் சொரூபத்த தாகவே
ஏதமி லாநிரு வாணம் பிறந்ததே. 2864

Progression of Soul's Journey to Five Muktis

Jiva reaches to (Jiva) Mukti first;
Then passes on to Param State;
And thence to Siva State;
In the Turiya practised therein,
Is the Primal Self-illumined Manifestness,
And having attained Svarupa,
Is reached the State of Nirvana,
(In Ariya Turiyatita State.)

பற்றற் றவர்பற்றி நின்ற பரம்பொருள்
கற்றற் றவர்கற்றுக் கருதிய கண்ணுதல்
சுற்றற் றவர்சுற்றி நின்றஎன் சோதியைப்
பெற்றுற் றவர்கள் பிதற்றொழிந் தாரே. 2865

He is the Finite Goal

He is Param that is reached
By those who desire Him,
Leaving their own desire behind;
He is Lord of Fore-Head Eye
Whom the learned who have learned all,
Still learn about;
He is the Transcendental Light
Whom those who have bonds none
Surround;
He is the One,
Whom those who have reached,
Have ceased to prattle about.

17. சூனிய சம்பாஷணை

SUNYA SAMBHASHANA (DIALOGUE OF SYMBOLISM)

காயம் பலகை கவறைந்து கண்மூன்றா
ஆயம் பொருவதோர் ஐம்பத்தோ ரக்கரம்
ஏய பெருமா னிருந்து பொருகின்ற
மாயக் கவற்றின் மறைப்பறி யேனே. 2866

Mystery of Lord's Play

Body the gambling board;
Five[1] the dice;
Three[2] the channels
Fifty-one[3] the squares
Thus the Jivas play the game;
He who thus leads them to it,
The mystery of His play
I know not.

---

1) Sense organs
2) Malas—anava, maya and karma
3) Fifty-one letters of nada pervading the body.

Chapter 17 is given the caption 'Sunya Sambhasana (Dialogue of Symbolism)", But it is more popular esoteric than symbolic, and resemble in this respect the popular "dohas' and other "sandabhasa", literature of Bengal which began to appear from about the 10th century onwards with the decay of Buddhism (See "Obscure Religious cults of Bengal" by Das Gupta). The verses in this chapter are typical siddhar poetry.

தூறு படர்ந்து கிடந்தது தூநெறி
மாறிக் கிடக்கும் வகையறி வாரில்லை
மாறிக் கிடக்கும் வகையறி வாளர்க்கு
ஊறிக் கிடந்ததென் உள்ளன்பு தானே. 2867

Holy Way is Strewn With Thorns

The Holy Way is by thorny bushes covered
They know not how to remove it;
They who know how to remove it
Are they for whom my heart yearns.

ஆறு தெருவில் அகப்பட்ட சந்தியிற்
சாறு படுவன நான்கு பனையுள
ஏறற் கரியதோர் ஏணியிட் டப்பனை
ஏறலுற் றேன்கடல் ஏழுங்கண் டேனே. 2868

Kundalini Yoga

Six are the streets
In their junction are juicy palm trees four;

With ladder difficult to climb,
I ascended the palm's heights;
And there I saw the seas seven.

Climb the four juicy palm trees (nadis—sun, moon, meru, and sushumna) in the junction of the six streets (adharas). Then you will behold the seven seas, sahasrara).

வழுதலை வித்திடப் பாகல் முளைத்தது
புழுதியைத் தோண்டினேன் பூசணி பூத்தது
தொழுதுகொண்டோடினோர் தோட்டக்குடிகண்
முழுதும் பழுத்தது வாழைக் கனியே. 2869

Abnegation of Desires Leading to Liberation Through Yoga

I sowed the seed of brinjal[1]
And the shoot of balsam-pear[2] arose;
I dug up the dust[3];
And the pumpkin[4] blossomed;
The gardner-gang[5] prayed and ran;
Full well ripened the fruit of plantain[6].

---

1) Renunciation (vazhu plus thalai means 'shaven head')
2) Bitterness—or world negation
3) The tattvas or the universals that constitute the body.
4) Siva (suggesting a Linga covered with holy ashes)
5) The indriyas or sense organs; may also refer to malas.
6) Mukti or liberation from birth. The plantain is thought of as being seedless (vazhai comes from 'vazh' and 'i'—creating a pun on the word to mean 'life-giving fruit').

ஐயென்னும் வித்தினில் ஆனை விளைப்பதோர்
செய்யுண்டு செய்யின் தெளிவறி வாரில்லை
மையணி கண்டன் மனம்பெறின் அந்நிலம்
பொய்யொன்று மின்றிப் புகஎளி தாமே. 2870

Sahasrara Centre of Liberation

With the seed of Lord
There is a field
Where the Jiva ripens
That field they know not;
If the Grace of Blue-throated Lord there is,
Easy to enter that field
In Truth it is.

பள்ளச்செய்யொன்றுண்டுபாடச்செய் இரண்டுள
கள்ளச்செய் யங்கே கலந்து கிடந்தது
உள்ளச்செய் யங்கே யுழவுசெய் வார்கட்கு
வெள்ளச்செய் யாகி விளைந்ததுதானே. 2871

Turiya State

A deep field there is one;[1]
Waste fields two[2] are there;
Another alien field[3] with them lay mingled;
Those that plough the field of heart
For them the field fed with water,[4]
Lay ripe in harvest rich.

---

1) Sushupti state
2) Waking and dream states
3) Turiya
4) Ambrosia

மூவணை யேரு முழுவது முக்காணி
தாமணி கோலித் தறியுறப் பாய்ந்திடு
நாவணை கோலி நடுவிற் செறுவுழார்
காலணை கோலிக் களருழு வாரே. 2872

Kundalini Yoga

In the Triangular Field,[1]
Are the Ploughs Three[2];
Yoke the bulls tight with rope[3];
Drive the ploughshare deep[4]
They who held not their tongue,[5]
Ploughed not in the Centre[6]
Closing their legs together,[7]
They plough the waste in vain.

---

1) Muladhara, the centre that is triangle-shaped.
2) Three nadis—ida, pingala, and sushumna
3) Control the breath.
4) Course breath through sushumna.
5) Thrusting the tongue upward into the uluva—a yogic practice for realisation known as kechari mudra.
6) Sahasrara in the cranium
7) Controlling breath.

ஏற்றம் இரண்டுள ஏழு துரவுள
மூத்தான் இறைக்க இளையான் படுத்தநீர்
பாத்தியிற் பாயாது பாழ்ப்பாய்ந்து போயிடிற்
கூத்தி வளர்த்ததோர் கோழிப்புள் ளாமே. 2873

Control of Breath

Two the picottahs[1], seven the wells[2];
The elder draws out[3], the younger waters[4];
If into field[5] the water flows not,
And into waste flows[6],
Verily is it like the fowl
That the harlot rears.

---

1) Nadis—ida and pingala
2) Seven centres—the six adharas leading to the seventh, sahasrara.
3&4) Breaths—exhalation and inhalation
5) The central sushumna nadi
6) Consumed any time as food in pleasure-seeking.

பட்டிப் பசுக்கள் இருபத்து நாலுள
குட்டிப் பசுக்களோ ரேழுள ஐந்துள
குட்டிப் பசுக்கள் குடப்பால் சொரியினும்
பட்டிப் பசுவே பனவற்கு வாய்த்ததே. 2874

Tattvas—Lower and Higher

Twenty and four the cows[1] that stray uncontrolled,
Other cows gentler are seven and five[2];
Well may the gentler ones a whole pot of milk give;

But Jiva has the straying uncontrolled ones alone.

---

1) Tattvas pertaining to jiva's body.
2) Higher tattvas—seven vidya tattvas and five Siva tattvas.

ஈற்றுப் பசுக்கள் இருபத்து நாலுள
ஊற்றுப் பசுக்கள் ஒருகுடம் பால்போதும்
காற்றுப் பசுக்கள் கறந்துண்ணுங் காலத்து
மாற்றுப் பசுக்கள் வரவறி யோமே. 2875

Yoga Way to Transcend Tattvas

Twenty and four the cows[1] that are in calf;
Better far a pitcher of milk from cows[2] that yield;
When you know how to milk the cows of breath (yoga)
The other cows[3] near not.

---

1) Tattvas of the body
2) Higher tattvas stated in Mantra above.
3) Sense organs.

தட்டான் அகத்தில் தலையான மச்சின்மேல்
மொட்டா யெழுந்தது செம்பால் மலர்ந்தது
வட்டம் படவேண்டி வாய்மை மடித்திட்டுத்
தட்டான் அதனைத் தகைந்துகொண் டானே. 2876

Yogic Kechari Mudra For Liberation

In the upper storey[1] of the house of smith[2]
Was a bud-like mass[3], that like copper[4] (sheet) expanded;
He shaped it round, folding it in Truth[5]
Thus the smith made it his own.

---

1) The cranium
2) Jiva's body-house—'thattan' is composed of 'thattu' and 'an,' creating a pun on the word which means, 'striking jiva.'
3) Mystic flower bud in sahasrara
4) Ruddy in color.
5) 'Vay' and 'mai' creates a pun on the word 'vay' to mean closing the uluva opening in the mouth.

அரிக்கின்ற நாற்றங்கால் அல்லற் கழனி
திரிக்கின்ற வொட்டஞ் சிக்கெனக் கட்டி
வரிக்கின்ற நல்லான் கறவையைப் பூட்டில்
விரிக்கின்ற வெள்ளரி வித்துவித் தாமே. 2877

Sublimate Bindu Within into Para Bindu

In the eroding seed bed
Of Sorrow's field,
Train the flowing water
And dam it tight;
Then plough with the good young bull,
And transplant the cucumber seedling;
That shall indeed into good seed ripe.

Plough the eroding seed bed (thoughts that are filled with sorrow) with the good young bull (yoga), and transplant the cucumber seedling (bindu). Truly, it will ripen into the good seed (macrocosmic bindu).

இடாக்கொண்டு தூவி எருவிட்டு வித்திக்
கிடாக்கொண்டு பூட்டிக் கிளறி முளையை
மிடாக்கொண்டு சோறட்டு மெள்ள விழுங்கார்
கிடாக்கொண்டு செந்நெல் அறுக்கின்ற வாறே. 2878

Liberation only for Those who Strive

Strewing the seed,
And applying manure in baskets full,
And ploughing with yoked bulls,
And digging out the weeds,
Thus producing rice,
And cooking in vessels big,
Gently should they consume it;
This they do not;
How then do they the sweet rice crop harvest,
Lying indifferent?

Strew the seed; apply manure; plough it; remove the weeds—then in produced rice (liberation). How can you reap a good harvest if you have not striven like this? Liberation will not be bestowed to those who do not strive in the yogic way.

விளைந்து கிடந்தது மேலைக்கு வித்தது
விளைந்து கிடந்தது மேலைக்குக் காதம்
விளைந்து விளைந்து விளைந்துகொள் வார்க்கு
விளைந்து கிடந்தது மேவுமுக் காதமே. 2879

Attaining the Triple Turiya States

The seed for future ripened
The seed ripened over quite a stretch,
For those whom the seed ripened in states three[1]
The three spaces[2] above, too, ripened.

---

1) Bindu
2) Mystic astral space within.
1) The three turiya states—jiva turiya, Para turiya, and Siva turiya.
2) The three space beyond, one in each of the three turiya states.

களருழு வார்கள் கருத்தை யறியோங்
களருழு வார்கள் கருதலு மில்லை
களருழு வார்கள் களரின் முளைத்த
வள்ரிள வஞ்சியின் மாய்தலு மாமே. 2880

Do not Cultivate the Waste of Worldly Pleasures

Why they plough the waste, we know not,
They who plough the waste have design none,
They who plough the waste perish,
Like the young weeds
That waste shoots.

கூப்பிடு கொள்ளாக் குறுநரிக் கொட்டகத்
தாப்பிடு பாசத்தை யங்கியுள் வைத்திட்டு
நாட்பட நின்று நலம்புகுந் தாயிழை
ஏற்பட இல்லத் தினிதிருந் தானே. 2881

Yoga Leads to Grace

Within the shed[1] where jackals[2] howl,
Rouse your call[3];
The binding Pasas to Fire[4] Consign;
Thus spend days continuous;
Then the great Mother appears
And there in the home, you shall be well.

1) Body
2) Passions
3) Chanting of the mantra, 'Aum.'
4) Kundalini

மலைமேல் மழைபெய்ய மான்கன்று துள்ளக்
குலைமேல் இருந்த கொழுங்கனி வீழ
உலைமேல் இருந்த உறுப்பெனக் கொல்லன்
முலைமேல் அமிர்தம் பொழியவைத் தானே. 2882

Experiences in the Mystic Sphere of Sahasrara

On the mountain it rained,
The young deer leapt;
The rich ripe fruit from bunch above dropped;
Like the metal on the smith's furnace,
It melted;
And over the heart, He made it flow.

It rained (nectar flowed) on the mountain (cranium), and the dear (Sakti) leapt. From the bunch (sahasrara) dropped the rich fruit (bliss of Grace). Like the metal in the furnace, it melted, and sweet ambrosia flowed.

பார்ப்பான் அகத்திலே பாற்பசு ஐந்துண்டு
மேய்ப்பாரும் இன்றி வெறித்துத் திரிவன
மேய்ப்பாரும் உண்டாய் வெறியும் அடங்கினாற்
பார்ப்பான் பசுஐந்தும் பாலாச் சொரியுமே. 2883

Control Senses

In Brahmin's home are Milk Cows Five
With none to herd them, they stray uncontrolled,
If a cowherd there is, and controlled they are,
The Five Cows will milk in abundance give.

If there is a cowherd (yogi) to control the five milky cows (senses) in the brahmin's home (yogi's body), they will give milk (ambrosia) in abundance. So hold firm control over your senses. You will remain youthful forever.

ஆமாக்கள் ஐந்தும் அரியேறு முப்பதுந்
தேமா இரண்டொடு திப்பிலி யொன்பதுந்
தாமாக் குரங்கொளிற் றம்மனத் துள்ளன
மூவாக் கடாவிடின் மூட்டுகின் றாரே. 2884

How to be Youthful

The five wild bulls[1] of Jiva,
And the fierce lions thirty[2],
The two mangoes sweet[3],
The fradulent nine[4]
And the mind within,
If yours they become, firm controlled,
The bull,[5] old becomes not;
If not, they put fire to it[6]

1) Senses
2) The other tattvas
3) Nadis—ida and pingala
4) Nine centres—the six adharas and the three spheres of sun, moon, and fire.
5) Body
6) Death—cremation.

எழுதாத புத்தகத் தேட்டின் பொருளைத்
தெருளாத கன்னி தெளிந்திருந் தோத
மலராத பூவின் மணத்தின் மதுவைப்
பிறவாத வண்டு மணமுண்ட வாறே. 2885

Immortality Through Yoga

The Truth of the Unwritten Book,
The Immaculate Virgin in clarity chanting,
The nectar of Flower, unopened until then,
Gushed forth;
As the Bee its fragrance drank,
Unborn it became.

When the immaculate virgin (kundalini) chants the truth of the unwritten book (Aum), the nectar of the flower (sahasrara) gushes out. When the bee (yogi) savours that fragrant liquid, immortality ensues.

போகின்ற பொய்யும் புகுகின்றபொய்வித்துங்
கூகின்ற நாவலின் கூழைத் தருங்கனி
ஆகின்ற பைங்கூழ் அவையுண்ணும் ஐவரும்
வேகின்ற கூரை விருத்திபெற் றாரே. 2886

Sure Death, if Breath is not Controlled

The deceptive one that leaves,[1]
The false seed that enters[2];
The Five[3] who eat of the broth[4] made
Of the ripe fruit[5] of flourishing Jamun tree;
—All, all, went the burning roof's way[6]

If breath is controlled through the yogic way, surely death can be vanquished.

1) Exhaling breath
2) Inhaling breath
3) Senses
4) Worldly pleasures, actually astringent in taste.
5) The Tamil word, 'naval,' also denotes a cry of pity.
6) Death.

மூங்கின் முளையில் எழுந்ததோர் வேம்புண்டு
வேம்பினிற் சார்ந்து கிடந்த பனையிலோர்
பாம்புண்டு பாம்பைத் துரத்தித்தின் பாரின்றி
வேம்பு கிடந்துவெடிக்கின்ற வாறே. 2887

Body Perishes if Yoga is not Practised

From the Bamboo Shoot arose a Margosa tree
Close on Margosa was a Palmyrah,
In that Palm is a Snake

Knowing not to drive that Snake and eat it,
The Margosa tree withered away.

From the bamboo shoot (karma) arose a margosa tree (body), and very close to that was a palmyrah (sushumna). Knowing not how to drive the snake (kundalini) that was in the palm, the margosa withered away (the body perishes if yoga is not practised).

பத்துப் பரும்புலி யானை பதினைந்து
வித்தகர் ஐவர் விநோதகர் ஈரெண்மர்
அத்தகு மூவர் அறுவர் மருத்துவர்
அத்தலை ஐவர் அமர்ந்துநின் றாரே. 2888

How the Body is

Ten[1] the tigers big,
Ten and Five[2] the elephants,
Five[3] the learned.
Ten[4] the jesters,
Three[5] that are upright
Six[6] the physicians,
Five[7] the lordly ones,
There they all stand.

1) Nadis
2) Ten sense organs (karmendriyas and jnanendriyas), and five sense potencies (tanmatras)
3) Antakarana (organs of intelligence)
4) Vayus
5) Sun, moon and fire spheres
6) Adharas
7) Avastas or experiences—waking, dreaming, etc.

இரண்டு கடாவுண்டு இவ்வூரி னுள்ளே
இரண்டு கடாவுக்கும் ஒன்றே தொழும்பன்
இரண்டு கடாவும் இருத்திப் பிடிக்கில்
இரண்டு கடாவும் ஒருகடா வாமே. 2889

Control Breath

Two the bulls in this hamlet,
One the servant for the bulls two;
Control the bulls two, firm,
As one they will then be.

Control the two bulls (breaths—right, pingala, and left, ida) in this hamlet (body). Then they will become one as prana coursing through the sushumna.

ஒத்த மனக்கொல்லை யுள்ளே சமன்கட்டிப்
பத்தி வலையிற் பருத்தி நிறுத்தலால்
முத்தக் கயிறாக மூவர்கள் ஊரினுள்
நித்தம் பொருது நிரம்பநின் றாரே. 2890

The Perfect Ones Practice Yoga Daily

Level up Mind-Garden in equanimity
In devotion's net, plant the cotton tree
By salvation's rope enter the place of Three,
Daily do they ascend thus,
Who perfection filled are.

Level up the mind-garden, and plant the cotton tree (coursing the thread-like prana through sushumna). Then enter the place of three (ajna) by liberation's rope (yoga practice), where Siva, Sakti and jiva are. Thus, by practising yoga, ascend daily. You will become perfect.

கூகையும் பாம்புங் கிளியொடு பூஞையும்
நாகையும் பூழும் நடுவில் உறைவன
நாகையைக் கூகை நணுக லுறுதலுங்
கூகையைக் கண்டெலி கூப்பிடு மாறே. 2891

The Six Evils Dwell Within and God's Warning to Them

The Owl, The Snake, the Parrot and the Cat,
The Mynah, and the Quail
They, all, within dwell;
As the Owl nears the Mynah
The Mouse warns Mynah, screeching loud.

The six base traits—lust, hatred, infatuation, avarice, arrogance (egoity), and malice (the owl, snake, parrot, cat, mynah, and quail) dwell within. The mouse (kundalini yoga power) warns the mynah (jiva) as the owl (lust) nears it.

1-6) Symbolisms for the six transgressions: kama (lust), kroda (hatred), lobha (miserliness), moha (greed), matha (ahankara—ego), matsarya (vengefulness). For the symbolism of birds as transgressions (avengers), vide—"The Book of Signs," by G.H. Mees, Vol.I, p.255.
7) The shrew-mouse is symbolic of the divine self which works in the 'unconscious" and interferes with man's ahankara stores, and in the plane for the future. One Ganapathi tradition says, "It is Isavara who enjoys all. He lives there like a thief. He is said to be a mouse." The shrew-mouse is the mount of Ganapathi, the guardian Mahadeva of the muladhara chakra, Vide "The Book of Signs," by G.H. Mees, Vol.I, pp.287-88, op.cit.

குலைக்கின்ற நன்னகை யாங்கொங் குழக்கின்
நிலைக்கின்ற வெள்ளெலி மூன்று கொணர்ந்தான்
உலைக்குப் புறமெனில் ஓடு மிருக்கும்
புலைக்குப் பிறந்தவை போகின்ற வாறே. 2892

Kundalini Yoga Alone Drives Away Triple Pasas

In the toddy measure[1] of foul smell
That a derisive laugh draws and (senses) to shambles sends,
He placed the white rats[2] three;
If on the fire[3] placed, they run;
Else they remain;
Of flesh-born,
How will they ever go?

Kundalini yoga alone drives away the triple pasas.

1) Body
2) Pasas—the rat (unlike the mouse which symbolises the divine) symbolises pasas. Vide G.H. Mees, op.cit.
3) Kundalini

காடுபுக் காரினிக் காணார் கடுவெளி
கூடுபுக் கானது ஐந்து குதிரையும்
மூடுபுக் கானது ஆறுள ஒட்டகம்
மூடு புகாவிடின் மூவணை யாமே. 2893

Liberation Possible Only By Renunciation

They enter the Forest dense,
No more will they see the Sky above,
The Five Steeds together entered,
The Six Camels were closed up, entire;
If they leave the Forest dense,
The Three will near come.

If the five steeds (senses), and the six camels (evils) leave the dense forest (thought), the three (Siva, Sakti and Grace) will near them. Renounce everything—you will be liberated.

கூறையுஞ் சோறுங் குழாயகத் தெண்ணெயுங்
காறையும் நாணும் வளையலுங் கண்டவர்
பாறையி லுற்ற பறக்கின்ற சீலைபோல்
ஆறைக் குழியில் அழுந்துகின் றாரே. 2894

Worldly Desires Lead to Perdition

Food, raiment and phialled unguents,
Necklace, waistband and bangles lovely,
They who (as goal) saw,
Fly away
Like a garment piece on a high rock laid,
Into the deep pit of six sins they fall
And there immersed are.

They who desire for earthly riches are like a fragile garment piece laid on a high rock. At the blow of the slightest wind, it falls into the deep pit of the six sins.

துருத்தியுள் ளக்கரை தோன்று மலைமேல்
விருத்திகண் காணிக்கப் போவார்முப் போதும்
வருத்தியுள் நின்ற மலையைத் தவிர்ப்பாள்
ஒருத்தியுள் ளாளவர் ஊரறி யோமே. 2895

Kundalini Removes Obstacles to Reach Sahasrara

Beyond the Islet beyond to the Mountain on the Bank
They daily thrice journeyed,
To superintend the Field there,
She there is, who moves the Mountain obstacle within stands;
Her place we know not.

Kundalini removes the obstacles to reaching the sahasrara. Her abode is beyond our cognition.

பருந்துங் கிளியும் படுபறை கொட்டத்
திருந்திய மாதர் திருமணப் பட்டார்
பெருந்தவப் பூதம் பெறலுரு வாகும்
இருந்திய பேற்றினில் இன்புறு வாரே. 2896

Kundalini Unites in Siva

The Kite[1] and Parrot[2] together beat the drum loud
The Shapely Virgin[3] her wedding[4] celebrated,
The Form of the holy Element she attained,
In that state, rapturous She remained.

---

1) The Tamil word for kite, 'parunthu,' also means bangle of conch shell worn by women.
2) Parrot held by Sakti symbolises good and evil in balance
3) Kundalini
4) Union in Siva in sahasrara

கூடும் பறவை இரைகொத்தி மற்றத
னூறுபுக் குண்ணடி யறுக்குறில் என்னொக்குஞ்
சூடெறி நெய்யுண்டு மைகான் றிடுகின்ற
பாடறி வார்க்குப் பயனெளி தாமே. 2897

Goal of Jiva is to Seek Liberation

The mating Bird[1] pecked at food[2]
And approaching its partner fed it
Like it easy is the Goal to reach
For those who eat of Ghee[3] in the melting Fire[4] within
And away the Darkness[5] drive.

Indeed, reaching the destined goal (liberation) is easy for those who eat of the ghee (Grace) in the melting fire (love of God) within, driving away the darkness.

1) Jiva
2) Enjoyments
3) Spiritual energy or ambrosia
4) Kundalini
5) Ignorance

இலையில்லை பூவுண் டினவண் டிங்கில்லை
தலையில்லை வேருண்டு தாளில்லை பூவின்
குலையில்லை கொய்யும் மலருண்டு சூடுந்
தலையில்லை தாழ்ந்த கிளைபுல ராதே. 2898

Mystic Flower Within

Leaves none, bees none, Flower there is;
Top none, sheath none, root there is;
Bunch none, Flower to pluck there is;
Head none to wear;
The Branch that bent withers not.

No leaves, no bees, but the flower (sahasrara) is there (in the cranium). No top, no sheath, but the root (Siva) is there. No head to wear that mystic flower. The branch (Grace) that bends does not wither.

அக்கரை நின்றதோர் ஆல மரங்கண்டு
நக்கரை வாழ்த்தி நடுவே பயன்கொள்வர்
மிக்கவரஞ்சு துயரமுங் கண்டுபோய்த்
தக்கவர் தாழ்ந்து கிடக்கின்ற வாறே. 2899

The Truly Great Vision the Lord in Cranial Cavity

Visioning the Banyan tree that stands Beyond,

They adore the holy Lord and in Him unite;
Those who transcend the Five Sorrows exceeding
Are the truly great;
Low at Lord's Feet they lie;
And there they remain.

Having visioned the banyan tree (Siva) that stands aloft (in sahasrara), they adore the Holy Lord and unite in Him. Truly great are those who rise above the five sorrows.

கூப்பிடு மாற்றிலே வன்கா டிருகாதங்
காப்பிடு கள்ளர் கலந்துநின் றாருளர்
காப்பிடு கள்ளரை வெள்ளர் தொடர்ந்திட்டுக்
கூப்பிடு மீண்டதோர் கூரைகொண் டாரே. 2900

Conquer Senses and Reach Siva

In the Way of Loud Call of Jiva
Is a Forest that stretches two leagues far;
Inside stand Robber that ceases and binds,
If the White Guard chases the Black thieves
And away shout them loud
Then does Jiva the Roof of Safety reach.

The robbers (senses) stand in the forest that is in the way of the loud call of jiva (seeking). If the white guard (yoga) chases these black thieves (senses), then jiva will reach the roof safely.

கொட்டியும் ஆம்பலும் பூத்த குளத்திடை
எட்டியும் வேம்பும் இனியதோர் வாழையுங்
கட்டியுந் தேனுங் கலந்துண்ண மாட்டாதார்
எட்டிப் பழத்துக் கிளைக்கின்ற வாறே. 2901

Sweet Ambrosia and Bitter Nux Vomica Within the Body

In the tank where bloomed Kotti and Lily
Are Neem and Nux Vomica, too;
They who eat not the Salad of Plantain sweet,
With candy and honey mixed,
Lo! hanker after the fruit of nux vomica.

Sweet ambrosia (liberation) and bitter nux vomica (passions) are both there within the body. They do not taste the salad of sweet plaintain mixed with candy and sugar (eternal life), but hanker after nux vomica (earthly life).

பெடைவண்டும் ஆண்வண்டும் பீடிகை வண்ணக்
குடைகொண்ட பார்சத்துக் கோலமுண் டானுங்
கடைவண்டு தானுண்ணுங் கண்கலந் திட்ட
பெடைவண்டு தான்பெற்ற தின்பமு மாமே. 2902

Sakti Grants Grace to Jiva

As He-Bee and She-Bee
The Lord is seated on the throne
The multi-hued umbrella aloft canopying,
The Lowly Bee, of Pasa embodied,
Drinks of (nectar), the She-Bee by Her glance grants;
That verily is rapture surpassing.

The Lord is seated on the (sahasrara) as He-bee (Siva) and She bee (Sakti). The lowly bee (jiva), of pasa embodied, swills the nectar which the She-bee grants by her glance (Grace).

கொல்லையில் மேயும் பசுக்களைச் செய்தவன்
எல்லை கடப்பித் திறையடிக் கூட்டியே
வல்லசெய் தாற்றன் மதித்தபி னல்லது
கொல்லைசெய் நெஞ்சங் குறியறி யாதே. 2903

Jivas Graze in the Backwood of Worldly Desires

What to do with those cows (Jivas)
In the backwoods of desires graze?
Take then beyond,
And lead them to the Feet of the Lord;
Discipline them in ways superior;
Thus manage the herd;
Untill then, their thoughts turn not
From the backwoods of worldly pleasures.

தட்டத்து நீரிலே தாமரை பூத்தது
குட்டத்து நீரிற் குவளை எழுந்தது
விட்டத்தி னுள்ளே விளங்கவல் லார்கட்குக்
குட்டத்தி லிட்டதோர் கொம்மட்டி யாமே. 2904

Lord in Sahasrara

In the Water Above, the Lotus blossomed,
In the Water Below, the Lily arose
To those who can see light in the Cross-beam above
The Lord is like a cool Watermelon,
That fruits even in regions low.

The lotus (sahasrara) and lily (kundalini) blossomed in the water above (cranium), and water below (muladhara) respectively. Vision the light in the crossbeam (ajna) above. You will find the Lord a cool watermelon that flourishes even in dry regions.

ஆறு பறவைகள் ஐந்தகத் துள்ளன
நூறு பறவை நுனிக்கொம்பின் மேலன
ஏறும் பெரும்பதி ஏழுங் கடந்தபின்
மாறுத லின்றி மனைபுக லாமே. 2905

Attaining Liberation in Sahasrara

Six[1] the Birds in the house of Five[2],
Hundred[3] the birds at the top of Tree,
Having ascended the Seven[4] Steps high,
You shall sure reach the Home[5]

---

1) The six base qualities—lust, hatred, greed, etc. Vide Mantra 2891, Tantra Nine, n. supra.
2) Body of the five senses
3) The sahasrara of 1,000 petals, sometimes indicated as one hundred petals also. Vide Mantra 2527, Tantra Eight, n.
4) The six adharas, and the seventh ultimate centre of sahasrara.
5) liberation.

கொட்டனஞ் செய்து குளிக்கின்ற கூவலுள்
வட்டனப் பூமி மருவிவந் தூறிடுங்
கட்டனஞ் செய்து கயிற்றால் தொழுமியுள்
ஒட்டனஞ் செய்தொளி யாவர்க்கு மாமே. 2906

Light Dawns in Sahasrara

Within the Bathing Well[1],
Where they water draw
The roundly Earth swells
And Water springs[2];
Bind your breath[3] and with Rope — Work
And centre your thoughts;
Well may the Light Divine dawn.

1) Body
2) Ambrosia
3) Coursing breath through sushumna

ஏழு வளைகடல் எட்டுக் குலவரை
யாழும் விசும்பினில் அங்கி மழைவளி
தாழு மிருநிலந் தன்மை யதுகண்டு
வாழ நினைக்கில தாலய மாமே. 2907

Reach the Holy Temple of Sahasrara

Seven the circling Seas, eight the Mountain ranges
In the depths of Space is Fire, Rain and Wind
And the Land expansive;
Visioning it, if you dwell in it
That verily a Holy Temple is.

This land (sahasrara) is expansively vast with seven circling seas (the spaces) and eight mountain ranges (the mystic flower with eight petals). Dwell in that land, for it is truly a holy temple.

ஆலிங் கனஞ்செய் தகஞ்சுடச் சூலத்துச்
சாலிங் கமைத்துத் தலைமை தவித்தனர்
கோலிங் கமைத்தபின் கூபப் பறவைகண்
மாலிங்கன் வைத்தது முன்பின் வழியே. 2908

Body Invaded by Indriyas

Embracing in warmth and pregnancy developing,
They made this body and (the couple) left;
The body-pole thus erected;
The bewitching Birds of Deep well invaded;
This way was it made, through lives successive.

This body-pole erected by man and woman has been sought after by the bewitching birds of the deep well (senses) through successive lives.

கொட்டுக்குந் தாலி இரண்டே இரண்டுக்குங்
கொட்டுக்குந் தாலிக்கும் பாரை வலிதென்பர்
கொட்டுக்குந் தாலிக்கும் பாரைக்கும் மூன்றுக்கும்
இட்டம் வலிதென்பர் ஈசன் அருளே. 2909

Lord's Love is Supreme

Two there are, the wedding drum and the wedding Thali;
Stronger than the wedding drum and thali is the crow-bar
Stronger than the drum, thali and crow-bar
Is the love that comes of Lord's Grace.

The Lord's Love and Grace is far superior and greater than the wedding drum, wedding 'thali', and the crowbar (sex-union).

கயலொன்று கண்டவர் கண்டே இருப்பர்
முயலொன்று கண்டவர் மூவரும் உய்வர்
பறையொன்று பூசல் பிடிப்பா னொருவன்
மறையொன்று கண்ட துருவம்பொன் னாமே. 2910

Vision Siva and Attain Golden Form

They who saw the Fish[1], remain looking at the fish;
They who saw the Hare[2], are of the Three[3] rid;
He who controlled the battle[4] turmultuous,
See the Hidden Truth[5],
His form golden becomes.

1) Woman
2) Astral vision of the mystic moon within.
3) Pasas
4) Indriyas
5) Siva

கோரை எழுந்து கிடந்த குளத்தினில்
ஆரை படர்ந்து தொடர்ந்து கிடந்தது
நாரை படுகின்றாற் போலல்ல நாதனார்
பாரை கிடக்கப் படிகின்ற வாறே 2911

Lord is Hidden Deep Within

In the Tank[1] where Reeds[2] flourished,
In Creepers[3] spread and entwined filled,
The Lord is not like the stork that on them gently walks
Deep into the Rocky Floor, He dives
For Jiva's redemption to grant.

1) Body
2) Pasas
3) Desires
4) Steadfast devotion

கொல்லைமுக் காதமுங் காடரைக் காதமும்
எல்லை மயங்கிக் கிடந்த இருநெறி
எல்லை மயங்கா தியங்கவல் லார்கட்
கொல்லை கடந்துசென் றூர்புக லாமே. 2912

Yoga Way to Liberation

Of three leagues is the Garden below,
Of half a league is the Forest above,
Frontiers blurring the two routes intermingled;
They who can see the Frontiers clear
Can quick cross the backyard

And reach the Hamlet safe.

The two routes (right and left breath) from the garden below (muladhara) and the forest above (sahasrara) intermingled, and they who can discern the blurring frontiers clearly reach the hamlet (liberation) safely and quickly.

உழவொன்று வித்து ஒருங்கின காலத்
தெழுமழை பெய்யா திருநிலச் செவ்வி
தழுவி வினைசென்று தான்பய வாது
வழுவாது போவன் வளர்சடை யோனே. 2913

No More Karmas if Yoga is Attained

When after Ploughing, Seed is cast,
And copious Rains fall,
And it soaks the Land,
No more will Karmas germinate;
Sure He comes,
The Lord of flourishing matted locks.

No more karmas will trouble you, if yoga is consummated. you will surely reach the Lord of Flourishing Matted Locks.

பதுங்கிலும் பாய்புலி பன்னிரு காதம்
ஒதுங்கிய தண்கடல் ஓதம் உலவ
மதுங்கிய வார்களி யாரமு தூறப்
பொதுங்கிய ஐவரைப் போய்வளைத் தானே. 2914

Jiva Vanquishes Indriyas by Yoga

The Tiger[1] that leaps twelve[2] leagues crouches,
The Billows[3] of the Hidden Sea soft spreads,
The nectar-sweet rapturous ambrosia wells up,
Thus did Jiva surround the Five[4] that harassed.

1) Prana breath
2) Twelve-finger measure of length
3) Mystic waters in the astral sphere
4) Indriyas

தோணியொன் றேறித் தொடர்ந்து கடல்புக்கு
வாணிபஞ் செய்து வழங்கி வளர்மகன்
நீலிக் கிறையுமே நெஞ்சின் நிலைதளர்ந்
தாலிப் பழம்போல் அளிக்கின்ற அப்பே. 2915

Jiva's Journey in Yoga Sea

He boarded a boat and launched into sea,
He traded well and flourished fast;
The good man,
To a She-devil gave his heart,
And in spirit lost dropped
To him as a rich fruit of nectar sweet
Is that Divine Water that flows.

The good man, jiva, while voyaging in the yoga sea, lost his heart to a she-devil (mayaic senses) and under her spell dropped in spirit. To him the divine water that flows (from cranium) is like a rich fruit laden with nectar.

முக்காத ஆற்றிலே மூன்றுள வாழைகள்
செக்குப் பழுத்த திரிமலங் காய்த்தன
பக்கனார் மிக்கார் படங்கினார் கன்னியர்
நக்கு மலருண்டு நடுவுநின் றாரே. 2916

Yoga's Triumph

In the river of Leagues Three
Are Plantain Trees Three;
Ruddy fruits of triple Malas they bore;
They who are with the Lord exceeding;
Hoisted their Flag;
And seeking the Virgin through Central Sushumna,
Inhaled the Flower's fragrance, divine sweet.

They who hail the name of the Lord and seek the virgin (Sakti Kundalini) through central sushumna will inhale the divine flower's (sahasrara) sweet fragrance.

அடியும் முடியும் அமைந்ததோர் ஆத்தி
முடியும் நுனியின்கண் முத்தலை மூங்கில்
கொடியும் படையுங் கோட்சரன் ஐயைந்து
மடியும் வலம்புரி வாய்த்ததவ் வாறே. 2917

Yoga Vanquishes Tattvas

There is an Athi tree[1] with root and top,
At the tip end high is the Bamboo[2] triple crested[3],
With flag and army are evil spies five times five[4]
Destroyed they shall be,
And the Sacred Conch in victory blow[5]

1) A tree (bauhina racemosa), whose flowers are dear to Siva. Here, it is symbolic of the body from muladhara to sahasrara.
2) The spinal column through which the sushumna nadi runs.
3) Ida, pingala, and prana nadis
4) The senses and the sense organs
5) Attainment of nada state in yoga.

பன்றியும் பாம்பும் பசுமுசு வானரந்
தென்றிக் கிடந்த சிறுநரிக் கூட்டத்துக்
குன்றாமை கூடித் தராசின் நிறுத்தபின்
குன்றி நிறையைக் குறைக்கின்ற வாறே. 2918

Conquer Indriyas and Reach Iruvinai-Oppu and Nalapari Pakam

Pig and Snake, Cow and Monkey
Together were in the lowly Jackal herd;
Joining them not and debasing himself not,
When, in balance, deeds good and bad are equal weighed
The Jiva, tinier than crab's-eye berry,
Its ego's diminution saw.

Give up the five senses. When good and bad deeds are weighed in balance, the jiva, tinier than the crab's eye, sees its ego diminishing.

1-5) Indriyas

மொட்டித்தெழுந்ததோர் மொட்டுண்டு மொட்டினைக்
கட்டுவிட்டோடின் மலர்தலுங் காணலாம்
பற்றுவிட் டம்மனை பாழ்பட நோக்கினாற்
கட்டுவிட் டார்க்கன்றிக் காணவொண் ணாதே. 2919

Freedom From Fetters

Unopened a Bud there is;
Freed from Fetters,
The bud soon blossoms, that you see
Give up desires, the Tattvas perish;
Unless they be from Fetters free,
They see not the Blossom.

The bud blossoms as soon as it is freed from the plant's fetters. Similarly, unless you are freed from the bonds you will not be liberated. So rend the fetters asunder and destroy the tattvas.

நீரின்றிப் பாயும் நிலத்தினிற் பச்சையாம்
யாவரும் என்றும் அறியவல் லாரில்லை
கூரு மழைபொழி யாது பொழிபுனல்
தேரினிந் நீர்மை திடரினில் லாதே. 2920

Uniqueness of Ambrosial Flow in Cranium

Green that Land, yet no water flows,
None know it ever;
The Water that flows rain devoid
Stands not in Land untilled.

Though no water flows, there is a land that remains ever green. The water that doesn't flow from rain (Grace, does not stand in the land (body) untilled (by yoga).

கூகை குருந்தம தேறிக் குணம்பயில்
மோகம் உலகுக் குணர்கின்ற காலத்து
நாகமும் ஒன்று நடுவுரை செய்திடும்
பாகனு மாகின்ற பண்பனு மாமே. 2921

Jiva Becomes Siva by Kundalini Yoga

When the Owl gets to the top of Kurunda tree
And realizes desire is the source of the world
Then the Snake standing in the Centre teaches (Jnana)
And Jiva, Siva becomes.

When the owl (jiva) on the top of the 'kurunda' tree (cranium) realises that desire is the source of the world, the snake (kundalini) standing in the centre (of sushumna) teaches jnana. Then jiva becomes Siva.

வாழையுஞ் சூரையும் வந்திடங் கொண்டன
வாழைக்குச் சூரை வலிது வலிதென்பார்
வாழையுஞ் சூரையும் வன்துண்டஞ் செய்திட்டு
வாழை யிடங்கொண்டு வாழ்கின்ற வாறே. 2922

Iruvinai Oppu Leads to Siva

The Plantain Tree and the Surai Creeper (pepper) together covered space;
The Surai creeper is stronger by far than the Plantain tree they say;
Cutting down the Plantain tree and Surai creeper, together,
The Plantain extending flourishes sure.

They say that the 'surai' creeper (pasa) is stronger than the plantain tree (jiva). Cut down the creeper — the plaintain flourishes well.

நிலத்தைப் பிளந்து நெடுங்கடல் ஓட்டிப்
புனத்துக் குறவன் புணர்ந்த கொழுமீன்
விலக்குமின் யாவர்க்கும் வேண்டிற் குறையா
தருத்தமு மின்றி யடுவது மாமே. 2923

Give up Worldly Pursuits and Practice Yoga

Digging not the Earth,
The upland Kurava sails seas
And catches fatty fish;
Let him give it up;
(Rather let him the Earth dig)
There is a way of a Rich Catch,
That is Wealth and Food for all.

Let the 'kurava' (inland fisherman) give up the fatty fish (sense enjoyment) which he has caught; for, there is a way to a rich catch that is wealth and food (liberation) for all.

தளிர்க்கும் ஒருபிள்ளை தட்டா னகத்தில்
விளிப்பதோர் சங்குண்டு வேந்தனை நாடிக்
களிக்குங் குசவர்க்குங் காவிதி யார்க்கும்
அளிக்கும் பதத்தொன் றாய்ந்துகொள் வார்க்கே. 2924

Reach Nada by Yoga and Attain Status of God

In the House of Goldsmith[1] a Child[2] flourishes,
A Conch of Call[3] there is;
Blow it and call the Lord in Joy;
To the Potter[4] and the Titled Minister[5] alike
Are granted the high state;
That do you seek.

1) Sahasrara
2) Jiva
3) Nada
4) Brahma (Creator)
5) Vishnu ('Kavi' and 'thi' means, 'Protector or Preserver')

குடைவிட்டுப் போந்தது கோயில் எருமை
படைகண்டு மீண்டது பாதி வழியில்
உடையவன் மந்திரி யுள்ளலும் ஊரார்
அடையா நெடுங்கடை ஐந்தொடு நான்கே. 2925

Indriyas Obstruct the Yoga Journey

The Temple buffalo left the Shed,
It saw the Army and half-way turned;

The Chief held counsel with Minister,
The Citizens closed the Gates,
Five and Four.

The temple buffalo (jiva) left the shed (yoga) and turned back seeing the army (senses). The chief (jiva) held counsel with the minister (Guru). The nine citizens (indriyas) closed the gates (orifices) by way of sense control. The indriyas are the impediments that obstruct the yoga journey

போகின்ற எட்டும் புகுகின்ற பத்தெட்டும்
ஆகிப் படைத்தன ஒன்பது வாய்தலும்
நாகமும் எட்டொடு நாலு புரவியும்
பாகன் விடாவிடிற் பன்றியு மாமே. 2926

The Lord Drives in the Tattvas into the Infant Body

The eight constituents of Body Subtle
That ultimately leave,
The eight and ten Tattvas that sneak in,
With Purusha in them immersed,
The orifices nine,
The Kundalini that serpent-like coils,
The life breath twelve finger-measure (angula) long,
—If these, the Divine Charioteer drives not in,
Verily may the infant less than human be (say, pig).

The eight constituents of the subtle body that leave ultimately, the eighteen tattvas with purusha immersed in them that enter at conception; the nine orifices, the kundalini, the twelve-finger measure long life-breath—if all these are not driven into the womb by the Divine Charioteer, truly the infant born will be far inferior to human (say, a pig).

பாசி படர்ந்து கிடந்த குளத்திடைக்
கூசி யிருக்குங் குருகிரை தேர்ந்துண்ணுந்
தூசி மறவன் துணைவழி எய்திடப்
பர்சங் கிடந்து பதைக்கின்ற வாறே. 2927

Pasa Disappears With Guru's Guidance

In the Lagoon that is Moss covered,
Gently walking, the Shy Heron feeds;
When the Marching Warrior's guidance got,
Pasa, to ground laid, fluttered away.

The shy heron (jiva) feeds in the lagoon (body) covered by moss (pasa). Pasa disappears with the guidance of the marching warrior (Guru).

கும்ப மலைமேல் எழுந்ததோர் கொம்புண்டு
கொம்புக்கும் அப்பால் அடிப்பதோர் காற்றுண்டு
வம்பாய் மலர்ந்ததோர் பூவுண்டப் பூவுக்குள்
வண்டாய்க் கிடந்து மணங்கொள்வன் ஈசனே. 2928

Siva Draws Jiva Like Himself

On the Peaked Mountain is a Summit High,
Beyond the Summit blows a Gusty Wind;
There blossomed a Flower that its fragrance spread
Within that Flower, a Bee its Nectar imbibed,
There the Lord like Himself Jiva draws.

A gusty wind (prana) blows beyond the high summit (cranium). There blossomed a fragrant flower (sahasrara). The Lord draws jiva towards Himself here.

வீணையுந் தண்டும் விரவி யிசைமுரல்
தாணுவும் மேவித் தகுதலைப் பெய்தது
வாணிபஞ் சிக்கென் றதுவடை யாமுன்னங்
காணியும் அங்கே கலக்கின்ற வாறே. 2929

Arouse Kundalini to Reach Cranium

Lute and Flute, their melody intermingling,
Jiva marched ahead in Cranium within;
Even before the Bargain was struck,
The Land was up there for Him to possess.

Jiva marched ahead within the cranium with the music of vina and flute that comes of yoga in the nada sphere. Even before the bargain talks began (between jiva and Siva), the land (liberation) was up there for jiva to possess.

கொங்குபுக் காரொடு வாணிபஞ் செய்தது
வங்குபுக் காலன்றி ஆய்ந்தறி வாரில்லை
திங்கள்புக் கால்இரு ளாவ தறிந்திலர்
தங்குபுக் கார்சிலர் தாபதர் தாமே. 2930

Reaching the Moon Sphere—A Mystic Secret

The trade with the One in Ambrosia
None know about,
But those who the Secret Cavern entered;
They know not,
When the Moon rises
No more darkness will be;
Some did reach there and remained ever,
They truly, are the holy beings devout.

போதும் புலர்ந்தது பொன்னிறங் கொண்டது
தாதவிழ் புன்னை தயங்கு மிருகரை
ஏதமில் ஈசன் இயங்கு நெறியிது
மாத ரிருந்தோர் மண்டலந் தானே. 2931

Dawn of Jnana in Sahasrara

The Day dawned, a golden hue it took,
On the banks high, the Mastwood shed its golden pollen;
Thus it is where the Holy Lord abides;
That Sphere the Damsel reached and remained.

The day dawned and shed its golden hue on the high banks (of sahasrara) where the Holy Lord abides. The damsel (kundalini) reached that sphere and remained there.

கோமுற் றமருங் குடிகளுந் தம்மிலே
காமுற்ற கத்தி இடுவர் கடைதொறு
மீவற்ற வெல்லை விடாது வழிகாட்டி
யாமுற்ற தட்டினால் ஐந்துண்ண லாமே. 2932

Properly Guided, Jiva Reaches the Final State

The tribes of Indriyas to Jiva belong
Each at his gate with swords fight;
If constantly guided,
Jiva takes the True Way to Frontier;
From that bourne none ever returns:
From that very plane shall he transcend;
The Five-States-Beyond.

Properly guided, jiva takes the true way to the frontier (sahasrara). From that plane he reaches the final state beyond the five states (of consciousness).

தோட்டத்தில் மாம்பழந் தோண்டிவிழுந்தக்கால்
நாட்டின் புறத்தில் நரியழைத் தென்செயும்
மூட்டிக் கொடுத்த முதல்வனை முன்னிட்டுக்
காட்டிக் கொடுத்தவர் கைவிட்டவாறே. 2933

Body No More Counts When Jiva-Siva Union is Effected

When in the Garden,
The Fruit of Mango, ripened, dropped,
What matters if Jackals outside howl?
When the Primal One was by Kundalini Fire reached,
The fleshy body that led to it,
Forever left.

The howling of the jackals (senses) outside matters little when the ripened mango fruit (Siva) drops within the garden (sahasrara). The body counts for little when the Primal One (Siva) is reached by kundalini fire.

புலர்ந்தது போதென்று புட்கள் சிலம்பப்
புலர்ந்தது போதென்று பூங்கொடி புல்லிப்
புலம்பி னவளோடும் போக நுகரும்
புலம்பனுக் கென்றும் புலர்ந்திலை போதே. 2934

Dawn of Jnana Eternal Day-Light

"Dawn[1] is it" — thus shrilled the Birds[2],
"Dawn is it" — thus, the flower-like Damsel[3]
Separation fearing, bewailed;
With Her in eternal union the Lord joyed;
And for Jiva no more the dawn
No more the separation.

1) Effulgent light of jnana in sahasrara
2) Indriyas
3) Kundalini

தோணியொன் றுண்டு துறையில் விடுவது
வாணி மிதித்துநின் றைவர்கோ லூன்றலும்
வாணிபஞ் செய்வார் வழியிடை யாற்றிடை
ஆணி கலங்கில் அதுவிது வாமே. 2935

When Pasas Leave Jiva Unites

A Boat there is in the River Ghat
The Five plant their feet and row;
Thus on the river route they trade;
If in the midst the Rudder wobbles,
That becomes This,
(No more the world trade).

The five boatmen (senses) row the boat (body) in the river ghat (life). If in the middle, the rudder wobbles (pasas leave), no more will there be world trade when pasas are sundered, jiva unites in Siva.

18. மோன சமாதி

MAUNA SAMADHI (TRANSCENDENTAL)

நின்றார் இருந்தார் கிடந்தார் எனவில்லை
சென்றார் தஞ்சித்த மோன சமாதியாம்
மன்றேயு மங்கே மறைப்பொருளொன்றுண்டு
சென்றாங் கணைந்தவர் சேர்கின்ற வாறே. 2936

Through Samadhi Being Within is Reached

They stood, they sat, they lay
—Thus their state can be described not;
Their thought is in Samadhi's Silence
There is a Being Hidden;
They who reach it (Samadhi),
Have reached Him indeed.

காட்டுங் குறியுங் கடந்தவர் காரணம்
ஏட்டின் புறத்தில் எழுதிவைத் தென்பயன்
கூட்டுங் குருநந்தி கூட்டிடி னல்லது
ஆட்டின் கழுத்தில் அதர்கிடந் தற்றே. 2937

Guru Alone Can Show the Way

He is beyond the Signs and Mudras
He is the Cause;
What avails describing Him in Books?
All those are like excrescence growth on Sheep's neck;
—Unless the Guru himself leads you to Him.

உணர்வுடை யார்கட் குலகமுந் தோன்றும்
உணர்வுடை யார்கட் குறுதுய ரில்லை
உணர்வுடை யார்கள் உணர்ந்தஅக் காலம்
உணர்வுடை யார்கள் உணர்ந்துகண் டாரே. 2938

Know the Finite Truth

They that the Truth know, see worlds all,
They that the Truth know, have sorrows none,

When they that the Truth thus saw
They indeed have seen the Truth Finite.

மறப்பது வாய்நின்ற மாயநன் னாடன்
பிறப்பினை நீங்கிய பேரரு ளாளன்
சிறப்புடை யான்திரு மங்கையுந் தானும்
உறக்கமில் போகத் துறங்கிடுந் தானே. 2939

Siva and Sakti are in Samadhi Union

Even in my forgetfulness He stands,
He is Lord of Maya-Land,
He is the Compassion vast,
He ended my birth,
He is of qualities great;
Himself and His Holy Sakti
Sleep in sleepless union.

துரியங்கள் மூன்றும் கடந்தொளிர் சோதி
அரிய துரிய மதில்மீது மூன்றாய்
விரிவு குவிவு விழுங்கி யுமிழ்ந்தே
உரையில் அநுபூ திகத்தினுள் ளானே. 2940

Lord is Beyond Turiyatita

He is the Light Transcendental
That shines beyond Turiyas Three,
In the Turiyatia that transcends them,
Beyond waking, dreaming sushupti states;
In that state, defying thought and speech.

உருவிலி யூனிலி யூனமொன் றில்லி
திருவிலி தீதிலி தேவர்க்குந் தேவன்
பொருவிலி பூதப் படையுடை யாளி
மருவிலி வந்தென் மனம்புகுந் தானே. 2941

Attributes of Siva

Formless is He,
Bodyless is He,
Blemishless is He,
Richless is He,
Harmless is He,
Celestial of celestials is He,
Contentionless is He,
Bhoota-army possessed is He,
Attachmentless is He,
He entered my thoughts.

கண்டறி வாரில்லைக் காயத்தின் நந்தியை
எண்டிசை யோரும் இறைவனென் றேத்துவர்
அண்டங் கடந்த அளவிலா ஆனந்தத்
தொண்டர் முகந்த துறையறி யோமே. 2942

Bliss of Devotees is Beyond Description

None have seen Him and known Him,
He, the Nandi, within the body is;
All, in directions eight,
Praise Him as Lord;
The unending bliss of His devotees many;
Surpasses universes vast,
—How much they enjoyed Him, little do we know!

தற்பர மல்ல சதாசிவன் தானல்ல
நிட்கள மல்ல சகள் நிலையல்ல
அற்புத மாகி யநுபோகக் காமம்போற்
கற்பனை யின்றிக் கலந்துநின் றானே. 2943

Felicity of Union of Jiva and Siva

Tat-Para He is not,
Sadasiva He is not,
Formless is He,
Formed is He not,
Wondrous indeed like felicity of sex-union enjoyed
Imagination baffling,
He in me in union stood.

முகத்திற்கண்கொண்டு காண்கின்ற மூடர்காள்
அகத்திற் கண்கொண்டு காண்பதே ஆனந்தம்
மகட்குத் தாய்தன் மணாளனோ டாடிய
சுகத்தைச் சொல்லென்றாற்
சொல்லுமாறெங்ஙனே. 2944

Divine Felicity Beyond Words

Thou fools who see with fleshy eyes
Know! To see with inner eye is bliss true;
How can mother tell the daughter
Of the felicity in the union with her husband?
In what terms will she that describe?

அப்பினில் உப்பென அத்தன் அணைந்திட்டுச்
செப்பு பராபரஞ் சேர்பர மும்விட்டுக்
கப்புறு சொற்பத மாளக் கலந்தமை
எப்படி யப்படி என்னுமவ் வாறே. 2945

Transcendental Union Beyond Word and Speech

As salt in water, in Lord I mixed,
Transcending Param and Paraparam states,
Beyond word and speech I in union merged;
"How was It?" — you ask
"It was It" — I say.

கண்டார்க் கழகிது காஞ்சிரத் தின்பழந்
தின்றார்க் கறியலாம் அப்பழத் தின்சுவை
பெண்டா னிரம்பி மடவிய ளானாற்
கொண்டான் அறிவன் குணம்பல தானே. 2946

Deceptive Ways of World

Lovely to look at is the fruit of nux-vomica,
Only those who eat know its taste (bitter)
When virgin matures and full woman becomes,
Only then will husband know her qualities diverse.

நந்தி யிருந்தான் நடுவுத் தெருவிலே
சந்தி சமாதிகள் தாமே யொழிந்தன

உந்தியி னுள்ளே யுதித்தெழுஞ் சோதியைப்
புந்தியி னாலே புணர்ந்துகொண் டேனே. 2947

Jiva Light Merges in Siva Light

Nandi He was, in Street-Centre (of Sahasrara),
Samadhi and other ways of union, of themselves went
Into the Light, within navel centre rises,
By my Jnana, I merged.

Jiva light merges into Siva Light of jnana that rises from below the navel centre.

விதறு படாவண்ணம் வேறிருந் தாய்ந்து
பதறு படாதே பழமறை பார்த்துக்
கதறிய பாழைக் கடந்தந்தக் கற்பனை
உதறிய பாழில் ஒடுங்குகின் றேனே. 2948

Merging into Space

Undistracted, I sit aloof and meditate,
Doubt-free, I follow the ancient Vedas,
I cross the awesome waste, this life is,
And beyond into the Space, that defies imagination,
I merge.

வாடா மலர்புனை சேவடி வானவர்
கூடார் அறநெறி நாடெறு மின்புறச்
சேடார் கமலச் செழுஞ்சுட ருட்சென்று
நாடார் அமுதுற நாடார் அமுதமே. 2949

The Celestials Seek Him Not

His Holy Feet bedecked in unfading blooms
The Celestials seek not;
To the Holy Way they take not;
To the radiance of the lovely lotus within,
They penetrate not,
They seek not to drink of the Divine Ambrosia.

அதுக்கென் றிருவர் அமர்ந்தசொற் கேட்டும்
பொதுக்கெனக் காமம் புலப்படு மாபோல்
சதுக்கென்று வேறே சமைந்தாரைக் காண
மதுக்கொன்றைத் தாரான் வளந்தரு மன்றே. 2950

Lord's Gushing Love

When for purposeful union the lovers sit and talk
Of a sudden gushes their passion;
When the Lord of fragrant Konrai flower beholds
Those who determined sit to meet Him,
He His Grace unhesitating grants.

தானும் அழிந்து தனமும் அழிந்துநீ
டூனும் அழிந்து உயிரும் அழிந்துடன்
வானும் அழிந்து மனமும் அழிந்துபின்
நானும் அழிந்தமை நானறி யேனே. 2951

Nature of Union in God

Myself perishing, my wealth perishing,
Body perishing and life perishing,
Heaven perishing and mind perishing,
My ego perishing
—This I knew not (is union in God).

இருளும் வெளியும் இரண்டையும் மாற்றிப்
பொருளிற் பொருளாய்ப் பொருந்தவுள் ளாகி
அருளால் அழிந்திடும் அத்தன் அடிக்கே
உருளாத கன்மன முற்றுநின் றேனே. 2952

Merging into Finite Reality

Darkness and Space I transcended,
As substance into Substance I merged,
To the Feet of Lord in Grace abounding,
Firm as rock immovable
My thoughts entire went.

ஒன்றிநின் றுள்ளே யுணர்ந்தேன் பராபரம்
ஒன்றிநின் றுள்ளே யுணர்ந்தேன் சிவகதி
ஒன்றிநின் றுள்ளே யுணர்ந்தேன் உணர்வினை
ஒன்றிநின் றேபல ஊழிகண் டேனே. 2953

Transcendental Awareness

Meditating in oneness, I visioned Paraparam,
Meditating in oneness, I realized Siva-State
Meditating in oneness, I experienced Awarene: Transcendental
Meditating in oneness, I witnessed aeons up aeons.

19. வரையுறை மாட்சி

GREATNESS OF LIMITLESSNESS BEYOND

தான்வரை வற்றபி னாரை வரைவது
தானவ னானபி னாரை நினைவது
காமனை வென்றகண் ணாரை யுகப்பது
தூமொழி வாசகஞ் சொல்லுமின் நீரே. 2954

State of Oneness in God

When you have, yourself, limitless become,
Who, in limit, are you to see?
When you have, yourself, He become,

Who are you to think of?
The Eyes that vanquished the God of Love,
Whom are they in longing to look for?
—Tell me, youself, the real Truth?

உரையற்ற தொன்றை யுரைசெய்யு மூமர்காள்
கரையற்ற தொன்றைக் கரைகாண லாகுமோ
திரையற்ற நீர்போல் சிந்தை தெளிவார்க்குப்
புரையற் றிருந்தான் புரிசடை யோனே. 2955

Thoughts Stand Still in the Beyond

You dumb ones!
They seek to speak,
Of the One beyond speech!
Can you ever reach the shores
Of the Shoreless Vast?
For them whose thoughts stand still,
Like the waveless waters,
Unreserved He appears;
He of the matted locks.

மனமாயை மாயைஇம் மாயை மயக்க
மனமாயை தான் மாய மற்றொன்று மில்லை
பினைமாய்வ தில்லை பிதற்றவும் வேண்டா
தனையாய்ந் திருப்பது தத்துவந் தானே. 2956

Maya Creates No Illusions There

Maya is but mind's work,
It creates the illusions;
When the mind's illusion disappears,
Nothing there left to worry about;
Death will not there be;
Chatter no more;
To seek the Self is Truth Divine.

20. அணைந்தோர் தன்மை

GREATNESS OF THE REALIZED

மலமில்லை மாசில்லை மானாபி மானங்
குலமில்லை கொள்ளுங் குணங்களு மில்லை
நலமில்லை நந்தி ஞானத்தி னாலே
பலமன்னி யன்பிற் புதித்துவைப் போர்க்கே. 2957

The Realized Souls Have No Possessions

Mala none; impurity none; pride and prejudice none;
Family none, excellences none; affluence none;
For them who in wisdom
Plant themselves in Nandi
—Firm in His love.

ஒழிந்தேன் பிறவி யுறுவென்னும் பாசங்
கழிந்தேன் கடவுளும் நானுமொன் றானேன்
அழிந்தாங் கினிவரு மாக்கமும் வேண்டேன்
செழுஞ்சார் புடைய சிவனைக் கண்டேனே. 2958

They Become God

Ended the birth; sundered the bonds;
God and I one became;
No more for me the way of rebirth;
I have met Siva the Auspicious.

ஆலைக் கரும்பும் அமுதும்அக் காரமுஞ்
சோலைத் தண்ணீரும் உடைத்தெங்கள்
பீலிக்கண் ணன்ன வடிவுசெய் வாளொரு
கோலப்பெண் ணாட்குக்
குறையொன்றுமில்லையே. 2959

They Want Nothing

Cane of sugar, rice of fineness, garments of richness
And water of green glades too,
Our and possesses;
By the Grace of lovely Mother
That is peacock shaped,
Nothing we want, nothing, indeed.

ஆராலும் என்னை அமட்டவொண் ணாதினிச்
சீரார் பிரான்வந்தென் சிந்தை புகுந்தனன்
சீராடி யங்கே திரிவதல் லால்இனி
யார்பாடுஞ் சாரா அறிவறிந் தேனே. 2960

They are Inseparable in God

None can intimidate me hereafter,
The Lord came and entered my thoughts,
There will I sport and wander in joy;
No more will I with anyone else be.

பிரிந்தேன் பிரமன் பிணித்ததோர் பாசந்
தெரிந்தேன் சிவகதி செல்லு நிலையை
அரிந்தேன் வினையை அயில்மன் வாளால்
முரிந்தேன் புரத்தினை முந்துகின் றேனே. 2961

How They Hastened to the City of God

I freed myself of fetters
The Creator bound me with,
I learned the way of reaching Siva;
I smote Karmas with the sharp sword of mind,
I stood ego lost;
And now I hasten toward the City of God.

ஒன்றுகண் டீர்உல குக்கொரு தெய்வமும்
ஒன்றுகண் டீர்உல குக்குயி ராவது
நன்றுகண் டீர்நல் நமச்சிவா யப்பழந்
தின்றுகண் டேற்கிது தித்தித்த வாறே. 2962

Sweetness of Namasivaya Fruit

One the God for worlds all,
One is He, the life of worlds all,
Lovely indeed in Namasivaya Fruit,
Sweet it is to them
Who of it tasted.

சந்திரன் பாம்பொடுஞ் சூடுஞ் சடாதரன்
வந்தென்னை யாண்ட மணிவிளக் கானவன்
அந்தமும் ஆதியும் இல்லா அரும்பொருள்
சிந்தையின் மேவித் தியக்கறுத் தானே. 2963

Doubt-Free State of the God Realized

The Lord who wears moon and serpent on His matted hair,
He, the jewelled lamp
That accepted me in His service,
The Being Rare,
Neither beginning nor end has,
He entered my thoughts and made me doubt-free.

பண்டெங்கள் ஈசன் நெடுமால் பிரமனைக்
கண்டங் கிருக்குங் கருத்தறி வாரில்லை
விண்டங்கே தோன்றி வெறுமன மாயிடில்
துண்டங் கிருந்ததோர் தூறது வாமே. 2964

Their Thought-Free State

Brahma and Vishnu, of yore,
Our Lord created;
And There He remains ever,
None know why;
If renouncing all,
Jiva There appears,
And empties its thoughts,
No more birth in carnal body will be.

அன்னையும் அத்தனும் அன்புற்ற தல்லது
அன்னையும் அத்தனு மாரறி வாரென்னை
அன்னையும் அத்தனு மியானும் உடனிருந்
தன்னையும் அத்தனை யான்புரந் தேனே. 2965

Siva-Sakti-Jiva Union

Unless the Heavenly Father and Heavenly Mother love me,
How shall the worldly father and worldly mother know me?
The Father, Mother and I were together seated;
My Father and Mother, I adoring.

கொண்ட சுழியுங் குலவரை யுச்சியும்
அண்டரும் அண்டத் தலைவரும் ஆதியும்
எண்டிசை யோரும்வந் தென்கைத் தலத்துளே
உண்டனர் நானினி உய்ந்தொழிந் தேனே. 2966

Prowess of Redeemed State

The seas vast,
The mountain peaks high,
The denizens of the universe,
And those who hold their sway there,
The Primal Sakti,
And the people in directions eight
—All, all, came within my grasp;
Redeemed am I, high above all.

தானே திசையொடு தேவரு மாய்நிற்குந்
தானே வடவரை யாதியு மாய்நிற்குந்
தானே யுடலுயிர் தத்துவ மாய்நிற்குந்
தானே யுலகில் தலைவனு மாமே. 2967

He is the Totality

Himself as space and Celestials stands,
Himself as body, life and matter stands,
Himself as sea, hill and dale stands;
Himself—all worlds' Lord Supreme.

நமன்வரின் ஞானவாள் கொண்டே எறிவன்
சிவன்வரின் நானுடன் போவது திண்ணம்
பவம்வரும் வல்வினை பண்டே யறுத்தேன்
தவம்வருஞ் சிந்தைக்குத் தானெதி ராரே. 2968

Their Thought Power

If God of Death comes,
I shall smite him with Sword of Jnana,
If Siva comes,
I am sure to go with Him;
Long back had I sundered Karma,
Which to birth leads;
Who can stand against Thought,
Of intense devotion born?

சித்தஞ் சிவமாய் மலமூன்றுஞ் செற்றவர்
சுத்தச் சிவமாவர் தோயார் மலபந்தங்
கத்துஞ் சிலுகுங் கலகமுங் கைகாணார்
சத்தம் பரவிந்து தானாமென் றெண்ணியே. 2969

They are in Nada and Bindu

Their thoughts are Siva-filled;
They have destroyed Malas three
Suddha Siva they have become;
To Mala's bondage they return not;
Shouts, confusion and fights (of this world),
They indulge not in;
Immersed are they in Nada and Para Bindu.

நினைப்பும் மறப்பும் இலாதவர் நெஞ்சம்
வினைப்பற் றறுக்கும் விமலன் இருக்கும்
வினைப்பற் றறுக்கும் விமலனைத் தேடி
நினைக்கப் பெறிலவன் நீளிய னாமே. 2970

Long They Live

They who cognize
Neither remembering nor forgetting,
In their thoughts,

The Pure One, who uproots Karmas,
Stand;
Seeking the Pure One,
Who uproots Karmas
They who think of Him, long long live.

சிவபெரு மானென்று நானழைத் தேத்தத்
தவபெரு மானென்று தான்வந்து நின்றான்
அவபெரு மானென்னை யாளுடை நாதன்
பவபெரு மானைப் பணிந்துநின் றேனே. 2971

Siva Appears as a Tapasvin

"O! Siva, my Great Lord" — thus I hailed Him;
And as a tapasvin the Holy Lord was before me;
He the Desired Lord, who accepted me in His service
Him I stood adoring, the Lord Eternal.

பணிந்துநின் றேன்பர மாதி பதியைத்
துணிந்துநின்றேன்இனி மற்றொன்றும்வேண்டேன்
அணிந்துநின் றேனுடல் ஆதிப் பிரானைத்
தணிந்துநின் றேன்சிவன் தன்மைகண்டேனே. 2972

Meek and Intense Prayer Leads to Siva

Him I adored, the Param, the Primal Lord,
Determined I stood, nothing else I seek;
In my body I held Him in union, the First One;
Meek in prayer I stood and I saw my Siva's Being.

என்னெஞ்சம் ஈசன் இணையடி தாஞ்சேர்ந்து
முன்னஞ்செய் தேத்த முழுதும் பிறப்பறுந்
தன்னெஞ்சம் இல்லாத் தலைவன் தலைவிதி
பின்னஞ்செய் தென்னைப் பிணக்கறுத் தானே. 2973

In the Presence of Siva

The Lord filled my thoughts,
His Feet I beseeched;
As I thus entered His Presence,
He ended my birth's whirl;
—He the Lord that has Thoughts none;
My Fate He fragmented,
My bonds He sundered.

பிணக்கறுத் தான்பிணி மூப்பறுத் தெண்ணுங்
கணக்கறுத் தாண்டனன் காணந்தி என்னைப்
பிணக்கறுத் தென்னுடன் முன்வந்த துன்பம்
வணக்கலுற்றேன்சிவம் வந்தது தானே. 2974

He Resolved My Contradictions

My contradictions He resolved;
Disease, age and life's reckoning He ended;
Thus He accepted me in His service,
He my Nandi;
My contradictions resolved,
My life's sorrows, I laid low;
And. Siva, of Himself appeared.

சிவன்வந்து தேவர் குழாமுடன் கூடப்
பவம்வந் திடநின்ற பாசம் அறுத்திட்
டவனெந்தை யாண்டருள் ஆதிப் பெருமான்
அவன்வந்தென் னுள்ளே யகப்பட்ட வாறே. 2975

How Siva Entered in Me

Siva with His Celestial retinue entered in me;
He severed my bonds that to births give rise;
He is my Father,
He the Primal Lord that in His service accepted me;
Into Grace my heart entered;
And there, imprisoned, remained.

கரும்புந் தேனுங் கலந்ததோர் காயத்தில்
அரும்புங் கந்தமு மாகிய ஆனந்தம்
விரும்பியே உள்ளம் வெளியுறக் கண்டபின்
கரும்புங் கைத்தது தேனும் புளித்ததே. 2976

Bodily Pleasures Ceased to Interest

In this body of pleasures
Like sugarcane and honey mixed,
Sprouted the Fragrance of Siva Bliss;
In eagerness my heart sought it
And I visioned the Void;
Then did the cane taste bitter
And honey sour.

உள்ள சரியாதி ஒட்டியே மீட்டென்பால்
வள்ளல் அருத்தியே வைத்த வளம்பாடிச்
செய்வன எல்லாஞ் சிவமாகக் காண்டலாற்
கைவள மின்றிக் கருக்கடந் தேனே. 2977

All My Doings Became Siva's

Having pursued the ways of Charya and the rest,
And having received the Bounteous Being's Grace,
I stand praising Him ever;
All that I do,
I see as of Siva's doings;
With no more Karma left,
I crossed the sea of births.

மீண்டார் கமலத்துள் அங்கி மிகச்சென்று
தூண்டா விளக்கின் றகளிநெய் சோர்தலும்
பூண்டாள் ஒருத்தி புவனசூ டாமணி
மாண்டா னொருவன்கை வந்தது தானே. 2978

Egoity Died and Siva Appeared

Into the thousand petalled lotus (in Sahasrara),
The Kundalini fire shot up fierce;

And as with the fat of my heart's love, I made it blaze,
She the Sakti appeared,
She the Jewel of worlds all;
The one, he died, my Egoity
And the One, He appeared, my Siva.

ஆறே யருவி யகங்குளம் ஒன்றுண்டு
நூறே சிவகதி நுண்ணிது வண்ணமுங்
கூறே குவிமுலைக் கொம்பனை யாளொடும்
வேறே யிருக்கும் விழுப்பொருள் தானே. 2979

Siva-Sakti in the Cranium Sphere

The Six streams (of Adharas)
Into one lake flow;
Thus in Way subtle
Into Siva-State penetrate;
There indeed is the Precious Truth,
Himself with Sakti stands,
—She of bouncing breasts and tender vine form.

அன்புள் உருகி அழுவன் அரற்றுவன்
என்பும் உருக இராப்பகல் ஏத்துவன்
என்பொன் மணியை இறைவனை யீசனைத்
தின்பன் கடிப்பன் திருத்துவன் தானே. 2980

Intense Devotion

My heart melting, I moan and rave,
My bones melting, I adore day and night,
My gold, my Guru, my Lord, my God,
Him I eat, bite and chew

மனம்வி ரிந்து குவிந்தது மாதவ
மனம்வி ரிந்து குவிந்தது வாயு
வனம்வி ரிந்து குவிந்தது மன்னுயிர்
மனம்வி ரிந்துரை மாண்டது முத்தியே. 2981

Mind Blossomed into Mukti

The mind blossomed and converged in tapas great;
The mind blossomed and converged in yoga breath;
The mind blossomed and converged for the Jiva;
When the mind blossomed beyond words to describe,
Then is Mukti Finale.

21. தோத்திரம்

LAUDATION

மாயனை நாடி மனநெடுந் தேரேறிப்
போயின நாடறி யாதே புலம்புவர்
தேயமும் நாடுந் திரிந்தெங்கள் செல்வனைக்
காயமின் னாட்டிடைக் கண்டுகொண் டேனே. 2982

Lord is in Body Land

Mounting the Chariot of Mind
They seek the Divine Juggler;
Knowing not whither He went,
They bewail;
Wandering in lands and kingdoms far and near,
I saw Him in this fleeting Body-Land

மன்னு மலைபோல் மதவா ரணத்தின்மேல்
இன்னிசை பாட இருந்தவ ராரெனில்
முன்னியல் கால முதல்வனார் நாமத்தைப்
பன்னினர் என்றே பாடறி வீரே. 2983

Glorious Reward of Prayer

Who were they,
Like mountain on kingly elephant sat,
And to sweet music accompanying, in procession we
Of yore, they chanted the Primal Lord's name in fervour
And so attained the status exalted.

முத்தினின் முத்தை முகிழிள ஞாயிற்றை
எத்தனை வானோரும் ஏத்தும் இறைவனை
அத்தனைக் காணா தரற்றுகின் றேனையோர்
பித்தன் இவனென்று பேசுகின் றாரே. 2984

I See not My Father

The Pearl of pearls,
The Lovely Sun rising at dawn,
The Lord whom all Celestials adore,
My Father;
I see not and rave;
A mad man, they think, I am.

புகுந்துநின் றானெங்கள் புண்ணிய மூர்த்தி
புகுந்துநின் றானெங்கள் போதறி வாளன்
புகுந்துநின் றானடி யார்தங்கள் நெஞ்சம்
புகுந்துநின் றானையே போற்றுகின் றேனே. 2985

He Entered in Me

He entered in me,
He our Holy Lord,
He entered in me,
He the Lord of Jnana's Flower,
He entered in the hearts of His devotees,
Him I adore, who entered in me.

பூதக்கண் ணாடியிற் புகுந்திலன் போதுளன்
வேதக்கண் ணாடியில் வேறே வெளிப்படு
நீதிக்கண் ணாடி நினைவார் மனத்துளன்
கீதக்கண் ணாடியிற் கேட்டுநின் றேனே. 2986

He is Seen in the Mind-Mirror

He appears not in the glasses of the fleshy eye;
He is in the Lotus of the Heart;
He appears in the glass of Vedic Jnana;
He is in the mind-glass of the righteous that think of Him,
Him I saw in the glass of songs
Listening to that Divine Music,
I enraptured stand.

நாமமோ ராயிரம் ஓதுமின் நாதனை
ஏமமோ ராயிரத் துள்ளே இசைவீர்கள்
ஓமமோ ராயிரம் ஓதவல் லாரவர்
காமமோ ராயிரங் கண்டொழிந் தாரே. 2987

Chant "Aum" Incessantly

Chant, the Lord's name, a thousand times,
A thousand blessings shall yours be;
They who chant the lovely "Aum" a thousand times,
Are rid of a thousand thousand passions, away.

போற்றுகின் றேன்புகழ்ந் தும்புகழ் ஞானத்தைத்
தேற்றுகின் றேன்சிந்தை நாயகன் சேவடி
சாற்றுகின் றேன்அறை யோசிவ யோகத்தை
போற்றுகின் றேன்எம் பிரானென்று நானே. 2988

Ajapa

I praise, I laud
Jnana that is our Refuge;
I adore the Holy Feet of the Lord,
Constant in my thought;
I expound Siva Yoga;
Hearken you!
I chant the One Letter (Aum),
Dear to our Lord.

நானாவிதஞ் செய்து நாடுமின் நந்தியை
ஊனார் கமலத்தி னூடுசென் றப்புறம்
வானோர் உலகம் வழிப்பட மீண்டபின்
தேனார வுண்டு தெவிட்டலு மாமே. 2989

Practise Yoga

In ways diverse, do seek Nandi;
Penetrating the Lotus within and going beyond,
You shall reach the Celestial world,
Having drunk of the nectar there, you shall return;
Sweet, sweet exceeding indeed, it is.

வந்துநின் றானடி யார்கட் கரும்பொருள்
இந்திர னாதி இமையவர் வேண்டினுஞ்
சுந்தர மாதர் துழனியொன் றல்லது
அந்தர வானத்தின் அப்புற மாமே. 2990

Devotees More Rewarded Than Celestials

He came and stood before His devotees,
He the Rare Truth;
Even if the Celestials and their King Indra ask
What will they get, but the music of lovely damsels?
But that which devotees get is beyond all their heaven.

மண்ணிற் கலங்கிய நீர்போல் மனிதர்கள்
எண்ணிற் கலங்கி இறைவன் இவனென்னார்
உண்ணிற் குளத்தின் முகந்தொரு பால்வைத்துத்
தெண்ணிற் படுத்த சிவனவ னாமே. 2991

Still Your Thoughts and Be Purified

Like muddied water these men's minds are,
Unclear in vision,
They see not and say, "This is Lord;"
From the heart's lake within,
Draw a pitcherful,
And keep it in stillness apart;
When you thus purify it,
You shall become Siva.

மெய்த்தவத் தானை விரும்பும் ஒருவர்க்குக்
கைத்தலஞ் சேர்தரு நெல்லிக் கனியொக்குஞ்
சுத்தனைத் தூய்நெறி யாய்நின்ற தேவர்கள்
அத்தனை நாடி அமைந்தொழிந் தேனே. 2992

Yearn For Him

He of the Penance Pure;
Transparent as amla fruit
On the palm of those who yearn for Him;
He the Pure One,
Whom Celestials seek in ways righteous;
Him, my Lord, I sought;
And thus ever remained.

அமைந்தொழிந்தேன் அளவில்புகழ் ஞானஞ்
சமைந்தொழிந் தேன்தடு மாற்றமொன் றில்லை
புகைந்தெழும் பூதலம் புண்ணியன் நண்ணி
வகைந்து கொடுக்கின்ற வள்ளலு மாமே. 2993

The Bounteous One

Thus remaining,
Limitless Jnana I attained;
No more wavering there is;
And as I reach the Holy One,
In the Land where Kundalini Fire burns,
The Bounteous One,
His choicest blessings gives.

வள்ளற் றலைவனை வானநன் னாடனை
வெள்ளப் புனற்சடை வேத முதல்வனைக்

கள்ளப் பெருமக்கள் காண்பர்கொ லோஎன்று
உள்ளத்தி னுள்ளே யொளித்திருந் தாளுமே. *2994*

He Hides in the Heart

The Bounteous Lord,
The Monarch of Heavenly Kingdom
The Lord of matted locks,
That carried Ganga waters flowing,
The Primal One of Vedas,
Lest them devoid of faith should see Him,
He hides in the heart within,
In the heart within.

ஆளும் மலர்ப்பதந் தந்த கடவுளை
நாளும் வழிபட்டு நன்மையுள் நின்றவர்
கோளும் வினையும் அறுக்குங் குரிசிலின்
வாளு மனத்தொடும் வைத்தொழிந் தேனே. *2995*

Divine Knight-Errant That Severs Karmas

Like me my God stretched His Flower-Feet in Grace
They, who adore Him daily in goodness, flourish;
He is the Divine Knight;
He severs my evil stars and Karmas,
Into His Sword of Jnana, my thoughts centred;
And no more cares I possess.

விரும்பில் அவனடி வீர சுவர்க்கம்
பொருந்தில் அவனடி புண்ணிய லோகந்
திருந்தில் அவனடி தீர்த்தமு மாகும்
வருந்தி யவனடி வாழ்த்தவல் லார்க்கே. *2996*

Seek His Feet

Seek His Feet,
They are the Valhalla warriors reach;
Do reach His Feet,
They are the haven of blessed deeds;
Do attain His Feet,
They are the confluence of holy waters;
Thus it is,
For those who constantly adore His Feet.

வானக மூடறுத் தானிவ் வுலகினில்
தானக மில்லாத் தனியாகும் போதகன்
கானக வாழைக் கனிநுகர்ந் துள்ளுறும்
பானகச் சோதியைப் பற்றிநின் றேனே. *2997*

Attain Jnana

In this world,
He pierced the overhanging Darkness of Ignorance;
Himself He has home none;
He is the Holy Preceptor of peerless grandeur;
I ate of the ripe fruit of His Jnana,
And I held on to the sweet Light within.

விதியது மேலை யமரர் உறையும்
பதியது பாய்புனற் கங்கையும் உண்டு
துதியது தொல்வினைப் பற்றறு விக்கும்
பதியது வவ்விட்ட தந்தமு மாமே. *2998*

Goal Ultima

That indeed is State Exalted,
That indeed is where Celestials have abode,
That indeed is where Ganga too-flows,
Sacred it is;
It is the State that severs,
Roots of Karmic desires,
That of yore come;
It is the Goal Ultima
Devoutly to be sought for.

மேலது வானவர் கீழது மாதவர்
தானிடர் மானுடர் கீழது மாதனங்
கானது கூவிள மாலை கமழ்சடை
ஆனது செய்யுமெம் ஆருயிர் தானே. *2999*

How Lord is Seated

The Celestials stand above,
Below them are Tapasvins great;
Below them are humans, by sorrow harassed;
Thus is He seated;
And the bilva garland fresh from forest,
Festoons the fragrant matted locks,
He does for Jiva what is appropriate.

சூழுங் கருங்கடல் நஞ்சுண்ட கண்டனை
ஏழும் இரண்டிலும் ஈசன் பிறப்பிலி
யாழுஞ் சுனையும் அடவியும் அங்குளன்
வாழும் எழுத்தைந்து மன்னனு மாமே. *3000*

He is in Five-Lettered Mantra

He quaffed poison that from oceans arose,
He pervades worlds seven times two,
Birthless is He the Lord,
He is seated where the Lute, the Spring and Forest are,
He is the King that reigns
In Five-Lettered mantra, Eternal.

உலகம் தொத்துமண் ணொத்துயர்காற்றை
அலர்கதிர் அங்கியொத் தாதிப் பிரானும்
நிலவிய மாமுகில் நீரொத்து மீண்டச்
செலவொத் தமர்திகைத் தேவர்பிரானே. *3001*

He is Pervasive in All Elements

Like Life is He,
Like Earth is He,
Like to Wind, Sun, Fire and Moon is He,
Like Water is He,
Like recurring Dissolution and Creation is He,
He the Lord of Gods in cardinal directions eight,
He the Primal One.

பரிசறிந் தங்குளன் அங்கி அருக்கன்
பரிசறிந் தங்குளன் மாருதத் தீசன்
பரிசறிந் தங்குளன் மாமதி ஞானப்
பரிசறிந் தன்னிலம் பாரிக்கு மாறே. 3002

He Confers Blessings According to Degree of Jnana Attained

In Fire and Sun He pervades,
In Wind He pervades,
In Moon He pervades,
Pervading all,
He gifts the Land True
To their Jnana according.

அந்தங் கடந்தும் அதுவது வாய்நிற்கும்
பந்த வுலகினிற் கீழோர் பெரும்பொருள்
தந்த வுலகெங்குந் தானே பராபரன்
வந்து படைக்கின்ற மாண்பது வாமே. 3003

He is the Object Mighty

Transcending all,
Yet immanent in each
He stands;
For the world here below in Pasa bound
He is the Object Mighty;
Himself the Parapara Supreme,
For all worlds He gave
That the Way His Greatness extends.

முத்தண்ட வீரண்ட மேமுடி யாயினும்
அத்தன் உருவம் உலகே ழெனப்படும்
அத்தனின் பாதாளம் அளவுள்ள சேவடி
மத்தர் அதனை மகிழ்ந்துண ராரே. 3004

His Cosmic Existence

His Crown is aloft pearl-like universes vast,
His Form engrosses seven worlds all,
His Feet descend deep like nether world;
The ignorant know these not,
And delight not.

ஆதிப் பிரான்நம் பிரானவ் வகலிடச்
சோதிப் பிரான்சுடர் மூன்றொளி யாய்நிற்கும்
ஆதிப் பிரான்அண்டத் தப்புறங் கீழவன்
ஆதிப் பிரான்நடு வாகிநின் றானே. 3005

Primal Lord is Everywhere—Above, Middle and Below

The Primal Lord is Our Lord,
He is the Light Resplendent of Spaces Vast,
He is the Lights Three—Sun, Moon and Fire;
The Primal Lord is beyond universes all,
He is below them and between them too.

அண்டங் கடந்துயர்ந் தோங்கும்பெருமையன்
பிண்டங் கடந்த பிறவிச் சிறுமையன்
தொண்டர் நடந்த கனைகழல் காண்டொறுந்
தொண்டர்கள் தூய்நெறி தூங்கிநின் றானே. 3006

Lord Seeks Those Who Seek Him

Great is He, rising above macrocosm vast,
Subtle is He, within the fleshy body to births an heir,
As His devotees see the vision of His Holy Feet,
And walk toward Him,
He goes seeking them,
On their way.

உலவுசெய் நோக்கம் பெருங்கடல் சூழ
நிலமுழு தெல்லா நிறைந்தனன் ஈசன்
பலமுழு தெல்லாம்படைத்தனன் முன்னே
புலமுழு பொன்னிற மாகிநின் றானே. 3007

He Created All

All worlds by vast oceans girt
He my Lord, filled pervasive;
In ominiscience over-seeing all;
Of yore He created, all, entire,
And stood diffusing His golden hue,
In worlds everywhere.

பராபர னாகிப்பல் லூழிகள் தோறும்
பராபர னாயிவ் வகலிடந் தாங்கித்
தராபர னாய்நின்ற தன்மை யுணரார்
நிராபர னாகிநிறைந்துநின் றானே. 3008

He Protects All

Through successive aeons several,
He stood as Paraparan Supreme;
All worlds He stood protecting
And this world too, as Paraparam Supreme;
This they know not;
He stood pervading the Jivas too,
Immanent in them and transcending them.

போற்றும் பெருந்தெய்வந் தானே பிறரில்லை
ஊற்றமும் ஓசையும் ஓசை யொடுக்கமும்
வேற்றுடல் தானென் றதுபெருந் தெய்வமாங்
காற்றது ஈசன்கலந்துநின் றானே. 3009

He Pervades as Prana Breath

He is the Mighty God to adore,
None beside Him are;
He is the Sense, the Feel, the Sound, and Sound's End;
He is the Body, too, of Jiva,
As Prana breath,
He the Lord is immanent in all.

திகையனைத் துஞ்சிவ னேயவ னாகின்
மிகையனைத் துஞ்சொல்ல வேண்டா மனிதரே

புகையனைத் தும்புறம் அங்கியிற் கூடு
முகையனைத் தும்எங்கள் ஆதிப்பிரானே. 3010

All Emanate From Him Alone

If directions cardinal are all of Siva,
Why speak of someone else, O! you men!
All smoke from Fire emanates,
All creation from our Primal Lord arises.

அகன்றான் அகலிடம் ஏழுமொன் றாகி
இவன்றா னெனநின் றெளியனு மல்லன்
சிவன்றான் பலபல சீவனு மாகி
நவின்றான் உலகுறு நம்பனு மாமே. 3011

The Pervasive Siva is Here as Well

The infinite spaces of the Seven worlds
He filled in oneness, expanding limitless;
Yet is He not easy of reach;
Siva Himself into myriad Jivas pervaded
In this world as well, He our Lord.

கலையொரு மூன்றுங் கடந்தப்பால் நின்ற
தலைவனை நாடுமின் தத்துவ நாதன்
விலையில்லை விண்ணவ ரோடும் உரைப்பன்
நரையில்லை யுள்ளுறு முள்ளவன் தானே. 3012

He is Transcendental and Immanent

Beyond the Kalas Three He stands,
Seek Him;
He is the Lord;
He is the Master of Tattvas,
Priceless is He;
Peerless is He;
Beyond Celestials all is He;
Ageless is He;
Yet is He within you,
You but seek Him.

1) The three kalas in Siva tattva: nivirti, pratista, and vidya. Beyond santi and santiyatita are the kalas of Sakti and Siva. Vide Mantra 2377, Tantra Eight, n.supra.

படிகால் பிரமன்செய் பாசம் அறுத்து
நெடியான் குறுமைசெய் நேசம் அறுத்துச்
செடியார் தவத்தினிற் செய்தொழில் நீக்கி
அடியேனை உய்யவைக்கத் தன்புகொண் டானே. 3013

He Redeems Jiva in Love

He severed Pasas
Of this world Brahma created;
He severed belittling desires
Vishnu to Jiva gives;
He severed Karmas interminable,
In His infinite divinity;
Thus me, the lowly, He redeemed,
And in endearment exceeding held me to Him.

ஈசனென் றெட்டுத் திசையும் இயங்கின
ஓசையி னின்றெழு சத்தம் உலப்பிலி
தேசமொன் றாங்கே செழுங்கண்டம் ஒன்பதும்
வாச மலர்போல் மருவிநின் றானே. 3014

He Spreads Like Flower's Fragrance

The Lord is the Light that moves in directions eight;
He is the source of all Sound;
He is the eternal;
As on one land,
The nine universes He pervaded;
Like the flower's fragrance,
He spreads everywhere.

இல்லனு மல்லன் உளனல்லன் எம்மிறை
கல்லது நெஞ்சம் பிளந்திடுங் காட்சியன்
தொல்லையன் தூயன் துளக்கிலன் தூய்மணி
சொல்லருஞ் சோதி தொடர்ந்துநின் றானே. 3015

He is Interminable Light Beyond Words

He is and He is not; my Lord;
Break your stony heart and there He is;
Ancient is He, Pure is He, Constant is He, Pure Gem is He;
He is Light beyond speech
Interminable is he.

உள்ளத் தொடுங்கும் புறத்துளும் நானெனுங்
கள்ளத் தலைவன் கமழ்சடை நந்தியும்
வள்ளற் பெருமை வழக்கஞ்செய் வார்கள்தம்
அள்ளற் கடலை அறுத்துநின் றானே. 3016

He is Bounteous

Within heart is He,
Without, too, He says, "I am;"
The inscrutable Lord;
Nandi of fragrant matted locks;
Those who adore Him constant
Their sea of birth He severs;
He, of Bounteous Magnificence.

மாறெதிர் வானவர் தானவர் நாடொறுங்
கூறுதல் செய்து குரைகழல் நாடுவர்
ஊறுவர் உள்ளத் தகத்தும் புறத்துளும்
வேறுசெய் தாங்கே விளக்கொளி யாமே. 3017

He Transforms Celestial Beings

The Devas and Danavas conflicting
Alike adore Him and daily seek Him;
They yearn for Him,
Within their heart and without;
He transforms them into Beings different,
He, the Lamp of Divine Light.

விண்ணிலும் வந்த வெளியிலன் மேனியன்
கண்ணிலும் வந்த புலனல்லன் காட்சியன்

பண்ணினில் வந்த பயனல்லன் பான்மையன்
எண்ணிலா னந்தமும் எங்கள் பிரானே. 3018

He is Endless Bliss

He appears not in heavenly space,
Yet Form He has;
He is not visible to naked eye,
Yet is He visible to inner eye;
He is the fruit of music;
He is the goodly One;
He is the fruit of all good deeds;
Endless Bliss is He,
He our Lord.

உத்தமன் எங்கும் உகக்கும் பெருங்கடல்
நித்திலச் சோதியன் நீலக் கருமையன்
எத்தனை காலமும் எண்ணுவர் ஈசனைச்
சித்தர் அமரர்கள் தேர்ந்தறி யாரே. 3019

None Knows Him Full Well

The Noble One is He,
A Sea of Joy beloved by all,
He is the Radiance of Pearl pure,
He is Dark-blue Throated,
Him they contemplate over time immeasurable,
The Siddhas holy and Celestials exalted,
Yet full well they know Him not.

நிறம்பல எவ்வண்ணம் அவ்வண்ணம் ஈசன்
அறம்பல எவ்வண்ணம் அவ்வண்ணம் இன்பம்
மறம்பல எவ்வண்ணம் அவ்வண்ணம் பாவம்
புறம்பல காணினும் போற்றகி லாரே. 3020

Adore Lord

Many are the hues, so is the Lord,
Many are the goodly deeds, so is the pleasure;
Many are the vile deeds, so are the iniquities
They see all these,
Yet they adore not the Lord.

இங்குநின் றானங்கு நின்றனன் எங்குளன்
பொங்கிநின் றான்புவ னாபதி புண்ணியன்
கங்குல்நின் றான்கதிர் மாமதி ஞாயி
றெங்குநின் றான்மழை போலிறை தானே. 3021

Lord is Benevolent Like Rain

Here He is, there He is, everywhere He is,
In all worlds He is, the Holy Lord;
In darkness He is, Light He is;
In sun He is, in moon He is, everywhere He is;
Benevolent is Lord,
Like the rain that falls.

உணர்வது வாயுமே யுத்தம மாயும்
உணர்வது நுண்ணறிவெம்பெரு மானைப்
புணர்வது வாயும் புல்லிய தாயும்
உணர்வுடல் அண்டமு மாகிநின் றானே. 3022

He is Cosmic Awareness

He is Sentience, He is Gracious
Wisdom subtle is to know Our Lord;
He is embrace, He is union
In divine awareness,
He stood as Body Cosmic.

தன்வலி யாலுல கேழுந் தரித்தவன்
தன்வலி யாலே யணுவினுந் தானெய்யன்
தன்வலி யான்மலை எட்டினுந் தான்சாரான்
தன்வலி யாலே தடங்கட லாமே. 3023

His Supreme Might

By His Might He supports the worlds seven,
By His Might He is subtler than atom,
By His Might He surpasses
The eight mountain ranges in directions eight,
By His Might, the oceans roar.

ஏனோர் பெருமைய னாகிலும் எம்மிறை
ஊனே சிறுமையுள் உட்கலந் தங்குளன்
வானோர் அறியும் அளவல்லன் மாதேவன்
தானே யறியுந் தவத்தின் அளவே. 3024

Lord Appears in Prayer and Penance

My Lord is of infinite greatness,
Yet is He within the littleness of this fleshy body;
Beyond the ken of Celestials is He;
Yet is prayer and penance
He Himself shall appear to you.

---

1) Vide Mantra 2012, Tantra Seven, supra.

பிண்டாலம் வித்தில் எழுந்த பெருமுளைக்
குண்டாலங் காயத்துக் குதிரை பழுத்தது
உண்டனர் உண்டார் உணர்விலா மூடர்கள்
பிண்டத்துட் பட்டுப்பிணங்குகின் றார்களே. 3025

Fruit of Jnana

The shoot of tiny banyan seed,
As a mighty tree within foul body grew,
And rich ripe fruit it bore;
They who ate, forever remained to be;
The fools who did not,
Remained in body,
Tossed about from birth to birth.

22. சர்வ வியாபி

THE ALL-PERVASIVE

ஏயுஞ் சிவபோக மீதன்றி யோரொளி
ஆயும் அறிவையும் மாயா உபாதியால்
ஏய பரிய புரியுந் தனதெய்துஞ்
சாயுந் தனது வியாபகந் தானே. 3026

When Jiva Unites in Siva

Siva Bhoga there will be;
Like it will be added a Light
That suffuses sentient knowledge;
The body by Mayaic experience harassed,
Will yours be, controlled full;
The Jiva's pervasiveness
Will everywhere spread.

நானறிந் தப்பொருள் நாடவிட மில்லை
வானறிந் தங்கே வழியுற விம்மிடும்
ஊனறிந் துள்ளே உயிர்க்கின்ற ஒண்சுடர்
தானறிந் தெங்குந் தலைப்பட லாமே. 3027

Omniscience and Omnipresence in Siva-Jiva Union

There is no one place where I can seek
That Object I have known;
Taking to the astral way,
There as Perfection, will it appear;
Seeking within the body,
There a Living Light will it be;
You then becomes omniscient and omnipresent.

கடலிடை வாழ்கின்ற கௌவை யுலகத்
துடலிடை வாழ்வுகொண் டுள்ளொளி நாடி
உடலிடை வைகின்ற உள்ளுறு தேவனைக்
கடலின் மலிதிரைக் காணலு மாமே. 3028

Seek Inner Light and Be One in Lord

In the sea-girt world filled with sorrows,
Seek Inner Light in life here led,
The Lord resides within this body,
May you meet Him ever,
On the waves of Seas High.

பெருஞ்சுடர் மூன்றினும் உள்ளொளி யாகித்
தெரிந்துட லாய்நிற்குந் தேவர்பிரானும்
இருஞ்சுடர் விட்டிட் டிகலிட மெல்லாம்
பரிந்துடன் போகின்ற பல்கோரை யாமே. 3029

His Infinite Compassion For Jiva

He is the Light within the Lights Three—
Sun, Moon and Fire;
He is their Body too
He the Lord of Celestials;
Yet leaving luminosities,
He follows Jivas in expanses vast
In compassion great;
He the One as several proliferates.

உறுதியி னுள்வந்த வுள்வினைப் பட்டு
இறுதியின் வீழ்ந்தார் இரணம தாகுஞ்
சிறுதியின் உள்ளொளி திப்பிய மூர்த்தி
பெறுதியின் மேலோர் பெருஞ்சுட ராமே. 3030

Jiva Becomes a Flaming Light

Entangled in crusted Karma;
That with their birth came;
They in the end realized Him,
And golden became;
He is the Spark within the spark of light,
The Being Divine,
If you reach Him,
A flaming Light you shall be.

பற்றி னுள்ளே பரமாய பரஞ்சுடர்
முற்றினு முற்றி முளைக்கின்ற மூன்றொளி
நெற்றியி னுள்ளே நினைவாய் நிலைதரு
மற்றவ னாய்நின்ற மாதவன் தானே. 3031

He is the Spark of Jnana in Ajna

He is the Divine Spark
Inside desires stands;
He is the Divine Spark,
Into the Three Lights—Sun, Moon and Fire-waxes,
He is the Divine Spark,
In the Fore-head Centre as our Thought seated,
The Tapasvins great, too, like Him stand.

தேவனு மாகுந் திசைதிசை பத்துளும்
ஏவனு மாம்விரி நீருல கேழையும்
ஆவனு மாமமர்ந் தெங்கு முலகினும்
நாவனு மாகி நவிற்றுகின் றானே. 3032

His is the Voice that Voices All

He is the Lord,
He is all in directions ten,
He is the seven expansive sea-girt worlds too,
Thus pervading,
He is the Speaker that speaks all.
(Thus the Jiva Siva Becomes.)

நோக்குங் கருடன் நொடியே மூலகையும்
காக்கு மவனித் தலைவனு மங்குள
நீக்கும் வினையென் நிமலன் பிறப்பிலி
போக்கும் வரவும் புணரவல் லானே. 3033

He Has No Entry, Exit and Stay

He is like the Garuda Bird, that in an instant sees all;

He protects the seven worlds entire,
He removes my Karmas,
He, the Pure One, the Birthless One,
He has Going, Coming and Mingling none.

செழுஞ்சடை யன்செம்பொ னேயொக்கு மேனி
ஒழிந்தன வாயு ஒருங்குடன் கூடுங்
கழிந்திலன் எங்கும் பிறப்பிலன் ஈசன்
ஒழிந்தில னேழுல கொத்துநின் றானே. 3034

He Pervades All Worlds Alike

He is of the rich matted locks,
He is of hue golden,
Unattached He is,
Yet immanent in all He is,
He is omnipresent, birthless, the Holy God,
Unintermittent He stands,
In all worlds seven.

உணர்வும் அவனே உயிரும் அவனே
புணர்வும் அவனே புலனும் அவனே
இணரு மவன்றன்னை எண்ணலும் மாகான்
துணரின் மலர்க்கந்தந் துன்னிநின் றானே. 3035

He is Within the Flower's Fragrance

Sentience He is, Life He is
Union He is, Senses He is
Continuity beyond Thought He is,
Within the Fragrance of the Flower He is.

புலமையின் நாற்றமில் புண்ணியன் எந்தை
நலமையின் ஞான வழக்கமு மாகும்
விலமையில் வைத்துள் வேதியர் கூறும்
பலமையில் எங்கும் பரந்துநின் றானே. 3036

He Comprehends All

The Holy One,
Devoid of odour of Senses Five,
My Father,
The Bounteous One, all Jnana gives;
In the precious wisdom of Vedic sages
Diverse He stands,
Comprehending all.

விண்ணவ னாயுல கேழுக்கு மேலுளன்
மண்ணவ னாய்வலஞ் சூழ்கடல் ஏழுக்குந்
தண்ணவ னாயது தன்மையின் நிற்பதோர்
கண்ணவ னாகிக் கலந்துநின் றானே. 3037

He is Light in the Eye of Jivas

He is Heavenly Being
He is beyond the worlds seven;
He is this earth too;
He is cool like seven ocean waters
That this globe girdles;
He stands in Jivas united,
As Light in their eye.

நின்றனன் மாலொடு நான்முகன் தானாகி
நின்றனன் தான்நிலங் கீழொடு மேலென
நின்றனன் தான்நெடு மால்வரை ஏழ்கடல்
நின்றனன் தானே வளங்கனி யாயே. 3038

His Limitless Expansiveness

He stood as Brahma and Vishnu,
He stood as heaven and earth,
He stood stretching
To the farthest mountains and seas seven,
He stood as Ripe Rich Fruit too.

புவனா பதிமிகு புண்ணியன் எந்தை
அவனே உலகில் அடர்பெரும் பாகன்
அவனே அரும்பல சீவனு மாகும்
அவனே இறையென மாலுற்ற வாறே. 3039

He is Jiva and Master of Jiva

He is Lord of Worlds,
The Holy One, my Father,
He is Master Mahout,
Of Jivas all,
He is Jivas themselves too,
He is the Lord,
Whom all in endearment hold.

உண்ணின் றொளிரும் உலவாப் பிராணனும்
விண்ணின் றியங்கும் விரிகதிர்ச் செல்வனும்
மண்ணின் றியங்கும் வாயுவு மாய்நிற்குங்
கண்ணின் றிலங்கும் கருத்தவன் தானே. 3040

He is the Spark of Life and Thought Within

He is Spark of Prana-breath within,
He is the Luminous Sun in firmament high,
He is the Breath of Wind that blows on land,
He is the Thought within all.

எண்ணும் எழுத்தும் இனஞ்செயல் அவ்வழிப்
பண்ணுந் திறனும் படைத்த பரமனைக்
கண்ணிற் கவருங் கருத்தில் அதுவிது
உண்ணின் றுருக்கியோர் ஆயமு மாமே. 3041

He Effected Union With Jiva

In the orderly way of numerals and letters
The Lord created music and melody;
In His Glance, in His Thought, from within
He effected rapturous union of Jiva and Siva,
Into one Family united.

இருக்கின்ற எண்டிசை அண்டம்பா தாளம்
உருக்கொடு தன்னடு வோங்கவிவ் வண்ணங்
கருக்கொடு எங்குங் கலந்திருந் தானே
திருக்கொன்றைவைத்தசெழுஞ்சடையானே. 3042

He is the Centre of All

The cardinal directions eight,

The worlds above and worlds below,
In Him centering stood;
Thus, immanent in all, He pervaded all;
He of the flowing matted locks,
Bedecked with fragrant Konrai blooms.

பலவுடன் சென்றஅப் பார்முழு தீசன்
செலவறி வாரில்லை சேயன் அணியன்
அலைவிலன் சங்கரன் ஆதிஎம் மாதி
பலவில தாய்நிற்கும் பான்மைவல் லானே. 3043

He is One and Many

The Lord is with creation all
None know His coming and going,
He is distant, He is near;
He is constant, He is Sankara,
He is the Primal Being;
Multiple He is, One He is,
He Our Primal Lord.

அதுவறி வானவன் ஆதிப் புராணன்
எதுவறி யாவகை நின்றவன் ஈசன்
பொதுவது வான புவனங்கள் எட்டும்
இதுவறி வான்நந்தி எங்கள் பிரானே. 3044

He Knows All; But None Knows Him

He is Jiva's knowledge,
He is the Ancient One,
Yet none know how He is;
In the universes eight all,
He knows all,
—He the Nandi, Our Lord Primal.

நீரும் நிலனும் விசும் பங்கி மாருதந்
தூரும் உடம்புறு சோதியு மாயுளன்
பேரும் பராபரன் பிஞ்ஞகன் எம்மிறை
ஊருஞ் சகலன் உலப்பிலி தானே. 3045

He is Deathless

Water, earth, sky, fire and wind,
The spark of light within the body,
—All these He is;
He is Paraparam, He is Siva, Our Lord,
He is the walking Jiva here below,
Deathless He is.

மூல னுரைசெய்த மூவா யிரந்தமிழ்
மூல னுரைசெய்த முந்நூறு மந்திரம்
மூல னுரைசெய்த மூன்பப துபதேசம்
மூல னுரைசெய்த மூன்றும் ஒன்றாமே. 3046

Tirumular's Songs, Mantras and Instructions Have But One Import

The Three times Thousand that Mula composed,
The Three Times Hundred Mantras that Mula chanted,
The Three Times Ten Instructions that Mula gave,
These Three that Mula said
Are all, all, of one import.

23. வாழ்த்து

BENEDICTION

வாழ்கவே வாழ்கஎன் நந்தி திருவடி
வாழ்கவே வாழ்க மலமறுத் தான்பதம்
வாழ்கவே வாழ்க மெய்ஞ்ஞானத் தவன்தாள்
வாழ்கவே வாழ்க மலமிலான் பாதமே. 3047

Long May They Be

Long may they be, Long may they be, our Nandi's Holy Feet!
Long may they be, Long may they be, the Feet of Him who severed Malas!
Long may they be, Long may they be, the Feet of Him of Divine Jnana;
Long may they be, Long may they be, the Feet of Him who has Mala none.

ஒன்பதாம் தந்திரம் முடிவு பெற்றது.
Tantra Nine Concluded